ANTIQUES
PRICE GUIDE 2006

Judith Miller

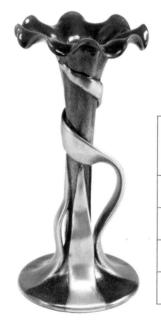

A DORLING KINDERSLEY BOOK

LONDON, NEW YORK,
MELBOURNE, MUNICH, DELHI

A joint production from DORLING KINDERSLEY
and THE PRICE GUIDE COMPANY

THE PRICE GUIDE COMPANY LIMITED

Publisher Judith Miller

Publishing Manager Julie Brooke

Senior Managing Editor Carolyn Madden

European Consultants Martina Franke,
Nicolas Tricaud de Montonnière

Sub-editors Jessica Bishop, Dan Dunlavey,
Sandra Lange

Digital Image Co-ordinator Ellen Spalek

Editorial Assistant Alexandra Barr

Design & DTP Tim & Ali Scrivens, TJ Graphics

Photographers Graham Rae, John McKenzie,
Andy Johnson, Byron Slater, Heike Löwenstein,
Adam Gault, Bruce Boyajian, Ellen McDermott

Indexer Hilary Bird

Workflow Consultant Bob Bousfield

Publishing Advisor Nick Croydon

DORLING KINDERSLEY LIMITED

Publishing Director Jackie Douglas

Managing Art Editor Heather McCarry

Managing Editor Julie Oughton

DTP Designer Adam Walker

Production Melanie Dowland

Production Manager Sarah Coltman

Front jacket shows:

A D'Argental cameo glass vessel, signed "D'Argental".
£1,000-1,500 **DRA**
A French tortoiseshell mantel clock.
£500-600 **GHOU**
A Chantilly lace fan.
£180-200 **BONM**

First published in 2005 by
Dorling Kindersley Limited
80 Strand, London WC2R 0RL

Penguin Group

The Price Guide Company (UK) Ltd
Studio 21, Waterside
44–48 Wharf Road
London N1 7UX
info@thepriceguidecompany.com

2 4 6 8 10 9 7 5 3 1

A CIP catalogue record for this book is available from the British Library.

ISBN: 1 4053 0881 8

Colour reproduction by Colourscan, Singapore
Printed and bound by MOHN media and Mohndruck GmbH, Germany

Discover more at

www.dk.com

CONTENTS

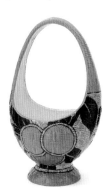

INTRODUCTION

Yes, the doom and gloom merchants are at it again. How many times over the last 30 years have I heard that antiques have had their day? And yet good specialist dealers and auctioneers adapt and their businesses continue to grow. Many are taking advantage of the Internet boom and trading online where they can reach a thriving global marketplace.

A full-colour annual price guide such as this one is an indispensable companion to online trading. My team travels the globe photographing antiques to ensure that all of the items featured are new each year. The prices featured are a guide – and nothing more – to the antiques pictured and tell you what you should expect to pay for a similar item in a similar condition.

My 'CARD' philosophy, that value is dependent on condition, age, rarity and desirability, has never been more true. I would also add to this the 'Two Ps' – provenance and prettiness. You may think prettiness is subjective, but in a climate where buyers are more discriminating, looks are vital. And when faced with a nervous and discerning market more people want to be absolutely assured of an item's authenticity.

The items that have shown the greatest growth in recent months are pieces designed by the greats of the 20thC such as Le Corbusier, Marcel Breuer and Charles and Ray Eames. These visionaries are beginning to rise to the same dizzy heights as Chippendale and Hepplewhite.

Tribal Art remains a growing market, and pieces from the Arts and Crafts movement are enjoying renewed popularity thanks to recent international exhibitions. The market for fine and unusual furniture is also extremely buoyant.

I think this is a great time to buy, with prices for good quality pieces, particularly from the 19thC, offering fantastic value. They will last you a lot longer than mass-produced tat from the superstores – and you could become the auctioneer's best friend.

Trust me – this is the time to buy and I for one am doing just that. Just please don't tell my husband!

Sincerely,

Judith Miller.

LIST OF CONSULTANTS

Bohemian Glass

Andrew Lineham
PO Box 465 Chichester
West Sussex PO18 8WZ

Ceramics

John Axford
Woolley & Wallis
51–61 Castle Street
Salisbury Wiltshire SP1 3SU

Christopher Spencer
Spencer Antiques Services
23a High Street
Falmouth TR11 5AB

Clocks

Paul Archard
Derek Roberts Fine Antique
Clocks
25 Shipbourne Road
Tonbridge Kent TN10 3DN

Commemoratives

John Pym
Hope & Glory
131a Kensington Church St
London W8 7LP

Decorative Arts

Michael Jeffery
Woolley & Wallis
51–61 Castle Street
Salisbury Wiltshire SP1 3SU

John Mackie
Lyon & Turnbull Ltd
33 Broughton Place
Edinburgh EH1 3RR

Furniture

Paul Roberts
Lyon & Turnbull Ltd
33 Broughton Place
Edinburgh EH1 3RR

Matthew Smith
Christie's
8 King Street, St. James's
London SW1Y 6QT

Glass

Jeanette Hayhurst
Jeanette Hayhurst Fine Glass
32a Kensington Church Street
London W8 4HA

Horst Ungar
Dr. Fischer Heilbronner
Kunst und Auktionshaus
Trappensee-Schlösschen
74074 Heilbronn
Germany

Jewellery

Joseph H Bonnar
72 Thistle Street
Edinburgh EH2 1EN

Oriental

Clive Stewart Lockhart
Dreweatt Neate
Donnington Priory Salerooms
Newbury Berkshire RG14 2JE

Robert McPherson
R & G McPherson Antiques
40 Kensington Church Street
London W8 4BX

Silver

Michael James
The Silver Fund
1 Duke of York Street
London SW1Y 6JP

Trevor Kyle
Lyon & Turnbull Ltd
33 Broughton Place
Edinburgh EH1 3RR

Toys

Glenn Butler
Wallis & Wallis
West Street Auction Galleries
Lewes
East Sussex BN7 2NJ

Tribal Art

Philip Keith

20th Century

Mark Hill
The Price Guide Company
(UK) Ltd

General Consultant

Keith Baker
The Price Guide Company
(UK) Ltd

HOW TO USE THIS BOOK

Running head – Indicates the sub-category of the main heading.

The introduction – The key facts about a factory, maker or style are given, along with stylistic identification points, value tips and advice on fakes.

Caption – The description of the item illustrated, including, when relevant, the period, the maker or factory, medium, the year it was made, dimensions and condition. Many captions have **footnotes** which explain terminology or give identification or valuation information.

The price guide – The price ranges in the Guide are there to give a ball-park figure of what you should pay for a similar item. The great joy of antiques is that there is not a recommended retail price. The prices guides in this book are based on actual prices – either what a dealer will take or the full auction price – and are then checked by consultants. If you wish to sell an item you may be offered much less; if you want to insure your items the insurance valuation may be considerably more.

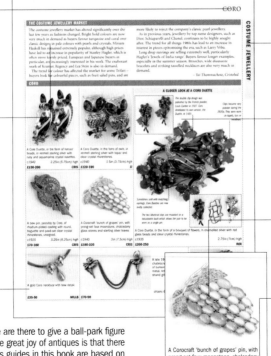

Page tab – This device appears on every spread and identifies the main category heading as indicated in the Contents List on pp.5–6.

A closer look at – Does exactly that. This is where we show identifying aspects of a factory or maker, point out rare colours or shapes and explain why a particular piece is so desirable.

The object – The antiques are shown in full colour. This is a vital aid to identification and valuation. With many objects, a slight colour variation can signify a large price differential.

The source code – Every item in *Antiques Price Guide 2006* has been specially photographed at an auction house, a dealer, an antiques market or a private collection. These are credited by the code at the end of the caption, and can be checked against the Key to Illustrations on pages 724–8.

THE PORCELAIN MARKET

Excitement rippled through the fraternity of European porcelain enthusiasts last year as a number of very significant lots went under the hammer. A pair of mid-18thC tawny owls by Bow secured a record price of more than £120,000 at Sotheby's in New York. In the UK, a seated Chinaman found in a box of bric-a-brac turned out to be the first ever recorded example of a figure by Limehouse, the short-lived and almost mythical London factory.

Strong and steady market demand for Welsh porcelain continued unabated. Philip Serrell, the Malvern auctioneers, sold a 19thC Nantgarw cabinet plate depicting the Three Graces for £26,000. Further afield, buyers from ex-Soviet states such as Russia, Latvia and Estonia have buoyed up demand for early Russian porcelain by factories such as St Petersburg and Gardner.

Continued economic uncertainty in the US has kept prices at the highest end of the market slightly lower than they might otherwise have been. The market still awaits the discovery of dinner services by the 18thC American China Manufactory.

As ever, buyers should be aware that it is invariably better to invest in a few quality pieces than in many mediocre items. Porcelain with damage or restoration should be avoided in all but the most exceptional cases.

– John Axford, Woolley & Wallis

BELLEEK

A Belleek oval covered basket, with three-strand centre and double-looped rim, applied with roses, thistles and shamrocks, impressed mark "Belleek Co Fermanagh", some damage and repair.

c1875   5.5in (14cm) high

£250-350   **HAMG**

A Belleek circular basket, the rim applied with roses, shamrocks and rose stems forming the handles, with impressed "Belleek" on a strap.

9.25in (23cm) wide

£500-700   **WW**

A late 19thC Belleek teapot and cover, moulded as a sea-urchin, the handle, spout and foot moulded as coral, with an impressed and moulded mark.

6.5in (16.5cm) wide

£250-300   **WW**

A Belleek 'Henshall's Twig' flower-encrusted basket, the flowers tinted in shades of pink, green and yellow, gold mark for post 1980, with a fitted box and cover.

11in (28cm) wide

£200-250   **DN**

A Belleek First Period globular teapot and cover, with basket moulded loop handle and bird mask spout, moulded with wheatsheaves, berries and leaves, picked out in enamels and gilt, printed mark in black, short crack to spout.

c1875   6in (15cm) high

£300-500   **LFA**

A late 19thC Belleek glazed parian planter, applied with flowers to the shoulders, below the wavy rim, the lobed body moulded with four sprays of prunus, on a petal-shaped foot, black hound, harp and Belleek mark.

9.75in (25cm) diam

£200-300   **CHEF**

BELLEEK

- Founded in 1857 in County Fermanagh by David McBirney and Robert Armstrong, Belleek initially produced earthenware.
- In 1863, a number of Stoke-on-Trent craftsmen joined the firm and it began to produce parian porcelain.
- The factory made a wide variety of vases, flower-pots and centrepieces, often decorated with flowers or marine motifs.
- Teaware is Belleek's most extensive product. Common colours are white, green and pink. Blue and butterscotch are rare.
- William Henshall originated the openwork baskets, with applied flowers, for which Belleek is famous.
- The earliest baskets were 'Convolvulus', 'Sydenham', 'Twig' and 'Shamrock'. The finest is thought to be 'Rathmore'.
- Covered baskets were particularly difficult to produce as both pieces were made at the same time and were prone to failure.
- The history of the factory has been divided into a number of periods and the marks change accordingly.
- The factory is still in operation today.

A Bow chinoiserie octagonal plate, painted with a mythical dragon and flaming pearl, painter's no. "13".

c1755   8.5in (21.5cm) diam

£800-1,200   **DN**

A Bow powder-blue ground plate, typically painted with circular and fan-shaped chinoiserie panels around a central river landscape, with painted Chinese-style marks, slight surface wear.

c1760   8.25in (21cm) diam

£300-500   **DN**

A Bow blue and white plate, painted with the 'Caddy' pattern of figures in a landscape, slight damage.

c1760   9.5in (24cm) diam

£300-500   **WW**

A Bow blue and white chinoiserie plate or stand, painted with flowers and shrubs issuing from rockwork, within a floral panel and diaper band border, rim chips and manufacturing faults.

c1760   9.25in (23.5cm) long

£150-250   **DN**

A Bow dish, of lobed lozenge form painted in underglaze blue with a chinoiserie scene of a pagoda.

c1760   11.25in (28.5cm) wide

£150-250   **SWO**

A rare Bow dish, in the form of two overlapping cabbage leaves, picked out in underglaze blue and painted with berries, within a feuille-de-choix border, Chinese style four character mark in blue.

c1770   11.5in (29cm) wide

£800-1,200   **LFA**

A documentary Bow blue and white cup, with a moulded flared top, the inner rim decorated with peony and lotus on a ground of dots and circles, the exterior painted with peony and willow, the base inscribed "Eliz.th Mackly. 1764", broken and re-glued and a large rim chip.

Despite the extensive damage, this cup is valuable because it is inscribed and dated. This is rare in a piece of Bow.

2.75in (7cm) high

£1,800-2,200   **WW**

A small Bow blue and white butter boat, with three feet and looped handle, decorated with flowers.

c1760   2.75in (7cm) wide

£500-800   **JN**

A Bow blue and white sauceboat, moulded in low relief with flowers and painted with floral panels, the interior with a diaper band border, small chips.

7in (18cm) wide

£250-300   **DN**

A Bow figure of 'Autumn', of a young boy holding up a bunch of grapes and sitting on a wicker basket, with appliqué details, on a scroll moulded base.

This piece was originally part of four-piece set depicting the seasons.

c1755   5.5in (14cm) high
£1,800-2,200   SHF

A pair of Bow figures of Arlecchino and Columbina, after Meissen, he wearing a motley suit and mask, she with a jacket decorated with playing cards, each raised on a rococo base applied with flowers, leaves and detailed in puce.

c1760   7.5in (19cm) high
£4,000-6,000   WW

A Bow figure of a seated nun, wearing a black headdress and holding a prayer book.

c1760   4.5in (11.5cm) high
£300-400   WW

A Bow figure of an abbess, wearing a black cloak and with her arms crossed, the circular base with applied flowers.

c1760   5.5in (14cm) high
£300-400   WW

A Bow coffee can, painted in enamel colours with floral sprays in red, blue and lime green, the cross-hatched border similarly painted.

2.25in (6cm) high
£200-300   HAMG

A Bow figure of 'Winter', the hunched figure warming his hands over a brazier, the base with four scroll legs, anchor and dagger mark.

c1770   6.5in (16cm) high
£400-600   SWO

A Bow mug, of baluster form, with a grooved strap handle, painted with chinoiserie decoration depicting two Chinese figures in a garden, in polychrome enamels.

c1760   4in (10cm) high
£3,000-4,000   SHF

A Bow mug, with a grooved strap handle, painted with chinoiserie decoration of exotic birds and branches in polychrome enamels, within an iron-red scroll border.

c1765   4in (10cm) high
£2,500-3,500   SHF

A circular Bow tureen and cover, painted with coloured flowersprays, the cover with a bird finial and raised flowerhead decoration, the body with a pair of naturalistic handles.

c1760
£700-900   SWO

CAUGHLEY

A Caughley heart-shaped dish, printed in blue with a sailing boat and Chinese pagoda landscape, unmarked.

c1770   11in (28cm) wide
£280-320   WW

A Caughley blue and white spoon tray, printed with a Chinese pagoda landscape, gilded rim, "Sx" mark.

c1780   6.25in (16cm) wide
£280-320   WW

A Caughley trefoil-shaped dessert dish, printed with figures in a pagoda landscape impressed "P" and printed "S" marks.

c1780   8in (20.5cm) wide
£200-250   WW

A Caughley blue and white printed shell-shaped dish, printed with the 'Full Nankin' pattern, some surface scratches.

c1790   8in (20.5cm) wide
£150-250   DN

BRITISH PORCELAIN

One of a pair of Caughley blue and white plates, printed with figures in a landscape, unmarked, small chips.

c1780   7.75in (20cm) diam

£120-180 pair   **WW**

A Caughley blue and white plate, printed with the 'Nankin' pattern, rim chip.

c1790   8in (20.5cm) high

£50-70   **DN**

A Caughley Low Chelsea ewer, moulded with acanthus leaves and painted with flowers, faint rim crack.

c1770   4.25in (11cm) long

£200-300   **WW**

A Caughley blue and white moulded bowl, printed with Chinese figures on a bridge, in a pagoda landscape, "S" mark, the gilt rim rubbed.

c1780   6in (15cm) diam

£100-200   **WW**

A CLOSER LOOK AT A CAUGHLEY DISH

The well-controlled printing in dark blue and the light straw coloured glaze is typical of Caughley. When held to a light, the body looks slightly orange, compared to the greenish tint found on Worcester.

Both Caughley and Worcester made versions of this design. They can be distinguished by the fact that the fisherman in the Worcester version has a larger fish and longer wiggly line.

Finely powdered black cobalt oxide is mixed with oil and painted onto the surface. When fired, it reacts with a lead glaze and turns blue.

Pieces are often marked with an "S" or an "S+" for the county of Salop, although a "C" was used between c1775-1795.

A Caughley blue and white water basin, printed with the 'Fisherman and Cormorant' pattern.

c1790   11.5in (29cm) diam

£700-1,000   **DN**

A rare Caughley lobed oval sauce tureen, cover, stand and ladle, with a loop knop, painted in underglaze blue with Chinese river landscapes within key fret and diaper panelled borders, gilded detail, the stand with a blue "X" inside the footrim, slight damage.

c1790   9in (23cm) wide

£1,200-1,800   **LFA**

A Caughley porcelain jug, moulded with cabbage leaves and a mask spout, transfer-printed blue floral decoration, underglaze blue crescent mark.

c1785   8.5in (21cm) high

£400-600   **S&K**

A Chelsea raised anchor deep fluted dish, painted with a central circular reserve of a wolf and a heron from Aesop's Fables.

c1750   4.5in (11.5cm) wide

£10,000-15,000   **SHF**

A Chelsea raised anchor deep fluted dish, painted with a central circular reserve of two tigers playing on a rock.

c1750   5in (13cm) wide

£10,000-15,000   **SHF**

A Chelsea lobed plate, with fluted cavetto, painted in a Kakiemon palette with the 'Hob in the Well' pattern within a scrolling border, red anchor mark.

c1750   9.5in (24cm) diam

£4,000-6,000   **LFA**

A Chelsea lobed plate, painted in coloured enamels with flowers, the rim with wave moulded panels and painted exotic birds, red anchor mark.

c1755   8.5in (21.5cm) diam

£250-350   **LFA**

A Chelsea plate, painted with sprays of flowers, red anchor mark, some surface scratches.

c1755   8in (20.5cm) diam

£200-300   **DN**

A Chelsea Hans Sloane botanical plate, of faceted form, painted with branches from the Arbutus tree and scattered insects, chocolate line rims, red anchor mark.

c1755   8in (20.5cm) wide

£7,000-10,000   **SHF**

A Chelsea plate, boldly painted in coloured enamels with an exotic bird perched on rockwork within a brown line rim, brown anchor mark, restored rim.

c1760   8.75in (22cm) diam

£400-600   **LFA**

A Chelsea figure of a dancing man, gold anchor mark.

c1760   7.75in (20cm) high

£6,000-8,000   **AA**

A Chelsea blue and white soup plate, painted with a pair of long-tailed fowl in a landscape, with a diaper and floral panel band and shaped rim, blue anchor mark.

c1755   8.75in (22.5cm) diam

£16,000-18,000   **DN**

A large pair of Chelsea masqueraders, modelled as a lady and gentleman in Turkish dress, he wears a turban, she with an ermine lined cloak, each raised on a gilded scrolling base applied with flowers, gold anchor marks.

c1760   13in (32.5cm) high

£6,000-8,000   **WW**

A 'Girl-in-a-Swing' factory porcelain scent bottle.

3in (7.5cm) high

£2,000-3,000   AA

A small 'Girl-in-a-Swing' factory fob seal, modelled and painted as a standing figure of Punchinello, the cornelian seal cut with a dove and a motto, the mounts of yellow metal.

'Girl-in-a-Swing' is the name attributed to a London factory established by Charles Gouyn in 1749. The name was inspired by a white figure of a girl, currently in the Victoria & Albert Museum, thought to be from Gouyn's factory.

1.25in (3cm) high

£200-300   CHEF

A Chelsea raised anchor tall beaker, of moulded faceted form, painted with a Ho Ho bird in blossoming branches on glaze enamel, the Phoenix bird to the reverse, small rim chip, unmarked.

c1750   3in (7.5cm) high

£7,000-10,000   SHF

Rear: A small Chelsea red anchor ashet, painted with Deutsche Blumen, the border relief decorated with scroll and diaper panel, painted red anchor mark.

13in (33cm) wide

£600-900   L&T

Front: A Chelsea red anchor circular pierced basket, painted with a central panel of Deutsche Blumen including roses and lilies, the exterior embossed with yellow flowerheads, exterior decoration of leaves and forget-me-not, faint painted red anchor mark, crack to rim.

16.75in (17cm) diam

£600-900   L&T

A Chelsea pierced oval two-handled basket, painted with floral bouquets and sprays, loop handles with flowerhead terminals, red anchor mark, repair to handles.

c1755   11.25in (29cm) long

£300-500   DN

A CLOSER LOOK AT A CHELSEA CREAMBOAT

Chelsea was founded by silversmith Nicholas Sprimont. Many early shapes, like this cream boat, were influenced by British silverware.

Jefferyes Hammett O'Neale enjoyed success at Chelsea, where he specialised in fable decoration and figures, as well as at Worcester. A named and highly regarded designer add to this piece's value.

Pieces from this period often feature Chelsea 'moons' - bubbles trapped in the body that appear as lighter spots when held to a strong light.

This cream boat dates from the 'Red Anchor' period (1752-56) when Chelsea was influenced by Meissen.

A Chelsea leaf-shaped creamboat, of fluted form, by Jefferyes Hammett O'Neale, with a solid loop handle, the reserve painted with birds in foliate and a landscape scene, red anchor mark, small cracks to rim.

c1780   4in (10cm) wide

£22,000-24,000   SHF

A John Rose Coalport oval sugar bowl and cover, with ring handles, painted with gilt, blue and iron red flower and leaf sprays.

c1805   5.5in (14cm) wide

£150-200   **WW**

An unusual Coalport drum-shaped inkwell, with three quill holes, brilliantly painted in coloured enamels with flowers and leaves, on a gold ground.

c1810   8.5in (21cm) diam

£250-300   **LFA**

A pair of English porcelain vases and covers, probably Coalport, in the Sèvres style, painted with panels of figures and flowers, on a turquoise ground, with rich floral gilding, unmarked, some restoration to the covers.

c1840   11.75in (30cm) high

£1,200-1,800   **WW**

A Coalport ovoid jug, with a flared neck and angular loop handle, painted in coloured enamels with flowers and leaves, within square canted gilt panels, the blue ground decorated in gilt, "W" mark in blue and "9" in gilt.

c1815   4.75in (12cm) high

£300-400   **LFA**

A 19thC Coalport coffee can and saucer, with angular handle, painted in iron red and gilt with flowers and leaves on a green ground, within gilt line borders, printed monogram in puce and retailer's mark for Daniell of London.

c1810

£180-220   **LFA**

A Coalport oval meat dish, the white ground reserved with foliate posies within moulded scroll and floral borders.

c1840   21.25in (54cm) diam

£300-500   **ROS**

A Coalport reclining dog, on a shaped green and gilt base.

4.5in (11.5cm) wide

£120-180   **JN**

A Coalport porcelain dessert service, with apple-green and gilt scroll-shaped borders and shaped rim centring a painted floral specimen, comprising 18 dessert plates, four square two-handled serving plates, four oval two-handled serving plates, one round plate and one square plate, bearing iron red pattern number "4174".

c1835

£1,000-1,500   **S&K**

DERBY

A Derby blue and white leaf pickle dish, with flower decoration, slight chip.

c1770   3.25in (8.5cm) wide

£280-320   **JN**

A Derby blue and white cream boat, painted in underglazed blue with a pagoda on an island.

c1765   3.5in (9cm) wide

£800-1,200   **JN**

DERBY

DERBY

- The Derby factory produced porcelain from c1750. From 1787 it operated under William Duesbury the younger.
- Early wares, including tea sets, tureens and baskets, aimed at the London market, were influenced by the designs of Meissen.
- During the Regency period, patterns were copied from Chinese and Japanese wares. The 'Old Witches', 'Tree of Life' and 'Kings' patterns from the Imari range were popular.
- The factory also produced many figures, often portraying pastoral scenes or Chinese and allegorical figures.
- Derby also produced a large range of ornamental pieces for display. The creamy white glaze gave pieces a unique, soft finish, making it popular today.
- Derby porcelain is sometimes called 'dry edge' because the glaze was removed from the base before firing to prevent pooling.
- Pieces were unmarked before 1770. After this, a model number was often added to the base.
- The company went into decline after Duesbury died in 1797.
- In 1870, the factory became home to Derby Crown Porcelain Co., which became Royal Crown Derby. It is still in operation today.

A Derby shepherd boy, with appliqué details, sitting on a wicker basket and holding flowers in a bow-shaped felt hat, unglazed, the flowers with blue glaze, the base impressed with "N 36".

c1770 · 6in (15.5cm) high · **£300-400** · **SHF**

A pair of Derby cupids, with appliqué details, one holding a falcon by a string and the other sitting under a tree with a dog, originally part of a four-piece sporting series, unglazed.

c1785 · 5in (13cm) high · **£300-500** · **SHF**

A Derby 'The Gardener' figure, with appliqué details, depicting a country gentleman leaning on a tree stump and holding a posy of flowers, on a Greek key base.

c1785 · 8in (20.5cm) high · **£300-400** · **SHF**

A Duesbury Derby group of two child musicians, with appliqué flowers, on a scroll moulded base, from a Tournai original by Nicholas Gauron, patch marks, incised number "140", glazed.

c1770 · 10in (25.5cm) high · **£1,800-2,200** · **SHF**

A pair of Derby models of the 'Welsh Tailor and his Wife', from the King Street Works, in the white, each astride a goat, on shell and scroll moulded oval mound base, painted marks in blue, some damage.

6.5in (16.5cm) high · **£250-350** · **LFA**

A Derby Longton Hall figure of a seated harlequin playing a set of bagpipes, decorated in polychrome enamels, on a scroll moulded base, slight damage and restoration, unmarked.

c1755 · 5.5in (14cm) high · **£3,500-4,500** · **SHF**

A Derby allegorical figure of Ceres, with appliqué details, holding a sickle and sheaves of wheat in her right arm, with a prancing infant by her side, on a scroll moulded base.

c1755 · 7in (18cm) high · **£1,500-2,000** · **SHF**

A Derby figure of a boy as Summer, his coat finely painted with sprays of flowers, on a scroll moulded base, once part of a four-piece set depicting the seasons.

c1755 · 5in (12.5cm) high · **£2,000-2,500** · **SHF**

A pair of Derby figures, with appliqué details, the lady holding a posy of flowers, the man with a floral-patterned vest, on scroll moulded bases.

c1755 · Man 5.5in (14cm) high · **£2,000-2,500** · **SHF**

A Derby figure of a dancing lady, in a classical pose, with appliqué flowers, wearing a painted enamelled floral dress, on a scroll moulded base, repairs to the forearms and hands.

c1760   *7in (18cm) high*

£3,000-3,500   **SHF**

A Derby group of lovers, with a gallant and maiden on a rocky base with a dog and a goat, restoration.

c1765   *5.5in (14cm) high*

£500-800   **WW**

A pair of Derby candlestick figures, modelled as a shepherd and shepherdess standing before white flowering trees, a dog and sheep at their feet, raised on scroll moulded bases.

c1765   *11in (28cm) high*

£1,500-2,000   **CHEF**

A Derby figure of a gardener, standing sharpening his scythe before a flowering tree, raised on a scroll moulded base.

c1765   *10in (25cm) high*

£350-450   **CHEF**

A pair of Derby figures of a shepherd and companion, the man modelled standing with a hound holding a basket of fruit, his companion with flowers in her apron and a lamb, on rocaille bases, incised marks "N55", chips and restoration.

c1770   *9in (23cm) high*

£500-800   **DN**

A pair of Derby figures of a shepherd and companion, the shepherd with a lamb under his arm, his companion with a basket of flowers and holding fruit in her apron, on scroll moulded bases, small chips and restoration.

c1770   *9in (23cm) high*

£400-600   **DN**

A pair of Derby small candlestick figures, in the form of a young boy and girl, decorated in coloured enamels, seated before floral bocage, the pierced shell and scroll moulded bases picked out in turquoise and gilt, sconces lacking, some damage.

c1780   *6in (15cm) high*

£120-180   **LFA**

A Derby 'Hairdresser' group, typically modelled with a seated woman and her hairdresser, incised "no 84", small chips and restoration.

c1770   *6.5in (16.5cm) high*

£180-220   **DN**

A Derby model of a dancing couple, raised on a scrolling base applied with flowers, incised "No.16", minor restoration.

c1775

£500-800   **WW**

A Derby 'Shoemaker' group, typically modelled with a woman having a shoe fitted by a kneeling man, impressed "no 78".

c1780   *6.75in (17cm) high*

£180-220   **DN**

A pair of Derby 18thC-style candlestick figures, in the form of a seated shepherd and shepherdess, each decorated in coloured enamels before floral bocage and flanked by two pierced sconces, the pierced shell and scroll-moulded base picked out in puce and gilt, blue crossed swords marks, minor restoration.

c1820   *8.25in (21cm) high*

£600-900   **LFA**

17

A pair of Derby 18thC-style candlestick figures, in the form of a gentleman and companion, each decorated in coloured enamels, with a flower-applied treestump and a pierced sconce, blue crossed swords mark, minor restoration.

c1820   9.75in (25cm) high

£800-1,200   LFA

A pair of early 19thC Derby figure groups of amorini in various playful gardening attitudes, incised "No. 48".

8.75in (22cm) high

£250-350   CHEF

A Derby model of Dr Syntax, standing holding a cane and raised on a circular base, painted King Street mark, small flakes to black enamel.

c1875   5.25in (13.5cm) high

£180-220   WW

A pair of Derby candlesticks figures, each in the form a female grape seller on a scallop-decorated plinth, blue painted Derby mark.

10.5in (26.5cm) high

£350-450   L&T

A pair of Derby models of recumbent cows, each before a flowering tree and raised on a base applied with leaves and flowers.

c1760   3.75in (9.5cm) wide

£600-900   WW

A Derby Imari porcelain shell-form serving dish, painted with a dragon before a flowering tree, gilt highlights, red enamelled mark.

c1815   9.5in (24cm) wide

£220-280   S&K

A Derby heart-shaped dish, painted in coloured enamels in the Dodson style with four exotic birds, within a gilt canted rectangular panel on a turquoise ground, crowned crossed batons mark in red, some wear to gilt rim.

c1815   10in (25.5cm) wide

£400-600   LFA

c1770   8.25in (21cm) diam

£800-1,200 pair   WW

One of a pair of Derby scallop-edged plates, decorated in gilt and coloured enamels in an Arita design, unmarked, one with crack.

Compare this example with the one in the Worcester section: both factories copied directly from Arita wares. Derby examples are slightly creamy in tone and are less popular with collectors.

A Derby leaf-moulded sauceboat, the stalk handle with flowerhead and fruit terminals, painted in colours with flower sprays, some small rim chips.

c1755   7in (18cm) wide

£350-400   DN

A Derby sauceboat, moulded with flowers, leaves and scrolling cartouches and painted with colourful flower sprays.

c1760   8.75in (22.5cm) wide

£400-600   WW

A Derby 'dolphin ewer' creamboat, of shell-moulded form with entwined dolphins beneath the spout, painted in coloured enamels with flower sprays.

c1765   4in (10cm) high

£200-300   DN

A pair of early 19thC Derby porcelain vases, each with gilt pierced border and grotesque masks, above a floral painted band, on quatriform base, red painted marks, covers missing.

4in (10cm) high

£180-220   **HAMG**

A garniture of three Derby 'Imari' campana, each with two gilt snake handles, iron-red script marks, minor damage and wear.

c1820   *largest 8in (20.5cm) high*

£400-600   **DN**

A pair of Derby porcelain twin-handled vases and covers, each of compressed circular shape with a domed cover and strap handles with gilt masks, printed marks including date code.

1884   *5in (13cm) high*

£250-300   **SWO**

A Victorian Derby inkstand decorated in Imari palette with pattern number 80, comprising a two handled tray, inkwell and cover, cylindrical box and cover and a taper stick, damaged.

£150-200   **CHEF**

A garniture of three Derby bough pots, painted with a still life of fruit, probably by Steele, in a rectangular panel on a green and gilt ground, raised on scroll feet, red printed marks.

c1820   *8.5in (21cm) high*

£2,200-2,800   **WW**

Part of an extensive composite Derby tea and coffee service, decorated in the 'Imari' palette, rust-painted factory mark, comprising teapot, cover and stand, sucrier and cover, cake plate, four bread plates, 24 tea cups, 16 coffee cans, 16 saucers, and a slop bowl.

£800-1,200 set   **L&T**

Two pieces from a part Derby fruit service, painted with cornflower sprays and a leaf and flower repeat border, rust painted factory marks, comprising five heart-shaped serving dishes with scroll handles, three plainer heart-shaped dishes, three lozenge-shaped dishes, two lozenge-shaped stands, sauce tureen and cover, and a large twin-handled serving bowl.

£200-400 set   **L&T**

A CLOSER LOOK AT A DERBY CUP & SAUCER

Trembleuses, saucers with a circular pierced gallery in the centre to hold the cup and prevent it from 'trembling' and spilling, were created in the early 18thC for drinking chocolate.

William Duesbury took over control of the factory from his father in 1786 and oversaw a period in which finely decorated display wares were produced for the higher end of the market.

This mark was used c1782-1825. Earlier Derby is generally unmarked. Since the introduction of marks, around 30 different versions have been used.

James Banford (1758--1798) worked at Derby from 1789 to about 1797. He specialised in fine quality figure subjects.

A rare Derby cabinet cup and trembleuse saucer, probably by James Banford, the cup with entwined handle, finely painted in coloured enamels with two female figures garlanding a bust of Pan, with inscription "Olim truncus eram ticulnus inutile lignum" (once upon a time I was a trunk, a useless log from a fig tree), crowned crossed baton marks in blue and titled beneath, saucer with restored rim chip.

This design is taken from an engraving by William Wynne Ryland, after Angelica Kauffman, 'Olim Truncus Elim', published by Ryland in 1776.

c1790

£5,000-8,000   **LFA**

A pair of Richard Chaffers & Co. Liverpool tea bowls and matching saucers, painted in underglaze blue with a scene of deer in a park, picked out in brown, red, green and gilt enamels, diaper border to the interior.

c1760   Bowl 2in (5cm) high

£180-220   **H&L**

A Liverpool finely potted bowl, probably by Philip Christian's factory, painted in underglaze blue with a crane in a Chinese river landscape of a fence, flowering branches and rockwork, the interior with a stylised leaf scroll within a diaper band.

c1760

£600-900   **LFA**

An 18thC Pennington's Liverpool blue and white coffee pot and cover painted with flowers on the lid and baluster body, the rims with alternating flower vignette, cell and coral diaper bands.

9.75in (25cm) high

£100-150   **CHEF**

A Pennington's Liverpool porcelain sparrow-beak jug, printed in blue with sprays of flowers.

c1785   3.75in (9.5cm) high

£150-200   **DN**

A rare Liverpool small cylindrical can, with notched loop handle, painted in underglaze blue with a Chinese angler in a river landscape, with a boat in full sail, tiny rim chip.

c1755   2.5in (6.5cm) high

£1,000-1,500   **LFA**

A Pennington's Liverpool porcelain sparrow-beak jug, printed in blue with sprays of flowers.

c1785   3.75in (9.5cm) high

£150-200   **DN**

LIVERPOOL

- In the 1750s a number of porcelain factories operated in Liverpool in close proximity.
- The key companies were: Richard Chaffers 1754-65, Philip Christian 1765-76, Samuel Gilbody c1754-61, William Reid and others c1755-70, John and James Pennington c1770-94 and Seth Pennington and John Part 1778-1803.
- Chaffers and Christian were leading makers. They produced blue and white porcelain tea wares, inspired by Chinese designs, which can be difficult to distinguish from Worcester.
- Liverpool porcelain is variable in quality and is often 'peppered' with small speckles on the glaze.
- Pieces were decorated in blue and white, coloured enamels or a harsh famille-rose palette.
- Pieces were left unmarked, making identification difficult today.
- Coffee services are popular today and figures are rare.

A Liverpool cylindrical mug, probably Richard Chaffers & Co., with a flattened loop handle, brightly painted in coloured enamels with flowering branches, a fence and rockwork, in Chinese famille rose palette.

c1760   4.5in (11.5cm) high

£2,000-3,000   **LFA**

A Richard Chaffers & Co. Liverpool coffee can, with a Chinese landscape painted in underglaze blue, iron red and gilt, interior with a diaper band.

c1760   2.5in (6.5cm) high

£700-1,000   **LFA**

A Liverpool coffee cup, with notched loop handle, painted in famille rose palette with Chinese figures, the interior with an iron red spearhead band.

c1760   2.5in (6.5cm) high

£400-600   **LFA**

A William Ball sparrow beak jug, enamelled in colours with fence and flowers, slight chip to rim.

An advertisement appeared for William Reid's porcelain in the Liverpool Advertiser of November 12th 1756. By June 1761, the company was bankrupt. It continued under William Ball until it was leased to James Pennington & Co. in 1763.

c1760   3in (7.5cm) high

£800-1,200   **JN**

A rare Longton Hall slender baluster milk jug, with a sparrow beak and loop handle, painted in underglaze blue with a Chinese river landscape of two buildings beneath a tree.

c1755   3.5in (9cm) high

£1,800-2,200   LFA

A Longton Hall blue and white bowl, painted with a Chinese landscape, small foot rim chip.

c1755   4.5in (11.5cm) diam

£400-600   WW

A Longton Hall 'Folly' pattern spoon tray, of modified leaf form, depicting an obelisk and figure with a walking stick.

1755   6.75in (17cm) long

£4,500-5,500   RTC

A pair of Longton Hall Strawberry leaf plates, painted with exotic birds in foliage, within a moulded border of strawberry leaves and fruit, tiny chip to rim, unmarked.

c1755   10in (25.5cm) wide

£2,500-3,500   SHF

A Longton Hall melon tureen and cover, of naturalistic form with a twig finial, on a triangular leaf-shaped foot, decorated in yellows and greens, painter's mark in black.

c1760   4in (12cm) high

£6,500-7,500   SHF

LOWESTOFT

A very rare Lowestoft blue and white cup, painted with a three-turret bridge and flowers.

c1760

£350-450   JN

A Lowestoft cylindrical mug, with an S-scroll handle, printed in underglaze blue, interior with a diaper band, chips.

c1785   5.5in (14cm) high

£220-280   LFA

A Lowestoft teabowl and saucer, painted in underglaze blue, teabowl with decorator's mark "X" and cracks.

c1780

£300-500   LFA

A large Lowestoft blue and white bowl, the exterior decorated with a Chinese figure, bird and two boats in a pagoda landscape, the centre with a flower spray, marked "5", hairline crack.

c1765   9.5in (24.5cm) diam

£1,200-1,800   WW

LOWESTOFT

- Robert Brown and partners founded the Lowestoft porcelain factory in Suffolk in 1757. It closed in 1802.
- The shapes of early underglaze blue ware tended to be based on salt-glaze stoneware.
- Foot-rims were usually marked with a numeral.
- After 1765, overglaze colours were used.
- Worcester became a major influence on designs, although the porcelain used at Lowestoft was coarser and prone to staining.
- The quality of the porcelain declined after 1770, when shapes and patterns were simplified and marks were seldom used.
- Rare Lowestoft birth tablets, painted with a baby's name, and pieces inscribed for the local market, are popular with collectors.
- Identification of Lowestoft largely relies on knowledge of patterns and shapes.

A Lowestoft bowl, painted in underglaze blue with two horses in a Chinese river landscape, the interior with a diaper band, short rim crack.

c1780   6.25in (16cm) diam

£200-300   LFA

A Lowestoft teapot cover, with ball knop, painted in underglaze blue with a Chinese river landscapes within a flower diaper band.

c1780   3.25in (8.5cm) diam

£100-150   LFA

A rare Lowestoft blue and white circular plate, decorated with a Chinese woman standing in a garden with a two-handled urn, flowers to the border.

c1770   8.75in (22cm) diam

£3,000-5,000   **JN**

A Lowestoft creamboat, of Low Chelsea ewer form, with a scroll handle, painted in underglaze blue with trailing flowers and leaves.

c1780   4in (10cm) long

£700-900   **LFA**

A Lowestoft globular teapot and cover, painted in colours and gilt with Chinese figures in a garden at various pursuits.

c1770

£600-900   **JN**

A Lowestoft baluster milk jug, with a sparrow beak and S-scroll handle, painted in coloured enamels.

c1785   3.25in (8.5cm) high

£700-900   **LFA**

A Lowestoft butter boat, of Low Chelsea ewer form, painted in coloured enamels with flowers and leaves beneath a brown line rim, crack, some discolouration.

c1785   4in (10cm) long

£200-300   **LFA**

MINTON

A pair of Minton biscuit porcelain figures, 'Flower-Seller' and 'Fruit-Seller', a country maiden carrying flowers in the apron of her dress, damage, and a youth carrying a basket of fruit, both on spiral moulded bases, unglazed.

c1810   7in (18cm) high

£500-600   **SHF**

A Minton bowl, part of a rare set comprised of two large plates, three side plates and three bowls, with illustrations of a chick and a wasp, the illustrations attributed to the Frenchman Pierre Mallet (1836-1898).

c1870   9.75in (25cm) diam

£300-400 set   **TCS**

A mid-Victorian inkwell and cover, possibly Minton, modelled as a bunch of flowers, the handle formed of the stalks tied by a pink ribbon, daisy head cover with morning glory tendril knop.

8.75in (22cm) wide

£250-300   **CHEF**

An unusual Minton Parian bust of Princess Mary of Teck, later Queen Mary, after H. Tyler, on a titled cylindrical socle and square base, impressed mark and incised "H. Tyler Sc. 1898".

10.75in (27cm) high

£400-600   **LFA**

A pair of Minton's china ewers, of Neo-Classical design, the loop handles with laurel leaf decoration and satyr mask terminals, with royal blue ground and oval beaded portrait medallions of Lady Hamilton (Romney) and Mrs Fitzherbert (Romney), both signed "F.N. Sutton" and with gilt printed mark.

c1900   11.5in (28.5cm) high

£1,000-1,500   **L&T**

A CLOSER LOOK AT A MINTON BOTTLE

Marc-Louis Solon (1835-1912) worked with the technique of pâte-sur-pâte whilst at Sèvres before introducing it to Minton, when he joined the company, in 1871. The importance of this artist makes this signed piece extremely valuable. —

The high quality porcelain of Minton is some of the finest produced in England during the 18th and 19thC. —

The decoration is inspired by Classicism and Renaissance styles. White slip is built up in layers against a dark background, to give the effect of depth.

A fine Minton pâte-sur-pâte olive green pilgrim bottle, the sides finely painted and hand-tooled in white slip with a seated nymph holding a cupid amongst stars, gold crowned globe mark, impressed "Mintons, N-Y, shape 1343", signed "L. Solon".

c1880   *10.5in (26cm) high*

£15,000-20,000   **FRE**

A pair of Minton blanc-de-chine four-light candelabra, with leaf-moulded sconces and scroll branches held aloft by a male and female figure, each with torch bearing putto and seated on a column, impressed mark and puce printed retailer's mark, some restoration.

c1885   *23.5in (59.5cm) high*

£300-500   **HAMG**

SPODE

A Spode perfume bottle, the mazarin blue ground enriched with gilt florate patterns.

c1805   *4in (10cm) wide*

£1,500-2,000   **SHF**

An early Victorian Spode scent bottle and stopper, the broad rim of the baluster shape in gilt, above applied flowers and shells on a pea green body, gilt mark.

     5in (13cm) high

£300-500   **CHEF**

A Spode scent bottle and cover, the mazarin blue ground overlaid with cisele figures of exotic birds in foliage, pattern number "4051".

Cisele is a technique where patterns are tooled into thickly applied gilding to create intricate decoration.

c1805   *4in (10cm) high*

£400-500   **SHF**

An early Victorian scent bottle and stopper, possibly Spode, the downswept neck and shoulders applied with flowers between gilt handles, gilt bands to the dished rim, rim of the body and the socle foot, marked "1664" in mauve.

     6.35in (16cm) high

£200-300   **CHEF**

A Spode spill vase, the pale blue mazarin ground enriched with with gilt scrolls and florate sprays, pattern number "4298".

c1810   *3in (8cm) high*

£150-200   **SHF**

A Spode pot-pourri vase and cover, with gilt crocodile handles, painted with applied white slip with figures of cherubs, on an aubergine ground.

c1805   *3in (8cm) high*

£350-450   **SHF**

A Spode teapot and cover, of swept-neck form, the mazarin blue ground painted in gilt enriched with Chantilly spray patterns and gilt line rims.

c1805   *7in (18cm) wide*

£250-350   **SHF**

SPODE

A Spode porcelain campana-shaped pastille burner and cover, painted with sprays of flowers reserved on a blue and gilt scale ground, the pierced cover with flamiform finial, iron-red mark and pattern number "1166".

c1820   4.75in (12cm) high
£2,500-3,000   **DN**

A Spode trio, comprising a teacup, coffee cup and saucer, with shaped handles, the mazarin blue ground enriched with gilt decoration and line rims, pattern "1166".

c1805   saucer 5.5in (14cm) diam
£2,500-3,000   **SHF**

A Spode chamberstick with snuffer, the mazarin blue ground enriched with gilt decoration, pattern "1166".

c1805   5in (13cm) wide
£2,000-3,000   **SHF**

A Spode watering can, with two handles, the mazarin blue ground with raised florate sprays and chrysanthemum sprigs, pattern "3153".

c1805   4in (10cm) high
£1,000-1,200   **SHF**

An early 19thC Spode inkwell, decorated with the 3993 pattern of birds and foliage on a claret ground, two quill holders and an inkwell within the oval rim.

4.75in (12cm) wide
£70-100   **CHEF**

STAFFORDSHIRE

A Staffordshire porcelain ovoid jug, the leaf-moulded scroll handle picked out in blue, painted in coloured enamels with flowers and leaves, and inscribed in gilt "F/R Lees, 1816".

5.5in (14cm) high
£200-300   **LFA**

A Staffordshire porcelain cottage-shaped pastille burner and stand, with a thatched roof and an oriel window to one end, painted in coloured enamels with climbing flowers and leaves, picked out in gilt, shallow chip.

c1820   5in (13cm) high
£600-800   **LFA**

A 20thC Staffordshire porcelain stirrup cup, modelled as a fox with a red coat and black eyes, the collar dressed with holly.

4.75in (12cm) long
£150-200   **S&K**

An early 19thC Staffordshire porcelain seated gentleman, holding a beer mug in his right hand.

c1840   5.25in (13.5cm) high
£120-180   **KGO**

An early 20thC Staffordshire porcelaineous elephant group of a leopard hunter, of William Kent type, modelled with a leopard slung over the elephant's withers and the mahout seated next to it in Eastern dress, tusks restored.

8in (20.5cm) high
£200-300   **DN**

A Swansea 'Carnation' or 'Peony Rose' pattern dinner plate, printed in blue with the floral centre and chinoiserie-type border, impressed "SWANSEA".

c1810   9.5in (24.5cm) diam
£500-800   DN

A Swansea plate, decorated in London, with flowers in coloured enamels, the border with a blue dot ground and trailing flowers within tooled gilt flower and leaf scroll loops, star crack.

c1815   7.25in (18.5cm) diam
£400-600   LFA

A good Swansea plate, painted in the manner of William Billingsley, in brightly coloured enamels with a loose garland of flowers, the rim gilded, red painted 'Swansea' mark.

c1820   8.5in (21.5cm) diam
£4,000-6,000   WW

A pair of Swansea porcelain dessert plates, the centres painted with a floral bouquet within a floral band ring, the pale-green-ground borders with C-scroll panels of flower sprays, iron-red "SWANSEA", slight wear.

c1820   8.25in (21cm) diam
£2,800-3,200   DN

A Swansea two-handled shaped rectangular serving dish, painted with scattered floral sprays, iron-red mark, cracked.

c1820   12.5in (32cm) wide
£300-500   DN

A Swansea porcelain plate, sparsely painted in green and gilt with scattered floral sprigs within a band of urns suspending husk swags and a gilt-line rim, gilt script mark, some wear.

c1820   8.25in (21cm) diam
£150-200   DN

One of a rare pair of porcelain candlesticks, possibly Swansea, with a ribbed stem picked out in gilt, the base painted in coloured enamels.

c1820
£3,000-5,000 pair   LFA

WORCESTER

An 18thC Worcester blue and white sparrow beak jug, the baluster sides with sprays of flowers, the interior with foliate rim band with diaper vignettes.

3.5in (8.5cm) high
£70-100   CHEF

An 18thC Worcester blue and white jug and cover, the baluster sides painted with sprays of flowers below diaper vignettes, crescent mark.

5in (13cm) high
£150-200   CHEF

A Worcester blue and white sparrow beak jug, printed with the so-called 'Three Flowers' pattern, blue crescent mark.

c1775   4in (10.5cm) high
£280-320   DN

A Worcester porcelain cabbage leaf jug, with a mask spout and floral decoration.

c1770   8.25in (21cm) high
£100-150   SWO

A Worcester blue and white sparrow beak jug, painted with the 'Cannonball' pattern.

c1775   3.75in (9.5cm) high
£200-300   DN

A Worcester white porcelain sparrow beak jug and cover, with a flower finial, moulded in low relief with the 'Chrysanthemum' pattern.

c1765   5.5in (14cm) high
£350-450   DN

An 18thC Worcester blue and white sauceboat, moulded with cartouches and fluted decoration and painted with scenes of fishermen in a boat.

5in (13cm) wide

£400-600   **GORL**

WORCESTER

- The first factory in Worcester was established in 1751. The major shareholder, Dr John Wall, acquired the stock and closely guarded steatite recipe of Lund's failed Bristol porcelain works.
- In 1783, Thomas Flight bought the factory to be run by Joseph and John Flight, his sons.
- The 'Flight' period was between 1783 and 1792.
- The 'Flight & Barr' period lasted from 1792 to 1804. The new, simpler forms of this period were characterised by fine painting.
- The 'Barr Flight & Barr' period was between 1804 and 1813.
- The 'Flight Barr & Barr' period lasted from 1813 to 1840.
- In 1840 the company was amalgamated with Chamberlain's, another Worcester porcelain firm.
- In 1862 the conglomerate became Royal Worcester Porcelain.
- The final amalgamation of the porcelain manufacturers in the area took place in 1889 when Grainger's was brought under the umbrella of the Royal Worcester Porcelain Company.

An 18thC Worcester blue and white chocolate cup and saucer, painted with the 'Fence' pattern within shaped rims, with ogee-handled cup.

5.5in (14cm) wide

£400-600   **GORL**

An 18thC Worcester teabowl and saucer, painted with a willow tree and a fence.

3.5in (8cm) wide

£400-600   **GORL**

An early 18thC Worcester blue and white teacup, painted with the 'Warbler' pattern.

2.5in (6cm) high

£280-320   **GORL**

One of a pair of Worcester blue and white butter boats, the painted inside with gooseberries and flowers, the exteriors moulded with three tiers of leaves about the stalk handles, one with crescent mark.

c1765   *3.5in (9cm) wide*

£500-700 pair   **CHEF**

A Worcester blue and white butter boat, painted on the interior with four sprays of flowers and a butterfly, the exterior moulded with three tiers of leaves, the stem handle continuing into the centre of the foot-rim, crescent mark.

c1765   *3.5in (9cm) wide*

£250-350   **CHEF**

A Worcester globular teapot, with loop handle, painted in underglaze blue with the 'Canonball' pattern, beneath a diaper band, script "W" mark, no cover.

c1770   *4.75in (12cm) high*

£150-200   **LFA**

A Worcester globular teapot and cover, with loop handle and flower knop, printed in underglaze blue with the 'Fruit and Wreath' pattern, within leaf and C-scroll bands, hatched crescent mark, small chip to tip of spout.

c1775   *6in (15cm) high*

£300-500   **LFA**

A Worcester flared basket, printed in underglaze blue with the 'Pine Cone' pattern, within a flower, scroll and diaper border, the exterior applied with flowerheads, picked out in blue, hatched crescent mark.

c1770   *7.25in (18.5cm) diam*

£400-600   **LFA**

A rare Worcester round chamberpot, with loop handle and turned over rim, printed in underglaze blue with the 'Three Flowers' pattern, the interior with Auriculas, beneath a cell diaper band, hatched crescent mark.

c1770   *5.25in (13.5cm) high*

£1,200-1,800   **LFA**

A Worcester blue and white slop bowl, of fluted form and painted with the 'Prunus Root' pattern, script mark.

c1770   6in (15cm) wide

£500-800   DN

A Worcester plate, printed in underglaze blue with the 'Carnation' pattern, the basket-moulded border with blue line rim, hatched crescent mark.

c1775   9.5in (24cm) diam

£150-200   LFA

A Worcester fluted lozenge shaped dish, printed in underglaze blue with the 'Caughley Floral Sprays' pattern, blue crescent mark.

c1780   11.75in (30cm) wide

£350-450   LFA

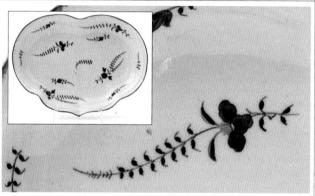

An unusual Worcester heart-shaped dish, painted in underglaze blue with the 'Chantilly Sprig' pattern, within a blue line rim, stylised horn mark in blue.

This pattern is rarely found on dessert ware.

c1780   10.5in (26.5cm) wide

£300-500   LFA

A Worcester deep sauce dish, printed in black with the second version of 'Tea Party No.2', by Robert Hancock, within a black line border, unmarked.

c1765   7.5in (19cm) wide

£800-1,200   SHF

A Worcester transfer-printed cylindrical mug, decorated with a vignette of 'The Milkmaids' by Robert Hancock, after a 1760s engraving by Robert Sayer, the reverse with a print of maidens dancing to a peg-leg fiddler, some fritting and minor stains.

c1770   5.5in (14cm) high

£400-600   DN

A Worcester tankard, by Robert Hancock, of cylindrical form, with a grooved strap handle, printed in black with the 'Whitton Anglers', the reverse with the "Diseuse D'Avanture".

c1770   5in (13cm) high

£1,000-1,500   SHF

A Worcester bell-shaped tankard, with a transfer print of the King of Prussia and a grooved strap handle, signed, anchor and helm for Richard Holtship.

c1755   3in (8cm) high

£1,000-1,500   SHF

An 18thC English porcelain coffee cup, possibly Worcester, painted in the famille verte palette with chrysanthemums and other foliage.

2.25in (6cm) high

£600-900   H&L

An 18thC English porcelain coffee cup, possibly Worcester, painted in the famille verte palette with chrysanthemums and other foliage, within red line borders.

This cup, and the one pictured above, fetched an unexpectedly high price at auction because they are examples of a rare Worcester pattern.

c1755   2.25in (6cm) high

£800-1,200   H&L

BRITISH PORCELAIN

A Worcester teabowl, brightly painted in coloured enamels with sprays of European scattered flowers and butterflies, within brown line borders.

c1760   4.5in (11.5cm) diam

£250-350   **AA**

A Worcester hexagonal teabowl, painted in colours with the '100 Antiques' pattern.

c1760   2.25in (5.5cm) wide

£800-1,200   **JN**

A Worcester bell-shaped cup, painted with English flowers, in the manner of James Rogers, two chips to the rim, unmarked.

c1760   3in (7cm) high

£500-700   **SHF**

A Worcester facetted coffee cup and saucer, the cup with a scroll handle, with Kakiemon-style decoration of growing flowers and orange and gilt bands, decorated in iron red with mons.

c1765

£250-350   **LFA**

A Worcester baluster shaped mug, with notched loop handle, printed in the Kakiemon style with a version of the 'Two Quails' pattern, beneath an iron red and gilt flowerhead and scroll band.

This pattern is much more uncommon than its Bow counterpart.

c1760   4.75in (12cm) high

£1,800-2,200   **LFA**

A Worcester coffee cup, with notched loop handle, boldly painted in coloured enamels with scattered flowers and leaves, the interior with an iron red and gilt looped band.

c1765   2.5in (6.5cm) high

£300-500   **LFA**

A Worcester coffee cup, with a scroll moulded handle, decorated in the Kakiemon style with flowers and leaves alternating with blue ground bands, roundels of gilt flowers and leaves, blue fret mark.

c1770   2.5in (6.5cm) high

£220-280   **LFA**

A Worcester fluted coffee cup, with ear shaped handle, painted in famille rose style with figures and flowers, alternating with orange and gilt diaper bands, decorated in iron red with mons.

c1770   2.5in (6.5cm) high

£200-300   **LFA**

A Worcester coffee cup, with a notched loop handle, painted in famille rose palette with numerous figures, the gilt scroll ground decorated in black and iron red with flowers and leaves.

c1770   2.5in (6.5cm) high

£220-280   **LFA**

A Worcester coffee cup, with a notched loop handle, painted in famille rose palette, probably in the London atelier of James Giles, the gilt scroll ground decorated in black, iron red and puce.

c1770   2.5in (6.5cm) high

£200-300   **LFA**

A Worcester coffee cup, decorated with fruit in the London atelier of James Giles.

c1770   3in (7.5cm) high

£500-700   **AA**

A Worcester 'Valentine' pattern coffee cup, with a loop handle.

c1770

£500-800   **JN**

A Worcester dish, of naturalistic form, moulded in the shape of a lettuce leaf, with overlapping handles, pencilled in lilac with a chinoiserie scene of two Chinamen outside a pavilion, slight rubbing to highlights, unmarked.

c1760   *10.5in (26.5cm) wide*

£1,200-1,800   **SHF**

A Worcester teapot stand, of hexagonal form, decorated with polychrome enamels depicting a Chinese family fishing in a lake, all within a scale red border and vignette of lakeside scenes, slight rubbing, unmarked.

c1765   *5.5in (14cm) wide*

£2,000-2,500   **SHF**

A CLOSER LOOK AT A WORCESTER DISH

This piece dates from the very first years of porcelain production at Worcester, making it of great interest to the collector.

James Rogers' painting is particularly celebrated. He is known to have specialised in the depiction of birds, but any decoration that can be attributed to his hand is very desirable.

The moulded edge of this dish is very vulnerable to chipping. This piece is remarkable in that it has survived intact.

Depictions of ruins are typical of the Neo-Classical period, during which the arts were suffused with the Graeco-Roman culture.

A Worcester dish, by James Rogers, of naturalistic form, moulded in the shape of a leaf with a short stalk, painted monochrome handles, decorated with a European landscape of ruins, and bouquets of flowers in a scrolled reserve edged with yellow, all within sprays and bouquets of flowers, unmarked.

c1755   *8in (20cm) long*

£7,000-10,000   **SHF**

A Worcester deep sauce dish, possibly by James Giles, painted in the chinoiserie style, with a central circular reserve depicting a Chinaman and a horse in a wooded Chinese garden, within a border enriched with gilt scrolls, unmarked, mint condition.

c1770   *7.5in (19cm) wide*

£2,200-2,800   **SHF**

A Worcester plate, with indented border, painted in coloured enamels in the London atelier of James Giles.

c1770   *9in (23cm) diam*

£500-700   **LFA**

A Worcester plate, with fluted border, painted in coloured enamels in the London atelier of James Giles.

c1770   *8.25in (21cm) diam*

£600-900   **LFA**

A Worcester scallop-edged plate, decorated in the Giles workshop, in gilt and coloured enamels with two cranes, peony, prunus and bamboo to an Arita design, no marks.

Provenance: *Raby Castle.*

c1770   *8in (20.5cm) diam*

£1,000-1,500   **WW**

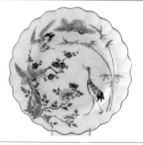

BRITISH PORCELAIN

JAMES GILES

- Operating from studios in Soho, London, James Giles (1718-80) was an outside decorator of English porcelain and glass.
- From 1749 he is recorded as a 'Chinaman' (i.e. a vendor or importer of porcelain) and from 1763 as a painter.
- From c1767 Worcester sent blank white porcelain, in many recently developed shapes, to be decorated by Giles.
- He decorated in the latest styles. This was extremely important to Worcester because, despite its commercial success, it had begun to neglect its fashionable London market.
- Designs were copied from Meissen and Sèvres and were very popular in London.
- He probably also decorated for Bow and Longton Hall and for the Falcon glassworks (est. 1693) in London.
- He painted in enamels and fuchsia flowers are characteristic.
- His work is not signed.
- Records suggest that in 1776, he went bankrupt.

A Worcester plate, painted in the London atelier of James Giles, with flowers.

c1770   8.25in (21cm) diam

£3,000-4,000   **AA**

A Worcester dessert plate, with fluted rims, painted with a central bouquet of cut fruit and flowers, raised gilding to the claret ground, cornucopia reserves.

c1770   7in (18cm) wide

£2,200-2,800   **SHF**

A Worcester plate, unusually decorated in the Imari style with flowering trees and a fence within a broad flower panelled border, with phoenix and leaf scrolls, restored rim chip.

c1770   8.75in (22cm) diam

£400-600   **LFA**

A Worcester square dish, painted in coloured enamels with flowers and leaves within a gilt C-scroll roundel, the blue ground with gilt dentil rim, crescent mark, glaze chip.

c1770   7.75in (19.5cm) wide

£180-220   **LFA**

A Worcester dish, of naturalistic form, in the shape of a leaf, painted with birds in foliage, puce-coloured veins and scatter insects, enriched with gilt line rims, unmarked, some sooting to glaze.

c1770   11in (28cm) wide

£500-800   **SHF**

A Worcester Imari pattern globular teapot and cover, painted with oblique panels of stylised plants and foliage and blue and gilt diaper oblique panels, finial glued.

c1770

£400-600   **DN**

A Worcester globular teapot and cover, polychrome decorated with chinoiserie scenes, the cover with a floral knop, unmarked, restoration to the finial and minor chips.

c1770   6.75in (17cm) high

£400-600   **WW**

A Worcester teapot and cover, printed and painted with Chinese figures, the cover with a floral knop.

c1770   5.5in (14cm) high

£500-800   **AA**

A Worcester teapot and cover, painted with coloured flower sprays and a ladybird.

c1770   7in (17.5cm) high

£300-400   **WW**

A small Worcester feather moulded cream jug, painted in the famille rose palette with a bird, a butterfly and a peony bush, underglaze blue inner rim, workman's mark.

c1755   3.5in (9cm) high

£1,200-1,800   **WW**

A large Worcester 'cabbage leaf' jug, decorated with the 'Two Quails' pattern.

c1770   6.75in (17cm) high

£1,200-1,800   **AA**

A Worcester cabbage leaf moulded sauceboat, with stalk loop handle, painted in coloured enamels.

c1755   8.75in (22cm) long

£150-200   **LFA**

A First Period Worcester cornucopia-shaped wall picket, with spiral moulding, painted on glaze, with bouquets of flowers and scattered insects, originally one of a pair.

c1755   9.5in (24cm) high

£3,500-4,000   **SHF**

A Worcester faceted circular bowl, painted in the Chinese style and depicting a corpulent monk holding a fan by a screen and three girls seated at a table, the interior with foliate sprays and gilt enriched dot border, unmarked.

c1765   6in (15cm) wide

£1,000-1,500   **SHF**

A Worcester sweetmeat basket, of pierced and circular form, the exterior with moulded florets, the interior interlaced with circlets, painted with bouquets of English flowers and insects.

c1770   8in (20.5cm) wide

£1,000-1,500   **SHF**

BARR, FLIGHT & BARR

An early 19thC Barr period Worcester teacup and saucer, from a trio, each piece finely decorated with a Japanese pattern, the cup and saucer Barr, Flight & Barr, the coffee can Barr period.

5.5in (14cm) wide

£300-400 trio   **GORL**

A Flight, Barr & Barr Worcester plate, painted in coloured enamels with an exotic bird, the shaped pale blue ground with butterflies and insects, within a gilt gadrooned rim, impressed mark and printed mark in brown.

c1815   8.5in (21.5cm) diam

£280-320   **LFA**

A CLOSER LOOK AT A BARR, FLIGHT & BARR WORCESTER DESSERT PLATE

As a result of Worcester's good standing and reputation at the time, members of the aristocracy commissioned services from the firm. This piece bears the crest of John Prendergast-Smythe, First Viscount Gort.

High quality gold adorned the factory's wares from the end of the 18thC. Following a visit by the king in 1788, Worcester abandoned its blue and white output to focus on higher-end pieces.

The landscape scene is well executed. Worcester was known for its fine hand-painted decoration during the Barr, Flight & Barr period.

The piece is marked BFB for the Barr, Flight & Barr period of 1804-1813.

A Barr, Flight & Barr Worcester dessert plate, made for John Prendergast, First Viscount, depicting a landscape scene, probably by Thomas Rogers, of the Wye near Goodrich Castle, within a border of gilt arabesques and line rims, with the crest of Viscount Gort, including Prince of Wales plumes, fine condition.

c1810   9in (23cm) wide

£3,000-5,000   **SHF**

BRITISH PORCELAIN

A Flight, Barr & Barr Worcester shell-shaped dish, with gilt anthemion handle, painted in coloured enamels, impressed and printed marks in brown.

c1815   8in (20.5cm) wide

£500-800   **LFA**

A Flight Barr & Barr Worcester ceremonial oval tureen cover and liner, with gilt strawberry leaf finial, painted on a white ground with a continuous band of Billingsley-type pink roses within gilt line rims, enclosing a griffon, impressed "FBB" mark.

c1820   32in (12.5cm) wide

£3,000-5,000   **SHF**

A Flight, Barr & Barr Worcester vase, with seed-pearl border, impressed crowned initials, full painted mark in puce with London House address.

c1825   5.25in (13.5cm) high

£800-1,200   **GORL**

CHAMBERLAIN'S WORCESTER

A Chamberlain's Worcester meat plate, painted with a central spray of garden flowers, the pale blue border with panels of flowers.

22in (56cm) wide

£280-320   **GORL**

A late 18thC Chamberlain's Worcester plate, possibly by the Worcester artist George Davis, the centre painted with peafowl within a landscape, the blue and gilt oval panel-band border suspending polychrome fruit and leaves, hairline crack.

8.25in (21cm) diam

£200-300   **DN**

Part of a Chamberlain's Worcester part dinner service, in underglazed blue with polychrome and gilt flower decoration, brown printed mark, comprising soup tureen and cover and 33 other pieces.

£300-500 set   **L&T**

A Chamberlain's Worcester Imari patterned inkwell, the cylindrical shape pierced at the top with three quill holders about the central funnel, marks in red.

2.5in (6.5cm) diam

£120-180   **CHEF**

OTHER WORCESTER

A garniture of three Grainger Lee & Co. Worcester two-handled campana urns, the rich blue ground painted with flowers, on a square base, mark in red.

Largest 10in (25.5cm) high

£700-1,000   **JN**

A rare Chamberlain's Worcester shallow round pot pourri bowl and cover, with a 'Vase of Flowers' knop, the interior painted in coloured enamels with a view of Windsor Castle, within applied bands of seashells and seaweed, on a gilt vermicelli ground, script mark in black, chips to finial.

c1840   6.25in (16cm) diam

£600-900   **LFA**

A pair of Kerr & Binns Worcester ovoid vases, each painted in coloured enamels and raised on a square base, printed marks in red, faint crack.

8.5in (21.5cm) high

£500-700   **LFA**

A pair of Worcester twin-handled urns, on stands, each with flared neck and dolphin decorated scroll handles.

13.25in (33.5cm) high

£1,500-2,000   **L&T**

A pair of Nantgarw oval dishes, each painted with a central bouquet within four small scattered floral sprays and a gilt dentil rim, one impressed "Nantgarw C.W.", wear to gilding.

c1820   *11.5in (29.5cm) wide*

£1,200-1,800   **DN**

A Nantgarw teacup and saucer, decorated in shades of iron-red, green and gilt with scrolling foliage, saucer fritted to underside.

Nantgarw porcelain is fine and translucent. It was difficult to fire and as a result, teaware is especially scarce. Many pieces were sent to London to be decorated in the fashions of the time, but this piece was decorated locally.

c1820   *55in (14cm) wide*

£700-1,000   **DN**

A Nantgarw shaped oval dish, with a gilt shell handle and painted in blue with scattered floral sprays, impressed "Nantgarw C.W."

c1820   *8in (20.5cm) wide*

£250-350   **DN**

A New Hall cream jug, of tapered form with fluted lower section and conical foot, painted in the Chinese export style with pattern N173, small foot rim chip, slight fritting.

c1800   *5in (12.5cm) high*

£80-120   **DN**

A New Hall plate, brightly printed and painted with three sprays of flowers and leaves, moulded border with black and green bands, pattern number 1749.

New Hall was the first factory to assign pattern numbers to its designs, helping collectors to identify and date pieces.

c1815   *8.25in (21cm) diam*

£120-180   **LFA**

A Wedgwood porcelain pot-pourri vase and cover, painted in polychrome enamels, with a long-tailed tit, dartford warbler and a group of bathers, with gilt ring handles and faceted rims, marked "Wedgwood" in script and titles in black.

c1820   *3.5in (9cm) wide*

£1,000-1,500   **SHF**

One of a set of seven early 20thC Wedgwood fish plates, painted by A. Holland with the W2582 pattern of named freshwater fish swimming within powder blue and gilt rim bands, printed marks.

8.75in (22.5cm) diam

£400-600 set   **CHEF**

A 20thC Wedgwood porcelain part dinner service, each piece with rich gilt foliate decoration on a deep red ground, comprising of 18 dinner plates, 18 side plates, 18 bread and butter plates, 18 cups, 18 saucers and four small dishes, printed brown and green marks.

Dinner plate 11in (27.5cm) diam

£2,200-2,800   **FRE**

A mid-19thC Wedgwood glazed parian figure of a lady reclining, with a blue drape over her knee and an anchor in her left hand, impressed mark.

9.5in (24cm) high

£200-300   **CHEF**

A Samuel Alcock Parian model of Arthur Wellesley, first Duke of Wellington, the base with a wreath surmounted with a ducal coronet and moulded with monogram "WW", the underside printed "Published by Saml. Alcock & Co., June 18 1852, Alfred Crowquill Designavit. G. Abbott. Sculpit", hands repaired, crack and blisters.

11in (28cm) high

£200-300   DN

A Copeland Parian bust of Napoleon Bonaparte, on a socle base, after an original by William Theed (1804-91), the reverse impressed "Copeland", small chips and cracks.

c1865   *11in (28cm) high*

£500-800   DN

A Copeland Parian bust of Enid, modelled after the original by F.M. Miller, with gilt highlights, on a column plinth base, the reverse with printed and impressed marks.

c1860   *16.5in (41cm) high*

£600-900   DN

A Parian bust of Ned Hanlan, the professional rowing world champion, raised on a socle base.

c1880   *11.75in (30cm) high*

£1,500-2,000   RTC

COMMEMORATIVE CERAMICS

A circular footed punch bowl, the oak leaf and acorn painted border with a pair of opposing swags, inscribed with "Nelson 22 April", the interior painted with central panel depicting the "Armorials of Vice Admiral Horatio, Viscount Nelson of the Nile, K B".

The armorial bearings allude to incidents in Nelson's life and the honours accorded him. This illustration of Nelson's arms is accurate and complete, in the highest late-Hanoverian artistic style.

9in (23cm) diam

£1,500-2,000   L&T

A cylindrical tyg, the oak leaf and acorn painted border with a pair of opposing swags, inscribed with "Nelson 22 April", the front painted with a panel depicting the "Armorials of Vice Admiral Horatio, Viscount Nelson of the Nile, K B".

5.25in (13.5cm) high

£1,500-2,000   L&T

An early 19thC Masonic Sunderland lustre jug, with black printed decoration, the Masonic print inscribed "Dixon & Austin Sunderland Pottery", a view of the cast Ironbridge verso and a monogram "WM".

£500-800   SWO

A black basalt rectangular commemorative teapot and cover, with everted rim, serpent loop handle and a lion mask spout modelled with Britannia garlanding a bust of Wellington, the reverse inscribed "India, Portugal and Spain, Vittoria 21st June 1813", rim chip to cover.

c1815   *5.75in (14.5cm) high*

£300-500   LFA

An 1825 Reform commemorative jug, of ornate Rococo shape printed in mulberry with the figure of Britannia and flags titled "UNION" and "REFORM", with union sprays around and inside the neck titled "COMMERCE AND FREEDOM" and "UNITY AND LIBERTY", unmarked.

1825   *7in (18cm) high*

£200-300   DN

An unusual earthenware cylindrical mug, with angular loop handle, printed in underglaze blue with "The Immortal Shakespeare", "Shakspeare's Mulberry Tree" and a figure of fame, beneath a band of figures.

c1830   *5.75in (14.5cm) high*

£400-600   LFA

A rare pearlware lobed plate commemorating "Our Amiable Queen Adelaide", printed in purple with a portrait and titled beneath, the gadrooned border with sprays of flowers and leaves, printed lion and crown mark, small chip to underside of rim.

c1830   8.5in (21.5cm) diam

£400-600   LFA

A nursery plate commemorating the wedding of Victoria and Albert, of octagonal shape with a portrait of the couple printed in black and enamelled in red, blue and green, the daisy moulded rim lined with pink lustre, unmarked.

c1840   6in (15cm) wide

£250-350   DN

A Sunderland lustre jug commemorating the Crimea, of typical Dutch shape with pink lustre lining and highlights, printed in black and enamelled in colours, one side with a pseudo coat-of-arms titled "Crimea", the other with a print titled "The Flag that Braved a Thousand Years", the front with a verse "England, England, Glorious Name ... ", unmarked, minor chip to spout.

c1855   7in (18cm) high

£350-450   DN

A CLOSER LOOK AT A COMMEMORATIVE BEAKER

A Minton & Hollins paperweight commemorating the golden jubilee of Queen Victoria, covered with green glaze and moulded with a portrait of the Queen, with monogram and "JUBILEE 1887", detailed impressed mark with maker's name and address, "Rd.68207", minor edge chipping.

1887   5in (12cm) high

£100-150   DN

A Copeland souvenir Edward VII loving cup, with flaring rim and gilt handles, printed shield mark to base "Souvenir Edward VII. 1910, Subscribers copy, T Goode & Co, South Audley St, London".

    7in (18cm) high

£600-900   SWO

Commemorative wares have crossover interest as they appeal to porcelain aficionados as well as people with an interest in history. This increases the desirability and value of an item.

Edward VII's coronation was postponed due to his appendicitis. Although this piece is not dated, many commemorative items on the market are incorrectly dated June 24th 1902. Pieces bearing the correct date – August 9th – are far harder to find.

This piece sold at auction for a sum considerably higher than estimated. In a highly specialised field such as commemorative ceramics, prices can fluctuate wildly, particularly if two collectors are interested in the same rare piece.

There is little if any evidence of rubbing to the attractive gilt decoration on this beaker, enhancing the value.

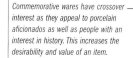

A Royal Doulton beaker commemorating the coronation of Edward VII, with an oval portrait and raised gilt foliage on a red ground.

1902   4in (10cm) high

£700-1,000   WW

FRENCH PORCELAIN

CHANTILLY

- The Chantilly factory was founded in 1725 by Louis-Henri of Bourbon, Prince of Condé. The factory started making soft-paste porcelain in the 1730s.
- Many of the early wares were decorated in the Kakiemon style or in designs copied from Chinese originals.
- Kakiemon style figures were a speciality before c1750.

- During the second half of the 18thC, pieces were decorated with scattered European flowers. Designs were typically painted in simple blue or coloured enamels following the 1753 edict limiting the use of gilded decoration to Vincennes.
- Pieces are marked with a hunting horn and sometimes with the word "Chantilly". The factory closed c1800.

A Chantilly cane handle, decorated in the Kakiemon style with figures and buildings.

c1740   3in (8cm) high

£700-1,000   **HFG**

A CLOSER LOOK AT A CHANTILLY BOX AND COVER

Before 1740, pieces had a yellowish body and an opaque tin glaze. After this time a transparent lead glaze was used.

The decoration on early Chantilly may have been inspired by pieces in the Prince of Condé's extensive Oriental ceramic collection.

The Kakiemon style became popular throughout Europe, but no other factory rivalled Chantilly for the quality of its imitation Kakiemon pieces.

A Chantilly magot figure, depicting a reclining Chinese figure, decorated with flowers in the Kakiemon style, gilt-bronze mounts.

c1740   12.5in (32cm) wide

£50,000-70,000   **GV**

A Chantilly oval box and cover, polychrome decorated in the Kakiemon style.

c1745   2.5in (6.5cm) wide

£1,000-1,500   **PIA**

A Chantilly bowl, decorated with flowers and insects in the Kakiemon style, with red hunting horn mark.

c1740

£1,500-2,000   **GV**

A Chantilly plate, polychrome decorated with floral bouquets, hunting horn mark.

c1760   9.5in (24cm) diam

£250-350   **HFG**

An 18thC Chantilly sucrier, cover and stand, decorated with naturalistic polychrome flowers and insects, hunting horn mark.

9in (23cm) wide

£2,000-2,500   **HFG**

An 18thC Chantilly plate, decorated with flowering sprigs, hunting horn mark.

9.5in (24cm) diam

£100-200   **HFG**

An 18thC Chantilly cream pot and cover, decorated with flowering sprigs, hunting horn mark.

3in (8cm) high

£200-300   **HFG**

A Chantilly square fruit dish, with 'à la brindille' decoration of flowering sprigs in monochrome blue.

c1770   8.75in (22cm) wide

£150-250   **GV**

A late 19thC set of four Samson figures of the gods, after Meissen, depicting 'Diana', 'Vulcan', 'Jupiter' and 'Apollo', marks in blue.

6in (15cm) high

£200-300   **CHEF**

A CLOSER LOOK AT A PAIR OF SAMSON 'MEISSEN' FIGURES

Edmé Samson (1810-1891) specialised in reproductions and copies of other popular ceramic manufacturers, such as Meissen, Worcester, Bow, Derby and Chelsea. This pair is modelled on a Meissen original. They were also copied by Derby in the 18thC.

Distinctions between an original and a Samson piece are evident. A grayish hard paste was used to copy creamy soft paste originals and the reproductions tended to be less sharply modelled.

Johann Joachim Kändler, on whose work this pair is based, was the most famous Meissen modeller. He produced a wide range of lively and flamboyant figures including a tailor - thought to be tailor to Count Bruhl, the director of the factory, who had many clothes - and his wife.

Despite being copies, Samson pieces are sought after today because they are highly decorative and were popular at the time.

A late 19thC Samson figure modelled as a lady playing a hurdy-gurdy, in a chinoiserie style.

11.5in (29cm) high

£150-200   **CHEF**

A pair of 19thC Samson goat groups, in the Meissen style, the subjects based upon the 'Tailor and Tailor's Wife' models by Kändler and Eberlein, on oval bases with mock Derby marks.

7in (18cm) high

£700-800   **GORL**

A late 19thC Samson shaped box and hinged cover, painted with a Watteauesque vignette and sprays of flowers, blue cross mark, glued mount.

2.5in (9cm) wide

£70-100   **DN**

A late 19thC Samson pill box and hinged cover modelled as a mouse, the cover painted with a cat chasing a mouse.

2.5in (6cm) wide

£50-80   **DN**

SÈVRES

One of a pair of Sèvres plates, painted with polychrome flower sprays within blue leaf scroll borders, marked with interlaced "L"s enclosing a "G".

c1760   *10.25in (25.5cm) wide*

£500-700 pair   **WW**

A late 18thC Sèvres dessert dish moulded as a flowerhead, painted with colourful flower sprays, marked with interlaced "L"s enclosing "M".

8.5in (21cm) wide

£400-600   **WW**

One of a set of twelve Sèvres porcelain portrait plates, retailed by Davis Collamore & Co., New York, each plate painted with portraits of 'Roi de Rome', several Bonaparte ladies and other French dignitaries, within apple green borders, enhanced with gilt lattice and jewelled decoration, printed marks "Chateau Des Tuileries" and "Sevres 1844", signed "Morin".

9.5in (24cm) diam

£6,000-9,000 set   **FRE**

A pair of 19thC Sèvres porcelain plates, painted with swags of summer flowers within gilt borders.

8.35in (21cm) diam

£200-300   **ROS**

FRENCH PORCELAIN

A Sèvres salad bowl, of lobed form, painted inside and out with colourful sprays of flowers, the rim and foot rim gilded, marked with interlaced "L"s enclosing a "G" for 1759.

9.75in (24.5cm) diam

£700-1,000   **WW**

A Sèvres oval monteith, with scrolled handles and a wavy rim, decorated with floral garlands and gilt, the handles detailed in mauve, marked with interlaced "L"s and an "I" for 1761.

11.75in (29.5cm) wide

£300-500   **WW**

A pair of Sèvres quatrefoil sauce tureens and covers, on fixed stands, painted by Jean-Jacques Pierre le Jeune, with bouquets of flowers within blue and gilt line rims, marked with blue interlaced "L"s, mark for 1767 and painter's mark.

9.25in (23.5cm) wide

£1,500-2,000   **CHEF**

One of a pair of 19thC Sèvres cachepots, finely painted with scenes of romantic dalliance within gilt reserves against a bleu celeste background.

6in (15cm) high

£1,200-1,800 pair   **GORL**

One of a pair of 19thC Sèvres cachepots, painted with figures and woodland panels in gilt reserves against a bleu celeste background, mock painted Sèvres marks, some restoration to one pot.

5in (19cm) high

£700-1,000 pair   **GORL**

A rare Sèvres biscuit three-part table ornament, in the form of three putti, on fluted plinth, incised monogram "BZ".

Provenance*: Aske Hall, Yorkshire.*

c1770   *10.5in (26.5cm) high*

£1,500-2,000   **LFA**

A large late 19th to early 20thC Sèvres porcelain and gilt bronze candelabra, with two oval panels, one depicting cherubs, the other an artist, the ornate rococo scroll openwork top with eight candelabra arms.

42in (105cm) high

£4,000-6,000   **FRE**

VINCENNES

- The Vincennes porcelain factory was established in 1738 by Robert and Gilles Dubois, former Chantilly workers, with the help of Orry de Fulvy, an official at the treasury.
- In 1745 Louis XV granted the company exclusive rights to produce porcelain for the next twenty years.
- Early pieces were decorated in a soft palette with small flower sprays, gilt trellis and scrollwork.
- More exclusive early output included porcelain flower models and figures, such as nymphs, produced on a limited scale.
- The painter Jean-Jacques Bachelier became artistic director in 1752 and introduced a wide range of Rococo designs.
- Following a period of financial difficulties, Vincennes was boosted by a 1753 Royal edict restricting the use of gilding and other techniques to the factory.
- In 1756, the company moved to Sèvres. It was at this time that date letters were added to the interlaced "L"s mark.

A Vincennes model of an oval jardinière with flowers, the front decorated with a polychrome scene after 'Le Feu', an engraving by Boucher, with two children playing in a landscape, the back is decorated wih a river scene, interlaced "LL" with date letter "D" for 1756-57, painter's mark for Vieillard.

11.5in (29cm) wide

£5,000-7,000   **PIA**

An 18thC Vincennes pot-pourri, decorated in relief with flowers and branches, interlaced "LL" mark.

c1750   *5.5in (14cm) high*

£800-1,200   **GV**

A Vincennes cup and saucer, polychrome decorated with flowers and garlands on a bleu celeste ground, interlaced "LL" and painter's mark for Pierre Rosset.

1754   *3.75in (9.5cm) diam*

£2,000-3,000   **GV**

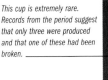

A pair of Vincennes plates, decorated with a cherub and with relief decoration to rims.

c1750

9in (23cm) wide

£1,200-1,800   **WW**

A CLOSER LOOK AT A VINCENNES CUP & COVER

This cup is extremely rare. Records from the period suggest that only three were produced and that one of these had been broken.

The flower decoration within the gilt panels is exquisitely crafted. Despite being 250 years old, it is in perfect condition.

The cup is likely to be one of two originally purchased in 1755 by Mercier Aulagnier, a dealer who sourced porcelain for the King. He would only have dealt with the finest pieces.

Dating from the early period of Vincennes-Sèvres, this cup is highly desirable.

A Vincennes cup and cover, of cylindrical form with a handle, the body decorated with colourful flowering vines, strawberry plants and currant bush branches in relief, within petal-shaped panels with gilded rims, the cover with a large mound of flowers and foliage, the cover with applied flowers, date letter "C" and interlaced "L"s.

1755

£120,000-150,000   **PIA**

OTHER FRENCH FACTORIES

An inkwell by J.L. Encrier Bascule, Paris, painted with flowers and rotating on brass arms, the open end resting against the gallery of the stand to prevent spillage.

4in (10cm) high

£80-120   **CHEF**

An early 19thC Paris porcelain inkwell, the gilt two-handled vase receiver flanked by a cherub climbing out of a shell on a matt blue rectangular base, gilt with foliage.

4.75in (12cm) wide

£150-200   **CHEF**

A Paris bisque candlestick, in the form of a kneeling Indian figure holding aloft a sconce, decorated in coloured enamels and gilt highlights, on a lobed blue ground, with base.

c1850   10.25in (26cm) high

£200-300   **LFA**

A rare Saint-Cloud porcelain box, modelled with a hunter and his dog reclining, painted in soft coloured enamels.

c1740   2.75in (7cm) wide

£700-1,000   **WW**

A pair of 19thC porcelain urns and covers, in the Sèvres style, the ormulu-mounted panels of lovers and flowers reserved against a pink background.

12in (30.5cm) high

£700-1,000   **GORL**

GERMAN PORCELAIN

BERLIN

- The Royal Porcelain Factory in Berlin (est. 1752) is highly regarded for its late 18thC and early 19thC Neo-classical wares.
- During the early 19thC, the company specialised in producing fine gilt wares. Dinner wares and vases were meticulously painted with scenes framed with an opulent gilt border.
- Topographical views of well-known buildings, Classical scenes and portraits were popular subjects.
- Berlin successfully adapted to the expanding middle class market by producing ornate display wares, particularly 'cabinet cups'.
- Vases, usually based on urns and kraters, and decorated with Classical motifs, formed a major part of the output from c1830.
- From c1840 the factory began to produce porcelain plaques enclosed in gilt frames. Blanks would be sent to decorators who would paint copies of Old Masters or sentimental subjects.
- Pieces are marked "KPM" (Königliche Porzellan-Manufaktur).
- The Berlin factory is still in operation today.

A large Berlin plaque, painted with the 'Penitent Magdalene', after Correggio, draped in blue velvet, lying in a wooded grotto reading a book, impressed sceptre and "KPM" marks.

c1860   22.25in (55.5cm) wide

£6,000-8,000   **FRE**

A large Berlin rectangular plaque, painted with a young girl sitting beside a river with a classical building in the distance, impressed "KPM" and sceptre marks, incised "13 1/4 - 11 1/4".

c1870   13.5in (34cm) wide

£6,000-8,000   **WW**

A good Berlin porcelain plaque, painted with a gypsy girl standing beside a tree with a tambourine at her feet, impressed "KPM" and sceptre mark.

c1880   13in (32.5cm) high

£4,000-6,000   **FRE**

A Berlin porcelain plaque, painted with a Pre-Raphaelite beauty wearing a Grecian gown, in a rose draped interior with mosaic floor, with an ornate carved gilt-wood rococo scroll frame, impressed "KPM" and sceptre mark.

c1880   13in (32.5cm) high

£4,000-6,000   **FRE**

A CLOSER LOOK AT A KPM PORCELAIN PLAQUE

Berlin was known for treating porcelain vases and plates as a medium for painted images. Plaques allowed further experimentation with painting.

Many plaques were copied from well-known paintings. This is after the work of the French religious artist Charles Landelle (1821-1908).

Berlin plaques had elaborately scrolling gilt frames. This intricate frame adds to the value.

Unmarked plaques can be worth up to 50 per cent less.

A good Berlin porcelain plaque, depicting 'Ruth' after Landelle, holding a wheatsheaf under one arm, in an ornate carved gilt wood Rococo scroll frame, impressed "KPM" and sceptre mark.

c1880   13in (32.5cm) high

£4,000-6,000   **FRE**

A good Berlin porcelain plaque, painted with young gypsy girl leaning against a brick wall and holding a lute, impressed "KPM" and sceptre mark.

c1880   13in (32.5cm) high

£4,500-5,500   **FRE**

A late 19thC Berlin porcelain plaque, depicting Madonna reading, framed, impressed "KPM" and sceptre mark.

17.5in (44cm) high

£2,000-4,000   **FRE**

A Berlin porcelain plaque, painted with 'Judith', after a painting by August Riedel, Rome, framed, signed, sceptre mark.

c1840   11.25in (28.5cm) high

£1,500-2,000   LPZ

A Berlin porcelain plaque, painted with a young woman wearing a black dress, framed, unsigned, stamped eagle and "P6".

c1840   6in (15.5cm) high

£500-1,000   LPZ

A 19thC Berlin painted porcelain plaque, in a carved and punched walnut frame, marked.

8.75in (22cm) high

£600-900   CHEF

A Berlin porcelain plaque, depicting 'Princess Louise' after G. Richter, signed indistinctly, impressed "KPM" and sceptre mark, inscribed "Königin Louise Richter".

c1880   16in (40cm) high

£8,000-12,000   FRE

A late 19thC Berlin porcelain plaque of 'Ruth', after Bouguereau, the figure holding a wheatsheaf, wearing a white head scarf and grey flowing dress, framed, impressed "KPM" and sceptre mark.

10.75in (27cm) high

£3,000-5,000   FRE

A late 19thC Berlin porcelain plaque, after 'Female Bust with a Head Scarf' by Hans Holbein, framed, impressed "KPM" and sceptre mark.

21.5in (54cm) high

£4,000-6,000   FRE

A late 19thC Berlin porcelain plaque, after 'Madonna and Child' by Raphael, signed by E. Dietrich, impressed "KPM" and sceptre mark.

9.75in (24cm) high

£1,500-2,500   FRE

A late 19thC Berlin porcelain plaque, depicting a saint holding an infant, framed, signed "F d Lapi, Dresden", impressed "KPM" and sceptre mark.

21in (52.5cm) high

£2,000-4,000   FRE

A late 19thC Berlin painted porcelain plaque, framed, "KPM" mark.

plaque 9in (23cm) high

£1,500-2,000   S&K

A late 19thC Berlin painted porcelain plaque, in a gilded wooden frame.

23in (59cm) high

£500-800   WW

A late 19thC Berlin painted porcelain plaque, in a gilded stucco frame, signed, marked, the back signed in pencil in English.

19in (48.5cm) wide

£3,000-5,000   BMN

A Berlin porcelain plaque, painted with views of Dessau, impressed marks and sceptre mark, dated, signed, in a new gilded stucco frame.

1908   5.5in (14cm) high

£800-1,200   BMN

41

A pair of Berlin porcelain 'Antique glatt' plates, the border with two decorative bands, gilded rim, sceptre mark and numbered.

c1785   9.75in (24.5cm) diam
£400-600   LPZ

A Berlin plate, with an autumnal vine border on a brown ground, gilded rim, sceptre mark, red painter mark, numbered.

c1800   9.5in (24cm) diam
£1,800-2,200   LPZ

A Berlin plate, depicting allegorical romantic scenes, with a gilded rim on a dark green ground, sceptre mark, red painter mark.

c1800   12.5in (31.5cm) diam
£2,800-3,200   LPZ

A pair of Berlin plates, painted with still life scenes of fruit, blossoms, and a wine glass and bottle, floral gilded border, blue sceptre mark, restored.

c1820
£4,000-6,000   BMN

A Berlin porcelain cup, with a view of a town, on four paw feet, sceptre mark.

c1825   5.25in (13cm) high
£300-500   BMN

A Berlin porcelain cup and saucer, with a blue oval portrait medallion in relief and gilt edging, eagle mark.

c1830
£200-300   BMN

A Berlin porcelain cup and saucer, with a blue oval portrait medallion in relief and gilt edging, eagle mark and sceptre mark.

c1830
£300-400   BMN

A Berlin cup and saucer, with floral and leaf decoration and gilding, the cup with a snake handle and three paw feet, the saucer with "den 20sten März 1829" in gold, blue sceptre mark, red painter mark.

£800-1,200   BMN

A Berlin gilded cup and saucer, the cup with a banner, sceptre mark.

c1830
£80-120   BMN

A Berlin cup and saucer, painted with vine tendrils on a green ground, gilding, blue sceptre mark.

c1840
£50-70   BMN

A Berlin cup and saucer, polychrome painted with flowers and insects and with a gilded mosaic border, the cup with branch handle, blue sceptre and penny mark.

c1860
£100-150   BMN

A Berlin lidded vase, with floral relief decoration, polychrome painted and gilded scenes by Watteau, the cover with rose finial, blue sceptre mark, restored.

c1770   11.75in (30cm) high

£800-1,200   **BMN**

A Berlin porcelain vase, with rich gold borders, the two octagonal gold reserves with birds in a landscape, blue underglazed sceptre mark with brown eagle and "KPM".

c1830   12.5in (31cm) high

£4,000-6,000   **MTZ**

A Berlin Biedermeier lidded jug, with floral and insects decoration, of ovoid shape with a raised handle and cambered mouth, blue sceptre mark and red "KPM" mark.

c1835

£200-300   **BMN**

A late 19thC Berlin Easter egg, with a Rococo reserve depicting a young couple in the woods, gilt floral decoration on a cobalt-blue ground, metal mounts.

3.75in (9.5cm) high

£1,200-1,800   **BMN**

A Berlin Art Nouveau porcelain vase and cover, with rich applied enamel and gilt decoration, the reserves depicting Sanssouci castle, putti handles, underglazed sceptre mark with orb and "KPM", Jubilee mark and letter mark for year.

1913   27.25in (68cm) high

£7,000-10,000   **MTZ**

A Berlin French-style porcelain vase, with griffin handles, engraved and polished gilt decoration and rectangular gold reserves to both sides with fine polychrome painted decoration, underglaze sceptre and penny mark.

This vase was presented to the court doctor and pediatrician to the young William II by his father William I.

c1860   27.25in (69cm) high

£18,000-20,000   **MTZ**

A Berlin Rococo lidded porcelain vase, with a silver monogram by Auguste Victoria, gilded relief decoration and two coat-of-arms cartouches under a crown, one with the Prussian eagle, the other with the coat-of-arms of Schleswig-Holstein-Sonderburg-Augustenburg, sceptre mark, red stamp, impressed marks, one handle slightly chipped.

c1880   22.75in (57cm) high

£6,000-9,000   **LPZ**

A Berlin porcelain figure of a shepherd, representing 'Air' from the series of 'The Four Elements' by Friedrich Elias Meyer, sceptre and orb mark, painter mark.

c1870   8.5in (21cm) high

£250-350   **BMN**

A Berlin Pierrot, with a guitar, glazed in white and painted in pink and brown, signed "WACKERLE", model number "9547", blue sceptre mark.

c1910   15.25in (38cm) high

£1,500-2,000   **QU**

GERMAN PORCELAIN

A Berlin porcelain teapot, in the Puce Caneill style.

c1780

£800-1,200 JF

A Berlin lidded soup tureen, with dish, gilded rims, sceptre mark, impressed marks, crack to dish.

c1780 8in (20cm) high

£1,800-2,200 LPZ

A Berlin chocolatière, with crimson flower decoration and a wooden handle, sceptre mark.

c1790 6.25in (15.5cm) high

£1,800-2,200 LPZ

A large Berlin tureen, with gilded bronze mounts, crowned with a putto, blue sceptre mark, restored.

c1830 19.5in (48.5cm) high

£3,000-4,000 BMN

A Berlin footed dish, with polychrome painted decoration of flowers and figures, blue sceptre mark, brown eagle mark, restored.

c1835 13.25in (33cm) diam

£2,800-3,200 BMN

A Berlin golden dish with handle, polychrome painted decoration of flowers and leaves, gilded brass mounting with relief floral decoration, brown eagle mark, blue sceptre mark.

c1830 10.25in (25.5cm) diam

£1,200-1,800 BMN

A rare Berlin tea caddy, with matted and polished gold decoration on a green ground, blue sceptre mark, red orb mark.

c1835 6.5in (16cm) high

£500-800 BMN

A Berlin easter egg flacon, decorated with violets and leaves, with a metal stopper, unmarked, gold slightly rubbed.

c1860 3.5in (8.5cm) high

£400-600 LPZ

A Berlin pastry dish, the brown ground with central floral decoration and a vine and blossom border, gilded, blue penny mark, blue sceptre mark.

c1860 9.75in (24.5cm) wide

£40-60 BMN

A Berlin Neo-Classical travel set, consisting of six cylindrical cups, one depicting the birth of Venus, six saucers, six Biedermeier cut-glass beakers, knifes and forks, six silver spoons, an oval silver teapot, a conical silver cocoa pot, a silver pear-shaped mocha pot, a casserole and a dark blue sugar bowl with a leaf border and gilded decoration, various marks, in a red leather case with bronze side handles and front lock, lined with saffian leather.

A Louis XVI Berlin oil lamp, designed by Johann Carl Friedrich Riese, some biscuit porcelain, gilded, sceptre mark, orb mark, gold painter mark.

c1900 11.25in (28cm) high

£800-1,200 BMN

c1800

£8,000-12,000

29in (72.5cm) wide

LPZ

A Dresden rectangular box, with polychrome flower decoration and a gilt edge, blue mark.

3.5in (9cm) wide

£100-150   **BMN**

A late 19thC Dresden flower-encrusted oval wall mirror, mounted with putti and musical motifs, blue cross mark, some small chips and repairs.

17.75in (45cm) high

£500-800   **DN**

A Dresden-style miniature salon suite, decorated with painted floral sprays in relief, the table with an impressed crossed swords mark and initials "DKE".

Chair 5in (12.5cm) high

£300-350   **H&L**

A Dresden porcelain figure of the Pied Piper of Hamlin, modelled dancing and playing his pipe.

8in (20cm) high

£80-120   **DN**

FRANKENTHAL

A Frankenthal pug bowl, with naturalistic painting and engraved gilded brass mounting with hinge and cambered thumb rest, blue crowned "CT" mark.

c1770   2.5in (6.5cm) high

£800-1,200   **BMN**

A Frankenthal porcelain figure of a seated pug, on a raised base, naturalistic design and decoration, impressed "PH", incised mark.

c1760   3.5in (8.8cm) high

£1,500-2,000   **MTZ**

A mid-18thC Frankenthal figure of a lady playing a mandolin, blue lion rampant mark and impressed marks.

4in (10cm) high

£400-600   **WW**

A Frankenthal figure of a country woman, model by Johann Wilhelm Lanz, standing on a gilded rocaille socle, holding a wheatsheaf with both arms and wearing a hat, a white blouse and a red and green striped skirt, blue "CT" mark, the hat restored.

c1760   6in (15cm) high

£1,000-1,500   **LPZ**

A Frankenthal porcelain tea caddy, with rounded shoulders and painted birds, blue lion mark and interlaced "JAH", incised mark with three dots.

c1760

£500-800   **MTZ**

A Frankenthal porcelain coffee-pot, on three scrolled feet, the domed lid with a pear knop, gilt-scroll borders, with painted scenes, blue underglaze lion mark, four dots in a square, letter "I".

This piece is part of a service originally made for the Court of Kurpfalz.

c1760   10in (25cm) high

£24,000-26,000   **MTZ**

A large Frankenthal plate, with 'Altozier' relief decoration, gilding, Indianische Blumen and rocks, blue lion mark.

c1760   13in (32.5cm) diam

£700-1,000   **BMN**

A Frankenthal plate, painted with flowers, the gold slightly rubbed, blue lion mark.

c1760   8.5in (21cm) diam

£120-180   **BMN**

GERMAN PORCELAIN

A Fürstenberg bullet-shaped teapot and cover, painted with coloured enamels and gilt, script "F" mark, chips.

c1770

£500-800   DN

A pair of Fürstenberg cups and saucers, decorated with floral paintings and scattered flowers, gilding, blue "F" mark.

c1800

£150-200   BMN

A Louis XVI Fürstenberg lidded vase, gilded and decorated with Camaieu-Sepia paintings of parkscapes, the lid partly restored, blue mark "A.B."

c1785   16.75in (42cm) high

£800-1,200   BMN

An early 19thC Fürstenberg 'Berliner Stummel' shape pipe bowl, with polychrome painted scene in a gold reserve, blue F-mark to inside.

4.5in (11cm) long

£300-500   BMN

A Fürstenberg porcelain oval snuff box, with gilt-metal mounts, the exterior with scroll and floral reliefs painted in purple, the inside lid and reserves painted with putti in landscape, unmarked.

c1770   3.25in (8cm) wide

£2,000-3,000   MTZ

An early 19thC Fürstenberg group of the drunken Silenus on a barrel, the putto with a flask at his feet, the barrel painted with panels of harbour scenes in the Meissen style, on a scroll-moulded base, partially coloured and with gilt, script "F" mark, some damage and restoration.

9.75in (25cm) high

£1,500-2,000   DN

HÖCHST

- In 1746, the elector of Mainz granted a privilege to Adam Friedrich von Löwenfinck (1746-58), a porcelain decorator who had once worked at Meissen, to establish a faience factory in Höchst. The factory produced porcelain from 1750.
- The factory became known for its figures, modelled by talented craftsmen including Simon Feilner (1726–98), who produced a range inspired by the Commedia dell'Arte, and Johann Peter Melchior (1742-1825), who created finely detailed figures on mound bases.
- Wares were painted with landscapes and figures, especially rustic scenes, or scattered flowers.
- Modelled details, such as scrollwork spouts, small animals details and wishbone handles, decorated many of the factory's wares, including trembleuse cups and saucers.
- From c1750, a blue wheel mark was used.
- The firm suffered from financial difficulties and political upheavals in the region, finally closing in 1796. The moulds were sold to the Damm Pottery (est. 1827) in Aschaffenburg and original Höchst pieces were reproduced in faience from c1830. These reproductions are also widely collected today.
- In 1946, the Höchst porcelain factory reopened at its original location in Höchst.

A Höchst porcelain group of three putti.

c1770   6.5in (16.5cm) high

£2,800-3,200   BMN

A Höchst porcelain jug, decorated with a landscape of buildings and a figure, restored, blue wheel mark.

c1770   5.5in (14cm) high

£800-1,200   BMN

A Höchst cup and saucer, decorated with rural scenes, the rims gilded, blue wheel mark.

c1770

£1,200-1,800   LPZ

A Höchst candlestick, ornately modelled as a couple kissing, minor restorations.

c1755   10.5in (26cm) high

£12,000-18,000   LPZ

A pair of Höchst porcelain figures of gardeners, each on a base with embossed foliage and a watering can, holding a basket filled with radishes, polychrome decoration, unmarked, iron-red painter's monogram.

c1750   7.8in (19.5cm) high

£3,000-5,000   **MTZ**

A Höchst porcelain figure of Poseidon, draped in cloth and holding a trident, a dolphin at his feet, on an oval raised base with embossed flowers, polychrome and gold decoration, reddish-brown wheel mark and incised mark.

c1755   13.5in (33.5cm) high

£3,000-5,000   **MTZ**

A Höchst porcelain figure of a Chinese man smoking a pipe, seated under a tree, on a scroll base with purple and gold decoration, overall polychrome decoration, iron-red wheel mark.

c1755   9in (22.5cm) high

£2,000-3,000   **MTZ**

A Höchst porcelain figure of an Oriental snake charmer, on an octagonal plinth, dressed in a kimono and playing a horn, polychrome decoration, blue wheel mark.

c1760   7.5in (18.5cm) high

£1,200-1,800   **MTZ**

A Höchst 'The Dance Master' porcelain group, standing on an oval scroll base, with purple and gold decorations, iron-red wheel mark.

c1760   6.75in (17cm) high

£3,000-5,000   **MTZ**

A Höchst porcelain figure of a girl holding a bird, with spice dishes either side, elongated naturalistic base, blue Kurhut mark on base, incised mark.

c1765   5.5in (14cm) high

£800-1,200   **MTZ**

A CLOSER LOOK AT A HÖCHST PORCELAIN GROUP

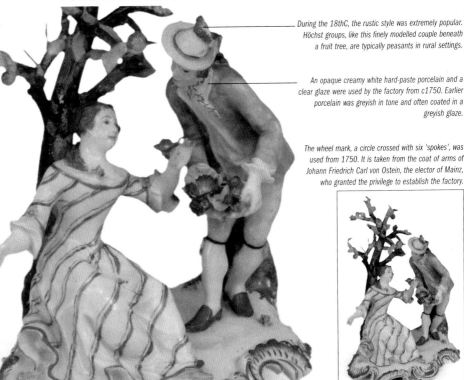

During the 18thC, the rustic style was extremely popular. Höchst groups, like this finely modelled couple beneath a fruit tree, are typically peasants in rural settings.

An opaque creamy white hard-paste porcelain and a clear glaze were used by the factory from c1750. Earlier porcelain was greyish in tone and often coated in a greyish glaze.

The wheel mark, a circle crossed with six 'spokes', was used from 1750. It is taken from the coat of arms of Johann Friedrich Carl von Ostein, the elector of Mainz, who granted the privilege to establish the factory.

A Höchst 'The Gallant Gardener' porcelain group, on an oval rocaille base with purple and gold decoration, the lady with a flower basket, iron-red wheel mark, incised mark.

c1755   7.5in (19cm) high

£3,000-5,000   **MTZ**

GERMAN PORCELAIN

A Höchst porcelain solitaire dish, with a scalloped rim and a gold and chequered border, painted with flower sprays, insects and a purple river landscape, impressed wheel mark.

c1765   13.6in (34cm) wide
£1,000-1,500   **MTZ**

A Höchst porcelain reticulated bowl, with two raised rope handles, painted in the centre with fruit, unmarked, incision.

c1770   10in (25cm) wide
£280-320   **MTZ**

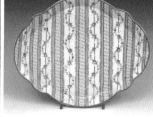

A Höchst porcelain 'English Façon' solitaire tray, painted in the 'wallpaper' pattern, the raised border with a gilt rim, blue wheel mark.

c1770   10in (25.2cm) wide
£600-900   **MTZ**

A Höchst porcelain solitaire tray, painted with a river landscape surrounded by insects, the quatrelobe shape with a raised rim, gilding, blue wheel mark, impressed mark.

c1770   11in (27cm) wide
£180-220   **MTZ**

A Höchst porcelain serving dish, with raised border and lowered centre, painted purple with merchant scene surrounded by butterflies, insects and flower trails, impressed wheel mark.

c1770   6.5in (16cm) wide
£500-800   **MTZ**

A Höchst porcelain serving dish, with raised border and lowered centre, painted purple with merchant scene and flower sprays impressed wheel mark.

c1770   6.5in (16cm) wide
£300-500   **MTZ**

A Höchst oval porcelain plate, divided in twelve sections, profiled gilded rim, with colourful scene in the centre, blue wheel mark.

c1775   11.5in (28.5cm) wide
£600-900   **MTZ**

A Höchst porcelain plate, with a central reserve decorated with garlands, the raised borders with gilt and 'Antique Blue Mosaic' decoration, inscribed iron-red "Genies", blue wheel mark.

c1780   10in (25cm) diam
£1,800-2,200   **MTZ**

A Höchst porcelain plate, with a garland-framed "L'Education d'Achille" reserve in iron red, the raised borders with gilt and the 'Antique Blue Mosaic' pattern, blue wheel mark.

c1780   10in (25cm) diam
£2,000-3,000   **MTZ**

A mid-18thC Höchst teapot and cover, with a clip handle and moulded spout, painted with flower sprays, unmarked.

6in (15cm) high
£550-650   **WW**

A pair of Höchst porcelain spice dishes, the figures on rectangular bases with round and quatrelobe dishes, blue wheel mark.

c1765   5.25in (13cm) high
£1,200-1,800   **MTZ**

A pair of Höchst porcelain potpourri vases, the rocaille cartouches with painted architectural and figural scenes, the lids with flower finials, ribbed and reticulated apertures, iron-red wheel mark, impressed letter 'IH'.

c1755   5.12in (12.8cm) high
£1,000-1,500   **MTZ**

A Höchst porcelain birds nest ozier-moulded box, with a pair of naturalistic goldfinches and a grassy cover, unmarked.

c1760   4.5in (11.5cm) high
£1,000-1,500   **MTZ**

A Höchst porcelain group of cherubs, on an oval grass base, an eagle with spread wings in their midst, blue wheel mark.

c1765   5.25in (13cm) high
£1,000-1,500   **MTZ**

A Meissen tea cup and saucer, painted with rural vignettes of cowherds and cows within ozier-moulded borders, blue crossed swords marks.

c1760

£300-500   **DN**

A late 19thC Meissen flower-encrusted cabinet cup and saucer, painted with scattered floral sprigs, blue crossed swords marks.

£300-500   **DN**

A late 19thC Meissen flower-encrusted cabinet cup and saucer, typically painted with flowers and insects within gilt-lined borders, cup and saucer with peg feet, blue crossed swords mark, minor chips.

4.5in (11.5cm) wide

£300-500   **DN**

A Meissen blue ground saucer, painted with a quatrefoil panel of a rural scene, within an elaborate gilt diaper panel cartouche surmounted with shells, within a gilt border, blue crossed swords mark, rubbed.

c1740   5in (12.5cm) wide

£300-500   **DN**

A Meissen Kakiemon plate, painted with the 'Lowe' pattern, within a 'Sulkowski' ozier border with insects and sprays of Indianische Blumen, blue crossed swords and dot mark, rivetted repair to rim.

c1740   9in (23cm) diam

£200-300   **DN**

A mid-18thC Meissen quatrefoil ozier-moulded tureen stand, painted with scattered Deutsche Blumen, gilt-line rims, blue crossed swords mark and dot mark, rubbing to gilt.

11in (28cm) wide

£250-300   **DN**

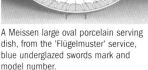

A Meissen large oval porcelain serving dish, from the 'Flügelmuster' service, blue underglazed swords mark and model number.

c1900   19.12in (47.8cm) wide

£300-500   **MTZ**

An important Meissen porcelain coffee and tea service, comprising of 25 pieces in the original wooden case, with coffee pot, milk jug, teapot, waste bowl, spoon cup, sucrier, twelve teacups, six coffee cups, 18 saucers, all with blue and coral red scrolling decoration and a central crested coat-of-arms, blue underglazed swords mark and "8".

c1740

£50,000-55,000   **MTZ**

A Meissen porcelain bowl and cover, with a button knop, with gilt and coral-framed cartouches of trading and equestrian scenes, gold to rims, blue swords mark, number in gold.

c1735   4.28in (10.7cm) diam

£2,000-3,000   **MTZ**

A Marcolini Meissen porcelain tureen, with moulded ram-head handles, painted panels and gold staffage, the cover with berry knop, blue underglazed swords mark with a star, painter's mark.

c1775   10.5in (26cm) wide

£1,000-1,500   **MTZ**

A Meissen porcelain tureen and cover with stand, with a baluster-shaped body and two weaved loop handles, heavily embossed with flower trails and painted with birds and insects, gold rims, blue underglazed swords mark.

c1745

£2,000-3,000   **MTZ**

A Marcolini Meissen porcelain tureen and stand, with a baluster-shaped body and a pine-cone knop, painted in rose and coral-red with colourful reserves, gilt-scroll borders, blue underglazed swords mark with star.

c1775

£2,800-3,200 MTZ

An Augustus Rex two-handled bowl, cover and stand, painted with panels of birds and butterflies, "A.R." mark in blue.

9.5in (24cm) wide

£800-1,200 JN

A Meissen sucrier and cover, with flower knop, decorated in coloured enamels with figures and panels of flowers, gilt scroll borders, cancelled mark in blue.

4.25in (10.5cm) high

£250-300 LFA

A 19thC Meissen sugar bowl and cover, with a matching milk jug, the bowl painted with a view of Bastei, the jug with a view of Wesenstein and further panels of colourful flowers and rich, gilt scrollwork, crossed swords mark and titled to bases.

4.5in (11.5cm) wide

£1,200-1,800 WW

A 19thC Meissen porcelain breakfast set, comprising an oval tray, teapot, milk jug, sucrier and a pair of cups and saucers, all with quatrefoil gold reserves painted with scenes and figures on a yellow ground, blue underglazed swords mark.

£1,500-2,000 MTZ

An early Meissen teapot, in white Böttger porcelain, of baluster shape with a domed lid and pointed finial, the slim curved spout with gilt and a mask, gilt-crested oval reserves of painted chinoiserie scenes in iron-red and purple.

c1725   5.5in (14cm) high

£5,000-8,000 MTZ

A Meissen coffee pot, in white Böttger porcelain, with a domed lid and pine-cone knop, decorated with quatrelobe reserves of landscape scenes in gilt-edged cartouches, gold cipher, blue underglazed swords mark, purple triangle and cross.

c1730   8in (20cm) high

£6,000-9,000 MTZ

A Meissen porcelain coffee pot, decorated with gilt-edged reserves of painted figural scenes and rich Böttger lustre, blue underglazed swords mark, gold cipher, turner's mark.

c1730   7.75in (19.5cm) high

£3,000-5,000 MTZ

A Meissen porcelain coffee pot, with a rocaille spout and domed lid with gilt pine-cone knop, gilt-scroll border and continuous painting of a river landscape, blue underglazed swords mark, gold cipher.

c1745   9.25in (23cm) high

£2,800-3,200 MTZ

One of a pair of 19thC Meissen porcelain 'Element' ewers, representing 'Air and Water', with an S-shape handle, richly decorated with putti, Neptune and a peacock, blue underglazed swords mark, damage and restoration.

26.5in (66cm) high

£6,000-9,000 pair MTZ

A 19thC Meissen porcelain vase, designed by H.A. Leuteritz, with scroll handles and a gilt-edged pâte-sur-pâte reserve of a woman holding a mirror, cobalt-blue ground, underglazed blue swords mark.

14.75in (37cm) high

£4,000-6,000 MTZ

A pair of Meissen 'Indian Yellow' vases, each with an ovoid body and bulbous neck, gilt-edged borders and painted with branches of Indian flowers, birds and a toad on stylised rocks, blue "AR" mark to base.

c1730   10in (25cm) high
£5,000-7,000   **BMN**

A Meissen amphora, in the style of Michel Victor Acier, with gold-plating and rectangular reserves to front and back, cover restored.

c1820   10.75in (27cm) high
£300-400   **BMN**

A pair of Meissen vases and covers, with scenes by Watteau, of ovoid baluster form with small domed covers and flower knops, decorated with painted Watteau court scenes of comical figures, above rocaille decoration in purple camaieu, flower sprays to neck, base and cover, gold to edges, gilded bronze mounts to bases in the form of rocailles and leaves, blue swords marks to unglazed base, flower knops restored.

c1760   9.5in (24cm) high
£8,000-12,000   **LPZ**

A Meissen cobalt-blue amphora, with applied floral and ornamental gilt decoration, the oval reserves to each side with scenes of 17thC Dutch Old Masters from the Dresden Picture Gallery, one 'Violin Player by the Window' the other 'Singing Lesson', gilt lion-head handles, blue swords mark, cover and the interior of the mouth restored, minor crack to handle.

c1860   16.5in (41cm) high
£5,000-8,000   **BMN**

A Meissen snake-handled vase, designed by Ernst August Leuteritz, with floral and ornamental relief decoration, slightly rubbed, blue swords mark.

c1860   15.25in (38cm) high
£500-800   **BMN**

An 18thC Meissen tea caddy, painted with flowers, the rectangular body with rounded shoulders, unglazed base, unmarked.

4in (10cm) high
£100-150   **BMN**

A Meissen tea caddy and lid, painted with 'Deutsche Blumen', the rectangular body with rounded shoulders, swords mark.

c1755   5in (12.5cm) high
£400-600   **WW**

A Meissen tea caddy and lid, decorated with landscape scenes, the rectangular body with rounded shoulders, the lid with a rose knop, unmarked, unglazed base, lid slightly chipped.

c1755   5.5in (13.5cm) high
£800-1,200   **BMN**

A Meissen tea caddy and lid, decorated with landscape scenes, the body with rounded shoulders, unmarked, unglazed base, lid slightly chipped.

c1755   5.5in (13.5cm) high

£800-1,200   **BMN**

A Meissen lidded tea caddy, painted with floral motifs, the lid restored.

c1775   5.25in (13cm) high

£320-380   **WW**

A large 19thC Meissen mantel clock, designed by Michel Victor Acier, blue swords mark.

22.5in (56cm) high

£3,000-4,000   **BMN**

A pair of Meissen figural candlesticks, modelled as tree trunks on bases with figures, probably by Victor Michel Acier, gilded, impressed mark, blue swords mark, restored.

c1860   9.25in (23cm) high

£1,800-2,200   **BMN**

A pair of Meissen pack of card candlesticks, shaped as a heart and a spade and decorated with flowers and gilding, impressed mark, blue swords mark, dated, restored.

1876   7.25in (18cm) high

£2,000-2,500   **BMN**

A Meissen walking stick handle, decorated with hunting scenes, engraved gold, rubbed and chipped.

c1740   2.75in (7cm) high

£1,000-1,500   **LPZ**

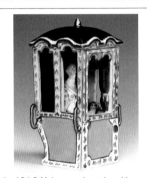

An 18thC Meissen palanquin, with a seated Rococo lady, probably designed by Peter Reinicke, gilded, unglazed base, blue swords mark, restored.

4in (10cm) high

£500-800   **BMN**

An 18thC Meissen walking stick handle, with a woman's head in a veil and polychrome painted scattered flowers and insects, gilded scrolling and rocaille relief decoration, blue swords mark.

5in (12.5cm) wide

£800-1,200   **BMN**

A Meissen snuff box, with scenes from Watteau, master Charles Rawlings, porcelain with enamel colours, vermeil mounting, rectangular box with rounded lid, all six sides decorated with court couples in park landscapes, gilded on the inside, left backside of lid restored.

c1750   3.5in (9cm) wide

£2,800-3,200   **LPZ**

MEISSEN FIGURES

A Meissen porcelain group, of a courting couple, unglazed base, unmarked, one foot restored and chip to flowers.

c1740   6in (15cm) high

£4,000-6,000   **LPZ**

A Meissen porcelain Japanese-style group, of a seated couple kissing over a table, their clothing decorated with Indian flowers, unglazed base with faded blue swords mark, restored.

c1745   4.5in (11cm) high

£8,000-12,000   **LPZ**

A Meissen porcelain figure of a seated harlequin holding a bagpipe, by Johann Joachim Kändler, the rocaille base encrusted with flowers and leaves.

c1740   5.5in (13.5cm) high
£800-1,200   **MTZ**

A Meissen porcelain figure of a female gardener holding a wicker basket, modelled by Johann Joachim Kändler, the base with flowers and leaves, blue underglazed swords mark.

c1745   7.8in (19.5cm) high
£1,200-1,800   **MTZ**

JOHANN JOACHIM KÄNDLER (1706-1775)

- The great porcelain factory at Meissen employed Johann Joachim Kändler to revitalise their modelling section in 1731.
- He became chief modeller two years later when Kirchner, his predecessor, left the firm.
- This position meant that he was responsible for sculpting original models out of wax or clay from which moulds were made.
- Kändler produced figures ranging from tinkers to lords, as well as more idiosyncratic ranges of harlequins and monkey bandsmen.
- His signature was complicated yet refined detailing in the Baroque style. He had an eye for fluid, naturalistic movement
- His most prestigious commission was to create a large collection of porcelain animals for Augustus the Strong – the most ambitious ceramic project ever attempted in Europe at the time.
- Kändler's work was much imitated by his contemporaries. If unsure about the authenticity of a piece, it is always best to examine it against one that is known to be genuine to compare the quality of the modelling and the colours.
- Groups, especially those that combine human figures with animals, are invariably more valuable than single figures.
- Kändler worked at the factory for 44 years.

A Meissen model of a baker, after a model by Johann Joachim Kändler, holding a baking bat, crossed swords mark to base, rubbing to gilt, restoration.

c1745   7in (17.5cm) high
£3,000-4,000   **WW**

A pair of Meissen figures of trinket sellers, after models by Johann Joachim Kändler from drawings by Edmé Bouchardon, unmarked, lacking box lids, some repairs.

c1745   7.25in (18.5cm) high
£3,000-5,000   **WW**

An 18thC Meissen 'Street Chef with Turkey' porcelain, modelled by Peter Reinicke and Johann Joachim Kändler, model no. 31, painted and gilded, blue crossed swords mark, restored.

5.5in (14cm) high
£700-1,000   **BMN**

An 18thC Meissen two-faced mythological porcelain figure, wearing a long robe, crown and bayleaf wreath, polychrome painted, gilded, unglazed base, blue crossed swords mark.

5in (12.5cm) high
£700-900   **BMN**

A Meissen porcelain 'Violinist' figure, modelled by Friedrich Elias Meyer, model no. 10, from the series 'Gallant Band', gilded, blue crossed swords mark, damage and restoration.

c1750   5.5in (13.5cm) high
£600-900   **BMN**

A Meissen 'Winter' putto figure, modelled seated on a plinth base and wearing an ermine-lined cloak and holding a small brazier, figure and base probably glued.

c1750   5in (12.5cm) high
£280-320   **DN**

A Meissen porcelain 'The Earth' putto figure, after an original by Johann Joachim Kändler, model no. C100, from the series 'The Four Elements', blue crossed swords mark, restored.

c1860   4.5in (11.5cm) high
£300-500   **BMN**

A Meissen porcelain figure of a gardening child, after an original by Johann Joachim Kändler, model no. 7x, painted and gilded, blue crossed swords mark, arms and hat restored.

c1860   5in (13cm) high
£400-600   **BMN**

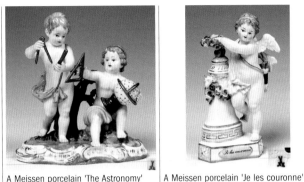

A Meissen porcelain 'The Astronomy' group, with star globe, compasses, triangle and levelling board, painted and gilded, on an oval base, blue crossed swords mark.

c1860   4.5in (11.5cm) high

£400-600   **BMN**

A Meissen porcelain 'Je les couronne' figure of a child, designed by Michel Victor Acier, model no. F3, painted and gilded, on a triangular base, blue crossed swords mark.

c1860   5.25in (13.5cm) high

£700-1,000   **BMN**

A Meissen figure of a young woman, holding flowers and wearing a feather muff, decorated in coloured enamels and gilt, painted mark in blue and incised "D.66", small chips.

c1860   8in (20cm) high

£300-500   **LFA**

A large Meissen porcelain articulated pagoda figure, with floral and gilt clothing and a nodding head and hands, blue underglazed cross sword mark, impressed "53".

c1880   12in (30cm) high

£8,000-10,000   **FRE**

A late 19thC Meissen group of seated lovers, modelled after an original by Johann Joachim Kändler, wearing court dress and with a pug dog, blue crossed swords mark, numbered, incised 778, slight damage.

6.5in (16.5cm) wide

£400-600   **DN**

A pair of late 19thC Meissen models of a shepherd musician and companion, with a hound and a sheep, on scroll-moulded bases, blue crossed swords marks, small chips and losses.

6in (15.5cm) high

£1,000-1,500   **DN**

A CLOSER LOOK AT A PAIR OF MEISSEN FIGURES

These large figures are also known as nodding buddhas. Although made by Meissen after an original by Johann Joachim Kändler, this pair was made long after the modeller's death.

The heads, tongues and hands are pivoted to rock rhythmically. It is thought that this function was originally used to detect earthquakes.

Meissen revived many of its successful 18thC pieces from the late 1840s to c1870 under director, Heinrich Gottlieb Kühn. The original mould was often used.

The originals were made in the mid-18thC and were inspired by blanc-de-Chine from Dehua in the Fujian province.

A late 19thC pair of Meissen articulated 'Pagoda' figures, after originals by Johann Joachim Kändler, the male and female figures in brightly coloured flower-painted robes, their heads, tongues and hand pivoted to rock rhythmically, underglazed blue cross sword marks.

12in (30cm) high

£15,000-20,000   **FRE**

A late 19thC large Meissen porcelain figure of Count Brühl's tailor, after an original by Johann Joachim Kändler, in the form of the tailor astride a billy goat, wearing a yellow floral-painted coat, black boots and a tricorn hat, the tools of his trade around him, blue underglazed cross mark.

17in (42.5cm) high

£12,000-18,000   **FRE**

A pair of Continental porcelain figures of a gentleman and companion, in the Meissen style, each holding a basket of flowers, decorated in coloured enamels, the round mound base with a gilt key fret band, marks in blue.

7.5in (19cm) high

£300-400   **LFA**

A late 19thC Meissen rustic group, of a gentleman and two companions, one modelled seated with a birdcage on her knee, the other standing with a bird in one hand and a basket of flowers in the other, gilt, blue crossed swords mark and incised "F94", damage and losses.

8.75in (22cm) high

£600-900   **DN**

A late 19thC Meissen group, of a boy escorting a maid with apples, a third figure, probably the boy's tutor, holding a book, the boy's books and a cane in a pile at their feet, painted with coloured enamels and gilt, on an oval base with a gilt ovolo band frieze, blue crossed swords mark and incised "J. 61", chips.

7.75in (21cm) high

£1,200-1,800   **DN**

A late 19thC Meissen group, of a seated lady holding a heart, with a male courtier, a female attendant offering manicure and a young male attendant with a tray, crossed swords mark, incised mark and incised numeral "100".

10.5in (27cm) wide

£700-1,000   **GORL**

A late 19thC Meissen allegorical group, modelled as a rocky mound base surmounted with figures wearing 18thC dress, sparsely coloured and with gilt, blue crossed swords mark, incised "D.93", damage, losses and restoration.

11.5in (29cm) high

£500-800   **DN**

A late 19thC Meissen model of a winged putto, probably Cupid, tied to a tree trunk with roses, blue crossed swords mark, "R123", restored.

7in (18cm) high

£400-600   **DN**

A late 19thC Meissen group, of dancing lovers, on a scroll-moulded base, blue crossed swords mark, incised "C.75", restored.

5in (14cm) high

£400-600   **DN**

A late 19thC Meissen group, of a shepherdess playing a lute and a companion with a bunch of flowers, blue crossed swords mark, "447", restored.

5.5in (14cm) high

£700-1,000   **DN**

A late 19thC Meissen Bacchic model, of a man wearing 18thC dress, with a flower-encrusted wine ewer, blue crossed swords mark, incised "907".

8in (20cm) high

£400-600   **DN**

A late 19thC Meissen figure of a woman, emblematic of 'Sight' from a series of 'The Senses', blue crossed swords mark, small chips to lace frills.

6in (15cm) high

£800-1,200   **DN**

A late 19thC Meissen group of three children, amongst ruined columns, on an oval mound base, blue crossed swords and cancellation marks, incised "G 32", numbered, restored.

8.5in (22cm) high

£500-800   **DN**

c1900

A Meissen porcelain figural group, of a faun caught by two nymphs, designed by Paul Helmig, polychrome painted and gilded, decorated with reeds, waterlilies and shells, model number Q 191, blue crossed swords mark.

15in (37.5cm) high

£1,500-2,000   **BMN**

A Meissen porcelain figure of a putto, 'The Summer', after an original by Johann Joachim Kändler, from 'The Seasons' series, blue jubilee crossed swords mark, "A 67", restored.

c1910   *5in (13cm) high*

£300-500   **BMN**

An early 20thC Meissen group of children, modelled holding hands dancing around a central tree, blue crossed swords mark, numbered and incised "2728", chips, losses.

13in (33cm) high

£1,000-1,500   **DN**

A Meissen porcelain figure of a jay with chicks, designed by Johann Joachim Kändler, perched on a naturalistic tree trunk, raised on a scrolled gilt bronze base, unmarked.

c1740   *18in (45cm) high*

£3,000-5,000   **MTZ**

A late 19thC Meissen model of pug, after an original by Johann Joachim Kändler, seated on its haunches and wearing a blue collar with gilt bells, blue crossed swords and cancellation mark, chips and damage to collar.

    9in (25cm) high

£1,000-1,500   **DN**

A Meissen figure of an aurochs attacked by hounds.

An aurochs is a type of ancient wild ox, which became extinct in Britain in the Bronze Age.

c1745   *7in (17.5cm) high*

£1,000-1,500   **MTZ**

A Meissen porcelain 'Deer Hunt' group, modelled by Johann Joachim Kändler, with jumping deer chased by three hounds, on an oval base encrusted with flowers and leaves, naturalistic painted decoration, blue underglazed swords mark.

c1770   *9.25in (23cm) high*

£300-500   **MTZ**

A Meissen figure of an aurochs, attacked by hounds, modelled by Johann Joachim Kändler, on an oval relief base with embossed flowers and leaves, unmarked, numbered, some restoration.

c1745   *7in (17.5cm) high*

£1,200-1,800   **MTZ**

A Meissen porcelain figure of a crowing cock, originally modelled by Johann Joachim Kändler, naturalistically decorated and raised on a round base with embossed flowers and foliage, faint swords mark.

c1750   *10in (25cm) high*

£3,000-5,000   **MTZ**

A mid-18thC Meissen model of a small hen pheasant, modelled by Johann Joachim Kändler, standing amidst corn with her three chicks, naturistically painted in coloured enamels, unmarked.

    5in (13cm) high

£3,000-5,000   **WW**

A pair of 20thC Meissen swans, originally modelled by Johann Joachim Kändler, each raised on a round base with reed decoration, blue underglazed swords mark and model number.

    8.8in (22cm) high

£700-1,000   **MTZ**

A late 19thC Meissen monkey band figure of a trumpeter, after an original by Johann Joachim Kändler, modelled with a trumpet, wearing 18thC dress, blue crossed swords mark, damaged.

    5.25in (13.5cm) high

£300-500   **DN**

A late 19thC Meissen model of a bullfinch, perched on a stump, blue crossed swords mark, wear to tip of beak.

    6in (15cm) high

£200-300   **DN**

A Vienna porcelain plate, decorated in polychrome enamels with a scene of a reclining woman, the border with floral decoration on a black ground, blue mark and titled verso.

10in (25cm) diam

£80-120   LFA

A 19thC Vienna porcelain cabinet service, decorated with scenes of figures on horses against a dark blue ground, with tray, milk jug, teapot, lidded sugar bowl, two teacups and saucers.

£400-600   CHEF

A Vienna porcelain serving plate, decorated with a painted scene titled "Cupid and Psyche", the rim in bordeaux red and blue.

9.75in (24.5cm) diam

£300-500   L&T

A 19thC Vienna porcelain cabinet plate, painted with scenes of Achilles and Thetis, the border with red enamels, blue underglazed mark.

9.75in (24.5cm) diam

£700-1,000   S&K

A 19thC Vienna porcelain vase, with two gilded handles, painted with bunches of flowers, on a square plinth, marked, restored.

13.25in (33cm) high

£120-180   CHEF

A 19thC Vienna porcelain plate, painted with scenes of Wotan and Brunhilde within in a dark red border, gilded.

15in (37.5cm) diam

£800-1,200   FRE

A Vienna porcelain mocha cup and saucer, painted by Franz Dörfl with relief scene of figures on a gold and red-brown ground, signed "J. Kohl", titled in red, blue mark, numbered.

c1880

£180-220   BMN

A Vienna porcelain wall plaque, painted with a portrait titled "Clementis", of a lady with flowers in her hair, on a dark red ground, gilded borders.

c1880   *19.75in (49.5cm) high*

£1,200-1,800   FRE

GERMAN PORCELAIN

A late 19thC Vienna porcelain portrait plate, depicting a woman with flowing hair, blue, brown and gilded border, titled "Innocence" and signed "Wagner".

10in (25cm) diam

£1,200-1,800   **FRE**

A late 19thC Vienna porcelain portrait plate, painted with a woman's bust, signed "Weigel", frame restored.

10in (25cm) diam

£800-1,200   **FRE**

A Vienna porcelain 'The Secret' plate, painted with a scene of two small boys, with gold to border, blue swords mark, signed "Storch", numbered.

9.75in (24.5cm) diam

£500-800   **L&T**

A lidded Vienna porcelain urn, with two handles, painted with scenes of "The Three Graces" and "Achilles and Agamemnon", signed "K Weh", red "Austria" mark, restored.

10.5in (26.5cm) high

£300-400   **FRE**

A Vienna porcelain model of a codfish seller, standing on a round base with green stripes and holding a fish basket under her left arm, a fish in her right hand, wearing a lilac dress with a darker flounce, blue mark, shield mark to glazed base, embossed "0", engraved "5", a finger restored.

c1755   *8in (20cm) high*

£1,200-1,800   **LPZ**

A Vienna porcelain wall plate, printed with mythological scenes, blue and gold rim.

c1900   *13.5in (33.5cm) diam*

£50-80   **LFA**

A pair of 20thC Vienna porcelain plates, in white, blue and red, with open-work gilded rims.

9.5in (23.5cm) diam

£70-100   **FRE**

A Vienna porcelain 'Mother and Child at the Breakfast Table' group, the lady wearing a crinoline skirt and supporting a child on her knee, a coffee service and parrot on the table, on a colourfully painted base with gold decoration and flowers, blue shield mark, parrot reglued.

7.5in (19cm) high

£280-320   **BMN**

A Vienna porcelain 'The Music' allegorical putti group, the two amorettes with a lyre, book and sheet of music, an eagle at their feet, reticulated rocaille-flower base, gilt decoration, blue shield mark, partially restored.

c1760   *10.75in (27cm) high*

£400-600   **BMN**

A small Ansbach bowl, with surrounding gilt decoration in the Turkish manner.

c1800   2.5 in (6.5cm) diam
£40-60   BMN

A rare Fulda porcelain pear-shaped jug, with a C-scroll handle, finely painted on both sides, underglazed "FF" mark.

c1785   6in (15cm) high
£1,200-1,800   MTZ

One of a set of 12 Heinrich & Co. 'Selby' service plates, each with central polychrome floral decoration and an extensive gold border with moulded details.

          10.75in (27cm) diam
£700-1,000 set   FRE

A Ludwigsburg large porcelain tureen, on a raised stand with rocaille handles, the cover with a naturalistic lemon knop, painted with birds and insects, blue underglazed crowned "CC" mark.

c1770   10.8in (27cm) high
£3,000-5,000   MTZ

A Nymphenburg porcelain plate, with a scalloped edge and double scroll handles, gilt rims and flower trails, the centre with a gilt-edged floral cartouche and two river landscapes, impressed diamond mark, impressed letters "QQL".

c1770   12.75in (32cm) wide
£700-1,000   MTZ

A Nymphenburg figure of a roe buck, model number 423, designed by Theodor Kärner, marks.

          5.25in (14cm) high
£70-100   BMN

A Nymphenburg large 'Ara spec' macaw, the red body with naturalistic decoration, perched on a pedestal with with a flower garland, diamond-shaped mark impressed to side of base.

c1910   23.25in (58cm) high
£2,000-3,000   MTZ

An early 20thC pair of Volkstedt figures, modelled as an 18thC gallant offering a rose to the lady, blue marks.

          15.75in (40cm) high
£300-500   CHEF

A pair of 19thC Sitzendorf figural four-light candelabra, with two wood nymphs beside a floral appliqué stump with four candle arms and a central candle holder, encrusted with flowers, on scrolled mounts.

c1880   19in (48cm) high
£1,500-2,000   SHF

A Continental porcelain oval plaque, painted with 'Ruth in the cornfield', mounted in an elaborate gilt scrollwork frame.

c1880   Frame 17.25in (43cm) wide
£1,200-1,800   WW

A late 19th to early 20thC German porcelain group, modelled as a young man in 18thC dress and two snarling hounds, incised underlined letter "A".

          14.75in (37cm) high
£600-800   L&T

EUROPEAN PORCELAIN

An early 20thC rectangular biscuit bowl, from Herend, Hungary, decorated with birds and insects, gilded wavy rim, blue mark and painter's mark.

7in (18cm) wide

£60-90   BMN

An early 20thC lidded bowl, from Herend, Hungary, polychrome painted with red roses and with gilding, raised on three scroll feet, blue mark and painter's mark.

3.5in (9cm) diam

£30-50   BMN

A Doccia plate, painted in coloured enamels and gilt with stylised flowers, the ozier-moulded border with scattered floral sprays, some surface wear.

c1760   9in (22.5cm) wide

£250-300   DN

A Doccia teapot and cover, decorated 'con basso relievo istoriato' with classical subjects including the goddess Diana, with richly gilt borders, some small losses, extensive damage and old repairs.

c1770   6in (15cm) high

£250-300   DN

A good pair of Naples Monteiths of rare form, the rims applied with six birds divided by short pillars, the bodies and interiors painted with flowers in coloured enamels above bands of flutes, each raised on three paw feet, incised marks.

These Monteiths are of the same form as the celebrated 'Servizio dell'Oca' made for the Bourbon court between 1793 and 1795, much of which is on display in the Capodimonte museum. Another example, decorated with figures, is in the Naples museum.

c1795   11.25in (28cm) diam

£7,000-10,000   WW

A Copenhagen figure of a young brown bear, naturalistically painted, with a green and blue mark.

3.75in (8.5cm) high

£30-40   BMN

A small vase, by Bing & Groendahl, Copenhagen, painted with floral motifs on blue ground, with a green and blue mark, "J.P.", "No 1058/8".

6.25in (16cm) high

£25-30   BMN

A set of five porcelain plates from St. Petersburg, each with a raised border and gilt-scrolled rim, the polychrome Asiatic floral decoration with butterflies on a turquoise ground, blue-grey interlaced mark, press mark.

c1850   9.25in (23.5cm) diam

£150-200   MTZ

A pair of Russian Imperial platters, each decorated with a central rosette surrounded by a black ground roundel with green scrolling vines and radiating leaves with stems on a gilt ground, within a beaded border, painted and printed marks.

14.25in (35.5cm) diam

£3,000-4,000   L&T

THE POTTERY MARKET

The demand for pottery at the middle and lower end of the market has slowed as buyers seek out high quality, unusual and rare pieces at the higher end of the market.

As far as Staffordshire figures are concerned, groups with historical themes – depicting military, political, religious and royal subjects – have fallen out of favour. Collectors specialising in these areas are predominantly British and are becoming fewer in number. They favour unusual, rare examples over easier to find pieces. Staffordshire animal groups, however, continue to sell well, largely because the US market for these is very strong.

New life has been injected into the market by buyers, such as

professional interior designers, looking for pottery to enhance the décor of their homes. Staffordshire dogs and hens on nests, as well as a wide variety of other subjects, have proved popular.

In the pre-1830 pottery market, the top end is holding up well. Creamware, lustreware and Delft – which is currently undervalued and becoming harder to find – remain popular. Walton, Obadiah Sherrat and Thomas Parr figures are also desirable.

In general, pottery that offers something extra is currently commanding the best prices. High quality pieces with appealing subjects or attractive colouring tend to perform well.

– *John Howard, Woodstock, Oxfordshire*

CREAMWARE

A large baluster-shaped creamware jug, with female mask spout, the reeded entwined loop handle with applied flower and leaf terminals, printed in black with 'The Tithe Pig', the couple and parson above the verse, old restoration.

c1780   9.5in (24cm) high

£400-600   **LFA**

A Liverpool double transfer-printed creamware jug.

c1790   7in (18cm) high

£1,200-1,800   **JHOR**

A large creamware jug, printed in black with two fat men en route to the tavern.

c1800   9.75in (24.5cm) high

£600-900   **WW**

A creamware jug, printed in black with an armorial titled "The Weaver's Arms".

c1800   7.25in (18cm) wide

£500-800   **WW**

A CLOSER LOOK AT A TRANSFER-PRINTED JUG

This jug is made from Queensware, a refined version of creamware introduced by Josiah Wedgwood in 1765 and named for Queen Charlotte, consort of George III.

Liverpool was among the first towns to apply transfer decoration to ceramics and remained the centre of this niche industry for years. Designs like this one were produced c1780-1830, making this jug one of the earliest examples.

The scene depicts the death of James Wolfe, a British general who enjoyed great success against the French in Canada. He died from wounds sustained in battle in 1759.

The encampment scene on the reverse of this jug is rare, adding to its value.

A Liverpool double transfer-printed creamware jug.

c1780   7in (18cm) high

£3,500-4,500   **JHOR**

A creamware jug, transfer-printed in black, with a village scene titled "The Church Militant", the reverse inscribed with a verse.

c1800 7.25in (18cm) high

£600-900 WW

A late 18thC creamware jug, double transfer-printed in black with a Classical lady and a verse "How Hard to Avoid Censure How Soon Get Applause".

11in (28cm) wide

£500-800 CHEF

A green glazed creamware jug, with floral motif finials, probably Yorkshire.

c1770 7in (18cm) high

£3,500-4,500 JHOR

A creamware teapot and cover, with a moulded handle and spout, one side printed with a rural couple and their child, the reverse with a beggar woman and a young lady holding a rake, good restoration.

c1765 7.25in (18.5cm) long

£300-500 WW

A rare William Greatbatch cylindrical creamware teapot and cover, with a cross-over handle and flower knop, brightly painted with Aurora in her chariot, the reverse with a rising sun, minor faults.

c1775 7.5in (19cm) high

£1,500-2,000 WW

A Staffordshire or Yorkshire bullet-shaped creamware teapot and cover, painted in coloured enamels with a rose spray and other flowers, the strap handle with flowerhead terminals, minor wear.

c1790 8in (20.5cm) wide

£200-300 DN

A creamware coffee pot and cover, printed with Thomas Rothwell-type prints of 'The Shepherd' and 'Tea Party No.1', the spout reduced.

c1790 9.75in (25cm) high

£300-400 DN

A late 18thC blue and white creamware jug painted with six foliage panels below pale green glazed leaves moulded on the rim.

c1780 3.75in (9.5cm) high

£200-300 CHEF

A creamware Toby jug, modelled in a seated position and holding a foaming jug of ale, painted in blue, brown and green coloured glazes, restored hat, lacks cover.

Toby jugs are modelled to show the full body, in contrast to character jugs which depict just the head and shoulders of a subject.

c1780 9.5in (24cm) high

£1,000-1,500 DN

CREAMWARE

- Staffordshire potters, led by Josiah Wedgwood, developed creamware c1750.
- By the late 18thC it had become the standard household pottery throughout Europe, undermining tin-glazed wares.
- The clay was mixed with flint to produce a fine, lightweight, close-grained surface that was then thinly glazed with a smooth, ivory-tinted lead solution.
- Production centred around Staffordshire and Yorkshire.
- Wedgwood coined the name 'Queensware' after Queen Charlotte granted him a Royal Warrant for his creamware in 1765.
- Creamware was versatile and could be finely moulded and printed or painted either under or over the glaze.

A Pratt-type creamware Toby jug, 'Hearty Good Fellow', typically modelled and painted, hat repaired.

c1800 9.75in (25cm) high

£600-900 **DN**

An early 19thC Dawson cylindrical creamware mug, printed and painted in polychrome with a view of the Iron Bridge at Sunderland, Lowford Pottery mark.

5.5in (14cm) high

£700-1,000 **WW**

A late 18thC cylindrical creamware mug, printed in brown with 'The Tea Party'.

4.75in (12cm) high

£200-300 **WW**

A late 18thC cylindrical creamware mug, printed in black with a scene depicting "The Tithe Pig" above a verse.

5.5in (14cm) high

£700-1,000 **WW**

A late 18thC cylindrical creamware mug, transfer-printed in black with "The Triple Plea" illustrating a priest, a doctor and a lawyer discussing their fees above a verse attacking the hypocrisy of their vows.

4.75in (12cm) high

£800-1,200 **WW**

A cylindrical creamware jug, printed in black with a view of the Iron Bridge over the River Wear.

c1800 5.75in (14.5cm) high

£500-700 **WW**

A cylindrical creamware mug, printed in black with a parson and a clerk above a verse.

c1800 6.25in (15.5cm) high

£500-700 **WW**

A cylindrical creamware mug, printed in black with the shipwrights' arms of a shield surmounted by an ark, flanked by two figures above a motto.

c1800 5.75in (14.5cm) high

£800-1,200 **WW**

A cylindrical creamware mug, printed in black with a view of the "Iron Bridge in Sunderland", the print signed "Barker".

c1815 4.75in (12cm) wide

£300-400 **WW**

An early 19thC cylindrical creamware mug, transfer-printed in dark brown with 'The Gypsy Fortune Teller'.

4.75in (12cm) wide

£200-300 **WW**

An early 19thC cylindrical creamware mug, printed in black with a ship in full sail flying the American flag.

6in (15cm) high

£800-1,200 **WW**

An early 19thC cylindrical creamware mug, printed in black with the verse "A little Health, A little Wealth, A little House and Freedom, And at the end a little Friend, And little cause to need Him", signed "Johnson Hanley".

3.5in (9cm) wide

£300-500 **WW**

A Liverpool creamware bowl, printed in black by Sadler & Green, the interior decorated with a gypsy woman telling the fortune of a young lady, the exterior with four further vignettes of figures.

c1770 *9.25in (23cm) high*

£400-600 **WW**

A round creamware bowl, the interior printed in black with "A First Rate Ship of War With Rigging etc At Anchor", and titled on a scroll beneath, the exterior with a family and young lovers seated on a bench, beneath a green line rim, slight damage.

c1800 *9in (23cm) diam*

£300-500 **LFA**

A Staffordshire or Yorkshire creamware slop bowl, extensively cracked and repaired.

c1790 *6in (15cm) wide*

£80-120 **DN**

A circular creamware sugar bowl and cover, probably Staffordshire or Yorkshire, painted with a spray of roses and other flowers, the cover with flower finial, the bowl with strap handles and flowerhead terminals, minor chips.

c1790 *5.5in (12.5cm) wide*

£350-400 **DN**

A flared oval two-handled creamware basket and stand, probably Yorkshire, of pierced form with winged masks suspending swags.

c1780 *11.25in (28cm) wide*

£400-600 **DN**

An English pierced oval creamware chestnut basket and stand, both parts ozier-moulded central section, the stand with rim chips.

c1790 *Stand 10in (25.5cm) wide*

£200-300 **DN**

A pair of creamware ice pails with liners, the domed covers with mauve detailed bud knops, the shallow lobed bodies painted with bands of green-leaved brown vines and mauve lines.

c1810 *9in (23cm) high*

£1,000-1,500 **CHEF**

A cylindrical creamware tea canister and domed cover, probably Staffordshire or Yorkshire, painted in coloured enamels with a spray of roses and other flowers, small foot rim chip.

c1790 *5.5in (12.5cm) high*

£400-600 **DN**

A cylindrical creamware tea canister, printed in black with figures in an interior, and titled "Conjugal Felicity", the reverse with figures and a book, in a river landscape, lacks lid, rim chips.

c1800 *9.75in (9.5cm) high*

£180-220 **LFA**

A cylindrical creamware tea canister, printed in black with female figures each beside a lion rampant, holding a sword and arrows, and inscribed "Voor Vryheid en Vaderland", lacks lid, chips.

c1800   *3.75in (9.5cm) high*

£150-200   **LFA**

A small Staffordshire creamware model of a seated monkey, splashed in brown, green and yellow, on an oval mound base, foot rim chip restored.

c1770   *2.75in (7cm) high*

£400-600   **LFA**

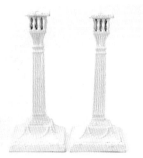

An early 19thC Staffordshire creamware model of a leopard, decorated in underglaze colours, seated on a green mound.

3.75in (9.5cm) wide

£500-700   **WW**

A pair of creamware candlesticks, the nozzles modelled with baluster columns, the stems fluted and raised on square bases cast with garrya swags and geometric borders, unmarked.

c1775   *10.5in (26cm) high*

£1,000-1,500   **WW**

A pair of Neale and Co. ozier-moulded creamware oval basket stands, impressed marks.

12.25in (31cm) wide

£280-320   **DN**

LEEDS

A creamware sweetmeats centrepiece, probably Leeds.

c1785   *17in (43cm) wide*

£3,000-4,000   **JHOR**

A late 18thC creamware figure of a lady representing Summer, standing on a green base next to a wheat sheaf, wearing a spotted dress.

11in (28cm) high

£80-120   **CHEF**

A Staffordshire creamware figure representing Autumn, modelled standing holding a bunch of grapes, painted in Pratt colours.

c1800   *7.5in (19cm) high*

£180-220   **DN**

A Leeds creamware teapot and cover, with flower knop, with reeded entwined loop handle and leaf-moulded terminals, unusually inscribed in iron red "Bohea Tea" and painted in famille verte colours, damaged.

c1770   *4.5in (11.5cm) high*

£700-1,000   **LFA**

A late 18thC creamware teapot and cover, possibly Leeds, printed by William Greatbatch with two scenes from the prodigal son, "The Prodigal Son In Excess" and "The Prodigal Son in Misery".

c1790

£300-500   **CHEF**

POTTERY

A late 18thC Leeds plate, decorated with a scalloped blue rim and blue, yellow and orange spotted peafowl.

8in (20cm) diam

£300-400   POOK

A Wedgwood creamware teapot and cover, with a leaf-moulded handle and spout, each side printed in black with hunting scenes, impressed "Wedgwood" mark.

c1765   7.5in (18.5cm) high

£700-1,000   WW

A Leeds creamware ewer and basin, pattern number 188, restored hairlines, bowl has chip.

c1780   14.5in (36.5cm) high

£4,000-6,000   JHD

A pair of Wedgwood Queensware navette-shaped cruet bottle stands, with shaped rims, impressed marks.

c1790   10.25in (26cm) wide

£350-400   DN

A Wedgwood creamware feeding pot.

c1785   4.75in (12cm) high

£500-700   JHD

A Wedgwood Queensware ozier-moulded oval basket and stand, with pierced rims, the interior of the basket painted in coloured enamels with a band of flowers, impressed marks, painted pattern number N899, some wear to stand.

Wedgwood's creamware was renamed 'Queensware' after Queen Charlotte's patronage was given to the line.

c1810   Stand 10in (25.5cm) diam

£200-300   DN

BRISTOL DELFT

A Bristol delft plate, chip to rim.

c1740   10in (25.5cm) diam

£500-700   AS

A Bristol pancake-shaped delft plate, with a pale manganese border and a central blue swan.

c1740   9in (23cm) diam

£700-1,000   AS

A mid-18thC Bristol delft plate, repaired chip and associated crack.

13.25in (33.5cm) diam

£800-1,200   AS

A Bristol delft charger, with an Oriental harbour scene.

c1760   13in (33cm) diam

£700-1,000   JHOR

A Bristol delft plate, with a portrait of Frederick the Great of Prussia, inscribed "KP".

c1755   8.75in (22cm) diam

£4,000-6,000   AS

A pair of Bristol bianco sopra bianco delft plates.

Bianco sopra bianco refers to the use of white enamel decoration on a white tin glaze.

c1760   9in (23cm) diam

£800-1,200   AS

A mid-18thC Bristol delft bowl, with crimped edge, decorated with foliage.

c1740　　　　　　　　　　*8in (20.5cm) diam*

£1,000-1,500　　　　　　　　　　**AS**

An English delft jar, with handles, probably Bristol.

c1705　　　　　　*6in (15cm) high*

£700-1,000　　　　　　**JHOR**

An English blue and white delft posset pot, probably Bristol, of baluster form, painted with stylized plants.

c1720　　　　　*5.5in (14cm) high*

£350-400　　　　　　**ROS**

A Bristol delft tulip charger, with blue dash border.

c1700　　　*13in (33cm) diam*

£3,500-4,500　　　　**JHOR**

A Bristol delft charger, with an Oriental figure on a lake.

c1730　　　*13in (33cm) diam*

£3,000-4,000　　　　**JHOR**

A Bristol delft dish, chipped.

c1740　　*11.75in (30cm) diam*

£1,000-1,500　　　　**AS**

A Bristol delft charger, painted with Oriental figures on a bridge.

c1740　　　*14in (36cm) diam*

£4,000-5,000　　　　**JHOR**

A Bristol delft charger.

c1740　　　*13in (33cm) diam*

£1,200-1,800　　　　**JHOR**

A Bristol delft charger.

c1760　　　*13in (39.5cm) diam*

£2,000-3,000　　　　**JHOR**

A CLOSER LOOK AT A PAIR OF ENGLISH DELFT PLATES

The body of English delft tends to be harder and coarser than that of the Dutch equivalent. Glazes are smoother and more prone to chipping. Small glaze chips do not therefore have a particularly detrimental effect on value.

The decoration on 18thC delft tended to be less formal than earlier pieces, which were influenced initially by Dutch and Italian and later by Chinese design. The cockerel image makes this pair of plates quirky and appealing.

Most English delft pieces are blue and white. Polychrome decoration is rarer and highly collectable.

This pair was probably made in Bristol, where delft was made between c1685-1770.

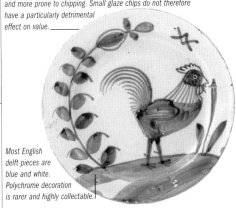

A pair of mid-18thC English delft plates, probably Bristol, each with painted design of a cockerel and a stylized flower in blue, green and orange.

9in (23cm) diam

£8,000-10,000　　　　**B&H**

A Bristol delft charger, with an Oriental scene of a figure in a garden.

c1740   13in (33.5cm) diam

£2,000-2,500   JHOR

A Bristol polychrome delft charger, boldly painted in blue, green, yellow and iron red with a Chinese figure and a parrot, in a fenced garden, within a flower-panelled blue and iron red diaper band, old restoration.

c1760   13.5in (34cm) diam

£200-300   LFA

A Bristol polychrome delft charger, painted in blue, green and iron red with a bird and an insect amidst flowering branches and rockwork, within a pendant flower and leaf scroll roundel, numeral "7" in blue verso.

c1760   13in (33cm) diam

£1,200-1,800   LFA

A Bristol delft charger, finely painted in manganese, blue and yellow with a Chinese woman holding a fan, within a leaf-panelled manganese diaper border, restored rim chip.

c1770   13.5in (34cm) diam

£500-700   LFA

LONDON DELFT

A London delft Act of Union plate, decorated with a thistle and a rose, marked "GR", with repaired chips.

In 1714, George I of the House of Hanover succeeded Queen Anne as monarch of Britain pursuant to the terms of the 1707 Act of Union.

c1715   8.75in (22cm) diam

£6,000-8,000   AS

An English blue and white delft Chinoiserie plate, minor rim chips.

c1750   8.75in (22.5cm) diam

£350-400   DN

A rare powder blue London delft plate, tiny chip repaired.

c1750   13in (33cm) diam

£1,200-1,800   AS

A large pair of Ann Gomm London delft plates.

c1770   13.5in (34.5cm) diam

£2,000-3,000   AS

A London octagonal delft charger.

c1730   9in (23cm) diam

£600-900   JHOR

A London ornamental delft charger.

c1765   13.5in (34.5cm) diam

£2,200-2,800   JHOR

A London delft charger, decorated with a landscape scene and stylized foliage.

c1790   13in (33cm) diam

£500-700   JHOR

An English blue and white delft punch bowl, probably London, painted with Chinoiserie landscapes, the interior with an 'oxo' band border, minor chips and cracks.

c1760   10.5in (27cm) diam

£220-280   **DN**

A mid-18thC London or Glasgow delft barber's bowl.

12in (30cm) diam

£1,500-2,000   **JHOR**

An early 17thC delft apothecary jar, probably Southwark.

6in (15cm) wide

£1,000-1,500   **JHOR**

An early 18thC English delft apothecary wet jar, probably London, inscribed "S. Croci".

7in (18cm) high

£200-300   **JHOR**

An early 18thC London delft apothecary wet jar, with a spout, inscribed "S Rubi Idaei".

7.5in (19cm) high

£2,000-3,000   **JHOR**

A CLOSER LOOK AT A DELFT CISTERN

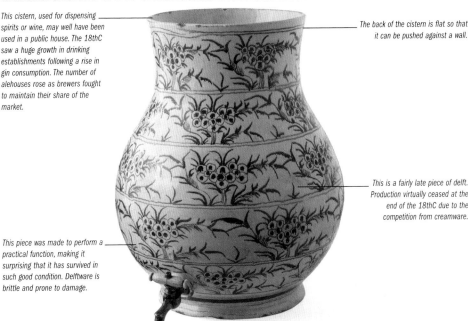

This cistern, used for dispensing spirits or wine, may well have been used in a public house. The 18thC saw a huge growth in drinking establishments following a rise in gin consumption. The number of alehouses rose as brewers fought to maintain their share of the market.

The back of the cistern is flat so that it can be pushed against a wall.

This is a fairly late piece of delft. Production virtually ceased at the end of the 18thC due to the competition from creamware.

This piece was made to perform a practical function, making it surprising that it has survived in such good condition. Delftware is brittle and prone to damage.

A mid-18thC London delft campana vase, with a landscape scene of a row of buildings with trees in the foreground.

6in (15cm) high

£2,000-2,500   **JHOR**

An English delft cistern, probably London, with a tap for wine or spirits with a bone handle, three cracks to rim.

c1780   11in (28cm) high

£6,000-8,000   **JHOR**

A London delft tavern bottle, with a looped handle, inscribed "Sack 1650".

1650   *7.5in (19cm) high*

£1,800-2,200   **JHOR**

A London delft tankard, with scroll and flower decoration.

c1725   *5.25in (13.5cm) high*

£4,000-5,000   **JHOR**

A London delft flower brick, with a scene of a walking couple.

c1750   *6in (15cm) wide*

£1,800-2,200   **JHOR**

An 18thC London delft flower brick, with a landscape scene of a seated shepherdess and her flock.

6.5in (16cm) wide

£1,800-2,200   **JHOR**

A pair of London delft flower bricks, with polychrome floral decoration.

c1735   *6in (15.5cm) wide*

£7,000-8,000   **JHOR**

LAMBETH DELFT

A rare Lambeth delft plate, decorated with figures in a landscape.

c1740   *12in (30.5cm) diam*

£2,000-2,500   **AS**

A mid-18thC Lambeth delft plate, decorated with people in a landscape, repaired rim chip.

13.75in (35cm) diam

£800-1,200   **AS**

A Lambeth delft charger, with a figure under a weeping willow tree.

c1765   *13in (33cm) diam*

£1,200-1,800   **JHOR**

LIVERPOOL DELFT

A Liverpool delft plate, depicting an Oriental lady in a landscape.

c1750   *6.75in (17cm) diam*

£700-1,000   **AS**

A rare Liverpool delft plate, decorated with a cartouche containing Masonic symbols including pillars, candles, compasses and a square, inscribed "Virtuti et Silentio".

c1760   *9in (23cm) diam*

£4,000-6,000   **AS**

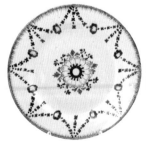

A pair of Lambeth delft plates.

c1780   *8.75in (22cm) diam*

£700-1,000   **AS**

A Liverpool delft plate, inscribed "Admiral Keppel Forever", cracked.

At the Battle of Quiberon Bay on 20 November 1759, Admiral Keppel commanded the 74 gun 'Torbay' and sank the French ship 'Thesée'.

c1760   *9in (23cm) diam*
£3,500-4,500   **AS**

A Liverpool octagonal delft ship's plate, the border decorated with flowers and four cherubs representing the four winds, inscribed "Vertrouwen" above the ship and "Pieter Pieters Eisen" below, dated.

1765   *8.75in (22cm) diam*
£5,000-8,000   **AS**

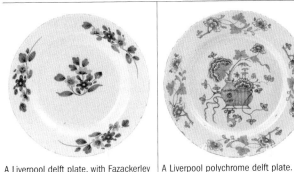

A Liverpool delft plate, with Fazackerley colours.

c1760   *8.75in (22cm) diam*
£700-1,000   **AS**

A Liverpool polychrome delft plate.

c1760   *8.75in (22cm) diam*
£700-1,000   **AS**

A Liverpool delft plate, with Fazackerley colours.

c1760   *10.75in (27.5cm) diam*
£700-1,000   **AS**

c1760
£700-1,000   **WW**

A rare double-ended delft sauceboat, after a Chinese shape with animal head handles, the interior well painted with a farmer and his wife feeding three goats and a cow in a field with buildings and a windmill beyond, probably Liverpool, some restoration.

8.25in (21cm) wide
WW

A rare delft sweetmeat dish, with six compartments and a scalloped edge, painted in blue with flowers and foliage within a hatched border, all raised upon five stump feet, probably Liverpool.

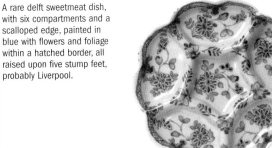

c1765   *8in (20.5cm) high*
£1000-1,500   **WW**

A mid-18thC Liverpool delft flower brick, decorated in blue and white.

6in (15cm) wide
£500-800   **AS**

A Liverpool delft tile by Sadler, printed in brown with a sleeping shepherd, the print signed "J. Sadler Liverp".

c1770   *5in (12.5cm) wide*
£250-300   **WW**

An early English blue and white delft plate.

c1720   9in (23cm) diam

£500-700   AS

A pair of English delft plates, decorated with Chinese figures in a landscape.

c1740   9in (23cm) diam

£1,000-1,500   AS

An English hexagonal delft plate, repaired chip.

c1750   8in (20.5cm) wide

£700-1,000   AS

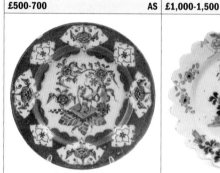

An English delft plate, chipped.

c1750   8.75in (22cm) diam

£500-800   AS

A dated blue and white delft plate, with a scalloped edge, painted with peony and bamboo and inscribed "I.P 1757".

8.75in (22.5cm) wide

£1,000-1,500   WW

A large English blue and white delft plate, painted with Chinese figures and insects in a landscape with trees and a building, rim chips.

c1760   13.5in (34.5cm) diam

£500-700   WW

An English blue and white delft plate, painted with a stag and a doe within a landscape, within an elaborate border of foliate devices, some rim chips.

c1770   9in (23cm) diam

£500-800   DN

c1730

£1,800-2,200   AS

An English delft plate, unusually painted in underglaze blue with a flowering tree, a fence and rockwork in the Chinese style, within a barbed panel, the powered brown ground with four panels of flowers and leaves, some glaze flaking.

c1760   8.75in (22cm) diam

£300-500   LFA

An English polychrome delft plate, painted with a bird chasing an insect, with floral detail.

8.75in (22cm) diam

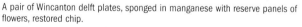

A pair of Wincanton delft plates, sponged in manganese with reserve panels of flowers, restored chip.

c1745   12in (30.5cm) diam

£1,000-1,500   AS

An English octagonal delft plate, finely painted in blue, green, yellow and manganese with flowering trees and fence and rockwork, restored.

c1770   8.75in (22cm) wide

£280-320   LFA

An English delft vase, with two twisted handles and floral decoration.

c1685   8in (20cm) high

£5,000-7,000   JHOR

An English delft vase, with a central cartouche of flowers flanked on either side by trellis.

c1765   10in (25cm) high

£2,500-3,000   JHOR

A pair of mid-18thC English delft vases, one with a rim repair.

                    7in (18cm) high

£1,800-2,200   JHOR

An English delft flower vase.

c1780   9in (23cm) wide

£1,800-2,200   JHOR

A small English polychrome delft bowl, painted with a naive landscape within a manganese dashed border, restored.

c1725   4.5in (11.5cm) diam

£200-250   WW

An English delft teabowl, decorated with trees and shrubs.

c1755   3in (7.5cm) wide

£1,200-1,800   JHOR

An English delft colander bowl, the dished top with a radiating design of holes, the sides painted with a Chinese figure, flowers and leaves, restored chip.

c1750   8.25in (21cm) high

£800-1,200   WW

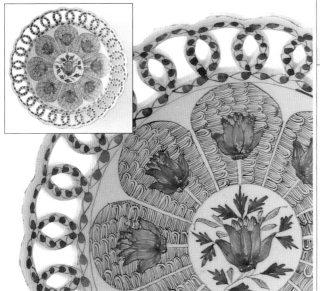

An English delft bowl with pierced borders.

c1765   8in (20cm) wide

£5,000-8,000   JHOR

An English heart-shaped delft sweetmeats dish, with a flower to the centre.

c1750   4.5in (11.5cm) wide

£600-900   JHOR

An English heart-shaped delft sweetmeats dish, with bands of floral decoration.

c1750   4.5in (11.5cm) wide

£800-1,200   JHOR

An English delft flower brick, decorated with sprigs of flowers.

c1740   6in (15.5cm)

£800-1,200   **JHOR**

An English delft flower brick, decorated with birds and flowers.

c1750   6in (16cm) wide

£800-1,200   **JHOR**

A delft flower brick with floral decoration to the sides, on raised bracket feet.

c1750   5in (13cm) wide

£1,200-1,800   **JHOR**

An English delft jar, with handles and polychrome flowers.

c1705   6.5in (16.5cm) wide

£1,800-2,200   **JHOR**

An English delft tankard, with polychrome landscape decoration.

c1760   5in (13cm) high

£3,000-4,000   **JHOR**

An English delft fuddling cup.

Fuddling cups were designed as a tavern joke. The drinker was 'befuddled' as to which of the three mouthpieces to drink from. Examples from the 17th and 18thC are particularly sought after.

c1640   4in (11.5cm) wide

£4,000-6,000   **JHOR**

An English delft stand, with foliate decoration and raised scroll feet.

c1725   5.25in (13.5cm) diam

£2,500-3,000   **JHOR**

IRISH DELFT

One of a pair of large blue and white delft meat plates, of chamfered rectangular form, possibly Irish, painted with a pine tree and building on a rocky island, a few small rim chips.

c1765   16.5in (42.5cm) wide

£1,200-1,800 pair   **WW**

An Irish delft plate.

c1750   9in (23cm) diam

£300-500   **AS**

An Irish delft plate, with a scalloped edge, painted with floral decoration.

c1750   9in (23cm) wide

£500-800   **AS**

A mid-18thC delft sauceboat, possibly Irish, with two handles and floral decoration, minor crack.

8in (20cm) wide

£5,000-6,000   **JHOR**

A delft posset pot, probably Irish, with double handles.

c1720 9.5in (29cm) wide

£3,000-4,000   **JHOR**

A blue and white Delft charger, painted in the Kraak style with Chinese figures seated beneath an arbour, within a border of figures and flowers.

c1700   12.5in (24.5cm) diam

£300-500   **DN**

One of a pair of Delft Chinese-style dishes.

c1720   13.25in (33.5cm) diam

£700-1,000 pair   **R&GM**

A blue and white lobed Delft dish, with a raised central boss painted with a stylized plant, within a dash border, minor rim chips.

c1700   8.75in (22cm) diam

£200-300   **DN**

An 18thC moulded Delft dish, decorated with a blue, yellow and ochre bird within a foliate band, rim section re-glued.

11.75in (30cm) diam

£200-300   **WW**

One of a pair of 18thC Delft plates, painted in polychrome with flowers, foliage and blue rockwork, small glaze chips to the rims.

12in (30.5cm) diam

£500-800 pair   **WW**

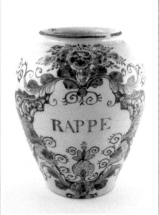

An 18thC ovoid Delft vase, inscribed "Rappe" in an elaborate floral cartouche, the base marked "Honl 9", minor faults.

10.5in (26.5cm) high

£800-1,200   **WW**

A ribbed hexagonal Delft vase and cover, with an animal finial, the body painted with a Chinese figure, animals, birds, insects and flowers.

c1750   13.25in (33cm) high

£300-500   **WW**

An 18thC blue and white Delft vase, the hexagonal moulded body decorated with flowers and fabulous beasts.

10.5in (26cm) high

£300-500   **WW**

An octagonal section Delft vase, painted with a peacock and other birds amidst chrysanthemum, the neck and the foot modelled with flutes, probably 18thC.

11in (27.5cm) high

£400-600   **WW**

A pair of early 18thC Delft drug jars, each painted with a cartouche surmounted by pheasants and a basket of flowers in blue, inscribed "Violarum" and "Nervinum".

7in (18cm) high

£1,000-1,500   **GORL**

An 18thC blue and white Delft drug jar, with a flared foot, the ovoid body inscribed "E. Catholicum" in a Baroque cartouche with cherub surmounts.

8.75in (22cm) high

£500-700   **WW**

An 18thC blue and white Delft tobacco jar, inscribed "No.5 Tonca" within a Baroque panel flanked by native Indians smoking pipes.

10.75in (27cm) high

£400-600   **WW**

POTTERY

IRONSTONE

- The first earthenware to be patented was produced by William and John Turner in 1800.
- Charles James Mason developed his successful 'Patent Ironstone China' c1810, as an alternative to imported porcelain.
- His recipe, patented in 1813, included ironstone slag and cobalt oxide, which gave the finished product a faint blue tinge.
- Mason's Ironstone was so strong that it was used to make fireplaces and even furniture, including four-poster beds.
- Mason's Ironstone was very successful and was exported in bulk to Europe and America.
- Ironstone was decorated with colours and patterns derived from Oriental designs, particularly the colours of Imari ceramics.
- A great deal of Mason's Ironstone bears a crown mark with the inscription "Mason's Patent Ironstone China".
- When Mason's patent expired in 1827 rival firms, including Spode and Davenport, began manufacturing similar wares.

A Mason's Patent Ironstone China two-handled vase, of ribbed form with a flared rim, richly decorated with the 'Old School House' pattern, impressed "Mason's Patent Ironstone China" mark.

c1820　　*8.25in (21cm) high*

£400-600　　**WW**

A Mason's Patent Ironstone China octagonal jug, with a winged dragon handle, decorated with the 'Japan Fence' pattern, impressed "Mason's Patent Ironstone China" mark, minor faults.

c1820　　*8.25in (21cm) high*

£400-600　　**WW**

A very large Mason's Patent Ironstone China jug, surmounted by two cherubs, rich gilt decoration with scrolled sides and mask mounts, on a black square base.

26in (66cm) high

£4,000-5,000　　**JN**

Three Mason's Patent Ironstone China octagonal hydra-shape jugs, with moulded serpent handles, decorated with a typical Japanese pattern in blue and iron-red with green on the handles, two with peach lustre rims, the largest with impressed mark "Mason's Patent Ironstone China", the others with blue-printed crown and drape marks.

c1830　　*9in (22cm) high*

£600-900　　**DN**

A pair of Mason's Patent Ironstone China wine coolers, of tapered shape with flared feet and blue-moulded leaf handles, rims moulded with flowers and leafy scrolls, decorated with a typical Japanese pattern in blue and iron-red, unmarked.

c1825　　*8.75in (22cm) high*

£400-600　　**DN**

A good pair of Mason's Patent Ironstone China dessert plates, of lobed form with gilt foliate decorated rims, the centres well painted with landscape views of Orford, Suffolk and Niton, Isle of Wight by Samuel Borne, impressed mark and titled in red.

c1820　　*9.25in (23.5cm) diam*

£1,500-2,000　　**WW**

A Mason's Patent Ironstone China covered sauce tureen with matching stand, of octagonal form with pedestal foot and moulded handles.

c1830　　*8in (20cm) wide*

£300-500　　**DN**

A large Mason's Patent Ironstone China mug, of octagonal form with a hydra handle, decorated with Chinoiserie scenes, black printed mark.

c1825　　*7.75in (20cm) wide*

£300-500　　**WW**

A Mason's Patent Ironstone China footbath, of twelve-sided shape with dog's head handles, decorated with the 'Table and Flower Pot' pattern.

c1825　　*19.5in (49cm) wide*

£800-1,200　　**DN**

A rare Mason's Patent Ironstone China orange ground vase, with gilt wreath handles, painted with two figures in a landscape, rare circular mark.

c1815　　*6in (15cm) wide*

£700-1,000　　**WW**

An early 15thC Italian earthenware bowl with handles.

5.5in (14cm) wide

£500-700 JHOR

A 15thC Italian earthenware bowl with handles, probably for drinking.

4.5in (11cm) diam

£500-800 JHOR

An unusual earthenware mug, with lion loop handle, applied relief of Wellington on horseback and soldiers, inscribed "Plunder".

c1815   4in (10cm) high

£400-600 LFA

A rare canaryware child's mug, depicting sheep, with lustre rim.

c1800   1.75in (4.5cm) diam

£300-400 PST

A German blue glazed cylindrical earthenware mug, decorated in gilt, red and black with foliage, the hinged pewter cover with bird thumbpiece.

c1760   10in (25.5cm) high

£300-400 LFA

A Sussex puzzle jug, the green splashed ochre sides with two birds and flowers in sgraffito, inscribed "God Save The King", initialled "Jn B" and dated.

1833   8in (20.5cm) high

£1,000-1,500 CHEF

An early 19thC bear jug and cover, possibly Nottingham, modelled standing holding a ring, the textured fur covered in a treacle brown glaze.

7.75in (20cm) high

£200-300 CHEF

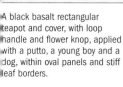

A 19thC country earthenware tobacco jar and cover, modelled as a young bear sitting holding a stick, the removable head with white details to the eyes and teeth.

6in (15.5cm) high

£300-500 WW

A Swansea-type cow creamer and cover, standing on a rectangular base.

c1820   5.75in (14.5cm) high

£400-600 AD

An earthenware cow creamer, standing on a rectangular base, painted with brown and blue patches, lacks cover, some losses and damage.

5.5in (14cm) high

£220-280 HAMG

A black basalt rectangular teapot and cover, with loop handle and flower knop, applied with a putto, a young boy and a dog, within oval panels and stiff leaf borders.

c1815   5.5in (14cm) high

£150-200 LFA

A rare pair of yellow slip-glazed lions, minor chips repaired.

c1820   10.75in (27.5cm) wide

£3,500-4,500 AS

FAIENCE

- Tin-glazed pottery first arrived in Europe during the Middle Ages, after invading Arabs introduced the technology to Andalusian Spain.
- Faience is a general term referring to earthenware products covered with a tin-enamelled, or stanniferous, glaze which became popular in Europe in the 16thC.
- Faience is made from a mixture of different clays, which are beaten and filtered to remove impurities, mixed with water and then sieved before drying.
- The tin glaze is prepared by combining molten siliceous sand and potash salt from wine sediment with lead and tin ashes. The resultant white enamel is applied to the prepared clay, painted and fired.

- Some pieces were glazed, fired at high temperature, then painted and fired again at a lower temperature. This method helps to seal the decoration more permanently.
- During the glaze firing the tin oxide creates a uniform white surface, which is more opaque and less glossy than a lead glaze, providing a superior foundation for coloured paints and enamels.
- The pigments used to decorate early tin-glazed ceramics were oxides of metals such as iron, which fired red, and manganese, which produced a purple colour.
- Faience reached the height of its popularity in France during the 18thC, when whimsical forms and decoration captured the imagination of the middle classes.

LUNÉVILLE

- The Chambrette family of Lunéville developed the art of tin-glazed earthenware during the 18thC under the patronage of the Dukes of Lorraine.
- They also manufactured 'faience fine' lead-glazed earthenwares in the English manner.
- In 1750 the Chambrettes adopted the 'petit feu' technique, which allowed a greater range of colour than the 'grand feu' method.
- Painted ornamentation consisted of flowers, birds, rustic scenes and decoration in the Chinese style.

A late 18thC Lunéville faience plate, with petit feu polychrome decoration of a bouquet of flowers outlined in the Strasbourg style in the centre, and pea pods and leeks in relief around a Rococo rim outlined in purple.

Pea pods and leeks in relief are typical of the first period of 'petit feu' decoration at Lunéville.

9.75in (25cm) diam

£400-600   **HFG**

A pair of late 18thC Lunéville faience oval wine coolers with Rococo handles, wavy rims outlined in purple and petit feu polychrome decoration of Chinese figures.

4.25in (11cm) high

£1,000-1,500   **HFG**

A late 18thC Lunéville faience cup and saucer, with petit feu polychrome decoration of flowers and forget-me-not buds, the rim outlined with purple.

4.75in (12cm) diam

£80-120   **HFG**

A late 18thC Lunéville faience plate, decorated with a bouquet of assorted flowers in the centre and florets scattered around the lobed rim.

9.5in (24cm) diam

£80-120   **HFG**

A late 18thC Lunéville oval faience wine glass cooler, with Rococo handles, undulating rim and petit feu polychrome Chinoiserie decoration.

14.5in (37cm) long

£800-1,200   **HFG**

A late 18thC Lunéville faience plate, with a moulded wavy rim outlined in green and petit feu polychrome decoration of a Chinese figure.

As Lunéville faience was not marked, pieces can be confused with those from neighbouring factories, notably Saint-Clément, which was also managed by the Chambrette family.

8.75in (22cm) diam

£120-180   **HFG**

A faience bowl by Gaspard Robert of Marseille, the undulating rim outlined in brown, with petit feu polychrome decoration of a maritime scene in the centre enclosed by flowering branches around the rim.

Gaspard Robert established himself as a manufacturer of both porcelain and faience in the 18thC. He became famous for his pastoral motifs and delicate landscapes.

c1760   8.75in (22cm) diam

£2,200-2,800   **HFG**

A late 18thC faience plate by La Veuve Perrin of Marseille, with petit feu polychrome decoration of bouquets and flowering branches.

9.5in (24cm) diam

£400-600   **HFG**

A late 18thC faience platter by La Veuve Perrin of Marseille, with petit feu polychrome decoration of bouquets and florets, scalloped and moulded rim.

14.25in (36cm) diam

£1,200-1,800   **HFG**

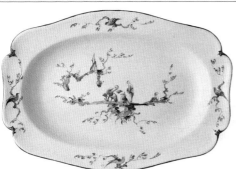

A large late 18thC Marseille faience platter, the undulating rim outlined with green, with petit feu polychrome decoration of Chinese figures in a landscape with branches, flowers and birds.

15.75in (40cm) long

£1,200-1,800   **HFG**

A pair of oval faience wine-coolers by La Veuve Perrin of Marseille, with everted scalloped rim, the handles formed as branches bearing cherries, with grand feu polychrome decoration of floral bouquets, maker's mark.

The mark of La Veuve Perrin, or 'Perrin's Widow' consists of a monogram formed from a "V" and a "P".

5.5in (14cm) high

£3,000-4,000   **HFG**

MOUSTIERS

■ The small town of Moustiers was one of the leading centres of French faience production from the end of the 17thC.

■ The first factory was founded here by the Clérissy family, and many rival firms followed, including that of Joseph Olérys who became famous for the fantasy figures he called 'Grotesques'.

A faience jardinière by Ferrat of Moustiers, with petit feu polychrome decoration of floral bouquets outlined in purple and handles formed as branches bearing cherries.

The technique of outlining painted decoration was developed by Joseph Hannong of Strasbourg. A black or manganese purple line accentuated the definition of the painting.

5.5in (14cm) high

£300-350   **HFG**

A late 18thC faience plate by Ferrat of Moustiers, with petit feu polychrome Chinoiserie decoration of two Orientals, the undulating rim outlined in purple and decorated with flowering branches.

9.75in (25cm) diam

£400-600   **HFG**

A faience sauceboat by Ferrat of Moustiers, with petit feu polychrome decoration of outlined flowers, the handles in the form of branches, the undulating border outlined in purple.

8.75in (22cm) long

£300-350   **HFG**

A late 18thC faience plate by Ferrat of Moustiers, with petit feu polychrome decoration of outlined floral bouquets, the moulded wavy rim edged in purple.

9.75in (25cm) diam

£180-220   **HFG**

An early 18thC oval Moustiers faience dish, with grand feu monochrome blue decoration of putti surrounded by a composition in the style of Bérain in a central medallion, and a band of lambrequins around the rim.

Jean Bérain's work was inspired by Renaissance and Classical designs. Arabesques, scrolled foliage, and fanciful scenes are all features of his work.

14.5in (37cm) long

£500-800   **HFG**

An oval Moustiers faience dish, with polychrome grand feu decoration of a hunting scene in a central medallion framed by a wreath of flowers.

c1755   13.5in (34cm) long

£5,000-7,000   **GV**

A Moustiers faience plate, with a wavy rim outlined in yellow and grand feu polychrome decoration of a mythological scene in a central circular medallion, framed by a wreath of flowers and garlands on the rim.

The painted scene depicts the centaur Nessos helping Hercules and his wife Deineira to cross the river Evenos.

c1760   9.75in (25cm) diam

£3,000-4,000   **GV**

A mid-18thC Moustiers faience cup and saucer, with wavy rim and grand feu green and manganese floral clusters.

c1750   Saucer 4.75in (12cm) diam

£300-500   **HFG**

An early 18thC Moustiers faience plate, with grand feu monochrome decoration of grotesques, birds, and insects.

9.75in (25cm) wide

£1,500-2,000   **HFG**

A late 18thC Moustiers faience plate, with grand feu monochrome green decoration of a Punchinello.

9.5in (24cm) diam

£300-500   **HFG**

A Moustiers faience dish, with grand feu monochrome yellow decoration of grotesques and clusters of flowers.

10.75in (27.5cm) diam

£300-500   **HFG**

A Moustiers faience covered porringer, with ear-shaped handles and grand feu monochrome green decoration of grotesques and floral clusters.

c1775   11.75in (30cm) wide

£800-1,200   **HFG**

A Moustiers faience plate, with grand feu polychrome floral decoration in blue, yellow and green, the rim lightly gadrooned and outlined in blue, marks for Olérys and Laugier of Moustiers.

c1740   9.75in (25cm) diam

£400-600   **HFG**

A Moustiers faience plate, with grand feu polychrome floral decoration in blue, yellow and green, the rim lightly gadrooned, marks for Olérys and Laugier of Moustiers.

c1750   9.5in (24cm) diam

£300-400   **HFG**

A mid-18thC Sceaux faience covered sugar bowl and stand, with petit feu polychrome decoration of outlined bouquets of assorted flowers and branches, the undulating border outlined in purple.

8.75in (22cm) long

£800-1,200   **HFG**

A Sceaux faience covered tureen with Rococo handles, the cover with a lemon finial, with petit feu polychrome decoration of delicate outlined flowers and bouquets.

c1780   11in (28cm) high

£800-1,200   **HFG**

A Sceaux half-moon faience wall jardinière, feathered with purple, blue and green petit feu polychrome decoration, with three rectangular panels of Chinese figures in landscapes.

c1780   7.5in (19cm) long

£1,500-2,000   **HFG**

A Sceaux faience wall jardinière, feathered with purple, blue and green petit feu polychrome decoration, with three rectangular panels depicting scenes from 'les Fables de La Fontaine'.

Jacques Chapelle took control of the Sceaux factory in 1759 after working there for a decade. The Duchesse du Maine, who held court nearby, was an early patron.

c1780   7.75in (20cm) long

£1,200-1,800   **HFG**

A Chapelle period Sceaux faience silver shape plate, painted with the 'Indian Flowers' pattern of scattered flower sprigs with a black outline, the rim outlined in manganese-purple.

9.5in (24cm) wide

£300-350   **HFG**

A Sceaux faience cabbage leaf tureen stand, painted with scattered flower sprays within a cabbage leaf-moulded border picked out in shades of green with yellow veins, fleur de lys mark in brown.

c1755   14.25in (36cm) wide

£1,200-1,800   **HFG**

A Sceaux faience plate with petit feu polychrome decoration of figures in a landscape, the moulded and scalloped rim feathered in blue.

c1760   9in (23cm) wide

£800-1,200   **HFG**

A Sceaux faience plate with petit feu polychrome decoration of an outlined bouquet of assorted flowers, the trompe l'oeil rim moulded with leaves.

c1770   9.5in (24cm) wide

£500-800   **HFG**

A Sceaux faience plate with petit feu polychrome decoration of naturalistic birds in imitation of Sèvres porcelain, inspired by the prints of Buffon.

c1770   9in (23cm) wide

£1,000-1,500   **GV**

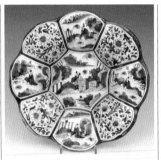

A Frankfurt faience dish with eight lobes, blue underglaze chinoiserie and floral painting on white ground, with factory number.

c1670   *12.5in (31.5cm) wide*

£220-280   **MTZ**

A Frankfurt faience plate, with blue underglaze landscape painting on milky grey ground, unmarked.

c1700   *13.75in (35cm) diam*

£150-200   **MTZ**

A Frankfurt faience fan plate, with raised, lobed border, blue underglaze Chinoiserie painting and off-white glaze, unmarked.

c1700   *13.5in (34.5cm) wide*

£300-500   **MTZ**

A Frankfurt faience fan plate, with Chinoiserie painting in manganese-violet and yellow under the off-white glaze, blue brush mark.

c1700   *13.75in (35cm) wide*

£300-500   **MTZ**

A Frankfurt faience plate, with raised border and manganese-purple Chinoiserie painting on milky grey ground with yellow highlights.

c1700   *13.75in (35cm) diam*

£400-600   **MTZ**

A Frankfurt faience fan plate, with raised wavy border and blue underglaze painting on white ground, with yellow highlights, unmarked.

c1700   *13.5in (34cm) wide*

£300-500   **MTZ**

An 18thC Frankfurt blue and white faience vase, with flared octagonal base, onion knop and neck with stiff leaf border, painted with a mounted Oriental warrior and figures in a garden, filled and converted into a lamp base, rim missing, cracks.

22.5in (57cm) high

£500-800   **HAMG**

A Kelsterbach faience inkstand in the shape of a Louis XVI commode, on four small feet, painted with architectural motifs to the sides, violet mark, inserts added later, minor damage.

c1780   *6in (15cm) wide*

£300-500   **MTZ**

A Rostrand faience plate, with a moulded border, painted with three large flower sprays, with painted mark, dated 29th July 1767.

10.5in (26cm) wide

£200-300   **WW**

A cylindrical Höchst faience pot, on three feet, the long handle in the form of a branch, heavily moulded tree-bark decoration with embossed acorns, leaves and a caterpillar, grey wheel mark and painter's mark.

c1750   *7.25in (18.5cm) high*

£1,500-2,000   **MTZ**

MAIOLICA

- Maiolica has its origins in the 14thC, when Italians began to manufacture their own version of the ceramics made by the Spanish Moors.
- The Moors exported cargoes of pottery to Pisa via Majorca. The European misconception that the pottery came from Majorca resulted in its name.
- From the start of the Renaissance, Italian maiolica entered a more decorative phase. The tin glaze gives the pottery a glassy white finish, which is an ideal base for painted decoration.
- The technique spread into northern Europe after Italian potters set up business in the Low Countries.
- Albarelli, or drug jars, are among the most prized maiolica forms. Plaques, tiles and plates were also produced in quantity.

A pair of Italian polychrome albarelli, with oak leaf decoration.

Albarelli were pharmacy jars, often made in sets for monasteries. The groove around the neck allowed a parchment lid to be tied on.

c1600   10in (26cm) high

£1,800-2,200   **JHOR**

A Sicilian polychrome albarello, with a Turk's head design.

c1600   12in (35cm) high

£2,500-3,000   **JHOR**

A pair of 17thC Sicilian blue and white albarelli, of waisted cylindrical form, titled across the body, one painted with a portrait and a bird picking berries, the other with a deer amidst foliage.

10in (25.5cm) high

£2,000-3,000   **ROS**

A garniture of three 17thC Sicilian blue and white albarelli, each titled diagonally across the body, the larger example decorated with a stylized lion amidst foliage.

Largest 10.25in (26cm) high

£1,500-2,000   **ROS**

A small Italian waisted albarello, inscribed in blue "Grand Citri" amidst a figure and buildings in a landscape, painted Savona mark.

4.25in (11cm) high

£150-200   **LFA**

A pair of 20thC Italian albarelli, of cylindrical form with narrow flared neck, portrait medallion on orange ground, trophy decoration and inscription, unmarked.

14.75in (37.5cm) high

£400-600   **MTZ**

A late 19thC Cantagalli waisted albarello in the Urbino style, painted with a figure of a Roman soldier in a landscape, cockerel mark, foot rim chip.

11.5in (29cm) high

£100-150   **DN**

An Italian rectangular maiolica plaque, probably 18thC, moulded in relief with the Madonna and child and decorated in blue, green, yellow and manganese.

15.25in (38cm) wide

£800-1,200   **WW**

An 18thC Savona maiolica tazza, painted in shades of green, ochre, manganese and blue with birds, trees and ruins, Genoa beacon-light mark, minor damage.

13.5in (34cm) diam

£600-900   **DN**

A 19thC Urbino-style maiolica crespina, painted in shades of ochre, green and blue in the Istoriato manner depicting Apollo with a lyre, surrounded by a centaur and figures from Classical mythology, rim chips.

11.5in (29cm) diam

£200-300   **DN**

A 17thC Calta Girone albarello, of cylindrical shape with flat shoulders, decorated with a coat-of-arms within a cartouche.

13.5in (34cm) high

£3,000-4,000   **WKA**

An 18thC Savona maiolica vase, decorated in blue and white, with mascarons to the side in relief, blue lighthouse mark.

13.25in (33cm) high

£300-400   **BMN**

A Spanish albarello, decorated with a blue and red bird, the back signed "V.O. 1778".

1778   *7in (17.5cm) high*

£150-200   **FIS**

An early 19thC Italian maiolica plate, with polychrome floral decoration, the rim decorated with openwork.

10.75in (27cm) wide

£50-80   **BMN**

A 19thC Italian albarello, with polychrome decoration on a cream glaze, the waisted body with a broad rim.

9.75in (24.5cm) high

£80-120   **BMN**

A 19thC Italian maiolica fruit plate, painted in polychrome with fruits, with blue painted wavy rim.

9in (22.5cm) wide

£80-120   **BMN**

A 19thC Spanish maiolica ledrillo, or foot bowl, decorated with blue, yellow and green cross pattern on a white ground, some chips.

25.5in (64cm) diam

£800-1,200   **LPZ**

A late 19thC Italian bowl by Ginori, with two swan handles to the sides, painted with ornaments in the Renaissance style, marked.

14.25in (35.5cm) wide

£320-380   **FIS**

An Italian two-piece maiolica plaque, relief-moulded with a figure of the infant Christ in the della Robbia style, mounted on wooden plates.

18.5in (46cm) high

£3,000-4,000   **LPZ**

A pearlware Toby jug, modelled seated, holding a jug of ale, painted in pale shades of ochre and manganese glazes, slight damage, lacks cover.

c1800   10.25in (26cm) high

£1,000-1,500   DN

A pearlware Toby jug, modelled seated holding a foaming jug of ale, painted with coloured enamels, hat restored, lacks cover.

c1800   9.75in (25cm) high

£600-900   DN

A pearlware 'Hearty Good Fellow' Toby jug, modelled with mug and pipe and painted in Pratt colours, restored.

c1810   6.75in (17.5cm) high

£300-500   DN

A Yorkshire pearlware standing Toby jug, modelled holding a flask and beaker, painted in Pratt colours, damaged.

c1825   7.75in (20cm) high

£500-800   DN

A rare pair of English pearlware candlestick groups, possibly by Ralph Wood, one with a boy playing a pipe, a girl, and animals against bocage, the other with a boy by a stream holding a birdcage, a girl and animals, impressed numbers "89" and "90", restored.

c1790   11in (28cm) high

£2,500-3,000   JN

A rare pair of early 19thC Staffordshire pearlware groups, in the manner of Obadiah Sherratt, depicting the 'Flight into Egypt' and the 'Return from Egypt', well coloured and raised on rectangular bases moulded with blue, red and yellow panels, minor repairs.

7.75in (20cm) high

£2,000-3,000   WW

A CLOSER LOOK AT A TOBY JUG

Toby jugs were first made by Ralph Wood in the 1760s and were imitated throughout Staffordshire and other parts of England.

The name 'Toby' comes from a famous engraving of a seated drinker holding a pipe and a mug of ale which was itself inspired by a popular song about one 'Sir Toby Philpott'.

Although Toby jugs in good condition are more desirable, some minor chipping and cracks are usually acceptable on older examples, like this one, because they were functional objects, well-used in the alehouses of their day.

A corner of the tricorn hat forms a spout for pouring. There would originally have been a cover, which sometimes doubled as a measure or cup, but these are missing from all but a very few Toby jugs on the market today.

A pearlware Toby jug, probably Yorkshire, typically modelled seated with a jug in one hand and a beaker in the other, painted in coloured glazes, restored, lacks cover.

c1825   9.75in (24cm) high

£1,200-1,800   DN

A Staffordshire pearlware model of a girl with a dove and a basket, partially painted with coloured enamels, minor flaking.

c1820   *7.25in (18.5cm) high*

£150-200   **DN**

A Staffordshire pearlware girl and sheep group, modelled before bocage, the sheep jumping up to her, painted with coloured enamels, chipped.

c1820   *5in (13cm) high*

£150-200   **DN**

A Staffordshire pearlware model of a gardener, modelled standing and preparing to graft a tree, painted with coloured enamels.

c1820   *7in (17.5cm) high*

£220-280   **DN**

An early 19thC pearlware figure of Elijah, seated beneath a tree with birds perched in the boughs, on a naturalistic mound base, some losses.

10.5in (26.5cm) high

£150-200   **HAMG**

A small pearlware model of a bird on a nest, sponged in brown, yellow, ochre and green, restored.

c1800   *3.5in (9cm) wide*

£150-200   **LFA**

A pearlware cow creamer, sponged in black and ochre, a seated milkmaid at its side, impressed number "13".

c1815   *5.5in (14cm) high*

£500-800   **LFA**

A small early 19thC pearlware model of a sheep, sitting on a grassy bank, decorated in grey and green.

3.25in (8cm) wide

£300-350   **WW**

A pair of Staffordshire pearlware recumbent sheep, modelled facing left and right with sponged puce patches and green bases, the ram with curly horns, the ewe with restored ears.

c1830   *5.5in (14cm) wide*

£400-600   **DN**

A pair of Staffordshire pearlware recumbent sheep, modelled facing left and right with sponged black patches and green bases, the ram with curly horns, restored.

c1830   *6.25in (16cm) wide*

£400-600   **DN**

An octagonal pearlware teapot and cover, perhaps Yorkshire, moulded with bands of acanthus leaves and painted with flower sprays in the famille rose style, restored.

c1790   *9.25in (23.5cm) high*

£100-150   **WW**

A rare pearlware jug, possibly Welsh, the spiral-fluted body printed in underglaze blue depicting an Oriental landscape, painted asterisk mark.

c1800   *7.25in (18.5cm) high*

£200-300   **ROW**

An ovoid pearlware jug, with angular loop handle, the diamond-moulded ground picked out in yellow and iron red, beneath a band of flowers.

c1810   *4in (10cm) high*

£50-80   **LFA**

An unusual ovoid pearlware jug, with angular loop handle, decorated in silver resist with a flower and leaf scroll band, within silver lustre line borders, small rim chip.

c1815   *5.5in (14cm) high*

£150-200   **LFA**

A Swansea baluster-shaped pearlware puzzle jug, with loop handle, the diamond-and roundel-pierced neck with three nozzles, painted with foliage within brown line borders, rim chip, one nozzle glued.

c1815   6.75in (17cm) high

£2,000-3,000   LFA

An early 18thC Staffordshire pearlware ladle, with a scalloped finial.

11in (30.5cm) long

£1,000-1,500   JHOR

A leaf-shaped pearlware dish, with loop handle, picked out in underglaze blue, on three short tapering feet.

c1790   7.5in (19cm) long

£80-120   LFA

A small pearlware plaque, modelled in relief with a putto riding a dolphin, picked out in yellow, brown and green within a reeded border.

c1800   4.5in (11.5cm) diam

£400-600   LFA

An unusual pearlware supper set, each piece printed in underglaze blue with a flower and fruit band, on an iron red vermicelli ground with brown rim, comprising four square dishes and a rectangular tray with two scroll and loop handles, rim chip.

c1815   11in (28cm) wide

£400-600   LFA

A 19thC transfer-printed and enamelled pearlware jug, the ovoid form printed on one side with "The Farmer's Arms – In God We Trust".

8in (20cm) high

£280-320   FRE

An unusual ovoid pearlware jug, with loop handle and straight neck, decorated in silver resist with vines, on a pale purple ground.

c1900   4.5in (11.5cm) high

£180-220   LFA

PEARLWARE & PRATTWARE

- Josiah Wedgwood is generally credited with the invention of pearlware, although a number of factories developed similar products from c1780. The name at least is derived from Wedgwood's version, which he called 'Pearl White'.
- Pearlware differs from factory to factory, but it is essentially an earthenware made with china clay to produce a white body, covered with a cobalt glaze which gives it a slight blue colour.
- Plain shell-edged pearlware was very affordable and purchased in quantity by those on lower incomes. Pearlware might also be decorated with transfer-printed designs.
- Prattware is a coloured and relief-moulded version of pearlware. Common forms include plaques, figures and pipes.
- The blue, yellow, brown and green pigments that could withstand high firing temperatures came to be known as 'Pratt colours'.
- Although named for William Pratt of Lane Delph in the Potteries, Prattware was made by a number of factories.

A pair of pearlware tea bowls and saucers, each printed with Chinese figures in landscapes, coloured in enamels.

c1800

£220-280   LFA

A Bristol pearlware spirit barrel, decorated in the manner of William Fifield, painted in coloured enamels with a central band of flowers between horizontal brown and green bands.

c1830   5in (12.5cm) high

£200-300   DN

A Bristol pearlware spirit barrel, decorated in the manner of William Fifield, painted in enamels with a band of flowers and the monogram "FAW" between coloured bands.

c1830   5in (12.5cm) high

£200-300   DN

POTTERY

A large Prattware plaque, moulded with a scene of the crucifixion, the border moulded with bands of small flower heads, decorated in blue, yellow, brown and ochre.

c1800   13.5in (34cm) high

£1,800-2,200   **WW**

An early 19thC Prattware money box, formed as a cottage flanked by two figures, with two children's faces at the bedroom windows, the sides moulded with trees.

5.25in (13cm) high

£180-220   **WW**

A small early 19thC Prattware figure of a man, possibly a Rabbi, standing holding a prayer book, on a green circular base.

3.75in (9.5cm) high

£200-300   **WW**

An early 19thC Prattware plaque, of arched form and moulded with a hunting scene, figures and trees, decorated in green, brown, yellow blue and ochre.

9in (23cm) wide

£1,800-2,200   **WW**

STAFFORDSHIRE FIGURES

A pair of Alcock and Co. Staffordshire spaniels on yellow bases.

c1840   5in (13cm) high

£1,200-1,800   **JHD**

A pair of Staffordshire spaniel and pup groups, minor flaking.

c1845   5.25in (13.5cm) high

£2,200-2,800   **JHD**

A Staffordshire spaniel, on black base.

c1845   5.5in (14cm) high

£800-1,200   **AD**

A pair of mid-19thC Staffordshire pottery models of spaniels, facing left and right, seated on their haunches, painted with iron red patches, some chips and flaking.

8.25in (21cm) high

£200-300   **DN**

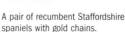

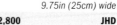

A pair of brown and white Staffordshire spaniels.

c1850   5.5in (14cm) high

£600-900   **AD**

A pair of recumbent Staffordshire spaniels with gold chains.

9.75in (25cm) wide

£2,200-2,800   **JHD**

A pair of Staffordshire spaniels on cobalt blue bases, well modelled with finely detailed faces, restored seam stresses.

Cobalt blue was the only colour able to withstand 'glost' firing and is a sign of quality.

c1850   8.25in (21cm) high

£2,000-3,000   **JHD**

An unusual Staffordshire pottery window rest, in the form of a spaniel's head, picked out in brown, and wearing a black collar, chipped.

c1850   4.5in (11.5cm) high

£700-1,000   **LFA**

One of a pair of mid-19thC Staffordshire penholders modelled as recumbent spaniels on cushion bases, partially painted with iron red patches and ochre collars, one damaged.

5.5in (14cm) long

£500-800 pair DN

A mid-19thC Staffordshire model of a spaniel with a pipe, modelled seated on its haunches on a turquoise base with a scrolling frieze, with black patches and pink muzzle, pipe missing.

9in (22cm) high

£600-900 DN

A pair of Staffordshire spaniels with children sitting on their backs.

c1855 *6.75in (17cm) high*

£2,000-2,500 JHD

A small pair of Staffordshire spaniels, restored.

c1855 *4.5in (11.5cm) high*

£300-350 JHD

A Staffordshire pen holder with three spaniels on a cobalt blue base.

c1855 *6.25in (16cm) high*

£300-500 JHD

A rare pair of Staffordshire spaniels on coloured bases, restored hairline crack.

c1855 *8.25in (21cm) high*

£2,200-2,800 JHD

A pair of Staffordshire spaniels with puppies, painted black and brown detail.

c1860 *6in (15cm) high*

£500-800 AD

A Staffordshire pottery clock group, the painted dial flanked by seated spaniels, picked out in black on brown, and surmounted by a standing poodle, the oval mound base with a gilt band.

c1860 *9.5in (24cm) high*

£300-500 LFA

A Staffordshire spaniel jug with black and white detail.

c1860 *10in (25.5cm) high*

£800-1,200 JHD

One of a pair of Staffordshire spaniels.

c1860 *9.5in (24cm) high*

£500-700 pair JHD

One of a pair of Staffordshire sporting spaniels.

c1860 *8.75in (22.5cm) high*

£1,200-1,800 pair JHD

A pair of Staffordshire spaniels with baskets of flowers in their mouths.

c1860 *8in (20.5cm) high*

£1,200-1,800 JHD

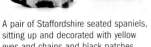

A pair of Staffordshire seated spaniels, sitting up and decorated with yellow eyes and chains and black patches.

c1875 *12.25in (31cm) high*

£300-500 WW

A pair of Staffordshire spaniel jugs, modelled seated on their haunches and painted with iron red patches.

7.5in (19cm) high

£200-300 DN

A pair of Staffordshire poodles with baskets.

c1840   3.25in (8.5cm) high

£200-300   **AD**

A pair of Staffordshire poodles on cushions.

c1860   3.5in (9cm) high

£300-400   **RDER**

STAFFORDSHIRE FIGURES

- The first Staffordshire figures were made c1740 and were intended to be budget versions of the fine porcelain models offered by European factories such as Meissen and Sèvres.
- The most popular animal figures were dogs, especially spaniels. Depictions of famous people were also popular – modellers copied likenesses from paintings and newspapers.
- From the 1840s many Staffordshire figures were produced with unmoulded and unpainted backs, designed to rest against walls.
- Staffordshire figures were made in plaster moulds, and painted over the glaze. More than 100 separate Staffordshire factories produced figures and very few bear maker's marks.

A pair of late 19thC Staffordshire poodle groups, each depicting a seated mother with her two pups, on blue rounded rectangular plinths.

5.5in (14cm) high

£700-1,000   **L&T**

A Staffordshire poodle trio clock group, restored.

7.75in (20cm) high

£500-800   **JHD**

A Staffordshire brown and white dog.

c1800   4.5in (11.5cm) high

£1,800-2,200   **JHOR**

A Staffordshire dog with bocage.

c1820   6in (15.5cm) high

£1,200-1,800   **JHOR**

A pair of Staffordshire greyhounds, seated on their haunches, painted with iron red coats and on blue gilt-lined bases, one with hairline cracks.

c1860   6in (15cm) high

£220-280   **DN**

A Staffordshire child with Afghan hound.

c1860   11.75in (30cm) high

£1,200-1,800   **JHD**

STAFFORDSHIRE FACTORIES

- The Staffordshire ceramics trade developed around the six towns of the Potteries in the mid-17thC, when local farmers developed a sideline manufacturing butter pots.
- The rich natural resources in the area include good seams of coal and red clay, close enough to the surface in some areas as to be dug from the road. White clays were brought to north Staffordshire from Dorset, Devon and Cornwall.
- The industry developed steadily throughout the 18thC, with literally hundreds of firms producing pottery in the area at various times. By 1800, the Potteries were home to the most prolific collection of ceramic factories in the world.
- It is very hard to ascribe a particular Staffordshire figure to any one factory. Pieces are rarely marked, and smaller factories often sold their moulds to rival firms when they went out of business.
- The ceramics industry has declined in more recent years, but a number of companies continue to thrive around Stoke-on-Trent.

A pair of Staffordshire St Bernards.

c1860   5in (13cm) high

£700-1,000   **JHD**

A pair of Staffordshire dogs with baskets, ridden by children.

c1860   9.75in (25cm) high

£2,500-3,000   **JHD**

A pair of late 19thC Staffordshire recumbent dalmatian pen holders, modelled facing left and right, on blue gilt lined bases.

6.25in (16cm) long

£280-320   **DN**

A pair of Staffordshire pottery models of hounds, each standing with mouth open, painted with liver markings, on white oval mound bases.

3.5in (9cm) high

£150-200   **HAMG**

A Staffordshire figure of a dog with a basket, ridden by a child.

c1860   9.75in (25cm) high

£500-800   **JHD**

One of a pair of Staffordshire models of dogs, possibly collies, seated on its haunches on a pink gilt-lined base, sparsely coloured and gilt, slight damage.

c1860   6in (15cm) high

£1,000-1,500 pair   **DN**

A Ralph Wood-type Staffordshire lion and cub group spill vase.

Ralph Wood, active 1781-1801, was from a family of Staffordshire potters. He became well known for his fine modelling and coloured glazes, and his work was much imitated. Some of his work is marked "RA. Wood Burlsem".

c1790   5.5in (14cm) high

£3,000-3,500   **JHOR**

A Staffordshire lion spill vase.

c1855   6.25in (16cm) high

£500-700   **JHD**

A Staffordshire lion spill vase.

c1855   6.25in (16cm) high

£500-700   **JHD**

A Staffordshire standing lion.

c1850   4.25in (11cm) high

£600-900   JHD

A Staffordshire lion and leopard pair.

c1855   6in (15cm) high

£2,000-2,500   JHD

A pair of Staffordshire models of standing lions.

c1860   6.75in (17cm) high

£1,500-2,000   HAMG

A pair of Staffordshire English lions overcoming Napoleon III.

c1860   9.75in (25cm) high

£1,800-2,200   JHD

A Staffordshire swan, by Alcock and Co.

c1840   4.75in (12cm) high

£700-1,000   JHD

A Staffordshire spill vase depicting hens fighting over a worm.

c1860   6in (15.5cm) high

£700-900   JHD

A pair of Staffordshire pigeon tureens and covers, modelled as nesting birds and painted in iron red, restored.

c1860   9in (22cm) long

£400-600   DN

A Staffordshire parrot.

c1855   9.25in (23.5cm) high

£400-600   AD

A pair of Staffordshire roosters.

c1860   4in (10.5cm) high

£500-700   JHD

A rare Staffordshire spill vase group, inscribed "The Milkmaid".

c1830   5.25in (13.5cm) high

£280-320   GCL

A rare Staffordshire seated monkey, on an inkwell base.

c1840   5.5in (14cm) high

£600-900   AD

A Staffordshire prancing fox, with restored ear.

c1850   6.5in (16.5cm) high

£500-800   JHD

A Staffordshire fox vase.

c1850   5in (13cm) high

£400-600   JHD

A Staffordshire pony on a textured base.

c1860   6.75in (17cm) high

£400-600   **AD**

A Staffordshire spill vase group with a zebra in flight chased by a fox, mostly coloured, on an oval gilt-lined base.

c1860   11in (28cm) high

£200-300   **DN**

A Staffordshire figure of a cow.

c1860   4.5in (11.5cm) high

£300-400   **AD**

One of a pair of Staffordshire lambs with flags.

c1860   3in (7.5cm) high

£400-600 pair   **JHD**

A Staffordshire horse and foal spill vase.

c1860   11.5in (29.5cm) high

£800-1,200   **JHD**

A pair of Staffordshire sheep and ram spill vases with some flaking paint, retouched on bases.

c1880   7.5in (19cm) high

£800-1,200   **JHD**

HUMAN FIGURES

A pair of Staffordshire rabbits.

c1860   3.5in (9cm) long

£700-1,000   **JHD**

A figure of a lady with a basket, probably Staffordshire.

c1800   10.75in (27.5cm) high

£2,500-3,000   **JHOR**

An early 19thC Staffordshire figure representative of Winter.

c1810   7.5in (19cm) high

£200-300   **AD**

An unusual Staffordshire buff earthenware figure of a man in Turkish costume, decorated in coloured enamels, and flanked by a gun and a game bird, on a mound base.

c1820   6in (15.5cm) high

£200-300   **LFA**

A Staffordshire group of children with their nanny and dog, before a flowering tree.
c1815
9in (23cm) high

£5,000-7,000   **JHOR**

An early 19thC Staffordshire figure of a man holding a book.
7in (18cm) high

£500-800   **AD**

An early 19thC Staffordshire figure inscribed "Autum", on a square base.
6.75in (17.5cm) high

£60-90   **CHEF**

An early 19thC Staffordshire figure of a trumpeter, modelled in Walton style.
6in (15.5cm) high

£300-400   **CHEF**

A pair of early 19thC Staffordshire figures of Elijah and the widow, both seated on rocks by streams and with square marbled bases, he with a raven and she with her arm around her child.
10in (25.5cm) high

£150-250   **CHEF**

A Staffordshire model of a man and a woman on a bench.
c1820   *8.5in (21.5cm) high*

£3,000-4,000   **JHOR**

A Staffordshire family group sitting on a bench, with bocage.
c1825

£4,000-6,000   **JHOR**

A Staffordshire figural group of a woman with children, bocage missing.
c1830

£120-180   **AD**

An unusual Staffordshire figure of a country woman.
c1850   *11.5in (29cm) high*

£300-500   **JHD**

A Staffordshire figure of Sir Robert Peel, modelled standing, holding a scroll in his right hand, decorated in coloured enamels, the rectangular base titled in gilt "S.R. Peel", restored.
c1850   *7.5in (19cm) high*

£280-320   **LFA**

A mid-19thC Staffordshire group of a man and companion, modelled wearing Jacobean dress, dancing.

7.5in (19cm) high

£120-180   **DN**

A 19thC Staffordshire model of the jockey Fred Archer, wearing an orange cap and a pink jacket.

9in (23cm) high

£150-200   **WW**

A mid-19thC Staffordshire group of a fisherman with wife and child, modelled seated in a boat with nets.

11in (28cm) high

£150-200   **DN**

A mid-19thC Staffordshire figure of a Highlander.

16.5in (42cm) high

£350-400   **SWO**

A 19thC Staffordshire flatback figural group of Samson and the lion, on an oval plinth base.

9in (23cm) high

£150-200   **SWO**

A Staffordshire pottery figure of a young woman, standing, wearing a plumed hat and holding a riding crop.

c1865   *12in (30.5cm) high*

£80-100   **GAL**

A CLOSER LOOK AT A LATE STAFFORDSHIRE GROUP

During the mid-19thC there was a demand for figures of famous people such as politicians, criminals, sportsmen and actors. Prior to this, Staffordshire groups had typically depicted allegorical figures, children or lovers.

The resemblance to the person portrayed was often poor as well-known personalities were modelled from drawings and prints rather than from life. Factories also used the same moulds for different characters.

Styles were generally copied from grand figures in stately homes, transferred to subjects that appealed to the working classes.

There are many fakes of Staffordshire figures on the market. Look out for artificially stained white porcelain, poor modelling and over-pronounced crazing.

Charlotte Cushman (1816-1876) was a famous American actress and patron who was particularly well known for playing male roles, including Romeo.

A late Staffordshire pottery group by Thomas Parr, depicting Charlotte Cushman as Romeo and Susan Cushman as Juliet, standing with arms entwined, the base with gilt painted title.

c1850   *10.5in (25.5cm) high*

£200-300   **HAMG**

POTTERY

A Staffordshire flatback watch stand group, the male standing beside a seated lady with a guitar.

12in (30.5cm) high

£30-50   **GORL**

A Staffordshire arbour group, of two lovers under a vine with Cupid to one side.

c1870   *12in (30.5cm) high*

£150-200   **SWO**

A Staffordshire figure of a huntsman and his dog.

18.5in (47cm) high

£400-600   **SWO**

A Staffordshire figure of Napoleon, his right arm resting on a cannon.

c1875   *16.25in (41cm) high*

£150-200   **SWO**

WHIELDON

A rare Whieldon-type model of a seated cat, decorated with a runny green and mottled brown glaze, small chip to one ear.

c1750   *4.5in (11.5cm) high*

£1,500-2,000   **WW**

A rare Whieldon-type commemorative box, the cover applied with a portrait bust, a canon, an eagle, an axe and the initials "K.P." for the King of Prussia.

c1755   *3.25in (8cm) high*

£400-600   **WW**

A CLOSER LOOK AT A WHIELDON FIGURE

The Staffordshire potter Thomas Whieldon (1719-95) made stoneware, agateware and cauliflower and pineapple-shaped moulded ceramics.

The earliest Staffordshire figures, made by Astbury or Whieldon, are scarce and valuable.

Whieldon created this mottled decoration by kneading together clays of various colours, or by applying splashes of coloured slip to the body.

These early figures are naively modelled compared to later examples. Figures became more refined during the second half of the 18thC.

A rare Whieldon-type creamware coffeepot and cover, with a moulded spout and strap handle.

c1760   *10.75in (27cm) high*

£600-900   **WW**

A Whieldon-type tortoiseshell glazed teapot and cover, with a bird knop and a crabstock handle and spout, raised on three mask-capped paw feet, some restoration.

c1765   *8in (20.5cm) high*

£800-1,200   **WW**

A Whieldon school teapot, restored finial.

c1765   *8.5in (21.5cm) long*

£800-1,200   **AS**

A rare Whieldon-type figure of a cobbler, seated mending a shoe on his knee and wearing an apron, raised on an oval base, the blade of his knife restored.

c1750   *4.5in (11.5cm) high*

£3,000-4,000   **WW**

THOMAS WHIELDON

- Thomas Whieldon (1719-95) worked from the Fenton Vivian potworks in Fenton, one of the Pottery towns in Staffordshire.
- He employed Josiah Spode from 1749 and went into partnership with Josiah Wedgwood c1755.
- Whieldon is associated most closely with the production of tortoiseshell ware, but he also produced agateware.
- Many Staffordshire potteries also produced tortoiseshell pieces, sometimes known as 'Whieldon-type' wares.
- Translucent coloured glazes, usually in manganese brown, copper green and cobalt blue, were applied to produce a mottled effect.
- Teaware forms in cream-coloured earthenware dominate the range, often with applied motifs.

A Whieldon-type miniature teapot with moulded decoration.

c1780   5.5in (14cm) long

£500-800   **AS**

A Whieldon-type lead-glazed earthenware tea canister, decorated with a figure of Flora, cover missing.

c1765   7in (18cm) high

£3,500-4,500   **JHOR**

A Whieldon-type 'Domino' caddy.

c1770   5in (12.5cm) high

£1,000-1,500   **AS**

AGATEWARE

A solid agateware teapot and cover, modelled as a shell, the handle modelled as a serpent, the knop as a lion, restored.

c1745   7.25in (18.5cm) high

£2,000-3,000   **WW**

A mid-18thC agateware teapot, with lion knop, restored.

6in (15cm) high

£3,000-5,000   **AS**

A shell-shaped agateware teapot, with lion knop.

c1755   5in (12.5cm) high

£3,000-5,000   **JHOR**

A Staffordshire agateware teapot, with applied chain and tripod feet.

c1755   8in (20.5cm) wide

£3,500-4,500   **JHOR**

An agateware cream jug, with three legs moulded as lion heads and claws.

c1755   3.5in (9cm) high

£2,200-2,800   **JHOR**

An agateware cat, salt-glazed with blue splashes, the eyes picked out in brown.

c1750   5in (13cm) high

£2,200-2,800   **JHOR**

A solid agateware model of a seated cat, marbled in cream and brown, on an oval mound base, chips to ears.

8in (20.5cm) high

£400-600   **LFA**

A 19thC solid agateware tobacco jar, the finial mounted lid above a cylindrical body applied with a panel incised "Major W.O. Wade".

1889   8.75in (22cm) high

£150-200   **ROW**

An agateware bowl.

c1750   4.25in (11cm) high

£3,000-4,000   **AS**

A Staffordshire salt-glazed stoneware teapot and cover, the branch handle issuing applied leafy branches, grapes and a squirrel, painted in polychrome with a bird chasing insects, restored.

c1760   7.5in (19cm) long

£280-320   **WW**

An English polychrome salt-glazed teapot with Chinoiserie decoration, restored chips to lid.

c1760   4.5in (11.5cm) high

£4,000-6,000   **AS**

A rare Staffordshire blue ground salt-glazed teapot and cover, painted in polychrome with two large and three small panels of flowers, restored.

c1765   7in (18cm) long

£1,200-1,800   **WW**

A polychrome salt-glazed inkwell and inner, inscribed "EM".

c1760   2.75in (7cm) diam

£2,500-3,000   **AS**

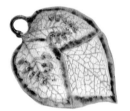

A Staffordshire salt-glazed stoneware leaf-moulded dish, with a green stalk handle, moulded with pink pea flowers and painted green, yellow and pink, restored.

c1760   7in (18cm) wide

£300-400   **WW**

A Staffordshire salt-glazed teapot.

c1750   6.5in (16cm) high

£2,500-3,000   **JHOR**

A Staffordshire salt-glazed teapot, on three lion feet.

c1750   3in (8cm) high

£700-1,000   **JHOR**

A CLOSER LOOK AT A SALT-GLAZED TEAPOT

Small Staffordshire teapots of this period are very scarce. This example features a rare faceted spout with moulded decoration, making it even more unusual.

This rose, with pink fading to white leaves, may have had Jacobite significance. This teapot was made around the time of the last great Jacobite Rebellion in 1745.

This teapot is exceptionally well modelled. It is of regular shape, is well proportioned and the lid fits snugly onto the body.

The enamels on this teapot remain extremely vibrant and attractive despite its age. Aside from a small patch of restoration to the spout, this piece is in perfect condition.

A mid-18thC English blue salt-glazed midget teapot, enamel rose decoration, restored spout.

7.5in (19cm) long

£8,000-10,000   **AS**

A Staffordshire salt-glazed stoneware sauceboat, of silver shape, moulded with scrolls on a diaper ground, a few faint hairlines.

c1750   6in (15cm) long

£200-250   **WW**

A Staffordshire salt-glazed stoneware butter tub, restored.

c1750   5in (13cm) wide

£1,200-1,800   **JHOR**

A pair of salt-glazed pot pourri containers, probably Leeds.

c1780   5in (13cm) high

£3,500-4,500   **JHOR**

REDWARE

- The Elers brothers introduced redware to Staffordshire c1685, not long after tea first went on sale in London.
- Redware was largely used to make tablewares for tea and coffee. The increasing consumption of these beverages provided a growing market for these types of ceramic.
- From c1700 redware was produced at various famous Staffordshire potteries including Wedgwood and Spode.
- Around 1765 the technology was developed that allowed the decoration of the hard body by turning it on an engine lathe.
- The Elers brothers may originally have been silversmiths by trade, and the decoration on many of their pots is reminiscent of the chasing and embossing seen on Continental silverware in the Renaissance style.
- In deference to the fashion for exotic eastern ceramics, Oriental-style marks appear on many pieces of English redware.

A rare Staffordshire octagonal redware teapot and cover, with a snake handle and leaf-moulded spout, the sides moulded with oriental figures amidst foliage, some damage.

c1760   *6in (15cm) long*

£600-900   **WW**

A CLOSER LOOK AT A REDWARE CADDY

This piece is very early, increasing its desirability. It was made by the Elers brothers, who first introduced redware to England. This historical significance adds to the value.

Redware commonly features lathe-turned or applied decoration such as these chrysanthemums.

This mark adds interest to this piece. Such marks were added to redware to enhance its desirability in the face of genuine Chinese imports.

A Staffordshire redware vase or tea caddy, made by the Elers Brothers, with chrysanthamum relief.

c1695   *2.5in (6cm) diam*

£6,000-8,000   **JHOR**

A Staffordshire redware teapot.

c1765   *5.5in (14cm) wide*

£600-900   **JHOR**

A Staffordshire redware teapot.

c1765   *6in (15cm) wide*

£500-700   **JHOR**

A Staffordshire hexagonal redware teapot, press-moulded with dragon handle and Oriental scenes, unglazed.

c1765   *7in (18cm) wide*

£1,200-1,800   **JHOR**

A large redware tea kettle, with twist handle.

c1775   *11in (28cm) wide*

£3,000-4,000   **JHOR**

A Staffordshire redware milk jug.

c1780   *5in (13cm) high*

£500-700   **JHOR**

A Staffordshire redware milk jug, with a face to the spout.

c1780   *3in (8cm) high*

£800-1,200   **JHOR**

An early 19thC mochaware pitcher, of ovoid form with moulded green bands at the neck and base, the mid section banded in taupe and tan with blue and brown earthworming, some roughness at spout.

7in (17.5cm) high

£3,000-4,000 **FRE**

A mochaware pitcher with green, ochre and brown banding.

4.25in (11cm) high

£700-1,000 **POOK**

A mochaware pitcher with green, black, ochre, blue and white banding and spotted decoration.

6in (15cm) high

£2,200-2,800 **POOK**

An early 19thC mochaware jug, decorated with concentric blue and brown bands with root designs.

8in (20cm) wide

£700-1,000 **WW**

A Staffordshire mochaware jug, of baluster form, painted with a sponged band of stylized trees.

c1840 *7.5in (19cm) high*

£300-400 **DN**

MOCHAWARE

■ Mochaware was produced by William Adams of Tunstall in Staffordshire during the late 18thC.

■ Its popularity was such that production spread throughout Europe and America during the 19thC. The technique is still used today.

■ The name is derived from the moss agate stone, which has thin, branching striations of colour. Many of these stones were shipped across the world from the port of Mocha in Yemen.

■ The process involves dripping a 'tea' of tobacco and a colouring agent, such as iron oxide, onto a ground of slip clay. The acidic tea reacts with the alkaline ground and causes a tree-like pattern to grow across the surface of the pot.

■ Mochaware is sometimes slip-decorated with designs known as 'cat's-eye', 'earthworm' and 'tobacco leaf'.

■ Popular and inexpensive at the time it was made, a wide variety of mochaware is available on today's market. However, its popularity means that prices are usually high and exceptional pieces are becoming more scarce.

■ Mugs and jugs are the most common forms, although other types of vessel such as canisters and pots can also be found.

■ Mochaware is not usually marked, making attribution to a specific factory or even an area difficult.

An early 19thC English mochaware cup, of baluster form with brick-red body decorated with brown and blue fans and brown stripe at neck, restored.

3.25in (8cm) high

£800-1,200 **FRE**

A 19thC mochaware mustard pot and cover, decorated with six blue designs within buff borders.

3.75in (9.5cm) wide

£100-150 **WW**

A large mochaware mug with earthworming on tan ground and green and black banding.

6.25in (16cm) high

£1,500-2,000 **POOK**

A mochaware canister with green band and multicolour mottled glazing.

5in (12.5cm) high

£400-600 **POOK**

An early 19thC Staffordshire money box, modelled as a house.

5in (13cm) high

£150-200   **ROS**

A Staffordshire triple house pastille burner, by Alcock, with restored finials.

c1830   *6in (15.5cm) wide*

£800-1,200   **JHD**

A Staffordshire model of Stanfield Hall, partially coloured in gilt, restored turret.

c1850   *6.25in (16cm) wide*

£280-320   **DN**

A 19thC Staffordshire model of a lighthouse beside a cottage, with a shepherd and his dog and four sheep.

7.25in (18.5cm) high

£180-220   **WW**

A Staffordshire Fair Hebe jug, modelled after John Voyez with three figures and a dog around a tree stump, inscriptions.

c1790   *10.5in (26cm) wide*

£400-600   **WW**

A Staffordshire basaltware teapot, with lion head spout and Duke of Wellington relief.

1813   *12in (30.5cm) high*

£700-1,000   **JHOR**

A Staffordshire frog mug, the interior modelled with a brown and black spotted frog perched on the base of the side, the exterior with rustic figures drinking.

c1850   *4.75in (12cm) high*

£50-80   **H&L**

A small late 18thC Staffordshire lead-glazed green leaf dish.

8.5in (22cm) wide

£400-600   **JHOR**

STONEWARE

A rare Waldenburg salt-glazed stoneware beaker, with tin mounts on a moulded brown body, the lid with relief border and ball-shaped knop.

10.5in (26.5cm) high

£4,000-6,000   **WKA**

A Creussen dark brown salt-glazed stoneware bottle, with short neck, floral relief between four oval fields, tin mounting and screw cap.

c1680   *7.75in (19.5cm) high*

£300-500   **BMN**

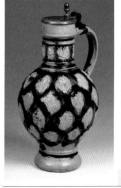

A late 17thC Westerwald salt-glazed stoneware jug, painted in blue, decorated with five stamped angels' heads, the tin mounting with flat lid and oak handle.

11.5in (29cm) high

£400-600   **BMN**

An early 18thC Westerwald salt-glazed stoneware tankard, painted in blue, the inside with a scale, tin mounting.

8.5in (21.5cm) high

£100-150   **BMN**

A 19thC Muskau salt-glazed stoneware jug, painted in blue, the tin mounting with flat lid and oak handle, engraved monogram and indistinct mark.

7.5in (18.5cm) high

£80-120   **BMN**

A large salt-glazed stoneware beer jug with tin lid, painted in blue, decorated with relief ornaments, the front with a circular medallion.

c1880   *15in (37.5cm) high*

£80-120   **FIS**

A pair of 19thC German beige stoneware ring jugs, with relief decoration, floral and geometrical borders and mascarons in the Renaissance style.

11.5in (28.5cm) high

£60-90   **FIS**

A late 19thC German Villeroy & Boch stoneware beer jug, designed by Christian Warth, glazed and with scored decoration, tin mounts, and silver-plated brass lid.

8.5in (21cm) high

£180-220   **BMN**

A German stoneware 'Studentika' jug, with polychrome enamel decoration of a student coat-of-arms and tin lid.

c1890   *6.5in (16cm) high*

£70-100   **FIS**

A German salt-glazed stoneware tankard, 'Nuremberg Tower' by Theodor Wiesler, painted in manganese and blue, with tin mounts in relief, marked.

c1900   *8in (20cm) high*

£120-180   **BMN**

A German Art Nouveau salt-glazed stoneware beer jug, designed by Richard Riemerschmid, the handle and feet in blue, with tin mounts.

c1910   *6in (15cm) high*

£300-500   **BMN**

A German Siegburg salt-glazed stoneware tankard, with a hallmarked silver lid, inscribed "A.H".

c1600   *3.5in (8.5cm) high*

£600-900   **JHOR**

A late 17thC German Westerwald salt-glazed stoneware tankard, decorated with views of Frankfurt, with a pewter lid.

5.5in (11cm) high

£2,500-3,500   **JHOR**

A late 17thC Westerwald salt-glazed stoneware tankard, with a Queen Mary plaque.

4.5in (11.5cm) high

£3,000-4,000   **JHOR**

A late 17thC Westerwald salt-glazed stoneware tavern jug.

£400-600   **JHOR**

A Westerwald salt-glazed stoneware tankard, with a pewter lid.

c1690   *6in (15cm) high*

£1,200-1,800   **JHOR**

An early 18thC Westerwald salt-glazed tankard, decorated with scenes of peasants dancing.

5in (12.5cm) high

£500-700   **JHOR**

A CLOSER LOOK AT A STONEWARE TANKARD

European stoneware was developed in the Rhineland region during the 12thC. Production eventually spread to Saxony, where this tankard was made.

This drinking vessel form with the pewter lid is typical of Annaburg stoneware, although flasks, table salts, inkwells and tureens were also produced.

A Bellarmine salt-glazed stoneware jug, from Cologne, with an old man's face, repairs to handle and rim.

The shape of Bellarmine flagons originated in mid-16thC Cologne and was used throughout the Rhineland, Flanders and London until the end of the 17thC.

c1580   7in (18cm) high

£700-1,000   **JHOR**

A Bellarmine salt-glazed stoneware jug, with an old man's face, damaged.

Bellarmine is a type of German salt-glazed stoneware used to make flagons, typically moulded with a representation of a bearded man who is believed to be Cardinal Bellarmine (1542-1621), a distinguished Jesuit theologian.

c1660   10in (25.5cm) high

£700-1,000   **JHOR**

The oil-based colours used to decorate Annaburg stoneware are prone to chipping, so pieces must be checked carefully for damage.

This type of stoneware usually has a smooth dark brown surface created by the application of slip containing a dye made from manganese oxide.

An Annaburg salt-glazed tankard, with further lead glazing.

1697   6in (15cm) high

£3,000-5,000   **JHOR**

A 17thC German stoneware Bartmankrug with later 19thC Baroque-style mounts.

11.5in (29cm) high

£350-450   **DN**

An early 17thC Bellarmine salt-glazed stoneware jug, with an old man's face.

9in (23cm) high

£200-250   **JHOR**

A Bellarmine salt glaze stoneware tavern jug, with an old man's face.

c1660   9in (23cm) high

£300-500   **JHOR**

A Westerwald salt-glazed stoneware jug, with a pewter lid.

c1680   10in (25.5cm) high

£1,200-1,800   **JHOR**

A Staffordshire white ovoid stoneware ewer, with loop handle and ribbed waisted neck, applied with a profile medallion of King George II, "GR" cypher, and underglaze blue leaf scrolls, damaged.

c1755   5in (12.5cm) high

£400-600   **LFA**

A Charles Meigh 'Bacchanalian Dance' mug, relief-moulded in stoneware with scenes after Poussin and Rubens, picked out with an unusual pink background, the inside rim with a broad band of gilding, brown-printed pseudo-medallion mark surrounded by a presentation inscription.

1847   5in (12.5cm) high

£120-180   **DN**

STONEWARE

- The first European stoneware was made in Germany towards the end of the Middle Ages. It was an improvement on earthenware as it was more durable and watertight.
- Stoneware is made by mixing clay with a stone flux and firing the mixture at a very high temperature in order to vitrify, or fuse together, the ingredients.
- Stoneware proved particularly suitable for making steins, the lidded drinking vessels popular in Germany.
- Although not required, stoneware is often given a decorative salt glaze. Famous unglazed stonewares include Wedgwood's Basalt and Jasper wares.
- White stonewares are made using ball clays, which are white-firing. These were very popular as they emulated the properties of elusive Oriental porcelain.
- Stoneware was eventually superseded in popularity by pale, opaque earthenwares such as creamware and pearlware.

POTTERY

A small Ralph & James Clews "Romantic Ruins" pattern dish, printed in blue with a Classical scene and foliage border, impressed crown mark with "GR" and "Clews Warranted Staffordshire", small chip.

c1820   11in (28cm) wide

£100-150   **DN**

A small Ralph & James Clews 'Indian Sporting' series tea plate, printed in blue with "Groom Leading Out" within a strip border of animals, impressed circular crown mark.

c1820   8in (20.5cm) diam

£100-150   **DN**

A Ralph & James Clews blue and white decorated plate, printed with "Doctor Syntax Taking Possession of his Living", with impressed and printed marks.

c1820   10.25in (25.5cm) diam

£100-150   **SWO**

A Ralph & James Clews 'Foliage and Scroll Border' series dessert plate, printed in dark blue with a scene identified as St. Catherine's Hill near Guildford, within irregular foliage border.

c1825   8.75in (22.5cm) diam

£100-150   **DN**

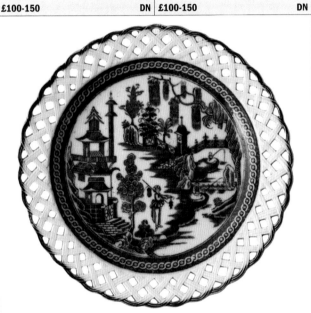

A 'Donovan' pattern pierced dessert plate, attributed to Davenport, the basketweave rim edged in blue, printed in blue with a Chinoiserie scene of fishermen by a temple, unmarked.

c1805   8in (20.5cm) diam

£120-180   **DN**

A Davenport 'Tudor Mansion' pattern well-and-tree meat dish, printed in blue with a country house scene and a border of running branches, impressed lower-case anchor mark.

c1815   18.5in (47cm) wide

£200-300   **DN**

A pair of Davenport 'Chinese River Scene' pattern dinner plates, printed in blue with a view identified as the Imperial Park at Gehol, impressed maker's name, one with cracked rim.

c1815   10in (25.5cm) diam

£80-120   **DN**

A Davenport 'Rustic Scenes' series dinner plate, printed in blue with the "Thatched Farmshed" scene within the usual floral border, impressed lower-case anchor mark.

c1820   9.75in (25cm) diam

£100-150   **DN**

A Davenport 'Fisherman' series dinner plate, printed in blue with the 'Fisherman's Tale' or 'Fisherman and Woman with Basket' scene within a geometric border, impressed anchor mark.

c1820   9.75in (25cm) diam

£50-80   **DN**

A rare Ridgway 'Net' pattern dinner plate, printed in blue with a Chinoiserie pattern and border, impressed "Ridgway" mark.

c1810   9.75in (25cm) diam

£100-150   **DN**

A Ridgway 'Angus Seats' series arcaded tea plate, printed in blue with Tong Castle in Shropshire, within a square frame and border, unmarked.

c1815   7.75in (19.5cm) diam

£100-150   **DN**

A Ridgway "Christ Church, Oxford" pattern dinner plate from the 'Oxford and Cambridge College' series, printed in blue with the titled view within an octagonal frame and border of cherub vignettes, printed mark.

c1820   9.75in (25cm) diam

£100-150   **DN**

A Francis Morley & Co. armorial well-and-tree meat dish, printed in green with the border from the 'Caledonian' pattern and a central crest of a rising sun with the motto "Quis Separabit", impressed mark "Real Ironstone China F. Morley & Co.", further printed marks with pattern title, maker's initials "RMW & Co." and registration diamond for 21 July 1846.

1846   19in (48.5cm) wide

£150-200   **DN**

A Ridgway stone china dinner plate, printed in blue with an Oriental-style pattern of a vase of flowers within a panelled border of flowers and other symbols, printed marks.

c1815   10in (25.5cm) diam

£80-120   **DN**

A pair of 'British Scenery' series dinner plates attributed to Ridgway, printed in blue with the scene known as 'Cottages and Castle' within flower and leaf border, printed series title mark.

c1820   10in (25.5cm) diam

£150-200   **DN**

A Ridgway 'Oxford and Cambridge College' series dinner plate, printed in blue with "Christ Church, Oxford" within an octagonal frame, printed mark.

c1820   10in (25.5cm) diam

£150-200   **DN**

A Ridgway 'Giraffe' pattern dinner plate, printed in blue with an animal group and open floral border, printed mark with title and maker's name.

c1830   10in (25.5cm) wide

£180-220   **DN**

A Ridgway blue and white 'Clare Hall' pattern dessert dish, of shell shape, with fruiting vine handle.

c1820   9.25in (23.5cm) wide

£100-150   **HAMG**

One of a pair of early 19thC Rogers' blue and white platters printed with the 'Monopteros' pattern of a buffalo being driven past towers and ancient ruins, impressed marks.

16.75in (42.5cm) wide

£120-180 pair   **CHEF**

A Spode 'Caramanian' series dinner plate, printed in blue with "Sarcophagi and Sepulchres at the Head of the Harbour of Cacamo", impressed mark.

c1815   10in (25.5cm) diam

£150-200   **DN**

A CLOSER LOOK AT A TRANSFER-PRINTED PLATE

Joseph Spode's 'Indian Sporting' series is one of the most famous patterns.

The illustrations are based on coloured engravings taken from Samuel Howitt's drawings in Thomas Williamson's 'Oriental Field Sports', published in 1807.

This blue and white meat dish displays the pattern to its best advantage. Dishes should not be hung using sprung metal grips as these can scratch or even crack the rim.

The pattern on this dish has been transfer printed via the application of a sheet of paper bearing a wet ink image from an engraved copper plate. The design is under the glaze.

A Spode 'Indian Sporting' series meat dish, printed in blue with "Shooting a Leopard", printed title and printed and impressed marks.

c1820   20.25in (51.5cm) wide

£2,200-2,800   **DN**

A Spode 'Indian Sporting' series dinner plate, printed in blue with the "Death of the Bear", printed title and printed and impressed marks.

c1820   9.75in (25cm) diam

£180-220   **DN**

A Spode 'Indian Sporting' series meat dish, printed in blue with "Dooreahs Leading Out Dogs", printed title and printed and impressed marks.

c1820   18.75in (47.5cm) wide

£1,800-2,200   **DN**

A Spode 'Indian Sporting' series meat dish, printed in blue with "Driving a Bear out of Sugar Canes", printed title and printed and impressed marks.

c1820   16.5in (42cm) wide

£800-1,200   **DN**

A 'Greek' series dish of Spode type, with ochre rim, printed in blue with a central scene known as 'Artemis Drawn by a Griffin and a Lynx' within a border.

c1820   18in (46cm) wide

£150-200   **DN**

A 'Greek' series well-and-tree dish, attributed to Spode, printed in blue with a central scene known as 'Cynisca Winning the Chariot Race' within a border of vases and Classical figure panels, unmarked.

c1830   20.75in (52.5cm) wide

£100-150   **DN**

A Spode printed and enamelled earthenware oval drainer, printed in blue with the 'Trophies-Etruscan' or 'Hundred Antiques' pattern within the 'Cracked Ice and Prunus' border, with details picked out in ochre enamel, printed and impressed upper-case marks.

c1825   12in (22cm) wide

£400-600   **DN**

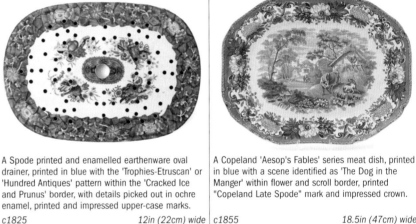

A Copeland 'Aesop's Fables' series meat dish, printed in blue with a scene identified as 'The Dog in the Manger' within flower and scroll border, printed "Copeland Late Spode" mark and impressed crown.

c1855   18.5in (47cm) wide

£300-400   **DN**

A 'Beehive and Vases' pattern dinner plate, attributed to Ralph Stevenson & Williams, printed in dark blue with a central still life scene and border.

c1825   10in (25.5cm) diam

£70-100   **DN**

A Stevenson 'Acorn and Oak Leaf Border' series cake or cheese stand, printed in blue with a scene identified as Windsor Castle, unmarked.

c1825   10.75in (27cm) diam

£300-400   **DN**

An Andrew Stevenson 'Culford Hall, Suffolk' pattern dinner plate from the 'Rose Border' series, printed in dark blue with the titled view and border.

c1825   10.25in (26cm) diam

£100-150   **DN**

A 'Beehive and Vases' pattern dinner plate, attributed to Stevenson & Williams, printed in dark blue with a central still life scene and a border.

c1825   10in (25.5cm) diam

£60-90   **DN**

A Stevenson 'Fig Tree' pattern mug, with ochre rim, printed with a Chinoiserie scene with a pavilion-like building and a fig tree with hanging lanterns.

c1800   5in (12cm) high

£80-120   **DN**

An Enoch Wood & Sons 'Gunton Hall, Norfolk' pattern tea plate from the 'Grapevine Border' series, printed in blue with the titled scene and border.

c1825   7.5in (19cm) diam

£120-180   **DN**

A 'Lady with Parasol' pattern soup plate, of octagonal shape, printed in blue with a Chinoiserie scene and running floral border, unmarked.

c1795 8.75in (22.5cm) wide

£50-80 DN

A Bovey Tracey 'Pagoda and Swan' pattern dessert plate, printed in dark blue with a Chinoiserie scene and a narrow geometric border.

c1800 8in (20.5cm) diam

£70-100 DN

A Wedgwood & Co. 'Elephant' pattern dessert plate, printed in blue with a Chinoiserie scene including an elephant and other figures, impressed marks.

c1800 8in (20.5cm) diam

£70-100 DN

A Leeds Pottery 'Great Wall of China' pattern dessert plate, printed in blue with a Chinoiserie scene and border, impressed mark.

c1810 8.5in (21.5cm) diam

£60-90 DN

A pearlware plate, printed in underglaze blue with the 'Grazing Rabbits' pattern, within a broad band of flowers and leaves.

c1815 8.5in (21.5cm) diam

£320-380 LFA

A Hartley Greens & Co. 'Scene After Claude Lorraine' pattern dinner plate, printed in blue with a Continental-style scene and strip border.

c1815 9.5in (24cm) diam

£50-70 DN

A Tams 'Floral City' series dinner plate, decorated in dark blue with an unidentified central scene framed by the usual irregular foliage border.

c1820 10in (25.5cm) diam

£50-80 DN

A 'Pashkov Palace' pattern soup plate, printed in blue with a Moscow scene and floral border, unmarked.

c1820 9.5in (24cm) diam

£120-180 DN

A pair of 'Parrot Border' series dinner plates, printed in blue with the "Mausoleum of Kausim Solemanee at Chunar Gur", printed title marks, one also with retailer's mark for "King's Warehouse Dundee", glaze crack.

c1820 10in (25.5cm) diam

£150-200 DN

An 'Audley End Essex' pattern dinner plate, possibly by Carey's, printed in blue with the identified country house scene and floral border, unmarked.

c1825 9.75in (25cm) diam

£150-200 DN

A John Denton Bagster 'Vignette' series dinner plate, printed with a scene depicting a Scottish shepherd, flowers and scroll and ribbon framing.

c1825 10in (25.5cm) diam

£50-80 DN

A Copeland & Garrett 'Caramanian' series dessert plate, printed in blue with the 'Necropolis' or 'Cemetery of Cacamo' pattern within series border.

c1840 8.5in (21.5cm) diam

£70-100 DN

A 'Gleaners' pattern soup plate, printed in blue with the genre scene and fruit and flower border, unmarked except for impressed date code "10/23".

9.75in (25cm) diam

£50-80 DN

A set of eight English transfer-printed soup plates, each printed in brown with a romantic river landscape of pavilions, castles, and a bridge.

c1825 9.5in (24cm) diam

£200-300 FRE

An early 19thC pearlware bowl, printed in blue with "The Ghost", a spectre appearing before four cowering characters, crack to border.

c1810   10in (25.5cm) wide

£200-300   **GORL**

A 'Temple with Panel' pattern meat dish, probably by Barker, printed in blue with a Chinoiserie scene and border, unmarked, damaged.

c1790   19in (48cm) wide

£150-200   **DN**

A 'Tall Pagoda' pattern dish, attributed to Lakin & Poole, printed in blue with a Chinoiserie scene featuring a tall pagoda, buildings and three junks.

c1795   12in (22.5cm) wide

£80-120   **DN**

A pair of oval pearlware dishes, each printed in underglaze blue with the 'Willow' pattern, the reeded pierced basketwork borders picked out in blue.

c1810   10.5in (26.5cm) wide

£150-200   **LFA**

A 'View of Brecknock' pattern dish from the 'Diorama' series, printed in dark blue with the titled view within the usual foliage border, printed title mark.

c1825   13.5in (34.5cm) wide

£300-400   **DN**

A Minton 'English Scenery' series meat dish, printed in blue with the scene identified as Windsor Castle within the usual floral scroll border, printed series title mark.

c1825   20.75in (53cm) wide

£400-600   **DN**

A 'Swiss Scenery' pattern well-and-tree meat dish, with moulded wavy rim, printed in brown with a typical Swiss-style romantic scene and open floral border, printed title cartouche mark.

c1830   20in (51cm) wide

£250-300   **DN**

An early Victorian blue and white platter printed with fishermen on and about a toll bridge with castle ruins in the distance, the rim with flowering vines over cherry leaves.

c1840   21.25in (54cm) wide

£150-200   **CHEF**

A 'Conversation' pattern teapot, of circular form with distinct shoulder and acorn knop to cover, printed in dark blue with a line-engraved Chinoiserie scene, unmarked, some restoration.

c1790   9in (22cm) long

£180-220   **DN**

A 'Chinaman with Rocket' pattern teapot, of spherical shape with flower-moulded knop to the cover, printed in blue with a Chinoiserie scene, unmarked, restored.

c1805   10in (25.5cm) long

£150-200   **DN**

A centrepiece from a supper set attributed to the Herculaneum Pottery, of oval shape with domed cover and internal pierced egg tray, printed in blue with an Italianate scene.

c1815   10in (25.5cm) wide

£200-250   **DN**

A Don Pottery 'Named Italian Views' series sauce tureen and cover, with a blue lion knop to the cover, printed with scenes and floral border, with flying putti beneath the handles, unmarked.

c1820   6in (15.5cm) wide

£100-150   **DN**

A 'Castle and Bridge' pattern tea plate with matching soup tureen stand, each printed in blue with a scene representing St. Albans and border of buildings and foliage, unmarked.

c1815   Stand 14.5in (37cm) wide

£150-200   **DN**

A printed blue and white pottery tureen, printed with the 'Piping Shepherd' pattern, damaged.

c1820   14in (35.5cm) wide

£300-500   **SWO**

A William Smith & Co. 'Select Views' series covered vegetable dish, of ornate oval shape, printed with romantic scenes and border of flowers, printed vignette mark with title and maker's name and impressed "Wedgwood" mark.

c1830   12.5in (24.5cm) long

£80-120   **DN**

A 'May Queen' pattern mug, with turned rim, foot and central band and simple strap handle, printed with a genre scene of the May Queen, a companion and a piper playing to dancers.

c1820   6in (15.5cm) high

£250-300   **DN**

A mid-19thC blue and white transfer-printed vomit pot or child's chamber pot, with strap handle, decorated with a Chinoiserie pattern beneath an elaborate floral border, unmarked.

5.5in (14cm) diam

£100-150   **H&L**

A Victorian blue and white 'Willow' pattern scent flask, of flat circular form, the silver lid marked "London 1886, Samson & Mordan" with printed number "29260".

2.25in (5.75cm) high

£150-200   **HAMG**

WEDGWOOD

A decorated Wedgwood vase, of twin-handled ovoid form, the encaustic decoration depicting two Classical figures within Greek key and laurel leaf borders.

c1790   9.5in (24cm) high

£1,200-1,800   **ROS**

A Wedgwood black basalt amphora, painted in Etruscan enamels with Classical figures between Greek key and anthemion band borders, impressed "Wedgwood" mark.

c1800   12.25in (31cm) high

£1,200-1,800   **DN**

A 19thC Wedgwood black basalt 'Bacchus' ewer, modelled with a strap handle with a satyr enveloping the neck and clutching the horns of a goat's mask, suspending swags of fruiting vine, on a pedestal stem and plinth foot, impressed "Wedgwood" mark, restored.

15.25in (39cm) high

£700-1,000   **DN**

An early 19thC Wedgwood black basalt bust of Shakespeare, the bearded bard wearing a buttoned jerkin and open-collared shirt, supported on a socle plinth.

12.5in (32cm) high

£500-800   **CHEF**

A large Wedgwood black basalt teapot or punch-pot, the frieze sprigged in relief with dancing Classical maidens, the cover with a finial of fruit, impressed mark, restored spout.

c1800

£150-200   **DN**

A rare Wedgwood black basalt model of a raven, modelled by E.W. Light, with glass eyes, on a shaped base, impressed mark.

c1915   8in (20.5cm) long

£300-500   **LFA**

A Wedgwood blue jasper dip canopic vase and cover, the cover moulded as a pharaoh's head, the body applied with Egyptian motifs, impressed "Wedgwood" mark and incised date.

1796   9.75in (24.5cm) high

£600-900   **WW**

A Wedgwood lidded jasperware jug, with relief decoration in white.

c1880   7.25in (18.5cm) high

£150-200   **GCL**

A late 19thC Wedgwood black jasper two-handled urn and cover, impressed mark.

9in (23cm) high

£250-300   **DN**

A 19thC Wedgwood black basalt bust of Mercury, the reverse impressed "Mercury" and "Wedgwood", on a socle base.

18in (46cm) high

£1,000-1,500   **DN**

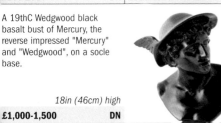

A Wedgwood white ware teapot and cover, moulded with two bands of foliate scrolls, the cover with a spaniel finial.

c1820   7in (18cm) long

£220-280   **ROS**

CHINESE DYNASTIES & MARKS

CHINESE REIGN PERIODS AND MARKS

Imperial reign marks were adopted during the Ming dynasty, and some of the most common are reproduced here. Most pieces with these marks were made in kilns at carefully controlled Imperial workshops. These workshops made ceramics for the Emperor's household and as tribute for foreign dignitaries. During periods when Imperial control was relatively lax, ceramics made outside the confines of these exalted workshops would sometimes be painted with reign marks. Many Chinese ceramics have reign marks that actually pre-date the object. A piece of Kangxi porcelain made in the late 17thC, for example, might bear the mark of the Emperor Chenghua who reigned between 1465-87. This was designed not to deceive, but to show reverence for a golden age of production.

Early periods and dates

Xia Dynasty	c2000 - 1500BC	Northern and Southern Dynasties	420 - 581
Shang Dynasty	1500 - 1028BC	Sui Dynasty	581 - 618
Zhou Dynasty	1028 - 221BC	Tang Dynasty	618 - 906
Qin Dynasty	221 - 206BC	The Five Dynasties	907 - 960
Han Dynasty	206BC - AD220	Song Dynasty	960 - 1279
Three Kingdoms	221 - 280	Jin Dynasty	1115 - 1234
Jin Dynasty	265 - 420	Yuan Dynasty	1260 - 1368

Ming Dynasty Reigns

Hongwu	1368 - 1398	Jingtai	1450 - 1457
Jianwen	1399 - 1402	Tianshun	1457 - 1464
Yongle	1403 - 1424	Chenghua	1465 - 1487
Hongxi	1425 - 1425	Hongzhi	1488 - 1505
Xuande	1426 - 1435	Zhengde	1506 - 1521
Zhengtong	1436 - 1449		

Ming Dynasty Marks

Jiajing	Longquing	Wanli	Tianqi	Chongzhen
1522 – 1566	1567 – 1572	1573 – 1619	1621 – 1627	1628 – 1644

Qing Dynasty Marks

Shunzhi	Kangxi	Yongzheng	Qianlong	Jiaqing	Daoguang
1644 – 1661	1662 – 1722	1723 – 1735	1736 – 1795	1796 – 1820	1821 – 1850

Republic Period

Xianfeng	Tongzhi	Guangxu	Xuantong	Hongxian (Yuan Shikai)
1851 – 1861	1862 – 1874	1875 – 1908	1909 – 1911	1915 – 1916

THE ORIENTAL CERAMICS MARKET

The market for Oriental ceramics is generally buoyant, although increasingly polarised. Buyers from mainland China are now beginning to dominate the world market and have forced up prices in many sectors. They are especially keen to acquire so-called 'mark and reign' pieces that bear the correct reign mark for their period. Kangxi and Transitional blue and white porcelain is proving extremely popular in China, where there has been a marked increase in the number of registered antique dealers in the last year. Figurative art has long been an important part of Chinese culture, and vases with figurative decoration are attracting particular interest at the moment.

A fundamental shift in the attitude of Chinese buyers is their newfound desire to acquire export ware, provided it does not deviate too far from the traditional Chinese aesthetic. Famille Rose decoration and ceramics based on European silver shapes, on the other hand, are not enjoying the same degree of success. The preference among European buyers for minimalist decorative arts is a contributory factor in the stagnation of this sector of the market.

Damaged pottery and porcelain has probably shown the most dramatic increase in value over the last year. Whereas a minute rim chip would once have been enough to consign an otherwise beautiful vase to the back shelf, buyers are increasingly willing to overlook such minor imperfections. Items with more obvious cracks are now attracting up to half the value one would expect for a pristine example, rather than the 10% that was previously the norm. Once confined to the very best examples of a particular genre, this trend is now affecting more ordinary pieces.

Robert McPherson, Oriental ceramics expert

EARLY CHINESE DYNASTIES

A Chinese Eastern Jin dynasty Yueyao ewer, the shoulders with a dragon head spout and faceted lugs, rim restored.

The kilns of Yueyao are situated in the Ningbo region of China, one of the starting points for the Silk Road.

cAD300   9in (22cm) high
£300-500   **DN**

A Chinese Eastern Jin dynasty Yueyao vase, with an olive green glaze, the shoulders with four taotie heads.

The taotie is a fearsome horned beast that has been used in Chinese decorative arts for 3000 years.

cAD300   6.5in (16.5cm) high
£300-500   **DN**

One of a pair of Chinese Tang dynasty mottled glaze tea bowls, with green and ochre glazes over a white slip ground, the feet unglazed.

2.5in (6.5cm) diam
£100-150 pair   **CHEF**

A Chinese Liao dynasty pottery cockscomb vase, with short neck and tapering sides incised with lotus, covered with an olive green glaze, losses.

cAD1000   10.5in (26.5cm) high
£280-320   **DN**

A Chinese Tang dynasty ovoid vase and cover, covered with an amber brown glaze falling short of the foot, with a single blue splash, rim chipped.

AD618-907   9in (22cm) high
£800-1,200   **DN**

A Chinese Tang dynasty pottery straw-glazed model of a princess, her hair tied up in a chignon, with traces of original black pigment, her shoes upturned at the front, restored.

£400-600   **WW**

A Chinese Tang dynasty ewer, the design based on metal work, made of dense iron-splashed stoneware.

AD618-907   7.5in (19cm) high
£500-700   **R&GM**

An unusually large pair of Chinese Song dynasty Qingbai jars and covers, of slender baluster form, the necks moulded with dragons, lingxhi fungus, deer and bands of accolytes, the covers with bird finials.

29in (74cm) high

£800-1,200 **DN**

A 12thC Chinese Song dynasty Qiangbai jar and cover.

These vessels were made in large numbers for use as storage containers.

8.25in (21cm) high

£200-250 **R&GM**

A Chinese Song dynasty Qingbai vase, with cylindrical neck incised with fluting and ovoid body moulded with bands of flowers beneath a pale ice blue glaze.

11in (28cm) high

£250-350 **CHEF**

A large Chinese Southern Song dynasty Henan bottle vase, with ribbed body, short neck and flared rim, covered in a black glaze falling short of the foot, restored.

12in (30.5cm) high

£350-400 **DN**

A Chinese Tang dynasty horse and rider burial piece, with cold painted decoration, losses and restoration.

This piece comes with thermoluminescence test results indicating its authenticity. There are many fakes on the market, often reassembled from mismatched fragments retrieved from the ground which are sometimes repainted.

AD618-907 *13.75in (35cm) high*

£1,300-1,500 **R&GM**

A 12th/13thC Chinese Southern Song dynasty moulded Qingbai box.

The Qingbai glaze was developed at the Xinping kilns. The blue tinge is from iron impurities in the glaze recipe.

2in (5cm) wide

£100-150 **R&GM**

An 11th/12thC Chinese Song dynasty fruit-form box and cover, restored.

In better condition, this piece would be worth around £250.

2.5in (6cm) high

£70-100 **R&GM**

A Chinese 12thC Song dynasty Qingbai bowl, with incised fish, chipped.

7in (18cm) diam

£500-600 **R&GM**

A Chinese late Ming dynasty celadon duck water dropper, with removable wing for filling the interior chamber, the bird's open beak forming the spout and its rocky perch the circular foot.

6.75in (17cm) high

£2,500-3,000 **CHEF**

A Chinese late Ming dynasty celadon monkey, modelled sitting, with a hole in his back open to an interior chamber, holding a sacred peach, the octagonal base with flange foot.

6.5in (16.5cm) high

£1,000-1,500　　　　**CHEF**

A CLOSER LOOK AT A CHINESE CUP STAND

Cup stands of this shape would have held small, straight-sided cups with slightly recessed bases and narrow feet.

The clarity of the glaze is excellent, with little of the typical greying or clouding associated with the aging process.

The copper underglaze used in this piece is relatively unsuccessful in the kiln, and few examples survive. An example with no firing faults is a real rarity.

A similar slightly smaller cup stand is owned by the British Museum, and another can be seen in the Avery Brundage Collection. Pieces of 'museum quality' are excellent illustrative examples of their type and invariably attract great interest.

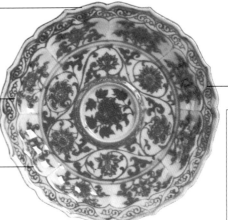

A Chinese Yuan period porcelain cup stand, decorated in underglaze copper red with peony blossom and ruyi heads, the scalloped border with fan-shaped panels decorated with lotus flower sprays, the unglazed base with a pale orange wash.

The ruyi is a stylized lotus flower whose name translates as 'as you wish'. It is a symbol of favour and a traditional birthday gift.

8in (20cm) diam

£40,000-45,000　　　　**L&T**

A Chinese Jin dynasty carved Yaozhou celadon bowl.

'Yaozhou' refers to the kiln group where this piece was made. The decoration was achieved by incising the bowl before the clay dried. When the green celadon glaze was applied it pooled in these depressions, creating a design in varying tones of green.

AD1115-1234　　*5in (13cm) diam*

£600-900　　　　**R&GM**

A 15thC Chinese Ming dynasty celadon dish.

10.5in (26.5cm) diam

£350-450　　　　**R&GM**

A Chinese late Ming dynasty earthenware table, from northern China, laid with food and drink offerings, lead glazed and cold painted, probably a burial piece, chipped.

1550-1600　*8.25in (21cm) wide*

£300-500　　　　**R&GM**

WANLI BLUE & WHITE

A mid-16thC Chinese blue and white dish, painted with a central floral rosette within a band of ruyi lappets and four mythical beasts on the rim, the reverse with five horse roundels and Buddhist objects, pseudo seal mark.

12.25in (31cm) diam

£500-800　　　　**CHEF**

One of a pair of Chinese Wanli period blue and white Kraak dishes, painted with birds and insects within floral panelled borders.

11.25in (29cm) diam

£500-800 pair　　　　**HAMG**

A Chinese Wanli period Kraak dish, decorated in underglaze blue with a panel of birds and flowers within a radiating panel of flowers and precious emblems.

1573-1619　　*11in (28cm) diam*

£500-800　　　　**DN**

ORIENTAL CERAMICS

A Chinese late Ming dynasty blue and white plate, with a central phoenix design.

1560-1620   7.75in (19.5cm) diam

£120-180   **R&GM**

A Chinese late Ming dynasty Kraak dish.

Kraak porcelain was made c1580-1640. It was named after the Portugese ships called 'carracks' in which it was carried.

1600-1630   7.75in (19.5cm) diam

£220-280   **R&GM**

A Chinese Ming dynasty dish, decorated with fowl on a white ground, for the Japanese export market.

1620-1640   6in (15cm) diam

£300-400   **R&GM**

A late 16thC Chinese blue and white jar, the sides painted with a band of dragons and phoenix amongst clouds, between lappet bands.

7in (17.5cm) high

£1,000-1,500   **CHEF**

An unusual Chinese Wanli period blue and white box and cover, painted with lotus flowers and scrollwork, restored.

This piece would originally have been part of a set that would fit together.

3in (7.5cm) high

£4,500-5,500   **BEA**

A Chinese Wanli period blue and white kendi.

A kendi is a Persian drinking vessel without a handle.

1575-1610   7.75in (19.5cm) high

£2,200-2,800   **BEA**

A Chinese Transitional period blue and white vase.

The price of this vase is relatively low as its cover has been lost and it has poor quality painting.

7.25in (18.5cm) high

£150-200   **CHEF**

A large mid-17thC Chinese Transitional period Wucai brush pot, the body incised with a band of five horizontal lines, damaged.

In perfect condition, a pot like this would be worth £3,500-5,000.

8.5in (21cm) diam

£2,500-3,000   **WW**

A Chinese late Ming dynasty moulded kraak dish, decorated with a cricket.

Kraak porcelain is prone to chips at the edges, caused by blisters that form under the glaze during firing.

1600-1630   5.25in (14cm) diam

£140-165   **R&GM**

A Chinese blue and white cylindrical vase, with waisted neck and flared rim, the shoulder and foot decorated with anhua bands, the body with figures and a horse beside a waterfall, rim chips.

c1640   18.75in (47cm) high

£12,000-15,000   **WW**

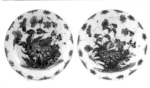

A Chinese Transitional period blue and white ewer, painted with a broad band enclosing a garden scene and a scholar with attendants, small chips.

8.25in (21cm) high

£1,500-2,000   BEA

A pair of Chinese Kangxi period blue and white dishes, chipped.

1662-1722   8.5in (21.5cm) diam

£1,200-1,500   R&GM

A CLOSER LOOK AT A KANGXI PERIOD BLUE AND WHITE DISH

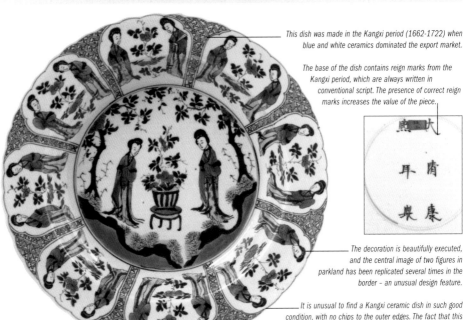

This dish was made in the Kangxi period (1662-1722) when blue and white ceramics dominated the export market.

The base of the dish contains reign marks from the Kangxi period, which are always written in conventional script. The presence of correct reign marks increases the value of the piece.

The decoration is beautifully executed, and the central image of two figures in parkland has been replicated several times in the border – an unusual design feature.

It is unusual to find a Kangxi ceramic dish in such good condition, with no chips to the outer edges. The fact that this example is pristine makes it especially valuable to collectors.

A Chinese Kangxi period dish, with a central roundel depicting figures in a landscape, with Kangxi reign marks.

c1690   13.5in (34.5cm) diam

£3,000-5,000   R&GM

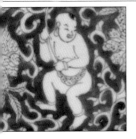

One of a pair of Chinese Kangxi period dishes, depicting a figure amid foliage.

1690-1710   11in (28cm) diam

£2,500-3,000 pair   R&GM

A Chinese Kangxi period dish, with a seascape scene, rim chips.

c1700   8.75in (22cm) diam

£400-600   R&GM

A Chinese Kangxi period Kraak dish.

This is late revival of Kraak decoration, usually associated with the Wanli period.

1662-1722   8.75in (22cm) diam

£500-700   R&GM

A pair of Chinese Kangxi period dishes, decorated with items representing cultural and artistic pursuits, including books and flowers arranged in vases.

This is a Chinese pair – the dishes are not identical, as they were probably worked on by several artists. They are hand painted to a similar theme and have the same border design.

c1700   11in (28cm) diam

£1,200-1,800 pair   R&GM

A Chinese Kangxi period reticulated saucer, with foliate decoration.

This highly delicate technique involves the pattern being cut out while the clay is semi-hard, before glazing. European factories such as Worcester experimented with similar techniques in the late 19thC.

c1700   4.25in (11cm) diam

£600-900   R&GM

A pair of Chinese Kangxi period blue and white plates, decorated with the eight horses of Mu Wang, with flower marks.

1662-1722   8.5in (21.5cm) diam

£2,000-3,000   **WW**

A pair of Chinese Kangxi period blue and white plates, each painted with the eight horses of Mu Wang.

8.75in (22cm) diam

£1,500-2,000   **WW**

A 17thC Chinese blue and white bowl, decorated with peony flowers and foliage, with six-character mark for the Hall of Admiring Frugality.

8.25in (20.5cm) diam

£500-700   **WW**

A Chinese Kangxi period bowl, with Chenghua reign marks.

1662-1722   5.5in (14cm) wide

£1,200-1,800   **R&GM**

A Chinese Kangxi period brush pot, decorated with figures, with chips to inner rim and footrim, unmarked.

In perfect condition, a pot like this would be £8,000-10,000.

7.5in (18.5cm) wide

£3,500-4,000   **WW**

A pair of Chinese Kangxi period blue and white bowls, decorated with a continuous hibiscus scroll above a band of lappets, with six-character Kangxi marks, chipped.

In perfect condition, a pair of bowls like this would be worth £3,000-4,000.

6.5in (16.5cm) high

£2,000-2,500   **WW**

A Chinese Kangxi period blue and white bowl, boldly painted with eight tribute bearers, the interior painted with a dragon in pursuit of a flaming pearl amongst clouds, seal mark.

In Chinese mythology, the dragon represents the powers of air and water, while the flaming pearl symbolizes the quest for virtue and wisdom.

8.75in (22cm) diam

£400-600   **WW**

A Chinese Kangxi period salt, decorated with a typical Chinese landscape.

This shape is based on European silverware. A complete pair in good condition would be worth around £1,400.

c1700   3.5in (9cm) wide

£350-450   **R&GM**

A Chinese Kangxi period blue and white moulded bowl, rim chips.

c1700   6in (15.5cm) high

£300-500   **R&GM**

One of a pair of Chinese European shape blue and white salts.

1710-1735   3in (7.5cm) long

£800-1,100 pair   **R&GM**

A small Chinese Batavia ware teabowl.

Batavia, now called Jakarta, was the trading centre of the Dutch East India Company. Batavia ware, recognisable by its iron red exterior, was particularly popular with the Dutch market. Tea bowls were small because the tax on tea made it expensive.

1720-40   3in (7.5cm) wide

£25-30   **R&GM**

A Chinese Kangxi period blue and white bombe censer, decorated with the Eight Daoist Immortals, small rim chip.

1622-1722   7.75in (20cm) high

£700-1,000   **WW**

A large Chinese Kangxi period blue and white moulded baluster vase and cover, decorated with panels of peony, the knop a wooden replacement.

23.25in (59cm) high

£3,500-5,000   **WW**

A Chinese Kangxi period goblet, based on the shape of a European wine glass.

1690-1700   5.75in (14.5cm) high

£1,000-1,500   **R&GM**

A Chinese Kangxi period blue and white oviform vase, some damage.

In perfect condition, this vase would be worth £2,000-3,000.

13.5in (34cm) high

£1,000-1,500   **ROS**

A Chinese Kangxi period gu vase.

The gu vase shape is based on the ritual bronze wine vessels of ancient China.

7.5in (19cm) high

£800-1,100   **R&GM**

A Chinese Kangxi period blue and white brushpot, decorated with the 'Hundred Antiques' pattern.

1690-1720   4.75in (12cm) high

£1,500-2,000   **R&GM**

A 17thC Chinese Kraak teapot, extensively damaged, lacking cover.

In perfect condition, a teapot like this would be worth £800-1,200 and more than double that with its cover.

7.75in (20cm) high

£120-180   **CHEF**

A rare Chinese Kangxi period blue and white teapot and cover, with raised handle and spout modelled as a snake, the spherical body raised on a domed foot.

7in (18cm) high

£2,500-3,000   **CHEF**

A Chinese Kangxi period blue and white ewer, decorated with two shaped panels containing figures.

10.5in (26.5cm) high

£800-1,200   **WW**

A Chinese Kangxi period blue and white teapot and cover, the ribbed sides painted with flowers below moulded key fret bands, the cover with a chrysanthemum knop.

5in (12.5cm) high

£100-150   **CHEF**

ORIENTAL CERAMICS

A Chinese Kangxi period blue and white ewer, the ovoid body painted with a band of flowers and foliage, swastika mark.

8in (20.5cm) high

£1,400-1,800   **WW**

A 17thC Chinese blue and white kendi, decorated with figures in a landscape beneath a scroll band, chipped.

7in (18cm) high

£300-500   **WW**

A Chinese Kangxi period incised jar and cover, made for the European market, with Chenghua mark.

The mark relates to the 15thC Emperor Chenghua. It denotes reverence for a bygone era.

1690-1720   *9.5in (24cm) high*

£2,000-3,000   **R&GM**

A Chinese Kangxi period European shape mug, with firing crack, chipped.

Although the form of this piece is European, the decoration is distinctly Chinese in style.

c1700   *3.25in (8cm) high*

£400-600   **R&GM**

A Chinese Kangxi period cruet, with 19thC Dutch silver mounts.

This shape is based on European glassware. It is in the form of two conjoined bottles, creating separate chambers for oil and vinegar.

1690-1710   *8.25in (21cm) high*

£3,000-5,000   **R&GM**

A Chinese Kangxi period blue and white porcelain candlestick, after a European silver shape, the canted square base painted with exotic birds, with a band of leaves on the column.

7in (18cm) high

£900-1,200   **HAMG**

YONGZHENG BLUE & WHITE

An Chinese Yongzheng period, with three feet, small chip to spout.

This teapot is desirable as it has three feet and is of good colour with varied tones of rich, strong blue.

1723-1735   *3.25in (8.5cm) high*

£1,200-1,800   **JES**

A Chinese Yongzheng period blue and white sugar castor, chipped.

Designs for these European shapes were sent to China for manufacturers to copy.

1723-1735   *4.75in (12cm) high*

£400-550   **R&GM**

A Chinese Yongzheng period blue and white baluster vase, painted with a broad band enclosing a garden scene with go players, repaired neck.

14.5in (37cm) high

£1,200-1,800   **BEA**

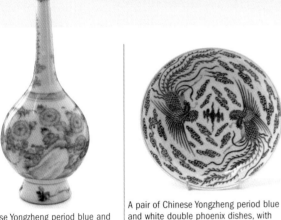

A Chinese Yongzheng period blue and white rosewater sprinkler.

The decoration here is made up of simple blue lines. Pieces decorated with different tones of blue are worth more.

1723-35   7.75in (20cm) high
£400-600   **R&GM**

A pair of Chinese Yongzheng period blue and white double phoenix dishes, with Yongzheng reign mark.

The phoenix, emblematic of the Empress, is one of the four supernatural creatures, along with the dragon, tortoise and kylin, symbol of Imperial power.

1723-35   7.75in (20cm) diam
£5,000-7,000   **R&GM**

A Chinese Qianlong period Pompadour plate, with fish vignettes, rim chips.

The fish refer to Pompadour's original surname, Poisson, and the crowned eagle to Louis XV, to whom she was mistress.

c1750   9in (23cm) diam
£300-500   **R&GM**

A Chinese Qianlong period blue and white export ware dish, made in imitation of a Dutch Delft herring dish.

c1765   9.5in (24cm) wide
£2,200-2,800   **R&GM**

A Chinese Qianlong period blue and white Ming-style bowl, heavily potted and decorated with a continuous flower and leaf scroll, beneath a band of jui heads.

8.75in (22cm) diam
£1,800-2,200   **WW**

A large 18thC Chinese blue and white vase, of archaic form, with moulded animal mask and ring handles, decorated with stylized bands of taotie masks, stiff leaves and key fret band.

18in (46cm) high
£6,000-8,000   **WW**

A CLOSER LOOK AT A CHINESE QIANLONG BLUE & WHITE VASE

A Chinese Qianlong period blue and white baluster vase and cover, painted with prunus issuing from rockwork, the domed cover with bud finial, damaged.

14.25in (36cm) high
£250-300   **ROS**

This vase has a six-character Qianlong period (1736-1795) reign mark, enclosed in a double circle. Having the correct reign mark can double the value of a piece.

This octagonal form is relatively unusual and marks this piece out from comparable Qianlong ceramics.

A large Chinese Qianlong period blue and white vase, the octagonal section body painted with exotic pheasants, cranes and ducks beneath a leafy tree flanked by peony and hydrangea, the reverse with sparrows and butterflies above chrysanthemums and rockwork.

£15,000-18,000

This vase has no manufacturing faults and is in excellent condition. The well-executed painting remains bright and clearly defined, further increasing the appeal of this vase.

Blue and white wares dominated the export market during this period and tended to imitate early Ming versions, with carefully spaced decoration. These formal and measured arrangements of scrolling foliage and animals are typical of the period.

22in (56cm) high
WW

QIANLONG BLUE & WHITE

A 17thC Chinese blue and white vase, with later metal lid, the gu-shaped body painted with birds amongst flowers.

This vase was originally taller, but has been cut down. The metal mount has been added to disguise the cut edge.

17.5in (44.5cm) high

£900-1,200 **CHEF**

A Chinese Qianlong period pear-shaped ewer, painted with the Flowers of the Four Seasons, with a later metal cover.

This is a piece of Imperial porcelain. The price is relatively low because it has been restored from fragments.

c1750 *11in (28cm) high*

£2,500-3,000 **WW**

An 18thC Chinese blue and white tureen, cover and stand, the lid with pomegranate knop and painted with two fallow deer in a landscape, the handles with rabbit masks, the stand with birds in a garden.

15in (38cm) wide

£300-500 **CHEF**

An 18thC Chinese blue and white Nanking tureen and cover, with animal head handles.

13in (33cm) wide

£300-500 **JN**

An 18thC Chinese soft paste porcelain jar, with an archaic pattern based on ancient bronze designs.

Soft paste Chinese porcelain is unusual.

3.5in (9cm) high

£500-650 **R&GM**

A late 18thC Chinese blue and white octagonal jardinière, painted with alternating reserves of landscapes and gardens on a cash diaper ground, with bracket feet.

14.25in (36cm) wide

£800-1,200 **CHEF**

LATE QING BLUE & WHITE

A 19thC Chinese porcelain tulip vase, painted with flowers in underglaze blue.

This form is also found in Delft ware and was used in Holland to display flowers, especially tulips.

10in (25.5cm) high

£450-600 **GORL**

A pair of late 19thC Chinese blue and white moon flasks, painted with mountainous landscapes.

8.5in (21.5cm) high

£1,000-1,500 **BEA**

A pair of late 19thC Chinese blue and white porcelain double-gourd vases, painted in underglaze blue with reserves enclosing birds and flowers.

20.75in (53cm) high

£700-1,000 **BEA**

A Chinese Qing dynasty blue and white beaker vase, painted with figures in a garden setting, four-character mark to the base.

14.25in (36cm) high

£500-800 **H&L**

A late 19thC Chinese blue and white cylindrical stick stand, decorated with a dragon amidst flowers.

23.5in (60cm) high

£250-300 **WW**

A 19thC Chinese blue and white wash stand, of circular form with a floral rim, painted with floral panels, in reserves on a blue ground, with crackle glaze.

15in (38cm) diam

£250-300 **ROS**

A rare and early Chinese Blanc-de-Chine figure of Guanyin, from Dehua in Fujian province.

1630-50   9.5in (24cm) high

£1,500-2,000   **R&GM**

A 17thC Chinese Blanc-de-Chine figure of Guanyin.

Guanyin, the goddess of mercy, is sometimes also represented with a child. In some pieces made for the European market the figure was modelled as the Virgin Mary.

4.25in (11cm) high

£600-800   **R&GM**

A large Chinese Kangxi period Blanc-de-Chine figure of Guanyin, seated on rockwork, a child on her lap.

15.75in (40cm) high

£600-900   **WW**

A late 19thC Chinese Blanc-de-Chine figure of Guanyin, sitting cross legged on a double lotus throne and holding a pearl.

13in (33cm) high

£70-100   **CHEF**

A late 19thC Chinese Blanc-de-Chine figure of Guanyin, holding a child and seated on a lotus.

9in (22cm) high

£100-150   **DN**

A pair of Chinese Kangxi period Blanc-de-Chine figures from Dehua in Fujian province, known as 'Adam and Eve'.

c1690   9in (23cm) high

£2,500-3,200   **R&GM**

A Chinese Kangxi period Blanc-de-Chine group.

The holes under the nose would have held a horsehair moustache.

1662-1722   9in (23cm) high

£800-1,200   **R&GM**

A Chinese Kangxi period Blanc-de-Chine Buddhist lion, from Dehua in Fujian Province.

This piece was made in a mould and hand-finished. Some pieces feature more hand-carved work.

c1700   2in (5cm) high

£220-280   **R&GM**

A pair of late 19thC Chinese Blanc-de-Chine Buddhist lions, each with a raised paw, on pierced ball and plinth bases.

9in (23cm) high

£180-220   **ROS**

A 17thC Chinese Blanc-de-Chine vase, from Dehua in Fujian province.

5.5in (14cm) high

£800-1,200   **R&GM**

A 17thC Chinese Blanc-de-Chine stem cup, from Dehua in Fujian province.

5.25in (13.5cm) diam

£1,200-1,500   **R&GM**

An 18thC Chinese An hua decorated stem cup, complete with leather, cotton and wicker carrying case.

'An hua' means 'secret decoration'. The design is only visible when held to the light.

5.5in (14cm) diam

£1,200-1,800   **R&GM**

FAMILLE VERTE

- Famille verte, literally meaning the 'green family', was adopted during the Kangxi reign (1662-1722), having evolved from the five colour Wucai style.
- The predominant famille verte colours are a bright apple green and iron red, combined with hues of blue, yellow and aubergine. These enamels pigments are painted over the glaze, with the exception of cobalt blue and copper red.
- Patterns often incorporate flowers, such as chrysanthemums, lotus and prunus, combined with black speckled diapers. Larger designs include rocky oriental gardens and landscapes, figures, the Eight Precious Things and the Eight Buddhist Emblems.
- Wealthy northern European clients commissioned large famille verte dinner services decorated with their own coat of arms.
- The production of famille verte continued well into the 20thC. The most sought after pieces, however, are those dating from the Kangxi period, and these command a premium.

A Chinese Kangxi period famille verte supper set, decorated with prunus sprays on a green ground, comprising 19 shaped dishes in a fitted wood tray, some damage.

16.25in (41.5cm) wide

£800-1,200 WW

A Chinese Kangxi period famille verte fluted saucer dish, decorated with a small kylin issuing from the breath of a larger kylin, within alternate radiating panels of birds and Imari iron red mons, chipped.

8in (20.5cm) diam

£500-700 DN

A Chinese Kangxi period famille verte charger, with shaped rim, decorated with a basket of flowers within radiating panels of flowers and cell borders.

14.5in (36cm) diam

£700-900 DN

One of a pair of Chinese Kangxi period famille verte plates, decorated with the Hundred Antiques.

c1700 *8.5in (21.5cm) diam*

£600-800 pair R&GM

A Chinese Kangxi period famille verte ovoid vase, decorated with cartouches containing fan-shaped panels of figures, flowers and buildings, with wooden cover, leaf mark.

10.5in (26.5cm) high

£1,000-1,500 WW

A 19thC Chinese famille verte vase, of baluster form painted with dignitaries and a rocky outcrop with a tree, painted marks.

8.5in (22cm) high

£400-600 HAMG

A pair of 19thC Chinese famille verte vases, converted as table lamps, each painted with eight figures conversing and holding fans and scrolls, with wooden stands, four-character Qianlong marks.

14in (36cm) high

£800-1,200 WW

A late 19thC Chinese famille verte ginger jar and cover, enamelled with panels of flowers and insects, on a celadon foliate scroll ground, within stylized borders, blue four-character marks to base, with wooden stand.

9.75in (25cm) high

£200-250 H&L

A Chinese Kangxi period famille verte jug, painted with birds and flowers on a green-seeded ground, the sides with panels of insects amongst lotus, roses, chrysanthemums and prunus, cover missing.

8.75in (22cm) high

£2,000-2,500 BEA

An early 18thC Chinese famille verte wine pot, with yellow arch handle, gilt metal lid and mounted spout tip, the bell-shaped sides painted with two reserves of ladies seated at tables.

7in (17.5cm) high

£800-1,200 CHEF

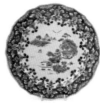

A pair of Chinese Yongzheng period famille rose plates, damaged.

1723-35   *8in (20.5cm) wide*
£550-650   **R&GM**

A pair of Chinese early Qianlong period famille rose plates.

c1740   *9in (23cm) diam*
£300-500   **R&GM**

A pair of Chinese Qianlong period famille rose plates.

1750-60   *9in (23cm) diam*
£100-125   **R&GM**

A Chinese Qianlong period famille rose dish, chipped.

This piece was made for the European market but with Chinese-style decoration.

1740-50   *15.5in (39.5cm) diam*
£2,000-2,500   **R&GM**

A Chinese Qianlong period famille rose plate, decorated with a roundel of recumbent boys with lotus, within a border of flowers on a cell ground.

1726-95   *9in (22cm) diam*
£150-200   **DN**

A large 18thC Chinese famille rose charger, decorated with a basket holding peonies, pomegranates and other flowers, surrounded by prunus and peony sprays.

21.75in (55.5cm) diam
£800-1,200   **L&T**

One of a set of four mid-18thC Chinese famille rose plates, painted with panels of flowers and foliage, rim chips.

9in (23cm) diam
£500-800 set   **WW**

A Chinese Qianlong period famille rose lotus pattern saucer dish, with celadon green back.

1740-50   *8in (20.5cm) diam*
£500-800   **R&GM**

A Chinese Qianlong period famille rose celadon ground dish, painted with a formal design of flowers and scrolling foliage, the reverse with five iron red bats, six-character Qianlong mark.

11in (28cm) diam
£500-700   **WW**

A Chinese Qianlong period famille rose saucer, with blue and white border.

c1785   *9.5in (24cm) diam*
£150-180   **R&GM**

One of a pair of 19thC Chinese famille rose chargers, painted with a five-clawed dragon and a cockerel fighting against a floral and gilt ground.

15in (38cm) diam
£800-1,200 pair   **HAMG**

A Cantonese famille rose dish, of shaped square form, painted with figures before a river within a gilt leaf border, reserved with iron red scenic panels.

c1800   *7.75in (20cm) diam*
£350-550   **ROS**

An 18thC Chinese famille rose bowl, painted with Chinese figures in various pursuits, inscribed "John Miller".

11.75in (30cm) diam
£800-1,000   **WW**

FAMILLE ROSE

A Chinese Qianlong period famille rose 'Hunting' punch bowl, the exterior decorated in the Mandarin palette with panels depicting huntsmen and hounds, the interior with a huntsman with two dogs and a pheasant, damaged.

c1770   11.75in (30cm) diam

£1,800-2,200   **H&L**

A pair of Chinese famille rose medallion bowls, decorated on the exterior with roundels of auspicious characters on a pink sgraffito ground, six-character Qianlong seal marks, one well repaired.

5.75in (14.75cm) diam

£1,000-1,500   **WW**

A Chinese Qianlong period famille rose bowl and cover, painted in the Meissen style with panels of female figures in a garden, the finial re-glued.

4.75in (12cm) diam

£200-300   **WW**

A 19thC Chinese Canton famille rose bowl, richly decorated with panels of figures, the borders with birds, butterflies and bats amid foliage.

5in (13cm) diam

£800-1,200   **WW**

FAMILLE ROSE

- Famille rose became popular in the Yongzheng period (1723-35), and virtually replaced famille verte. It is characterized by opaque rose-pink or purple overglaze, combined with greens and yellows.
- The palette was known to the Chinese as 'yang cai', meaning 'foreign colours', because the pink hue derived from the gold chloride first introduced to China by Jesuit missionaries.
- These new enamels were favoured due to their superior brightness, quality and opacity, which gave artists a greater range.
- Panels of figures, oriental landscapes or interior scenes were typical subjects for famille rose ceramics, often combined with rockwork, branches, flowers and birds.
- The porcelain was very popular throughout the 18th and 19thC, and many armorial designs were exported to Europe.
- Famille rose from the Yongzheng period, with its brilliant colours and the delicate painterly quality of its decoration, is the most highly prized amongst collectors.

A large 19thC Chinese famille rose jardinière, painted with panels of dragons and phoenix on a pink ground decorated with bats, shou characters, flowers and foliage, the interior painted with fish, on a wooden stand.

18.5in (47cm) high

£900-1,200   **WW**

A pair of Chinese Qianlong period export baluster vases, with panels of flowers in iron red and famille rose enamels, the ground with scrolling lotus, one neck damaged.

1726-95   11in (28cm) high

£800-1,200   **DN**

A pair of 19thC Chinese famille rose vases, decorated with birds, flowers and rocks on a turquoise ground, minor faults.

9.5in (24cm) high

£500-800   **WW**

A CLOSER LOOK AT A PAIR OF FAMILLE ROSE VASES

Famille rose was exported to Europe in vast quantities during the 18th and 19thC. This pair of vases date from the first half of the 19thC, before the quality of decoration began to deteriorate.

These vases bear iron red Jiaqing marks, which are correct for their period and therefore considerably increase their value.

The handles are in the form of animals, adding visual interest to this piece. The high overall quality of the decoration makes these vases highly collectable.

Although not from the Yongzheng period, which was the golden age of famille rose decoration, this pair of vases exhibits the intricate, painterly style associated with the very best famille rose work.

A pair of Chinese famille rose yellow ground vases, each with four animal handles and decorated with stylized foliage, flowers, bats, and endless knots, the rims with jui bands, the feet with blue key fret designs, each with an iron red Jiaqing mark.

c1810   10in (25.5cm) high

£4,500-6,500   **WW**

A pair of 19thC Chinese famille rose hexagonal vases, painted with figures, buildings and landscapes, one badly damaged.

11.5in (29cm) high

£200-300   **WW**

A large pair of 19thC Chinese Canton famille rose vases, decorated with panels of figures, flowers, birds and insects, the bases drilled.

21.75in (55cm) high

£1,500-2,000   **WW**

A 18thC Chinese famille rose mug, decorated with a lady at a window, birds, peaches and flowers.

5.25in (13.5cm) high

£200-300   **WW**

A Chinese famille rose barrel-shaped tankard, after a European shape, decorated with flowers and foliage.

5in (12.5cm) high

£200-250   **JN**

A pair of 19thC Chinese Canton famille rose jugs and covers, with cross-over handles, painted with figures, flowers and insects, minor faults.

8.75in (22.5cm) high

£2,500-3,000   **WW**

A Chinese Qianlong period famille rose teapot, after a European shape, small chips.

c1770   *4in (10cm) high*

£300-400   **R&GM**

An 18thC Chinese famille rose European silver shape sauceboat, decorated with the 'Peacock' pattern, rim crack.

9.75in (24.5cm) long

£300-400   **WW**

A mid-18thC Chinese famille rose tureen and cover, painted with peacocks standing upon rockwork amidst peony and bamboo.

10.75in (27cm) wide

£2,000-2,500   **WW**

A 19thC Chinese famille rose deskstand, painted with birds, flowers and ducks swimming amid lotus, the gilt edges rubbed.

7.25in (18.5cm) wide

£300-500   **WW**

An 18thC Chinese famille rose Compagnie-des-Indes model of a horse and rider, decorated with pink flower heads, minor faults.

The Compagnie des Indes Orientales was founded in 1664 to pursue French trading interests in India and across the Orient. In 1719 the foundering company was acquired by John Law and amalgamated into a new entity known as the Compagnie des Indes.

7.5in (19cm) long

£2,500-3,000   **WW**

A Chinese Qing dynasty famille rose model of a feng, modelled standing on pierced rockwork, painted with flowering peony.

11.75in (30cm) high

£200-300   **H&L**

A Chinese Qianlong period famille rose figure of Shoulou, holding a peach, cracked hand.

Shoulou represents long life and the peach is a symbol of life. These figures were usually made in sets of eight, but they are also collectable individually.

1736-1795   *9in (23cm) high*

£280-320   **R&GM**

ORIENTAL CERAMICS

One of a pair of Chinese late Kangxi period Imari plates.

1700-1720　　8.5in (21.5cm) diam
£300-400 pair　　**R&GM**

One of a pair of Chinese Qianlong period armorial plates, inscribed "RS".

c1750　　9in (23cm) diam
£800-1,100 pair　　**R&GM**

A Chinese Qianlong period Meissen-style dish, rim chips.

c1750　　14in (35.5cm) diam
£1,200-1,800　　**R&GM**

A Chinese Qianlong period export armorial dish, with flowers and floral garlands.

15.25in (38.5cm) diam
£800-1,200　　**BEA**

A Chinese Qianlong period Meissen-style dish, painted with overglaze enamels and gilding, rim chips.

c1750　　14.25in (36cm) diam
£1,200-1,800　　**R&GM**

One of a pair of Chinese enamelled dishes, decorated in green and aubergine with dragons on a yellow ground, six-character Kangxi marks.

6.75in (17cm) diam
£1,500-2,000 pair　　**WW**

An early 20thC Chinese saucer, finely enamelled with a water chestnut, gourd, cricket and bamboo shoot beneath a poem, with gilt rim and four-character "Eternal China Hall" mark.

5in (12cm) diam
£300-400　　**DN**

A Chinese Qianlong period oval dish, decorated with floral swags and sprays.

16in (40.5cm) long
£800-1,200　　**BEA**

A Chinese Qianlong period canted rectangular meat dish, boldly painted with flowering branches and rockwork in Imari colours, within a flower panelled scroll border.

17.25in (44cm) wide
£500-700　　**LFA**

A Chinese Qianlong period armorial plate, after a European shape, decorated with the arms of Seton.

c1780　　9.75in (25cm) long
£800-1,200　　**R&GM**

One of a pair of Chinese Qianlong period export meat dishes.

c1785 11.75in (30cm) wide
£2,000-2,500 pair　　**R&GM**

A rare 18thC Chinese celadon bowl, fitted at the neck and base with later ormolu borders incorporating scrolling foliate motifs and acanthus, on scrolling feet.

11.75in (30cm) diam
£18,000-20,000　　**BLA**

A Chinese cache pot, painted with peony and chrysanthemum sprays, with gilt ormolu mounts in Régence style, damaged.

c1750   *8.75in (22cm) high*

£700-1,000   **BEA**

A large 18thC Chinese shallow bowl, decorated with a pagoda landscape, damaged.

15.25in (38.5cm) diam

£100-150   **WW**

A CLOSER LOOK AT A CELADON GUAN

Celadon is a glaze derived from iron, with a distinctive blue-green colour. It was first adopted by craftsman over 2000 years ago in an effort to imitate nephrite jade, and is often carved or moulded.

This vase and cover dates from the Ming period (1368-1644), when exported celadon guans remained a vital source of revenue for the Chinese government. Ceramic forms were often dictated by the demands of the export market.

The ormolu mounts actually enhance the value of this piece as they have been executed to the highest standard and add to the original aesthetic of the guan vase.

During this period, decoration became increasingly ornate, which is evident here in the abundance of flowering lotus and chrysanthemum sprays carved into the body of the vase.

A fine Chinese Ming dynasty gilt bronze mounted celadon guan, carved with flowering lotus, camellia and chrysanthemum sprays and finely moulded in relief with 'qing xiang mei jiu' decoration, with later ormolu mounts in the Louis XV style.

20.5in (52cm) high

£20,000-25,000   **BEA**

An unusual late 18thC Chinese tureen and cover, with cone knop and cross-over handles, painted with four circular panels with views of mansions within formal border patterns, probably for the American market.

12.5in (31.5cm) diam

£1,000-1,500   **WW**

A Chinese bowl, the interior painted with figures, an ox, birds and cloud scrolls, the exterior with roundels of figures in landscapes, ground decorated with stylized flowers, six-character Daoguang mark.

c1835   *6in (15cm) diam*

£300-350   **WW**

A Chinese yellow ground jardinière, painted with flowering branches.

c1870   *13.5in (34cm) high*

£600-900   **SWO**

A late 19thC Chinese Canton porcelain bowl, decorated in coloured enamels with figures, birds, insects and flowers.

14.25in (36cm) diam

£500-800   **SWO**

A Chinese Guangxu period green glazed bowl, rising from a straight foot to rounded sides everted at the rim, Guangxu mark, small chip.

1875-1908   *5.75in (14.5cm) diam*

£600-900   **BEA**

A rare Chinese rice bowl, made during the Cultural Revolution, with a portrait of Dr Norman Bethune, with marks for Hunan Zijiang Porcelain Factory 1970, and inscribed "Never selfish, only to help others".

1970   *6.25in (16cm) diam*

£500-800   **BP**

ORIENTAL CERAMICS

A large Chinese Transitional period jar, decorated in underglaze blue, turquoise and rouge de fer enamels with figures and rocks, cover missing.

c1640   11.75in (30cm) high

£2,000-2,500   **BEA**

A Chinese Wucai baluster vase, decorated with branches of magnolia and peony, birds and insects in flight, the shoulders with peony and chrysanthemums.

c1650   11in (28cm) high

£1,000-1,500   **WW**

A Chinese Qianlong dynasty sang-de-boeuf vase, with an elongated tapering neck and deep speckled red glaze.

                             14.25in (36cm) high

£800-1,200   **CA**

A pair of Chinese Daoguang period Imperial yellow glazed vases, oviform with short cylindrical necks, on wooden stands, impressed Qianlong seal marks.

c1835   9.5in (24cm) high

£500-600   **HAMG**

A 19thC Chinese yellow ground bottle vase, decorated in bianco sopra bianco beneath a bright yellow glaze, four-character mark.

                              9.5in (24cm) high

£500-700   **DN**

A pair of 19thC Chinese yellow ground square section vases, decorated with writhing dragons, chrysanthemums and other flowers and leaves.

                               11in (28cm) high

£800-1,200   **WW**

A 19thC Canton celadon ground bottle and stopper, painted with two gilt daodieh framed reserves of ladies and attendants, on a jade green ground.

                             14.5in (37cm) high

£220-280   **CHEF**

A pair of Chinese porcelain baluster vases, with flaring necks and pomegranate handles, painted with birds and butterflies in fruiting and flowering gardens.

c1870   23.25in (59cm) high

£1,200-1,800   **BLA**

A pair of 19thC Chinese vases, each of lidded ovoid form, decorated in enamels with a bird on a prunus branch, the domed covers with rockwork issuing flowers, with six-character marks.

                               10in (25.5cm) high

£700-900   **ROW**

A late 19thC Chinese Canton famille rose porcelain vase, painted with floral and figural reserves, applied with qilin and fu dog handles.

                                35in (89cm) high

£2,500-3,000   **BEA**

A pair of Chinese Canton vases, each with waisted neck painted with two reserves of ladies and attendants on a cash diaper ground.

                           23.75in (60.5cm) high

£1,500-2,000   **CHEF**

A late 19thC Chinese bottle vase, moulded in relief with bats over flowering and fruiting peach, picked out in green and ochre on a brown ground, six-character Kangxi mark.

                             12in (30.5cm) high

£300-500   **DN**

A Chinese Qianlong period export coffee cup, in the form of a lotus flower.

c1750   2.5in (6.5cm) high

£50-80   **R&GM**

A Chinese porcelain coffee cup and saucer, with solid loop handle, painted in the style of James Giles, with landscape and ruins, unmarked.

1765-1768   *4in (12cm) wide*

£1,600-1,800   **SHF**

A 19thC Cantonese mug, with interlaced handle, decorated with figures and trophies.

5.5in (14cm) high

£400-600   **GORL**

A large Chinese Qianlong armorial tankard, decorated with famille rose sprays and a large crest with motto "Insperata Floruit".

7in (18cm) high

£400-600   **JN**

A late Chinese Kangxi period tea canister, with later Dutch decoration.

This canister would be worth around £700 if it was complete with its cover.

c1720   *3.75in (9.5cm) high*

£300-350   **R&GM**

A Chinese Yongzheng period teapot, with silver mounts, decorated in underglaze blue with iron oxide red and gilding, on a new stand, with later silver mounts.

This teapot is decorated in a Chinese version of the Japanese Imari palette.

1723-1755   *4in (10cm) high*

£300-500   **R&GM**

A pair of Chinese Ming dynasty sancai glazed rooftile figures, of officials wearing long green and yellow glazed robes.

17.5in (44.5cm) high

£1,800-2,200   **BEA**

A Chinese Qianlong period export group, fan restored.

The group is not from a shipwreck, but similar pieces found on the Nanking cargo help to date this piece to the Qianlong period.

c1750   *6.75in (17cm) high*

£500-800   **R&GM**

A pair of Chinese Jiajing period incense stick holders, in the form of dragons, damaged.

c1810   *9in (23cm) high*

£300-500   **R&GM**

A pair of late 19thC Chinese glazed models of roosters.

14.75in (37.5cm) high

£500-700   **BEA**

A 19thC Chinese 'spinach and egg' glazed incense stick holder, modelled as a two-tier corral with cows under a tree, the mottled glazes in blue, brown, yellow and green.

5in (13cm) wide

£200-300   **CHEF**

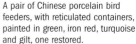

A pair of Chinese porcelain bird feeders, with reticulated containers, painted in green, iron red, turquoise and gilt, one restored.

c1800   *4.25in (11cm) high*

£400-600   **WW**

Two large 17thC Japanese Arita Kraak-style blue and white porcelain chargers.

17.75in (44.5cm) diam

£3,000-4,000   **NAG**

A 17thC Japanese Kakiemon porcelain dish, decorated in blue and white, with flashes of red and green enamel.

7.5in (19cm) diam

£400-600   **NAG**

One of a pair of early 18thC Japanese Arita blue and white dishes, painted in the Kraak style.

16.5in (42cm) diam

£2,500-3,000 pair   **WW**

A small Japanese Nabeshima dish, painted with cloud scrolls, the reverse with stylized brocade balls tied with ribbons, on a comb foot, with applied silver handle, restored.

6in (15cm) high

£400-600   **WW**

A Japanese blue and white Nabeshima-type dish, painted in blue with flowers and leaves issuing from rockwork, raised on a high comb foot.

8.25in (21cm) diam

£50-80   **WW**

A large Japanese blue and white dish, decorated with peony and prunus.

c1900   *21.5in (54.5cm) diam*

£200-300   **WW**

A Japanese blue and white porcelain sake ewer.

c1685   *8.75in (22cm) high*

£800-1,200   **NAG**

A 19thC Japanese Hirado blue and white porcelain ewer, moulded as a figure riding a carp through waves.

9in (23cm) long

£400-600   **WW**

A 19thC Japanese Hirado porcelain blue and white vase and cover, applied with three chrysanthemum sprays, the body painted with flowers floating on water, chipped.

4.25in (10.5cm) high

£700-1,000   **WW**

An 18thC Japanese Arita tokuri, of square form, painted in underglaze blue with a riverscape and swastika decoration.

7.25in (18.5cm) high

£1,500-2,000   **BEA**

An unusual Japanese porcelain condiment pot, after a German stoneware shape, with a loop handle, applied with prunts, cover missing.

c1700   *3.5in (9cm) high*

£300-400   **WW**

JAPANESE IMARI

- In the early 17thC ceramics were first made on Hyushu island, in the south of the Japanese archipelago. The largest city on Hyushu is Arita, which is served by the port town of Imari.
- Clay in the vicinity of Arita and Imari has the requisite high kaolin content for making porcelain. Wares made for export became known as Imari after the port from which they sailed.
- Imari potters first used enamels in the 1640s. Coloured pigments were eventually supplemented with the use of silver and gold.
- Production of Imari porcelain received a boost when instability in China disrupted the Dutch East India Company's supply of porcelain, and the Dutch turned to Japanese producers.
- Genuine Japanese Imari porcelain was rarely signed until the 20thC. Exceptions include rare pieces that are marked by the artist who decorated them.

A Japanese Imari blue and white dish, with a crab design.

1700-1730   *16.25in (41.5cm) diam*

£1,200-1,800   **R&GM**

A Japanese Imari dish, the central vase of flowers painted within three blue scrolls dividing chrysanthemums and peonies to rim.

c1800   *10.75in (27cm) diam*

£120-180   **CHEF**

An 18thC Japanese Imari circular dish, decorated in red and gilt.

12.75in (32.5cm) diam

£400-600   **JN**

A large 19thC Japanese Imari charger, decorated with three panels of dragons.

23.5in (59.5cm) diam

£500-700   **WW**

A large 19thC Japanese Imari charger.

22in (55cm) diam

£3,000-4,000   **NAG**

One of a pair of Japanese Imari chargers, painted with a vase of peonies, the fluted border with panels of flowers and foliate designs.

1880-1910   *18.5in (46.5cm) diam*

£700-1,000 pair   **HAMG**

An early 20thC Japanese Imari deep dish, painted with a phoenix.

12in (30.5cm) diam

£150-200   **CHEF**

A pair of early 20thC Japanese Imari chargers, decorated with bowls of flowers within fluted rims, painted with shishi panels alternating with peonies.

18.5in (47cm) diam

£500-800   **CHEF**

A late 17thC Japanese Imari covered standing bowl, with ruyi lappet handles, standing on a trumpet foot, the domed cover surmounted by a shishi and flower finial, the sides painted with flowers.

8.25in (21cm) high

£1,000-1,500 **CHEF**

A Japanese Arita Imari bowl and cover, decorated with flowers, foliage and fan-shaped panels, with later ormolu mounts comprising a foliate finial, scrolling side handles, reticulated rim and Rococo base.

c1700 *9in (23cm) wide*

£1,500-2,000 **WW**

A Japanese Imari porcelain bowl and cover, the later ormolu mounts probably French.

c1700 *12in (30cm) high*

£1,500-2,000 **NAG**

An 18thC Japanese Imari bowl and cover, decorated with vases of flowers, gilt highlights, chips to cover.

c1700 *10.25in (26cm) diam*

£1,500-2,000 **BEA**

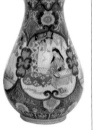

A pair of late 19thC Japanese Imari pear-shaped vases, painted with panels of birds and a geisha practising calligraphy, one with small drill hole.

12.25in (31cm) high

£300-500 **WW**

A large Japanese Imari vase, decorated with panels of pine, prunus and chrysanthemum.

c1900 *23.5in (60cm) high*

£200-300 **WW**

A Japanese Imari bush holder, painted in blue and gilt with chrysanthemums and prunus flowers.

c1700 *3.5in (9cm) high*

£600-900 **BEA**

A Japanese Imari teapot and cover, made for the European market.

1700-1730 *6.25in (16cm) wide*

£500-700 **R&GM**

A rare Japanese Imari tokkuri, modelled as Hotei seated on a gourd holding a fan, decorated in iron red and green enamels with flowers, body cracked.

'Tokkuri' is a generic term for sake flasks, which come in many different shapes and sizes. Figural forms are relatively scarce.

c1680 *8.25in (21cm) high*

£3,000-4,000 **WW**

A rare Japanese Genroku period Arita Imari porcelain wall vase, in the form of a standing bijin, restored.

c1700 *13.5in (34cm) high*

£1,800-2,200 **NAG**

A late 19thC Japanese Kakiemon style plate, painted with a phoenix, a pomegranate and prunus spray, the reverse with three cloud scrolls.

9.5in (24cm) diam

£200-300   **WW**

A 19thC Japanese foliate moulded bowl, decorated in the Kakiemon style, the interior a flowering prunus tree.

If this was an original 18thC piece it would be worth £8,000-10,000.

7.5in (19cm) wide

£1,500-2,000   **WW**

A small Japanese Kakiemon dish.

Kakiemon pieces from this period are rare. European porcelain factories copied this palette, particularly Chelsea and Chantilly.

1690-1710   *5in (12.5cm) diam*

£700-1,000   **R&GM**

A Japanese Hododa Satsuma bowl, of square shape, with an applied figure in one corner, painted with immortals in gilt and enamel, signed.

c1890   *4.5in (11.5cm) wide*

£120-180   **SWO**

A Japanese Meiji period Satsuma shallow bowl, on three feet, decorated with a water dragon rising from waves, overglaze blue Satsuma mon and two-character gilt mark, faint rim crack.

9in (23cm) high

£300-400   **WW**

A Japanese Kozan Satsuma bowl and cover, the cover painted with seated ceremonial figures, the interior painted with women in a garden, signed to the base.

c1900   *5in (12.5cm) diam*

£600-800   **HAMG**

A CLOSER LOOK AT A SATSUMA VASE

Satsuma ware ranges from high quality to decidedly mediocre pieces. The faces of figures on high quality Satsuma are very expressive.

Unsigned pieces are often considered inferior and were sold in department stores in the West. This piece has the gilt signature of its maker and therefore commands a premium.

This vase is similar in style to pieces made by the Kinkozan family, who made ornate, cream-coloured pottery in the Satsuma style, usually heavily embellished with gilding, for the Western market In the 19thC and early 20thC.

The exquisite decoration here represents the best of Satsuma ornamentation, with traders and warriors interacting in a busy marketplace, scrolling flowers and gilding.

A late 19thC Satsuma vase, of square section with re-entrant corners, painted with panels of figures in a landscape, birds and foliage, the shoulder decorated with flowerheads.

6in (15cm) high

£120-180   **ROS**

A large Japanese Meiji period Satsuma vase, in Kinkozan style, one side decorated with a samurai beneath wisteria wrapped around a ginko tree, the reverse with figures in a market place, the blue ground with a gilt scroll design, gilt signature.

c1890   *12.5in (31cm) high*

£2,500-3,000   **WW**

A Japanese Meiji period Satsuma vase, decorated with panels of figures and buildings, two-character mark, minor faults.

9.5in (24cm) high

£280-320   **WW**

A pair of Japanese Meiji period Satsuma vases, with elephant's head mask handles, painted with chrysanthemums and prunus trees, chipped.

7.25in (18.5cm) high

£150-200   **HAMG**

A pair of Japanese Meiji period Satsuma vases, each painted with a landscape panel and wild flowers.

9.5in (24cm) high

£220-280   **GORL**

A pair of Japanese Meiji period Satsuma vases, painted with bijin beneath maple trees before lakes and mountains, signed.

7in (18cm) high

£400-600   **WW**

A Japanese Meiji period Satsuma vase, formed as two conjoined square sections, decorated with butterflies above wild flowers and a banded hedge, signed "Hododa" and "Satsuma Yaki" with four-character blue enamel mark.

6.25in (16cm) high

£400-600   **WW**

A 19thC Japanese Satsuma vase, with a green decorated acorn top over a twin gourd style body, highly decorated with relief painted floral and crane patterns.

8.5in (21.5cm) high

£1,000-1,500   **FRE**

A Japanese Meiji period Satsuma jar and cover, decorated with flowering branches, with chrysanthemum knop, signed "Tozan", with impressed seal mark.

6.5in (16.5cm) high

£350-400   **BEA**

A late 19thC Japanese Satsuma pot and cover, of squat form, painted with landscape and figural panels against a maple tree ground, signed "Shizan".

3in (7cm) high

£500-800   **HAM**

A small Japanese Meiji period Satsuma koro and cover, with chrysanthemum knop and angled side handles, decorated with overlapping panels of figures in various pursuits, signed to the base.

3.25in (8cm) high

£1,000-1,500   **WW**

A late 19thC Japanese Satsuma earthenware lidded koro, with reticulated domed lid, fish handles, enamelled decoration and pierced sides, on three feet, with painted signature.

4in (10cm) high

£300-500   **ROW**

A Japanese Kiyozan period Satsuma koro and cover, with gilt elephant's trunk handles, painted with Japanese ladies seated on a terrace and landscape scenes, painted marks.

c1900   *6in (15cm) high*

£150-200   **HAM**

A Japanese Yasuda Satsuma baluster vase, with pierced cover and chrysanthemum knop, decorated with panels of ladies in gardens with flowering prunus, the red ground with gilt brocade decoration, with Satsuma mon, Yasuda factory mark and signature.

9in (23cm) high

£1,500-2,000   **DN**

A late 19thC Japanese vase, of shouldered form, painted with figures walking in a garden setting, signed "Kinkozan Zo".

4.75in (12cm) high

£300-500   **HAMG**

A late 19thC Fukugawa-style vase, painted in white with herons against a shaded blue ground.

7.25in (18.5cm) high

£150-200   **HAMG**

An early 18thC Japanese Arita charger, painted with peony and lotus plants in underglaze blue, iron-red and gilt, the reserve with floral sprays.

21in (62cm) diam

£1,000-1,500   **GORL**

A pair of Kutani Showa period chargers, of eight-petalled form, painted in blue and green with birds on camellia branches, within an aubergine decorated yellow ground.

11in (28cm) diam

£250-300   **ROS**

A small 17thC Japanese Arita tea bowl and saucer, printed in coloured enamels and gilt with flowers and leaves, within red, blue and gilt borders.

4.5in (11.5cm) diam

£250-300   **LFA**

A Japanese fluted pink lustre bowl, painted with a mythological hoho bird, with reeded moulding on the interior.

c1720   *4.25in (11cm) diam*

£200-250   **R&GM**

A Japanese earthenware lobed bowl, with a river landscape, wisteria floribunda, bridge and mountains, signed.

6.75in (17cm) high

£50-80   **DN**

OTHER JAPANESE CERAMICS

A pair of Japanese Arita fish vases, painted over a white nigoshide ground in red, black and green, damaged.

c1700   *11.5in (29.5cm) high*

£1,800-2,200   **BEA**

An unusual 19thC Japanese Hirado porcelain ewer, in the form of Hotei, the fat buddha.

7.5in (19cm) wide

£500-800   **NAG**

A large, early 20thC Japanese Kutani model of a sleeping cat, wearing a red and turquoise ribbon.

12.25in (31cm) high

£500-800   **WW**

IZNIK CERAMICS

LEFT: A 17thC Iznik circular footed bowl, loosely painted with tulips and chrysanthemums in blue, green, brown and black, the border with naive scroll and spiral motifs.

9.75in (24.5cm) diam

£1,000-1,500   **L&T**

RIGHT: A 17thC Iznik circular footed plate, decorated with tulips and chrysanthemums in blue, green, brown and black, the border with panels of spirals.

10.25in (26cm) diam

£1,500-2,000   **L&T**

A CLOSER LOOK AT AN IZNIK DISH

Iznik wares were the finest ceramics in the Ottoman Empire, and show the influence of China and Central Asia.

The term 'Iznik' describes the decorative scheme on this piece, characterised by long, curling, serrated saz leaves on thin spiralling stems, with flowers based on roses, tulips and carnations.

This sealing-wax red is in relief, demonstrating the artistic development in Iznik from the second quarter of the 16thC.

It is unusual for Islamic pottery to be marked. A potter's imprint would add considerable value to this piece.

A late 16thC Iznik dish, decorated with tulips, carnations and other flowers issuing from a tuft, with brown line borders, the reverse with ten leaf motifs and a shaped line border, damaged.

11.75in (30cm) diam

£1,800-2,200   **WW**

A glazed Persian tile, decorated with a male figure on horseback, holding a bird of prey in his left hand, surrounded by floral sprays, in blue, puce and green, on a rich blue ground.

8.75in (22cm) high

£100-150   **H&L**

A large early 20thC Middle Eastern moulded pottery panel, decorated with ten figures engaged in hunting an array of animals, amidst flowers and with buildings beyond.

18in (46cm) wide

£1,200-1,800   **WW**

A hexagonal Persian tile, decorated with a figure in a garden.

12.5in (32cm) high

£120-180   **CA**

late 19thC Japanese ivory
kimono, carved as an old
rmer with a young child by
s side, with a signed red
ablet to the base.

8.25in (21cm) high

300-500   **ROS**

A late 19thC Chinese ivory
figure, carved as a man holding
a child and lion mask above
his head, the base with red
two-character mark.

7.5in (19cm) high

£300-400   **ROS**

A Japanese Meiji period ivory
okimono, carved as a mythical
character with three Oni, red
lacquer seal, signature, slight
damage.

7in (18cm) high

£500-700   **WW**

A Japanese Meiji period ivory
okimono, carved as a Bijin
carrying a flower and a tea
kettle, damaged.

7.25in (18.5cm) high

£400-600   **WW**

A Japanese Meiji period ivory
okimono, carved as an elderly
man with his dog, red lacquer
signature seal.

7.25in (18.5cm) high

£600-900   **WW**

Japanese Meiji period ivory group,
arved as three men in a heated
rgument, their robes inset with lacquer
nd glass.

2in (5cm) high

500-700   **WW**

Two large Japanese Meiji period marine
ivory carvings, each carved with figures
and dragons, one with a shi shi, each
with a two-character signature.

14.5in (37cm) high

£1,000-1,200   **WW**

A large 19thC
Japanese ivory
carving of an
Immortal,
standing on a
dragon, signed
on a pad.

11in (28cm) high

£3,500-4,500   **WW**

A Japanese
Meiji period
ivory okimono,
carved as a
hunter, standing
holding a
tethered bird of
prey on his
shoulder,
holding a gun in
his other hand,
signed on an
inlaid tablet
"Isshi".

7.75in (20cm) high

£500-700   **ROS**

Japanese Meiji period ivory okimono, carved as a group of
ats, signed "Masatami".

3.75in (9.5cm) wide

4,000-6,000   **NAG**

An early 20thC Japanese ivory
okimono, carved as a geisha,
standing holding a songbird
and cage, with engraved
kimono, signed "Gyoku".

10.75in (27cm) high

£800-1,200   **HAMG**

An early 20thC ivory figure by Shizuo, carved as a man kneeling
with a basket of precious objects, signed on a red lacquer tablet.

3.75in (9.5cm) high

£1,800-2,200   **CHEF**

ORIENTAL IVORY FIGURES

A 19thC Chinese ivory figure, carved as an Immortal, carrying a basket of flowers, a writhing dragon at her feet.

8.25in (21cm) high

£1,500-2,000　　　**WW**

A Japanese Meiji period ivory okimono, carved as a fisherman, standing holding a basket of fish and a club, his coat with engraved, stained decoration, incised signature.

14in (35cm) high

£2,000-2,500　　　**HAMG**

A Japanese Meiji period ivory okimono, carved as an archer, standing holding a staff, a quiver of arrows on his back, his costume with engraved and stained detail.

21in (53.5cm) high

£2,000-3,000　　　**HAMG**

A Japanese Meiji period ivory okimono, carved as a musician with a basket of masks over his shoulder, his costume with engraved and stained detail, signed.

21in (53.5cm) high

£1,800-2,200　　　**HAMG**

A Japanese Meiji period ivory okimono, carved as a Samurai warrior standing beside a young boy fending off monkeys, signed.

9in (23cm) high

£4,000-6,000　　　**GOR**

A Japanese Meiji period ivory okimono, carved as a group of hunters trying to catch a giant crane, signed "Haruyoshi".

6.25in (16cm) high

£2,000-2,500　　　**BEA**

A Japanese Meiji period ivory okimono, carved as a woman playing flute, with three Oni, signed "Yoshi".

10.75in (27cm) high

£500-700　　　**BEA**

A Japanese Meiji period black wood and ivory okimono, carved as a farmer seated on a pile of wood, signed.

5in (12.5cm) high

£2,000-2,500　　　**BEA**

A Japanese Meiji period ivory okimono, carved as a fisherman carrying a cormorant in a basket, signed.

9.5in (24cm) high

£1,800-2,200　　　**BE**

A Japanese Meiji period ivory okimono, carved as a salesman, with horn and mother-of-pearl inlaid details, signed "Gyokuzan".

7.25in (18.5cm) high

£1,200-1,800　　　**BEA**

A CLOSER LOOK AT AN IVORY OKIMONO

The very dense structure of ivory prevents splintering, making it an ideal material for finely detailed carving such as this bundle of branches.

Despite its size, this okimono was carved from a single piece of tusk, requiring great skill on the part of the craftsman.

Japanese carved figures often feature flowing lines, animated poses and vividly expressed emotion.

Export pieces tend to have smooth surfaces, without chisel marks. This was preferred in the West, where highly finished pieces characterised good craftsmanship.

Genuine ivory has a dark cross grain that can be seen in strong light.

A Japanese Meiji period ivory okimono, carved as a woodsman seated on a pile of faggots, signed.

7.25in (18.5cm) high

£3,000-4,000　　　**BE**

Japanese ivory okimono, carved as a fisherman carrying boy, on a naturalistic plinth, signed "Nobuyuki".

7in (18cm) high

800-1,200 **BEA**

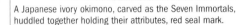

A Japanese ivory okimono, carved as the Seven Immortals, huddled together holding their attributes, red seal mark.

2.25in (5.5cm) wide

£500-700 **DN**

An early 20thC Japanese ivory figure, carved as a gold prospector, holding gold pieces in his hand and with a jar of gold on the ground, signed with red inset seal.

8.25in (21cm) high

£600-900 **WW**

A 20thC Japanese Meiji period carved ivory group, depicting an old fisherman and a young boy, with two-character mark to the base.

10.25in (26cm) high

£200-300 **ROS**

NETSUKE

late 18thC Japanese ivory netsuke, by Masanao, carved as a boar reclining on bed of leaves, signed on red coral tablet.

2.25in (5.5cm) wide

1,500-2,000 **CHEF**

19thC Japanese ivory netsuke, by Masatami, carved as a monkey singing and dancing to a drum while supporting youngster holding a peach stem on his back, the eyes and drum inlaid with annel coal, signed on the leg.

2.25in (5.5cm) high

1,200-1,800 **CHEF**

An early 19thC Japanese ivory netsuke, by Tomotada, carved as the dragon witch sitting on top of a temple bell, holding a lock of her hair in one hand and a crutch in the other, her tail coiled around the body of the bell, signed on the lip.

2.25in (5.5cm) high

£1,200-1,800 **CHEF**

A 19thC Japanese ivory netsuke, carved as Kinko reading as he rides a giant carp through the waves, the eyes of the fish inlaid.

2.25in (5.5cm) high

£1,800-2,200 **CHEF**

A 19thC Japanese ivory netsuke, carved as a group of warriors battling around a warhorse, signed.

1.75in (4.5cm) high

£2,500-3,000 **CHEF**

OTHER ORIENTAL IVORY

An early 19thC Chinese cricket cage, the ivory-rimmed gourd incised with a dragon amongst clouds, the pierced cover carved with flowering cherry.

4.25in (11cm) high

£280-320   **CHEF**

An early 19thC Chinese cricket cage, the vegetable gourd with ivory rim and domed tortoiseshell top pierced and carved with two phoenix amongst flowers.

5.75in (14.5cm) high

£500-700   **CHEF**

A CLOSER LOOK AT A CHINESE IVORY PUZZLE BALL

Puzzle balls are made up of numerous concentric spheres, all carved from the same piece of ivory. The painstaking piercing and carving required to produce this example would have taken many weeks.

Years of handling produces a patina that can vary in tone from golden to dark brown and is difficult to fake..

The production of ivory pieces is now strictly monitored due to dwindling elephant populations. Despite bans on the trade in elephant ivory, illicit dealing continues and purchasers should check the origin of ivory articles that are offered as 'antique'.

Only the finest puzzle balls were made of ivory, as opposed to jade or other materials, making this example particularly desirable.

A 19thC Cantonese ivory miniature table cabinet, carved with ptarmigan amongst undergrowth, the handles carved as insects, with a single-character signature tablet fitted to the stand, complete with wooden fitted carrying cabinet.

13in (33cm) high

£1,000-1,500   **ROS**

A 19thC Chinese Canton ivory tusk vase, intricately carved with peony flowers and leaves on a reticulated ground, with wooden stand.

9in (23cm) high

£300-400   **WW**

A Chinese ivory card case, carved and pierced with figures in a river landscape.

c1860   *4.5in (11.5cm) high*

£400-500   **DN**

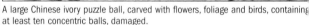

A large Chinese ivory puzzle ball, carved with flowers, foliage and birds, containing at least ten concentric balls, damaged.

4.75in (12cm) diar

£1,000-1,500   **WV**

A Japanese ivory Buddhist shrine, the roof bearing a swastika and dragons above opening doors with the goddess Kwannon flanked by acolytes on a stepped gallery, signed "Kuniaki".

c1880   *18.5in (47cm) high*

£800-1,200   **SWO**

A 20thC Japanese ivory book page turner, intricately engraved with monkeys chasing a fly, red single-character mark.

18in (45.5cm) long

£100-150   **ROS**

A Chinese ivory cylindrical box and cover, carved in low relief with flowers on the domed lid and decorated with figures by pavilions amongst trees on the sides.

3.75in (9.5cm) diam

£200-300   **CHEF**

A small Japanese engraved and gilded ivory table cabinet, with brass edges and hinges, the front with a small pair of double doors concealing four drawers, with one long drawer below.

5in (12.5cm) wid

£700-1,000   **J**

n 18thC Chinese carved jade hand of
uddha.

*'hand of Buddha' is a religiously
gnificant mutation of the citrus plant.*

3.5in (9cm) long

400-600   **JN**

A Chinese jade carving of two gourds,
with a gnarled stem and leaves upon
which a large bug crawls.

2in (5cm) high

£100-150   **WW**

A pair of Chinese soapstone seals, each
carved with a boy climbing on the back
of a water buffalo beside its calf as
they try to escape foaming waves.

2.75in (7cm) high

£700-1,000   **WW**

A 19thC Chinese celadon green jade
ewer and cover of, rectangular section,
the sides decorated with guei dragons.

6in (15.5cm) high

£700-1,000   **DN**

19thC Chinese jade carving of a large
each, encased by gnarled branches
nd leaves and with two small fruit
ats, symbolic of long life and
appiness, chipped.

4.75in (12cm) high

£7,000-10,000   **WW**

A Chinese carved soapstone figure of
Guanyin, depicted seated, holding mala
beads and a scroll.

5in (13cm) high

£600-900   **GORL**

An 18thC Chinese jade carving of two carp, leaping from waves, raised on a
carved wood stand.

8.75in (22.5cm) high

£18,000-22,000   **WW**

A Chinese carved pink quartz figure of
Guanyin, restored.

8.25in (21cm) high

£200-250   **ROS**

A Chinese agate vase and cover, carved
with taotie masks, surmounted by a
phoenix finial and raised on a flared
foot.

11in (28cm) high

£400-600   **WW**

A Chinese amethyst pendant, carved
with a bat clambering over a peach and
a pair of finger citron plants.

1.75in (4.5cm) high

£500-700   **WW**

A Chinese white jade carving of a
stylized fish.

2.25in (6cm) wide

£350-400   **WW**

A Chinese Canton enamel snuff bottle, with a lapis lazuli stopper, the body painted with butterflies and flowers above rockwork, with four-character Qianlong mark, restored.

2in (5cm) high

£100-200   **WW**

A 19thC Chinese rock crystal ovoid snuff bottle, carved with bands of lappets.

2.25in (6cm) high

£280-320   **WW**

A 19thC Chinese glass snuff bottle, with four colour overlay, carved with flowers and insects.

2.5in (6.5cm) high

£600-900   **WW**

A 19thC Chinese glass snuff bottle, with four colour overlay, carved with flowers and insects.

2.5in (6.5cm) hig

£400-600   **WW**

A 19thC Chinese jade snuff bottle, of mottled black and green colour, the sides carved with lion mask handles.

2.75in (7cm) high

£400-600   **WW**

A 19thC Chinese amber snuff bottle, of flattened oval shape, with gilded copper mounts and spoon.

2.75in (7cm) high

£150-200   **BMN**

A 19thC Chinese cut glass snuff bottle, painted in between two layers of glass, partially red lacquered, damaged.

2.75in (7cm) high

£150-200   **BMN**

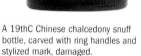

A 19thC Chinese chalcedony snuff bottle, carved with ring handles and stylized mark, damaged.

2.25in (6cm) hig

£40-60   **CHE**

A 19thC Chinese glass snuff bottle, black ground with five colour overlay, carved with fish and lotus.

3.25in (8cm) high

£400-600   **WW**

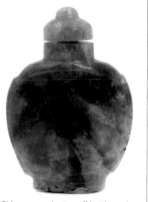

A Chinese amethyst snuff bottle and stopper, with flattened rectangular sides below a short neck, damaged.

2.25in (6cm) high

£40-60   **CHEF**

A Chinese pale jade snuff bottle, of fluted ovular form, with coral stopper.

2.25in (6cm) high

£1,500-2,000   **GORL**

A Chinese amber snuff bottle, carved with fish, lotus and calligraphy.

3.25in (8cm) hig

£800-1,200   **WW**

19thC Chinese circular footed cloisonné bowl, the exterior decorated with scrolling leaves and lotus flowers, the interior with two writhing dragons and the well with fruit.

8.25in (21cm) diam

700-1,000   **L&T**

A late 19thC Japanese simulated cloisonné vase, of tapered square section, with short flared turquoise ground neck, bronze ground body decorated with lotus flowers and mon, and narrow yellow frieze to base.

11in (28cm) high

£150-250   **L&T**

A pair of 19thC Chinese gu-shaped cloisonné beaker vases, with flared necks and feet, decorated with flowers, lotus scrolls and key fret borders.

14.75in (37.5cm) high

£500-700   **WW**

A pair of 19thC Chinese cloisonné hanging wall vases, formed as lanterns with quatrefoil bodies, decorated with lotus flowers and leaves on a turquoise ground.

12.25in (31cm) high

£1,200-1,800   **WW**

late 19thC Chinese cloisonné jardinière, enamelled with four alternating turquoise and red floral ovals on a lapis blue ground with scrolling flora.

10.25in (26cm) high

280-320   **CHEF**

A Japanese hexagonal cloisonné lobed tray, finely decorated with a mallard in snow-covered grasses, the back with a ground of scattered flowers, with monogram for Namikawa Sosuke.

c1900   *10.75in (27cm) wide*

£1,800-2,200   **DN**

A pair of Japanese Meiji period cloisonné vases, decorated with sparrows in flight above peony and chrysanthemums, all on a dark ground flecked with aventurine.

9.75in (24.5cm) high

£600-900   **WW**

A pair of Japanese Meiji period cloisonné vases, decorated with panels of birds amidst wisteria, chrysanthemums and phoenix, impressed koro marks.

7.25in (18.5cm) high

£800-1,200   **WW**

small Japanese ovoid cloisonné vase, with white metal mounted foot and rim, finely decorated with a bird in a flowering tree on a dark blue ground, in original fitted wooden case, with paper label printed "J. Ando, Cloisonné Ware, Tokyo, Nagoya, Japan".

3.25in (8cm) high

500-700   **LFA**

A pair of Canton enamel plant pots and stands, of tapered square section, decorated with figural panels reserved on a foliate scroll ground.

c1900   *3.5in (9cm) high*

£100-150   **H&L**

A Chinese Kangxi period silver and parcel gilt ewer and cover, with a lobed hexafoil body engraved with panels containing Chinese figures and trees on a matted ground, the knop formed as a curled prunus twig with three flower heads, the handle as a knotted pine branch, the spout modelled as bamboo, with detail picked out in gold, marked "Rui Long" in Chinese characters to the base.

The "Rui Long" inscription may be a Chinese personal name or an early Chinese rendering of a European surname. Oriental silver was popular in the West at this time and export items were sometimes marked to order.

6in (15.5cm) high

£7,000-10,000 **WW**

A CLOSER LOOK AT A CHINESE SILVER EWER

The word 'ewer' derives from the 14thC French word 'evier', signifying a stone sink. This large jug was originally designed to carry water and would have been placed on a table in a conspicuous place within the room.

The detailed ornamentation is crisp desp its intricacy, demonstrating the skill of t craftsman and adding considerabl value to this ewe

The use of precious metals such as silver and gold in the Far East was generally confined to decorative inlay. From the 17th to the mid-20thC, however, silver hollowware was produced specifically for export to the West.

The condition of silver should be checke carefully, as any holes, splits or cracks arour joined or pierced areas will have a negati effect on valu

A 19thC Chinese silver ewer and cover, the hexafoil body decorated with panels of figures and animals in landscapes, the gold knop formed as a lion dog.

6.75in (17cm) hig

£7,000-10,000 **W**

A 19thC Chinese bronze vase, cast with a band of stylized birds above formal lappets.

15.75in (40cm) high

£200-300 **WW**

A 19thC Chinese two-handled bronze censer, cast with archaic taotie masks on a keyfret ground, with a fitted wood cover and stand.

12.75in (32.5cm) hig

£400-600 **WW**

A Japanese late Edo period iron tsuba, signed "Echizen ju Kogitsune saku kore".

2.75in (7cm) high

€700-1,000   **NAG**

A Japanese late Edo period brass tsuba, with a depiction of Hotei, signed "Ichijosai Hironaga", in a wooden box.

3in (7.5cm) high

£2,000-2,500   **NAG**

A large Japanese Meiji period copper tsuba, signed "Masayuki".

3.5in (9cm) high

€3,000-4,000   **NAG**

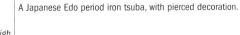

A Japanese Edo period iron tsuba, with pierced decoration.

3.5in (9cm) high

£3,000-4,000   **NAG**

145

A Japanese early Edo period iron tsuba.

2.75in (7cm) high

£500-700   **NAG**

A Japanese mid-Edo period sentoku tsuba, signed "Mori Terukazu", with artist's seal.

2.75in (7cm) high

£3,000-5,000   **NAG**

A Japanese mid-Edo period iron tsuba, with chrysanthemum design, inscribed "shin marugata, katachi niku bori sukashi".

3.5in (9cm) high

£700-1,000   **NAG**

A Japanese mid-Edo period iron tsuba.

3.5in (9cm) hig

£300-400   **NAG**

A Japanese Edo period iron tsuba, with dragon design.

2.75in (7cm) high

£200-300   **NAG**

A Japanese Edo period iron tsuba, with dragon design, inscribed "Kiyobo sanjin Jakushi Ryuunken Koretaka", with artist's seal.

3.75in (9.5cm) high

£200-300   **NAG**

A Japanese late Edo period iron tsuba, with cloisonné inlays, signed "Hirata Harunari".

3in (7.5cm) high

£1,500-2,000   **NAG**

A Japanese late Edo period shakudo tsuba, with dragon design.

Shakudo is an alloy of copper and gold.

3.25in (8cm) hig

£1,500-2,000   **NAG**

A Japanese late Edo period elaborate sentoku tsuba, with a depiction of Rakan Handaka Sonja, signed "Furukawa Genchin".

4in (10cm) high

£3,000-4,000   **NAG**

One of a pair of Japanese late Edo period daisho shakudo tsuba, in a wooden box.

3.25in (8cm) high

£3,500-4,500 pair   **NAG**

A Japanese late Edo period shakudo tsuba, in a wooden box.

2.75in (7cm) high

£1,000-2,000   **NAG**

A Japanese late Edo period iron tsuba, decorated with fishermen.

3.25in (8cm) high

£1,000-1,500   **NAG**

A large Japanese Meiji period copper tsuba, signed "Hitotsuyanagi Tomohisa", with artist's seal.

A tsuba is a hand guard placed above the handle of a Japanese sword.

3.5in (8.5cm) high

£4,000-5,000   **NAG**

A Japanese late Edo period sentoku tsuba, with a depiction of Rakan Handaka Sonja.

Tsuba give information about the owner's social standing and beliefs.

4in (10cm) high

£2,000-3,000   **NAG**

A fine Japanese iron casket, by Ryuunsai Yukiyasu, the cover inset with a copper panel decorated in silver and gold relief with a basket of flowers and with insects, the sides with aquatic scenes, flowering trees and a view of Mount Fuji, the inner rim with wisteria and grape vines, the interior silver lined, with five-character mark on a silver pad.

c1870

£10,000-15,000

7.25in (18.5cm) long

WW

A large Japanese Meiji period bronze figure, cast as a grotesque warrior with left hand held aloft supporting a domed bronzed gong, his right hand grasping a cudgel, set on a carved hardwood plinth with scroll-pierced apron.

Figure 15.5in (39cm) high

£2,000-3,000

L&T

A pair of Japanese bronze, metal-mounted and enamelled vases, the cylindrical sides decorated with butterflies and vines.

c1900

£1,000-1,500

DN

A Japanese Meiji period bronze vase, of swollen cylindrical form, with narrow scroll neck, decorated in high relief in silver, gold and copper with a cockerel and a hen on a naturalistic grassy ground, with printed mark and signature.

11.25in (28cm) high

£400-600

L&T

A Japanese Meiji period bronze model of a Bijin, playing a samisen, wearing a robe inlaid in gold with fans and petals, with two-character seal mark, raised on a wood stand decorated with a gilt karakusa scroll.

12.25in (31cm) high

£2,500-3,000

WW

A Japanese bronze ovoid vase, cast in shallow relief with three swimming carp, signed.

c1900

7in (18cm) high

£500-700

DN

A Japanese bronze circular pierced bowl, with swing handle.

13in (33cm) diam

£500-800

JN

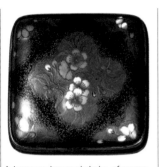

A Japanese lacquer kobako, of square section, the black nashiji lacquer ground decorated in gold hiramakie with inlays of mother-of-pearl depicting prunus flowers, restored.

c1600   *2.5in (6.5cm) wide*

£500-700   **BEA**

A Chinese Qianlong period red lacquer charger, carved with flowering branches and grasses.

12in (30.5cm) diam

£3,000-4,000   **BEA**

A 19thC Chinese lacquer table cabinet, the metal bound sides with Chinoiserie decoration, with two doors opening to reveal an arrangement of seven drawers, on scroll feet.

24.5in (62cm) wide

£2,000-3,000   **FRE**

An early 19thC Chinese black and gilt lacquer tray, of wavy outline, painted in gilt with attendants in a garden, within a stylized floral border.

26.5in (67cm) diam

£300-400   **ROS**

A late 19thC Japanese tortoiseshell lacquered cigar case, decorated in tones of gold, black and red with exotic birds in trees above rock pools.

4.75in (12cm) high

£50-80   **CHEF**

A 19thC Chinese gilt lacquered spice box and stand, the two-tier lobed container fitted with eleven black and floral gilt lacquered boxes, the exterior with a Buddhist lion and cubs, butterflies and flower heads.

5.25in (13.5cm) high

£150-200   **H&**

A 19thC Japanese lacquer box and cover, decorated in hiramakie and takamakie techniques with flowers, on a nashiji ground.

5.5in (14cm) wide

£200-300   **DN**

A Japanese Meiji period gold lacquer five-case inro, decorated with tsuba on a complex diaper ground, one end decorated with mother of pearl, with three-character signature for Kajikawa, together with a pink hardstone ojime.

£800-1,200   **WW**

A Japanese Meiji period Shibayama-inlaid lacquer box and cover.

13.25in (33cm) wide

£3,000-5,000   NAG

A Chinese lacquer inlaid box, of rectangular form, the pierced three-quarter gallery inlaid with a ship in port, within a parquetry border, enclosing drawers above a single drawer on bracket feet.

16in (40.5cm) wide

£500-700   L&T

A lacquered Chinoiserie box, in the form of a book, the hinged lid with relief lacquer panel depicting a Chinese scene of a temple in a garden on a black ground, with label.

23.25in (59cm) long

£150-200   L&T

A Japanese gold lacquer five-case inro, decorated in hiramakie with leafy plants, with nashiji interior, the base with signature.

4in (10cm) long

£500-700   HAMG

A Japanese lacquer box and cover, with lift-out tray.

4in (10cm) high

£700-1,000   JN

ORIENTAL COSTUME

A Chinese Qing dynasty fifu dress, embroidered with polychrome silk and metal thread on blue silk taffeta.

£1,000-1,500   **RSS**

A Chinese Qing dynasty fifu dress, embroidered with polychrome silk and metal thread on taffeta, faded.

£300-400   **RSS**

A 19thC Chinese long pao woman's court robe, decorated with silk embroidery on twill weave silk.

£700-900   **RSS**

A 19thC Chinese Mandarin long pao woman's court robe, of embroidered blue silk with couched gold threads depicting nine dragons and religious symbols.

£1,800-2,200   **BEA**

A CLOSER LOOK AT CHINESE CEREMONIAL ARMOUR

There is a contemporary depiction of the Emperor Kangxi (1662-1722) wearing a very similar outfit to this one, armed with a sabre and a bow. Kangxi's reign coincided with the height of the Qing dynasty's power.

This high headpiece was unsuitable in a battle situation. This outfit was made for ceremonial use, and was therefore made to a higher decorative specification than battle armour.

A Chinese xia pei woman's ceremonial court vest, of indigo satin silk embroidered with phoenix amid clouds, flowers and auspicious emblems above waves and mountains, with tassel fringes.

£200-300   **RSS**

A Japanese Meiji period lime-green silk kimono, with floral and bamboo pattern.

61.5in (154cm) high

£600-900   **NAG**

The dragon has long been a potent symbol in Chinese mythology. Lung, the Chinese dragon, is associated with heroism and bravery and so is particularly suited to use in a military context.

Suits of armour in better repair, with more vivid colours and more complete histories are generally worth more than this example.

A Chinese Qing dynasty ceremonial suit of armour.

£1,800-2,200   **RSS**

One of a pair of late 19thC Chinese carved and painted Buddhist lions, gilded and seated with paws raised on a brocade ball, on a fixed red plinth gilt with half florets.

6.25in (16cm) high

£150-200 pair   **CHEF**

A 19thC Chinese carved and gilt wood Buddhist lion, with one paw raised on a brocade ball, on a red two-tier stand of hexagonal section.

6in (15cm) high

£60-90   **CHEF**

A 19thC Japanese bamboo sake bottle.

10in (25cm) high

£500-800   **NAG**

A 19thC Chinese bamboo brushpot, deeply carved with figures beneath pine trees in a rocky landscape, damaged.

7.5in (19cm) high

£700-1,000   **WW**

A late 19thC Japanese carved wooden figure of a rat catcher, with a rat on his back, oval ivory seal signature.

3in (8cm) high

£1,200-1,800   **SWO**

A fragment of a Gandaharan grey schist figure of Buddha, wearing loose robes, the hair in a high chignon, the face with a serene expression.

cAD250   *9in (23cm) high*

£500-700   **S&K**

A fragment of a Indian sandstone relief, depicting a female wearing a diaphanous dhoti and jewellery.

cAD900   *15in (38cm) high*

£600-900   **S&K**

A Gandaharan grey schist stone figure of a Bodhisattva, with attendants.

cAD250   *18in (45.5cm) high*

£1,200-1,800   **S&K**

A large Chinese early Ming dynasty wood figure of Guanyin, her hands in vitarka mudra, seated in dhyanamudra, with an elaborate pendant necklace and tiara.

34in (86.5cm) high

£1,500-2,000   **S&K**

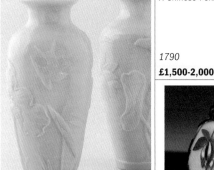

A pair of Chinese Peking glass vases.

c1880   *12in (30.5cm) high*

£800-1,200   **DB**

A Chinese Peking cameo glass bowl.

1790   *6.5in (16.5cm) diam.*

£1,500-2,000   **AL**

A pair of Chinese late Qing dynasty bowls of white Beijing glass, decorated with leaves and lotus in red overlay.

4.75in (12cm) diam

£700-1,000   **NAG**

A rare and important Chinese gouache on paper, depicting a Cantonese shop making furniture in the Western style.

This is the only known depiction of a Cantonese shop making Western-style furniture. Although caned recamiers, chests of drawers and Empire-style chairs made in China are well documented, few gate-leg tables and no candlestands have so far been identified with Chinese provenance.

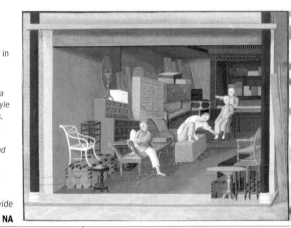

A rare Chinese gouache on paper, depicting the interior of a Cantonese shop selling ceramics.

c1820   14in (35.5cm) wide
£10,000-20,000   **NA**

c1820   14in (35.5cm) wide
£10,000-20,000   **NA**

A rare Chinese gouache on paper, depicting the interior of a Cantonese shop making Chinese-style furniture for the West.

The beds represented in this scene were not generally exported to the West. They were used by Westerners living at Macao and Canton. Trunks and desks, however, were common export items.

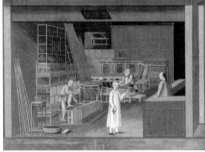

A rare and important Chinese gouache on paper, depicting the interior of a bamboo furniture shop.

c1820   14in (35.5cm) wide
£10,000-20,000   **NA**

c1820   14in (35.5cm) wide
£30,000-40,000   **NA**

A colour woodcut, 'Fireworks at Ryogaku Bridge', by Ando Hiroshige, from the series 'Famous Places in the Eastern Capital', published by Sanoki, unframed.

15in (38cm) wide
£300-400   **FRE**

A fan print, 'Hakone Tonosawa Yuba', by Ando Hiroshige, from the series 'Five Designs from an Untitled Series of Famous Places in Sagami Province', with aratame seal and date seal, published by Maruya Jinpachi, unframed.

A colour woodcut, 'Kanasugi Bridge and Shibaura', by Ando Hiroshige, plate 80 from the series '100 Views of Places in Edo', unframed.

A colour woodcut, 'The City Flourishing, Tanabata Festival', by Ando Hiroshige, plate 73 from the series '100 Views of Famous Places in Edo', unframed.

1855   10in (25.5cm) wide
£4,000-5,000   **FRE**

15in (38cm) high
£400-600   **FRE**

15in (38cm) high
£400-600   **FRE**

A colour woodcut, 'Yoshiwara', by Hiroshige, plate no 15 form the series 'Tokaido Goju-san Tsugi no Uchi' published by Hoeido.

1834   15in (38cm) wide

£600-900   **BEA**

A woodcut, 'Shono', by Ando Hiroshige, plate number 46 from the series 'Fifty Three Stations of the Tokaido', published by Hoeido, signed "Hiroshige ga".

This plate is considered the masterpiece of the series. In no other design does Hiroshige depict the raging elements more convincingly.

1835   15in (38cm) wide

£3,500-4,500   **BEA**

A woodblock print, 'The Hill at Kanagawa Station 4', by Hiroshige, from the series 'Fifty Three Stations of the Tokaido', published by Hoeido, the print depicts travellers climbing a hill lined with houses and restaurants facing Tokyo Bay.

1834   15in (38cm) wide

£400-600   **BEA**

A woodcut by Hokusai, from the series 'Hyakunin isshu uba ga etoki', signed "Zen Hokusai", published by Éijudo.

1835   15in (38cm) wide

£5,000-6,000   **BEA**

A colour woodcut, 'Nichiren Walking Barefoot Up a Steep Mountainside', by Kuniyoshi, plate 10 from the series 'The Life of Nichiren', printed by Iseya Rihe, signed "Ichiyusaï Kuniyoshi".

1836   15in (38cm) wide

£2,200-2,800   **BEA**

A 19thC Japanese colour woodcut, 'Mount Fuji From Midzukubo', by Takahashi Hiroaki, signed and sealed.

18.25in (46.5cm) wide

£200-300   **S&K**

A Japanese colour woodcut, 'Suzaku Gate Moon', by Taiso Yoshitoshi, plate 20 from the series '100 Views of the Moon', unframed.

1890   15in (38cm) high

£300-400   **FRE**

One of a set of five Japanese colour woodcuts, by Tsukioka Kogyo, from the series 'One Hundred Noh Pictures', unframed.

c1900   13in (33cm) high

£200-300 set   **FRE**

A Japanese mezzotint, 'Oiseau Et Poissons En Sympathie' by Kiyoshi Hasegawaon, signed and inscribed "ep. d'artiste" in the margin; also pencil titled, dated, and inscribed "maniere noire" along bottom edge of sheet, and with artist's blindstamp in lower margin, framed.

1964   14in (35.5cm) high

£3,000-4,000   **FRE**

A Japanese woodcut, 'Seated Deity', by Munakata Shiko, pencil signed, dated, and sealed in the margin, framed.

1961   11.75in (30cm) high

£2,000-3,000   **FRE**

A pair of Japanese Edo period red lacquer folding chairs, with brass fittings.

39.25in (98cm) high

£3,500-4,500   NAG

A pair of 18thC Chinese hard wood armchairs, with rectangular seats, open-work backs and ornamental armrests.

44.75in (112cm) high

£6,000-8,000   NAG

A Chinese Qing dynasty hardwood low stand.

c1780   *12in (30.5cm) high*

£250-300   DL

A 19thC Chinese hardwood ceremonial open armchair, the panelled back decorated with open scrollwork above similarly carved open arms and caned seat, with shaped and carved apron.

£700-1,000   L&

A large Chinese gilt and red lacquer cabinet, with two panel doors opening to an interior with one shelf, painted to depict precious objects.

81in (202.5cm) high

£300-500   S&K

A Chinese red lacquer and elmwood cabinet, from Shanxi province, with two doors opening to a single shelf.

c1850   *51in (127.5cm) high*

£300-500   S&K

An early 19thC Chinese red lacquer soft wood presentation case, divided into compartments of various shapes and sizes, on square legs terminating in hoof-shaped feet.

58.5in (146cm) high

£1,000-1,500   NAG

A Chinese black lacquer cabinet, the doors inlaid with mother-of-pearl foliage, with brass mounts.

31.5in (80cm) high

£1,000-1,500   BE

A Korean rosewood display cabinet, the rectangular framed structure supported on a base with ornamental panels, comprising two shelves and a shelf cover, with metal fittings, lock, hinges, corner pieces and handles.

c1850   *66.25in (168cm) high*

£200-300   NAG

A Japanese red lacquer cabinet, carved and painted with flowers and foliage, the panel doors decorated with bone and mother-of-pearl inlays of flowers and birds.

1880   *51.5in (131cm) high*

£1,500-2,000   BEA

A Chinese red lacquer whatnot, decorated with flowering trees, comprising five tiers, three with galleried open shelves and two enclosed by sliding panel doors, decorated with mountainous seascape scenes.

64.25in (163cm) high

£400-600   L&T

A Chinese Canton black lacquer paravent, decorated with young women and children in a pagoda garden, within a border of floral foilage.

90.5in (230cm) hig

£4,000-6,000   BE

A 19thC Korean travel cabinet, in two parts, with metal fittings, ornamental hinges, handles and corners, and fish-shaped locks.

41in (102cm) high

£300-400 **NAG**

A Chinese late Qing dynasty red and black lacquer soft wood cupboard, with a three-part brass lock plate and handles.

37.5in (93.5cm) high

£1,200-1,800 **NAG**

A Chinese hardwood medicine chest, overpainted in ochre, the rectangular top above six rows of seven drawers with three drawers below, each painted with Chinese symbols, the whole raised on square legs with decorative brackets.

47.25in (120cm) wide

£600-900 **L&T**

A late 19thC Japanese lacquer cabinet, decorated with combined lacquer and inlay techniques, in three parts, the four-legged stand a later addition.

58.75in (147cm) high

£5,000-6,000 **NAG**

A Japanese Meiji period two-panel black lacquer wood screen, with inlaid silk paintings and gilt mounts.

82.75in (207cm) high

£3,000-5,000 **NAG**

FURNITURE

As has been the case in recent years, antique furniture at the lower end of the market remains difficult to sell. For some pieces, prices have fall by as much as 50 per cent over the last two to three years. The outlook is particularly bleak for Victorian pieces, although George II and George III furniture, which enjoyed a boom a few years ago, is now also struggling to attract interest.

In contrast, the market for fine and unusual furniture is extremely buoyant, with exceptional pieces selling at auction for unprecedented prices. Buyers favour stylish, well-made pieces in good condition, particularly items by highly regarded makers, such as Gillows or Holland & Co. Provenance is important and furniture from a respected source can attract a premium.

Seat furniture, dining room furniture and bookcases remain popular, whilst bedroom furniture and sofa tables attract less interest. Bureaus have also fallen out of fashion, as buyers opt for flat surfaces to use as computer tables. Items needing restoration, except upholstered seat furniture, are generally fairing badly.

The downturn in the market makes the present an ideal time to invest, and middle market pieces are currently very good value. The strong pound has made furniture relatively inexpensive in the US and this has ensured the market remains lively.

– Paul Roberts, Lyon & Turnbull

18TH CENTURY SECRETAIRES & BOOKCASES

A George II kingwood and mahogany small secretaire bookcase, with simple parquetry veneering to sides and drawers, astragal glazed mirror doors enclosing adjustable shelves and fitted interior, on bracket feet.

74.75in (187cm) high

£8,000-12,000   **L&T**

A George II mahogany bureau bookcase, with a later Grecian bust above mirrored panel doors, the lower section with a fall front enclosing pigeonholes, drawers and a later leather writing surface, on ogee bracket feet.

96in (240cm) high

£7,000-10,000   **FRE**

An 18thC mahogany bureau bookcase, with bevelled mirror doors enclosing adjustable shelves above candle slides and a vitruvian scroll, the fall front with a fitted interior, on ogee bracket feet.

84in (210cm) high

£5,000-7,000   **L&T**

A George III mahogany secretaire bookcase, with rosewood banding and boxwood stringing, the astragal glazed doors enclosing adjustable shelves, the base with secretaire drawer and fitted interior, on shaped bracket feet.

96.75in (242cm) high

£2,500-3,000   **L&T**

A George III mahogany secretaire bookcase, with astragal glazed doors enclosing shelves, on a deeper base with an ebony-strung fall front and doors enclosing four drawers.

100.75in (252cm) high

£2,500-3,000   **L&T**

A Scottish George III mahogany secretaire bookcase, with boxwood and ebony stringing, the astragal glazed doors enclosing shelves, on a bowfront base with drawers and turned bun feet.

93.5in (234cm) high

£2,500-3,000   **L&T**

A George III mahogany secretaire bookcase, inlaid with a vase of flowers, the astragal glazed door enclosing shelves, the lower section with drawers and fitted interior.

102.5in (256cm) high

£5,000-6,000   **L&T**

An 18thC George III and later mahogany bookcase, with astragal glazed doors enclosing a later interior, the base with drawers and fluted columns, on ogee bracket feet.

93in (232.5cm) high

£5,000-7,000   **FRE**

FURNITURE

A George III mahogany library bookcase, with a dentil cornice over two astragal glazed doors, on splayed bracket feet.

c1810   90in (225cm) high

£3,000-5,000   **FRE**

A George III mahogany secretaire bookcase, the Greek key cornice over two glazed panel doors enclosing two adjustable shelves, the lower section with a fitted secretaire drawer over three long drawers, on bracket feet.

c1780

£6,000-7,000   **FRE**

A CLOSER LOOK AT A SECRETAIRE BOOKCASE

The moulding to the mirrored doors has a semi-circular section known as astragal, or bead moulding. This shape is often found on glazing bars of bookcases.

The decorative features on this bookcase were popular during the George III period, such as the breakfront (protruding central section) and the swan-moulded pediment.

The secretaire drawers open to create a writing surface and the panelled doors below conceal further bookshelves.

From the 1730s mahogany emerged as an increasingly popular material, particularly for larger items of furniture like this secretaire bookcase, due to its strength and the width of its boards.

A George III mahogany breakfront secretaire bookcase, the cornice with central swan neck moulded pediment above four astragal mirrored doors enclosing adjustable shelves, the lower section with central panelled secretaire drawer enclosing interior, flanked by panelled doors enclosing three drawers, over four further panelled doors, each enclosing adjustable shelves, the whole raised on a plinth.

Provenance: Gillingham Hall, Norfolk. Probably supplied for Francis Schutz of Gillingham who married in 1755; then by descent.

76.75in (192cm) wide

£25,000-35,000   **L&T**

A Georgian mahogany secretary-bookcase, with dentil-moulded cornice above two doors, the base with dovetailed and cockbeaded drawers, original brass hinges, ogee bracket feet.

c1800   90in (225cm) high

£6,000-8,000   **BRU**

An unusual George III mahogany and inlaid secretaire bookcase, probably from the Channel Islands, with bevelled mirror doors, the inlaid fall front with a fitted interior, above two further doors and drawers, bracket feet.

c1800   99in (247.5cm) high

£5,000-7,000   **FRE**

A Victorian mahogany bureau bookcase, of early George III style, with astragal glazed doors enclosing adjustable shelves, hinged fall front and graduated drawers, on carved ogee bracket feet.

98in (245cm) high

£3,000-4,000   **L&T**

A Dutch 18thC-style walnut veneer and marquetry bombé bureau bookcase, with glazed panel doors, the lower section with a fall front and three long drawers, on carved paw feet.

89in (222.5cm) high

£2,000-4,000   **FRE**

An early 19thC Gothic mahogany breakfront library bookcase.

127.25in (318cm) wide

£6,000-9,000   LC

An early 19thC mahogany dwarf breakfront bookcase, with four astragal glazed doors enclosing adjustable shelves, the projecting base with a frieze drawer and cupboard door enclosing further shelves, plinth base.

87.25in (218cm) high

£4,000-6,000   L&T

A Regency simulated rosewood library bookcase, with two Gothic arched astragal glazed doors enclosing shelves, the lower section with two conforming cupboard doors, on a plinth base.

c1820   *96in (240cm) high*

£3,000-5,000   FRE

An early 19thC Anglo-Indian rosewood bookcase cabinet, with leaf-moulded cresting above twin doors enclosing adjustable shelves, the lower section with two carved frieze drawers and two foliate and rosette panel doors, on carved bracket feet, bears maker's label "Deschamps & Co., Madras".

41in (104cm) wide

£8,000-12,000   L&T

A 19thC mahogany bureau bookcase, the moulded cornice with blind fretwork frieze, the astragal glazed doors with fluted Corinthian pilasters, on an associated bureau, ogee bracket feet.

89.5in (224cm) high

£2,000-3,000   L&T

A 19thC mahogany bookcase cabinet, with astragal glazed doors enclosing adjustable shelves, the base with panelled doors enclosing shelves, plinth with flattened bun feet.

88.5in (221cm) high

£1,200-1,800   L&T

A 19thC English mahogany secretary, the two doors with through muntins and enclosing three shelves, the base with a fold-down drawer, dovetailed drawers and cubbyholes, the two lower doors enclosing dovetailed drawers, on French feet.

89in (222.5cm) high

£3,000-4,000   BRU

A 19thC mahogany breakfront bookcase, the astragal glazed doors enclosing adjustable shelves, raised on a deeper base with panelled doors enclosing sliding trays, drawers and shelves, on shaped apron with ogee bracket feet.

96.5in (241cm) high

£2,500-3,000   L&T

A 19thC mahogany breakfront bookcase, with four astragal glazed doors enclosing shelves, the lower section with four panelled cupboard doors enclosing shelves, bracket feet.

100in (250cm) high

£4,000-6,000   L&T

A 19thC George III-style mahogany library breakfront bookcase, with four astragal glazed panel doors enclosing adjustable shelves, the lower section with four panel doors enclosing shelves, raised on plinth base.

89in (222.5cm) high

£1,500-2,000   FRE

FURNITURE

A French mahogany library bookcase, the acanthus and shell carved pediment over glazed panel doors enclosing adjustable shelves, the lower section with panelled doors enclosing shelves, on bracket feet.

c1860   109in (272.5cm) high

£4,000-6,000   **FRE**

·A Victorian mahogany Chippendale-style breakfront bookcase, with Gothic carving, the cornice with dentil moulding above four astragal glazed doors enclosing adjustable shelves, on a deeper base with a central drawer and pair of cupboards flanked by deeper cupboards enclosing sliding trays and drawers, with bracket feet.

The design for this bookcase appeared in Thomas Chippendale's "Gentleman and Cabinet-maker's Directory" of 1754.

114.5in (286cm) high

£14,000-16,000   **L&T**

One of a pair of Victorian mahogany bookcases, each with moulded cornice above adjustable shelves, on a deeper base with four panelled doors enclosing shelves, plinth base.

97.25in (243cm) high

£3,000-5,000 pair   **L&T**

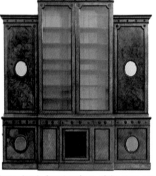

A late 19thC oak reverse breakfront bookcase, the moulded and projecting cornice above four glazed doors divided by fluted pillars, the base with four panel doors raised on a plinth.

94in (235cm) wide

£2,000-3,000   **L&T**

A burl walnut and ebonised library bookcase, by Lamb of Manchester, the moulded cornice above a frieze applied with rosettes, the two glazed doors with mirrored panels, enclosing shelves, the lower section with three frieze drawers, set with oval relief carved cameos depicting classical busts, on a plinth base, stamped "Lamb, Manchester 35207".

James Lamb, founder of one of the most successful 19thC English cabinet makers, commissioned work from a number of designer such as Bruce Talbert and Alfred Waterhouse who designed Manchester Town Hall. The trademark of the firm's work was consistently high quality pieces and as a result it won several prizes at International Exhibitions.

c1880

£8,000-12,000   **FRE**

A late 19thC breakfront bookcase, the stepped cornice above glazed doors enclosing adjustable shelves, deeper base with four flame-veneered panelled doors enclosing shelves and drawers, on plinth base.

129.25in (232cm) high

£3,500-4,500   **L&T**

An unusual George I walnut bureau-bookcase, incorporating an automaton musical clock movement by Christopher Pinchbeck, painted with a lady and her lover to the arch, with a glazed arched door above a pair of bevelled plate glass doors enclosing a cupboard, the base with a fall front enclosing drawers and pigeonholes, on squared cabriole legs, signed "CHRISTOPHER PINCHBECK, LONDON", the musical parts missing.

93.25in (233cm) high

£8,000-12,000   **L&T**

A 19thC Dutch walnut and marquetry bombé bureau bookcase, inlaid with scrolling foliage and exotic birds, two glazed panelled doors, the lower section with a fall front enclosing a stepped fitted interior, on square cabriole legs, alterations.

81in (202.5cm) wide

£3,000-5,000   **FRE**

An early 19thC waterfall bookcase, with a solid back and sides and three open shelves, on bracket feet and casters.

37.25in (93cm) wide

£1,200-1,800   **L&T**

A matched pair of George III mahogany bookcases, each freestanding with three shelves and brass drop handles to the ends, plinth bases and casters.

46in (115cm) wide

£3,000-5,000   **L&T**

A pair of Regency rosewood waterfall bookcases, each with boxwood strung decoration, open shelves, brass carrying handles and a drawer below, the turned legs with brass caps and casters.

40.5in (101cm) high

£8,000-12,000   **L&T**

A fine late 19thC Louis XVI-style kingwood and gilt-bronze mounted dwarf bookcase attributed to Francois Linke, with a moulded marble top, on turned legs and toupie feet.

37in (92.5cm) high

£2,000-3,000   **FRE**

CABINETS

A pair of Edwardian mahogany open bookcases, by Morison & Co., Edinburgh, each with adjustable shelves flanked by canted corners with carved terminals and scroll tops, stamped.

50.5in (126cm) wide

£2,000-3,000   **L&T**

An early 18thC walnut cabinet chest, with a cushion frieze drawer and twin cupboard doors inlaid with feather banded panels, the base with further drawers, labelled "Gill & Reigate Ltd, Oxford Street, London".

47.25in (118cm) wide

£2,000-3,000   **L&T**

A Queen Anne-style red japanned cabinet, of two sections, in gilt and colours with Chinese figures and flowers, the domed pediment above two cupboard doors, over a lower section with two cupboard doors, bun feet.

37.75in (96cm) wide

£2,000-3,000   **B**

A 19thC Swiss painted cabinet, the top and base each with a moulded cornice above two panelled doors enclosing three drawers, on end supports.

80.75in (205cm) high

£800-1,200   **DN**

A CLOSER LOOK AT A GOTHIC CABINET

This cabinet is in the Gothic style, which was revived in the 18th and 19thC. The 19thC Revival was far less fanciful than the 18thC Gothic style and tended to be more archeologically exact. The influence of medieval design can clearly be seen in this cabinet.

The superb quality of this piece is evident from the use of marquetry and the exquisitely carved arched top, depicting a host of mythological beasts. It is also in an excellent condition.

A 19thC Continental marquetry Gothic cabinet, probably Portuguese or German, with a frieze arched door and drawer finely inlaid with figures, lions and angels, flanked by Corinthian pilasters, the conforming lower section with a further cupboard door flanked by spiral turned pilasters, raised on block feet.

This piece has a distinctly architectural feel to it, with arches raised on Corinthian and spiral turned columns. Gothic motifs were used primarily in church architecture, such as tracery and columns.

Block feet are vulnerable and prone to water damage and wear. Original feet will increase the value of the piece. Inspect the base for different woods and new additions.

119in (297.5cm) high

A 19thC mahogany estate cabinet, with sliding doors enclosing pigeonholes and three short drawers below, on acanthus carved legs and brass casters.

£800-1,000   **SWO**   **£15,000-20,000**   **FRE**

FURNITURE

An early 20thC Louis XVI-style mahogany and gilt-bronze mounted side cabinet, in the manner of Francois Linke, the white moulded marble top above a pair of panelled doors applied with draped cherubs, three long drawers, on turned legs with toupie feet.

58.25in (145.5cm) high

£1,500-2,000   **FRE**

A lacquered Buddha cabinet, with an open shelf enclosed by carved and pierced panels centred by roundels of fighting warriors, three drawers and pair of cupboard doors below flanked by carved panels, on stile feet.

59.5in (149cm) high

£400-600   **L&T**

WRITING CABINETS

A Queen Anne walnut escritoire, with a moulded cornice, over a cushion frieze drawer, the crossbanded fall front opening to reveal a fitted interior with a cupboard flanked by drawers and pigeon holes.

44in (110cm) wide

£5,000-7,000   **SWO**

A Queen Anne-style walnut secretaire cabinet, the moulded cornice with a cushion frieze drawer, above a boxwood inlaid fall front enclosing drawers and pigeon holes, the base with two short and two long drawers, on turned feet.

65.25in (163cm) high

£1,500-2,000   **L&T**

A George II walnut secretaire cabinet, attributed to William Old and John Ody, with a cavetto cornice over two mirrored doors enclosing an arrangement of eleven drawers with herringbone bands.

£8,000-12,000   **SWO**

A George III mahogany and brass-inlaid library secretaire, with twenty-four small drawers each inlaid with a letter, the lower section with a fal-front with leather writing surface and pigeonholes.

74.5in (186cm) high

£5,000-7,000   **FRE**

A 19thC mahogany Biedermeier secretaire cabinet, with a mirror door, cupboards and Carrara marble columns with gilt-brass composite capitals, the base with marquetry inlaid fall front.

40.5in (103cm) wide

£2,000-3,000   **L&T**

A 19thC French mahogany secretaire abbatant, with a grey marble top above a gilt-metal mounted frieze drawer, the fall flap enclosing a fitted interior, above three drawers on plinth base.

58.25in (145.5cm) high

£1,200-1,800   **L&T**

DISPLAY CABINETS

An 18thC Dutch walnut and marquetry inlaid cabinet chest, the serpentine moulded cornice above twin astragal glazed doors enclosing shelves, the bombé base with two short above two long graduated drawers, raised on paw-carved front feet.

76.75in (192cm) wide

£3,000-4,000   **L&T**

A Louis XVI style D-shaped mahogany vitrine, with a marble top, brass gallery and three Vernis Martin rustic panels, glass shelves, turned toupie feet.

58.75in (147cm) high

£1,200-1,800   **L&T**

A Regency rosewood and brass-inlaid display cabinet, with a pair of glazed doors raised on later plinth, the reverse breakfront base with a frieze drawer, glazed doors and brass-inlaid consoles.

78.5in (196cm) high

£5,000-8,000   **L&T**

A Louis Phillipe walnut and gilt-brass mounted vitrine, with mahogany banding and boxwood and ebony stringing, the single glazed door and glazed sides enclosing glass shelves, with cast rams head brackets to the angles, on flattened bun feet.

54.5in (136cm) high

£5,000-7,000   **L&T**

A late Victorian elm and marquetry display cabinet, in the manner of Gillows & Co., the cornice above a floral marquetry frieze and four glazed doors enclosing velvet-lined interior with glass shelves, raised on a breakfront base with marquetry panel doors.

85in (216cm) wide

£2,500-3,000   **L&T**

A Victorian mahogany display cabinet, with inlaid decoration and gilt-metal mounts.

26.75in (67cm) wide

£800-1,000   **SWO**

An early 20thC Louis XV-style rosewood bombé vitrine, with gilt-brass mounts, a glazed door and glazed serpentine sides, the lined interior with glass shelves, above Vernis Martin panels of lovers in a landscape, on splayed legs with sabots.

73.5in (184cm) high

£3,000-4,000   **L&T**

An Edwardian satinwood display cabinet, the crossbanded top above a pair of astragal glazed doors enclosing velvet-lined shelved interior, bears label of Druce & Co., Baker Street, London.

42in (107cm) wide

£600-900   **L&T**

A mahogany and inlaid display cabinet, with boxwood stringing, the astragal glazed door and bowed glass panels enclosing glass shelves, the whole raised on square tapered legs.

72.5in (181cm) high

£1,500-2,000   **L&T**

CABINET-ON-STANDS

A 17thC-style walnut writing cabinet-on-stand, the fall front with geometric panelling enclosing a door and drawers, flanked by Mannerist pilasters, the stand with barley twist legs.

64.75in (162cm) high

£1,200-1,800   **L&T**

An 18thC black lacquered cabinet-on-stand, decorated with Chinoiserie panels to cupboard doors, enclosing eleven drawers, on square section legs.

42.75in (107cm) wide

£1,000-2,000   **L&T**

An 18thC or later William and Mary-style oyster veneer cabinet-on-stand, the two doors enclosing twenty drawers and a cupboard door, the stand with two drawers and bun feet.

47in (117.5cm) wide

£3,000-4,000   **FRE**

A George III mahogany writing cabinet-on-stand, with arched fielded panelled doors enclosing drawers and shelves, on a deeper base with writing slide and drawer, on moulded chamfered legs.

74in (185cm) high

£700-900   **L&T**

A George III mahogany cabinet-on-stand, with twin doors enclosing a shelf, on an 18thC Venetian gilt and silvered wood stand, the top with lion rampant and silvered lozenge with "S. G. de C."

25.5in (65cm) wide

£2,500-3,500   **L&T**

An 18th to 19thC Italian ebonised and ivory table cabinet-on-stand, with ten drawers and a cupboard door enclosing three further drawers, all inlaid with hunting scenes, on associated stand.

58.5in (146cm) high

£3,000-4,000   **FRE**

A Louis Phillipe mahogany and inlaid writing cabinet, with gilt-brass mounts, with a pierced gallery and 'verde antico' marble top, above a central door set with a Sèvres panel, the sides with galleried shelves, the base with a writing slide, raised on turned and fluted columns linked by a marble inset undershelf with a mirror back, on tapered engine-turned feet.

52in (130cm) high

£20,000-30,000   **L&T**

A walnut veneered display cabinet-on-stand, with early 18thC elements, the projecting cornice above twin astragal glazed doors enclosing a shelf, the sides with oyster veneered panelling above plain frieze, the base with barley twist supports linked by shaped stretcher, on bun feet.

38.75in (97cm) wide

£800-1,200   **L&T**

A 19thC tapestry cabinet on stand, in the 17thC style, the doors and sides depicting an English landscape with a king and his subjects, on a green-painted and parcel-gilt stand.

58.5in (146cm) high

£1,500-2,000   **FRE**

A 19thC Flemish ebony cabinet-on-stand, with tortoiseshell and ivory, the mirrored door enclosing shelves, the Spanish stand with bobbin turned legs and iron stretchers.

36in (90cm) wide

£3,000-4,000   **FRE**

CORNER CABINETS

A lacquered Chinoiserie cabinet-on-stand, with a stylised gilt landscape, the doors enclosing ten drawers, pierced brass hinges and corners, raised on plain ebonised stand.

60.75in (152cm) high

£700-1,000   **L&T**

A Danish Louis XVI mahogany corner cabinet, with panelled cupboard doors enclosing shelves, the lower section with a bow-fronted fluted frieze drawer above three drawers, on block feet.

c1785   *90in (225cm) high*

£8,000-12,000   **EVE**

A George III oak standing corner cabinet, with a moulded cornice and two panelled doors, on a plinth base.

41.5in (104cm) wide

£1,000-2,000   **SWO**

A George III black Japanned and chinoiserie standing corner cabinet, fitted with an arrangement of shelves, on bracket feet.

38.75in (97cm) wide

£2,000-3,000   **SWO**

An early 19thC provincial carved and stained corner cabinet, unusual sliding bolt mechanism to the door, hidden drawer to the interior and false bottom to base.

40.5in (102cm) high

£3,000-4,000   CATO

A late 19thC Dutch satinwood corner cabinet, with Neo-classical faux marquetry decoration and leaf-cast gilt-brass mounts, the shaped triangular top centred by oval panel of oak leaves, with padouk banding, the single door centred by a putti mask in a panel, raised on pyramidal legs with brass bun feet.

35.5in (89cm) wide

£5,000-7,000   L&T

A 19thC light oak and mahogany standing corner cabinet, with one astragal glazed door over two panelled doors.

44.75in (114cm) wide

£1,000-1,500   SWO

SIDE CABINETS

A 17thC and later Italian walnut side cabinet, moulded rectangular top over a frieze drawer, one panelled doors raised on bracket feet.

25in (62.5cm) wide

£500-700   FRE

An Italian walnut side cabinet credenza, probably 18thC, moulded top above three drawers with nailed construction, single door, later bracket feet.

34.25in (85.5cm) high

£2,000-3,000   BRU

An 18thC Dutch mahogany cabinet, with chequer stringing, the rectangular top with canted angles above a frieze drawer and pair of cupboard doors centred by shell paterae, on spade feet.

37.5in (95cm) wide

£1,200-1,800   L&T

A Louis XV-style mahogany and kingwood bombé cabinet, the serpentine marble top above a single door with floral marquetry and gilt-brass scrolling mounts enclosing shelves.

35in (89cm) wide

£3,000-3,500   L&T

An Italian Neo-classical-style painted and parcel-gilt side cabinet, the inverted breakfront top centred by a star motif, over two bead-moulded frieze drawers and two fielded panel doors carved with laurel wreaths, opening to reveal a shelf, raised on a plinth base.

57in (142.5cm) wide

£3,000-4,000   FRE

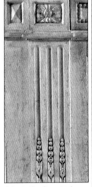

An adapted Scottish George III mahogany side cabinet, with boxwood stringing, the stage back with hinged top and shell and leaf paterae, above a pair of dummy fronted doors, on square section tapered legs.

36in (90cm) wide

£800-1,200   L&T

A kingwood marquetry and parquetry side cabinet, the centre panel with a scrolled cartouche, stamped "Gillows".

c1800   *48in (122cm) wide*

£4,000-6,000   LC

FURNITURE

A Regency rosewood side cabinet, the crossbanded top with burr wood banding and foliate marquetry, the two doors with later pleated silk panels, on carved and gilded paw feet.

43.75in (111cm) wide

£4,000-6,000   **L&T**

An early 19thC Dutch mahogany and marquetry inlaid side cabinet, of demi-lune form, the inlaid top above a single frieze drawer and pair of tambour action doors, raised on block feet.

36in (90cm) wide

£1,000-1,500   **L&T**

A William IV rosewood and brass-inlaid side cabinet, with a green marble top above serpentine sides with applied castings of Ceres and Flora, two Boulle-inlaid doors.

46.75in (117cm) wide

£800-1,200   **L&T**

A 19thC rosewood breakfront dwarf side cabinet, the green marble top above scroll brackets, the four doors with pleated silk panels, between a pair of shallow scroll pilasters.

70.5in (176cm) wide

£2,000-2,500   **SWO**

An 18thC-style painted Italian side cabinet, the canted top above a panelled frieze with two drawers and five further panelled doors, on bracket feet.

84.5in (211cm) wide

£2,000-3,000   **FRE**

A pair of Napoleon III ebonised gilt-bronze-mounted and 'pietra dura' side cabinets, each decorated in relief with exotic birds and foliage, the canted sides surmounted by female carytid and boulle panels, raised on a plinth base.

49in (122.5cm) high

£12,000-18,000   **FRE**

A Victorian ebonised parcel-gilt and gilt-metal side cabinet, with a white marble top, the panelled door between turned columns, on a plinth base.

43.25in (108cm) wide

£400-600   **SWO**

A Renaissance Revival walnut and part-ebonised side cabinet, attributed to Pottier and Stymus, with an inlaid central door, flanked by gilt-metal stylised acanthus capitals, with graffito-work and decorative burr veneers, on casters.

c1880   *61in (152.5cm) wide*

£3,000-4,000   **FRE**

A CLOSER LOOK AT A GOTHIC REVIVAL CABINET

This walnut cabinet is attributed to the designer Frank Furness, who is noted for working with gothic themes. A piece by such a reputable designer is desirable and commands a premium.

The two oval copper panels have been replaced. This does not dramatically affect value, as the repair has been executed in a sympathetic manner.

A Victorian Gothic Revival walnut side cabinet, attributed to Frank Furness, with two frieze drawers and panelled doors, raised on a plinth base, the two copper panels replaced.

Together with a copy of a letter from the Philadelphia Museum of Art discussing the piece.

£5,000-7,000   **FRE**

This piece is typical of the 'Eastlake' style, pioneered by English architect Charles Eastlake, who published "Hints on Household Tastes" in 1868. In this publication Eastlake brought incoming Gothic Revival forms to simple household furniture. The Eastlake style was particularly popular in the US.

The extended curvilinear hinges on the panelled doors play an important part in the decoration.

85.5in (214cm) high

FRE

A pair of 20thC George III-style satinwood and painted side cabinets, the cupboard door and panelled sides centred by oval panels depicting classical females, on carved square tapered legs with blocked feet.

48in (120cm) wide

£5,000-7,000   **FRE**

An Edwardian satinwood side cabinet, with open quadrant shelves and astragal glazed doors enclosing shelves, the base with grotesque marquetry.

42.5in (108cm) wide

£2,000-3,000   **L&T**

An Edwardian mahogany side cabinet, with boxwood and chequer stringing, kingwood crossbanding and an astragal glazed door, on square tapered legs.

19.25in (48cm) wide

£500-700   **L&T**

CREDENZAS

A pair of kingwood veneered serpentine side cabinets, each with a veined purple marble top and twin quarter-veneered and boxwood-strung serpentine doors, enclosing shelves, on square cabriole legs and cast sabots.

40.5in (103cm) wide

£5,000-7,000   **L&T**

A Victorian ebonised and gilt-metal mounted credenza, with an inlaid foliate frieze and four glazed doors, the turned and fluted columns with leaf-carved knops, the whole raised on a plinth base.

78.75in (200cm) wide

£1,000-1,500   **L&T**

A large Victorian ebonised credenza, with brass stringing and gilt-brass mounts, the frieze with metal panels decorated with applied floral sprays, carved from semi-precious stones, the central door with similar oval panel in ribbon-tied gilt-brass frame, flanked by glazed doors, framed by four fluted Corinthian columns and bases, on bun feet.

74.75in (190cm) wide

£1,500-2,000   **L&T**

A Victorian walnut inlaid and gilt-bronze mounted credenza, of serpentine form, the frieze inlaid with floral sprays, the door with a central inlaid oval flanked by shaped glazed doors, on a plinth base.

76in (190cm) wide

£3,000-5,000   **SWO**

FURNITURE

A Regency-style simulated rosewood chiffonier, with gilt decoration, the scrolling ledge back and single shelf on console supports, the base with a drawer, single panelled door and turned freestanding columns, on turned feet.

58.75in (147cm) high

£600-800   **L&T**

A George IV mahogany chiffonier, with two tier upper section above a rectangular top with frieze drawer and cupboard, flanked by reeded pillars and raised on reeded ball feet.

56.75in (144cm) high

£1,200-1,800   **B**

A William IV mahogany chiffonier, with a raised back, cushion moulded drawer and two panelled doors within turned columns.

44in (110cm) wide

£500-700   **SWO**

A William IV rosewood chiffonier, the mirrored back with an open shelf, pierced gilt-brass gallery and gilt-metal column supports, above a rectangular top with a plain frieze, supported on stiff leaf-carved columns and plinth base, on turned feet.

33.25in (83cm) wide

£800-1,200   **L&T**

A Victorian mahogany chiffonier, with a shaped back, over two frieze drawers and two panelled doors.

50in (125cm) wide

£400-600   **SWO**

SMALL CABINETS

A 19thC mahogany hanging cabinet, of pedimented form with a glazed pointed arch door enclosing lined shelves, flanked by spire-topped buttresses, plinth base.

38in (95cm) high

£800-1,200   **L&T**

A 19thC mahogany pot cupboard, the rectangular top with three-quarter gallery above a door enclosing a slatted interior, turned tapering legs.

33.5in (84cm) high

£180-220   **L&T**

A George III mahogany tray-top commode, the shaped gallery with pierced handles above a tambour door and slide out compartment with lid and commode aperture, on square legs.

19.5in (49cm) wide

£2,500-3,000   **L&T**

A George II mahogany bedside commode, the waved tray top above a pair of doors with a converted drawer below, shaped apron and square section legs.

28.5in (71cm) high

£500-700   **L&T**

A late George III mahogany and boxwood-strung commode, the top with a later pierced gallery and fan inlay, square tapering legs.

32in (80cm) high

£500-700   **DN**

An 18thC elm and pine commode armchair, with a shaped top rail, a tapering splat, outswept arms and a shaped apron.

A set of four George III painted softwood Darvel chairs, each with a shaped top rail, above a vase splat painted with ribbon-tied husk swags framing the coat of arms of Graham of Gartmore, outscrolled ash arms and saddle seat, on splayed turned legs joined by H-stretcher.

An 19thC English Windsor chair, probably Lancashire, in mixed hardwoods including ash and elm, with a shaped plank seat, turned cross-stretcher base and ring-turned legs.

41.5in (104cm) high

A English Windsor comb-back armchair, with bentwood arm rests, a hand-planed seat and an L-stretcher turned base, with hoof feet.

43in (107.5cm) high

| £300-500 | SWO | £7,000-10,000 | L&T | £500-700 | BRU | £300-500 | BRU |

A set of eight Victorian Windsor wheelback chairs, with elm sets, including a pair of armchairs.

A 19thC ash and elm rocking chair, with a spindle back and rush seat, on turned legs

A set of eight English plank-bottom chairs, with shaped elm seats, on turned legs and supports, old refinishing, small separations.

33in (82.5cm) high

| £500-700 set | SWO | £150-250 | SWO | £800-1,200 | BRU |

HALL CHAIRS

A mid-18thC mahogany hall chair, of Italian form with a shaped, waisted, dished back above a corresponding seat, on shaped trestle supports joined by a stretcher.

A pair of 19thC Black Forest hall chairs, each with stained and carved frames, inlaid with hunting scenes to the back and seat, the waisted, pierced, scrolling back above a shaped serpentine seat, on cabriole legs.

| £1,000-1,500 | L&T | £600-800 | L&T |

A pair of George III mahogany hall chairs, each waisted back with cut-out leaf decoration and a silvered roundel inscribed with a crest, above a rounded solid seat with dished centre, raised above cut supports with a dished roundel.

£3,500-4,000   **L&T**

A Regency mahogany hall chair, with a stylised crescent crest, a solid seat and sabre legs, some repairs and damage.

35.5in (88.5cm) high

£300-400   **DN**

A William IV mahogany hall chair, the scroll-carved back above a shaped seat on turned front supports.

34in (86.5cm) high

£300-400   **WW**

One of a pair of early Victorian mahogany hall chairs with shaped backs and seats.

£250-300 pair   **SWO**

A mahogany hall seat, by James Winter of 101 Wardour Street, Soho, London, with maker's stamp.

c1835

£10,000-14,000   **CATO**

A CLOSER LOOK AT A CHINA TRADE CORNER CHAIR

The corner chair was developed in England in the first half of the 18thC. This particular chair is based on a George II prototype.

Although this chair is clearly Georgian with its classically inspired urn/vase back splats, the curved and sloping rail reveals a distinctly Chinese influence

As this chair is designed for a corner the only decorative chair leg is the one on display at the front.

The front leg terminates in a ball and claw foot, which became popular in the early 18thC. This foot originates from Chinese bronzes where the dragon holds a flaming pearl of wisdom, showing the popularity of oriental design in furniture from this period

A mid-late 18thC China trade corner chair, Canton (Guangzhou), in Asian hardwood, probably rosewood, minor repairs.

34in (86cm) high

£10,000-15,000   **MJM**

One of a pair of early 19thC mahogany hall chairs, in the manner of Charles Heathcote Tatham, the back with a circular cartouche for a crest, with a solid seat, on architectural legs.

£3,000-5,000 pair   **CATO**

A Victorian cherry wood hall chair.

£400-500   **SWO**

A very rare early China trade side chair, Canton (Guangzhou), in Asian hardwood, probably rosewood.

c1730   42in (106 cm) high

£18,000-22,000   **MJM**

An 18thC-style side chair, in gros point and petit point fabric with floral panels, on carved cabriole legs with pad front feet, patches and repairs to upholstery.

43in (107.5cm) high

£800-1,200   **BRU**

A pair of George II walnut dining chairs, with yoked top rails above solid vase-shaped splats, with upholstered inverted bow front drop-in seats, on cabriole legs headed by carved shells.

£2,500-3,000   **L&T**

A mid-18thC mahogany side chair, possibly American, with a rolled crest and pierced splat, drop-in serpentine seat and pierced seat rail, on cabriole legs with claw and ball feet.

41.5in (103.5cm) high

£400-600   **DN**

A pair of 18thC Chippendale cherry chairs, with similar tapered rectangular backs, upholstered drop-in seats, stretcher bases and original circular glue blocks, variations in seat moulding, rail size and other construction details.

£1,000-2,000   **BRU**

THE INFLUENCE OF CHIPPENDALE

- Published in April 1754, Thomas Chippendale's "The Gentleman and Cabinet-Maker's Director", was the most influential Rococo pattern book, containing 161 engraved plates of furniture designs.
- Subscribers included several aristocratic patrons of the arts.
- Designs that imitated desirable imports from the East, called Chinese Chippendale, were highly sought after, resulting in many prestigious commissions for the business.
- "The Director" became the 'bible' for furniture makers in Britain and also gave impetus to the American Chippendale style.

A late 18thC rare Colonial Indian side chair, Asian hardwood.

The design for this chair would almost certainly have been derived from Manwaring (1765), Ince & Mayhew (1762) or Chippendale (1754-63). The closest associated Indian furniture is a small group of ivory chairs from Vizagapatam.

c1770   40in (100cm) high

£13,000-16,000   **MJM**

One of a set of six mahogany dining chairs, in the George III style, each with a pierced splat with pendant garrya, drop-in seat, on straight legs with H-stretchers.

£500-700 set   **DN**

Two of a set of six mahogany dining chairs, in the George III style, each with yoked top rail above a pierced vase-shaped splat, the drop-in seat on square legs joined by stretchers.

£1,500-2,000 set   **L&T**

A George III-style mahogany side chair, with a carved, pierced and interlaced wheat ear splat, upholstered serpentine seat, on square tapering legs with spade feet and an H-stretcher.

£400-600   **DN**

A pair of 19thC mahogany George III-style dining chairs, each with serpentine top rail and pierced scrolling vase splat above stuffover gros point seats, on moulded cabriole legs and pad feet.

£600-900   **L&T**

FURNITURE

One of a set of four mahogany chairs, in the George III style, with a pierced and interlaced vase splat, each with a drop-in seat, on straight chamfered legs with H-stretcher.

39.25in (98cm) high

£600-900 set   DN

A set of six early 20thC Chippendale-style mahogany chairs, with two armchairs and four side chairs, each with an openwork splat with shaped crest rail and scrolled ears, scrolled arms, drop-in upholstered seats and cabriole legs with ball-and-claw feet.

39in (97.5cm) high

£3,000-4,000   BRU

Two of a set of six 19thC mahogany dining chairs, in the George III Chippendale style, each with a serpentine top rail with moulded lugs above pierced vase-shaped splats and drop-in seat, on square chamfered legs with decorative brackets.

£1,200-1,800 set   L&T

Two of a set of eight 19thC mahogany dining chairs, in the Chippendale style, with two carvers, each with a serpentine top rail above pierced vase-shaped splats, above stuffover upholstered seat on square tapering and chamfered legs.

£2,500-3,000 set   L&T

Two of a set of four George III mahogany dining chairs, each with an arched back and anthemion pierced splat, above a drop-in needlework seat and chamfered square section legs joined by an H-stretcher.

£700-900 set   L&T

One of a set of ten walnut dining chairs, each with a moulded frame and pierced and shaped splat, with an upholstered seat, the turned and fluted legs with an X-stretcher, two with arms.

£2,000-3,000 set   DN

THE INFLUENCE OF HEPPLEWHITE

- English cabinet-maker George Hepplewhite (d. 1786) became known through his pattern book, "The Cabinet-maker and Upholsterer's Guide", posthumously published in 1788.
- Hepplewhite's designs, found in both his Guide and "The Cabinetmakers London Book of Prices" (1788), proved to be extremely influential in both Europe and America.
- Hepplewhite furniture is distinguishable by its lightness, grace and delicacy, especially when compared to Chippendale designs.
- The elaborately carved cabriole and square legs, preferred by Chippendale and his contemporaries, are greatly contrasted by the slender, tapered legs seen on Hepplewhite pieces.
- Characteristic features of the style include curvilinear forms, inlaid and painted decoration, shallow carving, motifs such as sunbursts, husks, scrolls and paterae.
- Chairs often have distinctive shield-shaped backs or square backs incorporating Prince of Wales feathers.
- Due to the difficulty in identifying an actual piece or design by Hepplewhite himself, his name has come to represent a particular style rather than the handiwork of one man.

Three of a harlequin set of eight mahogany dining chairs, including two carvers, in the Hepplewhite style, the serpentine top rails above pierced and waisted splats and drop-in seats, raised on square legs linked by stretchers.

£1,500-2,000 set   L&T

Two of a set of eight Georgian-style mahogany shield back dining chairs, with drop-in seats.

Two of a set of six 19thC Hepplewhite-style walnut dining chairs, including two carvers, each with a shaped top rail above carved uprights and three splats, one with pierced and carved Prince of Wales feathers, bowfront stuffover seat with plaid upholstery, on moulded square section tapering legs joined by H-stretchers.

Two of a set of six late 19thC Sheraton-style mahogany dining chairs, the square backs with three pierced splats with wheat ear capitals, above studded leather upholstered seats, on panelled square tapering legs.

£800-1,200 set **SWO**	£1,500-2,000 set **L&T**	£2,000-3,000 set **L&T**

EARLY 19TH CENTURY DINING & SIDE CHAIRS

Two of a set of eight Regency Trafalgar side chairs, in mahogany, the rope top rail above an anthemion inlaid panel, the caned seats on sabre legs.

£3,000-4,000 set **WW**

Two of a set of twelve George III mahogany dining chairs, each with yoke backs with purplewood stringing, the nailed stuffover horsehair seats above ring turned front legs, stamped "M.B."

£6,000-9,000 set **L&T**

Two of a set of six George III mahogany dining chairs, each with diamond lattice back, stuffover horsehair seat and chamfered square section legs.

£3,000-5,000 set **L&T**

Two of a set of eight early 19thC mahogany dining chairs, including two armchairs, each with incised bar back, three carved splats and reeded uprights, stuffover seat and square section legs.

£6,000-8,000 set **L&T**

Two of a set of four Regency simulated rosewood dining chairs, each with a pierced scrolling panel back centred by a palmette, drop-in seat and sabre legs.

£800-1,200 set **L&T**

A set of four English Regency side chairs, each with a crest rail with carved shells and scrolls, a carved back with fruit and floral decoration, tapered and reeded legs and cane seats below drop-in upholstered drop seats, carved "GB" under front rail.

34in (85cm) high

£400-600 **BRU**

Two of a set of eight Regency mahogany dining chairs, with curved and panelled top rail above bound leafy mid-rail, the stuffover seat raised on square tapering legs linked by stretchers.

£2,000-3,000 set   **L&T**

Two of a set of seven Regency mahogany dining chairs, including one carver, each with curved top rail above anthemion carved mid-rail and drop-in seat, on turned and sabre legs.

£1,500-2,000 set   **L&T**

Two of a set of six mahogany and satinwood crossbanded dining chairs, each with rectangular top rail above 'X' pierced mid-rail and stuffover seat, raised above square tapering legs.

£1,200-1,800 set   **L&T**

Two of a set of eight William IV mahogany dining chairs, including two carvers, each with leaf-carved and gadrooned top rails and drop-in seats, raised on sabre legs.

£800-1,200 set   **L&T**

One of a set of eight mahogany dining chairs, in late George III style, each with a satinwood crossbanded crest rail above a lattice back rail, upholstered seat and square tapering legs with spade feet, two with reeded arms.

£1,500-2,000 set   **DN**

Two of a set of ten Edwardian mahogany dining chairs, including two carvers, in the Regency style, each with twin panelled yoke back, raised on reeded uprights with pierced lyre splat, stuffover seat with serpentine front, on turned and reeded tapering legs.

£7,000-10,000 set   **L&T**

Two of a set of four Regency mahogany dining chairs, with tablet backs, carved splats and stuffover seats on reeded tapering legs.

£400-600 set   **SWO**

Two of a set of twelve Regency mahogany dining chairs, ten original and two modern reproductions, each with a curved back with inset upholstered panel, above stuffover seat and panelled frieze, raised on panelled sabre legs.

£6,000-8,000 set   **L&T**

Two of a set of eight Regency mahogany dining chairs, including two carvers, each with curved top rail above reeded uprights and panelled mid-rail, the drop-in seat raised on turned and tapering reeded legs.

£2,000-3,000 set   **L&T**

Two of a set of twelve Regency mahogany dining chairs, each with panelled yoke back supported by sabre uprights with Corinthian capitals, nailed stuffover leather seats, moulded seat rail and turned and reeded front legs.

£15,000-20,000 set   **L&T**

Two of a set of six early 19thC Japanned parlour chairs, each with curved top rail above slatted back, painted in gilt with mother of pearl inlay, the plush stuffover seat on square cabriole legs linked by a stretcher.

£2,000-3,000 set   **L&T**

VICTORIAN CHAIRS

One of a set of eight late Victorian mahogany dining chairs, each with reeded panels to the rail and supports, with blue leather buttoned upholstered seat, on fluted turned legs.

34.75in (87cm) high

£800-1,200 set   **DN**

A Victorian Carolean-style oak side chair, with beadwork panel and seat, the turned and blocked frame with pierced foliate decoration, H-stretcher.

£150-250   **L&T**

Two of a composite set of fourteen Victorian mahogany balloon back chairs, the moulded backs above stuffover seats with moulded rails, on turned and tapering front legs with toupie feet.

£4,000-6,000 set   **L&T**

Two of a set of six late Victorian mahogany parlour chairs, of George III style, each with vine carved and moulded back with damask upholstered panel, above stuffover serpentine seat, on square tapering moulded legs with rosette terminals and spade feet.

£7,000-10,000 set   **L&T**

A set of four oak and antler horn dining chairs, each with a oval upholstered back supported by an antler frame, above a stuffover seat and on antler supports.

£2,000-3,000   **L&T**

An early 19thC pair of mahogany inlaid shield-back chairs, with heart-back moulded crests, the inlaid fans flanked by heart-carved splats and inlaid lunettes, the moulded and curved back supports above over-upholstered seats with serpentine front rails, above string and bellflower-inlaid square tapering front legs ending in spade feet, with rounded rear legs.

c1800

38in (96.5cm) high

£18,000-22,000

SK

A set of six Victorian rosewood and tapestry-upholstered spoon-back side chairs, the shaped backs with shell and C-scroll carved crestings, over serpentine stuffover seats, raised on moulded cabriole legs and casters.

c1860

£4,000-6,000

FRE

A pair of Empire-style parcel-gilt mahogany chairs, each with a tapering padded back with curved panelled crest rail carved with berried laurel, above a shaped padded seat on acanthus carved tensed animal legs, upholstered in gold floral silk.

£7,000-10,000

FRE

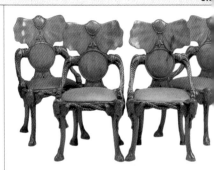

A set of four Continental carved walnut side chairs, the shaped backs modelled as elephants' heads with downswept rope-twist arms above drop-in seats, raised on outswept legs surmounted by elephant masks.

£2,000-3,000

FRE

Two of a set of five early 19thC Continental walnut parlour chairs, each with a caned back and serpentine seat, turned and stop fluted front legs with ball feet.

£2,000-3,000 set   **L&T**

A pair of Swedish Biedermeier birch side chairs, with cream upholstered seats.

c1840

£1,500-2,000   **LANE**

One of a set of four 19thC Dutch elm dining chairs, each with a panelled crest rail, the felt upholstered seat with brass studding, on turned tapering legs.

33.5in (85cm) high

£700-900 set   **DN**

A pair of Indian hardwood thrones, with applied brass and steel incised panels, chip carved decoration and stylised animal heads to the corners, panelled rope seat and columnar front legs.

£700-1,000   **L&T**

A set of six Italian Neo-classical walnut gondola chairs, each with a fluted backrest above a pierced stylised foliate border, the cane seat applied with a roundel to each side, raised on sabre legs.

£3,000-4,000   **NA**

OTHER SIDE & DINING CHAIRS

A mahogany child's high chair, of George III style, the turned removable bar with ball finials, close nail upholstered seat on square splayed supports.

40in (100cm) high

£700-1,000   **L&T**

An early 19thC mahogany framed child's high chair, with an upholstered close nailed back and scrolled arms, on swept square tapered legs.

17.25in (43cm) high

£600-900   **SWO**

A George III mahogany and upholstered reading chair, with upholstered ears, back and spoon seat, the back fitted with an adjustable hinged reading slope, on cabriole legs with pad feet.

£1,200-1,800   **L&T**

A pair of George VI upholstered coronation chairs, with invitation to the Coronation and five Union Jack flags.

£500-700   **L&T**

A George II mahogany armchair, with figural gros and petit point needlework upholstery, stuffover seat and moulded curved supports, on leaf-carved cabriole front legs with hairy paw feet.

£8,000-12,000   **L&T**

A George II mahogany armchair, with serpentine back, stuffover seat, shaped apron and scrolling arms with squabs, on leaf-carved cabriole French front legs, the rear legs with scroll toes.

£3,000-5,000   **L&T**

A George II mahogany armchair, with gros and petit point needlework upholstery, the stuffover seat with padded arms and cabochon carved supports, on cabriole front and rear legs with pad feet.

£6,000-9,000   **L&T**

A George II mahogany open armchair, the serpentine arms with scroll terminals, on cabriole legs and pad feet united by a turned and blocked stretcher.

£2,000-2,500   **L&T**

A pair of Hepplewhite-style mahogany open armchairs, each with rounded upholstered back, outscrolled arms with squabs and serpentine stuffover seat, on cabriole legs with scroll toes.

£1,200-1,800   **L&T**

A pair of mahogany open armchairs, in the Hepplewhite style, the shield-shaped backs carved with Prince of Wales feathers and drapery, stuffover seats, on square tapering legs and spade feet.

37in (94cm) high

£1,000-1,500   **WW**

A pair of mahogany framed Raeburn chairs, each with upholstered back, open arms and curved uprights with later carved blind fretwork panels, the upholstered seat on similarly carved square legs linked by stretchers.

£1,200-1,800   **L&T**

A late 18thC mahogany 'Drunkards' chair, probably Lancashire, with a pierced wavy top rail above spindle balustrade back, scrollover arms and a wide padded seat, on square tapering legs joined by stretchers.

£2,500-3,000   **CATO**

A George III mahogany carver, with a moulded serpentine top rail above pierced interlaced vase splat and open scroll arms, drop-in needlework seat, on acanthus-carved cabriole legs with ball and claw feet.

£600-900   **L&T**

A George III open armchair, the oval upholstered back above outscrolled padded arms with moulded uprights, stuffover serpentine seat and panelled square section tapering legs with collar feet.

£700-1,000   **L&T**

A George III mahogany elbow chair, the serpentine back and saddle seat with shaped arms, on chamfered moulded legs with an H-stretcher, later seat rails.

39in (97.5cm) high

£600-900   **DN**

A George III mahogany elbow chair, with a shaped crest rail and pierced interlaced splat, with shaped arms, a drop-in seat and straight legs.

38.75in (97cm) high

£200-300   **DN**

A late George III mahogany elbow chair, with a slatted splat, shaped arms, a drop-in seat and chamfered straight legs with an H-stretcher.

37.75in (94.5cm) high

£300-400   DN

A George III mahogany provincial Chinese Chippendale chair, the upholstered seat on square chamfered legs.

25in (63.5cm) high

£800-1,200   WW

A George III mahogany open armchair, with carved tablet top rail, pierced lattice back and upholstered seat, on reeded tapering legs and toupie feet.

£800-1,200   L&T

A George III mahogany tub armchair, with later drop-in 18thC needlework seat, on square section tapered legs.

£800-1,200   L&T

George III mahogany elbow chair, with n interlaced hoop back and swept rms, raised on moulded square apering legs.

600-900   SWO

A George III mahogany Gainsborough open armchair, with a serpentine back, swept arms and velvet upholstery, on square legs, united by an H-stretcher, casters lacking.

£1,200-1,800   SWO

A George III mahogany Gainsborough armchair, with replaced silk upholstery, outswept arms with carved scrollwork, and a serpentine fronted seat, on moulded square tapering legs.

£2,000-2,800   SWO

A pair of Regency mahogany carvers, each with a panelled yoke back above a single mid-rail, downscrolled arms with turned supports and a nailed stuffover leather seat, on sabre legs.

£1,200-1,800   L&T

Regency simulated rosewood tub-haped showframe chair, with caned ack and sides, on sabre legs with rass terminals and casters, paintwork orn and lacking carving to seat.

31.5in (79cm) high

300-400   DN

A Regency mahogany elbow chair, the ebony strung crest rail above a roundel centred X-back, with downswept arms and upholstered seat, on square tapering legs.

34in (85cm) high

£300-500   DN

A Regency mahogany open armchair, the brass line inlaid tablet toprail above a horizontal splat, channelled down scrolled arms and lemon upholstered seat, on channelled sabre legs.

£400-600   L&T

A pair of Regency ebonised and painted open armchairs, each with a pierced horizontal splat with a tablet painted with putti, the rattan seat with squab cushion, turned legs with toupie feet.

£2,500-3,000   L&T

FURNITURE

A Regency mahogany bergère armchair, the moulded frame with a caned back and seat, the caned arms with turned terminals, on turned tapering front legs with brass caps and casters, back and seat cushions.

£2,000-2,500　　　　**L&T**

A Regency caned bamboo armchair, in the Brighton Pavilion style, the back and sides filled with intricate fretwork, with a cane seat and cluster column legs, together with a similar hexagonal occasional table.

c1815

£1,200-1,800　　　　**SWO**

A William IV rosewood 'Wilkie Patent' armchair, with a leather upholstered back, armrests and seat cushion, the seat with a tin plate and spring patent slats, on brass casters.

£700-1,000　　　　**WW**

A George IV mahogany and ebony strung elbow chair, with a reeded frame, downswept arms and an upholstered seat, on turned tapering legs.

33.5in (84cm) high

£400-600　　　　**DN**

A pair of William IV rosewood upholstered library chairs, with button backs and scrolled padded arms, on turned legs with brass cappings and casters.

£2,500-3,000　　　　**SWO**

A dwarf oak Orkney chair, of typical form with curved rush back and drop-in seat, on square section tapering legs joined by stretchers.

£1,000-1,500　　　　**L&T**

A 19thC oak Orkney chair, of typical form with a curved rush back and open arms.

£800-1,200　　　　**L&T**

A George II-style mahogany open armchair, bearing the label of John Reid & Co, Buchanan Street, Glasgow, with leather upholstery and stuffover seat, on leaf carved cabriole legs with ball and claw feet.

£1,200-1,800　　　　**L&T**

A late 19thC Sheraton Revival mahogany and printed elbow chair, painted with garrya and flowers, the shield back centred with an urn of swags, with a caned seat, on square tapering legs with spade feet.

39.25in (98cm) high

£500-700　　　　**DN**

A mahogany open armchair, in the George II style, with a blue leather padded back, arm rests and seat, on cabriole legs and pad feet.

25.5in (64cm) hig

£300-500　　　　**D**

One of a pair of Orkney chairs, each with a rush back and domed top, on square tapering legs with stretchers.

26in (65cm) wide

£2,000-3,000 pair   DN

A 19thC pair of George III-style mahogany armchairs, with pierced fret-carved panel backs and arms over drop-in seats, on moulded square legs.

£1,000-1,500   FRE

An early Victorian stained beech bobbin-turned armchair, by John Maggs of Liverpool, the square brander back with separate squab cushion above a stuffover seat and turned front legs.

£200-400   L&T

A Victorian walnut upholstered open armchair, with button back and stuffover seats, on carved cabriole legs.

£800-1,200   SWO

A late 19thC mahogany Empire-style chair, the square back with a lyre splat with swans' mask carved downswept arms raised on square tapered legs.

£1,000-1,500   FRE

A late 19thC George II-style mahogany open armchair, with carved decoration and serpentine seat, on cabriole legs.

38.5in (96cm) high

£3,000-4,000   FRE

An Edwardian Sheraton Revival painted satinwood bergère armchair, with Gothic tracery, putti and a roundel with a mother and child.

£1,200-1,800   L&T

One of a pair of mahogany cockpen open armchairs, each with a typical lattice back, stuffover hollow seat and splayed front legs with bead to front.

£1,200-1,800 pair   L&T

A mahogany Raeburn chair, the upholstered serpentine back above open arms, stuffover seat and moulded square section front legs linked by H-stretcher.

£600-900   L&T

A mahogany cockpen armchair, the lattice back and open arms with leaf-carved terminals and serpentine supports, hollow stuffover seat and splayed front legs.

£500-700   L&T

A Chinese Chippendale-style mahogany elbow chair, the upholstered back and serpentine-shaped seat with open pierced arms and on blind fret-carved legs.

37in (94cm) high

£1,000-1,500   WW

The pierced vase splat beneath the carved top rail incorporates gothic-style elements, which is typical of Georgian design.

This impressive needlepoint upholstery is in very good condition, and this will add to the desirability and consequently its value.

The spandrels flanking the knee of the legs are carved from one piece of wood, indicating high quality.

Used by both Sheraton and Chippendale, Downswept arms became very fashionable in the second half of the 18thC.

A George II carved walnut reading armchair, with needlepoint upholstery.

c1760

£20,000-25,000

CATO

The classically inspired swags and ribbons that surround this coat of arms were popular motifs during the Renaissance Revival.

This inlaid shield back is a distinctive feature of the Hepplewhite style, which was clearly a source of inspiration for Wright and Mansfield.

These sunburst pieces are again typical of Hepplewhite's designs, which feature slender furniture with inlaid and carved decoration.

The crisply carved, mythological ram heads are inspired by Etruscan art, which was introduced by the architect Robert Adam.

One of an important pair of mahogany armchairs, in the manner of Robert Adam, attributed to Wright and Mansfield, each with an inlaid satinwood back and carved front.

c1860

£40,000-60,000 pair

CATO

An 18thC giltwood fauteuil, of Louis XVI style, the back with a leather panel and laurel and lappet-carved frame, the open arms with acanthus carving, on turned legs, upholstered seat damaged.

£500-700   L&T

An 18thC Spanish walnut savonarola-type folding chair, of slatted X-shape, the crest with a cartouche centred with an "S", the arms with patera terminals, on plinth ends with scored feet.

37.5in (94cm) high

£700-1,000   DN

A set of four Louis XVI giltwood and upholstered fauteuils, the rope twist-carved backs with musical or gardening trophies, the padded scroll arms over serpentine stuffover seats, on fluted turned legs, one lacking seat upholstery.

c1780

£2,000-3,000 set   FRE

A late 18thC Italian side chair, with a shield back and acanthus-carved arms, cane seat and back, on tapered and stop-fluted legs with serpentine cross-stretcher base.

37in (15cm) high

£1,200-1,800   BRU

Two late 18th to early 19thC Spanish Colonial leather chairs, with scroll arms and headcrests, ornately carved with abstract floral designs, Hapsburg eagles, and heraldry crests.

58in (147.5cm) high

£5,000-7,000   SK

An early 19thC Italian fruitwood elbow chair, with pierced interlaced back above arms with lion head terminals, stuffover seat, tapering legs.

£2,000-3,000   CATO

One of a set of three early 19thC Italian walnut elbow chairs, each with a moulded frame and upholstered back, the arms with stiff leaf-carved supports, drop-in seats, on stop-fluted square tapering legs.

41in (104cm) high

£2,500-3,000 set   DN

A Swedish Biedermeier birch chair, with arms and detailing to the back.

c1840   *22.5in (57cm) wide*

£400-600   LANE

A 19thC Danish mahogany armchair, the hoopback upholstered backrest raised on curved supports above an upholstered seat, on square tapered legs.

30in (75cm) high

£2,000-2,500   EVE

A rare early 19thC China trade armchair, Canton (Guangzhou), in Asian hardwood with a caned seat.

The Neo-classical design motifs and Greek key carved crest suggest the design for this chair originated from London pattern books. The shaped carved rail supports a family crest, possibly making the chair unique.

33in (84cm) high

£12,000-14,000   MJM

A late 17thC-style walnut elbow chair, carved with coronets and scrolls, the back with two caned panels flanked, with leaf-carved scroll arms, on turned legs and paw feet, some worm.

23.25in (59cm) wide

£1,000-1,500   DN

A Louis XV-style walnut fauteuil, with needlework upholstery and carved outscrolled open arms and seat rail, on cabriole legs with scroll toes joined by wavy X-stretcher.

£500-800 **L&T**

A 19thC Louis XV-style beechwood fauteuil, with foliate tapestry centred by two panels of lovers and a dog, padded arms and serpentine stuffover seat, raised on cabriole legs.

£600-900 **FRE**

A 19thC Louis XV-style beechwood and walnut fauteuil, the shaped back, padded arms and seat covered in figural and foliate tapestry, raised on cabriole legs.

£500-700 **FRE**

Three of a set of four 19thC walnut framed open armchairs, in the French 17thC style, each covered in 17thC verdure wool tapestry, the scrolling open arms with acanthus-carved terminals, above leaf-carved and pierced front stretchers and turned and blocked legs, on stylised paw feet.

£4,000-6,000 set **L&**

A pair of 19thC carved pine open armchairs, in the Louis XVI manner, each with ribbon-carved moulded frames with foliate crestings, the open arms and upholstered seats raised on turned and fluted front legs.

£800-1,200 **L&T**

A 19thC Spanish folding elbow chair, of folding savonarola form, the crest rail with a pierced motif, the slatted sides, seat and legs with rectangular bases.

32in (80cm) high

£1,000-1,500 **DN**

One of a set of three late 19thC French provincial open armchairs, each with a shaped crest rail and a pierced splat, with a drop-in seat, on cabriole legs.

22.5in (56cm) high

£300-500 set **DN**

One of a pair of 19thC Swedish Empire style painted open armchairs, with spool-turned X-form splats and an upholstered seat, on circular tapered legs with leaf banding.

36.5in (91cm) high

£3,000-4,000 pair **EV**

A pair of late 19thC Russian birch open armchairs, each with a stepped yoke backrest with a fan carving, scrolled armrests and an upholstered seat, raised on sabre legs.

36in (90cm) high

£4,000-6,000 **EVE**

A pair late 19th to early 20thC Louis XVI-style armchairs, of pegged construction, the shield backs with scrolled arms, tapered and fluted legs, old pale yellow and olive paint.

38in (95cm) high

£2,000-2,500 **BRU**

An Italian ivory inlaid Mooresque open armchair, the shaped back rail centred by an urn issuing flowers, with a panel seat and X-frame supports, on sled bases.

£500-700 **L&T**

A Selanese ebony planter's armchair, with a carved back and seat and carved and turned arm supports, on reeded seat rail and turned front legs.

£800-1,200 **L&**

An early George II upholstered wingback armchair, on shell and leaf-carved front cabriole legs, one back leg re-spliced, some restoration.

*1730

| £800-1,200 | B |

Regency upholstered and mahogany wing armchair, in foliate damask fabric, on ring and baluster turned legs with brass caps and ceramic casters.

| £2,000-2,500 | L&T |

A George III mahogany-framed bergère armchair, with an arched moulded back, padded armrests and upholstered seat, on square tapering legs.

| £800-1,200 | L&T |

A pair of Regency simulated rosewood and upholstered library armchairs, the uprights and rail with gilded reeding, raised on turned tapering front legs with gilded embellishments.

| £3,500-4,000 | L&T |

One of a pair of Regency mahogany library bergère armchairs, in the manner of Gillows, with reeded moulded frames, padded arm supports, reeded tapered uprights and upholstered panel seats, on turned and reeded tapered legs terminating in brass cappings and casters.

| £15,000-20,000 pair | H&L |

pair of Regency rosewood library tub hairs, each with scrollover moulded acks and arms with lappet terminals, he upholstered backs and seats with oose cushions, on leaf-moulded apering front legs with leaf-carved feet.

| 8,000-12,000 | L&T |

An early 19thC Regency mahogany wing chair, probably English, with carved hand rests, re-upholstered with blue vinyl, on turned front legs with porcelain casters and sabre rear legs.

49in (122.5cm) high

| £500-700 | BRU |

A George II-style walnut wing armchair, the back, seat and sides upholstered in yellow damask, the seat with an edge moulding, on scroll carved cabriole legs with pad feet.

43.75in (109.5cm) high

| £500-700 | DN |

A 19thC George III-style tapestry wing armchair, covered in 18thC fabric and raised on square tapered legs.

| £1,500-2,000 | FRE |

FURNITURE

A Victorian carpet chair, by John Taylor & Sons of Edinburgh, with velvet upholstery and turkey carpet panels, tassels and fringe, on turned front legs and casters.

£800-1,200　　　　**L&T**

A Victorian mahogany framed button-back upholstered chair, with scrolled arms, on cabriole legs terminating in brass casters.

£400-600　　　　**SWO**

A pair of Edwardian mahogany armchairs, of bergère form, with guilloche carved frames, squab seats and leaf and ribbon carved seat rails, the arms with leaf-carved terminals and baluster turned supports, on leaf clasped turned front legs.

£2,000-3,000　　　　**L&**

An Edwardian mahogany framed bergère library chair, with Vitruvian scroll-carved frame, double caned panels and twist column arm supports, on fluted turned legs and brass casters.
37in (94cm) high

£800-1,200　　　　**WW**

A matched pair of early 20thC Howard & Sons upholstered armchairs, one with outscrolled arms and gadrooned seat rail, the other with downscrolled arms and moulded seat rail, each stamped "Howard & Sons, Berners Street".

£800-1,200　　　　**L&T**

A mahogany patent self-reclining bath chair, with buttoned leather upholstery, by G. Minter, 33 Gerrard Street, Soho, London, with handle to rear and large spoked side wheels.

£1,000-1,500　　　　**L&**

A Swedish Biedermeier birch armchair, with black upholstery.

c1840　　*30in (75cm) high*
£1,800-2,200　　　　**LANE**

A Swedish Biedermeier birch armchair, with cream-lined upholstery.

30in (75cm) wide
£1,000-2,000　　　　**LANE**

A 19thC mahogany bergère library chair, the arms carved with angel heads, acanthus leaves and scrolls, on fluted front legs.

£1,800-2,200　　　　**SWO**

A late 19thC Danish mahogany and upholstered wing chair, with padded armrests and candle bracket.

48.5in (121cm) hig
£2,000-3,000　　　　**EV**

An 18thC mahogany settee, with panelled back and solid seat, on cabriole legs.

72.75in (182cm) wide

1,800-2,200   **SWO**

An early 18thC walnut double-chairback settee, the serpentine top rail above two crossbanded splats, with outscrolled arms and drop-in seat, on cabriole front legs with pad feet, later arms and restorations.

58in (145cm) wide

£1,000-1,500   **L&T**

An 18thC English oak bench, of mortise-and-tenon construction, with panelled back, on cabriole legs with pad feet, old refinishing, seat boards partially replaced.

73in (182.5cm) wide

£1,500-2,000   **BRU**

An 18thC Louis XVI painted and tapestry-upholstered settee, raised on top-fluted legs.

76.5in (191cm) wide

2,000-3,000   **FRE**

A George III mahogany and upholstered sofa, the arched back and sides with moulded framing, on moulded square tapering legs.

78.5in (196cm) wide

£5,000-7,000   **L&T**

A George III mahogany framed upholstered settee, with channelled top rail and arms, on square tapering legs and feet with brass caps and casters.

77.25in (193cm) wide

£2,000-2,500   **L&T**

A Regency rosewood framed sofa, with leaf-carved cresting, square upholstered arms and squab seat, on turned reeded feet with brass caps and casters.

85.25in (213cm) long

£1,500-2,000   **L&T**

A CLOSER LOOK AT A REGENCY WINDOW SEAT

This window seat was executed in the manner of William Trotter, the leading Scottish cabinet-maker of the period, who excelled in richly carved rosewood suites.

The quality and precision in craftsmanship in this piece is evident from the brass casters and mounts, which are exceptionally crisp and detailed.

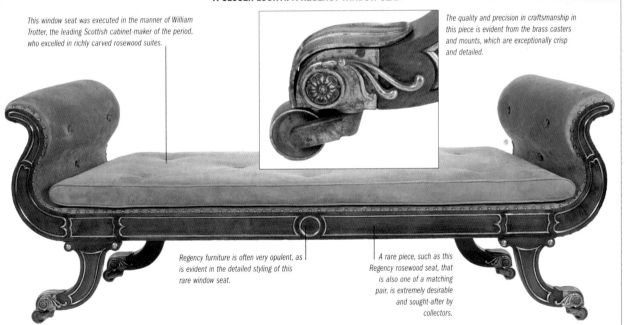

Regency furniture is often very opulent, as is evident in the detailed styling of this rare window seat.

A rare piece, such as this Regency rosewood seat, that is also one of a matching pair, is extremely desirable and sought-after by collectors.

One of a rare pair of Regency rosewood and brass-mounted window seats, in the manner of William Trotter, each with pronounced S-scroll arms, later upholstered in suede above a padded seat, on bold sabre legs and honeysuckle cast-brass cappings and casters.

68in (170cm) wide

60,000-80,000 pair   **CATO**

A Regency mahogany sofa, the framed scrolling back and outscrolled arms with reeded fronts, squab and bolsters, reeded seat rail, on splayed reeded legs with leaf cast-brass caps and casters.

90in (225cm) long

£1,500-2,000   **L&T**

A Regency ebonised and painted settee.

60.75in (152cm) wide

£2,500-3,000   **L&T**

A Regency mahogany and brass-inlaid settee, with a shaped back and scroll ends, raised on reeded legs.

77.25in (193cm) wid

£1,000-1,500   **SW**

A Regency mahogany chaise longue, with a scroll end and a reeded show frame.

£600-900   **SWO**

A William IV carved rosewood chaise longue, with a button upholstered back and end, on short cabriole legs, claw and ball feet and brass casters.

78.25in (195.5cm) wide

£3,500-4,000   **WW**

A 19thC George III-style mahogany and tapestry-upholstered settee, raised on gadrooned square legs with foliate-carved pierced angle brackets.

82in (205cm) wide

£2,000-2,500   **FRE**

A late 19thC George III-style mahogany triple back settee, with shell-carved scroll arms, raised on acanthus carved cabriole legs and paw feet.

65in (162.5cm) wid

£2,000-3,000   **FR**

A Victorian chaise longue, with a buttoned back, upholstered in green damask with fringe and piping, on ebonised turned legs with horn casters.

62.25in (158cm) wide

£700-1,000   **DN**

A late Victorian ebonised settee, with buttoned stuffover upholstery, the balustraded sides with ring-turned uprights, moulded front seat rail, on brass casters.

62.5in (156cm) wide

£600-900   **L&T**

A late Victorian painted satinwood settee, decorated with classical scenes and foliage.

139.25in (348cm) wid

£1,000-1,500   **L&**

A Victorian rosewood and tapestry-upholstered salon suite, comprising a serpentine-back settee and two armchairs, all raised on moulded cabriole legs, terminating in casters.

74.5in (186cm) wide

£2,000-3,000   **FRE**

An early 20thC Louis XV-style gilt-wood and painted salon suite, comprising a settee and two fauteuils, all raised o foliate-carved cabriole legs.

73in (182.5cm) wic

£1,000-2,000   **FR**

late Gustavian Swedish painted and upholstered settee, with turned uprights nd central X-form supports, above a Neo-classical frieze, three loose cushions nd upholstered cushion seat, on circular turned legs.

1805   75in (187.5cm) wide

8,000-12,000   EVE

A Danish Louis XVI elmwood daybed, the upholstered seat between outscrolled vertical slat armrests, raised on square tapered and fluted legs.

c1800   78in (195cm) wide

£4,000-6,000   EVE

STOOLS

walnut stool, of George I style, with val drop-in seat, moulded seat rail and our scrolled cabriole legs with pad feet.

23.25in (58cm) wide

400-600   L&T

A pair of 18thC-style carved giltwood X-frame stools, with tasselled striped loose cushion seats.

30in (75cm) wide

£1,000-1,500   FRE

George III mahogany piano stool.

A Regency rosewood stool, the later upholstered woolwork seat above four scrolling supports with acanthus-carved capitals.

19.25in (49cm) wide

A pair of mid-19thC rosewood stools, each with rectangular flamework squab above moulded curvilinear apron and legs with scroll toes.

22.5in (56cm) wide

150-200   SWO   £200-300   L&T   £1,000-1,500   L&T

A Regency style mahogany window seat, with sabre legs.

41.25in (103cm) wide

£400-600 SWO

A Victorian Gothic Revival pitch pine bench, the ends surmounted by crouching dragons, joined by a board seat with buttoned squab.

56in (140cm) wide

£2,000-3,000 L&T

A Victorian upholstered ottoman, with a hinged lid enclosing a lined interior, on a mahogany plinth and bun feet with casters.

41.5in (104cm) wid

£800-1,200 L&'

A massive Victorian serpentine ottoman, upholstered with burgundy felt and floral cross stitch panels, on a moulded maple plinth and lotus leaf-carved feet.

98in (245cm) wide

£1,800-2,200 L&T

A Victorian Rococo-style walnut framed stool, the square serpentine stuffover seat above a moulded seat rail and cabriole legs with scroll toes.

19.25in (48cm) wide

£500-700 L&T

A near pair of late Victorian Aesthetic oak and brass mounted hall benches, in the manner of James Schoolbred, each with brass balustrade back above scrolling arms, solid seat and slight cabriole legs united by stretchers, stamped registration marks.

£5,000-7,000 CAT

An English joined stool, with a saddle-shaped elm top, on splayed legs with stretchers, feet worn and chipped.

20in (50cm) wide

£200-300 BRU

A Swedish Biedermeier birch bench, with ebonised oak spheres.

c1840   *14.5in (37cm) wide*

£1,000-2,000 LANE

A Swedish Biedermeier birch bench, with a leopard skin seat, re-upholstered.

c1840   *24.5in (62cm) wide*

£500-700 LANE

A set of four Gothic-style oak hall benches, in the manner of Pugin, the moulded rectangular seats raised on twin supports united by chamfered stretchers.

c1840   *42.25in (105.5cm) wid*

£1,500-2,000 FR

A large 16thC oak stile chest, the four-panel hinged lid above a corresponding front, with strapwork carved panels.

71.5in (179cm) wide

£800-1,200   L&T

A 17thC oak stile chest, the three panel hinged lid above a corresponding front, with arcaded frieze and geometric incised panels.

56in (140cm) wide

£400-600   L&T

An early 18thC oak mule chest, the hinged top above chevron inlaid front with four arched foliate carved panels, above two carved short drawers, on ogee bracket feet, carved "WH 1716".

58.75in (147cm) wide

£1,500-2,000   L&T

A 17thC Italian walnut cassone, with a stepped panel hinged lid, above a dentil-carved frieze and panelled front, inlaid with satyrs, architectural and wooded landscapes, centred by a vacant cartouche, gadrooned apron, raised on carved paw feet.

72in (180cm) wide

£2,000-3,000   FRE

A late 18thC Dutch oak and ebony-strung mule chest, the hinged top with a moulded edge, the panelled front inlaid in fruitwood with fans and an urn, above two drawers, on square tapering channelled feet.

58.25in (148cm) wide

£600-900   DN

A Spanish 18thC walnut chest, the hinged lid above a chip-carved front decorated with central cross and rosettes.

35.25in (88cm) high

£800-1,200   L&T

An 18thC oak mule chest, the hinged lid above three shaped and fielded panels, within quarter turned columns, over two base drawers.

59in (150cm) wide

£400-600   SWO

A late 18thC to early 19thC large Spanish carved wood trunk with stand, of dome-topped form carved with a deep foliate pattern, with a Spanish crest to the lid and mirrored images and a Habsburg eagle to the interior, wrought iron hardware.

50in (125cm) wide

£2,000-3,000   SK

A mahogany mule chest, of George III style, the hinged rectangular top above a plain front, on earlier hairy claw and ball feet.

39.5in (99cm) wide

£700-1,000   L&T

An Eastern European pine marriage chest, with iron side handles, painted overall with urns of flowers in red and green on a gold ground within yellow borders.

25.5in (65cm) high

£300-500   DN

A 19thC oak kist, of plank construction, the hinged lid with a moulded edge above a front with crimped edges, the sides with cut-out feet.

35.25in (88cm) wide

£300-400   L&T

CHEST OF DRAWERS

A late 17thC oak chest of drawers, with an ogee moulded frieze, four long drawers with geometrical moulded panel fronts and applied mouldings, later cast brass handles and escutcheons.

45in (114cm) wide

£1,200-1,800   WW

A late 17th to early 18thC oak chest of drawers, with two short and three long graduated drawers with geometric panelling, on bun feet.

41.5in (104cm) wide

£700-1,000   L&T

An early 18thC oyster veneered walnut chest of drawers, with boxwood inlay and moulded edge, above two short and three long graduated drawers, on shaped bracket feet.

40.75in (102cm) wide

£2,500-3,000   L&T

An 18thC Italian chest of drawers, with four graduated dovetailed drawers and frame-and-panel sides and back, formerly a lift-top chest with faux drawer fronts, the drawers and front rebuilt.

41.5in (104cm) wide

£1,000-1,500   BRU

An inlaid English chest of drawers, probably late 18thC, with burlwood top and dovetailed drawers with banded inlay, openwork brass pulls and escutcheons, the secondary woods pine and oak, partially replaced bracket feet.

41in (102.5cm) wide

£800-1,200   BRU

A late 18thC walnut serpentine chest of drawers, the shaped top above three graduated drawers and a shaped apron, raised on splayed bracket feet.

42in (105cm) wide

£1,000-1,500   L&T

A late 18thC Indo-Portuguese rosewood serpentine chest of drawers, with two short and four long drawers, the brass handles stamped "W.I", the apron carved with scrolls and a flowerhead, on bracket feet.

45.75in (116cm) wide

£2,500-3,000   DN

A George III mahogany bowfront chest, with boxwood stringing, the crossbanded top above two short and three long graduated drawers, on shaped bracket feet.

32in (80cm) wide

£2,000-3,000   **L&T**

A George III mahogany bowfront chest of drawers, with ebony and boxwood stringing, bird's eye maple panel and two short over three long graduated drawers, shaped apron and bracket feet.

40.75in (102cm) wide

£1,000-1,500   **L&T**

A George III mahogany and crossbanded bowfronted chest of drawers, with two short and three long drawers and original handles, raised on splayed bracket feet.

42.25in (107cm) high

£800-1,200   **B**

A George III mahogany chest of drawers, of small proportions, with two short and three long drawers, raised on bracket feet.

31in (79cm) wide

£2,000-3,000   **B**

A George III mahogany bachelor's chest, the moulded top above a baize-lined brushing slide and four long graduated drawers, on bracket feet.

32in (80cm) wide

£2,500-3,000   **L&T**

A George III mahogany bowfront chest, the line-inlaid top above two short and three long drawers, with a shaped apron, on bracket feet.

42in (105cm) wide

£2,000-2,500   **L&T**

A George III mahogany serpentine chest, the moulded shaped top above four long graduated drawers, on bracket feet.

42.75in (107cm) wide

£4,000-6,000   **L&T**

A George III mahogany serpentine chest, with four long graduated drawers and a shaped apron, on splayed bracket feet.

46in (115cm) wide

£2,000-3,000   **L&T**

A George III mahogany serpentine chest, the moulded shaped top above a brushing slide and four long graduated drawers, on ogee bracket feet.

48.75in (122cm) wide

£5,000-7,000   **L&T**

A George III mahogany secretaire chest of drawers, the fall-front opening to reveal a fitted interior on bracket feet.

32in (80cm) wide

£800-1,200   **SWO**

A George III mahogany chest, with a moulded top over two short and three long drawers, flanked with canted corners, on ogee bracket feet.

36in (90cm) wide

£800-1,200   **SWO**

A Scottish early 19thC mahogany chest of drawers, with boxwood and ebony stringing, the three short and three long cockbeaded drawers flanked by bead and reel angles, on bracket feet.

49.5in (124cm) wide

£400-600 L&T

An early 19thC English mahogany chest, the dovetailed and cockbeaded drawers with original brass pulls, full dust panels and horizontal backboards with hand-wrought nails, on original bracket feet with stacked glue blocks.

44in (110cm) wide

£3,000-4,000 BRU

An early 19thC English mahogany chest, the moulded top over dovetailed drawers, on original bracket feet.

38in (95cm) wide

£1,000-1,500 BRU

An early 19thC overpainted pine Wellington secretaire chest, with six drawers and a secretaire drawer, opening to reveal an interior fitted with drawers and pigeonholes, enclosed by a hinged lockable faux pilaster, raised on a plinth.

30.25in (77cm) wide

£2,500-3,000 L&T

A fine Regency Egyptian Revival mahogany bowfront chest, possibly by Oakley.
c1815

£2,000-3,000 BAM

An early 19thC pitch pine chest of drawers, the rectangular top with a moulded edge, above two short and three long graduated drawers, raised on a plinth base.

48.75in (122cm) wide

£600-900 L&T

A 19thC teak campaign chest, with brass binding and sunken handles, two short and three long drawers, on turned feet, divided into two sections.

41.25in (103cm) high

£1,200-1,800 L&T

A 19thC oak chest of drawers, the rectangular top with a moulded edge, above four long graduated drawers with turned ebonised handles, on bracket feet.

32in (81cm) wide

£800-1,200 L&T

An unusual mid-19thC French Empire concave secretaire chest, the raised top with one drawer, compartment frieze drawer and two further ivory drawers, flanked by bobbin-turned pilasters, on conforming legs, formerly a dressing chest.

42in (105cm) wide

£2,000-3,000 FRE

FURNITURE

A Victorian Scottish mahogany chest, with boxwood stringing, with a frieze with a secret drawer, flanked by four short drawers, two long drawers below, all flanked by spiral turned columns with turned feet.

52in (132cm) wide

£600-900   **L&T**

A Victorian walnut Wellington chest with seven graduated drawers, raised on a plinth base.

£600-900   **SWO**

A late 19th or 20thC Italian pine chest, the three dovetailed drawers with side runners, vertically bowed front, drawers rebuilt, replaced brass pulls, old black-painted surface.

40in (100cm) wide

£1,500-2,000   **BRU**

An Edwardian painted satinwood bowfront chest of drawers, with Neo-classical decoration and oval vignettes, on splayed bracket feet.

36.5in (93cm) wide

£2,000-3,000   **L&T**

A mahogany chest of drawers, with three long graduated drawers and handles bearing Prince of Wales feathers, shaped apron with rosette, on bracket feet.

36.75in (92cm) wide

£200-300   **L&T**

CHEST-ON-CHESTS

A George III mahogany chest-on-chest, with three short over three long graduated drawers enclosed by canted and fluted angles, the base with three long graduated drawers, raised on bracket feet.

70.5in (176cm) high

£1,200-1,800   **L&T**

A George III mahogany chest-on-chest, with two short and three long graduated drawers flanked by fluted angles, the base with three long graduated drawers and shaped bracket feet.

73.5in (184cm) high

£2,500-3,000   **L&T**

A George III mahogany chest-on-chest, with graduated drawers flanked by inlaid canted angles, the base with three long graduated drawers raised on bracket feet.

48in (120cm) wide

£1,500-2,000   **L&T**

An English Regency two-part mahogany apothecary chest, with 22 drawers resting on a base with two drawers, above a scalloped skirt and straight bracket feet, stamped "W. Priest 17 & 24 Water St. Black Friars".

c1815   *69.75in (177cm) high*

£2,000-3,000   **POOK**

A Victorian burr-walnut tallboy, of George I style, with two short and three long graduated drawers with feather stringing, raised on a base with brushing slide and two further drawers, on shaped bracket feet.

75.25in (188cm) high

£1,000-2,000   **L&T**

An English mahogany chest-on-chest, with two over six dovetailed drawers, figured mahogany drawer fronts, dovetailed top and bottom cases, on bracket feet, replaced or reset brass pulls, possibly an old marriage.

69.5in (174cm) high

£1,500-2,000   **BRU**

A kingwood and marquetry inlaid semainiere, the veined rouge marble top above seven drawers, marquetry inlaid with figures, the whole raised on splayed legs with gilt-metal cast sabots.

26.75in (68cm) wide

£1,200-1,800   **L&T**

A late 17thC oak chest on later stand, with panelled drawers, marquetry inlaid with mother-of-pearl and stained wood, the stand with barley twist and blocked legs, linked by stretchers.

52in (130cm) high

£700-1,000   **L&T**

An 18thC oak tallboy, with graduated crossbanded drawers, on a base with a central drawer flanked by deeper small drawers, above shaped crossbanded apron and leaf-carved cabriole legs.

63.25in (158cm) high

£2,000-3,000   **L&T**

An early 19thC mahogany campaign dressing chest, the fitted interior above a brushing slide, with a writing slope and an arrangement of drawers, brass carrying handles, on removable turned legs.

£800-1,200   **SWO**

A French marble-top cabinet, with an openwork brass gallery, three drawers, a door opening onto two drawers, and a drop-front drawer concealing two further drawers, extensive geometric light and dark wood inlay.

c1900   54.5in (136cm) high

£1,000-2,000   **BRU**

A CLOSER LOOK AT AN INDO-PORTUGUESE CABINET-ON-STAND

The form and decoration of this cabinet is typical of a type of furniture made in India, probably Goa, under Portuguese patronage.

During the second half of the 17thC, large multiple drawers were very much in fashion in Europe .

High quality furniture of the period is also characterised by intarsia of various types, including seaweed marquetry named after the inlaid interlacing designs and dense arabesques.

The inlay pattern of stars and intersecting circles is recorded and is identical to a cabinet-on-stand in the collection of the Victoria and Albert Museum in London.

A rare late 17thC Indo-Portuguese cabinet-on-stand or contador, teak and rosewood inlaid with ebony and ivory.

49in (125cm) high

£35,000-40,000   **MJM**

A George III satinwood serpentine commode, with rosewood crossbanding and boxwood stringing, the shaped top with kingwood banding above four long drawers, on a plinth base.

46.5in (116cm) wide

£15,000-20,000 **L&T**

A George III mahogany serpentine commode, with three graduated cockbeaded drawers flanked by blind fret angles, on shaped bracket feet.

47.5in (119cm) wide

£3,000-5,000 **L&T**

A Scottish George III mahogany serpentine commode, with boxwood stringing and four graduated drawers, on shaped bracket feet.

44.75in (112cm) wide

£3,000-5,000 **L&T**

A George III mahogany and kingwood serpentine commode, inlaid with floral sprays and swags, with three long drawers, the top one still partially fitted, on gilt-brass cast mounts and sabots.

60in (150cm) high

£10,000-15,000 **L&T**

An Edwardian oak lacquered serpentine commode, in the mid-18thC style, with a marble top and two graduated drawers, painted in gilt and black with Chinoiserie scenes, gilt-metal mounts, on cabriole legs terminating in cast sabots.

37.5in (94cm) wide

£1,500-2,000 **L&T**

A pair of early 20thC George I-style walnut and parcel-gilt commodes, each with two cupboard doors enclosing shelves, the foliate-carved aprons centred by a shell motif, raised on cabriole legs with trefoil feet.

36in (90cm) wide

£5,000-7,000 **FRE**

A North Italian rosewood veneered and marquetry inlaid commode, with a frieze drawer decorated with birds and garlands of flowers above two further drawers, later brass handles, on square tapering supports, some losses to veneer, splits to sides.

c1800   *48.25in (122.5cm) wide*

£3,000-5,000 **WW**

A late 18thC French Provincial oak commode, with three long drawers and panelled sides, the whole raised on bracket feet.

48.5in (123cm) wide

£2,000-3,000 **L&T**

A French Louis XIV commode, in walnut, root wood, birch and other exotic woods, with inlaid ivory decoration of flowers and birds, three drawers and bronze mounts, on short cambered legs.

c1710   *52in (130cm) wide*

£40,000-60,000   **GK**

A French Louis XV commode, in veneered walnut, ash and plum wood, of bombé shape with marble top, banding and marquetry and pierced bronze decoration, original locks and keys, on splayed feet.

c1745   *49.2in (123 cm) wide*

£3,000-4,000   **KAU**

A mid-18thC Louis XV provincial walnut commode, with three long drawers, raised on squat cabriole legs.

                   50in (125cm) wide

£4,000-6,000   **FRE**

A mid-18thC Louis XV kingwood and crossbanded bombé commode, with gilt-bronze mounts, the marbled top over two short and two long drawers, raised on splated legs with sabots.

51in (127.5cm) wide

£7,000-10,000   **FRE**

A kingwood and marquetry inlaid commode, in the French mid-18thC style, the serpentine veined rouge marble top above three drawers, marquetry inlaid with figural panels, on tapering legs and cast sabots.

46in (117cm) wide

£2,000-3,000   **L&T**

A Transitional breakfront commode, in rosewood and satinwood with parquetry and marquetry and decorated with musical instruments, with gilded ormolu mounts and sabots, profiled 'Campan rubané' top, signed "Jean Girardau".

c1775   *54in (135cm) wide*

£25,000-35,000   **GK**

A small Transitional marquetry commode, in rosewood and satinwood and decorated with musical instruments, with a 'Brèche d'Alep' top, two drawers and ormolu mounts and sabots, signed "Louis-Noel Malle".

c1775   *31.25in (78cm) wide*

£25,000-35,000   **GK**

FURNITURE

A late 18thC Louis XV bombé kingwood and cross banded commode, with gilt-bronze mounts, the marble top over drawers, on square splayed legs and sabots.

51in (127.5cm) wide

£7,000-10,000   **FRE**

A good Louis XVI provincial mahogany commode, with drawers carved with drapery, ribbon-tied motifs and paterae, on square tapered legs.

c1780   55in (137.5cm) wide

£3,000-4,000   **FRE**

A Louis XVI kingwood and gilt-metal mounted commode, the later marble top above a frieze drawer with inlaid faux fluting and two quarter-veneered drawers, on turned tapering legs with cast gilt caps.

36.5in (93cm) wide

£1,800-2,200   **L&T**

A pair of French Transitional-style walnut and kingwood-banded commodes, with gilt-metal mounts, the marble tops over four long drawers, on bracket feet ending in sabots.

28in (70cm) wide

£2,000-3,000   **FRE**

A Louis XV kingwood marquetry bombé commode, with later gilt-metal mounts, the later marble top above two foliate-inlaid drawers, raised on square cabriole legs ending in sabots.

57.5in (144cm) wide

£1,000-2,000   **FRE**

A pair of mahogany Empire-style commodes, the drawers inlaid with sphinxes, foliage and reclining females, on squat square tapering legs.

28in (70cm) wide

£1,500-2,000   **FRE**

An early 19thC French walnut commode, with a marble top above three drawers flanked by a cupboard door, applied and inlaid brass stringing, on short square tapering legs.

£2,500-3,000   **SWO**

A Louis XV-style kingwood and cherrywood marquetry commode, with gilt-brass casts mounts, the rouge marble top above drawers, on splayed legs with sabots.

48.5in (121cm) wide

£3,000-5,000   **L&T**

A late 19thC Louis XV or Louis XVI gilt-bronze mounted commode, by Gouverneur, in mahogany, tulipwood and kingwood, the moulded marble top over two long drawers veneered with lattice parquetry panels and applied with cast gilt-bronze floral garlands, the hipped legs ending in massive paw feet, the apron applied with foliate scrolls and centred by Bacchic and angel masks, the lock plate signed "Gouverneur Fabricant, 68 Rue Street, Paris".

67in (167.5cm) wide

£50,000-60,000   **FRE**

Gilded ormolu mounts are typical of 18thC French decoration, particularly on the commode.

The surface has been decorated with veneered parquetry – inlays of small, coloured pieces of wood.

A French kingwood inlaid commode, by Noël Gerard of Paris, with five drawers and gilded ormolu mounts shaped as female busts, on scroll feet, restored.

c1720   *52in (130cm) high*

£65,000-85,000   **GK**

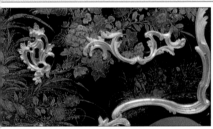

Luxurious Louis XV-style furniture often had decoration of Chinese-style figures in landscapes and an abundance of flowers.

This beautiful and detailed flower bouquet is of exceptional quality, making it highly desirable to collectors of French 18thC furniture.

A French Louis XV lacquered commode, with a 'Brèche d'Alep' top, two drawers decorated with flower bouquets and leaves, gilded ormolu mounts and sabots, signed "N. GREVENICH".

c1755   *38.5in (96.5cm) wide*

£100,000-200,000   **GK**

An early 18thC Baroque commode, from Dresden, Saxony, in veneered oak with three drawers and a shaped apron, with new locks and keys.

50in (125cm) wide

£1,500-2,000   **BMN**

An early 18thC Southern German Baroque commode, in veneered walnut and cherrywood, with fine banding throughout and original locks and fittings, on four bun feet.

48.75in (122cm) wide

£3,000-4,000   **KAU**

A German Baroque commode, in veneered walnut, with two drawers, carved apron, marquetry and bronze mounts, carved apron, with original locks, on two high cambered legs, restored.

c1750   *50.75in (127cm) wide*

£5,000-7,000   **BMN**

A CLOSER LOOK AT A BAROQUE COMMODE

The French term 'commode' was adopted in the 18thC, when French furniture became fashionable. The term is used to describe low, highly decorative chests of drawers with serpentine fronts.

This cabinet is symmetrical and has heavy ornamentation, which is typical of the Baroque style.

This piece is a product of Europe's fascination with oriental art and culture, which reached its heyday in the 18thC. Oriental motifs and forms were adapted to Western tastes. Japanese style furniture with a black lacquered ground and raised gilded decoration, consisting of oriental landscapes and pagodas, was particularly sought-after in the 18thC.

Antique chinoiserie furniture was manufactured from the early 18thC across Europe. Despite this, a quality piece in good condition, like this commode, is rare and therefore commands a premium.

An 18thC Baroque serpentine commode, in Japanese style, from Berlin or Dresden, with a gilded and idealised Pagoda and park landscape, four drawers and bronze mounts, raised on flattened ball feet.

36in (90cm) wide

£7,000-10,000   **GK**

A German Neo-classical walnut and crossbanded commode, inlaid with chequer banding, the moulded top over three long drawers, raised on bracket feet, reduced in height.

c1785   *51.5in (129cm) wide*

£2,000-2,500   **FRE**

A late 18thC German baroque commode, in veneered mahogany and birch, the two drawers with band inlays, original locks and gold-plated fittings, on four cabriole legs.

30.8in (77cm) high

£700-1,000   **KAU**

A late Baroque German oak commode, with seven drawers decorated with plaits and garlands and with fluted edges, a plaited garland on each side wall, original locks and fittings, on four compressed cylindrical feet.

c1780   *52in (130cm) wide*

£2,000-3,000   **KAU**

An 18th/19thC German Berlin or Bayreuth commode, veneered jacaranda, rosewood and fruitwood, on two bracket and two pointed feet, high rectangular six-drawer structure with projecting top-drawer, top-plate with ogee profile, rich inlays in the form of foliage, birds, vases and flowers.

28.8in (72cm) high

£800-1,200   **KAU**

A late 18thC and later German Baroque burl walnut crossbanded commode, the serpentine top above a conforming case, fitted with three drawers, on later compressed bun feet.

47in (117.5cm) wide

£1,500-2,000   **FRE**

An early 19thC Austrian or German satinwood commode, with parquetry decoration, three drawers within canted corners and ebonised columns.

50in (125cm) wide

£1,000-1,500   **SWO**

A rare Russian commode, in veneered mahogany and ormolu, bellied, three-drawer body with projecting top plate and rich bronze decoration, original locks, keys and ormolu fittings, on two stile feet and two bronze paw feet.

c1825   *28in (70cm) high*

£1,000-1,500   **KAU**

FURNITURE

A 19thC Biedermeier walnut and feather-banded commode, with three long drawers, raised on square feet.

49.5in (124cm) wide

£1,500-2,000   **FRE**

A Dutch 18thC mahogany and marquetry bombé chest of drawers, profusely inlaid with floral marquetry, the top with moulded edge and arc-en-abalette front, over four drawers flanked by corresponding canted angles, on bracket feet.

36in (90cm) wide

£2,000-2,500   **L&T**

A late 18thC to early 19thC Dutch walnut and floral marquetry bombé chest, with four long graduated drawers, on lion's paw feet.

36.75in (92cm) wide

£2,800-3,200   **SWO**

A late 18thC Danish Louis XVI mahogany commode, with fluted frieze drawer and roundel corners, above three lower drawers flaked by fluted quarter pilasters, raised on bracket feet.

31in (77.5cm) high

£5,000-7,000   **EVE**

A Danish Louis XVI mahogany commode, with three drawers flanked by fluted quarter pilasters, raised on bracket feet.

c1790   *28.5in (71cm) high*

£5,000-7,000   **EVE**

A Danish Empire mahogany and fruitwood inlaid commode, with a bow-front, frieze drawer with an inlaid fan and three long drawers, raised on short circular turned and tapered feet.

c1815   *31.25in (78cm) high*

£7,000-10,000   **EVE**

A Swedish late Gustavian painted commode, the top with canted forecorners above three long drawers flanked by fluted and canted sides, raised on conforming fluted legs.

c1820   *45in (112.5cm) wide*

£3,000-4,000   **EVE**

A Dutch 19thC mahogany serpentine bombé commode, with three drawers and Neo-classical brass handles, mounts and sabots, on splayed feet, possibly the base of a linen press.

£400-600   **L&T**

Two similar 19thC Dutch mahogany and marquetry inlaid bombé commodes, in the mid-18thC style, the serpentine top above two shaped drawers, on square tapering cabriole legs.

Provenance: Membury Court, Axminster.

28.5in (71cm) wide

£3,000-5,000   **L&T**

n 18thC Italian and walnut crossbanded commode, ith two short and three long drawers raised on racket feet.

58in (145cm) wide

5,000-7,000 **FRE**

A late 18thC Italian walnut commode, crossbanded and boxwood strung, the three drawers with floral marquetry and a marquetry architectural oval, gilt metal lion mask handles and escutcheons, on square tapering legs.

46.25in (117.5cm) wide

£4,000-5,000 **DN**

An 18thC-style Italian green-painted and parcel gilt bombé commode, the serpentine moulded marble top above two drawers, raised on cabriole legs united by a shaped apron.

58in (145cm) wide

£3,000-4,000 **FRE**

n Italian Neo-classical walnut and marquetry commode, the later marble above ree long drawers inlaid with flaring urns, foliate swags and a central circular anel inlaid with two draped maidens and a cupid, raised on square tapered legs.

1800 *53in (132.5cm) wide*

3,000-4,000 **FRE**

An early 19thC Italian olive wood and tulipwood crossbanded bedside commode, lift up lid above fall front and fitted interior, square tapering legs.

31in (79cm) high

£2,500-3,000 **CATO**

A 19thC Italian bombé kingwood parquetry commode, the moulded marble top above two chequer veneered drawers centred by flower-head motifs, raised on square cabriole legs ending in sabots.

47in (117.5cm) wide

£2,500-3,000 **FRE**

LINEN PRESSES

William and Mary ulberry wood and ossbanded linen ress, in the manner Coxed and Woster, th a pair of arched anel doors nclosing a part later terior, the lower ction with two ort and two long awers, raised on un feet.

A George II mahogany linen press, the dentilled cornice and cavetto frieze above a pair of doors with shaped fielded panels enclosing sliding trays, the base with two short and two long graduated drawers, on cut shaped bracket feet.

The exposed timber hinges are characteristic of the work of Francis & William Brodie, cabinet makers in Edinburgh.

65.25in (163cm) high

1690

15,000-20,000 **FRE** **£2,000-3,000** **L&T**

FURNITURE

An 18thC oak press, later carved in low relief, with two panelled cupboard doors flanking a central panel, enclosing a pegged interior, the lower section with three drawers, on bracket feet.

58.5in (146cm) wide

£1,000-1,500   L&T

A George III mahogany linen press, the dentilled swan neck pediment above a pair of panelled doors and three long drawers, the upper two now false concealing a well, on ogee bracket feet.

88in (220cm) high

£1,800-2,200   L&T

A George III mahogany and line-inlaid linen press, with panel cupboard doors enclosing four oak slide-out trays, the projecting base fitted with two short and one long drawer, on shaped bracket feet.

48.5in (123cm) wide

£800-1,200   B

A George III mahogany linen press, the swan neck pediment above two panelled cupboard doors, enclosing sliding trays, the lower section with graduated drawers, on splayed bracket feet.

51.25in (128cm) wid

£3,000-4,000   L8

A George III mahogany breakfront wardrobe, the moulded cornice above two oval and square panelled cupboard doors, flanked on each side by a further panelled cupboard door enclosing shelves, on plinth base.

Provenance: Purchased Mallet & Son, 40 New Bond Street, London, June 1929.

96in (240cm) wide

£6,000-9,000   L&T

A George III mahogany linen press, with two line-inlaid, panelled cupboard doors, over graduated drawers, on splayed bracket feet.

52in (130cm) wide

£1,800-2,200   L&T

A George III mahogany linen press, wit two panelled doors opening to reveal a hanging rail, over two false drawers an a long drawer, on bracket feet.

74.75in (187cm) hig

£1,000-2,000   SW

An 18thC George III mahogany linen press, converted to an armoire, the Greek key cut cornice over two panelled doors enclosing hanging space, the lower section with four dummy drawers, raised on shaped bracket feet.

£1,000-1,500   FRE

A George III mahogany and crossbanded linen press, the ogee moulded cornice above two fielded panel doors enclosing sliding trays, the lower section with drawers flanked by spiral-turned split pilasters, raised on later turned legs, stamped "W. Williamson & Sons, Guildford".

55in (137.5cm) wide

£3,000-5,000   FRE

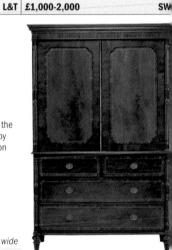

n 18thC George III chest-on-chest and later matching end cabinets, the Victorian
nds with moulded cornices over panelled doors, opening to reveal hanging
pace, the chest with a moulded cornice over two short and three long drawers,
ised on shaped bracket feet.

46.5in (116cm) wide

3,000-5,000   **FRE**

A 19thC mahogany linen press, the
moulded cornice with ebonised bands
above a pair of panelled doors
enclosing hanging, the base with
graduated drawers, on ebonised reeded
plinth and carved paw feet.

82.5in (206cm) high

£1,500-2,000   **L&T**

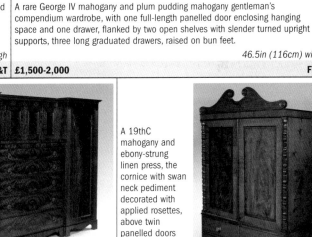

A rare George IV mahogany and plum pudding mahogany gentleman's
compendium wardrobe, with one full-length panelled door enclosing hanging
space and one drawer, flanked by two open shelves with slender turned upright
supports, three long graduated drawers, raised on bun feet.

46.5in (116cm) wide

£1,500-2,000   **FRE**

19thC mahogany gentleman's breakfront wardrobe,
e stepped cornice above seven graduated drawers
anked by panelled cupboards enclosing shelves and
anging space, on plinth base.

90in (225cm) wide

4,000-6,000   **L&T**

A 19thC gentleman's compactum, with a pair of full-
length panelled doors enclosing hanging space, flanking
a chest of five long graduated drawers, with small
recessed cupboard above, shaped apron and bracket
feet.

£800-1,200   **L&T**

A 19thC
mahogany and
ebony-strung
linen press, the
cornice with swan
neck pediment
decorated with
applied rosettes,
above twin
panelled doors
enclosing hanging
space, above
drawers.

48in (122cm) wide

£400-600   **L&T**

FURNITURE

An early Victorian rosewood wardrobe, by John Kendell & Co, with seven long graduated drawers and bowed hanging cupboards with panelled side doors, paper label "J Kendell & Co, No. 96388", workman's signature.

£2,500-3,000   SWO

A Victorian mahogany breakfront linen press, with an architectural cornice, two panelled doors enclosing slides and tw short and three long drawers, within full length double panel doors, on a plinth base.

96in (240cm) wide

£1,800-2,200   SW

An Edwardian mahogany bowfront liner press, with chequer and boxwood stringing, the panelled doors enclosing sliding trays, on a base with brushing slide and three long graduated drawers on splayed bracket feet.

80.75in (202cm) hig

£2,000-2,500   L&

A 19thC mahogany and crossbanded breakfront wardrobe, the moulded cornice with boxwood stringing, the central section with two panelled doors above two short and two long graduated drawers, the hanging sections to either side with twin panel doors, on shaped bracket feet.

81.25in (203cm) wide

£1,800-2,200   L&T

A mid-18thC Louis XV provincial oak armoire à deux corps, with a kingwood and chequer banded frieze and shaped fielded panelled doors, the lower section with three central drawers, flanked by two further cupboard doors, on squat cabriole legs.

92in (230cm) high

£5,000-7,000   FRE

A fine Louis XV provincial oak and kingwood banded armoire, with two panel doors centred by star motifs, opening to reveal hanging space, two apron drawers, moulded cabriole legs.

c1780   88.5in (221cm) hig

£3,000-4,000   FR

A CLOSER LOOK AT A DUTCH BOMBÉ BURL WALNUT LINEN PRESS

In the second half of the 17thC there was a demand for domestic furniture, like the linen press. Used to store linen and candles, they are traditionally in walnut or oak and were sometimes commissioned to celebrate a marriage.

The influence of the Rococo movement is evident in the curvaceous and organic form. The Rococo linen press is distinguished by a waved cornice, above serpentine, moulded panel doors and deep shaped aprons.

The division of the form into two parts, with a high waist, was the most important evolution from the 17thC linen press. The doors of the upper section were reduced considerably in size to allow for the introduction of a series of long drawers in the base. This arrangement provided a far more effective means of storage.

Look out for alterations. Linen presses have often been converted to make room for a hanging space by removing shelves or by cutting through a top drawer. An unaltered example will command a higher price.

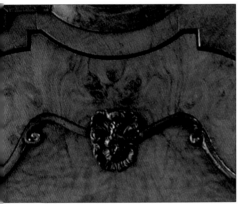

Dutch bombé burl walnut linen press, the shaped top centred by a shell and scroll carved surmount, below are two shaped panel doors enclosing shelves and five drawers, the lower section with two short and two long drawers, raised on scroll feet.

1760

68in (136cm) wide

7,000-10,000   **FRE**

A German oak and marquetry armoire, the moulded cornice above a parquetry frieze and sides, the panelled doors and sides inlaid with birds, cartouches and leaves.

Once owned by Stopford Brooke, who was Chaplain to the Kaiser in the mid-19thC and friend of William Morris.

116in (294cm) wide

2,500-3,000   **DN**

A French 19thC mahogany dwarf wardrobe, the pagoda top and moulded cornice above a frieze drawer, false fronted door and drawers enclosing hanging space, on moulded plinth and bun feet.

71.25in (178cm) high

£500-800   **L&T**

A Central European painted pine folk art marriage cupboard, initialled "A.F.R" and dated "Anno 1780".

Dated 18thC Folk Art furniture of this quality and condition is extraordinarily rare. This example, with fine painted panels depicting the Ages of Man through the symbolic representation of the four seasons, was probably made to commission as a wedding gift for a prominent family.

1780	75.75in (189cm) high
£20,000-25,000	R

A European painted marriage cupboard, in moulded pine, re-dated "1856".

It was a tradition in rural alpine communities for families to commission cupboards of this type as wedding gifts. Examples, such as this, were sometimes re-dated to serve as wedding gifts for a subsequent generation.

c1830	77.5in (194cm) high
£3,000-5,000	RY

An Italian 18thC Bombé painted commode, with three long drawers, decorated with the 'Arte Povera' technique including relief collages.

	32.75in (82cm) high
£5,000-7,000	

A French Directoire semainier, in cherrywood with an oak carcass and a marble top, original painted decoration.

c1810	59.5in (149cm) high
£5,000-7,000	R

Charles II oak press cupboard or Duodarn, the moulded cornice over a foliate-carved frieze dated "1673", the triple panel front carved with fleur-de-lys and scrolls, the two cupboard doors enclosing a void interior, three further cupboard doors, raised on style feet.

74in (185cm) wide

3,000-4,000 **FRE**

A small mid-18thC French Provincial walnut armoire, the later cornice over a panelled frieze centred by a flowerhead motif, below are two grill and fielded panel doors, opening to reveal later shelves, on a later shaped plinth base.

78in (195cm) high

£1,500-2,000 **FRE**

A Swedish Gustavian painted step-back cabinet, with leaf-tip carved cornice moulding, two fluted panel cupboard doors and a niche, the lower section with two conforming panel doors, on square fluted and tapered feet.

c1800 *101in (252.5cm) high*

£7,000-10,000 **EVE**

A George III oak press cupboard, the dentil moulded cornice over a pair of panelled doors, with two short dummy drawers over two short and one long drawer, on bracket feet.

52.75in (132cm) wide

£1,000-2,000 **SWO**

19thC English three-piece mahogany corner cupboard, the moulded cornice above two frame and panel doors, the interior with a faux marble grain-painted ace and three dovetailed drawers, the base with two doors, inlaid teardrop scutcheons and vertical pine backboards with rosehead nails, on bracket feet.

89in (222.5cm) high

3,000-4,000 **BRU**

An early 19thC Italian walnut bow-front cupboard, in two pieces, the figured walnut top with openwork lattice doors and four interior shelves, the base with a demilune top with conforming doors, on tapered and panelled legs.

88.5in (221cm) high

£2,000-3,000 **BRU**

211

An 18thC Welsh oak dresser, the plate rack with a lined back, the base with three large and three small drawers flanking an ogee arched apron, on ring turned front supports and a panelled pot board, on turned feet.

A 17thC oak dresser base with an associated plate rack, containing three short drawers above an undulating apron, on square legs.

71in (178cm) high

83.25in (208cm) high

An 18thC oak dresser, the drawers with inlaid herringbone banding, above an open pot board, later back.

92in (230cm) hig

£2,000-3,000   **SWO** | £2,500-3,500   **L&T** | £1,500-2,000   **SW**

A George III oak dresser base, the hinged top above three dummy drawers and a central fielded panel cupboard door, flanked by six crossbanded drawer, on moulded plinth with ogee bracket feet.

A George III mahogany dresser base, with seven crossbanded drawers, around a central cupboard with two arched panelled doors, flanked by fluted quarter columns, on a plinth with ogee bracket feet.

A George III oak dresser base, with three frieze drawers over a pot board, on square legs.

78.75in (200cm) wide

77.25in (196cm) wide

74.5in (186cm) wid

£1,500-2,000   **L&T** | £1,500-2,000   **L&T** | £1,000-2,000   **SW**

An Irish Regency mahogany dresser, the surmount with a scrolling pediment and lion mask panel, above a frieze and three graduated and reeded shelves, on cast brass paw feet, the base with three reeded half columns enclosing two drawers and two panelled doors, raised on carved paw front feet.

A 19thC oak dresse base, the plank top with a chamfered edge, above four drawers and a shaped apron, on square legs.

93.5in (234cm) high

67.25in (168cm) wid

£3,000-4,000   **L&T** | £1,500-2,000   **L&**

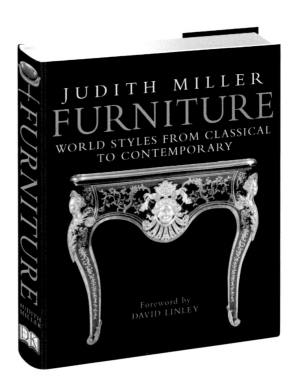

FURNITURE

A Queen Anne giltwood and gesso pier glass, with two bevelled mirror plates in an arched shell and harebell moulded frame.

75.25in (188cm) high

£4,000-6,000   **L&T**

An English Trumeau mirror, probably early 18thC, painting with village scene, losses to paint and silvering.

50in (125cm) high

£1,500-2,000   **BRU**

A Queen Anne mahogany looking glass, the scalloped crest with a gilt shell, ove a rectangular mirror plate with a gilt liner.

c1755   *42.5in (106cm) hig*

£1,500-2,000   **POO**

A late 18thC Danish Louis XVI giltwood mirror frame, with a beaded inner edge and a leaf carved outer edge, surmounted by a carved ribbon crest.

29in (72.5cm) high

£3,000-4,000   **EVE**

A late 18thC Russian Neo-classical brass-inlaid mahogany mirror, the flat frame with a Greek key brass inlay, and a flat frieze with a brass arch inlay, the corners with gilt metal mounts.

43.5in (109cm) high

£5,000-7,000   **EVE**

A large Regency-style convex wall mirror, the circular plate within reeded ebonised slip and gilt, the ebonised frame with ball spacers.

47.5in (119cm) diam

£1,000-1,500   **L&T**

A Regency giltwood mirror, the moulded cornice with ball spacers, the original plate flanked by latticework columns with shell cresting.

43.5in (109cm) hig

£1,500-2,000   **L&**

£7,000-10,000   **BRU**

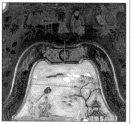

A pair of late 18th to early 19thC English mirrors, in the Chinese style, the top panels with raised and painted decoration of figures in a landscape, on red ground.

56in (140cm) high

A 19thC Continental looking glass, the carved wood and gesso frame with an openwork wreath pediment and leaf and berry decoration, mahogany backboard.

32in (80cm) high

£300-400   **BRU**

A Regency giltwood and gesso convex mirror, with an eagle surmount and sea serpent flanks, the leaf-carved frame with ball spacers, issuing twin wire branch sconces with crystal nozzles.

40in (100cm) wid

£2,800-3,200   **L&**

Regency giltwood and gesso convex all mirror, the circular mirror plate in eded ebonised slip and a ball oulded frame, surmounted by an gle and foliate scrolls, still leaf rving to the base.

49.5in (124cm) high

3,000-5,000   **L&T**

massive Philadelphia carved and ded mirror, with a flower and ears of rn frame, ending in winged griffins.

845   *141in (352.5cm) high*

20,000-30,000   **POOK**

A Regency carved giltwood convex wall mirror, the circular mirrored plate with a reeded ebonised slip and ball moulded frame, surmounted by a dragon, flanked by two sea serpents, above a leaf carved apron.

c1815   *46in (115cm) high*

£4,000-6,000   **FRE**

A German Biedermeier wall mirror, in cherry wood veneer, the ebonised columns with gilded bases and capitals, supporting a cornice and pediment, the central brass mount depicting the goddess Diana.

c1825   *68in (170cm) high*

£800-1,200   **BMN**

A 19thC Italian giltwood wall mirror, in carved pine and white gesso, with a red paint undercoat and gilt surface.

26.75in (67cm) high

£2,000-2,500   **CATO**

19thC giltwood convex mirror, the rcular plate within ebonised reeded p and rope-twist frame, eagle rmount and floral pendent, two spiral re sconces with cut glass drip trays.

31.5cm (79cm) high

1,200-1,800   **L&T**

A 19thC giltwood and gesso convex mirror, of Adam style, with a moulded frame surmounted by a gadrooned urn, the lower section with a green jasperware Wedgwood-style plaque.

30in (75cm) high

£600-900   **L&T**

A 19thC Italian Neo-classical-style giltwood and gesso pier mirror, decorated in relief with a classical scene, the bevelled plate within a scale moulded frame.

74in (185cm) high

£2,000-3,000   **FRE**

A Victorian carved giltwood and gesso overmantel mirror, the frame with curved canted angles, Neo-classical husk and guilloche and grotesque decoration, inset velvet border.

54.5in (138cm) high

£1,500-2,000   **L&T**

A late 19th or early 20thC Empire-style buffet mirror, in three panels, with half columns and corner bosses, traces of original gilding, losses and chips, replaced mirrors.

64in (160cm) wide

£300-400 **BRU**

One of a pair of Indian carved hardwood hall mirrors, each decorated with a bird crest, the frames with foliate scrolls and flowers, now painted white.

60.25in (153cm) high

£400-600 pair **DN**

A CLOSER LOOK A 19THC MICROMOSAIC MIRROR

The link between this piece and a prominent glassmaker like Salviati, who helped to revitalise the Venetian glass industry in the 19thC, adds considerable value to this mirror.

The exquisite quality and precision of decoration, seen in the micromosaic, is extremely desirable to collectors.

The depiction of popular Venetian sites, such as one of the columns of San Marco and the first floor arcading of the Palazzo Ducale, would be attractive to any Venetian or Murano glass enthusiast.

Replacing glass should be avoided, as this will reduce value. If the glass is cloudy it may be possible to have it re-silvered. A mirror with original glass and little sign of repair commands a premium.

A late 19thC Italian walnut framed micromosaic mirror, possibly by Salviati of Venice, with rectangular bevelled plate, the lugged frame decorated with scenes of Venice and relief moulded foliate sprays.

70in (175cm) hig

£12,000-14,000 **L&**

A faux bamboo overmantle mirror, of rectangular form with curved brackets to the base.

£600-900 **L&T**

A William and Mary-style oyster veneered mirror, the rectangular plate in bolection moulded frame.

31.25in (78cm) high

£400-600 **L&T**

An American or English giltwood mirror, with a spread-winged eagle crest atop a moulded cornice with spherules.

c1810 *52in (132cm) high*

£4,000-6,000 **POOK**

An American or English giltwood conve: mirror, with a spread-winged eagle pediment and two girondole arms.

c1800 *40in (100cm) hig*

£7,000-10,000 **POO**

A pair of walnut and marquetry mirrors, the bevelled plates with foliate and scroll inlaid frames.

29.5in (74cm) wide

£500-700   FRE

A pair of Continental gilt bronze wall mirrors, surmounted by an oval medallion with ribbon-tied drapery and flanked by two cherubs, the bevelled plates within pierced frames.

34in (85cm) high

£1,500-2,000   FRE

An oval oak gilt-framed mirror, mounted with gilt composition figures, the pediment with an angel and oval coat of arms.

58in (145cm) wide

£2,500-3,000   BRU

A Regency mahogany cheval mirror, with a moulded swing frame, ring turned supports and hipped reeded scroll legs with cast brass sabots and casters, later rectangular bevelled plate.

25.75in (65.5cm) wide

£1,000-1,500   WW

A Regency mahogany cheval mirror, with reeded uprights and Greek key decorated top, the sides with brass candle holders, on reeded sabre legs ending in brass caps and casters.

32in (80cm) wide

£3,000-4,000   L&T

A 19thC French rosewood cheval mirror, with a rectangular glass on turned columns and downswept legs united by a turned stretcher.

£3,000-5,000   SWO

A mahogany rectangular cheval mirror, the crossgrained frame flanked by moulded supports with brass sphere finials, on downswept square section legs with brass terminals and casters.

61.5in (154cm) high

£800-1,200   DN

A Regency faux bamboo dressing mirror, painted in black and grey on a green ground, the rectangular plate supported by turned and blocked uprights, on corresponding trestle base with bun feet.

24.5in (61cm) high

£400-600   L&T

An early 19thC mahogany and boxwood strung mirror, the oval plate on stepped supports, the bowfronted base with three drawers, on ogee bracket feet.

22.5in (56cm) high

£300-400   DN

A Victorian walnut and gilt-metal mounted toilet mirror, with serpentine uprights, on a crossbanded serpentine base inlaid with strapwork marquetry, serpentine apron and cast scrolling feet.

28in (71cm) wide

£1,500-2,000   L&T

An Edwardian Chippendale-style giltwood dressing mirror, within a moulded frame supported by fluted and turned leaf-carved uprights with acorn finials, on cabriole legs with scroll toes.

36.75in (92cm) wide

£200-300   L&T

FURNITURE

One of a pair of Regency framed chinoiserie canvas panels, each depicting an Oriental gentleman in garden setting on black ground, within gilt scrolled border.

78.5in (196cm) high

£3,000-5,000 pair L&T

A pair of late Regency rosewood pole screens, each with gilt brass pole supporting screen with gros point floral tapestry, on triform base and scrolling feet.

14.5in (36cm) wide

£2,500-3,000 CATO

A Regency rosewood pole screen, with floral needlepoint, turned and shaped standard above a footed base, the veneer with chips.

51.5in (129cm) high

£200-300 BRU

A William IV rosewood pole screen, the banner inset with a woolwork panel, on a turned and lappet carved column, with a concave base on paw feet.

59.5in (149cm) high

£400-600 DN

A 19thC four-fold Chinoiserie screen, decorated with panels of domestic scenes and vases of flowers, a border of birds and scrolling vine, the reverse with monochrome decoration.

72in (183cm) high

£400-600 L&T

A 19thC Louis XVI-style painted and giltwood four-fold screen, depicting figures in a church.

28in (70cm) wide

£4,000-6,000 FRE

A 19thC Dutch marquetry walnut fire screen, the shaped top inlaid with figures, exotic birds, insects and scrolling foliage, above a pleated fabric panel, raised on downswept legs.

49.5in (124cm) high

£1,500-2,000 FRE

A late 19thC carved mahogany three-fold screen, each section inset with a bevelled glass shaped panel with a blue silk lined panel below.

61.25in (153cm) high

£500-700 SWO

A pair of early 20thC Edwardian painted fire screens, the cartouche shaped panels painted with draped classical maidens and cherubs, raised on tripod bases.

61.5in (154cm) high

£1,500-2,000 FRE

A four-fold leather screen, with gilt tooling and brass nailing.

79.5in (199cm) high

£600-900 L&T

A four-fold Spanish polychrome gilt leather screen, each fold with a serpentine top, gilt nailing.

82.5in (206cm) high

£2,000-2,500 L&T

A George III mahogany silver table, the rectangular top with a dished edge and cusped corners, raised on cabriole legs with ball and claw feet.

37.35in (93cm) wide

£2,000-3,000   **L&T**

A Regency rosewood centre table, the circular top with plain frieze raised on bulbous octagonal column and concave triform base with paw feet and brass casters.

51.25in (128cm) diam

£1,800-2,200   **L&T**

A CLOSER LOOK AT A REGENCY CENTRE TABLE

This table has a tilt-top, an ingenious device that allowed circular tables to double up as a firescreen or to be stored neatly and compactly.

A true centre table is one without a specific purpose; designed purely to furnish the space in the middle of a room and to be the centre of attention. Therefore the centre table's function is largely ornamental.

Round and oval tables tend to be more popular than rectangular tables – as a result many table tops have been reshaped. Look out for poor reshaping, a lack of signs of real wear to the outside edges, or a top that is too small for its base. An original and unaltered centre table, like this piece, is worth considerably more.

The luxurious brass inlay and brass foliate banding typifies the rich ornamentation of the Regency style. This can also be seen on the reeded stem and the fine rams head cappings and casters.

A Regency rosewood and brass inlaid centre table, the circular tilt-top with brass foliate banding, reeded stem and four bold s-scroll supports with fine rams head cappings and casters.

48.5in (123cm) diam

£15,000-20,000   **CATO**

A Regency mahogany centre table, with a bead and reel frieze, on square section tapering column with bead and reel collar, raised on quadruped base with corresponding mouldings, on spherical feet.

51.5in (129cm) diam

£1,500-2,000   **L&T**

A 19thC mahogany Chippendale-style centre table, the rectangular veined green marble top with moulded edge, scrolling pierced corner brackets and blind fret frieze, on chamfered legs with Chinese blind fret.

48.5in (121cm) wide

£3,200-3,800   **L&T**

An early Victorian yewwood octagonal table, probably Irish, the top with radiating veneers, crossbanding and stringing, with four drawers to the frieze, on a turned column and triform base, with turned feet and recessed casters.

28.25in (72cm) wide

£800-1,200   **DN**

A Victorian rosewood loo table, the circular tilt-top with shallow frieze, raised on a bulbous octagonal baluster with a leaf-carved saucer and circular plinth, on three carved paw feet with casters.

51.5in (129cm) diam

£700-1,000   **L&T**

A mid-Victorian rosewood centre table, the shaped oval top with moulded edge above a central column with a turned pendant drop, the whole raised on leaf-carved scrolling supports.

59in (150cm) wide

£1,500-2,000   **L&T**

A Victorian mahogany drum table, with inset leatherette writing surface above alternating cockbeaded and dummy drawers, raised on four baluster turned legs with brass caps and casters.

53in (135cm) diam

£700-1,000   **L&T**

A late 19thC Victorian Aesthetic ebonised and marquetry centre table, attributed to Herter Brothers, New York, inlaid with foliage and a musical trophy, on four turned legs.

£2,000-3,000   **FRE**

An early 20thC mahogany centre table, in the manner of Robert Lorimer, the oval top raised on scrolling trestle supports joined by a central cross-frame.

58in (145cm) wide

£1,200-1,800   **L&T**

A Victorian Grecian Revival marquetry and ebonised centre table, attributed to Herter Brothers, New York, inlaid with a marquetry musical trophy panel and decorated with gilt incised graffito work, raised on elaborate carved trestle supports joined by a turned stretcher, on bun feet with recessed casters.

c1880

£5,000-7,000   **FRE**

A Blackamoor and simulated marble table, the geometric top inlaid with flowerhead motifs within a Greek key border, raised on twin figural carved end supports.

72in (180cm) wide

£3,000-4,000   **FRE**

An early 19thC Austrian Neo-classical thuya wood and kingswood veneer centre table, the circular top above a waisted support, raised on giltwood paw feet.

51in (127.5cm) diam

£7,000-10,000   **FRE**

A pair of Louis XV-style mahogany and gilt-bronze mounted centre tables, the white marble inset tops above a shaped frieze with lions' mask motifs, raised on square cabriole legs ending in sabots.

23in (57.5cm) wide

£1,000-1,500   **FRE**

A Louis XV-style malachite and bronze centre table, the circular top supported by a figural column modelled as the Three Graces, ending in three claw feet and a triform base.

35in (87.5cm) high

£8,000-12,000   **FRE**

A Louis XV-style marble and gilt-bronze Sèvres-style porcelain table, the top inset with transfer-printed porcelain panels depicting lovers, centred by a panel of Louis XV, the turned marble column and triform base applied with gilt-bronze mounts.

45in (112.5cm) diam

£6,000-9,000   **FRE**

A French Empire-style mahogany and specimen marble centre table, raised on a bulbous turned column support ending in five outswept legs with lowerhead motifs.

36in (90cm) diam

£3,000-4,000   **FRE**

A Charles X mahogany and marble centre table, the circular reeded top above a wavy frieze on three reeded turned supports ending in downswept legs with paw feet.

41.5in (104cm) diam

£3,000-4,000   **FRE**

A 19thC French carved giltwood and gesso centre table, the top with a faux marble inset supported by three cherubs and a naturalistic hexagonal base.

From an important Hollywood studio.

34in (85cm) wide

£4,000-6,000   **FRE**

17th to 18thC Italian walnut table, he hexagonal top raised on a baluster urned column and three scale-carved croll feet.

30.5in (76cm) high

6,000-9,000   **FRE**

A Russian mahogany and parcel-gilt centre table, the octagonal top above a conforming frieze, raised on curved supports with gilded eagle heads, on gilded ball and paw feet ending with a concave quatripartite plinth base.

c1825   *41.75in (104cm) diam*

£8,000-12,000   **EVE**

A 19thC Russian birch centre table, the marble top with a raised rim and reeded edge above a chamfered frieze and leaf-clasped column, with three anthropomorphic legs and paw feet with sunken casters.

38.75in (97cm) diam

£1,200-1,800   **L&T**

Swedish Neo-classical birchwood edestal table, the top with a onforming apron, on a waisted stem nd concave tripartite base ending in crolled feet.

1830   *30.75in (77cm) high*

7,000-10,000   **EVE**

A Swedish Biedermeier birch circular table, raised on a column support and four feet.

c1835   *33.5in (85cm) diam*

£3,000-4,000   **LANE**

A 19thC Swedish Gustavian-style painted centre table, with a bead and leaf frieze and panelled rosette corners, the laurel leaf swags between tapered fluted legs headed with leaf banding and ending with acanthus leaves.

34.75in (87cm) wide

£3,000-4,000   **EVE**

A pair of Neo-classical-style marble and gilt-bronze centre tables, each with two graduated tiers supported by scaly cast scroll legs headed by rams' masks and terminating in hairy hoof feet.

30in (75cm) wide

£4,000-6,000 pair   **FRE**

A CLOSER LOOK AT A CONTINENTAL WALNUT TABLE

This luxurious walnut table is richly decorated with seaweed marquetry, oyster veneering, and ivory and ebony starbursts. The quality in ornamentation in this example makes it a particularly desirable piece.

This table has been executed in a 17thC style. The bun feet, spiral turned legs, X-stretcher and seaweed marquetry were all popular features. These characteristics were adopted in the 19thC, when all things 'Jacobethan' enjoyed a revival.

It is common for rosewood or calamander crossbanding and decorative inlay to have been added at a later date, as this will boost the table's commercial appeal. Therefore examine the table carefully: a table with original crossbanding will command a higher price.

Oyster veneering is so-called because the grain resembles an oyster shell. This type of veneering was executed by slicing the veneer transversely across the end grain of smaller branches.

A Continental walnut table in the 17thC style, with panels of seaweed marquetry and oyster veneers, with an ivory and ebony starburst to each corner, rosewood crossbanding and chequer bands, on spirally turned legs and bun feet.

80in (200cm) lon

£1,500-2,000　　　　　　　　　　　　　　　　　　　　　　　　**D**

A mid-19thC Continental giltwood centre table, the serpentine veined carrara marble top above a scrolling frieze carved with alternate shell and floral cartouches, supported on cabriole legs with foliate carving and linked by moulded stretchers centred by a leafy rosette.

57.5in (146cm) wide

£8,000-12,000　　　　　　　　　　　　　**L&T**

A 19thC Continental ebonised carved centre table, the circular top raised on three crane form supports, terminating on a triform base with bun feet.

23in (57.5cm) dia

£700-1,000　　　　　　　　　　**FR**

Pietre Dure, an Italian term meaning 'hardstones', was traditionally used in ancient Rome, and later in the Renaissance period. As a result of the 19thC Renaissance Revival, Italian furniture of the late 1860s and 1870s often feature pietre dure such as the lapis lazuli and black marble seen here.

This scene shows the Temple of Vespasian in the Roman Forum, and the extraordinary precision and detail in its execution is evident. These exquisite micro-mosaic tables were widely exported during the 19thC century and today a piece of this quality, in such a good condition, is extremely valuable.

The Doves of Pliny motif was a popular design in Italy. It is named after an ancient mosaic by Sosos of doves on the rim of a drinking bowl, mentioned by Pliny the Elder as 'the finest ever found.'

late 19thC Italian micromosaic table top, centred with the Doves of Pliny, encircled with eight scenes of ancient Roman structures including the Panthenon, the Arch of Titus, the Capitoline Hill, the Colosseum, St. Peter's Basilica and Square, the Temple of Vespasian in the Roman Forum, the Tomb of Cecilia Metella and the Temple of Vesta, with three bands of lapis lazuli or African Blue, within an outer Greek key border, on a black marble ground, later black marble base.

32.75in (83cm) diam

30,000-40,000

DN

A rare Regency rosewood, ebonised and parcel gilt console table in the manner of George Smith, the mottled red marble top above twin animal legs, the supports united by a foot board.

49.5in (126cm) wide

£12,000-18,000   CATO

A Scottish Regency mahogany side table, in the manner of William Trotter, the veined white marble top with ledge back, above twin scrolling front consoles carved with acanthus leaves and with bead and reel panels, raised on a plinth with bead and reel mouldings.

46.5in (118cm) wide

£2,200-2,800   L&T

A William IV mahogany pier table, the top with a moulded edge above a crossbanded frieze with gilt moulding, raised on octagonal spreading columns and a mirrored back, on a platform base with pad feet.

39.25in (98cm) wide

£2,200-2,800   L&T

An early Victorian rosewood and scagliola-topped console table, with two scrolled consoles, each carved with acanthus leaves, mirrored back, raised on a plinth base.

44.5in (113cm) wide

£4,000-6,000   L&T

A Rococo-style giltwood pier table, with auricular C-scroll carving, the serpentine moulded marble top, above base with four floral carved cabriole legs joined by shaped X-stretcher.

45.25in (113cm) wide

£1,800-2,200   L&T

A late 19thC French carved walnut console table, the serpentine top with leaves and berries and a lappet and lunette moulded borders, the pierced frieze centred by a bird group, on scroll legs with lion masks, shells and foliage, all united by a shaped stretcher centred by foliage.

76in (190cm) wide

£4,000-6,000   WW

A late 18th to early 19thC Swedish Neo-classical worn giltwood and painted console, the rectangular faux marble top above a foliate and bird painted frieze, raised on fluted supports ending with a faux marble stepped plinth base.

47in (117.5cm) wide

£7,000-10,000   EV

A 19thC French or Italian Neo-classical painted sarcophagus console table, the faux painted marble with applied parcel-gilt fruiting vine decoration, the back with one cupboard door, raised on a plinth base.

113in (282.5cm) wide

£1,500-2,000   FRE

A Portuguese Rococo jacaranda console, with a serpentine top and a frieze drawer, raised on cabriole legs.

41.5in (104cm) wide

£5,000-7,000   FRE

A pair of Charles X mahogany console tables, each rounded rectangular marble top over an ogee moulded frieze drawer, raised on scroll supports ending in a shaped platform base, with carved claw feet.

42in (105cm) wide

£4,000-6,000   FR

A Regency rosewood breakfast table, with mirror veneers and shallow frieze, above a leaf clasped pedestal and concave tripod base, on scroll feet with leaf cast brass caps and casters.

51.25in (128cm) diam

£6,000-9,000   **L&T**

A Regency mahogany breakfast table the hinged rectangular top with a reeded edge, on a column, circular platform and four sabre legs, reeded legs and brass caster caps, base worn.

38.5in (96cm) wide

£700-1,000   **SWO**

A Regency mahogany, crossbanded and boxwood-strung breakfast table, the hinged top on a turned column and quadruped base terminating in brass foliate cappings and casters, stamped "W & C Wilkinson, 14 Ludgate Hill, 19395".

£2,800-3,200   **SWO**

A William IV mahogany turnover top pedestal table, with a carved foliate column over a quatreform base, supported by foliate carved feet.

48.75in (122cm) wide

£600-900   **SWO**

A mid-19thC Gothic Revival oak foldover supper table, the crossbanded top with rounded angles above a panelled frieze with lancet decoration and pendants turned to the angles, on a moulded square tapering column and concave quadruped base with turned feet.

48in (122cm) wide

£2,200-2,800   **L&T**

An Irish Chippendale mahogany hunt table, with a drop-leaf top, supported by eight square legs with beaded edges.

c1780   *78in (198cm) wide*

£5,000-7,000   **POOK**

A George III mahogany drop-leaf dining table, the central legs opening to support the extending leaves, on slight cabriole legs and pad feet.

50in (125cm) wide

£500-800   **SWO**

A George III-style mahogany drop-flap table, the oval top with reeded edge above a frieze and four club legs with reeded panel terminals and brass feet.

57.5in (144cm) wide

£600-900   **L&T**

A George III mahogany drop-leaf table, the oval top raised on four club legs with pad feet.

64.75in (162cm) wide

£4,000-6,000   **L&T**

A large modern mahogany 'wake' table, with two leaves opening to an oval, on eight legs.

90.75in (227cm) wide

£1,200-1,800   **SWO**

A George II-style mahogany gateleg table, the oval top raised on four club legs, with pad feet.

42.5in (106cm) diam

£300-500   L&T

A Regency mahogany, dining table, on turned urn pedestals above three reeded sabre legs with brass cuffs and casters, with two sets of poles for extension.

46in (115cm) wide

£3,000-4,000   BRU

A Regency-style mahogany triple pedestal dining table, the rosewood crossbanded top, on baluster turned pedestals with reeded sabre legs and brass paw cast caps and casters, includes two further leaves.

143in (363cm) wide

£3,000-4,000   L&T

A Victorian mahogany three pedestal dining table, with re-entrant corners on a plain frieze, raised on octagonal tapering stems, quadripartite bases and claw feet, each section with drop flaps.

£2,200-2,800   SWO

A George III D-end dining table, with boxwood stringing, the central gateleg section with drop leaves, above a panelled frieze with chequer stringing, raised on tapered legs with spade feet, brass caps and casters.

111.75in (284cm) wide

£2,200-2,800   L&T

A George III mahogany dining table, in the manner of Morgan and Sanders, the rectangular top with a reeded edge above a plain frieze, brass handle to each end, raised on six turned and reeded tapering legs with brass caps and casters, two legs unscrewing and stowing in the table, includes two further locking leaves.

139.25in (348cm) wide

£15,000-20,000   L&T

An early 19thC mahogany dining table, with a plain cockbeaded frieze, the central gateleg section with six legs and a pair of D-ends, the legs turned and reeded with brass caps and casters.

124.75in (312cm) wide

£7,000-10,000   L&T

An early 19thC dining table, with a central gateleg section, on ring turned and reeded tapering legs, toupie feet.

118.5in (301cm) long

£1,200-1,800   L&T

A Regency D-end mahogany dining table, the central gateleg section with one hinged leaf, one end with a further hinged leaf and one additional leaf, with reeded edge above ebony lined panelled frieze and coromandel crossbanded tablets, raised on ring turned and reeded tapering legs and toupie feet.

142in (355cm) wide

£3,500-4,000   **L&T**

A 19thC mahogany D-end dining table, with extensive boxwood stringing, two extra leaves, and a panelled frieze above panelled square section tapering legs.

52in (130cm) high

£2,000-3,000   **L&T**

An early Victorian mahogany telescopic dining table, with D-ends and reeded edge, on rosette headed lobed baluster legs, brass caps and casters, including five leaves.

163.25in (408cm) wide

£4,000-6,000   **L&T**

An early Victorian mahogany telescopic dining table, with four leaves, the top with D-ends and moulded edge, raised above a plain frieze and five moulded and bulbous baluster legs, brass caps and casters.

156.25in (397cm) wide

£10,000-15,000   **L&T**

A Victorian mahogany extending dining table, the top with moulded edge and rounded angles, raised on four carved and fluted baluster legs with sunken brass casters, includes three leaves.

121.2in (303cm) wide

£4,000-6,000   **L&T**

A Victorian mahogany telescopic dining table, the top with demilune ends and moulded edge, raised on paired baluster trestle supports with scroll feet and casters, includes three leaves.

80.75in (202cm) wide

£3,000-5,000   **L&T**

A Victorian mahogany dining table, the rectangular top with D-ends above a plain frieze, the telescopic pull out action with central leg, on turned and buckle carved tapering legs with brass caps and casters, six extra leaves with frieze to each leaf.

17.25in (44cm) wide

£6,000-8,000   **L&T**

SIDEBOARDS

A Scottish George III mahogany sideboard, with boxwood and purplewood stringing and inlaid rosewood panels to the uprights, the stage back with tambour, above central frieze drawer, single drawers, dummy fronted cupboard and cellaret drawer, on carved square section tapering legs with collar feet.

79.5in (202cm) wide

£2,200-2,800   **L&T**

A George III mahogany demilune sideboard, with a central drawer and kneehole, flanked by dummy fronted deep drawers and similar cupboard doors, on tapering legs with spade feet.

88.25in (224cm) wide

£4,000-6,000   **L&T**

A Maple & Co. mahogany sideboard, in the neo-classical style, with a semi-bowed central drawer, faux tambour drawer and two cupboard doors, carved with husk swags and with rams' heads to the angles, raised on square tapering legs on leaf-carved feet.

79.25in (198cm) wide

£1,500-2,000   **L&T**

A George III style mahogany serpentine sideboard, with boxwood and ebony stringing, with a central drawer lined for cutlery, recessed drawer and deeper cupboard and drawers, on square section tapering feet with spade feet.

60.75in (152cm) wide

£800-1,200   **L&T**

A George III mahogany sideboard of serpentine outline, the top with purpleheart crossbanding above drawers, on six square tapering legs and spade feet.

43.75in (111cm) wide

£8,000-12,000   **CATO**

A Scottish George III serpentine sideboard, with boxwood stringing, the shaped top with reeded edge and corresponding stage back with tambour doors, above three frieze drawers and square section tapered legs.

54.25in (138cm) wide

£800-1,200   **L&T**

A George III stageback bowfront sideboard, with turned brass gallery, the upper section with marquetry panels and sliding doors, the base with drawers, on fluted tapering legs and cushion feet.

84.5in (211cm) wide

£10,000-15,000   **L&T**

A George III mahogany bowfront serving table, with turned brass gallery, the line inlaid D-shaped top above an oval inlaid frieze drawer flanked by two further drawers, on ring turned tapering legs with toupie feet.

72in (180cm) wide

£5,000-7,000   **L&T**

A George III mahogany bowfront serving table, with turned brass gallery, the breakfront D-shaped top above an oval inlaid and quarter veneered frieze drawer, on stiff leaf-carved and reeded tapering legs with toupie feet.

73.5in (184cm) wid[e]

£6,000-9,000   **L&[T]**

George III mahogany bowfront sideboard with a central frieze drawer flanked by two drawers, on square tapering legs.

67.25in (168cm) wide

£1,500-2,000   SWO

A George III mahogany bowfront sideboard, with an inlaid and crossbanded central drawer, flanked by a drawers and cupboards, raised on turned tapering legs.

54in (135cm) wide

£1,500-2,000   SWO

A Regency mahogany serving table, the panelled ledge back above a rectangular top and deep frieze, with three cushion drawers, on turned and reeded legs with toupie feet.

81.25in (203cm) wide

£2,200-2,800   L&T

A Regency-style mahogany pedestal sideboard, with a pair of panelled drawers and scrolling panelled ledge back, flanked by taller pedestals with a drawer and cupboard containing sliding trays, on carved and turned feet.

75.5in (189cm) wide

£1,500-2,000   L&T

A Scottish Regency mahogany sideboard, with brass stringing, the breakfront stage with tambour doors and rosewood panels surmounted by a gallery, with drawers, cupboards and arched kneehole, on tapering legs with spade feet.

79.5in (199cm) wide

£4,000-6,000   L&T

A Regency mahogany bowfront sideboard.

71.25in (178cm) wide

£1,800-2,200   GIL

Regency mahogany bowfront sideboard, with an ebony line-inlaid frieze drawer, curved deep drawers and two cupboard doors, line-inlaid spandrels, on ring turned tapering legs with toupie feet.

61in (152.5cm) wide

£3,000-4,000   L&T

A Regency mahogany pedestal sideboard, with three central moulded frieze drawers, flanked by two tapered pedestals, raised on outswept carnel paw feet.

c1820   90in (225cm) wide

£3,000-4,000   FRE

A Regency mahogany pedestal sideboard, with a raised shell and acanthus carved back over four frieze drawers, the breakfront pedestals carved with lions paw feet and opening to reveal shelves and a cellarette drawer, on plinth bases.

c1820   88.5in (221cm) wide

£2,000-3,000   FRE

A William IV mahogany serving table, of large proportions, possibly Scottish, with a raised gallery to the back, the top with gadrooned border, on reeded turned legs with beaded bands and carved with leaves.

95.25in (242cm) wide

£6,000-9,000   DN

A William IV mahogany serving table, the scrolling ledge back centred by a floral spray above a moulded top with plate rack to rear, plain deep frieze and monopodial supports.

76in (190cm) wide

£2,800-3,200   L&T

A William IV mahogany twin pedestal sideboard, the semi-bowed top with a reeded edge above drawers and panelled doors, enclosed by spirally reeded columns, on a plinth.

Provenance: Membury Court, Axminster.

67.25in (168cm) wide

£1,800-2,200   L&T

FURNITURE

A 19thC English diminutive mahogany sideboard, breakfront top with three conforming dovetailed drawers, central drawer with compartments, secondary woods pine and mahogany, black line inlay on legs and drawer edges.

45in (112.5cm) high

£1,000-1,500 **BRU**

A mid-19thC Anglo-Indian hardwood serving table, the ledge back elaborately carved with central anthemion and acanthus motifs, on leaf and bird carved brackets with foliate fretwork, on carved paw feet.

48in (122cm) wide

£2,200-2,800 **L&T**

An Edwardian inlaid mahogany sideboard, the crossbanded top with a moulded cornice and chequer-banded frieze, two inlaid pagoda topped cupboards flanking a lower serving surface.

£2,000-3,000 **SWO**

A late 19thC mahogany satinwood crossbanded and marquetry inlaid sideboard, in the late 18thC-style, of serpentine form, with arched brass rail above a central drawer flanked by a deep lead-lined cellar drawer and single door enclosing a shelf, on square tapering legs terminating in spade feet.

73.25in (183cm) wide

£2,800-3,200 **L&T**

A 17thC and later oak refectory table, the plank top with cleated ends, on a later base with turned legs, united by square stretchers.

80.5in (201cm) wide

£1,200-1,800 **SWO**

A 17thC and later Italian walnut refectory table, the top and base associated, the rectangular top raised on twin shaped open end supports united by a bowed stretcher.

31in (77.5cm) wide

£2,000-2,500 **FRE**

A Regency mahogany D-end table, on a square tapering column and three downswept legs with brass paw caps and casters.

54.75in (137cm) wide

£400-600 **L&T**

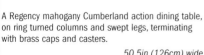

A Regency mahogany Cumberland action dining table, on ring turned columns and swept legs, terminating with brass caps and casters.

50.5in (126cm) wide

£1,200-1,800 **SWO**

A Danish Neo-classical mahogany pedestal extending table, raised on a plain circular stem and ending with three graduating curved and rounded feet, on casters.

c1840 *43in (107.5cm) diam*

£6,000-9,000 **EVE**

George III mahogany, tulipwood and satinwood crossbanded dressing table, the top with oval panels enclosing a bowl recess and a mirror, drawer with a fitted interior and two doors, on square tapering legs.

34.25in (87cm) high

400-600   **DN**

A George III mahogany dressing table, the double hinged top enclosing an adjustable mirror and fittings, above a false drawer front, on square tapering legs with an H-stretcher.

33.5in (85cm) high

£400-600   **DN**

A George III mahogany gentleman's washstand, the hinged lid opening to reveal a mirror and lidded compartments, over three false and three deep drawers, on square tapering legs, with caps and casters.

£800-1,200   **SWO**

China Trade Huang Hua Li wood metamorphic combined dressing and writing table, the hinged lid enclosing a fitted interior, mirror and candle slides, a drawer to the reverse, fluted legs, brass casters.

1800   *29in (72.5cm) high*

2,000-3,000   **FRE**

An early 19thC mahogany kneehole dressing table, the top with a banded edge above an arrangement of five drawers, raised on ring turned tapering legs with brass caps and casters.

48.75in (122cm) wide

£800-1,200   **L&T**

An early 19thC mahogany kidney-shaped dressing table, the top with a reeded edge above a plain frieze and turned and reeded tapering legs, with brass caps and casters.

48.75in (122cm) wide

£3,000-5,000   **L&T**

19thC mahogany dressing table, the top with apertures for bowl, cups and counterbalanced mirror, the kneehole flanked by drawers and pedestals containing panelled doors concealing a toilet bowl and bidet, sprung handles.

48.75in (122cm) wide

1,200-1,800   **L&T**

A Victorian bird's eye maple dressing table, with purplewood stringing, the mirror with pierced strapwork cresting, raised on a reverse breakfront kneehole desk with nine drawers and a recessed panelled cupboard, on plinth base.

69.25in (173cm) high

£800-1,200   **L&T**

A late 19thC French mahogany and kingwood poudreuse, with banding and boxwood stringing, the top with a marquetry urn of flowers, the triple section hinged top enclosing a mirror and two recesses, on square tapering legs.

29.75in (74.5cm) wide

£800-1,200   **DN**

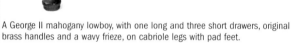

A Queen Anne solid walnut lowboy, the rectangular moulded top above three drawers and a shaped apron, raised on circular tapering legs and pad feet.

29.25in (74cm) high

£2,200-2,800　　　　　　　　　　　　　　**B**

A George II mahogany lowboy, with one long and three short drawers, original brass handles and a wavy frieze, on cabriole legs with pad feet.

30in (76cm) wid

£7,000-10,000　　　　　　　　　　　　　　**CAT**

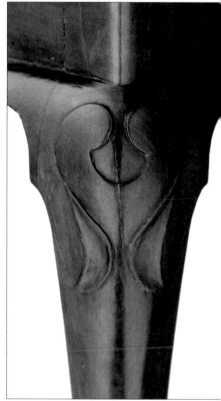

A late 18thC fruitwood country lowboy, the twin drawer frieze with oak lining above heart and scroll carved cabriole legs and pad feet.

30.5in (77.5cm) wid

£3,000-5,000　　　　　　　　　　　　　　**CAT**

A George II mahogany foldover tea table, the rectangular top raised on cabriole legs with pad feet.

34in (85cm) wide

£1,200-1,800 **L&T**

A George III mahogany foldover tea table, the rectangular top with astragal edge above a frieze drawer, on square section tapering legs.

35.5.in (89cm) wide

£600-900 **L&T**

A Scottish George III mahogany tea table, with boxwood stringing, the crossbanded foldover top above a frieze drawer with divided interior, on square section tapered legs with round dot terminals and tapered legs.

39in (99cm) wide

£400-600 **L&T**

An early George III mahogany foldover tea table, the rectangular top with a moulded edge, on turned tapering legs with scroll caps and pad feet, warped top.

29.5in (74cm) wide

£400-600 **SWO**

A George III padouk wood folding tea table, on a mahogany stand with a central frieze drawer, the square tapering legs with concave spade feet.

33.5in (83.5cm) wide

£500-800 **SWO**

A Regency rosewood and crossbanded tea table, the rectangular top above a strung frieze with a central raised tablature, on a stepped column support with four downswept feet and lapette carved knees, on brass casters.

£1,200-1,800 **SWO**

An early 19thC mahogany tea table with a crossbanded edge, on four columns and four reeded sabre legs, the legs and base repaired.

36.75in (92cm) wide

£600-900 **SWO**

A 19thC Scandinavian birch tea table, the rectangular folding top with rounded corners and a plain frieze, on square tapering legs.

35in (89cm) wide

£400-600 **DN**

An early Victorian mahogany foldover tea table, on a turned column, outswept legs and paw feet.

£500-700 **SWO**

FURNITURE

A George III mahogany foldover card table, with boxwood and ebony stringing, the demilune top with satinwood crossbanding, above a panelled frieze, on stop-fluted and leaf carved turned tapering legs, toupie feet.

33.5in (84cm) wide

£1,800-2,200   **L&T**

A Regency mahogany and brass-strung card table, the rosewood crossbanded foldover top raised on a spreading pair of pierced trestle supports, on a plinth with four sabre legs, paw cast brass caps and casters.

36.5in (91cm) wide

£4,000-6,000   **L&T**

A Regency mahogany and satinwood banded foldover card table, with boxwood stringing, hinged top and lion masks to the frieze, on bamboo form supports and a quadripartite base with sabre legs, ending in brass paw caps and casters.

36.75in (92cm) wide

£2,200-2,800   **L&T**

A George IV rosewood card table, the hinged top on turned legs with acanthus leaf ornament.

37.5in (94cm) wide

£1,800-2,200   **SWO**

A 19thC Dutch walnut and floral marquetry card table, on square tapering legs with gilt-metal feet.

32.75in (83cm) long

£800-1,200   **DN**

A 19thC Gillows foldover amboyna card and writing table, the top with inset tooled leather skiver, opening to reveal a baize-lined interior, the panelled frieze with a gilded band raised above two twin columnar supports, on scrolling sabre legs, stamped 'Gillows & Co. 4362'.

37in (94cm) wide

£4,000-6,000   **L&T**

A 19thC Colonial campaign card table, probably padouk wood, the foldover top with a brass inlaid central medallion, the interior with a circular baize within brass inlaid scrolling foliage and birds, detachable legs, brass fittings.

£1,000-1,500   **SWO**

An early Victorian rosewood foldover card table, with an anthemion decorated frieze, on an octagonal tapering column and quadruped platform base.

£500-700   **SWO**

One of a pair of Edwardian painted demilune foldover card tables, each decorated with gilt lattice work, flowers and figural panels of 18thC lovers, on club legs with pad feet.

35.5in (89cm) wide

£2,800-3,200 pair   **L&T**

An Edwardian rosewood and gilt-metal mounted foldover card table, the quarter-veneered and crossbanded top with a baize-lined interior, on cabriole legs with scrolled mounts, cast sabots.

35.75in (91cm) wide

£2,500-3,000   **L&T**

An Edwardian mahogany painted demilune foldover card table, the top with peacock feather border and a panel of a goddess and cherubs, above festoon frieze, tapering legs, spade feet.

36.5in (91cm) wide

£4,000-6,000   **L&T**

An Edwardian mahogany and inlaid card table, the hinged top inlaid with a satinwood and harewood patera within a foliate border, on square tapered legs, terminating in spade feet.

A Dutch floral marquetry folding card table, the serpentine top with outset corners, enclosing a baize-lined surface with marquetry playing card motifs, over a frieze drawer, on carved cabriole legs with claw and ball feet.

A walnut crossbanded card table, with a single frieze drawers, on cabriole legs.

36.5in (91cm) wide

29.5in (75cm) high

33.5in (84cm) wide

£800-1,200   SWO   £2,000-3,000   B   £700-1,000   SWO

A CLOSER LOOK AT A CHINA TRADE BACKGAMMON TABLE

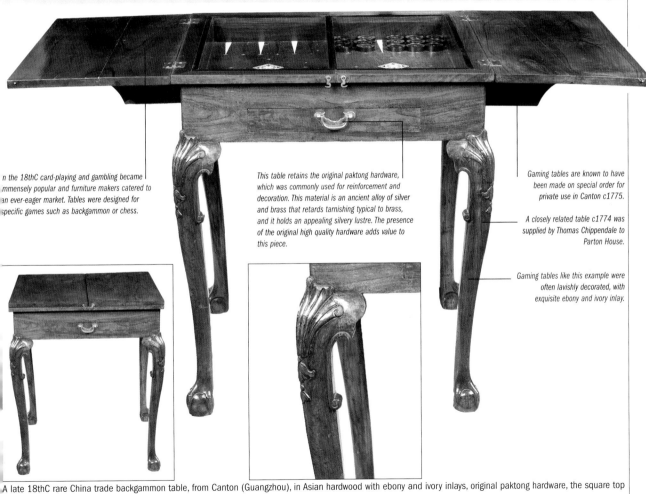

In the 18thC card-playing and gambling became immensely popular and furniture makers catered to an ever-eager market. Tables were designed for specific games such as backgammon or chess.

This table retains the original paktong hardware, which was commonly used for reinforcement and decoration. This material is an ancient alloy of silver and brass that retards tarnishing typical to brass, and it holds an appealing silvery lustre. The presence of the original high quality hardware adds value to this piece.

Gaming tables are known to have been made on special order for private use in Canton c1775.

A closely related table c1774 was supplied by Thomas Chippendale to Parton House.

Gaming tables like this example were often lavishly decorated, with exquisite ebony and ivory inlay.

A late 18thC rare China trade backgammon table, from Canton (Guangzhou), in Asian hardwood with ebony and ivory inlays, original paktong hardware, the square top divided into two hinged flaps.

c1775

54.75 (137cm) long

£30,000-40,000   MJM

235

A Regency square penwork chess table, the squares with alternating flowers and chinoiserie scenes of oriental buildings and figures in landscapes, within a wide foliate border, inscribed "Drawn by James W Beeson, Derby", on later column.

£2,500-3,000   **SWO**

A Regency mahogany games table, the crossbanded foldover top enclosing a baize playing surface, on a stepped column, sabre legs with hairy paw caps and casters.

c1820   *35.5in (89cm) wide*

£1,500-2,000   **FRE**

A 19thC Damascus games table, with a mosaic inlay of exotic woods, mother of pearl and ivory, the top swivelling and opening to reveal a card surface, chessboard and backgammon board.

£400-600   **SW**

A George IV rosewood games table, with a moulded edge and reversible chequerboard, the base with parcel gilt gesso husks and scrolls, on slender end supports with a turned stretcher, with gilt metal scroll and paw terminals with brass casters.

66.5cm wide

£1,000-1,500   **DN**

A 19thC Louis XV-style kingwood and marquetry games table, the rectangular top with outset corners above two lateral frieze drawers, raised on square cabriole legs ending in sabots.

33in (82.5cm) wide

£3,000-4,000   **FRE**

A Victorian burr walnut games and work table, the hinged top enclosing a backgammon and chequer board, above a frieze drawer and sliding wool bag, on turned end supports with a double stretcher and carved outswept cabriole legs, ceramic casters.

29.25in (73cm) high

£500-700   **DN**

Regency figured work table, the top inlaid with ebony bellflowers over one frieze drawer and two opposing dummy drawers, raised on a lyre shaped support, terminating in sabre legs with hairy paw cappings and casters.

18in (45cm) wide

1,500-2,000   **FRE**

A George IV yew sewing table, the hinged cover inlaid with stringing to canted corners, revealing a lift-out tray, the turned and moulded walnut stem to a quatreform base with bun feet and sunken brass casters, old worm to base and lifting to veneer.

29in (73.5cm) high

£2,800-3,200   **WW**

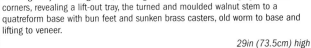

19thC Louis XV-style kingwood inlaid work table, the quarter-veneered, kidney-shaped top over a brushing slide and three cloth-lined drawers, raised on shaped end supports ending in downswept legs.

23in (57.5cm) wide

1,500-2,000   **FRE**

A Victorian burr walnut combination work and games table, the top with a Tunbridgeware tesserae mosaic view of Eridge Castle within a tesserae mosaic view and a broad band of flowers, the folding and revolving top inlaid for chess, backgammon and cribbage, on turned stems and carved cabriole legs with white china caster feet.

23.25in (59cm) high

£3,000-4,000   **B**

An early 19thC mahogany work table, the dropleaf top above a frieze drawer, on three reeded sabre legs.

12.5in (32cm) wide

£700-1,000   **L&T**

An early 19thC mahogany work table, with two drawers, raised on baluster turned pedestal, triform plinth, bun fee

20in (50cm) wid

£400-600   **L&**

A Louis XV-style marquetry work table, by Edwards & Roberts, with floral marquetry decoration, the cherrywood panels set in rosewood veneered frame, the serpentine hinged top with gilt brass banding, on square section cabriole legs joined by concave undershelf.

14.25in (36cm) wide

£700-1,000   **L&T**

A William IV rosewood work table, the top with rounded corners, with a drawer and sliding wool bag, on fluted end supports and acanthus casters.

28.75in (72cm) high

£700-1,000   **DN**

A William IV rosewood work table, with two false drawers and a cotton wool bag, on an octagonal column and a concave platform base, with bun feet.

28.5in (71cm) hig

£400-600   **D**

A 19thC parquetry specimen wood ladies' work table, containing a single frieze drawer, with a sliding silk-covered bag below, on standard end supports united by a stretcher.

22.5in (56cm) wide

£1,200-1,800   **SW0**

A Victorian burr walnut games and work table, the hinged serpentine shaped top enclosing a backgammon and chequer board, above a frieze drawer and sliding wool bag, on turned end supports with carved outswept cabriole legs and ceramic casters.

29.25in (73cm) high

£500-700   **DN**

A Victorian or Edwardian inlaid rosewood work table, with a carrying handle and bevelled glass opening to reveal a buttoned silk interior, on square tapering legs, united with an undertier.

£700-1,000   **SW**

late 18thC Chinese export lacquered tilt-top occasional table, the top decorated with a scene of maidens at play in a pastoral setting, tripod base and scroll feet.

41in (102.5cm) wide

8,000-12,000

CATO

A English penwork oval top occasional table.
c1825

£10,000-15,000

CATO

An English burr elm lamp table, supported on a plain turned column.
1835

£4,000-6,000

CATO

A Victorian walnut and gilt-brass mounted occasional table, the tulipwood crossbanded top with floral inlay of convallaria, with a single frieze drawer, on cabriole legs.

28in (73cm) high

£3,000-4,000

CATO

A George II mahogany envelope table, the hinged triangular top swivelling to become hexagonal, on turned tapering legs and pad feet.

26in (65cm) wide

£4,000-6,000 L&T

A George III rosewood occasional table, with satinwood crossbanding and box stringing, on dual pierced supports, wavy stretcher and overscrolled legs.

32.5in (81.5cm) wide

£3,500-4,000 CATO

A Swedish Karl Johan gilt-metal mounted mahogany side table, with a frieze, raised on a stem ending in a tripartite base with scrolled feet.

c1825 *31in (77.5cm) high*

£2,800-3,200 EVE

A pair of Directoire-style mahogany guerdons, each with a marble top, pierced brass gallery, panelled frieze and drawer and gilt-brass mounts, on turned legs and brass toupie feet.

36.5in (91cm) hig

£1,200-1,800 L&

A Chippendale-style mahogany occasional table, the top with serpentine sides above a pierced apron and cluster column legs with blind fret blocks, joined by corresponding X-stretcher, on brass casters.

29.25in (73cm) high

£800-1,200 L&T

A Victorian lacquered teapoy, decorated with flowers and giltwork, the hinged lid enclosing a velvet lined interior with a pair of glass decanters and wells for mixing bowls, on scroll feet and casters.

32in (80cm) high

£300-500 L&T

A Victorian coromandel and rosewood occasional table, the veneered top with crossbanded edge, the fluted column with jewelled knop and tripod legs.

24.5in (62cm) wid

£800-1,200 L&

A pair of mahogany and brass-inlaid bijouterie tables, each with hinged glass lids and sides, on square tapered legs ending in brass feet.

32in (80cm) wide

£1,500-2,000 FRE

An Edwardian mahogany bijouterie table, with chequer and boxwood stringing, the hinged top above a frieze, on square section tapering legs.

28.75in (72cm) high

£400-600 L&T

A Brazilian monkey puzzle wood lamp table, the circular top with a leather inset, labels to the underside.

23.5in (58.5cm) dian

£200-300 SW

A CLOSER LOOK AT A GEORGE III DWARF SIDE TABLE

...rom the 15thC side tables, which ...ere intended to stand against the ...all, were used as an additional ...urface at meal times or for holding ...rnaments. They became fashionable ...the mid-18thC, when they were ...cluded in grand sets of furniture ...nd were also used as writing and ...ressing tables.

...uring the George III period, furniture ...esigners were inspired by the ...lassical world and used delicate ...ecorative motifs. There was a move ...a further refinement of form, which ...an be seen in this example, where ...ewly imported timbers from all over ...e world, like satinwood and ...urpleheart, were used for ...ophisticated veneers.

...urpleheart is a dense hardwood (of ...e genus Peltogyne) from the ...aribbean and is so-called due to the ...urplish colour it becomes when ...eshly cut.

The spade feet seen here are typical of the period. Check that none of the feet have been replaced – a side table which has its original feet will command a premium.

...n George III English satinwood veneer dwarf side table, crossbanded in purpleheart.
1790

8,000-12,000   **CATO**

...Queen Anne oak ...ide table, with ...urned legs linked by ...tretchers.

28in (71cm) wide

3,000-4,000   **EP**

A George III mahogany bowfront side table, the shaped rectangular top with a moulded edge above frieze drawers, on square section tapering legs.

36in (90cm) wide

£800-1,200   **L&T**

A George III mahogany bowfront side table, with ebony stringing and a pair of frieze drawers, on square section tapering legs with collars.

53.5in (134cm) wide

£800-1,200 L&T

A George III mahogany serpentine serving table, the rectangular top with an astragal edge above a fluted frieze with rosettes, raised on fluted square section tapering legs with block feet.

67in (170cm) wide

£12,000-18,000 L&T

A George III mahogany serpentine side table, the shaped top over one frieze drawer, raised on fluted square tapered legs.

c1790 *35.5in (89cm) wid*

£2,000-2,500 FR

A Scottish late Regency oak lobby table, the top with a pedimented ledge back above an ogee frieze and scrolling leaf-carved consoles, turned rear legs.

51.25in (128cm) wide

£500-700 L&T

An early 19thC mahogany side table, the rectangular top above a small frieze drawer, raised on square section legs joined by H-stretcher.

36.75in (92cm) wide

£800-1,200 L&T

An early 19thC mahogany side table, the rectangular top with a moulded edge above a frieze drawer, on square section tapering legs.

30in (75cm) wide

£400-600 L&T

A pair of Regency walnut and beechwood tables, with gilt-metal mounts and stimulated ebony inlay, on twin trestle supports and scroll feet.

39in (97.5cm) wid

£1,500-2,000 FR

A 19thC mahogany serving table, the rectangular top with a reeded edge above a vertically reeded frieze, on turned and reeded tapering legs.

64.5in (161cm) wide

£3,000-4,000 L&T

A Victorian oak hall table and a matching pair of hall chairs, the table with a shaped ledge back and serpentine moulded top, above shaped apron and moulded cabriole front legs with scroll toes, each chair with waisted panel back, shaped spreading seat and cabriole front legs.

Table 48.75in (122cm) wid

£800-1,200 L&

A pair of Victorian overpainted tables, each with faux marble tops above friezes carved with Vitruvian scrolls and rosettes, the whole raised on square tapering legs with deep fluting, terminating in left carved feet.

52.75in (134cm) wide

€4,000-6,000   **L&T**

A pair of early Victorian burr oak side tables, the modern marble tops above a panelled frieze, on square tapering baluster front and pilaster rear legs.

Provenance*: Haggerston Castle, Northumberland.*

66in (165cm) wide

£5,000-7,000   **L&T**

An Edwardian oak side table, the breakfront top with rounded angles and verde antico marble, inset above a plain frieze, on turned and fluted supports joined by a shaped undershelf, on corresponding feet.

47.25in (118cm) wide

£400-600   **L&T**

A late 17thC Iberian walnut side table, the rounded rectangular plank top above two frieze drawers, raised on bobbin turned legs united by a peripheral stretcher.

62in (155cm) wide

€2,000-2,500   **FRE**

A late 18thC French mahogany table, with a frieze drawer and panelled sides, on square tapering legs with brass terminals and casters, stamped "MBF".

28.25in (71.5cm) high

£2,200-2,800   **DN**

A 19thC Scandinavian pine rectangular table, with a leather inset top and moulded border, above a dentil and fluted frieze of shaped form, on fluted square tapering legs, some repairs.

33.75in (86cm) wide

£200-300   **DN**

A pair of Louis XVI-style walnut and brass inlaid side tables, with gilt-metal mounts, each rectangular top above a frieze drawer, raised on square tapered legs ending in toupee feet.

29in (72.5cm) wide

€1,500-2,000   **FRE**

A 19thC Dutch marquetry and parquetry mahogany and satinwood side table, the cubic-veneered top centred by a coat of arms, above conforming veneered sides, with one drawer, raised on faceted tapered legs joined by a wavy tri-form stretcher terminating in bun feet.

44.5in (111cm) wide

£3,000-4,000   **FRE**

A Scottish George III mahogany Pembroke table, with boxwood stringing, the satinwood crossbanded top above a frieze drawer, on square section tapering legs with 'round dot' terminals, brass caps and casters.

44in (110cm) wide

£2,200-2,800 **L&T**

A George III mahogany and satinwood-banded Pembroke table, attributed to Young and Trotter, Edinburgh, with a single drawer and opposing dummy drawer, on square tapering legs, terminating in brass caps and casters.

38.5in (98cm) wide

£1,200-1,800 **L&T**

LEFT: A George III mahogany Pembroke table, with boxwood and ebony stringing, the oval top above a bowed frieze drawer and opposing dummy drawer, on square section tapered legs with brass caps and casters.

35.5in (90cm) wide (oper

£800-1,200 **L&**

RIGHT: A George III mahogany Pembroke table, with boxwood and purplewood stringing, the crossbanded oval top above a bowed frieze drawer and opposing dummy drawer, on square section tapered legs with collars.

45.25in (115cm) wide (oper

£800-1,200 **L&**

A George III mahogany Pembroke table, the hinged oval top on turned and tapered legs terminating in claw and ball feet.

65.6in (164cm) wide

£600-900 **SWO**

A George III mahogany oval Pembroke table, with a single frieze drawer on square tapering legs.

33.5in (83.5cm) wide

£800-1,200 **SWO**

A George III satinwood and crossbanded Pembroke table with a hinged oval top, containing one true and an opposing dummy drawer, on square tapering legs terminating in brass cappings and casters.

40.75in (102cm) wid

£1,200-1,800 **SW**

A late 18th to early 19thC English Pembroke table, with a single board top and a bowfront dovetailed drawer with inlaid borders, on tapered legs with oval, floral and string inlay, original glue blocks and iron hinges, pit-sawn surface under top.

30.5in (76cm) wide

£1,500-2,000 **BRU**

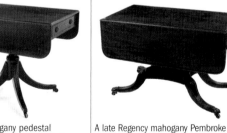

A Regency mahogany pedestal Pembroke table, the figured twin flap top above an end frieze drawer and false verso, on a turned column, four reeded and fluted splay legs and brass casters.

48.75in (122cm) wide

£1,200-1,800 **WW**

A late Regency mahogany Pembroke supper table, the top with a pair of drop flaps above a shallow frieze fitted with two opposing drawers, on a ring-turned column, four fluted legs, brass lion paw caps and casters.

42.5in (107cm) wid

£600-800

A Regency rosewood sofa table, with a drop-leaf top above two frieze drawers opposed by false drawers, on dual standard ends, brass cappings and casters.

This is a good example of the effect of sunlight on rosewood. The back of the table has been hidden from sunlight and has a richer colouring.

59in (150cm) wide

€12,000-18,000   **CATO**

A Regency mahogany sofa table, possibly Scottish, with boxwood stringing and satinwood banding, two frieze drawers and dummies, raised on trestle supports with scroll toes and inlaid decoration.

62.5in (156cm) wide

€5,000-7,000   **L&T**

A Regency mahogany sofa table, with satinwood crossbanding and boxwood and ebony stringing, two frieze drawers with opposing dummy drawers, on trestle supports with downswept legs, brass caps and casters.

52.75in (132cm) wide

£1,200-1,800   **L&T**

A late Regency rosewood sofa table, with a pair of frieze drawers and opposing dummies, on leaf-clasped trestle supports and sled bases, with carved scroll toes and casters.

59.25in (148cm) wide

£2,000-3,000   **L&T**

A Regency mahogany sofa table, with ebony inlay and opposing frieze and dummy drawers, on balustraded trestle supports joined by an arched stretcher, with splayed feet with cast paw caps and casters.

65.5in (164cm) wide

£1,000-1,500   **L&T**

A Regency mahogany sofa table, the hinged top above two freeze drawers, on twin turned column ends and reeded dual splayed legs, united by a turned stretcher, terminating in brass cappings and casters.

68in (173cm) wide

£4,000-6,000　　　　　　　　**H&L**

A Regency coromandel wood sofa table, with satinwood crossbanding and two frieze drawers opposing dummy drawers, raised on rectangular section supports on inlaid sabre legs terminating in anthemion cast brass caps and casters.

57.5in (146cm) wide

£2,000-3,000　　　　　　　　**L&T**

A Regency mahogany pedestal sofa table, the top with rounded angles above two frieze drawers opposing alternate dummy drawers, on an anthemion carved column, raised on base with gadrooned apron and boldly carved lions' paw feet.

59.75in (152cm) wid

£1,000-1,500　　　　　　　　**L&**

A Regency mahogany sofa table, the crossbanded top above a pair of frieze drawers with opposing dummies, raised on pierced lyre trestles joined by pot stand, on sabre legs with coromandel panels, cast brass paw feet and casters.

61.5in (154cm) wide

£2,000-3,000　　　　　　　　**L&T**

A Regency mahogany and ebony-lined sofa table, with hinged flaps, above two frieze drawers opposed by two dummy drawers, raised on curved and reeded legs with brass caps and casters.

46in (115cm) wid

£800-1,200　　　　　　　　**L&**

A Danish Empire mahogany ebonised sofa table, with fruitwood inlay and parcel-gilt the D-shaped drop-leaves above a rectangular frieze with a rootwood drawer, the end supports flanked by curved giltwood and ebonised bird head supports with paw feet.

c1815　　　　　　　　*59.5in (149cm) wide*

£10,000-12,000　　　　　　　　**EVE**

A 19thC rosewood sofa table, the frieze drawer with applied beading, raised on baluster turned supports and downscrolled sled bases with a turned and blocked stretcher with urn finial.

53.5in (136cm) wide

£700-1,000　　　　　　　　**L&T**

A 19thC Continental mahogany sofa table, the oval drop-leaf top with ripple moulded edge above two frieze drawers raised on spiral supports joined by a conforming stretcher, terminating in downswept legs.

62in (155cm) wid

£1,000-2,000　　　　　　　　**FR**

George III style mahogany tilt top tripod table, the dished top with thumbnail edge, raised on bird cage and cannon pedestal, the cabriole legs with elongated ball and claw feet.

28in (70cm) high

400-600   **L&T**

A George III mahogany tilt-top tripod table, the dished circular top raised on bird cage and cannon pedestal with cabriole legs.

28.75in (72cm) diam

£600-900   **L&T**

A George III mahogany tilt-top tripod table, the circular top raised on canon support and cabriole legs.

34.75in (87cm) diam

£300-500   **L&T**

A George III mahogany birdcage tripod table, raised on a tapering gun barrel column and pad feet.

30.25in (75.5cm) diam

£800-1,200   **SWO**

George III mahogany circular top tripod table, with a birdcage undertier, raised on a baluster column and pad feet.

800-1,200   **SWO**

A Regency mahogany tilt-top table, the circular hinged top on a baluster turned column and three ebony line-inlaid downswept legs with brass paw caps and casters.

37.5in (94cm) diam

£1,200-1,800   **L&T**

19thC mahogany tripod table, the circular pie-crust top above a birdcage, raised on a fluted column with spirally fluted knop, on acanthus carved cabriole legs with ball and claw feet.

29.6in (74cm) high

1,200-1,800   **L&T**

A pair of 19thC green and gilt painted wine tables, the oval satinwood crossbanded tops raised on reeded columns, above three hipped legs on paw feet.

27.5in (69cm) high

£4,000-6,000   **B**

A mahogany tripod table, the top with a pie-crust border, on a turned and fluted column above leaf-carved cabriole legs with claw and ball feet.

28.75in (72cm) diam

£600-900   **DN**

late 18th to early 19thC mahogany block and shell carved bureau, with oak and pine, the fall-flap above an interior with a well lined with a paper label inscribed Ezekiel Baker, weight and diameter of lead balls 1821; R Haseldine Sculpt, 7 Upper Rathbone Place", three long drawers on stepped ogee bracket feet.

39in (99cm) high

35,000-40,000

CATO

A George I walnut bureau, the fall-front revealing a pigeonhole interior and well, above two short and two long drawers, on bracket feet, some alterations.

37in (94cm) high

£3,000-5,000   **B**

A George II burr elm veneered and mahogany banded bureau, the sloping fall enclosing an interior fitted with five pigeonholes above ten short drawers, with a green baize lined writing surface, above four cock-beaded drawers, on shaped bracket feet, restorations.

43.5in (110.5cm) high

£800-1,200   **B**

An early George III mahogany bureau, the fall front enclosing a fitted interior above four long graduated drawers and lopers, on panelled bracket feet.

37.75in (96cm) wide

£700-1,000   **L&T**

A small George III mahogany bureau, with a fitted interior over four long drawers, original brass handles and oak lined drawers, on bracket feet.

30.5in (76cm) wide

£1,800-2,200   **SW**

A George III painted and satinwood bureau, with ribbon-tied foliate swags and scrolling foliage, the fall front centred by an oval panel depicting a classical female with two cherubs, opening to reveal a fitted interior with pigeonholes, drawers, a central cupboard door and inset leather writing surface, over two short and three long graduated drawers, raised on bracket feet.

c1800   *42.5in (106cm) high*

£5,000-7,000   **FRE**

A George III oak bureau, the slope front opening to reveal a pigeonholed interior, over four graduated long drawers, on shaped bracket feet.

33.5in (83.5cm) wide

£500-700   **SWO**

An 18thC North Italian walnut and sycamore marquetry bureau, of small size, the banded and quarter-veneered sloping fall enclosing fitted interior with three small central drawers, two long drawers below, on cabriole legs.

32.25in (82cm) wide

£1,200-1,800   **H&**

A mid-18thC French Provincial Louis XV walnut bureau, the panelled fall centred by a marquetry medallion, with a stepped interior and covered well, below is one central frieze drawer flanked by two cupboard doors, on square cabriole legs.

35in (87.5cm) wide

£4,000-6,000   **FR**

250

A CLOSER LOOK AT A NAPOLEON II BUREAU MAZARIN

Louis XV tulipwood and kingwood bureau, the shaped fall enclosing a stepped fitted interior inset with a writing surface, two frieze drawers and one long ogee-moulded drawer, raised on square cabriole legs, stamped "R. onssell J M E".

1760   38in (95cm) wide

7,000-10,000   **FRE**

The bureau Mazarin was made from the late 17thC through to the early 18thC and experienced a revival in the 19thC. Bureau Mazarins are usually supported on legs joined by double X-shaped stretchers to allow for leg room.

The quality of this bureau is evident from the exquisite boullework, with brass and pewter inlay, and popular classical motifs such as carytids, exotic birds and foliate scrolls, which were typical of the era.

This piece is a 19thC copy, but unlike most of these revival pieces it has a boullework top (a type of marquetry) rather than the more common leather inset top. The best copies show a good understanding of the originals and command a premium.

Examine the boullework as the brass should be engraved – if it is not it may have been rubbed off through wear. Beware of damage because this will be extremely expensive to repair and has a negative impact on its value.

late 18thC Dutch mahogany and floral marquetry cylinder fronted bombé bureau, with foliage decoration, the fall with a sliding pull-out writing surface inset with a panel of tooled leather, shaped and fitted interior, three long drawers below, on splayed bracket feet.

48in (122cm) wide

4,000-6,000   **H&L**

A 19thC Napoleon II bureau mazarin, inlaid in brass and pewter with figures, carytids, exotic birds and foliate scrolls, with one central frieze drawer and recessed fall front cupboard with six further drawers, flanked and divided by outset scroll corners, raised on four square tapered legs joined by wavy stretchers and ending in toupie feet.

54in (135cm) wide

£15,000-20,000   **FRE**

BONHEUR DU JOUR

A George III satinwood bonheur du jour in the Sheraton manner, with tulipwood crossbanding and box and ebony stringing, two open shelves above three small drawers, foldover green baize lined writing surface above single frieze drawer, on slender tapering legs and brass cappings and casters, later baize and metalware.

40in (100cm) high

£15,000-20,000   **CATO**

A rare George III black and gilt floral painted bonheur du jour, with a wavy top above a shelved space enclosed within interlaced pierced oval metal grilles, frieze drawer below, on square tapering legs and spade feet.

46.5in (116cm) high

£5,000-7,000   **CATO**

FURNITURE

A 19thC Louis XV-style rosewood bonheur de jour, with a brass gallery, inlaid decoration and a fitted interior with well.

56in (140cm) high

£1,200-1,800   **SWO**

A late 19thC French kingwood bonheur du jour with gilt-metal mounts, the top with two glazed doors and two drawers, the serpentine base with a velvet-lined writing surface, on cabriole legs.

48.5in (123cm) high

£1,200-1,800   **DN**

A late 19thC quarter-veneered kingwood and tulipwood bonheur de jour, with gilt-brass mounts, the pagoda top with a gallery above doors centred by Sèvres-style panels, raised on serpentine base with frieze drawer enclosing a writing slide, on square section tapered cabriole legs with scrolled sabots, stamped "Tahana, Paris".

31.5in (80cm) wid

£3,000-5,000   **L&**

CYLINDER DESKS

A George III mahogany roll-top desk, with a tambour front enclosing a fitted interior with sliding writing surface, above two short drawers, on square tapering legs joined by stretchers, with brass caps and casters.

40.5in (101cm) wide

£3,000-4,000   **L&T**

A George III mahogany roll-top desk, the tambour top opening to reveal a fitted interior with candle slides, drawers, pigeonholes and a leather writing surface, two frieze drawers, raised on square tapered legs terminating in brass cappings and casters.

c1790   *37in (92.5cm) wide*

£3,000-5,000   **FRE**

A George IV mahogany twin pedestal roll-top desk, the three-quarter galleried reeded top above solid ebony-strung roll front enclosing a fitted interior with sliding writing surface, above a frieze drawer and kneehole flanked by two columns of four graduated drawers, on bracket feet, stamped "T Willson 68 Great Queen Street London".

Thomas Willson is entered in directories as a furniture broker and appraiser at 68 Great Queen Street between 1821 and 1829. He was also a cabinet maker from 1818 The business was continued by his widow Mary from 1830 and his son Matthew from 1838, when the stamp 'M Willson' was used.

54in (135cm) wid

A George III mahogany roll-top desk, the tambour fall, opening to reveal a ratchet adjustable inset leather brushing slide, small drawer and pigeonholes, below are two frieze drawers, raised on square tapered legs, ending in brass cappings and casters.

c1790   *36.5in (91cm) wide*

£3,000-4,000   **FRE**

£6,000-9,000   **L&**

A Victorian mahogany cylinder desk, the three-quartered gallery top above a fall-front, enclosing a fitted interior and brushing slide with pigeonholes, drawers, inkwells, and a leather inset writing surface, each pedestal with four graduated drawers and moulded plinth bases, stamped "maple and co."

c1860   60in (150cm) wide

£4,000-6,000   FRE

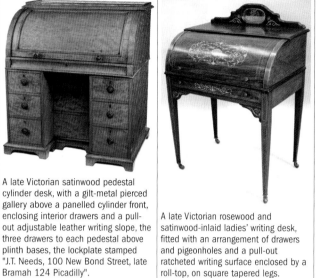

A late Victorian satinwood pedestal cylinder desk, with a gilt-metal pierced gallery above a panelled cylinder front, enclosing interior drawers and a pull-out adjustable leather writing slope, the three drawers to each pedestal above plinth bases, the lockplate stamped "J.T. Needs, 100 New Bond Street, late Bramah 124 Picadilly".

45in (114.5cm) high

£1,800-2,200   DN

A late Victorian rosewood and satinwood-inlaid ladies' writing desk, fitted with an arrangement of drawers and pigeonholes and a pull-out ratcheted writing surface enclosed by a roll-top, on square tapered legs.

£500-700   SWO

An Edwardian rosewood cylinder bureau, with boxwood stringing and floral marquetry, the ledge back with an hexagonal panel, above an interior with a sliding writing surface and drawers, on square section tapering legs.

43.5in (109cm) high

£800-1,200   L&T

A mahogany and brass-inlaid Directoire cylinder bureau, with gilt-bronze mounts, the marble top over three frieze drawers and a cylinder fall, the fitted interior with drawers and a central shelf and a pigeonhole, the lower section with three long drawers, and fluted pilasters, on a shaped plinth base.

c1800   51in (127.5cm) wide

£7,000-10,000   FRE

A Dutch mahogany marquetry bombé cylinder bureau, inlaid with scrolling foliage, urns and exotic birds, the brushing slide and rising fall opening to reveal a serpentine fitted interior with pigeonholes, drawers and a secret compartment, over three further long drawers, on outswept feet.

c1800   47.5in (119cm) wide

£4,000-6,000   FRE

A Louis XV gilt-bronze-mounted bureau à cylindre, in kingwood, tulipwood and rosewood, with a three-quarter pierced galleried top above a cylinder fall enclosing a fitted interior with an inset leather brushing slide, over three shaped frieze drawers, on square cabriole legs ending in sabots, some later mounts.

c1760   32in (80cm) wide

£10,000-15,000   FRE

FURNITURE

A 19thC Dutch burr satin walnut bureau à cylinder, with boxwood and ebony stringing, the top above counter-balanced cylinder fall with a slide, enclosing a fitted interior above two long drawers, on square section tapering legs.

41.25in (103cm) wide

£1,200-1,800 **L&T**

A late 19thC French walnut and parquetry cylinder bureau, the marble top with a pierced brass gallery over three drawers, the cylinder enclosing a fitted interior, over a pull-out writing surface, five frieze drawers and shaped tapering legs, all with ornate gilt bronze mounts.

51in (130cm) wide

£4,000-6,000 **SWO**

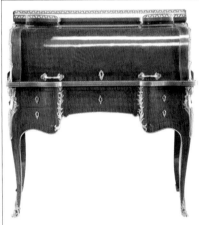

A late 19thC Louis XV-style mahogany parquetry bureau à cylindre, in the manner of Francois Linke, with a breakfront marble top, gallery and a fitted interior with leather-lined writing slide, over four frieze drawers with rocaille-cast handles, on cabriole legs headed by gilt-bronze ram mask heads, terminating in scrolled sabots.

40in (100cm) wide

£8,000-12,000 **FRE**

DAVENPORTS

A Regency mahogany Davenport, with a brass gallery above a pen drawer and sloping hinged fall with inset writing surface, the interior fitted with drawers and pigeonholes, over four drawers, opposed by dummy drawers, on divided bun feet with casters.

34.75in (87cm) high

£1,200-1,800 **L&T**

A Victorian burr walnut veneer harlequin piano-top Davenport, with pierced front frets, three small drawers, and a curved hinged fall enclosing a sliding tooled leather-inset writing surface, the side with four maple veneer drawers, on a plinth base with casters.

23.25in (59cm) wide

£2,200-2,800 **H&L**

A CLOSER LOOK AT A POLLARD OAK VENEER DAVENPORT

The Davenport is a small writing desk, usually with real and dummy drawers to the sides. Davenports made between c1800 and 1820 are usually narrow and compact, such as this British pollard oak example with its sloping desktop. The Davenport broadened in width from the 1830s.

This piece has cedarwood drawer linings, which adds value. Good-quality Davenports are always well finished on all sides, including the inside.

This example is linked with the best-known furniture maker of the 18thC and early 19thC, Gillows of Lancaster, and therefore commands a premium. Gillows of Lancaster made and, perhaps, invented this sort of desk, which was named after its customer Captain Davenport.

Due to the Davenports free-standing nature, they should be well veneered and are often fitted with casters. The top section slides forward to accommodate the writer's legs and is anchored by simple iron rods that slide into holes. The finest examples have ingeniously concealed hinged drawers.

A pollard oak veneer Davenport, with cedarwood drawer linings, possibly by Gillows of Lancaster.

c1800

£12,000-14,000

CATO

PEDESTAL DESKS

A George III mahogany kneehole desk, the rectangular moulded top above two columns of three graduated drawers enclosing kneehole with single cupboard door, the whole raised on bracket feet.

37.5in (94cm) wide

£3,000-4,000

L&T

A Swedish Late Gustavian painted kneehole desk, the overhanging rectangular top above three fluted frieze drawers and three short drawers to each side, raised on block feet.

c1815

51.5in (129cm) wide

£3,000-4,000

EVE

A Victorian burl walnut kneehole desk, the moulded top with an inset tooled green leather writing surface over three frieze drawers, each pedestal with three further drawers, raised on plinth bases and ceramic casters.

41in (102.5cm) wide

£1,800-2,200

FRE

255

FURNITURE

A George IV rosewood pedestal library desk, the moulded top over an arrangement of eight drawers and a central frieze drawer, with blind Gothic tracery to the canted corners, an open bookcase to each end.

£8,000-12,000   SWO

An Edwardian satinwood pedestal desk, with tulipwood banding and ebony stringing, the top with inset gilt tooled skiver, above three frieze drawers to two sides and writing slides to each end, raised on pedestals with three drawers and opposing false-fronted cupboards.

£2,800-3,200   L&T

An early 20thC directoire-style mahogany and gilt-metal pedestal desk, with an inset leather writing surface, above three drawers, each pedestal with three further drawers, raised on plinth bases and turned bun feet.

57in (142.5cm) wide

£3,000-4,000   FRE

A Victorian mahogany pedestal desk, the inset red leather writing surface over nine drawers.

55.25in (138cm) wide

£1,800-2,200   SWO

A George III mahogany partner's desk, the top with a reeded edge and later inset writing surface, the frieze with twelve alternate dummy and real drawers, raised on acanthus-carved cabriole legs ending in trefoil feet.

60in (150cm) wide

£3,000-4,000   FRE

A George III mahogany architect's desk, the moulded top with an easel action, above a secretaire frieze drawer with inset baize and pigeonhole interior, raised on three long graduating drawers flanked by blind fretwork panels, on bracket feet.

37.75in (96cm) wide

£6,000-9,000   B

A Regency mahogany Carlton House desk, the flat rectangular stage with a pierced brass gallery and drawers to front and centre, framing a central writing slope, above three frieze drawers and reeded and ring turned tapering legs, with brass caps and casters.

56in (140cm) wide

£15,000-20,000   L&T

A 19thC English mahogany folding writing desk, constructed as a games table, a swing-leg supporting one leaf, the other leaf with a rising leather writing surface and three dovetailed drawers with brass clips and hinges, on tapered legs with moulded feet and brass casters.

38in (95cm) wide

| £2,000-2,500 | BRU |

A late Victorian mahogany writing desk, with a brass pierced three-quarter gallery and seven short drawers with blind fret-carved decoration, on carved cluster legs, stamped "Edwards and Roberts".

| £800-1,200 | SWO |

A massive Edwardian oak partner's desk, with a green gilt tooled leather top and rounded angles, above frieze drawers and kneeholes to each side, flanked by drawers and cupboards, on plinth base.

106.5in (266cm) wide

| £3,000-4,000 | L&T |

An Italian walnut, ivory and inlaid desk, by Ferdinand Pogliani, the raised back with two small drawers, above a hinged top centred by a panel depicting four figures and a flaming urn, baize writing surface and one frieze drawer, raised on spiral-turned legs, stamped "Ferd Pogliani E Banista Milano".

c1880   *37in (92.5cm) high*

| £1,200-1,800 | FRE |

WRITING TABLES

A Regency rosewood library table, with a tooled inset skiver, the three frieze drawers opposed by dummy drawers, on belt-waisted supports with gilt-decorated milled panels in the manner of John Maclean, later brass feet and pot casters.

c1825   *60in (152.5cm) wide*

| £15,000-20,000 | CATO |

A Milanese mid-19thC ebony penwork and ivory-inlaid library table, the top with intricate floral inlay, over four frieze drawers, on fluted turned tapering legs.

35in (89cm) wide

| £20,000-25,000 | CATO |

FURNITURE

A Regency mahogany and rosewood crossbanded library table, in the manner of Gillows of Lancaster, with two drawers opposed by dummy drawers, above dual spindle-filled ends, brass cappings and casters.

42in (105cm) wide

£25,000-30,000   **CATO**

A Regency rosewood library table, with an inset writing surface above two frieze drawers opposing dummy drawers, raised on spindle-filled supports with sabre legs, united by a stretcher, terminating in brass caps and casters.

49in (124cm) wide

£2,800-3,200   **L&T**

A late Regency rosewood and brass-inlaid library table, the top inlaid with a band of foliage, above two frieze drawers on tapering supports, raised on sabre legs with applied cast rosettes and terminating in leaf cast caps and casters.

39.5in (99cm) wide

£2,200-2,800   **L&T**

A Victorian mahogany library table, with a leather inset top and two frieze drawers, on turned tapering legs and brass caps and casters.

48in (120cm) wide

£500-700   **SWO**

A Victorian Aesthetic walnut and burl walnut library table, possibly Philadelphia, with an inset writing surface over one frieze drawer, raised on twin open-end supports united by a turned stretcher and ending in scroll feet.

c1880   *47in (117.5cm) wide*

£2,000-3,000   **FRE**

A mahogany library table, with a gilt tooled leather skiver, above a panelled frieze with two drawers to each side, on tapering moulded legs with scrolled and carved brackets, block feet with brass caps and casters, lacking one drawer.

59.75 (152cm) wide

£800-1,200   **L&T**

A mahogany Chippendale-style writing table, with a blind fret frieze and drawers to each end, on square section tapered chamfered legs with tassel feet.

48in (122cm) wide

£800-1,200   **L&T**

An 18thC Continental writing table, with marquetry decoration of a banded panel, trees and baskets of fruit, secret drawer, on cabriole legs and hoof feet.

33.75in (86cm) wide

£700-1,000   **L&T**

A Directoire-style brass-inlaid mahogany writing table, the top with an urn of flowers in a cartouche, above a single frieze drawer and turned and fluted legs, joined by a stretcher with a central tablet, on toupie feet.

44in (110cm) wide

£1,200-1,800   **L&T**

An Italian writing table, probably late 18thC and from the Duchy of Parma, with an ornate burlwood inlay, four side drawers with hand-wrought nails and original brass pulls, pencil inscription in one drawer "Carolina Lorenzetti", old paper label to base "Camera Della Franducclessa(?)".

42.5in (17cm) wide

£2,200-2,800   **BRU**

A Regency mahogany writing table, inset with a tooled leather writing surface, above three opposing drawers, one with fitted interior, the whole raised on turned and reeded tapering legs.

54in (137cm) wide

£2,200-2,800   **L&T**

A George IV mahogany writing table, the leather-inset top above two frieze drawers, on bold reeded legs and original brass cappings and casters.

48in (122cm) wide

£4,000-6,000   **CATO**

A William IV mahogany writing table, with a moulded top over two frieze drawers, raised on turned and gadrooned legs, brass caps and casters.

52.5in (131cm) wide

£1,500-2,000   **SWO**

A 19thC mahogany writing table, the three frieze drawers with panelled brackets, on ring turned tapering legs.

36.5in (91cm) wide

£400-600   **L&T**

A Gothic Revival mahogany and ebonised writing desk, the inlaid top with inset rounded angles above a twin panel frieze drawer, on four turned and blocked legs joined by pierced H-stretcher, brass casters, stamped "Johnston and Jennings".

54.75in (137cm) wide

£1,500-2,000   **L&T**

A mid-19thC satin birch writing table, in the manner of Gillows of Lancaster, with an inset writing surface, ebony stringing and a frieze drawer, on cabriole legs.

44.5in (113cm) wide

£1,500-2,000   **L&T**

A 19thC Louis XVI-style mahogany and gilt-bronze-mounted writing table, with an inset leather writing surface, three frieze drawers, on turned fluted tapered legs.

17.25in (43in) wide

£2,000-3,000   **FRE**

A mid-Victorian walnut and marquetry inlaid kidney-shaped writing table, the top with moulded and crossbanded edge inlaid with sprays of flowers and enclosing a tooled leather writing surface, on cabriole legs with gilt-metal Rococo mounts.

49in (114cm) wide

£1,500-2,000   **L&T**

A Regency-style tortoiseshell and boulle work bureau plat, the top with cast brass mounts and gilt tooled leather lining above a frieze drawer and opposing dummy, on square section cabriole legs with cabochon mounts and sabots.

52.5in (131cm) wide

£800-1,200   **L&T**

A Louis XVI-style kingwood walnut and gilt-brass-mounted bureau plat, the top with leather inset writing surface, above five drawers and a kneehole, on turned fluted tapering legs with gilt-brass sabots.

68in (170cm) wide

£2,200-2,800   **L&T**

A 19thC kingwood crossbanded and gilt-bronze-mounted bureau plat, by Paul Sormani, the serpentine quarter-veneered top with a rockwork and shell-cast edge.

69.5in (174cm) wide

£15,000-20,000   **FRE**

A late 19thC Louis XV-style parquetry bureau plat, in kingwood and rosewood, the top with flowers and a marquetry courting couple panel, one drawer, on square cabriole legs and sabots, "Forest, Paris" label.

39in (97.5cm) wide

£4,000-6,000   **FRE**

FURNITURE

An early Victorian rosewood dwarf folio stand, the two fixed splayed folio supports with scrolling brackets, above a base with two pierced sides and open ends, on a plinth with scroll feet and sunken casters.

28in (70cm) high

£2,200-2,800   **L&T**

A pair of satinwood Biedermeier-style torchère stands, with octagonal columns and ebonised moulding.

46.5in (116cm) high

£800-1,200   **SW**

A near pair of 19thC Dutch mahogany ice buckets or jardinières, with slatted, tapered sides raised on triform bases and bun feet.

16in (40cm) high

£1,500-2,000   **FRE**

A pair of French Empire-style burl walnut, veneered and gilt-metal jardinières, raised on Egyptian Revival gilt-metal-mounted legs.

22.5in (56cm) high

£1,200-1,800   **FRE**

A George III mahogany basin stand, the divided hinged caddy top enclosing apertures for basin and cups, over an undershelf with single drawer, on square section tapering legs joined by a shaped X-stretcher.

32.75in (82cm) high

£300-500 **L&T**

A 19thC mahogany canteen on stand, with ebony stringing, the top with fitted drawers and crossbanded doors, on splayed bracket feet resting on stand with a frieze drawer and square section tapered legs, fitted with cutlery by the Eagle Plate Company, Sheffield.

48in (120cm) high

£1,200-1,800 **L&T**

A George III mahogany kettle stand, the serpentine gadrooned top above frieze with slide to the front, on channelled and moulded chamfered square legs with acanthus carved spandrels.

13.25in (33cm) wide

£3,000-4,000 **L&T**

A Regency mahogany teapoy, with ebony and boxwood stringing and satinwood banding, the hinged lid with canted angles enclosing interior, raised on turned and spirally reeded pedestal with gadrooned foot, the base with gilt-brass ball and claw feet.

12in (30cm) wide

£800-1,200 **L&T**

A mid-19thC English adjustable walnut candle stand, with a six-sided pedestal above three heavily carved tapered square legs with lions' head, iron adjusting mechanism.

31in (77.5cm) high

£400-600 **BRU**

A 19thC octagonal burlwood candle stand, probably Italian, the top with inlaid frieze, on four tapered legs with pad feet and shaped returns, lacking original slide-out tray for candle.

25.5in (64cm) high

£1,200-1,800 **BRU**

A Victorian walnut folio stand, the hinged open sides locked by brass fittings with leaf castings, the whole raised on a baluster 'jewelled' column, on four scroll supports terminating in scroll feet.

40in (100cm) wide

£3,000-4,000 **L&T**

A late Victorian Sheraton Revival satinwood and chequer-strung pedestal, of square tapering form with a stepped plinth and shaped apron, painted with floral and garrya motifs.

44.75in (112cm) high

£500-700 **DN**

An early 19thC overpainted wood grotto stand, carved with a clam shell held by three caryatids, their tails wreathed with foliage, extending to three outswept legs linked by a lower tier.

29in (74cm) wide

£3,000-4,000 **L&T**

A Dutch 19thC mahogany jardinière, with floral marquetry decoration, pierced leaf supports, lift-out liner and hinged handle, on a turned foot and circular base with ball feet.

13.75in (35cm) diam

£800-1,200 **L&T**

261

FURNITURE

A George II mahogany two-tier dumb waiter, with moulded octagonal tiers, on cannon turned columns and octagonal base with cabriole legs, adapted.

29.25in (73cm) high

£600-900   **L&T**

A George III mahogany three-tier dumb waiter, the graduated shelves of dished form, with baluster columns, cabriole legs and pad feet with casters.

40.5in (101cm) high

£400-600   **DN**

An early 19thC gilt-brass and mahogany dwarf whatnot, with turned supports and brass edging, acorn finials and casters.

28.5in (71cm) deep

£2,800-3,200   **L&T**

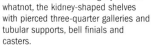

A 19thC brass and mahogany two-tier whatnot, the kidney-shaped shelves with pierced three-quarter galleries and tubular supports, bell finials and casters.

30in (75cm) high

£600-900   **L&T**

A Victorian rosewood whatnot, with a fret cut gallery, on turned supports and a base drawer.

£800-1,200   **SWO**

An early Victorian mahogany three-tier whatnot, on roundel and lotus carved supports, brass cappings and casters.

30in (75cm) high

£5,000-7,000   **CATO**

A Victorian rosewood whatnot, with a pierced fretwork gallery and raised on turned circular supports above a single drawer, on brass casters.

37in (94cm) high

£1,500-2,000   **B**

A Victorian mahogany whatnot, the four serpentine-fronted shelves on turned supports, the lower shelf with a drawer.

27.5in (69cm) wide

£500-700   **SWO**

A Victorian walnut four-tier whatnot, with pierced fret-cut gallery and spiral twist supports.

46.75in (117cm) high

£300-500   **SWO**

ÉTAGÈRES

A late 19thC rosewood and marquetry inlaid étagère, in the French mid-18thC manner, the kidney shaped top with pierced gilt-metal gallery, the crossbanded top with floral marquetry inlay above a single inlaid drawer, on cabriole legs with gilt-metal cast mounts.

27.25in (69cm) wide

£1,500-2,000   **L&T**

A pair of mahogany and gilt-metal mounted étagères, each with three tiers with bamboo-cast mouldings, supported by cast faux bamboo uprights, terminating in outswept feet.

24.75in (93cm) wide

£2,000-3,000   **L&T**

A George III mahogany Canterbury, with an unusual six section top, above two cedar-lined drawers, brass cappings and casters.

26.5in (66cm) wide

£5,000-7,000   **CATO**

A Victorian rosewood Canterbury or whatnot, with serpentine front, with pierced three-quarter gallery and trestle support, above Canterbury with spiral-turned outer supports and single drawer, on turned feet, brass caps and castors.

24in (61cm) wide

£1,200-1,800   **L&T**

A William IV rosewood Canterbury, the X-shaped superstructure with three divisions, above a single frieze drawer, on lotus-carved turned supports with brass casters.

19.75in (50cm) wide

£800-1,200   **B**

An early 19thC mahogany Canterbury, with downswept dividers, pierced handle and two shallow drawers, on ring turned feet with brass caps and casters.

20.5in (51cm) wide

£1,200-1,800   **L&T**

A Victorian walnut Canterbury, with four fret-cut divisions over a drawer, on turned legs.

£600-900   **SWO**

A 19thC French rosewood Canterbury, with five fret-carved divisions.

18in (45cm) wide

£500-700   **SWO**

FURNITURE

A George III mahogany cellaret, with a crossbanded hinged top and astragal moulded edge, enclosing a lead-lined divided interior, raised on chamfered square section legs joined by turned and blocked H-stretcher.

17.25in (44cm) wide

£1,200-1,800   **L&T**

A Scottish George III octagonal mahogany cellaret, with brass banding, the hinged lid with satinwood band, lead-lined interior, on stand with fluted frieze and square section tapered legs, with brass caps and casters.

18in (46cm) wide

£1,800-2,200   **L&T**

A late George III mahogany and brass-bound octagonal cellaret, the lid hinged to enclose a lead-lined interior, on a later base.

26.5in (66cm) high

£800-1,200   **DN**

A George III mahogany cabinet cellaret, with boxwood and ebony stringing, the domed lid enclosing a divided interior, above two cupboard doors, on splayed bracket feet.

23.5in (59cm) wide

£1,200-1,800   **L&T**

A George III mahogany and brass-bound cellaret, the hinged top with marquetry inlay depicting an urn and demilune line inlay to the border, on square tapering legs with brass caps and casters.

29.5in (74cm) wide

£2,800-3,200   **L&T**

A George III mahogany and brass-bound wine cooler of oval shape, with a hinged lid, lead-lined interior and brass carrying handles, on square tapered legs, terminating in brass casters.

£3,200-3,800   **SWO**

A CLOSER LOOK AT A PAIR OF GEORGE III WINE COOLERS

This tapering box style is typical of the mid- to late 18thC wine cooler. Rectangular pieces found favour from the beginning of the 19thC, with the sarcophagus form becoming common from the late Regency onwards.

This piece has retained some of its original lead lining, which considerably increases the value.

The bold lion heads seen here are typical of Regency design. The lion mask, with a ring in its mouth for a handle, derives from ancient Roman furniture. The motif enjoyed a revival from the early to mid-18thC.

Mahogany or walnut wine coolers from this era, especially pairs, are highly desirable to collectors.

A pair of George III or Regency mahogany wine coolers, each of octagonal form with a lead-lined interior and modern brass liner, bold lion head handles to the sides, on a finely reeded tripod base with brass cappings and casters.

27.5in (69cm) high

£20,000-30,000   **CATO**

A Regency mahogany cellaret, the hinged top enclosing divided interior, on rope turned plinth and ring turned legs with brass caps and casters.

27.25in (68cm) high

£1,500-2,000   **L&T**

A Regency mahogany and bronze-mounted cellaret, of sarcophagus form, with a fitted interior, the sloping sides with cast foliate beading and anthemion motifs to the angles, on turned and gadrooned feet with brass caps and casters.

29in (74cm) wide

£5,000-6,000   **L&T**

A Regency mahogany cellaret, the moulded and reeded top with canted corners, above a line-inlaid and crossbanded front with a central gadrooned boss, on hairy paw feet with brass casters.

22.75in (57cm) wide

£2,000-3,000   **L&T**

An early 19thC George III mahogany sarcophagus cellaret, with a pyramidal hinged top, lead-lined interior and a tapering body, on later bun feet.

The tapering wine cellaret with pyramidal lid evolved from a 'sarcophagus' pattern in Thomas Sheraton's 'The Cabinet Dictionary', London, 1803.

34.5in (86cm) wide

£1,200-1,800   **FRE**

A William IV mahogany sarcophagus cellaret, with a raised top above a cavetto moulded border, scroll moulded corner brackets with palmette incised carving, on four lion paw feet.

29in (74cm) wide

£4,000-6,000   **WW**

A George IV mahogany wine cooler, with an everted rim and lead lining, the plinth base with a nulled border, gilt-metal side handles and recessed casters.

29.25in (73cm) wide

£2,800-3,200   **DN**

A Victorian mahogany sarcophagus cellaret, the pyramidal hinged lid enclosing a baize-lined interior above panelled sides, on a moulded plinth base with sunken casters.

30.5in (76cm) wide

£2,000-3,000   **L&T**

A Victorian sarcophagus mahogany cellaret, the domed hinged top with a band of beaded decoration above tapering sides, standing on turned feet.

29in (74cm) wide

£600-900   **ROW**

An Edwardian mahogany cellaret on stand, with chequer stringing and fan medallions, the hinged top inlaid with musical trophy, enclosing divided interior later lined for sewing, the legs inlaid with ribbon tied husk drops.

26.5in (66cm) high

£800-1,200   **L&T**

An octagonal mahogany cellaret, the satinwood crossbanded hinged lid with an inlaid rosette, over a lead-lined interior and brass bound sides with carry handles, on splayed square section tapering legs with brass caps and casters.

28in (70cm) high

£2,200-2,800   **L&T**

An English mahogany spirits cabinet, the panel lift top above an interior compartment, above a dovetailed drawer with wood pulls, on compressed turned bun feet, secondary woods pine and ash.

31in (77.5cm) wide

£400-600   **BRU**

A mahogany and brass-bound oval jardinière, with lion mask handles and a metal liner, on a stand with cabriole legs and pad feet.

27.25in (68cm) wide

£1,200-1,800   **DN**

FURNITURE

A 19thC Louis XVI-style kingwood and parquetry bed, attributed to Francois Linke, with a gilt bronze wreath and an oval jasperware panel, the geometric veneered ends raised on turned legs ending in toupie feet.

61in (152.5cm) high

£2,000-3,000 FRE

A Whytock and Reid elmwood double headboard and footboard, of arched form with shallow leaf carved decoration and moulded panelling, enclosed by carved panelled angles.

60.75in (152cm) wide

£600-900 L&T

Part of a 1920s mahogany bedroom suite, comprising a wardrobe, with a central mirrored door enclosing twin panelled doors, a dressing chest with ogee arched frame, a chest of drawers, a pot cupboard, and two double bed ends to match.

Part of an Edwardian mahogany chequer-strung bedroom suite, by A. Gardner & Son, Glasgow, comprising a dressing table with an arrangement of five drawers and a washstand with a dentilled ledge back above a pair of panelled doors, a wardrobe with a pair of doors, four short graduated drawers and a full-length mirror.

88in (220cm) high

£1,200-1,800 set L&T   **£2,200-2,800 set**   L&T

BUCKETS

A George III mahogany and brass-bound peat bucket, of elliptical form, with a dished rim and brass carrying handle, above staved sides held by four straps.

13.75in (34cm) high

£800-1,200 L&T

A late 18th to early 19thC oak and brass-bound plate bucket, with a swing handle above a staved tapering body.

36in (90cm) diam

£3,200-3,800 CATO

An early 19thC brass bound mahogany bucket, the tapering cylindrical sides with two brass bands and a handle, the interior with metal liner.

10in (25cm) diam

£600-800 CHEF

An Edwardian mahogany coal bin, of tapering form, with lion's head carrying handles.

£200-300 SWO

TRAYS

A rosewood inlaid tray.

c1840   4in (10cm) wide
£80-120   MB

A 19thC black papier mâché tray, by Jennens and Bettridge, painted with a central bouquet of coloured flowers within mother-of-pearl borders, impressed mark to reverse.

33.25in (83cm) wide
£300-400   SWO

A black lacquer papier-mâché tray, painted with a stable interior with two horses, within a gilt running-leaf border, stamped trademark "TH".

16.5in (42cm) wide
£500-700   HAMG

A papier mâché tray, painted with a hunting scene.

26.5in (66cm) wide
£800-1,200   SWO

267

FURNITURE

A Flemish oak book press, with ebony-veneered frieze and finial surmounts and a moulded rectangular press, raised on leaf-carved cup-and-cover supports linked by stretchers, the drawer inscribed "Anno 1630".

1630   *31in (79cm) wide*

£3,000-4,000   **L&T**

An 18thC French oak dough bin, with a hinged top above a tapering body, on turned and linked legs joined by chamfered H-stretcher, adapted as a jardinière with fitted tin liner.

37.5in (94cm) wide

£1,200-1,800   **L&T**

A set of Regency mahogany library steps, with two carpeted steps, on turned tapering legs and toupie feet.

16.5in (41cm) wide

£800-1,200   **L&T**

A Regency rosewood table-top book tray, with beaded moulding, a baluster column H-shaped gallery and a frieze drawer, the handles damaged.

18in (45cm) wide

£1,200-1,800   **L&T**

A 19thC English walnut burlwood bracket, the top with rectangular well and brass hangers, with tag "From the Estate of Jim Jefferson".

15in (37.5cm) wide

£200-400   **BRU**

A 19thC mahogany cheval towel rail, with two hinged sections, a plinth base and down scrolled feet.

40.75in (102cm) high

£300-400   **L&T**

A set of Victorian oak and ash library steps, with a ring turned support above three leather-inset steps.

58.5in (146cm) high

£1,800-2,200   **CATO**

A Victorian double dome top birdcage, with a single opening, lacking lock and two base trays.

35.5in (88.5cm) wide

£220-280   **SWO**

An Edwardian mahogany strung and crossbanded drinks trolley, the hinged top opening to reveal a lift-up section with a detachable tray, labelled "Chapman, Son & Co, London E C".

22.75in (57cm) wide

£1,200-1,800   **SWO**

A mahogany terrarium, with turned wood and brass rod supports, a pagoda top with urn finial, the base with tapered and fluted legs and copper liner, damage and wear.

72in (180cm) high

£1,200-1,800   **BRU**

268

An 18thC Italian miniature walnut and crossbanded commode, with three drawers, on squat bun feet.

14.5in (36cm) wide

£2,000-3,000   **FRE**

A 19thC miniature burr yew and parquetry crossbanded chest of drawers, fitted with two short and two long drawers, with turned ivory handles, one handle missing.

9.5in (24cm) high

£600-900   **ROS**

A miniature inlaid mahogany dining table.
c1830   *12in (30.5cm) diam*

£500-700   **MB**

A 19thC German Baroque-style miniature inlaid commode, in walnut and fruitwood, with three moulded drawers, on four splayed feet.

14.75in (37cm) wide

£400-600   **KAU**

A pair of 19thC miniature yew wood stools, each with four turned legs.

5in (12.5cm) high

£200-300 pair   **CA**

19thC Dutch miniature walnut china cabinet, with a pair of astragal glazed doors enclosing shaped shelves, on a bombé base with three long drawers, on carved claw feet.

40in (100cm) high

£600-900   **WW**

A Scottish miniature stained pine chest of drawers, with an ogee moulded frieze drawer and four further drawers flanked by carved brackets, on a plinth and turned legs, labelled "These drawers were bought at the Franchise Demonstration which took place at Falkirk on 27th September 1884", inscribed.

15.5in (39.5cm) wide

£1,800-2,200   **L&T**

A late Victorian miniature oak linen press, with a pair of panelled cupboard doors enclosing three slide-out trays, the base fitted with two short and two long drawers with brass drop handles, on a stepped plinth and shaped bracket feet.

26.5in (67cm) high

£700-1,000   **B**

A Victorian miniature mahogany chest, with two short and three long graduated drawers and turned bone handles, on a plinth base.

6in (15cm) high

£400-600   **B**

FURNITURE

A late 17thC yellowwood kist, from the Cape of Good Hope.

c1705   62.5in (156cm) wide

£4,000-5,000   **PRA**

A 19thC yellowwood wagon kist, from the Western Cape.

32.75in (82cm) wide

£1,800-2,200   **PRA**

A late 18thC stinkwood and satinwood cabinet, from the Cape of Good Hope, with two doors to the top section and four drawers below.

Known colloquially as armoires, these cabinets were essentially Baroque in construction and form throughout the 18thC. Only the decorative overlay – such as the key blocks, plates and drawer pulls – tended to reflect stylistic changes.

c1785   112in (280cm) high

£25,000-30,000   **PRA**

A late 18thC unusual corner cabinets, from the Cape of Good Hope, in five exotic timbers, including satinwood, partridge wood, ebony, teak and amboyna, the shelf in indigenous yellowwood.

c1790   48in (120cm) wide

£18,000-22,000   **PRA**

An early 19thC stinkwood and yellowwood cupboard, Eastern Cape.

c1825   67.5in (169cm) high

£5,000-6,000   **PRA**

A 19thC amboyna, stinkwood and satinwood low cabinet, from the Cape of Good Hope.

42in (105cm) wide

£7,000-9,000   **PRA**

An early 19thC stinkwood and yellowwood cupboard, South Eastern Cape (Langkloof).

c1810   65.25in (163cm) high

£8,000-12,000   **PRA**

A late 18thC stinkwood and yellowwood corner chair, in the manner of Chippendale, Cape of Good Hope.

c1790   33.25in (83cm) high

£3,000-4,000   **PRA**

A late 18thC stinkwood armchair, from the Western Cape.

c1795   38in (95cm) high

£3,000-4,000   **PRA**

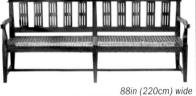

A late 18thC stinkwood settee, Western Cape.

c1795   88in (220cm) wide

£7,000-10,000   **PRA**

An early 19thC stinkwood and bone settee, South Western Cape.

c1815   82.75in (207cm) wide

£4,000-6,000   **PRA**

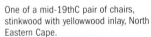

One of a mid-19thC pair of chairs, stinkwood with yellowwood inlay, North Eastern Cape.

c1835   33.5in (84cm) high

£3,000-4,000 pair   **PRA**

A mid-19thC teak and Oregon pine settee, South Western Cape (Elim).

c1865

72in (180cm) wide

£1,800-2,200   PRA

A mid-19thC Transvaal teak corner chair.

c1870

32.5in (81.5cm) high

£700-1,000   PRA

A late 18thC teak tea table, Cape of Good Hope.

c1775

28.5in (71cm) high

£5,000-6,000   PRA

A late 18thC teak and marble sideboard table, Cape of Good Hope.

c1775

55.25in (138cm) wide

£12,000-18,000   PRA

A 19thC stinkwood tea table, Western Cape.

c1800

34in (85cm) wide

£4,000-5,000   PRA

A 19thC stinkwood and satinwood tea table, Cape Town.

c1800

32.5in (81.5cm) wide

£2,000-3,000   PRA

One of an early 19thC pair of half-moon tables, South Western Cape.

Most of the half-moon tables from the region were made by country craftsmen using a combination of light wood – in this case yellowwood – for the table-top and apron and dark wood – in this case stinkwood – for the legs. On many of these tables, it is the construction and decoration of the legs that gives the best indication of the craftsman's skill and sense of proportion.

c1815

40in (100cm) diam

£10,000-15,000 pair   PRA

One of an early 19thC pair of half-moon tables, South Western Cape.

c1815

50.5in (126cm) diam

£7,000-9,000 pair   PRA

A round stinkwood table, Eastern Cape.

c1835

60.75in (152cm) diam

£7,000-10,000   PRA

A 19thC Oregon pine trek table, the base with a wooden peg pivot, West coast (Sandveld).

The table is collapsible so it could be stored underneath a wagon when the owner's family was on the move.

£800-1,200   PRA

FURNITURE

An 18th or 19thC carved wooden figure of woman, wearing flowing gown and holding musical pipes, one finger missing, damage.

42.5in (106cm) high

£3,200-3,800   BRU

A pair of early 19thC carved oak allegorical figures, in the manner of Richard Bridgens, depicting Justice and Plenty, raised on plinths carved with blind strapwork and figural panels.

largest 66in (168cm) high

£4,000-6,000   L&T

A pair of 19thC Continental carved limewood figures, depicting a portly couple on shaped bases.

largest 14.5in (37cm) high

£150-200   ROW

A pair of Continental Blackamoor figures, each modelled as a man in 18thC costume holding a flaming torch and standing on a pillow, raised on a square base terminating in carved paw feet.

71.75in (179cm) high

£7,000-10,000   FRE

A Continental carved walnut figurehead, modelled as an admiral.

30in (75cm) high

£2,000-3,000   FRE

An 18th or 19thC gilt-wood sconce, with eagle and lion's head boss.

27in (67.5cm) high

£2,000-3,000   BRU

A 19thC Black Forest oak figure of a bear, with a rocky naturalistic base.

26in (66cm) high

£800-1,200   L&T

A 19thC Black Forest oak stick stand, carved as a bear with a 'branch' hoop.

36in (91cm) high

£3,000-4,000   L&T

A late 19thC German carved boxwood inkwell, modelled as a hound's head with a hinged lid and glass eyes.

8.5in (21.5cm) wide

£220-280   GORL

A Black Forest carved bear liqueur set, modelled holding a staff and carrying a young bear, the basket with glass decanter and six glasses.

10in (25.5cm) high

£1,500-2,000   GORL

A carved wooden tobacco jar, in the form of a skull, with an entwined carved snake and a lid.

7.5in (19cm) high

£150-200   GORL

An 18thC carved and painted wood relief, with a bishop and angels, signed "Joseph Go..." and dated "Ano de 1745", later frame.

11in (27.5cm) high

£800-1,200   CHE

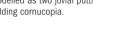

A pair of late 19thC bronze figural twin branch candelabra, modelled as two jovial putti holding cornucopia.

16.25in (41.5cm) high

£700-1,000　　　　**SWO**

A set of four 19thC Continental Popeian-style iron and brass candlesticks, the knop moulded stems raised on triform openwork bases.

A pair of Italian 18thC-style blackamoor torchères, modelled as figures holding cornucopia, with vine branch candelabra, on scrolled triangular bases.

A pair of Regency gilt and patinated bronze candelabra, modelled as angels holding candelabra with flaming sconces, on pedestal with applied maidens.

28.25in (73cm) high

One of a pair of bronze Barbadienne five-branch candelabra.

36in (91.5cm) high

69.5in (176.5cm) high

| **£1,500-2,000** **SWO** | **£6,000-8,000** **L&T** | **£700-1,000 pair** **JN** | **£1,200-1,800** **FRE** |

LAMPS

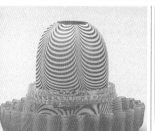

A Nailsea-type 'fairy-size' dome fairy lamp, with a red ground, clear Clarke lamp cup and matching base.

5in (13cm) high

£350-400　　　　**JDJ**

A rare Victorian double student lamp, the brass body with lion's heads and scrolls, topped with two ribbed pink shades cased with white interiors, shades probably later, lamp drilled and electrified.

24in (61cm) diam

£1,500-2,000　　　　**JDJ**

Two miniature fluid finger lamps, with applied handle and drop-in burner, deeply indented pontil mark.

1.75in (4.5cm) high

£500-700　　　　**JDJ**

An American cut glass table lamp and bowl.

17.5in (44.5cm) high

£350-400　　　　**JN**

A Mt. Washington Crown Milano lamp, decorated with seven snow geese and a sunburst, base signed with purple "CM", crown mark.

19in (48cm) high

£2,500-3,000　　　　**JDJ**

A cobalt blue pear-shaped table lamp, the font mounted on a crystal-stemmed foot, with no.1 burner.

9.75in (25cm) high

£100-150　　　　**JDJ**

An amethyst pear-shaped table lamp, the font mounted on a brass and marble foot, size zero coronet burner and old flange chimney.

9.25in (23.5cm) high

£150-200　　　　**JDJ**

A pair of brass table lamps, in Victorian ecclesiastical style, with glass cabochons and round bases, each with three feet.

31in (79cm) high

£400-600　　　　**DN**

A 19thC pair of Federal giltwood sconces, each with a ribbon crest above a shaft with a profile bust portrait on a blue reserve, some losses.

28in (71cm) high

£1,500-2,000 **POOK**

An 18thC-style silvered electrolier, with branches and sconces supported on a turned column cast with caryatid figures, together with four matching two branch sconces.

31in (79cm) diam

£3,000-5,000 **L&T**

A CLOSER LOOK AT A PAIR OF WALL SCONCES

The popular French maker Henry Dasson worked in the aesthetic style, which has become very desirable in recent years. Henry Dasson expertly copied the Louis XV and Louis XIV style and the fact that these sconces are signed and dated by Dasson increases the value.

The animated grotesque is crisp and detailed and the gilt-bronze is bright.

The quality of casting is substantially better than many 20thC reproduction pieces, which tend to be a bit ragged around the edges.

These lights are of grand proportions, made for a large house. This increases value.

A pair of gilt-bronze wall sconces, each cast with a horned grotesque mask issuing three acanthus cast s-scroll branches, terminating in candle nozzles, with leafy drip trays and drapery aprons, signed "Henry Dasson" and dated.

1887 *23.5in (59cm) high*

£6,000-9,000 **FRE**

A two socket wall sconce, with cast-brass mounts and two blown-glass elongated bell-shaped globes with rolled rims.

16in (40.5cm) high

£500-800 **BRU**

A pair of Cornelius & Sons wall sconces, each for a single candle or burner, tôle painted, impressed mark to back "Cornelius Philad Patent, April 1st 18(?)3", replaced glass globes.

11.5in (29cm) high

£1,200-1,800 **BRU**

Two 19thC English brass-mounted candle sconces, with glass globes, brass acorn drop finials and chevron-shaped wall mounts.

14.25in (36cm) high

£1,500-2,000 **BRU**

CEILING LIGHTS

A late 19thC cast-brass chandelier, attributed to Cornelius & Baker of Philadelphia, the shaft and arms with cast leafage and bosses, restored and electrified.

46in (117cm) high

£2,500-3,000 **FRE**

A late 19thC Continental Gothic Revival hall lantern, in wrought iron, with fleur-de-lys finials, scrolling pendant and pierced frieze, electrified.

52in (132cm) high

£1,200-1,800 **L&T**

A late 19thC Swedish alabaster chandelier, with a hand-carved flower design.

25in (63.5cm) diam

£4,000-6,000 **LANE**

A late 19thC Swedish amber alabaster chandelier, carved with leaf design.

24in (61cm) diam

£3,000-4,000 **LANE**

An 18thC mahogany tea caddy, of Chippendale design, with an ornate brass handle and escutcheon.

£280-320   SWO

A George III mahogany tea caddy, the rectangular top with concave sides and a brass handle, enclosing divisions, and a secret drawer to one side, on ogee bracket feet, restored.

9.5in (24cm) wide

£300-500   DN

A George III black lacquer tea caddy, of oval form, painted with bands of anthemion and harebell, the hinged lid above two glazed ovals with Wedgwood Jasperware style Neoclassical figure panels.

4.25in (11cm) high

£800-1,200   L&T

A George III burr fruitwood tea caddy, of octagonal form, the lid with chevron and rope-twist inlay.

4.25in (11cm) high

£500-700   SWO

A George III mahogany tea caddy, the hinged lid concealing a compartmented interior, on bracket feet.

9in (23cm) wide

£200-300   SWO

A George III mahogany tea caddy, the six sides and lid with inlaid ovals and narrow crossbanding.

£600-900   SWO

A George III inlaid satinwood octagonal tea caddy, with rope-twist inlay to the corners, the body with alternate inlay of fluted columns and ovals with floral sprays.

£800-1,200   SWO

A George III inlaid mahogany elliptical tea caddy with crossbanded and rope-twist inlay to the edges and urn and husk inlay to the front, opening to reveal two lidded compartments.

7.25in (18.5cm) wide

£2,000-2,500   SWO

A George III inlaid mahogany tea caddy.

c1800   *10.25in (26cm) wide*

£300-500   MB

A Regency tortoiseshell and mother-of-pearl tea caddy, of square shape with canted corners and geometric lozenge design, with silver escutcheon and initialled mount.

6in (15cm) wide

£6,000-8,000   GORL

A Regency mahogany and line-inlaid tea caddy, of sarcophagus form, the hinged cover enclosing three lidded canisters, the sides mounted with pressed brass handles, on four compressed bun feet.

12.25in (31cm) wide

£200-300 B

A Regency oak and marquetry sarcophagus-shaped three division tea caddy, inlaid with satinwood and rosewood geometric motifs, on bracket feet.

11.25in (28.5cm) wide

£100-150 GORL

A Regency rosewood and tulipwood crossbanded sarcophagus-shaped tea caddy, with chequer banding and foliate brass loop handles, on bun feet.

12in (30.5cm) wide

£150-200 GORL

An early 19thC rectangular mahogany tea caddy, with a hinged lid enclosing two lidded compartments and a cut glass mixing bowl.

12in (30.5cm) wide

£100-150 GORL

A Regency tortoiseshell tea caddy of rounded sarcophagus shape, with white metal stringing and ball feet, the interior with two lidded compartments with white metal stringing and ivory knobs.

6.75in (17cm) high

£2,500-3,000 SWO

An early 19thC mahogany, boxwood and ebony-strung tea caddy, of plain rectangular shape, with an elliptical handle and ivory escutcheon, fitted with two lidded compartments and a later glass bowl.

£70-100 SWO

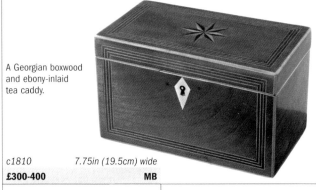

A Georgian boxwood and ebony-inlaid tea caddy.

c1810 *7.75in (19.5cm) wide*

£300-400 MB

A late 18thC mahogany framed paper scroll tea caddy, of six-sided section, the hinged lid and sides inset with panels of scrolled paper formed as floral sprays, under glass.

7.25in (18.5cm) wide

£600-900 L&T

A late Georgian blonde tortoiseshell and pewter-strung tea caddy, of rounded rectangular form, the dome hinged cover enclosing a pair of lidded zinc-lined compartments standing on four metal bun feet, restored.

6.25in (16cm) wide

£800-1,200 B

A Regency giltwood and papier mâché tea caddy, of oval section, the top with dragons in the Chinoiserie style on a black lacquer ground, opening to reveal the interior fitted with a hidden caddy, the gadrooned body raised on a leaf-carved pedestal.

£1,500-2,000 L&T

A William IV blonde tortoiseshell bombe sarcophagus-shaped two division tea caddy, the hinged lid opening to reveal two zinc-lined compartments, the covers with turned ivory knops, on brass ball feet.

6.5in (16.5cm) wide

£2,000-3,000 B

small 19thC tortoiseshell tea caddy, ised on ivory bun feet.

5in (13cm) wide

300-400   **CHEF**

A 19thC tortoiseshell tea caddy, the interior with two lidded compartments.

7.75in (20cm) wide

£600-900   **CHEF**

A 19thC tortoiseshell and mother-of-pearl tea caddy, of serpentine outline.

5.5in (14cm) wide

£400-600   **CHEF**

19thC black Japanned papier mâché a caddy, with painted floral decoration.

14.25in (36cm) wide

100-200   **B**

A mid-19thC Cantonese lacquered tea caddy, of canted rectangular form, the exterior decorated in gilt with panels and borders of birds amongst trees and flowers, the domed cover enclosing a pair of engraved pewter canisters and covers, above a bombe-shaped body, on four carved and stylized bat feet.

8.5in (21.5cm) wide

B   £2,000-3,000

A Victorian mahogany tea caddy, with two lidded compartments and a glass mixing bowl.

12.75in (32.5cm) wide

£100-150   **GORL**

WRITING BOXES

large Georgian mahogany entleman's writing box, ilaid with a compass star.

1800 *14in (35.5cm) wide*

400-600   **MB**

n early 19thC coromandel travelling riting box of rectangular form, profusely arved with flowering and scrolling foliage, e interior inlaid in bone with dotted lines nd enclosing a folding writing surface.

16.5in (41cm) wide

200-300   **L&T**

A Regency rosewood and mother-of-pearl inlaid stationery cabinet, the hinged lid and twin doors enclosing a tray and three drawers, on gadrooned plinth and bun feet.

12.5in (32cm) wide

£300-400   **GORL**

A William IV rosewood ladies' compendium, inlaid with mother-of-pearl and pewter, with jewellery and writing compartments.

c1830   *12.25in (31cm) wide*

£1,000-1,500   **MB**

A late 19thC boullework inkstand, fitted with two glass inkwells, box and pen tray, on button feet.

16in (40.5cm) wide

£150-200 **GORL**

A 19thC Jennings & Bettridge papier mâché stationery box, black lacquered finish with sloped lid and swept sides enclosing fitted interior, impressed mark and crown cypher to base.

6.5in (16.5cm) wide

£100-150 **GORL**

A Victorian walnut writing slope, the hinged lid concealing a removable fitted tray, with a secret sprung writing slope below.

15.25in (39cm) wide

£300-400 **SWO**

An early Victorian writing slope with brass bindings and inlay, hinged to enclose a leather writing inset, recesse and a pen tray.

20in (50.5cm) wic

£150-200 **D**

An early Victorian rosewood writing box, of rectangular form, with a pair of hinged covers flanking a turned carrying handle, enclosing an interior fitted with a single lidded compartment.

37.5in (95cm) wide

£150-200 **B**

A Victorian mother-of-pearl writing and ink box.

3in (7.5cm) wide

£120-180 **MB**

A Victorian mahogany artist's box, the compartmentalised interior with watercolour blocks in a labelled tray together with other artist's materials and equipment, stamped "Reeves and Sons", inscribed with owner's name and dated "March 24th 1860".

11.5in (29cm) wide

£150-200 **GORL**

A Victorian Isle of Man stationery box, in bird's-eye maple and inset rosewood, th hinged top and fall-front enclosing a well stand and bone pen rack, with two spring-loaded drawers and carved bone Manxman device initialled "EL".

15in (38cm) wic

£150-200 **GOR**

A rosewood drawing box.

c1870 *8in (20.5cm) wide*

£120-180 **MB**

A Victorian brass-bound coromandel desk inkstand.

c1870 *11.5in (29cm) wide*

£300-500 **MB**

A Victorian inlaid rosewood stationary cabinet.

c1890 *12in (30.5cm) wide*

£700-1,000 **MB**

An ivory and shagreen writing box and cover, with turquoise-coloured exterior, the handle gilt-embossed "London Made".

13in (33cm) wic

£1,500-2,000 **RO**

n early 19thC penwork work basket, the
d decorated with a view of Brighton
avilion within a foliate border, the front
anel decorated with two harbour scenes,
ith turned ivory handle and feet.

10in (25.5cm) wide

600-900   **GORL**

A Regency penwork work box, with
foliage decoration and later lined
interior, the sides with brass petal plate
ring handles, on foliate paw feet.

13in (33cm) wide

£300-400   **WW**

A Regency tooled Morocco leather work
box, with gadrooned hinged lid revealing
a compartmented interior with seven
mother-of-pearl and treen spools, on gilt
metal scroll feet, damaged.

11in (28cm) wide

£70-100   **GORL**

An early 19thC octagonal penwork box,
the lid decorated with a harbour scene
within a scrolling acanthus leaf border.

11in (28cm) wide

£150-200   **GORL**

An early 19thC penwork work box, the
lid decorated with Oriental figures in a
garden within a foliate border, the sides
with scrolling acanthus leaves, on gilt
metal scroll feet.

9.5in (24cm) wide

£200-300   **GORL**

Regency painted boxwood work box, decorated with a rustic landscape with
owers and leaves.

10in (25.5cm) wide

500-700   **GORL**

An early 19thC penwork work box, the
moulded lid decorated with a lion and
four music-making cherubs, with a
compartmented interior housing various
sewing accessories, on gilt ball feet.

9in (23cm) wide

£200-300   **GORL**

A William IV satinwood and ebony
banded sarcophagus-shaped work box,
the interior with a compartmented tray,
on gilt metal paw feet.

12.5in (32cm) wide

£80-120   **GORL**

19thC mother-of-pearl inlaid and gilt-
ainted papier mâché toilet or work box,
e cover inset and painted with a scene
f Windsor castle from the river below,
e inside with six matched jars, with
tted stationery drawer to the base.

11in (28cm) wide

150-200   **ROS**

A late 19thC Anglo-Indian work box, of sarcophagus shape, veneered in ivory and
sadeli work, the hinged cover enclosing a detachable mirror and various dedicated
compartments, above a pull-out slide containing a plush-lined writing surface.

Sadeli work is a mosaic of ivory, pewter and wood inlaid in geometric patterns.

16.5in (43cm) wide

£800-1,200   **WW**

A 19thC burr elm and steel pique work
box, with fitted interior tray housing
various bone and glass accessories.

*Pique work makes use of gold and silver
pins to create an inlaid design.*

9.75in (25cm) wide

£400-600   **GORL**

A 19thC stained pine workbox, in the form of a cottage, with a hinged lid, damaged.

10in (25.5cm) wide

£600-900   **SWO**

A Victorian rosewood sarcophagus-shaped work box, the lid inset with a mother-of-pearl presentation plaque, inscribed "Presented to Miss Bower by her pupils 1838".

11.5in (29cm) wid

£200-300   **GOF**

A 19thC Chinese export lacquer work box, decorated throughout with shaped reserves depicting Oriental figures and buildings within foliate borders, the hinged lid opening to reveal a compartmented tray with ivory fittings and sewing accessories, on carved lion's head feet.

14.5in (37cm) wide

£200-300   **GORL**

A walnut oyster-veneered lace box, the top with an inlaid circle and crossbanding.

£400-600   **SW**

JEWELLERY BOXES

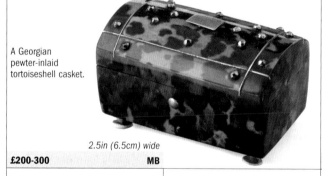

A Georgian pewter-inlaid tortoiseshell casket.

2.5in (6.5cm) wide

£200-300   **MB**

A William IV mother-of-pearl inlaid rosewood box.

c1830   *11in (28cm) wide*

£300-400   **MB**

A William IV mother-of-pearl inlaid coromandel cigar case.

5.25in (13.5cm) wid

£150-200   **M**

An Austrian burr cedar, ebony and specimen agates box.

c1870   *2.75in (7cm) wide*

£100-150   **MB**

A Victorian walnut jewellery box.

12in (30.5cm) wide

£200-300   **MB**

An Edwardian walnut jewellery box, with inscription.

c1905   *9.75in (25cm) wide*

£300-400   **MB**

A CLOSER LOOK AT A JEWELLERY BOX

Pulling the small brass handles on the left- and right-hand sides reveals two circular-shaped jewellery compartments lined with fabric.

The miniature watercolour in the centre depicts an Alpine lake landscape. If the artist were identified the value of the piece would increase.

Tulipwood is a hard, dense wood from Brazil and Peru, known in France as 'bois de rose'.

The front and sides are decorated with delicate, floral ormolu mounts.

A French tulipwood jewellery box, with watercolour scene to the lid.

10.5in (26.5cm) wide

£300-400   **MB**

TOILET BOXES

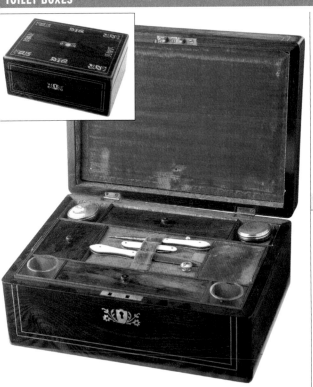

A William IV mother-of-pearl inlaid rosewood vanity box.

c1830   12in (30.5cm) wide

£300-400   **MB**

A 19thC brass-bound coromandel vanity case, the lid and fall-front enclosing a velvet-lined compartmented interior with base drawer.

13.75in (35cm) wide

£200-300   **GORL**

A Victorian brass-bound coromandel toilet box, with compartmented interior housing nine glass jars and boxes with plated tops, with side and base drawers.

12in (30.5cm) wide

£100-150   **GORL**

A Victorian brass-bound rosewood toilet box, with compartmented interior.

12in (30.5cm) wide

£150-200   **GORL**

An Oriental coromandel toilet box, with hinged lid enclosing a compartmented tray above two doors housing three drawers, on plinth base.

7.5in (19cm) wide

£120-180   **GORL**

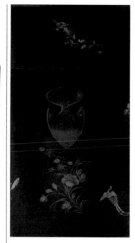

A George III mahogany and chequer-strung knife box, the tulipwood crossbanded slope top enclosing a fitted interior, flanked by brass handles.

14.5in (37cm) high

£600-900   **DN**

A George III mahogany knife box with brass handles and escutcheon, converted with a plush-lined open interior.

13in (33cm) high

£180-220   **SWO**

A Regency japanned knife box, in the form of a Classical urn with rising lid and fitted interior, with gilt and mother-of-pearl decoration.

29.5in (75cm) high

£1,500-2,000   **CHEF**

GAMES BOXES

An early Victorian games box.

c1840   *8in (20.5cm) wide*

£300-400   **MB**

A 19thC 'Royal Cabinet of Games', in a burr walnut and ebony case, of rectangular form with hinged lid and opening front, the leather-lined interior enclosing a leather chequer and backgammon board, turned chess and draughts pieces, a cribbage board, whist and bezique markers, counters, tumblers and a book of rules bearing retailer's label for "Charles Henry, 22 King St, Manchester".

13.25in (33cm) wide

£1,800-2,200   **L&T**

A late Victorian games compendium, housed in a brass-mounted coromandel box, with a hinged top and front and a fitted interior with two lift-out trays, including bone chess pieces, draughts, dominoes and dice, a cribbage board, bezique markers and original instruction book.

12.5in (32cm) wide

£1,500-2,000   **SWO**

STOCK
LONDON

An early 19thC mahogany domestic medicine chest, the hinged lid with an ivory plate marked "Stock London", containing a glass-spouted mortar and pestle, tumbler, brass tweezers and blood-letting blades in cases, the front of the chest with a door enclosing six clear glass bottles above six labelled drawers, the reverse enclosing twelve further bottles and an apothecary's balance scale in a Japanned tin case, with brass side handles, on bracket feet.

11in (28cm) high

£700-1,000   **CHEF**

A Tunbridgeware work box, by Thomas Barton, the domed lid decorated with a central floral spray within a foliate border, with similar decoration to side panels, with paper label.

11in (28cm) wide

£450-650   **GORL**

A large Tunbridgeware parquetry box, by Edmund Nye, the dark ground with geometric inlay with tesserae banding, with maker's paper label on base.

11in (28cm) wide

£800-1,200   **B**

An early 19thC Tunbridgeware rosewood work box, the hinged lid with perspective cube panel between a pair of green velvet pin cushions.

12in (30.5cm) wide

£180-220   **B**

A Victorian Tunbridgeware inlaid walnut writing slope.

c1880   *10.25in (26cm) wide*

£120-180   **MB**

A Victorian Tunbridgeware mosaic snuff box.

c1820   *3.25in (8.5cm) diam*

£70-100   **MB**

A 19thC Tunbridgeware rosewood box, with eight-point star design.

c1820   *1.5in (4cm) diam*

£70-100   **MB**

A William IV Tunbridgeware stickware box, with geometric design.

4.25in (11cm) wide

£80-120   **MB**

A 19thC Tunbridgeware rosewood jewellery box, the top inlaid with a stag, with a silk-lined interior.

6in (15cm) wide

£120-180   **SWO**

A Victorian Tunbridgeware inlaid brush, with floral design.

c1860   *6.25in (16cm) wide*

£30-40   **MB**

A Victorian Tunbridgeware rosewood box, with perspective cube design.

c1870   *3.75in (9.5cm)*

£80-120   **MB**

A Victorian Tunbridgeware inlaid rosewood box, with floral design.

4.5in (11.5cm) wide

£70-100   **MB**

Victorian Tunbridgeware mosaic
alnut box, with floral design.

1870   *3.5in (9cm) wide*

80-120   **MB**

A Victorian Tunbridgeware inlaid walnut
box.

10.75in (27.5cm) wide

£100-150   **MB**

Victorian Tunbridgeware
osewood box, with floral
esign, inscribed
Christmas 1881".

4in (10cm) wide

80-120   **MB**

A Tunbridgeware inlaid mahogany tea caddy, of rectangular shape, the body with
chequered band inlay, fitted with two tea compartments and a moulded glass
mixing bowl.

c1870   *13in (33cm) wide*

£180-220   **ROS**

Tunbridgeware bird's-eye maple
ewellery box, by Thomas Barton,
tained with Chalybeate springwater,
he cushion-shaped top with central
ose spray on a white wood ground
vithin stylized tesserae banding, with
haker's paper label, damaged.

*he Chalybeate Spring in Tunbridge Wells
vas famed for its medicinal properties.*

9in (23cm) wide

280-320   **B**

A Tunbridgeware rosewood box, the
cushion-shaped lid with a tesserae
mosaic view of Hever Castle within
flower tesserae banding, with interior
panel of Edward, Prince of Wales,
damaged.

10.75in (27cm) wide

£500-700   **B**

A Tunbridgeware rosewood
folding watchstand, with
stylized tesserae mosaic
leaf banding.

3.25in (8.5cm) wide

£150-200   **B**

Tunbridgeware rosewood glove box, by
dmund Nye, the pin hinge lid with
crolling leaf and rose mosaic band
vithin geometric crossbanding, with
riginal turned ivory peg handle, the
ase with paper label.

9.25in (23.5cm) wide

220-280   **B**

An early Tunbridgeware rosewood
blotter, one cover with a gaugework view
of Tonbridge Castle within half square
and tesserae mosaic banding, the other
with a tesserae mosaic panel of a bird,
damaged.

£280-320   **B**

A Tunbridgeware rosewood thread
wheel, with eight-point stars to both
ends.

1.25in (3cm) diam

£200-300   **B**

A Tunbridgeware coromandel writing box
by Thomas Barton, the cushion-shaped
top with perspective cube panel within
tesserae mosaic stylized banding.

12.5in (32cm) wide

£1,000-1,500   **B**

An early 19thC Tunbridgeware bird's-eye maple netting box, possibly by the Wise family, the oblong lid with central perspective cube panel within half square and chequer-strung cross banding, enclosing fitted interior including four Cantonese carved reel holders.

10.25in (26cm) wide

£700-1,000   **B**

An early Tunbridgeware burr yew writing box, by George Wide of Tunbridge, the sloping lid with lozenge-shaped colour print of Wellwark in Cheltenham, the concave sides with penwork borders, complete with inkwell and key, damaged.

£1,000-1,500   **B**

A Tunbridgeware Hungarian ash folding writing box, stained with Chalybeate springwater, the sloping fall with a tesserae view of Bayham Abbey ruins, the sides with parquetry roundels.

Water from the Chalybeate Spring imparts a red stain to the wood.

11in (28cm) wide

£1,500-2,000   **B**

A Tunbridgeware rosewood desk stand, fitted with a candle sconce between tw tesserae-topped cylindrical seal boxes, and other accessories, the sloping side with tesserae mosaic stylized flower banding, on stickware bun feet.

8.25in (21cm) wid

£500-700

A Tunbridgeware coromandel stationery box, by Thomas Barton, the domed lid with perspective cube panel within stylized tesserae mosaic banding, the sides with tesserae mosaic band of hops, the base with partially torn label.

9in (23cm) wide

£700-1,000   **B**

A Tunbridgeware burr walnut glovebox, the domed top with a tesserae mosaic view of Eridge Castle, the waisted sides with fine tesserae scrolling flower border on a black ground, the base with wavy tartan paper, damaged.

9.5in (24cm) wide

£400-600   **B**

A Tunbridgeware tesserae mosaic architectural view of Penshurst Place, attributable to Henry Hollamby, the view of Solar and Buckingham Buildings, Penshurst Place on a whitewood ground within a tesserae mosaic banded frame.

7in (18cm) wid

A Tunbridgeware rosewood bookslide, by Thomas Barton, one folding end with a tesserae mosaic rose and the other with a gaugework picture of a bullfinch.

c1855

13in (33cm) long

£800-1,000   **B**

A Tunbridgeware rosewood tea caddy, the cushion-shaped lid with tesserae mosaic view of Battle Abbey within mosaic banding, the waisted sides with a broad black ground mosaic band of roses, the interior with frames for a tea caddy and suga bowl, with eight-point sta key escutcheon and rosewood bun feet.

9.5in (24cm) wid

£400-600

Tunbridgeware rosewood ewing companion, the rned central stem with a rcular pin cushion with an Dyke inlay, the middle er with a smaller incushion, thread waxer, pe measure and imble stand, etween four cotton el pegs.

'an Dyke' inlay is a attern of elongated iangles in contrasting olours.

6.75in (17cm) high

800-1,200   **B**

A novelty Tunbridgeware pin wheel, by Thomas Barton, modelled as a table, the ebony top inlaid with a Barton star on a stickware baluster-turned stem and tesserae mosaic decorated circular base, losses.

3.25in (8cm) diam

£500-700   **B**

A Victorian Tunbridgeware inlaid frame.

c1880   *6.25in (16cm) high*

£60-90   **MB**

A Tunbridgeware oblong rosewood box, with sloping sides and pin cushion top. the sides with a tesserae mosaic band of daffodils.

9.75in (24.5cm) wide

£150-200   **B**

Tunbridgeware rosewood box, the blong-shaped lid with tesserae mosaic se banding within chequer stringing, e cedar-lined interior with single boat-haped division.

5.75in (14.5cm) wide

120-180   **B**

A Tunbridgeware inlaid rosewood box.

2in (5cm) wide

£60-80   **MB**

A Victorian Tunbridgeware stamp box.

1.75in (4.5cm) wide

£70-100   **MB**

A Tunbridgeware 'saucepan' caddy spoon, with turned handle.

3.5in (9cm) long

£200-300   **WW**

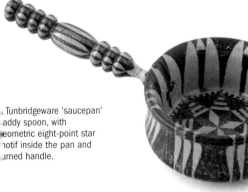

Tunbridgeware 'saucepan' addy spoon, with eometric eight-point star notif inside the pan and urned handle.

3.5in (9cm) long

200-300   **WW**

A Tunbridgeware 'saucepan' caddy spoon, with turned handle.

4in (10cm) long

£200-300   **WW**

A Tunbridgeware 'saucepan' caddy spoon, with turned handle.

3.5in (9cm) long

£200-300   **WW**

A Tunbridgeware 'saucepan' caddy spoon, with turned handle.

3in (7.5cm) long

£200-300   **WW**

A Victorian Mauchlineware watch case.

c1850   2.75in (7cm) high

£50-80   **MB**

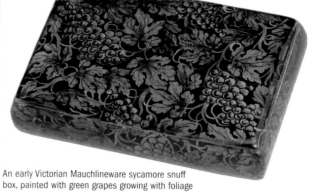

An early Victorian Mauchlineware sycamore snuff box, painted with green grapes growing with foliage on brown vines against a black background.

2.75in (7cm) wide

£150-200   **CHEF**

A Mauchlineware miniature saucepan, with a print of the Parade at Skegness. c1860

£40-60   **M**

A Victorian Mauchlineware larch and sycamore box, with a print of Porthcawl.

2.75in (7cm) wide

£50-80   **MB**

A Victorian Mauchlineware sycamore box.

4in (10cm) wide

£30-50   **MB**

A Victorian Mauchlineware hat pin box, with a print of York Minster.

4in (10cm) wide

£40-60   **MB**

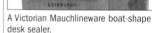

A Victorian Mauchlineware boat-shape desk sealer.

4.75in (12cm) wide

£80-120   **M**

A Mauchlineware larch and sycamore watch barrel.

c1880   3.25in (8.5cm) high

£50-80   **MB**

A Mauchlineware cylindrical box and cover, the lid with a print of Hawkhurst in Kent, the side with a print of the Queens Hotel in Hawkhurst.

3.25in (8cm) diam

£50-80   **B**

A Mauchlineware hexagonal hinged box, containing a glass inkwell.

2in (5cm) high

£80-120   **GORL**

A Mauchlineware string box, with a print of Campbeltown harbour.

3.5in (9cm) diam

£80-120   **GORL**

A Mauchlineware napkin ring.

2.25in (5.5cm) wide

£20-30   **MB**

A Mauchlineware ruler, with a print of Wimborne Minster in Dorset.

12in (30.5cm) wide

£30-40   **MB**

A Mauchlineware sycamore watch box.

£50-80   **MB**

An early Mauchlineware cigar case, with a portrait print.

5in (13cm) wide

£120-180   **MB**

TARTANWARE

A tartanware specimen wood snuff box, with a hinged lid and presentation inscription, dated 1849.

£400-600   **CHEF**

A mid-19thC tartanware snuff box, possibly from Mauchline.

Tartanware boxes were made by the Smith works at Mauchline from 1825.

£70-100   **CHEF**

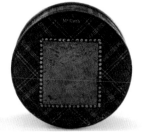

A tartanware stamp box, printed with the 'McBeth' tartan.

1.5in (4cm) diam

£40-60   **WW**

A tartanware go-to-bed, printed with the 'MacDuff' tartan.

2.75in (7cm) high

£40-60   **WW**

A tartanware string box, printed with the 'Caledonia' tartan.

3in (7.5cm) diam

£50-80   **WW**

BOXES & TREEN

A rare 17thC carved beech Friesland mangle board, carved with traditional decoration and with date "Anno 1670".

30.75in (78cm) long

£400-600   **L&T**

The lion is an important motif in Norwegian folk art, and a crowned standing lion features on the Norwegian coat of arms. It appears in medieval wood carving and can be found as a frequent motif in the 19thC. In a religious context, the lion is the symbol of good in the fight against evil.

Apart from a patch to the side and repairs to the base, this tankard appears to be in good condition. Both the scroll handle and the crowned lion are still intact.

The lid is beautifully carved with traditional Norwegian motifs and chip-carved, or 'karverskurd', ornament.

An early 18thC wrought iron rush light, on a bell-shaped wood base.

8.25in (21cm) high

£300-400   **DN**

A mid-19thC Norwegian birch peg tankard, the domed hinged lid carved with a crowned lion, with a scrolled handle and stylized lion feet, restored.

Peg tankards were used for communal drinking. Each drinker had to drain the tankard down to the next peg.

The lion motif is repeated on the base in the form of four stylized pressed lions supporting the vessel

9.5in (24cm) wide

£800-900   **DN**

A rare 18thC carved beech Friesland mangle board, carved with traditional decoration, initialled "HM BV" and dated 1728.

34.75in (88cm) long

£600-900   **L&T**

An early 18thC wrought iron rush light, on a round oak base, traces of paint.

10.75in (27cm) high

£300-400   **DN**

A lignum vitae goblet and cover, with later silver mounts inscribed "To friendship, Mirth & good Humour, ever Sacred", hallmarks undated, maker's marks for Thomas Phipps and Edward Robinson II.

c1785   *10in (25cm) high*

£8,000-12,000   **L&T**

An early 19thC mahogany and laburnum egg epergne, the central baluster column supporting two graduated tiers with removable egg cups and with lidded finial above, the whole raised on a spreading turned base.

19.25in (49cm) high

£1,000-1,500   **L&T**

A 19thC turned lignum vitae string barrel, with brass tap and cutter.

3.5in (9cm) high

£150-200   **WW**

A 19thC knitting sheath, inlaid with heart, star and diamond shapes and inset with a paper label inscribed "Miss M Brown, White House, March 16th 1838".

8.25in (21cm) long

£80-120   **WW**

A 19thC continental yew wood nut cracker, modelled as a squirrel, with a screw handle.

7in (18cm) high

£80-120   **WW**

A 19thC fruitwood pen box, the carved sliding top with a button release.

9in (23cm) long

£50-80   CA

A 19thC turned fruitwood glove powder box.

4.25in (11cm) high

£50-80   CA

A late 19thC Swiss carved pine gnome coat hook, with glass eyes and two ibex horns, dated.

1887   *14.25in (36cm) long*

£500-700   DN

A Victorian fruitwood chemist's jar and cover with stoppered glass bottle, by S. Mawson & Sons.

5.5in (14cm) high

£50-80   CA

A Victorian turned fruitwood box and cover, containing a small measuring glass and a phial measure, by S. Mawson & Sons.

3.25in (8.5cm) high

£70-100   CA

An Edwardian turned mahogany urn, on a concave-sided square base, with brass paw feet.

20.5in (52cm) high

£300-400   WW

A 19thC turned olive-wood wool winder, the baluster stem with clamp, adjustable arms with pegs, and a wool bowl.

10in (25.5cm) high

£80-120   WW

An antique treen cup and cover.

4.75in (12cm) high

£100-150   CA

A treen money box, in the form of a round castle.

3.5in (9cm) high

£100-150   CA

A fruitwood boot in the 18thC style, with a spur.

3in (7.5cm) high

£40-60   CA

A treen campana-form pin cushion stand.

4in (10cm) high

£80-120   CA

A treen glove powder box.

4.75in (12cm) high

£50-80   CA

A treen barrel-form box and cover.

3.25in (8.5cm) high

£50-80   CA

A mandoline-style music box on stand, probably by Bremond, with six changeable cylinders, in a rosewood veneered case, with Aesthetic Movement style inlays to the lid and front, on a matching writing table.

30in (76cm) wide

£3,000-5,000   **EG**

A tortoiseshell singing bird box, the lid enamelled on the top with an Egyptian bust flanked by winged serpents, the interior with a sphinx, the bird with moving parts driven by a fusee movement, with ratchet key and leather travelling case.

3.75in (9.5cm) wide

£3,000-5,000   **EG**

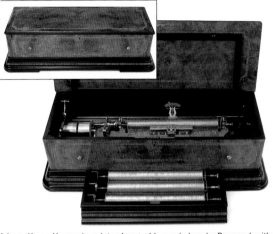

A large Harpe-Harmonique interchangeable music box, by Bremond, with four cylinders playing eight airs each, double-spring motor, tune indicator, speed regulator and zither attachment, in a walnut veneered case with a cylinder drawer.

50in (127cm) wide

£3,000-5,000   EG

A CLOSER LOOK AT A REGINA UPRIGHT MUSIC BOX

The Regina Music Box Co. was founded in 1892 by Gustav Brachhaussen and based in New Jersey. Originally the company sold imported music boxes from Polyphon of Leipzig, but later they began producing their own. Between 1894 and 1921 Regina was the most prominent maker of music boxes in America.

This piece is one of Regina's earlier music boxes, made in 1899, and retains original features such as the automatic changer and an original paper plate printed with the patent date. A music box in this condition is extremely desirable.

The mechanism is in good, unrestored condition, which is essential if a music box is to realise the best possible price.

The upright case has been skillfully constructed from fine mahogany and the legs remain undamaged despite frequent movement, which further enhances its value.

A Regina mahogany upright case music box, with automatic changer, original paper plate with patent date "Nov. 21, '99" and partial paper label "Regina Music Box Co.", complete with 50 discs.

27in (68.5cm) wide

£8,000-10,000   FRE

An automaton music box, by Karrer, with one cylinder playing six airs, further bells struck by a monkey, three-piece comb and silvered zither attachment signed "S. Karrer, Manufacturer of Musical Boxes, Teufenthal, Switzerland", in an ebonized case, the lid painted with a three-masted schooner, signed and dated "Capt. Elisha Jonas 1876", on an associated ebonised writing table by Hernedon.

40in (101cm) wide

£2,500-3,000   EG

A Sublime Harmony music box, by Mermod, with one cylinder playing 12 airs, nickelled movement, tune indicator, speed regulator, Jacot safety check and coin mechanism, in an oak case with carved front, panelled lid and bead and reed moulding.

38in (96.5cm) wide

£1,500-2,000   EG

A Regina music box, in a serpentine mahogany case, with 71 steel discs.

A Nicole Frères music box, the rosewood case inlaid with a classical bust, stamped "Nicole Frères a Geneve" on the brass bed, with serial number.

18in (46cm) wide

£2,500-3,000   H&L

18in (46cm) wide

£3,000-5,000   BRU

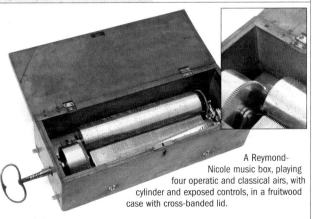

A Reymond-Nicole music box, playing four operatic and classical airs, with cylinder and exposed controls, in a fruitwood case with cross-banded lid.

12in (30.5cm) wide

£3,000-5,000   EG

MUSICAL

A Reymond-Nicole music box, playing six airs, with cylinder and exposed controls, in a fruitwood case with cross-banded lid, winding key and manuscript tune list.

11.75in (30cm) wide

£1,000-1,500 EG

A German upright walnut polyphon, inlaid in brass with the name "Polyphon", with a plaque to the side of the case stamped with retailer's label "H. Peters & Co. London. Made in Leipzig", complete with 12 discs.

c1870 *42.25in (107cm) high*

£3,500-4,500 H&L

A German upright walnut polyphon, with a crank-wound movement and coin slots, a bone plaque to the door stamped with retailer's label "T. Rhodes and Sons Ltd 18 Silver Street Halifax", complete with 20 discs.

c1870 *50.5in (128cm) high*

£4,000-5,000 H&L

A 19thC Swiss musical box, with lever-operated mechanism, one silvered metal cylinder playing 30 airs and coloured lithographic card to the lid, contained in a rosewood inlaid case transfer-decorated with floral sprays.

26.5in (67.5cm) long

£1,500-2,000 H&L

A late 19thC Visible Bells Swiss music box, with one cylinder playing eight airs on a comb and three bells, the rosewood lid with marquetry inlay, the sides painted to simulate rosewood.

16.5in (42cm) wide

£250-350 CHEF

A Swiss carved wood musical log cabin, with pitched roof and embellishments, in original pine box.

7.5in (19cm) high

£100-150 GORL

A Sublime Harmonie musical box, with one cylinder playing eight airs, double comb and winding lever, stamped with the serial number "12411", with decorated tune sheet, in a burr walnut case with brass and ebonised inlay.

28.75in (73cm) wide

£2,000-3,000 H&I

A musical sewing box, with a two air movement under a glazed cover, contained in a walnut case with inlaid central cartouche and cross banding, the base with tune card.

9.5in (24cm) wide

£80-120 EG

A singing bird cage, containing a pair of birds with moving heads, beaks and tails, on a gilt gesso square base with floral and foliate decoration.

18.5in (47cm) high

£1,200-1,800 EG

A Griesbaum whistling organ grinder, the carved wood figure with brass whistling movement, the barrel organ with Manivelle movement.

13in (33cm) high

£800-1,200 EG

An Edison Model B Fireside phonograph, with four-minute gearing, Diamond B reproducer, oak case and No.10 Cygnet horn.

£700-1,000   EG

An Edison Opera phonograph, with Diamond A reproducer, traversing mandrel, brown enamelled top plate and upper works, oxidized fittings, mahogany case, and self-supporting Music Master horn.

£3,000-5,000   EG

An Edison Model G Triumph phonograph, with Diamond B reproducer, double-spring motor, oak case with corner columns, and oak Music Master horn.

A Victor Type C phonograph, with Concert sound box, oak travelling arm, nickelled extension arm, wood dust ring, brass-belled horn, chromed turntable and oak case.

£1,800-2,200   EG

A Victor MS phonograph, with Exhibition sound box, goose-neck tone arm, oak case with fluted corner columns, and fluted oak 'spear tip' horn.

21.5in (54.5cm) diam

£1,800-2,200   EG

£6,000-9,000   EG

A Victor Type P phonograph, with Exhibition soundbox, metal top plate, oxidized extension arm, oak case and travelling arm and brass-belled horn.

11in (28cm) diam

£500-800   EG

An early 20thC zinc figure of Nipper, with glass eyes, studded collar and realistic features, repainted.

Nipper the dog (1884-1895) became a world famous icon after he was immortalised in Francis Barraud's painting 'Dog looking at and listening to a phonograph', later renamed 'His Master's Voice'.

18in (45.5cm) high

£2,200-2,800   EG

A Zonophone Concert phonograph, with Universal soundbox on tapering tone arm, double-spring motor, oak case and blue Morning Glory horn, retailer's label "So. Cal. music Co., Los Angeles, Cal."

23in (58.5cm) diam

£800-1,200   EG

Four items of phonograph paraphernalia, comprising a record case by Hawthorne & Sheble, a framed advertisement for Columbia Art Models, a modern ceramic Nipper money bank, and a plastic Nipper.

£80-120   EG

MUSICAL

An Edison Amberola V phonograph, with Diamond reproducer on telescoping arm, above bedplate mechanism, in a mahogany case with metal grille and canted corners.

£300-500 EG

A Columbia type AJ disc graphophone, with single-spring motor, needle-clip sound box, aluminium travelling and extension arms, oak case with carrying handle and black horn with gilt lining and brass elbow.

8.5in (21.5cm) diam

£400-600 EG

A mahogany bow-front music stand, with foliate-carved front corners and claw feet, with slots for sixty discs.

42in (106.5cm) high

£180-220 EG

INSTRUMENTS

A carved giltwood harp, the main support carved with winged maidens, capitals and a turned and fluted column, signed "Browne G. Buckwell Makers New York".

65.75in (167cm) high

£2,500-3,000 POOK

An eight-string Orheum No. 1 inlaid banjo, with case, pick and tuner, label for Rettberg & Lange of New York City.

The head is signed by alumni of The Catholic University of America.

c1920   23.5in (59cm) long

£120-180 FRE

A Mason & Hamlin Model BB grand piano, with 88 ivory keys and restored ebony finish, on fluted and tapered legs terminating in heavy brass casters, serial number 11770, with bench.

c1900   84in (213.5cm) long

£4,000-6,000 BRU

A Heckel stained beech and silvered contra bassoon, stamped number "229", with a canvas carrying case.

The Heckel factory have records for the sale of this instrument in 1898.

51in (130cm) high

£2,000-3,000 L&

THE GLASS MARKET

A quiet and uneventful year in the antique glass market has been a mixed blessing for collectors. Values have remained relatively stable and predictable, but the lack of quality glass reaching the market is beginning to stifle certain areas of this sector.

Colour continues to spell popularity. Antique wine glasses with colour-twist stems and the enamelled and brightly painted armorial glasses of William Beilby have been market leaders for some time now. However, even in these popular areas of the market, price rises have not been particularly dramatic. This may well be because so few pieces are offered for sale that collectors abandon hope of acquiring them and move on to other fields.

Glimmers of hope were afforded by the publication of an authoritative book on decanters by Andy McConnell and the final sale of the late Wing Commander Ron Thomas' stock in trade at Dreweatt Neate. An influx of new knowledge and good quality glass will recruit new collectors and re-enthuse those already familiar with antique glass.

Buyers should concentrate their resources on acquiring one or two pieces of top quality glass rather than a greater number of inferior items. Above all, it is important to buy pieces as much for their intrinsic appeal as for their investment value.

Margaret Hopkins, Frank Dux Antiques

AIR-TWIST WINE GLASSES

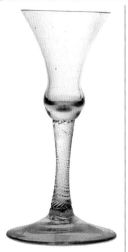

A mid-18thC Continental wine glass, with a bell bowl and incised twist stem, made from soda glass.

6.5in (16.5cm) high

£100-150   **JH**

An air-twist wine glass, the flared bucket bowl supported on a stem with a pair of multi-ply tapes, on a conical foot.

c1750   6.5in (16.5cm) high

£500-700   **DN**

A mid-18thC engraved air-twist wine glass, the bell bowl decorated with a stylized foliate band, on a folded conical foot.

6in (15cm) high

£600-800   **DN**

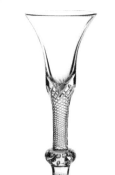

A mid-18thC wine glass, the bell bowl supported on an air-twist stem filled with spiral threads.

7in (18cm) high

£100-150   **DN**

A mid-18thC engraved air-twist wine glass, the bell bowl on an annular knop and decorated with a rose, bud and a thistle.

7in (17.5cm) high

£300-400   **DN**

An air-twist wine glass, the bell bowl supported on a shoulder-knopped stem filled with spiral threads, on a conical foot.

c1750   7in (18cm) high

£400-600   **DN**

A mid-18thC Jacobite air-twist wine glass, of drawn trumpet form, engraved with a rose and thistle, the stem with a pair of entwined cables, on a conical foot, inscribed "Fiat".

7.5in (19cm) high

£1,400-1,800   **DN**

A wine glass of drawn trumpet form, with a solid plain section supported on an air-twist inverted baluster stem and conical foot, foot-rim chip.

c1750   *7in (18cm) high*

£400-600   **DN**

A mercury-twist wine glass, of drawn trumpet form, the stem with a pair of spiral tapes, on a conical foot.

c1750   *6.5in (16.5cm) high*

£600-900   **DN**

A mid-18thC air-twist wine glass, the round funnel bowl supported on an annular cushion knop, on a conical foot.

6.5in (16.5cm) high

£600-800   **DN**

A mid-18thC pan-top wine glass, with multi-spiral air-twist stem.

6in (15cm) high

£120-180   **JH**

A small mid-18thC air-twist wine glass, the round bowl with a gilt dentil rim, supported on a stem with central swelling knop, on a conical foot.

4.5in (11.5cm) high

£500-800   **DN**

An air-twist wine glass, the round funnel bowl supported on a shoulder-knopped stem, with a basal-knopped lower section on a conical foot.

c1750   *6in (15cm) high*

£300-400   **DN**

A pair of engraved air-twist wine glasses, the round funnel bowls with a band of fruiting vine, the centrally knopped stems filled with spiral threads.

c1750   *6in (15cm) high*

£700-900   **DN**

An engraved air-twist wine glass, the round bowl with everted rim and engraved with a floral band, the stem filled with spiral threads.

c1750   *6in (15cm) high*

£500-800   **DN**

A mid-18thC engraved air-twist wine glass, the round funnel bowl decorated with a floral band, on a domed foot.

6.25in (16cm) high

£700-900   **DN**

An air-twist goblet, the ogee bowl with honeycomb-moulded lower section, on a conical foot.

c1760   *8in (20cm) high*

£400-600   **DN**

An opaque-twist toasting glass or ale flute, of drawn trumpet form, with double-series stem and conical foot.

c1770   *7.5in (19cm) high*

£400-600   **DN**

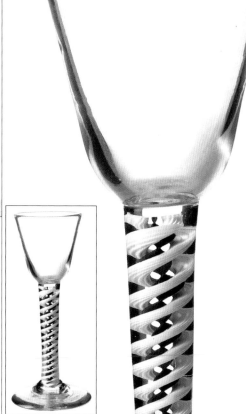

A colour-twist wine glass, the round funnel bowl supported on a stem with a red corkscrew core entwined by a broad opaque spiral, on a conical foot.

c1765

£2,200-2,800   **DN**

An opaque-twist wine glass, of drawn trumpet form, with a double-series stem and conical foot.

c1770   6.25in (16cm) high

£400-600   DN

An engraved opaque-twist ale glass, the tall ogee bowl decorated with hops and barley, supported on a double-series stem and conical foot.

c1770   7in (18cm) high

£350-400   DN

One of two similar opaque-twist wine glasses, the round funnel bowls supported on a double-series stem and conical foot.

c1770   6in (15.5cm) high

£300-350 pair   DN

A Jacobite air-twist wine glass, the bell bowl engraved with a rose and bud, supported on a multi-knop double-series stem.

c1770   8in (20.5cm) high

£1,000-1,500   DN

An opaque-twist wine glass, the bell bowl on a double-series triple-knopped stem and conical foot, foot-rim chips.

c1770   6.5in (16.5cm) high

£350-400   DN

An opaque-twist wine glass, the round funnel bowl supported on a centrally knopped stem filled with spiral threads.

c1770   5.75in (14.5cm) high

£200-300   DN

An opaque-twist cordial glass, the tapered bucket bowl supported on a tall double-series stem and conical foot.

c1770   7in (17.5cm) high

£600-900   DN

An opaque-twist wine glass, the ogee bowl supported on a double-series stem and conical foot.

c1770   6.25in (16cm) high

£300-350   DN

An opaque-twist wine glass, the round funnel bowl supported on a double-series stem and conical foot.

c1770   6in (15cm) high

£280-320   DN

An opaque-twist firing glass, the ogee bowl supported on a double-series stem and terraced foot.

c1770   4in (10cm) high

£350-500   DN

An opaque-twist goblet, with a generous bucket bowl supported on a double-series stem and conical foot.

c1770   7.25in (18.5cm) high

£400-600   DN

An opaque-twist 'Lynn' wine glass, the round funnel bowl moulded with four horizontal bands, supported on a double-series stem and conical foot.

c1770   5.5in (14cm) high

£800-1,000   DN

299

BALUSTER WINE GLASSES

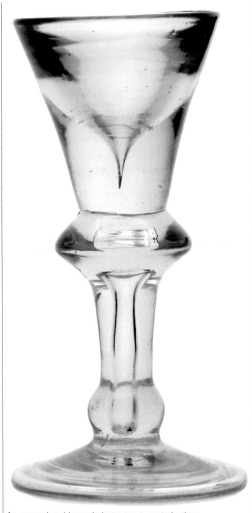

An unusual and heavy baluster toast master's glass.

c1710   *5in (13cm) high*

£1,800-2,200   **JH**

A heavy baluster goblet, the funnel bowl with solid lower section, supported on an inverted baluster stem with tear inclusion and folded foot.

c1710   *7.5in (19cm) high*

£2,500-3,000   **DN**

A balustroid wine glass, of drawn trumpet form, the plain stem above an inverted acorn knop with bead inclusions, on a domed foot.

c1730   *6.5in (16.5cm) high*

£800-1,200   **DN**

A balustroid wine glass, the bell bowl supported on a short plain section above an inverted baluster stem with a tear inclusion, on a conical foot.

c1730   *7in (18cm) high*

£600-900   **DN**

A balustroid wine glass, the bell bowl supported on a centrally knopped stem with tear inclusion, on a domed foot.

c1730   *7in (18cm) high*

£600-900   **DN**

A baluster wine glass, the funnel bowl supported on a cushion knop above a plain section, on a folded conical foot.

c1740   *4.5in (11.5cm) high*

£400-600   **DN**

A baluster gin glass, the bell bowl supported on an inverted baluster stem with basal knop, on a domed folded foot.

c1740   *5in (13cm) high*

£280-320   **DN**

A mid-18thC baluster wine glass, the bell bowl supported on a cushion knop, plain section and basal knop, on a folded conical foot.

4.25in (11cm) high

£220-280   **DN**

A mid-18thC light baluster wine glass, of drawn trumpet form with a solid section and tear inclusion, supported on an inverted baluster stem.

7in (18cm) high

£700-1,000   **DN**

An engraved light baluster goblet, the round funnel bowl decorated with floral swags and diaper panel festoons, on a multi-knopped stem.

c1750   *7in (18cm) high*

£1,500-2,000   **DN**

A mid-18thC balustroid wine glass, the bell bowl supported on a centrally knopped stem and conical foot.

7.5in (19cm) high

£220-280   **DN**

An engraved balustroid wine glass, the round funnel bowl engraved with a foliate lappet band border, on an inverted baluster stem with basal knop.

c1750   *7.5in (19cm) high*

£1,200-1,800   **DN**

A large plain-stemmed goblet, of drawn trumpet form, with tear inclusion, on a folded conical foot.

c1710   9.25in (23.5cm) high

£500-700   **DN**

A plain-stemmed wine glass, of drawn trumpet form, on a folded conical foot.

c1740   7in (18cm) high

£250-300   **DN**

A Jacobite plain-stemmed engraved goblet, with remnants of original gilding.

c1745   6.25in (16cm) high

£1,500-1,800   **JH**

A mid-18thC plain-stemmed wine glass, the bucket bowl with everted rim, on a folded conical foot.

6.25in (16cm) high

£400-600   **DN**

A mid-18thC plain-stemmed toasting glass, of drawn trumpet form, with short plain stem and basal knop, on a folded conical foot.

8in (20cm) high

£600-900   **DN**

A mid-18thC Dutch engraved plain-stemmed wine glass, of drawn trumpet form, engraved with a Classical figure with a winged helmet and an anchor, on a conical foot, initialled "FPH".

6in (15cm) high

£200-300   **DN**

An engraved Chinoiserie plain-stemmed wine glass, of drawn trumpet form, with a Chinese figure in a garden landscape.

c1760   6.25in (16cm) high

£1,000-1,500   **DN**

OTHER WINE GLASSES

A mid-18thC Continental wine glass, with hollow moulded pedestal stem, on a folded foot.

6.25in (16cm) high

£120-180   **JH**

A Dutch engraved armorial goblet, the funnel bowl engraved with arms of the United Provinces of Holland above the inscription "Concordia Resparvae Crescunt", on a cushion knop, hexagonal moulded tapering stem and folded conical foot.

c1750   7in (17.5cm) high

£1,000-1,500   **DN**

A mid-18thC Dutch engraved pedestal-stemmed goblet, the round funnel bowl engraved with Classical figures.

7in (17.5cm) high

£300-500   **DN**

One of a set of five 19thC German champagne flutes.

7in (17.5cm) high

£100-150 set   **FIS**

One of a set of six 19thC French red wine glasses.

5in (13cm) high

£220-280 set   **FIS**

A small mid-18thC wine glass, with funnel bowl, double-knopped stem and folded foot.

4.5in (11.5cm) high

£180-220   **DN**

A facet-stemmed Masonic wine glass, the ovoid bowl engraved with initial "G" within a set-square and compasses.

c1790   5.5in (14cm) high

£280-320   **DN**

A Riesengebirge allegorical armorial tumbler, chipped.

c1700 3.75in (9.5cm) high

£2,000-2,500 **FIS**

An 18thC enamelled tankard with the arms of Saxony and Poland.

c1720 9in (23cm) high

£1,000-1,500 **FIS**

A CLOSER LOOK AT AN ENGRAVED TUMBLER

Johann Wolfgang Schmidt was a glasscutter who worked in Nuremberg during the late 17thC.

Glass made from potash lime was developed in Germany at around this time. It was far more suitable for this kind of engraved decoration than soda glass.

The fleeing doe and captured buck is a romantic take on the hunting motif, which was typical of the German decorative arts throughout the medieval period and into the Renaissance.

Nuremberg was a centre of the European glass industry during this period, and was especially famed for detailed Baroque engraving such as this.

An engraved tumbler by Johann Wolfgang Schmidt of Nuremberg, depicting a hunting scene.

c1680 3in (7.5cm) high

£4,000-6,000 **FIS**

A late 18thC 'Lynn' tumbler, typically worked with horizontal ribs on tapering cylindrical sides.

4.5in (11.5cm) high

£400-600 **CHEF**

An early 19thC commemorative shipping tumbler, with fluted lower section, engraved with a single-masted fishing boat, inscribed "Adelaide", and "JH".

4in (10.5cm) high

£400-600 **DN**

GOBLETS & RUMMERS

An engraved tumbler, decorated with a hunting scene in a continuous band.

c1820 4in (10cm) high

£250-300 **DN**

A Riesengebirge goblet with a mirror monogram.

c1730 6.75in (17cm) high

£1,500-2,000 **FIS**

A goblet by the Glasburger Hütte, with the arms of the Prince of Fulda.

9.75in (24.5cm) high

£4,000-6,000 **FIS**

A mid-18thC Dutch light baluster marriage goblet, the round funnel bowl engraved with a rocaille cartouche with love-hearts on an altar and a cornucopia of fruit and flowers, the reverse inscribed, on a stem with cushion knop above an inverted baluster section with bead inclusions, on a conical foot.

8in (20.5cm) high

£2,500-3,000 **DN**

An early 18thC armorial goblet with the coat of arms of 'Old France', Potsdam, engraved with a band of leaves.

9.25in (23.5cm) high

£2,500-3,500 FIS

A mid-18thC Flemish soda glass goblet, the thistle-shaped bowl engraved with seven crowned armorial shields above faceting, on a knop and hollow inverted baluster stem, the circular foot folded.

8in (20.5cm) high

£800-1,200 CHEF

A German trumpet-shaped goblet, engraved with the arms of the British-Hanovarian Alliance, depicting a crowned lion and unicorn.

c1760   8.25in (21cm) high

£700-1,000 FIS

A goblet from Osterwald or Emde, engraved with the arms of the British-Hanovarian Alliance, depicting a crowned lion and unicorn, on a baluster honeycomb-cut double-knop stem.

c1760   10.5in (26.5cm) high

£2,500-3,500 FIS

A goblet with the arms of the Count of Schwerin, from northern Germany or Holland.

c1760   8.25in (21cm) high

£700-1,000 FIS

A dark emerald-green goblet, the generous ovoid bowl supported on a swollen knopped stem, moulded with vertical flutes, on a domed foot applied with radiating spiral ornament.

c1760   6.25in (16cm) high

£800-1,200 DN

A Lauenstein goblet with golden rim, depicting the four seasons.

c1765   9.25in (23.5cm) high

£1,800-2,200 FIS

A friendship goblet with gilded rim, on a honeycomb-cut double-knop baluster stem.

c1765   9.75in (25cm) high

£2,500-3,500 FIS

A Lauenstein trumpet-shaped goblet, with gilded rim.

c1770   6.5in (16.5cm) high

£220-280 FIS

A Lauenstein trumpet-shaped goblet, with gilded rim.

c1770   7.5in (18.5cm) high

£300-400 FIS

A Lauenstein trumpet-shaped goblet, with armorial engraving.

c1770   6.5in (16.5cm) high

£500-700 FIS

A late 18thC trumpet-form 'Wachtmeister' wine glass, from Solling in northern Germany, with a blue rim and flat foot.

5in (13cm) high

£200-250 FIS

A late 18thC trumpet-shaped goblet, with a band of engraved decoration.

8.5in (21.5cm) high

€800-1,200 | **FIS**

A pair of engraved rummers, the barrel-shaped bowls with foliate sprigs above fluted lower sections, on centrally knopped stems and circular feet, initialled "RAK".

c1820 *5in (13cm) high*

£150-200 | **DN**

A large early 19thC Admiral Lord Nelson commemorative rummer, the round funnel bowl engraved with the HMS Victory under sail, the reverse with the Admiral's funeral barge, on a knopped stem and conical foot, inscribed "Nile", "Trafalgar" and "Victory", cracked.

8.5in (21.5cm) high

£1,000-1,500 | **DN**

A large coin rummer, the bucket bowl with a fluted lower section, the hollow stem with a George III coin insert, on a conical foot, engraved "WAL".

c1820 *6.75in (17cm) high*

£300-400 | **DN**

A commemorative rummer, the tapered bucket bowl engraved with the London to York mail coach with figures and horses, on a facet-knopped stem and square foot, initialled "GC".

c1825 *6in (15cm) high*

£700-1,000 | **DN**

An engraved rummer, the tapered bucket bowl with a two-masted ship sailing beneath Sunderland Bridge, on a capstan stem and circular foot, inscribed "Sunderland Bridge River Wear" and initialled "EB".

c1825 *6in (15cm) high*

£300-500 | **DN**

Two of a set of six Edwardian rummers, with tall bell bowls on stepped plinth bases.

£350-500 set | **L&T**

OTHER GLASSES

A mid-19thC German rummer, with octagonal tapered bowl, faceted knop and strawberry-cut octagonal foot, engraved with a Munich landscape, inscribed "Baberte" and "Zur Erinnerung" amidst vine motifs.

6.25in (16cm) high

£180-220 | **L&T**

An engraved crested rummer, the generous bucket bowl with a crest of an anchor entwined with a serpent, on a plain stem and conical foot.

6.25in (16cm) high

£280-320 | **DN**

A mid-18thC ribbed sweetmeat glass, with moulded pedestal stem and folded foot.

6in (15cm) high

£400-600 | **JH**

A mid-18thC baluster sweetmeat glass, the round bowl with everted and notched rim and fluted lower section, supported on a centrally knopped stem and domed foot.

7in (18cm) high

£300-500 | **DN**

A mid-18thC sweetmeat glass, the fluted ogee bowl supported on a tapered octagonal pedestal stem and a domed, folded and pincered foot.

6.5in (16.5cm) high

£300-500　　　　**DN**

A sweetmeat glass, the shallow bowl supported on a stem with central knop and tear inclusion, on a domed foot.

c1760　　6.5in (16.5cm) high

£150-200　　　　**DN**

An 18thC British panel-moulded jelly glass with handle, chipped.

In this instance the small chip halves the value of this piece.

4.25in (11cm) high

£120-150　　　　**JH**

An 18thC British air-beaded jelly glass, with pan top and domed foot.

4.25in (11cm) high

£120-150　　　　**JH**

A late 18thC British jelly glass, with folded foot.

3.75in (9.5cm) high

£20-30　　　　**JH**

An unusual 19thC lidded custard cup.

4.75in (12cm) high

£80-120　　　　**JH**

An early 19thC slice-cut jelly glass.

3.75in (9.5cm) high

£20-30　　　　**JH**

A small mid-18thC British hexagonal glass.

3.5in (9cm) high

£80-120　　　　**JH**

A small mid-18thC glass, with gilded rim and initials.

3.75in (9.5cm) high

£80-120　　　　**JH**

A ribbed dram glass, with oversewn foot.

1770　　4in (10cm) high

£120-180　　　　**JH**

Two mid-18thC glasses, with jagged rims, one with a handle.

Largest 4.25in (11cm) high

£120-180　　　　**JH**

One of a set of six late 18thC northern German glasses, probably Lauenstein.

7in (17.5cm) high

£1,500-2,000 set　　　　**FIS**

An unusual late 18thC drinking glass, with hops and barley decoration and folded foot.

5in (13cm) high

£50-80　　　　**JH**

An 18thC German olive-coloured trumpet glass.

5in (13cm) high

£300-500　　　　**FIS**

A CLOSER LOOK AT A FAÇON DE VENICE GLASS

'Façon de Venice' means 'in the manner of Venice'. Factories all over Europe emulated the lampwork designs of the Venetian master glassblowers.

Belgium and southern Holland, from where this piece originates, were the great centres of Façon de Venice production during the 17thC. Most examples are made from clear glass combined with these characteristic blue colours.

The delicacy, age and technical accomplishment of this piece combine to make it a valuable and desirable item.

Most of the Façon de Venice glass on the market today dates from the 19thC revival. This piece is a far more valuable 17thC original.

A very rare 17thC 'Façon de Venice' stemmed glass, from the southern Netherlands.

12.25in (31cm) high

£2,000-3,000   **FIS**

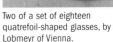

A 19thC ruby-flashed German rummer.

7in (17.5cm) high

£280-320   **FIS**

Two of a set of eighteen quatrefoil-shaped glasses, by Lobmeyr of Vienna.

c1890 Largest 6in (15cm) high

£1,500-2,000 set   **AL**

A set of three green wine glasses, with clear stems.

4.75in (12cm) high

£50-80   **H&L**

One of a set of eight cranberry champagne glasses.

£70-100 set   **H&L**

DECANTERS

A Victorian oak and silver-plated tantalus, by Walker & Hall, with three square cut-glass decanters for gin, whiskey and brandy.

c1890   *13.75in (35cm) wide*

£220-280   **CSA**

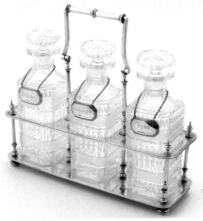

A Sheffield silver decanter carrier, by James Deakin & Sons, with three cut-glass decanters and later silver labels.

1904   *12in (30cm) wide*

£800-1,200   **CSA**

Three mid-19thC slender coloured decanters, with silver-plated stoppers and a plated tripartite stand, in amethyst, blue and green glass.

13.75in (35cm) high

£300-500   **DN**

A CLOSER LOOK AT A TANTALUS

Invented in the mid-18thC, the tantalus is a wooden frame used to display decanters whilst keeping them locked away from the servants. The name is taken from Greek mythology. Tantalus abused the hospitality of the gods and was punished by being surrounded by inaccessible food and drink for eternity.

In order to attract a good price, it is essential that a tantalus be complete with original, matching decanters and stoppers in good condition, without chips or losses.

This good quality example has many compartments and features good carving, making it appealing to collectors.

The cigars, cards, dice and gambling tokens stored in this bottom drawer provide a fascinating insight into the less improving past-times of the Victorian era.

A carved oak tantalus, with nickel mounts, panels for cigarettes and cigars, four lidded compartments, and bottom drawer with catch containing two packs of cards, dice, gambling tokens, cribbage and dice.

c1900   14.5in (37cm) wide

£500-800   **CSA**

A pair of blue club-shaped decanters and stoppers, each inscribed in gilt with faux bottle labels and chains "Hollands" and "Brandy", with later papier-mâché stand.

c1800   9in (23cm) high

£300-400   **DN**

An Irish engraved club-shaped decanter and stopper, with a pair of notched neck rings, decorated with fruiting vine above a flute-moulded lower section.

c1800   9.75in (25cm) high

£400-600   **DN**

An early 19thC mallet-shaped toddy lifter, of decanter form, with fluted neck and inscribed "Bitters" within a foliate cartouche.

7.75in (20cm) high

£150-200   **DN**

An Irish mallet-shaped decanter and stopper, with three notched annular neck rings, the body with a band of engraved and polished stars.

c1810   10.25in (26cm) high

£600-900   **DN**

A turquoise club-shaped decanter, stopper and bottle coaster, the neck applied with three plain rings, the stopper with radiating flutes.

c1820   10.75in (27.5cm) high

£300-500   **DN**

A pair of club-shaped decanters and stoppers, with triple rings over fluted necks, the shoulders cut with fan-shaped bands above diamond fields, chipped.

c1840   9.75in (25cm) high

£200-300   **DN**

A pair of plain mallet-shaped decanters and stoppers, with flattened disc stoppers, stoppers replaced.

12.25in (31cm) high

£500-800   **DN**

BOWLS

A rare 17thC German Maigelein cup.

4.5in (11.5cm) high

£1,200-1,800   **FIS**

A cut glass pedestal bowl, of ogee form, cut with a fan-shaped rim above a field of large strawberry and hobnail diamonds, on a knopped stem and circular foot, chipped.

c1820   8.75in (22cm) diam

£300-400   **DN**

A bowl from a Whitefriars 'straw opal' sixteen-piece port service.

c1850   5.75in (14.5cm) high

£300-400 set   **AL**

A Salviate & Co. Venetian revival bowl and underdish.

c1890   3in (8cm) high

£200-300   **AL**

Two of a set of ten early 20thC dimpled and ribbed bowls and stands, possibly Venetian, gilded with rural scenes.

Stands 6in (15cm) diam

£200-300   **AG**

A Victorian cut glass and gilt bronze mounted comport, by F. & C. Osler, the circular lattice-cut bowl with rim mounts supporting twin handles cast as exotic birds, the base with cast curved paw feet.

c1890   14in (35cm) diam

£800-1,200   **L&T**

A circular cranberry bowl and cover, the bowl with a flared rim, the domed cover with a clear glass finial.

6in (15cm) diam

£40-60   **H&L**

BOTTLES & JUGS

An unusual pair of early 18thC green wine bottles, the flattened oval bodies with slim conical necks and string rims, with kick-in bases.

7in (18cm) high

£400-600   **H&L**

An 18thC purple Alpine bottle, with flattened fluted body and narrow neck.

6.25in (15.5cm) high

£220-280   **FIS**

A rare 18thC flat bottle, by Lauenstein, with a hunting scene relief.

5.75in (14.5cm) high

£280-320   **FIS**

A 19thC blue Alpine bottle, with flat body, narrow neck and wide rim.

7.5in (19cm) high

£80-120   **FIS**

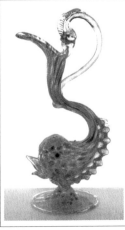

A 19thC miniature sample pressed glass jug, with applied handle.

3.25in (8.5cm) high

£8-12   **AG**

A Salviati & Co. Venetian revival dolphin pitcher.

c1890   9.5in (24cm) high

£600-900   **AL**

A cranberry glass ewer with a reeded clear glass handle and tear-shaped stopper.

7in (18cm) high

£30-40   **H&L**

An early 19thC Nailsea-type olive green shouldered jug, with white inclusions, cracked.

7in (18cm) high

£280-320   **DN**

A beaker by Johann Joseph Mildner, with the arms of Joseph Edlen von Fürnberga in gilt within a red lacquered medallion.

c1790   4.5in (11.5cm) high

£3,000-4,000   FIS

A late 19thC gilded beaker, by J. Pohl, depicting riding and hunting scenes.

3.75in (9.5cm) high

£700-1,000   FIS

A beaker by Anton Kothgasser of Vienna, with gilded edges and a depiction of Cupid, inscribed "Blühe immer".

c1825   4.25in (11cm) high

£5,000-8,000   FIS

A dark red lithyalin cup, by Friedrich Egermann, with gilded decoration.

Lithyalin glass resembles semi-precious stones.

c1830   4.25in (11cm) high

£1,800-2,200   FIS

An enamelled beaker, by Friedrich Egermann, with checkered decoration and faceted stepped mouth.

c1835   4.25in (10.5cm) high

£800-1,200   FIS

A rare clear glass Artel beaker, decorated in colours with a church, animal grotesques and symmetrical arabesques.

c1925   4.25in (10.5cm) high

£800-1,200   FIS

A tall goblet and cover by August Böhm, clear and red engraved glass with deep-cut engravings depicting stags in a woodland setting.

c1850   20.75in (53cm) high

£3,000-4,000   FIS

A tall green glass rummer, by Harrach, with gilded rim and enamelled coat of arms, on a trumpet-shaped foot.

c1880   12.5in (31.5cm) high

£500-800   FIS

A red overlay goblet, by F.P. Zach of Munich, engraved with a hunting scene.

c1850   8.75in (22cm) high

£4,000-6,000   FIS

A light green 'Emanuel' goblet and cover, by the Rhineland Glassworks, on a footed base, stamped.

1893   17.75in (45cm) high

£1,200-1,800   FIS

A 'Jodphur' wine glass, by Fritz Heckert, engraved with silver, gold and polychrome enamel.

c1900   7.5in (19cm) high

£150-200   FIS

An enamelled wine glass, by Meyr's Neffe, with green stem and clear bowl with polychrome enamelling and gilding.

c1900   9in (22.5cm) high

£500-800   FIS

An enamelled wine glass, by Meyr's Neffe, the light blue bowl with polychrome enamels and gilding, signed "S.F.".

c1900   9in (22.5cm) high

£600-900   **FIS**

A German amethyst flash chalice, with engraved decoration, clear stem with amethyst striped foot, chipped.

11.25in (28.5cm) high

£200-300   **JDJ**

A German glass tankard with a pewter mount, depicting a lady wearing traditional dress, framed with foliage.

c1800   9.75in (24.5cm) high

£700-1,000   **FIS**

An early 18thC green glass oxhead tankard, enamelled with an oxhead motif in a woodland alpine landscape, with gilt band under lid, cracked.

13.25in (34.5cm) high

£7,000-10,000   **FIS**

A large mid-19thC Bohemian glass vase and cover, decorated with eight oval panels painted with flowers, on a ground of gilt scrolling foliage.

12in (30cm) high

£800-1,200   **WW**

A green glass handled vase, by Max Rade for Fritz Heckert of Petersdorf, decorated with branches of leaves and fruit, outlined in black enamel.

c1900   4.75in (12cm) high

£300-500   **FIS**

An iridescent glass vase, of baluster form with flared foot and rim, in shades of orange, green, blue and purple.

c1900   11in (28cm) high

£120-180   **FIS**

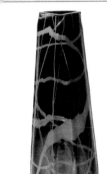

An iridescent Kralik vase, dark purple glass decorated with broad irregular bands of silver foil, damaged.

1902   10.5in (26.5cm) high

£100-200   **FIS**

A Zwiesel vase, designed by Bruno Mauder, clear glass overlayed in blue, with a faceted design.

c1910   6.75in (17cm) high

£70-100   **FIS**

A vase by Beyermann & Co. of Haida, decorated with stylized blossoms, marked on the side "Beyermann".

c1915   6in (15cm) high

£300-500   **FIS**

A vase by Hermann Pautsch of Haida, clear glass painted in gold and polychrome, with gilded lip and foot.

c1915   10.5in (26cm) high

£180-220   **FIS**

A vase, by Hermann Pautsch of Haida, clear glass enamelled with gold, black and polychrome colours.

c1915   7.25in (18cm) high

£80-120   **FIS**

A clear blown vase, designed by Adolf Beckert for Steinschönau, with a black and gold frieze depicting the hunting god Pan, above a faceted lower section.

c1915   4.5in (11cm) high

£400-600   **VS**

A blue glass vase, by Jean Beck of Munich, with stylized silver floral decoration, numbered on underside "472" in orange-red enamel.

c1920   7.75in (19.5cm) high

£120-180   **FIS**

A lidded purple glass vase, by L. Moser & Sons of Karlsbad, with an etched and gilded frieze of musicians.

c1920   12.25in (30.5cm) high

£300-500   **FIS**

A purple glass faceted vase, by L. Moser & Sons of Karlsbad, with gilded decoration of fighting Amazons and centaurs, etched signature.

c1920   9.5in (24cm) high

£300-500   **FIS**

A green cased glass vase, by the Josephinen glassworks in Schreiberhau, with original label, chipped.

c1925

£150-200   **FIS**

A rare Steinschönau cameo vase, clear glass overlayed in purple, etched, engraved and cut with stylized blossoms and leaves.

1928   6.5in (16.5cm) high

£2,500-3,000   **FIS**

A vase, by Karl John of Haida, with polychrome painting and inlay between layers of clear glass, signed "Jonolith".

c1930   6in (15cm) high

£400-600   **FIS**

An etched and lacquered Eisenbrod vase, decorated with a female nude in a winter landscape with blossoms.

c1940   9in (22.5cm) high

£280-320   **FIS**

A Haida yellow stained and etched lidded glass jar, decorated in black enamel with stylized blossoms, leaves and geometrical ornaments.

c1920   7.5in (18.5cm) high

£800-1,200   **FIS**

A Haida lidded jar, with polychrome translucent enamel medallions of stylized blossoms.

c1920   6.75in (17cm) high

£800-1,200   **FIS**

A CLOSER LOOK AT A BOHEMIAN LIDDED CUP

Cups of this size complete with their original covers are an increasingly rare commodity. The combination of complex decorative techniques make this piece of even greater interest to collectors.

This cup has been decorated with fired-on enamels made from metallic oxides and ground glass. This is longer lasting than cold-painted decoration and produces these vibrant, translucent colours.

The yellow colour visible at the knop and elsewhere on this piece has been applied by flashing, which involves applying metallic oxides and reheating the glass.

The 1920s saw a renaissance in Bohemian glass-making after the collapse of the Austro-Hungarian empire and the establishment of a free market led to a surge in exports.

A rare Haida lidded cup, clear and honey-yellow stained glass, decorated with stylized flowers in polychrome enamel.

c1920   10.5in (26cm) high

£1,500-2,000   **FIS**

A Haida lidded cup, clear glass painted in black with a geometrical pattern.

c1920　　*10in (25cm) high*

£400-600　　　　　**FIS**

A small lidded jar, by the Lorenz brothers of Steinschönau, dark purple cut glass painted with gold figures.

c1925　*5.75in (14.5cm) high*

£150-200　　　　　**FIS**

A faceted glass jar, by Hermann Eiselt of Steinschönau, clear underlayed with ruby-red glass, decorated with gilding, etched to underside "Radierung hest".

c1925　　*4.5in (11cm) high*

£250-350　　　　　**FIS**

A Friedrich Egermann decanter and stopper, clear glass with schwarzlot enamel, cracked.

c1840　　*14in (35cm) high*

£700-1,000　　　　**FIS**

A lidded jug, by the Buquoysche Glassworks, black hyalith glass with fine gilded floral and ornamental motifs.

c1830　　*8in (20cm) high*

£1,000-1,500　　　**FIS**

A Moser purple faceted glass jar, chipped.

c1920　*6.5in (16.5cm) diam*

£120-180　　　　　**FIS**

A clear glass Steinschönau bowl, painted with stylized floral motifs in black and coloured enamels, with gilded rim.

c1915　　*5.5in (14cm) high*

£150-200　　　　　**FIS**

A clear glass lidded Steinschönau bowl, painted with a female nude and dog in black and polychrome enamels.

c1915　*3.75in (9.5cm) diam*

£200-300　　　　　**FIS**

A clear etched glass Steinschönau bowl, stained yellow and painted with stylized floral motifs and spiral ornaments in black and gold, with gilded rim, cracked.

c1920　　*6in (15cm) high*

£180-220　　　　　**FIS**

A miniature J.&L. Lobmeyr sweet dish, by Meyr's Neffe of Vienna, with gilded foot and rim, signed.

c1880　　　　　　*2.75in (7cm) high*

£1,200-1,800　　　　　　　　　　　**FIS**

One of a set of seven glass brandy bowls, red cut to clear glass, with circles and cross-hatching in panels, the base star-cut, with a clear loop handle, chipped.

7.25in (11cm) diam

£60-90 set　　　　**FRE**

A Haida desk lamp, by Hermann Pautsch, clear etched glass with stylized blossoms and leaves in gilding and polychrome enamels.

c1920　　*12in (30cm) high*

£400-600　　　　　**FIS**

A faceted Baccarat paperweight, with two interlocking garlands of blue and red millefiori canes between small flowers, large white flower to centre.

c1845   3in (7.5cm) diam

£1,000-1,500   WKA

A mid-19thC French concentric paperweight, possibly Baccarat, the central green and red millefiori cane within two rings of coloured canes, scratched.

2.5in (6cm) diam

£300-350   DN

A Clichy scattered millefiori paperweight, with coloured flowers on a clear ground.

c1845   2.5in (6.5cm) diam

£800-1,200   WKA

A large Clichy paperweight, set with various coloured canes on a lace ground.

c1845   3.25in (8cm) wide

£1,800-2,200   WW

A Clichy paperweight, set with concentric canes and a border of white stars and rose canes.

c1845   2.5in (6.5cm) wide

£800-1,200   WW

A CLOSER LOOK AT A BACCARAT PAPERWEIGHT

These 'Gridel' silhouettes are named for Emile Gridel, the nephew of a Baccarat manager, whose paper animals inspired the deceptively simple designs.

Densely packed millefiori canes are a signature feature of Baccarat paperweights, which are considered among the very best on the market.

Date canes like this one were first used by Baccarat in 1846. Genuine date canes will not be placed centrally.

A mid-19thC Clichy chequer paperweight, set with coloured millefiori canes on a ground of latticinio tubing, some surface scratches.

2.5in (6.5cm) diam

£600-900   DN

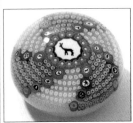

£300-500

A 20thC Baccarat paperweight, decorated with a central deer 'Gridel' silhouette and alternate green and yellow concentric rows of canes within a twist of blue canes.

3in (7.5cm) diam

GORL

A complex St. Louis millefiori paperweight, with coloured flowers and one figure on clear ground.

1845   2.75in (7cm) diam

£800-1,200   WKA

A 19thC St Louis glass paperweight, with central red and white cogwheel design surrounded by rows of blue, red and white wavy cut canes.

3in (7.5cm) diam

£600-900   GORL

A mid-20thC Paul Ysart paperweight, with thirteen polychrome canes on a green ground, complete with original presentation box.

3in (7.5cm) diam

£300-500   GORL

A 20thC Perthshire paperweight, dark blue glass base with yellow and pink millefiori canes, centred with a flower and a butterfly, with signature "P" cane to the base.

2.75in (7cm) diam

£300-400   WKA

An early 17thC heraldic stained glass section, decorated in polychrome enamel colours with the supper at Emmaus, beneath a Renaissance cartouche with a four-line inscription, dated "1619", restored.

1619   *14in (5.5cm) high*

£1,200-1,800   **LPZ**

A baluster coin mug, with a trailed band beneath the rim and fluted lower section, supported on a domed and folded foot and applied with a loop handle, containing a George II coin dated 1758.

7in (17.5cm) high

£150-200   **DN**

A pair of 19thC northern English green glass dumps, each of typical knob form enclosing a frosted effect mushroom.

3.75in (9.5cm) high

£120-180   **H&L**

A mid-19thC glass vase with a trailed and draped pattern.

7.75in (20cm) high

£150-200   **JH**

One of a pair of Victorian satin glass moulded light shades.

11.5in (29cm) high

£200-300 pair   **SWO**

A mid-Victorian cameo glass plaque, attributed to Thomas Webb, acid-etched with entwined ivy in white against a deep blue ground, unsigned.

4in (10cm) wide

£600-900   **GORL**

A Salviate & Co. Venetian revival sweetmeat dish.

c1890   5.75in (14.5cm) high

£300-400   **AL**

An amber millefiori vase, with green, blue and amber highlights and two applied handles, the gold stand with ram's head capitals and hoof feet, chipped.

16in (40.5cm) high

£300-500   **JDJ**

A covered Anfora goblet, with applied daisies over a latticework body, the knop handle with applied mythical creatures.

Based on a historical design found in a museum, this piece was made to show the virtuosity of the Anfora glassmakers.

17in (43cm) high

£5,000-6,000   **ANF**

A German enamelled glass vase and cover, of conical form with prunts above a spread foot, painted in polychrome colours with a warrior, his wrists encircled with serpents.

23.5in (60cm) high

£200-300   **HAMG**

A pair of cobalt blue overlay candlesticks, with vertical ribbing and fleur-de-lys mark.

12in (30.5cm) high

£600-900   **JDJ**

A cranberry glass and gilt metal swing-handled basket, decorated with fruiting vine.

4.25in (11cm) diam

£30-40   **H&L**

THE SILVER & METALWARE MARKET

Over the last few years, buyers have become increasingly knowledgeable and are more selective about what they buy. Silver and metalware at the lower ends of the market is being rejected in favour of high quality and unusual pieces without restoration.

As well as 20thC pieces by designers such as Jensen and Ramsden, smaller Victorian items, including boxes and vinaigrettes, have remained popular, particularly examples with unusual decoration. Highly regarded 19thC makers, such as Hennell, Hunt Roskell and Storr, have also held their appeal.

With earlier pieces, buyers look for good, simple, Georgian silver with original engraving. Bright-cut tea sets are popular.

Traditionally, silver with engraved coat-of-arms and inscriptions have attracted little interest but buyers, increasingly fascinated by provenance, now intentionally seek out original examples.

Scottish silver is also in demand, especially provincial hollow-ware. Lyon & Turnbull in Edinburgh recently sold a rare Tain c1710-20 whisky cup for a staggering £22,000. To command high prices, Scottish pieces should bear distinct hallmarks.

The market is poor for pieces of low quality, including mass-produced 20thC silver. Victorian tea sets currently attract little interest, unless they feature unusual decoration.

– Trevor Kyle, Director, Lyon & Turnbull

SILVER BOWLS & BASKETS

A pair of George II 'Duty Dodgers' pomanders, by Abraham Buteux, each with a hinged body, reticulated design and engraved crest of Bernard of Dunsinnan and Buttergask of Perthshire, on spreading circular foot, marks for London.

'Duty dodgers' inserted hallmarks from lighter pieces into new silver to avoid paying the tax levied from 1719 to 1758.

1727   *3.75in (9cm) high*

£7,000-10,000   **FRE**

A matched group of four 19thC French small silver comports, each of circular form, inscribed with various mottos, applied Napoleonic bee motifs and engraved Heroic inscriptions, dated 1811 and 1808.

7in (17.5cm) wide

£600-900   **L&T**

A pair of George III silver oval dishes, by Paul Storr, the wavy rim with engraved frieze of floral and C-scrolls forming four cartouches, on a bold cast base of four scrolling leaf-form feet, with marks for London, formerly with armorial bearings.

1817   *12.5in (31.5cm) wide*

£1,500-2,000   **L&T**

A 19thC Continental silver gilt and enamel urn, of campana form, the ornate foliate chased sides with twin ram's mask handles and applied bloodstone lobes, set with rubies, on a spreading oval base.

5.5in (14cm) high

£5,000-7,000   **FRE**

A Victorian Irish silver melon-fluted sugar bowl, by J. Mahoney, with a shell and leaf chased border, embossed with foliate sprays and cartouches, marks for Dublin.

1868   *6in (15cm) diam*

£350-400   **DN**

A Victorian silver monteith, by Elkington and Co., of traditional form, demi-fluted with a cartouche and engraved monogram, a spreading foot and gilt interior, marks for Birmingham.

1898   *10.5in (26.5cm) diam*

£800-1,200   **L&T**

A set of four Victorian silver baskets, each with cast interwoven handles, reticulated sides and a floral swag, pierced oval back, by "JC" and marks for London.

1893   *7in (17.5cm) wide*

£1,200-1,800   **L&T**

A George III silver vinaigrette, by Samuel Pemberton, the hinged cover engraved with "J.C." within a repeating leaf border, gilt interior with filigree and scrollwork grille, marks for Birmingham.

1802   *1.25in (3cm) wide*

£180-220   **B**

A George III agate inset silver snuff box, by "WH" of London, the hinged lid with a raised panel of pink and brown banded stone, on an overall vermicular, stippled and engraved ground.

1806   *3in (7.5cm) wide*

£150-200   **CHEF**

A George III silver gilt snuff box, made by Matthew Linwood of Birmingham, of rectangular form with basket weave decoration.

1810   *3in (7.5cm) wide*

£350-400   **HAMG**

A silver snuff box, made by Nathaniel Mills of Birmingham, the cover cast and chased with a foliate border, the base and sides with engine-turned decoration.

1839   *3.5in (9cm) wide*

£450-500   **HAMG**

A silver table snuff box, by Nathaniel Mills of Birmingham, the cover engraved with an inscription to "William Hardman" dated "May 1849", with red velvet lining, marks for Birmingham.

1846   *3.25in (8.5cm) wide*

£1,500-2,000   **B**

A Russian Niello silver cigarette case, the cover engraved with figures in a wagon pulled by three horses, against a scrolling foliate ground, with a letter of provenance.

c1870   *5.5in (14cm) wide*

£500-800   **HAMG**

A silver and parcel-gilt cornucopia vinaigrette, by Sampson Mordan and Co., applied with die-stamped and pierced borders, the cover enclosing a foliate pierced grille, London.

1873   *8cm (3.25in) long*

£400-600   **B**

A Victorian oval tobacco box, by John and Frank Pairpoint, embossed with scrolls and a later inscribed cartouche, the cover with a figure in a rural landscape, marks for London.

1883   *6in (15cm) wide*

£250-300   **DN**

A late Victorian silver and enamel cigarette case, with an oval panel depicting a Boer War soldier at a carriage-mounted machine gun, engraved verso "T.B.S", marks for Birmingham.

1899   *3.5in (9cm) high*

£350-400   **DN**

An Edwardian silver snuff box by The Goldsmith's and Silversmith's Company of London, with central "FM" initials and a wavy edged hinged lid, gilt interior.

     3.5in (9cm) high

£120-180   **CHEF**

A CLOSER LOOK AT A VICTORIAN SILVER SNUFF BOX

The inscription adds to the desirability, as silverware collectors are increasingly interested in historical context. Pieces that have a strong link with a historical figure can command a premium.

The crisp high relief decoration, depicting specific military campaigns, adds to the unique nature of the piece, which appeals to both collectors of snuff boxes and of militaria.

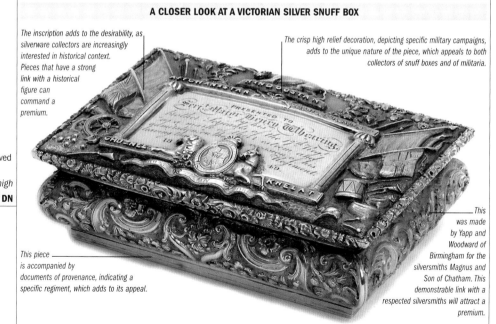

This piece is accompanied by documents of provenance, indicating a specific regiment, which adds to its appeal.

This was made by Yapp and Woodward of Birmingham for the silversmiths Magnus and Son of Chatham. This demonstrable link with a respected silversmiths will attract a premium.

An early Victorian silver military table snuff box, a unique commission by Yapp & Woodward of Birmingham for silversmiths Magnus & Son of Chatham, with inscription to Sergeant Major Henry Whearing on retirement in 1849, cast in high relief depicting his campaigns and regimental details, with documents of provenance.

     4.25in (10.5cm) wide

£3,500-4,500   **B**

One of an early 20thC pair of sterling silver five-light candelabra, in the Louis XV style, with scroll arms with floral hand-chased bobeches, on cast scroll feet, base marked "Goldis Blum".

19in (47.5cm) high

£5,000-7,000 pair   FRE

A pair of George III silver candlesticks, by John Carter of London, with hexagonal scroll edged foot embossed with shells below a knopped stem, spool socket with detachable shell decorated nozzle.

1775   10.5in (26.5cm) high

£2,000-3,000   CHEF

A pair of George II cast silver candlesticks, by Ebenezer Coker, of traditional knopped form with removable sconce, the base engraved with crest and motto, marks for London.

1748   8.25in (21cm) high

£2,500-3,000   L&T

A pair of George II candlesticks, by William Gould, with vase shaped capitals, leaf chased knopped stems and shaped square bases with anthemion corners, engraved armorials, marks for London.

1749   8.75in (22cm) high

£1,800-2,200   DN

A set of four early George III silver cast candlesticks, by Ebenezer Coker, with spiral fluted knopped columns and nozzles and stepped square bases, numbered 1 to 4, with scratch weights beneath "21: 7", "21: 14", "21: 10" and "21: 2", marks for London.

1766   10.5in (26.5cm) high

£7,000-10,000   DN

A CLOSER LOOK AT A PAIR OF SILVER CANDLESTICKS

These detachable nozzles are discreet, conforming with the outline to the base of the candlestick, and with the decoration to the stem.

Nozzles have been added at a later date; they are detachable and prevent the wax from pouring down the stem of the candlestick. By the 1740s these were a regular feature on candlesticks.

These candlesticks are in very good condition. Cast silver candlesticks are stronger and less prone to damage than those stamped from sheet and are therefore especially attractive to the buyer.

The production of cast candlesticks became rare after the 1770s. Therefore, cast candlesticks are much more desirable and command a premium.

A pair of George II cast silver candlesticks, by Edward Feline, the round leaf chased capitals with later nozzles, knopped stems headed with oval medallion busts, sunk centres with armorials, the bases with concave corners, engraved scale-work panels and applied cherubs, scratch weights beneath 28 and 28-15, London.

Provenance: Rushbrooke Hall, Suffolk.

1743   9in (23cm) high

£10,000-15,000   DN

A pair of George III silver table candlesticks, by John Green & Co., of circular tapered form, with removable sconces and spreading feet, marks for Sheffield.

1800   11.75in (30cm) high

£800-1,200   L&T

A pair of George II cast silver candlesticks, by John Pollock, of traditional knopped form with removable sconce, the base with engraved crest, marks for London.

1750   8.25in (21cm) high

£2,500-3,000   L&T

A George I hexagonal taperstick, by Gabriel Sleath, with a knopped stem and moulded base, with a later monogram, marks for London.

1718   4.25in (11cm) high

£1,500-2,000   DN

A pair of silver mounted tortoiseshell candlesticks, on turned spreading bases, marks for Birmingham.

1921   4.75in (12cm) high

£700-1,000   L&T

A pair of George III pierced oval pedestal salt cellars, by Robert Hennell, with scroll handles, beaded rims, and engraved with bright cut floral swags, blue glass liners, marks for London.

1783	4.75in (12cm) wide
£500-800	**DN**

One of a pair of George IV round salt cellars, by Emes and Barnard, each on a triform paw stem and round base, marks for London.

1822	3.5in (9cm) diam
£150-200 pair	**DN**

A pair of salt cellars modelled as ducks, by E. & J. Barnard, with silver gilt interiors, one marked beneath "Thomas's, Bond St, London", marks for London.

1862	4.75in (12cm) wide
£1,200-1,800	**DN**

A pair of Danish silver salt and pepper pots, each in the form of a squirrel with a bushy tail crouching on a circular removable base, "NM" maker's marks and "925S".

	2.5in (6.5cm) high
£100-150	**DN**

A set of four Victorian silver gilt salt cellars, by John S. Hunt, of lobed-oval trencher form on eagle supports, engraved with scrolls, cartouches and arms, marked to base with "Hunt and Roskell Late Storr and Mortimer", blue glass liners, London.

The arms are an early and unauthorised shield and motto used by Wells City Council in Somerset, England.

1856	4in (10cm) long
£3,000-5,000	**DN**

SILVER MARKS

- During the 14thC laws were passed to fix the purity of English silver at 925 parts in every thousand. A London Assay Office was set up to test and mark silver. This type of silver was known as 'sterling' – a term thought to derive from Easterling, a part of Germany known for the quality of its silver.
- A maker's mark was introduced in 1363 and in 1478, the date letter, which changed every year, was added.
- Assay offices opened all over the country to test the quality of silver. Each had its own mark. Important English assay marks include: leopard's head - London (est. 1544), sword and three wheatsheaves - Chester (1686-1962), castle - Exeter (1701-1883), three castles - Newcastle (est.1702), anchor - Birmingham (est.1773), crown - Sheffield (est. 1773).
- Assay offices were established in Russia from 1700 and a standard system was introduced in the USA in 1869, although in both these countries other marks had been used prior to these dates.
- Be aware of fake marks that are badly punched or incorrectly positioned, or marks that have been lifted from other pieces.

CASTERS

A Queen Anne silver caster, with a pierced and engraved domed top and ball finial, the baluster body engraved with initials 'VSH', with marks for London.

Provenance: Purchased at Spink & Son of 5 King St, St James's, London, October 1929.

1705	8.25in (21cm) high
£1,800-2,200	**L&T**

A George I caster, probably by Glover Johnson, engraved with an armorial, on a stepped foot, the foliate pierced cover with a finial, London, maker's mark rubbed.

The arms are those of Townshend of Raynham, Norfolk with a crescent for a second son.

1718	7in (18cm) high
£1,800-2,200	**DN**

A George II vase-shaped caster, by John White, with a moulded girdle and borders, later chased with leaf scrolls and rocaille, a crest within a cartouche, pierced cover with vase shaped finial, cover unmarked, London.

1731	6.75in (17cm) high
£800-1,200	**DN**

A matched pair of silver casters, by Samuel Wood, of plain vase form, with pierced cover and turned finial, together with a facsimile, with marks for London.

1742	6.25in (16cm) high
£500-800	**L&T**

A George II vase-shaped caster, by Samuel Wood, later embossed with foliate scrolls, the pierced cover with a turned finial, the cover with lion passant only, London, the body repaired.

1744	5.5in (14cm) high
£80-120	**DN**

SILVER & METALWARE

A George III pear-shaped caster, by Robert Pearcy, with beaded borders and bright-cut engraved cover with a flame finial, London.

1777   6in (15cm) high
£200-250   DN

A George III vase-shaped sugar caster, by Hester Bateman, with beaded border, diaper engraved cover and acorn finials, on a round foot, London.

1788   6in (15cm) high
£250-300   DN

A George III vase-shaped caster, possibly by William Abdy, with spiral fluted and foliate embossed body, the shaped cover with acorn finial on a reeded foot, London.

1798   6.75in (17cm) high
£120-180   DN

A pair of George III casters, with urn-shaped fluted bodies and crests, gadrooned borders on spreading reeded feet, the domed top pierced covers with ball-turned finials, London, maker's marks indistinct.

1819   3in (8cm) high
£180-220   DN

An urn-shaped silver caster, by George Fox, with a bead and reel border, part spiral fluted and chased with shells and scrolls, the pierced cover with a finial, London.

1901   8.25in (21cm) high
£350-450   DN

A vase-shaped caster, embossed with spiral flutes and leaves, the cover with spiral turned finial, on a moulded foot, Birmingham.

1904   5.5in (14cm) high
£80-120   DN

A Scottish vase-shaped sugar caster on a moulded foot, Edinburgh.

1914   7.5in (19cm) high
£180-220   DN

A William IV silver oval cylindrical nutmeg grater, by Rawlings and Sumner, with two hinged covers, engraved with script initials, London.

1835   2.75 in (7cm) long
£500-800   DN

A Victorian silver egg epergne, probably by Rawlings and Sumner or Reily and Storer, with acanthus-clasped base, hands and rims to the six gilt egg cups, each engraved with a crest, the whole on C-scroll feet, London.

1840   11in (28cm) high
£500-800   L&T

SILVER CUPS & GOBLETS

A Charles II silver porringer and cover, embossed with lions and gazelles amidst leaves, makers mark "WW" and a fleur-de-lys below, London.

1668
£4,000-6,000   DN

A William III silver porringer, possibly by Alexander Roode of London, the lower body fluted below a rope twist girdle, initialled "EL SS".

1696   3.25in (8.5cm) high
£1,000-1,500   CHEF

A Queen Anne silver porringer and cover, initialled by William Keat, part swirl fluted with a ropework band around the cover, the body engraved on one side with a later lozenge-shaped cartouche, London.

1711   5.75in (14.5cm) high
£1,500-2,000   WW

A Queen Anne porringer, by William Gamble, the part spiral lobed and fluted bowl with an embossed ropework band and an acanthus cartouche with pricked initials "B" over "W S", London.

1713   3.5in (9cm) high
£500-800   DN

, silver caddy spoon, by Omar Ramsden, with pale chalcedony osses, with commemorative allmarks for London.

'935   3in (8cm) long

£2,200-2,800   **WW**

A silver caddy spoon, with a grotesque mask and turquoise cabochon, pseudo-marks, unascribed, probably Chinese.

2.25in (5.5cm) long

£120-180   **WW**

A CLOSER LOOK AT A SILVER CADDY SPOON

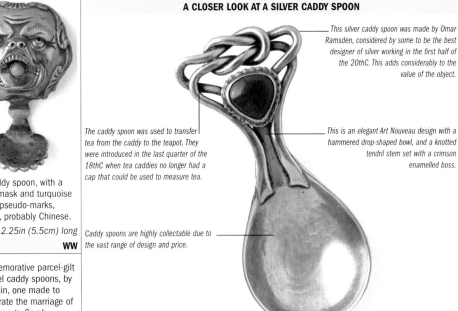

This silver caddy spoon was made by Omar Ramsden, considered by some to be the best designer of silver working in the first half of the 20thC. This adds considerably to the value of the object.

The caddy spoon was used to transfer tea from the caddy to the teapot. They were introduced in the last quarter of the 18thC when tea caddies no longer had a cap that could be used to measure tea.

This is an elegant Art Nouveau design with a hammered drop-shaped bowl, and a knotted tendril stem set with a crimson enamelled boss.

Caddy spoons are highly collectable due to the vast range of design and price.

Two commemorative parcel-gilt and enamel caddy spoons, by Stuart Devlin, one made to commemorate the marriage of Prince Andrew to Sarah Ferguson, hallmarked London 1986, the other for the birth of William, Prince of Wales and hallmarked London 1982.

2.5in (6.5cm) long

£400-600   **WW**

A silver caddy spoon, by Omar Ramsden of London, with a hammered drop-shaped bowl and a knotted tendril stem set with a crimson enamelled boss.

1919   3.5in (9cm) long

£3,500-4,500   **WW**

SPOONS

An Elizabeth I unascribed provinicial silver maidenhead spoon, the terminal with traces of gilding, struck once in the bowl with as fleur-de-lys within a shaped punch.

c1580   6.5in (16.5cm) long

£2,800-3,200   **WW**

A rare James I ascribed Cornish silver seal top spoon, by John Parnell of Truro, the fluted terminal with gilding, maker's mark "PARN" and the 'silver ship of Truro' in bowl, later initials.

c1620   6.5in (16.5cm) long

£2,000-2,500   **WW**

A Charles I silver-gilt seal top spoon, by David Cary of London, with a large decorated terminal, pricked "IA" over "MB".

1638   7in (18cm) long

£4,000-6,000   **WW**

A rare Henry VIII silver maidenhead spoon, with faint traces of gilding on the finial, pheon maker's mark, London.

1540   6in (15cm) long

£7,000-9,000   **WW**

A Charles I ascribed West Country silver apostle spoon of St Bartholomew, by Robert Wade II of Bridgewater, the gilt figure with a large nimbus, pricked "IM" over "1647" over "HM", maker's mark.

1647   7.25in (18.5cm) long

£2,000-2,500   **WW**

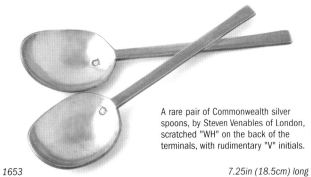

A rare pair of Commonwealth silver spoons, by Steven Venables of London, scratched "WH" on the back of the terminals, with rudimentary "V" initials.

7.25in (18.5cm) long

1653   £6,000-7,000   **WW**

A rare Commonwealth or Charles II provincial silver spoon, by one of the William Dodsons of Lewes, scratched "SR", town mark, crowned "D".

c1655   6.75in (17cm) long

£2,500-3,000   **WW**

A rare early Charles II inscribed puritan silver spoon, by Jeremy Johnson of London, with a rudimentary "V" rattail, the front of the stem inscribed "William Taunton borne Good Friday the 13th April 1655 Baptised the 24th of the same month 1655", the back of the terminal scratched "S" over "AD" over "1708".

1662   7.5in (19cm) long

£4,000-6,000   **WW**

A Charles II laceback silver trefid spoon, probably by Nicholas Brassey or Bracey of London, maker's mark "NB", a mullet and two pellets.

1679   7.5in (19cm) long

£800-1,200   **WW**

A pair of Charles II trefid spoons, with ribbed rattails and swollen terminals, initialled, by Lawrence Coles of London.

1684   7.5in (19cm) long

£1,000-1,500   **WW**

A rare James II large silver trefid spoon, by John King of London, with a plain moulded rattail and a flared terminal with a tongue-like projection, the stem of plain tapering form struck with an additional punchmark.

1686   10in (25.5cm) long

£3,500-4,000   **WW**

A Japanese silver spoon, modelled as a bijin with a samisen under a parasol.

5.75in (14.5cm) long

£500-800   **WW**

An extremely scarce Queen Anne marrow fork, by Lawrence Jones of London, crest, "1=19".

1705   8in (20.5cm) long

£1,000-1,500   **WW**

A pair of George III scissor-action chop servers, by W. Eley and W. Fearn of London.

1805   9.75in (25cm) long

£500-800   **WW**

A 19thC French fiddle and thread pattern sugar sifter ladle, with scratchwork piercing in the bowl, maker's mark "Irstein", Strasbourg.

9in (23cm) long

£280-320   **WW**

An extremely rare William III Scottish provincial knife, fork and by-knife, decorated with corded wire inlay, the blades with cutler's mark, the silver end caps with maker's mark "DB" within a heart-shaped punch for David Bigger or Biggart of Kilmaurs, in original tooled leather travelling case.

knife 8.25in (21cm) long

£5,000-8,000   **WW**

A set of King Edward sterling silver flatware, by Gorham, with 227 pieces, including a fish set, cocktail forks, 29 serving pieces, some monograms.

£3,500-3,000   **BRU**

A set of Kirk Repousse flatware, with 101 pieces, some with monograms, together with a serving spoon marked "Steiff", in two-drawer wood case.

£1,500-2,000   **BRU**

A set of Francis I sterling silver flatware, by Reed & Barton, with 179 pieces, including 29 serving pieces, six teaspoons with "S" monogram, in fitted brass-mounted oak case with two drawers and brass pulls on Chippendale-style stand, some monograms.

stand 33in (84cm) high

£4,000-6,000   **BRU**

An early 18thC Scottish silver circular stand, by Robert Luke, with a domed centre and on a circular foot, initials "MR" in script, marks for Glasgow.

725   7.75in (19.5cm) diam

£2,500-3,000   L&T

A George II Scottish small silver waiter, by Robert Luke, with shell and acanthus-carved inner border on four hoof feet, marks for Glasgow.

c1725   6.5in (16.5cm) wide

£1,200-1,800   L&T

A George II silver salver, by Edward Pocock, with chased decoration and a C-scroll and floral border, on four scroll feet, with marks for London.

1732   12.5in (32cm) diam

£500-700   L&T

A George III Scottish small silver waiter, maker James Hewitt, with gadrooned edge and engraved inner leaf border, on short cabriole legs with hoof feet, marks for Edinburgh.

1770   7in (18cm) diam

£350-450   L&T

A William IV silver tray, by J.E. Terry, with a heavy cast deep border of C-scrolls and flowers and vine-clasped handles, blank central cartouche surrounded by a deep chased border on a diaper ground and two C-scroll cartouches, one with armorial bearings and a shield, on heavy-cast shell feet, with marks for London.

1833   32.75in (83cm) wide

£7,000-10,000   L&T

INTEGRAL DECORATIVE TECHNIQUES

- The term 'integral decoration' refers to decoration that is formed from the body of the piece.
- Engraved decoration is cut into the surface with a 'graver' or 'burin'. Bright-cut engraving is angled to reflect the light.
- Embossing or 'repoussé' creates raised (relief) or hollow (incuse) designs. Hammers are used to bulge the material to one side. The technique also adds strength to the object.
- Chasing is often used to add definition to embossing and involves drawing a design on silver and then hammering it with a blunt ball-point chisel to distort the surface.
- In the 19thC, the technique of die stamping, where sheets of silver were sandwiched between shaped metal moulds, was developed, making it easier to mass-produce decorative silver.
- When buying, check that the style of the decoration matches the date of the hallmark. Engraved and chased designs may be later than the date of a piece, as decoration was sometimes added during the Victorian period to suit the tastes of the time. Earlier coats of arms and initials were also occasionally removed.
- Be aware of decoration that conceals repairs to silver, particularly where a worn area has been patched or replaced.

A George III silver gilt sideboard dish, by William Pitts, the base later engraved with "Presented to William Rome Corporation of the City of London Chairmanship 1892", London.

1789

£1,500-2,000   L&T

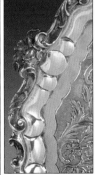

A pair of Victorian silver salvers, by Rawlings & Sumner or Reily & Storer, with a C-scroll border, inner decorated border of acanthus scrolls and flowers and a blank central cartouche, on three bracket feet, with marks for London.

1843   13.5in (34cm) wide

£1,200-1,800   L&T

A Scottish George II circular stand, by Archibald Ure, assaymaster Edward Penman, with marks for Edinburgh.

1728   8in (20.5cm) diam

£2,500-3,000   L&T

SILVER & METALWARE

A George III Irish helmet-shaped silver cream jug, by John Shields, embossed with rocaille cartouches, with a moulded girdle, double scroll handle and chased lion's mask, on paw feet, Dublin.

c1765	4in (10cm) high
£400-600	**DN**

A George III vase-shaped cream jug, by Hester Bateman, embossed with panels of fruit and vines and a scroll cartouche, punched rim, loop handle and square base, London.

1789	5.75in (14.5cm) high
£300-500	**DN**

A George III silver wine jug, of large helmet shape, with an engraved full armorial and demi-fluted oval foot, hardwood handle, marks for London.

1801	11in (28cm) high
£700-1,000	**L&T**

A Regency Scottish silver ewer, by Robert Gray & Son of Glasgow, of baluster form, the body embossed with flowers above a gadrooned circular foot, the flared spout chased with acanthus and anthemion, over a hinged cover.

1819	
£1,200-1,800	**CHEF**

A Victorian silver claret jug, probably by Rawlings & Sumner or Reily & Storer, of classical ewer shape, horn scroll handle, the body engraved with classical figures, on a pedestal foot, with marks for London.

1840	12.5in (32cm) high
£1,000-1,500	**L&T**

APPLIED DECORATIVE TECHNIQUES

- The term 'applied decoration' indicates designs which are not part of the basic form of a piece.
- Cut-card decoration, most common on Huguenot silver, refers to designs cut from plates of silver and then soldered to an object.
- Gilding is used to give silver the appearance of gold. The term 'parcel gilt' refers to gilding in a limited area rather than an all-over coating. The process of mercury gilding is highly toxic and was replaced with electrogilding in the mid-19thC.
- Electrogilding involves coating silver objects with a film of gold using an electric current. The gold can be brassy in colour.
- Other types of applied decoration was also used, such as beaded rim wires or cast foliate, figural and shell decoration.

An early 19thC silver ewer, with a later engraved crest, central band of applied foliate grotesques and chased acanthus base and stem, with a pedestal base on ball feet, inscription, probably contemporary, to crest "This formerly belonged to the... 1st EMPEROR NAPOLEON, AT FONTAINBLEUE".

Provenance: *Purportedly once the property of Napoleon Bonaparte.*

	7.5in (19cm) high
£1,500-2,000	**ROS**

A Victorian Irish silver presentation claret jug, by "P.L.", inscription, Dublin.

1844	12.25in (31cm) high
£1,000-1,500	**L&T**

A Victorian silver hot water jug, with a scroll capped handle, London.

1892	6.5in (17cm) high
£150-200	**SWO**

A late Victorian helmet-shaped cream jug, by J. Millward Banks, embossed with flowers, birds and animals and with a shaped rim, moulded girdle and lion mask and paw feet, Birmingham.

1895	
£180-220	**DN**

A late 17thC Scandinavian silver peg tankard, with a beaded scroll handle and shield terminal, the hinged lid with lion and ball thumbpiece, engraved with 'Olle Peders * Anne Nielsd 1680" and shields with scrolling flowers, on floral capped melon feet.

6.5in (16.5) high

£2,800-3,200　　　　**DN**

A Queen Anne silver tankard, by Gabriel Sleath, London, with moulded foot, edge and girdle, S-scroll handle and peaked cover with scrolled thumbpiece, later embossed presentation inscription, dated "24 June 1842".

1710　　　　7.5in (19cm) high

£700-1,000　　　　**CHEF**

A CLOSER LOOK AT A SILVER TANKARD

Thumbpieces with little sign of wear, like this one, contribute to the value of a piece. Although the thumbpieces were for use, the silversmith combined practicality with beauty when crafting them.

The tapered cylindrical sides and shallow domed lid is emblematic of pre-1765 tankard design. Chased and embossed foliate and fruit decoration, along with the chased décor on the S-scroll handle is typical of tankards from the William and Mary period, which tend to have plain shapes and simple decorative borders.

The floral ornamentation was typical of the William and Mary style of decoration. The style was heavily influenced by the French Louis XIV style, whose classical motifs and formality were brought to England by the Huguenot refugees.

Between the two mullets are the initials "H.I." Tankards were expensive purchases and were recognised as a symbol of the owner's wealth, therefore most were marked with the owner's initials.

A William and Mary silver tankard, the lid and tapered cylindrical sides with chased and embossed foliate and fruit decoration, the S-scroll handle with chased decoration, "H.I." between two mullets, London.

1693　　　　8in (20cm) high

£6,000-8,000　　　　**FRE**

A George III English provincial silver quart tankard, by John Langlands I, with a moulded border and band, the scroll handle with a heart-shaped terminal, inscribed "H" over "I.M", Newcastle.

1770

£2,000-3,000　　　　**DN**

A William and Mary silver mug, by John Sutton, with moulded borders and a scroll handle with two armorials, the sides engraved with a shield and crest, inscribed, London.

The shield and crest of George Donnington, Armiger, and an inscription marking this gift to the Town of Wells in Somerset.

1693

£3,500-4,000　　　　**DN**

A George II silver baluster-shaped mug, by Thomas Whipham II and Charles Wright. with a leaf-capped double scroll handle and broad spreading foot, London.

1757　　　　5in (13cm) high

£250-350　　　　**DN**

A late George II baluster mug, by John Wilks, with leaf capped scroll handle on a moulded spreading foot, London.

1758　　　　6in (14.5cm) high

£500-800　　　　**DN**

A Victorian drum-shaped silver mustard pot, by Henry Wilkinson & Co., with a shaped foot-rim, engraved with a bird and vines on a diaper ground, the cover with a cartouche and presentation inscription, green glass liner, Sheffield.

1843　　　　2.75in (7cm) diam

£220-280　　　　**DN**

A George III silver three piece tea service, by J.E. Terry, the teapot lid with a fluted ivory finial, the body with an engraved crest in a C-scroll and floral ground, reserve panels of an oriental person fishing and eagle surmount, with marks for London.

1819

£1,200-1,800 CHEF

A Scottish Victorian three piece silver tea service, comprising teapot, sugar bowl and cream jug, engraved with birds and C-scrolls, floral finial to teapot, "JM" maker's marks, marks for Glasgow.

1857

£600-900 CHEF

A four-piece silver tea service, by Barraclough and Barraclough, with fluted covers, shell-chased and formal engraved bands and borders, the teapot and hot water jug with ivory handle and finial, London.

1939 *Teapot 6.25in (16cm) diam*

£800-1,200 DN

A George I small bullet-shaped teapot, by Abraham Buteux, with a moulded spout and foot, a fruitwood scroll handle and a turned finial, the rim with and engraved band and with a later crest, London 1721.

The Irish crest and coronet are those of Earl Winterton of Gort in the county of Galway, Ireland. Buteux married Eliza Godfrey, one of the most prolific silversmiths of the time.

1721

£7,000-10,000 DN

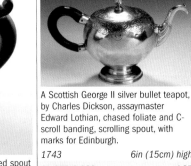

A Scottish George II silver bullet teapot, by Charles Dickson, assaymaster Edward Lothian, chased foliate and C-scroll banding, scrolling spout, with marks for Edinburgh.

1743 *6in (15cm) high*

£2,000-3,000 L&T

A George III silver teapot and matching stand, with bright-cut decoration and blank cartouche, the base similarly engraved and with a mahogany base. "G.B." marks for maker, London.

1800 *11.75in (30cm) wide*

£600-900 L&T

A George III Irish silver teapot, with bold Rococo chased decoration, the lid with later butterfly finial, the scroll spout with eagle and mask support, with marks for Dublin.

1816 *6in (15cm) long*

£1,200-1,800 L&T

A Victorian oval silver teapot, by Thomas Smily, with an angular handle, engraved cartouches with an elephant crest and presentation inscription dated 1871, hinged cover with knop finial, London.

1869 *12in (31cm) wide*

£250-300 DN

An early Victorian silver melon-shaped teapot, London.

1844

£200-300 SWO

A George III silver coffee pot, by John Swift of London, with embossed decoration and engraved coat of arms.

1776 *11.5in (29cm) high*

£1,200-1,800 WW

A fine Maltese silver coffee pot, by Gio Andrea Azzopardi, hinged dome cover, ebonised handle, raised on caprine legs.

c1800 *10.5in (27cm) high*

£2,500-3,000 HAMG

A silver coffee pot, wooden handle and Duncan crest, Goldsmiths & Silversmiths Company marks, Sheffield.

1918 *11in (28cm) high*

£1,000-1,500 L&T

A George III silver tea urn on stand, with a hinged wicker handle, the spout with an ivory handle, marks for "IS", London.

1795 *18in (46cm) high*

£2,800-3,200 L&T

A George III large lidded silver ewer, by Robert William, with a cartouche and crest, marks for Dublin.

1796 *11.5in (29cm) high*

£3,000-4,000 L&T

One of a pair of late George II silver sauceboats, by William Homer, with leaf capped flying scroll handles, shaped borders and hoof feet, London.

1755

£1,200-1,800 pair **DN**

A George III small sauceboat, by William Skeen, with a leaf capped flying scroll handle and a punched rim, later embossed with flowers, London.

1775

£120-180 **DN**

A pair of oblong sauceboats, with shell and gadrooned rims, leaf capped flying scroll handles and pad feet, marked "Sharman.D.Neill Ld, Belfast", Chester 1915.

1915

£280-320 **DN**

A pair of George III silver oval sauce tureens and covers, the bowls by Daniel Smith and Robert Sharp, the covers probably by Thomas Ellis, with beaded borders and armorials, London.

1782

£1,500-2,000 **DN**

One of a pair of George III silver vegetable tureens and covers, of squat octagonal form, the lid with curled branch handle and initials "JME", the dish with gadrooned rim, marks for "DS RS", London.

1786 9.5in (24.5cm) wide

£1,200-1,800 pair **L&T**

A George III silver soup tureen and cover, the domed lid with boat finial, the base with ball cast rim and scrolling handles, on an oval foot with ball cast edge, with marks for Paul Storr, London.

1812 18.5in (47cm) wide

£1,200-1,800 **L&T**

9in (23cm) wide

OTHER SILVER

An early Victorian inkstand, of waisted oblong outline, by Messrs Barnard of London, with naturalistic decoration, foliate shell handles and two applied cartouches, one crested and one inscribed "The Gift of the Rev Cr Wordsworth D D Master of Trinity Col Cam to E&D Quillinan July 6 1841", internal glass liners with covers, central detachable taperstick.

1840 15in (38cm) wide

£2,500-3,000 **WW**

An early Victorian silver desk stand, the pierced scrolled gallery and divisions with two silver mounted glass jars, on four silver feet with marks for "EA", London.

1848 7.5in (19cm) wide

£1,000-1,500 **L&T**

An Edwardian silver inkstand by Charles Stewart Harris, beaded and scroll pierced gallery, cylindrical box with a chamber taperstick cover, the two cut glass bottles with silver tops, London.

1903 9.5in (24cm) wide

£400-600 **CHEF**

A William IV silver toast rack, the threaded hoops on a shaped acanthus-clasped base with shell terminals and a central handle, with "E", "E", "J", "W. Barnard" and marks for London.

1832 8.75in (22cm) wide

£600-900 **L&T**

SILVER & METALWARE

A silver cucumber slicer, the open framework supporting a screw with moving back plate opposing a rotating blade, set on an ogee form base, London.

£250-300   ROS

A Britannia silver photograph frame, of rectangular form, enriched with repoussé putti playing among flowering vines, London.

11in (28cm) high   1897

£280-320   ROS

A late Victorian Irish dish ring, by Charles Lamb, pierced and embossed with figures and animals, the rocaille cartouche with a presentation inscription dated "1913", blue glass liner, Dublin.

1902

£1,200-1,800   DN

A silver and mother-of-pearl child's teether, by Crisford & Norris, in the form of spaniel's head, Birmingham.

4.75in (12cm) long

£100-150   DN

A Dutch silver miniature longcase clock, the hood cast with a figure and scrolls, the white enamel dial painted with a harbour scene, 18thC London pocket watch movement, on a Bombay shaped base, the case 833 standard with date letter.

1904   *9.75in (24.5cm) high*

£350-450   B

A silver mounted pin cushion, by Adie and Lovekin Ltd., in the form of a Venetian gondola decorated with scrolls, Birmingham.

1906   *3.75in (9.5cm) long*

£280-320   DN

A silver fluted and engraved rattle, by Crisford and Norris, hung with six bells and with a coral teether, Birmingham.

1910

£200-300   DN

A pair of silver mounted glass vesta holders, of ribbed globular form, with marks for "JG&S", London, 1912, and another larger, Birmingham, 1911.

largest 4.75in (12cm) high

£1,000-1,500   L&T

A silver desk ruler, with loop handle, engraved with initials "J A L D" with marks for Asprey & Co., London.

1917   *10in (25.5cm) long*

£700-1,000   L&T

A Continental articulated model of a salmon, with scale detail, textured fins, hinged head with glass eyes, the hinged mouth with realistic teeth, English import marks for London.

1927   *26in (66cm) long*

£7,000-10,000   WW

An Eastern silver scent bottle, modelled as an articulated fish, the head hinged to reveal a bottle, jewelled eyes, chain with finger ring, unmarked.

4.5in (11.5cm) wide

£120-180   CHEF

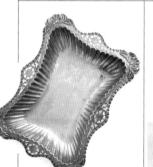

An Edwardian silver pastry dish, by C Westwood & Sons, Birmingham.

1903   *11in (28cm) wide*

£80-120   CHEF

An 18ct gold goblet, engraved to commemorate the Royal Silver Wedding, by A. T. Cannon, numbered "12", Birmingham.

1972

£1,500-2,000   DN

SILVER PLATE

An early 19thC Old Sheffield plate tea urn, the chamber with a cast iron frog.

15.75in (40cm) high

£500-800   CHEF

An early Victorian silver-plated tea kettle on a stand, with a lamp, embossed with scrolls and cartouches and with a bird of prey finial.

£300-400   DN

A Victorian silver-plated on copper double tea caddy, of bombé form and serpentine body, decorated with C-scrolls and scroll feet, divided interior, the lid with floral finial and lock.

8.25in (21cm) wide

£350-400   L&T

A large Victorian silver-plated soup tureen and cover, of oval shape, with all-over bright-cut decoration and cast mounts.

19.25in (49cm) wide

£700-1,000 | **L&T**

An early 20thC tortoiseshell mounted vesta/match case, in the form of a tortoise with a plated base and a press-moulded tortoiseshell hinged cover.

3.25in (8.5cm) wide

£400-600 | **DN**

A pair of Old Sheffield plate candelabra, each with a central gadrooned urn finial, the scrolled candle branches with trumpet sconces, the swag embossed tapering column on a spreading circular foot.

14.5in (37cm) high

£1,000-1,500 | **L&T**

An electroplate reproduction of an Old Sheffield plate ewer by Walker & Hall, the body of scrolled and fluted form, with foliate handle, hinged cover with acanthus thumbpiece.

13.5in (34cm) high

£150-200 | **CHEF**

Two of a set of four Old Sheffield plate extending candlesticks, with gadrooned borders, round columns and oblong bases and nozzles.

£100-150 set | **DN**

WINE ANTIQUES

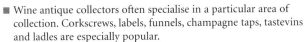

A George III beaded silver wine label, probably provincial or Scottish, in the shape of a narrow kidney, incised "Port", maker's mark "WS" struck twice, unascribed.

c1785

£150-200 | **WW**

A George III English silver oval-shaped port label, by John Whittingham of London.

1791 | *2in (5cm) wide*

£50-70 | **CSA**

A rare George III Irish silver wine label, of canted oblong form with a moulded border, incised "Tenerif", maker's mark "JT" possibly for J. Teare of Dublin.

c1800

£500-800 | **WW**

A George III English silver oblong brandy label, by John Angel of London, with cut corners.

1806 | *1.75in (4.5cm) wide*

£40-60 | **CSA**

WINE ANTIQUES

- Wine antique collectors often specialise in a particular area of collection. Corkscrews, labels, funnels, champagne taps, tastevins and ladles are especially popular.
- Wine labels, made from ivory, wood or silver, were produced to hang around the neck of bottles and decanters to identify the contents. When legislation was introduced in 1860 forcing retailers to label their own bottles prior to sale, the use of hanging wine labels declined.
- Wine funnels, used for pouring liquid into decanters for serving, were made from the mid-17thC. The curve to the base of the spout allowed wine to pour gently against the side of the decanter. Early funnels are rare and often valuable.
- Tastevins were a professional tool designed for wine tasting to assess colour and clarity.
- The corkscrew became popular from the 18thC when wine producers began to seal bottles by driving the cork well into the neck. Major manufacturers include Thomason, James Heeley, Dowler and Robert Jones. Types include peg and worm, concertina and waiter's friends.

A cast silver madeira wine label, by Charles Rowlings and William Summers, with grapevine border.

c1809 | *2.75in (7cm) wide*

£120-180 | **CSA**

A George III silver wine label, probably Scottish, of plain oblong form, incised "Soterne", maker's mark "PG" in an oval, unascribed.

c1815

£700-1,000 | **WW**

SILVER & METALWARE

A George III provincial silver wine label, by John Walton of Newcastle, canted oblong with a reeded border, incised and filled "Rum".

1815

£120-180 WW

A George III English silver sherry label, by George Knight of London.

1819 *1.75in (4.5cm) long*

£30-50 CSA

A 19thC Colonial mounted tiger claw wine label, probably Indian, with engraved decoration, incised "Port", unmarked.

c1850

£100-150 WW

A pair of Birmingham silver decanter labels, by Yapp & Woodward, with pierced lettering "port" and "sherry", in the form of vine leaves, hallmarked "Birmingham".

1852 *3.5in (9cm) wide*

£150-200 CSA

A Birmingham silver Scotch whiskey label, by C.H. Cheshire, escutcheon-shaped with scrolled border.

c1865 *2in (5cm) wide*

£100-150 CSA

A Victorian stamped-out silver wine label, by Edward Charles Brown of London, with a decorative border of husks and scrolls and pendant thistles, pierced "GIN".

1868

£80-120 WW

A pair of English Victorian silver spirit decanter labels, marked "Rum" and "Gin", with "Free (trade)" on the ribboned edge frame, among cornucopia, wheatsheaves and farming tools.

2.25in (6.5cm) wide

£200-300 CSA

A Dutch cast-silver corkscrew, with cavorting ladies and cherubs, the base with piped hamper.

c1760 *3in (8cm) long*

£300-350 CSA

An English silver pocket corkscrew, by Samuel Pemberton, stamped "SP".

c1780 *3.5in (9cm) long*

£220-280 CSA

A CLOSER LOOK AT A CORKSCREW

The brush is used to remove remaining lead and debris from the label, the bottle top and neck.

This corkscrew was also made with an open barrel. The open version commands a premium.

The corkscrew is complete with the two original handles and patent mark.

The top handle is used to insert the worm into the cork whilst the side handle operates a rack and pinion mechanism to remove the cork from the bottle.

A Birmingham silver-sheathed corkscrew, by Wardell and Kempson, with a two-finger ivory grip.

c1790 *3.25in (8.5cm) long*

£500-700 CSA

An English bronze-barrelled wide-rack king's screw, with a turned bone handle and a lion and unicorn tablet inscription "Dowler Patent".

c1820 *Extended 11in (28cm) wide*

£500-700 CSA

n English straight-pull corkscrew, with arved turned bone handle and dusting rush, mobed stem, helical worm.

1840   *4.25in (11cm) long*

50-70   **CSA**

An English six-tool steel folding bow, with horse hoof pick, button hook, corkscrew, screwdriver, gimlet and spike.

The more tools and the larger the piece, the more this type of tool is worth.

c1850   *2.75in (7cm) long*

£120-180   **CSA**

c1860

£150-200   **CSA**

A rare English silver roundlet corkscrew, with folding baluster stem, fluted steel worm, hallmarked "TJ" by Thomas Johnson of Birmingham.

3in (8cm) long

CSA

steel concertina-type corkscrew, with opper finish, marked "Weir's Patent 2804, 25 Septr 1884".

Extended 12.5in (32cm) long

50-70   **CSA**

An English two-part cast steel level corkscrew, with hinge plate bearing the inscription "Lund Patentee, 24 Fleet Street and 57 Cornhill, London 1884".

Lund was a retailer in Cornhill who was known to sell stationery and gentlemen's accessories and accoutrements. There are some pieces marked "Lund".

8.25in (21cm) long

£70-90   **CSA**

An English steel concertina-type corkscrew, inscribed "H.D. Armstrong Patent", with bladed worm.

c1885   *Ext. 10.5in (27cm) long*

£50-80   **CSA**

A French steel bladed corkscrew, with rivetted cow horn handle and corkscrew helix.

c1890   *3in (8cm) long*

£12-18   **CSA**

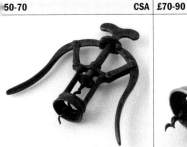

A double-lever steel corkscrew, with copper finish, stamped "'A1' Heeley's Double Lever".

c1900   *6.75in (17cm) long*

£50-80   **CSA**

An Italian four-pillar, open-frame bladed worm corkscrew, fixed brass 'T'-shaped driving handle on a threaded shaft.

c1920   *5.5in (14cm) long*

£50-70   **CSA**

A French nickel-plated concertina-type corkscrew, marked "Perfect Revete S.G.D.G.".

c1920   *ext. 7.75in (20cm) long*

£20-25   **CSA**

A George III part-fluted wine funnel, by Thomas Johnson, with gadrooned and moulded borders, London.

1810   *6in (15cm) long*

£300-400   **DN**

A Scottish silver wine funnel and drip stand, by J. McKay, Edinburgh, with pierced pattern, one-shell tab, family crest and motto.

1826   *5in (12.5cm) long*

£400-600   **CSA**

A George III silver wine funnel, by Thomas James of London, with a deep circular bowl, reeded borders and a shaped tang.

1805   *6in (15.5cm) high*

£600-700   **WW**

An English George III silver-gilt toddy ladle, with a turned bone handle.

c1820   *12in (30.5cm) long*

£120-180   **CSA**

SILVER & METALWARE

A Scottish silver toddy ladle, with turned rosewood handle, hallmarked "F.F." for Finlay and Field.

1828   *18.5in (47cm) long*

£150-200   **CSA**

A French silver tastevin on a chain with a French 50 cents coin, rim engraved with stars and "Dieu protege la France".

1872   *2.5in (6.5cm) diam*

£350-450   **CSA**

A French miniature silver-plated tastevin, marked "juva fruit" under the thumbpiece.

c1905   *2.75in (7cm) diam*

£12-18   **CSA**

A 1960s French chromium-plated tastevin.

4.25in (10.5cm) wide

£5-8   **CSA**

A George III silver tumbler cup, by Benjamin Brewood of London, initialled "RGL" below a crest.

1764   *3.25in (8.5cm) diam*

£500-600   **WW**

A George I silver tumbler cup, by Richard Bailey of London, with slightly tapered sides and a gilt interior.

1719   *2.75in (7cm) diam*

£2,000-3,000   **WW**

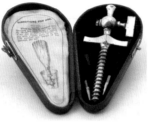

An English silver-plated leather-cased champagne tap, with two detachable spikes and a silk case lining printed with directions for use.

c1890   *4in (10cm) long*

£60-90   **CSA**

A pair of electroplate on copper wine coolers, each on a circular reed edged fluted foot supporting a half-fluted vase-shaped body with two foliate and shell scroll handles, reed-edged removable liner.

10.5in (26.5cm) high

£250-350   **CHEF**

An Old Sheffield silver-plate wine cooler or planter, of plain serpentine form raised on four bun feet and fitted with two ram's mask and ring handles, crested.

8.75in (22cm) diam

£280-320   **CHEF**

A pair of George III large silver wine coasters, by Edward Farrell of London, with cast husk and scroll rims and turned wooden bases, engraved with a coat of arms within an embossed scene, one depicting men and riders apprehending a man in the woods and conveying another back on a horse, the other with putti on a boar hunt in the woods.

1818   *6.75in (17cm) diam*

£1,500-2,000   **WW**

An 18thC Dutch brass hexagonal wedding presentation foot warmer, the pierced and embossed body with decoration of hearts, flowers, and busts of man and woman.

7in (18cm) high

£1,800-2,200   **POOK**

A penny foot brass trivet, with pierced decoration.

c1800

£600-900   **BP**

A pair of George II silver waiters, with pie crust borders and the coat of arms of a lady or widow in the centre, by William Tuite of London.

1733   *6.25in (16cm) diam*

£700-1,000   **WW**

A 19thC Boulle inkstand, with covered inkwells and raised on scroll feet cast with female masks.

14.5in (37cm) wide

£500-800   **CHEF**

A late 19thC gilt brass urn, with two handles cast with double head finials, above boar's heads, the body with bands of oak, shell and Greek key decoration, on a fluted foot and square base.

22.75in (57cm) high

£1,200-1,800   L&T

A massive brass and copper wine cooler, in the form of a Renaissance goblet, with mask handles and circular armorial and figural panels.

42.75in (107cm) high

£2,200-2,800   L&T

A copper and brass log bin, of cylindrical form with a rolled edge and two lion mask handles, on three paw feet.

18.75in (47cm) diam

£150-200   L&T

BRONZE

An American 'The Pioneer Woman' bronze group, by Bryant Baker, with a brown patina, on a marble base, inscribed and dated "Bryant Baker c 1927" and stamped "R. B. W. INC.".

1927   *11in (27.5cm) high*

£3,000-5,000   FRE

A Franz Bergman Austrian cold-painted bronze model of a woodcock, vase stamp.

8in (20.5cm) high

£1,000-1,200   WW

A Franz Bergman cold-painted bronze figure of a cock pheasant, in a standing posture, stamped monogram.

10.5in (26cm) high

£1,200-1,800   L&T

A Franz Bergman cold-painted bronze model of a golden pheasant, marked "B" within a vase stamp, and "Gesch 5724".

17.5in (44.5cm) wide

£800-1,200   WW

BRONZE FIGURES

- Bronze figures were either sand-cast or cast using the 'lost wax' (cire perdue) technique which involves moulding an object in wax, covering it with a clay or plaster mould and then heating it to allow the wax to run out and leave a shaped mould.
- The fluidity of bronze makes it particularly well suited to casting sculpture and decorative objects.
- In 1830, the pantograph was invented. This tracing instrument allowed artists to accurately scale down large antique sculptures and produce copies to meet the increased demand for decorative objects of a domestic size.
- During the 19thC Paris was considered the centre of sculpture and attracted sculptors from all over the world. Many based work on Classical statues until the advent of the Art Nouveau movement.
- Austria was also a centre for the production of high quality miniature bronzes. Several makers had studios in Vienna, including Franz Bergman.
- Known for its bronze groups, birds and animals, the Bergman factory was founded in Austria by Franz Bergman. Many pieces were exported and were extremely popular in the UK.
- Bergman signed some of his work with a "B" inside a two handled vase. The word "Namgreb" (Bergman spelled backwards) is also found.

A French 'Racehorse with Jockey Up' bronze group, by Isidore Bonheur, with a brown patina, on marble base, inscribed "I. Bonheur" and stamped "28/100".

23.5in (59cm) high

£5,000-8,000   FRE

A Maurice Bouval figure, of a bronze hunter, with birds strapped to his waist, shielding his eyes and holding a sling, with a greenish brown patination.

12in (31cm) high

£550-650   CHEF

SILVER & METALWARE

A French Jean Baptiste Auguste Clesinger 'Tauredo Romain' bronze standing bull, signed "J. Clessinger Rome, F. Barbedienne".

10in (25.5cm) wide

£1,000-1,500   JN

A French Paul Edouard Delabrierre bronze group of two fighting bulls, one standing over the other, on a rocky ground with branches, signed.

10.5in (26.5cm) wide

£1,200-1,800   JN

A 19thC French calling stag bronze, by Christophe, lying on a naturalistic base, signed.

12.5in (32cm) wide

£1,000-1,500   JN

A rare French Emmanuel Fremiet group of goats, the large goat feeding two kids, on a shaped naturalistic base, stamped "Fremiet".

7.75in (19.5cm) long

£1,200-1,800   JN

A Ferdinand Frick 'Male Cryer' bronze figure, with a rich dark brown patina, inscribed "Frick fec.".

24.5in (61cm) high

£1,800-2,200   FRE

An Austrian cold-painted bronze model of a bulldog, stamped "Gesch".

4.5in (11.5cm) wide

£300-350   WW

A Russian Ievgueni Alexandrovitch Lanceray 'Cossack on Horseback' bronze group, inscribed "Lanceray" in Cyrillic.

11.25in (28cm) high

£4,000-6,000   FRE

A German Hugo Lederer 'Man With Sword' bronze figure, with a brown patina, on a marble base, inscribed "H. Lederer fec".

37.5in (94cm) high

£3,000-4,000   FRE

An American 19thC Kate Lizard 'Shepherd Boy' bronze group, with a brown patina, inscribed "K. Lizard", stamped "Bronze Garantiau Titre C & L Déposée" and "12 6649".

20.25in (50.5cm) wide

£2,000-3,000   FRE

A 19thC French Jules Moigniez 'Merinos Nes A Wildeville' cast group, of a family of sheep, signed.

15.5in (39.5cm) wide

£3,500-4,000   JN

A CLOSER LOOK AT A BRONZE GROUP

The 19thC French sculptor Pierre Lenordez specialised in the medium of bronze. He was very popular among the socially elite in the French Riviera, especially those within horseracing circles.

Lenordez' equestrian bronzes were often portraits of specific thoroughbreds or the favourite horses of prominent horse owners. This bronze is signed, in script, and is accompanied by an inscription.

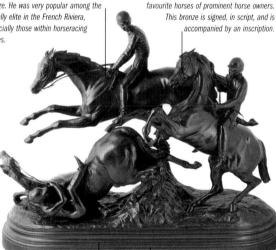

This particular bronze, 'Graux Marley', demonstrates the artist's skill in the medium, and his firm knowledge of the anatomy of horses.

The quality of the casting is flawless, with no sign of foundry marks, as is typical of Lenordez.

A 19thC Jules Moigniez large bronze stallion, standing before a rustic fence, signed.

20.5in (52cm) high

£7,000-8,000   JN

A 19thC bronze figure of Cupid, his hands tied by a ribbon, on a tree trunk, his bow and arrows on the oval base at his feet, dark brown patination.

8.25in (21cm) high

£80-120   CHEF

A 19thC French Pierre Lenordez 'Graux Marley' large bronze group, with three horses and riders at fence, the first horse fallen, the second leaping clear of the fence and the third startled, the bronze signed and inscribed.

30in (76cm) wide

£10,000-15,000   JN

An early 19thC 'The Dancing Faun' bronze figure, after the Antique, in a naked contraposto pose, standing on a square plinth, dark green patination.

12.75in (32cm) high

£400-600 **L&T**

A bronze figure of a naked male after the Antique, on a rectangular base, with a brown patina.

20.5in (51cm) high

£1,500-2,000 **FRE**

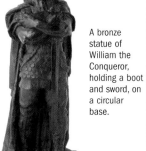

A bronze statue of William the Conqueror, holding a boot and sword, on a circular base.

19in (58cm) high

£400-600 **JN**

A bronze figure of Cupid, with a staff and tambourine, on a circular base.

22.5in (57cm) high

£1,500-2,500 **JN**

A small Vienna bronze of a native American on horseback, wearing full length head feathers and carrying a club, signed.

10.5in (26.5cm) wide

£2,000-2,500 **JN**

A pair of Marly rearing horses, with attendants, each on an ovoid naturalistic base.

15.75in (40cm) high

£700-1,000 **DN**

A large bronze group of a Chinese pheasant and lizard, on a rectangular base, signed.

29in (73.5cm) wide

£700-1,000 **JN**

A 19thC gilt-bronze table lamp, the stem and circular foot heavily cast in relief with leaves, fitted for electricity.

19.75in (50cm) high

£800-1,200 **CHEF**

A mid 19thC painted bronze tazza, with twin handles, cast with a frieze of Neo-Classical male and female figures, raised on a spreading foot, cast marks "ART UNION OF LONDON 1851".

1851 *16.75in (42cm) diam*

£300-400 **L&T**

A pair of slate and bronze urns, each with campana body centred by lion masks, fitted with bronze liner and leaf cast scroll handles, on acanthus socle base and stepped square slate base with brass feet.

13.5in (34cm) wide

£1,500-2,000 **L&T**

A copper strong box, weighing nine pounds, with a key.

c1820 *9.5in (24cm) wide*

£300-400 **BP**

A late 19thC copper wash basin of circular form, with flattened rolled rim.

12.5in (32cm) diam

£50-70 **BP**

A late 19thC rectangular copper pan and zinc drainer, with rounded corners and brass handles.

21.75in (55cm) wide

£250-300 **DN**

A set of twelve graduated 'Crosby' copper measures, each of tapering cylindrical form with brass banding and applied handles, ranging from 20 litres to 25 millilitres.

Largest 18.5 in (47cm) high

£3,000-4,000 **L&T**

LONGCASE CLOCKS

THE CLOCKS & SCIENTIFIC INSTRUMENTS MARKET

Demand continues to be very strong for the best examples of the clockmaker's art, with exceptional prices being paid for rare and unusual pieces by the likes of Tompion and Knibb, makers from the 'Golden Age' of British clockmaking. There are also signs that the low- to mid-range market is beginning to recover after a dip.

Good early British bracket clocks have been one of the strongest performing areas recently, with five and even six figure sums being realised for top examples in good condition.

With longcases, condition, quality and market freshness are important and good movements with nice dials in smart cases are doing well. Pieces by known London or Edinburgh makers

are a wise investment. Watch out for 'marriages', although attractive and contemporary examples are finding buyers.

Prices for carriage clocks remain steady, with the highest figures being paid for those with more elaborate cases and unusual movements. Rarer London pieces by makers such as Jump are hotly contested to top selling prices.

Things have cooled somewhat in the scientific instrument market, although rarer and unusual things continue to be in strong demand. If you are starting to collect, steer clear of more mass-produced 20thC items and watch out for fakes.

– *Gavin Strang, Lyon & Turnbull*

LONGCASE CLOCKS

A walnut and floral marquetry longcase clock, by John Lowe of London, with month duration six-pillar movement.

c1690   *81in (205cm) high*

£25,000-35,000   **DR**

A walnut and Arabesque marquetry longcase clock, by Joseph Bates of Holborn, with fretwork to the sides and front of the hood, walnut spiral-twist columns and giltwood capitals, the trunk door with three panels of Arabesque marquetry and a lenticle in the centre, five-pillar movement with internal count.

c1700   *84in (213.5cm) high*

£18,000-22,000   **DR**

An early 18thC longcase clock, the square brass dial with seconds and date apertures, inscribed "Richard Fennell, London", with an eight day striking five-pillar movement.

£1,200-1,800   **SWO**

An early 18thC walnut longcase clock, the square brass dial with cherub and crown spandrels, subsidiary seconds dial, winding holes and date wheel, inscribed "Sam. Townson, London".

£2,800-3,200   **SWO**

An early 18thC walnut and floral marquetry longcase clock, the brass dial cast with woman's head spandrels and silvered Roman numeral chapter ring.

81in (206cm) high

€6,000-8,000   **B**

A George I mahogany longcase regulator, by George Graham of London, with a silvered circular regulator dial, the six-pillar month-long movement numbered "622".

The dial of this regulator was formerly square, and has been filed into its current shape.

82in (208cm) high

£10,000-12,000   **WW**

A walnut longcase clock, by Edward Cockey of Warminster, with five-pillar rack-striking movement and subsidiary lunar phase dial, signed.

c1735   *89in (226cm) high*

£30,000-35,000   **DR**

A walnut longcase clock, by John Thomas of Crewkerne, the triple-train six-pillar movement plays one of three tunes every four hours.

c1735   *73in (262cm) high*

£35,000-38,000   **DR**

A Japanned oak longcase clock by George Langford of London, the twin-train eight day movement with anchor escapement striking on a bell.

100in (250cm) high

£3,000-4,000   **L&T**

A George III mahogany longcase clock, with painted dial and two subsidiary dials, the spandrels and arched top painted with British military figures and inscriptions.

86.5in (216cm) high

€1,200-1,800   **FRE**

A Louis XV-style kingwood and marquetry bombe longcase clock, with embossed and enamel dial, the case inlaid with a flowering urn and scrolling foliage, eight day chiming movement.

79.5in (199cm) high

£1,500-2,000   **FRE**

An 18thC walnut veneered longcase clock, the eight day five-pillar movement striking on a bell to a brass arched dial with subsidiary moon phase and seconds dials and date aperture, inscribed "John Gordon, London".

99in (251.5cm) high

£7,000-10,000   **WW**

A mid-18thC oak longcase clock, the eight-day movement striking on a bell to a brass arched dial with silvered chapter ring, subsidiary seconds dial and date aperture, applied plaque inscribed "James Tanqueray, London".

79in (200.5cm) high

£1,000-1,500   **WW**

An extremely rare longcase automaton clock, by Samual Toumlin of London, the trunk door decorated with mahogany veneers.

c1770   *95in (241cm) high*

£25,000-28,000   **DR**

A mahogany longcase clock, by Lawson of Newton, with conventional striking movement, rotating moon disc and lunar calendar.

c1770   *87in (221cm) high*

£14,000-16,000   **DR**

A CLOSER LOOK AT A LONGCASE CLOCK

John Benson won admiration in his day for the tidal, lunar, musical and astronomical mechanisms he fitted to his clocks.

The fine mahogany case is well proportioned with good quality carving, and has acquired an attractive dark patina

This chapter ring giving the relative altitude of the sun is an unusual feature of great interest to collectors

Fewer than two dozen clocks by this maker are known to exist today, making them very rare and valuable commodities

A very rare mid-18thC astronomical longcase clock by John Benson of Whitehaven, the dial with Rococo engraving and stylized dolphins, two further chapters show the rising and setting sun, signed.

89in (226cm) high

£35,000-40,000   **DR**

A George III mahogany longcase clock, the twin-train eight day movement with anchor escapement striking on a bell, the false plate inscribed "Walker & Finemore, Birmingham".

84.5in (211cm) high

£1,500-2,000   **L&T**

A George III oak longcase clock, the twin-train eight day movement with anchor escapement striking on a bell, false plate inscribed "Dallaway & Son, Edinburgh".

88in (220cm) high

£1,000-1,500   **L&T**

A George III mahogany longcase clock, the twin-train eight day movement with anchor escapement striking on a bell.

81.5in (204cm) high

£1,000-1,500   **L&T**

An early 19thC painted satinwood longcase clock, with Adams-style decoration, the face marked "Ogeden, Darlington", losses.

83in (211cm) high

£3,000-4,000   **BRU**

A George III mahogany longcase clock, by John Hamilton of Glasgow, the twin-train eight day movement with anchor escapement striking on a bell.

78.75in (200cm) high

£800-1,200   **L&T**

A George III oak longcase clock, by Charles Barclay of Montrose, the twin-train eight day movement with anchor escapement striking on a gong, the arched brass dial with cast spandrels, subsidiary seconds dial and date aperture.

80.5in (205cm) high

£1,000-1,500   **L&T**

A George III mahogany longcase clock, the eight day movement striking on a bell to an arched brass dial with subsidiary seconds and date dials, the silvered chapter ring inscribed "Wm Evill, Bath".

85in (216cm) high

£3,000-4,000   **WW**

A provincial George III oak longcase clock, with cherub mask spandrels, the thirty hour movement striking in a bell stamped "W.H. & Co. Bristol", silvered chapter ring inscribed "Jno Ettry, Horton".

75.5in (192cm) high

£1,000-1,500   **WW**

A George III oak long case clock, by Thomas Hampton of Wrexham, the twin-train eight day movement with anchor escapement striking on a bell.

92.25in (234cm) high

£1,500-2,000   **L&T**

A George III oak and mahogany crossbanded longcase clock, the twin-train eight day movement with anchor escapement striking on a bell, unmarked false plate.

89.75in (228cm) high

£2,000-3,000   **L&T**

A George III marquetry inlaid satinwood and mahogany longcase clock, with eight day striking movement, the spandrels decorated with figures emblematic of the seasons, the centre of the dial signed "Vincent Topham, Ashton".

89.5in (227cm) high

£3,000-5,000   **ROW**

A George III mahogany and satinwood inlaid longcase clock, the twin-train eight day movement with anchor escapement striking on a bell, the dial inscribed "Alexander Millar, Montrose", false plate inscribed "Osborne".

86.25in (219cm) high

£2,500-3,000   **L&T**

A George III mahogany longcase clock, by James McCulloch of Auchterarder, the twin-train eight day movement with anchor escapement.

85.75in (218cm) high

£2,500-3,000   **L&T**

A George III longcase clock, by George Suggate of Halesworth, the single-train thirty hour movement with brass dial, the red lacquered case painted with Chinoiserie figural scenes, decoration of a later date.

84.75in (215cm) high

£2,000-3,000   **L&T**

A mahogany longcase clock, by James Gray of Edinburgh, the painted dial by Hipkiss & Harrold.

c1800   *88in (224cm) high*

£6,000-9,000   **DR**

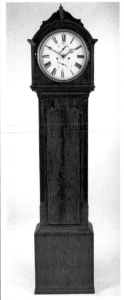

A rare early 19thC longcase regulator by John Moore & Sons of Clerkenwell, the movement with chain fusees for the striking and chiming trains.

74.5in (189cm) high

£15,000-18,000   DR

A small mahogany longcase regulator by Markwick Markham Perigal of London, the month duration movement with shouldered plates, six bar-shaped pillars and six spokes.

Markwick Markham Perigal specialized in clocks for export markets.

c1800   *72in (182.5cm) high*

£30,000-36,000   DR

A shallow break-arch mahogany longcase regulator, with four-pillar movement, inscribed on the dial "Regulator, presented to Sir John Rae Reid Bart. by RJ Eaton Esq. MP".

c1820   *75in (190cm) high*

£18,000-22,000   DR

An early 19thC mahogany longcase clock, the twin-train eight day movement with anchor escapement striking on a bell, false plate inscribed "Osborne".

83in (207cm) high

£800-1,200   L&T

An early 19thC mahogany longcase clock, iron face with original paint and floral spandrels, indistinctly marked, damaged.

84.5in (214.5cm) high

£2,000-3,000   BRU

A George IV mahogany longcase clock, the broken arched pediment above a shaped door, raised on splayed bracket feet, the painted dial signed "Robinson Dewsbury".

92in (233.5cm) high

£1,200-1,800   FRE

A 19thC mahogany longcase clock, by R. Cunninghame of Edinburgh, the twin-train eight day movement with anchor escapement striking on a bell.

88in (220cm) high

£800-1,200   L&T

A 19thC mahogany longcase clock, the twin-train eight day movement with anchor escapement striking on a bell, with false plate inscribed "Beilby & Hawthorn, Newcastle".

79.5in (199cm) high

£1,000-1,500   L&T

A small 19thC walnut and marquetry longcase clock, with oyster veneer in the William-and-Mary style, with a striking twin-train eight day five-pillar movement.

62in (155cm) high

£3,000-4,000   FRE

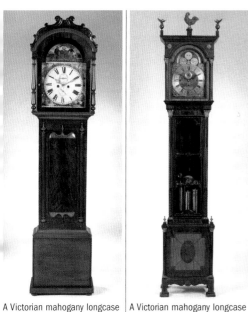

A Victorian mahogany longcase clock, the twin-train eight day movement with anchor escapement striking on a bell, decorated with mottos:"By this we live" and "United we stand, Divided we fall".

89in (226cm) high

£1,000-1,500   **L&T**

A Victorian mahogany longcase clock, by George Graham, the triple-train eight day quarter-chiming movement with anchor escapement striking on four and eight bells, inscribed "George Graham, Clock Maker".

99.5in (253cm) high

£7,000-10,000   **L&T**

An oak longcase clock by Jason Duncan of Old Meldrum, the twin-train eight day movement with anchor escapement striking on a bell, with subsidiary seconds and date dials.

85.5in (217cm) high

£800-1,200   **L&T**

An oak and floral marquetry longcase clock, with eight day four-pillar movement to dial, the silvered chapter ring signed "George Booth", lacking bell and weight.

83in (211cm) high

£4,000-6,000   **WW**

An oak longcase clock, by Hubbard of Louth, the white enamel dial enclosed by an arched panelled door with stellar inlay, the twin-train movement striking on a bell.

85.5in (217cm) high

£1,500-2,000   **SWO**

BRACKET CLOCKS

A George I repeating bracket clock, by Joseph Windmills, the twin-fusee movement striking on six bells, the back plate inscribed "Jos Windmills London", the date dial inscribed "J Windmills London".

24.25in (61.5cm) high

£20,000-25,000   **WW**

An 18thC walnut bracket clock, the twin-train eight day fusee movement with anchor escapement striking on a bell.

20.5in (52cm) high

£2,500-3,000   **L&T**

A George III mahogany bracket clock, by J. Y. Hatton of London, with twin-train fusee movement and engraved back plate.

18.75in (47cm) high

£2,000-3,000   **L&T**

A George III mahogany bracket clock by Webster of London, the double-fusee movement striking on a bell, with a shaped and engraved back plate inscribed "Webster, London".

£2,000-3,000   **SWO**

A George III mahogany bracket clock by Robert Ward of London, the musical movement striking on bells, the domed case with glazed door enclosing an arched silvered dial, with dial to the arch for a selection of jigs and airs.

16.75in (42.5cm) high

£5,000-8,000   **L&T**

A Regency mahogany and brass inlaid bracket clock, by Wieland of Watworth, with enamel dial, stepped gadrooned rectangular top and gilt brass pineapple finial.

19in (48cm) high

£3,000-5,000   L&T

An English Regency mahogany bracket clock, the painted dial signed "Sutherland, Davies and Co. Liverpool", with twin-train striking anchor escapement mechanism.

c1830   *18.5in (47cm) high*

£1,000-1,500   ROS

A 19thC Gothic stained oak bracket clock, by Barraud & Lund of Cornhill, London, the twin-train movement striking on two gongs, numbered "1872".

25.5in (64cm) high

£3,000-5,000   L&T

A Victorian burr walnut bracket clock, by John Creed Jennens of Clerkenwell, with Gothic arched silvered dial with triple-fusee movement striking the quarters on eight bells.

1,800-2,200   SWO

An Edwardian bracket clock, by Marshall & Sons of Edinburgh, the triple-train movement with circular silvered dial, and subsidiary dials.

24.5in (62cm) high

£2,000-3,000   L&T

A George I-style ebonised bracket clock, the triple-train movement striking on eight bells and Westminster chimes on bells and a gong, the brass dial with silvered Roman chapter ring and subsidiary tune dials.

29.25in (73cm) high

£2,000-3,000   L&T

MANTEL CLOCKS

A 19thC French ormolu mantel clock, the case with a Classical female figure seated on a naturalistic base, with pink and floral painted porcelain dial flanked by trophies, gilt stand and ebonised plinth.

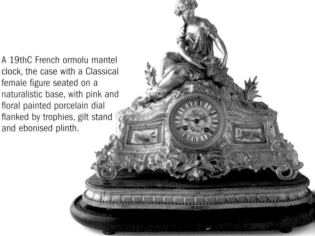

15.25in (39cm) wide

£400-600   CHEF

A 19thC French gilt metal and porcelain-mounted mantel clock, with floral painted dial and panels.

15in (38cm) high

£300-500   CHEF

A 19thC French ormolu timepiece, within a sunburst-topped lyre frame on a variegated marble base.

15.75in (40cm) high

£800-1,200   CHEF

A 19thC French mantel clock, the eight-day movement striking on a bell inscribed "Leroy à Paris".

19in (48cm) high

£300-500   WW

A 19thC ebonised amboyna and gilt-metal-mounted mantel clock, of Louis XV-style, with circular silvered dial.

13.75in (35cm) high

£600-900   L&T

A large 19thC rosewood mantel clock, with brass dial, silvered chapter ring and triple-train musical movement.

£1,800-2,200   SWO

An early 19thC marble and ormolu mounted mantel clock, the eight day striking movement with an external count wheel, the enamel dial inscribed "Jeannin à Paris", the case with a flaming urn finial, flanked by reeded pilasters with urns, on turned feet.

13in (33cm) high

£400-600   **WW**

A 19thC gilt brass and champlevé decorated mantel clock, the circular dial surmounted by a cherub holding a torch and flanked by urns, on two caryatid supports.

18.5in (47cm) high

£800-1,200   **L&T**

An early 19thC French bronze and ormolu-mounted pillar clock, the dial marked "Angevin à Paris", with silk suspension countwheel movement, case entwined with fruiting vine, upon a canted base with leaf and beaded bands.

14.5in (37cm) high

£800-1,200   **CHEF**

A late 18thC Swiss Carrara marble mantel clock, with a musical mechanism incorporating eleven bells and twenty hammers, the white enamel numeral ring with Arabic numbers and decorated hands.

18.5in (46cm) high

£5,000-8,000   **NAG**

A late 19thC French bronze mantel clock, the convex porcelain dial with a striking drum movement, on a marble base.

15.75in (40cm) high

£300-500 SWO

A 19thC gilt bronze mantel clock, with ornate Gothic decoration, enamel plaque and enamel dial supporting a French striking movement.

17.25in (44cm) high

£500-800 SWO

A 19thC walnut mantel clock, the silvered dial with Arabic numerals, with striking French drum movement.

9.25in (23.5cm) high

£400-600 SWO

A 19thC French gilt metal mantel clock, with black enamel dial and Vincenti '1855' striking movement, the case stamped "Camus".

16.25in (41cm) high

£280-320 CHEF

A late 19thC French bronze and gilt mantel clock, the twin-train movement with circular enamel dial, the case cast as a figure of a putto on a cloud.

12.25in (31cm) high

£800-1,200 L&T

A late 19thC French Empire-style parcel gilt and patinated metal and onyx mantel clock, with twin-train striking movement, the dial signed "Bergmiller à Paris".

23in (57.5cm) high

£1,200-1,800 S&K

A late 19thC decorative porcelain mantel clock, designed as an artist's palette upon a brass easel, painted with a Neo-classical harbour scene, with drum movement.

17.75in (45cm) high

£500-800 CHEF

A French porcelain mantel clock, movement by S. Marti & Cie, mounted in a pink, white and gilt cartouche-form case with a painted figural reserve.

c1900 *11in (27.5cm) high*

£300-500 S&K

A CLOSER LOOK AT A TRIPOD CLOCK

This stamped signature and serial number helps to confirm authenticity and can be checked against original records to ensure that the clock is a genuine Cole piece.

Thomas Cole is known for his fine engraving, which appears here around the dial and on the base of this clock.

This tripod clock is a rare form. It would be worth up to twice as much if it still had its original glass dome.

This clock features Cole's own pendulum locking system, which holds the heavy pendulum in place to prevent damage when the clock is inactive.

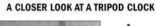

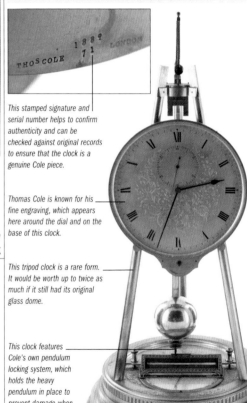

A Victorian brass tripod clock, by Thomas Cole of London, the dead beat escapement to a circular floral engraved dial, the base with a barometer and thermometer, the back plate stamped "Thos Cole 1882 71 London", and numbered on back support.

1882 *20in (51cm) high*

£6,000-9,000 WW

An early 20thC French ormolu and champlevé enamel clock, retailed by Tiffany & Co., with paste-set bezel and pendulum, twin-train brass movement and stamped back plate, restored.

13.75in (35cm) high

£800-1,200 B

A 1920s silver gilt and enamelled mantel clock, possibly by George Stockwell, with single-train movement, enamelled dial, English silver import marks for 1924 and Continental sterling mark.

9.25in (23cm) high

£3,000-4,000 L&T

A Meissen figural clock, modelled by Paul Scheurich, depicting a cherubic conductor seated on a cushion, with Mozart sheet music and a baton.

1939 *15in (38cm) high*

£5,000-7,000 DA

An Atmos mantel timepiece, by Jaeger-LeCoultre, the temperature-sensitive movement turning a suspended balance wheel, bears presentation plaque dated 1952, in original marbled paper-covered box with hinged doors.

1952   *9.5in (24cm) high*

£800-1,200   **L&T**

An Empire-style bronze and ormolu mantel clock, the striking movement with external count-wheel.

17in (43cm) high

£700-1,000   **DN**

A brass lantern clock, the twin-train fusee movement with circular dial, inscribed "John Ebsworth".

13.75in (35cm) high

£1,000-1,500   **L&T**

A cut brass, tortoiseshell enamel and mother-of-pearl inlaid mantel timepiece, by Payne of London, signed.

16in (40.5cm) high

£800-1,200   **WW**

An ebonised mantel clock, by Charles Frodsham of London, the signed silvered dial with Roman numerals, the single-train movement with a lever platform escapement.

9in (23cm) high

£1,000-1,500   **SWO**

A modern inclined plane clock, by Dent of London, the lacquered brass drum timepiece marked to reverse "Dent for Eustace Hope 1973", engraved dial, the heavy brass sloping stand with red leather surface, mounted with red perspex, marked for days of the week.

28.25in (72cm) wide

£600-900   **CHEF**

An Edwardian tortoiseshell and 15ct gold mounted small carriage timepiece, the French eight day movement with platform lever escapement, signed "Drew & Sons, Piccadilly Circus, London W", the case with a Viscount's coronet over initials "MM".

3.25in (8cm) high

£700-1,000   **DN**

A gilt brass carriage clock with alarm, by E. Maurice & Co. of Paris, the silvered chapter ring with gong-striking movement numbered "1993", replacement platform lever escapement.

6.25in (16cm) high

£1,500-2,000   **CHEF**

A brass carriage timepiece, by Charles Frodsham of London, the lever platform escapement striking on a bell.

7.75in (20cm) high

£600-900   **SWO**

A 19thC Louis XV-style slate and gilt bronze clock garniture, the silvered dial with a black chapter ring and an eight day striking movement, bases stamped "H. Ferrat".

Candelabra 26in (65cm) high

£4,000-6,000   **FRE**

A 19thC Louis XV-style onyx and gilt bronze clock garniture, the rock crystal dial with eight day movement, flanked by a pair of conforming figural candelabra.

Candelabra 33.5in (84cm) high

£3,000-5,000   **FRE**

CLOCKS

A 19thC French malachite and gilt bronze clock garniture, the clock with white enamel dial and eight day movement, with a pair of later figural five-light candelabra.

Candelabra 31in (77.5cm) high

£7,000-10,000   **FRE**

A 19thC French gilt metal clock garniture, the urn-topped case moulded with scrolls, masks and flowers, with numbered Marti movement, restored.

Clock 13in (33cm) high

£300-500   **CHEF**

A 19thC ormolu and bronze clock garniture, the eight day striking timepiece set within an ornate case with strapwork and artistic trophies.

20.25in (51.5cm) high

£1,000-1,500   **ROW**

POCKET WATCHES

An early 20thC French 18ct gold, diamond and enamel round pendant watch by Le Roy & Sohn of Paris, signed "Grand Prix Paris 1900".

£600-900   **DN**

An 18ct gold cuckoo clock coat pin, set with diamonds in platinum mounts, with movable weights and pendulum winding mechanism, marked on face "Walser Wald".

3in (7.5cm) long

£1,000-1,500   **BRU**

A George IV open-faced gold pocket watch, the granulated gold dial with gold Roman numerals, centred with a three-colour gold wreath, applied with turquoise cabochons, marks for Chester.

1820

£600-900   **WW**

An early 20thC silver cased triangular Masonic fob watch, the pyramidal case decorated with a temple and Masonic symbols, with conforming mother-of-pearl dial.

1.75in (4.5cm) high

£600-900   **ROW**

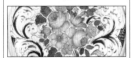

A gold open-faced fob watch, the silvered dial with black Roman numerals, engraved with foliate scroll decoration, the reverse decorated with enamel painted flowers, the gold dust cover signed "Mare Dupan", with watch key.

1in (2.5cm) diam

£300-400   **WW**

An open-faced pocket watch, signed "Patron", the scroll hands and bezel set with small diamonds, the back cover painted with an enamel scene within a guilloche and scroll enamel border, signed and numbered "2263".

1.5in (4cm) diam

£1,200-1,800   **WW**

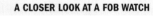

A CLOSER LOOK AT A FOB WATCH

These appendages are similar to those found on charm bracelets, which are currently in vogue. Popular fashions can have a substantial effect on the market value of any antique.

Natural pearls have a thicker nacre — the shiny outer surface — than the cultured variety. Intensive harvesting has devastated natural pearl beds, with the result that they are extremely valuable today.

The hands are encrusted with diamonds – a luxurious touch that adds to the general opulence of this fine piece of jewellery.

A gold, enamel and half-pearl fob watch and chatelaine, the cover enamelled, with white enamel face, diamond hands and half-pearl bezel, the fob suspension mounted with natural pearls, with four appendages, comprising a pair of tassels, a watch key and a monogrammed seal.

c1800

£3,000-4,000   **WW**

A Victorian oak wall regulator by Stewart of Glasgow, the single-train eight day fusee movement with dead beat escapement.

15.5in (39cm) diam

£300-500   **L&T**

A Victorian mahogany trunk dial wall clock, the dial marked "Honeybone Nottingham", the trunk with glass panel and pierced side mounts, the four-pillar brass fusee movement with tapered plates.

23.25in (59cm) high

£600-900   **CHEF**

A George III mahogany banjo barometer, by Lione & Somalvico of London, with silvered circular dial and brass frame, spirit level at base in corresponding dial, engraved "Lione & Somalvico, 125 Holborn Hill, London".

42.75in (107cm) high

£800-1,200   **L&T**

A George III mahogany stick barometer, by A. Trony, with chequer stringing, broken pediment, vernier slider and narrow shaft with circular reservoir panel and domed cover.

38in (97cm) high

£1,000-1,500   **L&T**

A George III mahogany barometer, by A. Lione of London, with a silvered circular dial, subsidiary humidity dial, thermometer and spirit level.

41.25in (105cm) high

£1,500-2,500   **L&T**

A George III mahogany stick barometer, with boxwood stringing and silvered scale, the body with exposed mercury tube and square reservoir cover inlaid with oval shell patera.

38.25in (97cm) high

£1,000-1,500   **L&T**

A George III cased stick barometer, by F. Bird of London, the rubbed silvered dial above a rectangular body with exposed mercury tube.

36.25in (92cm) high

£1,200-1,800   **L&T**

A Regency mahogany stick barometer by Adie & Son of Edinburgh, with silvered vernier slider and thermometer.

42.5in (106cm) high

£8,000-10,000   **L&T**

A mid-19thC bird's-eye maple stick barometer, by Adie & Son, the square silvered scale with glass mercury tube, the bowed case with dual apertures and two ivorine adjusters.

41.75in (106cm) high

£5,000-8,000   **L&T**

BAROMETERS

An early 20thC lacquered brass barograph, with clockwork drum, stylus arm and chamber, in glazed mahogany case with retailer's label "L. E. Knott Apparatus Co., Boston" and 1902 British patent number, losses.

14in (35.5cm) wide

£100-150 EG

A 19thC rosewood stick barometer, by T.B. Winter of Newcastle, with canted ivory scales, applied thermometer and panelled reservoir case.

39.25in (100cm) high

£800-1,200 L&T

A Victorian walnut wheel barometer, the silvered dial inscribed "Chadburn, Optician, Liverpool".

39.25in (100cm) high

£200-300 SWO

A Victorian stained wheel barometer, with a thermometer flanked by columns, inlaid with husks and cornucopia.

£200-300 SWO

A pocket barometer, cased in gilt metal and fitted in a red leather travelling case, inscribed "Hicks London".

1.75in (4.5cm) wide

£200-300 ROS

NAVIGATIONAL INSTRUMENTS

A mahogany sextant, by Gregory & Wright of London, with brass vernier arm, tangent screw, telescope, triple pin-holes, six shades and adjustable mirror, with later ivory label for "H. Duren, New York", restored.

Duren worked in New York from c1865. It is probable that he updated this sextant by replacing the handle and possibly the scale.

c1785 *16.25in (41.5cm) long*

£1,500-2,000 EG

A late 18thC English mahogany octant, with ivory divided scale, brass vernier carrier, twin pin-holes, shades and mirrors with clamps, in a shaped mahogany case with paper-lined interior, restored.

15in (38cm) long

£1,000-1,500 EG

An ebony octant by Spencer, Browning & Rust of London, with original mahogany case and rare "Janet Taylor" label on box lid.

c1790 *11in (28cm) long*

£300-500 CSA

An English brass, ebony and ivory three-filter octant, by Benjamin Walter of London, with ivory scales and original oak case.

c1810 *14.25in (36cm) long*

£500-700 CSA

An early 19thC mahogany cased chronometer, by Eggert & Son, with engraved silver dial and applied ivory plaque inscribed with maker's name.

17.75in (45cm) high

£2,200-2,800 SK

A late 19thC mahogany cased two-day marine chronometer, by Francis M. Moore of Dublin and Belfast, with silvered dial, brass case and gimbal.

4.75in (12cm) diam

£1,800-2,200 L&T

A Continental circular brass-cased magnetic compass, with folding sundial gnomon and paper card background.

c1780   2.25in (6.5cm) wide

£120-180   CSA

An English circular magnetic compass, with paper dials showing the time in over fifty world locations, with original boxwood case.

c1850   2in (5cm) wide

£70-100   CSA

An early 20thC pocket barometer and compass, by Queen & Co. of Philadelphia, with silvered dials, in brass case and leather outer case.

2.75in (7cm) diam

£60-90   EG

A brass circular protractor, with two folding radius arms and engraved vernier scale, signed "W.C. Cox of Devonport", with original mahogany case.

c1830   6in (15.5cm) wide

£300-350   CSA

SUNDIALS

A Victorian bronze and brass sextant, by the Elliott Brothers of London, with engraved platinum scale at the bottom and original leather case, signed "W.D. Lindley".

c1870   2.75in (7cm) wide

£220-280   CSA

A Charles I medium-sized bronze square sundial, showing hour and quarter scales, initialled "E.R.".

c1630   5.5in (14cm) wide

£300-350   CSA

A Charles II bronze square sundial, by John Nash.

c1680   4in (10cm) wide

£150-200   CSA

An English brass circular sundial, by J. Springer of Bristol, with folding gnomon and engraved hour scale.

c1760   3in (8cm) wide

£150-200   CSA

An English bronze circular sundial, by W. & S. Jones of Holborn, London, showing watch correction scale.

c1800   12.25in (31cm) wide

£700-900   CSA

An early 19thC Dollond brass compass sundial, of circular form, inscribed to the reverse with latitudes of world cities.

4.25in (11cm) diam

£300-400   L&T

A silver Butterfield-pattern sundial, the octagonal plate with four engraved scales, inset compass with blued-steel needle, and engraved floral centre, on three ball feet, with marks for Birmingham and maker's mark "D&F".

1899   2.25in (5.5cm) long

£400-600   EG

A wooden diptych sundial, by Stockert of Bavaria, with printed coloured hour scales and latitude table, string gnomon and fifty-two cities listed with their latitudes.

c1840   3in (7.5cm) long

£220-280   EG

OPTICAL INSTRUMENTS

A Brewster-pattern stereoscope, by the New York Stereoscopic Co., the tapered leather-covered body with gilt-tooled decoration and hinged reflector, lacking ground glass, together with a stereograph entitled "New Year's Calls".

c1860   *7.5in (19cm) high*

£400-600   **EG**

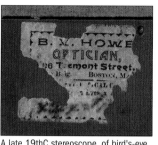

A late 19thC stereoscope, of bird's-eye maple with herringbone inlay, with main lens, sliding easel and partial retailer's label for "B.M. Howell, Optician, Tremont St. Boston".

10in (25.5cm) high

£150-200   **EG**

A Magic Mirror by McLoughlin Bros., with mercury-glass anamorphic viewer, chromolithographic views and wooden box, with sliding illustrated lid, numbered 22 of 24.

10.75in (27.5cm) high

£1,200-1,800   **EG**

A pair of scissor spectacles, probably early 19thC, of wire construction, with loop handle.

3.25in (8.5cm) long

£150-200   **EG**

An early 19thC walnut-framed gallery glass, probably English, with lens and turned handle.

13.5in (34.5cm) high

£150-200   **EG**

TELESCOPES & MICROSCOPES

A late 19thC refracting telescope, the cylindrical tube with star finder and presentation inscription, on a tripod base, in a fitted mahogany case.

46.75in (119cm) long

£2,000-3,000   **DN**

An English brass and baleen six-draw cased telescope, by R. Field of Birmingham, with stand and leather case.

c1830   *15.75in (40cm) long*

£200-250   **CSA**

A CLOSER LOOK AT A MICROSCOPE

The skin of the ray was used by many manufacturers of scientific instruments during the 19thC as it is attractive, provides good grip, and is waterproof.

This original oak case houses and protects the microscope and accessories. These cases often have fitted interiors specially designed for their contents.

This kind of tripod microscope is named after Edmund Culpeper, an 18thC instrument maker who helped to popularise the microscope.

This microscope is complete with a number of original accessories, including tools, lenses, specimen plates made from bone and a powder box carved from ivory.

A compound Culpeper-type microscope, with biconvex eye and field lens, the barrel sheathed in ray skin, with original pyramid-shaped oak case.

c1730   *14.25in (36cm) long*

£5,000-7,000   **CSA**

An early 19thC pocket globe.

1.5in (4cm) diam

£400-600 SWO

A celestial globe, by Malby & Sons of London, raised on a turned column with three downswept legs.

c1860 *40in (100cm) high*

£2,800-3,200 FRE

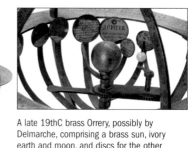

A late 19thC brass Orrery, possibly by Delmarche, comprising a brass sun, ivory earth and moon, and discs for the other planets and asteroids, most with paper labels, in a horizon ring with engraved calendar and zodiac, and meridian ring marked for the solstices and equinoxes, on a turned stand.

13in (33cm) high

£3,000-5,000 EG

OTHER SCIENTIFIC INSTRUMENTS

A farmer's boxwood cattle gauge, by J. Tree of Charlotte Street, London.

c1830 *9in (23cm) long*

£80-120 CSA

A 19thC English ship chandler's brass and boxwood slide gauge, with engraved tables showing weights, fathoms and circumferences of various ropes, hawsers and shrouds.

5in (13cm) wide

£50-80 CSA

A chondrometer by Harris and Co. of Holborn, London, with beam scale, used to calculate the weight of seed, with original printed directions for use on the inside of box lid, dated 1826.

7.75in (20cm) long

£300-350 CSA

A brass telegraph key by Partrick, Bunnel & Co. of Philadelphia, with knife and ebonite grips, on a later wood base.

c1875 *5.5in (14cm) long*

£600-900 EG

A plaster phrenology bust, made by D.P. Butler for Fowler, Wells & Co. of Boston, with maker's label, together with a copy of "Faces We Meet", published by Wells of London, and three 19thC phrenological reports, published in New York, Foxboro Massachusetts and England.

9.5in (24cm) high

£200-300 EG

EARLY BROOCHES

THE PRECIOUS JEWELLERY MARKET

The very top end of the jewellery market is extremely buoyant and prices for the most attractive, finely crafted pieces made from the best materials remain high. Unusual items and signed jewellery by well-known designers, such as Cartier and Van Cleef & Arpels, continue to attract a great deal of attention.

Jewellery buyers currently tend to favour wearable pieces that sit happily with contemporary dress and can be worn for both day and evening. This has lead to an increase in demand for jewellery from the 1940s and 1950s, particularly that made in America by companies such as Rubel and Trabert & Hoeffer Mauboussin. Bold jewels, such as rubies, and semi-precious stones that create a striking visual effect, including amethyst and aquamarine, are very desirable, although diamonds remain enduringly popular.

Interest in pieces from the 1960s and 1970s, that were largely ignored until recently, has also grown and prices have risen accordingly. Grima and Charles de Temple pieces from this period have recently fetched startling prices. In comparison, Victorian jewellery has somewhat fallen out of fashion and can struggle to attract interest.

In terms of types of jewellery, earrings are the most sought after and prices tend to be high because they are also the most difficult to come by. Bracelets and pendants are also popular, whilst brooches move in and out of fashion.

The market for middle and lower end pieces is faring less well. Buyers are rejecting poor quality, unsigned and semi-mass-produced jewellery.

– Ian Harris, N. Bloom & Son

An antique Egyptian winged scarab brooch, with carved blue glazed ceramic from the Middle Empire (2000 BC) and French set in the 1880s.

5.75in (14.5cm) wide

NBLM

£5,000-8,000

An early 19thC gold en-tremblant brooch, in the form of a filigree bird with a ruby eye and drop, mounted on a spring within a flowerhead and turquoise surround, with a small hair-glazed back panel, in a fitted case.

£600-900   **DN**

An early 19thC gold pendant brooch, the heart-shaped locket with wirework floral motifs and a repoussé scroll border, suspended by snake chain inter-links, set with rubies and emeralds, one stone a later green paste.

£300-500   **DN**

An early 19thC serpent brooch, set with graduated half-pearls and a ruby eye, the glazed centre with needlework, hinged glazed locket section to reverse.

1.5in (3.5cm) wide

£700-1,000   **WW**

An early Victorian gold and gem cruciform brooch, with a round hessonite garnet, four oval mixed-cut Imperial topaz and chrysolite spacers and terminals.

£1,500-2,000   **DN**

An early Victorian coiled serpent brooch, partly set with graduated turquoise cabochons and garnet eyes, set in gold, missing pin.

1.75in (4.5cm) wide

£400-600   **WW**

A mid-19thC architectural micromosaic brooch, depicting the Vatican and St. Peter's Church in Rome, in a rectangular gold mount.

2in (5cm) wide

£600-800   **CHEF**

A 19thC oval cameo pin, carved with an image of a Roman soldier, surrounded by a bead-decorated silver frame.

2in (5cm) high

£40-60   **FRE**

A Victorian gold and garnet brooch, in the form of entwined hoops, with an oval drop and a hair-glazed back panel, later pin.

£220-280   **DN**

A Victorian diamond-set star brooch, with graduated cushion-shaped diamonds and larger diamonds set in gold, in a fitted case.

In the Victorian era, there was a revival of interest in 18thC court jewellery which typically used star or sunburst motifs.

1.25in (3cm) wide

£1,500-2,000   **WW**

A gem-set butterfly brooch, with a diamond and emerald body, sapphire and diamond wings and cabochon ruby eyes, set in silver on gold.

Insect jewellery, using forms such as bees, wasps, butterflies and dragonflies, first became popular in the 1860s. Butterfly brooches are very popular with collectors.

2in (5cm) wide

£2,500-3,000   **WW**

A Victorian owl and moon brooch, set with graduated circular-cut diamonds, the owl with cabochon ruby eyes, set in silver on gold.

2.25in (5.5cm) wide

£3,000-3,500   **WW**

A late Victorian gold brooch, with a fox walking into a bush, set with diamonds.

1.75in (4.5cm) wide

£1,500-2,000   **NBLM**

A late Victorian rose diamond and enamel brooch, in the form of a cockerel and two hens, on a knife-edge bar with pearl terminals, set throughout in silver and gold, in a Hancock's case.

£1,500-2,000   **DN**

A late Victorian moonstone and diamond brooch or pendant, with a heart-shaped moonstone carved with a classical cameo of Apollo, set within an old-cut diamond border with a ribbon tied bow surmount, set in silver and gold, removable brooch fitting.

This brooch has all the classic ingredients of late Victorian sentimentality, the 'lovers knot' surmount, the use of moonstone with its reference to night and dreams and carved to depict Apollo, a god legendary for his love affairs, all neatly wrapped up in a brooch of heart-shaped outline set with diamonds, the eternal gemstone.

£3,000-5,000   **DN**

A late Victorian frog brooch, set with rose-cut diamonds, a line of demantoid garnets and cabochon ruby eyes, set in silver on gold, French control mark to the pin.

1in (2.5cm) wide

£1,000-1,500   **WW**

A late Victorian diamond horseshoe brooch, pavé-set throughout in silver and gold with graduated old-cut diamonds in three rows, in a case.

£1,200-1,800   **DN**

A late Victorian jewellery model, with two gold rabbits, running over a hill of pearls.

1in (2.5cm) wide

£1,000-1,500   **NBLM**

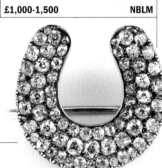

A late Victorian closed crescent diamond brooch, the graduated old-cut stones set in silver and gold.

£800-1,200   **DN**

An Art Nouveau scroll and diamond platinum brooch, adaptable as a pendant, with openwork.

The design is Art Nouveau, but the use of materials is typical of the Edwardian era.

2in (5cm) wide

£5,000-8,000   **NBLM**

A Belle Epoque pierced brooch, set with graduated circular and rose-cut diamonds in platinum, with a border of untested pearls, detachable pin and pendant loop.

1.75in (4.5cm) wide

£3,500-4,000   **WW**

A French gold brooch, with a winged chimera holding a diamond in her mouth

c1900   1.75in (4.5cm) wide

£1,000-1,500   **NBLM**

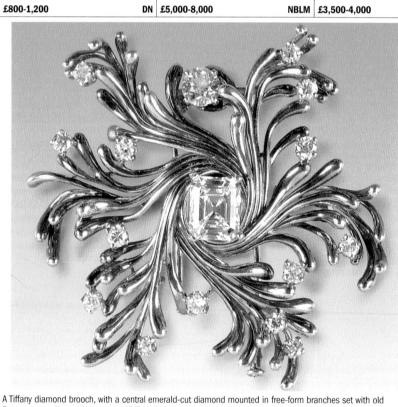

A Tiffany diamond brooch, with a central emerald-cut diamond mounted in free-form branches set with old European-cut diamonds, stamped "Tiffany Schlumberger".

French master jewellery designer Jean Schlumberger opened his salon at Tiffany & Co. in 1956.

£12,000-18,000   **BRU**

An Edwardian gold and pearl shield-shaped openwork brooch, the central flowerhead with a small old-cut diamond, scroll work surmount and a half-pearl collet swag and drop, removable brooch fitting, unmarked.

£800-1,200   **DN**

An Edwardian Caduceus brooch, with red enamelled wings, old-cut diamond entwined snakes and pearl terminals, set throughout in silver and gold.

The Caduceus was the magic staff of Greek god Hermes, or Roman god Mercury. The messenger gods were also associated with incantations and conducting the dead.

£800-1,200   **DN**

An Edwardian gold brooch, with three cushion-shaped rubies, probably of Burmese origin, spaced by pairs of old-cut diamonds.

£9,000-11,000   **DN**

An Edwardian diamond openwork brooch, with a lobed lozenge-shaped outline, millegrain set throughout with old-cut diamonds.

£2,200-2,800   **DN**

An Edwardian opal and diamond brooch, centred with a round white opal, millegrain set within an open-lobed border with old-cut diamonds.

£600-900   DN

An Edwardian gold crescent brooch, set with two rows of graduated seed pearls.

1in (2.5cm) wide

£150-200   WW

An Edwardian bicycle lapel pin, with articulated wheels and set with small diamonds.

1.5in (4cm) wide

£1,500-2,000   NBLM

An enamelled brooch.

c1910   *1.5in (4cm) wide*

£30-40   GKA

A French tree in a bucket brooch, with carved emerald leaves and ruby and diamond fruit.

The carved emerald detail suggests an Indian influence.

c1930   *2.25in (6cm) high*

£5,000-7,000   NBLM

A French fintail fish brooch, set with sapphires and diamonds.

c1940   *3in (7.5cm) high*

£4,000-6,000   NBLM

An hourglass watch drop brooch, set with rubies.

c1940   *3in (7.5cm) high*

£1,500-2,000   NBLM

A fine plique-a-jour enamel bird of paradise brooch, with a blue feathered body and perched on a diamond branch, signed 'Mellerio Dits Mellers Paris'.

c1945   *2.75in (7cm) high*

£5,000-8,000   NBLM

A 'sunshine and clouds' gem-set brooch, in the style of Simon Schepps, American-set with blue and yellow sapphires and diamonds.

c1940   *3in (7.5cm) high*

£5,000-8,000   NBLM

A 20thC opal and moonstone 'bumble bee' pin, with brushed gold wings inset with small diamonds, the head with garnet eyes, stamped "BBB".

1.5in (4cm) wide

£300-500   FRE

JEWELLERY

A 20thC 14ct gold and enamel duck pin, with a green enamelled hat, jade dangle, yellow enamelled body, green and blue enamelled wings.

1.75in (4.5cm) long

£150-200   **FRE**

A 20thC yellow gold and diamond 'Rooster' pin, with inset diamond eye.

1.75in (4.5cm) long

£120-180   **FRE**

A CLOSER LOOK AT AN OSCAR HEYMAN DIAMOND BROOCH

Oscar Heyman & Brothers, founded in New York in 1912, hand-produced precious stone jewellery in the European style to the very highest standard. Pieces are produced with great skill using the best materials and are thus extremely desirable.

The firm produced jewellery for Cartier, Van Cleef & Arpels and other prestigious brands. Elizabeth Taylor and the Sultan of Brunei have featured on its list of clients. Pieces by such an important company attract a premium.

Until relatively recently, the firm's work was generally not signed. However, many pieces have registration numbers that can help with identification.

The unique design makes this brooch extremely versatile and thus very appealing to collectors. The brooch can be worn alone or with one of the two detachable bars.

An Oscar Heyman diamond set spray brooch, with two adaptable bars, one in sapphire and diamonds, the other in emerald and diamonds.

c1950

2.25in (6cm) wide

£20,000-25,000   **NBLM**

A gem-set flower spray brooch, with 4ct of rubies and 7ct of diamonds.

c1950   *2.25in (6cm) high*

£5,000-8,000   **NBLM**

A Tiffany double-heart brooch set, with two diamonds.

c1950   *1.5in (4cm) wide*

£1,200-1,800   **NBLM**

A Tiffany brooch pendant set with diamonds, 4.5ct.

c1950   *3in (8cm) high*

£8,000-12,000   **NBLM**

A Meister secretary bird brooch, with spectacles and emerald eyes.

1965   *1.75in (4.5cm) high*

£3,000-3,500   **NBLM**

An onyx and lapis lazuli duck brooch, with a small diamond eye.

c1980   *0.75in (2cm) wide*

£400-600   **NBLM**

A jade and diamond leaping fish brooch, with maker's mark "WAD" for Wendy Anne Dan, Birmingham.

c1986   *2.25in (6cm) high*

£3,000-3,500   **NBLM**

A late 20thC 18ct gold brooch, set with a panel of agate, marked "750".

£300-400   **GS**

A late 20thC seated hound brooch, with an enamelled head.

1.5in (4cm) high

£1,000-1,500   **NBLM**

A late 20thC carved labradorite 18ct moonface brooch, by Stephen Webster, with cabochon sapphires, emeralds and cultured pearls.

2.5in (5cm) wide

£3,000-4,000   **NBLM**

A jade brooch, mounted with pierced jade in the form of a dragon, the shaped gold frame decorated with enamel.

2.75in (7cm) wide

£2,000-2,500   **WW**

A fox mask stick pin, designed as a riding crop and applied with a realistically formed fox mask with ruby eyes, fitted case.

3.25in (8.5cm) wide

£180-220   **WW**

A goshawk stick pin, with a realistically formed bird, pavé-set with graduated turquoise cabochons, with ruby eyes and two small rose-cut diamonds to the beak, set in gold, the fitted case by Mappin and Webb.

3.75in (9.5cm) high

£600-900   **WW**

A Cartier 18ct gold turtle brooch, set with turquoise cabochons and sapphire eyes, signed "Cartier Paris no 7383".

1.5in (3.5cm) high

£1,000-1,500   **WW**

A French gold pheasant brooch, with a ruby eye, rose-cut diamond feathers and a polychrome enamelled body, indistinct lozenge-shaped maker's mark.

£700-1,000   **DN**

A Royal Artillery diamond regimental badge brooch, in the form of a cannon, set with eight-cut diamonds, enamelled ribbon mottos and an enamelled crown.

£400-600   **DN**

A CLOSER LOOK AT A RARE KASHMIR SAPPHIRE AND DIAMOND NECKLACE

The sapphire mines of Kashmir are situated in the Padar region of the Himalayas. When sapphires were first discovered there after a landslide in 1881, they were so plentiful that locals used the hard blue rocks as flints for their rifles, starting fires and as cutting tools.

The quality of these Kashmir stones is such that they reveal their rich yet 'velvety' quality under a range of light sources.

The necklace can be converted in to five brooches, and this adaptable quality, together with provenance, adds to its desirability.

Kashmir sapphires of this size and colour rarely come onto the open market. They have been catalogued by the London Precious Stone Laboratory.

A rare Kashmir sapphire and diamond necklace, formed of eight graduated oval 'target' clusters, with sapphire and diamond five stone saltire-shaped inter-links, each oval cluster centred with a sapphire within two old-cut diamond graduated borders, each silver and gold mounted cluster with two suspension loops and screw apertures, with five removable screw-in brooch fittings, the diamonds weigh 37ct, in a fitted case.

With the necklace is a contemporary hand-written note from the vendor's grandmother; "Marjorie's sapphire and diamond necklace, given to me to give to her by Mama on March 30th 1888".

c1885

£250,000-300,000

DN

A George III flat garnet cruciform pendant, set with five garnets, half-pearls and turquoise cabochons to the gold canetille mount, later gold chain.

1.5in (4cm) wide

£250-350 WW

A Victorian diamond riviere necklace, set with graduated circular-cut diamonds in cut down silver and gold collets, the clasp with eight similar diamonds, 7ct.

16.25in (41.5cm) long

£5,000-7,000 WW

A Victorian black pearl and diamond pendant, the half-pearl in a surround of circular diamonds suspending a pear-shaped diamond, set in silver and gold.

1.25in (3cm) high

£1,800-2,200 WW

An unusual Victorian gem-set gold horseshoe pendant, with a carved amethyst and assorted stone beads, set with a small diamond to the pendant hoop.

2.5in (6.5cm) high

£350-450 WW

A late 19thC gilt-metal ship pendant, in the Renaissance style, mounted with pearl and decorated with emeralds, rubies and smaller pearls.

1.75in (4.5cm) wide

£400-500 WW

An American necklace pendant, with moonstones and moonstone drops.

c1900   *drop 1.5in (4cm) high*

£800-1,200 NBLM

An Edwardian diamond trefoil pendant necklace, designed as leaf scrolls with old-cut diamonds, set in silver and gold, with a small pearl drop, later chain.

£700-1,000 DN

An Edwardian diamond pendant necklace, millegrain set with old-cut and rose diamonds, with three graduated diamond drops, on a fine trace-link back chain.

£2,000-2,500 DN

An Edwardian pendant watch, in blue enamel and platinum set with small rose-cut diamonds, the dial signed 'Agassiz'.

Agassiz supplied movements to Tiffany.

1.75in (4.5cm) high

£8,000-12,000 NBLM

An Edwardian winged cherub pendant, set with rubies, diamonds and pearls, adapts as a brooch.

1.75in (4.5cm) wide

£2,200-2,800 NBLM

A pink satin glass drop necklace.

c1930   *drop 2.75in (7cm) high*

£30-40 GKA

A mid-20thC 6.5ct diamond swirl pendant.

2.5in (6.5cm) high

£5,000-7,000 **NBLM**

A suite of seed pearl and peridot jewellery, with a necklace, earrings and a brooch, each with gold framing, the brooch and earrings with tear-drop shaped stones.

£500-800 **ROW**

A rope design necklace, by Mellerio Dits Mellers of Paris, with a watch pendant set with diamonds, adaptable as a bracelet.

c1950 *1in (2.5cm) wide*

£8,000-12,000 **NBLM**

A unique Van Cleef & Arpels triple rope-twist necklace, with an articulated gem set centre, diamonds, emeralds and rubies.

c1950 *panel 2.5in (6.5cm) wide*

£10,000-15,000 **NBLM**

BRACELETS

An early 19thC hardstone itaglio yellow metal bracelet, formed from seven hardstone itaglio links, each carved with a classical maiden.

£220-280 **ROW**

A Victorian cased demi-parure, in the Etruscan style, comprising a hinged bangle, brooch and drop earrings, each with a pink foiled back cabochon stone and white coral beads to the gold filigree mounts.

Bangle 2.25in (5.5cm) wide

£800-1,200 **WW**

A CLOSER LOOK AT AN EDWARDIAN PEARL & DIAMOND BRACELET

The quality of this piece is evident in the standard of the materials and the smoothness, delicacy and strength of the connections and settings.

Millegrain, popular in the Edwardian period, is a setting in which stones are subtly held in place by small beads or grains of metal. It also refers to a surface that is decorated with tiny beads of metal.

Edwardian jewellery tended to be delicate and feminine with dainty and intricate decoration that would compliment the fashions of the period. Diamonds were a favoured stone.

Higher quality pearls, like these, have less imperfections. Examples with blemishes should be avoided.

An Edwardian pearl and diamond bracelet, adaptable as a choker, with openwork and millegrain.

7.75in (20cm) long

£8,000-12,000 **NBLM**

A Victorian garnet and gold hinged bangle, mounted with three garnet cabochons, each centred with a diamond to the star mount.

2.5in (6.5cm) wide

£400-600   **WW**

An Edwardian ruby calibre sapphire and diamond bracelet.

2.75in (7cm) wide

£5,000-8,000   **NBLM**

A honeycomb-patterned belt bracelet, in pink gold, with a sapphire and diamond set buckle.

c1940

£5,000-7,000   **NBLM**

A modern 18ct gold erotic hinged bangle, by Carrera y Carrera, chased with a group of nudes, with a gold ring with associated subject, in original fitted cases.

bangle 2.5in (6.5cm) wide

£1,500-2,000   **WW**

RINGS

A Russian Imperial presentation ring, with a black opal and eleven cushion-shaped diamonds, inscription, cyrillic maker's mark "AR", St Petersburg marks for 1856.

The inscription probably refers to the botanist Henry Bradbury (1831-1860).

1in (2.5cm) wide

£2,000-3,000   **WW**

A Victorian 18ct gold 'Mizpah' ring, with a plain tapering band and letters chased in high relief on a textured ground, Birmingham 1876.

'Mizpah' is an Hebraic salutation, translating as 'watch tower', meaning 'May God watch between us when we are apart'. The Victorians often used it on sentimental jewellery.

£120-180   **DN**

An early 20thC Prussian gold and iron ring, chased with laurel, the front with a coronet above an initial "E", applied to a gold inner band, the back marked "1915".

The crown is that of a German Duke or Prince. The date and the laurel wreath suggests this ring may have been made for followers of a noble general, maybe to mark a victory.

£250-350   **DN**

An Art Deco carved emerald and diamond platinum ring, the Indian emerald probably 19thC.

c1930   *0.5in (1.5cm) wide*

£10,000-15,000   **NBLM**

A retro cocktail ring, with sapphire and diamonds, set in pink gold.

c1945   *1in (2.5cm) wide*

£3,000-4,000   **NBLM**

An American gold ring, shaped as a pelican forming a square.

c1965   *1.5in (4cm) wide*

£1,000-1,500   **NBLM**

A 9ct Tanzanite set cluster ring, with a 5ct diamond pave border.

Only discovered in 1967 in Tanzania, Tanzanite was championed by Tiffany's as the gemstone of the 20thC.

c1980   *1in (2.5cm) wide*

£10,000-12,000   **NBLM**

A carved emerald ring, depicting a female face, the emerald carved in the 1920s, in a modern setting.

1in (2.5cm) long

£3,000-4,000   **NBLM**

A diamond cluster ring, by Boucheron, with a central 2ct brilliant-cut diamond and baguette and brilliant-cut diamonds to the shoulders, 18ct yellow gold, signed and numbered "885795".

1in (2.5cm) wide

£6,000-8,000   **WW**

EARRINGS

A pair of 19thC gold and woven hair pendant earrings, each with a floral chased cap and similar round surmount.

3.25 in (8cm) high

£200-300   DN

A pair of Late Victorian Egyptian Revival earrings, with antique Egyptian glazed ceramic beads.

3.5in (9cm) high

£2,000-3,000   NBLM

A pair of late 19thC large baroque natural pearl drop earrings, with rose-cut and brilliant diamonds.

2in (5cm) high

£15,000-20,000   NBLM

A pair of Edwardian emerald pear-shaped drop earrings, diamond set, with an openwork top.

1.75in (4.5cm) high

£7,000-9,000   NBLM

A night and day ear clip set, with 6ct of diamonds and a cultured pearl, with a detachable lower half.

Night and day earrings have detachable elements to make them simpler or more elaborate, as appropriate for the time of day. Some earrings had 'day' covers to hide valuable gems from public view when travelling.

c1955   *1.75in (4.5cm) high*

£10,000-15,000   NBLM

A pair of tiger ear clips, with black enamel stripes.

c1975   *1.25in (3cm) wide*

£1,200-1,800   NBLM

OTHER PRECIOUS JEWELLERY

A rare Victorian lady's chatelaine, in silver gilt, with notebook, perfume bottle, locket, letter opener and smelling salt pot.

c1885   *4.75in (12cm) high*

£600-900   TRIO

A pair of Cartier platinum and diamond cufflinks and studs, in original fitted case.

c1930   *cufflink 0.5in (1.5cm) wide*

£5,000-8,000   NBLM

An unusual pair of gold skunk cufflinks by Van Cleef & Arpels, set with a line of brilliant cut diamonds, signed "VCA", engraved with initials.

1.25in (3cm) wide

£1,500-2,000   WW

THE COSTUME JEWELLERY MARKET

The costume jewellery market has altered significantly over the last few years as fashions changed. Bright bold colours are now very much in demand as buyers favour turquoise and coral over classic designs in pale colours with pearls and crystals. Miriam Haskell has remained extremely popular, although high prices have led to an increase in popularity of Stanley Hagler, which is often more keenly priced. European and Japanese buyers in particular, are increasingly interested in his work. The exuberant work of Kramer, Regency and Lea Stein is also in demand.

The trend for colour has affected the market for some Trifari – buyers look for colourful pieces, such as fruit salad pins, and are more likely to reject the company's classic pearl jewellery.

As in previous years, jewellery by top name designers, such as Dior, Schiaparelli and Chanel, continues to be highly sought after. The trend for all things 1980s has lead to an increase in interest in pieces epitomising the era, such as Larry Vrba.

Long drop earrings are selling extremely well, particularly Hagler's 'Jewels of India range'. Buyers favour longer examples, especially in the summer season. Brooches, wide diamanté bracelets and striking tasselled necklaces are also very much in demand.

– Yai Thammachote, Cristobal

CORO

A Coro Duette, in the form of horses' heads, in vermeil sterling silver with ruby and aquamarine crystal navettes.

c1940 — 2.25in (5.75cm) high

£150-200 — **CRIS**

A Coro Duette, in the form of owls, in vermeil sterling silver with topaz and clear crystal rhinestones.

c1940 — 1.5in (3.75cm) high

£120-180 — **JJ**

A CLOSER LOOK AT A CORO DUETTE

The double clip design was patented by the French jeweller, Louis Cartier in 1927. Coro developed its own version, the Duette, in 1931.

Clips became very popular during the 1920s. They were worn on lapels, furs or necklines.

Sometimes sold with matching earrings, Coro Duettes are now avidly collected.

The two identical clips are mounted on a detachable back which allows the pair to be worn as a single pin.

A Coro Duette, in the form of a bouquet of flowers, in enamelled silver with red glass beads and clear crystal rhinestones.

c1935 — 2.75in (7cm) high

£200-250 — **ROX**

A bow pin, possibly by Coro, of rhodium-plated casting with round, baguette and pavé-set clear crystal rhinestones, unsigned.

c1935 — 3.25in (8.25cm) high

£70-100 — **CRIS**

A Corocraft 'bunch of grapes' pin, with prong-set faux moonstone, chalcedony glass stones and sterling silver leaves.

c1940 — 3in (7.5cm) high

£180-220 — **CRIS**

A gold Coro necklace with bow detail.

£30-50 — **MILLB**

A late 1940s Coro chatelaine pin, with a pair of ballerinas in gold-tone metal, linked by a a twin-strand gilt metal chain.

chains 6in (15.5cm) long

£70-90 — **JJ**

A pair of Coro Native American chief earrings, in pewter-tone white metal castings.

c1960 — 1in (2.5cm) high

£30-40 — **MILLB**

A Cristobal butterfly pin, from the 'Butterfly' collection, ruthenium-plated, with navette-cut, round and square-cut clear rhinestones.

c1995   3.75in (9.5cm) wide

£70-100   CRIS

A Cristobal butterfly pin, from the 'Butterfly' collection, ruthenium-plated with round and navette-cut sapphire and lime green and aurora borealis rhinestones.

c1995   3in (7.5cm) wide

£50-70   CRIS

A Cristobal apple pin, from the 'Secret Garden' collection, with prong-set ruby, fuchsia, aquamarine, amethyst and emerald rhinestones of various cuts, mostly dating to the 1950s.

c1995   3in (9cm) h

£80-120   CRIS

A Cristobal sunflower pin from the 'Secret Garden' collection, ruthenium-plated, with Swarovski jet, emerald, peridot and rainbow rhinestones.

c1995   4.75in (12cm) high

£70-100   CRIS

A Cristobal necklace, with 1950s amber and topaz rhinestones, in a ruthenium-plated casting.

c1995   15.25in (39cm) long

£100-150   CRIS

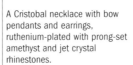

A Cristobal necklace with bow pendants and earrings, ruthenium-plated with prong-set amethyst and jet crystal rhinestones.

c1995   17.25in (44cm) long

£100-150   CRIS

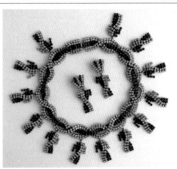

A Dior pendant necklace with earrings, of gilt metal with rectangular-cut jonquil pastes, black enamel cabochons, faux pearls and clear rhinestones.

c1965

14.5in (37cm) long

£1,000-1,500   FM

A Dior necklace with bracelet and earrings, of interlinked hoops of gilt metal with topaz rhinestones.

c1955   14.5in (37cm) long

£600-800   FM

A pendant tassel necklace and earrings, by Mitchell Maer for Dior, of faux gold with round-cut haematite stones.

c1955   pendant 4in (10cm) long

£700-900   WAIN

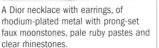

A Dior necklace with earrings, of rhodium-plated metal with prong-set faux moonstones, pale ruby pastes and clear rhinestones.

c1960   14in (35.5cm) long

£700-1,000   FM

A Dior stylised floral necklace, with textured gilt squares, triangles and black and fluorescent blue pastes.

c1965   16.75in (43cm) long

£700-1,000   FM

An Eisenberg Original bowtie pin, of rhodium-plated metal, set with unfoiled, square, round and oval-cut Swarovski crystal clear rhinestones.

c1940   3.5in (9cm) wide

£150-200   **ABIJ**

An Eisenberg Original stylised floral pin, of rhodium-plated metal with sapphire, turquoise and clear Swarovski crystal rhinestones.

c1940   3in (7.5cm) wide

£150-200   **ABIJ**

An Eisenberg Original flower pin, of gilt metal with emerald poured glass, with a prong-set, oval-cut, Austrian ruby crystal cabochon and four further pear-cut ruby crystal rhinestones.

c1940   4in (10cm) wide

£500-800   **SUM**

An Eisenberg Original fur clip, of rhodium-plated metal with prong, bezel-set, rectangular, round and oval-cut Swarovski emerald and clear crystal rhinestones.

c1945   3in (7.5cm) high

£200-250   **ABIJ**

An early Hobé necklace, unsigned.

£800-1,200   **ROX**

A large Hobé roses and pendant heart locket pin, in sterling and vermeil sterling silver with metallic faux pearls and white metal tassels.

c1945   5.5in (14cm) high

£300-400   **BY**

A Hobé necklace and earrings with rose motifs and bow in vermeil sterling silver, metallic faux pearls and white on red carved cameo, unsigned.

c1945   15.5in (40cm) long

£300-400   **BY**

A Hobé necklace and earrings, of flower form, with iridescent glass petals and inset diamanté, the pendant detachable from the mesh necklace.

c1965   Pendant 2in (5cm) high

£100-150   **BY**

A Joseff Russian gold floral pin, with central ruby red cabochon and navette-cut clear rhinestones.

c1945   3.5in (9cm) wide

£300-350   **SUM**

An unusual Joseff floral motif necklace and earrings, Russian gold with navette-cut ruby and round-cut clear rhinestones.

c1945   Earrings 3.5in (9cm) high

£600-900   **SUM**

A large Joseff Russian gold tassel pin, of middle Eastern inspiration, with a faux silver finish.

c1945   6.5in (16.5cm) high

£300-500   **SUM**

A Russian gold 'Joseff' retail display logo, by Joseff of Hollywood.

c1940   3in (8cm) high

£100-150   **CRIS**

COSTUME JEWELLERY

A L'Atelier de Verre bracelet, with four strands of dark amethyst poured glass beads and a pansy clasp with black, amethyst and green poured glass.

c2000   8in (20.25cm) long
£250-300   **SUM**

A L'Atelier de Verre floral pendant necklace, with faux pearls, yellow poured glass and mother-of-pearl petals, with green glass cabochons and clear crystal rhinestone centre.

c2000   16in (41cm) long
£250-300   **SUM**

A L'Atelier de Verre flower pin, in gold-plated metal with yellow and green poured glass and clear crystal rhinestones.

c2000   2.5in (6.5cm) high
£250-300   **SUM**

A L'Atelier de Verre floral pin and earrings, with emerald green poured glass leaves and pavé-set clear crystal rhinestone petals in gilt metal settings.

c2000   Pin 3in (7.5cm) wide
£600-900   **SUM**

A Made in Austria fruit pin, with a single blue glass strawberry, gilt-metal stalks and leaves and a lilac crystal rhinestone.

c1940   2.25in (5.75cm) high
£50-80   **CRIS**

A Made in Austria fruit pin, with yellow glass strawberries, green glass and gilt leaves, gilt metal stalks and a rose pin crystal rhinestone.

c1940   2.5in (6.5cm) high
£70-100   **CRIS**

A late 1940s Made in Austria fruit and leaf pin, gold-plated with amber-yellow and green glass.

2.5in (6.5cm) high
£50-80   **CRIS**

An early 1950s Made in Austria fruit and leaf pin, with red and amber glass, gold-plated leaf and a rose pink crystal rhinestone highlight.

1.4in (3.5cm) high
£50-80   **CRIS**

A Made in Austria fruit pin, with opaque red cherries, green glass leaves and yellow diamanté, stamped AUSTRIA.

c1955   2in (5cm) wide
£40-60   **BY**

A large Made in Austria fruit pin, with a single orange glass fruit and four green glass leaves.

c1955   2.5in (6cm) wide
£30-50   **BY**

A Made in Austria fruit pin, in the form of a large red glass fruit, with two green glass leaves and a single centre-set red diamanté.

c1955   1.5in (4cm) high
£30-50   **BY**

An Austrian fruit pin with black glass cherries, green glass leaves, japanned metal stalks and a clear crystal rhinestone.

c1955   2in (5cm) long
£30-50   **BY**

A Made in Austria fruit pin, with a single opaque green glass pear, green and white enamelled leaves, gilt metal stalks and two green crystal rhinestones.

c1955   2.25in (5.75cm) high
£30-50   **BY**

A Made in Austria fruit pin, with clear glass wild strawberries, clear crystal rhinestones flowerheads and japanned metal stalks.

c1955   2.25in (5.75cm) high
£30-50   **BY**

A CLOSER LOOK AT A MAISON GRIPOIX ORNAMENT

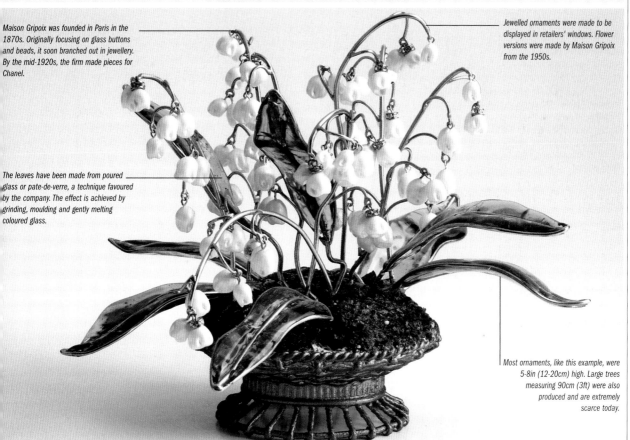

Maison Gripoix was founded in Paris in the 1870s. Originally focusing on glass buttons and beads, it soon branched out in jewellery. By the mid-1920s, the firm made pieces for Chanel.

Jewelled ornaments were made to be displayed in retailers' windows. Flower versions were made by Maison Gripoix from the 1950s.

The leaves have been made from poured glass or pate-de-verre, a technique favoured by the company. The effect is achieved by grinding, moulding and gently melting coloured glass.

Most ornaments, like this example, were 5-8in (12-20cm) high. Large trees measuring 90cm (3ft) were also produced and are extremely scarce today.

Maison Gripoix basket of flowers ornament, in antiqued gold-tone metal with emerald poured glass and faux baroque pearl drops.

1955

6.25in (16cm) high

500-700

CRIS

Maison Gripoix flower pin, with poured glass leaves and turquoise, emerald and black glass cabochons in an antiqued gilt-metal frame.

1945   3.25in (8.25cm) high

500-700   **SUM**

A Maison Gripoix berries and leaves necklace, with green poured glass leaves and cherry poured glass beads.

c1985   17.5in (45cm) long

£400-600   **RITZ**

A late 1930s Maison Gripoix glass bracelet, the clasp marked "MADE IN FRANCE".

3.25in (8cm) wide

£100-200   **ROX**

MIRIAM HASKELL

MIRIAM HASKELL (1899-1981)

- Miriam Haskell made glamorous and fashionable costume jewellery from the mid-1920s.
- She helped to establish costume jewellery as a valued art form in its own right. Her pieces were worn by high profile individuals, such as Joan Crawford.
- Although not a designer herself, she possessed a talent for spotting good designs and skilled designers.
- Frank Hess was appointed Chief Designer of the company from 1926. He introduced innovative designs well into the 1960s.
- Talented designers included Robert Clark and Peter Raines in the 1960s, Larry Vbra in the 1970s and Millie Petronzio in the 1980s.
- Haskell's pieces broke with traditional jewellery design.
- Materials included Japanese faux pearls, Murano glass beads and Austrian faceted crystals.
- Pieces were finished to high standards, often by hand. The appeal today rests with the high quality and the innovation of designs.
- The company is still in production today.

A Miriam Haskell pin, with large French jet cabochons set in antiqued gilt metal with rings and clusters of clear rose montées.

c1945   3.25in (8.5cm) high

£400-600   SUM

A Miriam Haskell two-tier pendant pin, of antiqued gilt metal with clusters of clear rose montées and three faux baroque pearl drops.

c1950   3.75in (9.5cm) high

£400-600   SUM

A Miriam Haskell floral motif pin, of antiqued gilt metal with lavender, amethyst and moonstone glass cabochons and clear rose montées.

c1950   4in (10cm) high

£400-600   SUM

A Miriam Haskell floral motif pin and bracelet, with clear and aurora borealis rose montées and antiqued gilt metal leaves.

c1950   bracelet 7.5in (19cm) long

£600-900   SUM

A Miriam Haskell festoon necklace, of filigree gilt metal, clusters of faux seed pearls and round-cut clear rhinestones.

3.5in (9cm) long

£1,200-1,800   SUM

A Miriam Haskell necklace, with five strands of faux pearls of various size, terminating in gilt metal plates with small, faux pearl floral motifs.

c1950   10.5in (26.5cm) long

£400-600   SUM

A Miriam Haskell floral pin, of antiqued gilt metal with rings and rows of faux seed and baroque pearls and clear rose montées.

c1950   2.25in 5.75cm) diam

£300-500   SUM

A Miriam Haskell pin, with bands of antiqued gilt metal and faux baroque pearls, topped with antiqued gilt-metal leaves covered with clear rose montées.

c1960   3in (7.5cm) high

£400-600   SUM

A Miriam Haskell parure, with a pendant necklace, two pins and earrings, all with black resin beads and cabochons and square-cut clear rhinestones.

c1960   Necklace 14.75in (38cm) long

£2,200-2,800   SUM

A pair of Miriam Haskell large floral motif earrings, with seed pod and foliate pendants, of filigree and textured silvered metal.

c1975   4.25in (10.5cm) high

£70-100   ABIJ

A pair of Miriam Haskell earrings, of antiqued gilt metal with clusters of small faux baroque pearl beads and prong-set clear rhinestones.

c1950   2in (5cm) high

£250-300   SUM

An Elsa Schiaparelli demi-parure, with necklace, bracelet and earrings, of gold-plated metal with prong-set smoked topaz and amber crystal stones and beads.

c1955   Necklace 16in (40.5cm) long

£400-600   **CRIS**

An Elsa Schiaparelli necklace and earrings, with gilt metal links, faux pearls and prong-set lilac, amethyst and dusty pink pastes and aurora borealis rhinestones.

c1955   Necklace 14.5in (37cm) long

£300-400   **SUM**

An Elsa Schiaparelli demi-parure, with necklace, bracelet and earrings, with gilt metal links and prong-set faux amber and dark amethyst glass stones and aurora borealis rhinestones.

c1955   Necklace 14.5in (37cm) long

£700-1,000   **SUM**

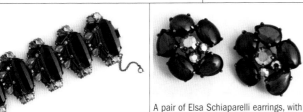

A late 1940s Schiaparelli glass and diamanté bracelet, unsigned.

          7.75in (20cm) long

£100-200   **ROX**

A pair of Elsa Schiaparelli earrings, with prong-set reddish-brown and ruby glass stones encircling aurora borealis rhinestones.

c1955   1.75in (4cm) wide

£70-100   **SUM**

TRIFARI

- Trifari was established by an Italian goldsmith, Gustavo Trifari, in New York in 1904. It became one of the largest costume jewellery makers and made pieces for all sections of the market.
- Glamorous clientele, including Mamie Eisenhower, helped raise the profile of the firm.
- Pre-eminent chief designer Alfred Philippe introduced techniques that had previously been used only for precious jewellery.
- Phillipe's high-end pieces are sought-after today, while his popular 'Jelly Belly' and crown pins are also desirable.
- Early Trifari tends to be more valuable, with many exceptions.
- Trifari is now part of Liz Claiborne Inc.

A Trifari 'jelly mould' necklace, bracelet and earrings.

c1945   Earrings 1in (2.5cm) high

£200-300   **ROX**

A Trifari necklace and earrings, of rose-gold-plated base metal with carved, pale yellow glass flowers.

c1955   Necklace 15in (38cm) long

£70-100   **CRIS**

A Trifari floral pendant necklace, rose-gold-plated with a cluster of plum-black cabochons.

c1955   Pendant 1.5in (3.75cm) wide

£70-100   **TR**

A Trifari necklace with multiple gun-metal links, strands of tourmaline glass beads and a gold-plated clasp.

c1965   Clasp 2.5in (6.25cm) wide

£100-150   **TR**

A late 1930s Trifari large lily pin, of vermeil sterling silver with semi-translucent white Lucite leaves and clear rhinestones.

          4in (10cm) high

£1,000-1,500   **ROX**

A Trifari bow pin, of gold vermeil over sterling silver, with ruby red baguette and pavé-set clear rhinestones.

c1945   3.5in (9cm) wide

£400-600   **LYNH**

A Trifari pin, with matte-finish gold-plating and elongated faux pearls.

c1955   4in (10cm) high

£50-70   **CRIS**

A gilt floral spray pin, the three flowers centred with red, green, and blue pavé and clear stones, unsigned, possibly Trifari.

          2.5in (6.5cm) high

£50-70   **JJ**

A Weiss floral wreath pin and earrings, in antiqued silvertone metal with topaz, sapphire and aurora borealis rhinestones.

c1955   *Pin 3.5in (9cm) diam*

£30-50   **ABIJ**

A Weiss floral pin and earrings, with clusters of yellow enamel, topaz and aurora borealis rhinestone flowerheads.

c1955   *Pin 1.5in (4cm) diam*

£40-60   **JJ**

An unusual early 1970s Weiss fantasy coloured pin, with goldtone metal casting, set with inverted 3-D aurora borealis crystal rhinestones.

1.75in (4.5cm) diam

£30-50   **ABIJ**

A Weiss cross pin, of japanned base metal set with 'black diamond' Austrian crystal beads.

c1975   *2.5in (6.5cm) high*

£30-40   **MILLE**

A Weiss necklace, bracelet and earrings, of solid and meshed goldtone metal, with pink and aurora borealis crystal rhinestones.

c1965   *Necklace 15in (38cm) long*

£70-90   **JJ**

A CLOSER LOOK AT A VIVIAN WESTWOOD CROWN

Westwood has been designing clothes and accessories since the early 1970s. Her high profile helps make this piece desirable.

Emblems of royalty frequently feature in Westwood's work and are indicative of her irreverent and witty style - at its most subversive during the Punk era.

Most Westwood pieces are made with goldtone metal and decorated with faux pearls and clear crystals.

The large size of this crown increases the value.

A Vivian Westwood 'royal' crown, with black velvet lining and fake fur trim, the goldtone metal frame with fleur-de-lis and a royal orb finial set with faux pearls, baquette-, lozenge-, round- and pear-cut clear pastes and crystal rhinestones.

c1985   *6.25in (16cm) high*

£400-600   **REI**

A Vivian Westwood faux pearl choker, with a royal orb and clasp of silvertone metal studded with pavé-set clear crystal rhinestones.

c1985   *Necklace 13.5in (34cm) long*

£70-90   **REL**

A Vivian Westwood choker, with four chains of gilt metal, three strands of faux pearls and a gilt metal clasp with a royal orb motif.

c1985   *12.5in (32cm) long*

£80-120   **REL**

A Vivian Westwood necklace, the 'royal' orb with a large round faux pearl above a pendant faux pearl, clear rhinestone highlights and goldtone metal chain.

c1985   *Necklace 30.5in (78cm) long*

£70-100   **REL**

A pair of Vivian Westwood goldtone metal 'royal' orb earrings, with round faux pearls and pendants and clear rhinestone highlights.

c1985   *3in (7.5cm) high*

£80-120   **REL**

A pair of Vivian Westwood bow and heart pendant earrings, of silvertone metal with black and pavé-set clear rhinestones.

c1985   *1.5in (3.75cm) high*

£50-70   **REI**

An Alcozer 'vase of flowers' pin, with semi-precious stones, cultured pearls and clear and ruby rhinestones, on a rose-gold-plated casting.

c1995   4.5in (11cm) high

£180-200   **CRIS**

A Fred A. Block cat pin, of vermeil sterling silver, with turquoise glass beads to the whiskers and tail and clear crystal rhinestone eyes.

c1945   4cm (10cm) high

£200-250   **BY**

A Chanel flower and bow pin, with poured glass stones, glass beads, clear crystal rhinestones and faux pearls, in gilt-metal settings.

c1935   2.5in (6.5cm) high

£300-400   **BY**

A Chanel pendant pin, with green and blue glass stones and faux pearls, in gold-plated settings.

c1955   3.25in (8cm) high

£250-300   **RITZ**

A pair of Chanel pendant earrings, of antiqued, stamped gilt metal with faux pearls, green glass cabochons and glass drops.

c1975   3.75in (9.5cm) high

£250-300   **SUM**

A De Rosa bowl of flowers pin, in vermeil sterling silver with red enamelled roses.

c1945   2in (5cm) high

£200-250   **ROX**

A Deposé necklace, with strands of faux pearls, faux pearl drops, clear crystal rhinestones and a silver clasp.

c1920   15in (39cm) long

£200-250   **CRIS**

A German black and silver pin, possibly by Fahrner.

      2in (5.5cm) wide

£1,000-1,500   **TR**

An Art Deco Fahrner pin, in silver and marcasite with amazonite bars, blue glass cabochons and a pink quartz stone.

c1925   1.75in (4.5cm) wide

£700-1,000   **TR**

A Fahrner stylised leaf pin, in silver and marcasite with a single pearl highlight.

c1925   1.75in (4.5cm) wide

£280-320   **RBRG**

A 1930s Fischel and Nessler necklace, in sterling silver and carved glass.

      2.5in (6.5cm) wide

£150-200   **RG**

A Fahrner floral motif bar pin, in silver with matte black enamel and an aventurine quartz cabochon.

c1925   2.75in (7cm) wide

£400-600   **RBRG**

A Har pendant bracelet, the oriental Lucite head with jade glass cabochons and small aurora borealis crystal rhinestones, on a silver-plated chain.

c1955   Pendant 1.5in (3cm) high

£80-120   **CRIS**

COSTUME JEWELLERY

A pair of Har cobra heads earrings, with aurora borealis lava stones, green enamel and topaz crystal rhinestones, on gold-plated castings.

c1955   1.5in (3.5cm) high

£120-180   **CRIS**

A Har serpent bangle, gold-plated with green enamel and green and aurora borealis glass stones.

c1955   2.5in (7cm) wide

£300-500   **CRIS**

A 1950s Hattie Carnegie plastic and diamanté 'Aztec Man' pin, the plastic imitating jade and coral.

2.25in (6cm) high

£180-220   **ROX**

A Hattie Carnegie leaf pendant necklace and earrings, of gold-washed metal with faux pearl highlights.

c1965   Necklace 17in (43cm) long

£120-150   **JJ**

A 1940s Schreiner pink glass and faux pearl pin and earrings, unsigned.

Pin 3in (7.5cm) wide

£200-300   **ROX**

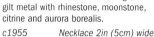

A Schreiner necklace and earrings, in gilt metal with rhinestone, moonstone, citrine and aurora borealis.

c1955   Necklace 2in (5cm) wide

£700-900   **SUM**

An Ian St. Gielar tasselled scarf of mauve, cranberry, red and pale green glass beads.

c1995   44in (112cm) long

£300-350   **CRIS**

A Larry Vrba vase of flowers pin, in glass, mother-of-pearl, jade and coral.

c1995   4.75in (12cm) high

£150-200   **CRIS**

A Larry Vrba vase of flowers pin, in mother-of-pearl, glass and rhinestones.

c1995   4.5in (11.5cm) high

£150-200   **CRIS**

A CLOSER LOOK AT A SCHREINER BUSH PIN

Schreiner jewellery, like this striking red and green pin, is characterised by unconventional combinations of colours and paste stones.

Output was limited as pieces were made by hand. This increases their desirability today.

Glamorous and exuberant, Schreiner pieces were worn by stars such as Marilyn Monroe during the 1940s and 1950s.

This piece was made shortly after Henry Schreiner's death in 1951, when the firm was taken over by his daughter, Terry Schreiner.

A Schreiner bush pin, in gilt wire backing with prong-set ruby, emerald and clear crystal rhinestones, square-cut aquamarine pastes and carved, pear-cut emerald glass drops.

c1955   4.25in (11cm) wide

£1,000-1,500   **SUM**

A Marcel Boucher pin, in scrolling sterling silver with clear crystal rhinestone highlights, around a faux ruby paste.

c1935　　　*2.25in (5.75cm) wide*

£120-180　　　**ABIJ**

A 1930s Mazer ruby glass and diamanté inset necklace and earrings.

Centrepiece 2in (5cm) diam

£400-600　　　**ROX**

A 1940s figural Nettie Rosenstein brooch, in faux ivory inset with diamanté inset.

1.75in (4.5cm) high

£150-200　　　**ROX**

A Pennino Bros. bow with pendant tassels necklace and earrings, rhodium-plated with clear crystal rhinestones.

c1940　　*Necklace 14.5in (37cm) long*

£400-500　　　**CRIS**

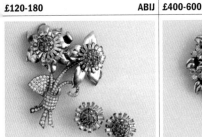

A Pennino Bros. bouquet of flowers pin and earrings, of rose-gold vermeil sterling silver with rose-pink and clear crystal rhinestones.

c1945　　*Pin 2.75in (7cm) high*

£400-450　　　**CRIS**

A Pennino Bros. stylised flower pin, with trailing tendrils, of vermeil sterling silver with aquamarine and clear crystal rhinestones.

c1945　　　*2.75in (7cm) wide*

£200-250　　　**CRIS**

A Regency butterfly pin, gold-plated with prong-set round and navette aurora borealis and aquamarine and jade rhinestones.

c1955　　　*1.75in (4.5cm) wide*

£60-90　　　**CRIS**

A Canadian floral pin, in the style of the Regency company, with green navettes, aquamarine, emerald, clear and aurora borealis rhinestones, unsigned.

c1960　　　*3in (7.5cm) wide*

£40-60　　　**CRIS**

A Regency flower and leaf motif necklace and earrings, silver-plated with navette and round-cut aurora borealis and clear rhinestones.

c1955　*Necklace 15.3in (39cm) long*

£120-180　　　**CRIS**

A Robert horse pin, in silver gilt-metal, the head set with polychrome crystal beads and rhinestones.

c1955　　　*5in (12.5cm) wide*

£150-200　　　**ROX**

A Robert de Mario floral motif pin, of gilt-metal with large, faceted emerald green crystal stones and small clear crystal rhinestone highlights.

c1955　　　*2.25in (95.5cm) wide*

£70-90　　　**ROX**

A 1940s Sandor plastic pin, in the form of a bunch of green berries or grapes.

2.5in (6.5cm) high

£150-200　　　**ROX**

A Secrett brooch, in the form of a butterfly, custom made from black opal for the Lieutenant Governor of Ontario.

c1980　　　*2in (5cm) wide*

£2,500-3,000　　　**TCF**

A 1950s Selro glass bracelet and earrings.

Bracelet 7in (18cm) long

£100-200　　　**ROX**

A Stanley Hagler diamanté brooch and earrings, with faux pearls.

c1955　　*Brooch 2.5in (6.5cm) wide*

£100-200　　　**PC**

A Stanley Hagler necklace, with strands of filigree gilt-metal capped faux pearls and rose montées.

c1975　　　*15.75in (40cm) long*

£200-250　　　**CRIS**

A gilt-metal snake necklace, the head with an inset faceted faux amethyst and faux sapphire eyes, unsigned.

c1925　　　　　　　　　　　　　　*11.5in (29cm) long*

£180-220　　　　　　　　　　　　　　**BY**

An unsigned necklace, with faceted crystal spheres, silver filigree work in the form of flowers.

c1925　　　*19.25in (49cm) long*

£120-180　　　　　　**BY**

A necklace, with faceted clear crystal stones and three emerald green poured glass stones, unsigned.

c1935　　　*15.25in (39cm) long*

£100-150　　　　　　**BY**

A pendant necklace, attributed to Rousselet, with cranberry coloured glass beads and clusters of faux pearls, unsigned.

c1935　　　　　　　　*Necklace 20in (51cm) long*

£300-400　　　　　　　　　　　　　　**BY**

A Murano glass fruits and leaves necklace and bracelet, with aquamarine cabochons, orange and red fruits and unusual opaque green leaves, unsigned.

c1955　　　　　　*Necklace 16.25in (42cm) long*

£200-250　　　　　　　　　　　　　　**BY**

A necklace, bracelet and earrings, of gilt metal with faux amethysts, faux coral glass beads and green crystal rhinestones, unsigned.

c1965　　　　　　　*Necklace 17in (43cm) long*

£120-180　　　　　　　　　　　　　　**BY**

An 18thC genuine pinchbeck necklace, with oval links and a barrel clasp.

c1770   37.5in (96cm) long

£1,000-1,500   RBRG

A Berlin ironwork necklace with alternating s-scroll and cross motifs.

c1810   37in (95cm) long

£1,500-2,000   RBRG

A 'Mariner's Art' nut necklace, carved with floral and foliate motifs and lacquered.

c1840   17in (44cm) long

£1,200-1,800   CSAY

A Murano glass necklace, with alternating clear and opaque blue glass beads.

c1925   33in (85cm) long

£200-250   RBRG

An Austrian lariat necklace with woven ropes of jet and white glass beads.

c1955   44in (110cm) long

£220-280   CRIS

A floral motif necklace, with clear Lucite links and drops and clusters of clear crystal rhinestones.

c1955   32in (82cm) long

£300-500   CSAY

A mid-19thC multiple-pendant necklace and earrings, with inlaid gold and silver piqué.

14.5in (37cm) long

£4,000-5,000   CSAY

A gilt metal butterfly pendant necklace, with blue plique-à-jour and a baroque pearl drop.

c1910   Pendant 1.5in (3.75cm) wide

£500-700   RBRG

A silver pendant, with red and green plique-à-jour and diamond and ruby pastes.

c1915   1.5in (3.75cm) wide

£300-350   RBRG

An Egyptian Revival gilt-metal pyramids pendant necklace, bracelet and earrings, with enamelling.

c1935   Pendant 2in (5cm) high

£150-200   CRIS

An Egyptian Revival female head pin and earrings, in vermeil sterling with faux pearls.

c1935   Pin 2.25in (5.75cm) high

£120-180   RITZ

A Egyptian Revival camel pin.

This piece is typical of the animal figurals popular from the late 1920s to late 1930s.

c1930   1.5in (4cm) high

£25-35   ABAA

A mid-Victorian eagle belt buckle, with faux diamond pastes set in a brass casting.

c1865   6in (15cm) w

£150-250   RITZ

A pair of gilt metal floral earrings, with red, green and yellow plique-à-jour and pearls.

c1910　　　　1.5in (3.75cm) long

£500-700　　　　**RBRG**

A Berlin ironwork ring, in gilt-metal with an inscribed band of iron.

c1915　　　0.25in (0.75cm) wide

£400-500　　　　**CSAY**

A Georgian cut-steel tiara, with a four-prong tortoiseshell hairgrip.

c1800　　　　6.25in (14cm) wide

£400-600　　　　**CSAY**

An Edwardian circular flower motif pin, gold-plated with red, blue, green, amber and clear crystal rhinestones.

　　　　　　2.5in (6cm) diam

£100-125　　　　**CRIS**

A French 'Fruit Salad' pot of flowers pin, with polychrome French carved glass and clear crystal rhinestone baguettes, on a sterling silver casting.

c1920　　　1.75in (4.25cm) high

£100-150　　　　**CRIS**

A Moorish-style pin, of antiqued gilt-metal with a large faux amethyst, turquoise and pale blue glass cabochons and white, red, turquoise and black enamel, unsigned.

c1925　　　　2.5in (6cm) diam

£100-150　　　　**BY**

A 1930s French pendant, the geometric design in blue enamel and paste.

　　　　　　2.5in (6cm) long

£400-600　　　　**TR**

An large green and clear diamanté grape and vine leaf belt buckle, unsigned.

c1935　　　　15cm (6in) wide

£100-150　　　　**BY**

One of a pair of 1930s Czechoslovakian faceted glass clips.

　　　　　1.75in (4.5cm) high

£80-120 pair　　　　**ROX**

An unsigned 'Retro' bow pin, in sterling silver with clear crystal rhinestones and a large aquamarine glass stone.

c1945　　　　2.75in (7cm) wide

£70-100　　　　**CRIS**

A glass and diamanté inset bracelet, unsigned.

Possibly a copy of a David Webb piece.

c1945　　　　3in (8cm) wide

£700-1,000　　　　**BY**

A very rare unsigned cat and 'jelly belly' goldfish bowl pin and earrings, in vermeil sterling silver with clear crystal rhinestones and Lucite bowls with reverse-carved goldfish.

c1945　　　Pin 2.25in (5.75cm) high

£1,000-1,500　　　　**BY**

An unsigned ballroom dancer pin, in vermeil sterling silver with black enamelling and faux sapphires, ruby baguettes and emeralds.

c1945　　　　3.5in (9cm) high

£200-250　　　　**BY**

A woman's torso and head pin, with flowing hair in vermeil sterling silver and pavé-set clear crystal rhinestones, unsigned.

c1945 2.75in (7cm) high

£150-200 BY

An eye pin, of vermeil sterling silver with pavé-set clear and sapphire crystal rhinestones, a black glass cabochon and two faux pearl drops, unsigned.

c1945 2in (5cm) wide

£220-280 BY

A Lucite and gilt-metal pin, with painted red fingernails holding a trembling enamelled gilt-metal lily with a faux pearl centre, unsigned.

c1945 3.5in (9cm) high

£500-800 BY

A Lucite and gilt sterling pin, with a Lucite crescent and fans, unsigned.

c1945 3in (7.5cm) wide

£200-250 BY

A pin in the form of a winged serpent, the body and wings set with tiny diamanté, unsigned.

c1945 3in (7.5cm) high

£150-200 BY

A flower pin with open and close 'night-and-day' mechanism, of gilt metal with blue enamelling and clear crystal rhinestones, unsigned.

c1955 3.5in (9cm) high

£200-250 BY

A tree pin, with enamelled leaves and flowers, applied faux pearls and inset diamanté, unsigned.

c1955 2.75in (7cm) high

£100-150 BY

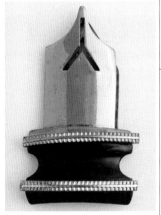

A brass pin, in the form of a fountain pen nib with enamelled section, unsigned.

c1955 2in (5cm) high

£50-80 BY

A 1950s plastic and gilt metal pin, in the form of a fish, the plastics imitating ivory and turquoise.

2in (5cm) wide

£80-120 ROX

A pair of shield-shaped earrings, with asymmetrical faceted citrine and ruby coloured glass, prong-set in white metal.

c1965 1in (2.5cm) high

£30-50 ROX

A Scottish silver and pebble-set target brooch, with central facet-cut stone, surrounded by bands of agate and acanthus engraving.

2in (5cm) diam

£100-200 B&H

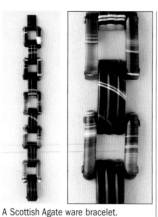

A German enamel pendant.

1.75in (4.5cm) high

£220-280   **TR**

A Scottish Agate ware bracelet.

c1895   8.25in (21cm) long

£120-180   **CRIS**

A faceted faux amethyst bracelet, with silver filigree work in the form of flowers and leaves, unsigned.

c1925   7in (18cm) long

£150-200   **BY**

A French bracelet, with a design of oval blue paste, unsigned.

c1930   0.5in (1cm) wide

£300-500   **TR**

A gilt-metal and mesh bracelet, with translucent plastic, clear crystal rhinestones and a faceted glass faux amethyst, unsigned.

c1930   2.5in (6.5cm) wide

£700-1,000   **BY**

A paste bracelet, with red ridged paste stones, unsigned.

c1935

£200-300   **ROX**

A gilt-metal bracelet, with red and green 'fruit salad' glass stones, green baguettes and clear crystal rhinestones, unsigned.

c1945   6.75in (17cm) long

£200-250   **BY**

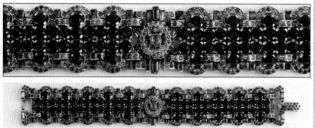

A faux ruby bracelet, with faceted faux rubies and faceted and baguette-cut diamanté, unsigned.

c1945   6.25in (16cm) wide

£220-280   **BY**

A gold-plated metal bracelet, with prong-set aquamarine, blue aurora borealis and sapphire crystal rhinestones, unsigned.

c1955   6.75in (17cm) long

£30-50   **BY**

A Blackinton bangle, of gold-washed sterling silver with graduated bead moulding and turquoise glass cabochons.

c1890   3in (7.5cm) diam

£120-180   **CGPC**

A Blackinton bangle, of gold-washed sterling silver with scrolling leaf motifs and amethyst glass cabochons.

c1895   3in (7.5cm) diam

£200-250   **CGPC**

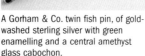

A Gorham & Co. twin fish pin, of gold-washed sterling silver with green enamelling and a central amethyst glass cabochon.

c1900   2.25in (5.75cm) wide

£400-600   **CGPC**

A rare Gorham & Co. 14ct gold pin, with a miniature, enamelled romantic bacchanalian portrait.

1906   1in (2.5cm) wide

£700-900   **CGPC**

A Howard & Co. belt buckle, of sterling silver with applied sterling silver flowers.

c1885   3.25in (8.25cm) high

£80-120   **CGPC**

A Howard & Co. circular buckle, of goldwashed and textured sterling silver, with ruby and amethyst glass stones and a blister pearl centre.

c1900   1.5in (3.75cm) diam

£200-250   **CGPC**

A Kerr & Co. belt buckle, with coiled cobras in silver plated metal and a central ruby red crystal rhinestone.

c1900   5in (12.75cm) wide

£300-400   **CGPC**

A rare Kerr & Co. gold-wash over sterling silver necklace, comprising floral swags intertwined with cherubs.

c1900   15in (38cm) long

£400-600   **CGPC**

A very rare Kerr & Co. two-part cherub belt clasp, in silver-plated metal, the male and female cherubs dancing when fastened.

c1900   2.75in (7cm) wide

£300-500   **CGPC**

A Kerr & Co. belt buckle, adapted to a pin, of engraved silver bordered with enamel.

c1905   3in (7.5cm) wide

£200-250   **CGPC**

A La Pierre belt buckle, the sterling silver frame with scrolling leaves and two romantic celluloid miniatures.

c1905   4in (10cm) wide

£400-600   **CGPC**

An S. & B. Lederer & Co. medal pin, of hand-beaten and textured sterling silver with copper and gold-plated dragon and antiqued gold soldier's face.

c1900   1.5in (3.75cm) wide

£800-1,200   **CGPC**

A Pryor Novelty Co. sterling silver belt pin, in the form of a bust with stylised flowing hair and floral motifs.

1903   2.5in (6.25cm) wide

£300-350   **CGPC**

AMERICAN SILVER

A pair of Reddall & Co. Inc. winged suspender or garter clips, in gold-washed sterling silver.

c1900   *1in (2.5cm) wide*
£120-180   **CGPC**

A Reddall & Co. Inc. buckle, with scrolling leaf forms in gold-washed sterling silver with a faceted, dark amethyst-coloured centre stone.

c1900   *2.25in (5.75cm) diam*
£200-250   **CGPC**

A CLOSER LOOK AT A SHIEBLER SILVER BELT PIN

The frog and snake decoration on this belt pin exemplify Shiebler's use of naturalistic motifs, which he realised with great attention to detail. He also favoured Classical motifs, like this bust.

Known for their creativity and fine workmanship, pieces by silversmith George W. Shiebler of Brooklyn, New York, are hotly collected today.

A Shiebler twin leaf pin, of engraved sterling silver with applied insects, one in sterling silver, the other in matt-finish copper alloy.

c1900   *2.75in (7cm) high*
£300-500   **CGPC**

A Shiebler cross pin, of asymmetrical shape, with sterling silver casting and a large, faceted, sapphire blue crystal cabochon.

c1900   *2.25in (5.75cm) wide*
£400-600   **CGPC**

Pieces are marked with an "S" within a circle and flanked by wings.

The influence of the Aesthetic Movement can be seen in Shiebler's pieces, while the overall shape and scrolling forms are Art Nouveau in style.

A Shiebler sterling silver belt pin, with a frog, snakes and wings encircling a gilded neo-classical-style bust of a female.

c1900   *5in (12.75cm) wide*
£1,000-1,500   **CGPC**

A very rare Unger Bros. bonnetted lady head belt pin, in sterling silver, with naturalistic detail.

c1905
£600-700   **CGPC**

A Shiebler open cuff bangle, of sterling silver with applied, highly naturalistic floral and foliate imagery.

c1900   *2.5in (6.25cm) diam*
£1,000-1,500   **CGPC**

A Thomas F. Brogan buckle, with looped wire border, gold-washed sterling silver scrolls and a dark amethyst-coloured centre stone.

c1900   *2.25in (5.75cm) high*
£100-150   **CGPC**

An Unger Bros. gold-wash over sterling silver bracelet, with filigree scrolling leaf and flower cartouches.

c1900   *7.5in (19cm) long*
£250-300   **CGPC**

An Unger Bros. belt pin, with a duck or goose head bursting out of an egg, in textured sterling silver with a ruby red glass cabochon eye.

c1905   *1.75in (4.5cm) wide*
£300-500   **CGC**

A rare pair of Unger Bros. eagle head cufflinks, in gold-wash over sterling silver castings, with ruby red glass cabochon eyes.

c1905   *0.75in (2cm) high*
£400-500   **CGC**

A rare pair of Unger Bros. owl head cufflinks, of sterling silver with amber and dark brown glass cabochon eyes.

c1905   *0.5in (1.5cm) diam*
£300-500   **CGPC**

An English enamel snuff box, the cover painted with a piper, the sides with flowers.

c1750   2.75 (7cm) wide

£150-200   **ROS**

An 18thC enamel box, in the form of a goldfinch, the hinged lid painted with a dog chasing birds.

3.5in (8.5cm) wide

£500-800   **WW**

A late 18thC enamel box, with a hinged mirrored lid, painted with two birds in a garden and inscribed, "Keep this for my sake", within a jewelled border.

1.75in (4.5cm) high

£300-400   **WW**

A late 18thC enamel box, with a hinged mirrored lid, printed in puce with a view of a harbour, inscribed "Sold at Thompson & Co. on the Corn Hill, Bridgewater".

2in (5cm) high

£300-400   **WW**

An 18thC erotic enamel box, the hinged lid painted with two figures and concealing two erotic panels, the sides with figures and landscape vignettes.

3.5in (9cm) wide

£700-900   **WW**

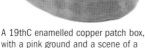

A South Staffordshire enamel box, the cover depicting a house in a landscape within pink borders, the base and sides with flowers and diaper panels.

c1800   2in (5cm) wide

£100-150   **DN**

A 19thC enamelled copper patch box, with a pink ground and a scene of a cottage and tree.

£150-200   **WW**

A 19thC enamelled copper patch box, with a trophy of arms and the inscription "May British Valour Conquests Gain and Make our Foes our Friends Again".

£200-300   **WW**

A 19thC enamelled copper patch box, with a pink ground and the inscription "Who Opens this Will have a Kiss".

£100-150   **WW**

A 19thC enamelled copper patch box, with a floral design and inscribed "Present from Dover".

£200-300   **WW**

A 19thC to 20thC enamel pill box, the lid decorated with an English sailing ship in battle.

1.5in (4cm) wide

£150-200   **FRE**

A South Staffordshire enamelled patch box, with "Constant to thee I'll ever be" and two ladies in a landscape, the base in pink, restored.

£100-150   **DN**

A 19thC Limoges enamel on brass beaker, made for the Persian market, of flared form with enamel decoration of vignettes depicting mother and child, within floral borders.

3.25in (8.5cm) diam

£200-300 **ROS**

A Limoges silver and enamel jewellery box, decorated with three young women in Rococo dress, signed "A. Juan', marked for Paris and Limoges.

c1900 *6in (15.5cm) wide*

£300-400 **VZ**

An early 20thC French enamelled mirror pendant, with a portrait, set in a paste frame.

1.5in (4cm) diam

£150-200 **WW**

A Viennese enamelled ladies' cigarette case, with mauve, black and white stripes, heightened with gilding, English import marks for London.

1923 *3.5in (9cm) wide*

£400-600 **WW**

CLOISONNÉ

A silver cloisonné-enamelled milk jug, sugar pot and tong, made in Moscow, silver mark "GK", maker's mark "A.A", dated.

1896 *3.25in (8.5cm) high*

£1,500-2,000 **HMN**

A Russian silver and gilded cloisonné-enamelled spoon, 84 zolotnik mark.

1850 *5.5in (14cm) long*

£100-200 **KAU**

A Russian cloisonné-enamelled caddy scoop, decorated in shaded polychrome within a white pelleted border and a toffee-coloured ground, with state marks for 1896 to 1908.

4in (10cm) long

£800-900 **WW**

Six silver and gilded cloisonné-enamelled spoons, silver mark.

1850 *5.5in (14cm) long*

£200-300 **KAU**

A Russian cloisonné-enamelled and amethyst silver-gilt beaker, of trumpet form, decorated with polychrome fruiting and flowering vines bordering floral panels, below four cabochon amethysts, on a cream ground.

c1885 *5.25in (13.5cm) high*

£500-700 **ROS**

An early 20th Russian cloisonné-enamelled kovsch, decorated in blues, mauve, white and red, with state marks for 1908-1917.

4.25in (10.5cm) wide

£400-500 **WW**

An early 19thC papier-mâché snuff box, the lift off lid painted with a character smiling as he holds a foaming jug of ale in one hand and a glowing clay pipe in the other.

4in (10cm) diam

£250-350 **CHEF**

An early 19thC German papier-mâché box, the lift-off lid painted with a world weary man wearing a tricorn hat, with a newspaper inscribed "A Lame Duck".

4in (10.5cm) diam

£300-400 **CHEF**

An early 19thC papier-mâché snuff box, the lid painted with a young couple walking.

4in (10.5cm) diam

£300-500 **CHEF**

An early 19thC "Pedestrianism or Foote Travelling" snuff box, the lid bearing a hand-coloured print of a lady about to spit a joint and talking to a traveller, their words printed within the footrim.

3.5in (9cm) diam

£180-250 **CHEF**

An early 19thC papier-mâché snuff box painted with a man, possibly Moses, crowned by a gold circlet below a hooded grey robe.

3.5in (9cm) diam

£300-400 **CHEF**

An early 19thC papier-mâché snuff box, the lift-off lid painted with a 17thC Dutch scene of figures drinking and talking around a campfire.

4in (10.5cm) diam

£200-300 **CHEF**

An early 19thC papier-mâché snuff box, the lid painted with a dandy wearing a top hat and blue striped white waistcoat.

3.75in (9.5cm) diam

£400-600 **CHEF**

An early 19thC German papier-mâché snuff box, the lid painted with an elderly couple kissing over their meal.

3.75in (9.5cm) diam

£200-300 **CHEF**

An early 19thC papier-mâché snuff box, the lift-off lid bearing two black engravings on straw yellow paper, the exterior scene inscribed "Le Riche a Besoin du Pauvre", the erotic scene inside partially scratched out.

£100-150 **CHEF**

An early 19thC papier-mâché snuff box, the lid painted with a shepherd and travellers on their way home from market, signed and inscribed inside "Patronised by HRH the Duke of Sussex and Prince Leopold".

4in (10cm) diam

£800-1,000 **CHEF**

An early 19thC "Les Boxeurs" papier-mâché snuff box, the lift-off lid with a black and white engraving of bare fisted pugilists, a cock fight and a man racing a horse.

9in (23cm) diam

£200-300 **CHEF**

A commemorative Coronation papier-mâché snuff box, the circular lift-off lid bearing a partially hand-coloured print of the interior of Westminster Abbey, titled "Coronation of George IV 19 July 1821".

3.75in (9.5cm) diam

£200-300　　　　**CHEF**

A William IV papier-mâché snuff box, the lid painted with a miser counting his money.

4in (10cm) diam

£300-400　　　　**CHEF**

A CLOSER LOOK AT A PAPIER-MÂCHÉ SNUFF BOX

Hunting scenes were particularly popular in the 18thC and early 19thC. This miniature painting by Samuel Raven is of very high quality and shows the painter's attention to detail.

Prince Leopold was popular in his country following his marriage to Charlotte, daughter of George IV, in 1816. She died in childbirth in 1817. This indicates that the box could have been painted around 1816.

The box is signed and inscribed by Samuel Raven, which adds to the value of this piece.

An early 19thC papier-mâché snuff box, by Samuel Raven, with a hunting scene, inscribed "Patronised by HRH The Duke of Sussex and Prince Leopold of Sax-Coburg", signed and inscribed inside.

£800-1,200　　　　**CHEF**

A William IV papier-mâché snuff box, 'The Proposal', by Samuel Raven after Harlow and Meyer, signed.

The accompanying note states that the box is likely to date from c1815-31.

4in (10cm) diam

£800-1,200　　　　**CHEF**

A mid-19thC German papier-mâché snuff box, the rectangular hinged lid with an overpainted theatrical print of a tearful mother with her two children by a cave mouth.

3in (8cm) wide

£150-200　　　　**CHEF**

A mid-19thC German papier-mâché snuff box, the rectangular lid printed and overpainted with a deer-shooting scene.

3.75in (9.5cm) wide

£120-180　　　　**CHEF**

A mid-19thC Russian papier-mâché snuff box, the rounded hinged lid with a gilt Rococo cartouche, inscribed about an Imperial eagle on the simulated tortoiseshell interior.

3.5in (9cm) wide

£80-120　　　　**CHEF**

A mid-19thC German snuff box, the hinged lid printed and overpainted with a lady choosing flowers to dress her hair.

3.25 (8.5cm) wide

£150-200　　　　**CHEF**

An early Victorian papier-mâché census snuff box, the lid printed on the straw yellow top with population figures radiating about the central portrait of Prince Albert.

4in (10.5cm) diam

£300-400　　　　**CHEF**

A 19thC German papier-mâché box, the lid painted with a bearded man wearing a red cloak and a green tunic.

3.5in (9cm) diam

£200-300　　　　**CHEF**

An early Victorian papier-mâché snuff box, the hinged lid inscribed "J H Gray", decorated overall with coloured stripes over an engine turned gilt ground.

3.25in (8.5cm) wide

£150-200　　　　**CHEF**

A late 19thC papier-mâché snuff box, possibly Russian, painted with a fisherman's cottage by a lake, the interior with traces of two circular seal marks.

3.25in (8.5cm) wide

£200-300　　　　**CHEF**

STOBWASSER

- Johann Heinrich Stobwasser was born in 1740 in Lobenstein, Germany.
- After an apprenticeship at a lacquer factory, he began to experiment with new techniques with the help of his pharmacist brother.
- He soon became famous for his delicate miniature paintings on lacquered papier-mâché snuff boxes. These were produced at his father's Brunswick factory.
- His boxes became the height of fashion among the German bourgeoisie in the late 18thC.

- His erotic snuff boxes were also very popular and were sold all over the world.
- The company soon branched out into other areas, producing furniture and royal carriages.
- In 1772, Johann Heinrich founded a subsidiary in Berlin with J. Guérin, a French carpenter who had married into the Stobwasser family.
- In 1818, Johann Heinrich's son moved the entire Stobwasser business to Berlin. It was taken over in 1829 and closed after WWI.
- The snuff boxes are often signed.

An early 19thC Stobwasser snuff box, painted with 'Mile Lundens la...de Rubens', numbered "906", with a note giving the history of Stobwasser, taken from "The Connaisseur", by PAS Phillips.

£2,500-3,500   **CHEF**

An early 19thC Stobwasser snuff box, painted with 'Le Credo D'apres Raphael', a lady holds up a chalice and witnesses transubstantiation, numbered "13904", signed in red inside.

4in (10cm) diam

£1,500-2,000   **CHEF**

An early 19thC papier-mâché snuff box, attributed to Stobwasser, the lid painted with a Dr Syntax-like figure about to carve into 'The Tythe Pig' on a table backed by decanters on shelves, the interior with later gilding possibly obscuring inscription.

4.25in (10.5cm) diam

£300-500   **CHEF**

A Stobwasser snuff box, with 'Stowe Buckinghamshire in England', "5430".

The firm probably made this snuff box after an 1806 visit by the Prince of Wales to Sir John Soane's new library at Stowe.

3.75in (9.5cm) diam

£2,500-3,500   **CHEF**

A John Obrisset pressed tortoiseshell and silver snuff box.

c1690   *3.75in (9.5cm) wide*

£500-800   **MB**

A Neopoleonic horn snuff box, modelled as a cocked hat, with an ivory rosette to one side and moulded on the other with Napoleon and plans by a camp fire, titled "La Veillee D'Austerlitz".

3in (8cm) wide

£300-500   **CHEF**

An 18thC French Vernis Martin snuff box, the circular lift-off lid inset with a brass framed watercolour miniature of a lady, the interior and exterior lacquered to simulate tortoiseshell.

3in (8cm) diam

£150-250   **CHEF**

A late 18thC French mother-of-pearl mounted snuff box, of panelled form with reeded cagework borders, inlaid with mother-of-pearl flowers and a butterfly, maker's mark "AD" probably for Antoine Daroux of Paris.

c1765   *3in (7.5cm) wide*

£2,000-3,000   **WW**

A Queen Anne tortoiseshell snuff box, with ridged decoration.

c1705   *3.75in (9.5cm) wide*

£400-600   **MB**

An oval tortoiseshell snuff box, with gold standaway hinges and gold pique-work decoration, the cover depicting cranes, peacocks and exotic foliage, the base with a small bird, unmarked.

c1715   *3in (7.5cm) long*

£1,500-2,000   **WW**

A Napoleonic snuff box, the lid inset with glazed-over yellow metal, embossed by Morel with Napoleon urging his troops on up a pass, titled "Napoleon au Mont St Bernard".

3.25in (8.5cm) diam

£250-350   **CHEF**

An 18thC painted mahogany table snuff box.

3.5in (9cm) wide

£200-300   **MB**

An early 19thC Japanned tole snuff or tobacco box, possibly Pontypool, the lid with a magnifying glass, inscribed "Bright Sol Through This Your Pipe will Light and Help Old Age to Read and Write".

£300-400   **CHEF**

An early 19thC snuff box, the hinged lid slightly arched and printed with an overall stipple of yellow crosses on a green ground.

2.5in (6cm) wide

£150-200   **CHEF**

An early 19thC penwork snuff box, the cover depicting a steeplechase, titled "A Slap at a Stone Enclosure".

3.25in (8.5cm) wide

£250-300   **DN**

An oval horn snuff box, possibly American.

c1830   *3.5in (9cm) wide*

£300-400   **MB**

A mid-19thC black Wellington boot snuff box, the hinged lid inlaid with a mother-of-pearl flowerspray.

2.75in (7cm) high

£100-150   **CHEF**

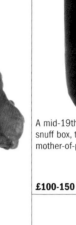

A mid-19thC tortoiseshell and horn snuff box, with central white metal and mother-of-pearl flower enclosed by a tortoiseshell edge.

2.75in (7cm) wide

£70-100   **CHEF**

, burr wood and sycamore snuff box, by William Graham of Ayr, painted with a British soldier carrying the standard, inscribed "Church & King".

he 1841 records shows William Graham maker of boxes in Ayr High Street.

1.75in (4.5cm) wide

£300-400   **CHEF**

An early 19thC Boxiana brass-mounted hardwood snuff box, the quatrefoil lid rotating to open, one half pierced and the other engraved with boxers, the reverse initialled "JW".

2.75in (7cm) wide

£150-250   **CHEF**

An early Victorian horn and tortoiseshell snuff box, the top veneered with tortoiseshell over dark brown horn cavetto sides.

2.75in (7cm) wide

£80-120   **CHEF**

A Continental silver-gilt snuff box, engraved with scrolling decoration.

3in (7.5cm) wide

£150-200   **MB**

A Continental silver-gilt snuff box, with an ornate engraved design.

3in (7.5cm) wide

£150-200   **MB**

An amboyna and tortoiseshell circular table snuff box, with a lift-off lid.

2.75in (7cm) diam

£150-200   **MB**

A German commemorative enamel snuff box, the lid inscribed with names and dates of victorious Prussian battles of the Seven Years war, around a silver appliqué profile of Frederick the Great, the interior of the lid with a Prussian allegory of victory.

3.25in (8.5cm) wide

£500-600   **ROS**

CARD CASES

A 19thC tortoiseshell card case, with inlaid mother-of-pearl foliate decoration.

4.25in (11cm) high

£70-100   WW

An early 20thC Cantonese carved ivory card case, intricately carved with figures in a garden.

4.25in (11cm) high

£150-200   ROS

An Anglo-Indian sadeli work card case, with floral decoration.

4in (10cm) high

£70-100   WW

An engraved mother-of-pearl card case.

4.25in (11cm) high

£150-200   MB

OTHER BOXES

A straw work thread box.

c1780   9in (23cm) long

£200-300   ATL

An early 19thC parcel-gilt tubular bodkin/needle case, decorated with floral filigree against a gilt ground, a flowerhead motif to each end, pull-off cover, unmarked.

3.75in (9.5cm) long

£150-200   WW

A handpainted Victorian ladies' leather purse, with brass casing, brass glove clasp and a porcelain plaque depicting a lady painted in the Italian style.

4in (10cm) high

£150-200   AGO

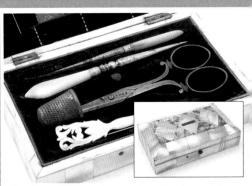

A Victorian mother-of-pearl necessaire, with an inlaid abalone shell top and fitted velvet interior containing sewing accessories.

5in (12.5cm) long

£100-150   GORL

A Moser-type blue glass and brass-mounted casket, enamelled with birds amidst foliate swags, enriched in gilt.

5in (13cm) wide

£700-900   ROS

An early 20thC novelty tortoise box, with a hardwood head and feet, the hinged lid with parquetry interior.

10.75in (27.5cm) long

£300-400   GORL

A Moser-type turquoise blue glass casket, enamelled with leaves and with gilt metal mounts.

4.75in (12cm) diam

£500-800   ROS

A late 18th to early 19thC ivory pique canted box, with an ivory folding ruler and a carved bone cylindrical bodkin case.

Box 3.25in (8cm) long

£150-200   DN

An early 18thC French mounted ivory patch box, with a pique-work cover and base and a stand-away hinge, the cover opening to reveal a symbolic miniature portrait of a lady with a bow and arrow, above a further portrait of a young lady at her toilette and a portrait of a young gentleman in a powdered wig, struck with charge and discharge marks.

c1710

£1,000-2,000   WW

A 19thC Dieppe ivory triptych figure of the Empress Josephine, with glass jewels, her dress revealing a scene of her coronation by Napoleon, with another figure, probably Joan of Arc.

9.5in (24cm) high

£1,200-1,800 pair   L&T

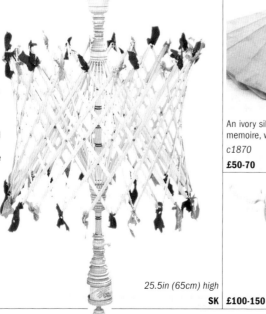

A 19thC sailor-made ivory and bone yarn swift, the ring-turned ivory axis topped with a yarn cup and with an engraved eagle and turned thumbscrew, highlighted with red and black wax, expanding carved whale bone cage joined by metal rivets and red and blue silk ribbons, dovetail constructed mahogany case with hinged lid.

25.5in (65cm) high

£10,000-15,000   SK

An ivory silver-mounted ladies' aide memoire, with six sheets.

c1870   *3in (7.5cm) wide*

£50-70   CSA

An ivory circular box and cover, carved in relief with roses and briars and stylised bands of foliage.

3.5in (9cm) diam

£100-150   GORL

A Victorian carved bone sewing Jenny, formed as a classical urn with a pin cushion and a table screw mechanism to base.

8in (20.5cm) long

£100-150   GORL

MINIATURES

An 18thC English School portrait of a gentleman, wearing a rust-coloured jacket, watercolour on ivory, mounted in a gold brooch setting.

Provenance by descent from Frank Arthur Cecil Richardson (1874-1940) and Winifred Eva Richardson (1878-1945).

1.5in (4cm) high

£300-400   **DN**

An American oil on ivory miniature sepia landscape, in a locket, of Germantown near the Schuylkill river, mother and children in the foreground, the reverse with a later Victorian photograph of a lady.

c1800   2in (5cm) high

£5,000-7,000   **POOK**

An American miniature portrait on ivory of a baby, in a long dress, in a gold leaf mount with a pin and necklace loop.

c1840   2.25in (5.5cm) high

£1,000-1,500   **PST**

A 19thC oils on ivorine portrait miniature, painted with a young lady in a white dress, with moulded gilt frame.

c1840   8.75in (22cm) high

£1,000-1,500   **L&T**

A 19thC American School miniature portrait of Margaretta Rentz Benfer, watercolour on ivory, indistinct initials.

2.75in (7cm) wide

£400-600   **FRE**

A 19thC Anglo-American School miniature portrait of Mrs. Holbrook, watercolour on paper, framed, unsigned.

5in (12.5cm) high

£100-200   **FRE**

A late 18thC English School portrait of a gentleman, wearing a wig and a brown coat, watercolour on ivory, in a rose gold clasp mount with later brooch pin and loop.

1.5in (4cm) high

£200-300   **DN**

An 18th to 19thC miniature portrait of George Washington, watercolour on ivory, framed, unsigned.

2.75in (7cm) diam

£2,000-3,000   **FRE**

A CLOSER LOOK AT A MINIATURE PORTRAIT

Miniature portraits became fashionable in the second half of the 18thC. They were a popular way of recording the faces of family members and were worn as jewellery, given as gifts or displayed around the home.

Mary Jane Simes was a member of the Peale family of successful American artists. She was taught to paint by her nieces, the artists Anna and Sarah Peale. Her mother was a daughter of James Peale.

The work of Mary Jane Simes is thought to be the rarest of the Peale family, and this is a very good example.

Ivory was used in many miniature portraits as they were produced as treasured and decorative objects, in the same way as precious jewellery.

A miniature portrait by Mary Jane Simes, watercolour on ivory, gold locket setting, the back with an oval of woven hair, signed and dated "Mary Jane Simes 1834", Baltimore, Maryland, in a fitted red leather case.

1.5in (4cm) high

£7,000-10,000   **FRE**

A 19thC English School portrait of a lady, half length, probably Lady de Grey, watercolour on ivory, in an ebonised and gilt metal mounted frame.

2.5in (6.5cm) high

£300-400   **DN**

A 19thC portrait miniature, of a gentleman wearing a black coat.

5in (12.5cm) high

£80-120   **ROW**

A portrait of the Duchess of Kent and Princess Victoria, by G. Cruickshank after Sir William Beachey, watercolour on ivory, in an ebonised frame.

4.5in (11.5cm) high

£300-500   **DN**

A portrait of a young lady, wearing a low-cut dress and a turquoise hair-ribbon, after Cosway, bust length, watercolour on ivory, inscribed verso "Lady Selina, Sir J. Laurence".

3in (7.5cm) high

£100-200   **DN**

A miniature portrait on ivory, depicting a woman wearing a dress with a high lace collar, in an ivory frame.

3.5in (9cm) high

£100-150   **AAC**

A watercolour on ivory miniature portrait of a gentleman, enclosed with a lock of his hair and enamelled initials "F.C." within a seed pearl border, all within a fitted leather case.

2in (5cm) high

£1,500-2,000   **POOK**

A late 19thC silhouette of Mrs. Overton, (nee Betty Stoddart), painted on the reverse of the oval glass, within a wood frame with embossed brass coverlet.

5in (13cm) high

£150-200   **CHEF**

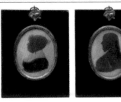

A pair of silhouettes, by Auguste Edouart, signed and "1842 Hartford".

5.5in (14cm) high

£2,000-4,000   **POOK**

A pair of Regency miniature painted silhouettes, of "Mr. and Mrs. Whitty", each mounted in an ebonised frame and inscribed on the reverse.

5.25in (13.5cm) high

£200-300   **ROW**

A 19thC wax commemorative portrait medallion, of Mrs Steward, Greco-Roman dress, by F. Tathe, encased in a mahogany box frame against a velvet background.

c1815   *7in (17.5cm) high*

£150-200   **AGO**

A 19thC wax commemorative portrait medallion, encased in a mahogany diamond frame against a velvet background, inscription reads "Courijuer".

c1815   *6.25in (16cm) high*

£150-200   **AGO**

A 19thC wax commemorative portrait medallion, encased in a mahogany hexagonal frame against a velvet background, inscribed "F/Uni Aequus Virtute 1799", possibly James Tassie.

c1815   *6.5in (16.5cm) high*

£200-300   **AGO**

OTHER OBJETS DE VERTU

A pair of 19thC waxwork figures of maids in a garden, under white muslin linen blossom, in glass domes.

8.5in (21.5cm) high

£100-200   **AG**

A 19thC Continental mosaic, depicting a saint in profile.

15in (37.5cm) high

£150-200   **S&K**

A 19thC octagonal sailor's 'valentine', the mahogany box with reeded framed hinged lid enclosing concentric geometric arrangement of shells.

10.75in (27cm) wide

£2,000-3,000   **L&T**

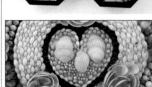

A shell sailor's 'valentine', contained in a hinged wooden octagonal case.

8.5in (21.5cm) wide

£800-1,000   **WW**

A late 19thC tortoiseshell parasol handle, in the form of a bust of a winking bald headed man.

£500-700   **DN**

A Victorian game of Whist.

2in (5cm) wide

£700-1,000   **JBS**

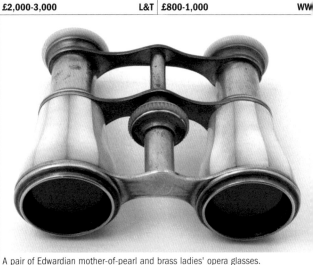

A pair of Edwardian mother-of-pearl and brass ladies' opera glasses.

c1890   *4in (10cm) wide*

£50-100   **CSA**

A Victorian pair of mother-of-pearl and brass opera glasses.

c1880   *3.75in (9.5cm) wide*

£80-120   **MB**

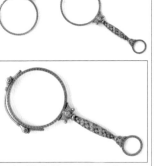

A pair of Belle Epoque diamond set platinum lorgnettes, the handle set overall with graduated circular cut diamonds, the spring loaded eyepieces release with a button to the upper section.

3.75in (9.5cm) high

£1,500-2,000   **WW**

A Pietra Dura framed plaque, depicting two chickens in mottled white and orange stone, frame with wear and two missing beads.

7in (12.5cm) wide

£700-900   **JDJ**

A Victorian double-ended cranberry glass scent bottle, with a faceted tubular body, embossed caps, unmarked.

c1870   4in (10cm) long
£70-90   WW

A Victorian English cranberry glass perfume bottle, with white enamelling.

c1890   4in (10cm) high
£220-280   TRIO

An English Georgian clear glass perfume bottle, in a typical shape.

c1830   5.5in (14cm) high
£120-180   TRIO

An English Georgian clear glass perfume bottle, probably for a man, in a typical shape with a simple stopper and silver top.

c1830   3in (7.5cm) high
£150-200   TRIO

A Georgian gold and cornelian flat scent bottle, with original chain.

1.25in (3cm) wide
£200-300   SSP

A 19thC clear glass perfume bottle, with blue overlay, silver top, probably English.

5.5in (14cm) high
£220-280   TRIO

A Victorian scent bottle, in black enamel on gilt silver, with cupid and floral detail, hinged cover, glass liner and stopper, interior flaw.

2.5in (6.5cm) high
£1,000-1,500   RDL

A mid- to late 19thC English latticino blue and white perfume bottle, with a pinchbeck stopper.

2.5in (6.5cm) high
£150-200   TRIO

An Victorian English green smelling salts bottle.

Smelling salts were often worn on a chain around the neck.

c1870   4in (10cm) high
£150-200   TRIO

A 19thC shell perfume bottle, with pinchbeck stopper, chain and ring.

c1875   3.5in (9cm) high
£100-150   TRIO

An English Victorian smelling salts bottle, with a silver top.

c1870   5in (13cm) high
£150-200   TRIO

An English Victorian clear cut-glass perfume bottle, with blue enamelling and silver top.

c1870   3.75in (9.5cm) high
£250-350   TRIO

397

19TH CENTURY PERFUME BOTTLES

OBJETS DE VERTU

A 19thC English double-ended clear glass perfume bottle, with silver tops.

c1880   3.25in (8.5cm) high
£220-280   **TRIO**

A Victorian mounted ruby glass perfume bottle, with a screw cover and cut decoration to the body, by G.E.W. LTD, Birmingham.

c1880   2.75in (7cm) high
£200-300   **WW**

A Victorian white opaline cut-glass perfume bottle, with blue overlay and silver tops.

c1870   3.5in (9cm) high
£220-280   **TRIO**

A mid-Victorian silver-mounted and amethyst cut-glass scent bottle, of tapering form, the clear glass cut all-over with ovals, the mounts embossed with a flowerhead and 'C'-scrolls.

4.5in (11.5cm) high
£200-300   **DN**

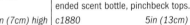

An English Victorian green double-ended scent bottle, pinchbeck tops.

c1880   5in (13cm) high
£150-200   **TRIO**

A late 19thC English clear glass perfume bottle.

c1885   10.75in (27.5cm) high
£150-200   **TRIO**

A Birmingham scent bottle, painted with flowers.

1890   3in (8cm) high
£150-250   **JBS**

A late 19thC English silver miniature perfume bottle, with a clear glass bottle inside.

1899   2in (5cm) high
£220-280   **TRIO**

398

A Lalique 'L'Effleurt' perfume bottle for Coty, in clear and frosted glass with gray patina, moulded "LALIQUE", stopper edges slightly ground.

c1910

4.5in (11.5cm) high

£3,000-4,000

RDL

A Lalique 'Panier de Roses' perfume bottle, in clear and frosted glass with blue patina, engraved "R. Lalique".

c1910   *4in (10cm) high*

£2,000-3,000   **RDL**

A Lalique 'Flausa' perfume bottle for Roger et Gallet, in clear and frosted glass with sepia patina, moulded "LALIQUE" to stopper.

c1915   *4.75in (12cm) high*

£2,500-3,500   **RDL**

A Lalique 'L'Elegance' perfume bottle for D'Orsay, in clear and frosted glass with sepia patina, moulded "R. LALIQUE".

c1915   *3.25in (9cm) high*

£1,500-2,000   **RDL**

A Lalique 'Salamandres' perfume bottle, in clear and frosted glass with blue patina, engraved "R. Lalique France".

c1915   *3.5in (9.5cm) high*

£1,000-1,500   **RDL**

LALIQUE PERFUME BOTTLES

A Lalique 'Styx' perfume bottle for Coty, in clear and frosted glass with sepia patina, a variation with a central stopper, moulded "LALIQUE".

c1910   *5in (12.5cm) high*

£1,000-1,500   **RDL**

A Lalique 'Ambre' perfume bottle for D'Orsay, in black glass with a whitish patina, moulded "LALIQUE".

c1910   *5.25in (13.5cm) high*

£800-1,000   **RDL**

A Lalique 'Au Coeur des Calices' perfume bottle for Coty, in blue glass with grey patina, moulded and impressed "LALIQUE".

c1915   *2.25in (6cm) high*

£4,000-5,000   **RDL**

A Lalique 'Mystère' perfume bottle for D'Orsay, in black glass, engraved "R. Lalique", label, chip to one corner and stopper.

c1910   *3.75in (9.5cm) high*

£300-500   **RDL**

A Lalique 'Pan' perfume bottle, in clear and frosted glass with sepia patina, moulded "R. LALIQUE".

c1920   *5in (12.5cm) high*

£1,000-2,000   **RDL**

A Lalique 'Lepage' perfume bottle, in clear and frosted glass with green patina, moulded "R. LALIQUE", engraved "France".

c1920   *4.5in (11.5cm) high*

£2,500-3,000   **RDL**

A Lalique 'Le Parisien' atomiser for Molinard, in clear and frosted glass with sepia patina and gilt metal, with moulded "R. LALIQUE MADE in FRANCE".

c1925   *5in (13cm) high*

£600-800   **RDL**

A Lalique 'Figurines No. 1' atomiser for Marcas et Bardel, in clear and frosted glass with blue patina and gilt metal, moulded "R. LALIQUE MADE in FRANCE".

c1925   *5in (12.5cm) high*

£500-600   **RDL**

A Lalique 'Le Jade' perfume bottle for Roger et Gallet, in green glass, with silk display box, paper label on box, bottle moulded with "RL FRANCE" mark.

3in (7.5cm) high

£5,000-6,000   **RDL**

A Lalique 'Toutes les Fleurs' perfume bottle for Gabilla, in clear and frosted glass with red patina, moulded "LALIQUE MADE in FRANCE", stopper frozen and hairline to neck.

c1925   *3.75in (9.5cm) high*

£500-700   **RDL**

A Lalique 'Bouquet de Faunes' perfume bottle for Guerlain, in clear and frosted glass with grey patina, moulded "MADE in FRANCE".

c1925   4.25in (11cm) high

£600-800   RDL

A Lalique 'La Belle Saison' perfume bottle for Houbigant, in clear and frosted glass with sepia patina, in a large size, moulded "R. LALIQUE MADE in FRANCE".

c1925   5.75in (14cm) high

£1,000-2,000   RDL

A Lalique 'Pavots d'Argent' perfume bottle for Roger et Gallet, in clear glass, sealed, with card box, numbered, box printed with "RL" mark.

c1925   3.75in (9cm) high

£700-1,000   RDL

A Lalique 'Calendal' atomiser for Molinard, in clear and frosted glass with sepia patina, with gilt metal top, moulded "R. LALIQUE", engraved "Molinard Lalique France".

c1925   5.5in (14cm) high

£600-800   RDL

A Lalique 'Le Parfum des Anges' perfume bottle for Oviatt of Los Angeles, in clear and frosted glass with sepia patina, moulded "R. LALIQUE FRANCE".

c1930   3.25in (8cm) high

£1,000-2,000   RDL

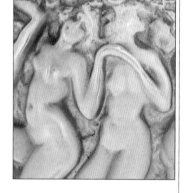

A Lalique 'Myosotis Flacon No. 3' perfume bottle, in clear and frosted glass with green patina, engraved "R. Lalique France".

c1930   9in (23cm) high

£3,000-4,000   RDL

A Lalique 'Sans Adieu' perfume bottle for Worth, in green glass, on chrome and wood stand, moulded "R. LALIQUE".

c1930   5.5in (13.5cm) high

£500-700   RDL

A Lalique 'Habanito' perfume bottle for Molinard, in clear and frosted glass with sepia patina, with original box, with stencilled "R. LALIQUE MADE in FRANCE, MOLINARD PARIS FRANCE" mark.

4.5in (11.5cm) high

RDL

£1,000-2,000

A Lalique 'Je Reviens' perfume bottle for Worth, in blue glass with chromed metal case, with stencilled "R. LALIQUE WORTH MADE in FRANCE" mark.

c1930   5.5in (14cm) high

£500-700   RDL

A Lalique 'Danae' perfume bottle for Magasin du Louvre, Paris, in clear and frosted glass with sepia patina, with moulded "LALIQUE" mark.

c1930   3.25in (8.5cm) high

£1,000-1,500   RDL

A Lalique 'Rosace Figurines' perfume bottle, originally designed 1912, in clear and frosted glass, with stencilled "LALIQUE" mark.

c1940   5in (12.5cm) high

£1,500-2,000   RDL

A Lalique 'Fille d'Eve' miniature perfume bottle for Nina Ricci, in frosted glass with screw cap and hang tag, in wicker basket, with moulded "LALIQUE" mark.

c1950   2.5in (6cm) high

£700-1,000   RDL

BACCARAT PERFUME BOTTLES

A Baccarat 'Parfum des Champs-Elysees' perfume bottle for Guerlain, in clear and frosted crystal with grey stain, label and display box, slight stain.

c1900   4.5in (11.5cm) high

£1,500-2,000   **RDL**

A Baccarat 'Le Parfum D'Antan' perfume bottle for D'Orsay, in clear and frosted crystal, with grey stain, with label and box.

c1915   3in (7.5cm) high

£1,000-1,500   **RDL**

A Baccarat 'Moda' perfume bottle for Gabilla, in clear crystal with recessed and enamelled detail, stencilled "Baccarat".

c1920   3.75in (8.5cm) high

£2,000-3,000   **RDL**

A Baccarat 'Toquade' perfume bottle for Silka, in clear and frosted crystal with recessed name labels, stencilled "BACCARAT".

c1925   4in (10cm) high

£700-1,000   **RDL**

A Baccarat 'Le Secret de Dieux' perfume bottle for Yardley, in clear and frosted crystal, with recessed gilt detail.

c1915   4.5in (11.5cm) high

£3,000-4,000   **RDL**

A Baccarat 'Mitsouko' perfume for Guerlain, with a label and box.

This perfume was used by many celebrities of the time including De Agalef, the ballerina. Guerlain used a variety of glassmakers to make their bottles.

c1920   4.75in (12cm) high

£120-180   **LB**

A Baccarat 'Le Dandy' perfume bottle, designed by Louis Sue for D'Orsay, in black crystal with label and seal in box.

c1920   3.5in (9cm) high

£300-400   **RDL**

A Baccarat 'L'Heure Bleu', perfume bottle for Guerlain, in clear crystal with a label, seal and display box, stencilled "BACCARAT" mark.

c1920   4.75in (12cm) high

£400-600   **RDL**

A Baccarat 'Sleeping' perfume bottle for Schiaparelli, in clear and red crystal with gilded details and a stencilled "Baccarat".

c1940   8in (20cm) high

£400-600   **RDL**

A Baccarat 'It's You' perfume bottle for Elizabeth Arden, in clear and frosted crystal with an enamelled ring, on a display stand, with stencilled "BACCARAT" mark.

c1940   6.5in (16.5cm) high

£600-800   **RDL**

A Baccarat 'Cyclamen' perfume bottle for Elizabeth Arden, in white and clear crystal with gold detail, with stencilled "Baccarat".

c1940   5.5in (13.5cm) high

£1,500-2,000   **RDL**

A Hoffman perfume bottle, in clear and frosted green crystal, with stencilled oval "MADE in CZECHOSLOVAKIA" mark.

c1920   *5.75in (14.5cm) high*

£500-600   **RDL**

A Hoffman perfume bottle, in pink crystal, mounted with jewels and an ivory miniature, with "HOFFMAN" intaglio mark, the metal marked "AUSTRIA".

c1920   *5.5in (13.5cm) high*

£1,000-1,500   **RDL**

A Hoffman perfume bottle, in black crystal with applied green crystal plaque and unusual stopper of St. George slaying a dragon, stopper edge flaked.

c1920   *6.5in (16.5cm) high*

£1,500-2,000   **RDL**

A CLOSER LOOK AT A HOFFMAN PERFUME BOTTLE

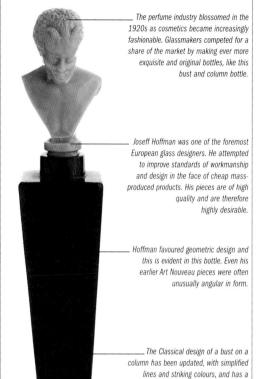

The perfume industry blossomed in the 1920s as cosmetics became increasingly fashionable. Glassmakers competed for a share of the market by making ever more exquisite and original bottles, like this bust and column bottle.

Joseff Hoffman was one of the foremost European glass designers. He attempted to improve standards of workmanship and design in the face of cheap mass-produced products. His pieces are of high quality and are therefore highly desirable.

Hoffman favoured geometric design and this is evident in this bottle. Even his earlier Art Nouveau pieces were often unusually angular in form.

The Classical design of a bust on a column has been updated, with simplified lines and striking colours, and has a distinctive 1920s look.

An Ingrid perfume bottle, in clear and frosted amber crystal, with stencilled oval "MADE in CZECHOSLOVAKIA" mark.

c1920   *5.75in (14.5cm) high*

£1,500-2,000   **RDL**

An Ingrid perfume bottle, in opaque black crystal, with frosted stopper and dauber.

c1920   *5.25in (13cm) high*

£1,000-2,000   **RDL**

An Ingrid perfume bottle, in opaque green crystal with clear and frosted stopper.

c1920   *6.5in (16.5cm) high*

£1,000-2,000   **RDL**

A Hoffman perfume bottle, in black and opaque green crystal, with stencilled divided circle marked with "FBS" and "FRANCE".

c1920   *9.5in (23.5cm) high*

£3,000-5,000   **RDL**

A Czechoslovakian perfume bottle, in blue crystal, with stencilled oval "MADE in CZECHOSLOVAKIA" mark, and silver paper label.

c1930   *7.75in (19.5cm) high*

£500-600   **RDL**

A Czechoslovakian perfume bottle, in amber crystal, with blue and pearl jewelled metalwork, stencilled circle "CZECHOSLOVAKIA" mark, missing jewels.

c1920   *4.5in (11.5cm) high*

£500-600   **RDL**

A Czechoslovakian perfume bottle for Shimy, in green crystal with enamelled details and metal filagree cap, with metal plaque, marked "CZECHOSLOVAKIA".

c1930   *6in (15cm) high*

£600-800   **RDL**

OTHER PERFUME BOTTLES

An 'Apres L'Ondee' perfume bottle for Guerlain, in clear glass with enamelled detail, paper label and display box, box lid loose.

c1900   *3in (7.5cm) high*

£600-800   **RDL**

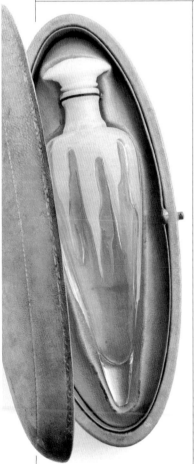

A Cristallerie De Pantin 'Parfum Precieuse' perfume bottle, a J. Viard design for Caron, in opal and white crystal with deluxe leather box.

c1915   *6in (15cm) high*

£2,000-3,000   **RDL**

A 'Giardini' perfume bottle for Babani, in green glass with gilded and enamelled detail.

c1920   *4.5in (11cm) high*

£1,000-2,000   **RDL**

A Devilbiss Imperial perfume bottle, with dauber, in yellow glass shading to opal, with glass jewels in metal filagree.

c1920   *7.75in (19.5cm) high*

£5,000-6,000   **RDL**

A continental silver-gilt and mauve enamelled scent bottle, the translucent enamel on an engine turned ground, the interior fitted with a stoppered glass bottle, with English import marks for London.

c1910   *1.5in (4cm) high*

£500-600   **WW**

A Devilbiss atomiser, in decorated glass with amber glass foot and finial, removable insert and paper label.

c1920   *6.75in (16cm) high*

£400-600   **RDL**

A 'Miss Kate' Saint-Louis perfume bottle for Bourjois, in clear and black crystal, with label and box.

c1920   *4.75in (12cm) high*

£700-900   **RDL**

A rare 'Heure Exquise' perfume bottle for Breyenne, in blue glass with gilt detail and label to base, in velvet cushion box, chip, missing stopper.

c1925   *3.5in (9cm) high*

£2,000-3,000   **RDL**

A Depinoix perfume bottle, a J. Viard design for Dubarry, in clear and frosted glass with stained and painted details, stencilled "MADE in FRANCE" mark.

c1920   *3.5in (9cm) high*

£2,000-3,000   **RDL**

A 'Chypre' perfume bottle for Sauze, of cube form, in clear glass, with screw cap, bakelite cover, label and display box.

c1920   *3in (7.5cm) high*

£2,000-3,000   **RDL**

A J. Viard 'Ambre de Carthage' perfume bottle for Isabey, in clear and frosted glass with grey stain and faux Spanish leather box, moulded "J. VIARD".

c1925   *5in (12cm) high*

£1,500-2,000   **RDL**

A J. Viard 'Vers la Joie' perfume bottle for Rigaud, gilt details and black pearl finished cover, Art Deco box, stencilled "J. Viard" mark, lacking stopper.

c1925   *2.5in (6cm) high*

£2,000-3,000   **RDL**

A Depinoix 'Lune de Miel' perfume bottle for Sari, in opaque black glass with silver-gilt detail and label.

c1925   *4.5in (11cm) high*

£1,000-2,000   **RDL**

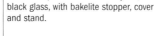

A 'Bibelot' perfume bottle for Lydes, in black glass, with bakelite stopper, cover and stand.

c1925   *4.5in (11.5cm) high*

£1,000-1,500   **RDL**

A 'Jicky' perfume bottle for Guerlain, in French opaline crystal with bronze neck, gilt stopper, and enamelled decoration signed by R. Noirot, slight gold wear.

c1950   *6.5in (16.5cm) high*

£1,000-2,000   **RDL**

TEXTILES

THE TEXTILES MARKET

A relative dearth of important textiles auctions in the last year has dampened the market in rugs, curtains and tapestries. Dealers, and consequently collectors, have been struggling to source top quality items and these are snapped up quickly when they do surface. Run-of-the-mill fabrics, on the other hand, can be found in abundance and as such are failing to realise anything but rudimentary prices. The weak dollar is contributing to this general malaise, as the US has traditionally been one of the main markets for antique European textiles. American collectors of Colonial and Federal needlework samplers, on the other hand, remain unaffected by international financial markets and are very active right now. Prices over £20,000 are not unheard of for the finest early American textiles.

Buyers should be especially aware of condition when purchasing textiles. A degree of sun damage is acceptable, although examples with bright colours that have been protected from ultra-violet radiation invariably attract a premium. Many fabrics, such as silk, will begin to rot after too much exposure to sunlight, and this can be a particular problem with curtains.

Many collectors are now showing interest in ethnographic pieces in preference to traditional French, Flemish and American textiles. This new trend looks set to continue as the tribal art market attracts more devotees who find that tribal forms and motifs gel well with modern interiors.

Joanna Booth, antique textiles dealer, London

PERSIAN RUGS & CARPETS

A late 19thC Heriz carpet, from northwest Persia.

167in (417.5cm) long

£3,000-5,000 FRE

A Heriz carpet, from northwest Persia.

c1940   *129in (322.5cm) long*

£2,200-2,800 FRE

A late 20thC Heriz carpet, from northwest Persia.

74in (185cm) long

£3,000-5,000 FRE

A Heriz rug, with a large central medallion on a salmon and blue field, with corner work in blue and olive and rebound selvedge.

129in (327.5cm) long

£3,000-5,000 BRU

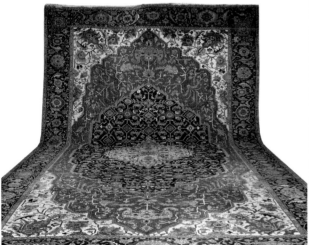

A large Heriz carpet, the brick red field with indigo and sky blue medallions and ivory spandrels, within an indigo turtle palmette border.

236.25in (600cm) long

£16,000-18,000 L&T

A Heriz carpet, the brick red field with a small central medallion, flanked by large palmettes and surrounded by angular yellow vines, within an indigo scrolling vine border.

141.75in (360cm) long

£2,000-3,000 L&T

A late 19thC Mohtashem Kashan rug, from central Persia.

79in (197.5cm) long

£600-900 **FRE**

An Indo-Kashan prayer rug, from central Persia.

c1900 60in (152.5cm) long

£2,000-3,000 **FRE**

A CLOSER LOOK AT A MOHTASHEM KASHAN CARPET

Kashan, in northern Iran, has been a centre of carpet production for many years. Before the 1930s, Kashani weavers actually used wool spun in Manchester.

This medallion repeats the 'Tree of Life' pattern in miniature, attesting to the cyclical nature of creation.

There are records relating to a prolific carpet factory known as Mohtashem, but the name has now become a by-word for any high quality rug of the Kashan region.

Unlike most Persian rugs, which are symmetrical, this 'Tree of Life' pattern has a top and a bottom. It is decorated with many varieties of flowers and foliage.

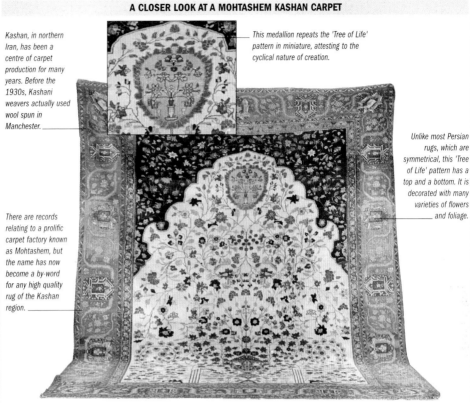

A late 19thC Mohtashem Kashan carpet, from central Persia.

116in (290cm) long

£14,000-16,000 **FRE**

A Mohtashem Kashan carpet, the indigo field with a central medallion suspending pendants and rose and ivory spandrels, within an indigo hunting border between bands decorated with birds.

118.5in (301cm) long

£6,000-9,000 **L&T**

A Kashan rug, the cream field with a central medallion suspending pendants and similar spandrels, within a cream palmette and angular vine border between bands.

66.25in (168cm) long

£1,200-1,800 **L&T**

A Kashan carpet, from central Persia, the red ground with a central medallion, the corners decorated with multicoloured flowers and leaves.

123.5in (314cm) long

£1,000-1,500 **SWO**

A Kashan carpet, from central Persia, the red ground with a central medallion, the corners decorated with multi-coloured flowers, leaves and motifs.

123.5in (314cm) long

£1,200-1,800 **SWO**

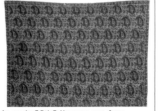

An early 20thC Kerman rug, from southeast Persia.

83in (207.5cm) long

£6,000-8,000 **FRE**

A Lauer Kerman rug, from Persia.

c1920 81in (202.5cm) long

£1,200-1,800 **FRE**

A late 19thC Ziegler Mahal wagireh rug, from west Persia.

146in (371cm) long

£1,800-2,200 FRE

A Mahal carpet, from west Persia.

c1920 *149in (372.5cm) long*

£1,800-2,200 FRE

A late 19thC Sarouk Fereghan carpet, from west Persia.

119in (297.5cm) long

£8,000-10,000 FRE

A Sarouk Fereghan rug, from west Persia.

c1910 *80in (203cm) long*

£1,000-1,500 FRE

A Sarouk Malayer rug, with an ivory medallion on a rust field, with overall floral design.

c1920 *81in (205.5cm) long*

£1,500-2,000 POOK

A Sarouk carpet, from west Persia.

c1930 *257in (642.5cm) long*

£2,200-2,800 FRE

A Sarouk Fereghan rug, from west Persia.

c1940 *50in (125cm) long*

£2,200-2,800 FRE

A Sarouk Fereghan rug, with rows of boteh designs on an ivory field, worn.

59in (150cm) long

£500-800 BRU

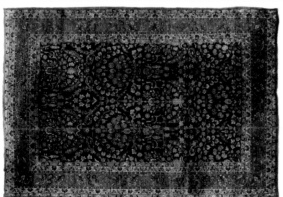

A finely woven Sarouk or Kashan rug, with repeating floral designs on a blue field, within ivory and red borders, worn.

188in (477.5cm) long

£1,800-2,200 BRU

A Sarouk Fereghan rug, with a central medallion on an ivory field, with repeating floral and geometric motifs.

77in (195.5cm) long

£1,000-1,500 BRU

A Sarouk rug, the rose field with central red and ivory medallions and indigo spandrels, within an ivory rosette palmette and scrolling vine border, between similar bands.

80in (203cm) long

£800-1,200 L&T

An early 20thC Serapi rug, with a blue and green central medallion on a pale salmon field, stepped corner work, restored.

176in (447cm) long

£5,000-8,000 **BRU**

A late 19thC Serapi carpet, from northwest Persia.

177in (442.5cm) long

£12,000-14,000 **FRE**

A large Serapi rug, with a central ivory medallion on a red ground, with ivory corners.

c1900 *145in (362.5cm) long*

£6,000-8,000 **POOK**

A Zeigler carpet, the cream field with overall pattern of palmettes, within rust palmette and scrolling vine borders, between three guard bands.

Zeiglers are 'trophy' carpets, made in Sultanabad for the Western market.

281.5in (704cm) long

£120,000-150,000 **L&T**

A late 19thC Bidjar carpet, from northwest Persia.

149in (372.5cm) long

£4,000-6,000 **FRE**

A 19thC Hamadan runner, with four medallions on a striped field, within camel borders, damaged.

133in (338cm) long

£300-500 **BRU**

A Hamadan rug, with a repeating design on a dark central field, within a border.

75in (190.5cm) long

£300-500 **BRU**

A late 19thC Karadja carpet, from northwest Persia.

143in (363cm) long

£2,000-3,000 **FRE**

A Lavar Kermin rug, with an elaborate central medallion and corner work, on a pale red field, with signature cartouche at one end, restored.

216in (548.5cm) long

£3,000-5,000 **BRU**

A Lori Pambak Kazak rug, with three medallions on a rust field, within a running dog border, from Caucasus.

c1910 *90in (228.5cm) long*

£4,000-6,000 **POOK**

A Mosul rug, with a multiple diamond ivory central medallion on a red field with blue corner work, damaged.

74in (188cm) long

£300-500 — **BRU**

A Mushkabad rug, with repeating geometric and blossom designs on an ivory field, damaged.

139in (353cm) long

£1,000-1,500 — **BRU**

A Shahsavan runner, from northwest Persia.

c1900 — *173in (439.5cm) long*

£800-1,200 — **FRE**

A Shiraz rug, with three stepped central medallions on a brown field, with ivory, blue and salmon borders and a flat-woven fringe with alternating stripes.

88in (223.5cm) long

£500-800 — **BRU**

A Tabriz carpet, from northwest Persia, the claret ground with a central blue medallion, the inner field with quarter medallion corners, decorated with multicoloured flowers and motifs.

156in (396cm) long

£2,500-3,000 — **SWO**

A late 19thC corridor carpet, from northwest Persia.

Corridor carpets, also known as 'runners', are designed for use in entranceways and hallways.

201in (510.5cm) long

£600-900 — **FRE**

CAUCASIAN RUGS & CARPETS

A Kazak throw rug, with three central medallions on a blue field, with multiple borders.

c1900 — *96in (240cm) long*

£3,000-4,000 — **POOK**

A Kazak Karatchopf rug, the red field with a central ivory and indigo square panel, flanked by two similar blue and cream panels, within ivory rosette borders between bands.

85in (216cm) long

£2,800-3,200 — **L&T**

A Kazak rug, the lemon field with three hooked medallions, within ivory hooked lozenge borders between skittle bands.

80in (203cm) long

£3,500-4,500 — **L&T**

A 19thC Shirvan rug, from east Caucasus.

56in (140cm) long

£3,000-5,000 — **FRE**

A late 19thC Shirvan throw rug, with four central medallions on a navy field, with a kufic and running dog border.

82in (205cm) long

£4,000-6,000   **POOK**

A Daghestan prayer rug.

c1910   *70in (175cm) long*

£800-1,200   **POOK**

An Erivan rug, the rust field with an olive lozenge medallion suspending pendants and similar spandrels, within a red and blue script style, border between scrolling bands.

78in (198cm) long

£250-300   **L&T**

A late 19thC Karabagh runner, from south Caucasus.

242in (605cm) long

£1,800-2,200   **FRE**

A late Karagashli rug, from northeast Caucasus.

60in (152.5cm) long

£2,200-2,800   **FRE**

A late 19thC Leshgi rug, from south Caucasus.

76in (190cm) long

£1,800-2,200   **FRE**

An Oushak carpet, from west Anatolia.

187in (467.5cm) long

£1,500-2,000   **FRE**

A Perpedil rug, the dark indigo field with a ram's horn pattern, within an indigo kufic border between various bands, signature cartouche.

73.25in (186cm) long

£700-1,000   **L&T**

A Sechour throw rug, with two central lime and ivory medallions, on a blue field within an elaborate running border.

c1900   *81in (202.5cm) long*

£1,800-2,200   **POOK**

An early 20thC Sivas carpet, from Anatolia.

150in (375cm) long

£1,500-2,000   **FRE**

A Caucasian rug, the rust red field with large flowerheads, within multiple borders.

114.25in (290cm) long

£1,000-1,500   **L&T**

A 20thC French Aubusson carpet.

189in (472.5cm) long

£10,000-12,000   **FRE**

A French Aubusson carpet, with a floral design.

c1900   *117in (292.5cm) long*

£2,000-3,000   **FRE**

An Aubusson-style needlepoint rug, with a central oval medallion with floral bouquet, and panels with stitched seams.

162in (411.5cm) long

£700-1,000   **BRU**

An early 20thC Turkish rug.

73in (182.5cm) long

£700-1,000   **FRE**

An Agra rug, with repeating floral designs on an ivory field, within green, ivory and red minor borders, damaged.

129in (327.5cm) long

£4,000-6,000   **BRU**

An Agra rug, the claret field with a palmette and scrolling vine pattern, within a claret palmette border.

80in (203cm) long

£500-800   **L&T**

A mid-20thC Indian runner.

237in (592.5cm) long

£1,200-1,800   **FRE**

An 19thC Ikat panel, from central Asia.

61in (155cm) long

£1,000-1,500   **FRE**

A 19thC Tibetan saddle rug, mounted on linen, affixed to a wood stretcher.

51in (127.5cm) wide

£1,200-1,800   **FRE**

A Chinese carpet.

c1900   *116in (290cm) long*

£4,000-6,000   **FRE**

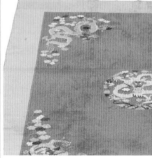

A Chinese carpet.

c1930   *140in (350cm) long*

£1,200-1,800   **FRE**

A 17thC French Royal Aubusson verdure tapestry, in silk and wool on a linen foundation, depicting a woodland scene, within a ribbon-bound floral border.

136.25in (346cm) wide

£8,000-10,000   **RSS**

A 17thC French Aubusson historical verdure tapestry, within a later foliate border, restored.

80.75in (205cm) high

£3,000-5,000   **RSS**

A 17thC French Aubusson mythological tapestry, woven in silk and wool.

95in (241cm) high

£1,000-1,500   **RSS**

A Louis XIV Aubusson mythological tapestry, woven in silk and wool, depicting warriors, within a scrolling foliate and flower head border, restored.

114.25in (290cm) high

£2,500-3,500   **BEA**

An early 18th French Royal Aubusson verdure tapestry, in silk and wool on a linen foundation, depicting woodland scenes, within a ribbon-bound floral border.

112.25in (285cm) wide

£1,500-2,000   **BEA**

A French Aubusson verdure tapestry, woven in silk and wool, depicting a wooded landscape within a ribbon-bound floral border.

109.5in (278cm) high

£2,000-3,000   **BEA**

An 18thC French Aubusson verdure tapestry, woven in silk and wool, depicting a wooded landscape within a ribbon-bound floral border.

114.25in (290cm) wide

£2,000-2,500   **BEA**

An18thC French Royal Aubusson verdure tapestry, woven in silk and wool on a linen foundation, depicting woodland scenes, within a ribbon-bound floral border, in the manner of Pillement.

91.25in (232cm) high

£3,000-5,000   **RSS**

An 18thC French Royal Aubusson verdure tapestry, woven in silk and wool on a linen foundation, depicting woodland scenes, within a ribbon-bound floral border.

100.5in (255cm) high

£2,000-3,000   **RSS**

An 18thC French Aubusson pastoral tapestry, woven in silk and wool, depicting a group hunting game birds, restored.

80.75in (205cm) high

£4,000-6,000   **RSS**

An 18thC French Royal Aubusson verdure tapestry, woven in silk and wool on a linen foundation, depicting a woodland scene with birds, within a ribbon-bound floral border, restored.

98.75in (251cm) wide

£3,000-5,000   **RSS**

A French Royal Aubusson verdure tapestry, woven in silk and wool on a linen foundation, depicting an exotic woodland scene, within a ribbon-bound floral border, restored.

75.5in (192cm) wide

£2,200-2,800   **RSS**

An 18thC French Royal Aubusson verdure tapestry, woven in silk and wool on a linen foundation, depicting an autumnal woodland scene, within a ribbon-bound floral border, restored.

88.5in (225cm) high

£3,000-5,000   **RSS**

An 18thC French Royal Aubusson verdure tapestry, woven in silk and wool on a linen foundation, depicting a woodland scene with two figures, within a blue border.

108.25in (275cm) wide

£5,000-7,000   **RSS**

An 18thC French Royal Aubusson verdure tapestry, by Finet, woven in silk and wool on a linen foundation, depicting a woodland glade, within a ribbon-bound floral border, restored.

151.5in (385cm) wide

£5,000-6,000   **RSS**

An 18thC French Royal Aubusson verdure tapestry, woven in silk and wool on a linen foundation, depicting a woodland scene with birds and buildings, within a ribbon-bound floral border, restored.

106.75in (271cm) high

£3,000-5,000   **RSS**

An 18thC French Royal Aubusson verdure tapestry, woven in silk and wool on a linen foundation, depicting a woodland scene with farmland, within a ribbon-bound floral border, in the Pillement style, restored.

81in (206cm) wide

£2,000-3,000   **RSS**

An 18thC French Royal Aubusson verdure tapestry, woven in silk and wool on a linen foundation, depicting a woodland scene with buildings in the distance, within a ribbon-bound floral border, restored.

99.25in (252cm) high

£3,000-4,000   **RSS**

A French Aubusson tapestry, woven in silk and wool, depicting urns, trophies, flowers and scrolling foliage, with a central cartouche depicting a romantic scene.

102in (259cm) high

£8,000-12,000   **BEA**

A late 18thC French Royal Aubusson verdure tapestry, woven in silk and wool on a linen foundation, depicting a woodland scene, within a ribbon-bound floral border, restored.

114.25in (290cm) high

£3,000-4,000   **BEA**

A late 18thC French Royal Aubusson verdure tapestry, woven in silk and wool on a linen foundation, depicting a woodland scene.

198.75in (505cm) high

£3,000-5,000   **BLA**

A late 18thC French Royal Aubusson verdure tapestry, woven in silk and wool on a linen foundation, depicting a woodland scene.

169.25in (430cm) wide

£4,000-5,000   **BLA**

A late 18thC French Royal Aubusson verdure tapestry, woven in silk and wool on a linen foundation, depicting a woodland scene, within a ribbon-bound floral border.

193in (490cm) wide

£4,000-6,000   **BEA**

An 18thC French Royal Aubusson verdure tapestry, woven in silk and wool, depicting a woodland scene.

95.25in (242cm) wide

£2,000-2,500   **BEA**

An 18thC French Aubusson mythological tapestry, woven in silk and wool, restored.

72in (140cm) wide

£2,000-3,000   **BEA**

A pair of 19thC Aubusson pastoral tapestries, depicting hunting scenes.

112.25in (285cm) high

£8,000-10,000   **PIL**

A 19thC French Aubusson pastoral tapestry fragment, in the 18thC manner, woven in silk and wool.

47.25in (120cm) wide

£700-1,000   **RSS**

A 19thC French Aubusson pastoral tapestry, in the 18thC manner after Téniers, woven in silk and wool, depicting a gypsy fortune teller with peasants in a wooded landscape, within a simulated picture frame border, signed "Aubusson Manufacture Royale 1847".

106in (269cm) high

£3,000-5,000   **RSS**

A 19thC French Aubusson pastoral tapestry, woven in silk and wool, in the 18thC manner after Téniers, within a simulated picture frame border.

113.5in (288cm) wide

£3,000-5,000   **RSS**

A 19thC French Aubusson verdure tapestry, in the 18thC manner, within a foliate and flower border and a grey outer slip.

73.5in (187cm) wide

£2,000-3,000   **RSS**

A 19thC French Aubusson verdure tapestry, with blue outer slip.

121.75in (309cm) wide

£3,000-4,000   **RSS**

A 19thC French Aubusson pastoral tapestry, woven in silk and wool in the 18thC manner, within a simulated picture frame border.

85.75in (218cm) wide

£2,200-2,800   **RSS**

A 19thC Aubusson verdure tapestry, in the 18thC manner, depicting an idyllic waterside dwelling, within a brown outer slip.

115in (292cm) wide

£2,500-3,000   **RSS**

A French Aubusson historical tapestry, woven in silk and wool in the 16thC manner, depicting a hunting scene, within a rich decorated border and blue outer slip.

85in (216cm) wide

£3,000-5,000   **RSS**

A late 19thC French Aubusson tapestry, woven in silk and wool, in the 18thC manner after Braquenié, depicting a pastoral scene with figures.

93.25in (237cm) high

£2,000-3,000   **RSS**

A 20thC French Aubusson tapestry, 'La Biche au Drapeau', by Jean Lurçat of the Tabard factory in Aubusson, numbered "2252" and signed by the artist.

c1940   *91in (231cm) high*

£3,000-5,000   **RSS**

A French Aubusson tapestry, 'Le Vannier', by F. Schlegel of the Braquenié factory.

90.5in (230cm) wide

£1,500-2,000   **PBA**

AUBUSSON SEAT PANELS

An 18thC French Aubusson tapestry sofa cover, woven in silk and wool, depicting La Fontaine's fables.

52.25in (133cm) wide

£700-1,000   **RSS**

One of a pair of 19thC French Aubusson settee panels, woven in silk and wool in the 18thC manner after Lancret and Oudry.

55.5in (141cm) wide

£500-800 pair   **RSS**

A 19thC French Aubusson tapestry settee panel for a cabriolet armchair, in the Louis XVI style.

30.75in (78cm) wide

£400-600   **RSS**

A CLOSER LOOK AT AN AUBUSSON SEAT PANEL

The carpet-weaving industry at Aubusson was founded to compete with Turkish carpets, which were very highly regarded in early 18thC France. They used Turkish designs and techniques, and were initially marketed as Turkish products.

This piece has been woven in wool and silk, which was a very expensive luxury import available only to the wealthy.

Tapestries like this were created from actual size mock-ups made of board, with the design hand-painted in reverse to aid the weavers in their work.

Complete sets of tapestry cycles like this appear on the market only occasionally, and always attract far more attention than single pieces or part collections.

Four of a set of eight French Régence Aubusson tapestry seat covers, with Classical border designs and romantic central scenes with birds, animals and flowers.

Each of these panels contains a cartouche with a bird surrounded by verdure garland within an ornate border of flowers and lozenges.

Each of the scenes is set in summer, as indicated by the flowers in full bloom and the early fruit on the vine.

The backgrounds depict the natural habitats of the birds. The eagle is in a mountain landscape, and the peacock in woodland.

30.25in (77cm) long

£25,000-28,000 set   **RSS**

A 19thC French Aubusson settee panel, in the Louis XVI style, unused.

33.75in (86cm) wide

£200-300   **RSS**

A 19thC French Aubusson settee panel for a cabriolet armchair, in the Louis XVI style, unused.

29.25in (74cm) wide

£400-600   **RSS**

A 19thC French Aubusson settee panel for a cabriolet armchair, in the Louis XVI style, unused.

28.75in (73cm) wide

£400-600   **RSS**

A 19thC French Aubusson settee panel for a cabriolet armchair, in the Louis XVI style, unused.

30in (76cm) wide

£400-600   **RSS**

OTHER FRENCH TAPESTRIES

A 17thC Parisian mythological tapestry, woven in silk and wool, depicting Renaud and Armide in a woodland scene, restored.

'Armide' premiered at the Paris Opéra in 1686.

133.75in (340cm) wide

£4,000-6,000   **BLA**

One of a set of six early 18thC French chair covers, woven in wool with a red, blue, cream and brown floral pattern, damaged.

16.5in (42cm) wide

£70-100 set   **RSS**

A late 17thC French silk and wool needlepoint chair cover, with a central image surrounded by scrolling foliage and large flowerheads.

27.5in (70cm) wide

£300-400   **RSS**

An early 18thC French verdure tapestry, manufactured by De la Marche, woven in silk and wool on a linen foundation, depicting woodland scenes.

96in (244cm) wide

£2,000-2,500   **RSS**

An 18thC Beauvais mythological tapestry panel, woven in silver thread, silk and wool, in a gilt frame.

85.75in (218cm) high

£8,000-10,000   **BEA**

An early 18thC verdure tapestry, by Felletin, woven in silk and wool on a linen foundation, depicting woodland scenes, within a ribbon-bound floral border.

193in (490cm) wide

£4,000-6,000   **BEA**

An 18thC pastoral tapestry, by Felletin, woven in silk and wool, within a large ribbon-bound floral border, restored.

93in (236cm) high

£3,000-4,000   **RSS**

An 18thC French silk and wool needlepoint panel, restored.

57.5in (146cm) wide

£800-1,200   **RSS**

A pair of 18thC French wool needlepoint seat covers, in the Regence style.

32.25in (82cm) wide

£1,200-1,800   **RSS**

A French 18thC silk and wool needlepoint chair cover, depicting a mythological scene.

29.25in (74cm) high

£700-1,000   **RSS**

A 19thC French tapestry, woven in silk and wool in the 18thC manner, depicting a woman picking flowers.

The floral swags and garlands that frame this scene are typical motifs of 18thC Neoclassicism. A rural French twist is provided by the use of native wild flowers and sheaves of wheat.

99.25in (252cm) high

£4,000-5,000   **RSS**

FLEMISH TAPESTRIES

A 16thC Flemish tapestry, woven in silk and wool on a linen foundation, depicting a hunting scene.

64.5in (164cm) wide

£2,000-3,000   **RSS**

A 16thC Flemish mythological tapestry, woven in silk and wool, depicting a hunting scene with archers, cavalry and spear bearers bringing down a large boar within a later blue outer slip, restored.

Hunting was a favourite pastime of the European aristocracy in the 16thC. In Belgium, one of the greatest prizes was a wild boar.

74.75in (190cm) wide

£3,000-5,000   **RSS**

A 16thC Flemish mythological tapestry, woven in wools and silks, within a scrolling foliate and flower head border, restored.

147.75in (375cm) wide

£16,000-19,000   **RSS**

A Flemish Audenarde mythological tapestry, woven in wools and silks, depicting a scene from the war of Troy, within a scrolling foliate and flowerhead border, restored. *c1590*

167.25in (425cm) wide

£4,000-6,000   **RSS**

A late 16thC Flemish Audenarde mythological tapestry fragment, restored.

A Flemish mythological tapestry fragment, within a later simulated picture frame border, restored.

A late 16thC Flemish mythological tapestry fragment, woven in silk and wool, within a later beige and grey outer slip, restored.

80.75in (205cm) high

£3,000-5,000   **RSS**

74.75in (190cm) high

£3,000-5,000   **RSS**

74.75in (190cm) high

£1,500-2,000   **RSS**

A 17thC Flemish mythological tapestry, woven in silk and wool, depicting Diane, goddess of the hunt, within a scrolling foliate and flower head border, restored.

214.25in (544cm) wide

£15,000-17,000   **RSS**

A 17thC Flemish mythological tapestry, woven in silk and wool, within a rich decorated border, restored.

107in (272cm) high

£3,000-5,000   **RSS**

A 17thC Flemish mythological tapestry, woven in silk and wool, within a rich decorated border, restored.

107in (272cm) high

£3,000-5,000   **RSS**

TEXTILES

A 17thC Flemish historical tapestry fragment, woven in silk and wool, depicting Julius Caesar and Cleopatra, within a later simulated picture frame border, restored.

96.5in (245cm) high

£2,000-3,000   RSS

A 17thC Flemish verdure tapestry, woven in silk and wool on a linen foundation, depicting a dense woodland scene, within a ribbon-bound floral border.

118in (300cm) wide

£2,000-4,000   RSS

A 17thC Flemish mythological tapestry fragment, woven in silk and wool, within a later outer slip.

94.5in (240cm) high

£3,000-4,000   RSS

A 17thC Flemish mythological tapestry fragment, within a later outer slip, restored.

117in (297cm) high

£4,000-6,000   RSS

A four-fold screen, inset with Louis XIV Flemish tapestry panels, woven in silk and wool, depicting foliage and flowers.

59in (150cm) wide

£3,000-5,000   RSS

A late 17thC Flemish garden tapestry, depicting trees in a landscape.

102in (255cm) high

£3,000-5,000   POOK

A late 17thC Brussels mythological tapestry, woven in silk and wool, signed "BB" for Bruxelles-Brabant and "MA" for Manufacture ROS.

128in (325cm) high

£4,000-6,000   BLA

An 18thC Brussels tapestry, signed "BB" for Bruxelles-Brabant.

£6,000-9,000   BEA

4 lot page

An early 18thC Brussels allegorical tapestry, 'The Feast of the Continents' by Jasper van der Borght, woven in wool, depicting men and women of four continents seated at a banquet, with a puppet show, musicians and dancers to one side, the border woven to resemble a carved frame, bearing the Brussels town mark "BB" and signed "I V D BORGHT".

Jasper van der Borght was born into one of the leading families of Brussels weavers, and two further generations continued the family business after him. This tapestry represents one of a set of five known as 'The Four Continents', the others in the series each focusing on a single continent. Nine sets of tapestries on this theme are believed to exist — the only extant full set is at the Kunsthistorisches Museum in Vienna. In Britain there are examples in the Royal Collection at Holyrood House in Edinburgh, which has two panels, and Mereworth Castle in Kent, which has four.

157.5in (400cm) wide

£60,000-90,000   L&T

An 18thC Flemish verdure tapestry, woven in silk and wool on a linen foundation, depicting a woodland scene, within a ribbon-bound floral border, restored.

88.25in (224cm) high

£2,000-3,000 **RSS**

An 18thC Brussels tapestry, woven in silk and wool, depicting a fishing port scene, within a simulated picture frame border and brown outer slip.

115.75in (294cm) high

£6,000-8,000 **BEA**

A 19thC Continental tapestry, depicting a pastoral landscape with figures.

74in (185cm) wide

£2,000-3,000 **FRE**

A 16th Continental tapestry, depicting a courting scene with figures beside a river, with traffic in the harbour beyond.

131in (327.5cm) high

£17,000-20,000 **FRE**

A 17thC tapestry of a hunting scene.

80.75in (205cm) high

£1,000-1,500 **BEA**

A 17thC millefleurs tapestry panel, woven in wools and silks, restored.

41.75in (106cm) high

£2,000-2,500 **RSS**

An 18thC silk and wool needlepoint panel, depicting a Court scene.

88.5in (225cm) high

£4,000-6,000 **RSS**

One of a set of four French Aubusson tapestry curtains, woven in silk and wool.

118in (300cm) high

€4,000-6,000 set   **RSS**

A pair of 19thC curtains, made from 16thC Italian red velvet, with silvered threads.

123.25in (313cm) high

£2,000-3,000   **RSS**

A red silk and velvet valance, Spanish or Italian, with applied motifs in silk, embroidered with metal thread.

95.75in (243cm) wide

£2,000-3,000   **RSS**

A late 16thC Flemish tapestry portière, woven in silk and wool.

126.75in (322cm) high

£1,500-2,000   **RSS**

One of a pair of late 19thC French Aubusson cantonnières.

92.5in (235cm) high

£2,000-3,000 pair   **RSS**

A late 19thC damask valance, in the Regence style, with applied ivory and satin border.

166.25in (422cm) long

£500-800   **RSS**

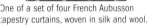

FABRIC

A length of 17thC Italian furnishing velvet.

47.25in (120cm) long

€300-400   **RSS**

A length of late 17thC French green and gold damask, with a scrolling pattern of stylized flowers.

213.5in (542cm) long

£200-300   **RSS**

A French Abbeville damask furnishing panel, with a floral pattern.

c1710   *27.25in (69cm) long*

£1,000-1,500   **RSS**

A French Regence silk panel, with a cream and green floral pattern on a red ground.

551.25in (1400cm) long

£1,500-2,000   **RSS**

A length of French Lyon naturalist brocaded lampas silk.

c1740   *204in (518cm) long*

£200-300   **RSS**

A piece of 18thC French furnishing fabric, from the Rhône valley, with flower and urn motifs on a blue ground.

140.25in (356cm) long

£300-400   **RSS**

A French linen and silk bed cover.

111.5in (283cm) long

£500-800   **RSS**

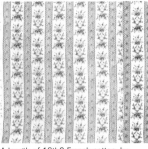

A length of 18thC French cotton, by Haussmann, with a woodblock print.

82.25in (209cm) long

£200-300   **RSS**

A piece of 18thC furnishing fabric panel, in blue woven silk damask.

245.25in (623cm) long

£500-600   **RSS**

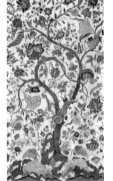

An section of 18thC Indian quilting, painted and printed with a tree of life.

96in (244cm) long

£5,000-6,000   **RSS**

A section of French Jouy printed cotton, by the Oberkampf factory, with a repeating pattern of flowers and birds.

This design was created for Christophe-Philippe Oberkampf's bedroom.

c1775   *106.25in (270cm) long*

£1,800-2,200   **RSS**

TOILE DE JOUY

- 'Toiles peintes', literally translated as 'painted fabrics', first arrived in France along the Silk Road in the 17thC. They were also known as 'Indiennes' because of their Eastern origin.
- French workshops soon began to make their own versions to meet demand but small textile producers, fearful for their livelihoods, successfully lobbied for a ban on this enterprise.
- Christophe-Philippe Oberkampf established the Manufacture Royale at Jouy-en-Josas in 1760, a year after the ban was lifted.
- The Jouy factory used French cotton as well as fabric imported from India, the Middle East and Britain.
- Chief designer Jean-Baptiste Huet produced floral and allegorical patterns, primarily in monochrome red, blue, green or yellow on white, although combinations of these colours were also used.
- Jouy became especially well known for printed fabrics designed for use as furniture coverings and wall hangings. The generic term 'toile de Jouy' came into use to describe these wares.
- Oberkampf's factory was closed in 1843 after the hardships of the Napoleonic Wars irreparably eroded his business.

A piece of French Jouy Indienne cotton, printed from a wooden matrix, depicting stylized flowers, by the Oberkampf factory.

c1780   *67in (170cm) long*

£700-1,000   **RSS**

A piece of French Jouy furnishing cotton, printed from copper plates, by the Oberkampf factory, entitled 'Pagode sur un pont de rochers'.

c1780   *41in (104cm) long*

£300-400   **RSS**

A piece of furnishing cotton, by the Oberkampf factory, printed from copper plates.

c1785   *22.75in (58cm) long*

£300-400   **RSS**

A length of French Lyon woven silk lampas.

This pattern was created in 1784 for the games salon at Versailles.

55in (140cm) long

£500-700   **RSS**

A French furnishing cotton, printed from copper plates, by Petitpierre Frères of Nantes, entitled 'Panurge dans l'île des lanternes'.

c1785   *85.75in (218cm) long*

£500-700   **RSS**

A French furnishing cotton, printed from copper plates, by the Gorgerat factory in Nantes, entitled 'A la gloire de Louis XVI'.

c1790   *35.5in (90cm) long*

£100-150   **RSS**

A French Indienne quilt, manufactured by Hartmann of Alsace, printed from woodblocks with an Indian tree of life design and flowers.

c1800   *112.25in (285cm) long*

£700-1,000   **RSS**

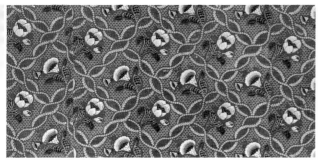

A French cotton quilt, manufactured in Jouy or Beautiran, printed from wood blocks with flowers on a patterned red ground.

c1800   *109.5in (278cm) long*

£500-700   **RSS**

A 19thC French Lyon brocade sample, in the Grand Frères manner, the cream ground brocaded in blue with flowers.

50.75in (129cm) long

£250-350   **RSS**

A French 19thC lampas sample, woven in silk with grotesques, in the 18thC manner, marked "TC".

58.75in (149cm) long

£300-400   **RSS**

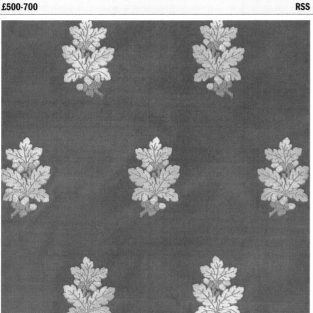

A 19thC French Empire-style Gros de Tours panel and runners, with gold embroidery.

£8,000-12,000   **RSS**

A 19thC French Lyon woven silk lampas sample, based on a late 18thC design.

87in (221cm) long

£300-400   **RSS**

A 19thC French Lyon woven silk lampas brocade, in the 18thC manner.

230in (584cm) long

£220-280   **RSS**

A length of 19thC French Lyon woven silk and satin furnishing brocade, in the Byzantine style.

25.25in (64cm) long

£200-300   **RSS**

A 19thC French silk lampas seat cover, manufactured by La Maison Grand Frères for the Vice King of Egypt, after an 18thC design by Gaudin.

1862   *100in (254cm) long*

£700-1,000   **RSS**

A late 19thC French table runner, embroidered in silk with bullion cruciform appliqué, stamped dedication to Tsar Nicholas II and Tsarina Alexandra Fedorovna, restored.

94in (228cm) long

£8,000-10,000   **RSS**

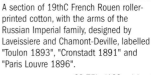

A section of 19thC French Rouen roller-printed cotton, with the arms of the Russian Imperial family, designed by Laveissiere and Chamont-Deville, labelled "Toulon 1893", "Cronstadt 1891" and "Paris Louvre 1896".

63.75in (162cm) long

£300-400   **RSS**

A section of 18thC French Régence wallpaper, manufactured by Les Associé of Paris.

33.75in (86cm) long

£500-700 RSS

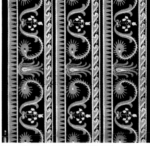

A French wallpaper, designed by Jean-Baptiste Réveillon, with flowers and love birds on a cream ground.

c1786 *23.25in (59cm) wide*

£1,500-2,000 RSS

One of a set of 11 late 18thC French wallpaper strips and borders.

£500-800 set RSS

A French wallpaper, by Jacquemart and Bénard, printed from wood blocks in gouache with flowers, on a blue ground.

c1795 *20.75in (53cm) long*

£200-300 RSS

A French wallpaper, by Jacquemart et Bénard, printed from wood blocks in gouache with laurels and a landscape, on a blue ground with 'Directoire' motifs.

1796 *20.75in (53cm) long*

£200-300 RSS

A French wallpaper, printed in colour from wood blocks with flocks, with 'Directoire' motifs and a bust of Barras in grey, on a blue ground.

1798 *139.75in (355cm) long*

£300-400 RSS

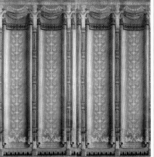

A pair of French wallpaper panels, designed to imitate drapery.

c1800 *100.5in (255cm) long*

£2,000-3,000 RSS

An early 19thC Belgium scenic wallpaper, block-printed with a landscape scene with trees.

145in (368cm) long

£150-200 RSS

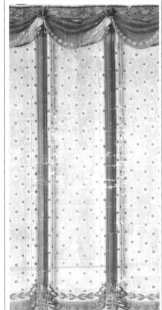

A block-printed wallpaper, with drapery.

c1820

£4,000-5,000 RSS

A 19thC French block printed wallpaper.

87.75in (223cm) wide

£1,500-2,000 RSS

One of a pair of 19thC French scenic wallpaper rolls.

39.25in (100cm) long

£150-200 pair RSS

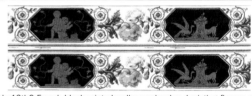

An early 19thC French block printed wallpaper border, depicting flowers and antic scenes in reserves, in the style of Dugourc.

78.75in (200cm) wide

£200-300 RSS

A 19thC wallpaper strip, probably designed by Défossé and Karth.

91.25in (232cm) long

£150-200 RSS

One of a set of 22 scenic wallpaper panels, after designs by Merry-Joseph Blondel and Louis Laffitte.

c1870

£3,000-4,000 set RSS

A George I linen needlework sampler, embroidered in polychrome cross and satin stitch with verse "Mary Price look well to what you take in hand..." and floral motifs supported by columns, framed and glazed.

1714   *13.5in (34cm) wide*

£700-1,000   **HAMG**

A CLOSER LOOK AT A NEEDLEWORK SAMPLER

This shepherdess is part of an idyllic pastoral scene, typical of later needlework samplers with their emphasis on industry and piety.

Girls in the 18thC were encouraged to stitch samplers as a sign of their virtue. Needlework was an important part of a young woman's education.

This extensive verse includes meditations on the nature of God's love and how to live a righteous life.

The standard of needlework on this sampler is particularly high. It has been thoughtfully composed and is an attractive ornament as well as an interesting document of social history.

A linen needlework sampler, embroidered in silk with the alphabet, decorative bands and the inscription "Abigail Bond Her Sampler Age 15 in Year 1753 MB MH RB", framed.

21.25in (53cm) high

£1,500-2,000   **FRE**

A woollen needlework sampler by Mary Susannah Lambeth, embroidered in silk with rows of stylized flowers, the alphabet and numerals, above a pictorial band with shepherdess and flock, angels, pious verse and the inscription "Mary Susannah Lambeth works this in the 10th year of her age, 1789", framed.

1789

£22,000-24,000

27.5in (69cm) high

FRE

A Scottish linen sampler, embroidered in silk with 12 lines of alphabet, numerals and the inscription "AIHLBI anno 1757", in a modern wood frame, worn.

12in (30.5cm) wide

£280-320   **BRU**

A New York linen sampler, embroidered in silk with a tree of life, Adam and Eve, a Federal house and the inscription "Elizabeth Vermillya, aged 13 years, New York June in the year 1796", within a strawberry border.

17.5in (44.5cm) high

£2,200-2,800   **POOK**

A woollen sampler, embroidered in silk with four verses, rows of alphabet, numerals, weeping willow and decorations, with the inscription "Mary Burbery's Work Finished October 27th in the year 1796", in a simple painted wooden frame.

16.5in (42cm) high

£600-900   **BRU**

A Maine linen sampler, embroidered in silk with multiple alphabets above central potted trailing floral vines, within a vine border, with the inscription "Sophronia Robinson's sampler, wrought in the twelfth year of her age".

18in (45.5cm) wide

£4,000-6,000   **POOK**

A Connecticut linen sampler, embroidered in silk with a floral and ribbon swag garland above the Wells family record, over a landscape of the village of Wethersfield, wrought by Hannah Wells, losses.

20in (51cm) wide

£2,200-2,800   **POOK**

A 19thC American linen sampler, embroidered in silk with the Gallison family genealogy, wrought by Julia A. Gallison, the central record with a floral and vine border.

20.5in (52cm) wide

£1,200-1,800   **POOK**

TEXTILES

A George III sampler, embroidered in silk and chenille with moral sentiments and decorative devices, within a floral border.

c1800   *21in (53.5cm) high*

£500-800   **GORL**

An early 19thC canvas sampler, embroidered in coloured silks with alphabets, religious verses and motifs.

1802   *17.75in (45cm) high*

£100-150   **DN**

A linen sampler, embroidered in silk with a stylized floral vine enclosing rows of alphabet and decorative items, framed.

1806   *17.5in (44cm) high*

£1,500-2,000   **FRE**

An English Adam and Eve linen sampler, embroidered in silk and wool, with two lines of alphabet and initials.

1808   *15.75in (40cm) high*

£220-280   **BRU**

An early 19thC linen sampler, embroidered in coloured silks with verses, biographical details, a prayer, a self-portrait and motifs including trees and a horn of plenty.

     21.75in (55.5cm) wide

£300-500   **DN**

An American linen sampler, embroidered with rows of alphabet and a stylized floral vine above pious verse, framed.

c1810   *1,500-2,000*

£1,500-2,000   **FRE**

An early 19thC Scottish linen sampler, embroidered in silk and wool, with the alphabet, rows of initials, and verse.

     23.25in (59cm) high

£250-300   **BRU**

An English linen sampler, embroidered in silk with a central verse above a house and trees, within a red scrolling border.

1821   *12in (30.5cm) wide*

£600-900   **POOK**

A linen sampler, embroidered in silk with rows of alphabet, numerals and stylized flowers.

1822   *18in (45cm) high*

£400-600   **FRE**

A sampler, embroidered with rows of alphabet, numerals and verses, in a modern gilt wood frame, faded.

     17.5in (44.5cm) high

£200-300   **BRU**

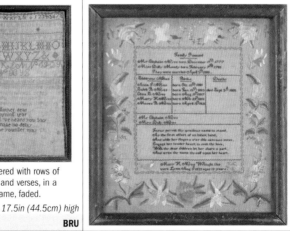

A Massachusetts linen family record, embroidered in silk with a central record and verse within a scrolling border, surrounded by large flowers and a sawtooth border, with the inscription "Mary H. Noyes Lynn Aug. 3 1823 aged 12 years".

     19.25in (49cm) high

£1,500-2,000   **POOK**

An English linen sampler, embroidered in silk with a central verse, birds in trees, baskets and pots of flowers, within a strawberry vine border, with the inscription "Charlotte Haviland Harrison 20th of 12th month 1827 aged 8 years & 8 months".

     17.25in (44cm) wide

£1,500-2,000   **POOK**

A North Carolina linen sampler, embroidered in silk with the alphabet and numerals above the inscription "M H Bell Tarboro Academy NC", damaged.

1833   *16.75in (42.5cm) wide*

£700-1,000   **BRU**

A pair of linen samplers, one embroidered in silk with verse over twin homes and the inscription "Ellen Wood May 29, 1835", the other with verse above a building flanked by flowers, trees and other designs, within a vine border and the inscription "Hannah Wood 1835".

1835   *14.5in (37cm) wide*

£1,800-2,200   **POOK**

A linen sampler, embroidered in wool with rows of alphabet above a house flanked by trees, animals and rectangular reserves enclosing initials.

c1835   *17.5in (44cm) high*

£400-600   **FRE**

A linen sampler, embroidered in silk with rows of alphabet, flowers and trees above the inscription "Ann Jane Coldwells sampler made in 1839", in a modern painted wood frame.

1839   *23.75in (60.5cm) high*

£800-1,200   **BRU**

A woollen family record sampler, embroidered with verse, a domed church and birds in flight, inscribed with maker's name, restored.

1840   *16.25in (41.5cm) high*

£400-600   **BRU**

A linen sampler, embroidered with a petit-point floral border, religious poem and maker's name, framed.

1843

£150-200   **TA**

An Irish linen sampler, embroidered in silk with the inscription "Sarah Gowan, Belfast January 1844", in a wooden frame, faded.

1844   *11.75in (30cm) high*

£180-220   **BRU**

A Pennsylvania linen sampler, embroidered in wool with a basket of flowers, a church, birds, a heart, trees and a strawberry vine border enclosing verse, with the inscription "Sarah Knight's Work Aged 10 1848", framed.

1848   *21in (52.5cm) wide*

£600-900   **FRE**

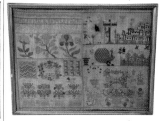

A mid-19thC needlework sampler, embroidered in colours with the alphabet, spring flowers, potted fruit trees, biblical subjects, a peacock and vases of flowers, in a giltwood frame.

16in (40.5cm) wide

£250-300   **S&K**

A Victorian needlework sampler, embroidered with a figure in front of a house and a verse, in a simulated rosewood frame.

1850   *28.25in (72cm) high*

£400-600   **SWO**

A 19thC linen marking sampler, embroidered with alphabets in four lettering styles.

17in (43cm) high

£120-180   **BRU**

A linen needlework sampler, embroidered in silk with an alphabet, potted flowers and birds, in a decorated frame.

12in (30.5cm) high

£300-500   **POOK**

An Adam and Eve linen sampler, embroidered in silk with a verse entitled "The Fall of Adam", with Adam and Eve, cupids, flowers, birds, butterflies and dogs.

16in (40.5cm) high

£400-600   **BRU**

A 17thC stumpwork panel, with raised sculptural forms on an ivory silk ground, alluding to a period of political calm and prosperity, depicting a lady with a musical instrument, encased in an oak box with sloping mirrored sides.

16in (40.5cm) wide

£2,500-3,500   **GORL**

A 17thC stumpwork panel, with a central oval cartouche depicting a young woman gathering a posy in a castle and country landscape, flanked by leopard, deer, insects, flowers and foliage.

11.5in (29cm) wide

£2,000-3,000   **GORL**

A 17thC woolwork panel, worked in coloured wools, depicting the angel Gabriel and Mary at the scene of the Annunciation.

9.75in (25cm) wide

£400-600   **L&T**

A late 18thC needlework map of Ireland, by A. Wolfe, the county borders worked in silks and their names in black thread, within numbered degrees of latitude and longitude, in a verre eglomise slip, framed.

16.5in (42cm) high

£800-1,200   **CHEF**

An early 19thC silk pictorial needlework, 'Rebecca at the well with Eliezer', probably American, in silk chenille satin stitch on a silk ground, the facial features and sky painted in watercolours, in a painted wood and composition frame with oval eglomise mat, damaged.

14in (35.5cm) high

£500-800   **BRU**

An early 19thC silk on silk oval pictorial needlework, possibly Folwell School, depicting a young girl wearing a white dress, petting a lamb in a pastoral landscape.

7in (17.5cm) wide

£500-800   **POOK**

A pair of 19thC English silkwork pictures, one depicting a mother with her two children in a wooded landscape, the other a harvest scene, framed.

A late 19thC sailor's woolwork picture, depicting a ship in full sail, inset with a Victorian photograph of a sailor and his wife.

23.5in (60cm) wide

£2,500-3,500   **SWO**

A Charleston woollen needlework, embroidered in silk chenille and wool crewelwork with a basket of flowers and the inscription "Worked by Mary E. Ward at the Academy of the Sisters of Our Lady of Mercy, Charleston SC", worn.

28in (70cm) wide

£1,200-1,800   **FRE**

15.25in (38.5cm) wide

£1,500-2,000   **BRU**

An 18thC Continental cut velvet panel, the plum ground decorated with raised embroidered silk work and silver threads, depicting a stylized tree of life, with exotic flowers, peacocks and smaller birds.

101.25in (253cm) long

£1,500-2,000 **L&T**

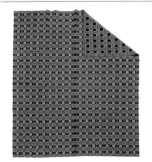

An American four-colour overshot coverlet, comprising two panels, with multicoloured wool on cotton.

87in (221cm) long

£250-300 **BRU**

A set of three jet and black bead decorative panels.

Longest 14in (35.5cm) long

£40-60 each **PSA**

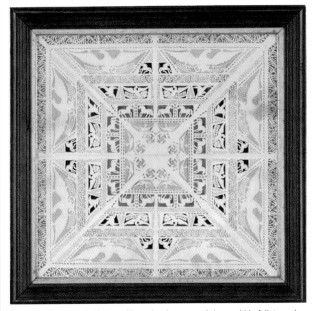

A Pennsylvania cut-work picture, with eagles, horses, and doves within foliate and geometrically patterned borders, backed with painted pale blue, green and yellow paper, framed.

This picture is backed with newspaper dated 1859.

c1860 *21in (52.5cm) wide*

£20,000-22,000 **FRE**

An orange paisley coverlet, with tassels.

£180-220 **DRA**

A multicoloured paisley shawl.

£300-400 **DRA**

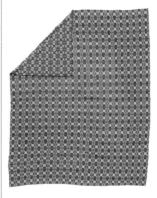

A late 19thC American green overshot coverlet, comprising two hand-sewn panels, with three shades of green wool on cotton.

A coverlet was used as a bed covering. The term 'overshot' refers to a method of weaving popular from the late 17thC.

98in (249cm) long

£150-200 **BRU**

A 19thC baby's white work bonnet, with fine needle lace insert.

£300-500 **BONM**

A Victorian jet and black bead collar.

18in (45.5cm) high

£70-100 **PSA**

A mid-19thC black lace parasol, with cream silk lining and elaborate ivory handle.

26in (66cm) high

£300-400 **GMC**

431

A 15thC English dalmatic garment, in red velvet with embroidery in silk and silver gilt thread.

41in (104cm) long

£3,000-3,500   RSS

A formal French ensemble, in embroidered satin with Beauvais needlepoint in silver thread.

c1780

£1,000-1,500   CSB

A late 18thC French waistcoat, in embroidered silk.

£700-1,000   CSB

A late 18thC French formal breeches and coat ensemble, in aubergine silk velvet, embroidered with polychrome silk and metal thread, backed with ivory linen.

A French Empire Court suit, comprising breeches and coat, in silk and velvet embroidered with silk and metallic thread, backed with ivory linen.

A late 18thC French green taffeta coat.

£500-700   CSB

£2,000-2,500   RSS

A late 18thC French waistcoat, in iridescent silk, the collar with large lapels.

c1790

£700-1,000   RSS

£300-400   RSS

WOMEN'S CLOTHING

An early 18thC French silk and linen jacket and billowing skirt, embroidered with flowers, insects and birds.

£2,000-2,500   RSS

An 18thC dress, in iridescent green and pink silk taffeta.

c1745

£3,500-4,500   CSB

An 18thC French woven silk dress.

£2,000-2,500   RSS

A French silk taffeta waistcoat and skirt.

c1795

£700-1,000　　　　**RSS**

An early 19thC French silk taffeta dress, with very high waist and long sleeves.

£700-1,000　　　　**RSS**

An 18thC French Regence coat, worn with a dress, in silk woven with taffeta.

£1,800-2,200　　　　**RSS**

A 19thC French dress, in Gros de Tours heavy tartan silk with a matt finish, on a blue ground.

c1860

£500-700　　　　**RSS**

OTHER CLOTHING

An Italian or French silk cape, with a multicoloured pattern on a green ground.

c1735

£5,000-6,000　　　　**RSS**

A pair of French Louis XV gloves, of hand stitched leather with silk thread.

c1750

£1,800-2,200　　　　**RSS**

A late 18thC French bicorne hat, with applied satin rose detail.

£400-600　　　　**RSS**

An early 19thC Russian hat, of red velvet embroidered with gold.

£300-400　　　　**RSS**

An Italian hat, with a wooden hat box.

c1835

£1,000-1,500　　　　**CSB**

A pair of 19thC gloves, of hand stitched leather with silver thread.

These gloves were made for Napoleon III, Emperor of France.

£2,500-3,000　　　　**BEA**

433

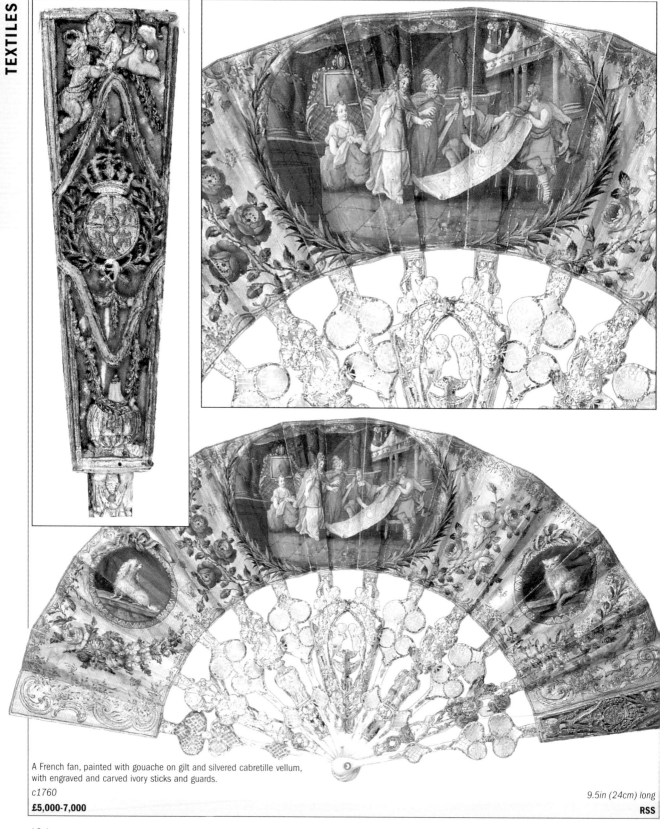

A French fan, painted with gouache on gilt and silvered cabretille vellum, with engraved and carved ivory sticks and guards.

c1760

9.5in (24cm) long

£5,000-7,000

RSS

A 17thC French fan, painted in gouache on vellum, with later carved and pierced mother-of-pearl sticks and guards, inlaid with silver and gold, restored.

c1660   9.5in (24cm) long

£1,200-1,800   **RSS**

An 18thC French fan, "Le commerce du Levant", painted in gouache on cabretille, with painted, varnished engraved and carved sticks and guards, restored.

c1750   10.75in (27.5cm) long

£3,000-4,000   **RSS**

A 18thC French fan, painted in gouache with a mythological scene, with carved and pierced mother-of-pearl sticks and guards, inlaid with silver and gold.

c1760   10in (25.5cm) long

£2,000-2,500   **RSS**

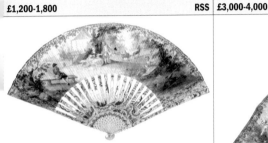

An 18thC French fan, painted in gouache on cabretille leaf, with carved and pierced sticks and guards.

c1765   9.5in (24cm) long

£2,000-3,000   **RSS**

An 18thC French fan, painted in gouache on cabretille leaf, with carved and pierced ivory sticks and guards.

Cabretille a is very fine vellum made from kid leather.

c1770   10in (25.5cm) long

£5,000-7,000   **RSS**

An 18thC French fan, "Les mariages dans l'île de Cayenne", painted in gouache on paper, with wooden sticks and guards inlaid with bone.

c1775   10in (25.5cm) long

£800-1,200   **RSS**

A French fan, "Le banquet champêtre", painted in gouache on paper with a pastoral scene, with carved and gilt painted ivory sticks and guards.

c1780   10in (25.5cm) long

£700-1,000   **RSS**

A late 18thC French fan, painted in gouache on silk leaf, with ivory and tortoiseshell sticks and guards.

c1780   10.5in (26.5cm) long

£800-1,000   **RSS**

A late 18thC French fan, painted in gouache on vellum with three medallions of romantic and pastoral scenes, with carved, pierced and varnished ivory sticks and guards, inlaid with gilt.

c1780   9.5in (24cm) long

£500-700   **RSS**

An 18thC French fan, painted in gouache on silk, with pierced ivory sticks and guards inlaid with silver, dated.

1783   10in (25.5cm) long

£2,000-2,500   **RSS**

A late 18thC French fan, the paper leaf decorated with a printed and gouache military scene depicting Lafayette, with wooden sticks and guards.

c1790   10in (25.5cm) long

£700-1,000   **RSS**

A French fan, "La quiétude de la campagne", painted in gouache on vellum, with pierced mother-of-pearl sticks and guards with metal pique.

c1820   *7in (18cm) long*

£1,500-2,000   **RSS**

A 19thC French fan, painted in gouache on vellum, with carved, pierced and engraved mother-of-pearl sticks and guards, with a cut crystal scent bottle.

c1850   *9.75in (25cm) long*

£800-1,000   **RSS**

A 19thC French lace fan, decorated with golden sequins and spangles, with gilt and pierced ivory sticks and guards.

11.75in (30cm) long

£300-500   **BO**

A 19thC French fan, designed by Alexandre, painted in gouache on silk leaf with a pastoral scene, with ivory sticks and guards, signed "Marius b.d.".

c1870   *10.5in (26.5cm) long*

£300-400   **RSS**

A late 19thC French fan, painted in gouache on cabretille, with carved and pierced mother-of-pearl sticks and guards, signed "Mok Revers" and "MM".

c1875   *10.5in (26.5cm) long*

£700-1,000   **RSS**

A French fan, lithograph on paper after John Lewis Brown, with carved wooden sticks and guards, signed "Buissot" and dated "May 1889", restored.

1889   *12in (30.5cm) long*

£700-1,000   **RSS**

A French vellum fan, "Nonchalance", with carved and pierced wooden sticks and guards, signed "Jacques Blanche" and "MM", dated.

1878   *10in (25.5cm) long*

£2,000-2,500   **RSS**

A late 19thC French fan, painted in gouache on cabretille leaf, with ivory sticks and guards, signed "b.d. Cécile Chennevière" and "A. Rodien Paris", restored.

c1890   *13in (33cm) long*

£2,500-3,500   **RSS**

A 19thC French fan, of lace leaf and gouache on paper, with carved and gilt painted ivory sticks and guards.

c1890   *13in (33cm) long*

£300-400   **RSS**

A late 19thC French vellum fan, painted with an Italian palazzo, with carved and pierced bone sticks and guards, dated.

1898   *6in (15cm) long*

£1,000-1,500   **RSS**

A French Art Nouveau fan, of silk leaf with gouache and gilt scroll decoration, with pierced and carved mother-of-pearl sticks and guards.

c1900   *9in (23cm) long*

£200-300   **RSS**

A 20thC French fan, painted in gouache on silk, with carved horn sticks and guards, signed "E Kees".

c1905 · 6in (15cm) long

£300-500 · RSS

A French black Chantilly and Bayeux lace fan, the lace leaf painted with a romantic scene on gauze, with tortoiseshell sticks and guards.

c1905 · 10in (25.5cm) long

£200-300 · RSS

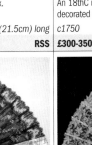

A French Duvelleroy fan, of gauze leaf decorated with silk, lace and silvered sequins, with horn sticks and guards engraved with gilt and silver designs, the reverse signed "Duvelleroy".

c1900 · 8in (20.5cm) long

£500-700 · RSS

A French Duvelleroy fan, painted in gouache on silk, with a peacock painted by Adolphe Thomasse, with tortoiseshell sticks and guards, signed to the reverse.

c1905 · 10in (25.5cm) long

£1,500-2,000 · RSS

A French Duvelleroy feather fan, with mother-of-pearl sticks and guards, complete with original box.

c1910 · 8.5in (21.5cm) long

£700-1,000 · RSS

An 18thC ivory fan, decorated with muses.

c1750 · 18in (45.5cm) wide

£300-350 · GMC

A fine Brussels point-de-gaze fan, with gilded mother-of-pearl sticks.

c1870 · 26.5in (67.5cm) wide

£400-600 · GMC

A bird fan, with yellow mother-of-pearl sticks.

c1880 · 21in (53.5cm) wide

£200-300 · GMC

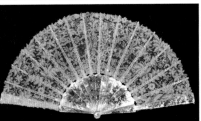

A 19thC fan, possibly Romanian, with Brussels lace leaf and mother-of-pearl pierced sticks and guards, damaged.

c1880 · 12in (30.5cm) long

£2,500-3,500 · RSS

A late 18thC Japanese Edo period fan leaf, from the school of Tosa, painted in gouache on paper with a landscape scene.

21in (53.5cm) wide

£200-300   **RSS**

A 19thC Chinese export fan, painted in Cantonese gouache on paper, depicting a Mandarin family, with mother-of-pearl sticks and guards carved and engraved with flowers and figures, with "LDC" monogram.

c1840   *10in (25.5cm) long*

£700-1,000   **RSS**

A cream silk embroidered Chinese fan, with carved ivory guards and original box, restored.

c1850   *21.5in (54.5cm) wide*

£200-250   **GMC**

A 19thC Japanese Edo period fan leaf, from the school of Kano, painted in gouache on paper with a phoenix.

19in (48cm) wide

£200-300   **RSS**

A 19thC Canton Mandarin fan, in vibrant colours, with lacquer sticks and original box.

This type of fan is known as a 'fan of a thousand faces' because of the many small applied ivory faces that adorn the figures on the fan. It also has applied silk detail.

c1860   *20.75in (52.5cm) wide*

£300-400   **GMC**

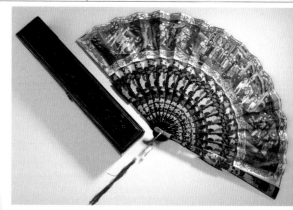

A circular Chinese Canton cockade fan, with carved ivory sticks, restored.

c1790   *13.5in (34.5cm) diam*

£1,200-1,800   **GMC**

A late 19thC Chinese erotic fan, painted in gouache on paper, with wooden sticks and guards.

11.5in (29.5cm) long

£700-1,000   **RSS**

A Japanese novelty cockade cigar fan.

c1860   *8.75in (22cm) long*

£20-30   **GMC**

A 19thC French Duvelleroy fan, "La première indiscrétion aérienne", painted with gouaches on silk on gauze leaf, depicting the commemoration of the first dirigible in 1783, with carved bone sticks and guards.

8in (20.5cm) long

£2,000-2,500   **RSS**

A French fan, "Souvenir of The Paris Exhibition 1867", lithograph on paper by Guilletat, printed by Truillot, with wooden sticks and guards.

1867   10in (25.5cm) long

£250-350   **RSS**

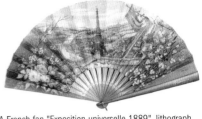

A French fan "Exposition universelle 1889", lithograph on paper, depicting a view of Paris with the Eiffel Tower and the Champ de Mars, with wooden sticks and guards, dated.

1889   13in (33cm) long

£200-300   **RSS**

A French fan, "Les Grands Boulevards", for the 1889 Paris Exhibition, lithograph on paper depicting a street scene, printed by Dupuis and Son, with wooden sticks and guards.

13in (33cm) long

£1,000-1,500   **RSS**

A French advertising fan, "Le Grand Hôtel de Monte-Carlo", lithograph on paper, printed by Buissot, with wooden sticks and guards.

c1890   12.75in (32.5cm) long

£120-180   **RSS**

An early 20thC French advertising fan, "Chemins de fer de l'Ouest", lithograph printed paper after Steinlen, with wooden sticks and guards.

11in (28cm) long

£400-600   **RSS**

ADVERTISING FANS

- Businesses eager to find new ways of communicating with potential clients issued fans printed with advertising material from c1890-1935, during the Art Nouveau and Art Deco periods.
- Despite their ephemeral nature, many of these fans were prized for their highly decorative designs and collections have survived through the years, maintaining a lively secondary market.
- Typical subjects include international exhibitions, upmarket hotels and restaurants and brands of liqueur or spirits. Souvenir fans were also issued at society balls and on cruise liners.
- These fans appeal to many collectors not just for their intrinsic beauty but also as valuable documents of social history.
- The majority of these fans were given away free, so they are predominantly made of cheap materials such as lithographed paper with wooden guards, although more elaborate examples with metallic gilding can be found.
- Historically the leading producers of fans, the French were particularly enthusiastic in their adoption of the fan as an advertising medium, and many examples on today's market hail from Paris.

Three of a set of seven French advertising fans, lithograph on paper, after Abel Truchet, with wooden sticks and guards.

c1903   9in (24cm) long

£600-900 set   **RSS**

An early 18thC French brisé fan, of painted and varnished ivory.

c1720   7.5in (19cm) long

£1,200-1,800   **RSS**

A CLOSER LOOK AT A BRISÉ FAN

Antique French fans are among the most desirable on the market due to their good construction and excellent design. Examples this old are becoming increasingly rare as they are particularly fragile objects.

Fans were made for a variety of social purposes. The opulence of this piece suggests luxury and high fashion, making it appealing to collectors of both fans and vintage costume generally.

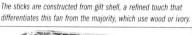

The turquoise cabochons that decorate these guards are a costly addition and therefore increase value.

The sticks are constructed from gilt shell, a refined touch that differentiates this fan from the majority, which use wood or ivory.

A French brisé fan, with pierced gilt shell sticks held together with silk ribbon, the guards encrusted with turquoise.

c1830   6in (15cm) long

£5,000-8,000   **RSS**

An 18thC French brisé fan, of painted and varnished ivory, with carved and engraved sticks, the guards decorated with Chinoiseries, restored.

c1720   8in (20.5cm) long

£1,000-1,500   **RSS**

A 19thC French brisé fan, in the Gothic style, with carved and engraved horn sticks and guards, inlaid with metal.

c1830   7in (18cm) long

£200-300   **RSS**

A 19thC French brisé fan, in the Gothic style, with carved and engraved horn sticks and guards, inlaid with metal.

c1830   7in (18cm) long

£200-300   **RSS**

A Viennese carved ivory brisé fan.

c1875   15.25in (38.5cm) wide

£200-300   **GMC**

A late 19thC French brisé fan, "Les fêtes du Pont Neuf en 1789", in lacquered bone.

7.5in (19cm) long

£1,000-1,500   **RSS**

A French brisé fan, "L'Alsace recouvrée", in painted bone, depicting an Alsacian woman holding the French flag.

1918   9in (23cm) long

£1,000-1,500   **RSS**

A microbeaded handbag, with a floral design.

c1910   *8in (20.5cm) high*

£300-400   **AHL**

A 1920s beaded handbag, with a multicoloured organic design, triangular beaded fringing and circular base, faux-tortoise Lucite clasp and Lucite chain strap.

7.5in (19cm) wide

£300-400   **AHL**

A 1930s French hand-beaded evening purse, with clear beadwork over floral satin, lined with ivory satin, marked "Made in France, Hand made".

7.35in (18.5cm) wide

£50-70   **RG**

An Art Deco beaded evening bag, in cream.

c1920   *6in (15cm) wide*

£30-50   **TDG**

An Art Deco beaded bag, in cream and white.

c1925   *6.25in (16cm) wide*

£30-50   **TDG**

A 1930s Belgian woven beadwork purse, with cream silk lining and label reading 'HANDMADE IN BELGIUM', metal frame, sprung cover and beadwork handle.

8.5in (21.5cm) high

£100-200   **PC**

A 1930s beadwork handbag, in gold, cream and white, with a sprung top lip and white beadwork handle.

8in (20.5cm) wide

£80-100   **PC**

A 1930s beadwork bag, with curling thread motif, circular catch and cream fabric lining, woven label reading "Bags by Josef HAND BEADED IN FRANCE".

9.25in (23.5cm) wide

£100-200   **BY**

A 1930s black beadwork purse, with a woven basketwork pattern, on a gilt metal frame with inlaid bands of tiny rhinestones, beadwork handle, the interior lined with black silk.

6.75in (22cm) wide

£150-200   **BY**

A 1940s black satin and hand-embroidered evening purse, with a beaded and enamel frame, yellow satin lining and a satin handle, unmarked, probably French.

11.75in (30cm) wide

£200-250   **RG**

A 1940s Fre-Mor hexagonal beaded box bag, with relief metal surround and five internal compartments.

7in (18cm) high

£150-200   **FAN**

A 1950s beaded evening bag, the flamingo with gem detail to its tail, satin interior and chain handle.

12in (30cm) wide

£150-200   **AHL**

A 1940s copper-coloured beaded clutch handbag, with an etched clasp and frame.

7in (18cm) wide

£150-200   **AHL**

A 1950s French beaded bag, made for the American market, with a beaded frame and clasp, lined with ivory satin, marked "Davids Fifth Avenue".

8.25in (21cm) wide

£80-100   **RG**

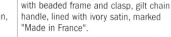

A 1950s French beaded evening bag, with beaded frame and clasp, gilt chain handle, lined with ivory satin, marked "Made in France".

7.5in (19cm) wide

£80-100   **RG**

A CLOSER LOOK AT A BEADED TAPESTRY BAG

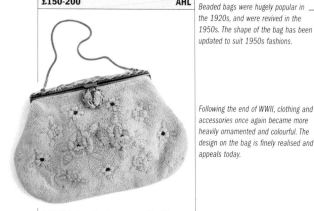

A 1950s beadwork purse, with gilt metal frame, cream silk lining and swinging circular catch.

9in (23cm) wide

£100-150   **ROX**

Beaded bags were hugely popular in the 1920s, and were revived in the 1950s. The shape of the bag has been updated to suit 1950s fashions.

Following the end of WWII, clothing and accessories once again became more heavily ornamented and colourful. The design on the bag is finely realised and appeals today.

Based in New York, Austrian-born Nettie Rosenstein was an influential designer between the 1930s and 1960s. The value of this bag is increased by the known maker, as well as the high quality.

The bag is made from thick tapestry fabric. Glass beads have been carefully embroidered onto the cloth to highlight the woven design.

A 1950s tapestry bag, by Nettie Rosenstein, USA, with applied glass beads and satin lining, made in Florence, Italy, minor bead loss.

c1950   *9.5in (24cm) wide*

£600-800   **MGL**

A Jolles Original bag, applied with beading, leaves and a bunch of large plastic cherries, pink felt interior.

12.5in (32cm) high

£100-200   **FAN**

A hand-beaded bag, by Veldore of Texas, with a country scene.

11in (28cm) wide

£50-80   **FAN**

A Belgian beaded purse, in white silk, overlaid with faceted iridescent glass and rope beads, gilt metal frame, acorn shaped clasps and cream silk lining, fabric label "MADE IN BELGIUM".

7.75in (19.5cm) wide

£50-100   **BY**

A beaded handbag, with black and cut steel beads.

6in (15cm) wide

£200-300   **AHL**

An Art Deco embroidered handbag, in the style of Sonia Delaunay.

c1925   15.75in (40cm) high

£300-400   **MOD**

A black silk evening bag, with a bakelite clasp.

c1930   8in (20.5cm) high

£100-200   **TDG**

A French satin handbag, custom made, with double self handles.

c1950   9.5in (24cm) wide

£300-400   **GOL**

A 1960s carpet bag, in the style of Pucci.

12in (30.5cm) wide

£50-100   **CHA**

A mid-1970s Jeanesse white ostrich bag, with shoulder strap of cut steel, lined in gold leather.

7.5in (19cm) wide

£300-400   **GOL**

A 1980s Diane Love 'Envelope' handbag.

12in (30.5cm) wide

£200-300   **GOL**

A 1930s Argentine brown crocodile bag, marked "Industria Argentina".

11.75in (30cm) wide

£100-150   **RG**

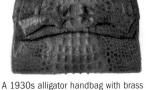

A 1930s alligator handbag with brass hardware.

12in (30.5cm) wide

£150-200   **AHL**

An Art Deco-style small suedette bag, with integral geometric pattern, brass clasp and fabric handle.

c1940   6.75in (17cm) wide

£150-200   **AHL**

A British Art Deco leather bag, with a stitched geometric design, silver frame, with integral leather purse fixed to frame.

c1930   7in (18cm) wide

£300-400   **AHL**

A 1930s French lizard bag, with enamelled and cut steel silver frame.

8.5in (21cm) wide

£700-800   **GOL**

TEXTILES

A 1940s Brazilian Aveda ponyskin bag, with lanyard hand-stitched detail, and a clear Lucite and brass clasp.

12.5in (31.5cm) wide

£200-300 **AHL**

A 1940s Gucci black lizard clutch bag.

7.5in (19cm) wide

£300-400 **GOL**

A 1950s lizard handbag.

11.5in (29cm) wide

£150-200 **AHL**

A rare 1950s calfskin bag, by Holzman, USA, lucite clasp and lucite circle handles.

c1950 *11.25in (28.5cm) wide*

£200-400 **MGL**

An early 1960s Gucci leather bag, with woven effect.

9.5in (24cm) wide

£80-100 **CHA**

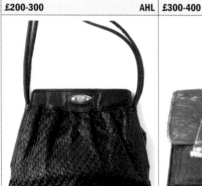

A 1960s ponyskin handbag.

11in (28cm) wide

£100-200 **AHL**

A 1960s calfskin handbag, by De Leon, USA, of elongated circular design with satin lining.

20in (51cm) wide

£200-400 **MGL**

A 1960s Hermes 'Kelly' calfskin box handbag, with lock, keys and clochette.

11.25in (28.5cm) wide

£1,000-2,000 **MGL**

A 1970s red calfskin clutch handbag, with a Gucci shoulder strap.

10.5in (26.5cm) wide

£100-200 **MGL**

A 1960s Hermes leather handbag, known as the 'piano bag'.

10in (25.5cm) wide

£1,000-2,000 **MGL**

A 1950s Llewellyn grey shell Lucite handbag, in a a rare shape, with grey handles.

9in (23cm) wide

£500-600   **DJI**

A 1950s Wilardy black Lucite travel bag, with hand-painted decoration.

11in (28cm) wide

£300-500   **DJI**

A 1950s Wilardy pearl grey Lucite handbag, of 'beanpot' design, with rhinestones.

5in (13cm) wide

£400-800   **DJI**

A 1950s Rialto Lucite handbag, with a clear top and hand-carved decoration.

6.5in (16.5cm) wide

£200-300   **DJI**

An early 1950s Myles Original Lucite handbag, in caramel and striated butterscotch, with clear plastic hand-carved rose and leaf decoration.

8.25in (21cm) wide

£400-600   **DJI**

A 1950s Lucite handbag, with a caramel waffle-carved body and apple juice coloured top.

4.5in (11.5cm) wide

£200-300   **DJI**

A CLOSER LOOK AT A LUCITE HANDBAG

This wedding handbag has a clear plastic top that can be filled with brightly coloured flowers to compliment an outfit. Other popular 1950s bags had clear sides that could be lined with coloured fabrics of the owner's choice.

Plastic box bags were very popular in the 1950s and come in a wide range of shapes and styles. Additional decorative features, such as the clear top, add value.

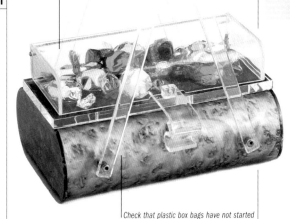

Check that plastic box bags have not started to decay. Look out for warping and damage as they will affect value.

A 1950s Lucite wedding handbag, unsigned, with a clear lid for removable flowers or other decoration.

7.5in (19cm) wide

£300-400   **DJI**

A 1950s Llewellyn Lucite handbag, the grey circular panel with a tapestry of pearls and rhinestones.

9in (23cm) wide

£300-500   **DJI**

A 1950s Tyrolean Lucite handbag, basket-shaped, with gold decoration.

8in (20.5cm) wide

£200-300   **DJI**

A 1950s Rialto bone-colour pearl Lucite handbag, with an amber and aurora rhinestone disc.

7in (18cm) wide

£800-1,000   **DJI**

A late 1950s Wilardy black Lucite handbag, with aurora rhinestones to the base of handle and clasp.

10in (25.5cm) wide

£400-600   **DJI**

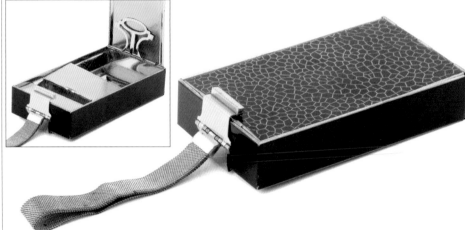

A French cut-steel beaded handbag, with rose decoration.

c1910   *8in (20.5cm) high*

£200-300   **AHL**

A 1930s evening compact bag, with a fitted interior and strap.

5in (13cm) wide

£100-200   **TDG**

A 1970s Judith Leiber bag, in brushed gold over metal, with coral accents and diamonds, the clasp with coral top, strap inside, the back with a concave shape to follow the line of the hand.

7.5in (19cm) wide

£800-1,200   **GOL**

A 1970s Karung box purse handbag by Judith Leiber, with sleeper bag, mirror and tassel comb.

6.75in (17cm) wide

£200-300   **MGL**

A purse, by Holzman, USA, design probably in silkscreen on leather, the wrapped frame with piped edges and silk lining, with signature "Holzman" ball clasp.

1960   *8in (20.5cm) wide*

£200-400   **MGL**

A CLOSER LOOK AT A NOVELTY HANDBAG

Novelty bags are popular with collectors, especially animal examples like this poodle.

It is rare to find a bag like this in such good condition as the beadwork is vulnerable to breakage and loss.

Poodles were a fashionable 1950s motif as they symbolised glamour and sophistication. Today they appear rather kitsch, but continue to have great appeal.

A 1960s American Telephone bag, in black patent leather.

10in (25cm) wide

£400-500   **AHL**

A 1950s black poodle beaded handbag, by Walborg, Belgium.

8in (20.5cm) wide

£1,000-2,000   **DJI**

A 1970s red plastic telephone bag, by Dallas Handbags, USA, with a working telephone.

9.75in (25cm) wide

£200-300   **DJI**

A 1960s unusual wooden box handbag, in a satchel style, with brass handles and fittings, probably French.

5.5in (14cm) wide

£200-300   **GOL**

A Paco Rabanne purple metal handbag, branding applied to metal.

c1990   *9in (23cm) wide*

£700-900   **MGL**

WAX DOLLS

THE TOYS MARKET

Whilst the market for some antiques has been fairly subdued in the last year, the toy market has been extremely buoyant. The reasons for this are diverse: as well as being a fun collecting area and having great nostalgic appeal to a wide range of buyers, toys have the potential to rise in value in the future, making them an alternative investment to stocks and shares. Toys are also particularly appealing to collectors who are focused on completing sets, as many were produced in numbered series.

Television and film related toys of all kinds are currently very desirable, and this trend seems likely to continue as cult figures, such as James Bond and Batman, are continually re-invented and introduced to new audiences. Diecast toys in mint condition are also performing well, especially examples by the well-known makers Corgi and Dinky. Condition is increasingly essential.

Tinplate continues to be desirable and early, clockwork pieces can command huge prices. The market for later Japanese tinplate remains strong, particularly for space related toys. Collectors are also increasingly expressing interest in Chinese tinplate, although prices are generally yet to reach the levels of Japanese toys.

Teddy bears and dolls, especially examples by well-known German and English makers, such as Steiff, Simon and Halbig and Merrythought, are continuing to fetch high prices.

Model railways are almost always popular, although interest tends to tail-off to some extent during the summer. As was the case around five or six years ago, the market for Wrenn trains has become very strong over recent months.

– Glenn Butler, Partner, Wallis & Wallis

An early 18thC wax carved creche doll, with painted features, wearing a full-length dress and underwear, inscribed in French, hands and legs missing.
11in (28cm) high
£80-120　　　　　　　**GORL**

A mid-Victorian poured wax shoulder doll, possibly Montanari, with inset blue glass paperweight eyes, inserted hair, cloth body with wax lower limbs, clothed.
c1860　　　*20.5in (52cm) high*
£200-300　　　　　　　**GORL**

A Victorian wax doll, dressed as a Christmas fairy in a silk layered dress, displayed under a glass dome.
17in (43cm) high
£180-220　　　　　　　**ROS**

A poured wax Lucy Peck-type fashion doll, with rare sleep eyes.
c1880　　　*17in (43cm) high*
£700-800　　　　　　　**BEJ**

COMPOSITION DOLLS

A Biedermeier shoulder head doll, with a waxed papier-mâché shoulder head and fixed blue glass eyes, fabric body, blonde mohair wig and painted yellow boots, damage.
20.75in (52cm) high
£150-200　　**WDL**

A very rare Biedermeier doll, with waxed papier-mâché shoulder head on a horn shaft, painted blue eyes and black hair, the dress with cardboard stars, remains of a hat.
c1840　　*10.75in high*
£350-400　　**WDL**

A pair of 19thC wax over composition shoulder dolls, with inserted real hair, inset glass eyes and cloth bodies with leather forearms.
Largest 25.5in (65cm)
£300-400　　　　　　　**GORL**

A large wax over composition shoulder doll, with fixed glass paperweight eyes, cloth body and painted composition limbs, in a velvet dress.
c1880　　　*38in (96cm) high*
£150-200　　　　　　　**GORL**

A tall Dressel wax doll, with fixed brown eyes, an old blonde mohair wig, papier-mâché limbs and a fabric body, in a faded train dress with an old brooch, stamped mark.
26in (65cm) high
£600-700　　　　　　　**WDL**

A wax composition old crone doll, with a mask-like face and stick legs, carrying a child by the hand.
16.5in (42cm) high
£400-500　　　　　　　**GORL**

A Jumeau bisque character doll, dressed as a nun with a pendant rosary, fixed glass eyes, open mouth and pierced ears, on a jointed wood and composition body, wearing original leather shoes.

19in (48cm) high

£1,000-1,500 **GORL**

A Jumeau bisque doll, with fixed glass eyes, open mouth and a jointed composition body with voice box, label attached to lower back "Bebe Jumeau, Diplome d'Honneur".

26in (66cm) high

£800-1,200 **GORL**

A Jumeau bisque 'closed mouth' character doll, with fixed blue glass paperweight eyes, pierced ears and a jointed wood and composition body, printed mark in red "Tete Jumeau 8".

c1885 *22in (56cm) high*

£1,000-1,500 **GORL**

A French Jumeau bébé, in original woollen dress.

c1880 *16in (40.5cm) high*

£3,500-4,000 **BEJ**

449

An Armand Marseille 'My Dream Baby' baby doll, mould 341, with closed mouth, sleep eyes and a jointed composition body.

16in (41cm) high

£120-180   **GORL**

An Armand Marseille bisque 'My Dream Baby' doll, mould 351, with sleep eyes, an open mouth with two teeth and a jointed composition bent-limb body, chipping.

16in (40.5cm) high

£120-180   **W&W**

An Armand Marseille black bisque 'My Dream Baby' doll, mould 351, with sleep eyes, open mouth showing two teeth and a composition body, wearing a long white dress.

14in (35.5cm) high

£120-180   **W&W**

An Armand Marseille bisque 'My Dream Baby' doll, with weighted blue eyes, open mouth and a five piece curved limb composition body, impressed "A M 351 /3 1 /2 K", firing speck.

1926   *14in (36cm) high*

£120-180   **VEC**

An Armand Marseille bisque 'My Dream Baby' doll, mould 353, with sleep eyes, closed mouth and a bent-limb composition body, wearing a hand-woven outfit.

15in (38cm) high

£600-800   **GORL**

An Armand Marseille 'Puppet Dream Baby', in original bedding.

c1920   *Doll 10in (25.5cm) high*

£600-700   **BEJ**

A bisque doll, by Armand Marseille, mould 390n, with sleep eyes, open mouth and a jointed wood and composition body, seated within an early 20thC steel push chair.

26in (66cm) high

£400-500   **GORL**

A large Armand Marseille porcelain bisque doll, mould 390, with sleep eyes, open mouth and a jointed composition body, impressed "A 15 M", on an Edwardian mahogany chair.

31in (79cm) high

£300-400   **GORL**

An Armand Marseille child doll, mould '390', dressed as a goose girl in an apron and plaits.

c1920   *19in (48.5cm) high*

£350-400   **BEJ**

A late 19thC French bisque fashion doll, with fixed glass eyes, pierced ears, a closed mouth and a kid leather body, in a lace-trimmed dress, some damage.

13in (33cm) high

£400-500   **GORL**

A 19thC French bisque fashion doll, the swivel head with fixed blue glass eyes, closed mouth and pierced ears, on a kid leather body, in a satin and lace dress.

15in (38cm) high

£800-1,200   **GORL**

A French fashion doll, attributed to Madame Huret, with a bisque shoulder head, glass eyes, closed mouth and a kid leather body, dressed as a bride, chemise with "S & S Hibernia" label.

c1860   *19in (48cm) high*

£700-1,000   **GORL**

A French Simonne young lady fashion doll, with rare neck articulation, wearing original clothes with red trim.

c1870   *20in high*

£3,000-4,000   **BEJ**

An early Bru fashion doll, wearing an original outfit with ribbons and bonnet, in display case, the head marked "C".

c1870   *14in (35.5cm) high*

£3,000-3,500   **BEJ**

A very rare French mignonette with rare peach boots, in original red outfit and bonnet, with box.

c1880   *6in (15cm) high*

£3,000-3,500   **BEJ**

A late 19thC French bisque fashion doll, with fixed glass eyes, pierced ears, closed mouth and a kid leather body, in a lace-trimmed dress, cracks to neck.

13in (33cm) high

£400-500   **GORL**

SIMON & HALBIG

A Simon & Halbig character toddler girl doll, with a white dress and shoes.

c1900   *20in (51cm) high*

£800-900   **BEJ**

A German bisque shoulder doll, attributed to Simon & Halbig, with fixed glass paperweight eyes and closed mouth, on kid leather body, clothed in blue silk, unmarked.

18in (46cm) high

£300-400   **GORL**

A CLOSER LOOK AT A SIMON & HALBIG DOLL

Most Simon & Halbig dolls are marked. The mark was changed slightly in 1905 – dolls with marks without an ampersand were generally produced prior to 1905.

Dolls made by Simon & Halbig before the 20thC tend to have open mouths, while the mouths on later examples are usually closed.

Simon & Halbig, established in Thüringia in Germany in 1839, began producing dolls in the early 1870s. This makes this c1880 doll a fairly early example.

Collectors look for all original dolls, especially attractive examples in outstanding condition.

A Simon & Halbig all original child doll, in a white dress.

c1880   *17in (43cm) high*

£800-1,000   **BEJ**

A Simon and Halbig bisque-headed doll, model number 126.

£200-300   **JN**

A Simon & Halbig character doll, model number 126, with composition body, flirty eyes and tremble tongue, inactive voice box.

18in (46cm) high

£200-300   **ROS**

TOYS, DOLLS & MODELS

A 19thC bisque shoulder doll, with moulded hair, blue eyes, fabric body and bisque limbs, in original outfit.

13.5in (34cm) high

£300-400 ROS

A Parian sailor boy shoulder doll, with moulded hair and painted features, cloth body and bisque arms and legs.

c1870 *12in (31cm) high*

£120-180 GORL

A Parian shoulder doll, with moulded hair and painted features, above a cloth body and bisque arms and legs.

c1870 *12in (31cm) high*

£400-500 GORL

A Parian shoulder doll, with moulded hair and painted features, cloth body and bisque arms and legs, in a green satin dress and carrying a violin.

c1870 *12in (31cm) high*

£400-500 GORL

A Parian 'Annie' shoulder doll, with moulded hair and painted features, wearing a white dress and a pink hat, unmarked.

c1895 *12in (31cm) high*

£400-500 GORL

OTHER DOLLS

An Altbeck & Gottschalk 'Sweet Nell' character doll.

c1890 *25in (63.5cm) high*

£800-1,200 BEJ

An A. M. of Austria character boy, with a hat and sword.

c1890

£1,000-1,200 BEJ

25in (63.5cm) high

BEJ

A rare French Belton child, with a box and extra clothes.

c1880 *13in (33cm) high*

£2,000-2,500 BEJ

A German double-ended doll, possibly by Karl Bergner, with one smiling and one serious face, fixed glass eyes and closed mouths, on kid leather body with bisque forearms, in a velvet suit.

12in (31cm) high

£300-400 GORL

A Chad Valley 'Princess Margaret Rose' doll, with original clothing.

c1930   *17in (43cm) high*

£300-400   **BEJ**

An Eden Baby bisque character doll, impressed "no.8, Paris Depose", with fixed glass eyes, open mouth and pierced ears, on a jointed composition body, in a black velvet suit.

c1900   *22in (56cm) high*

£500-600   **GORL**

A CLOSER LOOK AT A FRENCH EDEN BÉBÉ

French Bébés, popular between 1860 and 1900, are among the most sought-after bisque dolls. This is a medium-sized example – Eden Bébés were produced up to 34in (86cm) high and larger examples tend to command more.

Eden Bébé is a trade name for the Fleischmann and Bloedel Doll Factory, of Bavaria and France. This doll predates the firm becoming part of the Société Francaise de la Fabrication de Bébés et Jouets (S.F.B.J.) in 1899.

Heads are made from bisque and bodies are composition. Eyes are usually paperweight and mouths are slightly open.

Minor repairs will not have a great effect on price. Damage to the porcelain however, could reduce value by up to fifty per cent.

A French Eden bébé, wearing a cream suit with velvet trim.

c1885   *16in (40.5cm) high*

£2,000-2,500   **BEJ**

An Eden Bébé porcelain bisque doll, with fixed paperweight eyes, open mouth and pierced ears, on a five-piece composition body, in hand-embroidered clothes, impressed size "11".

25in (64cm) high

£600-900   **GORL**

An Farnell Alpha Toys Princess Elizabeth cloth doll, with side glancing painted blue eyes, blonde mohair wig and a velveteen jointed body, in an original cotton dress, blue label to foot.

1930   *14in (36cm) high*

£200-300   **VEC**

A Max Handwerck bisque headed No. 3 doll, with wood and composition jointed body.

21.75in (55cm) high

£200-300   **ROS**

A Heubach Koppelsdorf child doll, dressed as Alice in Wonderland, wearing a white apron and plaits.

17in (43cm) high

£500-600   **BEJ**

A Gebruder Heubach bisque Piano baby girl, wearing a blue bonnet and pinafore.

c1910   *8.5in (21.5cm) high*

£200-300   **BEJ**

A Kämmer and Reinhardt/Halbig bisque doll, with sleeping eyes, open mouth and pierced ears, on a jointed composition body, in blue velvet with under garments.

18.5in (37cm) high

£400-600   **GORL**

A Kämmer and Reinhardt German girl doll, with a dark wig and wearing a blue dress.

7in (18cm) high

£200-250   **BEJ**

A very large Kämmer & Reinhardt doll, with a bisque head, sleeping eyes, open mouth with teeth, pierced ears and a mohair wig, on a wooden and papier-mâché 15-part body, red mark "192".

c1905　　　28.75in (72cm) high

£1,000-1,500　　　　**WDL**

A rare Käthe Kruse number 1 doll, the painted head with one seam.

c1910　　　18in (45cm) high

£2,000-3,000　　　**WDL**

An early Käthe Kruse type VII boy, 'Kleines Du mein' (My little darling), with a wood wool-stuffed body, stamped "Käthe Kruse 34...4".

c1930　　　14in (35cm) high

£2,000-3,000　　　**WDL**

A 1950s Käthe Kruse 'German Child' doll, the plastic head with painted eyes and a real hair wig, on a fabric body.

20.5in (51cm) high

£600-900　　　**WDL**

A 1950s Käthe Kruse 'Friedebald' doll, with a plastic head, painted eyes and blonde hair, on a fabric body, later cardigan, stamped "...a.d. Saale".

20.5in (51cm) high

£700-1,000　　　**WDL**

A German Max Oscar Arnold child doll.

c1900　　　18in (45.5cm) high

£350-400　　　**BEJ**

A Pintel & Godchaux French bébé.

c1880　　　17in (43cm) high

£1,500-2,000　　　**BEJ**

A German Recknagel child, with painted shoes and socks.

13in (33cm) high

£300-350　　　**BEJ**

A doll with a Schildkröt celluloid head, with an open mouth with teeth, white leather body with wooden arms and original worn silk dress, socks and black wax shoes, marked "Germany SiR Schutz-Marke 12", damaged eyes.

16in (40cm) high

£50-100　　　**WDL**

A Schoenau and Hoffmeister bisque headed doll, with jointed composition body, marked "1909, 6".

21.75in (55cm) high

£200-300　　　**ROS**

A S.F.B.J. bisque doll, with brown sleep eyes, open mouth with teeth and a brown mohair wig, on a composition body with national costume, paper tag to wrist, marked "Unis 60", some mottling.

19in (48.5cm) high

£200-300　　　**W&W**

An S.F.B.J. bisque boy doll, mould 227, with painted hair to the domed head, fixed glass eyes and an open mouth, on clothed composition body.

c1900　　　21in (53cm) high

£1,200-1,800　　　**GORL**

A large French Steiner 'C' series bébé, dressed in layered white clothing and a bonnet.

A Jules Steiner bisque doll, with fixed blue glass eyes, closed mouth and a jointed composition body, in a cotton dress with elaborate lacework and bonnet.

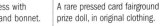

A rare pressed card fairground prize doll, in original clothing.

A French Steiner 'A' series bébé.

c1880	17in (43cm) high	
£3,000-4,000		**BEJ**

c1880	30in (76cm) high	
£8,000-12,000		**BEJ**

	9.5in (24cm) high	
£2,000-3,000		**GORL**

c1920	18in (45.5cm) high	
£400-500		**BEJ**

A Japanese brocade and bisque play doll.

c1920	12in (30.5cm) high	
£150-200		**BEJ**

A composition baby doll, in a knitted outfit and hat.

c1930	22in (55.75cm) high	
£250-300		**BEJ**

DOLL'S HOUSES & FURNITURE

A large mid-19thC three-story doll's house, with furniture.

This house was originally built in a closet in the Morris Longstreth Hallowell House in Philadelphia in 1840. In 1917, the house was razed and the interior walls were saved and stored until 1929 when they were placed in the present cabinet and donated to Stenton House museum. The contents, original to the doll's house, include period furniture, cutlery, portraits, and porcelain accessories.

	79in (197.5cm) high	
£15,000-20,000		**POOK**

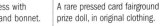

A British Georgian-style wooden doll's house, the lift-off front revealing four rooms, a wooden staircase, a fitted range and open cast-iron fireplaces, with glazed windows, damaged.

c1900	38in (97cm) high	
£800-1,200		**VEC**

A Triang Tudor-style doll's house, with half-timbered gables, five rooms, staircase, opening metal-framed windows with imitation shutters, electric wall lights with switches, repainted.

1938	47in (120cm) wide	
£220-280		**VEC**

An unusual American Gothic wooden doll's house, with a papered brick finish, a tinplate spiral staircase and extensive fittings, with spare panes of glass and Pollock's wallpaper, damage.

c1920	42in (107cm) high	
£1,000-1,500		**VEC**

A Triang-type doll's house, with four rooms, a staircase and 14 windows.

	23.5in (60cm) w	
£40-60		**VEC**

TOYS, DOLLS & MODELS

A French musical 'L'Ecole' schoolroom automaton, with a clockwork mechanism, six bisque-headed schoolchildren and a teacher, possibly Jumeau.

c1900   *17in (43cm) wide*

£1,200-1,800   **GORL**

A German wooden Noah's ark, brightly painted with gothic-style windows, 23 animals and five figures, some missing, replacement hinged roof, damage.

c1900   *23in (59cm) wide*

£120-180   **VEC**

A late 18thC miniature oak refectory table with skillets.

22in (56cm) wide

£400-500   **BEJ**

A French wrought iron miniature doll's bed, all original.

c1880   *12in (30.5cm) wide*

£600-700   **BEJ**

A rare French boxed porcelain doll's tea service, with original teacups, plates and teaspoons.

c1890   *box 22in (56cm) wide*

£850-1,000   **BEJ**

A miniature Landau carriage.

c1880   *24in (61cm) wide*

£1,500-2,000   **BEJ**

A Lines Bros. child's cart with original paintwork.

c1890   *36in (91.5cm) wide*

£400-500   **BEJ**

TEDDY BEARS

- The first teddy bears are attributed to German seamstress Margarete Steiff (b1847), who started producing toys in 1884.
- The first Steiff bear appeared at the 1903 Leipzig fair. An American visitor ordered three thousand, knowing that, after President Roosevelt well-publicised refusal to shoot a bearcub, American children would love the new 'Teddy bear'.
- Steiff bears are the most sought after teddy bears. Pre-1930s bears have humped backs and long arms. Glass eyes replaced boot buttons after WWI, and following WWII, artificial and wool plush was used. White and cinnamon colouring are rare.
- British bears have grown in popularity. Chiltern introduced its famous 'Hugmee' bear in 1923, Chad Valley made bears from the 1920s, and Merrythought began production in the 1930s, releasing its well-known 'Cheeky' bear in 1957.
- Bears by Dean's, Farnell and Schuco are also collectable, as are Pre-WWII bears by other makers.
- An attractive faces tends to command a premium.
- Condition is crucial to value, especially on more recent bears.

A Chad Valley golden mohair teddy bear, with vertically stitched black nose and shaven muzzle, fully jointed, with black claw stitching and cloth pads, replacement eyes, inoperative growler, damage and wear.

c1920   *17in (43cm) high*

£150-200   **VEC**

A pre-WWII English teddy bear, probably Chad Valley, with gold mohair plush and wood-wool filling, glass eyes, stitched snout and jointed limbs some wear.

Wood-wool stuffing indicates an early teddy bear.

43.5in (110cm) high

£200-300   **GORL**

An early post-WWII Chad Valley teddy bear, with gold plush, glass eyes and a stitched snout, the jointed body with brown velour pads, maker's label to foot.

27in (69cm) high

£300-400   **GORL**

A 1920s to 1930s Chiltern golden mohair teddy bear, with clear glass eyes and vertically stitched nose, fully jointed, with black claw stitching and cloth pads, growler inoperative, wear.

16in (41cm) high

£150-200   **VEC**

A Chiltern pink mohair and wool teddy bear, with vertically stitched nose, fully jointed, remains of black claw stitching and velveteen pads, replacement glass eyes, inoperative squeaker, some wear.

c1930   *14in (35cm) high*

£120-180   **VEC**

A pink mohair Chiltern Hugmee teddy bear, with a vertically restitched nose with longer upward stitches, fully jointed, replacement glass eyes, repairs, damage.

c1930   *20in (51cm) high*
£180-220   **VEC**

An English cinnamon plush mohair teddy bear, with plastic eyes, a stitched snout, growler and jointed limbs, labelled "Le Fray".

c1950   *31in (78cm) high*
£120-180   **GORL**

A CLOSER LOOK AT A MERRYTHOUGHT TEDDY BEAR

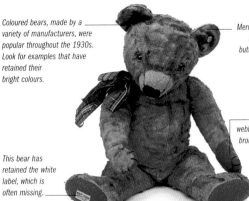

Coloured bears, made by a variety of manufacturers, were popular throughout the 1930s. Look for examples that have retained their bright colours.

Merrythought bears were made with metal ear buttons as well as white labels until WWII.

This bear has retained the white label, which is often missing.

The claw stitching is webbed. This feature was brought to Merrythought c1930 by Director A.C. Janisch, who had previously worked for J.K. Farnell.

A Merrythought red artificial silk plush teddy bear, with a shaven muzzle, fully jointed, with a metal button and white embroidered label to foot, replacement plastic eyes, wear.

Although Merrythought was known for making coloured bears, red is hard to come by.

1936-38   *17in (43cm) high*
£300-400   **VEC**

A Merrythought blonde mohair teddy bear, with amber and black glass eyes and vertically stitched black nose with long downward stitches, fully jointed, squeaker, missing label, some wear.

c1930   *19in (48cm) high*
£80-120   **VEC**

A large blonde mohair Steiff teddy bear, with extensive restoration and replacements, with notes and photographs relating to the restoration process, stains.

c1910   *22in (56cm) high*
£500-700   **VEC**

A Steiff limited edition Alfonzo red mohair teddy bear, number 440 from an edition of 5000, white tag "406195", for Teddy Bears of Whitney, box and certificate.

14in (35cm) high
£500-700   **VEC**

An English golden mohair teddy bear, with glass eyes and jointed limbs, wear.

28in (71cm) high
£250-350   **GORL**

A golden mohair American teddy bear, with black boot button eyes and horizontally stitched black nose, fully jointed, black claw stitching and felt pads, inoperative growler, wear.

c1920   *11.5in (29cm) high*
£150-200   **VEC**

An American blonde mohair teddy bear, with boot button eyes and horizontally stitched black nose, fully jointed, remains of black claw stitching, in a tailor-made tweed suit, wear and repairs.

c1920   *14in (36cm) high*
£200-300   **VEC**

A British curly blonde mohair teddy bear, with pronounced hump and remains of horizontally stitched black nose, fully jointed, replacement eyes and repairs.

c1920   *16in (40cm) high*
£200-300   **VEC**

A British golden mohair teddy bear, with black boot button eyes, fully jointed, restoration and losses to mohair.

c1910   *13in (33cm) high*
£200-300   **VEC**

A large golden blonde teddy bear, stuffed with wood wool, with long arms, brown glass eyes and a black stitched nose.

c1920   *24in (60cm) high*
£250-300   **WDL**

A rare French curly plush teddy bear, with a red ribbon, probably Jopi or Helvetica.

c1920
£800-1,000   **BEJ**

A British Farnell golden mohair teddy bear, with glass eyes and a small hump, growler inoperative, repairs, with photographs of owner and a tinplate box.

1930   *19in (48cm) high*
£400-500   **VEC**

OTHER SOFT TOYS

A Merrythought mohair plush monkey, with a cloth face, paws and feet, jointed.

22in (56cm) high

£150-200   **GORL**

A good Roullet et Descamps 'Springing' lion, with glass eyes, a fur mane and beard, whiskers and a skin covered body and tail, the mechanism partly inoperative.

This lion is classed as an automaton, it winds up and 'jumps' forward. The body and legs are rigid.

17in (43cm) wide

£800-1,200   **ROS**

A Schuco 'Biego Bello' plush crow, with original label, slightly dirty.

10in (25cm) high

£50-70   **LAN**

A Steiff soft toy terrier, with glass eyes, a squeak and spotted white mohair plush.

16in (40.5cm) wide

£120-150   **GORL**

A Steiff curly plush lamb.

c1950   *16in (40.5cm) high*

£400-450   **BEJ**

A British black mohair Felix the Cat, with boot button eyes, black painted metal nose, embroidered mouth simulating teeth and an internal wire frame, inoperative squeaker, wear, restitched.

c1920   *9in (23cm) high*

£50-70   **VEC**

DINKY TOYS

A Dinky No.504 second cab Foden 'Mobilgas' tanker, with a red body, filler caps and supertoy hubs, in a dark blue box with an orange and white label.

£400-600   **VEC**

A Dinky No.982 Bedford Pullmore car transporter, with large baseplate print and model number to base, in a blue striped box, card packing and No.994 ramp.

£280-320   **VEC**

A CLOSER LOOK AT A DINKY TRUCK

This No.935 Leyland flatbed truck with chains was produced by Dinky between 1964 and 1966.

The blue version of this truck is rare and can be worth up to twice as much the green.

Scratches, bruises and damage can reduce value significantly, particularly on post-WWII models.

Correct boxes in excellent condition increase the value of Dinky vehicles.

A Dinky No.935 Leyland Octopus flat truck, with chains, in a rare colourway, dark blue cab and chassis, primrose yellow cab band and bumper, silver radiator grille, in a yellow box with a detailed picture panel.

£4,000-6,000   **VEC**

A Dinky No.31c trade box of six 'Chivers Jellies' Trojan vans, all dark green with mid-green ridged wheels, in a repaired trade box with repro dividers.

Before c1953 most Dinky toys were sold from retailers packs like this, and were not individually boxed.

£700-1,000   **VEC**

A Dinky No.23f trade box of six Alfa Romeo racing cars, five with No.23f baseplate, and one with No.232 baseplate, trade box with repro dividers.

£400-600   **VEC**

A rare Dinky No.141 Vauxhall Victor estate car, a promotional issue with "Lightning Fastners Ltd Technical Service", in maroon, with a blue interior, paper labels, sun-faded.

The colourway and transfers are rare and appeared as part of a US promotion.

£700-800   **VEC**

A Dinky No.140a Trade Box of six Austin Atlantic convertibles, two pink and four light blue, in a yellow trade box complete with original dividers.

£400-600   **VEC**

A rare Dinky Set No.3 Private Automobiles, with No.30d Vauxhall Saloon, No.36b Bentley Coupe, No.36d Rover Streamlined Saloon, No.38a Fraser Nash, No.38c Lagonda, boxed.

£2,500-3,000   **VEC**

A Corgi 'Mister Softee' Smiths Karrier van, with spun hubs, in a blue and yellow card box.

£400-500   **VEC**

A Corgi No.471 'Joe's Diner' Smiths Karrier mobile canteen, with spun hubs, in a blue and yellow carded box.

£250-300   **VEC**

A Corgi No.413 'Family Butchers' Smiths Karrier Bantam Mobile Shop, with flat spun hubs, in a blue box with a folded leaflet.

£400-500   **VEC**

A Corgi No.803 'The Beatles' Yellow Submarine, in yellow with a red front and rear hatches, in an inner plastic stand and picture window box.

£400-500   **VEC**

A Corgi No.207m Standard Vanguard, in yellow with flat spun hubs, in a blue box with a colour folded leaflet.

£300-400   **VEC**

A CLOSER LOOK AT A CORGI MONKEEMOBILE CAR

Corgi made the 'Monkeemobile' between 1968 and 1972, at the height of the TV pop group's popularity.

This car was also sold in a box without a header card. The version with the card tends to command a premium.

The theme of the car appeals to fans of cult TV and retro collectors as well as Dinky enthusiasts. This increases its desirability and value.

The car featured figures of Mike, Mickey, Davey and Pete. During the 1960s Corgi were known for producing especially detailed models.

A Corgi No.277 The Monkees 'Monkeemobile' car, with a red body, white roof and blue and yellow windows, cast hubs, the box with a colourful detachable header card.

£1,000-1,500   **VEC**

A Corgi No.422 'Corgi Toys' Bedford van, with flat spun hubs, in a blue and yellow box with a folded leaflet.

£600-700   **VEC**

A Corgi No.1109 Bristol Bloodhound guided missile, on a loading trolley, with an inner carded tray and blue and yellow lift-off lid box, complete with correct 'Rocket Age' folded leaflet.

£300-400   **VEC**

A Corgi No.GS31 'Riviera' gift set, with a Buick in pale blue, with a red interior and wire wheels, a boat on a trailer, and a figure and Skier on skis, pictorial stand, packing, box and instruction sheet.

£400-500   **VEC**

A Corgi No.303s Mercedes Benz 300SL Open Roadster, in blue with a yellow interior, figure, spun hubs and racing number "7", in inner packing ring and blue and yellow box.

£250-300   **VEC**

A Corgi No.300 Austin Healey sports car, in cream with red seats and flat spun hubs, in blue box with colour folded leaflet.

£500-600   **VEC**

SCHUCO

- German factories led the toy market for much of the 19thC and early 20thC, and Schuco was one of the country's most influential firms.
- The company was established as Schreyer & Co. in 1912 by Heinrich Schreyer and Heinrich Muller, who had worked at Bing.
- Despite mass producing toys for a wide range of markets, Schuco is known for the relative high quality of its products.
- Vehicles, such as cars, fire engines and lorries, tended to be highly detailed and were sold with accessories. Boxes were well-made with fitted compartments.
- Look out for the pre-war gear-operated open Mercedes, the rare 'Turn-About Motor Car' of 1935, the 'Radio-Auto' and Sir Malcolm Campbell's 'Bluebird'.
- Vehicles were marked on the base plate. Examples produced between 1945 and 1952 read "Made in the US zone Germany", while later models are marked "Made in Germany".
- The company is still in production today.

A Schuco tinplate No.5306 Elektro-Fernlenk truck, based on the MAN Diesel open lorry, with a red cab, dropdown rear tailgate and electric operation, in an illustrated box, wear.

13.75in (35cm) wide

£300-400 VEC

A Schuco tinplate No.6084 Elektro Lastomat truck, based on the MAN Diesel open lorry, in various shades of red, with a black chassis and electrically operated loading ramp, wear, missing parts.

14.25in (36cm) wide

£150-200 VEC

A Schuco tinplate No.6080 fire engine presentation set, with a turntable ladder and a long bonnet, two firemen figures in cab, steering control, battery compartment, in box with a card base, parts missing.

11.75in (30cm) wide

£800-1,200 VEC

A Schuco tinplate fire engine, with a turntable ladder and a long bonnet, back rest, silver platform and four-sectional ladder, plated parts, missing elements, wear.

11.75in (30cm) wide

£400-600 VEC

A Schuco tinplate No.5720 Mercedes Hydro-car sports car, with an open top, battery operation and plated parts, lacks control wire and accessories, box for No.5311.

10.25in (26cm) wide

£500-600 VEC

A Schuco tinplate No.2095 Mercedes 190 SL sports car, with a printed dashboard, clockwork operation and plated parts, missing cable, illustrated card box.

9in (23cm) wide

£150-200 VEC

A Schuco tinplate No.5509 Mercedes Elektro Razzia police car, with plated parts, clockwork and battery operation and two interior policeman figures, in an illustrated box with key and instructions.

8.75in (22cm) wide

£200-300 VEC

A Schuco tinplate No.5720 Electro Hydro-car sports car, with a printed dashboard, steering wheel, opening boot with battery compartment and remote control wire, with two wooden bollards, in correct box.

10.25in (26cm) wide

£700-1,000 VEC

A Schuco tinplate No.5307 Mercedes 230SL electric sports car, with ignition key, printed dashboard and plated parts, battery compartment, in a card box, lacks control cable.

11in (28cm) wide

£500-600 VEC

A Schuco tinplate No.4003 combination car, in beige with a red interior and clockwork operation, key, some wear.

8in (20cm) wide

£400-500 VEC

A Schuco tinplate No.5509 Elektro Razzia car, with clockwork and battery operation, red revolving roof beacon and plated parts, with two plastic uniformed figures, illustrated card box.

9in (23cm) wide

£400-600 VEC

An Arnold tinplate No.2500 military jeep, with clockwork operation and key, dashboard mounted semaphore, jerry can and three figures, card box.

6.75in (17cm) wide

£700-1,000 VEC

An Arnold tinplate No.11500 lorry-mounted crane, with an orange cab and body, detailed tin printed interior, on an illustrated card box with instructions slip, wear.

10.25in (26cm) wide

£400-600 VEC

An Arnold tinplate MAN diesel breakdown lorry, with a long bonnet, pale yellow plastic cab and detailed tin printed interior, plated parts and friction drive, light wear and retouching.

12.5in (32cm) wide

£500-700 VEC

An Arnold tinplate container lorry, with control cab and friction drive, the wheeled plastic tank with "Esso" to sides, light wear, hard to find variation.

11in (28cm) wide

£500-700 VEC

An Arnold tinplate DAF high-sided open-backed truck, with a long wheel base, drop down tailgate and red hubs, a rare friction drive model, in a plain card box.

17.25in (44cm) wide

£500-700 VEC

An Arnold tinplate Dutch Post Office delivery van, in yellow and light grey with opening rear door, friction drive and plated parts, printed interior, light wear.

11.75in (30cm) wide

£500-700 VEC

EARLY TINPLATE TOYS

TINPLATE

- Tinplate was the most widely used toy material from c1850.
- German factories, such as Lütz, Rock & Gräner, Tipp & Co., Bing and Märklin, led the tinplate market during the late 19thC and early 20thC. Early hand-painted German toys were made to high standards and are among the most sought-after today.
- 'Penny toys', produced inexpensively in the early 20thC and sold by street vendors throughout Europe, are also collectable. Look for early complex examples in good condition and by a recognised maker, such as Meier, Distler or Fischer.
- By the end of WWI, tinplate designs had generally become less complex and lithography had replaced painted decoration.
- After the 1930s, the American Marx company became the world's largest toy manufacturer and produced popular tinplate models.
- Japan established its own toy industry after WWII and successfully reached European markets with its exciting array of new and cheap products.
- By the late 1960s plastic had largely replaced tinplate.

An early Bing tinplate Kiddy Phone Junior Gramophone, with clockwork operation, turntable, stylus and key, selection of early records and a tin of HMV stylus needles, the horn detached.

Gebruder Bing, one of best known tinplate makers, made several of these children's gramophones.

£120-180 VEC

A rare Branko tinplate clockwork acrobat, with a celluloid doll and original box.

c1920

16in (40.5cm) high

£500-700 BEJ

A Bub tinplate limousine, with driver and battery-operated motor, in green with chromolithography decoration and two faux lamps.

Limousines are particularly popular with collectors.

10.75in (27cm) wide

£800-1,200   LAN

A CLOSER LOOK AT A MÄRKLIN ZEPPELIN

This airship is made by Märklin, one of best known tinplate toy manufacturers.

The D-LZ-127 Graf Zeppelin was launched in 1928 and set a number of flying records. The historical interest of this and other airships makes items depicting them desirable.

The hand-painted rather than lithographed finish suggests an early date and increases the value.

The airship is complete with its box and has a working movement. It therefore commands a premium.

A Märklin 'Zeppelin D-LZ 127' hand-painted airship, with working movement, propeller and original hangings, in original box.

16in (40cm) wide

£3,000-5,000   LAN

A DRG tinplate wind-up musical model of Cologne Cathedral, with lithographed detail, plays church-organ-style music when handle is rotated, the box with colourful illustration to lid.

6.75in (17cm) high

£200-300   VEC

A DRG tinplate 'Buckingham Palace' clockwork diorama, with Coldstream Guards marching at Palace gates on operation, in an illustrated box.

8.75in (22cm) wide

£500-700   VEC

An unusual DRG tinplate 'Hitler's Palace' clockwork diorama, modelled as Buckingham Palace, with German sentries holding rifles and marching on operation, includes key.

£600-900   VEC

An S. Guntherman tinplate clockwork double decker bus, with printed decoration, some rubbing and wear.

13.75in (35cm) wide

£600-900   SWO

A Lehmann No.445 'Tame Seal' model, hand-painted, the movement in working order, with original key.

7.5in (19cm) wide

£300-400   LAN

A Lehmann No.770 'Express Boy' with cart, chromolithographed decoration.

6.5in (16cm) wide

£250-300   LAN

A Märklin No.1151 constructor low-wing monoplane, with lithographed decoration and "D-ALBA", tail fatigue, in original box with instruction manual.

21in (53cm) wide

£500-700   GORL

A large 1950s Marx tinplate clockwork racing car, with single seat and driver.

13.5in (34.5cm) wide

£300-400 W&W

A Modern Toys tinplate 'Moon Explorer' vehicle, with clear perspex cockpit and tinplate astronaut, battery operated with mystery action, light wear, Japan.

14.25in (36cm) wide

£180-220 VEC

A rare Rock & Graner tinplate castle landscape, with rope bridge and lake with fountain, hand-painted, partly restored.

11.5in (29 cm) wide

£800-1,200 LAN

A TN Toys tinplate and plastic Pinocchio with xylophone, battery operated and lithographed, in an illustrated card box, Japan, dated, damage.

1962 *9in (23cm) high*

£200-300 VEC

A TN Toys tinplate 'Bartender' toy, the figure makes a cocktail on battery operation, with smoke and sound effects, in illustrated box with card inserts, Japan.

11.75in (30cm) high

£50-70 VEC

A tinplate clockwork figure at a snooker table, lacks ball and accessories, man's arm detached but present.

£120-180 VEC

ROBOTS

A rare Yoshiya 1950s tinplate 'Planet Robot', with battery-operated remote control box and cable, light corrosion, Japan.

8.75in (22cm) high

£400-600 VEC

An early Ideal plastic 'Robert the Robot', with manual remote control operating movement and voice, card box, lacks antenna, USA.

13.75in (35cm) high

£120-180 VEC

A Horikawa tinplate 'Swivel-o-matic Astronaut', battery operated, with firing guns, in an illustrated card box, Japan.

11.5in (29cm) high

£180-220 VEC

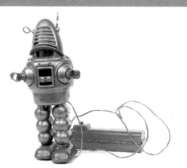

An early Marx tinplate and plastic 'Mr Mercury' robot, with battery operated remote control and sponge pads to hands, light wear.

c1960 *13in (33cm) high*

£400-600 VEC

An SH Toys for Horikawa tinplate 'Fighting Robot', battery operated, in a colourful illustrated box, small crack, Japan.

11.5in (29cm) high

£200-300 VEC

An SH Toys tinplate 'Attacking Martian' robot, battery operated, with plastic lights to front, in a colourfully illustrated box, Japan.

11.5in (29cm) high

£120-180 VEC

An early Britains 'The Mikado' flywheel toy, in brightly painted hollow-cast lead, with parasol, paper fan missing.

4in (10cm) high

£300-500 **GORL**

A rare Britains diecast No.234 'The Meet' hunt set, with nine mounted huntsmen and women and nine hounds, in original box.

£400-600 **W&W**

A rare Britains diecast No.235 'Full Cry' hunt set, with seven huntsmen and women, 12 hounds and a fox, in original box.

£500-700 **W&W**

An Excella 'Walt Disney's Three Little Pigs and the Big Dad Wolf', in hollow-cast lead, painted, original box.

c1935-40 *wolf 3in (8cm) high*

£600-900 **GORL**

An early Johillco 'Miniature Fire Engine', with six firemen and bell, in original card box, wear.

3.5in (9cm) wide

£120-180 **W&W**

A rare Meccano early No.5A accessory outfit, with "Meccano 5A" in gold to outside and inside of lid, in correct wooden box.

c1915

£80-120 **VEC**

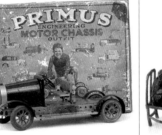

A Rare Primus Engineering 'Motor Chassis Outfit', constructed in metal and wood, with screen, mud guards and very rare AA badge, in original box with rare instructions.

£200-300 **VEC**

A Taylor and Barrett 'Chimpanzees' Tea Party', with three chimpanzees and a zoo keeper, in original labelled box.

Chimpanzees 1in (2.5cm) high

£180-220 **GORL**

A rare Spot-On No.116 'Caterpillar D9 bulldozer', in standard yellow, with original rubber tyres, the blade in working order, in box with data sheet and packing.

£800-1,200 **W&W**

A rare 19thC French wooden hand-painted diorama, with a Chinese castle, and firing war ships.

39.25in (98cm) wide

£500-700 **LAN**

A Scandinavian wooden toy horse, with a rich patina, some wear.

c1890 *3in (7.5cm) wide*

£600-700 **BEJ**

A wooden puppet, with a carved head and dressed as a pierrot.

c1890 *18in (45.5cm) high*

£500-700 **BEJ**

TOYS, DOLLS & MODELS

A Bing for Bassett-Lowke 1-gauge L&NWR No.44 'Precursor' tank locomotive, clockwork, complete with winding handle, wear.

£600-900 VEC

A CLOSER LOOK AT A BASSETT-LOWKE LOCOMOTIVE

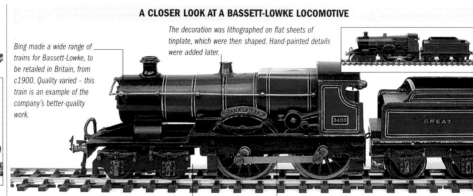

Bing made a wide range of trains for Bassett-Lowke, to be retailed in Britain, from c1900. Quality varied - this train is an example of the company's better-quality work.

The decoration was lithographed on flat sheets of tinplate, which were then shaped. Hand-painted details were added later.

As a relatively early Bing train, the bearings and springs are visible outside, rather than within, the wheels.

Look out for repainting and replacement part as these will reduce value.

A Bing for Bassett-Lowke 4-4-0 No.3433 'City of Bath' locomotive and tender, in Great Western green, clockwork, with nameplate and running number "3433", wear and crazing.

£6,000-8,000 VEC

A Bassett-Lowke O-gauge 4-6-2 LMS No.6232 'Duchess of Montrose' locomotive and tender, 12v electric, with LMS lettering, some restoration and repainting.

£1,000-1,500 VEC

A Bassett-Lowke 2-6-0 LNER No.33 'Mogul' locomotive and tender, 12v DC electric, with running number "33".

£500-700 VEC

A Bing cast iron 1-gauge 2-B steam locomotive and '1012' tender, hand-painted, with cow catcher and bell, working movement, restored.

£300-400 LAN

A Craigard Railway Collection 4-6-2 LMS No.6200 'The Princess Royal' locomotive and tender, three-rail Electric, skate pick-up, some repainting.

£1,000-1,500 VEC

HORNBY

- Established in 1907 by Frank Hornby, the Hornby company initially concentrated on producing Meccano construction toys.
- A range of 0-gauge trains were introduced in 1920. Trains made before 1923 had a simple nut and bolt construction, while Hornby Series trains made after this time were tinplate.
- From 1925 trains were made with clockwork and electric motors. Clockwork motors were phased out after WWII.
- In 1938, the smaller Hornby Dublo 00-guage range was launched. Locomotives had diecast bodies and were well-made and more affordable. They became the most popular toy train.
- Pre-war Hornby Dublo is hard to come by and can be identified by its blue boxes with date codes and distinctive coupling.
- Southern Railway trains are the most popular with collectors and tend to fetch higher prices.
- Sets that have not been played with command a premium.
- Hornby still produces trains, largely for the collector market.

A Hornby O-Gauge 0-4-0 No.1 Southern B343 Special locomotive and tender, clockwork, retouching and coupling replaced.

£700-1,000 VEC

A Hornby O-Gauge E320 Riviera train set, consisting of a 20v electric 4-4-2 No.3 locomotive and tender, two coaches, 12 pieces of electric three-rail track, three boxes of connecting plates and one corridor connector, in box.

£1,500-2,000 VEC

A Hornby O-guage 4-4-0 No.2 Special 'Yorkshire' locomotive and No.234 LNER tender, clockwork, some restoration and re-wheeled.

£1,200-1,800   VEC

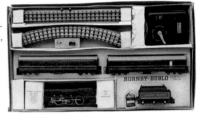

A Hornby Dublo 'EDP2' passenger train set, with a 4-6-2 Canadian Pacific locomotive, tender and coaches, instructions dated "7/52".

This train, a British 'Duchess of Atholl' in Canadian colours for the Canadian market, was a financial disaster.

£1,000-1,500   VEC

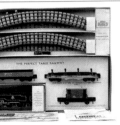

A Hornby Dublo EDG16 tank goods train set, with a 2-6-4 BR black standard class tank No.80054 locomotive, bogie brick wagon and bolster wagon, BR brake Van and track, instructions dated "9/54", boxed.

£500-700   VEC

A Pre-WWII Hornby Dublo LNER Gresley teak 1st/3rd Coach, with minor rusting around windows and some bare metal parts.

The Gresley was one of the first Hornby Dublo issues.

£120-180   VEC

A Hornby O-Gauge No.2 Special Pullman set, with a 4-4-0 locomotive and tender, clockwork, an early version with "Hornby Made in England limited Liverpool" transfer to front, with two Pullman coaches, box, guarantee and instructions, dated "11/29".

£2,000-3,000   VEC

A Hornby O-Gauge 4-4-0 No.2 locomotive and 'L1' "Southern 1759" tender, 20v electric, overpainting.

£1,000-1,500   VEC

A Hornby O-Gauge 0-4-0 No.1 Special tank locomotive, in green with "Southern 516", clockwork.

£500-700   VEC

A Hornby O-Gauge 0-4-0 No.1 Special tank locomotive, with "Southern A129", clockwork.

This version was only issued in 1929 and 1930.

£2,500-3,000   VEC

MÄRKLIN TRAINS

- The German Märklin company produced high quality and expensive toys from 1859. It introduced regular gauge trains at the 1891 Leipzig toy fair.
- After 1900, Märklin trains became more realistic and sophisticated.
- Electric motors were introduced in 1898.
- Live steam trains are fairly rare. Produced for only a short time around 1900, they were dangerous and messy.
- Trains can often be dated by the coupling. A tin loop was used 1904-1909, a hook was used 1909-1913 and, between 1913 and 1954, a sliding drop was used.
- A wide range of buildings and other accessories were produced. Post-WWI examples tend to be less detailed.
- After WWI, Märklin produced trains for all levels of the market. Collectors look for high quality realistic examples.
- Early paintwork had a tendency to craze. By the 1930s, paint was finely applied.
- The guage was changed from '00' to a smaller 'H0' in 1948.
- Märklin is still in production today.

A Märklin 1-gauge 2-B steam 'Queen of Scots' locomotive 1443 and a 3-A LNER tender, electric, painted in green, wear.

£400-500   LAN

A Märklin 1-gauge 2-B steam locomotive EE1021 and a 4-A tender, electric, with two electrified headlights, one tender cover missing.

£400-600   LAN

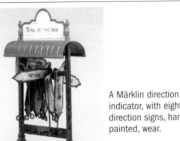

A Märklin direction indicator, with eight direction signs, hand-painted, wear.

8.75in (22cm) high

£180-220   LAN

A Märklin 1-gauge mail carriage 1802, hand-painted in green, with gothic windows, replaced footboards.

4.75in (12cm) wide

£200-300   LAN

A Märklin 1-gauge canvas-covered carriage, hand-painted in green, with three wax cows.

8.75in (22cm) wide

£200-300   LAN

TRAINS

A rare Märklin 1-gauge handcar 1100, hand-painted, with three original figures, the movement in working order, flags replaced, one hat restored.

£7,000-10,000   **LAN**

A Märklin 2-C-1 PLM steam locomotive H 64/13021 and a 4-A tender, electrified, hand-painted in green, two electrical headlights, cover of tender missing.

£3,000-4,000   **LAN**

A Märklin 1-gauge platform carriage 1766, carrying two cars, tinplate wheels, hand-painted.

9.75in (24.5cm) wide

£1,000-2,000   **LAN**

A Märklin 0-gauge carriage 1886, with 4-A tinplate wheels, no interior decoration.

8.5in (21.5cm) wide

£80-120   **LAN**

A Märklin 0-gauge luggage carriage 1846, hand-painted, with interior decoration and 4-A tinplate wheels, one axis and wheels missing, old finish, buffer replaced.

6.5in (16cm) wide

£800-1,200   **LAN**

A Märklin 0-gauge 2-B-1 tender locomotive TCE 66/12920, electric, partly restored.

£1,000-1,500   **LAN**

A Märklin 0-gauge 2-B-1 electro-locomotive CS 66/12920, chromolithographed, with two moving panthographes and two electric lanterns, some wear.

£1,500-2,000   **LAN**

A Märklin 0-gauge carriage 1983, with a Sarrasani animal cage and a lion, 2-A tinplate wheels, lion's tail missing.

6.5in (16.5cm) wide

£300-400   **LAN**

A Rocket and three wagon set, consisting of 0-2-2 locomotive and tender, three-rail electric, four-wheeled Liverpool to Manchester coach, four-wheeled two container open wagon and a flat wagon with Landau.

£1,500-2,000   **VEC**

A Triang D31 station set, part assembled, with a T32 island platform set labelled "Plymouth" and a T28 Engine Shed.

£50-70   **VEC**

A Trix No.1540 4-6-2 BR 'Scotsman' blue A3 class locomotive and tender No.60103, three-rail AC, with box and some internal packaging.

£300-400   **VEC**

A Trix No.244 diesel shunter three-rail Set, comprising 0-6-0 green shunter and shunter's match truck, box.

£150-200   **VEC**

A Wren W2296 (ins) 4-6-2 BR 'Dartmoor' West Country class locomotive and tender No.34021, box.

£500-600   **VEC**

A Wren W2278 (ins) 4-6-2 SR 'Blue Funnel' Wartime black Streamlined Merchant Navy class locomotive and tender No.21C13, box.

£400-500   **VEC**

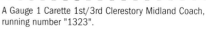

A Gauge 1 Carette 1st/3rd Clerestory Midland Coach, running number "1323".

£400-500   **VEC**

A Bing steam brewery, hand-painted, with two brew kettles and a small steam engine with boiler, on a wooden base, complete.

20in (50cm) wide

£8,000-12,000   **LAN**

A Bing steam factory, with working clockwork drive, in tinplate with chromolithographed and hand-painted decoration, on a wooden base.

9.25in (23cm) wide

£1,500-2,000   **LAN**

A Doll et Cie ship steam engine, hand-painted, with two boilers, two flights of stairs, two burners and a chimney, some losses and damage.

12in (30cm) wide

£1,000-1,500   **LAN**

A Kraus and Mohr steam engine, with boiler, boiler house and cylinder, on a wooden base, missing burner.

10.75in (27cm) wide

£1,000-2,000   **LAN**

A Markie live steam traction engine, approximately 1in scale, with a single cylinder and slip eccentric valve gear, spirit fired copper boiler with under tubes.

£700-1,000   **W&W**

A Markie live steam showman's tractor, approximately 1in scale, with a single cylinder and Stephenson's link valve gear, canopy with barley twist supports.

£800-1,200   **W&W**

A Märklin '4149/7' steam engine, hand-painted, with a boiler and a tiled base, complete with accessories, in original wooden box.

14in (34cm) wide

£1,000-1,500   **LAN**

A Schoenner locomotive, with boiler, one fly wheel with cylinder and outlet, complete with burner and chimney.

11.25in (28cm) wide

£4,000-5,000   **LAN**

A spirit locomotive, with brass boiler, chimney and a pair of tender wheels, burner missing, replaced parts to driver's cabin.

7.5in (19cm) wide

£500-700   **LAN**

CHESS & GAMES

A 19thC Jaques Staunton boxwood and ebony chess set, the white king stamped "Jaques London", wooden box with green label "Jaques & Son, London", label scuffed.

King 3.25in (8.5cm) high

£200-300   **CO**

A late 19thC English large weighted Staunton-style boxwood and ebonised chess set, in a mahogany hinged box with brass escutcheon plate, velvet interior.

King 4.75in (12cm) high

£1,000-1,500   **CO**

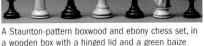

A Staunton-pattern boxwood and ebony chess set, in a wooden box with a hinged lid and a green baize interior.

King 4in (10cm) high

£600-900   **CO**

470

A Staunton-pattern weighted boxwood and ebony chess set, together with a 19thC leather covered chessboard.

King 4in (10cm) high

£500-700   CO

A 19thc Jaques Staunton ivory chess set, the white king stamped "Jaques London", the pieces with Victorian registration lozenges, with a Jaques Cartonpierre box with separate lid.

King 3.5in (9cm) high

£1,500-2,000   CO

A Jaques Staunton boxwood and ebony chess set, both kings stamped "Jaques London", boxed, some damage.

King 3.5in (9cm) high

£1,000-1,500   CO

An ivory Macao-type 'bust' chess set, probably Cantonese.

c1830   *King 3.5in (9cm) high*

£1,000-1,500   CO

An ivory Burmese-type chess set, probably Cantonese, boxed, the pieces varnished.

c1840   *King 3.5in (9cm) high*

£600-800   CO

An ivory Burmese-type chess set, probably Cantonese.

c1840   *King 3.25in (8.5cm) high*

£400-600   CO

An ivory Burmese-type set, Cantonese.

c1840   *King 4.25in (10.5cm) high*

£400-600   CO

A 20thC German large Volksteder porcelain 'Crusader' chess set, marked on underside of base.

King 7in (18cm) high

£3,000-4,000   CO

A Schoenhut Manufacturing Co. indoor golf game, with Tommy Green and Cissy Lofter figures, three clubs and balls, papier-mâché and wood hazards, sand traps, mounds and felt fairways, Philadelphia.

c1920

£1,000-1,500   FRE

A Victorian table croquet game, in original wooden box with pictorial chromolithographic label to inside of lid, with mallets, balls and other equipment.

£120-180   FRE

A Victorian mahogany travelling chess set, by Pearce and Maker, with inlaid chequering, and boxwood and ebony pieces.

8in (20.5cm) wide

£120-180   GORL

A Victorian boxwood and ebony chess set and board.

13in (33cm) wide

£100-150   MB

A boxed set of building bricks.

c1890   *box 18in (45.5cm) wide*

£100-150   BEJ

A boxed set of wooden ninepins with jack.

c1895   *pins 8in (20.5cm) high*

£120-180   BEJ

TRIBAL ART

THE TRIBAL ART MARKET

The higher end of the tribal art market has remained buoyant over the last year. Early, rare and fine pieces in good condition tend to perform extremely well at auction and can far exceed even optimistic sales estimates. Provenance is crucial. The most desirable pieces can be traced back, through prominent owners or museums, to the original point of collection by missionaries or military men. The market is polarised, however, and pieces in the £50-500 bracket can struggle to attract much interest.

The falling number of UK collectors is currently balanced by interest from the many serious European and American collectors who tend to favour sculptural pieces with classic forms. Casual buyers seeking attractive or striking pieces to decorate their homes, as well as professional interior designers, make up a large section of the market.

The market for ethnographic objects, including domestic items such as weapons, bowls and staffs, is continuing to grow. A Tsonga headrest from Mozambique that would have made around £100-200 ten years ago could well be worth over £1,000 today. As traditionally popular forms of tribal art become increasingly expensive, buyers on a smaller budget look for other types of object to invest in, such as Tanzanian art, which is currently enjoying greater interest.

Many of the better works of African tribal art are now to be found in Europe, as they were largely removed from the continent in the late 19th and early 20th century. Examples found in Africa today are recent and crude, or produced for the tourist market, or in poor condition due to termite damage.

Philip Keith

A rare prehistoric Anasazi Chaco upright pottery pitcher, decorated in black on a white ground with fine line designs, restored.

7in (18cm) high

£200-300   **ALL**

A prehistoric Anasazi water olla, of layered corrugated construction, cracked.

11.5in (29cm) high

£300-400   **ALL**

A small prehistoric Anasazi Salado Gila pottery olla, decorated in black and white on a red ground with a continuous geometric band, restored.

6in (15cm) high

£150-200   **ALL**

A prehistoric Anasazi Chaco pottery pitcher, decorated in black on a white ground, as excavated.

5in (12.5cm) high

£200-300   **ALL**

A prehistoric Pueblo Anasazi pottery olla, of speckled redware, with wide rim, as excavated.

10in (25.5cm) high

£200-300   **ALL**

A rare prehistoric Ho Ho Kam pottery water olla, with native repair.

14.5in (37cm) high

£150-200   **ALL**

A rare prehistoric Casas Grandes figural pottery vessel, with polychrome exterior design and human head effigy.

7.5in (19cm) high

£350-400   **ALL**

CHOKWE

- The Chokwe are made up of four sub-tribes living in Angola and the Democratic Republic of Congo, formerly called Zaire.
- Their history goes back to the 15thC, when an alliance between a Lunda queen and a Luba prince prompted a section of the Lunda aristocracy to resettle in what is now Angola.
- Chokwe society is administered by the Mwanangana, a ruler who apportions hunting and farming plots, supported by societies for male and female subjects called Mugonge and Ukule respectively.
- Art in Chokwe society is divided into two distinct schools. Folk art, for use in everyday family life, is made by craftsmen called Songi. Higher status artists, known as Fuli, craft artifacts for the royal court.
- Chokwe chief's chairs are based on Western forms – a consequence of contact with Portuguese colonialists. They are often elaborately carved symbols of power, with caryatid supports.
- A great deal of Chokwe figurative art depicts venerated ancestors. Typical subjects include the prince Tshibinda Ilunga and deceased Mwanangana.

A CLOSER LOOK AT A CHOKWE MASK

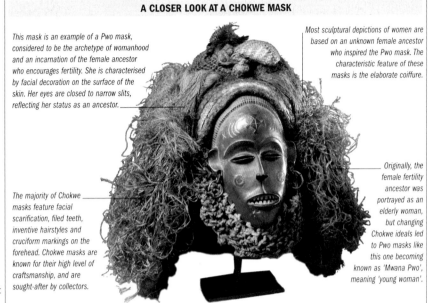

This mask is an example of a Pwo mask, considered to be the archetype of womanhood and an incarnation of the female ancestor who encourages fertility. She is characterised by facial decoration on the surface of the skin. Her eyes are closed to narrow slits, reflecting her status as an ancestor.

Most sculptural depictions of women are based on an unknown female ancestor who inspired the Pwo mask. The characteristic feature of these masks is the elaborate coiffure.

Originally, the female fertility ancestor was portrayed as an elderly woman, but changing Chokwe ideals led to Pwo masks like this one becoming known as 'Mwana Pwo', meaning 'young woman'.

The majority of Chokwe masks feature facial scarification, filed teeth, inventive hairstyles and cruciform markings on the forehead. Chokwe masks are known for their high level of craftsmanship, and are sought-after by collectors.

An early 20thC Chokwe mask, with a headdress made of loofah and an overlay of raffia hair.

12in (30cm) high

£4,000-6,000   **BLA**

A late 19thC Chokwe Pwo dance mask, from Angola or the Democratic Republic of Congo.

9in (22.5cm) high

£1,500-2,000   **BLA**

An early 20thC Chokwe dance mask, with elaborate hairstyle, keloid facial scarification patterns, remnants of kaolin pigment around the eyes and cruciform on forehead, from the Democratic Republic of Congo.

7.5in (19cm) high

£2,000-2,500   **BLA**

A late 19thC Chokwe carved wooden cane, from Angola.

33in (84cm) high

£500-800   **BLA**

An early 20thC Chokwe figure, from Angola.

9.25in (23.5cm) high

£400-500   **BLA**

An early 20thC wooden Chokwe chief's chair, from Angola.

£800-1,200   **BLA**

An early 20thC small carved Chokwe chief's chair, with enthronement scenes.

24.5in (61cm) high

£1,000-1,500   **BLA**

A mid-19thC wooden Kuba figure, from the Democratic Republic of Congo.

10.5in (26cm) high

£800-1,200   **BLA**

A late 19thC Kuba wooden medicine cup, from the Republic Democratic of Congo.

8.5in (21cm) high

£1,500-2,000   **BLA**

LUBA

- Luba artists and craftsmen carry a ceremonial axe as a symbol of their high status in society. Members of the clan with birth defects are thought to have a propensity for magic, and are often inducted into the artistic community for this reason.
- The Luba have a special reverence for women and believe that the clan was established by Vilie, a female spirit who assures fertility.
- Luba chieftains would offer women from their family lines as wives to neighbouring rulers, forging alliances cemented by female influence.
- When a Luba ruler died, his spirit traditionally transferred to a woman who would move into the deceased chief's residence and continue his reign by proxy.
- Luba stools, supported by a kneeling or standing female caryatid figure, are very distinctive. They are invariably carved from a single tree trunk and display a high degree of craftsmanship.
- The power of Luba rulers is demonstrated by flaunting art objects, including stools and canes. The coiffure and scarification patterns depicted on a chief's artifacts relate to his own prestige.

A 19thC Luba stool, supported by a female caryatid, from the Democratic Republic of Congo.

18in (45cm) high

£2,000-2,500   **BLA**

A late 19thC Luba Suku wooden fetish figure, from the Democratic Republic of Congo.

12.75in (32cm) high

£1,500-2,000   **BLA**

A late 19thC Luba male ancestral Hemba figure, from the Democratic Republic of Congo.

8in (20cm) high

£800-1,200   **BLA**

A late 19thC Luba ancestral wooden medicine cup, in the form of a woman, from the Democratic Republic of Congo.

6.25in (15.5cm) high

£200-300   **BLA**

An early 20thC Luba figure of a crouching woman, holding her breasts, from the Democratic Republic of Congo.

6.75in (17cm) high

£200-300   **BLA**

An early 20thC Luba stool, supported by female caryatids, from the Democratic Republic of Congo.

17.25in (43cm) high

£4,000-6,000   **BLA**

An early 20thC Luba stool, supported by a female caryatid, from the Democratic Republic of Congo.

6in (15cm) high

£1,200-1,800   **BLA**

An early 20thC wooden Luba chief's cane, with a bust in the form of a female figure, from the Democratic Republic of Congo.

59.5in (149cm) high

£500-800   **BLA**

An early 20thC Luba ceremonial wooden Kasai figure, in the form of a female, from the Democratic Republic of Congo.

12.5in (31cm) high

£500-700   **BLA**

An early 20thC Luba Hemba ancestral male figure, in wood, from the Democratic Republic of Congo.

12.75in (32cm) high

£4,000-6,000   **BLA**

An early 20thC Luba wooden female figure, from the Democratic Republic of Congo.

10in (25cm) high

£300-500   **BLA**

An early 20thC Luba Hemba stool, supported by a female caryatid, from the Democratic Republic of Congo.

12in (30cm) high

£800-1,200   **BLA**

An early 20thC eastern Pendé Giphogo ceremonial dance mask, in the form of a helmet, the wood decorated with mineral pigments, from the Democratic Republic of Congo.

10in (25.5cm) high

£2,000-3,000　　　**BLA**

An early 20thC Pendé chief's mask, with a woven raffia headdress, from the Democratic Republic of Congo.

18in (45cm) high

£800-1,200　　　**BLA**

An early 20thC wooden Pendé dance mask, decorated with mineral pigments, from the Democratic Republic of Congo.

10in (25.5cm) high

£500-800　　　**BLA**

An early 20thC Pendé mask, in wood and polychrome pigments, from the Democratic Republic of Congo.

10.5in (26cm) high

£500-800　　　**BLA**

An early 20thC Songyé Kifwébé mask, layered with kaolin and pigments, from the Democratic Republic of Congo.

£3,000-4,000　　　**BLA**

An early 20thC wooden Songyé fetish figure, from the Democratic Republic of Congo.

4.5in (11.5cm) high

£100-150　　　**BLA**

An early 20thC Songyé wooden initiation mask, the face covered with linear pigmented incisions, from the Democratic Republic of the Congo.

This is a very rare Songyé mask used for the initiation of adolescent boys. The abstract face is Cubist in form, with outsize eyes and a protruding mouth.

25.75in (64.5cm) high

£8,000-10,000　　　**BLA**

A late 19thC wooden Téké fetish figure, from the Democratic Republic of Congo.

15.5in (39cm) high

£1,800-2,200　　　**BLA**

A late 19thC wooden Téké fetish figure, from the Democratic Republic of Congo.

17.25in (43cm) high

£3,000-4,000　　　**BLA**

An early 20thC oblong wooden Téké fetish figure, from the Democratic Republic of Congo.

13.25in (33cm) high

£500-800　　　**BLA**

A Téké Fumu fetish, in wood with traces of white mineral pigments, from the Democratic Republic of Congo.

13.25in (33cm) high

£300-400　　　**BLA**

A late 19thC dance mask, from the Democratic Republic of Congo.

12.5in (31cm) high

£3,000-4,000   **BLA**

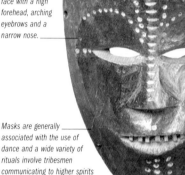

A CLOSER LOOK AT A NGBAKA DANCE MASK

Many African tribes believe masks to be the faces of gods and spirits. This mask conforms to an ideal of an aesthetically pleasing narrow, well-proportioned face with a high forehead, arching eyebrows and a narrow nose.

These scarification marks are a reference to bodily scarification, a process that holds important societal value in some tribes. A scarificator is used to pierce the skin and aid blood-letting, possibly as an initiation ritual or a way of preparing girls for the ordeal of childbirth.

Masks are generally associated with the use of dance and a wide variety of rituals involve tribesmen communicating to higher spirits through dance and song.

Masks were predominantly made from wood due to the large amount and variety of available timber. The carver of the mask would often undergo a purification ritual before the felling of a tree that was intended for a dance mask.

A rare early 20thC Ngbaka wooden dance mask, of Cubist form, from the Democratic Republic of Congo.

10.5in (26cm) high

£7,000-9,000   **BLA**

An early 20thC wooden Ngbaka dance mask, with facial scarification patterns, from the Democratic Republic of Congo.

10.5in (26cm) high

£7,000-9,000   **BLA**

An early 20thC oblong Lélé helmet mask, from the Democratic Republic of Congo.

18in (45cm) high

£1,000-1,500   **BLA**

An early 20thC Lega wooden chief's mask, decorated with white pigment, from the Democratic Republic of Congo.

7.25in (18cm) high

£300-400   **BLA**

An early 20thC Salampasu wooden dance mask, decorated with polychrome pigments, from the Democratic Republic of Congo.

10.75in (27cm) high

£1,500-2,000   **BLA**

A rare mid-19thC patinated Mbole ivory figure, from the Democratic Republic of Congo.

4.25in (10.5cm) high

£800-1,200   **BLA**

An early 20thC wooden Kongo fetish figure, from the Democratic Republic of Congo.

9in (22.5cm) high

£1,000-1,500   **BLA**

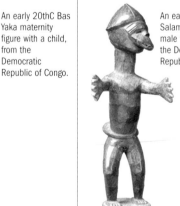

An early 20thC Bas Yaka maternity figure with a child, from the Democratic Republic of Congo.

£800-1,200   **BLA**

An early 20thC Salampasu wooden male figure, from the Democratic Republic of Congo.

11.5in (28.5cm) high

£600-900   **BLA**

An early 20thC wooden Vilie fetish, encrusted with mirror and metal splinters, form the Democratic Republic of Congo.

25.5in (63.5cm) high

£7,000-9,000 BLA

An early 20thC statue of a Kusu ancestral male figure, from the Democratic Republic of Congo.

18.75in (47cm) high

£3,000-4,000 BLA

An early 20thC Bassikassingo fetish figure, with an elongated oblong face terminating in a stylized beard, marked with sacrifice symbols, from the Democratic Republic of Congo.

14.5in (36cm) high

£800-1,200 BLA

An early 19thC ivory pounder, with carved geometric design, from the Democratic Republic of Congo.

£150-200 BLA

A wooden Yaka hand drum, the carved head with pierced ears, above an open cylinder, from the Democratic Republic of Congo.

11in (27.5cm) high

17in (42.5cm) high

£500-700 FRE

GABON

An early 20thC wooden Punu dance mask, decorated with kaolin pigments, from Gabon.

11.5in (29cm) high

£1,000-1,500 BLA

A 19thC iron and carved ivory Mangbetu battle knife, from the Central African Republic.

A late 19thC Kota reliquary figure, with oval face, crescent crest and lobed lateral flanges, all covered with brass, from Gabon.

16in (40cm) high

£800-1,200 BLA

22.5in (56.5cm) high

£5,000-7,000 BLA

An early 20thC miniature Punu wooden mask, from Gabon.

8in (20cm) high

£1,000-1,500 BLA

An early 20thC wooden Fang Byeri reliquary figure, from Gabon.

19.5in (48.5cm) high

£10,000-15,000 BLA

BURKINA FASO

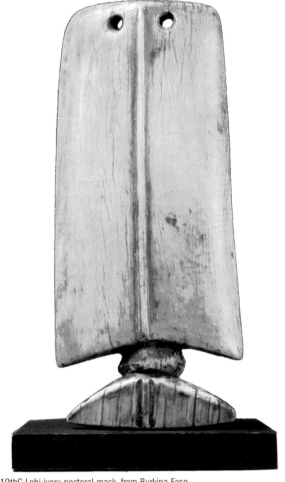

A 19thC Lobi ivory pectoral mask, from Burkina Faso.

8.5in (21cm) high

£3,000-4,000   **BLA**

An early 20thC wooden Bobo Molo dance mask, decorated with white and red paint, from Burkina Faso.

51.25in (128cm) high

£5,000-7,000   **BLA**

An early 20thC female Lobi wood carved figure, from Burkina Faso.

11.25in (28cm) high

£200-300   **BLA**

CAMEROON

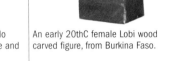

A mid-19thC Bamgwa chief's stool, from Cameroon.

13.25in (33cm) high

£300-500   **BLA**

A late 19thC wooden Bamiléké chief's stool, with traces of white pigment, from the Cameroon grasslands.

27.5in (69cm) high

£700-1,000   **BLA**

A Namji fertility figure, crafted from hard wood and decorated with metal, from Cameroon.

10.75in (27cm) high

£300-500   **BLA**

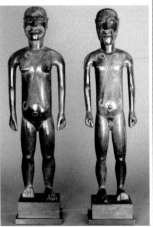

A pair of early 20thC Fang statues, made from exotic wood, from the border of Gabon and Cameroon.

14.75in (37cm) high

£3,000-4,000   **BLA**

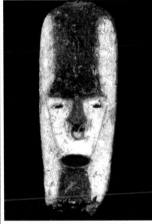

An early 20thC wooden Kwélé dance mask, with white kaolin pigment, from Gabon.

15.25in (38cm) high

£1,800-2,200   **BLA**

An early 20thC Bamiléké boubou, woven from hemp, from Cameroon.

52in (130cm) high

£700-1,000   **BLA**

BAOULÉ

- Originally from Ghana, the Baoulé people migrated westwards with their queen Aba Pokou when the Asante tribe rose to influence in their traditional territory during the 18thC.
- Now settled in the Ivory Coast, the Baoulé are one of the most prolific and culturally dominant tribes in Western Africa.
- Craftsmen used carved wood with gold and brass castings to produce an abundance of artwork including masks, statues and everyday decorative objects such as carved doors and boxes.
- The Baoulé use a variety of mask forms. One of them, known as Bonu Amwin, represents a buffalo head. Its heavy, stylized features inspired Picasso and the Cubist movement. Other mask types include the Goli festival mask, used to celebrate the harvest.
- Spirit statues have great importance in Baoulé culture. Asie Usu statues help ensure fruitful harvests and hunting, whereas Blolo Bian and Blolo Bla statues symbolize male and female spouses from the spirit world. These statues are characterised by detailed coiffures and keloid scarification marks.

A CLOSER LOOK AT A BAOULÉ MASK

This mask was made by the Baoulé people, who account for around a quarter of the population of the Ivory Coast. The Baoulé tribe was greatly influenced by the neighbouring Senufo and Guro tribes, particularly in the design of masks and figure carving.

This example is typical of a Baoulé mask, with its realistic rounded face, pointed chin, T-shaped nose, raised scarification marks, semi-circular eyes and distinctive coiffure.

This mask does not appear to have had a specific sacred function and was probably worn during festivals held for important dignitaries. The ownership of masks was usually restricted to powerful and specially trained individuals and families.

Masks were designed for specific people and it was believed that when a person's face came into contact with the inside of a mask, the individual would become the entity that the mask represented. It was therefore dangerous for others to wear ceremonial masks because each one had received an individual's soul.

A 19thC wooden Baoulé mask, representing a dignitary, with scarification marks, from the Ivory Coast.

9.75in (24.5cm) high

£3,000-4,000   **BLA**

An early 20thC hardwood Baoulé or Guro mask, with traces of vegetable and mineral pigments, from the Ivory Coast.

16.5in (41cm) high

£800-1,200   **BLA**

A late 19thC male Baoulé Blolo Bian figure, from the Ivory Coast.

21.5in (54cm) high

£3,000-4,000   **BLA**

A late 19thC Baoulé figure of a dignitary or important ancestor, from the Ivory Coast.

17.5in (44cm) high

£1,000-1,500   **BLA**

An early 20thC abstract Baoulé figure, from the Ivory Coast.

8.25in (20.5cm) high

£200-300   **BLA**

An early 20thC Baoulé anthropomorphic Blolo Bla figure, from the Ivory Coast.

16.75in (42cm) high

£1,000-1,500   **BLA**

An early 20thC Baoulé wooden masculine figure, from the Ivory Coast.

18.75in (47cm) high

£500-700   **BLA**

An early 20thC Baoulé wooden figure, from the Ivory Coast.

13.25in (33cm) high

£500-800   **BLA**

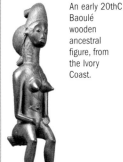

A pair of early 20thC ancestral Baoulé figures, from the Ivory Coast.

20in (50cm) high

£5,000-7,000   **BLA**

An early 20thC Baoulé wooden ancestral figure, from the Ivory Coast.

18.5in (46.5cm) high

£2,000-3,000   **BLA**

An early 20thC Baoulé wooden figure, from the Ivory Coast.

13.25in (33cm) high

£500-800   **BLA**

TRIBAL ART

DAN MASKS

- The characteristic features of Dan masks include a concave face, protruding mouth and high-domed forehead.
- The rich brown patina on these masks is achieved by applying vegetable extracts. Once dry, these extracts act like a varnish or lacquer, imparting a dark hue to the wood.
- Most Dan masks are produced and kept by powerful societies such as Poro, a men's society, and Sande, a secret women's society.
- As well as ritual and ceremonial use, Dan masks are used for education and entertainment. They also provide an important social function by helping to arbitrate in disagreements.
- Dan masks are vessels for an essence known as 'du', bestowed by the creator god Zlan on all living things. Bodiless du appear in dreams to initiates of Dan societies to reveal how they want to be represented.
- The business of bridging the gap between the village and the dark forest, where the formless du reside, is considered very dangerous in Dan society, and is therefore a serious undertaking.

A CLOSER LOOK AT A DAN MASK

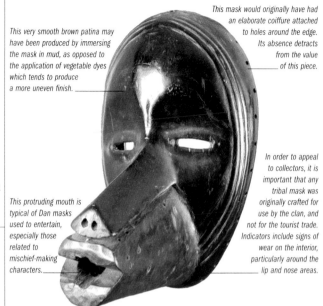

This very smooth brown patina may have been produced by immersing the mask in mud, as opposed to the application of vegetable dyes which tends to produce a more uneven finish.

This mask would originally have had an elaborate coiffure attached to holes around the edge. Its absence detracts from the value of this piece.

This protruding mouth is typical of Dan masks used to entertain, especially those related to mischief-making characters.

In order to appeal to collectors, it is important that any tribal mask was originally crafted for use by the clan, and not for the tourist trade. Indicators include signs of wear on the interior, particularly around the lip and nose areas.

An early 20thC anthropozoomorphic wooden Dan mask, from the Ivory Coast.

9.75in (24.5cm) high

| £1,000-1,500 | | BLA |

A Dan mask, from the Ivory Coast.

c1870	9.5in (24cm) high
£3,000-5,000	JBB

A late 19thC Dan mask, from the Ivory Coast or Nigeria.

16in (40cm) high

| £1,500-2,000 | BLA |

A late 19thC Dan mask, from Liberia.

10in (25cm) high

| £800-1,200 | BLA |

An early 20thC Dan mask, from the Ivory Coast.

9.5in (24cm) high

| £300-500 | BLA |

An early 20thC Dan dance mask, from the Ivory Coast.

8.5in (21cm) high

| £300-400 | BLA |

An early 20thC wooden Dan mask, from the Ivory Coast.

8in (20cm) high

| £500-800 | BLA |

A carved wood Dan mask, of hollowed oval form, pierced around the rim for attachments, with pointed chin, broad mouth, pierced slit eyes, traces of kaolin, cowrie shell, and yellow trade bead attachments.

10.5in (27cm) high

| £200-300 | SK |

A carved wood Dan mask, of hollowed oval form, pierced around the rim for attachments, with pierced protruding mouth, triangular nose, narrow pierced eyes, incised frame lines and a dark patina.

9.25in (23.5cm) high

| £200-300 | SK |

A late 19thC male wooden Dan figure of an ancestor, from the Ivory Coast.

21.25in (53cm) high

| £1,800-2,200 | BLA |

An early 20thC Dan figure, from the Ivory Coast or Liberia.

10.25in (25.5cm) high

£700-1,000　　　　**BLA**

An early 20thC male Dan figure, from the Ivory Coast.

18in (45cm) high

£800-1,200　　　　**BLA**

A mid-19thC Bambara ritual mask, from Mali.

12.75in (32cm) high

£800-1,200　　　　**BLA**

An early 20thC wooden Marka Bambara dance mask, with hammered brass, from Mali.

11.25in (28cm) high

£3,000-4,000　　　　**BLA**

An early 20thC Bambara dance mask, from Mali.

11.5in (29cm) high

£500-800　　　　**BLA**

An early 20thC ceremonial Bambara mask, the eyes marked by porcelain pieces, with applied mirror splinters, from Mali.

21.5in (54cm) high

£2,500-3,000　　　　**BLA**

An early 20thC anthropozoomorphic Bambara wooden mask, from Mali.

£800-1,200　　　　**BLA**

25.25in (63cm) high

An early 20thC Bambara dance mask, from Mali.

11.25in (28cm) high

£400-600　　　　**BLA**

An early 20thC female Bambara figure, from Mali.

24.75in (62cm) high

£1,800-2,200　　　　**BLA**

A 19thC carved wood female Dogon figure, with traces of ritual marks, from Mali.

11.5in (29cm) high

£800-1,200　　　　**BLA**

A 19thC hermaphrodite Dogon Nommo figure, with traces of sacrificial marks, from Mali.

11.5in (29cm) high

£500-800　　　　**BLA**

A 19thC Dogon or proto-Dogon autel, representing a Nommo with bowl, from Mali.

9.5in (24cm) high

£500-800　　　　**BLA**

A late 19thC Dogon maternity figure, from Mali.

15in (37.5cm) high

£1,800-2,200　　　　**BLA**

A late 19thC Dogon door lock, from Mali.

20in (50cm) high

£700-1,000   **BLA**

A late 19thC Dogon carved wood hermaphrodite figure, from Mali.

19.25in (48cm) high

£2,000-3,000   **BLA**

An early 20thC Dogon wooden mask, from Mali.

The symbolism behind Dogon masks is a closely guarded secret, available only to initiates of the secret mask societies.

29.25in (73cm) long

£2,200-2,800   **BLA**

NIGERIA

An early 20thC Eket hardwood dance mask, from Nigeria.

6.5in (16.5cm) high

£200-300   **BLA**

An early 20thC Eket wooden solar mask, from Nigeria.

6.5in (16.5cm) high

£800-1,200   **BLA**

A monolithic Ekoi stone sculpture, depicted with scarification patterns.

42.75in (107cm) high

£8,000-12,000   **BLA**

A late 19thC wooden Ekoi ritual dance head, decorated with paint and bronze, from Nigeria.

14.5in (36cm) high

£500-800   **BLA**

A late 19thC Ekoi Janus helmet mask, the wooden base covered with leather, from Nigeria.

23.5in (59cm) high

£3,000-5,000   **BLA**

A pair of Ibeji carved wood figures, one with beaded belt, the other with beaded necklace.

10.5in (26cm) high

£150-200   **FRE**

A set of three Ibeji carved wood figures, all with beaded necklaces, two with beaded belts.

11in (27.5cm) high

£300-500   **FRE**

An early 20thC Idoma ritual female figure, from Nigeria.

32.5in (81cm) high

£6,000-8,000   **BLA**

An early 20thC Idoma painted wooden dance mask, on a cane stand.

14.5in (36cm) high

£800-1,200   **BLA**

A rare early 20thC Ijo wooden dance crest, from Nigeria.

21.75in (54.5cm) long

BLA

An early 20thC Ijo wooden ceremonial crest, from Nigeria.

25.5in (64cm) high

£500-700   **BLA**

An early 20thC wooden female Mumuye figure, from Nigeria.

45.5in (114cm) high

£5,000-8,000   **BLA**

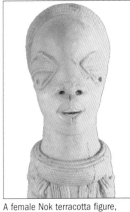

A standing carved Mumuye-style figure, with angular legs, cylindrical torso and abstract head with helmet-like headdress, overall dark patina, on a black wooden base.

38.5in (96cm) high

£300-500   **FRE**

A Katsina pottery head, from Nigeria.

cAD100   *6.75in (17cm) high*

£700-1,000   **BLA**

A Nok clay terracotta head, from Sokoto in Nigeria.

cAD200   *20in (51cm) high*

£4,000-5,000   **BLA**

A female Nok terracotta figure, from Nigeria.

32.75in (82cm) high

£15,000-20,000   **BLA**

A Nok terracotta head, on a stand, from Nigeria.

4.75in (12cm) high

£500-800   **BLA**

A rare Sokoto terracotta bust, from Nigeria.

c200BC   *16in (40cm) high*

£1,000-1,500   **BLA**

A CLOSER LOOK AT A NOK TERRACOTTA FIGURE

Remnants of the Nok civilisation were discovered in 1943 in tin mines located near the town of Nok in Nigeria. All of the archeological finds from this area have been dated between 500BC and AD300.

These mysterious terracotta sculptures are of great artistic quality, and are valued very highly by collectors.

This sculpture is of typical Nok style, characterised by the full-length figure, elongated head, high smooth forehead, eyes with linear upper and curved lower brows and distinctive coiffure. The bodies are often decorated with rows of terracotta necklaces.

The exact function of these sculptures is unknown, but the huge variety of Nok terracotta artifacts indicates various uses. One function may have been to mark graves, and these sculptures may have represented Nok deities, acting as intermediary icons.

A seated Nok terracotta figure, from Nigeria.

12in (30.5cm) high

£3,000-4,000   **BLA**

A 19thC Yoruba Ibeji male figure, made from cauri wood, decorated with fibres and imported pearls.

10.5in (26cm) high

£300-500   **BLA**

An early 20thC ivory Yoruba sceptre, with concentric decoration and a central figure of a kneeling female, from Nigeria.

11.25in (28cm) high

£300-500   **BLA**

An early 20thC female Yoruba figure representing a priestess, from Nigeria.

30in (75cm) high

£3,000-4,000   **BLA**

A late 19thC Yoruba dance mask, from Nigeria.

34.75in (87cm) high

£3,000-4,000   **BLA**

YORUBA MATERNITY FIGURES

- The Yoruba people inhabit the southwest region of Nigeria and the Republic of Benin, in Africa. Yoruba civilisation is centred around the sacred city of Ife, which is considered the birthplace of all humanity and has a prestigious artistic heritage.
- Among the most celebrated Yoruba carvings are Ibjebu figures, representing deceased twins. The Yoruba region has the highest dizygotic twinning rate in the world, although premature births and living conditions mean high infant mortality. Yoruba maternity figures, signifying fertility and lineage, are therefore of great importance.
- The maternity figure represents the ideal of feminine beauty, fertility and character. The archetypal mother is often depicted seated, suckling an infant and surrounded by other children.
- The worship of these statues, by way of sacrificial ceremonies and offerings, appeases the maternal spirit and brings the Yoruba people many children and good fortune, particularly during pregnancy and labour.

An early 20thC Yoruba maternity fetish figure, with traces of blue indigo pigments on the hair, from Nigeria.

14.25in (35.5cm) high

£1,800-2,200   **BLA**

An early 20thC Yoruba Gelede dance mask, from Nigeria.

11.5in (29cm) high

£500-800   **BLA**

A Yoruba Shango carved wood staff, with a figure holding a drum with a traditional double axe form, from Nigeria.

19.5in (49cm) high

£1,000-1,500   **FRE**

A pair of Yoruba carved wood figures, each supported by a staff with leather straps and cowrie shells, with traces of white pigment, from Nigeria.

14.5in (36cm) high

£700-1,000   **FRE**

A late 19thC Ogoni bronze ritual Edan sceptre, from Nigeria.

9.25in (23cm) high

£800-1,200   **BLA**

A large early 20thC Wurkum Anyang hardwood dance mask, from the border of Nigeria and Cameroon.

42.75in (107cm) high

£1,800-2,200   **BLA**

An early 20thC wooden Igbo Alusi figure, from Nigeria.

42.75in (107cm) high

£1,500-2,000   **BLA**

An early 20thC Igbo wooden dance mask, from Nigeria.

9in (22.5cm) high

£500-800   **BLA**

An early 20thC wooden anthropomorphic Bassa mask, from Sierra Leone.

10in (25.5cm) high

£1,500-2,000   **BLA**

An early 20thC Mendé Bundu helmet dance mask, from Sierra Leone.

16in (40cm) high

£500-800   **BLA**

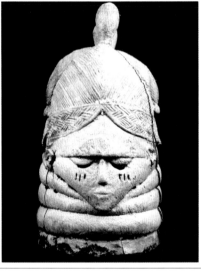

An early 20thC female Mendé dance mask, representing the head of a young high-ranking female, from Sierra Leone.

16in (40cm) high

£1,000-1,500   **BLA**

An early 20thC Baga wooden sculpture, from Sierra Leone.

11.75in (29.5cm) high

£300-500   **BLA**

An early 20thC archaic wooden Ashanti figure, from Ghana.

14in (35cm) high

£800-1,200   **BLA**

An early 20thC Ashanti wooden figure, from Ghana.

£800-1,200   **BLA**

An early 20thC Fon wooden depiction of Mami Wata, from Benin.

6in (15cm) high

£150-200   **BLA**

A late 20thC West African carved wood walking stick, the shaft with a ring-carved finial over two similar faces, terminating in a snake at the base of the shaft.

35in (87.5cm) long

£70-100   **FRE**

An early 20thC Zulu ceremonial war shield, of wood covered with buffalo hide and monkey skin, painted with pigments, from South Africa.

24in (61cm) high

£500-700   **BLA**

An early 20thC Zulu ceremonial shield, of wood covered with monkey skin and buffalo hide, from South Africa.

25.25in (64cm) high

£500-700   **BLA**

A carved Zulu female figure, with linear carving to the head and neck, from South Africa.

16in (40cm) high

£700-1,000   **FRE**

A late 19thC Mbunda wooden divinity figure, from Angola.

28in (71cm) high

£3,000-4,000   **BLA**

A Bapende carved wood mask, highlighted with pigments, from the Democratic Republic of Congo.

10in (25.5cm) wide

£40-60   **GORL**

A late 19thC Kwere wooden ancestor buti figure, from Tanzania.

15.5in (39.5cm) high

£3,000-5,000   **BLA**

An early 20thC wooden Makondé figure, from Tanzania or Mozambique.

33in (84cm) high

£2,000-2,500   **BLA**

A large carved wood drum, of hollow cylindrical form, with pegged animal hide skin, depicting a kneeling mother nursing an infant, with encrusted patina, damaged.

46in (117cm) high

£300-400   **SK**

MODERN AFRICAN ART

An African carved monkey, with bent knees, long cylindrical torso, heart-shaped face and carved teeth, standing on a base, damaged.

31in (79cm) high

£300-400   **SK**

A Bernard Matemera stone bust, unsigned.

15in (37.5cm) high

£500-700   **FRE**

A Fanizani Akuda stone bust, with carved signature "Fanizani".

13in (32.5cm) high

£300-400   **FRE**

A 20thC Luizi Purumero stone bust, with carved signature "Luizi".

16in (40cm) high

£300-400   **FRE**

An early 19thC Totokia carved wooden chief's war club, from Fiji.

The sharp beak was designed to deliver a fatal blow while preserving the enemy's skull as a trophy. The mass of the club head meant that even a weak swing was enough to kill a foe.

35.5in (90cm) high

£3,000-4,000   **BLA**

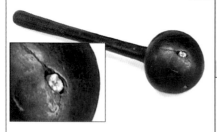

A Polynesian carved wood throwing club, with chip-carved hand grip, two teeth inlaid in the head and a dark patina, from Fiji.

14in (35.5cm) long

£300-400   **SK**

A Polynesian carved wood headrest, the long cylindrical form with flared ends, two sets of arched legs lashed on with braided fibres and dark patina, from Fiji.

28.5in (72.5cm) long

£300-400   **SK**

A Polynesian carved wood throwing club, with bulbous head, chip-carved handle and dark patina, from Fiji.

16in (40.5cm) long

£150-200   **SK**

A Fijian gunstock club and a Samoan club with serrated edge, elaborate chip-carving and dark patina, "Fana Fana" incised on the handle.

38in (96.5cm) long

£150-200   **SK**

A Polynesian carved wood throwing club, with a heavy bulbous head, chip-carved grip and dark patina, from Fiji.

15.5in (39.5cm) long

£200-300   **SK**

IRIAN JAYA

An early 20thC Asmat wooden pole, from Irian Jaya.

59.5in (151cm) high

£10,000-15,000   **BLA**

An early 20thC Asmat pole, from Irian Jaya.

43.25in (110cm) high

£500-700   **BLA**

An early 20thC carved wood gobi, from the Santini Lake area of Irian Jaya.

22.75in (57.5cm) high

£800-1,200   **BLA**

A 20thC tapa, from the Lake Sentani area of Irian Jaya.

27.5in (70cm) high

£1,000-1,500   **BLA**

An early 20thC Asmat ceremonial pole, from Irian Jaya.

47.5in (120.5cm) high

£800-1,200   **BLA**

MARQUESAS ISLANDS

An early 19thC carved wooden canoa stirrup, engraved with stylized and geometric motifs, from the Marquesas Islands.

These symbolic wooden stirrups were used by children and young adults for a sport that was practiced on stilts.

15in (38cm) high

£3,000-4,000   **BLA**

An early 19thC carved wooden canoa stirrup, shaped as a tiki figure, engraved with stylized and geometric motifs, from the Marquesas Islands.

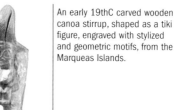

11.5in (29.5cm) high

£2,000-3,000   **BLA**

An early 19thC carved wooden canoa stirrup, shaped as a tiki figure, engraved with stylized and geometric motifs, from the Marquesas Islands.

13in (33cm) high

£1,500-2,000   **BLA**

MAORI

- The Maori people probably arrived in New Zealand from eastern Polynesia over a thousand years ago.
- Favoured materials for Maori art are timber from the toa and other native trees, whale bone and nephrite, a jade mineral known in New Zealand as 'greenstone'.
- Rival Maori sects were engaged in intermittent warfare for many years, and this is reflected in their art. Weapons reserved for the best warriors were decorated with representations of Tu Matuenga, the war deity.
- Hei-Tiki, or greenstone pendants, were among the first Maori artifacts given to Westerners. They generally represent stylized human figures, and have become symbolic of Maori culture.
- The art of Moari carving is known as Te Toi Whakairo, and is subject to Tapu, the series of laws that govern many aspects of traditional Maori culture.
- The lizard is the only animal to feature in Maori sculpture, and represents the fearsome god Whiro, representative of evil.

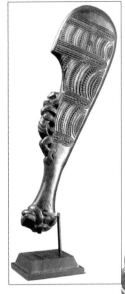

A late 19thC Maori Wahaika club, of toa wood, carved in relief with stylized motifs and incised ornament, with a dark glossy patina.

'Wahaika' is a Maori word that means 'mouth of the fish'. The first enemy killed in battle was often referred to as 'the first fish'.

A mid-19thC Maori greenstone Hei Tiki pendant, with pierced, bowed legs and arms and circular eyes filled with red wax.

6.25in (16cm) high

£3,000-4,000   **BLA**

14.5in (37cm) high

£3,000-4,000   **BLA**

A late 19thC Maori club, of toa wood, each side carved in relief with a Janus head and further incised ornament, with a dark glossy patina.

This end of the club would be used in a dummy attack against an enemy. The club would then be spun around to deliver a blow to the opponent's skull with the heavier end.

A Maori jade Hei Tiki pendant, the head tilted to the left, with recessed round eyes, pierced at the top for suspension.

61.5in (156.5cm) high

£800-1,200   **BLA**

3in (7.5cm) high

£2,000-3,000   **SK**

489

An early 20thC carved wood pigmented gobi, from the Papuan Gulf of Papua New Guinea.

36.25in (92cm) high

£5,000-7,000   **BLA**

An early 20thC male Ramu river figure, from Papua New Guinea.

5.5in (14cm) high

£3,000-4,000   **BLA**

An early 20thC Biwat wooden ancestral figure, in the Mundugumor style, from South Sepik in Papua New Guinea.

28.75in (73cm) high

£1,000-1,500   **BLA**

A mid-20thC carved wood ancestor board, with traces of red and white pigment, from the Wapo Creek area of Papua New Guinea.

44in (110cm) high

£300-400   **FRE**

A carved wood ancestor board, painted with red and white pigment, from the Papuan Gulf of Papua New Guinea.

62in (155cm) high

£220-280   **FRE**

A carved wood skull rack, with brown and white pigment, from the Papuan Gulf of Papua New Guinea.

39in (97.5cm) high

£300-400   **FRE**

A carved and painted wood Bioma figure, with traces of white and red pigment and plaited fibre, from the Papuan Gulf of Papua New Guinea.

46in (115cm) high

£400-600   **FRE**

An early 20thC Abelam wooden mask, decorated in polychrome pigments, from Maprik village in Papua New Guinea.

22in (56cm) high

£700-1,000   **BLA**

An early 20thC Baba helmet mask, with polychrome pigments, from the Maprik area of Papua New Guinea.

16.5in (42cm) high

£800-1,200   **BLA**

An early 20thC Tambuan mask, with pigments, from the Ramu River in Papua New Guinea.

16.5in (42cm) high

£800-1,200   **BLA**

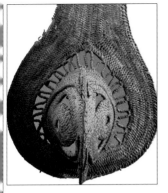

An early 20thC Abelan ceremonial yam mask, from Papua New Guinea.

22.5in (57cm) high

£200-300   BLA

A CLOSER LOOK AT A MALANGGAN HEADDRESS

'Malanggan' is a generic term for ceremonies honouring the dead on New Ireland. The spirits of the ancestors attend these ceremonies, arriving in visible form, often in a 12 foot long boat.

Malanggan headdresses exhibit some of the most sophisticated carving to be found in the South Pacific Islands. They are indigenous to northwest New Ireland.

This intricately carved sculpture was designed to decay over time as a symbolic representation of the dead. The majority of Malanggan sculptures were left to rot in the traditional fashion. They are therefore rare, and early examples in particular command a premium.

The pigments used on this headdress are unique to Oceanic tribal art. Although faded in places, much of the polychrome colouring remains, increasing the value of this piece.

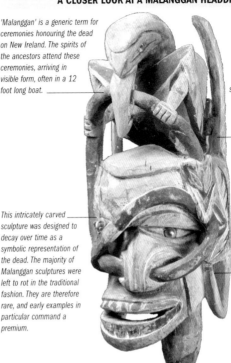

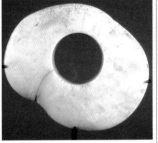

An early 19thC Boiken giant kina shell currency, from Papua New Guinea.

8.25in (21cm) diam

£1,000-1,500   BLA

An early 20thC Mendi Gam pakol pectoral shell ornament, worn by elders in the Mendi Valley area of Papua New Guinea.

9.75in (25cm) diam

£300-400   BLA

An early 19thC Malanggan wooden headdress, with polychrome pigments, used in ceremonies to honour the dead, from New Ireland.

23.75in (60.5cm) high

£8,000-10,000   BLA

An early 20thC shell disk ornament, with filigree turtleshell.

Commonly known as 'kapkaps', these ornaments were made in the Solomon Islands. They are worn as far west as the Papuan Gulf in Papua New Guinea.

4.5in (11.5cm) diam

£700-1,000   BLA

An early 20thC Sepik figural food hook, from Papua New Guinea.

30in (76cm) high

£1,800-2,200   BLA

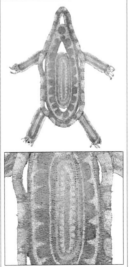

An early 20thC cult banner, of stylised animal form, woven from multicoloured fibres, from New Guinea.

32.75in (83cm) high

£1,500-2,000   BLA

A 20thC Sepik spirit hook, of carved wood coloured with pigments, from the Sepik River area of Papua New Guinea.

13.75in (35cm) high

£200-300   BLA

A carved wood drum, of hourglass form, with stylized animals at the waist, geometric carving on the reptile skin drum head and a dark patina, damaged, from New Guinea.

31.5in (80cm) high

£700-1,000   SK

A rare 19thC Rapanui kohau rongorongo tablet, from Easter Island.

10.25in (26cm) wide

£1,800-2,200   **BLA**

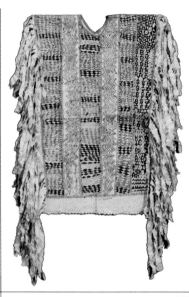

A 19thC tapa cloth poncho, the rectangular pullover with wide pinked fringe down the sides, decorated on both sides with handpainted panels of dark brown geometric patterns, traces of light yellow details, inscribed "Litfelika Makila Meleke Lalotoga Tahiti", from Tahiti.

53in (135cm) long

£400-600   **SK**

A 19thC wooden carved club, from the Solomon Islands.

46.75in (119cm) high

£700-1,000   **BLA**

A mid-19thC bird's head club, with triangular head, carved motifs, cylindrical grip and glossy patina, from New Caledonia.

3.5in (9cm) high

£3,000-4,000   **BLA**

A late 19thC Polynesian carved wood and stone adze, the handle a stylized figure holding the tail of a lizard, with elaborate carvings and abalone inlaid eyes, the dark stone blade lashed with fibre.

16.5in (42cm) long

£2,500-3,500   **SK**

A late 19thC wooden canoe paddle, with carved geometric patterns, from the Austral Islands.

33in (84cm) high

£1,800-2,200   **BLA**

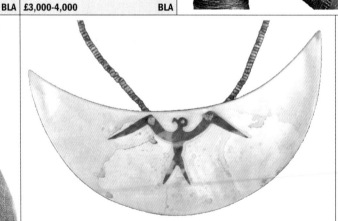

An early 20thC kina shell pectoral, encrusted with tortoiseshell, from the Solomon Islands.

7in (18cm) long

£1,000-1,500   **BLA**

A Melanesian carved wood club, of anthropomorphic form, with highly stylized faces and the remains of a rattan wrap at the handle.

38in (96.5cm) long

£200-300   **SK**

A George III pine and gesso fire surround, with Neo-Classical decoration, the leaf-moulded reverse breakfront mantel above a central tablet with cherub and ribbon tied swag, with panelled pilaster uprights.

59.5in (149cm) wide

£3,000-5,000   **L&T**

An American Federal or Federal-style pine fire surround, with a stepped cornice and a frieze of applied composition swags, tassels, classical figures and putti, some elements hand-planed, restored, some later elements.

56in (142cm) wide

£1,800-2,200   **BRU**

A CLOSER LOOK AT A LOUIS XV-STYLE FIRE SURROUND

Louis XV style is characterised by grandeur, luxury, formality and symmetry. Pieces convey wealth, power and magnificence.

Antique architectural features can fetch huge prices as buyers look for unique items to furnish grand period buildings in an authentic manner.

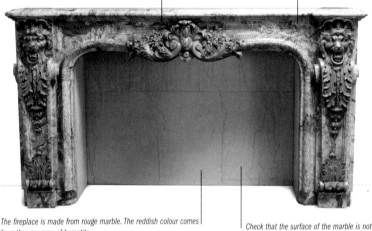

The fireplace is made from rouge marble. The reddish colour comes from the presence of hematite.

Check that the surface of the marble is not stained and that no damage or 'etching' has been caused by acidic substances.

A 19thC Louis XV-style rouge marble and gilt bronze fireplace, the serpentine moulded mantel above an ornate frieze centred by a foliate scroll cast cresting, flanked by two lions masks and acanthus-cast, caryatid-form supports.

82in (205cm) wide

£40,000-50,000   **FRE**

An early 19thC Tennessee fire surround, in poplar and yellow pine, with a stepped and moulded cornice above a carved frieze, three panels with oval and circular fluted elements and herringbone borders, reeded pilasters, cut nails, old black paint.

68in (172.5cm) wide

£1,800-2,200   **BRU**

A Garfield fire surround, the cypress cove and dentil-moulded cornice above two tapered and reeded Ionic columns, the centre with 14 panels with chamfered sides and fluted moulding at surround, paint chipped.

79in (200.5cm) wide

£1,500-2,000   **BRU**

ANDIRONS

A pair Federal-style andirons, the urn finials with acorn tips, matching log stops, pad feet, unpolished surface, dents, scratches.

27in (68.5cm) high

£350-400   **BRU**

An 18thC pair of iron and brass 'knife-edge' andirons, with a brass urn top, on slender vasiform 'knife-edge' shafts supported by an inverted-form base with penny feet.

22in (55cm) high

£300-500   **FRE**

A late 18thC pair of brass and wrought iron andirons, with urn tops on slender column shafts, spurred cabriole legs, on claw and ball feet.

27in (67.5cm) high

£3,000-4,000   **FRE**

A pair of Federal brass andirons, probably from Philadelphia, on ball feet.

c1810   13in (32.5cm) high

£300-400   **FRE**

An early 19thC pair of brass andirons, baluster-turned shafts, on ball feet.

16.5in (41cm) high

£150-200   **FRE**

A 19thC pair of 'Button'-end iron andirons, with baluster-turned shafts and raised on three ball feet.

17.25in (43cm) high

£200-300   **FRE**

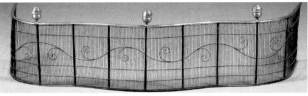

An early 19thC wirework fender, the serpentine front with scrolled wire decoration, brass rims and finials, scattered light rust.

59in (150cm) wide

£800-1,200   **BRU**

A steel fire fender, in cast and laminated iron with copper mounts, the central section with tool rests and handle rests to sides.

53in (135cm) wide

£120-180   **BRU**

FIREMARKS & OTHER ACCESSORIES

A wrought iron fender stool, by Thomas Hadden of Edinburgh, of rectilinear three-quarter form, the green leather padded seats with studded decoration above a slatted frieze enhanced with panels of entwined foliage.

71in (180cm) wide

£1,500-2,000   **L&T**

A 'Sun Fire Office 1710' firemark, embossed in relief and gilded with the wording above a sun on a black ground, mounted on a mahogany plaque.

7.25in (18.5cm) diam

£100-150   **CHEF**

Two 19thC American firemarks, the first, from Baltimore, of iron cast in oval form enclosing a figure of a fireman blowing a horn and holding a burning torch, the second, from Philadelphia, with a cast-lead tree mounted on a painted pine shield.

Provenance: The first mark was originally issued in 1848 by the Associated Fireman's Insurance Company of Baltimore. The second mark, the "Green Tree", was originally issued by the Mutual Insurance Company for Insuring Houses, Philadelphia, from 'Loss by Fire' in 1784.

Larger 15.75in (39cm) high

£700-1,000   **FRE**

A 'British' painted and gilt firemark, worked in relief with a gold lion resting a paw on a union shield, on a red ground with "British", mounted on mahogany plaque.

8.5in (21.5cm) diam

£200-300   **CHEF**

A 17thC cast iron Coat-of-Arms fire back, dated.

Provenance: Sorber Collection.

1635   *26in (65cm) wide*

£1,800-2,200   **POOK**

A cast iron stove plate, the two arched panels with the inscription "God's well has water in plenty", dated.

Provenance: Sorber Collection.

1748   *27.5in (69cm) wide*

£3,000-4,000   **POOK**

An 18thC Pennsylvania cast iron stove plate, depicting Samson and Delilah inscribed "When at last Delilah..."

Provenance: Sorber Collection.

24.75in (62cm) wide

£2,500-3,500   **POOK**

A cast iron stove plate, with a rampant horse above a foliate cartouche, dated.

Provenance: Sorber Collection.

1758   *26in (65cm) high*

£200-300   **POOK**

A Pennsylvania cast iron stove plate, with tulips and hearts, inscribed "George Ross Ann Mary Ann Furnace".

Provenance: Sorber Collection.

1763   *26in (65cm) wide*

£1,200-1,800   **POOK**

A Pennsylvania cast iron 'Depart from Evil' stove plate, inscribed "John Potts Warwick Furnace", dated.

Provenance: Sorber Collection.

1764   *26.75in (67cm) wide*

£2,500-3,500   **POOK**

An ornate cast iron parlour stove, with open central bay flanked by lyre-shaped supports, one central burner, removable cabriole legs and pad feet, damage.

86.5cm (34in) wide

£300-500   **BRU**

A painted leather fire bucket, of tapering cylindrical form, painted in dark green with a red trim and inscribed "No. 2 H. Eldridge" in yellow, dated, wear.

1831

9.5in (24cm) high

£800-1,200   **FRE**

A Victorian overpainted cast iron garden bench, in the form of oak branches and leaves, the legs with entwined rope stretchers, open arms.

52in (130cm) wide

£500-800   **L&T**

A Coalbrookdale-style fern and berry pattern cast iron garden bench, overpainted in forest green, with a slatted timber seat.

The Coalbrookdale foundry was established in Shropshire in 1708. It specialised in cast-iron furniture and exported to the US and Europe. Christopher Dresser designed some of pieces for the company and these were widely copied.

61.2in (153cm) wide

£800-1,200   **L&T**

A cast iron bench, the ends formed as swans, with board seat and back, old white and orange paint, scattered rust, boards probably replaced, repainting.

38in (96.5cm) wide

£3,000-5,000   **BRU**

A three-tier baker's rack, in iron with scrolled and rodded supports, sectional removable shelves, one foot repaired, lacking one finial.

79in (200.5cm) wide

£300-400   **BRU**

An 18thC stone bust of a gentleman, in a wig, his coat bearing a garter star, the face damaged.

32.75in (82cm) high

£1,000-1,500   **L&T**

MARBLE & ALABASTER

A 19thC stone bust, of a Roman soldier.

16.75in (42cm) high

£6,000-9,000   **L&T**

A 19thC patinated plaster bust of James Watt, raised on a turned socle base.

26.5in (67cm) high

£2,000-3,000   **L&T**

A 19thC terracotta bust of a French gentleman in 17thC dress.

26in (66cm) high

£1,200-1,500   **SWO**

An Italian white marble bust of Augustus, by L. Clerici, signed "L. Clerici, Roma, 1874".

22in (55cm) high

£2,000-3,000   **FRE**

A pair of white marble figures of a boy and girl, by Pietro Barzanti.

c1880   *34in (86cm) high*

£5,000-7,000   **L&T**

A 19thC plaster bust of Professor John Wilson, by James Fillans, with classical figures and portrait medallions.

James Fillans (1808-1852) was born in Lanarkshire. The National Portrait Gallery in Edinburgh has a version of this bust, derived from the 1845 marble original he exhibited at the Royal Academy.

34in (86cm) high

£2,000-3,000   **L&T**

An Italian carved alabaster urn, the shoulder with winged grotesque masks, swags and reliefs of nymphs and putti emblematic of the Four Seasons, raised on a giallo antico marble fluted socle, with "Prof. A. Petrilli/Firenze".

Provenance: *The Maxwell family, founders of the Maxwell House Coffee Company.*

29.25in (73cm) high

£4,000-6,000   **S&K**

A lidded marble urn, the lid with artichoke finial, damage, repairs.

36in high

£2,000-3,000   **BRU**

An early 19thC lead garden figure, cast in lead as a young girl in a smock dress, raised on a turned socle base.

26.75in (67cm) high

£700-1,000   **L&T**

A green patinated bronze figure of a Bacchic faun, after the Antique, with arms aloft and tail to rear, on stepped base.

32 (81cm) high

£2,000-3,000   **L&T**

A Gothic-style cast iron bird bath, the basin mounted with openwork twig decoration, the pedestal base formed as a tree trunk with roots, marked "Miller Iron/Prov./RI", rust, central rod replaced.

46in (117cm) high

£5,000-8,000   **BRU**

An American School life-size portrait of a gentleman wearing a frock coat, in bronze with a dark brown patina, on a circular wooden base supported by casters.

An early Victorian tole urn and cover, with a pineapple knop, the flattened ovoid body and footed socle painted with flowers, the lion mask and ring handles in gilt.

11.5in (29cm) high

£300-400   **CHEF**

An Alexander the Great bronze and marble bust, in military dress, the breastplate with silhouette medallion, bronze doré fringed chlamys, head and helmet in figured red marble, chest and base of grey/dark red mottled marble, losses, chips and corrosion.

48in (122cm) high

£22,000-24,000   **BRU**

66in (165cm) high

£10,000-15,000   **FRE**

A 19thC English church bell, inscribed "Thomas Mears of London, Founder 1836".

24in (60cm) diam

£800-1,200   **L&T**

An 18thC Dutch church bell, foliate cast bands, inscribed "Mr GR Van Kingschoten, Amstelodam", dated.

1739   *26.75in (67cm) diam*

£1,200-1,800   **L&T**

A cast iron window grille, of scrolled construction, overall rust and pitting.

24in (61cm) wide

£60-90   **BRU**

A Regency tole peint plate warmer, painted with gilt borders on a black ground, with a dome top above a door enclosing shelves and an open back, flanked by gilt metal handles, on cabriole legs with pad feet.

27.5in (70cm) high

£200-300   **DN**

A painted metal horse head, probably French, with an open mouth, covered with traces of old yellow and red paint, once used as a sign, wear and damage.

17in (43cm) high

£1,200-1,800   **BRU**

A terracotta horse head, probably French, with an open mouth, painted, with chips and losses.

25in (63.5cm) high

£1,000-1,500   **BRU**

A terracotta horse head, with an open mouth and flowing mane, minor surface chips and paint loss, repairs.

22in (56cm) high

£700-1,000   **BRU**

A pair of terracotta lion head architectural plaques, probably French, the rims with large losses, traces old red paint.

18in (46cm) diam

£1,200-1,800   **BRU**

A piece of 19thC Blue John, of solid circular vase shape.

Blue John is a type of flurospar found in Derbyshire. Its violet blue bands have made it a popular form of ornamentation for centuries.

5.5in (14cm) high

£500-800   **H&L**

A piece of 19thC Blue John, of solid circular vase shape.

4.75in (12cm) high

£500-800   **H&L**

A sandstone armorial ornament, with coronet and uncarved shield.

£400-600   **L&T**

A marbled post box, of drum form, with aperture above door enclosing shelves, plinth base.

44.75in (112cm) high

£1,200-1,800   **L&T**

A mid-Victorian pietra dura urn, the Belgian black slate thistle-shaped bowl inlaid with malachite, shark's tooth and ochre, with a marble band of flowers, the socle on square foot.

14.75in (37.5cm) high

£500-800   **CHEF**

A late 19thC massive Victorian carved and painted bird house, the wood and wire frame with painted turrets, faux brick accents and an elaborate entrance.

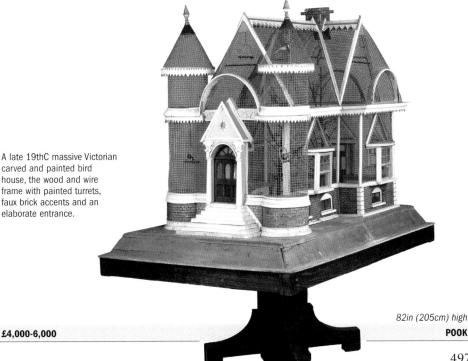

82in (205cm) high

£4,000-6,000   **POOK**

497

BOOKS

THE BOOKS MARKET

The increased public and press attention given to literary awards has had repercussions for the market in modern first editions over the last year. Crime and mystery fiction, traditionally the strongest genres in this sector, have lost ground to 21stC literary fiction.

Many collectors now specialise almost exclusively in first novels by contemporary authors. Inclusion on the Booker, Orange or Whitbread prize shortlist tends to fuel an increase in value, a situation exacerbated by the lower print runs now favoured by risk-wary publishers. Other areas to watch include foreign language writers, such as Turkey's Orhan Pamuk, and books aimed at young adults, such as 'Mortal Engines' by Phillip Reeve.

Up to 80 percent of the value of a first edition book is in its dust wrapper, so it is vital that buyers choose examples with intact dust wrappers in the best possible condition.

It is also worth bearing in mind that, despite the booming market in books still warm from the press, one of the most successful titles at auction in the last year was J.R.R. Tolkien's "Lord of the Rings" trilogy. Allen & Unwin's 1954-5 editions have enjoyed steady growth for more than a decade, and are now outperforming J.K. Rowling's early Harry Potter titles.

Chris Fruin, LMS Books

CLASSIC BOOKS

Aretz, Gertrude, "Napoleon and his Women Friends", first English translation, cover set with five watercolour on ivorine portraits by C.B. Currie, Cosway binding, inner gilt doublures, t.e.g., by Riviere, in original fleece-lined slipcase, Allen & Unwin, London.

1927

£15,000-20,000   **L&T**

Austen, Jane, "The Novels", Winchester edition in 12 volumes, red cloth boards, spines with gilt decoration, Grant, Edinburgh.

1911-12

£3,000-5,000   **L&T**

Bacon, Francis, Viscount St. Alban, "Essays, Moral, Economical, and Political", cover with watercolour on ivorine portrait of Bacon by C.B. Currie, Cosway, Sharpe, London.

1828

£7,000-10,000   **L&T**

Beardsley, Aubrey, "The Savoy: An Illustrated Monthly", with original bands and wrappers, volumes 1-8, cover decorations and other illustrations by Beardsley, London.

1896

£1,000-1,500   **FRE**

Couch, Jonathan, "A History of the Fishes", first edition, in four volumes, 252 coloured plates, 8vo., Groombridge, London.

1862-65

£1,800-2,200   **L&T**

Beebe, William, "A monograph of the pheasants", first edition, in four volumes, with 90 chromolithographed plates, 88 photogravure plates by Thorburn and others, and 20 maps, Witherby, London.

No. 35 of 600 copies, this was one of the last books printed using chromolithography.

c1920

£3,000-5,000   **L&T**

Burns, Robert, "Poems chiefly in the Scottish dialect", with a watercolour on ivorine portrait miniature of Burns by C.B. Currie, inner gilt doublures, by Riviere, Cosway binding, in fleece-lined slipcase, John Smith, Glasgow.

1927

£7,000-10,000   **L&T**

Colley, Cibber, "She wou'd and she wou'd not; or, the kind imposter", with a watercolour portrait on ivorine by C.B. Currie of Mrs Jordan as Hypolita, engraved frontispiece and titlepage, Cosway binding, inner gilt doublures, t.e.g., by Riviere, in its original slip case, published by Bell, London.

1792

£7,000-10,000   **L&T**

Crutwell, Maud, "Madame de Maintenon", first edition, covers with watercolour on ivorine portraits of Madame de Maintenon, Cosway binding no. 848, signed by John Stonehouse and C.B. Currie, inner doublures, a.e.g., by Riviere, in fleece-lined slipcase, Dent, London.

1930

£10,000-15,000　　**L&T**

Curtis, William, "Flora Londinensis" first edition, 435 hand-coloured engravings, six volumes, morocco binding.

Issued in 72 parts, the "Flora Londinensis" could be regarded as the first colour-plate national flora.

£8,000-12,000　　**L&T**

Dickens, Charles, "Sikes and Nancy", Cosway morocco binding, with watercolour on ivorine portrait of Dickens by C.B. Currie, in fleece-lined slipcase, Sotheran, London.

No 60 of 250 copies for sale, signed by the publisher.

1921

£3,000-5,000　　**L&T**

Dickens, Charles, "David Copperfield, a reading in five chapters", Cosway morocco binding, with watercolour portraits on ivorine of Dickens and Maria Beadnell by C.B. Currie, inner doublures, t.e.g., by Riviere, in fleece-lined slipcase, Sotheran, London.

1921

£10,000-15,000　　**L&T**

Dresser, H.E. "A History of the Birds of Europe", 1st edition, 9 volumes, 721 hand-finished lithographic plates, covers with the arms in gilt of Edward 4th Baron Sherborne, with the Sherborne Library bookplate, 4to., London.

1871-81

£12,000-14,000　　**L&T**

Forrester, A.E., "The City Hall, Baltimore: History and Construction", first edition, morocco cover, gilt-lettered spine, double-page colour lithographic frontispiece, with ten lithographic plates.

1877

£150-200　　**FRE**

Foxe, John, "Actes and monuments of these latter and perilous dayes", 1st edition, Black Letter, woodcut of the burnings in front of Windsor Castle and 47 other woodcuts in the text, full morocco cover, 4to., John Day.

1563

£7,000-9,000　　**L&T**

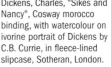

Tommaso Garzoni, "L'Hospidale de Pazzi Incurabili", Venice, first edition, limp vellum cover.

This is the first book devoted to the classification of mental disease.

1586

£1,200-1,800　　**FRE**

Godman, Frederick Du Cane, "A monograph of the petrels", first edition, 106 hand coloured plates, morocco cover, 4to., London: Witherby, 1907-10.

No. 46 of 225 copies, originally issued in 5 parts.

£2,500-3,000　　**L&T**

Graham, Kenneth, "The Wind in the Willows", first edition, frontispiece by Graham Robertson, original green pictorial cloth, 8vo., published by Methuen, London, t.e.g., other edges uncut, wear.

1908

£1,500-2,000　　**L&T**

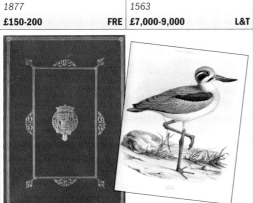

Gray, Robert, "The Genera of Birds...", illustrated by David Mitchell, first edition, 338 lithographed plates finished by hand, 3 volumes, Longman, London.

1849

£7,000-10,000　　**L&T**

Hayley, William, "The poetical works of John Milton with a life of the author", in 3 volumes, with 5 engraved portraits by Houbraken and Westall, printed by Bulmer, for J. & J. Boydell, and George Nicol, London.

1794

£2,500-3,000　　**L&T**

Herschel, Sir John Frederick William, "Results of Astronomical Observations Made During 1834, 5,6,7,8 at the Cape of Good Hope", first edition, gilt-lettered spine, raised bands, London.

1847

£400-600　　**FRE**

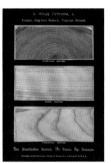

Hough, Romeyn Beck, "American Woods", green cloth portfolios with cloth sleeves, gilt lettered portfolio spines and metal clasps, with six text volumes in original wrappers and 468 wood samples window-mounted in 156 card mounts, New York.

c1890

£2,200-2,800　　　　**FRE**

Humphreys, H.N. & Westwood, J.O. "British moths and their transformations", 2 volumes, 124 hand-coloured plates, Smith, London.

1848

£1,500-2,000　　　　**L&T**

Ireland, W.H., editor, "Life of Napoleon Bonaparte...", first edition, four volumes, engravings by G. Cruikshank, first edition, four volumes, engraved titlepages, hand-coloured plates, 8vo., Fairburn, London.

1823-28

£1,000-1,500　　　　**L&T**

Takeji Iwamiya, "Forms, Textures, Images: Traditional Japanese Craftsmanship in Everyday Life", first English-language edition, original red cloth, gilt, colour and black and white photo plates.

1979

£60-90　　　　**FRE**

Lawrence, TE, "Seven pillars of wisdom: a triumph", Cosway morocco binding no. 691, cover with watercolour portrait of Lawrence on ivorine by C.B. Currie, t.e.g., by Riviere, in original fleece-lined slipcase, 4to., Cape, London.

1935

£7,000-10,000　　　　**L&T**

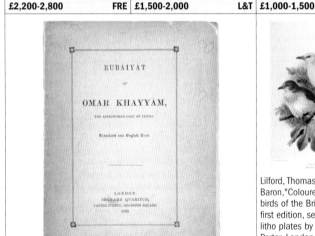

Fitzgerald, Edward, editor and translator, "Rubáiyát of Omar Khayyám", first edition, one of 250 copies, original printed wrappers, preserved in a brown morocco solander case, gilt, 4to., published by Bernard Quaritch, London, wear.

Many copies of this edition were unsold and remaindered, making this book rare.

1859

£8,000-12,000　　　　**BLO**

Lilford, Thomas L. Powys, Baron, "Coloured figures of the birds of the British Islands", first edition, seven volumes, litho plates by Thorburn et al, Porter, London.

1885-87

£1,800-2,200　　　　**L&T**

Lipscomb, George, "The history and antiquities of Buckingham", first edition, four volumes, 38 engraved plates, nine maps, 940 hand-coloured coats of arms, Nichols, London.

1831-47

£1,800-2,200　　　　**L&T**

Macdonald, George, "Phantastes: A Faerie Romance for Men and Women", first edition, original embossed cloth, 8vo., wear.

1858

£300-500　　　　**BLO**

Nicholson, William, "The History of the Wars Occasioned by the French Revolution", folio, 21 colour plates, London, back cover detached.

1820

£300-500　　　　**FRE**

Drummond, Comte de Melfort, "Trait sur la Cavalerie", folio, gilt-panelled spine, raised bands, red morocco spine label, red-stained edges, Paris.

1776

£120-180　　　　**FRE**

Millican, Albert, "Orchid Hunting: The Adventures of an Orchid Hunter", gilt-lettered and pictorial blue cloth, black and white plates, London.

1891

£400-600　　　　**FRE**

Pilkington, Matthew, "A general dictionary of painters", new edition, two volumes, with 450 engravings, morocco binding, McLean, London.

1824

£3,000-5,000　　　　**L&T**

Pollock, Jackson, "A Catalogue Raisonne of Paintings, Drawings and other Works", beige cloth, colour plates, gilt-lettered spines.

1978

£800-1,200 FRE

Riolan, Jean, "Discours sur les Hermaphrodits", first edition, gilt-panelled spine, morocco spine label, author's name in old ink on title-page, Paris.

1614

£600-900 FRE

Rosenthal, Leonard, "The Kingdom of the Pearl", white cloth and silver-decorated grey bands, paper cover label, spine gilt, ten mounted colour plates, London.

1920

£200-300 FRE

Rothschild, Lionel Walter, Baron, "Extinct birds" first edition, 45 coloured plates, four outline plates, green morocco binding, signed by the author, Hutchinson, London.

1907

£3,000-5,000 L&T

Rothschild, Lionel Walter, Baron "The Avifauna of Laysan", first edition, three parts, two volumes, 55 hand-finished cromolitho plates, 20 collotype and 8 uncoloured plates, full dark green morocco, Porter, London.

1893-1900

£6,000-9,000 L&T

Schäuble, Peter Lamber, "The First Battalion: The Story of the 406th Telegraph Battalian Signal Corps, US Army", gilt-pictorial blue cloth, photo illustrations and maps, Philadelphia.

1921

£25-30 FRE

Schoonhovius, Florentius, "Emblemata", first edition, full contemporary vellum, engraved title page, portrait and 74 engraved emblems, A. Burier, Gouda, old ink annotations on front free endpaper.

1618

£600-900 FRE

Scott, Walter, "The Poetical Works of Sir Walter Scott", Albion Edition, morocco bindings, fore-edge painted with "Pike Fishing" to one side and "Salmon Fishing" to the other, published by Frederick Warne & Company, London, wear.

8.5in (21.5cm) high

£600-900 BRU

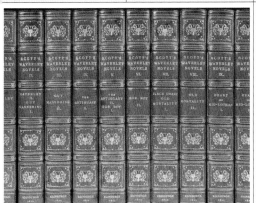

Scott, Sir Walter, "Works ... [with] Lockhart's Memoirs of the life of Sir Walter Scott", 64 volumes, illustrated plates, bound in half brown morocco, 8vo., Constable, Edinburgh.

1822-94

£2,800-3,200 L&T

Shelley, Percy B., "Adonais: an elegy on the death of John Keats", Cosway morocco binding, cover with watercolour miniatures on ivorine of St. Peter's Cathedral, Shelley and Keats, by C.B. Currie, inner gilt doublures, in original fleece lined slipcase, 4to., Noel Douglas, London.

1927

£8,000-12,000 L&T

Stevenson, Robert Louis, "A Child's Garden of Verses", London, first illustrated edition, red cloth, with gilt-decorated pictorial and lettered green cloth doublures.

1896

£400-600 FRE

Dana, Mrs. William Starr, "How to Know the Wild Flowers: A Guide", silver and green stamped brown cloth, illustrations by Marion Satterlee, with 30 watercolour drawings of American wild flowers, unsigned, dated, New York.

1895

£280-320   **FRE**

Stock, St. George H., "The Romance of Chastisement: Select Tales form the Original Manuscript", London, cloth-backed bands, paper spine label, text with ornamental red borders, edge wear.

1869

£60-90   **FRE**

Strutt, Joseph, "A biographical dictionary containing an historical account of all the engravers", first edition, two volumes extended to four, with 19 original plates, two hand-coloured, 450 additional engravings, 4to., Robert Faulder, London.

1785

£5,000-8,000   **L&T**

Tennyson, Alfred, Lord, "A selection from the works... (Moxon's miniature poets)", Cosway binding no. 911, with a watercolour portrait on ivorine of Tennyson by C.B. Currie, in original fleece-lined slipcase, 8vo., Moxon, London.

1865

£6,000-9,000   **L&T**

Thackeray, William Makepeace, "The Virginians", first edition, original printed pictorial yellow wrappers, 48 plates, adverts, custom cloth box, Bradbury and Evans, London.

1858

£200-300   **FRE**

Thackeray, William Makepeace, "The History of Henry Esmond", first edition, three volumes, half calf cover patterned boards, 8vo., wear.

1852

£300-500   **BLO**

Twain, Mark, "The Writings", memorial edition, with a manuscript leaf in Mark Twain's hand tipped-in, levant morocco binding, marbled bands, gilt, gilt-panelled spines, maroon morocco spine labels, plates, Harpers & Brothers, New York.

1929

£8,000-12,000   **FRE**

Whitman, Walt, "Memories of President Lincoln and Other Lyrics of the War", on vellum, signed by Thomas Mosher, unbound and unopened, Thomas B. Mosher, Portland, Maine.

1906

£600-900   **FRE**

Williamson, George C., Cosway, Richard, R. A. et al., "Miniaturists of the 18th century", first edition, one of 350, Cosway binding no. 889, with watercolour portrait miniatures on ivorine by C.B. Currie, inner gilt doublures, in fleece-lined slipcase, 4to., Bell, London.

1897

£17,000-19,000   **L&T**

The "Holy Bible containing the Old Testament and the New ", John Baskett, Oxford.

This edition is known as the "Vinegar Bible", infamous as "A Baskett-ful of Errors", including the misprint "vinegar" for "vineyard".

1717

£4,000-6,000   **L&T**

"The New Cries of London", printed stiff wrappers, 22 engraved vignettes and vignettes on each title and front wrapper, London.

1813

£500-800   **FRE**

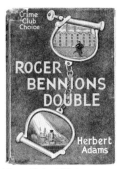

Adams, Herbert "Roger Bennions Double", first edition, published for the Crime Club, original cloth, dust jacket, discoloured, worn and repaired, 8vo.

1941

£150-200   **BLO**

Bellow, Saul, "Dangling Man", first English edition, original cloth, dust jacket, 8vo.

This was the first book by the author of "Herzog".

1946

£100-150   **BLO**

Baker, Josephine, "La Revue des Folies Bergere, 1926-1927", blue wrappers, gilt and colour illustrations, Paris.

1926

£250-300   **FRE**

Blake, Nicholas, "The Beast Must Die", first edition, original cloth, dust jacket, repaired on verso, 8vo, extremities worn, spine ends chipped, together with two other titles by Blake.

1938

£400-600   **BLO**

A CLOSER LOOK AT A MODERN FIRST EDITION

This world famous and much-loved tale, published in 1900, was an immediate bestseller. The story was further popularised by the 1939 movie starring Judy Garland as Dorothy.

The Wizard of Oz is a hugely popular collecting area making competition for items fierce and prices relatively high.

As a first edition of a popular title in excellent condition, this book is very desirable.

This first edition book is in its second state. An older, first state, first edition could command £20,000 or more.

Baum, Frank L., "The Wonderful Wizard of Oz", first edition, second state, published by George M. Hill, Chicago.

1900

£12,000-18,000   **BRB**

Blixen, Karen, (Isak Dinesen), "Out of Africa", first edition, original burgundy cloth, dust jacket, 8vo., soiled, rubbed at extremities, small tears to spine ends.

1937

£250-300   **BLO**

Buchan, John, "The Dancing Floor", first edition, with original cloth, 8vo., tanned, faded and rubbed at extremities.

1926

£120-180   **BLO**

Burgess, Anthony, "A Clockwork Orange", first edition, first issue dustwrapper, original cloth, 8vo., published by Heinemann, London, spotting.

1962

£1,200-1,800   **L&T**

Burroughs, William S., "The Naked Lunch", No. 76, The Traveller's Companion Series, first edition, original printed wrappers, 8vo., published by Olympia Press, Paris.

1959

£400-600   **BLO**

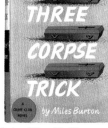

Burton, Miles, "The Three Corpse Trick", first edition, published for the Crime Club, original cloth, dust jacket, 8vo., slightly rubbed and soiled.

1944

£120-180   **BLO**

Carroll, Lewis, "Alice's Adventures in Wonderland and Through the Looking Glass", photo-play edition, stamped pictorial grey cloth, light edge wear.

1918

£100-150   **FRE**

Chesterton, G.K., "The Secret of Father Brown", first edition, ink signatures on front endpaper, slight peripheral and end foxing, original cloth, dust jacket, 8vo., creased and chipped.

£500-800   **BLO**

Chesterton, G.K., "Tales of the Long Bow", first edition, half-title, original cloth, dust jacket, 8vo., edge and end foxing, worn and internally strengthened.

1925

£300-400   **BLO**

Christie, Agatha, "A Pocket Full of Rye", early edition, Collins.

This early edition, printed one year after the first edition, is rare.

£100-150   **BIB**

Agatha Christie, "The Moving Finger", first edition, published by Collins/The Crime Club.

1943

£300-500   **BIB**

Christie, Agatha, "Why Didn't They Ask Evans?", first edition, published by Collins/The Crime Club.

This is a rare dust jacket.

1950

£300-500   **BIB**

Churchill, Sir Winston, "The Eve of Action: A Verbatim Report of Mr. Churchill's Speech", first edition, original red printed wrappers, 4to., published by W. & G. Baird Ltd., Belfast.

1944

£600-900   **BLO**

Conrad, Joseph, "The Arrow of Gold, first English edition, published by T. Fisher Unwin.

1919

£200-250   **BLO**

Dexter, Colin, "The Dead of Jericho", first edition, published by MacMillan.

1981

£300-400   **BIB**

Dinesen, Isak, "Seven Gothic Tales", first English edition, colour frontispiece, original cloth, dust jacket, printer's band still present, 8vo., tanned at edges and spine.

The frontispiece and dust jacket were designed by Rex Whistler.

1934

£220-280   **BLO**

Conan Doyle, Arthur, "The Memoirs of Sherlock Holmes", first edition, published by George Newnes.

1892

£700-1,000   **BIB**

Conan Doyle, Arthur, "The Return of Sherlock Holmes", first edition in book form, 16 plates by Sidney Paget, advertisements at end, published by George Newnes.

1905

£1,000-1,500   **BLO**

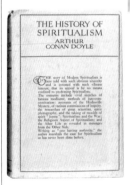

Conan Doyle, Arthur, "The History of Spiritualism", first edition, two volumes, original cloth, dust jackets, with "Pheneas Speaks", original publisher's wrappers, foxed.

1926

£300-500   **BLO**

Conan Doyle, Arthur, "The Hound of the Baskervilles", first edition, frontispiece and 15 plates by Sidney Paget, half-title, original gilt pictorial cloth, 8vo., bubbling of cloth, slight scuffing to extremities.

1902

£1,200-1,800 BLO

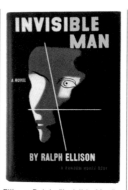

Ellison, Ralph, "Invisible Man", first edition, published by Random House, New York.

1952

£1,500-2,000 BRB

Faulkner, William, "The Wild Palms", first English edition, original cloth, 8vo., dust jacket a little tanned, rubbed at extremities.

1939

£100-150 BLO

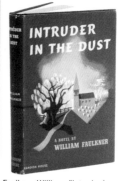

Faulkner, William, "Intruder in the Dust", first edition, first printing, original gilt and blue lettered and decorated black cloth, Random House, New York.

1948

£280-320 FRE

Fleming, Ian, "Moonraker", first edition, later printing, published by Jonathan Cape.

1955

£200-300 BIB

Fleming, Ian, "Diamonds are Forever", first edition, published by Jonathan Cape.

1956

£1,000-1,500 BIB

Fleming, Ian, "Goldfinger", first edition, original embossed boards, gilt, 8vo., dust jacket slightly soiled.

1959

£300-500 BLO

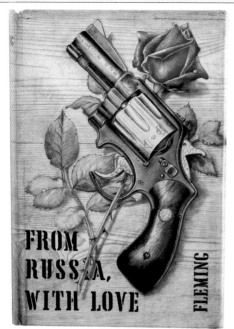

Fleming, Ian, "From Russia With Love", first edition, published by Jonathan Cape.

1957

£1,500-2,000 BIB

Francis, Dick, "Nerve", first edition, 8vo., remains of small labels on front endpaper, original boards, dust jacket worn.

1963

£500-800 BLO

Francis, Dick, "For Kicks", first edition, original boards, dust jacket, 8vo., worn at extremities.

1965

£500-800 BLO

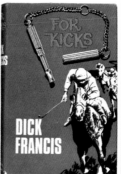

Francis, Dick, "Flying Finish", first edition, original boards, dust jacket, 8vo., ink inscription on front endpaper.

1966

£200-300 BLO

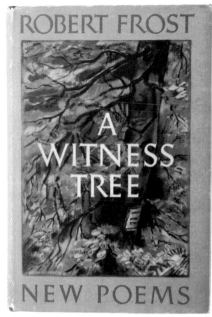

Robert Frost, "A Witness Tree", first trade edition, published by Henry Holt & Co., New York, Pulitzer Prize winner, inscribed by the author.

1942

£5,000-7,000 BRB

Golding, William, "Lord of the Flies", first edition, published by Faber & Faber, London.

1954

£4,000-6,000 BRB

Gray, Alasdair, "Lanark, A Life in Four Books", first edition, original cloth, gilt spine, dust jacket, 8vo., slightly creased at spine ends, Edinburgh.

1981

£200-300 BLO

Greene, Graham, "Stamboul Train", first edition, published by Heinemann, with rare dust jacket, distressed.

1932

£1,500-2,000 BIB

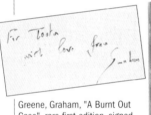

Greene, Graham, "A Burnt Out Case", rare first edition, signed by the author, published by Heinemann.

1960

£800-1,200 BIB

Greene, Graham, "It's A Battlefield", and eight other English first editions including "Stamboul Train", "The Quiet American", "Our Man in Havana" and "A Burnt Out Case", published by Heinemann, London.

1932-1961

£700-1,000 set L&T

Greene, Graham, "The Third Man and The Fallen Idol", first edition, original cloth, dust jacket, 8vo., edges slightly creased, tape repairs to jacket.

1950

£220-280 BLO

Greene, Graham, "The Lost Childhood", first edition, original cloth, dust jacket, 8vo.

1951

£280-320 BLO

Grogan, E.S. and Sharp, A.H., "From Cape to Cairo: The First Traverse of Africa from South to North", first edition, illustrated by A.D. McCormick, published by Hurst and Blackett, wear.

1990

£250-300 L&T

Hammett, Dashiell, "The Maltese Falcon", first edition, published by Alfred A. Knopf, New York and London.

1930

£1,200-1,800 BRB

Heinlein, Robert A., "Stranger in a Strange Land", first edition, original cloth, Putnam's, New York.

1961

£1,000-1,500 FRE

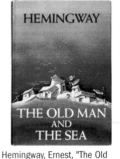

Hemingway, Ernest, "The Old Man and the Sea", first edition, publisher's seal and "A" to copyright page, original cloth, dust jacket, 8vo., rubbed, New York.

1961

£700-1,000 BLO

Herrick, Robert, "One Hundred and Eleven Poems", from an edition of 500, with eight extra plates, signed by the author, illustrated by Sir W. R. Flint, Golden Cockerel Press.

1955

£300-500 BLO

A CLOSER LOOK AT A MODERN FIRST EDITION

This is one of the first two novels to be written by Haggard, who is best known for "King Solomon's Mines" and "She".

First editions by emerging authors were often produced in small print runs to minimise the risk to the publisher's finances. Only 500 first edition copies of this novel were printed, making it scarce and increasing its desirability.

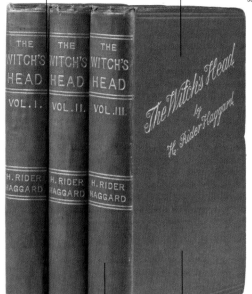

Age does not necessarily influence the value of books. Books dating from after the mid-19thC are fairly common. Value is determined by edition, author, rarity and condition.

This novel is typical of Haggard's adventure fantasies and explores the evil magic surrounding a witchdoctor's severed head. This subject matter would have appealed to mid-Victorian Colonial and Gothic sensibilities.

Haggard, H. Ryder, "The Witch's Head", first edition, three volumes, half-titles, eight pages of advertisements at end of volume three, original grey/green cloth, 8vo., endpapers splitting, knocked, fraying to spine-ends and fore-corners.

1885

£7,000-10,000 BLO

Huxley, Aldous, "Brave New World", first edition, original cloth, gilt spine, 8vo., some foxing, rubbed at extremities, worn, creasing.

1932

£600-800 BLO

Ishiguro, Kazuo, "A Pale View of Hills", first ed., Faber & Faber.

The first novel by the author of "The Remains of the Day".

1982

£450-550 BIB

James, P.D., "The Black Tower", first edition, published by Faber & Faber.

1975

£220-280 BIB

Knowles, John, "A Separate Peace", with "Morning in Antibes" and "Double Vision", first editions, dust jackets.

1959

£200-300 BLO

Kennedy, John F., "Why England Slept", first edition, second printing, in first printing dust jacket, signed "Jack Kennedy", published by Wilfred Funk, Inc., New York.

1940

£7,000-10,000 BRB

Lee, Harper, "To Kill a Mockingbird", first English edition, original boards, dust jacket, 8vo., stained.

1960

£120-180 BLO

Mailer, Norman, "The Naked and the Dead", first edition, original cloth, dust jacket, New York, with "Barbary Shore", first English edition, ownership inscription on front endpaper, original cloth, worn.

1957

£200-250 BLO

Masterman, Walter, "The Green Toad", first edition, original cloth, dust jacket by E. McKnight Kauffer, slight foxing, rubbed and worn, 8vo.

1928

£500-800 BLO

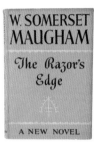

Maugham, W. Somerset, "The Razor's Edge", first English edition, inscribed by the author, published by Heinemann, London.

1944

£2,800-3,200   **BRB**

Miller, Arthur, "Death of a Salesman", first edition, winner of the Pulitzer Prize, inscribed by the author, published by The Viking Press, New York.

1949

£4,000-6,000   **BRB**

Miller, Henry, "Black Spring", first edition, first issue, from an edition of 1,000, original wrappers, 8vo., browned, worn, uncut.

1936

£500-600   **BLO**

Miller, Henry, "Max and the White Phagocytes", first edition, first issue, from an edition of 1,000, 8vo., original wrappers, neat ink ownership signature on half-title, slight edge creasing.

1938

£500-600   **BLO**

Miller, Henry, "The Rosy Crucifixion Book Two Plexus", first edition, two volumes, from an edition of 2,000 for private circulation, original wrappers, Olympia Press, Paris.

1953

£300-350   **BLO**

Morrison, Toni, "The Bluest Eye", first edition, the cover with a text design, published by Holt, Rinehart & Winston, New York.

1970

£2,800-3,200   **BRB**

Murdoch, Iris, "The Flight from the Enchanter", first edition, original cloth, 8vo., dust jacket in protective wrapper, creasing to head of spine.

1956

£500-800   **BLO**

Murdoch, Iris, "The Bell", first edition, original boards, 8vo., dust jacket, price clipped, slight top edge creasing.

1958

£50-80   **BLO**

Murdoch, Iris, "The Sea, The Sea", first edition, original boards, 8vo., dust jacket, slight creasing to head of spine.

1978

£80-120   **BLO**

Orwell, George, "Nineteen Eighty-Four", first edition, original cloth, green dust jacket, 8vo., ink ownership signature on front free endpaper, wear and restoration.

1949

£600-900   **BLO**

Pasternak, Boris, "Doctor Zhivago", first English edition, original cloth, dust jacket, 8vo., very slightly rubbed, spine slightly darkened and chipped at head.

1958

£150-200   **BLO**

Plath, Sylvia, "The Bell Jar", original boards, dust jacket, small ink signature on front free endpaper, Faber & Faber.

This is the first edition published under the author's true name.

1966

£220-280   **BLO**

Pynchon, Thomas, "V.", first English edition, original boards, dust jacket, a little rubbed, tanned, head of spine a little creased.

This was Pynchon's first book.

1963

£200-300   **BLO**

Rossetti, Christina, "Speaking Likenesses", first edition, wood-engraved frontispiece, title vignette, plates and illustrations by Arthur Hughes, original blue cloth, gilt, wear.

1874

£200-300   **BLO**

Rhys, Jean, "Voyage in the Dark", first edition, slightly darkened, original cloth, 8vo., a little faded at spine, worn at extremities and head of spine.

1934

£400-600 BLO

Saint-Exupery, Antoine de, "Le Petit Prince", first French-language edition, from a limited edition of 260, signed by the author, published by Reynal & Hitchcock, New York.

Issued simultaneously with the English limited edition, which was a larger run, the French edition is rarer and more desirable.

1943

£10,000-15,000 BRB

Sayers, Dorothy L., "The Unpleasantness at the Bellona Club", first edition, original purple cloth, name in pencil on front endpaper, wear, tape repaired at folds, price clipped, New York.

1928

£150-200 BLO

Tom Sharpe, "Riotous Assembly", first edition, original boards, dust jacket, 8vo.

1971

£120-180 BLO

Steinbeck, John, "The Red Pony", first edition, from an edition of 699 copies, numbered and signed by the author, in original numbered cardboard slipcase, published by Covici-Friede, New York.

1937

£3,000-5,000 BRB

Steinbeck, John, "Of Mice and Men", first English edition, frontispiece and pictorial headpieces by Michael Rothenstein, original cloth, 8vo., dust jacket, wear and tear, spine trimmed.

1937

£300-500 BLO

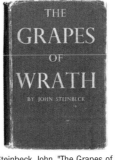

Steinbeck, John, "The Grapes of Wrath", first English edition, original cloth, 8vo., worn at peripheries, slightly tanned, small chips to spine ends, New York.

1939

£100-150 BLO

Steinbeck, John, "Cannery Row", first edition, first issue, original mustard cloth, 8vo., wear and restoration, New York.

This is the true first state first edition with the mustard coloured cloth as opposed to the brighter yellow cloth of the second state first edition.

1945

£300-400 BLO

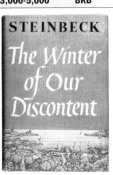

Steinbeck, John, "The Winter of Our Discontent", first edition, original publisher's boards, 8vo., dust jacket, spine tanned, price clipped, uncut, New York.

1961

£120-180 BLO

Thomas, Dylan, "Under Milk Wood", first edition, original cloth, dust jacket, 8vo.

1954

£250-300 BLO

Trevor, William, "A Standard of Behaviour", first edition, wear.

This was the Whitbread award winner's first book.

1958

£180-220 BLO

Verne, Jules, "The Purchase of the North Pole", first English edition, engraved frontispiece and illustrations throughout, tissue-guard, quires loose, several plates detached.

1891

£1,500-2,000 BLO

Wharton, Edith, "Italian Villas and Their Gardens", first American edition, published by The Century Co., New York.

1904

£1,200-1,800 BRB

Gould, J. and E., "Sparrow Hawk", a hand-coloured lithograph, folio sheet, matted.

c1835   19in (47.5cm) high
£180-220   FRE

Roberts, David, "Oblique View, Hall of Columns, Karnak", a hand-coloured lithograph, framed.

c1845   19in (47.5cm) high
£500-800   FRE

A CLOSER LOOK AT A LITHOGRAPH

Royal Academy of Arts alumni, Thomas Rowlandson, portrayed political subjects and London characters. He also illustrated a number of contemporary books by the likes of Henry Fielding and Oliver Goldsmith.

These high quality works were produced for Samuel Fores, one of the top dealers at the higher end of the market, although Rowlandson also produced some cheaper, less well-executed work.

COMFORTS of BATH.

Currier, N., a hand-coloured lithograph of "Young America", after James Butterworth, by Frances Flora Palmer, New York.

Palmer was a prominent 19thC graphic artist and one of the few women in her field.

27.75in (69cm) wide
£4,000-6,000   FRE

Cogniaux, Alfred, "Dictionnaire Iconographique des Orchidées", six volumes of text and 768 chromolithographic plates, wrappers preserved, the plates and accompanying text arranged by genus.

c1900
£2,500-3,000   FRE

This series of plates satirizes the activities of the affluent in the fashionable town of Bath. This one, 'The Portrait', shows a gentleman sitting for his portrait, while the viewer can see the couple behind the door.

Satirical prints became popular during the period as a result of political volatility, social excesses and a lack of censorship. The print captures the feeling of an age and is desirable.

Rowlandson, Thomas, "The Comforts of Bath" 12 hand coloured plates loosely inserted into a full red crushed morocco over-bevelled boards album, with white watered silk endpapers, 4to., Fores, London.

1798
£4,000-6,000   L&T

Wawra von Fernsee, Heinrich, "Botanische Ergebnisse der Reise Seiner Majestät des Kaisers von Mexico Maximillian I nach Brasilien", folio, original printed bands, 104 lithographic plates, 32 of which are partially coloured, Vienna.

1866
£2,500-3,000 set   FRE

Cappiello, Leonetto, "Cognac Pellisson", colour lithographic poster by, linen-backed, Vercasson, Paris.

1907   46in (115cm) high
£220-280   FRE

Pennell, Joseph and Robins, Elizabeth, "Lithography and Lithographers", with three original lithographs by Joseph Pennel, original gilt-lettered white vellum and gilt-lettered white vellum portfolio, in worn and soiled original box.

1916
£200-300   FRE

Sabartes, Jaime, "Picasso Toreros", with four original lithographs by Picasso, one in colour, other plates, original pictorial black stamped red cloth, New York.

1961
£800-1,200 set   FRE

Munting, Abraham, 'Ananas', a hand-coloured engraving, folio sheet, framed.

1696   *12.25in (30.5cm) high*

£150-200   **FRE**

Catesby, Mark, "Pseudoo & C. Flos. Passionins", a hand-coloured engraving, matted, depicting a Catesby snake.

c1745   *14in (35cm) high*

£300-500   **FRE**

An 18thC Persian "Anthology of Poems" manuscript, with contemporary flexible red morocco, double-page richly gilt and colour illuminated title and 176 pages with gold borders, Khate Shikest script, scuffed.

£400-600   **FRE**

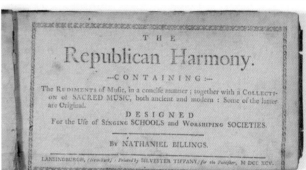

Billings, Nathaniel, "The Republican Harmony", unrecorded 18thC American Song writer, with ink inscription on front paste-down, Lansingburgh.

1795

£1,000-1,500   **FRE**

Piranesi, Giovanni Battista, "A Sua Eccellenza...", an etching of a perspective view of candelabrum.

1778   *27in (67.5cm) high*

£120-180   **FRE**

Michaux, Francois Andre and Nuttall, Thomas, "The North American Sylva", gilt-pictorial green cloth, 278 hand-coloured engraved plates, Philadelphia.

1855

£2,500-3,000   **FRE**

Beaton, Cecil, an original watercolour costume design drawing on paper.

c1950   *14.5in (36cm) high*

£600-900   **FRE**

Arp, Hans and Ernst, Max, "Geh durch den Spiegel", small folio, original pictorial red and white cloth, light wear, Cologne.

1960

£200-300   **FRE**

Thornton, Dr. Robert John, "The Night Blowing Cereus", a mezzotint engraving printed in colour and finished by hand, original colour, London.

1800   *19in (47.5cm) high*

£3,000-5,000   **FRE**

THE ARMS AND ARMOUR MARKET

The antique arms and armour market remains buoyant. High quality arms, such as guns and swords which are decorative and show the skill of the maker, attract a great deal of interest. Good pieces from Europe and the US almost always sell, and outstanding examples often command far above the estimate at auction.

The best firearms, particularly unrestored examples, are continuing to make record prices. The technically excellent pieces of John & Joseph Manton, dating from the late 18th to early 19thC are desirable, as are the early works of makers still in production, such as Purdey. Wheel-lock firearms from the 16th and 17thC are also valuable, especially decorative examples.

Since the 1990s, Scottish swords have become very popular, especially in the US and Canada, particularly basket hilted examples complete with scabbards. English swords are also sought after and highly decorative pieces can command high prices. Lyon and Turnbull recently sold an elaborate Teed, City of London, sword with an ornate gilded hilt and gold grip for £70,000, well exceeding all expectations. All types of 17th and early 18thC arms remain desirable, largely because this was a period of great craftsmanship. Cannons attract a great deal of interest in the US.

Early armour from the 14th and 15thC is extremely desirable. Pieces in good condition with maker's marks, such as that of Helmschmidt of Augsberg, sell for a premium.

In general, buyers favour pieces with strong provenance. Items that have a connection to an important historical figure or event lead the field. Condition is also crucial. Reproductions, or arms with missing parts and severe damage struggle to attract interest.

– John Batty, Consultant, Lyon & Turnbull

GUNS

A pair of flintlock duelling pistols, by W. Dupe of Oxford, with sawback handles, gold touch holes, filled lettering and octagonal barrels, in an adapted case with tools.

9.75in (24.5cm) long

£6,000-8,000   **LC**

An Austrian 20 bore flintlock holster pistol, by Georg Keiser of Vienna, with flat lock, swan neck cock and burr walnut fullstock, the plate engraved with a horseman, the top flat inlaid "Georg Keiser in Wienn".

c1730   *19.5in (49.5cm) long*

£1,500-2,000   **W&W**

A four-barrelled .32 Sharps' Patent pocket pistol, the barrels stamped "Address Sharps & Hankins, Philadelphia, Pa", the steel frame with "C. Sharps Patent Jan 25 1859", numbered "113366", in wooden case with modern accessories.

6in (15cm) long

£350-400   **W&W**

A pair of brass framed flintlock boxlock pocket pistols, the turn-off barrels with Birmingham proofs, with plain rounded walnut barrels, engraved with a Union shield, flags and owner's initials "FB", some wear.

c1820   *6in (15cm) long*

£700-1,000   **W&W**

A pair of flintlock pistols, with brass furniture, the belt clips with crown marks, marked with "GR" cypher.

12in (30.5cm) long

£1,800-2,200   **LC**

A pair of officer's double-barrelled 24 bore flintlock holster pistols, by Twigg, dark walnut halfstocks with chequered butts, engraved steel mounts, top ribs engraved "Twigg London", in original oak case, lid marked in ink "Major Hewett 22nd Regt", with tools.

c1785   *14.5in (37cm) long*

£8,000-12,000   **W&W**

A pair of Belgian percussion boxlock muff pistols, with turn-off damascus barrels and plain ivory grips, in a rosewood case with brass escutcheon and tools.

4.5in (11.5cm) long

£800-1,200   **W&W**

A pair of 11.4mm Belgian percussion target pistols, with blue fluted octagonal barrels, walnut halfstocks carved with vine leaves and fluted grips, in a rosewood veneered case.

16.75in (42.5cm) long

£4,000-6,000   W&W

A six shot self-cocking percussion pepperbox revolver, with polished walnut grips, fluted cylinder and round white metal frame, engraved "Bond, London, Improved revolving pistol".

7.25in (18.5cm) long

£700-1,000   W&W

A six shot .44 Colt Model 1860 Army percussion revolver, the walnut grips with inspector's marks and numbered "48787".

14in (35.5cm) long

£1,000-1,500   W&W

A French double-barrelled 20 shot 7mm pinfire double action revolver, by Lefaucheux, with chequered walnut grips and lanyard ring on butt, engraved "E. Lefaucheux Paris".

10in (25.5cm) long

£500-800   W&W

A six shot .44 Russian Smith & Wesson New Model Number 3 SA revolver, with address and patent dates on top rib, lower butt frame regimentally marked "892".

11.5in (29cm) long

£1,000-1,500   W&W

A six shot .44 Starr Arms Co. DA Army percussion revolver, the walnut butt with impressed stamp "Naval Yard Richmond VA Ins 1862", frame and cylinder marked "22503".

11in (28cm) long

£500-800   W&W

A pair of Holland & Holland Royal 12 bore side-lock ejector guns, with scroll-engraved hand detachable locks and figured dark walnut straight stocks with leather butt extensions, in original oak case.

£18,000-20,000   L&T

An ornate North Carolina long rifle, attributed to William Lamb, with full-stock flintlock, silver and brass engraved decoration and inlay, the lock plate marked "Phila," brown patina, restored.

c1820   *44.75in (113.5cm) long*

£6,000-9,000   BRU

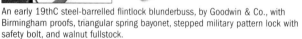

An early 19thC steel-barrelled flintlock blunderbuss, by Goodwin & Co., with Birmingham proofs, triangular spring bayonet, stepped military pattern lock with safety bolt, and walnut fullstock.

Many blunderbusses are fitted with a spring bayonet, used for mêlée combat.

34.5in (87.5cm) long

£1,200-1,800   W&W

A mid-19thC Northwest Trade gun, with brass serpent side plate and a large trigger guard, dark patina.

This piece bears signs of Native American use, including a cut-down barrel, hole in the stock for attachments, missing butt plate, and traces of tack decoration.

37in (94cm) long

£1,500-2,000   SK

SWORDS

A Georgian naval officer's dirk, by R. Clark & Son of London, the blued diamond-section blade with gilt arms and foliate decoration, with ribbed ivory hilt and engraved gilt scabbard.

9in (23cm) long

£700-1,000   W&W

A Georgian naval officer's dirk, with stylized dragon's head pommel, stylized crocodile crosspiece, ivory grip, and engraved gilt copper sheath.

12.5in (32cm) long

£400-600   W&W

MILITARIA

A Georgian naval officer's dirk, the diamond-section blade etched with floral decoration, with gilt bonnet-type pommel and ivory grip, in an embossed gilt sheath with Classical Greek medallion.

9in (23cm) long

£800-1,200 **W&W**

A Georgian naval officer's dirk, the flattened diamond section blade etched with foliage, with circular copper gilt guard, copper gilt mounts, turned ivory hilt with circular pommel, and copper gilt sheath.

c1810 *6in (15cm) long*

£350-400 **W&W**

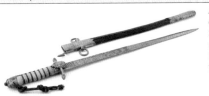

A George V naval officer's dirk by Gieve, Matthews & Seagrove, etched with regimental motifs, with lion's head pommel and fishskin covered grip.

17.75in (45cm) long

£320-380 **W&W**

An early 19thC Irish dirk, with diamond section blade, turned ebony grip, pommel carved with roped coil and steel mounted leather sheath, the locket engraved "Archer Dublin".

6in (15cm) long

£300-400 **W&W**

A Third Reich 1933 pattern NSKK dagger, by Eickhorn of Solingen, the hilt with solid nickel alloy mounts, in a painted sheath with steel mounts.

8.5in (21.5cm) long

£350-400 **W&W**

A French Ecole de Mars pupil's sidearm, the diamond section blade cut with three half-length fullers, in a brass-mounted scabbard, the blade blunted.

19.5in (49.5cm) long

£350-400 **W&W**

A Chinese Boxer period executioner's sword, the broad glaive-shaped blade cut with twin fullers, engraved with Chinese characters, with cord-bound grip and leather scabbard.

21.5in (54.5cm) long

£200-250 **W&W**

MEDALS

A Suakin 1884 medal from the Egyptian campaign, together with Khedive's star, dated.

1884 *2.5in (6.5cm) high*

£150-200 **W&W**

A Boer War Victoria Cross miniature dress group, comprising Victoria Cross, two campaign medals and a long service medal, unattributed.

1.75in (4.5cm) high

£280-320 **B**

A group of 11 miniatures, including a French Croix de Guerre.

3in (7.5cm) high

£180-220 **W&W**

A framed collection of medals awarded to Rifleman Fredrik Maskell, during the First World War.

13in (33cm) high

£350-400 **W&W**

A group of medals awarded to the Commander of HMS Foresight, comprising fifteen medals, among which are the O.B.E. and the US Bronze Star.

Commander Salter scuttled the HMS Edinburgh in 1942 to prevent its cargo of £40million in Russian gold from falling into the hands of the Germans.

2.75in (7cm) high

£22,000-28,000 **W&W**

Four medals awarded to Lieutenant R.B. St. O'Wall, including Victory, Defence and War, mounted as worn.

2.5in (6.5cm) high

£80-120 **W&W**

A rare 1768 Pioneer Infantry fur mitre cap, brown fur against dark red cloth, with large red-painted silver plated ear-to-ear plate, embossed with Royal Crest on a trophy of axes and handsaws with "GR", all within an ornamental motto scroll inscribed "Nec Aspera Terrent".

4in (10.25) high

£7,000-10,000   **W&W**

A Victorian Rifle Volunteers officer's shako, with patent leather peak top and headband, brass star helmet plate bearing a bugle horn with crowned laurel wreath and a leather plume.

8in (20.5cm) high

£600-900   **W&W**

A Victorian Northamptonshire Regiment officer's blue cloth spiked helmet, with rounded back peak, gilt peak binding, top mount and velvet backed chinchain with ear rosettes.

8.5in (21.5cm) high

£500-800   **W&W**

A Victorian 2nd Volunteer Battalion of the Royal Fusiliers officer's helmet, with rounded back peak, silver-plated peak binding, top mount, and helmet plate with rose and title circle.

8.75in (22cm) high

£500-800   **W&W**

The 1869 pattern shako, with patent leather peak, gilt shako plate with stencilled "24" in centre, lion's head ventilation hook and gilt plume socket with "VR" cypher on the ball, in a tin case with brass nameplate.

7.75in (19.5cm) high

£4,000-6,000   **W&W**

A scarce Victorian Military Prisons Staff officer's helmet, of ball-topped blue cloth, with Royal Arms helmet plate and leather and padded silk liner.

8.5in (21.5cm) high

£800-1,200   **W&W**

A Royal Air Force officer's full dress busby, leather skull with black fur trim, pale blue and gilt plaited cord, gilt and silver plaited badge, in round japanned tin case, inscribed to lid.

8.25in (21cm) high

£500-800   **W&W**

An Imperial German Saxon Garde Reiter regiment officer's helmet, with Saxon arms and a silvered lion parade crest with royal cypher on shield.

8.75in (22cm) high

£6,000-8,000   **W&W**

A WWI felt pickelhaube, from Saxony, the rear peak with regimental strap, with brass spike, leather chinstrap and cockades.

8in (20.5cm) high

£350-400   **W&W**

A Japanese Kabuto helmet, composed of twelve lacquered plates with applied copper gilt ribs and fittings, with foliate engraved decoration, the peak and protective fukigayeshi with gilt studs, the matching face mask with removable nose and laced throat lames.

13in (33cm) high

£1,500-2,000   **W&W**

WALLIS & WALLIS   Est. 1928

WEST STREET AUCTION GALLERIES, LEWES, SUSSEX, ENGLAND BN7 2NJ
TEL: +44 (0)1273 480208 FAX: +44 (0)1273 476562

Britain's Specialist Auctioneers of Arms, Armour, Medals & Militaria

*An emotive group of Orders and Medals to Commander Salter of HMS Foresight,
who in 1942, sank HMS Edinburgh. This group was sold in the Connoisseur
Collectors' Autumn 2004 auction and realized £21,000.*

2006 AUCTION DATES

SALE	DAY	LAST ENTRIES
488	January 10th	November 26th, 2005
489	February 14th	January 14th
490	March 21st	February 18th
491	May 2nd & 3rd, includes -	March 25th
	SPRING CONNOISEUR COLLECTORS' AUCTION	**March 21st**
492	June 13th	May 6th
493	July 18th	June 17th
494	August 29th	July 22nd
495	October 10th & 11th, includes -	September 2nd
	AUTUMN CONNOISEUR COLLECTORS' AUCTION	**August 29th**
496	November 21st	October 14th

Monthly Sale catalogue £8.50, Overseas airmail £9.50. Full colour
Connoisseur Sale catalogue £13.50 worldwide (all prices include postage)
*'Get to know the real value of your collection' - Our last 10 Sale catalogues
are available, price £30.00 inc. postage, complete with prices realised.*

Entry forms available on request
No charge for payment by credit card

email: auctions@wallisandwallis.co.uk   web site: http://www.wallisandwallis.co.uk

A Georgian officer's gilt gorget, engraved with crowned "GR" cypher.

4.5in (11.5cm) wide

£350-400　　**W&W**

A CLOSER LOOK AT A SCRIMSHAW POWDER HORN

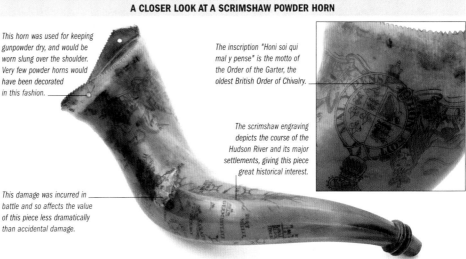

This horn was used for keeping gunpowder dry, and would be worn slung over the shoulder. Very few powder horns would have been decorated in this fashion.

The inscription "Honi soi qui mal y pense" is the motto of the Order of the Garter, the oldest British Order of Chivalry.

The scrimshaw engraving depicts the course of the Hudson River and its major settlements, giving this piece great historical interest.

This damage was incurred in battle and so affects the value of this piece less dramatically than accidental damage.

A Georgian scrimshaw powder horn, engraved with a map showing the river and settlements between Fort Stanwix, Fort Edward and New York, the lower part showing the Royal Arms, some battle damage.

c1760　　　　*13.5in (35cm) long*

£1,000-1,500　　**W&W**

A rare Indian 44th Infantry officer's gilt shako plate, with numerals "XLIV" on a mother-of-pearl backing and a wreath of laurel and palm leaves on a ten-pointed star, beneath a crown, inscribed "Auspicio Regis et Senatus Angliae".

c1845　　　　*4in (10cm) high*

£500-800　　**W&W**

A Victorian East Lothian Yeomanry Cavalry officer's pouch, of blue velvet with silver lace border, embroidered with a crown and "ELYC".

8in (20.5cm) wide

£120-180　　**W&W**

A Victorian Royal Artillery officer's full dress sabretache, embroidered with the Royal Arms, oak and laurel sprays and a solid gilt cannon.

A sabretache was a flat, long-strapped satchel, worn on the left side of a cavalryman's waist belt.

10in (25.5cm) high

£600-900　　**W&W**

A good Victorian Royal Artillery officer's shoulder belt set, comprising gilt lace belt, embroidered pouch with gilt lace border, gilt lace waistbelt with sword and sabretache slings, gilt snake clasp and lion's head buckles, in a tin case.

7in (18cm) wide

£400-600　　**W&W**

An Elizabeth II State Trumpeteers two-part embroidered trumpet banner, the damask embroidered with the Royal Arms, with flying angels and "ER", the floral border with a Union spray at each corner, gilt tasselled edges and suspension dees to top edge.

20in (51cm) wide

£800-1,200　　**W&W**

A rare 8th Bengal Cavalry officer's black pouch, the badge crowned "BC" over "VIII" over "Bengal Cavalry", with scrolls and brass mounts.

8in (20.5cm) wide

£120-180　　**W&W**

A London Scottish other ranks' sporran, with leather cantle, multi-coloured goatshair and two black tassels in white metal sockets with chains, the white metal cantle badge depicting a Glengarry cap.

9in (23cm) high

£150-200　　**W&W**

A Third Reich blockade runner's badge, by Otto Paczek of Berlin, complete with velvet lined box.

1.5in (4cm) diam

£300-400　　**W&W**

A German WWII period camera, painted in Afrika Korps colours, the lens mount stamped "Schneider Gottingen Xenon", the nameplate stamped "Handkammer".

11.25in (28.5cm) long

£500-600　　**W&W**

THE GOLF MARKET

The market for golfing antiques is less buoyant than during its heyday a decade ago. Despite this, pieces at the high end of the market are commanding greater prices than ever before. Buyers are currently attracted to golfing ceramics, particularly examples dating from c1900 and made by well-known factories such as Royal Doulton, Doulton Lambeth and Spode. Pieces need to be in good condition without restoration. Ceramics produced in Germany for the American market by makers such as Gerz, are also popular. Books and pictures also continue to perform well.

In terms of equipment, golf clubs have perhaps suffered the most from a declining market. Prices have come down for many examples, although this has enabled collectors on smaller budgets to buy quality clubs that have the potential to rise in value. Clubs at the very top of the market however, are attracting high prices. Examples by Hugh Philips of St. Andrews can sell for £10,000 or more, while clubs and balls by Tom Morris are also desirable. At the lower end of the market, collectors are becoming increasingly keen on other types of memorabilia, such as scorecards and Open programmes – even recent ones – and favour examples signed by players.

– Manfred Schotten, Manfred Schotten Antiques

CLUBS

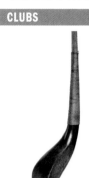

A long nose putter, by John Allan of Westward Ho, scared fruitwood head, horn insert and lead counterweight, hickory shaft, replacement grip.

Allen was the golf professional at Prestwick. This piece is rare as he only made a few clubs.

c1870

£1,800-2,200　　L&T

A B.W. Day long nose play club, with horn insert to sole, lead backweight and hickory shaft, the scared head stamped with maker's name, replacement wrapped leather grip, toe of head clipped.

£800-1,200　　L&T

An R. Dickson long nose putter, with horn insert to sole, lead backweight and hickory shaft, the scared head stamped with maker's name, replacement wrapped leather grip.

£400-600　　L&T

A one-piece straight-faced brassie, in hickory, a John Dunn patent for B.G.I. Co., the sole with ebony insert and brass plate, the face with a leather insert, lead counterweight, wrapped smooth leather grip.

£700-1,000　　L&T

A long nose wood, by Tom Dunn of Musselburgh, with a horn insert to sole, leather insert to face and a hickory shaft, lead counterweight, the head stamped "T Dunn".

c1880

£1,000-1,500　　L&T

A long nose play club, by R. Forgan of St. Andrews, with horn insert to sole, hickory shaft, and lead counterweight, the face mounted with an inscribed white metal plaque, with wrapped soft leather grip, the scared head stamped "R. Forgan" and with Prince of Wales feathers.

£10,000-15,000　　L&T

A long nose play club, by W. Frier of Edinburgh, the scared head with horn insert to sole, lead counterweight, hickory shaft and wrapped leather grip.

£1,200-1,800　　L&T

A William Gibson anti-shank Putter, with a wry neck, hickory shaft and wrapped leather square section grip, the head stamped "Lillywhite's London Woodfaced Putter, Special" and with star mark.

£1,500-2,000　　L&T

An early Karsten Co. 'Ping' putter, No. 1A, the brass head with a central shaft.

£1,000-1,500　　L&T

A rare Pro-swing practice club, with leaded brass ball head, hickory shaft and wrapped smooth leather grip.

£800-1,200   **L&T**

A hand-forged iron, by George Nichol of Leven, with gutta percha crimped hosel, hickory shaft and wrapped leather grip, stamped with patent number.
c1900

£2,500-3,500   **L&T**

A patent iron, by R.L. Urquhart, of conventional form, with an adjustable head and marked face, hickory shaft and wrapped leather grip, loose.

£800-1,200   **L&T**

An early unfinished blacksmith iron head.

£5,000-8,000   **L&T**

BALLS

A 'The Lunar' bramble rubber core ball, by the Scottish Golf Ball Manufacturing Co., with dot and crescent markings.
1912

£1,800-2,200   **L&T**

A Faroid 75 rubber core ball, with raised concentric circles, stamped at each pole in red.

£2,500-3,000   **L&T**

A hand-hammered gutta ball, by Andrew Patrick of Leven, stamped "A. Patrick, 27 1/2".

£10,000-15,000   **L&T**

A rare feather ball, of unusual proportions, inscribed in ink "Presented to Rev. H.M. Lamont by J.W.. Inglis C.B (?), an old student in St. Andrews, 18**" and "This ball was made by Wil. Robertson, 1790, Father (?) of Allan, the famous golfer", with protected lacquer to ball.

£25,000-30,000   **L&T**

BOOKS

Robert Clark, "Poems on Golf", first edition, privately printed in Edinburgh for subscribers and one of a limited edition of 58, illustrated with printer's vignettes, gilt stamped and lettered ribbed green cloth, inscription.

This work includes poems such as Mathison's "The Goff" and Carneigie's "Golfiana".
1867

£1,200-1,800   **L&T**

Bernard Darwin, "The Golf Courses of the British Isles", first edition, published by Duckworth, London, illustrated with sixty-four colour plates from paintings by Harry Rowntree, original gilt-decorated green cloth and grey cloth dust jacket.

This famous book covers the courses of Scotland, England and Ireland.

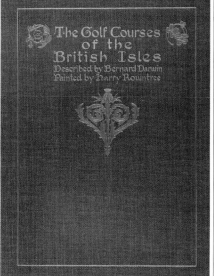

1910

£5,000-7,000   **L&T**

H.S.C. Everard, "A History of the Royal & Ancient Golf Club: St. Andrews from 1754-1900", first edition, published by William Blackwood, Edinburgh, illustrated, gilt-decorated green cloth cover.
1907

£800-1,200   **L&T**

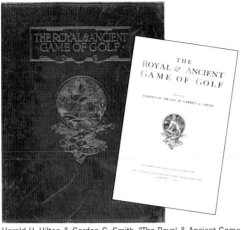

Harold H. Hilton & Garden G. Smith, "The Royal & Ancient Game of Golf", first edition, published by London & Counties Press, London, No. 40 of 900 copies, the Subscriber's edition, illustrations from paintings and photographs, the red vellum cover with gilt-tooled lion, gilt lettering to cover and spine.

1912

£1,500-2,000   **L&T**

E.C. Potter, "Midlothian Melodies, Mnemonic Maunderings of the Merry Muse", first edition, by appointment by the Midlothian Country Club, red cloth cover, gilt lettering, Chicago.

1900

£1,000-1,500   **L&T**

W.W. Tulloch, "The Life of Tom Morris, with Glimpses of St. Andrews and its Golfing Celebrities", first edition published by T. Werner Laurie, London, illustrations from 27 photographs, original pictorial green cloth cover, the spine lettered in gilt.

1908

£800-1,200   **L&T**

An Amateur Championship at St. Andrews "Official Programme", for 28th May 1930, with brown paper wrappers.

£3,000-5,000   **L&T**

OTHER GOLFING MEMORABILIA

A lithographed "Life Association of Scotland" advertising calendar, printed by Banks & Co., Edinburgh, with a golfing view of North Berwick and further golfing vignettes to the border.

1893   *22in (54cm) wide*

£2,000-3,000   **L&T**

John Blair, "North Berwick From The West", watercolour, with the links in the right middle distance, signed and inscribed lower right.

(10.25in) 26cm wide

£1,800-2,200   **L&T**

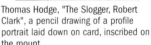

Thomas Hodge, "The Slogger, Robert Clark", a pencil drawing of a profile portrait laid down on card, inscribed on the mount.

(4.25in) 11cm high

£1,500-2,000   **L&T**

Life Magazine, "Fore! Life's Book for Golfers", first edition, published by Life Publishing, New York, illustrated with green cloth-backed pictorial boards and a cover design of a female golfer in the style of Charles Dana Gibson.

1900

£600-900   **L&T**

A Gerz salt-glazed stoneware jug and stopper, relief-moulded with golfers and caddies.

9in (23cm) high

£1,500-2,000   **L&T**

A pair of Bohemian iridescent glass vases, with enamel and gilt decoration of lady golfers.

(12.5in) 32cm high

£8,000-10,000   **L&T**

A pair of Copeland pottery golfing tygs, the body with relief moulding, decorated in white in the round with a scene of golfers and caddies, printed and impressed marks.

5.5in (14cm) high

£2,000-3,000   **L&T**

A Lenox pottery tobacco humidor, with a golfing scene in shades of green, the sterling silver cover by Shreve & Co., printed mark.

6in (15.5cm) high

£4,000-6,000   **L&T**

THE DECORATIVE ARTS MARKET

A landmark exhibition at the Victoria and Albert Museum last summer attracted media attention to the Arts and Crafts style, which has been mustering strong market interest for some time now. Decorative arts designed by giants of the movement, including William Morris, Charles Robert Ashbee and the Martin Brothers, are hot commodities right now.

Prestigious sales of silverware by Christopher Dresser and Omar Ramsden highlighted the desire among the buying public to acquire pieces by recognised designers. Generic products, or items done in the style of a known designer but lacking identifying marks, are consequently pushed to the sidelines. At the top and bottom ends of the market, anything that is representative of its period can be expected to find a buyer. Mid-range pieces, on the other hand, are proving slightly more difficult to sell.

Following the runaway success of pottery by Poole and Troika in recent years, interest in other small potteries is growing as buyers try to secure a stake in the next big thing. Carn and Hornsea, for example, have been subject to increasing market speculation in the last year. Studio pottery from the second half of the 20thC is a particularly buoyant sector and there is a very wide range available to choose from.

Inter-war Lalique glass has been the subject of healthy interest in recent months. This trend looks set to continue as a new generation starts to build specialist collections of perfume bottles and car mascots. The quantity of Lalique glass on the secondary market is actually dwindling while demand increases, and this potent combination of factors can only lead to higher prices at auction and in dealers' salerooms.

AMPHORA

An Amphora cylindrical vase, of tapering form with inverted rim, painted with cattle in a landscape, the base with stylised flowerhead frieze in relief, the rim with gilt decoration, printed and impressed marks "3731".

15.25in (38cm) high

£300-500   **L&T**

A large Amphora shouldered vase, of ovoid form, with everted rim, painted with cattle in a landscape, stylised flowerhead frieze to base, the rim with gilt decoration, printed and impressed marks "3760".

17in (42.5cm) high

£500-700   **L&T**

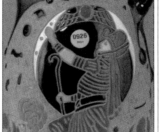

A tall Amphora water jug, with crossed handles, enamel-decorated with Egyptian motifs in polychrome, stamped numbers.

14.5in (37cm) high

£300-350   **DRA**

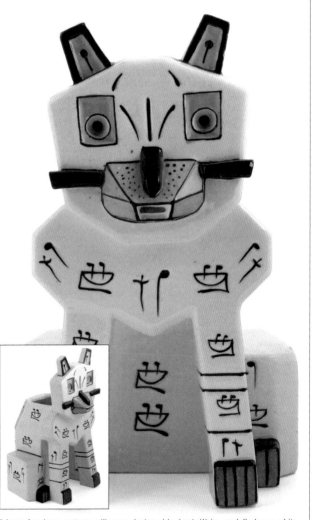

A large Amphora pottery spill vase, designed by Louis Wain, modelled as a white cat, with printed mark and impressed facsimile signature.

10.25in (26cm) high

£4,000-6,000   **WW**

A Boch Frères 'Gres Keramis' blue vase, with a cockerel design.

c1925   *11.5in (29cm) high*

£1,000-1,500   **MOD**

A Boch Frères 'Gres Keramis' green vase, with a cockerel design.

c1925   *6.75in (17cm) high*

£700-1,000   **MOD**

BOCH FRÈRES

- Boch Frères was founded by Pierre-Joseph Boch in Luxembourg in 1767 and was passed down through subsequent generations.
- It became Villeroy and Boch in 1836.
- In 1841, the Belgium branch of the Boch family set up a factory at La Louvière and traded as Boch Frères.
- The Boch Frères company became well known for its Art Deco ceramics. Pieces were of high quality and simple in form.
- Charles Catteau (1880-1966) was one of the factory's leading designers. He had worked as a potter at Sèvres and Nymphenburg before joining Boch Frères as Design Director in 1907. He was influenced by Japanese and African design as well as the Avant Garde and Bauhaus movements.
- Catteau joined the 'Circle of Friends of the Fine Arts' in 1908. His Art Deco work won him a grand prix at The International Exhibition of Decorative Arts in 1925.
- The company is still in production today.

A rare and early Boch Frères 'Gres Keramis' stoneware vase, by Charles Catteau, in brown and beige.

c1925   *7.75in (20cm) high*

£700-1,000   **MOD**

An early Boch Frères bulbous vase, by Charles Catteau, stamped "Boch Frères Keramis/Ch. Catteau", numbered.

8.75in (22cm) high

£1,800-2,200   **SDR**

A Boch Frères bulbous stoneware vase, by Charles Catteau, green ink stamps, "Boch Frères/Keramis/Made in Belgium/CH. Catteau" with numbers, and incised "Gres Keramis".

10.25in (26cm) high

£1,200-1,800   **SDR**

An early Boch Frères 'Keramis' vase, designed by Charles Catteau, in green and white with a stylised deer design.

c1925   *12.5in (32cm) high*

£2,000-2,500   **MOD**

A CLOSER LOOK AT A BOCH FRÈRES VASE

Boch Frères Keramis produced some of the finest ceramics in Belgium during the Art Deco period. With its geometric detailing, this is a classic Art Deco design.

Pieces identified as being by the renowned designers Arthur Finch or Charles Catteau will usually attract a premium. The maker of this vase is unknown.

Boch Frères Keramis often used enamels to decorate its ceramics. As well as the coloured metal mounts seen on this vase, the company also produced cloisonné work.

The colours on this vase have lost none of their vibrancy, so it has held its value particularly well.

A Boch Frères Keramis pottery vase, with geometric flowers on a craquelure ground, printed "Keramis" mark.

10.75in (27.5cm) high

£400-600   **WW**

A very rare Art Deco Boch Frères faceted vase, covered in Persian blue crackled glaze, with French enamelled metal mounts, black ink stamp to body, metal stamped "France", some wear to enamel.

10in (25.5cm) high

£2,500-3,500   **SDR**

A Carlton ware 'Chevron' Handcraft vase, pattern number 3657, with printed and painted marks.

4.25in (10.5cm) high

£300-400 WW

A Carlton ware 'Heron and Magical Tree' vase, with printed factory mark.

5in (13cm) high

£300-500 WW

A Carlton ware 'Fantasia' vase, pattern number 3406, with printed and painted marks.

7in (17.5cm) high

£600-800 WW

A Carlton ware oviform lustre jug, painted with highly stylised flowers and foliage against a mottled orange lustre ground, with a gilded handle, factory marks to base.

7.75in (19.5cm) high

£400-600 DN

An Art Deco Carlton ware 'Fantasia' wall plaque, pattern number 3388, printed and painted marks, paper label, repair to foot rim.

15.75in (40cm) diam

£800-1,200 WW

CLARICE CLIFF

A Clarice Cliff Bizarre 'Applique Avignon' octagonal plate, with printed mark, restored.

8.75in (22cm) diam

£700-900 WW

A Clarice Cliff Bizarre 'Applique Palermo' octagonal plate, with printed mark.

8.5in (21.5cm) diam

£1,000-1,500 WW

A Clarice Cliff Fantasque Bizarre two-handled grapefruit bowl, painted in coloured enamels with a version of the 'Autumn' pattern, printed marks in black.

6.75in (17cm) wide

£220-280 NEA

A Clarice Cliff Bizarre 'Autumn' cachepot, painted with a pattern of trees with sinuous trunks and a small cottage, black printed marks.

c1930

6.25in (16cm) high

£400-600 HAMG

CLARICE CLIFF

CLARICE CLIFF

- Clarice Cliff (1899-1972) joined A.J. Wilkinson, Staffordshire, in 1916 and, following the firm's acquisition of Newport Pottery in 1920, she was given her own studio. Here she began to decorate discarded stock with distinctive bright designs over a honey glaze.

- The 'Bizarre' range of pottery for everyday use was launched in 1928. Early pieces were decorated with triangular shapes. In the same year, the 'Fantasque' range was introduced. Cliff went on to design over 500 shapes and 2,000 patterns.

- Cliff became Art Director of A. J. Wilkinson's in 1931 and continued to design pieces into the 1950s, although her pre-war work is considered more innovative.

- As well as tableware, she also produced novelty pieces, including figures and wall masks, which are sought after today.

- Clarice Cliff pieces are hotly collected and widely available. The 'Inspiration' pattern is rare, as is the 'Circus' series produced with Laura Knight.

A Clarice Cliff Fantasque Bizarre 'Blue Chintz' Archaic vase, with printed mark.

12.25in (31cm) high

£1,200-1,800   **WW**

A Clarice Cliff Bizarre 'Blue W' Coronet jug, with printed mark.

6.5in (16.5cm) high

£1,200-1,800   **WW**

A Clarice Cliff Bizarre 'Crocus' pattern honey jar and cover, the beehive shape typically painted, an orange-striped grey bee as cover finial, printed marks.

3in (7.5cm) high

£250-300   **CHEF**

A large Clarice Cliff Bizarre 'Crocus' conical bowl, with printed mark.

9in (23cm) diam

£800-1,200   **WW**

A Clarice Cliff Fantasque Bizarre 'Farmhouse' candlestick, printed mark.

3.25in (8cm) high

£200-300   **WW**

A Clarice Cliff Bizarre 'Gay Day' cylindrical preserve pot and cover, printed and painted marks, damage.

3in (7.5cm) high

£150-200   **WW**

A Clarice Cliff Bizarre 'Gay Day' conical bowl, on a base of four triangles, printed marks in black.

7.5in (19.5cm) diam

£400-600   **NEA**

A Clarice Cliff Bizarre 'Latona Flowerheads' 358 vase, with printed and painted marks.

8.25in (21cm) high

£800-1,200   **WW**

A Clarice Cliff Bizarre 'The Laughing Cat' figure, painted with green, black and orange spots, with printed mark.

4.75in (12cm) high

£1,500-2,000   **WW**

A Clarice Cliff 'Mango' basket vase, with a brown café au lait background, the orange double skinned fruit with stylised bold black leaves, printed mark to underside.

14.25in (36cm) high

£400-600 ROS

A Clarice Cliff Fantasque Bizarre 'Mondrian' Tankard coffee pot and cover, with printed mark, restoration.

7.5in (19cm) high

£800-1,200 WW

A Clarice Cliff 'Newlyn' vase, with flared rim and pedestal foot, the interior with Delecia runnings, black printed mark "Clarice Cliff Newport England" and raised numbers "709/5".

c1935   5.25in (13cm) high

£600-900 HAMG

A Clarice Cliff 'Orange Chintz' sugar sifter, with electroplated pierced lid, printed mark "Newport Pottery Co. Ltd."

£400-500 L&T

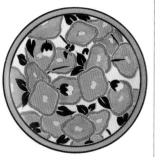

A Clarice Cliff Fantasque Bizarre 'Orange Chintz' wall plaque, with printed mark.

13.25in (33.5cm) diam

£800-1,200 WW

A Clarice Cliff Fantasque Bizarre 'Orange House' biscuit barrel and cover, with printed mark, hairline crack to rim.

5.5in (14cm) high

£1,800-2,200 WW

A pair of Clarice Cliff Bizarre 'Pansies' pattern vases, factory mark to the underside.

4.75in (12cm) high

£400-600 ROS

A Clarice Cliff Bizarre 'Orange Trees and Houses' Stamford tea set for two, with printed marks.

4.75in (12cm) high

£3,000-4,000 WW

A Clarice Cliff 'Patina Country' vase, painted with a rolling landscape of trees with a pink speckled patina glaze, black printed marks and moulded shape number.

1933   9.5in (24.5cm) high

£400-600 HAMG

A Clarice Cliff Bizarre 'Rhodanthe' pattern vase, the inverted bullet shape supported on three buttress feet and painted with orange, ochre and yellow flowers, printed marks, shape 452.

9in (21.5cm) high

£300-500 CHEF

A Clarice Cliff Fantasque Bizarre 'Rudyard' conical sugar sifter, with printed mark.

5.5in (14cm) high

£1,200-1,800 **WW**

A Clarice Cliff Bizarre 'Rudyard' single-handled Isis vase, with printed mark.

10in (25.5cm) high

£1,500-2,000 **WW**

A Clarice Cliff conical sugar sifter, in the 'Secrets' pattern, printed mark.

5.5in (13.5cm) high

£500-700 **L&T**

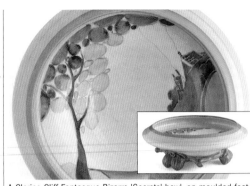

A Clarice Cliff Fantasque Bizarre 'Secrets' bowl, on moulded feet, with printed mark.

9.75in (25cm) diam

£250-350 **WW**

A Clarice Cliff Fantasque Bizarre 'Sunrise' conical bachelor set, comprising a teapot and cover, milk and sugar, one cup, saucer and side plate, with printed marks.

4.75in (12cm) high

£1,500-2,000 **WW**

A Royal Staffordshire Clarice Cliff 'Water-Lily' bowl, printed mark.

8.75in (22cm) wide

£70-100 **WW**

A CLOSER LOOK AT A CLARICE CLIFF PLAQUE

Large wall plaques like this one are among the most highly sought-after Clarice Cliff pieces.

Large, plain designs provide an ideal canvas on which to show off Fantasque Bizarre patterns.

Produced in smaller numbers than the utility ware, wall plaques are harder to come by and therefore more valuable.

The 'Red Tulip' pattern is one of the rarer designs found on the market today. An example as large and well preserved as this one is an exceptional find.

A Clarice Cliff Fantasque Bizarre 'Tulip' wall plaque, with printed mark.

13.5in (34cm) diam

£2,500-3,000 **WW**

A Clarice Cliff pierced roundel, decorated with moulded stylised flowers in yellow and orange with black leaves, black printed mark.

c1930 *8in (20cm) diam*

£200-300 **HAMG**

A Clarice Cliff pierced roundel, decorated with moulded stylised flowers in yellow and orange with green leaves, blue printed mark.

c1930 *13.25in (33.5cm) diam*

£200-300 **HAMG**

A Clarice Cliff Original Bizarre 'Isis' vase, impressed and printed marks.

c1930 *10in (25.5cm) high*

£400-500 **HAMG**

A Clarice Cliff Original Bizarre 366 vase, with printed mark.

6in (15.5cm) high

£800-1,200 **WW**

A William de Morgan 'BBB' ruby lustre tile, painted with a fan-shaped flower and foliage against a white background, impressed mark "DIP" for partnership between de Morgan, Iles and two Passenger brothers.

6in (15.5cm) wide

£200-300 — **DN**

A William de Morgan 'Persian' rectangular tile, decorated in soft greens, turquoises and blues with scrolling foliage, florets and buds, impressed Sands End rosette mark.

8in (20.5cm) wide

£150-250 — **DN**

A William de Morgan two-handled urn and cover, the body painted with birds perched among fruiting trees in a landscape, impressed Sands End mark, painted mark "FULHAM 2249 JH 19".

£3,000-3,500 — **L&T**

A William de Morgan 'Iznik' bowl, of deep circular form, decorated outside with curled fronds, flowers and leaves and inside with a circular panel of tulip flowers within a stellar band, painted mark "W DE MORGAN, FULHAM, JJ".

10.5in (26cm) diam

£2,000-3,000 — **L&T**

A William de Morgan 'Persian' pottery vase, by Joe Juster, painted with carnation sprays, impressed Sands End mark, painted "JJ", minor damage and restoration.

8.25in (21cm) high

£3,000-4,000 — **WW**

DE PORCELEYNE FLES

- De Porceleyne Fles was established c1635 at Delft, the Dutch home to over 30 ceramic factories during the period. The company name translates as 'The Porcelain Jar' and jar-shaped marks were applied to its wares. It was one of best-known companies operating in the area and survived longer than most of the region's great earthenware factories.
- In 1876 it was purchased by engineer Joost Thooft. He added the mark "Delft" and began to experiment with new designs.
- Earlier output consisted of blue and white wares, but by the start of the 20thC, De Porceleyne Fles under Thooft and then Abel Labouchere was producing pieces in the Arts and Crafts and Art Nouveau styles, including dinner services, object d'art and decorative tiles.
- By the end of 1919, the factory had received royal designation and it is still in operation today.

A De Porceleyne Fles "Kerstmis 1946" Christmas tile, with two people walking in the snowy town of Delft at night, stamped bottle mark "TL, Delft".

7.75in (19cm) high

£100-150 — **DRA**

An early De Porceleyne Fles vertical tile with a white ostrich by a fruit tree, minor damage, unmarked.

8.25in (20.5cm) high

£200-250 — **DRA**

A De Porceleyne Fles fine vertical tile with a white rooster, stamped bottle mark "J, Delft".

8.75in (22cm) high

£350-400 — **DRA**

A rare De Porceleyne Fles horizontal tile with two owls by a ruin, small firing flaw to corner, damage, stamped bottle mark "TL, Delft".

9in (22.5cm) wide

£350-400 — **DRA**

A rare De Porceleyne Fles tile, light abrasion, stamped bottle mark "TL, Delft".

13.5in (34cm) wide

£300-400 — **DRA**

DOULTON LAMBETH

A Doulton Lambeth stoneware vase by Hannah Barlow, of shouldered cylindrical form with applied foot, decorated with a frieze of children, goats and donkeys, impressed and incised marks, restored base.

10.75in (27cm) high

£800-1,200　　　　**L&T**

A Doulton Lambeth stoneware biscuit barrel and cover by Florence Barlow, with electroplated mounts and hinged cover, decorated with a frieze of horses, impressed and incised marks, cracks under mounts.

8in (20cm) high

£400-600　　　　**L&T**

A Doulton and Watts Lambeth stoneware spirit barrel, the sides decorated in relief with bands of fruiting vine and the Royal Coat of Arms.

c1840　　*15in (38cm) high*

£150-200　　　　**H&L**

A large Doulton Lambeth stoneware vase, by Hannah Barlow, incised with a band of grazing horses between foliate borders, on a buff ground, impressed mark, incised monogram.

17in (43cm) high

£1,000-1,500　　　　**WW**

A Doulton Lambeth stoneware jardinière, by Mark V. Marshall, incised with mythical beasts below a band of scrolling foliage, impressed marks, incised monogram.

6.5in (16.5cm) high

£700-900　　　　**WW**

A Doulton Lambeth candlestick designed by Edith Lupton, incised and impressed marks with date "1876".

8.75in (22cm) high

£180-220　　　　**CHEF**

ROYAL DOULTON

A pair of Royal Doulton stoneware vases, of shouldered baluster form, tubeline decoration with white roses and foliage, on a mottled blue ground, impressed mark and "MB" monogram.

14in (36cm) high

£300-400　　　　**HAMG**

A pair of Royal Doulton vases, by Hannah Barlow, incised with grazing donkeys in a landscape between applied foliate borders, incised marks, one with restored chip to base rim.

11in (28cm) high

£1,200-1,800　　　　**WW**

A Royal Doulton 'Seaweed' stoneware baluster vase, by George Tinworth, with applied and incised foliage decoration, and white tubelining, factory marks and signed with "GT" monogram.

10.5in (27cm) high

£380-420　　　　**DN**

A Royal Doulton 'Calumet' figure, number HN2068, by C.J. Noke.

6.5in (16cm) high

£180-220　　　　**DN**

A Royal Doulton figure, 'The Wizard', designed by A. Maslankowski, HN 2877.

9.75in (25cm) high

£120-180   **CHEF**

A Royal Doulton 'Mamselle' figure by L. Harradine, with printed and painted marks, HN786, chip to hat.

7in (17.5cm) high

£2,500-3,000   **WW**

A Royal Doulton figure, 'The Welsh Girl', designed by E.W. Light, in bronze finish, repaired neck and plinth.

13.5in (34cm) high

£280-320   **GORL**

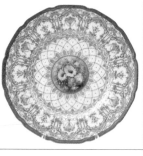

A Royal Doulton plate, painted by R. Carnock, with coloured enamel flowers within raised paste gilded trellis and vase bands, signed, printed green mark and retailer's mark for "Davis Collamore & Co Ltd, New York".

8.75in (22cm) diam

£100-150   **LFA**

An unusual Royal Doulton tea trio, modelled in low relief with fish amongst waterweed, the cover modelled with a seated frog, comprising teapot and cover, milk and sugar, impressed marks.

5in (13cm) high

£1,500-2,000   **WW**

GOLDSCHEIDER

- Goldscheider was established in Vienna in 1885. It produced Art Nouveau figures in a variety of materials including terracotta.
- During the 1920s and 1930s, the factory became one of the few Austrian ceramic firms to concentrate on Art Deco pieces.
- The company produced a wide range of models, many depicting female figures in elaborate modern costumes decorated in rich bright colours. Pieces, many of which are marked "Goldscheider", included ballerinas, Pierrettes, and cast plaster copies of bronze sculptures.

- The boldly coloured wall masks made by the company during the Art Deco period are highly collectable. They are hand-painted with stylised and simplified features and typically have curled hair. They were made from terracotta and are prone to chipping and damage.
- The Staffordshire firm Myott, Son & Co. produced Goldscheider from the late 1930s. These pieces, marked "Goldscheider made in England", are less sought-after than Austrian examples.
- The Goldscheider factory closed in 1954.

A large Goldscheider ceramic sculpture of Diana the Huntress, by Latour, with polychrome glaze, mounted on a bow-front base, black ink stamp "Goldscheider Wien/Made in Austria", with numbers and artist's signature, restoration, missing bow and arrow.

23.25in (33.5cm) high

£700-1,000   **SDR**

A Goldscheider pottery figure of a dancer, by Josef Lorenzl, signed to the skirt, base with black stamp and model number "5715/49/8".

c1930

16in (40cm) high

£1,500-2,000   **DOR**

A Goldscheider pottery figure of a girl standing on a drum, from a model by Josef Lorenzl, printed and impressed marks, restored.

14.5in (37cm) high

£1,000-1,500   **WW**

A Goldscheider figure, by Dakon, depicting a lady holding aloft the trail of her red floral skirt.

15in (38cm) high

£2,000-2,500   **BEV**

A Goldscheider figure, by Joseph Lorenzl, of an elegant lady in white hat and red dress.

13in (33cm) high

£1,200-1,800   **BEV**

A Goldscheider pottery figure of a dandy, designed by Lorenzl, with printed and impressed marks.

11.5in (29cm) high

£450-550   **WW**

A Goldscheider figure, 'Mephistopheles', by Josef Lorenzl, printed marks.

14.25in (36cm) high

£1,200-1,800   **WW**

A Goldscheider Art Deco figure of 'The Captured Bird', modelled as a dancing girl wearing batwing sleeves outstretched, painted and impressed marks, restored leg.

12.75in (32cm) high

£800-1,200   **L&T**

A large Goldscheider terracotta group, modelled as a woman and lion on an architectural base with lion masks, impressed factory marks and a metal retail label from Bordeaux.

20in (51cm) high

£700-1,000   **DN**

A Goldscheider ceramic bust of a woman with wavy hair, holding a flower in her hand, stamped "Goldscheider / Wien / Made in Austria", with incised numbers and remnant of foil label, restoration.

8.75in (22cm) high

£400-600   **SDR**

A Goldscheider earthenware head of a woman in dark brown clay, her features in turquoise and orange glaze, mounted on an ebonised wood block, marked with metal tag, minor damage.

10.75in (27.5cm) high

£400-600   **SDR**

A Goldscheider figure modelled as a draped maiden holding a conch to her ear, impressed marks, artist's signature, glaze flakes and chip to base rim.

26in (66cm) high

£450-500   **WW**

A CLOSER LOOK AT A GOLDSCHEIDER CLOCK

Goldscheider sculptural models are very popular. Rare examples will attract a premium, especially if they bear the mark of Ludwig Goldscheider.

Cabochons are precious stones that have been polished but remain uncut, and so have no facets. Opal cabochons of various colours have been applied to this piece.

This clock was made as a unique exhibition piece, which increases its market value substantially.

The large scale and dramatic subject matter of this clock makes it an impressive and unusual commodity.

A monumental Art Nouveau sculptural clock, by Ludwig Goldscheider, with a semi-nude maiden and an eagle, with grey glaze, glass and genuine opal cabochons, marked "Ludwig Goldscheider/Wien", with stamped numbers, chip to one corner and replaced works.

c1870   *25in (64cm) high*

£2,500-3,000   **DRA**

A Katshutte pottery figure, modelled as a nude maiden feeding a deer, with printed mark.

13in (33cm) wide

£450-500 WW

A Katshutte pottery figure, modelled as a naked dancer, printed mark.

11in (28cm) high

£400-600 WW

A Lenci figure, by A. Jacopi, painted marks, impressed artist's signature, glaze nick.

18.5in (47cm) high

£500-800 WW

A Lenci figure of an Alpine walker, her gloves with Tyrolean motifs, painted mark "Lenci Made in Italy" and impressed number "697".

17in (43cm) high

£1,800-2,200 HAMG

A Lenci figure of a nude sea nymph, encircled by a rainbow-coloured ribbon, painted marks.

18.75in (47cm) high

£3,000-4,000 L&T

A Lenci figure of a girl in culottes, standing on a lozenge base, painted marks, impressed mark "698".

18in (45cm) high

£2,000-3,000 L&T

A Lenci earthenware figure of a lady holding a parasol and wearing a blue-check crinoline dress, painted mark and date "15.2.29".

1929   *12in (30cm) high*

£350-400 GORL

A large Czechoslovakian wall mask, modelled as a girl screaming, with printed mark, restored.

10.75in (27cm) high

£800-1,200 WW

A Czechoslovakian wall mask, modelled as a girl screaming, with printed mark.

8.75in (22cm) high

£700-900 WW

A Keramos terracotta wall mask, modelled as a young girl holding a mask, with printed mark.

9.75in (25cm) high

£800-1,200 WW

A Czechoslovakian wall mask, modelled as a girl wearing a beret, with printed mark.

8.75in (22cm) high

£400-600 WW

A Minton majolica nut dish, leaf-moulded with a squirrel handle, date code, repaired damage.

1870   *9.5in (24cm) wide*

£150-200   **GORL**

One of a set of three Minton majolica lily leaf dishes, shape number 1086, realistically modelled, with impressed marks.

6in (15.5cm) long

£60-90 set   **HAMG**

A Minton majolica leaf dish, realistically modelled, unmarked.

9in (23cm) long

£60-90   **HAMG**

A CLOSER LOOK AT A MINTON MAJOLICA PIE DISH

Minton majolica was the brainchild of Joseph Arnoux, who sought to replicate the work of the 16thC French artist Bernard Palissy. It was launched at the Great Exhibition of 1851.

Game pie dishes were particularly significant in the Victorian era as they alluded to the wealth of the hostess who was able to provide such delicacies for her guests.

Naturalistic motifs, such as the animal decoration and mushroom finial, are typical of Victorian majolica.

Despite the many delicate protrusions, this piece is intact and in unrestored condition.

A Minton majolica game pie dish and cover, the body moulded with ducks amongst green ferns and ivy, fox mask handles, the interior in white, the cover with two central mushrooms and flowers, impressed marks, date code.

1880   *15.74in (40cm) wide*

£7,000-9,000   **CHEF**

A Minton green-glazed basket-moulded platter, with ears of corn handles.

16in (41cm) wide

£350-450   **GORL**

A Minton majolica oval game pie tureen and cover, the ozier-moulded base with trailing oak leaves, the cover moulded with a coot, rabbit and mallard, damaged.

c1865   *12.75in (32cm) wide*

£200-300   **DN**

A Minton majolica 'Tower' jug with a hinged cover, moulded with dancing medieval figures, the scallop-shell moulded cover with a jester's head finial, impressed marks, shape 1231, date code for 1868, cover cracked.

£300-500   **DN**

A Minton majolica jug, moulded in relief with oak leaves and acorns on a bark effect ground, the pewter cover with a porcelain thumbpiece.

5.5in (14cm) high

£200-300   **ROS**

A Minton majolica floriform vase, applied with sprays of bluebells, on three bulb feet, painted with typical coloured glazes, impressed marks, date code, chipped and repaired.

1865   7in (18cm) high

£1,000-1,500   DN

A Minton majolica nautilus vase, the pink-rimmed shell supported on a seaweed column with two dolphins, on an aubergine socle within a mottled green and brown gadrooned oval foot, impressed marks, date code, damaged.

1863   19.5in (24cm) high

£700-900   CHEF

A pair of Minton majolica figural wall sconces, modelled as two half-length figures of men in Renaissance dress, each within a laurel-wreath bordered oval frame, impressed marks, one with date code and model number "1222".

1866   18.5in (46cm) high

£5,000-8,000   DN

GEORGE JONES MAJOLICA

A matched pair of Minton majolica character jugs, modelled as a man and woman in 18thC dress, impressed marks, date codes for 1864 and 1867, some damage and repairs.

11.5in (29cm) high

£1,800-2,200   DN

A pair of Minton majolica tiles, relief-moulded with birds on a lavender ground, framed, raised mark "Minton Hollins & Co".

9.75in (24.5cm) wide

£200-400   HAMG

A George Jones majolica 'Monkey' teapot and cover, moulded in relief with a flowering shrub, with faux bois spout, the handle modelled as a monkey, impressed monogram and indistinct registration lozenge, damage and repairs.

c1875   11in (28cm) wide

£800-1,200   DN

A George Jones majolica cheese stand and cover, the cover moulded with a band of leaves and ropetwist border on a lavender ground, the knop modelled as a cow, impressed mark "GJ" and painted number 2200, slight damage.

c1875   9in (23cm) high

£1,500-2,000   HAMG

A George Jones majolica faux bois strawberry dish, with two bluetits on a trellis handle, moulded in relief with strawberry plants, impressed marks and registration lozenge for February 1875, lacks sugar and cream bowl, small chips.

15in (38cm) wide

£2,500-3,000   DN

A Georges Jones majolica ozier-moulded sardine box and cover, of typical form, the cover with a sardine finial, painted with coloured glazes, impressed marks.

c1875   8.25in (20.5cm) wide

£300-500   DN

A George Jones majolica jardinière stand, in the Neoclassical style, waisted top with tortoiseshell glazed disc insert and anthemion cast frieze, on a fluted column with spiral laurel leaf decoration, above a beaded plinth, impressed mark and impressed letter "L".

c1880   36in (90cm) high

£1,000-1,500   L&T

A late 19thC Wedgwood majolica japanesque jug, moulded in relief with fans, birds and flowering prunus, impressed marks, date code.

1883   *9.25in (23cm) high*

£100-150   **DN**

A late 19thC Continental majolica mug, decorated with a bird in flight above a border of green leaves, the handle modelled as a branch.

£80-120   **DN**

A late 19thC Continental majolica basket, modelled as a log with intertwined leaves, the interior with a pale pink glaze.

£80-120   **DN**

A Wedgwood majolica green-glazed and pierced chestnut basket, of flared ozier-moulded form, impressed marks and date code.

1880   *8in (20cm) wide*

£100-150   **DN**

A Wedgwood majolica salad bowl and servers, the interior printed with flowers and the exterior moulded with three winged lion's feet, the electroplate servers by James Dixons and Sons, date letter.

1887   *bowl 10.25in (26cm) diam*

£220-280   **CHEF**

An unusual English majolica miniature ewer, in the form of a frog, perched on a blue glazed ball, probably Copeland, small chips to lip.

c1870   *2.75in (7cm) high*

£700-900   **LFA**

A Joseph Holdcroft majolica nut dish, with two oval sections and a branch handle, painted with coloured glazes, impressed mark, restored.

c1880   *11in (28cm) wide*

£80-120   **DN**

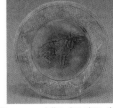

An Etruscan majolica dog plate, the green centre with an incised dog, surrounded by a swag-moulded border, impressed roundel and star.

c1875.   *9in (23cm) diam*

£80-120   **DRA**

A majolica oval bread tray, moulded with a carp on a bed of leaves, the rim inscribed "EAT THY BREAD WITH THANKFULNESS", glazed in tones of green, brown and yellow.

c1870 12.5in (32cm) wide

£300-500 NEA

A late 19thC Continental majolica four-tier oyster stand, of tapered form with eel-loop handle and revolving base, painted with coloured glazes, old metal rod repair through the middle.

12in (22cm) high

£300-500 DN

A pair of continental majolica urns, attributed to Bodenbowl, each of the baluster-shaped bodies glazed in blue, decorated with a stag and a boar chased by hounds, the handles in the form of huntsmen, unmarked.

12.75in (32.5cm) high

£500-700 CHEF

A German majolica blue-ground two-handled urn-shaped jardinière, moulded in relief with satyr masks suspending swags of oak leaves and acorns, the handles modelled as dragons, impressed "T.S", some chips.

c1880 18in (46cm) wide

£250-350 DN

A late 19thC Russian majolica smoking companion, modelled as a peasant washer woman beside a river with her basket, behind her a hollow tree stump, painted with coloured glazes, impressed marks.

6in (15cm) high

£180-220 DN

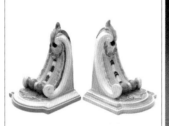

A pair of Royal Worcester majolica wall brackets, modelled as volutes supporting an architrave, painted with coloured glazes, impressed marks, one with chips to reverse.

c1865

£250-350 DN

A Continental majolica cushion-form terrace stool, modelled as three graduated tasselled cushions with floral 'embroidery'.

21.5in (54.5cm) wide

£300-350 S&K

MARTIN BROTHERS

- The Martin Brothers' studio was founded in 1873 at Fulham before moving to Southall in 1877.
- Each of the four brothers had different roles – Robert, the driving force behind the enterprise was the modeller, Walter took charge of throwing and glazing, Edwin was assigned to decoration, whilst Charles ran the shop.
- Martin Brothers produced stoneware table and ornamental pieces, influenced by the Gothic Revival movement. In keeping with the Arts and Crafts ethos, each piece was handcrafted.
- Vases and tableware are usually decorated with incised and carved foliage or aquatic scenes in muted tones.
- Pieces were fashionable at the time and Queen Victoria featured on their list of clients.
- The firm is best known for its grotesque 'Wally' birds, modelled as tobacco jars with separate heads and expressive faces. Also sought-after are the company's wide range of whimsical creatures and eccentric sculpted jugs with carved human faces.
- Production slowed in 1915 after a fire. The studio closed in 1923.

A tall Martin Brothers vase, painted and incised with birds and oak branches, incised "R.W. Martin Bros./London Southall/3-1883", firing lines, restoration to hairline crack.

20in (51cm) high

£2,500-3,500   **DRA**

A massive Martin Brothers stoneware vase, incised with intwined, fighting dragons and serpents in shades of brown, incised "11-1892, RW Martin & Bros, London & Southall".

18.5in (47cm) high

£4,000-6,000   **WW**

An important Martin Brothers stoneware clock, bearing the coat of arms for the Nettlefold family, glazed in shades of blue, green and brown, with clock movement, incised "Martin London 8-1875" and "32".

Frederick John Nettlefold was an enthusiastic promoter of the Martin Brothers.

15.75in (40cm) high

£7,000-10,000   **WW**

A Martin Brothers stoneware vase, the square section modelled to each side with sea creatures, incised "2-1903, Martin Bros, London & Southall", minor factory chip to top rim.

6.25in (16cm) high

£400-600   **WW**

A Martin Brothers stoneware vase, the swollen square section incised with dragons amongst scrolling foliage, incised "8-1892 Martin Brothers, London & Southall".

8.5in (21.5cm) high

£800-1,200   **WW**

A Martin Brothers stoneware vase, incised with three dragons and a serpent fighting, in shades of brown incised "Martin, London & Southall", drilled through base.

10.75in (27cm) high

£1,000-1,500   **WW**

A Martin Brothers stoneware vase, of compressed globular shape with a short neck, incised with flowering shrubs and a butterfly, signed "R.W. Martin & Brothers, London & Southall" dated "5-1890".

7in (18cm) high

£800-1,200   **DN**

A Martin Brothers posy vase, splashed with a scale-effect in blue, green and cream, incised marks and dated "6-1907".

3.25in (8.5cm) high

£400-600   **GORL**

A Martin Brothers large gourd-shaped vase, of tapering oviform, the textured surface incised with vertical lines, against a brown ground, signed "Martin Bros, London & Southall", dated "1-1906".

9in (22.5cm) high

£500-800   **DN**

A Martin Brothers stoneware jug, the sides incised with three roundels depicting grotesque faces, beneath a mottled blue frieze, later pewter cover, the handle with a ram's head and shield embellishment, the base incised "R.W. Martin, Southall - 74".

8.75in (22.5cm) high

£500-800   **H&L**

A Martin Brothers stoneware jardinière, the drum form modelled in low relief with a ruined landscape on an ochre ground, incised "RW Martin, London & Southall", minor glaze nicks to base rim.

8in (20cm) high

£1,000-1,500   **WW**

A Martin Brothers stoneware bird, modelled as an owl with rosette eye feathers and a metal collar to inside rim, incised "Martin Bros, London & Southall 11-1899" to head and base.

9.25in (23.5cm) high

£15,000-20,000   **WW**

A Martin Brothers stoneware 'Monk' bird, with shaved head and solemn features, a metal collar to rim, incised "R W Martin & Bros, London & Southall 10-1905", restoration to base rim.

9.5in (24cm) high

£8,000-12,000   **WW**

A Martin Brothers stoneware bird, with a broad beak and squinting eyes, incised "R W Martin & Bros, London & Southall 19.2.1909", minor restoration.

9.75in (25cm) high

£8,000-12,000   **WW**

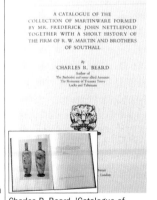

A CATALOGUE OF THE COLLECTION OF MARTINWARE FORMED BY MR. FREDERICK JOHN NETTLEFOLD TOGETHER WITH A SHORT HISTORY OF THE FIRM OF R. W. MARTIN AND BROTHERS OF SOUTHALL

By

CHARLES R. BEARD

Charles R. Beard, 'Catalogue of Martinware in the collection of F. J. Nettlefold', privately published in 1936.

14.5in (37cm) high

£600-800   **WW**

An important Martin Brothers stoneware 'Beak' bird, with a hooked beak and deeply modelled staring eyes, in shades of green ochre and brown, incised "R Wallace Martin & Brothers, London & Southall 5-1894", small glaze chip to beak.

7in (43cm) high

£40,000-45,000   **WW**

A Minton moon flask, painted with Cupid delivering a love letter, the reverse with love letter, quill and spray of roses, impressed and puce printed mark, hairline crack.

c1880   8in (20.5cm) high

£180-220   **HAMG**

A Minton Gothic Revival tile, designed by Augustus Welby Pugin, showing lilies issuing from a Gothic vase embellished with fleur-de-lys within a sexafoil panel, factory marks on reverse, in oak frame.

8in (20.5cm) wide

£400-600   **DN**

A Minton cloisonné tea caddy, designed by Christopher Dresser, in the form of a tea bundle tied with ropes and decorated with Oriental calligraphic characters, the drop-on cover similarly decorated, unmarked.

9in (10.5cm) high

£500-700   **DN**

A Minton cloisonné vase, decorated with masks amongst scrolling foliage, on a turquoise ground, restored.

10.35in (26cm) high

£700-900   **WW**

A Minton faience twin-handled bottle vase, of tapering form with applied foot, painted with panels of flowering branches in the 'Persian' style.

This piece was illustrated in 'Art Studio design for a 'Persian' bottle', c1872, and was based on a 16thC model in the Minton Archives. A pencil note to the top right side suggests it was loaned to the then South Kensington Museum.

c1870   21in (53cm) high

£1,000-1,500   **L&T**

A Minton 'The Fair Maid of Perth' tile, by John Moyr Smith, impressed mark, facsimile signature, chips to rim.

8in (20.5cm) wide

£100-150   **WW**

A Minton secessionist vase, the body slip-traced in brown with a cursive key fret pattern over a mauve splashed celadon ground, printed and impressed marks, date code.

1903   8in (20.5cm) high

£150-200   **CHEF**

MOORCROFT

A Walter Moorcroft 'African Lily' pattern vase, dated.

1949   13.25 (33.5cm) high

£1,000-1,500   **RUM**

A Moorcroft 'Anemone' pattern ovoid ginger jar and cover, tubelined on a shaded blue and green ground, impressed and painted initials, paper label.

6.25in (16cm) high

£180-220   **NEA**

MOORCROFT

WILLIAM AND WALTER MOORCROFT

- William Moorcroft (1872-1945) joined James Macintyre's factory in Staffordshire in 1898. Here he designed the well-known Aurelian and Florian ranges.
- Moorcroft started his own company in 1913 and produced handmade Art Nouveau ceramics.
- He decorated pieces with distinctive designs of stylized flora.
- Tubelining – a technique that involves trailing slip on a surface and filling the enclosed area with glaze – was extensively used.
- During the 1920s, the company partnered with Liberty & Co. and a highly fired flambé glaze was introduced.
- Success led to the firm receiving a Royal Warrant in 1929 and William's son, Walter, took over the pottery in 1945.
- Pieces can be dated by their shape, design and marking. Designs such as Pomegranate, Wisteria, Hazeldine, Moonlit Blue, Eventide and Claremont are hotly collected today. Earlier pieces are generally more valuable and damage usually reduces value.

A William Moorcroft Bara ware jardinière, made for Liberty & Co.

c1905　　　　7.5in (19cm) high
£700-900　　　　　　RUM

A Moorcroft 'Claremont' pattern bowl and oasis, decorated in shades of green, yellow and red against a mottled background, oasis unmarked, slight damage.

c1915　　　12in (31cm) wide
£500-800　　　　GORL

A Walter Moorcroft 'Clematis' pattern flambé vase.

c1950　　　　4in (10cm) high
£600-700　　　　　RUM

A Walter Moorcroft 'Clematis' pattern vase.

c1955　　　5.75in (14.5cm) high
£450-500　　　　RUM

A Walter Moorcroft 'Clematis' pattern vase, with a dark blue ground.

c1950
£250-300　　　RUM

A Moorcroft 'Clematis' pattern ovoid vase, with a slightly flared neck, with a shaded blue and brown ground, impressed and painted signature marks, paper label.

8.25in (21cm) high
£400-600　　　　NEA

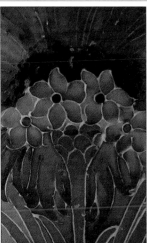

A William Moorcroft 'Cornflower' pattern vase, dated.

1914　　　　9.5in (24cm) high
£3,000-3,500　　　　　RUM

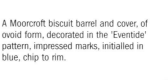

A Moorcroft biscuit barrel and cover, of ovoid form, decorated in the 'Eventide' pattern, impressed marks, initialled in blue, chip to rim.

7in (18cm) high
£700-1,000　　　L&T

A William Moorcroft 'Finches' charger, designed by Sally Tuffin, decorated in shades of blue, green and ochre against a blue background.

14in (35cm) wide
£250-300　　　GORL

A William Moorcroft Florianware egg cup, decorated with stylized poppies.

2in (5cm) high

£500-800   **GORL**

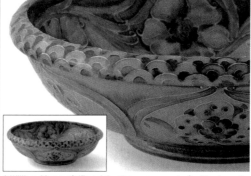

A William Moorcroft 'Freesia' pattern vase, made for Liberty and Co.

c1900   *9in (23cm) diam*

£1,500-2,000   **RUM**

A Walter Moorcroft 'Fuchsia' pattern silver flambé vase, dated.

1949   *11.5in (29cm) high*

£1,300-1,500   **RUM**

A Moorcroft 'Hibiscus' vase, impressed and painted initials, paper label.

9.75in (25cm) high

£300-500   **NEA**

A William Moorcroft Flambé 'Landscape' vase.

c1925   *7in (18cm) high*

£2,500-3,000   **RUM**

A modern William Moorcroft 'Hibiscus' pattern box and cover, painted against a brown background.

5.5in (13.5cm) wide

£40-60   **GORL**

A Moorcroft Pottery 'Leaf and Berry' flambé preserve pot, with a Liberty & Co. Tudric pewter cover, painted blue signature, stamped "Tudric Moorcroft".

4in (10cm) high

£400-600   **WW**

A Moorcroft cylindrical vase, of tapering form with inverted rim, decorated in the 'Moonlit Blue' pattern, impressed marks, signed in blue.

10.5in (26cm) high

£1,800-2,200   **L&T**

A Moorcroft Pottery 'Moonlit Blue' vase, with a painted green signature, minor restoration to interior.

£1,200-1,800   **WW**

A William Moorcroft 'Orchid' pattern flambé vase.

c1930   *12.25in (31cm) high*

£2,500-3,000   **RUM**

A miniature William Moorcroft 'Orchid' pattern flambé vase, decorated in shades of red, yellow, green and blue.

3in (8cm) high

£120-180   **GORL**

A Moorcroft 'Orchid' pattern ovoid jug, with loop handle, tube-line decorated in coloured enamels on a mottled blue ground, impressed and painted initial marks, paper label.

8.25in (21cm) high

£400-600   **NEA**

A Moorcroft circular bowl, decorated in the 'Plum Wisteria' pattern, impressed marks, signed in blue.

10.5in (26cm) wide

£1,800-2,200   **L&T**

A William Moorcroft 'Pansy' pattern vase.

c1914   *5in (12.5cm) high*

£1,200-1,400   **RUM**

A William Moorcroft 'Pomegranate' pattern vase.

c1930   *6in (15cm) high*

£450-500   **RUM**

A William Moorcroft 'Pansy' pattern vase, dated.

1913   *(29.5cm) high*

£3,500-4,000   **RUM**

A Moorcroft 'Pomegranate' flambé vase, with a painted blue signature.

10in (25.5cm) high

£1,200-1,800   **WW**

A Moorcroft candlestick, decorated in the 'Pomegranate' pattern, cylindrical form with spreading base, impressed marks, initialled in green.

8.25in (21cm) high

£200-300   **L&T**

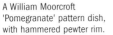

A William Moorcroft 'Pomegranate' pattern dish, with hammered pewter rim.

11in (29cm) high

£300-500   **GORL**

A William Moorcroft 'Pomegranate' pattern inkwell, with plated mount.

4.5in (11cm) wide

£500-800   **GORL**

A William Moorcroft 'Poppy' pattern tobacco jar.

c1900   *3.5in (8.5cm) high*

£600-800   **RUM**

A William Moorcroft 'Spanish' design vase.

c1910   *8.75in (22cm) high*

£4,500-5,000   **RUM**

A William Moorcroft 'Willow' pattern vase.

c1930   *9in (23cm) high*

£2,000-2,500   **RUM**

PILKINGTON

- The Pilkington factory was founded in Manchester in 1891 to produce architectural ceramics.
- From 1912, it was also known as Royal Lancastrian.
- At the advice of William Burton, a chemist for Josiah Wedgwood & Sons, it began to produce tiles which had become increasingly fashionable. Burton later took over as manager of the company.
- Pilkington soon expanded its range to include decorative vases. Distinctive glazes included Sunstone, Eggshell, Lustre and Lapis.
- The respected illustrator Walter Crane (b. 1845) produced a number of designs for the company in the early 20th century.
- Talented artists, including Lewis F. Day, C.F.A. Voysey, Gordon Forsyth and W.S. Mycock, also contributed to the firm.
- An impressed 'P' and bees mark and date marks were used between c1904 and 1914. A 'P' within a rose was used after c1914.
- The company is still in operation today.

A Pilkington's Lancastrian vase, by Annie Burton, decorated with scrolling foliage, impressed mark, painted "B".

4in (10cm) high

£300-500　　　WW

A Pilkington's Lancastrian vase, by Charles Cundall, painted with a hunting scene, impressed mark, painted monogram, date mark.

1910　　　8.25in (21cm) high

£2,000-3,000　　　WW

A CLOSER LOOK AT A LANCASTRIAN VASE

A Pilkington's Lancastrian vase, by Walter Crane, painted by William S. Mycock, decorated with a band of heraldic lions, impressed mark, painted Crane monogram, artist monogram.

5in (13cm) high

£1,500-2,000　　　WW

Pilkington's Lancastrian ware is named for the county where its clay seam was discovered.

Pilkington is best known for its glazes, which came in a dazzling variety of colours and textures.

Walter Crane was an illustrator, political activist and academic who had links with William Morris. This vase is more valuable because it was designed by Crane.

Richard Joyce was one of Pilkington's most successful artists. His signature on this piece is another indication of its superior quality and value.

A Pilkington's Lancastrian vase, designed by Walter Crane and painted with maidens by Richard Joyce, impressed mark "RJ", monogram date mark, probably "1912".

9in (23cm) high

£2,000-3,000　　　WW

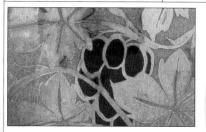

A Pilkington's Lancastrian vase, by Charles Cundall, decorated with grapevines in shades of copper and ruby lustre, painted monogram and date mark.

1909　　　5.75in (14.5cm) high

£1,500-2,000　　　WW

A Pilkington's Lancastrian vase, by Gordon Forsyth, painted with winged classical figure and horses between cypress trees, impressed mark.

9in (23cm) high

£1,800-2,200　　　WW

A Pilkington's Royal Lancastrian vase and cover, by Richard Joyce, decorated with Classical figures, inscribed "North Staffordshire Regiment 1918, Britain, France, Belgium", painted monogram, date mark, cover repaired.

1919　　　*11.75in (30cm) high*

£1,000-1,500　　　**WW**

A large Pilkington's Royal Lancastrian vase, by Richard Joyce, modelled in low relief with three kings, impressed mark, painted monogram.

12.5in (32cm) high

£1,200-1,800　　　**WW**

A Pilkington's Royal Lancastrian vase by Richard Joyce, decorated with classical female figures amongst cypress trees, in blue on a silver ground, impressed mark, incised monogram "41", chips to base rim.

11.5in (29cm) high

£250-350　　　**WW**

A Pilkington's Royal Lancastrian vase, modelled in low relief with a frieze of deer, impressed marks, incised signature "R Joyce".

8.25in (21cm) high

£250-300　　　**WW**

A Pilkington's Royal Lancastrian Lapis vase by Richard Joyce, decorated with simple geometric design under pale blue glaze, impressed mark, incised "RJ", monogram "6419".

2in (5cm) high

£100-150　　　**WW**

A Pilkington's Royal Lancastrian vase, by Richard Joyce painted with an ibex, impressed mark, artist monogram.

6.25in (15.5cm) high

£1,000-1,500　　　**WW**

A Pilkington's Royal Lancastrian vase, by William S. Mycock, decorated with geometric foliate design, impressed mark, incised monogram, date mark.

1932　　　*6.75in (17cm) high*

£180-220　　　**WW**

A Pilkington's Royal Lancastrian vase, by Gladys Rogers and E.T. Radford, decorated with foliate design, impressed marks, painted monogram and incised "E.T.R" mark.

9in (23cm) high

£100-150　　　**WW**

A Pilkington's Royal Lancastrian bottle vase, by Richard Joyce, painted with a floral motif in lustre, painted monogram, restored rim.

13in (33cm) high

£800-1,200　　　**WW**

A Pilkington's Royal Lancastrian vase, by William S. Mycock, with cranes flying through foliage, impressed mark, incised monogram, dated "Dec 28 1911".

8.25in (21cm) high

£500-800   WW

A Pilkington's Royal Lancastrian book end, modelled as a gazelle, impressed marks.

6.5in (16.5cm) high

£100-150   WW

A Pilkington's Royal Lancastrian limited edition figure, by David Evans, modelled as a cherub with a galleon, impressed marks "19/36", restored shell.

9in (22.5cm) high

£220-280   WW

A Pilkington's Royal Lancastrian leopard, probably designed by Richard Joyce, impressed marks, small chip to inside rim.

5in (12.5cm) high

£250-350   WW

A pair of Pilkington's Royal Lancastrian book ends, probably by David Evans, modelled as Classical dolphins, impressed marks.

6in (15.5cm) high

£300-400   WW

An early 20thC Pilkington's Royal Lancastrian scarab paperweight, with turquoise glaze, on an oval base, impressed mark.

4in (10cm) long

£150-200   HAMG

A Pilkington's Royal Lancastrian box and cover, by Dorothy Dacre, painted with a tudor rose inside an ivy border, impressed marks, painted "DD" monogram, "Fawcett Cave Southport" paper label.

4in (10cm) diam

£600-900   WW

POOLE

- In 1921, the Poole-based manufacturer of architectural ceramics, Carter & Co., established the subsidiary Carter, Stabler and Adams to produce decorative domestic pottery. The company became known as Poole Pottery.
- Truda Adams (later Truda Carter), wife of the Managing Director John Adams, became a leading designer for the company. She produced ceramics painted with stylised flowers and animals in the 1920s and 1930s. Pieces by Ruth Pavely, who became head of the painting department after WWII, are also widely collected.
- Pieces from the 1920s and 1930s tend to command the highest prices, especially those decorated with stylised geometric patterns in bright colours that exemplify the style of the period. 'Ship Plates', based on a series of drawings by Arthur Bradbury and made from the 1930s are also desirable.
- During the 1950s, Poole introduced an innovative 'Freeform' range of contemporary pieces, designed by Alfred Read and Guy Sydenham. Large examples in popular patterns such as 'PRP' are particularly sought after and valuable.
- The words "Poole England" appear on early pieces, occasionally with "Carter, Stabler & Adams Ltd". A dolphin was added to the mark in the 1950s and from c1956 the words and dolphin image appear within a box. Special wares produced after c1963 are marked "Poole Studio".
- The company is still in operation today.

A Poole Pottery hand-thrown vase, painted in the 'WL' design by Gwen Haskins.

6in (15cm) high

£120-180   C

A 1930s Poole pottery vase, painted by Iris Skinner, with blue bell flowers on a downswept neck and an hemispherical body, incised "267", impressed and painted marks.

5.75in (14.5cm) high

£100-150   CHEF

POOLE

A 1930s Poole pottery vase, painted by Hilda Hampton, with jazzy blooms on each side, the downswept shoulders above a hemispherical body, incised "443", impressed and painted marks,

7in (17.5cm) high

£100-150   **CHEF**

An Art Deco Poole pottery hand-thrown vase, decorated in the DU pattern by Ruth Paveley.

£200-300   **C**

A Carter, Stabler & Adams Poole Pottery 'The Bull' group, by Harold and Phoebe Stabler, depicting two children with garlands sitting on a bull above a shaped canted base, impressed factory marks.

13in (33cm) high

£1,200-1,800   **DN**

A Carter, Stabler & Adams Poole Pottery 'The Buster Boy' and 'The Buster Girl' pair of figures, designed by Phoebe Stabler, both with impressed factory marks.

Largest 7in (17.5cm) high

£800-1,200   **DN**

A pair of 1930s Poole pottery pair of Springbok bookends, No. 831, with brown glaze.

£200-300   **C**

A Poole pottery 'Atlantis Helmet' lamp, by Guy Sydenham, with internal grotesque face and outward chainmail carving.

12in (30.5cm) high

£1,500-2,000   **C**

A Poole Studio vase, No. 20, finished in turquoise-blue glaze on a white ground, impressed Poole Studio mark.

9.5in (24cm) high

£1,500-2,000   **C**

A 1930s Poole pottery ship bookend, designed by Harold Stabler and modelled by Harry Brown, minor chip.

£220-280   **C**

ROYAL DUX

A Royal Dux table centrepiece, modelled as a maiden sitting on a large shell, triangular pad mark and printed mark.

11in (28cm) high

£250-350   **HAMG**

A Royal Dux pottery centrepiece, modelled as a Classical girl catching fish and wearing pale green and gilt robes, between a pair of large shell-shaped bowls, raised on a rockwork and seaweed base, pink triangle mark.

14in (35.5cm) high

£500-800   **DN**

A Royal Dux Art Deco figure of a snake charmer.

9.5in (24cm) high

£300-500 **GCL**

A Royal Dux figure group, modelled as an eastern dancers, applied pink triangle mark.

14.25in (36cm) high

£500-800 **WW**

An unusual Royal Dux figure of a Chinese man with a cart.

c1915 *10in (25.5cm) wide*

£400-600 **GCL**

A pair of Royal Dux figures of musicians, on mound and scroll bases.

22in (56cm) high

£800-1,200 **GORL**

A large late 19thC Royal Dux figural vase, in the form of a woman holding a amphora beside a palm tree, raised on a naturalistic base, triangular seal and impressed "12800, 111/59", repairs to rim.

37in (92.5cm) high

£700-1,000 **FRE**

A Royal Dux Art Nouveau pottery vase, with basket weave texturing, embellished in shallow relief with blossom, olive green strapwork, gilded angular handles and female masks near the base, pink triangle mark on base.

10.5in (27cm) high

£350-400 **DN**

ROYAL WORCESTER

A Victorian Royal Worcester pedestal ewer, relief-moulded with birds and flowers against an unusual petrol-iridescent ground of crimson blue, shoulder and handle modelled with masks, date code.

1897 *9in (23cm) high*

£700-1,000 **GORL**

A Royal Worcester two-handled globular pot-pourri vase and cover, with painting of Durham Cathedral by Harry Davis, inscribed "Durham Cathedral", puce printed marks, date code, shape number 1515.

1912 *8.5in (21cm) high*

£3,500-4,000 **DN**

ROYAL WORCESTER

HARRY DAVIS

- Harry Davis (1885-1970) is considered to be one of greatest 20thC Royal Worcester artists.
- Davis joined the company as an apprentice in 1898 at the age of 14 and continued to work until 1970.
- He is known for meticulously hand-painted landscapes, highland scenes and architectural views, which are usually found on richly gilded vases and decorative services.
- A number of Harry Davis' designs are still in production today, including 'Lavinia', which was originally designed in 1946.
- Because his pieces date from the 20th century and were made for display rather than use, many have survived in good condition. This means that any damage greatly affects value.
- Pieces are marked "Royal Worcester". A dot was added to this mark for every year between 1892 and 1916. After this time, an asterix was added to the dots.
- Royal Worcester continues to operate today.

A CLOSER LOOK AT A ROYAL WORCESTER EWER

The shape is complex and thus suitable for display.

Harry Davis worked for Worcester for 70 years and was awarded the MBE for his work.

Although the date code is for 1902, when Davis was just 18, this ewer may have been painted later, after a period of storage.

Davis's landscape scenes are particularly admired by collectors for their restraint and attention to detail.

A Royal Worcester ewer, painted by Harry Davis, with sheep in a Highland landscape, puce printed marks, shape no.1209, date code, restored handle.

1902	17in (42.5cm) high
£5,000-7,000	DN

A Royal Worcester two-handled oviform vase and cover, painted by Harry Davis, with sheep in a Highland landscape, shape no. 2158, puce printed marks, date code, restored cover.

1912	11in (28cm) high
£3,500-4,500	DN

A Royal Worcester two-handled globular pot pourri vase and cover, with Durham Cathedral painted by Harry Davis, puce printed marks, date code, shape no.1515, the underside inscribed "Durham Cathedral".

1912	8.5in (21.5cm) high
£3,500-4,500	DN

A Royal Worcester slender ovoid vase, painted by Harry Davis with hill sheep in a Highland landscape, shape no.2217, puce printed marks, date code.

1914	9in (22cm) high
£3,500-4,000	DN

A Royal Worcester oviform vase, painted by Harry Davis, with sheep in a Highland landscape, puce printed marks, shape no.287/H, date code.

1922	8in (20.5cm) high
£2,500-3,000	DN

A Royal Worcester two-handled vase and cover, painted by Harry Davis, with Highland cattle, puce printed mark, shape no.2701, date code, finial gilt restored.

1922	5in (12.5cm) high
£800-1,200	DN

A Royal Worcester cylindrical spill vase, painted by Harry Davis, with sheep in a landscape, with a pierced gilt japanesque lower section, puce printed mark, shape no.6/161, date code.

1922	6.5in (16cm) high
£1,800-2,200	DN

A Royal Worcester ovoid vase with flared neck, painted by Harry Davis, with sheep in a landscape of bluebells, puce printed mark, shape no.202/H, date code.

1926	6.5in (16cm) high
£5,000-7,000	DN

A Royal Worcester bottle vase, painted and signed by Harry Stinton, with highland cattle, gilt rims, shape no. 2491, printed crown and circle mark in puce, date code.

1915

£300-400 NEA

A Royal Worcester ewer, painted with a heron in a desert landscape, gilt handle with mask terminal, signed "A. Shuck", date code, shape 2441, lip damage.

1909 *8in (20cm) high*

£600-900 GORL

A Royal Worcester two-handled vase, painted with two herons in a desert landscape in bright enamels against a sky blue background, signed "G. Johnson", date code.

1917 *9in (23cm) high*

£1,200-1,800 GORL

A Hadley Royal Worcester vase, painted with soft roses in pink and yellow.

c1910 *5.25in (13.5cm) high*

£300-400 GCL

A Royal Worcester pot-pourri vase, liner and cover, painted with fruit by M. Johnson, shape no. 2048, black printed post-war marks.

13.5in (34cm) high

£1,500-2,000 DN

A Hadley Worcester pot pourri.

c1910 *5in (12.5cm) wide*

£400-600 GCL

A pair of Royal Worcester pot-pourri vases, liners and covers, painted with fruit by Freeman, post-war black printed marks, shape no. 2048.

9.75in (25cm) high

£3,000-5,000 DN

A Royal Worcester ovoid two-handled vase, painted by P. Stanley, with fallen fruit, black printed marks and date code, small scratch.

1969 *12in (20.5cm) high*

£800-1,200 DN

A pair of Royal Worcester baluster vases in the Sèvres style, with applied loop handles, painted with an 18thC couple, purple printed mark and date code.

1869 *10.25in (25.5cm) high*

£500-800 L&T

A late 19thC Royal Worcester reticulated vase, raised on a flared foot, with pierced panels between stylised jewelled borders, printed and moulded marks.

4.75in (12cm) high

£800-1,200 WW

A Royal Worcester blush ivory vase, decorated with flower posies.

c1905 *10.75in (27.5cm) high*

£400-600 GCL

DECORATIVE ARTS

A pair of Royal Worcester vases, each of twin-handled shouldered form, painted on both sides with birds, beneath a beaded border, unmarked.

4in (10cm) high

£150-200   **HAMG**

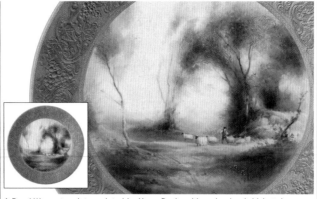

A Royal Worcester plate, painted by Harry Davis, with a shepherd driving sheep across a common, within a sage green low-relief ground decorated with fruiting vine, puce printed marks, date code.

1912   *8.75in (22cm) wide*

£1,000-1,500   **DR**

A Royal Worcester plate, painted by Harry Davis, with a rustic figure and a hound in a landscape, within a sage green low-relief ground decorated with fruiting vine, puce printed marks, date code.

1912   *8.75in (22cm) wide*

£800-1,200   **DN**

A Royal Worcester plate, painted by Harry Davis, with a view from the shore across Derwentwater, within a tooled gilt-line bordered rim, blue printed mark, date code, minor surface scratches.

1940   *10.75in (27cm) wide*

£800-1,200   **DN**

A Royal Worcester plate by Walter Powell, painted with storks, the shaped circular gilt outline with heart-shaped cartouches, green printed mark "CH" and "No. 224 H8554", dated.

1909   *10in (25.5cm) diam*

£1,500-2,000   **HAMG**

A Royal Worcester plate painted with fruit by R. Sebright, the border painted in blue, pink and gilt with stylised foliage, c-scrolls and shell motifs, puce marks, a date code, faint hairline cracks.

1912   *9in (23cm) diam*

£500-800   **DN**

A Royal Worcester blush ivory trio.

c1900   *6.75in (17cm) diam*

£180-220   **GCL**

A Royal Worcester gilt-ground coffee cup and saucer, painted by W. Ricketts and G. Cole, puce marks, date code.

1912

£300-400   **DN**

A Royal Worcester trio, painted with sheep in a landscape by E. Barker. puce marks, date code.

1919

£800-1,200   **DN**

A 20thC Royal Worcester teapot and cover, painted with fruit by Peter Platt, with richly gilt borders, spout and handle, black printed mark.

10in (25.5cm) wide

£700-900   **DN**

A Royal Worcester wall bracket, moulded in high relief with putti amid fruiting vine, puce printed mark, dated.

1865   *9.5in (24cm) high*

£300-400   **HAMG**

A Royal Worcester Aesthetic movement teapot and cover, of tapering square section, moulded to the sides with flowering plants and printed in blue on white with Japanese-style motifs.

7in (18cm) high

£80-120   **L&T**

A Ruskin Pottery high-fired stoneware vase and cover, with a mottled and running sang-de-boeuf, lavender and silver glaze, impressed marks, dated, repaired finial.

1909   10.5in (26cm) high
£2,000-3,000   WW

A Ruskin stoneware vase covered in a speckled silver and grey lustre glaze, impressed mark, dated.

1923   6in (15.5cm) high
£800-1,200   WW

A Ruskin high-fired stoneware vase mottled sang-de-boeuf and purple glaze, impressed mark, painted scissor mark, dated.

1905   8.5in (21cm) high
£1,200-1,800   WW

A Ruskin high-fired stoneware tyg, in mottled sang-de-boeuf and lavender on white, impressed marks, dated.

1933   8in (20cm) high
£1,200-1,800   WW

A Ruskin high-fired stoneware candlestick, of hexagonal section, mottled sang-de-boeuf and lavender on a white ground, impressed mark.

4in (10cm) high
£600-900   WW

A Ruskin high-fired stoneware stand, with streaked lavender and sang-de-boeuf on silver, impressed mark.

4.75in (12cm) high
£600-900   WW

A Ruskin high-fired stoneware vase, applied with silver mount to base rim, mottled pink, purple and turquoise on a white ground, impressed marks, silver marked "S*B Birmingham 1906".

9.5in (24cm) high
£1,500-2,000   WW

WEDGWOOD

A Ruskin lamp base, of hexagonal section raised on bracket feet, covered in streaked and crystalline blue, yellow, orange and buff glazes, impressed marks.

10.5in (26cm) high
£300-400   L&T

A Wedgwood Fairyland lustre 'Amherst Pheasant' bowl, designed by Daisy Makeig-Jones, printed mark, minor wear.

8.75in (22cm) diam
£1,500-2,000   WW

A Wedgwood lustre 'Flying Humming Birds' bowl, painted in gilt with birds against a mottled blue ground, the mottled red interior with orange border, gilt Portland vase mark.

c1925   11.5in (29cm) diam
£250-350   HAMG

A Wedgwood Fairyland lustre 'Willow' vase, designed by Daisy Makeig-Jones, pattern number Z5760, on flame lustre ground, with printed and painted marks, missing cover, wear to ground.

7.75in (20cm) high

£1,200-1,800   **WW**

A CLOSER LOOK AT A WEDGWOOD FAIRYLAND BOWL

Fairyland lustre pieces portray magical landscapes inspired by fairytales. They are highlighted in gold. The distinctive style of the pieces inspired other manufacturers to produce similar ranges.

Daisy Makeig-Jones designed Wedgwood's Fairyland lustre range during the 1920s. Along with Keith Murray, she was one of the many innovative designers employed by the company during the early 20thC.

Lustreware has been produced since the 8thC. The iridescent effect is made using a mixture of metallic oxides in oil that forms a thin film of metal on the surface of the pot when fired at a temperature of 750°C.

A Wedgwood Fairyland lustre 'Moorish' octagonal bowl, designed by Daisy Makeig-Jones, pattern number Z5125, the interior decorated in the 'Smoke Ribbons' pattern, printed and painted marks, minor ware to gilt interior.

7.75in (20cm) diam

£3,000-4,000   **WW**

A Wedgwood Fairyland lustre 'Willow' coral and bronze vase, designed by Daisy Makeig-Jones, with printed mark, missing cover, wear to bronze.

8.75in (22cm) high

£1,200-1,800   **WW**

A Wedgwood moon flask, by Norman Wilson, covered in a pale blue glaze, impressed and printed mark "NW".

8.75in (22cm) high

£300-400   **WW**

A Wedgwood earthenware 'Matt Blue' vase, designed by Keith Murray, of flaring shoulder form, with printed mark and "KM" monogram, slight damage.

11.75in (30cm) high

£400-600   **WW**

A Wedgwood sculpture, 'Duiker', by John Skeaping, covered in an ochre glaze, impressed "Wedgwood J Skeaping", minor overpainting to one ear.

7in (18cm) high

£80-120   **WW**

A Wedgwood earthenware Moonstone coffee set for four, designed by Keith Murray, various marks.

Pot 8.25in (21cm) high

£500-800   **WW**

Two of a set of six Wedgwood coffee cans and saucers, with Houses of Parliament design in gold and green band below rim.

Saucer 4.75in (12cm) diam

£30-40 set   **B&H**

WEMYSS

- Wemyss ceramics were made at Robert Heron's pottery in Sinclairtown, Fife, from 1882.
- The firm was named after local patrons, the Wemyss family.
- It produced everyday tableware, affordable household items and the famous decorative cats and pigs.
- Chief decorator from the mid-1880s, Karel Nekola, is well known for his cabbage rose designs.
- Pieces signed by Nekola attract a premium today.
- Heron closed his factory in 1929 and Bovey Pottery bought the right to produce Wemyss.
- Large quantities were made to order by Bovey for the London wholesaler Jan Plichta, many pieces from this period are marked with his name.
- In the 1950s, Wemyss ware returned to Fife, where it is still produced today.
- Early Wemyss has been immensely collectable since the 1960s.

A large Wemyss circular bowl, of tapered cylindrical form, decorated with 'Cabbage Roses', printed retailer's mark.

14.5in (36.5cm) diam

£500-800   **L&T**

A large Wemyss 'Roses' circular bowl, painted with branches of cabbage roses, restored chip to rim, impressed mark "Wemyss".

11.25in (28cm) diam

£300-500   **L&T**

A Wemyss 'Roses' jardinère, painted with a frieze of cabbage roses, yellow painted mark "Wemyss".

6.75in (17cm) high

£300-500   **L&T**

A Wemyss 'Roses' small ewer and basin, painted with branches bearing cabbage roses, green painted marks "Wemyss".

11.5in (29cm) diam

£400-600   **L&T**

A Wemyss medium-sized pig, decorated with roses and leaves on a white ground, with pale pink decoration to ears, snout and trotters.

11in (28cm) diam

£800-1,200   **RDER**

A Wemyss cat, the body painted with large roses and leaves against a white ground, with black glass eyes and painted whiskers.

12in (30cm) high

£2,500-4,000   **RDER**

A large early 20thC Wemyss pig, modelled seated on its haunches, painted with pink cabbage roses, painted green mark "Wemyss Ware no 5 Made in England", damage to tail.

16in (41cm) wide

£2,000-3,000   **HAMG**

A Wemyss 'Dog Roses' circular cake plate, painted with branches of dog roses, green painted mark "Wemyss", also a Wemyss 'Dog Roses' tea cup, saucer and side plate, each painted with dog roses, green painted marks "Wemyss".

Large plate 9.25in (23cm) diam

£400-600   **L&T**

A Wemyss 'Dog Roses' Lady Eva vase, impressed mark "Wemyss", yellow painted mark "Wemyss".

8in (20cm) high

£300-400   **L&T**

A pair of Wemyss candlesticks, each decorated in the 'Dog Roses' pattern, impressed marks.

7.5in (18.5cm) high

£1,000-1,500   **L&T**

A Wemyss Gordon plate, decorated with a yellow iris.

8.25in (21cm) diam

£400-600   **RDER**

A Wemyss quaich, decorated with a yellow iris.

c1900   *10.75in (27.5cm) wide*

£400-600   **RDER**

A small Wemyss Plichta pig money bank, painted with clover, signed "NEKOLA PINET".

c1930   *6.25in (16cm) wide*

£550-650   **RDER**

A Wemyss pottery pig, for Goode & Sons, painted with clover leaves, impressed "Wemyss Ware", printed retail mark, damages.

6.25in (16cm) wide

£400-600   **WW**

A small Wemyss pig, painted with green shamrocks, impressed "RH & S" mark.

6.75in (17cm) wide

£500-800   **L&T**

A CLOSER LOOK AT A WEMYSS PIG

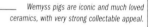

Jan Plichta was a wholesaler who bought up large quantities of Wemyss ware in the early 20thC. Pieces pre-dating this period tend to sell for a much higher price.

Wemyss pigs are iconic and much loved ceramics, with very strong collectable appeal.

Repeated designs inspired by flora and fauna, like these shamrocks, are typical Wemyss motifs.

Wemyss animals were made in various sizes. This large pig is more valuable than smaller examples, except the small rare sleeping pig.

A large early 20thC Wemyss Plichta pig, modelled seated on its haunches, painted with scattered shamrocks, some crazing, printed green mark.

16in (41cm) wide

£1,000-1,500   **HAMG**

A large early 20thC Wemyss Plichta pig, modelled seated on its haunches, painted with thistles, some crazing, printed green mark.

16in (41cm) wide

£2,000-3,000   HAMG

A Wemyss tankard, 'Thistles', of cylindrical form with applied handle, impressed mark.

5.5in (14cm) high

£220-280   L&T

A Wemyss candlestick, impressed "RH" and "S" mark.

12in (30cm) high

£180-220   L&T

A Wemyss ring holder, painted in the 'Sweet Peas' pattern, impressed and painted marks.

3in (7.5cm) high

£500-800   L&T

A Wemyss 'Apples' dog bowl, of tapering cylindrical form painted with apples and bearing inscription "Qui aime Jean Aime son chien", impressed mark "Wemyss".

8.5in (21.5cm) diam

£500-800   L&T

A late 19thC Wemyss pottery mug, painted in colours with apples hanging from a branch, impressed Heron mark.

5.5in (14cm) high

£250-350   DN

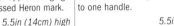

A Wemyss ware three-handled mug, decorated with raspberries, restoration to one handle.

5.5in (14cm) high

£500-800   RDER

A Wemyss preserve pot, decorated with raspberries.

5in (13cm) high

£300-400   RDER

A Wemyss breakfast plate.

c1900   *3.75in (9.5cm) diam*

£200-250   RDER

A Wemyss 'Plums' Low Kintore candlestick, painted with plums on branches, impressed mark "Wemyss", re-glued chip to rim.

4.5in (11.5cm) high

£180-220   L&T

A Wemyss 'Strawberries' footed comport, of circular form painted with a bands of fruiting strawberries on a black and white ground, impressed mark and painted mark "Wemyss".

9.25in (23cm) wide

£1,000-1,500   L&T

A Wemyss Gordon plate, decorated with oranges.

c1895   8in (20.5cm) diam

£700-900   RDER

A Wemyss cylindrical preserve jar and cover, painted with sprays of lemons, impressed and script marks, retailer's stamp for "T. Goode and Co", slight damage.

5.75in (14.5cm) high

£300-400   H&L

A Wemyss small pig, decorated in black and white, minor restoration to ear and trotters.

6.5in (16.5cm) wide

£400-600   RDER

A Wemyss small pig, with sponged black and white decoration.

c1930   6in (15cm) wide

£500-700   RDER

A Wemyss pottery vase painted with hens, impressed Wemyss mark.

4.5in (11.5cm) high

£200-300   WW

A Scottish Methuen mug, decorated with peacocks and cockerels.

c1890   6in (15cm) high

£300-500   RDER

A Wemyss commemorative mug, painted with "Nae Sic Queen was ever seen", restoration to handle.

1897   6in (15cm) high

£700-900   RDER

A Wemyss square plate, decorated with bees, by Karel Nekola.

7.5in (19cm) wide

£180-220   RDER

A Zsolnay faience vase, with landscape decoration depicting a coastal scene with boat and a gliding swan, glazed in red, purple and green, marked on base "Zsolnay Pécs", model no. 5282 S 49 56.

c1900   13in (33.5cm) high

£7,000-10,000   **QU**

A rare Art Nouveau Zsolnay trumpet vase with ruffled rim in lustered red glaze, surrounded with gold leaves, stamped "ZSOLNAY PECS" with "Castle/53/83/M".

9.5in (24cm) high

£6,000-9,000   **DRA**

A Zsolnay vase and cover, painted with butterflies and foliage in shades of blue, red and gold lustre, printed Zsolnay circular mark, painted "3252", small glaze frit to base.

7in (17cm) high

£1,500-2,000   **WW**

A tall Art Nouveau Zsolnay reticulated vase, with blood-red blossoms alternating with lustered green-gold leaves, over an incised matte green base, small chips and drilled hole to base, stamped "ZSOLNAY/6531/M".

14.5in (36cm) high

£18,000-22,000   **DRA**

A large Zsolnay moonflask vase, with a moulded, glazed and gilt peacock on a flowering branch, above a Chinese style base, impressed marks.

16.75in (42cm) high

£1,000-1,500   **L&T**

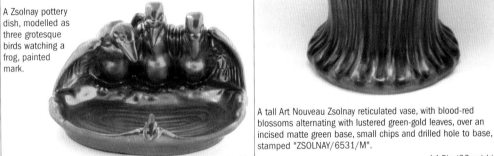

A Zsolnay pottery dish, modelled as three grotesque birds watching a frog, painted mark.

6.25in (16cm) wide

£350-450   **WW**

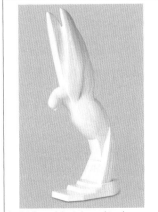

An Art Deco Adnet dove, signed.

c1925   19in (48cm) high

£450-500   **TDG**

A rare Adnet bowl, in cream, with a floral design.

Adnet is better known as a furniture maker.

c1925   10.25in (26cm) diam

£500-800   **MOD**

A circular vase, with green, olive and grey decoration, marked "EF Alsace".

c1925   14.5in (37cm) diam

£1,500-2,000   **MOD**

DECORATIVE ARTS

An Arabia ceramic vase, with glazed and painted decoration, red script mark "Made in Finland Arabia".

c1910   12in (30cm) high

£300-500   **FRE**

A large John Bennett bulbous vessel, painted with red hibiscus and amber leaves on a mottled indigo ground, signed "J. Bennett/1889/Apt 30/W.C.L./N.Y."

12.5in (32cm) high

£3,000-4,000   **DRA**

A large Art Deco Paul Bogatay terracotta plaque, in cuerda seca with polo players in glazes, incised "Bogatay/34 on reverse", minor damage.

The technique of cuerda seca uses an oil-based slip to separate different colours.

1934   16in (40.5cm) diam

£1,800-2,200   **DRA**

A Bretby vase with two pierced handles, in blue, green, cream and brown glaze.

c1905   13in (33cm) high

£300-400   **TCS**

A pair of Arts and Crafts Burmantoft vases.

c1885

£500-800   **PUR**

A Lotte Calm stoneware group of children, on a naturalistic base, red stoneware polychrome painted, manufacturer's mark and "MADE IN AUSTRIA 944".

c1925   6.75in (17cm) high

£800-1,200   **QU**

A CLOSER LOOK AT AN ARTS AND CRAFTS JARDINIÈRE

This jardinière and stand is typical of turn of the century Bretby, when the company was very influenced by the prevalent Arts and Crafts and Art Nouveau styles.

Bretby often applied wooden and metallic effect glazes to its wares. This copper glaze is one of many imitation finishes the company developed.

Bretby Art Pottery, or Tooth & Co., produced a line of cheap pressed ceramics alongside its more expensive thrown pots such as this jardinière.

Faux cabochons like these are another feature for which Bretby ceramics is well known. Their appearance here enhances the value of this piece to collectors.

An Arts and Crafts Bretby faux copper porcelain jardinière and stand, with four handles and four faux turquoise cabochons, hairline crack and chip.

c1905   33.5in (85cm) high

£6,000–8,000   **PUR**

One of a pair of large Burmantoft terracotta jardinières and stands, each with four lug handles, relief panels of hops and foliage and resting on separate waisted circular stands, impressed factory marks and numbered "2294" and "2295".

35.5in (90cm) high

£1,000-1,500 pair   **DN**

A Burmantoft earthenware jardinière and stand, decorated in relief with chrysanthemums, on a moulded base, with impressed and with painted factory marks '2021'.

42in (107.5cm) high

£350-450   **L&T**

A Hancock & Sons 'Morrisware' vase, by George Cartlidge, painted with purple poppies on a blue ground, printed mark, painted "C8.10" and signature, restored rim.

7in (17.5cm) high

£1,000-1,500 WW

A Hancock and Sons 'Morrisware' vase, of pedestal shape, tube-lined with blue and mauve foliage against a mottled green background.

7in (18cm) high

£500-700 GORL

A Hancock & Sons 'Morrisware', vase by George Cartlidge, painted with red cornflower on a mustard ground, printed mark, painted "C2.4".

9.75in (25cm) high

£1,000-1,500 WW

A Hancock & Sons 'Morrisware' vase, by George Cartlidge, painted with bell flowers in purple on a blue ground, printed mark, painted "C28.2" and signature, restored top rim.

14.5in (37cm) high

£1,000-1,500 WW

A Crown Devon 'Fairy Castle' jug, pattern number 2406, with printed and painted marks.

9.5in (24cm) high

£1,000-1,500 WW

A Royal Crown Derby urnular vase, painted and signed by W. E. J. Dean, painted marks in red, date code.

1920   *5in (13cm) high*

£550-650 NEA

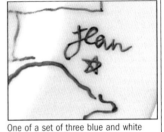

One of a set of three blue and white Jean Cocteau plates.

c1925   *9.75in (24.5cm) diam*

£500-800 each MOD

An Auguste Delaherche high-fired stoneware vase covered in brown microcrystalline 'tea glaze', restoration to chip at rim, inscribed "Aug Delaherche".

6.5in (16.5cm) wide

£400-600 DRA

An Arts and Crafts ceramic jug, painted with stylised flowers and scrolls against a mottled green background, painted mark and artist's initials "GP", by Anthony Della Robbia.

7.5in (19cm) high

£400-600 GORL

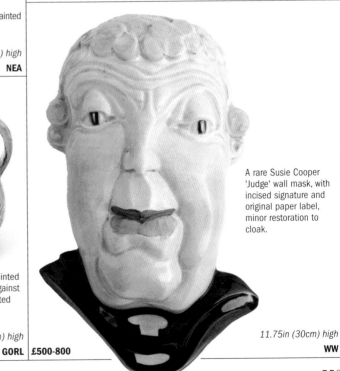

A rare Susie Cooper 'Judge' wall mask, with incised signature and original paper label, minor restoration to cloak.

11.75in (30cm) high

£500-800 WW

DECORATIVE ARTS

An Art Nouveau pair of Denbac porcelain vases, each with a circular neck surrounded by three openings and embossed with stylised sprigs of flowers, covered in flowing microcrystalline glaze, stamped "Denbac/89".

8in (20cm) high

£300-400   **SDR**

An Ault vase, designed by Christopher Dresser, with one tall neck surrounded by four smaller necks, each moulded with owls, the body moulded with stars and clouds, glazed, applied and impressed marks, "Ault England 365."

15.25in (38cm) high

£2,500-3,000   **L&T**

A CLOSER LOOK AT AN AULT 'PROPELLER' VASE

Between 1892 and 1895, the influential designer Christopher Dresser produced designs for Ault pottery, based in Derbyshire. Pieces were made in earthenware, sometimes with a shimmering glaze like this vase.

Inspiration for Dresser's organic pieces came partially from his training as a botanist.

The swirling shape of this vase pre-empts the Art Nouveau movement, whilst its simplicity looks forward to more minimalist Modernist design.

Ault continued to produce Dresser pieces after the designer died in 1904, but these later pieces usually lack the facsimile signature.

A large Ault pottery 'propeller' vase, designed by Dr Christopher Dresser, impressed facsimile signature, minor nicks to glaze.

14in (33.5cm) high

£2,000-3,000   **WW**

An earthenware plate by J. Selwyn Dunn, painted with a galleon at full sail, painted marks, Johnson Bros plate mark.

12.25in (31cm) diam

£70-100   **WW**

A Sunflower Pottery tyg, by Sir Edmund Elton, modelled with monkey mask above handles, applied and incised with foliate panels, unmarked.

8.5in (21cm) high

£180-220   **WW**

An Editions Etling of Paris porcelain box and cover, the cover modelled with a female figure, printed marks and original paper label, cover restored.

9in (23cm) wide

£350-400   **WW**

A Sunflower Pottery ewer by Sir Edmund Elton, incised and applied with flowers, in a blue glaze, painted "Elton" mark.

19.75in (50cm) high

£300-400   **WW**

A Sunflower Pottery vase and cover, by Sir Edmund Elton, covered in a gold craquelure glaze, painted signature.

10.5in (26.5cm) high

£400-600   **WW**

An Art Nouveau Rorstrand porcelain vase, designed by Algot Erikson, factory marks, numbered "6031" and with "AE" initials, some restoration.

12.25in (31.5cm) high

£150-200   **DN**

A pottery mug and cover, probably Ferrybridge, freely painted with floral sprays in green and puce with black lines, cracked.

c1810   5.5in (14cm) high

£30-50   **H&L**

A Foley Intarsio two-handled vase, of double gourd shape, painted with a band of geese within stylised foliate bands, printed marks with shaped number 3074, some restoration.

11.75in (30cm) high

£300-400   **H&L**

A 'St Cecilia' Foley Intarsio vase, number 3024, designed by Frederick Rhead, printed marks.

16.75in (42cm) high

£1,200-1,800   **WW**

A Foley Intarsio stickstand, model number 3118, decorated with panels of flowers in colours on a brown ground, printed marks.

28.5in (71cm) high

£800-1,200   **WW**

A Gallé pottery figurine with clamshell centre, the base with hand-painted bird, signed on the back "Galle Nancy", minor repair.

9.75in (24.5cm) high

£250-350   **JDJ**

A Gallé pottery inkwell, with separate insert, decorated with flowers and leaves, marked on base "E", with Cross of Lorraine, "G" "DEPOSE" and signed "E Galle Nancy", minor damage.

2.5in (6.5cm) wide

£100-150   **JDJ**

A Piero Fornasetti rectangular tray, transfer-decorated with a house of cards motif against a mountainous landscape, remnant of Fornasetti label.

23in (58cm) wide

£300-500   **SDR**

A Guerin large stoneware baluster vase, covered in blue-grey amber and ivory crystalline glaze, mounted in a wrought-iron frame with flowers and curlicues, "821H Guerin" in script, original patina, chip to base.

19.5in (49cm) high

£700-1,000   **DRA**

A pair of Arts and Crafts ebony tiles, with bird scenes, designed by E.W. Godwin.

£500-800   **PUR**

An Art Deco ceramic lion sculpture, made in France by Marcel Guillard, marked "Prost".

c1925   17.25in (44cm) wide

£2,000-3,000   **MOD**

A fine and large Mettlach tankard, with hinged pewter lid, carved and painted by M. Hein, with Renaissance floral design, stamp mark and artist's signature.

14in (35.5cm) high

£500-700   **DRA**

An Art Deco Gustavsberg Argenta cigarette box, designed by Wilhelm Kage, the matte aqua green pottery with silver overlay figural decoration.

c1935   *6in (15.25cm) wide*

£1,000-1,500   **DD**

An Art Deco Gustavsberg Argenta bowl, designed by Wilhelm Kage, with a silvered lady amongst fronds and holding a bird, a dentil edge to the green-glazed conical body, silvered marks.

9in (23cm) diam

£180-220   **CHEF**

A 1930s Art Deco lady's head, by Katshutte, stamped to base.

8in (20cm) high

£450-500   **TDG**

A Kenton Hills rare four-sided flaring vase, squeeze-bag decorated by Alza Stratton, with amber and gunmetal leopards on a red Coromandel base, stamped "KH 174, Alza Stratton, Unica".

7in (17.5cm) high

£500-700   **DRA**

A Berlin porcelain vase, designed by Arnold Krog, model number 51, the glaze by Sren Berg, signed with wave mark, artist's signature "SB" and "26-8-1925A", "51".

1925

£500-700   **QU**

An unusual Berlin porcelain figure of a clown or Pierrot, abstractly modelled with cubist influences, printed blue sceptre mark, red orb and "KPM".

6.5in (16.5cm) high

£350-450   **DN**

A French Fevola ceramic vase, fish design, marked "Fevola" and "Ceramique Lachenal".

c1925

£1,800-2,200   **MOD**

A Max Lauger pottery vase, tubeline decorated with grasses, impressed "ML" monogram, restored neck.

14.25in (36cm) high

£700-900   **WW**

An Otto Lendecke porcelain figure of a girl, holding down her flowing skirt, on a stepped base, sceptre mark, Wiener Werkstätte mark and dated.

c1910   *6.75in (17cm) high*

£300-350   **QU**

A Maria Likarz vase, depicting a polychrome landscape, stamped "MADE IN AUSTRIA, 107".

c1925   *7.25in (18.5cm) high*

£1,000-1,500   **QU**

A pair of Linthorpe footed vases, with moulded feather sunbursts, pattern no. 1790, restored.

c1885   *7in (18cm) high*

£700-1,000   **TCS**

A German china jug and bowl, designed by Raymond Loewy for Rosenthal.

Jug 4.25in (11cm) high

£250-300   **MOD**

A blue, black and white plate by J. Lurçat.

c1925   *9.75in (25cm) diam*

£500-800   **MOD**

A pair of Linthorpe moulded 'Iris' baluster vases, in green, brown and blue glaze, pattern no. 168, "SL" monogram for William Sheldon Longbottom, design attributed to Christopher Dresser, chip on base.

c1880   *19in (48.5cm) high*

£2,000-3,000   **TCS**

A CLOSER LOOK AT A BERNARD MOORE VASE

This vase dates from the period when Moore had his own ceramic firm and was experimenting with new glazes.

The deep red oxblood or 'sang-de-beouf' glaze was a Ming Dynasty glaze that Moore revived in his own work.

A signature invariably adds value to any item, particularly if the maker is known to have employed other potters or decorators.

The large size of this piece and its fine proportions add to its value.

An Art Deco plate by J. Lurçat of Sant-Vicens, with brown and white design.

c1925   *9.75in (25cm) diam*

£500-800   **MOD**

A Clement Massier vase, of tapered form with four loop handles, covered in lustre glaze, impressed and painted marks, chips.

4in (10cm) high

£60-80   **WW**

A group of mallards, by Leo Mol (Leonid Moludizhanyn), signed and dated "Canada 58" in the glaze to base.

This important painter and sculptor began modelling clay in his father's pottery workshop in Ukraine at the age of six. After moving to Canada in 1948, Leo began producing ceramic dancers, skiers and wildlife figurines which were exhibited in Winnipeg from 1949.

8.5in (21.5cm) high

£300-400   **WAD**

A tall Bernard Moore bottle-shaped vase with cylindrical body and ringed neck, covered in a fine lustred oxblood glaze, signed Bernard Moore.

18.5in (47cm) high

£1,000-1,500   **DRA**

An Art Deco pottery stand, with butterfly design, Monbijou stamp.

c1925   6.25in (16cm) diam

£80-120   **MOD**

One of a pair of owl candelabra, Moore Brothers, Staffordshire.

c1885   11.5in (29cm) high

£300-400 pair   **AL**

A Bernard Moore ginger jar and cover, painted with swimming fishes and underwater vegetation in lustre against a deep blue-black ground, printed mark.

c1910   6.75in (17cm) high

£700-1,000   **GORL**

A Bernard Moore lustre plate, with a design after the Laughing Cavalier.

c1905   8.5in (21.5cm) diam

£400-500   **TCS**

A Bernard Moore 'Diakokan' figure, the squat figure in a rich red glaze, with glass eyes, impressed mark "BM".

c1910   2.5in (6.5cm) high

£300-500   **HAMG**

A French pottery plate, after a design by Alphonse Mucha, printed factory mark, artist facsimile signature, minor wear to surface.

12in (31cm) diam

£700-900   **WW**

An Art Deco figure by the E. A. Muller factory, Thringia, Germany.

7.5in (19cm) high

£400-600   **GCL**

A French fish ceramic vase by Orchies, with fish design, maker's stamp.

c1925   9.75in (25cm) high

£1,200-1,800   **MOD**

A Crown Devon figure by Kathleen Parsons, with printed mark and facsimile signature, restored.

11in (28cm) high

£500-700   **WW**

A stoneware charger by Alfred Powell, painted with a tree motif, painted monogram "m55", firing crack to well and small chips to rim.

13in (33cm) diam

£1,800-2,000   **WW**

A Burleigh Ware plaque, by Charlotte Rhead, painted with a galleon in full sail within a wide border of speckled oblongs, painted and printed marks.

10.25in (26cm) diam

£1,000-1,500   **HAMG**

A large Primavera Art Deco bulbous vessel with four oval panels depicting nude women, covered in brown and gunmetal glaze against a celadon ground with cobalt sponged pattern, incised "Primavera/France/550", with "48-62" in ink.

16.5in (42cm) high

£1,500-2,000   **SDR**

A Crown Ducal vase, by Charlotte Rhead, of flared octagonal form decorated with stylised carnations in shades of blue and mauve, painted signature, number "4016" and printed mark.

7in (18cm) high

£180-220   **HAMG**

A Rorstrand porcelain bulbous vase, decorated in pâte-sur-pâte, with celadon branches and red berries against a grey and pure white ground, ink mark "Rorstrand/NL/23".

8in (20.5cm) high

£500-700   **DRA**

A Rosenthal porcelain 'Watching torso' figure, designed by Rudolf Kaesbach, model number 1603, signed and green mark.

c1945   *9.75in (25cm) high*

£150-200   **BMN**

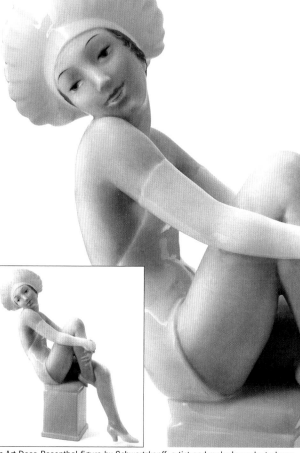

A Rosenthal Art Deco figure of a dancer with a snake.

10.5in (26.5cm) high

£500-700   **GCL**

A 1920s Rosenthal gilded porcelain figure, designed by Ernst Wenck, model number 746, green mark, signed.

c1940   *12.25in (31cm) high*

£400-600   **BMN**

An Art Deco Rosenthal figure by Schwartzkopff, artist and maker's marks to base.

c1930   *27.5cm high*

£1,000-1,500   **JES**

A large Royal Copenhagen porcelain bowl, of flared form, the inside naturalistically painted with a frieze of fish, waves and aquatic foliage, the exterior painted with further aquatic foliage and bubbles, painted factory marks, artist's monogram "GR" and dated "28/1" and "1919".

13.75in (35cm) diam

£800-1,200   **DN**

A 19thC Continental porcelain plateau, probably Royal Copenhagen, of canted rectangular form, the mirrored base within a flower-encrusted guilloche-pierced gallery, with gilt scroll feet.

20.5in (51cm) wide

£2,200-2,800   **FRE**

A pair of Royal Vienna covered urns, with handpainted scenes of women and Cupid, intertwined serpent handles and maroon trim with gold filigree decoration, artist signed in red "J. Tfuhl", blue beehive and stamped "Germany", indistinguishable signatures, some repairs.

12in (30.5cm) high

£1,500-2,000   **JDJ**

A Royal Crown Derby lobed ovoid pot-pourri vase and pierced flat cover, decorated in Imari palette with trailing flowers and leaves, on a pale yellow ground, printed mark in red for 1905 and pattern number 2553/574.

4.25in (11cm) high

£150-200   **LFA**

DECORATIVE ARTS

A Rozenburg 'Dutch Royal House' plate, decorated with a queen holding an orb of the earth and a palm frond in her hands, marked "Rozenburg/Denhaag".

1913   *10.75in (27.5cm) diam*

£600-900   **DRA**

A Sèvres porcelain Art Nouveau oviform vase, painted green ivy leaves with scrolling tendrils and berries against white, factory marks, "S" in triangle, dated "1905" and "RF Decore a Sèvres" and dated "1906", hairline crack.

8.5in (21.5cm) high

£300-400   **DN**

A Weller Sicard pottery vase decorated with foliage on an iridescent ground, signed in script 'Weller Sicard'.

c1905   *4.5in (11.5cm) high*

£400-600   **SL**

A pair of French Art Deco pottery bookends, modelled as a bust of a male whispering and a female listening, glazed, on rectangular bases, inscribed beneath "Sevein", other marks in triangles include "Paris, France".

7in (18cm) high

£150-200   **H&L**

A pair of Susi Singer figures, a boy and girl, stamped "SS".

c1940   *21.5cm high*

£500-800   **QU**

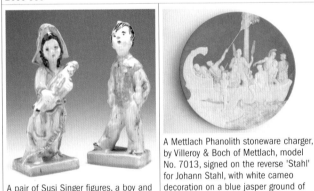

A Mettlach Phanolith stoneware charger, by Villeroy & Boch of Mettlach, model No. 7013, signed on the reverse 'Stahl' for Johann Stahl, with white cameo decoration on a blue jasper ground of Roman figures and gondola.

18.25in (46.5cm) diam

£250-350   **RTC**

A Henry Clemens Van Der Velde stoneware vase, with four handles, grey ground with mauve and turquoise drip glaze, with concentric scored border, insignia impressed to base with model number.

7.5in (19cm) high

£400-600   **ROS**

A Continental pottery pig, designed by Louis Wain, painted in colours, with printed mark "The Lucky Pig - I Charm All Your Ills Away", impressed marks to base, some paint wear.

5in (12.5cm) high

£800-1,200   **WW**

An Art Deco ceramic bust, by Elly Strobach, modelled as a woman holding a cigarette, on a geometric base, impressed "Czechoslovakia" and "Elly Strobach".

7in (17.5cm) high

£220-280 DN

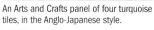

A handpainted plate, by Scottie Wilson, entitled 'Bird Tree and Fish' and painted in colours on a turquoise ground, signed "Scottie", with Aitken Dott label verso.

10.25in (25.5cm) diam

£400-600 L&T

An Arts and Crafts panel of four turquoise tiles, in the Anglo-Japanese style.

c1880

£500-700 PUR

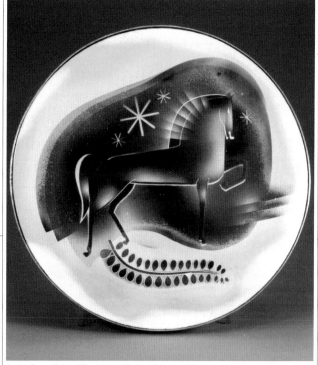

An Art Deco Edgar Winter stencilled and enamelled circular tabletop, of a stallion under stars, unmarked.

24.25in (62cm) diam

£1,800-2,200 SDR

A German pottery figure, impressed factory mark, minor glaze nicks.

10.75in (27cm) high

£300-500 WW

An Art Nouveau-style plaster floor vase, with gold figure on a matte black ground.

18in (45.5cm) high

£30-40 TA

An Art Deco vase, with mermaid design in a gold seascape on a white ground.

c1925   *11.5in (29cm) high*

£800-1,200 MOD

A turquoise and white glazed vase, stamped "OEH".

c1925   *11.75in (30cm) high*

£300-500 MOD

An Art Deco two-handled blue vase, unsigned.

c1925   *15in (38cm) high*

£500-700 MOD

A Belgian Art Deco vase, with blue, yellow and green design, with stamp.

c1925   *12.5in (32cm) high*

£700-1,000 MOD

A Daum Frères 'Mugets' clear glass vase, with three layers of coloured glass and etched lilies-of-the-valley, the base and rim painted gold, signed in gold to base "Daum", "Nancy" and with Cross of Lorraine, rim damaged.

c1895   5in (13cm) high

£400-600   **FIS**

A Daum Frères 'Rose de noel' glass vase, with with layers of gold and red overlaid with blue-green glass, engraved "Daum" signature rubbed with gold to base, Cross of Lorraine and "NANCY", the silver mounting marked with Minerva with "M" and "V".

c1900   4.5in (11.5cm) high

£3,000-5,000   **FIS**

A Daum Frères 'Chandelles' glass goblet vase, with three glass layers in azure, green and white, etched decoration of dandelions, signature to base engraved and rubbed with gold "DAUM", Cross of Lorraine and "NANCY".

c1900   9in (23cm) high

£2,500-3,500   **FIS**

A Daum Frères 'Chandelles' glass vase, overlaid in orange and green, etched dandelion decoration, the base with an incised and rubbed with gold "DAUM", Cross of Lorraine and "NANCY".

c1900   12in (30cm) high

£3,500-4,500   **FIS**

DAUM

- The Daum company was established when Jean Daum (1825-85) acquired a glassworks in Nancy, France.
- His two sons, Auguste (1853-1909) and Antonin (1864-1931), transformed the firm with innovative glass designs and made it commercially successful.
- Inspired by Gallé, the company made cameo, wheel-carved and acid-etched glass in the Art Nouveau and then Art Deco styles.
- Cameo glass is made from layers of coloured glass. The top layer or layers are then etched or carved to reveal the contrasting colour below.
- Brightly coloured acid-etched Daum is desirable, particularly examples with high quality decoration.
- Pieces are marked in gilding, engraving, intaglio or enamel "Daum" and "Nancy" in a variety of styles.
- A number of fakes are on the market. They tend to be inferior in quality and are often moulded rather than etched.

A Daum Frères 'Pavots et étoiles' glass vase, overlaid in violet and with engraved poppies, the gilded silver mount with stylized poppyheads, engraved signature "Daum Nancy", Cross of Lorraine, the silver mounting stamped with a head of Minerva in an octagon, "CARDEILLAC PARIS" and "0690".

c1900   10.5in (26.5cm) high

£20,000-25,000   **FIS**

A Daum Frères 'Eglantine' glass vase, with white overlay over two further layers, etched decoration of a bush rose, partially polished, signed, engraved and rubbed with gold "DAUM", Cross of Lorraine, "NANCY" and "13".

c1900   7.4in (18.4cm) high

£3,000-4,000   **FIS**

A Daum Frères cameo vase, with enamel etched decoration of berries and leaves, signed.

c1900   14.75in (37.5cm) high

£3,000-4,000   **FIS**

A Daum Frères vase with clematis, in purple and green with dark purple overlay and cut decor, signed "Daum Nancy" and with the Cross of Lorraine.

c1900   20.5in (51cm) high

£5,000-7,000   **DOR**

A Daum Frères squat cameo vase, with four sides, depicting a mountainous lake landscape against a red and yellow mottled ground, signed "Daum Nancy" in cameo.

5.5in (14cm) high

£1,800-2,200   **DRA**

A rare Daum Frères vase, in clear and green glass overlaid in blue with etched and cut branches, signed "Daum Nancy" with Cross of Lorraine.

c1900   *12.5in (31cm) high*

£6,000-9,000   **DOR**

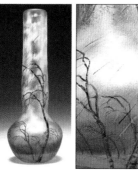

A Daum Frères 'Une Pluie' or 'Arbres sous l'Averse' etched vase, designed by Henri Bergé for the Paris World's Fair, with overlaid glass and coloured powder inclusions, signed "DAUM NANCY", Cross of Lorraine and "5".

c1900   *12.5in (31cm) high*

£6,000-9,000   **QU**

A Daum Frères 'Arbres Roux' vase, designed by Henri Bergé, the bell-shaped body in overlaid clear glass, with blue and purple powder inclusions, enamelled in brown and green, etched decoration, signed "Daum Nancy", Cross of Lorraine.

c1905   *5.5in (13.5cm) high*

£12,000-18,000   **QU**

A Daum Frères glass vase, with apple blossoms and yellow, orange and dark-brown inclusions, overlaid in brown and white, etched cut blossom and leaves, signed "Daum Nancy" with Cross of Lorraine.

c1910   *12.25in (30.5cm) high*

£5,000-7,000   **DOR**

A Daum Frères cameo vase, decorated with brown stems and padded white cameo flowers, all against a mottled blue background, incised signature to side "Daum Nancy".

7.5in (19cm) high

£6,000-9,000   **JDJ**

A Daum Nancy cameo vase, decorated with a butterfly, flower blossoms and leaves in gold enamel on a green and amber background, signed "Daum Nancy" on base.

3.75in (9.5cm) high

£1,000-1,500   **JDJ**

A CLOSER LOOK AT A DAUM FRÈRES VASE

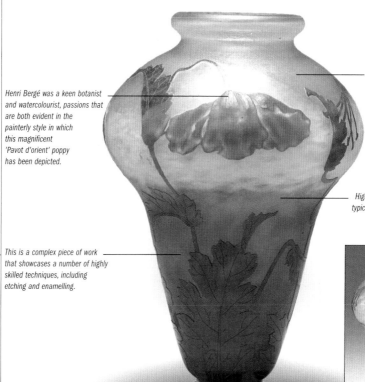

Henri Bergé was a keen botanist and watercolourist, passions that are both evident in the painterly style in which this magnificent 'Pavot d'orient' poppy has been depicted.

This is a complex piece of work that showcases a number of highly skilled techniques, including etching and enamelling.

The landscape background and the flowers have been etched onto the surface of the glass case, revealing the colours beneath.

Highly stylized subject matter like this is typical of Daum's early production during the Art Nouveau period.

A Daum Frères 'Pavot d'orient' baluster vase, designed by Henri Bergé, in clear overlaid glass with blue, white and yellow powder inclusions, enamelled in dark-blue with etched decoration of poppies, signed "DAUM NANCY", Cross of Lorraine.

£20,000-25,000   **QU**

DECORATIVE ARTS

A Daum Frères 'Paysage rose' vase, in clear glass over stained glass, an etched and enamel painted landscape with birches, signed to base "DAUM", Cross of Lorraine and "NANCY".

9.5in (3.75cm) high

£3,500-4,500   FIS

A Daum Frères cameo vase, with enamel decoration of blossoms with green leaves on a mottled background, signed "Daum Nancy".

13.75in (35cm) high

£2,500-3,500   JDJ

A Daum Frères cameo vase, with enamel decoration of amethyst flowers and green leaves on a mottled green and white background, signed to side "Daum Nancy".

4.25in (11cm) high

£1,000-1,500   JDJ

A Daum Frères enamelled vase, with blue enamel decoration of a scene with windmills and boats, signed to base "Daum Nancy".

4in (10cm) high

£700-1,000   JDJ

A Daum Frères dragonfly ewer, with cameo and enamel decoration of dragonflies and flower blossoms, applied handle, partial gold signature to base, minor wear to gold paint.

4.5in (11.5cm) high

£4,000-6,000   JDJ

A Louis Majorelle for Daum Frères 'verre de jade' and wrought iron glass vase, with an ovoid body in overlaid glass and green, milky and purple powder inclusions, signed "Daum Nancy", Cross of Lorraine and "L. Majorelle".

c1920   5.5in (14cm) high

£1,000-1,500   QU

A Louis Majorelle for Daum Frères 'verre de jade' vase, in overlaid glass with pink, white and blue inclusions, mounted with open-work wrought iron, signed "Daum Nancy" and "Louis Majorelle".

c1920   10in (25cm) diam

£800-1,200   QU

A Daum Frères green acid-etched vase, signed.

c1925   11.75in (30cm) high

£1,200-1,800   TDG

A Daum Frères 'rose de noel' salt pot, with opaque white underglaze, gold acid-etching and enamel Christmas roses, signed to base "Daum", Cross of Lorraine and "Nancy".

c1900   4in (10cm) high

£2,000-3,000   FIS

A Daum Frères 'Mûres' ceiling light, with coloured powder enamel, etched blackberry branches, etched "DAUM NANCY" and Cross of Lorraine.

c1910   18.5in (46cm) diam

£7,000-10,000   FIS

A Daum Frères 'Fraisier' glass bowl, with trailing green overlay, decorated with gold etching and enamel fruits, the French silver mount with relief decoration, signed to base "Daum", Cross of Lorraine, "Nancy", head of Minerva stamp to mount and "M" and "V".

c1895   4in (10cm) high

£700-1,000   FIS

A Daum Frères mottled glass shade, of bell form in orange, pink and yellow glass, engraved "Daum/Nancy" with Cross of Lorraine.

c1910   5.5in (14cm) high

£200-300   S&K

A Daum Frères 'Verreries marbrées pailletée d'or' desk lamp, with coloured enamel powder and single gold foil inclusions, iron assembly, engraved "DAUM", Cross of Lorraine, "NANCY".

c1915   13.2in (33cm) high

£1,200-1,800   FIS

GALLÉ

An Emile Gallé vase, with a narrow neck and ornamental handles, in honey-yellow blown glass with silver, decorated with scattered blossoms and leaves, painted "E. Gallé à Nancy".

c1885   8.8in (22cm) high

£3,000-4,000   FIS

An Emile Gallé jug, in brown smoky glass and decorated with an applied glass spiral and engraved stylized lily, etched signature to base within stylized blossom "Cristallerie d'Emile Gallé Nancy" and etched "modèle et décor déposés".

c1890   13.5in (34.5cm) high

£1,500-2,000   FIS

An Emile Gallé vase, in clear glass with black-brown overlay and engraved thistles, the base with stylized floral decoration in relief enamel on gold.

c1890   5in (13cm) high

£4,000-6,000   FIS

An Emile Gallé blown glass vase, decorated with venus shoe flowers, fern leaves and ornamental reserves, etched and relief painted, etched signature to base "Emile Gallé" and bud of flower, painted mark "Déposé".

c1890   10.5in (26.5cm) high

£700-1,000   FIS

GALLÉ

- Emile Gallé (1846-1904), the son of a prosperous glass factory owner, opened his own workshop in Nancy, France in 1874.
- He quickly established himself as a leading designer and glass technician and experimented with many new techniques.
- He is best known for his hand-carved work.
- Gallé introduced the technique of acid-etching cameo glass. Pieces were covered with a design in an acid resist and then plunged into acid which ate away at exposed areas of the surface. It was quicker and more economical than hand-carving pieces.
- Mass-produced acid-etched pieces were known as 'Standard'.
- Marqueterie-sur-verre and other techniques were also used.
- Unique and limited edition pieces are extremely valuable.
- Most Gallé glass is signed but signatures vary. From 1904 to 1914, after his death, pieces were marked with a star and "Gallé".

An Emile Gallé glass bowl, with a poppyhead, butterfly and etched star decoration, relief painting, the rim folded, painted signature to base "Emile Gallé modèle et décor déposés".

c1890   2.75in (7cm) high

£1,200-1,800   FIS

An Emile Gallé glass bowl, in moss-green and decorated with four blossoms, fern leaves and etching, signed to base "Emile Gallé déposé Série C" and a mushroom.

c1890   3in (7.5cm) high

£1,500-2,000   FIS

An Emile Gallé cylindrical glass vase, in two sections, with red overlay, etched decoration of a grasshopper and fern, signed to lower wall "Gallé", etched Cross of Lorraine, etched "Modèle et Décor Déposés".

c1895   8in (20.5cm) high

£3,000-5,000   **FIS**

A tall Gallé 'Pavonina' floor vase, in clear glass overlaid in auburn, with etched blossoms, flower buds and leaves, etched "Gallé" to inside and outside.

c1895   17.4in (43.5cm) high

£1,500-2,000   **FIS**

A Gallé enamelled and acid-etched amber glass vase, the ovoid, textured surface decorated with thistles and gilt highlights, engraved to base "Gallé/depose" within a stylized star.

c1895   7in (18cm) high

£2,000-3,000   **S&K**

An Emile Gallé 'Pâques Fleuries' glass vase, with overlay in three colours and silver inclusions, painted "Pâques Fleuries", etched and painted "Gallé Nancy déposé G.G.", silver mounting with head of Minerva, "M" and "V".

c1895   4in (10cm) high

£3,000-5,000   **FIS**

A rare Emile Gallé large vase, in clear glass with a four layers of semi-opaque overlay, etched decoration of lilies, rim formed as a blossom with five leaves, signed on the lower wall, etched "Gallé", cracked.

c1895   41.5in (105.5cm) high

£10,000-15,000   **FIS**

A Gallé floral cameo vase, in opalescent on clear glass decorated with spider chrysanthemum and pink, blue yellow and brown enamel, signed within the decoration "Galle".

5in (12.5cm) high

£3,000-4,000   **JDJ**

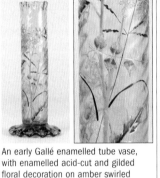

An early Gallé enamelled tube vase, with enamelled acid-cut and gilded floral decoration on amber swirled glass, engraved signature "E. GALLE NANCY".

8in (20.5cm) high

£1,000-1,500   **JDJ**

A Gallé vase, with orange overlay and marqueterie-sur-verre anemones, one green and two purple, engraved "Gallé", crack, restoration.

c1895   7.2in (18cm) high

£1,500-2,000   **FIS**

An Emile Gallé 'Pervincia' small vase, with an irregular oval section, buds of Vinca applied in violet and blue marqueterie-sur-verre, cracked, signed "Gallé".

c1900   4.25in (11cm) high

£6,000-8,000   **FIS**

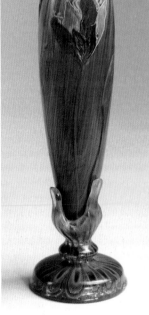

A rare Gallé marqueterie-sur-verre cameo glass vase, on a cushion foot, with a freeform three-pronged connector decorated with a wheel-carved martelé finish, the background glass internally streaked with russet, sienna, and green shading and decorated in marqueterie-sur-verre with crocus blossoms and foliage, with engraved signature "Gallé" to side.

14in (35.5cm) high

£55,000-60,000   **JDJ**

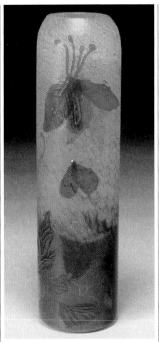

An important Emile Gallé post vase, in clear glass with applied coloured powder, the leaves and buds in marqueterie-sur-verre with engraving, the glass thread stamens with underlaid foil, matt etched, signed "Gallé Etude", cracks.

c1900   *7.75in (19.5cm) high*

£8,000-12,000   **FIS**

A CLOSER LOOK AT A GALLÉ VASE

Gallé developed the technique of glass marquetry c1898. It was named after the decorative wood effect which involves creating patterns with inlaid woods.

Gallé also used the marquetry technique to decorate furniture at his carpentry shop.

At the heart of Gallé's work was nature. The daffodil - symbol of spring, freedom and hope - is very well suited to Gallé's Art Nouveau stylization.

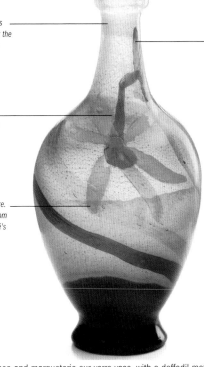

To make this magnificent piece, hot coloured glass, cut to shape, was inserted into the body of the vase while it was still molten. The whole was then rolled to embed the inclusions in place.

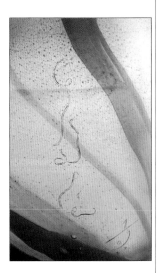

An important Emile Gallé cameo and marqueterie-sur-verre vase, with a daffodil motif in blue, green and yellow shades, signed and dated.

1900   *7in (18cm) high*

£15,000-20,000   **FIS**

A Gallé bowl 'Crete de coq', overlaid in dark amber, with foil and powder inclusions, decorated with plants, signed "Emile Gallé ft Nancy", Cross of Lorraine, "Exposition 1889".

£7,000-10,000   **QU**

An Emile Gallé vase with spiral tendrils, in clear glass with ruby overlay, signed to base "Cristallerie de Gallé Nancy" and etched "Modèle et Décor Déposés".

c1895   *10.75in (27.5cm) high*

£2,000-3,000   **FIS**

An Emile Gallé vase, with opalescent green-white inclusions, red overlay in an etched lily design, signed to base "Cristallerie de Gallé" and etched "Modèle et Décor Déposés", cracked.

c1895   *5in (13cm) high*

£800-1,200   **FIS**

A Gallé mould-blown cameo lamp base, with vivid blue-purple clematis flowers on a yellow background, signed in cameo "GALLE" to side.

c1900   *6.5in (16.5cm) high*

£2,500-3,500   **JDJ**

A Gallé mould-blown vase, decorated with purple plums with deep amber coloured leaves and stems, against a shaded yellow background, signed to side in cameo "Gallé".

c1900   *13in (33cm) high*

£10,000-12,000   **JDJ**

GALLÉ

A CLOSER LOOK AT A GALLÉ GOBLET

This was the first of a range of 'Etude' pieces designed by Gallé that were intended to represent the pinnacle of his virtuosity. Unfortunately, the firing cracks associated with this piece gave the range a bad name and 'Etude' became a byword for defective experimentation.

The overlay colours include a difficult to achieve ruby red at the base of the bowl, providing the illusion that the goblet contains blood.

Some twenty years after Gallé designed this piece, Orrefors perfected a method of encasing overlay glass with a protective layer of clear glass. It was a great success and became known as 'Grail glass'.

This is an unusual and highly conceptual example of Gallé's work.

An important Emile Gallé 'Etude St. Gral' goblet, the foot and cup in clear glass overlaid with three layers, with a high trumpet foot and two clear handles, signed to base, etched between two branches with berries, "Emile Gallé" in the Cross of Lorraine and "Etude St. Gral", crack.

c1895   *14in (35.5cm) high*

£15,000-20,000   **FIS**

A Gallé cameo glass vase, of compressed ovoid form in amber tinted glass overlaid in cranberry and cut with floral vines, signed in cameo "Gallé".

c1900   *3in (7.5cm) high*

£600-900   **S&K**

A small Gallé vase, with an etched clematis over matt glass, overlaid in blue and purple, etched signature to lower wall "Gallé".

c1900   *3.8in (9.7cm) high*

£500-700   **FIS**

An Emile Gallé cameo vase, with purple violets and green leaves on a pink ground, signed "Gallé".

14in (35cm) high

£1,500-2,000   **DRA**

A Gallé glass vase, on a trumpet-shaped foot, overlaid in amber, white, blue and purple, etched crocus design, signed "Gallé".

£1,000-1,500   **QU**

A Gallé cameo glass vase, with red cyclamen flowers on a yellow background, etched signature "GALLE" to side.

7.5in (19cm) high

£1,500-2,500   **JDJ**

A Gallé glass vase, overlaid in amber, white and red, etched decoration of an orchid with blossoms and buds, signed "Gallé", original paper label with "EMILE GALLE NANCY-PARIS".

£1,000-1,500   **QU**

An Emile Gallé cameo vase, with a tall neck and three-lobed rim, decorated with red blossoms, signed "Gallé".

10.25in (25.5cm) high

£700-1,000   **DRA**

An Emile Gallé tall tapering cameo vase, with branches of green leaves and pods on a russet ground, signed "Gallé".

24.5in (61cm) high

£2,000-3,000   **DRA**

A signed Gallé cameo vase, with red anemone flowers on an amber background, signed in cameo "GALLE" to side.

5in (13cm) high

£1,500-2,500 JDJ

A Gallé cameo vase, decorated with amethyst leaves and blossoms over clear frosted glass, signed to side "Gallé".

5.25in (13.5cm) high

£1,000-1,500 JDJ

A Gallé cameo vase, decorated with green and amethyst flower blossoms and leaves, signed on side "Gallé", ground top.

18in (45.5cm) high

£1,500-2,500 JDJ

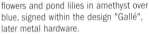

A Gallé fluid lamp, decorated with flowers and pond lilies in amethyst over blue, signed within the design "Gallé", later metal hardware.

10in (25.5cm) high

£1,200-1,800 JDJ

A Gallé cameo vase, decorated with amethyst and blue fuchsia blossoms, leaves and stems on a frosted amber background, signed "Gallé" on the side.

18.25in (46.5cm) high

£3,000-5,000 JDJ

A Gallé cameo bowl, with amethyst over pink over clear glass, decorated with flower blossoms, leaves and stems, matt finish, signed "Gallé" on the side.

6in (15cm) diam

£1,200-1,800 JDJ

A Gallé cameo bowl, with overlaid brown over pink over yellow and white, decorated with blossoms and leaves, signed within the design, the side collapsed during manufacture, four open bubbles to base.

6in (15cm) diam

£800-1,200 JDJ

A large Gallé wheel-carved, fired and polished cameo solifleur vase, the grey glass overlaid in shades of purple and acid-etched with clematis, lacks signature, base hollowed.

53in (135cm) high

£3,000-4,000 L&T

A Gallé cameo table lamp, decorated with chrysanthemum sprays, cameo signature, small chip to top rim of base.

20in (51cm) high

£7,000-10,000 WW

A pair of Gallé cups, with redcurrants, in the shape of a stylized calyx, on a trumpet-shaped foot, overlaid in orange and red, etched decoration, signed "Gallé".

1.5in (2cm) high

£1,500-2,000 QU

A Gallé cameo vase, overlaid with green amethyst and white on a frosted background, floral decoration with signature to base, signed "Gallé" with a star, two chips to cameo signature.

10in (25.5cm) high

£1,000-1,500 JDJ

A 1920s Gallé 'Gentiane' disc-shaped vase, overlaid with amber and blue glass, etched decoration of a gentian, signed "Gallé".

£1,500-2,000   QU

A Gallé cameo vase, decorated with amber pine cones on a mottled green background, signed "Gallé" with a star.

6in (30.5cm) high

£1,200-1,800   JDJ

A Gallé cameo vase, overlaid decoration of green leaves and purple lilac blossoms, signed on side of vase "Gallé" with a star.

11in (28cm) high

£800-1,200   JDJ

LALIQUE

A Lalique frosted glass centrepiece, with two disc-like handles moulded with an openwork design of antelopes leaping through foliage, with leaves extending on to the plain elliptical vessel, marked "R. Lalique".

19in (48cm) long

£1,500-2,000   DN

A Lalique 'Sirenes' frosted glass perfume burner and cover, moulded with a frieze of naked female forms, the domed lid moulded with their flowing hair, includes original wick, etched mark "R. Lalique, France".

£1,200-1,800   L&T

A Lalique 'Ceylan' frosted and opalescent glass vase, of tapering cylindrical form, moulded with a frieze of budgerigars, wheel-etched marks, traces of blue staining, "R.Lalique, France", "No.905".

9.5in (24cm) high

£2,500-3,500   L&T

A CLOSER LOOK AT A LALIQUE VASE

This decanter was mould blown, probably in a four-piece steel mould. These moulds were expensive to produce, making Lalique glass a luxury commodity at the time.

The stopper, depicting a kneeling female figure, is particularly vulnerable to chipping or loss. The fact that this one remains in excellent condition enhances the value of this decanter.

These diaphanous figures almost seem to melt into the body of the decanter. This kind of sophisticated design marks Lalique out as a master of his art.

Look for crispness in the moulded figures.

This is a very complex design depicting an amorous couple in six different poses.

A Lalique 'Moissac' opalescent, clean and frosted glass vase, number 992, with remains of blue staining, moulded mark "R Lalique France".

5in (13cm) high

£1,000-1,500   WW

A Lalique 'Domremy' amber glass vase, number 979, with etched signature.

8.75in (22cm) high

£2,000-3,000   WW

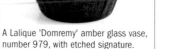

A Lalique 'Douze Figurines avec Bouchon' vase, with stopper, in clear and frosted glass, engraved "R. Lalique" mark.

c1920   *11.5in (29.5cm) high*

£5,000-7,000   RDL

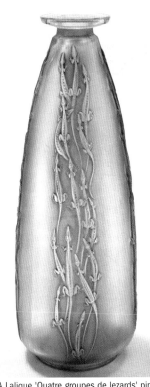
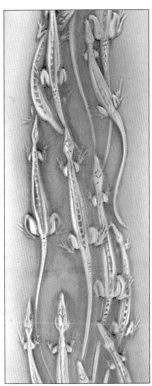

A Lalique 'Quatre groupes de lezards' pink glass vase, of elongated ovoid shape, moulded with vertical bands of running lizards, engraved mark "Lalique".

12.5in (32cm) high

£8,000-10,000   **GORL**

A large Lalique 'Sauterelles' ovoid glass vase, with a design of moulded crickets stained in green pigment, against a blue stained ground, designed in 1912, etched mark "R. Lalique".

11in (28cm) high

£5,000-8,000   **GORL**

A Lalique 'Milan' ovoid glass vase, with a design of moulded leaves and stalks stained in blue pigment, engraved mark "R. Lalique France".

c1930   *11.25in (28.5cm) high*

£2,000-3,000   **GORL**

A Lalique 'Spirales' glass vase, of tapering shape with moulded design of raised spirals, etched mark "R. Lalique".

c1935   *6.5in (16.5cm) high*

£700-1,000   **GORL**

A reissued Lalique 'Danseuse Bras Baisse' statuette, after an earlier figure, with engraved "No. 11910" mark.

c1975 9.5in (19cm) high

£400-600 RDL

A Lalique 'Longchamps' frosted glass car mascot, modelled as a horse's head with highly stylized mane, the glass with a pale amethyst tint, with a chromed collar mounted on a rectangular marble base, marked "R.Lalique", some trimming and nicks.

7in (17.5cm) high

£2,500-3,500 DN

A Lalique 'Ato Pendule électrique Moineau' frosted glass timepiece, with a curved top, the front moulded with sparrows resting on prunus, 'Ato' glass dial, moulded 'R. Lalique' near the base.

This model was created for and sold exclusively by 'Ato' and never appeared in the commercial catalogues of Maison Lalique.

6in (15.5cm) high

£1,200-1,800 DN

A Lalique clear and frosted opalescent box, with a later enamelled silver top depicting cherry blossom, inscribed "R. Lalique France", English silver marks Birmingham 1933.

5.5in (14cm) wide

£400-600 ROS

LOETZ

A Loetz-style enamelled iridescent glass vase, the spirally ribbed and dimpled ovoid body in pale green glass, painted with flowering clover and a gilt border, inscribed "Loetz/Austria".

10in (25.5cm) high

£150-200 S&K

A Loetz iridescent Art Nouveau vase, designed by Friedrich Adler, with a gilt pewter mount, signed "Orion", model number 315.

c1905 6in (15cm) high

£3,000-4,000 BMN

An overlaid vase, attributed to Loetz, of lustred glass with silver blossoms, etched number "21309".

8in (20cm) high

£800-1,200 DRA

A Loetz glass vase, of dimple ovoid form with everted rim, the green body covered in a tracery of peacock iridescence.

7.75in (19.5cm) high

£300-400 L&T

A Loetz-Witwe 'Gre 29' vase, in light olive-green glass with wide bands of silvery yellow, engraved "Loetz Austria".

c1900 10in (25cm) high

£2,500-3,000 FIS

A Loetz iridescent glass, vase with incised leaf veining.

c1905 8.75in (22cm) high

£7,000-10,000 LN

A Loetz iridescent small vase, with sterling silver overlay.

c1905 5in (13cm) high

£2,500-3,000 LN

A Loetz iridescent glass vase.

c1905   11.75in (30cm) high

£2,000-3,000   LN

An iridescent dimpled baluster vase, attributed to Loetz, in a wavy pull-feather motif of lustred blue-green and burgundy glass, unmarked.

8.25in (20.5cm) high

£1,500-2,000   DRA

A Loetz tapered vase, with a squat base and dimpled neck, lustred silver pull-feather pattern on celadon ground, engraved "Loetz Austria".

9.75in (24cm) high

£1,500-2,000   DRA

A Loetz Witwe vase, in iridescent light-green glass with purple string decoration and dark-red dots.

c1900   9.5in (24cm) high

£1,500-2,000   FIS

A large Loetz-style glass vase, of slender baluster form, the body covered with speckled peacock iridescence.

14in (35cm) high

£400-600   L&T

A pair of early 20thC 'Papillon' iridescent vases, attributed to Loetz, the waisted cylindrical necks flaring to the shoulders and tapering to the feet, the amber coloured glass spotted with iridescence.

13.5in (34cm) high

£700-1,000   CHEF

A CLOSER LOOK AT A LOETZ VASE

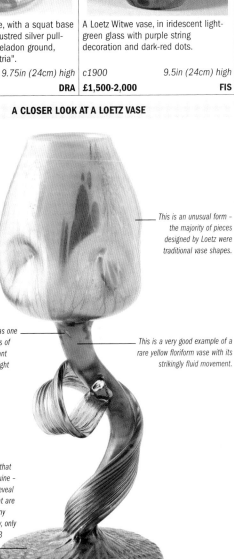

This is an unusual form – the majority of pieces designed by Loetz were traditional vase shapes.

Loetz is widely regarded as one of the very best producers of iridescent glass. The vibrant colours of this vase highlight the company's expertise in this area.

This is a very good example of a rare yellow floriform vase with its strikingly fluid movement.

It is important to ensure that Loetz signatures are genuine - close inspection should reveal the horizontal strokes that are made up of a series of tiny vertical strokes. Generally, only pieces made before 1903 were signed.

A Loetz iridescent decorative vase, in the form of a tulip with a twisted stem, overlaid by a leaf curling up from the base.

c1905   9.75in (24cm) high

£40,000-60,000   LN

A Loetz iridescent glass vase, the lobed body on a circular foot, with cylindrical rim, oil-spot decoration, unsigned.

c1900   10in (25.5cm) diam

£600-900   S&K

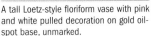

A tall Loetz-style floriform vase with pink and white pulled decoration on gold oil-spot base, unmarked.

13.5in (34cm) high

£300-400   DRA

A pair of Loetz-style gilt-decorated iridescent glass vases, with oil-spot decoration and gilt thistles, unsigned.

c1900   4.75in (12cm) diam

£200-300   S&K

DECORATIVE ARTS

A Loetz Witwe 'Phänomen' vase, overlaid with pulled decoration of silvery threads, lustred in gold and mother-of-pearl, signed "Loetz Austria".

c1900   10.5in (26cm) high
£1,500-2,000   QU

A Loetz Witwe 'Phänomen Gre 258' vase, in clear glass underlaid with yellow, orange and dark-brown, signed "Loetz Austria".

c1900   7in (17.5cm) high
£7,000-8,000   DOR

A Loetz Witwe footed 'Phänomen Gre 166' clear glass vase, with dark blue underlay, silver pulled feather decoration, engraved "Loetz Austria".

c1900   13.25in (33cm) high
£3,000-5,000   FIS

An iridescent Loetz 'Phänomen' vase, lustred amber coloured glass with pulled iridescent pearl coloured bands, signed "Loetz Austria".

c1900   6.75in (17cm) high
£2,000-3,000   QU

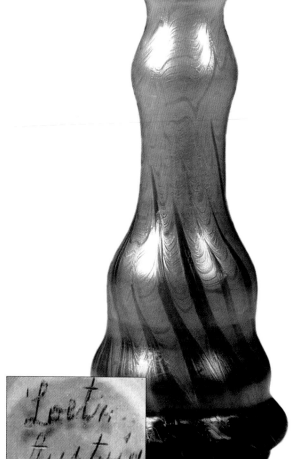

An important Loetz vase 'Phänomen Gre 388', with thin yellow underlay and wide silver thread decoration, overlaid with black to base, engraved "Loetz Austria".

c1900   8.5in (21.5cm) high
£6,000-8,000   FIS

A Loetz Witwe "Phänomen Gre 1/84" octagonal iridescent vase, in green glass with overlaid silvery yellow.

c1905   6in (15cm) high
£1,200-1,800   FIS

A Loetz Witwe 'Argus' vase, in clear, brown and light-green glass, with pulled decoration and silvery yellow dots, signed "Loetz Austria".

c1900   7in (17.5cm) high
£2,200-2,800   FIS

A pair of Loetz-style threaded green glass squat vases, unmarked, small nicks to rim.

4.25in (11cm) high
£50-70   DRA

A Loetz dimpled and ribbed glass vase with ruffled rim, in a gold and blue lustred finish, unmarked.

7in (18cm) high
£500-700   DRA

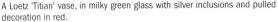

A Loetz 'Titian' vase, in milky green glass with silver inclusions and pulled decoration in red.

c1905   14.75in (37.5cm) high
£3,000-5,000   QU

A large Loetz Witwe glass vase, overlaid with red and milky white, etched quince decoration, signed "C. a. Loetz".

c1925   15.5in (39cm) high
£1,200-1,800   QU

A Loetz table lamp, the opalescent glass shade with a pattern of red and silver inclusions and a pearl finish, electrified.

c1900   17in (43.5cm) high
£1,000-1,500   QU

A Loetz ceiling light, with floral decoration in multicoloured glass, electric, marked "Genre Gallé", signed.

c1925   16in (41cm) diam
£2,000-3,000   QU

A Loetz glass and jadeite letter opener, the handle of iridescent green glass with coloured trailings, the Russian silver neck mounted with opals and rubies, on a stippled ground, mounted with a jadeite blade, the glass unsigned, the silver signed "Cartier", hallmarked and numbered.

c1900
£1,800-2,200   S&K

A Loetz goblet designed by Hans Bolek, in opaque-white glass with a frieze of black etched heart-shaped decoration, minor damage to foot.

c1915   6in (15cm) high
£3,000-4,000   QU

A Monart glass vase, of cylindrical form with blue and green cloisonné finish.

13.5in (34cm) high

£400-600 | **L&T**

A Monart tapering glass vase, the mottled pea green body with aventurine and blue inclusions to the rim.

8.5in (21.5cm) high

£100-150 | **L&T**

A Monart tapering glass vase, the mottled green body with aventurine inclusions, bears paper label.

7.5in (19cm) high

£100-150 | **L&T**

A Monart baluster glass vase, the mottled green body with blue and mica inclusions to the rim.

7.5in (19cm) high

£150-200 | **L&T**

MONART

- The Monart range was made by the Moncrieff glassworks (c1864-1996) from 1924-61 by the Spanish glassworker Salvador Ysart and his sons.
- Free-blown coloured glass shapes were rolled over specks of enamels, aventurine, metallic foil or mica and then cased in clear glass. Decoration was usually concentrated to the top of pieces.
- Most pieces are large vases, but bowls, jugs, lamps and other objects are also found.
- Forms tend to be heavy, with bubbled surfaces created by adding crushed charcoal to the body which then burns off when heated.
- Monart was sold at fashionable shops, such as Liberty & Co.
- Paul Ysart, eldest son of Salvador, took over production of Monart after WWII and specialized in paperweights. His father and two brothers set up their own company named Vasart.
- Post-WWII pieces tend to be paler and subtler in colour.
- Monart glass has a distinctive pontil mark of a ground disc surrounded by a ground circle. Paper labels are most commonly marked with the Monart trademark in a circle with "Moncrieff".

A large Monart glass vase, of baluster form with an everted rim, the green glass body with turquoise spiral ribbed decoration and aventurine inclusions.

11.5in (29cm) high

£1,200-1,800 | **L&T**

A Monart tapering glass vase, the swirling white and yellow body with multicoloured pulled inclusions to the rim.

6.5in (16cm) high

£150-200 | **L&T**

A Monart ovoid glass vase, with a mottled red body and mottled lemon yellow rim, bubble inclusions, bears paper label "UBVIII".

9in (22.5cm) high

£700-900 | **L&T**

A Monart ovoid glass vase, the swirling white and yellow body with multi-coloured pulled inclusions to the rim, bears paper label "No. VII*390".

150-200 high

£150-200 | **L&T**

A Monart tapering glass vase, the red, orange and mottled body with amethyst inclusions to the rim.

8.5in (21cm) high

£100-150 | **L&T**

A Monart tapering glass vase, in mottled orange and amethyst.

8.5in (21cm) high

£120-180   **L&T**

A Monart glass vase, of bulbous tapering form with cylindrical neck, the mottled orange body with amethyst inclusions to the rim.

8.5in (22cm) high

£250-300   **L&T**

A Monart posy vase, with broad flaring rim, the mottled pea green body with amethyst and aventurine inclusions to the rim

5.5in (14cm) diam

£30-50   **L&T**

A rare Monart cameo glass lamp, the domed shade above a baluster shaped body, the mottled orange glass overlaid with green and brown glass, acid-etched with a frieze of trees, possibly unique, bears paper label "etched lamp".

18.75in (47cm) high

£4,000-6,000   **L&T**

A Vasart pink glass basket, with handles.

£20-30   **L&T**

A Monart circular tapering bowl, the red, orange and mottled body with amethyst inclusions to the rim, bears paper label "No.MC.VII".

5.25in (13cm) high

£40-60   **L&T**

ORREFORS

ORREFORS

- Glass was first manufactured at Orrefors, Småland, Sweden in 1898.
- Simon Gate (1883-1945) was taken on as artistic director in 1916 and was joined by Edward Hald (1883-1980) a year later. The company then gained an international reputation for high quality glass.
- Graal, a type of cased engraved glass, was introduced by Gate in 1916.
- At the 1925 Paris International Exposition Orrefors was awarded the Grands Prix and gold medals.
- Ariel glass, sandblasted with intaglio decoration and cased, was introduced by Edvin Öhrström (b.1906) in 1937, and developed by Vicke Lindstrand (1904-83).
- Two other notable designers were Sven Palmqvist (1906-84), who produced abstract designs, and Ingeborg Lundin (b.1921) who used a variety of techniques including engraving and latticino.
- Orrefors continues to produce quality glass today and became part of Royal Scandinavian in 1997.

An Orrefors jug, by Simon Gate, engraved with a female dancer.

c1925   *8.75in (22cm) high*

£1,500-2,000   **LN**

An engraved glass vase, probably Orrefors, designed by Vicke Lindstrand, engraved with a classical nude, etched "L. 1935".

6.5in (16.5cm) high

£150-200   **WW**

A 1930s Orrefors 'Ariel' bright blue glass vase, by Öhrström.

6.75in (17cm) high

£3,000-5,000   **LN**

DECORATIVE ARTS

A 1930s Orrefors 'Mermaid' vase.

8.5in (22cm) high

£1,000-1,500   LN

An engraved Orrefors decanter, by Nils Landberg, with an image of a sailor.

c1940   9.5in (24cm) high

£200-300   JH

An Orrefors 'Graal' glass vase, by Edward Hald, in clear glass with green and brown overlay, acid-etched decoration of fishes and water plants, signed.

1944   7.5in (19cm) high

£500-800   FIS

A 1950s Orrefors engraved vase, by Palmqvist, with a scene of a boy and a bird.

9in (22.5cm) high

£80-120   JH

A 1950s Orrefors 'Utopia' vase, by Boran Varsh.

10.5in (27cm) high

£500-800   JH

An Orrefors window cut vase.

c1935   5in (13cm) high

£100-150   JH

An Orrefors glass bowl, on a trefoil foot, incised "Orrefors/ No 3516/211".

13in (33cm) diam

£100-150   S&K

A CLOSER LOOK AT AN ORREFORS VASE

The designer of this vase, sculptor Edvin Öhrström, was hired in 1936 to develop new designs before the world exhibition in Paris in 1937.

Öhrström, together with Vicke Lindstrand, developed a technique known as Ariel, which was named after the spirit of the air in Shakespeare's The Tempest.

A design is cut into multi-layered glass, revealing the colours beneath. The whole piece is then cased in clear glass, trapping air in the cavities.

Due to the way light is reflected in the cased cavities, the design has a silvery finish.

An Orrefors 'Ariel' pink glass vase, by Edvin Öhrström.

c1940   6.25in (16cm) high

£12,000-18,000   LN

STEVENS & WILLIAMS

- Established in 1847 in Stourbridge, Stevens & Williams started developing new types of art glass in the late 19thC.
- The high relief decorative technique of 'Mat-Su-Noke' ('The Spirit of the Pine Tree') was registered in 1884. This expensive process was widely copied.
- Innovations included the Silveria range, developed by John Northwood c1900. The technique involved carefully encasing thin sheets of silver foil between layers of glass. The range was only produced for a short period and is highly sought after today.
- As well as attractive decoration, collectors look for the work of particular craftsmen such as Joshua Hodgetts and Frederick Carder, who went on to found Steuben Glass Works in New York.
- The firm later employed Keith Murray who produced over 150 designs, including the Cactus vase, before he joined Wedgwood.
- Still in production today as Royal Brierley.

A Stevens & Williams double case hock glass.

c1900   8in (20cm) high

£300-400   AL

A Stevens & Williams two colour 'Hock' glass, in yellow and orange.

c1905   8in (20cm) high

£300-500   AL

A Stevens & Williams two colour 'Hock' glass, predominantly purple.

c1905   8in (20cm) high

£300-500   AL

A Stevens & Williams 'transparent cameo' decanter.

c1900   9.5in (24cm) high

£300-500   AL

A Stevens & Williams 'Mat-su-noke' glass vase.

c1885   7in (18cm) high

£500-800   AL

A Stevens & Williams 'rainbow stripe' fluted vase.

c1885   12in (31cm) high

£100-150   AL

A Stevens & Williams 'Jewell' threaded posy vase, registered design 55693.

c1890

£100-150   AL

A Stevens & Williams cased and intaglio cut glass bowl and stand.

c1920   Stand 6.25in (15.75cm) diam

£100-150   JH

A Stevens & Williams carved glass vase.

c1935   5.25in (13cm) high

£100-150   JH

TIFFANY

A Tiffany Favrile tall floriform glass vase, with a bulbous base and tulip-form top, in amber glass with pink and green iridescent pulled feather decoration, inscribed "L.C.T/V4476".

c1905   20.5in (52cm) high

£2,500-3,000   S&K

An early 20thC Tiffany Favrile glass vase, of trumpet shape, with a short knopped stem and domed base, signed "L.C. Tiffany Favrile/1509-9850L".

10in (25.5cm) high

£400-600   S&K

A Tiffany Furnaces Favrile amber glass and gilt-bronze trumpet-form vase, glass inscribed "L.C.T./Favrile", bronze impressed "Louis C. Tiffany Furnaces Inc./160" with company monogram.

c1925   14.25in (36cm) high

£1,200-1,800   S&K

A Tiffany Gold Favrile glass bud vase, with a gently flaring and facetted stem, inset in a circular base of green enamel, base stamped "LOUIS C. TIFFANY FURNACES INC. 151".

13.5in (34cm) high

£1,000-1,500   DRA

TIFFANY

- Louis Comfort Tiffany (1848-1933), son of the founder of the successful luxury goods business Tiffany & Co., was one of the most important figures in the American Art Nouveau movement.
- Tiffany trained as a painter and later studied glass. In the 1880s he patented his own type of iridescent glass, know as 'Favrile' meaning handcrafted.
- In 1892, Tiffany's freeblown glass went on sale. The majority of pieces were vases in a wide variety of forms and colours.
- Tiffany is best known for his commercially successful leaded lamps. Shades tended to be hemispherical in shape and designs ranged from simple geometrical patterns to complex designs of flowers and foliage. By 1906 over 125 types of lamps were on sale.
- As the price of Tiffany has increased, many pieces of art glass with fake Tiffany signatures have appeared on the market.

A Tiffany wheel-carved Favrile glass vase, with a shaped lip, in iridescent amber glass with trailing vines and carved leaves, inscribed "L.C. Tiffany. Favrile/2352K", numbered "14178".

c1915   6in (15cm) high

£3,000-5,000   S&K

A Tiffany glass vase, of iridescent gold with vertical ribbing and five folded petals, button pontil, signed "L.T.C. Y2390".

4.25in (11cm) high

£700-900   JDJ

A Tiffany blue iridescent vase, with silver decoration of leaves and vines with iridescent flashes of green, gold and blue, signed on base "Louis C. Tiffany LCT D1420".

4.5in (11.5cm) high

£4,000-6,000   JDJ

A Tiffany bulbous vase, in opaque yellow Favrile glass with threaded blue leaves and opaline dogwood blossoms, etched "L.C.T./T5284".

6in (15cm) high

£8,000-12,000   DRA

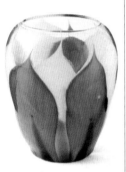

A small Tiffany paperweight vase, with a pink floral decoration.

c1910   6.25in (16cm) high

£10,000-15,000   LN

A Tiffany floriform vase with broad flat rim and pulled feather decoration, two manufacturing bubbles to rim, etched "L.C.T./T3241".

11.25in (28cm) high

£7,000-10,000   DRA

A large Tiffany iridescent wine glass, with carved vines.

c1910   6in (15cm) high

£500-700   LN

A CLOSER LOOK AT A TIFFANY CAMEO VASE

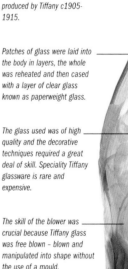

Paperweight vases were produced by Tiffany c1905-1915.

Patches of glass were laid into the body in layers, the whole was reheated and then cased with a layer of clear glass known as paperweight glass.

The glass used was of high quality and the decorative techniques required a great deal of skill. Speciality Tiffany glassware is rare and expensive.

The skill of the blower was crucial because Tiffany glass was free blown – blown and manipulated into shape without the use of a mould.

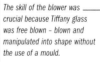

A small Tiffany iridescent wine glass, with carved vines.

c1910   5in (13cm) high

£300-400   LN

A Tiffany pastel wine glass.

c1910   6.25in (16cm) high

£1,000-1,500   LN

A pair of Tiffany Favrile pastel glass candlesticks, each of tapering form with flaring scalloped rim, in opalescent shading to teal green glass, inscribed "L.C. Tiffany. Favrile/1901", one numbered "993T".

c1925   9.5in (24cm) high

£1,500-2,000   S&K

A rare Tiffany cameo carved paperweight vase, inlaid with different colours and then engraved.

c1910   7in (18cm) high

£28,000-30,000   LN

DECORATIVE ARTS

A Tiffany Favrile glass candlestick, with reeded tapering stem, vasiform candle cup with foliate-moulded bobeche, base inscribed "L.C. Tiffany. Favrile/1953" with a Favrile Glass trademark paper label, bobeche inscribed "L.C.T. Favrile".

c1915   *14.5in (37cm) high*

£600-900   **S&K**

A Tiffany gold favrile glass shade, oviform with a flaring lip, the rim incised "LCT".

c1910   *9in (22.5cm) high*

£1,200-1,800   **S&K**

ALMÉRIC WALTER

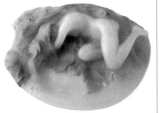

A pair of Alméric Walter pâte-de-verre book ends, each moulded as seated squirrels in green glass, moulded marks "A Walter, Nancy" and "Bergé Sc".

5.5in (13.5cm) high

£600-900   **L&T**

An Alméric Walter oval bowl with chameleon, designed by Henri Bergé, pâte-de-verre in opaque moulded glass, sculpted chameleon, signed on the inside wall "A WALTER NANCY", and "Bergé Sc.", restored.

c1910   *7in (18cm) long*

£6,000-9,000   **FIS**

ALMÉRIC WALTER

- Alméric Walter (1859-1942) was renowned for his pâte-de-verre work which he first made at Daum Frères.
- The pâte-de-verre technique involved adding flux and colour to ground glass and refiring.
- Walter also produced plaques and sculptural pieces. He collaborated with Daum's talented master decorator, Henri Bergé (1880-1937), who sculpted a number of pieces.
- Naturalistic and three dimensionally modelled chameleons and salamanders often feature in his work.
- Many pieces are marked "A Walter, Nancy" and sculptural pieces also feature a "B" for Bergé.
- Pate-de-verre is fragile and prone to cracking. Pieces can be restored. To check for restoration use a strong light.

An Alméric Walter pâte-de-verre sculpture, designed by A. Finot.

c1915   *9in (23cm) wide*

£3,000-5,000   **LN**

A 1920s Alméric Walter pâte-de-verre yellow bowl, designed by M. Corrett.

4in (10cm) high

£2,000-3,000   **LN**

An Alméric Walter pâte-de-verre vase, by Henri Bergé, decorated with thistles, with impressed marks and signatures.

4in (10cm) high

£1,200-1,800   **WW**

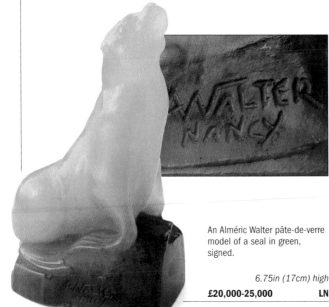

An Alméric Walter pâte-de-verre model of a seal in green, signed.

6.75in (17cm) high

£20,000-25,000   **LN**

An Alméric Walter pâte-de-verre vase, designed by Henri Bergé, impressed mark "H. Bergé Sc. A. Walter, Nancy".

8in (20.5cm) high

£2,500-3,500   **L&T**

An Alméric Walter pâte-de-verre scarab pendant, the glass bead and string possibly later.

Pendant 1.5in (4cm) long

£2,000-3,000   **LN**

A Thomas Webb three colour cameo vase, with cameo floral decoration of roses and leaves, signed "Tiffany & Co. Paris Exposition 1889 Thomas Webb & Sons Gem Cameo".

7.5in (19cm) high

£2,500-3,500   **JDJ**

A cameo glass vase, in the style of Thomas Webb, of bulbous form in ruby glass overlaid with branching flowers and butterflies.

13in (33cm) high

£3,000-4,000   **S&K**

A Thomas Webb cameo scent bottle, with original silver cover, decorated in white over red with lily of the valley, base signed "Thomas Webb & Sons".

5.25in (13.25cm) high

£3,000-4,000   **JDJ**

A Webb cameo perfume bottle, with white cameo vines and leaves, silver top marked "Gorham Sterling".

10.5in (26.5cm) long

£1,500-2,000   **JDJ**

A Webb cameo glass bowl, in Moorish style.

c1890   *4.5in (11.5cm) diam*

£1,000-1,500   **MW**

A pair of Webb cameo glass salad servers.

c1890   *11.5in (29cm) long*

£1,000-1,500   **MW**

A Webb vaseline glass fruit dish.

c1905   *5.5in (14cm) high*

£300-500   **MW**

A Webb Burmese vase, with a bulbous body and rolled rim, enamelled with red flowers and green leaves, marked on underside "Thomas Webb & Sons Queen's Burmeseware Patented Rd 67648".

4.75in (12cm) high

£300-500   **JDJ**

A 1930s Thomas Webb vase, designed by Anna Fogelberg, decorated with cacti.

Anna Fogelberg was married to the Managing Director of Thomas Webb.

£1,200-1,800   **JH**

A 1930s Webb cut and acid-etched vase.

This vase is similar to Webb's 'Cameo Fleur' but has a single casing.

8in (20.5cm) high

£200-300   **JH**

A Webb Corbett decanter, original label.

The ban on the production of luxury goods for the British market following WWII suggests that this was made for export.

c1945   *13in (34cm) high*

£300-400   **JH**

A late 1930s Whitefriars bottle shaped vase with horizontal bands, pattern number 9136.

8.5in (21.5cm) high

£250-350   JH

A Whitefriars footed vase, with diagonal cut lenses and waves, pattern number C3 or C4, probably by William Wilson.

c1940   7.5in (19cm) high

£500-600   JH

A Whitefriars Studio range 'Peacock' ancient urn vase, designed by Peter Wheeler, in colours of green and gold with silver nitrate random strapwork to centre band, pattern no. S8.

c1970   5.5in (14cm) high

£700-900   TCS

A Whitefriars bulbous lamp in sky blue with wave ribbon.

c1930   9.5in (24cm) high

£120-180   TCS

A Whitefriars emerald cased, five-lobed tall lamp, designed by William Wilson.

c1955   15in (38cm) high

£100-150   TCS

A Whitefriars ruby-cased, five-lobed tall lamp, designed by William Wilson, signed "camping 1963".

16in (40.5cm) high

£100-150   TCS

WHITEFRIARS

- Whitefriars glassworks was founded in the 17thC on the banks of the Thames, in London.
- in 1834, London vintner James Powell purchased the works and produced stained glass windows.
- Powell fostered ties with the Arts and Crafts movement and worked with William Morris on the Red House, in 1859. Historic Venetian forms provided much of the firm's output in this period.
- James Powell's grandson, Harry, joined the firm in 1875 and developed new techniques and forms such as 'straw opal'. Whitefriars became a leading maker of art glass.
- The company moved to Wealdstone in 1923 and produced Art Deco glass with geometric designs.
- Royal College of Art graduate, Geoffrey Baxter, was appointed as designer in 1954. He introduced colourful textured glass such as the banjo vase.
- Today, Whitefriars of all periods is hotly collected. Prices for Baxter have risen steeply in recent years.

A CLOSER LOOK AT A WHITEFRIARS VASE

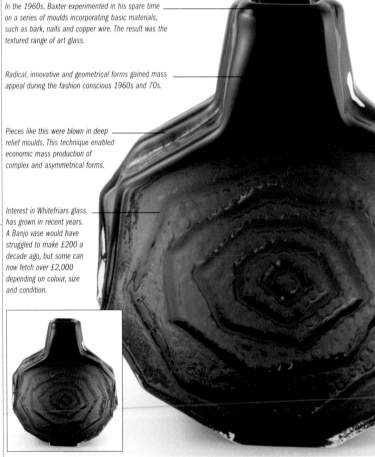

In the 1960s, Baxter experimented in his spare time on a series of moulds incorporating basic materials, such as bark, nails and copper wire. The result was the textured range of art glass.

Radical, innovative and geometrical forms gained mass appeal during the fashion conscious 1960s and 70s.

Pieces like this were blown in deep relief moulds. This technique enabled economic mass production of complex and asymmetrical forms.

Interest in Whitefriars glass has grown in recent years. A Banjo vase would have struggled to make £200 a decade ago, but some can now fetch over £2,000 depending on colour, size and condition.

A rare Whitefriars cinnamon banjo vase, designed by Geoffrey Baxter, unmarked, small bruise to base rim.

c1965   12.5in (32cm) high

£700-1,000   WW

A rare Whitefriars knobbly green-streaked lamp, designed by Harry Dyer, with original metal fitting.

A unique Whitefriars cased lamp made by Harry Dyer.

Dyer made this for Muriel Green, a PA at Whitefriars 30 years.

A Whitefriars gold coloured, full-lead crystal bed lamp, designed by Geoffrey Baxter.

Two of a set of six Whitefriars wine glasses, by Harry J. Powell, in Vaseline glass with a twist finish.

| c1965 | 10in (25.5cm) high | c1965 | 13.5in (34.5cm) high | c1980 | 16in (40.5cm) high | c1900 | | 4.5in (11.5cm) high |
| **£150-200** | **TCS** | **£200-300** | **TCS** | **£120-180** | **TCS** | **£800-1,200 set** | | **MW** |

ENGLISH CAMEO

An English cameo scent bottle, in white over amethyst over blue, with morning glory decoration and original silver top.

An English cameo scent bottle, in blue glass with flowers and butterfly, silver screw top monogrammed "CLM" and marked "Gorham Sterling".

An English cameo claret jug, overlay colours of white over blue with cameo decoration of morning glories, leaves and vines, silver handle and top.

An English cameo miniature lamp base, with light blue cameo flowers and leaves against a dark blue background.

An English cameo biscuit jar, with a silver-plated collar and apple blossom, handle and lid marked with a cupid within a shield and "6101".

| 2in (5cm) high | 10in (25.5cm) long | 8.75in (22cm) high | 4.75in (12cm) high | 6.5in (16.5cm) high |
| **£2,500-3,000** | **JDJ** | **£2,000-2,500** | **JDJ** | **£1,000-1,500** | **JDJ** | **£800-1,200** | **JDJ** | **£2,000-3,000** | **JDJ** |

STAINED GLASS

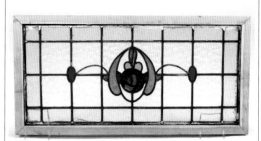

An Arts and Crafts leaded glass window, with a stylized red Glasgow rose on hammered clear and amber panes, mounted in a new pine frame.

34in (85cm) wide

A pair of Arts and Crafts leaded glass windows, in polychrome glass with different textures, one window depicting a medieval youth with hand-painted face and hands, the other with "Welcome the coming Speed the parting guest" and a beer tankard, mounted in original sashes, framed.

Frames 33 x 23in (84 x 58.5cm)

| **£200-250** | **DRA** | **£1,000-1,500 pair** | **DRA** |

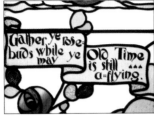

A pair of Arts and Crafts leaded glass windows, in polychrome glass with different textures, one depicting a medieval maiden with hand-painted face and hands, the other with "Gather ye rosebuds while ye may, Old Time is still a-flying", in original sashes.

Frames 33 x 23in (84 x 58.5cm)

£2,200-2,800 pair DRA

A late 19thC stained, painted and leaded glass panel, inscribed "Literature", the central panel painted with an allegorical female figure within an archway, surrounded by panels of foliage, within foliate borders, unframed.

112in (280cm) wide

£4,000-6,000 L&T

A leaded glass panel, depicting a medieval maiden in flowing robes and collecting flowers, with a poem.

10.5in (26.5cm) high

£700-900 WW

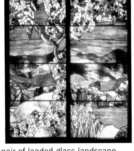

A pair of leaded glass landscape windows, in the manner of Louis Comfort Tiffany, blown, mottled, striated, drapery and confetti glass with lead, iron, oak, each in oak frames with protective clear glass to one side.

66in (165cm) high

£2,200-2,800 FRE

An Arts and Crafts stained glass panel, with a scene from Lewis Carroll's 'Alice in Wonderland', showing the rabbit looking at his watch.

c1930 *36in (91.5cm) high*

£20,000-30,000 PUR

An Arts and Crafts stained glass panel, with a scene from Lewis Carroll's 'Alice in Wonderland', showing the rabbit at the court of the Queen of Hearts.

c1930 *36in (91.5cm) high*

£15,000-20,000 PUR

An Arts and Crafts stained glass panel, with a scene from Lewis Carroll's 'Alice in Wonderland', showing Alice's first encounter with the Cheshire cat.

c1930 *36in (91.5cm) high*

£40,000-60,000 PUR

OTHER GLASS FACTORIES

An Arts and Crafts stained glass panel, with a woodland scene of a dark-haired nymph sitting by a stream.

c1930   *36in (91.5cm) high*

£20,000-30,000   **PUR**

An Arts and Crafts stained glass panel, with a woodland and setting sun scene.

c1930   *36in (91.5cm) high*

£5,000-10,000   **PUR**

An Arts and Crafts stained glass panel, depicting a scene from Lewis Carroll's Alice in Wonderland.

c1930   *36in (91.5cm) high*

£10,000-15,000   **PUR**

An Argy Rousseau pâte-de-verre nightlight, with cast iron mounts, signed "G Argy Rousseau".

8.25in (21cm) high

£2,000-3,000   **WW**

An Argy-Rousseau pâte-de-verre vase, embossed with prunus, minor nicks, stamped "G. Argy-Rousseau, 8874".

6in (15cm) high

£3,500-4,000   **DRA**

An Argy-Rousseau pâte-de-verre vase, embossed with thistles in purple and red on a mottled ground, stamped "G. Argy-Rousseau, France".

4in (10cm) wide

£2,200-2,800   **DRA**

An Argy-Rousseau table lamp 'La Coupe Fleurie', pâte-de-verre and relief decoration, wrought-iron mounting, signed "G.Argy-Rousseau France".

c1925   *6.25in (16cm) high*

£2,500-3,000   **FIS**

A Baccarat vase decorated with a grasshopper with coloured wings.

c1885

£1,000-1,500   **MW**

An Art Deco Baccarat glass box and cover, the pressed lid moulded with a naked couple, the body decorated with a white metal filigree band set with carved jadeite panels on reeded jadeite feet, moulded butterfly monogram.

5in (12cm) high

£350-400   **L&T**

A 1920s or 1930s Bimini Workshop blue and white vase, with decorative birds.

9in (23cm) high

£600-900   **LN**

Two Bimini glasses, of blown glass lampwork, with glass roosters inside.

Taller 8in (20cm) high

£200-250 each   **LN**

A Burgun marquetry pink glass cameo carved vase, with gilt details.

c1900   *8in (20cm) high*

£7,000-10,000   **LN**

DECORATIVE ARTS

A Burgun marquetry purple glass, cameo carved vase, with gilt details.

c1900   8.75in (22cm) high

£8,000-12,000   **LN**

A Leerdam 'Serica' series glass vase, designed by A.D. Copier, the clear glass internally decorated with tiny blue bubbles arranged in horizontal rows, etched triangular mark with "Serica Copier" and scratch numbered "108".

4.5in (11.5cm) high

£220-280   **DN**

A 'Boy's Head' badge, attributed to Henri Cros, Paris, pâte-de-verre in opaque colours, with a boy's face in relief, signature verso, inscribed "Cros" in a rectangle.

c1885   3in (7.5cm) diam

£2,200-2,800   **FIS**

A d'Argental cameo vase, decorated with rust-coloured floral blossoms and leaves on an amber background, signed on body "d'Argental".

14in (35.5cm) high

£1,800-2,200   **JDJ**

A D'Argyl amethyst vase, with frosted and silver paint decorated with tulips, the applied metal top with handles, metal foot and band, signed on the side in silver paint "D'Argyl", minor scratches.

14in (35.5cm) high

£400-600   **JDJ**

An Emil Dugay Art Deco table lamp, with flaring pink glass shade on a bright chrome hemispheric base, from the Chateau de Grenany in Lyons, France, unmarked.

13.5in (34.5cm) high

£700-1,000   **DRA**

An Art Deco opaque milk glass vase with aquatic design, by Pierre D'Avesn.

c1925   9.5in (24cm) high

£1,500-2,000   **MOD**

An Art Deco opalescent glass vase, by H. Dieupart.

c1925   13.5in (34cm) high

£800-1,200   **MOD**

A 1920s or 1930s Marcel Goupy enamelled vase, with gilt details.

9.75in (25cm) high

£3,500-4,500   **LN**

A 1920s or 1930s Marcel Goupy enamelled vase, the design of blue and green trees with gilt details.

7in (18cm) high

£3,000-3,500   **LN**

A Marcel Goupy clear glass decanter and stopper, of teardrop form, painted in green and red enamels with stylized leaves, signed on the base.

11in (28cm) high

£250-300   **L&T**

A 1930s Czechoslovakian pressed glass vase, overlaid with yellow and decorated with six female nudes and a vine.

5in (13cm) high

£20-30   **BMN**

A Wiener Werkstätte purple glass bowl, by Josef Hoffmann.

c1915   9.75in (25cm) diam

£3,000-4,000   LN

An opalescent glass bowl, with dragonfly decoration, frosted patina, pressed mark on base "Verlys France".

c1930   9.75in (24.5cm) diam

£1,200-1,800   QU

A French vase, by Auguste Jean, with enamel work in Japanesque style.

c1880   6.75in (17cm) high

£1,500-2,000   MW

A 1930s clear glass Mermaid vase, by Kjellander.

Kjellander was the workshop manager at Kosta but later set up his own factory. This vase was made in heavy and lightweight versions. This is a heavy example.

6.5in (16.5cm) high

£250-350   JH

An important floor vase, by Auguste Jean, Paris, in brown smoke glass, the rim with bright blue moulding, with gilded and auburn decoration, painted on base with gold "T. Ducy, 53 Rue de Chateaudun" and painted in red "A Jean", restored.

c1880   22.4in (55.9cm) high

£5,000-7,000   FIS

A 1920s enamelled vase, by Josephinen glassworks, Silesia, in blue glass with opaque enamelling depicting a bird perched on stylized golden branches surrounded by butterflies.

4.25in (10.5cm) high

£300-500   VS

A Stuart flared vase, designed by L. Kny, cut and engraved with a stylized seascape of rain clouds over seagulls and waves, pattern number 1934/25, marked "Stuart England".

c1935   7in (18cm) high

£600-800   JH

A mid-1930s cut glass bowl, designed by Ludwig Kny for Stuart.

11.75in (30cm) diam

£400-600   JH

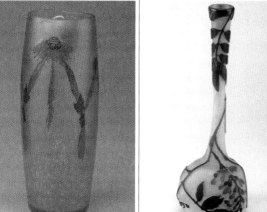

A Legras tall cameo glass vase, decorated with swags of ribbons and flowers in dark pink on a light pink mottled ground, signed "Le Gras".

13.5in (34.5cm) high

£400-600   DRA

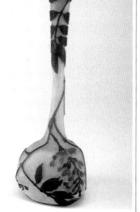

A Legras tall-necked cameo bottle, with purple wisteria and brown branches on a pearl grey ground, signed "Legras".

13in (32.5cm) high

£800-1,200   DRA

One of a pair of 1950s intaglio and engraved decanters, designed by Jack Lloyd for Crystal.

13.75in (35cm) high

£300-400 pair   JH

An extremely rare Maurice Marinot bottle with stopper, with enamelling around the rim.

c1915   6.25in (16cm) high

£12,000-14,000   LN

A school of Von Eiff vase, by M. Hagel and designed by Martlegh.

c1925 6.75in (17cm) high

£200-300 JH

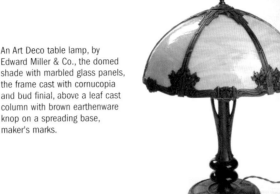

An Art Deco table lamp, by Edward Miller & Co., the domed shade with marbled glass panels, the frame cast with cornucopia and bud finial, above a leaf cast column with brown earthenware knop on a spreading base, maker's marks.

22.5in (56cm) high

£1,500-2,000 L&T

A Moser three-sided vase, amethyst shading to clear glass with a wheel-carved decoration of flowers and leaves, unsigned, small chip to base.

4.5in (11.5cm) high

£500-800 JDJ

A L. Moser & Sohne stem glass, in purple glass with an etched, gilded Amazonian frieze, signed.

c1920 7.75in (19cm) high

£180-220 FIS

A pair of Moser Jack-in-the-pulpit vases, with cranberry opalescent glass to clear body, gold and handpainted floral decoration, some wear to gold.

16in (40.5cm) high

£600-900 JDJ

A Moser cut-glass vase, of square section, the clear glass tinted amethyst at the neck with gilded decoration and deeply cut with irises and foliage.

9.5in (24.5cm) high

£300-400 DN

A Moser covered jar, in cranberry glass with gold, handpainted and enamel decoration.

4in (10cm) high

£200-300 JDJ

A Muller cameo vase, with etched autumn leaves and stag beetle decoration, narrow conical form, opalescent glass, signed on the base "Muller Croismare".

c1900 6.25in (15.5cm) high

£700-1,000 QU

A Muller Frères African vase, in moss green glass with a figure of an African figure and an elephant, signed on base "Muller Frères Luneville".

5.5in (14cm) high

£500-800 JDJ

A Muller Frères cameo glass vase, of moon-form, carved with passion flowers on leafy branches, signed "Muller Fres./Luneville".

c1895 7in (18cm) high

£1,500-2,000 S&K

A 1930s unmarked bowl, by Keith Murray.

£300-400 JH

A Muller Frères cameo floor vase, with layers in golden ruby-rosé and grey-green, etched chrysanthemum decoration, signed to base, with circle, butterfly and "Muller Croismare près Nancy".

c1905 34.4in (51.5cm) high

£1,200-1,800 FIS

A Muller Frères chandelier with a bowl and three fixtures of mottled frosted glass in yellow, orange and indigo, with original brass mount, signed "Muller Fres Luneville".

34in (85cm) high

£1,200-1,800 DRA

One of a pair of Keith Murray Royal Brierley decanters, with flat stoppers.

c1935 8.25in (21cm) high

£700-900 pair JH

A glass vase, attributed to Mechold or Adolf Rasche, Haida, with multicoloured layers and stylized floral engravings.

c1930   4.75in (12cm) high
£150-200   FIS

A Josef Riedel asymmetric vase, in clear glass with overlay in red, brown and yellow, etched decoration of stylized blossom and branches, with embossed gold, the rim gilded.

c1890   4.25in (11cm) high
£600-900   FIS

A large Rousseau footed vase, in crystal glass with orange, yellow, white and amethyst spattered decoration, the interior with crackle finish, signed on base "Rousseau".

10in (25.5cm) high
£2,000-3,000   JDJ

An important Eugène Rousseau jardinière, of smoky-brown glass with enamelled detail in reddish gold and white, with copper-coloured overlay, decorated with Japanesque quince, engraved signature to oval base "E Rousseau Paris".

c1880   6.3in (15.8cm) high
£2,000-3,000   FIS

A rare Eugène Rousseau pedestal vase, in smoky-brown glass with gold-ruby overlay, decorated with engraved chrysanthemums in the Japanesque style, the stand of smoky pressed glass, engraved signature to base "E Rousseau Paris".

c1885   7in (18cm) high
£12,000-14,000   FIS

A Eugène Rousseau 'plat à tête de chimère' vase, in ice glass overlaid with multicoloured oxide and gold foil-inclusions, glass blobs, two stylized heads of Chimera, signed, diamond-engraved "E. Leveillé Paris".

c1880   12.75in (32.5cm) high
£800-1,200   FIS

A Royal Flemish vase, with geometric background panels framed with raised gold enamel lines depicting a winged griffin to front and a dragon to back, outlined in gold enamel and highlighted with gold.

10in (25cm) high
£3,000-4,000   JDJ

A 1930s Royal Brierley cut glass jug.

7in (17.5cm) high
£80-120   JH

A Royal Brierley barrel vase, cut with a leaf design, marked "Royal Brierley".

c1940   8.5in (21.5cm) high
£400-600   JH

A Royal Flemish cologne bottle, decorated with gold outlined flowers and highlighted by three butterflies with wings enamelled in gold and rich colours, the neck and stopper decorated with purple wash and raised gold filigree, minor wear to gold rim.

5.5in (14cm) diam
£4,000-6,000   JDJ

A globular Sabino vase, in opalescent pressed glass with stylized etched rays, engraved signature to base "Sabino France".

c1925   10in (25cm) high
£1,200-1,800   QU

A Sabino vase, in frosted opalescent pressed glass with an engraved decoration of ornamental leaves, signed on base "Sabino Paris".

c1930   5in (12.5cm) high

£150-200   QU

A Sabino 'La Danse Gaité' vase, in frosted opalescent pressed glass with clear overlay and engraved decoration of eight dancing girls, diamond carved signature on base "Sabino Paris" .

c1930   14.75in (37cm) high

£600-900   QU

A Saint-Louis vase, decorated with flat-etched vine tendrils and two flying butterflies, signature to base "St. Louis".

c1900   7in (18cm) high

£300-400   FIS

A Murano bowl, by Salviati & Co, decorated with dogs between stylized buds and tendrils, rim gilded, signed "Salviati Venezia (...)" and round etched stamp mark.

c1900   3.75in (9.5cm) high

£1,000-1,500   FIS

A Le Verre Francais footed butterfly vase, by Charles Schneider, overlaid with blue and turquoise coloured powder-inclusions, decorated with acid-etched butterflies, the foot with etched signature "Le Verre Francais".

c1925   12.75in (32cm) high

£2,500-3,000   VS

A Schneider Art Deco oviform vase, in smoky-grey glass, with an acid-etched polished surface and a broad geometric frieze of frosted banding, on a solid circular foot, signed on foot "Schneider".

12.5in (31.5cm) high

£350-400   DN

A late 1930s Stuart vase of blown glass, on solid foot cut with outlined horizontal bands, marked "Stuart England".

7in (18cm) high

£300-400   JH

A wine glass by Theresienthal Glassworks, Bavarian Forest, Germany, in clear and green glass, the bowl with green enamel and gilt.

c1900   8.5in (21cm) high

£200-300   VS

An ovoid vase, by United Glass Manufacturers, Weisswasser, the overlaid glass with etched hawthorn branches, etched signature "Arsall".

c1920   16in (41cm) high

£500-800   QU

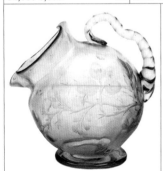

A Tutbury Glassworks lop-sided jug, with foliate decoration and a twisted handle.

c1935   8in (20cm) high

£200-300   JH

A Val Saint Lambert bowl, the orange body above a circular base and decorated with a bat design.

c1900   4in (10cm) high

£2,500-3,500   MW

A rare Val Saint Lambert vase, the green glass body with gold and red overlay and an etched village scene with a grouse in the foreground, the gilded mounts with embossed oak leaves, marked "ORIVIT", 2570".

c1905   14in (35cm) high

£2,500-3,500   FIS

A Val Saint Lambert double-cased footed vase.

c1915   8.75in (22cm) high
£800-1,200   AL

A Val Saint Lambert vase, in clear glass with cobalt blue overlay, etched decoration of tendrils of wild vine with blue grapes.

c1910   12in (30.5cm) high
£1,000-1,500   FIS

An important Vallerysthal vase, the clear glass with copper overlay and stylized etched tendrils of wild vine, a butterfly and stars, the rim decorated with a geometric design, etched signature to base "Vallerysthal".

c1905   14in (35.5cm) high
£4,000-6,000   FIS

A Walsh Walsh vaseline glass vase, with a ruffled rim.

c1905   4.25in (10cm) high
£300-500   MW

A pair of enamelled vases, designed by Wally Weisenthiel for Wiener Werkstätte.

c1915   8.25in (21cm) high
£8,000-12,000   LN

A rare WMF 'Myra-Kristall' footed bowl, by Karl Wiedmann, in opaque red glass with yellow flashes and etched decoration of stylized pine leaves.

c1930   10in (25.5cm) diam
£400-600   FIS

A WMF green crystal cut glass bowl, number '3172', with silver-plated lid and glass knop.

c1935   8.5in (21cm) high
£150-200   QU

An Arts and Crafts hanging lantern, in caramel and green slag glass with a wrought copper frame, original reddish brown patina, line to one panel.

15in (37.5cm) high
£2,000-3,000   DRA

A pair of Arts and Crafts Aesthetic Movement red glass vases, with birds and a spider painted in gold.

c1885
£500-800   PUR

An English vaseline glass shade.

c1900   7.25in (18.5in) high
£1,000-2,000   MW

A bell-shaped vaseline glass shade.

c1900   6.75in (17cm) high
£100-150   MW

One of a set of six naturalistically enamelled drinking glasses.

c1890 set   6.75in (17cm) high
£600-800   AL

DECORATIVE ARTS

A vaseline opalescent and enamelled shade.

c1900   5.75in (14.5cm) high

£100-150   **MW**

One of a pair of English glass water jugs, the silver mounts by John Grinsell & Sons, stamped marks for London.

1901   7in (18cm) high

£800-1,200 pair   **WW**

A 1920s mushroom top millefiore table lamp.

15.5in (39.5cm) high

£350-450   **GCC**

An Art Deco glass vase, with green and gold swirls.

c1925   8.25in (21cm) high

£400-600   **MOD**

An Art Deco Décorchement glass bowl, in brown and smoky glass, with an angular design.

c1925   4.75in (12cm) wide

£7,000-10,000   **MACK**

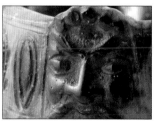

An Art Deco Décorchement glass bowl, in greens, brown and black, decorated with a male face.

c1925   4.75in (12cm) high

£3,000-5,000   **MACK**

A CLOSER LOOK AT AN ART DECO DÉCORCHEMENT GLASS BOWL

The French glassmaker François-Emile Décorchemont (1880-1971) set up a workshop in Coches in 1902. Here he produced thick-walled pâte-de-verre vases and bowls.

Décorchemont's pieces tended to have smooth interiors and textured exteriors.

Décorchemont pieces were coloured with metallic oxides and decorated with pâte-de-crystal. In this technique, a paste of adhesive substance and powdered glass was applied to a mould in layers and then fired. The technique is fairly rare as it was prone to failure.

An Art Deco Décorchemont glass bowl, in blue, black and turquoise, with a stylized flower design.

c1925   11in (28cm) wide

£1,500-2,000   **MACK**

A 1930s blue cut glass Czech cased and cut vase, with a diamond pattern.

9.75in (25cm) high

£220-280　　　　　　　　　**JH**

A 1930s Iittala engraved vase, with stopper and boat scene.

10.35in (26cm) high

£150-200　　　　　　　　　**JH**

An Art Deco glass liqueur set, comprising a decanter, stopper and six glasses, the decanter of bulbous facetted form with facetted stopper decorated with black enamelled panels and incised motifs, the glasses with similar decoration.

9in (22cm) high

£280-320　　　　　　　　　**L&T**

A Bohemian matt iridescent vase, in purple and blue glass with delicate waves of applied red-brown glass.

c1900　　　　　　11in (28cm) high

£120-180　　　　　　　　　**FIS**

A Bohemian matt iridescent vase, with applied silvery yellow and purple bands and irregular clear threads, asymmetrical rim.

c1900　　　　12in (30.5cm) high

£150-200　　　　　　　　　**FIS**

An English Art Nouveau vaseline and cranberry glass shade.

13.25in (34cm) diam

£1,200-1,800　　　　　　　　**MW**

A Swiss Art Deco burgundy and clear stem glass, sold by Pauly and C., Murano.

5.5in (14cm) high

£150-200　　　　　　　　　**S&K**

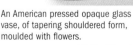

An American pressed opaque glass vase, of tapering shouldered form, moulded with flowers.

12.5in (31cm) high

£80-120　　　　　　　　　**L&T**

An Arts and Crafts brass-washed hammered metal chandelier, with five cylindrical fixtures lined in caramel slag glass hanging from a ring frame, minor wear, unmarked.

30in (75cm) high

£1,200-1,800   **DRA**

An Arts and Crafts hammered copper hanging fixture, with four pendant lanterns of yellow slag glass, suspended by hanging chains from a square ceiling plate, original patina, unmarked.

30in (76cm) high

£1,000-1,500   **DRA**

An Arts and Crafts table lamp, with a four-sided oak base and flaring shade inset with four panels of newer caramel slag glass, one loose, refinished, unmarked.

22in (55cm) high

£400-600   **DRA**

Three Arts and Crafts wicker shades, each lined in new silk, two conical, one with a flat top.

Largest 18in (45.5cm) diam

£350-400   **DRA**

Two Arts and Crafts wicker shades, each lined in silk with a flat top, one with original silk.

16in (40.5cm) diameter

£250-300   **DRA**

An Arts and Crafts brass and copper extending standard lamp, in the manner of W.A.S. Benson, with a turned column and applied tendril decoration, three scrolling and twisted brackets on a tripod base.

57.5in (144cm) high

£300-400   **L&T**

HANDEL

- The Handel factory (1885-1936), Meriden, Connecticut, is famed for its extensive range of decorative glass lamps.
- The factory is known for its reverse-painting – a painstaking technique that involved sandblasting the shade, coating it with glue and firing it, before painting the interior with a design.
- It also produced leaded shades and a range with a 'pebbled' texture achieved by melting glass beads on the surface of a lamp.

- Lamps are typically hemispherical and are usually signed. Early versions have holes to the top to allow for oil or kerosene.
- From 1902, the company began to design and produce its own bases – usually in white metal, but sometimes in bronze.
- Shades by named and well-known designers are particularly valuable. Look for examples painted by John Bailey.
- It also made glassware and china, which are rare and valuable.

An Arts and Crafts Handel oak leaf lamp, with overlay style leading.

c1910   *14in (35cm) high*

£3,000-5,000   **GAL**

An Arts and Crafts Handel lamp, bronze leading on a mixed metal base, simulated rivet detail to the shade.

c1910   *21.75in (55cm) high*

£3,000-5,000   **GAL**

An Arts and Crafts Handel boudoir lamp.

c1910   *13.75in (35cm) high*

£2,000-2,500   **GAL**

An Arts and Crafts Handel desk lamp, with a band of roses design.

14.25in (36cm) high

£2,000-2,500   **GAL**

An Arts and Crafts Handel lamp, with a painted floral band.

c1910   *20.5in (52cm) high*

£2,500-3,000   **GAL**

An Arts and Crafts Handel reverse-painted scenic lamp.

c1910   *23.5in (60cm) high*

£7,000-9,000   **GAL**

An Arts and Crafts Handel hanging lamp, in frosted and hand-painted etched glass with a hammered copper mount.

c1910   *26in (66cm) high*

£4,000-6,000   **GAL**

A CLOSER LOOK AT A HANDEL LAMP

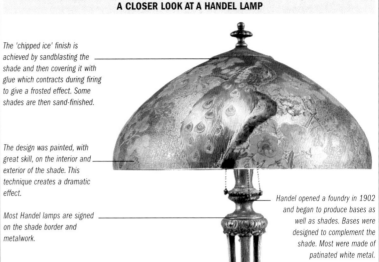

The 'chipped ice' finish is achieved by sandblasting the shade and then covering it with glue which contracts during firing to give a frosted effect. Some shades are then sand-finished.

The design was painted, with great skill, on the interior and exterior of the shade. This technique creates a dramatic effect.

Most Handel lamps are signed on the shade border and metalwork.

Handel opened a foundry in 1902 and began to produce bases as well as shades. Bases were designed to complement the shade. Most were made of patinated white metal.

Rare Handel lamps can rival Tiffany lamps in value.

A Handel table lamp, with bronzed base and reverse-painted chipped glass shade, cloth label and "Handel 7039".

23.5in (60cm) high

£4,000-6,000   **DRA**

A Handel reverse-painted table lamp, with a Winter dusk landscape, marked "Handel".

24.5in (62.5cm) high

£1,000-1,500   **DN**

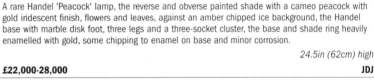

A rare Handel 'Peacock' lamp, the reverse and obverse painted shade with a cameo peacock with gold iridescent finish, flowers and leaves, against an amber chipped ice background, the Handel base with marble disk foot, three legs and a three-socket cluster, the base and shade ring heavily enamelled with gold, some chipping to enamel on base and minor corrosion.

24.5in (62cm) high

£22,000-28,000   **JDJ**

A rare Handel 'Bird of paradise' table lamp, reverse-painted against a black background with chipped ice exterior, enamelled gold base, with original amber glass prisms and matching glass finial, shade signed "Handel 7026" and artist signed "Broggi".

24in (61cm) high

£12,000-18,000   **JDJ**

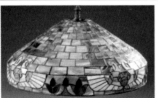

An early 20thC Handel leaded glass chandelier, composed of tiles with stylized cornucopia and flowers, impressed "HANDEL".

20.5in (51cm) diam

£1,000-1,500   **S&K**

An early 20thC Handel glass and patinated metal desk lamp, cloth label on felt base, shade inscribed "No 6577".

13.25in (33.5cm) high

£600-900   **S&K**

A Handel hanging chandelier, the chipped ice shade, the mounting fixture in bronze, marked "5-66827".

2in (30.5cm) diam

£2,500-3,500   **JDJ**

A Handel table lamp, with apple blossom leaded slag glass shade, new base patina, new cap, stamped "HANDEL".

22in (55cm) high

£1,000-1,500   **DRA**

DECORATIVE ARTS

A Handel piano lamp with cylindrical caramel leaded glass shade, overlaid with brick pattern and lyre, bronze-patinated adjustable base, unmarked.

12in (30cm) high

£800-1,200   **DRA**

A Handel floor lamp stand, with a new art glass shade by Lundberg Studios, the adjustable harp-shaped shade holder with original mottled, bronzed patina, base unmarked.

57in (142.5cm) high

£1,200-1,800   **DRA**

A Handel double student lamp, the base with bronze finish and two high sweeping arms supporting contemporary damascene replacement shades, base signed with cloth tag "Handel Lamps", minor blistering.

20in (51cm) high

£1,000-1,500   **JDJ**

TIFFANY

A Tiffany 'Crocus' table lamp, with a leaded glass shade, the patinated bronze foot decorated with 'Celtic knobs', signed "TIFFANY STUDIOS NEW YORK 25904".

c1910   23.5in (58.5cm) high

£22,000-24,000   **QU**

An unusual Tiffany table lamp, with a feather-pull twin-socket glass base, copper foot and a painted and quilted mesh Chinese shade, stamped "Tiffany Furnaces", damage.

22in (55cm) high

£3,000-5,000   **DRA**

TIFFANY

- Louis Comfort Tiffany founded an interior design firm in 1879. Designs included stained-glass windows. In the 1890s he established Tiffany Studios to produce his own glass.
- Tiffany had been fascinated by stained glass since visiting Byzantine churches in his youth, in particular, the effects of daylight on coloured glass.
- By making lamps, he was able to experiment with decorative glass and artificial light while bringing his work to a wider domestic audience.
- The first leaded shades included Nautilus, Dragonfly and Wisteria. By 1906, over 125 types were on sale.
- Shades tended to be hemispherical in shape and designs ranged from simple geometrical patterns to complex depictions of flowers, foliage and insects.
- The lamps were handmade by laying stained glass onto wooden moulds.

A CLOSER LOOK AT A TIFFANY LAMP

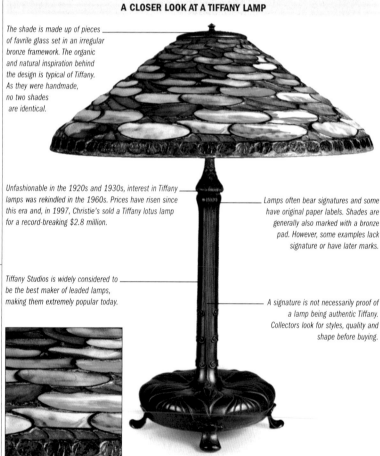

The shade is made up of pieces of favrile glass set in an irregular bronze framework. The organic and natural inspiration behind the design is typical of Tiffany. As they were handmade, no two shades are identical.

Unfashionable in the 1920s and 1930s, interest in Tiffany lamps was rekindled in the 1960s. Prices have risen since this era and, in 1997, Christie's sold a Tiffany lotus lamp for a record-breaking $2.8 million.

Lamps often bear signatures and some have original paper labels. Shades are generally also marked with a bronze pad. However, some examples lack signature or have later marks.

Tiffany Studios is widely considered to be the best maker of leaded lamps, making them extremely popular today.

A signature is not necessarily proof of a lamp being authentic Tiffany. Collectors look for styles, quality and shape before buying.

A Tiffany 'Lily Pad' mushroom-shaped table lamp, with a shallow, conical, leaded glass shade, the slender reeded stem with bud ornaments above a bronze foot with four leaf-like feet, stamped on underside "TIFFANY STUDIOS NEW YORK 357".

c1910   *25.25in (64cm) high*

£45,000-50,000   **QU**

A Tiffany lamp, with a tapering Arabian Favrile glass shade, the base with original Bakelite switch, shade marked "L.C.T.", base stamped "Tiffany Studios New York, 606", slight damage.

16in (40cm) high

£3,000-5,000　　　　**DRA**

A Tiffany Studios bronze and glass lamp, the shade etched "L.C.T." and base stamped "TIFFANY STUDIOS NEW YORK 424," original finial and one foot missing.

18in (45cm) high

£4,000-6,000　　　　**FRE**

A Tiffany bronze lamp, with fluted base and single-socket adjustable harp top around a grapevine shade with green glass lining, stamped "Tiffany Studios New York, 419".

13.5in (34cm) high

£3,000-5,000　　　　**DRA**

A Tiffany table lamp, with bronze and a Corona art glass feather-pulled shade, base stamped "Tiffany Studios New York, 424", shade unmarked, damage, restoration.

17.25in (43cm) high

£1,500-2,500　　　　**DRA**

A Tiffany bronze fluted table lamp base with adjustable harp top with a single socket, brass acid-etched finish, stamped "Tiffany Studios, New York".

13.5in (34cm) high

£1,200-1,800　　　　**DRA**

A rare Tiffany student oil lamp, with an adjustable bronze base with an Oriental-style rope pattern, two hemispherical gold Damascene glass shades, original patina, shades etched "L.C.T.", base unmarked, electrified.

37in (92.5cm) wide

£10,000-12,000　　　　**DRA**

A Tiffany Studios bronze and leaded glass double student lamp, with blown glass shades, old fittings, each shade with a tag stamped "TIFFANY STUDIOS NEW YORK".

29in (72.5cm) high

£10,000-12,000　　　　**FRE**

A Tiffany counter-balance floor lamp, with a five-legged bronze base topped by an adjustable arm with a ball and a Favrile glass shade, original patina, shade marked "L.C.T.", base stamped "Tiffany Studios, New York, 468".

52in (130cm) high

£7,000-10,000　　　　**DRA**

A Tiffany Studios bronze light fixture, with six lights and bronze balls on chains, some flaking to original verdigris patina, unmarked.

18in (45cm) diam

£15,000-20,000　　　　**DRA**

ART GLASS

A pair of Quezel shades, in iridescent green with white pulled feather decoration, signed on fitter "QUEZEL", one fitter has small chip.

9.5in (24.25cm) high

£700-1,000　　　　**JDJ**

One of a pair of art glass shades, attributed to Luster Art, with iridescent gold and green pulled feather decoration with iridescent gold interior, minor wear.

6in (15cm) high

£600-900 PAIR　　　　**JDJ**

One of a pair of Quezel sconces, each with a shaped arm supporting a signed gold iridescent Quezel shade, possible repairs.

Shade 5in (13cm) high

£250-300 pair　　　　**JDJ**

An iridescent gold art glass shade, with vertical ribbing and a scalloped edge, unsigned.

5.25in (13.5cm) high

£80-120　　　　**JDJ**

ART DECO

A rare Austrian Secessionist table lamp, with two sockets, its embossed and pierced bronze base with Glasgow roses on a mahogany frame and blown art glass stem, topped by an art glass shade with oilspot pattern, re-wired, unmarked.

27in (68.5cm) high

£5,000-7,000   **DRA**

An Art Deco decorated lamp, by Oscar Bach.

26in (66cm) high

£3,000-5,000   **MOD**

One of a pair of Art Deco candlestick-style lamps, by Edgar Brandt, with dove, berries and foliage decoration.

Frenchman Edgar Brandt (1880-1960) began creating metalwork from an early age. He became famous for his 'Oasis' screen which took a prize at 1925 Paris Exhibition. Brandt opened a studio, Ferrobrandt, in New York, to complete commissions for skyscrapers and domestic ware. His work captured the essence of the machine age.

c1925   16.25in (41cm) high

£7,000-9,000 pair   **MOD**

An Art Deco silver and glass lamp by Desny.

c1925   5in (13cm) high

£2,000-2,500   **MOD**

An Art Deco lamp, in glass and metal by Marc Erol.

c1925   15.75in (40cm) high

£1,500-2,000   **MOD**

An Art Deco three-lamp set, by Marc Erol.

c1925   20.75in (53cm) wide

£2,000-3,000   **MOD**

An Art Deco wrought iron lamp base by Serva, with leaf and berry decoration, the orange glass shade by Muller Frères.

c1925   17.75in (45cm) high

£2,000-2,500   **MOD**

An Art Deco dinanderie lamp, with original shade, with floral decoration.

c1925   12.25in (31cm) diam

£1,500-2,000   **MOD**

A French Art Deco wrought-iron and bronze lamp, unsigned.

c1925   17in (43cm) high

£2,000-2,500   **MOD**

A large Art Deco lamp, in wood and metal, with a bird design.

c1940   23.25in (59cm) high

£600-900   **MOD**

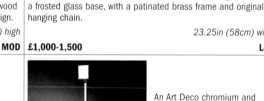

A large Art Deco glass ceiling light, of canted square form, the frosted glass sides with deeply moulded and ribbed glass blocks, a frosted glass base, with a patinated brass frame and original hanging chain.

23.25in (58cm) wide

£1,000-1,500   **L&T**

A Samuel Yellin wrought iron lantern and bracket, Philadelphia, with brass fittings.

Provenance: *This lantern flanked an entrance to the Central Savings Bank in New York City, one of Yellin's largest bank commissions.*

c1925   85in (212.5cm) high

£4,000-6,000   **FRE**

A Swedish Art Deco alabaster chandelier, with angular design.

c1925   16in (40.5cm) diam

£2,000-2,500   **LANE**

A Swedish Art Deco alabaster chandelier, with angular design.

c1925   17in (43cm) diam

£2,000-2,500   **LANE**

An Art Deco chromium and black lacquered electrolier, with four stepped branches, each with square section nozzles and cube pendants, a square column with cube pendant and box ceiling fixture.

195.5in (77cm) high

£200-300   **L&T**

An Arts and Crafts ebonized mantel clock, in the Anglo-Japanese style, inset with satsuma tiles.

c1885   16in (40.5cm) high

£2,000–3,000   **PUR**

An Arts and Crafts ebonized clock with red pillars, in the style of Bruce Talbert.

c1880   20in (51cm) high

£500–800   **PUR**

An Arts and Crafts oak bracket clock of architectural form, attributed to George Walton, with Queen Anne top, tapering sides and the stylized intertwined initials "GWB" carved above clock face, with Camerer Cuss movement.

c1900   23in (59cm) high

£2,000–3,000   **PUR**

An English Arts and Crafts hammered copper mantel clock, with Ruskin cabochons and dial, rivetted faceted top and sides, inscribed "Dum Spectas Fugit" in repoussé, some damage, unmarked.

17.5in (44cm) high

£2,000–3,000   **DRA**

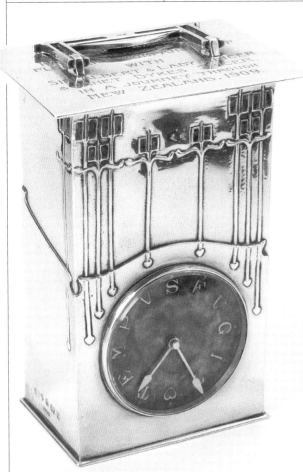

A Liberty & Co. silver Magnus clock of architectural form, with overhanging top, enamelled face with "Tempus Fugit" about the dial in silver letters, with inscription to the top.

1903   5in (13cm) high

£18,000–20,000   **VDB**

An Arts and Crafts silver-plated mantel clock with a copper face, brass plaque inscription reads "Presented to Mr. H.V.H. Everard by the members of the Ramblers Club of the Southwestern Polytechnic, Chelsea, S.W., on the occasion of his marriage, 1909".

14in (36cm) high

£1,000–1,500   **PUR**

A Liberty & Co. silver clock with blue and green enamelled face and hands, inscribed "Festina Lente" in silver letters.

c1905   3.5in (9cm) high

£6,000–8,000   **VDB**

A Liberty & Co. silver repoussé mantel clock, of swept rectangular form with blue and green enamelled dial.

4in (10cm) high

£2,000–3,000   **GORL**

An Arts and Crafts longcase grandfather clock, by Robert 'Mouseman' Thompson.

c1930   77in (195.5cm) high

£10,000–15,000   **PUR**

An Art Deco 'ATO' black and silver clock.

c1925   7.5in (19cm) wide

£1,200-1,800   **MOD**

A Garrad-Le Cautre clock with green face, British made with French movement.

1925   4in (10cm) high

£500-800   **TDG**

A Jaeger Le Coultre mantel timepiece, the double-sided green glass dial with pierced filigree border and pierced hands, raised on shaped base with stepped and pierced trefoil terminals.

9.25in (23cm) high

£400-500   **L&T**

An Art Deco clock by Kienzle, with a bronze case with glazed front and back, resting on a ribbed rectangular base, 8-day ruby movement.

7.5in (19.5cm) high

£250-300   **DN**

A CLOSER LOOK AT AN ART DECO CLOCK

The relief decoration around the top and sides of this clock is known as 'monnaie de pape' after the plant it portrays. Lalique also used it frequently.

The pierced gilt bronze case over the face of this clock carries exceptional sculptural detailing.

Simonet Frères was an important French bronze manufacturer specializing in light fittings. Henri Dieupart was an occasional collaborator who contributed some of their best designs.

A French Art Deco bronze and enamel clock by Simonet Frères, designed by Henri Dieupart, with impressed signature.

c1925   11.5in (29cm) high

£6,000-8,000   **MOD**

An Art Deco wooden clock by Paul Follot, carved with a leaf pattern and stained with red, brown and silver.

c1925   18.5in (47cm) wide

£2,000-2,500   **MOD**

An Art Deco frosted blue glass mantel timepiece, the machine-turned silvered dial enclosed by frame moulded with scantily clad maidens kneeling on a reeded bed.

43in (17cm) high

£450-500   **L&T**

An Art Deco electric clock by Herman Miller, attributed stylistically to Gilbert Rohde, burr-wood veneered case applied with three chromed bands, dial with abstract numerals in black, maker's mark to dial and stamped underneath with number "4082B".

The stamped number corresponds closely to design numbers known to be by Rohde.

12.5in (33cm) wide

£120-180   **DN**

An Art Deco marble-faced clock, the stepped base with a geometric dial and numerals, surmounted with two spelter models of German shepherd dogs.

26in (68cm) wide

£180-220   **DN**

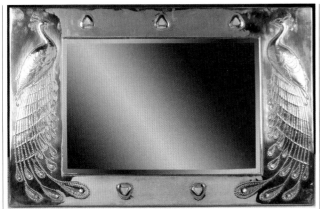

A Scottish School Arts and Crafts brass wall mirror, in the manner of Talwin Morris, the bevelled plate enclosed by repoussé decorated frame with opposing peacocks enclosing five triangular turquoise Ruskin panels, inset to repoussé bosses.

34.75in (87cm) wide

£2,500-3,000   L&T

A Scottish School Arts and Crafts brass wall mirror, of octagonal outline, the circular bevelled plate enclosed within a repoussé decorated frame with winged angels and meandering flowering tendrils.

23.5in (59cm) wide

£300-500   L&T

A Scottish Arts and Crafts brass wall mirror, of rectangular outline with lobed angles, the bevelled plate enclosed by a repoussé decorated frame with flowering branches.

24in (60cm) wide

£150-200   L&T

A Scottish Arts and Crafts brass candle sconce, in the manner of Margaret Gilmour, repoussé decorated with a dragonfly on a beaten ground with candle nozzle and drip tray below.

14in (35cm) high

£280-320   L&T

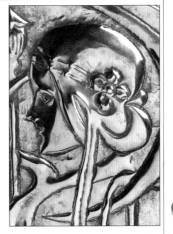

A Scottish Arts and Crafts brass candle sconce, by Agnes Bankier Harvey, the shaped backplate repoussé decorated with the profile of a girl amidst poppies, above twin candle nozzles and drip tray.

15in (37.5cm) high

£800-1,200   L&T

A pair of copper and brass candlesticks, decorated with flowerheads and tendrils, unmarked.

10.5in (26cm) high

£400-500   WW

An Arts and Crafts brass ceiling light, with three tulip-shaped lamp sockets on curved stems and five brass petal-like extensions radiating from the ceiling rose.

14.5in (37cm) wide

£150-200   DN

A Scottish Arts and Crafts brass jardinière, of hexagonal form, repoussé decorated with panels of poppy flowers, raised on square feet.

9.5in (24cm) diam

£220-280   L&T

A Scottish Arts and Crafts brass jardinière, of square tapering form with projecting rim and ring handles, repoussé decorated to two sides with Celtic galleons in full sail.

12in (30cm) wide

£220-280   L&T

A fluted brass bowl, attributed to the Artificers' Guild and a design by Edward Spencer, internally decorated with radiating flutes with a relief medallion of a sickle and branches of mistletoe.

6.25in (16cm) diam

£280-320   DN

A Jan Eisenloeffel tea service, by J.K.C. Sneltjes of Haarlem, Holland, made in brass, wicker and glass, comprising a kettle on warming stand, creamer, sugar bowl and associated tray, kettle and creamer both marked.

Jan Eisenloeffel's metalwork was considered avant-garde for its purity of form and functionalist aesthetic. He drew influences from Eastern and Western traditions, all of which contributed to his native Dutch 'Neue stile'.

c1905 Tray 12in (30cm) diam

£700-1,000 FRE

An Alexander Ritchie circular brass tray on stand, the pierced gallery with a broad repoussé band decorated with Celtic knotwork and centred with a roundel bearing the inscription "Iona", on a mahogany barley-twist column, the base inset with a brass panel.

38.5in (96cm) high

£700-900 L&T

A Scottish Arts and Crafts brass wall clock, the square dial repoussé decorated with a chapter ring enclosed by four roundels depicting fairy nymphs, includes pendulum and weights.

13.5in (33.5cm) wide

£700-1,000 L&T

A brass box and cover, design attributed to Edward Spencer, with fine wirework banding, centred with a circular silvered medallion showing a pelican in piety, engraved on base "From three not ungrateful young pelicans", dated "Christmas 1925".

3in (8cm) high

£400-600 DN

A large Lucien Bazar brass paper knife, decorated with a female figure.

c1930 10in (25.5cm) long

£300-500 TDG

A Cotswold School Arts and Crafts brass fender, pierced and repoussé decorated with a frieze of opposed red squirrels eating nuts, held at the angles by brackets with decorative screws.

The squirrel motif resembles a wrought iron radiator grille by C.A. Llewellyn-Roberts for The Birmingham Guild. Ernest Gimson also produced metalwork with squirrel and oak leaf designs, in particular a pair of brass andirons now in Cheltenham Museum.

49.25in (123cm) wide

£2,500-3,000 L&T

BRONZE

A French bronze group, 'Souviens', by Henri Allouard, brown patina with golden brown highlights, inscribed "H. Allouard".

29in (72.5cm) high

£1,500-2,500 FRE

A bronze sculpture of an athlete, with dark brown patina, on a marble base, with "R. Bellair & Co. Friedrichstr 182 Berlin" foundry seal.

12.75in (32cm) high

£800-1,200 FRE

An early 20thC cold-painted Austrian bronze group by Franz Bergman, of two Arabs seated playing chess at a table on a rug base, a lamp hung from a bamboo pole above them, stamped "Bergman" under the base.

16in (40cm) high

£600-900 GORL

A cold painted bronze figure in the style of Bergman, modelled as an Egyptian seated flanked by panthers, on red marble desk tidy base, unmarked.

15.75in (40cm) wide

£1,500-2,000   **WW**

A silvered bronze group, 'First Prize Bull', by Isidore Jules Bonheur, on silver mounted marble base, stamped "Christofle & Cie. 1274706".

18.75in (47cm) high

£2,500-3,000   **FRE**

A French Art Nouveau bronze and dore bronze plate, with fully moulded dore chestnut leaves and nuts on a patinated ground, signed "A. Bouny".

c1910   10.5in (26cm) diam

£280-320   **S&K**

A bronze figure of 'Moses', after Michelangelo Buonarroti, medium brown patina, with "Reduction Meccanique a Collas" foundry seal.

This piece is after the original, executed in 1515 in San Pietro, Rome.

16.5in (41cm) high

£1,500-2,000   **FRE**

A CLOSER LOOK AT A FRENCH GILT-BRONZE VASE

This woman's features have an Asian aspect. Chalon was very influenced by Japanese style, so it is not surprising that he looked East for his idealised depiction of feminine beauty.

The iris is often used as a representation of night and sleep. The irises around this woman's face seem to suggest that she is waking from a dream.

This figure is decorated with multiple patinas, ranging from the rose-coloured background to the golds on the body.

This woman's dress and stance are evocative of a pre-Raphaelite painting. The erotic undertones of this vase make it an enticing piece.

A French silvered and gilt-bronze vase, by Louis Chalon, of flaring stylized heart form with relief decoration of a smiling maiden, on a shaped square base, signed "L. Chalon".

40cm high (26cm) wide

£10,000-12,000   **MACK**

A bronze group, 'Classical Woman', by Henri Michel Antoine Chapu, brown patina, set on a marble base, inscribed "H. Chapu" and "F. Barbedienne Fondeur" and stamped "HH Made in France MM".

27.75in (69cm) high

£2,000-3,000   **FRE**

A bronze figure, 'La Zingara', by Jean Baptiste Auguste Clesinger, golden brown patina, inscribed "J. Clesinger Rome 1858" with foundry seal.

1858   41in (102.5cm) high

£4,000-6,000   **FRE**

A bronze figure, 'The Shipwreck', by Georges Colin, signed on the base and inscribed on the reverse "To Frank Bailey 1885-1914".

34in (85cm) high

£3,000-5,000   **L&T**

A bronze figure, 'Gladiator', from the Continental School, with rich dark brown patina, on marble base.

26in (65cm) high

£600-900   **FRE**

Two 19thC Continental School bronzes, Diomedes and a classical Greek head, with dark brown patina.

4.75in (37cm) high

£1,500-2,000   **FRE**

A bronze bust of a young woman, the drapery signed "G. Coudray", the plinth inscribed "Bakie" in relief.

c1900   63cm (24.75in) high

£3,000-5,000   **RGA**

A 20thC bronze figure, by Le Couflet, of a female nude reclining in a rocking chair.

£600-900   **ROS**

A bronze group, 'The Last Drop', cast by T. Curts, with a standing cavalry officer giving his horse a drink from his hat, on naturalistic base, with signed and impressed foundry marks and stamped mark "Made in Austria".

11.5in (29cm) high

£1,000-1,500   **L&T**

A bronze group by Antoine Coysevox, depicting a classical maiden with a cherub on a bronze base with inlaid champlevé panels, brown and gilt patinas, signed by the artist and stamped "F. Barbedienne Fondeur".

1710   27.5in (69cm) high

£2,000-4,000   **FRE**

A bronze, 'Porteur d'Eau Tunisien', by Jean Didier Debut, brown and reddish brown patinas, inscribed "Debut".

24.75in (62cm) high

£1,500-2,000   **FRE**

A bronze figure, 'Maiden with Pitcher', by Anatole J. Guillot, golden brown patina, inscribed "A. Guillot".

29.75in (74cm) high

£1,000-1,500   **FRE**

A gilt bronze figure, 'Pan', cast from a model by Emmanuel Fremiet, on a marble base, signed in the bronze "F Barbedienne, Fondeur Paris".

13.5in (34cm) wide

£800-1,200 **WW**

A bronze, 'Nymph With Two Dogs', by Amadeo Gennarelli, greenish-gold patina, signed "A. Gennarelli" on the base.

31in (77.5cm) wide

£2,000-3,000 **S&K**

A bronze with silver patina, 'Stella', by Maurice Guiraud-Riviere, on a marble base, inscribed "Guiraud-Riviere" and "Etling Paris".

23in (57.5cm) high

£2,800-3,200 **FRE**

A bronze with silver patina, 'Danseuse à La Boule', Maurice Guiraud-Riviere, inscribed "Guiraud-Riviere" and "Etling Paris".

24.5in (61cm) high

£2,800-3,200 **FRE**

A pair of Hafenrichter Art Deco bronze figures of nude dancers, on green onyx bases, each signed "Hafenrichter".

7.5in (19.5cm) high

£400-600 **HAMG**

A pair of Hagenauer bronze figures, cast as warriors with raffia skirts and polished brass spears, stamped marks.

5.5in (14cm) high

£200-300 **L&T**

A Heintz silvered bronze ashtray and matchbox holder with overlay of golfer and golf course on green patinated ground, some damage, stamped "HAMS".

7in (17.5cm) wide

£100-150 **DRA**

A bronze crocodile, by Barry Jackson, brown and green patinas, on wood base, inscribed and numbered "Barry Jackson 5/10".

35in (87.5cm) long

£2,000-3,000 **FRE**

A bronze figure, 'La Rosee', by E. Herbert, signed in the bronze.

25.5in (64cm) high

£1,500-2,000 **L&T**

A bronze figure, 'Retour de Peche', by Henryk Kossowski II, brown patina with golden brown highlights, inscribed "Kossowski Eleve de Math. Moreau".

43.75in (109.5cm) high

£2,000-4,000 **FRE**

A bronze fish sculpture, by Georges Lavroff.

c1925 *15.5in (39.5cm) high*

£1,000-1,500 **TDG**

A bronze figure, 'Christ in Majesty', cast from a model by Jean Lambert-Rucki, original wooden base, signed "Lambert-Rucki" with foundry mark.

17.75in (45cm) high

£3,000-4,000 **WW**

BRONZE

A 20thC female bronze nude, by F. de Luca, verdigris patina, signed by the artist.

64in (160cm) high

£6,000-9,000   **FRE**

A bronze group, 'Man with Child', by Gaston Veurenot Leroux, with brown patina, inscribed "G. Leroux" and "Boyer Fres Fondeur à Paris".

37in (92.5cm) high

£2,000-4,000   **FRE**

A bronze eagle, by Jules Moigniez, with a brown patina, inscribed "J. Moigniez".

30in (75cm) high

£1,000-1,500   **FRE**

A bronze group, 'Retour de Moisson' by Mathurin Moreau, with brown patina, on a marble base, inscribed "Moreau Math".

33.5in (84cm) high

£3,000-4,000   **FRE**

A CLOSER LOOK AT A BRONZE GROUP

Mathurin Moreau flourished during the French Second Empire, a period marked by the Classical revival which can be seen at work in this piece.

Moreau is particularly famous for his depictions of women, including a massive statue of Marguerite, the 13thC Countess of Anjou. This figure demonstrates the confidence with which he approached the female form.

The multiple patinas on this piece are a sign of technical expertise and an eye for subtle yet effective decoration.

Moreau's work often has a strong symbolic and allegorical content. This group is no exception, and has been modelled to depict 'Harmony'.

A bronze group, 'Les Harmonies', by Mathurin Moreau, inscribed "Math. Moreau", medium and dark brown patinas.

41.5in (104cm) high

£7,000-10,000   **FRE**

A French Art Nouveau bronze and dore bronze ink stand, by Marionnet, with patinated beach nuts and leaves surrounding the single ink well, signed "A. Marionnet".

c1910   7.5in (19cm) diam

£300-500   **S&K**

A French Art Nouveau bronze and dore bronze ink stand and letter opener, the stand with oak leaves and acorns, the two inkwells with acorn finials, signed "A. Marionnet".

c1910   13in (32.5cm) wide

£600-900   **S&K**

A gilded bronze figure, 'Priestess of Bacchus', by H. Moreau, on wooden base, signed in the bronze, with "AG Paris" foundry mark.

21.75in (55cm) high

£1,200-1,800   **WW**

A French Art Nouveau bronze inkstand of horseshoe shape, with dore bronze ground and patinated poppies, and a vide poche with dore bronze violas on a patinated ground, the stand signed "H. Risch", the vide poche "Van Roy".

c1910

£300-500   **S&K**

A Dutch bronze ashtray and match holder, signed "P. Teresczuk".

1900   *4.75in (11.5cm) high*

£350-400   **MW**

A 1930s bronze patinated figure of a girl, by Bruno Zach, on an onyx socle base, unsigned.

15.5in (39.5cm) high

£1,500-2,000   **DOR**

A pair of 19thC bronzes, both naked males, possibly Pan and Narcissus, one a satyr playing two pipes, the other in contraposto pose carrying a goatskin flask over his shoulder, dark green patination.

11.5in (29cm) high

£600-900   **L&T**

A pair of French bronze Art Nouveau maidens, with mild brown patina, on back marble socle bases.

c1880   *13.5in (34cm) high*

£3,000-5,000   **RGA**

An Art Deco bronze figure, 'Dancera', by Titze, brown and golden brown patina, on a white marble and slate pedestal, inscribed "1923 Titze" and stamped "Austria".

1923   *19in (47.5cm) high*

£800-1,200   **FRE**

A 19thC bronzed tazza, cast with a border of trailing leaves and pierced handles, supported by three putto figures with entwined fish tails.

24.75in (62cm) diam

£2,000-3,000   **L&T**

A late 19thC bronze statue of Daniel Webster, after Thomas Ball, mounted on a marble base, unsigned.

30in (75cm) high

£1,500-2,000   **FRE**

A late 19thC bronze inkstand, with hinged top and glass liner, cast with stylized foliage and berried branches.

9in (23cm) wide

£150-200   **S&K**

A bronze Art Nouveau candlestick holder, unsigned.

c1905   *7in (18cm) high*

£180-220   **TDG**

A bronze figure of crouching girl, on a base decorated with mother-of-pearl.

c1905   *5.25in (13.5cm) wide*

£700-900   **TDG**

BRONZE

A French bronze and onyx ash tray, signed.

c1910   4.5in (11.5cm) high

£400-600   MW

An early 20thC Austrian erotic bronze figure, modelled as a female wearing a fur coat, opening to reveal her nude figure, on an onyx base.

9in (22.5cm) high

£1,500-2,000   FRE

One of a pair of bronze Art Deco bookends in the form of nude female figures, with green patination.

c1925   6.75in (17cm) high

£300-500 pair   TDG

A bronze figure, modelled as a female figure balancing two balls, on a marble base, unmarked.

6in (15.5cm) high

£300-500   WW

A pair of bronze figures taken from the Parthenon frieze, each cast as a rearing horse led by a Classical maiden, raised on naturalistic bases, the stepped slate plinths inset with bronze palquettes cast with sections of the Parthenon frieze, brass bracket feet, stamped foundry marks "Graux Marly".

13in (32.5cm) high

£1,000-1,500   L&T

One of a pair of patinated bronze lions, depicted seated with their heads turned to one side.

35in (87.5cm) wide

£1,200-1,800 pair   FRE

A gilt bronze sculpture, 'San Jorge', after Salvador Dali, depicting St. George and the dragon, mounted on a black marble base, marked with limited edition number "586/650".

11.5in (29cm) high

£600-800   ROS

A Russian bronze group, 'Chorist', depicting a horse struggling to drag a cart from mud, with brown patina.

11.5in (29cm) long

£1,000-2,000   FRE

BRONZE & IVORY FIGURES

A green patinated bronze figure, 'Androcles and the Lion', on ebonized wood base, unsigned.

17.25in (44cm) high

£3,000-5,000   WW

A bronze and ivory figure, 'Ball Game', cast from a model by Demêtre Chiparus, on a shaped marble base, signed in the bronze "DH Chiparus", minor losses and damage.

15.25in (39cm) high

£2,000-3,000   WW

A bronze and ivory figure, 'Tennis Player', cast from a model by Demêtre Chiparus, on a shaped marble base, signed in the bronze "DH Chiparus", missing racquet, minor losses to ivory.

15.25in (39cm) high

£2,500-3,000   WW

A gilt and patinated bronze figure, 'Vedette', cast from a model by Demêtre Chiparus, on a stepped marble base, etched signature to the base, foundry mark in bronze.

31.5in (80cm) high

£15,000-17,000   WW

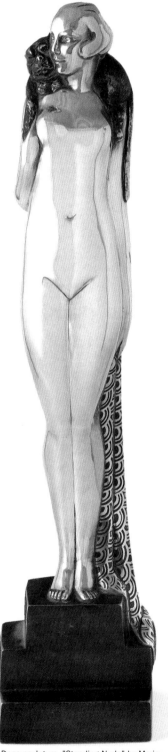

An Art Deco bronze figure, by Fayral, modelled as an exotic dancer holding a pose, on a lozenge-shaped black figured marble base, signed.

15in (38cm) high

£400-600   **ROS**

An Art Deco bronze and ivory figure, "Elegante au Levrier", by Solange Bertrand.

c1935   *11.75in (30cm) high*

£8,000-10,000   **JES**

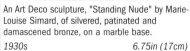

An Art Deco sculpture, "Standing Nude" by Marie-Louise Simard, of silvered, patinated and damascened bronze, on a marble base.

1930s   *6.75in (17cm) high*

£6,000-8,000   **JES**

A bronze and ivory figure of a Spanish dancer, on a rectangular marble base.

11.75in (30cm) high

£1,200-1,800   **WW**

DECORATIVE ARTS

An Art Deco bronze and ivory figure, by Dakon, on marble base with alabaster dish, signed in the bronze "Dakon".

7.5in (19cm) high

£1,200-1,800   **WW**

A CLOSER LOOK AT A DEMÊTRE H. CHIPARUS FIGURE

Chryselephantine is the Classical technique of combining ivory with metals in sculpture. It was revived in the Art Deco period, and Chiparus was a particularly skillful exponent.

A figure with bronze hands, face and naval would not be worth as much as this example. The ivory is carved to an extremely high standard.

Kapurthala is a district in the Punjab. Artists working within the Art Deco idiom frequently looked East for inspiration.

This dual-tone onyx base is very attractive and adds interest to this piece.

A cold-painted bronze and ivory figure, 'Dancer on Points', cast and carved from a model by Joe Descomps, engraved to the base "Joe Descomps".

£10,000-15,000   **WW**

An Art Deco bronze and carved ivory figure, 'Dancer of Kapurthala', by Demêtre H. Chiparus, the figure raised on a stepped brown and green onyx base, signed to the base "Chiparus".

c1925

22in (55cm) high

£20,000-25,000   **L&T**

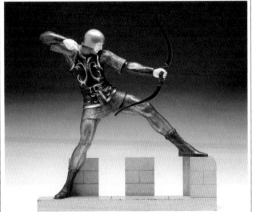

A bronze figure, 'Archer', by Pierre Le Faguays, brown and silver patinas with ivory, on marble base, inscribed "Le Faguays".

23.75in (59cm) high

£18,000-20,000   **FRE**

A cold-painted bronze and ivory figure, cast from a model by Hafenrichter, on alabaster base, signed in the bronze.

9.75in (25cm) high

£800-1,200   **WW**

A cold-painted bronze and ivory figural lamp, 'Woman with Two Urns', from a model by S. Lipchytz, signed in the bronze.

22.5in (57cm) high

£6,000-8,000   **WW**

A Lorenzl bronze and ivory figure, modelled as a dancing girl, signed in the bronze.

11in (28cm) high

£1,200-1,800   **WW**

A bronze figure, cast from a model by Josef Lorenzl, on an alabaster base, signed in the bronze "Lorenzl".

15in (38cm) high

£2,000-3,000   **WW**

A bronze figure, cast from a model by Josef Lorenzl, modelled as a female holding flowers, signed "Lorenzl".

9in (23cm) high

£1,200-1,800   **WW**

An Art Deco bronze and carved ivory figure, 'Grecian With Torch', by Ferdinand Preiss, signed in the bronze "F. Preiss".

11.25in (28cm) high

£2,500-3,500   **L&T**

A cold-painted bronze and ivory figure, 'Mandolin Player', cast and carved from a model by Ferdinand Preiss, signed.

23.25in (59cm) high

£12,000-18,000   **WW**

An Art Deco spelter lamp base, modelled as a figure with arched back, with frosted glass shade, unsigned.

25.5in (65cm) high

£800-1,200   **WW**

COPPER

An Arts and Crafts copper goblet, the circular hammered bowl with three curved supports with stylized leaf terminals joined by a pierced band, bearing the legend "Then Came Spring" and with stamped mark "Geo. Spencer Baker".

6.5in (16cm) high

£200-300   **L&T**

A Benham & Froud galleried copper tray, the design attributed to Christopher Dresser, of rectangular form, the frilled rim enclosing central brass panel, engraved with a stork flying above rocks in a silver finish, apparently unmarked.

12.25in (30.5cm) wide

£280-320   **L&T**

A pair of Aesthetic movement copper candle sconces, in the manner of W.A.S. Benson, each formed as a leaf stamped with veining and embossed with a frog chasing a fly, with detachable curved branches with candleholders, stamped registration mark, number 17801.

11.25in (28cm) high

£400-600   **L&T**

A brass, copper and steel kettle stand, by W.A.S. Benson, the circular top pierced and cast with flowering branches raised above baluster columns resting on a floret-embossed circular base.

7.5in (19cm) wide

£150-200   **L&T**

W.A.S. BENSON

■ William Arthur Smith Benson was born in 1854 and died in 1924. Between 1880 and the outbreak of World War I, he produced art metalware of an extremely high standard from his studios in Kensington.

■ His 1883 pamphlet, 'Notes on some of the minor arts', explained his personal aesthetic, illustrated with a number of his designs.

■ Unlike many of his Arts and Crafts contemporaries, Benson succeeded in making his work accessible to the mass market. He did this by embracing industrialisation and mass production techniques such as machine tooling.

■ Benson's signature materials were copper and brass, the reflective properties of which he used to great effect in his light fittings.

■ Pieces by Benson are often marked, sometimes with a monogram featuring his initials separated by metalworking tools.

A copper and brass twin-branch candlestick, by W.A.S. Benson, the curved branches resting on a foliate support with circular copper drip-pans, counter-balanced by a fluted brass bud-shaped weight, stamped "W.A.S. Benson" in a shaped panel.

12.5in (32cm) long

£1,800-2,200   **DN**

COPPER

A copper and brass plate warmer, by W.A.S. Benson, with riveted decoration, the domed hinged lid with insulated handle enclosing divided interior for plates, the whole raised on shaped supports with pointed pad feet, raised on a rectangular platform base.

17.5in (43.5cm) wide

£300-500   **L&T**

A dished copper tray by W.A.S. Benson, of circular form, embossed with divided panels, the lobed edge enclosing a repoussé decorated band of flowering rose branches, stamped mark.

19.25in (48cm) wide

£500-800   **L&T**

A Birmingham Guild copper plate, with mark.

c1920   *8.25in (21cm) diam*

£70-100   **HBK**

A Duchess of Sutherland's Cripples' Guild copper box, of rectangular shape, the hinged domed cover with an embossed geometric border, applied with silver florets, shells and an oval plaque, stamped "D.S.C.G." with coronet.

8.75in (22.5cm) wide

£300-500   **DN**

A Duchess of Sutherland's Cripples' Guild copper goblet, based on a vessel from antiquity, with deep bowl, twin handles and spreading circular foot, with applied silvered winged cherubs, swags and other Classical motifs, stamped "D.S.C.G." below a coronet.

7.5in (19cm) high

£300-500   **DN**

A Newlyn copper tea caddy, of oval section, finely embossed with a seascape, lighthouse and sailing ship, the drop-in cover embossed "Tea" and stamped "H. Dyer".

4.25in (10.5cm) high

£280-320   **DN**

An Art Nouveau brass and copper box, with enamel decoration, stamped "Fisher 188 Strand".

c1905   *8.5in (21.5cm) wide*

£500-700   **TDG**

A Fivemiletown copper tray, of rectangular form with raised edges, decorated with two peacocks flanking a fruiting tree, unmarked.

16in (40cm) wide

£150-200   **WW**

A Birmingham Guild of Handicraft silvered copper mug, with scrolling frieze, inscribed "R.W.R. Nov.24 1912", stamped "BGH 41".

1912   *5in (12.5cm) high*

£200-250   **WW**

A Hagenauer copper ice bucket with applied brass trim and rivetted handle, stamped "Handmade Hagenauer Wien WHW Made in Austria".

14in (35.5cm) high

£1,200-1,800   **SDR**

A rare Keswick School of Industrial Arts charger, the rim hammered in relief with a stag hunt frieze, the well with a Tudor rose, stamped "KSIA".

18.75in (47cm) diam

£2,200-2,800   **WW**

A Joseph Heinrichs hammered copper samovar, with sterling bands and wooden handles, stamped "Jos. Heinrichs, Paris, New York", replaced finials.

13.5in (34cm) high

£100-150 **DRA**

A Keswick lidded copper flagon, by W. H. Mawson, with applied strap handle, the hammer tapering body repoussé worked with the inscription "More Friends And Less Need of Them", stamped mark "W. H. Mawson".

8.5in (21cm) high

£300-500 **L&T**

A large Newlyn copper bowl, hammered in relief with a frieze of fish, stamped Newlyn mark.

Newlyn metalware is the product of fishermen from the Cornish coast who took to metalwork when bad weather prevented sailing.

11.5in (29cm) diam

£600-900 **WW**

A Newlyn twin-handled copper vase, of tapering cylindrical form with applied beaten handles, the body repoussé decorated with fish, unmarked.

£150-200 **L&T**

A John Pearson copper jardinière, with repoussé scrolling floral motifs on a hammered ground, numbered 2326 and incised "J Pearson 1897".

8in (20cm) high

£250-300 **HAMG**

A CLOSER LOOK AT A COPPER CHARGER

John Pearson's stylized bird designs are typical of pieces produced at the Newlyn Copper Class, where Pearson taught in the 1890s.

The slightly irregular line around the rim of this charger shows that it was cut and beaten by hand. This kind of detail appeals to enthusiasts of the Arts and Crafts look.

The oak leaves and and foliage depicted on this plate are typical of the Arts and Crafts style as it was practised in England.

Pearson pioneered the use of lead as a bed on which to beat copper — a closely guarded secret that allowed the development of ever more intricate designs.

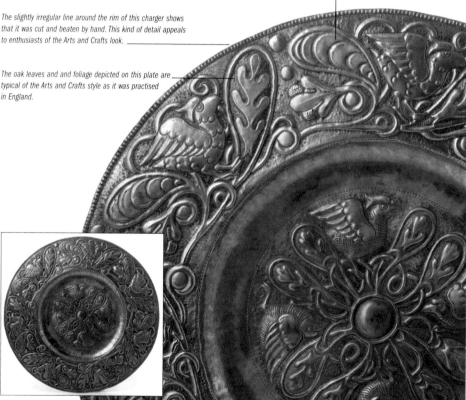

A large John Pearson copper charger, repoussé hammered with birds amongst foliage and incised "Jpearson", dated.

1896

25.25in (63cm) diam

£2,000-3,000 **WW**

An embossed copper jardinière, by John Pearson, the bulbous body with collar rim, initials "JP" and "1909" inscribed to underside.

1909   7.75in (20cm) high

£400-600   ROS

An Artificers' Guild silver and copper box and cover, designed by Edward Spencer, the finial formed as a bat with outspread wings, with mark for London.

1831   4.75in (12cm) high

£500-800   DN

An Artificers' Guild rectangular copper tray, the design attributed to Edward Spencer, the raised edge with silvered border and applied with silvered handles embellished with interwoven vines and foliage.

21.5in (55cm) wide

£280-320   DN

A copper picture frame, inset with a ceramic heart, on easel-support leather back, stamped "JS Vickery, Regent Street".

13.25in (33cm) high

£400-600   WW

An Artificers' Guild copper wall sconce, the design attributed to Edward Spencer, the back plate embossed and pierced with stylized branches of foliage, florets and buds, the drip-pan with two wavy-edged cylindrical sconces.

10.5in (27cm) high

£1,200-1,800   DN

A Scottish Arts and Crafts copper mantel timepiece, by Marion Henderson Wilson, with repoussé decorated dial and case, the dial with Roman chapters, the case decorated with a flock of birds, a galleon and an angel, signed "MHW".

16.5in (41cm) high

£3,500-4,500   L&T

An Arts and Crafts copper timepiece, in the form of a miniature longcase clock with an overall stippled surface, the central panel embossed with Glasgow-style roses and tendrils.

14.5in (36.5cm) high

£280-320   DN

An Arts and Crafts silvered copper vase, the copper body overlaid with silver ivy leaves and tendrils.

c1910   8in (20.5cm) high

£60-90   S&K

An Arts and Crafts hammered copper jardinière, with stylized flowers in repoussé on a rutile patinated ground, some damage, unmarked.

10in (25cm) wide

£300-500   DRA

An Arts and Crafts large hammered humidor with riveted hinges and corners, on ball feet, original zinc lining and excellent dark patina, unmarked.

10in (25cm) wide

£500-800   DRA

An Arts and Crafts hammered copper hinged miniature chest, with pewter rivets, latch and handles, new felt lining, original patina, unmarked.

7in (17.5cm) wide

£400-600   DRA

An Arts and Crafts copper kettle on stand, the kettle of ovoid form, repoussé decorated with a band of flowering foliage, raised on a scrolling wrought iron stand.

23.5in (59cm) high

£180-220　　　　**L&T**

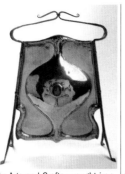

An Arts and Crafts wrought iron and copper firescreen, repoussé decorated with a domed central panel surrounded by scrolled foliage and centred with an enamel roundel, the frame with beaten finish and scrolling handle.

28in (70cm) high

£600-900　　　　**L&T**

An Arts and Crafts copper and wrought iron plant holder, the copper vessel of tulip shape embossed with heart shapes and lily-of-the-valley, supported on an iron stem decorated with naturalistic leaves, spreading to form feet.

16.25in (41cm) high

£300-500　　　　**DN**

A Gothic style copper candlestick, the lobed drip tray above a knopped column on a domed base.

6.5in (16cm) high

£150-200　　　　**L&T**

A Continental Art Nouveau copper and brass mounted kettle and stand, embossed with stylized foliate motifs, with wicker covered carrying handle on tripod stand with burner, stamped marks.

13.25in (33.5cm) high

£100-150　　　　**L&T**

A Scottish Arts and Crafts copper charger, of circular form, the central panel decorated with the profiled head of a girl enclosed within a rim, decorated with knotted tendrils and iridescent rounded inlay.

16.25in (40.5cm) wide

£800-1,200　　　　**L&T**

A Swedish Art Deco copper and wicker coffee set.

c1925　　*Tray 11.5in (29cm) diam*

£500-700　　　　**MOD**

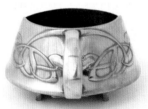

A pair of Art Deco copper picture frames, with a geometric design, unsigned.

c1925　　*13.75in (35cm) high*

£500-700　　　　**MOD**

PEWTER

A Liberty & Co. pewter bowl, with green glass liner, cast with foliate motif, model number 0320, stamped marks.

8.75in (22cm) diam

£400-600　　　　**WW**

A Liberty & Co. Tudric pewter slop bowl, designed by Archibald Knox, model number 0231, stamped marks.

6.5in (16cm) wide

£350-400　　　　**WW**

A hammered copper tray, of rounded rectangular form, hammered with Tudor rose motif.

21.75in (54.5cm) wide

£70-100　　　　**WW**

A Liberty & Co. Tudric pewter footed bowl, probably designed by Oliver Baker, model number 067, stamped marks.

11.25in (28cm) diam

£400-600　　　　**WW**

A Liberty & Co. pewter and enamel rose bowl, designed by Archibald Knox, with green glass liner, model number 0320, stamped "English Pewter" mark.

9in (23cm) diam

£1,000-1,500   **WW**

ARCHIBALD KNOX

- Archibald Knox (1864-1933) was inspired by the history and landscape of the Isle of Man, where he grew up.
- Knox worked primarily with pewter and silver, but also with other metals, textiles, ceramics and graphics.
- Plain metalware by Knox is often more valuable than hammered, and pieces that incorporate glass by famous makers such as Whitefriars or Clutha are very sought-after.
- Knox's rarer designs include some of his clocks and belt buckles, particularly those with enamel or semi-precious stone inclusions.
- Although popular in his lifetime, Knox has only recently been recognised for the instrumental role he played in the development of the British Art Nouveau scene.
- Knox was a driving force behind the Celtic Revival at the turn of the 20thC.

A Liberty & Co. Tudric pewter bowl, designed by Archibald Knox, of ovoid form with single applied handle, cast with Celtic whiplash budding foliage, model 0231, stamped marks.

6.25in (16cm) diam

£200-300   **L&T**

A Liberty & Co. pewter biscuit barrel and cover, designed by Archibald Knox, of square form, the cover with twin fin handles, the sides cast with stylized plant forms, model 0237, stamped mark.

4.75in (12cm) high

£1,200-1,800   **L&T**

A Liberty & Co. Tudric enamelled pewter vase, designed by Archibald Knox, cast with foliate decoration at the neck, with blue and green enamel bosses, model 0927, impressed marks.

c1905   *11.25in (28.5cm) high*

£500-800   **S&K**

A Liberty & Co. Tudric enamelled pewter vase, designed by Archibald Knox, cast with foliate decoration at neck with blue and green enamel bosses, model 0927, impressed marks.

c1905   *11.25in (28.5cm) high*

£500-800   **S&K**

A Liberty & Co. Tudric bullet-shaped pewter vase, designed by Archibald Knox, cast with entwined and stylized foliage and with applied bracket supports, model 0927, stamped marks.

11.5in (29cm) high

£600-900   **L&T**

A Liberty & Co. Tudric bullet-shaped pewter vase, designed by Archibald Knox, cast with entwined and stylized foliage, with three applied bracket supports, unmarked.

7.5in (19cm) high

£150-200   **L&T**

A Liberty & Co. Tudric single-handled tankard, designed by Archibald Knox, of tapering ovoid form cast with entwined foliage and seed heads, model 0228, stamped marks.

6in (15cm) high

£200-300   **L&T**

An unusual pair of Liberty & Co. pewter solifleur vases, designed by Archibald Knox, model number 0819, stamped marks.

6in (15cm) high

£500-800   **WW**

A Liberty & Co. pewter chamberstick and sconce, designed by Archibald Knox, indistinct marks.

7.5in (18.5cm) long

£300-500   **WW**

A Liberty & Co. Tudric pewter inkwell, designed by Archibald Knox, of flattened ovoid form, the hinged lid enclosing a void for a missing inkwell, the body cast with stylized fruiting tendrils, number 0521, stamped marks.

5.25in (13cm) wide

£300-500   **L&T**

One of a pair of Liberty & Co. Tudric pewter candlesticks, with a stylized ivy pattern on reticulated base and shaft, stamped "Tudric Pewter Made By Liberty & Co.", damaged.

10.5in (26cm) high

£2,000-3,000 pair   **DRA**

A Liberty & Co. twin-light candelabrum, designed by Archibald Knox, the column embellished with an openwork design of stylized leaves and berries, the rectangular base with similar leaf decoration, with separate drop-in sconces, numbered 0530, stamped "English Pewter".

11in (28cm) high

£1,200-1,800   **DN**

A Liberty & Co. pewter inkwell and pen tray, designed by Archibald Knox, unmarked.

11.5in (29cm) wide

£300-500   **WW**

A Liberty & Co. Tudric pewter clock, with a copper and enamel face.

c1910   *6.5in (16.5cm) high*

£1,200-1,800   **TDG**

A Liberty & Co. pewter wall plate.

c1905   *12.75in (32.5cm) diam*

£300-400   **TO**

A Liberty & Co. Tudric pewter timepiece, designed by Archibald Knox, embossed on the front with Roman numerals punctuated with plaques of abalone shell, with eight-day movement with cylinder escapement, marked on underside "Tudric" and "096".

11.5in (29.5cm) high

£7,000-10,000   **DN**

A Liberty & Co. Tudric pewter circular dish, with a sunken centre and broad everted rim punctuated with seven foliate motifs in relief and set with heart-shaped plaques of abalone shell, number 0113, stamped "Tudric".

13in (33cm) diam

£300-500   **DN**

A Liberty & Co. pewter wall mirror, designed by Archibald Knox, the tapering rectangular frame with arched top, repoussé decorated with a Celtic knot motif reserved on a hammered ground with riveted decorations enclosing a mirrored plate.

c1900   *28.75in (72cm) high*

£4,000-6,000   **L&T**

A W.M.F. Jugendstil pewter plate, the rim cast with panels of flowering whiplash foliage and centring the head of an Art Nouveau maiden in profile, stamped marks.

12.75in (32cm) wide

£400-600   **L&T**

A W.M.F. pewter tray, stamped in low relief with an Art Nouveau couple kissing, model number 196, stamped marks, minor scratches and wear.

11in (28cm) wide

£150-200   **WW**

A W.M.F. pewter card tray, decorated with stylized motifs.

c1905   *10in (25.5cm) high*

£800-1,000   **TO**

A W.M.F. Art Nouveau pewter claret jug, the green glass tapering body within mounts cast with maidens and flowering whiplash foliage, stamped marks.

16.5in (41.5cm) high

£400-600   **L&T**

A W.M.F. pewter vase, decorated with dragons amongst scrolling foliage, stamped marks.

12.75in (32cm) high

£200-250   **WW**

A CLOSER LOOK AT A PEWTER CLARET JUG

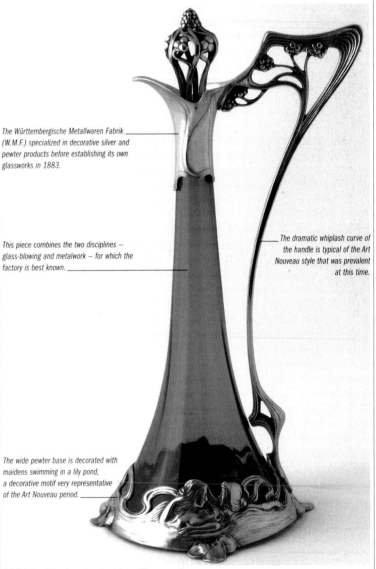

The Württembergische Metallwaren Fabrik (W.M.F.) specialized in decorative silver and pewter products before establishing its own glassworks in 1883.

This piece combines the two disciplines — glass-blowing and metalwork — for which the factory is best known.

The dramatic whiplash curve of the handle is typical of the Art Nouveau style that was prevalent at this time.

The wide pewter base is decorated with maidens swimming in a lily pond, a decorative motif very representative of the Art Nouveau period.

A W.M.F. polished pewter claret jug, with green glass.

c1900   *13.75in (35cm) high*

£1,200-1,800   **STY**

A W.M.F. pewter and green glass vase, of Classical urn form, cast with griffin amongst foliate swags, stamped marks.

15.5in (39cm) high

£300-400   **WW**

A W.M.F. pewter flower dish.

c1905   *14in (35.5cm) wide*

£300-400   **TO**

A W.M.F. pewter syphon stand.

c1905   *8.5in (21.5cm) high*

£220-280   **TO**

A W.M.F. pewter flower dish.

c1905   10in (25.5cm) wide
£300-400   **TO**

A pair of W.M.F. pewter and glass napkin holders.

c1905   5.25in (13.5cm) high
£220-280   **TO**

A W.M.F. pewter picture frame.

c1905   9.5in (24cm) high
£300-500   **TO**

A German Jugendstil pewter liquor set, comprising seven pieces, including tray, flagon and cups.

c1900   Tray 13.5in (34cm) wide
£600-900   **FRE**

A Kayzerzinn pewter novelty ewer, modelled as a kangaroo, with glass eyes, unmarked.

10.5in (26cm) high
£500-700   **WW**

A Danish pewter covered vase, designed by Edvin Ollers, of broad cup shape on a spreading circular foot, with scroll handles and drop-in cover domed in the centre with a fluted ribbon and ball finial, maker's marks and signed "Ollers" in oval.

5in (13cm) high
£100-150   **DN**

A set of six Sheffield pewter flaring cordials in the style of Desny, on buttressed bases with cones, one has small separation on stem, stamped "Manor Period" with trademark.

4.5in (11cm) high
£400-600   **SDR**

A Scottish School Arts and Crafts pewter wall mirror, of rectangular form, the mirrored plate enclosed by a frame repoussé decorated with sinuous tendrils and flowering rose plants.

22.75in (57cm) wide
£1,200-1,800   **L&T**

SILVER

C.R. ASHBEE AND THE GUILD OF HANDICRAFT

- Charles Robert Ashbee (1863-1942) founded the Guild of Handicraft in 1888. It was conceived as a co-operative based on the medieval guild system, and trained many apprentices.
- Originally concerned with carpentry, the Guild was soon successful enough to expand its interests and build a forge for metalwork on its east London premises.
- The Guild moved to Chipping Camden in 1902. Craftsmen from east London relocated and settled permanently in the Cotswolds, taking apprentices from the local community.
- The hand-hammered finishes and simple designs of the Guild's silverware were very popular and much imitated.
- The Guild was wound up in 1908 after a period of decline. Many of its members remained in Chipping Camden working in the decorative arts.
- Ashbee held large retailers such as Liberty & Co., who sold mass-produced goods, responsible for the failure of his experiment.

A Guild of Handicraft silver porringer and spoon, designed by Charles Robert Ashbee, the twin-handled form set with green chrysoprase stones, with later glass liner, stamped marks "GofHLtd, London 1902".

1902   10.75in (27cm) wide
£8,000-10,000   **WW**

A silver vase, set with garnets, by C.R. Ashbee.

c1900   7in (18cm) high
£3,000-5,000   **VDB**

A silver vase, by C.R. Ashbee.

c1900   7in (18cm) high
£2,500-3,000   **VDB**

DECORATIVE ARTS

An Arts and Crafts silver chalice and cover, designed by C.R. Ashbee for the Guild of Handicraft, with enamelled dolphins on the lid and base, the amethyst finial supported by three dolphins.

1901   18in (46cm) high

£26,000-28,000   VDB

An Arts and Crafts two-piece silver coffee set, designed by C.R. Ashbee for the Guild of Handicraft, with agate finial.

c1905   9.5in (24cm) high

£10,000-12,000   VDB

A pair of silver café-au-lait pots, by C.R. Ashbee, with original Guild of Handicraft box.

c1905   Larger 7.5in (19cm) high

£10,000-15,000   VDB

An enamel and silver stone-set tazza, by C. A. Beumers of Dusseldorf.

c1910   7in (18cm) diam

£3,000-4,000   VDB

A Deakin & Francis silver hand mirror.

c1905   10.75in (27cm) wide

£150-200   TO

An Arts and Crafts silver goblet and cover by Charles Boyton, stamped marks for London, with maker's signature and initials.

1936   9.75in (25cm) high

£800-£1,200   L&T

A silver and ivory vase and cover, with stamped maker's mark and mark for Birmingham.

1936   12.25in (31cm) high

£500-600   WW

An Irish Arts and Crafts silver vase, by William Egan of Cork, of tapering cylindrical shape with a flared wavy rim supported by three square section openwork legs, the body set with gems and engraved with a Celtic knot to the girdle, marks for Dublin.

1928   5.5in (14.25cm) high

£1,500-2,000   CHEF

An Arts and Crafts silver fruit bowl, by Elkington & Co. of Birmingham, raised on a hexagonal foot with incurved edges.

1908   8.5in (21.5cm) diam

£200-250   CHEF

An Arts and Crafts silver circular centrepiece bowl, by Kate Harris for Goldsmiths and Silversmiths Co., with stylized scrollwork, maker's marks and hallmarks for London, replaced glass liner.

1901   8in (20.5cm) wide

£1,500-2,000   VDB

A CLOSER LOOK AT A SILVER AND ENAMEL VASE

Eugene Feuillâtre was head enameller at Lalique before he began to make jewellery and silverware under his own name. The skills he developed at Lalique are evident in this piece.

The handles of this vase are done in pliqué-à-jour, a difficult technique of backless enamelling that had been revived in France by Thesmar.

The naturalistic modelling of this vase is a good example of the Art Nouveau aesthetic which was dominant at the turn of the 20thC.

The fact that this piece bears a stamped mark attests to its authenticity and so increases its value.

A small silver and enamelled twin-handled vase, by Eugène Feuillâtre, of artichoke form, with pliqué-à-jour handles, stamped mark.

3in (7.5cm) wide

£10,000-15,000   MACK

An Arts and Crafts symbolist silver and enamel panel, by Alexander Fisher, depicting William Morris' lyric poem 'Sigurd the Volsung', mounted in a silver pediment frame flanked by columns, unsigned.

The inscription is based on Morris' and Eirikr Magnusson's translation of the Icelandic 'Volsunga Saga'.

c1900   *13in (33cm) high*
£10,000-15,000   **VDB**

An Art Nouveau silver bonbon dish, by W.H. Haseler, of shaped oval form with pierced sides and floral border set with blue enamelling and chased foliage, marks for Birmingham.

1905   *5.5in (14cm) diam*
£300-400   **L&T**

A Liberty & Co. silver bowl set with turquoise, by W.H. Haseler, design attributed to Archibald Knox, marks for Birmingham.

1905   *7in (18cm) diam*
£3,000-5,000   **VDB**

An Art Deco silver coffee pot, by the International Silver Company.

c1925   *8.75in (22cm) high*
£200-300   **MOD**

A Georg Jensen sterling grape tazza, marked "263A Georg Jensen Denmark".

5in (12.5cm) high
£800-1,200   **POOK**

A Georg Jensen cigar ashtray, designed by Georg Jensen, design number 22.

c1910   *6.25in (16cm) long*
£1,000-1,500   **SF**

GEORG JENSEN

- Georg Jensen (1866-1934) established his business in April 1904 on Bredgade, a fashionable street in central Copenhagen.
- He became well-known for his elegant and simple designs which were influenced by the Arts and Crafts movement.
- Johan Rohde first worked with Jensen in 1906 when he engaged the firm to manufacture silver from his own drawn designs.
- Rohde is particularly celebrated for his forward-looking holloware. His '432A' pitcher was held back from production for a number of years as it was considered 'too modern'.
- Harald Neilsen started work for Jensen as a chaser in 1909. After leading the apprentice school for a period, he was appointed a director and also served as artistic director from 1958-62.
- After Jensen's death Neilsen trained a new generation, including Henning Kopel, to uphold the traditions of the Jensen brand.
- Sigvard Bernadotte, second son of King Gustav VI of Sweden, joined Jensen in 1930 after studying at Uppsala University.
- His 1939 'Bernadotte' cutlery is considered a classic, featuring his trademark motif of parallel lines.
- The Jensen factory continues to produce silverware from classic Jensen patterns and contemporary designs.

A Georg Jensen grape-style wine coaster, designed by Georg Jensen, design number 229.

1927   *5.5in (14cm) diam*
£3,000-4,000   **SF**

A set of 12 Georg Jensen 'Acorn' pattern gilded coffee spoons, each with an oval bowl, reeded handle and scroll-and-acorn finial, marked "Sterling Denmark" and "Georg Jensen & Wendel A/S", in the original fitted case.

3.75in (9.5cm) long
£300-400   **DN**

A Georg Jensen sterling silver salad fork and spoon, with fluted handles and pineapple tips, stamped "Georg Jensen Stainless" and "Sterling Denmark".

7.75in (19cm) long
£250-350   **DRA**

A Georg Jensen cigarette case, designed by Sigvard Bernadotte, design number 712.

1935   *5.25in (13.5cm) wide*
£1,000-1,500   **SF**

A Georg Jensen preserve jar, designed by Harald Nielsen, design number 891.

c1925   *5in (12.5cm) high*
£1,000-1,500   **SF**

A Georg Jensen vase, designed by Harald Nielsen, design number 676.

c1925   7in (17.5cm) high

£1,200-1,800   **SF**

A tall Georg Jensen vase, designed by Harald Nielsen, design number 757.

c1935   8.75in (22cm) high

£1,000-1,500   **SF**

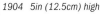

A Georg Jensen bowl, decorated with leaves and berries, designed by Johan Rohde, design number 17.

c1925   4in (10cm) high

£300-500   **SF**

An Arts and Crafts silver candlestick by A.E. Jones, with cylindrical sconce and broad drip-pan on a strapwork stem above a slightly domed circular base punctuated with four tiny turquoise-glazed Ruskin pottery studs, fixed to a turned wooden base, maker's mark and mark for Birmingham.

1904   5in (12.5cm) high

£600-900   **DN**

A silver muffin dish, by A. E Jones of Birmingham.

1935   5.5in (14cm) high

£800-1,200   **VDB**

A Liberty & Co. Cymric silver flower vase, the design attributed to Archibald Knox, with broad rim, tapering cylindrical body, cast with stylized leaf forms and supported by three curved brackets raised on a dished circular base, stamped marks "L & Co.", "Cymric" and hallmarked for Birmingham.

1903   5.5in (14cm) high

£2,500-3,000   **L&T**

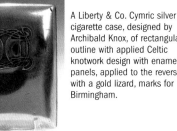

A Liberty & Co. Cymric silver cigarette case, designed by Archibald Knox, of rectangular outline with applied Celtic knotwork design with enamelled panels, applied to the reverse with a gold lizard, marks for Birmingham.

3.5in (9cm) long

£400-600   **L&T**

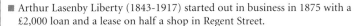

LIBERTY & CO

- Arthur Lasenby Liberty (1843-1917) started out in business in 1875 with a £2,000 loan and a lease on half a shop in Regent Street.
- Liberty & Co. soon became the most fashionable department store in London, catering to the wealthy elite and aspiring middle classes alike.
- Arthur Liberty sourced much of his merchandise from the near and far East, particularly Japan. The basement of the store was called the 'Eastern Bazaar'.
- By the 1890s, Liberty had forged links with many of the most prominent English designers, including Archibald Knox and Dr Christopher Dresser.
- Arthur Liberty strived to make good design affordable for the masses, and to this end he championed manufactured and even mass-produced goods.
- The distinctive Tudor-style building that Liberty & Co. now occupies was built in 1924 from timber salvaged from HMS Impregnable and HMS Hindustan.

Two silver vases, designed by Archibald Knox for Liberty & Co.

c1905   Largest 8.75in (22cm) high

LEFT: £20,000-25,000 RIGHT: £15,000-20,000   **VDB**

A pair of Liberty & Co. Cymric silver candlesticks, design attributed to Archibald Knox, the drip trays and sockets above nozzles cast with stylized buds and applied with tapering tendrils, Birmingham hallmarks.

1905   8.5in (21cm) high

£6,000-9,000   **L&T**

A Liberty & Co. Cymric silver coffee service, designed by Archibald Knox, comprising a lidded coffee pot with ivory handle, a cream jug, a sugar bowl and a twin-handled tray, set with turquoise cabochons, bearing hallmarks for Birmingham.

1906   Coffee pot 8.5in (21.5cm) high

£24,000-26,000   **L&T**

A pair of Liberty & Co. silver and enamel napkin rings, designed by Archibald Knox, design number 2107, marks for Birmingham.

1906 *2in (5cm) diam*

£300-400 **WW**

A silver and copper caddy spoon, probably designed by Archibald Knox and retailed by Liberty & Co., heart-shaped bowl with pierced handle.

3.5in (9cm) long

£300-500 **WW**

A Liberty & Co. Cymric silver and enamel buckle, of circular form cast and enamelled with a forest scene, stamped marks for Birmingham.

1904 *1.5in (3.5cm) wide*

£200-300 **WW**

A Liberty & Co. silver clock.

1903 *4.75in (12cm high)*

£6,000-8,000 **VDB**

A Liberty & Co. silver timepiece, the face enamelled in shades of blue and green, model number 5308, stamped marks for Birmingham.

1907 *3.25in (8cm) high*

£1,000-1,500 **WW**

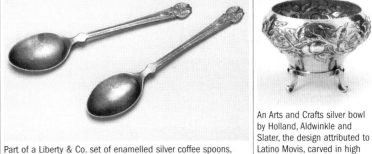

Part of a Liberty & Co. set of enamelled silver coffee spoons, resembling copper, each with a foliate motif picked out with green enamelling, marked "L & Co" with Birmingham hallmarks, in a fitted case.

1947 *3.75in (9.5cm) long*

£100-150 set **DN**

An Arts and Crafts silver bowl by Holland, Aldwinkle and Slater, the design attributed to Latino Movis, carved in high relief with bunches of fruit, on raised scrolled feet, marked.

1902 *7.2in (18cm) wide*

£1,800-2,200 **VDB**

A silver rose bowl, by Harold E. Landon, with finely engraved foliate motifs, amethyst and moonstone cabochons, amethyst finial and open foliate cutouts on the lid, base hallmarked.

1920 *10in (25.5cm) wide*

£10,000-15,000 **VDB**

A pair of silver candlesticks by Orivit.

c1905 *3.5in (9cm) high*

£300-350 **TO**

A Porter Blanchard hammered sterling silver flaring bowl, with wide, sweeping, angular handles, stamped "Sterling Silver Porter Blanchard", some scratches.

14in (35.5cm) wide

£2,000-3,000 **DRA**

A Ramsden & Carr silver and enamelled Arts and Crafts bowl, of trefoil shape with incurved rim, having three twin-branch wirework handles each punctuated with a red enamelled heart-shaped plaque and supported on a circular foot, maker's marks and marks for London, stamped on base "Designed and Made by Ramsden & Carr, London".

1902 *4.75in (12cm) high*

£5,000-8,000 **DN**

DECORATIVE ARTS

A silver Arts and Crafts hand mirror by Omar Ramsden and Alwyn Carr, marks for London.

1907   *11.75in (30cm) long*

£2,000-3,000   **VDB**

A silver and enamel box by Omar Ramsden, with blue enamel.

5.5in (14cm) wide

£2,500-3,000   **VDB**

An Arts and Crafts silver tea urn, by Omar Ramsden and Alwyn Carr, with an ivory handle and bands of foliate motifs, raised on six lion's paw feet.

1908   *12.5in (32cm) high*

£2,500-3,000   **VDB**

A silver and electroplated presentation goblet, by Omar Ramsden, surmounted by a naked boy and set with moonstone cabochons, with marks for London.

1931   *21.25 (53cm) high*

£3,000-4,000   **L&T**

An Artificers' Guild silver tureen spoon, by Edward Spencer, the tapering long handle with applied ropework decoration, with catch to reverse, stamped marks for London.

1922   *9in (23cm) long*

£400-600   **WW**

An Artificers' Guild circular silver box and cover, designed by Edward Spencer, with a wirework rim and a domed drop-in cover centred with a lion finial, maker's mark for London and designer's mark.

1928   *4in (10cm) diam*

£800-1,200   **DN**

A set of four silver goblets, by the Artificers' Guild of London, design attributed to Edward Spencer.

1923   *3.5in (9cm) diam*

£3,000-5,000   **VDB**

An Artificers' Guild silver 'Scorpio' napkin ring, the design attributed to Edward Spencer, with a relief medallion of a scorpion flanked by beading and two pink coral studs, maker's marks and marks for London.

1915   *1.75in (4.5cm) diam*

£120-180   **DN**

A Tattorini & Sons Ltd solid silver tray, with ivory handles.

c1925   *15in (38cm) wide*

£1,000-1,500   **TDG**

A pair of silver candlesticks, by Williams of Birmingham.

1906   *11in (28cm) high*

£6,000-8,000   **VDB**

A silver W.M.F. sugar basket.

c1900   *5in (12.5cm) wide*

£150-200   **TDG**

An Arts and Crafts silver cigar box, with handpainted enamel panel of a wooded glade, by Fleetwood Vardley for the Guild of Handicraft.

c1904   *8in (20cm) long*

£4,000-6,000   **VDB**

A London silver and glass perfume bottle, by Walter Thornhill.

1894   *7.5in (19cm) high*

£3,000-4,000   **JBS**

An Arts and Crafts silver mounted oak and leather writer's travelling aid, the front mounted with a silver panel depicting an owl amongst flowers and foliage, stamped "JA & S", marks for Birmingham.

1905   *13.5in (34cm) high*

£300-400   **WW**

An Edwardian silver photo frame, bearing embossed inscription "Parting is such sweet sorrow", and embossed with the figures of Romeo and Juliet, marks for Birmingham.

1906   *10in (25.5cm) high*

£80-120   **L&T**

A German silver mounted glass inkwell and penrest, the square inkwell set with a red stone finial, inscribed "Eisenbahn-Regiments No3 23 Marz 1907", stamped marks.

4.5in (11.5cm) high

£300-500   **WW**

A Finnish silver coffee pot, engraved with an Art Nouveau floral design, stamped marks.

10in (25cm) high

£280-320   **WW**

A pair of Arts and Crafts silver bonbon dishes, each with a dished oval bowl with hammered finish, applied scroll handles and base cast with a grotesque fish, marks for London.

1922

£1,000-1,500   **L&T**

A CLOSER LOOK AT AN ARTS AND CRAFTS CRUCIFIX

Henry Wilson was an architect who also worked with jewellery and metal. His skill and attention to detail have assured his lasting reputation as a master craftsman.

These cabochons are formed from semi-precious stones. Many Arts and Crafts jewellers and metalworkers shunned the use of more expensive stones as elitist.

The enamel panel at the centre of this cross depicts the 'Agnus Dei' — the 'Lamb of God' who is called upon during the mass to redeem the sins of mankind.

Many Arts and Crafts silversmiths designed and made church silver. The unassuming Arts and Crafts aesthetic matched the tenets of humility espoused by the Church.

Wilson's book 'Silverwork and Jewellery' was published in 1902 and became a seminal text. The author's virtuosity is apparent in the number and range of techniques he demonstrates within its pages.

An Arts and Crafts silver altar crucifix by Henry Wilson, with a central painted enamel panel of the Agnus Dei or Lamb of God in green and white, applied twisted wirework and open leaf motifs on the stem, resting on four feet.

1908   *14.5in (37cm) high*

£10,000-15,000   **VDB**

SILVER PLATE

An Art Deco silvered bronze figure by Adolph, the nude female study on a black marble base, signed "Adolph" on the base.

11.5in (29cm) high

£500-800   **ROS**

A Guild of Handicraft electroplated muffin dish and cover, designed by Charles Robert Ashbee, unmarked.

9.5in (24cm) diam

£1,200-1,800   **WW**

A W.A.S. Benson electroplated hot water jug, of tapering cylindrical form, with hinged lid.

9.5in (24cm) high

£50-80   **L&T**

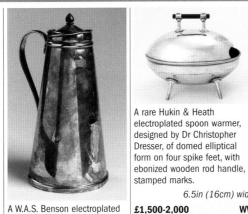

A rare Hukin & Heath electroplated spoon warmer, designed by Dr Christopher Dresser, of domed elliptical form on four spike feet, with ebonized wooden rod handle, stamped marks.

6.5in (16cm) wide

£1,500-2,000   **WW**

A Birmingham Guild of Handicraft electroplated teapot and milk jug, probably designed by Arthur Dixon, hammered finish, stamped mark.

6.5in (16cm) wide

£280-320   **WW**

An Art Deco silvered Spelter figure of a female with discus, by Fayral, on a green and black marble base, signed "Fayral" on the base.

Fayral was a noted French Art Deco sculptor. He worked alongside other important artists for the house of sculptor Le Verrier, producing models of popular decorative items using cheaper materials, which were sold in the rue du Théâtre, Paris.

8in (20.5cm) high

£320-380   **ROS**

A Christopher Dresser electroplated toast rack, for Hukin & Heath, the hinged dividers with sphere angles supported on a domed base with flattened bun feet, number 2555, impressed marks.

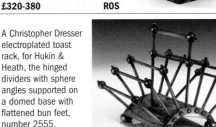

4.75in (12cm) high

£500-800   **L&T**

DECORATIVE ARTS

A fine silver-plated Art Deco teapot and creamer, by Paul Follot, of sweeping fluted design, marked "Pfollot", teapot inscribed "3050 XII" and creamer inscribed "3050 VI", slight damage.

11.5in (29cm) high

£3,000-5,000 — **SDR**

A silver-plated chocolate set and tray, by Hukin & Heath.

The stylized geometric form of this set is typical of Hukin & Heath. Pieces were usually electroplated or pure silver.

c1920 — *Tray 10.75in (27.5cm) wide*

£280-320 — **TDG**

A CLOSER LOOK AT A SILVER-PATINATED BRONZE

Maurice Guiraud-Rivière is considered one of the finest sculptors of the Art Deco period, and this is among his best-known works.

The streamlined form and strong sense of motion imparted by this sculpture make it instantly recognizable as a classic Art Deco image. A strong visceral association with a popular look will often enhance the value of a piece.

Different versions of this sculpture can be found — some are cold-painted, whereas this example is of unadorned, silver-patinated bronze.

The simple geometry of the lozenge-shaped base and the stylized clouds linking the figure to the base add to the Deco feel of this piece.

A silver-patinated bronze, 'The Comet', by Maurice Guiraud-Rivière.

c1925 — *24in (61cm) wide*

£20,000-25,000 — **TDG**

A Hukin & Heath electroplated lamp base, converted from a candle stick, the circular drip-tray above a rusticated turned column with frilled knop, on spreading domed base with frilled rim and stamped marks.

12in (31cm) high

£100-200 — **L&T**

A silver-plated cocktail shaker, formed as the Boston lighthouse, marks for "Meridien Silver Plate", light scratches, both lids with small dents on edge.

c1920 — *13.5in (4.5cm) high*

£4,000-6,000 — **BRU**

A Keswick School of Industrial Arts electroplated bowl, of circular form with braided edge, centred by repoussé worked rose motif, stamped marks.

11.25in (28cm) wide

£200-300 — **L&T**

One of two silver-gilt pedestal bowls, by Nathan & Hayes, designed in the Gothic style and part lobed, inscribed "in Dona Suis Srme Bene Dictus", marks for Chester.

c1910 — *4.25in (11cm) high*

£600-800 pair — **ROS**

A tazza-shaped sweet dish by Saunders & Shepherd Ltd of London, with a round bowl and a stem in the form of 'The Spirit of Ecstasy', on a stepped round foot, with initials "GB".

1930 — *5.5in (14cm) diam*

£1,000-1,500 — **DN**

An early 20thC Mappin & Webb silver-plated desk inkwell stand and pen tray, on lion paw feet.

7.25in (18.5cm) wide

£60-90 — **EPO**

A hexagonal part engine-turned table lighter, by Saunders & Shepherd Ltd of London, in the form of a petrol pump surmounted with a model of 'The Spirit of Ecstasy', with initials "GB".

1934

£3,000-5,000　　　　　**DN**

An Arts and Crafts silver-plated brass vase, designed by Edward Spencer, of broad trumpet shape with horizontal ribs in relief edged with ropework banding, decorated with simple florets and foliage near the base, number 216.

6.75in (17.5cm) high

£400-600　　　　　　**DN**

A W.M.F. Jugendstil electroplated 'Echo' strut mirror, the rectangular shaped frame cast with sinuous flowering tendrils and an Art Nouveau maiden with a hand cupped to her ear, enclosing a mirrored plate, stamped marks.

14.75in (37cm) high

£1,200-1,800　　　　**L&T**

A W.M.F. Art Nouveau electroplated ewer, of tapering form with hinged lid set with leafy tendrils, the applied handle cast as a mermaid, her tail flowing into the foliage of the body, case with entwined iris, stamped marks.

15in (37.5cm) high

£1,200-1,800　　　　**L&T**

A W.M.F. table lamp, with original plating.

c1900　　16in (41cm) high

£3,000-5,000　　　　**STY**

A pair of W.M.F. silver-plated figural candelabra, in the form of maidens holding stylized sconces.

c1900　　　19.25in (49cm) high

£10,000-15,000　　　　**STY**

A W.M.F. liquor service, with original glass.

c1900　　14in (36cm) high

£1,500-2,000　　　　**STY**

A W.M.F. electroplated jardinière and liner, the etched clear glass liner enclosed within an oval frame cast and pierced with fruiting whiplash foliage and with similarly cast twin handles, number 352, stamped and cast marks.

12.5in (31cm) wide

£250-350　　　　**L&T**

A W.M.F. silver-plated celery vase.

c1905　　7.5in (19cm) high

£200-250　　　　**TO**

A W.M.F. biscuit barrel.

c1905　　10in (25.5cm) high

£200-250　　　　**TO**

A W.M.F. silver-plated tea and coffee set on a tray.

c1905　　　　　Tray 28.25in (72cm) wide

£3,000-4,000　　　　**TO**

A W.M.F. Art Nouveau silver-plated wall plaque, with W.M.F. mark.

c1910   *17.25in (44cm) diam*

£400-600   **TDG**

A W.M.F. silver-plated biscuit barrel and glass liner, with sinuous stems and berries.

9in (23cm) high

£400-500   **DN**

A W.M.F. electroplated desk set, in the Secessionist style, comprising an inkstand, a paper clip, a pen tray and a blotter, each with stamped mark.

£200-250   **L&T**

Two knives from a W.M.F. plated metal 12-piece dessert service, comprising six knives and six forks with steel blades and prongs, the handles embellished with geometric foliate motifs, in a fitted case for Zurich retailer A. Wiskemann-Knecks.

Knife 6.75in (17cm) long

£200-300 set   **DN**

A silver-plated Arts and Crafts wine cooler, with maker's marks.

c1900   *7.5in (19cm) high*

£280-320   **TDG**

An Arts and Crafts white metal bowl, with deep rounded sides embossed with a band of foliage and berries, with applied green enamel roundels centred with a plaque of mother-of-pearl, on ball feet.

9in (23cm) high

£500-800   **DN**

An Arts and Crafts plated circular hand-mirror, with central green and blue enamelled plaque flanked by a wirework band, the mirror secured by florets and rivets.

5.25in (13.5cm) diam

£300-400   **DN**

A silver-plated Art Deco plate, with a mermaid design and bakelite handles.

c1930   *15in (38cm) diam*

£280-320   **TDG**

A Continental metal and enamel inkwell and desk tidy, the central inkwell with cloisonné enamel maiden, stamped "AE 9307".

10.25in (25.5cm) wide

£300-400   **WW**

WROUGHT IRON

An Artificers' Guild wrought iron trivet, the openwork design of a stylized plant with sinuous scrolling stems, with plain tapering handle, raised on three loop feet.

14.75in (37.5cm) long

£300-500   **DN**

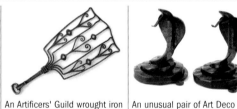

An Artificers' Guild wrought iron toasting frame, of almost rectangular outline with scrolling stems extending from a flattened handle with brass hanging loop.

18.25in (46.5cm) long

£220-280   **DN**

An unusual pair of Art Deco hand-wrought iron snake paperweights, by Edgar Brandt.

c1925   *4.75in (12cm) high*

£3,000-5,000   **MOD**

An English chrome and bakelite kettle and urn, stamped "Regd 849217" for 1946.

16.5in (42cm) high

£400-600   **WW**

A pair of Art Deco wrought iron gates in the style of Wilhelm Hunt Diederich, with leaping hounds and stags in a stylized landscape, within radially planished border, unmarked.

62.75in (159.5cm) high

£12,000-17,000   **SDR**

A wrought iron fender stool, by Thomas Hadden of Edinburgh, of rectilinear three-quarter form, the green leather padded seats with studded decoration above a slatted frieze enhanced with panels of entwined foliage.

72in (180cm) wide

£2,000-3,000   **L&T**

A CLOSER LOOK AT A PAIR OF BRANDT WROUGHT IRON GATES

Edgar Brandt is widely regarded as one of the most accomplished manipulators of iron in the 20thC.

Brandt's oeuvre includes lighting, tableware, furniture and decorative items. Large architectural pieces like this are particularly sought after as they make a bold statement.

The stylized symmetry of the fountain at the centre of the gates provides a counterpoint to the leaves and tendrils swirling around it.

'L'Oasis', a brass and iron five-panel screen by Brandt, sold for £1million in June 2000. These gates date from the same period of Brandt's work.

An Art Deco wrought iron hook, by Paul Kiss.

c1925   *9.5in (24cm) high*

£1,500-2,500   **MOD**

A pair of Art Deco wrought iron interior gates by Edgar Brandt, with stylized water fountain and swirling stems of leaves and pierced flowers, above vines along the base, stamped "E. Brandt France".

c1925   *51in (129.5cm) high*

£6,000-9,000   **SDR**

A pair of Art Deco hand-wrought iron candlesticks by Maury.

c1925   *11in (28cm) wide*

£800-1,200   **MOD**

A German Art and Crafts wrought iron casket, stamped with "FW" cipher and "GERMANY", retains original hand-wrought key.

11in (27.5cm) wide

£1,000-1,500   **FRE**

A pair of Arts and Crafts wrought iron fireirons, each with applied copper entwined banner on tripod base.

20.75in (53cm) high

£280-320   **L&T**

An Arts and Crafts cast-iron fireplace, in the manner of the Glasgow School and Margaret McDonald Mackintosh, with a high relief maiden's head with long, flowing hair, and stylized floral details either side and below the face.

c1905   *49.5in (126cm) high*

£8,000-10,000   **PUR**

A French Art Deco magazine rack, unsigned.

1925

£500-800   **MOD**

DECORATIVE ARTS

A unique Art Deco wrought iron and bronze aquarium, unsigned.

c1925   *15.25in (39cm) wide*

£600-900   **MOD**

A French Art Deco fish sculpture, unsigned.

c1925   *15.75in (40cm) wide*

£1,200-1,800   **MOD**

A gilt metal erotic figure of a dancer, after a model by Bergman, with hinged skirt, cast marks.

7in (18cm) high

£600-800   **WW**

An Art Deco spelter figure of a female in a flowing dress holding hoops.

c1925   *10in (25.5cm) high*

£400-600   **TDG**

A spelter figural lamp base, on a marble base, unsigned.

31.5in (80cm) high

£600-900   **WW**

A pair of French Art Deco metal vases with embossed decoration, signed "C. Terrers Lyon".

c1925   *6.25in (16cm) high*

£800-1,200   **MOD**

A Scottish Arts and Crafts tin jardinière, of circular form, repoussé decorated, with ring handles.

10in (25cm) diam

£250-300   **L&T**

A polished steel candlestick, designed by Ernest Gimson, probably made by Alfred or Norman Bucknell, stamped with bands of geometric decoration, on three shaped feet, unmarked.

9.5in (24.5cm) high

£1,500-2,000   **WW**

A Scottish Arts and Crafts polished tin hairbrush, by Margaret Gilmour, repoussé decorated with a panel of stylized flowers, stamped monogram.

9.25in (23cm) long

£400-600   **L&T**

An Arts and Crafts multistone silver necklace, for the Artificer's Guild, with wirework, leaves, beads and set cabochons.

c1910 *8.5in (21.5cm) long*
£3,500-5,500 **VDB**

An Arts and Crafts heart-shaped necklace, by Child & Child, with silver and gold citrine and pale aquamarine, the semi-precious stones encased in rubover settings.

c1890 *12in (30.5cm) long*
£1,500-2,500 **VDB**

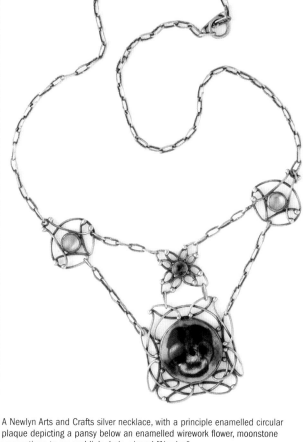

An Arts and Crafts silver necklace, by Katie Eadie, of intricate intertwining foliate and floral design, with moonstone and a mother-of-pearl drop.

c1905 *19in (48cm) long*
£4,000-6,000 **VDB**

An English Arts and Crafts necklace, by Arthur and Georgina Gaskin, having a central amethyst cabochon within a foliate mount, flanked by mother-of-pearl and with similar drops, signed 'G'.

c1900 *Pendant 2in (4.5cm) long*
£800-1,200 **PC**

A Newlyn Arts and Crafts silver necklace, with a principle enamelled circular plaque depicting a pansy below an enamelled wirework flower, moonstone connections to an oval link chain, signed "Newlyn".

Plaque 2in (5cm) high
£1,800-2,200 **WW**

An enamelled necklace, by Charles Horner, with a pendant of elliptical shape with blue-green enamelling and a plain openwork winged top, enamelled drop and spacer to chains above, marked "C.H" and Birmingham marks for 1908.

2.75in (7cm) long
£450-550 **DN**

An Arts and Crafts silver necklace, with sealed butterfly wing pendant, by Henry William King.

c1905 *12in (31cm) long*
£120-180 **AVW**

A Liberty & Co. silver and enamel necklace, with set mother-of-pearl, in an organic design.

9in (23cm) long
£2,200-2,800 **VDB**

A silver pendant necklace, in the style of Liberty & Co., blue and green enamel, set with a blister pearl and a Mississippi pearl, unmarked, new chain.

c1900 *12in (31cm) long*
£200-250 **AVW**

An Arts and Crafts silver repoussé pendant necklace, with blue and green enamel, a blister pearl, seed pearls and Mississippi pearl drop, unmarked.

c1900　　12in (31cm) long

£300-350　　　　　　**AVW**

An Arts and Crafts heart-shaped silver and enamel pendant necklace, with blister pearl drop.

c1900　　12.5in (32cm) long

£300-350　　　　　　**AVW**

An Arts and Crafts silver blue and green enamel pendant necklace, with a blister pearl and a Mississippi pearl, enamel work verso, foliate motifs, unmarked.

c1900　　10.5in (27cm) long

£300-350　　　　　　**AVW**

An Arts and Crafts silver pendant necklace, with three enamel squares and a drop pearl, enamel work verso, unmarked.

c1900　　12in (30.5cm) long

£150-200　　　　　　**AVW**

An Arts and Crafts silver and turquoise pendant necklace, with three set turquoise stones.

c1900　　9.5in (24cm) long

£100-150　　　　　　**AVW**

An Arts and Crafts turquoise and moonstone necklace, attributed to The Guild of Handicraft, the pendant with a plaque of turquoise within a foliate mount with three moonstone cabochon drops, suspended on chains with turquoise matrix pebbles and moonstones.

Pendant 2in (5cm) long

£700-1,000　　　　　　**DN**

An Arts and Crafts necklace, with a central malachite cabochon and drop below within fine wirework mounts, on a chain with two oval jade cabochon spacers.

£180-220　　　　　　**DN**

A Swedish Arts and Crafts silver pendant necklace, with iridescent central blue enamel panel surrounded by enamelled decoration, hallmarked "NM".

c1920　　11.5in (29cm) long

£180-220　　　　　　**AVW**

A CLOSER LOOK AT AN ARTS AND CRAFTS NECKLACE

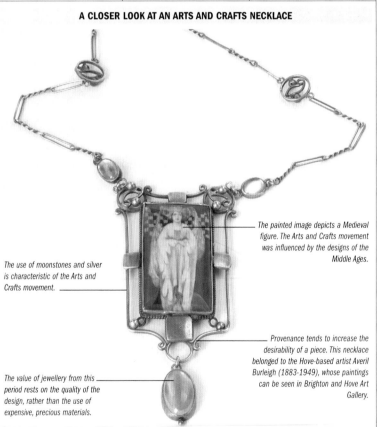

The painted image depicts a Medieval figure. The Arts and Crafts movement was influenced by the designs of the Middle Ages.

The use of moonstones and silver is characteristic of the Arts and Crafts movement.

Provenance tends to increase the desirability of a piece. This necklace belonged to the Hove-based artist Averil Burleigh (1883-1949), whose paintings can be seen in Brighton and Hove Art Gallery.

The value of jewellery from this period rests on the quality of the design, rather than the use of expensive, precious materials.

An Arts and Crafts silver and ivory necklace, with foiled moonstones and painted ivory panel.

Provenance: This piece belonged the 20thC artist Averil Burleigh.

1901　　　　　　15in (38cm) long

£4,000-6,000　　　　　　**VDB**

A Child & Child aquamarine and citrine pendant, of open-work double-scroll form, collet set with cushion, round and oval mixed-cut pale blue aquamarines and similarly cut citrines, with an hexagonal citrine drop, maker's mark only, adapted as a brooch.

£500-700 DN

A W.H. Haseler enamelled pendant, with a spray resembling a fleur-de-lys extending from a blue and turquoise enamelled band, stamped "W.H.H" and "Silver", suspended on chain.

1.5in (3.5cm) long

£400-600 DN

A Murrle Bennett white metal, enamel and abalone shell pendant, with a garland of flowers and leaves, stamped "MB" mark.

£300-400 WW

An Arts and Crafts pendant in silver and aquamarine, attributed to Rhoda Wager.

c1900 *1in (2.5cm) long*

£120-180 TDG

An Arts and Crafts pendant, with a plaque of blister pearl, the mount embellished with foliate stems and with a Swiss lapis cabochon drop, suspended from chain.

Pendant 2in (5cm) long

£220-280 DN

An Arts and Crafts enamelled pendant, formed as a stylized flowerhead with radiating petals and three simulated pearls in the centre.

1.75in (4.5cm) long

£150-200 DN

An Arts and Crafts silver pendant, with chalcedony chrysoprase, garnets, blister pearls and a crystal heart.

c1890 *3in (7.5cm) long*

£380-420 TDG

A heart-shaped 9ct gold and amethyst pendant, marked "HM" with Birmingham marks for 1908.

1.5in (3.5cm) long

£120-180 DN

An Arts and Crafts pendant, with abalone shell and a scrolling wirework mount, four mother-of-pearl studs, chain.

1.5in (3.5cm) long

£120-180 DN

An Arts and Crafts citrine pendant, with four faceted stones and wire ropework borders, linked by a foliate mount, the suspension loop engraved with foliage.

2in (5cm) long

£200-250 DN

An Arts and Crafts silver brooch, by C.R. Ashbee, of hexagonal shape with a large set agate cabochon.

1902 *1.75in (4.5cm) wide*

£3,000-3,500 VDB

An Arts and Crafts silver and turquoise brooch, by C.R. Ashbee for the Guild of Handicraft Ltd., shaped as a butterfly.

c1900 *3in (7cm) long*

£3,000-5,000 VDB

An Arts and Crafts silver repoussé brooch, in the style of James Fenton, in the shape of an insect's wings, with blue and green enamel work, a blister pearl and a drop pearl, unmarked.

c1900   *1.5in (3.5cm) wide*

£200-250   **AVW**

An Arts and Crafts silver pin, by Arthur and Georgina Gaskin, with leaves, florets, four set green pastes and a central blister pearl

c1910   *3in (7.5cm) long*

£700-1,000   **VDB**

An Arts and Crafts silver brooch, designed by Max Gradl and made by Theodor Fahrner, with two stained oval agate cabochons, unsigned.

c1900

£2,000-2,500   **VDB**

A Guild of Handicraft silver enamel brooch, with a painted pansy, of hexagonal form.

1902   *1.8in (4.5cm) wide*

£2,000-2,500   **VDB**

An Arts and Crafts Skonvirke brooch, by Bernhard Hertz, embossed with leaves and set with a green cabochon stone, a similar pendant below, stamped marks.

£120-180   **L&T**

A George Hunt white metal, enamel and moonstone pin, stamped "GH".

4in (10cm) long

£250-350   **WW**

An English Arts and Crafts oval brooch, by Bernard Instone, set with a central faceted citrine and flanked by slender leaves and pale smoky quartz.

c1920   *1.5in (4cm) wide*

£250-300   **PC**

A citrine and peridot brooch, by Bernard Instone, the oval faceted citrine within a mount of leaves, tendrils and berries punctuated with three peridots.

c1920   *1in (2.5cm) wide*

£200-300   **DN**

An English Arts and Crafts bar brooch, by Bernard Instone, with a plaque of abalone shell within a ropework border and flanked by a floret and leaves.

c1920   *2.5in (6cm) long*

£100-150   **PC**

An Arts and Crafts Dorrie Nossiter gem-set circular brooch, arranged around the outer edge with citrines and other stones of autumnal colours flanked by golden vine leaves.

c1905   *1.5in (4cm) wide*

£400-600   **PC**

An Arts and Crafts silver brooch, by Bernard Instone, with a set cornelian and foliate decoration, unmarked.

c1920   *1.5in (3cm) wide*

£100-150   **AVW**

An Arts and Crafts silver brooch, designed by Georg Kleeman, with three oval chrysoprases, unsigned.

c1900   *1.75in (4.5cm) wide*

£1,500-2,000   **VDB**

A Dorrie Nossiter gem-set clip, with golden wirework scrolls flanked by garnets, turquoise cabochons and half-pearls.

1.25in (3.5cm) high

£250-300   **DN**

An Arts and Crafts silver brooch, with blister pearls and foliate decoration, unmarked.

c1900   1.25in (3cm) wide
£50-80   AVW

An Arts and Crafts silver repoussé lady's brooch, with an orange Ruskin pottery roundel, unmarked.

c1900   1.75in (4cm) wide
£50-80   AVW

An Arts and Crafts silver repoussé diamond-shaped lady's brooch, with blue Ruskin pottery roundel, unmarked.

c1900   2.5in (6.5cm) wide
£40-60   AVW

An Arts and Crafts silver brooch, with a large cabochon labradorite, flowers and serpents, hallmarked.

1905   3.5in (9cm) wide
£700-1,000   VDB

An Arts and Crafts citrine brooch, centred with a faceted citrine flanked by foliage, stems and berries.

1.5in (4cm) wide
£150-200   DN

An Arts and Crafts silver and turquoise repoussé bar brooch.

c1900   3in (7.5cm) wide
£50-70   AVW

An Arts and Crafts silver brooch, with a blister pearl and stylized wheatsheaves, unmarked.

c1910   2.75in (7cm) wide
£70-100   AVW

An Arts and Crafts silver, gold and amethyst brooch, with four thistles around the central cabochon, unmarked.

c1900   1.9in (4.5cm) wide
£100-150   AVW

An Arts and Crafts silver, gold and chalcedony brooch, with stylized foliate scrollwork and three cabochons, unmarked.

c1900   3in (7.5cm) wide
£300-350   AVW

An Arts and Crafts carnelian and fire opal brooch, with a central pale carnelian plaque within an openwork foliate mount punctuated with four faceted fire-opals.

1.75in (4.5cm) wide
£180-220   DN

An Arts and Crafts silver lady's ring, by Bernard Instone, with a square central amethyst and detailed wheatsheaf motifs, unmarked.

c1920   1in (2.5cm) wide
£500-800   AVW

An Arts and Crafts silver lady's ring, by Bernard Instone, with a Swiss lapis lazuli and grapevine motifs, unmarked.

c1920   1in (2cm) wide
£500-700   AVW

BERNARD INSTONE

- Bernard Instone (1891-1987) won a scholarship to the Birmingham Central School of Art when he was still only 12 years old.
- He continued his training in Birmingham's jewellery district, before working as a journeyman. He spent time with Emile Lettré in Berlin and John Paul Cooper in Kent.
- Instone established Langstone Silver Works in the West Midlands in 1920. Here, he specialised in jewellery and made custom pieces for clients.
- Despite the quality, he aimed to keep his work affordable. Semi-precious stones reduced costs.
- The English countryside inspired designs and wheatsheaves and berries are common motifs.
- In 1937, he became president of the Birmingham Jewellers' Association.

An Arts and Crafts silver ring, with chrysoprase, chalcedony and opal stones, attributed to Bernard Instone.

1.5in (4cm) wide
£500-700   TDG

An Arts and Crafts silver and gold repoussé ring, with a large, square aquamarine, unmarked.

c1900   1in (2.5cm) wide
£500-800   AVW

An Arts and Crafts silver and turquoise enamel ring.

c1900   0.5in (1.5cm) wide
£300-350   TDG

A Liberty & Co. silver buckle, with a central set abalone plaque, with stylized floral scrollwork on the sides, hallmarked "Cymric", designed by Oliver Baker.

1901 4.5in (11.5cm) wide

£1,200-1,800 VDB

An Arts and Crafts silver buckle, by Theodor Fahrner, with two oval stained agate cabochons and enamel details.

c1900 3.5in (8.5cm) wide

£2,000-2,500 VDB

An Arts and Crafts silver belt buckle, of shaped outline with a beaten finish, applied with whiplash tendrils and centred by a turquoise stone, hallmarks for Birmingham.

1901 4in (10cm) wide

£200-300 L&T

An Arts and Crafts silver and enamel belt buckle, with stylized plant form decoration set with turquoise enamel and reserved on a hammered ground, hallmark for Birmingham, with later black silk belt.

1910 3.75in (9.5cm) wide

£400-600 L&T

A pair of drop earrings, in the manner of Jessie M. King and probably retailed through Liberty & Co, the foliate plaques picked out with turquoise enamelling and centred with a pearl.

£400-600 DN

A pair of Arts and Crafts silver and ivory 'Flora' earrings, with two intricately carved female figures, set in silver, unmarked.

c1910 1in (2.5cm) wide

£120-180 AVW

A rare Newlyn silver napkin ring, made by Reginald Dick, having a pierced oval aperture with wirework embellishment and set with a blue-green enamelled boss, London hallmarks for 1911 and marked "Newlyn" and "Newlyn Enamel".

1.75in (4cm) diam

£400-600 PC

ART NOUVEAU

A Georg Jensen pendant, designed by Georg Jensen, design no. 15.

c1910 2in (5cm) long

£2,000-3,000 SF

A Liberty and Co. silver repoussé pendant and necklace, with stylized swirling motifs and blister pearls.

c1900 9.5in (24cm) long

£300-500 AVW

A set of six Liberty & Co. silver and enamel buttons, designed by Archibald Knox, each with enamelled whiplash motif, in original fitted case, stamped marks "Birmingham 1903".

1in (2.5cm) diam

£1,500-2,000 WW

A bead belt with an Art Nouveau buckle.

c1900 28.5in (72cm) long

£60-90 TDG

A CLOSER LOOK AT AN ART NOUVEAU PENDANT

The difficult technique of plique-à-jour involves filling gaps in a metal framework with enamel, which is held in place by surface tension. The piece is then fired so that the enamel hardens

Innovative design in jewellery became more important during the Art Nouveau period as pieces became art forms in their own right, rather than a display of wealth.

There is usually no backing to the enamel so light is allowed to stream through and create a stained glass effect.

Freshwater pearls are formed by shellfish found in fresh water and rivers. They are duller and less iridescent than saltwater pearls

A Heinrich Levinger plique-à-jour enamel and pearl pendant, of foliate form with three freshwater pearls flanked by pale blue translucent enamelled panels and with a freshwater pearl drop, marked "HL 900 depose".

1.25in (3cm) wide

£800-1,200 DN

A CLOSER LOOK AT AN ART DECO BROOCH

A Lalique 'Cabochon Pommier du Japon' glass brooch, of domed form moulded with prunus blossom heightened with dark staining and held in a gilt metal mount, with internal green-tinted foil which reflects light, mount stamped "Lalique" and "RL".

1.5in (4cm) diam

£600-800   **DN**

This brooch is platinum - more rare and expensive than gold and silver and generally used only in the finest jewellery. It was the most popular setting for diamonds.

Many of the best Art Deco pieces are signed or numbered by the maker.

Brooch designs became bigger and bolder during the Art Deco period to accommodate large, striking designs.

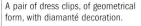

Good quality emeralds have fewer flaws and are deep in colour. It is rare to find an example with very few or no inclusions. They are prone to chipping, so jewellery should be checked for damage.

An Art Deco platinum, diamond and sapphire bow pin.

c1925   *1.75in (4.5cm) wide*

£7,000-10,000   **MACK**

A rare Art Deco platinum brooch, by Marchale of Paris, set with a 5ct sugarloaf-cut emerald and 2ct diamonds, with onyx flower design, signed.

c1925   *2.25in (6cm) wide*

£15,000-20,000   **MACK**

An Art Deco platinum and diamond bow pin.

c1925   *2.5in (6.5cm) wide*

£10,000-12,000   **MACK**

A Continental Art Deco platinum brooch set with diamonds and rubies.

c1925   *1.75in (4.5cm) wide*

£5,000-8,000   **MACK**

A French-cut sapphire and diamond clip brooch, of openwork tapering shape, the banded mounts engraved with fine foliate decoration.

1.25in (3cm) long

£500-800   **DN**

A French silver brooch with marcasite decoration.

c1935   *2in (5cm) wide*

£70-100   **TDG**

A pair of dress clips, of geometrical form, with diamanté decoration.

c1925   *1in (2.5cm) long*

£70-100   **TDG**

A pair of Art Deco dress clips with paste decoration.

c1930   1in (2.5cm) long

£30-40   **TDG**

An Art Deco platinum semi-curve clip, set with a 12ct diamond.

c1930   1.75in (4.5cm) wide

£10,000-15,000   **MACK**

A pair of Art Deco sapphire and diamond double clips.

c1930   1.5in (4cm) long

£12,000-18,000   **MACK**

An Art Deco platinum clip, with a French mark.

c1935   2.25in (5.5cm) wide

£5,000-7,000   **MACK**

An Art Deco platinum ring, with filigree decoration, set with calibré rubies and diamonds.

c1925   1in (2.5cm) high

£5,000-7,000   **MACK**

An Art Deco platinum ring, with filigree work, set with old European-cut diamonds and sapphires.

c1925   0.5in (1.5cm) high

£10,000-15,000   **MACK**

An Art Deco platinum ring, of buckle design, set with one carat diamonds and rubies, with cabochon-cut sapphires to the side.

This style of ring was often worn on the little finger.

c1935   1in (2.5cm) high

£3,000-4,000   **MACK**

An Art Deco Burmese platinum ring, set with rubies and diamonds.

c1935   1in (2.5cm) high

£7,000-10,000   **MACK**

An Art Deco platinum Van Cleef and Arpels calibré ruby ring.

c1940   1in (2.5cm) high

£4,000-6,000   **MACK**

An Art Deco platinum and ruby ring, signed by F. Folgert.

c1940   0.75in (2cm) high

£2,500-3,000   **MACK**

An Art Deco diamond, ruby and platinum ring, by Oscar Heyman, diamonds 50ct.

c1950   1in (2.5cm) high

£5,000-8,000   **MACK**

An Edgar Brandt necklace, with a mistletoe design, signed.

This is an extremely rare piece as Brandt, who specialised in ironwork, made jewellery only in his early years. Only two pieces of jewellery by Brandt are known to have come to market. The Brandt family also have some examples and other pieces were photographed during the period.

c1905

3.25in (8.5cm) high

£12,000-18,000   **MOD**

An Art Deco pendant, by Edgar Brandt.

c1925   2in (5cm) high

£7,000-10,000   **MOD**

An Art Deco platinum bracelet, set with old European-cut diamonds and French-cut sapphires.

c1925   7in (18cm) long

£12,000-18,000   **MACK**

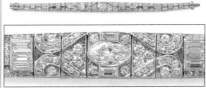

An Art Deco platinum bracelet, set with 32ct diamonds and emeralds.

c1925   7in (18cm) long

£18,000-22,000   **MACK**

An Art Deco articulated platinum bracelet, set with mixed-cut diamonds and hand-cut rubies.

c1935   7in (18cm) long

£40,000-45,000   **MACK**

An Art Deco celluloid bangle in shape of a serpent, with diamanté details.

c1930   3in (7.5cm) diam

£70-90   **TDG**

A gilt metal headdress, in Egyptian style, with a serpent.

c1920   7in (18cm) diam

£300-400   **TDG**

A pair of Art Deco earrings, with large central diamonds.

c1920   2.25in (6cm) long

£20,000-25,000   **MACK**

A pair of Art Deco diamond and sapphire pendant earrings.

c1925   2.5in (6.5cm) long

£12,000-18,000   **MACK**

A Cartier black onyx and diamond round dress set, in Art Deco style, comprising a pair of twin-panel cufflinks, four buttons and two collar studs, the buttons and two of the cufflink panels engraved "Cartier", the studs stamped "18c", in a case.

£4,000-6,000   **DN**

A Mexican silver bracelet, with green gem.

c1940   9in (23cm) long

£180-220   **TDG**

A 20thC amber bead necklace, with beads of varying size.

40in (101cm) long

£450-500   **TDG**

A 1950s brooch, silver metal formed as a stylized figure.

£120-180   **MOD**

An Arts and Crafts mahogany bookcase, by Shapland and Petter of Barnstaple, the cavetto frieze with applied and embossed copper foliage, with leaded glazed doors and linen fold panelled doors, on square supports, inscribed "Reading Maketh a Full Man".

84.5in (211cm) high

£3,000-4,000   **L&T**

An Arts and Crafts oak bookcase, in the manner of the Scottish school, by Wylie and Lochhead of Glasgow, with stained glass floral panels flanked by angular stylized copper repoussé panels, above drawers and a bottom cabinet.

c1900   *72in (183cm) high*

£6,000–8,000   **PUR**

A Cotswolds Arts and Crafts oak compendium, retailed by Heal and Son, with a chest of drawers, bookcase and wardrobe.

79in (197.5cm) high

£400-600   **FRE**

An Arts and Crafts standing oak bookcase, retailed by Liberty & Co., of three tiers, with stylized floral repoussé panels and cut-outs to the sides.

c1905   *35in (89cm) high*

£500–800   **PUR**

An Arts and Crafts oak bookcase, by Harris Lebus, the flaring cornice with shaped supports, open bookcase and drop-down writing surface, above a single drawer with stylized heart fretwork to the sides and two open bookshelves below.

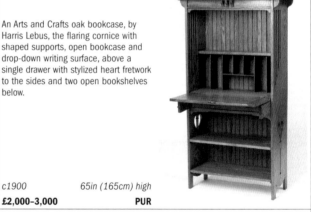

c1900   *65in (165cm) high*

£2,000–3,000   **PUR**

CABINETS

An Arts and Crafts oak bookcase, retailed by Liberty & Co., with adjustable shelves, stylized heart fretwork at the top, three long top shelves and a single central bottom cabinet flanked by two small short shelves.

c1900   *70in (70cm) high*

£18,000–22,000   **PUR**

An Arts and Crafts oak music cabinet, attributed to Bruce Talbert for Gillows of Lancaster.

c1885   *43in (109cm) high*

£1,500-2,000   **PUR**

An Arts and Crafts mahogany music cabinet in the Anglo-Japanese style, with string ebony and boxwood inlay.

c1895   *49in (125cm) wide*

£3,000-4,000   **PUR**

An Arts and Crafts mahogany bow-front cabinet, by Shapland and Petter of Barnstaple, with boxwood stringing, mother-of-pearl and abalone inlay, and a glazed door flanked by glazed panels.

75in (191cm) high

£800-1,200 DN

An Arts and Crafts champagne drinks cabinet, attributed to Liberty & Co., with carved square detailing and a painted Dickensian figure on one side, copper serving top.

c1900 *44.5in (113cm) high*

£1,200-1,800 PUR

An Arts and Crafts mahogany display cabinet, attributed to Ernest Archibald Taylor, of architectural form, with silver-plated repoussé fenestration, a butterfly centrepiece and floral designs in sycamore and tulipwood inlay.

c1905 *69in (175cm) high*

£8,000-10,000 PUR

An Arts and Crafts oak cabinet, designed by Sir Robert Lorimer, with three sloping hinged falls enclosing compartments, supported on curved brackets, the rectangular top above drawers, each with a curved handle.

52.5in (129cm) wide

£2,000-3,000 L&T

An overpainted and leaded glass table cabinet, attributed to E. A. Taylor, the moulded cornice above a single door with leaded and glazed panel depicting a flowering rose.

14.5in (37cm) high

£600-900 L&T

SIDEBOARDS

An Arts and Crafts ebonised oak bureau, the shaped three-quarter gallery with pierced sides enclosing an open shelf above a fall with decorative silvered hinges, with an open shelf and two panelled doors.

54.75in (134.5cm) wide

£180-220 L&T

An Arts and Crafts mahogany sideboard, by Shapland and Petter, with embossed and stylized copper floral repoussé upper panel, twin bevelled mirrors and curved drawers above cupboards with ring-pull handles.

c1905 *68in (173cm) high*

£3,000–5,000 PUR

An Arts and Crafts mahogany buffet, with a curved top carved with foliage, shelves and a mirror, slender spindles and panels pierced with hearts, frieze drawers with floral metal pulls, and cupboards with carved floral motifs.

60in (152cm) wide

£600-900 DN

An Arts and Crafts oak and inlaid sideboard, by Wylie and Lochhead of Glasgow, with mirrored back and open shelves, the base with bow-front top, drawers and inlaid doors, with maker's label.

75.25in (188cm) high

£800-1,200 L&T

An Arts and Crafts sideboard, designed by E.A. Taylor for Wylie and Lochhead of Glasgow, with a marquetry panel depicting a knight before a medieval castle in flames.

c1900   70in (170cm) wide

£8,000–10,000   **PUR**

A CLOSER LOOK AT AN ARTS AND CRAFTS SIDEBOARD

Godwin worked on commissions from many of the great and good in his lifetime, including studios for Princess Louise and James Whistler, a house and costumes for actress Lily Langtry, and interiors for Oscar Wilde.

Godwin's celebrated Anglo-Japanese styling can clearly be seen in this sideboard, especially in the pagoda-style detailing and the use of lacquer panels.

The lacquer panels are decorated with trees and birds, in imitation of the Japanese style.

Godwin was keen to make his furniture as light as possible. Combined with the delicate fretwork, that makes this a fragile piece that has survived in remarkably good condition.

An Arts and Crafts Anglo-Japanese mahogany sideboard, designed by E.W. Godwin and made by William Watts, with Japanese lacquer panels set in embossed leather, lattice top with pagoda-style detailing, two drawers flanked by lacquer panels, engraved handles, hinges and escutcheons, on splayed feet.

1878   50in (127cm) wide

£80,000-100,000   **PUR**

WYLIE AND LOCHHEAD

- In 1829 brothers-in-law Robert Wylie and James Lochhead founded a company in Glasgow to retail furniture and upholstery. In the 1860s the firm became increasingly involved in designing and producing their own products, establishing workshops at Kent Road and Mitchell Street.
- Wylie and Lochhead produced stylish but commercial and affordable Arts and Crafts furnishings for the middle classes. Typical Wylie and Lochhead furniture is in solid oak, with stylized inlaid detail and cut-out or carved decoration.
- Many talented craftsmen and designers produced pieces for the firm, including George Logan and Ernest Archibald Taylor, husband of illustrator and jewellery designer Jessie M. King. Shapland and Petter also supplied them with stock.
- The company survived until 1957, when it became part of The House of Fraser.

An Arts and Crafts ebonized sideboard by Collcut, with bone inlay.

54in (137cm) high

£3,000-5,000   **PUR**

DRESSING TABLES

A William Watt ash dressing table, designed by E.W. Godwin, the top with hinged extensions and fold-out supports, drawers with brass handles, and an enamelled metal 'Heirloom' label, together with an en-suite washstand table, some damage.

39.5in (100cm) wide

£10,000-15,000 set   **WW**

An Arts and Crafts walnut lady's desk, by Shapland and Petter, with a leather writing surface and a stained glass back panel with stylized floral motifs, above two drawers and a shaped slatted bottom gallery.

1903   42in (107cm) wide

£2,000-2,500   **PUR**

A Gordon Russell 'Ilmington' cherrywood dressing table, designed by W.H. Russell, with hinged triptych mirror, semi-bowed twin pedestals and oak-lined drawers with inset handles, bears maker's label.

This dressing table design differs from the standard stock and was probably made as a special commission for a client.

c1935   54.75in (137cm) wide

£800-1,200   **L&T**

An Arts and Crafts iron stick stand, in the Anglo-Japanese style.

30in (76cm) high

£3,000-4,000   PUR

An Arts and Crafts oak umbrella stand, by Shapland and Petter, with copper thistle repoussé panel, single drawer, three shaped spindles and central heart cut-out to the slatted bottom gallery, raised on square capped supports.

c1905   43in (109cm) high

£700-1,000   PUR

An Arts and Crafts oak stick stand, by Shapland and Petter, with stylized upper and lower copper floral repoussé panels, three umbrella compartments and lower slatted front and sides, raised on square supports.

c1905   41in (106cm) high

£1,200-1,800   PUR

An Arts and Crafts oak stick stand, retailed by Liberty & Co., with three compartments each decorated with a pierced heart, on capped feet.

c1905   32.5in (83cm) high

£300-400   PUR

An Arts and Crafts Gothic Revival oak hallstand, with angular pediment and stylized floral cut-outs above a mirror, butterfly fretwork detail at top corners, a row of tiles by Christopher Dresser above the serving area and a central drawer flanked by two Star of David roundels, raised on ring-turned front legs with ebony dot detailing.

c1880   97in (246cm) high

£2,000-3,000   PUR

An Arts and Crafts hallstand, by Harris Lebus, with dentil cornice above stylized floral carvings, with central mirror above a panel of tiles, stylized tubular floral motifs, seven stylized coat hooks, and central drawer flanked by side stick compartments, on stile feet.

c1905   82.5in (210cm) high

£2,000-2,500   PUR

An Arts and Crafts Gothic Revival oak hall seat with central mirror, ebonized floral details at the top and sides and chevron inlays to the front edges, with six ring-turned coat hooks and a lift-up store seat, raised on stile feet.

c1880   85in (216cm) high

£2,000-3,000   PUR

An Arts and Crafts oak hallrobe by Shapland and Petter, with classical carved panels at the top, stylized copper hinges and handles, and fitted interior.

c1905   82in (209cm) high

£2,500-3,500   PUR

WARDROBES

An Arts and Crafts oak wardrobe, by Brown and Lamont of Chester, of joined type construction with chamfered edges, two parquetry doors with pierced brass hinges, sliding trays and hanging space above two short drawers.

83.5in (212cm) high

£1,200-1,800   DN

An Arts and Crafts oak wardrobe by Maple and Co., in the form of a house, the roof-shaped cornice with stylized eaves.

86in (220cm) high

£400-600   DN

An Arts and Crafts mahogany wardrobe, designed by Barry Parker and Sir Raymond Unwin for Goodall, Lamb and Heighway Ltd. of Manchester, the doors with tongue-and-groove panelling and plant-form cut-outs, the canted sides with leaded glass doors, the doors containing shelves and drawers, with beaten copper fittings, raised on a plinth.

This wardrobe once belonged to the designer and ceramicist Clarice Cliff and stood in the bedroom of 'Chetwynd', her house in Northwood, Staffordshire. Designed by Parker and Unwin between 1899 and 1902 for C.F. Goodfellow, the house was bought and renamed in 1926 by Colley Shorter who lived there with his first wife before his marriage to Clarice Cliff in 1940. Clarice Cliff remained at 'Chetwynd' until her death in 1972.

8.75in (220cm) wide

£2,000-3,000　　　　　　　　　　　　**L&T**

A three-fold Arts and Crafts oak screen with brass disc detailing and gilded leather panels embossed with grapes, lemons, apples and passion fruit.

69in (175cm) high

£8,000–12,000　　　　　　　　　**PUR**

A CLOSER LOOK AT A MORRIS & CO. SCREEN

The combination of well-worked wood and attractive silk embroidery make this an important and appealing document of the work done by Morris & Co.

Each of these three silk panels is decorated with a different pattern, significantly enhancing the interest of this piece. J.H. Dearle's textile designs for Morris & Co. were among the best they produced.

This piece could be put to practical use in a contemporary setting, perhaps to divide a large loft-style interior. Utility will invariably increase the value of an antique.

The pierced detail on these panels is typical of Arts and Crafts furniture, with decoration primarily used to display the skill of the maker and highlight the inherent charm of the wood.

A Morris & Co. three-fold mahogany draught screen, each fold with a silkwork embroidered glazed panel, possibly designed by J. H. Dearle, with foliage worked in coloured silks, enclosed by a frame with shaped top and finials, the frieze below decorated with waved piercings, on turned feet.

74.75in (187cm) high

£13,000-15,000　　　　　　　　　**L&T**

An embroidered oak framed firescreen, the embroidered panel depicting two peacocks.

33.5in (84cm) high

£220-280　　　　　　　**WW**

A two-fold firescreen, in the style of Morris & Co., embroidered with panels of flowers and foliage.

40in (100cm) high

£280-320　　　　　　　**WW**

CHAIRS

A leather-upholstered armchair by Ogden Farago.

c1900　　　　　　*41.5in (105.5cm) high*

£3,000-5,000　　　　　　　　　　**LM**

E.W. GODWIN

- Edward William Godwin was an architect who designed furniture in the mid-19thC. His work is characterized by careful choice of materials and meticulous construction – the central tenets of the Arts and Crafts movement.
- Godwin embraced Japanese principles of design, as is evident in the balance of vertical and horizontal members in his furniture.
- His distinctive furniture is elegant, with a light touch and refined proportions.
- Ebonized woods were left unadorned, or else simply decorated with inset panels of embossed Japanese paper. A few pieces bear painted or stencilled stylized geometric patterns.
- Godwin submitted his designs for production by various cabinet-makers, including William Watt, John Gregory Crace, and the firm of Collinson and Lock.
- Furniture by Godwin is unmarked, making attribution problematic. Surviving sketches have helped identify a number of his designs.

An Arts and Crafts Anglo-Japanese armchair, by E.W. Godwin, with lattice details to the back support centred with an embossed leather back.

c1875   *40in (101.5cm) high*

£4,000-6,000   **PUR**

An Arts and Crafts oak armchair, attributed to E.W. Godwin, with slatted back and sides, and embossed leather back support.

c1875   *44in (112cm) high*

£3,000-4,000   **PUR**

An Arts and Crafts Jacobean ebonized all-round stretcher armchair, by E.W. Godwin.

c1875   *34in (86.5cm) high*

£2,000-3,000   **PUR**

An Arts and Crafts office chair, by E.W. Godwin.

40in (101.5cm) high

£4,000-6,000   **PUR**

An Arts and Crafts oak open armchair, possibly for Heal & Son, with a pierced splat and a padded seat.

£220-280   **DN**

A Swedish birch armchair, designed by Carl Malmsten.

c1900   *23.5in (60cm) wide*

£2,000-3,000   **LANE**

A Morris & Co. 'Sussex' ash armchair with rush seat, damaged.

33.5in (85cm) high

£280-320   **WW**

One of two similar late 19thC ebonized elbow chairs, by Morris and Co., each with a spindle back and caned seat.

34in (86cm) high

£120-180 pair   **DN**

A Morris & Co. 'Rossetti' chair, the design attributed to Dante Gabriel Rossetti, damaged.

35.5in (89cm) high

£150-200   **WW**

A mahogany armchair in the style of E.W. Godwin, possibly manufactured by James Peddle, with retailer's mark

35.25in (88cm) high

£300-400   **WW**

DECORATIVE ARTS

An Arts and Crafts mahogany revolving chair, by James Peddle, attributed to E.W. Godwin, with curved slatted back and shaped seat on tripulitic legs.

c1880   *34in (86.5cm) high*

£1,000–2,000   **PUR**

An Arts and Crafts walnut armchair, by E. Punnet for William Birch of High Wycombe, the shaped back with stylized heart cut-out, slatted sides, solid bow-fronted seat, and elongated square tapering legs, on sledge feet.

c1905   *32in (82cm) high*

£2,000–3,000   **PUR**

A 'Gnomeman' oak armchair, with leather seat and carved gnome, signed.

36in (90cm) high

£250-300   **WW**

A pair of Arts and Crafts ladder-back dining room chairs with rush seats, associated with Charles Rennie Mackintosh.

c1895   *46in (117cm) high*

£3,000–5,000   **PUR**

One of a set of six Arts and Crafts mahogany dining room chairs, designed by George Walton.

c1900   *38in (96cm) high*

£1,500-2,000 set   **PUR**

One of six oak and leather dining chairs by Robert 'Mouseman' Thompson, each carved with a mouse signature.

34in (85cm) high

£2,800-3,200 set   **FRE**

A CLOSER LOOK AT A MORRIS & CO. CHAIR

Ebonizing was one of the few treatments that Morris & Co. used, as it enhanced rather than disguised the grain and texture of the woods the company worked with.

The original upholstery adds a great deal of value to this chair, as it is the most perishable part. This 'Bird' pattern is typical of Morris & Co. textile designs, and was very popular in its day.

The slatted sides and long, curving back legs that meet the front seat rail are classic components of the William Morris chair.

An Arts and Crafts walnut armchair, designed by Philip Webb for Morris & Co., with original fabric upholstery depicting birds, of ebonized wood, with slatted sides.

c1865   *36.5in (92cm) high*

£7,000-10,000   **PUR**

A Heal & Son rush-seated oak child's chair, of slat back form.

36in (90cm) high

£80-120   **WW**

A mahogany chair, retailed by Liberty & Co., the back carved with a Celtic panel, with original paper label.

40.5in (101cm) high

£600-900   **WW**

A Swedish birch side chair, designed by Carl Malmsten.

c1900   17.75in (45cm) wide

£800-1,200   LANE

A Morris & Co. 'Sussex' chair, in ebonized beech, the spindle-filled back above a rush seat on turned legs.

£200-300   L&T

An Arts and Crafts mahogany high-backed side chair, by Shapland and Petter, in the Glasgow style, with a cherub head in pewter on the central slat, the upholstered seat not original.

c1905   42in (107cm) high

£1,000-1,500   PUR

A late 19thC Arts and Crafts walnut side chair, in the manner of George Walton or Arthur Simpson, with curved top rail, heart-pierced splat, and rush seat.

£350-400   DN

SHAPLAND AND PETTER

■ Cabinet-maker Henry Shapland initially founded his furniture company c1855 at Barnstable in Devon. Accountant Henry Petter soon joined Shapland, and the firm rapidly expanded.

■ Shapland had been impressed by an innovative wave-moulding machine on a trip to America. He recreated this technology on his return, and his company continued to combine sophisticated machine production with skilled hand craftsmanship.

■ Shapland and Petter's Arts and Crafts pieces are typically in mahogany or oak with inlaid decoration and carving. Designs often feature piercing, arches, stained panels and cabochons.

■ Shapland and Petter employees trained for many years to become fully qualified. Their mastery is evident in the work they produced for the company. The quality of their designs brought commissions from highly regarded retailers such as Morris & Co

■ When the market for hand-finished furniture declined after WWII, the firm began to focus on producing functional items.

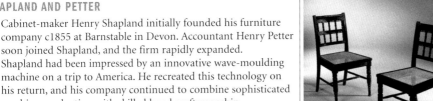

A pair of 19thC ebonized side chairs, designed by Bruce Talbert, the curved spindle-filled back above a caned seat on turned and tapering legs linked by stretchers.

£180-220   L&T

A Morris & Co. 'Sussex' sofa, in ebonised beech, with spindle back, horizontally spindled open arms above later cord seat, on turned legs linked by stretchers.

54.75in (137cm) wide

£600-900   L&T

An Arts and Crafts Moorish settee, retailed by Liberty & Co.

c1890   34in (86.5cm) high

£2,000-3,000   PUR

An Arts and Crafts settee, designed by George Jack for Morris & Co.

c1900   37in (94cm) high

£6,000-8,000   PUR

A Scottish Arts and Crafts stained pine and pokerwork decorated hall settle, with moulded top rail, tongue-and-groove back decorated with coloured pokerwork roses, and electroplated seat on square supports, with rose and chequer decoration and decorative brackets.

74.75in (187cm) wide

£1,500-2,000   L&T

An Arts and Crafts cast-iron garden bench, by Christopher Dresser for the Coalbrooke Dale, with an intricate and stylized floral cut-out panel.

c1875   76in (193cm) wide

£7,000-10,000   PUR

655

DECORATIVE ARTS

A Swedish birch bench, designed by Carl Malmsten.

Malmsten (1888-1972) was an important Swedish designer who promoted a more craft-orientated and functional approach to furniture design.

c1900   14.25in (36cm) wide

£500-800   **LANE**

An oak stool with embroidered seat, the uprights with overhanging arm rails, linked by a single stretcher

24.5in (61cm) wide

£80-120   **WW**

A Scott Morton oak stool, designed by Sir Robert Lorimer, with chamfered shaped trestle ends joined by a waved stretcher with exposed peg joints, bears maker's label.

17.5in (44cm) wide

£600-900   **L&T**

A pair of Arts and Crafts oak Thebes stools, retailed by Liberty & Co., with carved Egyptian and astrological motifs.

c1890   13.5in (34cm) high

£2,000–3,000   **PUR**

TABLES

A French 1930s limed oak dining table.

59in (150cm) wide

£2,500-3,000   **LM**

A mahogany side table, in the style of M.H. Baillie Scott, the circular top inlaid to the edge.

29.25in (73cm) high

£200-300   **WW**

A CLOSER LOOK AT AN ARTS AND CRAFTS TABLE

The simple, robust form of the table is typical of Webb's Gothic sensibility.

The symmetrical form of the table and its stretchers mean that it retains its aesthetic interest from every angle.

This table was commissioned by Sir William Beale for use at Drumlamford House in Ayrshire. The link to this illustrious family provides this piece with solid provenance.

Philip Webb designed this table while working for Morris & Co. An architect by trade, Webb also produced important designs for interiors, including metalware, furniture and textiles.

A large Morris & Co. mahogany dining table, designed in the 1860s by Philip Webb, the oval top with incised edge above a central turned support surrounded by six ring-turned legs linked by ring-turned stretchers.

Provenance: *Sir William Beale was the Liberal M.P. for Galloway. His younger brother James Beale commissioned Philip Webb to build 'Standen' at East Grinstead in 1891 and he in turn engaged Morris & Co. to furnish the interior with textiles, wallpapers and furnishings. William Morris became a personal friend of the Beale family and consequently his influence can be felt at all of their residences, including 32 Holland Park in London, 'Bryntirion' near Dongelan in Wales, and 'Drumlamford' in South Ayrshire.*

70.5in (176cm) long

£35,000-40,000   **L&T**

A pair of Arts and Crafts side tables by E.W. Godwin for Heal & Son, with open fretwork and staggered shelves, in the Anglo-Japanese style.

c1890   Tallest 27in (68.5cm) high

£2,500-3,000   **PUR**

An Arts and Crafts mahogany occasional table, probably Heal & Son, with chequer banding, the rectangular top above an arched frieze and single drawer raised on six square supports linked by stretchers and raised on a trestle base.

39.5in (99cm) long

£500-800   **L&T**

An Arts and Crafts rosewood side table, by Collinson and Lock.

27in (68.5cm) wide

£5,000-6,000   **PUR**

An Arts and Crafts ash bobbin side table, by E.W. Godwin.

22in (56cm) high

£1,500-2,500   **PUR**

An Arts and Crafts walnut three-leg bobbin side table, by E.W. Godwin.

22in (56cm) high

£2,000-2,500   **PUR**

An Arts and Crafts rosewood side table, in the style of William Morris.

26in (66cm) high

£4,000-6,000   **PUR**

A white painted Arts and Crafts occasional table, the rectangular top with moulded edge above square tapering legs linked by a lower stretcher and with pierced heart supports to the sides.

21.5in (55cm) high

£120-180   **L&T**

STANDS

An Arts and Crafts whatnot, attributed to Philip Webb for Morris & Co.

c1855   *60in (152.5cm) high*

£6,000-8,000   **PUR**

A Liberty and Co. oak étagere designed by Leonard Wyburd, the top above two lower galleried tiers linked by turned and blocked supports, the sides with latticed grilles, on bobbin-turned legs linked by stretchers.

31.25in (78cm) high

£400-600   **L&T**

An Arts and Crafts walnut plant stand, retailed by Liberty & Co., in the Anglo-Moorish style, with ebonized Moorish brackets and mushrabia bobbin turnings, on an angled kickout.

c1890   *33in (84cm) high*

£1,000-1,500   **PUR**

MIRRORS

An Arts and Crafts copper mirror, retailed by Liberty & Co., with six turquoise Ruskin pottery roundels and stylized floral embossing to the frame.

c1900   *19in (48cm) long*

£800–1,200   **PUR**

An Arts and Crafts Glasgow School repoussé brass mirror, with interlaced Celtic details.

c1905   *22.5in (57cm) long*

£1,200–1,500   **PUR**

An Arts and Crafts oak swing mirror, in a plain rectangular frame, held between two tapering uprights, on splayed feet united by a stretcher.

23.25in (59cm) high

£120-180   **DN**

An Arts and Crafts ebonized burr and walnut mirror, with painted top.

c1885   *32in (81.5cm) high*

£2,000-3,000   **PUR**

DECORATIVE ARTS

A pair of Arts and Crafts embossed metal fireplaces, the central roundels depicting peacocks with spread feathers.

36in (91.5cm) high

£3,000-5,000   **PUR**

An Arts and Crafts oak cradle, attributed to Sir Robert Lorimer, with spindle gallery, thistle finials and a canopy, the sides carved in bas relief with circular panels of animals, on a rocker base with scrollwork carving.

36in (91cm) long

£1,500-2,000   **L&T**

An Arts and Crafts iron radiator cover with ornate grillwork.

60in (152.5cm) wide

£2,500-3,000   **PUR**

A stained birch day bed, designed by Charles Rennie Mackintosh for the Ladies' Common Room in the Glasgow School of Art, with open arms and loose squab cushion upholstered in dark grey corduroy, raised on block feet with applied panels, restored.

c1910   *85.5in (214cm) long*

£7,000-9,000   **L&T**

A pine easel, designed by Charles Rennie Mackintosh for the Glasgow School of Art, of tapering outline with horizontal and vertical adjustable supports.

This very tall easel was designed to compliment the spacious interiors of the studios in the Glasgow School of Art. This example retains all of its original features.

c1910   *83.25in (208cm) high*

£3,000-5,000   **L&T**

An Arts and Crafts brass gong, by E.W. Godwin, with 'pagoda' frame.

30in (76cm) high

£6,000-8,000   **PUR**

AESTHETIC MOVEMENT

An Aesthetic movement oak wall cabinet, of semi-bowed form, the spindle galleried surmount above two central glazed doors and two doors with panels of flowers painted in colours and gilt, supported by decorative brackets.

53.25in (133cm) wide

£2,200-2,800   **L&T**

An Aesthetic Movement fireplace, by Talbert Thomas Jeckyll, with side tile panels.

£5,000-6,000   **PUR**

An Aesthetic Movement ebonized coal helmet, designed by Christopher Dresser, of triangular form with hinged sloping lid, with brass carrying handle and detachable coal shovel.

21.25in (53cm) deep

£400-600   **L&T**

A Gothic Revival oak armchair, in the style of Charles Bevan, with entrelac scrolled terminals, the leather upholstered swing seat with curved armrests and adjustable front legs carved with trefoil roundels, the rear legs linked by stretchers.

£1,200-1,800   **L&T**

AESTHETIC MOVEMENT

- The Aesthetic Movement flourished during the last 40 years of the 19thC, when it evolved as a reaction against the strict morality of Victorian art and design.
- The Aesthetes valued art for its own sake, prioritizing beauty over social purpose and function.
- Influences were diverse, ranging from Oriental to Moorish design and incorporating elements of the Pre-Raphelite and Gothic Revival movements.
- Earlier Aesthetic Movement pieces tend to be simple in form while later designs are characterised by a more decadent style.
- Key figures associated with the movement are the writer Oscar Wilde and the artist James McNeill Whistler.

An octagonal occasional table in the manner of Bugatti.

58cm (23in) wide

£1,800-2,200   LC

A corner chair in the manner of Bugatti.

£1,800-2,200   LC

A Carlo Bugatti side chair, in wood, copper, parchment, rope, pewter and bone, label of "C.LONATI - FIRENZE" under seat, restored.

36in (90cm) high

£2,800-3,200   FRE

A Carlo Bugatti stool, in wood, pewter, bone and wool, upholstered with a Soumac rug, some losses.

18in (45cm) high

£1,200-1,800   FRE

CARLO BUGATTI

- Carlo Bugatti was an Italian designer trained at Brera Academy of Fine Arts who worked c1880-1910. He was to become the head of a very creative household, with a sculptor and a legendary automobile designer as sons.
- Bugatti's prodigious output included metalware, textiles and ceramics, but it is for his furniture that he is most remembered today.
- Celebrated in his day, Bugatti was the recipient of a silver medal at the Exposition Universelle in Paris in 1900. His work is currently enjoying a revival in popularity after a period of relative neglect.
- Bugatti's work is indebted to the writing of Eugène Viollet-le-Duc, in particular his ideas on the use of decorative elements to draw attention to rather than disguise the structure of a piece.
- Some of the materials used by Bugatti were unorthodox – he incorporated brass, bone, silk and parchment into his furniture design.

MOORISH STYLE

- Notable for his rejection of the predominant European tradition of design, Bugatti instead looked to the East, especially to Islamic and Oriental cultures, for his inspiration.
- The use of ropework and tassels of silk and wool highlights the strong Moroccan influence running through Bugatti's design. Moorish forms, such as small side tables with multi-sided tops, also feature strongly in his work.
- Dark woods offset by bold colours and strong, geometric designs are also features of Moroccan furniture design that Bugatti appropriated in the search for his own unique aesthetic.

A Carlo Bugatti low table, in wood, copper, pewter, bone and parchment.

38.5in (96cm) wide

£3,500-4,500   FRE

A Carlo Bugatti settee, in wood, parchment, copper and pewter.

47in (117.5cm) long

£3,500-4,500   FRE

CABINETS

A Scottish School Art Nouveau mahogany sideboard, the central concave drawer with arched mouldings, enclosed by four drawers above panelled doors flanking a void and raised on bracket feet.

43in (109cm) high

£200-300   L&T

A Louis Majorelle oak pantry, with a two-door lower part divided by carved columns and a glazed two-door display case on curved consoles, part of an eight-piece dining room suite also including an extendable table and six upholstered chairs.

c1900   *100in (250cm) high*

£1,000-1,500 set   QU

An Art Nouveau mahogany and inlaid display cabinet, by Shapland and Petter, the D-shaped top with spindled gallery centred by a shelf and floral marquetry plaque, with glazed doors, on square legs and feet.

70in (175cm) high

£2,800-3,200   L&T

DECORATIVE ARTS

An Art Nouveau dressing chest, with a rectangular mirror above three short and one long drawer on square supports linked by a platform stretcher, part of a suite along with a three-drawer wardrobe.

45in (114cm) wide

£400-600 set   **L&T**

An Art Nouveau mahogany writing desk, the rectangular top above an asymmetrical glazed door and open shelf with heart piercings and a sloping fall, the sides pierced with tulips, on a stile base with bracket supports.

56.75in (144cm) high

£450-550   **L&T**

A CLOSER LOOK AT AN ART NOUVEAU ARMCHAIR

This slender chair frame with its sweeping curves is an excellent example of high Art Nouveau furniture.

Many dealers and collectors would prefer to buy a chair like this in unrestored condition, rather than one that has mismatched replaced upholstery.

A pair of Art Nouveau armchairs, by J.S. Henry, each with a mahogany frame, the tall backs with leaf finials above curving open arms, on turned and tapering legs linked by stretchers, one bearing a maker's label.

£1,800-2,200   **L&T**

An early J. and J. Kohn side chair, with bentwood back and tapering legs, by Josef Hoffmann, with four spheres under the seat rail, and tacked-on brown leather upholstery, the stamp mark obscured.

38.75in (98.5cm) high

£800-1,200   **SDR**

Jallot's monogram signature is visible here, as the upholstery is missing. The mark of such a revered designer cannot fail to enhance value.

The exquisite sculpting on these front rails has acquired a fine patina and is free of chips and other losses.

A French Art Nouveau sculpted armchair, by Leon Jallot.
c1910   *32in (81.5cm) high*

£9,000-11,000   **LM**

TABLES

A French Art Nouveau Ecolé de Nancy tea table, in walnut, brass and glass, with a tray top and four fold-down sides.

c1900   *31.5in (79cm) wide*

£700-900   **FRE**

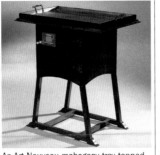

An Art Nouveau mahogany tray-topped tea table, with brass carrying handles and a pewter and copper inlaid panel depicting a teacup and saucer.

29in (74cm) high

£320-380   **L&T**

An Art Nouveau mahogany foldover card table, probably by J.S. Henry, inlaid with stylized bands in specimen woods, brass, copper and mother-of-pearl.

27.25in (68cm) high

£1,200-1,800   **L&T**

A giltwood 'Aubepin' occasional table by Louis Majorelle, the circular marble top above moulded frieze and tapering moulded legs with foliate carving.

32in (81cm) high

£1,200-1,800   **L&T**

An Austrian or German Jugendstil glazed ceramic tile-top table, unknown cabinet maker's stamp, original finish.

c1900 29.5in (74cm) high

£1,000-1,500 FRE

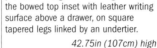

An Art Nouveau oak writing desk, with pierced brass grilles and ledge back, the bowed top inset with leather writing surface above a drawer, on square tapered legs linked by an undertier.

42.75in (107cm) high

£1,000-1,500 L&T

An Art Nouveau steel and applied brass duet stand, the music stops with sunburst decoration, applied candle sconces with cast and embossed leaf and floral decorations, on a tripod base with whiplash foliate embellishments.

49.5in (126cm) high

£1,200-1,800 L&T

An Art Nouveau mahogany jardinière stand, the canted square tapering supports linked by two further tiers and with decorative bracket supports.

47.25in (120cm) high

£120-180 L&T

A Gallé wooden marquetry tray, depicting elephants and banana trees, signed "Gallé" in marquetry.

22.75in (58cm) wide

£2,000-2,500 JDJ

An Art Nouveau gilt and gesso picture frame, moulded with a fringe of waterlilies and whiplash foliage on a ribbed ground.

37.5in (95cm) wide

£280-320 L&T

CABINETS

A Swedish Art Deco sideboard in birch, with typical Swedish sunburst motif and detailing in ebony and dark and light mahogany.

c1930 59in (150cm) wide

£2,500-3,000 LANE

A Swedish Art Deco bookcase in birch with fleur-de-lys detail to top.

c1920 39.25in (100cm) wide

£1,000-1,500 LANE

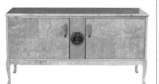

A Swedish Art Deco sideboard in birch, with ebony and burled ash detailing, the geometric dark wood motif influenced by Asian style.

c1930 59in (150cm) wide

£1,500-2,000 LANE

A red lacquer cabinet, by Maurice Jallot.

42in (106.5cm) wide

£4,000-6,000 LM

A cabinet by Guglielmo Ulrich of Milan, comprising a goat vellum-bound box on a rosewood veneered plinth, the doors with circular ivory fittings, the interior with a tuja-root veneer and fourteen drawers with ivory knobs.

c1930 60in (150cm) high

£3,000-4,000 QU

A wooden desk with a leather writing surface, by Maurice Jallot.

47in (119.5cm) wide

£5,000-6,000 **LM**

A desk by John Pascand, the surface and drawer fronts in blonde wood.

1931 *44.25in (112.5cm) wide*

£5,000-7,000 **LM**

A Swedish Art Deco desk in birch, marked with maker's name "A.B. Axel Beckmans Möbelfabrik, Norrköping".

c1930 *58.25in (148cm) wide*

£3,500-4,500 **LANE**

A Swedish Art Deco desk cabinet in rosewood and birch.

c1920 *35.5in (90cm) wide*

£2,000-2,500 **LANE**

A 1930s Belgian black lacquer desk and chair, by De Coene Frères.

68in (172.5cm) wide

£9,000-11,000 set **LM**

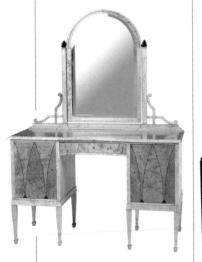

A Swedish Art Deco vanity unit, in birch with a mirror on top.

c1925 *47.75in (121cm) wide*

£2,000-2,500 **LANE**

An Art Deco skyscraper vanity unit.

c1930 *61in (155cm) high*

£1,200-1,800 **LOS**

A Swedish Art Deco birch vanity desk, of unusual design incorporating a lift-up desk, missing leg.

c1925 *35.75in (91cm) wide*

£1,200-1,800 **LANE**

One of a pair of Art Deco open armchairs with prominent reversed C-shape armrests on squat sabre legs.

c1930

£1,800-2,200 pair　　　　　**BL**

A Swedish Art Deco birch club chair, with curved arms and black leather upholstery.

c1930　　　*25.25in (64cm) wide*

£1,200-1,800　　　　　**LANE**

One of a pair of mid-1920s French Art Deco mahogany armchairs.

31.5in (80cm) high

£3,000-4,000 pair　　　　　**LM**

One of a pair of red chequered upholstered bridge chairs, by De Coene Frères.

c1930　　　*32.25in (82cm) high*

£2,000-2,500 pair　　　　　**LM**

A French wood and ropework chair by Wibo.

c1935

£600-900　　　　　**LM**

An Art Deco walnut framed three-piece suite, comprising a sofa and two armchairs, upholstered in red and buff uncut moquette, the backs and arms in walnut veneer, the arm uprights with fishscale carving, on stepped block feet.

Sofa 71.25in (178cm) wide

£2,500-3,000　　　　　**L&T**

One of a set of six Art Deco chairs with red plush upholstery fastened to the frame with studs, with scroll back and slightly outswept legs.

A Swedish Art Deco chair, with brown leather upholstery and burled elm and satinwood detailing to back.

c1925

24in (61cm) wide

£1,200-1,800　　　　　**LANE**

c1935　　　*35in (89cm) high*

£5,500-6,500 set　　　　　**LM**

One of a set of eight French chairs, with red leather upholstery.

c1935   *34.5in (87.5cm) high*
£7,000-10,000 set   **LM**

A Swedish Art Deco chair, with abstract design to roundel in central slat.

19in (48cm) wide
£400-600   **LANE**

One of a set of four American Art Deco patinated steel stools, with upholstered padded seats above pierced aprons cast with scrolling foliage, with maker's label "Edge-Lite, Chicago, Illinois".

£500-800 set   **L&T**

A Swedish Art Deco stool, with a leopard skin seat.

22.5in (57cm) wide
£400-600   **LANE**

A Belgian wood and cowhide vanity stool.

c1935   *6.25in (16cm) long*
£600-900   **LM**

An Art Deco three-seat sofa, its frame and loose seat cushions re-upholstered in blue patterned fabric with black trim, on black enamelled wood base, unmarked.

c1930   *80in (203cm) high*
£300-500   **SDR**

TABLES

A French mahogany dining table, by Michel Roux Spitz.

c1935   *39.5in (100.5cm) wide*
£5,500-6,500   **LM**

An Art Deco extendable dining table of exotic wood veneers inlaid with an oval band to top, on a double-pedestal base, unmarked.

80in (200cm) wide
£400-600   **SDR**

Part of an eleven-piece Art Deco dining suite in ebonized oak, consisting of a large double-pedestal dining table with rectangular top and ten dining chairs, each upholstered in lavender leather, unmarked.

98.5in (250cm) long
£3,000-4,000 set   **SDR**

A CLOSER LOOK AT AN ART DECO TABLE

Eugene Printz was an important French furniture designer who won numerous public commissions, including an office suite for the 1931 Exposition Coloniale Internationale.

This table has a strong but not overpowering design, making it ideal for use in any number of situations. This versatility makes it a desirable piece.

Limed oak is treated with a white pigment that fills the gaps in the grain of the timber. Originally used to prevent insect infestation, it became a fashionable decorative finish.

A Eugène Printz limed oak dining table, signed to the underside.

c1935   *50.5in (128.5cm) wide*
£25,000-27,000   **LM**

A CLOSER LOOK AT AN ART DECO TABLE

This table was part of a suite by Carl Malmsten. If it had a factory mark or signature its value would be doubled.

The table top is made of bookmatched birch, the four quadrants set at 45 degree angles so as to reflect light differently.

This stylized fleur-de-lys is inlaid in mahogany. It is indicative of earlier Art Deco with its freeform style.

This kind of symmetrical, geometric pattern, especially in monochrome, is a hallmark of a more mature Art Deco style.

A Swedish Art Deco birch occasional table, attributed to Carl Malmsten.

c1925 37.75in (96cm) wide
£2,000-2,500 **LANE**

A Swedish Art Deco birch table, with palisander veneer strips.

c1925 11.5in (29cm) wide
£1,200-1,800 **LANE**

A rectangular wooden coffee table in blonde wood.

c1940 31.5in (80cm) wide
£2,200-2,800 **LM**

A late 1940s French oak coffee table, with a black glass top.

32in (81.5cm) diam
£3,000-4,000 **LM**

A sculpted walnut and leather gueridon.

c1925 28.5in (72.5cm) diam
£2,500-3,000 **LM**

A Swedish Art Deco birch occasional table, with sunburst design to the top and chunky turned legs.

c1920 35.5in (90cm) wide
£1,000-1,500 **LANE**

A French round oak and leather table.

c1945 29.5in (75cm) diam
£3,000-3,500 **LM**

A 1940s French coffee table, with curved legs supported by pointed feet.

23.5in (59.5cm) diam
£3,000-3,500 **LM**

A Belgian end table with a mahogany coloured finish, inspired by Joseph Hoffmann's 'Fledermaus' model.

c1925 31in (78.5cm) high
£1,000-1,500 **LM**

A French Art Deco walnut marquetry gueridon.

c1935 24.25in (61.5cm) diam
£3,000-3,500 **LM**

A Swedish Art Deco birch table.

c1925 23.5in (60cm) wide
£700-1,000 **LANE**

A French padouk wood table.

c1925   31in (78.5cm) wide

£2,000-2,500   **LM**

An Belgian Art Deco lyre console, by De Coene Frères.

c1935   29.5in (75cm) high

£1,800-2,200   **LM**

An early 1930s rosewood coffee table, by De Coene Frères, with walnut veneer and chrome tubing.

24.5in (62cm) high

£1,200-1,800   **LM**

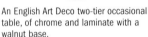

An English Art Deco two-tier occasional table, of chrome and laminate with a walnut base.

c1925   14.5in (36cm) wide

£800-1,200   **JK**

DE COENE FRÈRES

- De Coene Frères was a Belgian furniture manufacturer working during the inter-war period from Les Ateliers d'Art de Courtrai De Coene Frères in Brussels.
- The brothers specialized in producing elegantly designed furniture to extremely high standards, in contrast to the mass-produced Art Deco style that began to fill department stores as the movement gained momentum.
- High gloss finishes such as lacquer and polished veneers feature on a lot of De Coene furniture. They also used bright metals such as nickel and chrome to amplify this high sheen effect.
- Simple symmetry, and the contrast between straight lines and tight curves, are quintessential Art Deco motifs that the brothers made their own.
- The influence of tribal art and of Oriental aesthetics – both of which had an impact on the Art Deco scene – can be seen at work in some pieces by De Coene Frères.

A Swedish Art Deco sewing table in ash.

24in (61cm) wide

£800-1,200   **LANE**

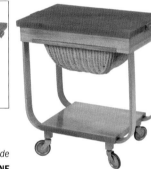

A Swedish Art Deco rectangular birch side table, with a black glass top.

c1930   26in (66cm) wide

£1,000-1,500   **LANE**

A rare Samuel Yellin wrought-iron side table, with a tripod base curled around a screw shaft and topped by a single four-sided tile covered in green crystalline glaze, fine original patina, stamped "Samuel Yellin 1933".

24in (60cm) high

£15,000-20,000   **DRA**

A Swedish Art Deco side table, in ash and dark wood, with curved edges.

13.5in (34cm) wide

£1,000-1,500   **LANE**

A pair of Art Deco style two-tier bedside tables, in blonde wood with ebonized supports and plinth bases.

24in (60cm) high

£300-400　　　　　　**S&K**

An Art Deco wood veneer and black lacquered mantelpiece of asymmetric design, with rectangular and round-edged pedestals, unmarked.

59.5in (151cm) wide

£700-900　　　　　　**SDR**

A pair of Swedish Art Deco birch bedside tables, with inlaid detailing and white marble tops.

15.75in (40cm) wide

£1,000-1,500　　　　　　**LANE**

A lacquer screen comprising four hinged panels, by Paul-Etienne Sain of France, of lacquered wood with brass fittings, signed in red "Paul Sain 32", some chipping.

63in (157.5cm) high

£3,000-5,000　　　　　　**FRE**

One of a pair of wooden lyre bedroom chests, with a single drawer.

c1920　　　　　　*23in (58.5cm) high*

£2,000-2,500 pair　　　　　　**LM**

A CLOSER LOOK AT A BOOKSHELF

These shelves are part of a suite with which Printz won a design competition in 1932. Other entrants included Emile Ruhlmann and Maurice Jallot.

The brief was to design a study and bedroom suite for halls of residence at La Cité Internationale Universitaire de Paris, an institution founded in the 1920s to provide international students in Paris with suitable lodgings.

The symmetrical design is very simple, allowing for relatively cheap construction. Printz made a virtue of the necessity to create something simple, and produced a very elegant, understated piece of work.

The elongated sides allowed for the storage of books above the cupboard.

A well-designed piece of furniture like this, in unrestored condition with an attractive patina, can be put to good use in a modern interior. This versatility increases desirability and, as a consequence, value.

Antique shelves or cabinets that have been modified to accommodate modern equipment, such as televisions, will invariably be worth less, particularly if these amendments are visible from the front.

One of a pair of bookshelves, designed by Eugène Printz for students' quarters at La Cité Internationale Universitaire de Paris.

1931　　　　　　*71in (180.5cm) wide*

£10,000-12,000 pair　　　　　　**LM**

Two of three Arts and Crafts crewelwork panels, each rectangular panel worked in coloured wools by Lady Phipson Beale, unbleached linen ground.

c1880   *largest 63.6in (159cm) wide*

£1,000-1,500   **L&T**

One of a set of eight Arts and Crafts crewelwork seat covers, worked in coloured wools by Lady Phipson Beale with sprays of flowering foliage on an unbleached linen ground.

Provenance: Sir William Phipson Beale, Drumlamford House, Ayrshire.

The Beale family became close friends with Morris after he was commissioned to design and furnish their East Grinstead home, Standen. Lady Phipson Beale was inspired by Morris' work and embroidered many pieces after his designs. One of a pair of Lady Phipson Beale's hangings in Morris' 'Artichoke' design now hangs in the Victoria and Albert Museum, London.

17.5in (44cm) high

£1,500-2,000 set   **L&T**

An Arts and Crafts embroidered panel, the design attributed to Walter Crane, possibly executed at the Royal School of Needlework, in ivory-coloured silks, with panels of winged putti, one holding a scrolling foliate branch, another resting beside a dolphin and a third feeding a plumed bird from a bowl, flanked by ribbons and foliage, framed and glazed.

51.25in (130cm) wide

£400-600   **DN**

A CLOSER LOOK AT A MORRIS TAPESTRY

A Glasgow school net panel, by Irene Cherry, depicting a stylized flower, framed, with a pencil inscription to the reverse.

Irene Cherry studied at the Glasgow School of Art.

16.5in (41cm) high

£150-200   **WW**

The trees and animals are species native to and commonly associated with the English countryside in keeping with the rural idyll that inspired the Arts and Crafts movement.

The banners are inscribed with 'Verses for Pictures', a poem by William Morris that featured in his 1891 collection entitled 'Poems by the Way'.

This tapestry was originally commissioned by Percy Wyndham, a member of the intellectual 'Souls' society, formed in the 1880s to counteract perceived philistinism in the aristocracy.

This is a remarkable example of verdure tapestry and its provenance places it at the very heart of the Arts and Crafts movement, making it a truly exceptional piece.

A Morris & Co. 'Greenery' tapestry, designed by John Henry Dearle, woven in coloured wools and mohair by John Martin and William Sleath, with a woodland glade, millefleurs and animals in the foreground, the trees woven with banners bearing inscriptions.

Provenance: The Hon. Percy Scawen Wyndham, Clouds, East Knoyle, Wiltshire.

A pair of Aesthetic Movement curtains, designed in the manner of Christopher Dresser.

94in (235cm) high

£400-600   **L&T**

1892   *184.5in (461cm) wide*

£200,000-225,000   **L&T**

A pair of Morris & Co. 'Strawberry Thief' chintz curtains, each with buff linen borders, lined and interlined.

100in (250cm) high

£800-1,200 pair   **L&T**

A pair of lined cotton curtains, designed by William Morris, wear and losses.

84.75in (212cm) high

£200-300 pair   **WW**

Five pairs of Morris & Co. 'Compton' printed cotton curtains, each pair lined.

92.5in (235cm) high

£4,000-6,000 set   **L&T**

Two pairs of Morris & Co. 'Acanthus' woven silk damask curtains, in Celadon green, lined, pelmets and bedspread.

96in (240cm) high

£2,800-3,200 set   **L&T**

A pair of Morris & Co. 'Vine and Pomegranate' wool curtains, each lined and lengthened with red woollen cloth, braided edges and tie backs.

Provenance: *Sir William Phipson Beale, Drumlamford House, Ayrshire.*

92in (230cm) high

£1,000-1,500 pair   **L&T**

One of three Morris & Co. 'Peacock and Dragon' upholstered footstools, each of rectangular form, covered in woven wool fabric with braided edges, rexine bases.

13.25in (33cm) wide

£300-500 set   **L&T**

An Arts and Crafts woven cotton rug, printed in colours with a Persian-style design of entwined foliage, in the manner of Morris & Co.

73.5in (184cm) long

£300-500   **L&T**

An Arts and Crafts Wilton carpet, in the style of Morris & Co., machine woven, the field with allover scrolling and flowering foliage in shades of green, a meandering foliate border with guard bands.

191.25in (478cm) long

£700-1,000   **L&T**

A pair of Alexander Morton 'Isphurhan' velveteen and cotton curtains, with opposed bird motifs, each with buff linen borders, lined and interlined.

£1,000-1,500 pair   **L&T**

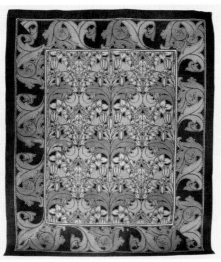

An Arts and Crafts Wilton carpet, designed by C.F.A. Voysey, woven by Tomkinson and Adam for Liberty & Co., with allover luxuriant flowering foliate design within a scrolling foliate band.

108.5in (271cm) long

£4,000-6,000   **L&T**

Three Arts and Crafts pillows, stencilled and embroider, one with shamrocks, one with dog roses and the other with the motto "Smoke a Pipe for Luck".

19.5in (49.5cm) wide

£180-220 set   **DRA**

A woven cotton blanket, decorated in reds and greens with paisley design.

£120-180 WW

An embroidered linen tablecloth, embroidered with bird panels in gold and black.

84in (210cm) wide

£80-120 WW

An embroidered velvet bookcover.

9.25in (23cm) wide

£80-120 WW

A Scottish silk embroidery, decorated with a medieval maiden picking roses in a garden setting, framed, unsigned.

11.25in (28cm) high

£500-800 WW

An Art Deco belt, with red and white beads.

c1935   *36in (91.5cm) long*

£70-90 TDG

WALLPAPER

A roll of Morris & Co. 'Acorn' wallpaper, printed "Morris & Co."

22in (56cm) wide

£300-400 per repeat PC

WILLIAM MORRIS TEXTILES

- William Morris established his company in 1861 under the name Morris, Marshall, Faulkner & Co., later renamed Morris & Co.
- The firm produced wallpapers, stained glass, textiles, furniture, tapestries and illustrations.
- The first two wallpapers were 'Trellis' and 'Daisy'. In 1887 Morris designed a wallpaper for Queen Victoria's Balmoral residence.
- Other than Morris, John Henry Dearle (1860-1932) was one of the firm's leading designers. He joined Morris & Co. in 1878 and designed wallpaper, textiles and tapestry, taking over as artistic director of the firm after Morris's death in 1896.
- Wallpapers were printed by hand using wooden blocks. This technique made them comparatively expensive. The number of different blocks used tended to correlate to the price of the paper.
- Morris & Co. closed in 1940. Arthur Sanderson & Sons Ltd, who had been producing Morris & Co. wallpapers since the 1920s, continued to make Morris wallpaper designs.

A panel of Morris & Co. 'Celadine' wallpaper, printed "Morris & Co."

Wallpaper produced by block printing was often retouched by hand. On this piece, hand painting marks and inconsistencies in the pattern can clearly be seen.

22in (56cm) wide

£300-400 per repeat PC

A roll of Morris & Co. 'Golden Lily' wallpaper, designed by John Dearle, printed "Morris & Co."

This pattern was designed after Morris' death.

22in (56cm) wide

£400-500 per repeat PC

A roll of Morris & Co. 'Foliage' wallpaper, unmarked.

This is a later example of a Morris & Co. design – there is no mark and the design has Art Deco elements in 1940s colours.

22in (56cm) wide

£100-150 per repeat PC

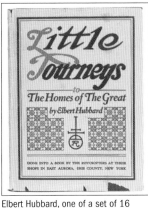

Elbert Hubbard, one of a set of 16 'Little Journeys' books.

8.5in (21.5cm) high

£200-250 set   GAL

One of a selection of volumes of 'The Magazine of Art' 1881-1884, 1886, 1891 and 1895-1897, with various bindings.

£150-200 set   WW

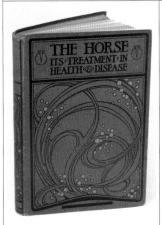

One of nine volumes of 'The Horse', with cover designs by Talwin Morris, published by The Gresham Publishing Company.

11in (27.5cm) high

£80-120 set   WW

One of six volumes of 'The Architectural Review', this one for 1897-1899.

£300-400 set   WW

PRINTS & PAINTINGS

Gustave Baumann, 'Eagle Ceremony at Tesque Pueblo', colour woodblock print, matted and mounted in a new Arts and Crafts frame, initialled in print only.

1932   Image 6.5in (16.5cm) high

£180-220   DRA

Ethel Isadore Brown, brown pen and ink with watercolour of a cityscape in winter, matted and mounted in a new Arts and Crafts frame.

1904   6.75in (17cm) high

£150-200   DRA

Sir Edward Coley Burne-Jones, 'Pan and Psyche', signed print.

17.5in (44cm) wide

£600-900   L&T

Waldo Chase, 'Tall Timbers', oil painting on board, mounted in a new Arts and Crafts-style frame, signed "Waldo S. Chase".

18in (45.5cm) high

£200-300   DRA

William S. Coleman, etching on paper, depicting a maiden playing a pipe, framed, signed in the print "WSC", pencil signature and blindstamp.

11.5in (29cm) high

£300-500   WW

Arthur Wesley Dow, 'Modern Art' lithograph, matted and framed, image signed.

Image 10in (25.5cm) high

£500-800   DRA

DECORATIVE ARTS

J. Foord, chromolithograph print of chestnut blossoms, from 'Decorative Flower Studies', stamped "J. Foord" and dated, new mat and frame, tears and losses.

1899   10in (25.5cm) high

£120-180   DRA

J. Foord, chromolithograph print of peace rose, from 'Decorative Flower Studies', stamped "J. Foord" and dated, new mat and frame, tears and losses.

1899   9.5in (24cm) high

£120-180   DRA

May Gaerhart, 'St. Laurence Islanders', colour etching depicting an Inuit family, matted and mounted in a new Arts and Crafts frame, pencil signed.

c1925   3in (7.5cm) high

£150-200   DRA

Clarence Hotvedt, 'Two Pines', colour woodblock print, mounted and matted in new Arts and Crafts frame, pencil titled, signed and monogrammed in print.

1929   9.75 (25cm) high

£150-200   DRA

Dard Hunter, 'Entrance to Roycroft Inn', published as a cover of a Roycroft menu, menu intact within frame.

c1920   5.25in (13.5cm) wide

£200-300   DRA

Leonard Hutchinson, 'Road to Niagra', colour woodblock print, 20/50, matted and mounted in new Arts and Crafts frame, pencil titled and signed.

c1935   8.5in (21.5cm) high

£220-280   DRA

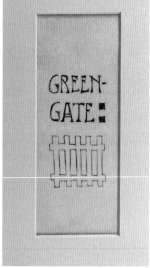

Jessie M. King, 'Green Gate', design for a bookplate, ink on vellum.

Provenance: *The Estate of Merle Taylor.*

4.75in (12cm) high

£300-400   L&T

Blanche Lazzell, woodblock print depicting a Providence dock scene in black on white paper, framed.

This piece featured as cover art for Ms. Lazzell's exhibition.

1928   8in (13cm) high

£300-400   DRA

Sidney Lee (British 1866-1949), colour woodblock print of fishermen and nets by a lighthouse, matted and mounted in new Arts and Crafts frame, signed.

c1925   15in (38cm) high

£300-400   DRA

Jessie M. King, 'Rose Trellis', ink on vellum.

8.5in (21cm) high

£180-220   L&T

Berta Lum, 'Snowballs', colour woodblock print, matted and mounted in new Arts and Crafts frame, pencil signed, chop mark and No. "133", water stains to bottom left corner.

10in (25.5cm) high

£300-500   DRA

W. Palmer, 'Seven Ages of Man', two of a set of seven prints of various sizes, in ebonised wood frames, signed in the print.

£1,000-1,500 set
WW

Henry van de Velde, 'Tropon', French version, a lithograph on cream-coloured paper, artist's signature lower right and "l'Aliment le plus concentre", framed.

1898
11.25in (28cm) high
£300-500
QU

German School, 'Flowers with Tree and House' woodblock print, mounted and matted in new Arts and Crafts frame, pencil titled and signed.

11.25in (28.5cm) high
£150-200
DRA

Eva Watson, 'Gull Rock', colour linocut, matted and mounted in new Arts and Crafts frame, pencil titled and signed.

8.5in (21.5cm) high
£600-900
DRA

A German School woodblock print of a house and garden, mounted and matted in a new Arts and Crafts frame.

4.25in (11cm) wide
£150-200
DRA

Two framed stained glass window sketches, one depicting an angel, the other as the Virgin, pencil, ink and ink wash.

£700-1,000 pair
L&T

A Russian Arts and Crafts woodblock print of an industrial scene by mountains, matted and mounted in period Arts and Crafts frame, illegible pencil signature, some foxing and folds.

16.75in (42.5cm) wide
£200-300
DRA

674

THE MODERN DESIGN MARKET

Modern design, encompassing movements from the mid-20thC onwards such as the Bauhaus, Pop Art and Post-modernism, has consistently been one of the fastest growing sectors of the art market. While sales of some antique furniture and glass have struggled in recent years, many modern pieces such as 'Wassily' armchairs and contemporary studio glass have performed extremely well.

In our increasingly self-referential culture, iconic post-war design, whether from the 1950s or 80s, is perpetually stylish. The current taste for all things 1970s has led to price increases for original versions of designs first produced in that era, such as Verner Panton's 'Relaxer' rockers. Japanese design is another popular area, and contemporary reproductions of classic Japanese design from the late 20thC have made them accessible

to a wider audience. Sculpture by Clive Barker was a runaway success at a sale in February 2005 and may be a sign that further recognition is on the way for the 1960s Pop Art sculptor.

Faded plastic and air bubbles underneath veneers will have a detrimental effect on value and can be difficult to restore. Despite this, it is important to be aware that furniture and accessories made in the first years of production are invariably worth far more than later pieces. A Bertoia barstool made by Knoll in 1952 will carry a very different price tag from one made in 2004, despite being made by the same company and to the same design. Most sought-after of all are unique commissions and prototypes by revered designers such as George Nakashima and Ercole Barovier.

Lilian Fawcett, Themes & Variations

MARCEL BREUER

MARCEL BREUER

- Marcel Breuer (1902-1981) moved from Hungary to Weimar in Germany in 1920 to study at the Bauhaus.
- A central tenet of Bauhaus teaching was the combination of good engineering with craftsmanship. This ideal, along with the commercial awareness instilled by the school, proved to be a great influence on Breuer throughout his career.
- In 1925, Breuer accepted a teaching post in the furniture workshop of the Bauhaus, which by then had relocated to Dessau. There he experimented with new materials such as plastics, laminated woods, aluminium and tubular steel.
- Breuer won critical acclaim with the Wassily chair, a functional, low cost and sleek design that lent itself to mass production.
- Breuer taught alongside his former mentor Walter Gropius at Harvard's architecture faculty from 1937.
- He is remembered today primarily as an architect and for pioneering the use of tubular steel in furniture.

A pair of 'B-34' armchairs, by Marcel Breuer, one in chromium plated steel, the other in tubular aluminium, both with canvas Eisengarn upholstery.

Eisengarn is a strong yarn developed by the Bauhaus to ensure that seat coverings maintained their shape.

c1930   32in (81cm) high
£1,000-1,500   SK

A pair of 'Wassily' armchairs, by Marcel Breuer, with tubular chromium frames and tan leather strapwork.

This iconic chair, designed at the Bauhaus in 1925, was named after the Russian artist Wassily Kandinski.

30.5in (77.5cm) wide
£400-600   ISA

A late 20thC 'B-35' lounge chair, by Marcel Breuer, in chromium-plated tubular steel, with black painted armrests, leather seat and paper label.

c1960   32in (81cm) high
£800-1,200   SK

A 'B-10' table, by Marcel Breuer, in chromium-plated tubular steel, with blue painted wood table top.

c1925   26.25in (67cm) high
£1,000-1,500   SK

LEFT: A single pedestal desk, by Marcel Breuer, with four drawers with recessed pulls, marked "Rhoads".

RIGHT: A wall-hanging shelf unit, by Marcel Breuer.

These items were designed for the Rhoads Dormitory at Bryn Mawr College.

Shelf unit 72in (183cm) high
£800-1,200   SDR

WENDELL CASTLE

WENDELL CASTLE

- Born in Kansas in 1932, Wendell Castle obtained a BFA in industrial design and an MFA in sculpture from the University of Kansas. He went on to teach at the School of American Craftsmen in New York and set up his own studio.

- Castle describes himself as a furniture artist, and his playful designs explore the aesthetic qualities and technical possibilities of wood and metal, as well as contemporary materials such as fibreglass and plastics.

- Castle's designs are simultaneously sculptural and functional, for public and residential space. He has exhibited his work in galleries and also taken commissions from private clients.

- As a leading light of the Pop Art movement, Castle's work is infused with irreverence and a sense of the absurd, and takes inspiration from everyday objects and the human form.

- His 'Molar' line of furniture from the late 1960s, coated with fibreglass plastic, was inspired by human teeth. This is typical of Castle's playful style, also evident in later works such as the 'Star' series.

- Castle's innovative and imaginative designs have won him international awards such as the 1994 Visionaries of the American Craft Movement prize, which was sponsored by the American Craft Museum, and a gold medal from the American Craft Council.

A 'Molar' coffee table, by Wendell Castle, with scalloped top, in black fibreglass, marked "WC".

40in (101.5cm) wide

£2,500-3,000   **SDR**

A 'Cloud' wall-hanging shelf, by Wendell Castle, in white fibreglass, marked "W.C. 69 03".

65.75in (167cm) wide

£2,500-3,000   **SDR**

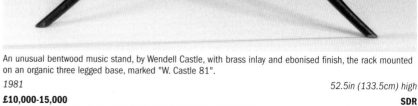

An unusual bentwood music stand, by Wendell Castle, with brass inlay and ebonised finish, the rack mounted on an organic three legged base, marked "W. Castle 81".

1981   *52.5in (133.5cm) high*

£10,000-15,000   **SDR**

A lounge chair, by Charles and Ray Eames, constructed from moulded mahogany plywood.

This is the famous 'LCW' chair, named as the best design of the 20thC by 'Time' magazine.

c1950   26in (66cm) high

£1,000-1,500   SK

EAMES

- Charles and Ray Eames helped to define post-war American design through their work with important companies and institutions such as IBM and the Smithsonian.
- The couple met in 1940 when they collaborated with Eero Saarinen on a competition design for the Museum of Modern Art. Their personal and professional partnership continued until Charles' death in 1978. Ray's death came exactly ten years later.
- Their goal to design a chair without joints or individual component parts was eventually realised after the emergence of fibreglass as a consumer material in the post-war years.
- Many Eames designs were distributed through Herman Miller, a company that continues to manufacture furniture to their original specifications today.
- Many of their pieces, such as the '670' lounge chair and '671' ottoman, have become word famous and entered the canon of modern design.
- True to Charles' maxim that "recognizing the need is the primary condition for design", utility is key to the Eames' work.

A 'DKW' wire chair, by Charles and Ray Eames, on dowel legs with a bikini pad.

c1950   33in (84cm) high

£200-300   SK

A 'DKW' wire chair, by Charles and Ray Eames, on dowel legs.

c1960   32.5in (82.5cm) high

£500-800   LOS

A rocker, by Charles and Ray Eames, with a plastic tub seat.

26.5in (67.5cm) high

£400-600   LOS

A set of six 'Aluminium' group swivel chairs, by Charles Eames for Herman Miller, with black hessian upholstery.

£1,500-2,000   L&T

A pair of reproduction lounge chairs, by Charles and Ray Eames, with black leather seats on moulded plywood shells with walnut finish, with paper labels.

This design was first produced in 1956 for the film producer Billy Wilder.

33in (84cm) high

£2,000-2,500   SK

A rare child's stool, by Charles Eames for Herman Miller, in bent plywood, unmarked.

This is an early design and was never a commercial success.

12in (30.5cm) wide

£800-1,200   SDR

A folding table, by Charles Eames for Herman Miller.

c1955   33.75in (85.5cm) wide

£700-1,000   LOS

A rare dowel leg table, by Charles Eames for Herman Miller, with a square wood veneer top, unmarked.

21.5in (54.5cm) wide

£1,500-2,000   SDR

An 'ESU' desk, by Charles Eames for Herman Miller, with three drawers in black and white laminate with birch fronts and early Herman Miller label.

60in (152.5cm) wide

£2,000-2,500   SDR

MOLLY GREGORY

One of a set of eight dining chairs, by Molly Gregory, with low back, single vertical slat, flared arms and hard brown leather sling upholstery, unmarked.

24in (61cm) high

£1,500-2,000 set   **SDR**

A Molly Gregory highchair, with low back, single vertical slat, flared arms and hard brown leather sling upholstery, unmarked.

18.25in (46.5cm) wide

£150-200   **SDR**

A pair of blonde wood occasional tables, by Molly Gregory, with triangular tops and graduated stretchers, unmarked.

28in (71cm) wide

£350-450   **SDR**

A small A-frame stepstool, by Molly Gregory, of pinned construction, with arched handle and two graduated steps, unmarked.

11in (28cm) wide

£300-400   **SDR**

VLADIMIR KAGAN

One of a pair of library chairs, by Vladimir Kagan for Dreyfus, upholstered in dark green leather on a sculptural walnut frame, unmarked.

1953   *24in (61cm) wide*

£3,000-4,000 pair   **SDR**

A mid-20thC chaise-longue, by Vladimir Kagan, with low rounded armrests, upholstered in brown and beige fabric on a sculptural walnut base, unmarked.

54in (137cm) wide

£3,500-4,500   **SDR**

A rare '175SS' rocker and ottoman, by Vladimir Kagan, on highly polished stainless steel frames, upholstered in high grade elephant grey leather.

25.5in (65cm) wide

£10,000-12,000   **SDR**

An unusual drop-leaf dining table, by Vladimir Kagan, with an oblong top on a seven-legged wood base, unmarked.

66.5in (169cm) wide

£2,500-3,000   **SDR**

JOHN MAKEPEACE

- John Makepeace trained under Keith Cooper in Dorset during the late 1950s before establishing his own workshop in the Midlands.
- Makepeace eventually returned to Dorset and founded Parnham College, a school for furniture designers housed in a country manor.
- Taking a lead from Arts & Crafts teachings, Parnham espouses a holistic approach and teaches design, craft and entrepreneurial skills. An on-site arboretum supplies native British woods for research and timber.
- Makepeace favours English hardwoods such as oak, yew, holly, and sycamore. Some of these timbers are rarely seen in contemporary furniture design.
- The majority of Makepeace designs are bespoke, one-off commissions.

A 'Bird' personal desk, by John Makepeace, of burr elm and wych elm with Lebanon cedar drawer linings, with adjustable writing slope, two paper drawers and five revolving trays, on a bronze tripod base.

45.75in (116cm) wide

£25,000-35,000   **JM**

A 'Mollusc' desk, by John Makepeace, of washed oak, with a suede-lined pull-out writing surface, on laminated curving legs.

The oak used for this desk was planted at Longleat in Wiltshire in the 1760s and harvested in 1980 to coincide with the late Lord Bath's 80th birthday.

c1980   *74.75in (190cm) wide*

£40,000-45,000   **JM**

A chest of 18 drawers, by John Makepeace, of English cherry, hornbeam and burr elm, with cast bronze handles.

32.25in (82cm) wide

£70,000-80,000   **JM**

A rosewood coffee display table, by John Makepeace, the rectangular framed glass top enclosing a green baize-lined well interior.

30.5in (76cm) wide

£3,000-4,000   **L&T**

A 'Desert Sand' chest of drawers, by John Makepeace, with solid ripple ash carcass, three shallow stationery drawers, suede-lined writing slide and six deep drawers.

The undulating pattern was computer-generated so that the peaks conclude at the corners of the drawers and the hollows coincide with the maximum extent of the handles.

42.5in (108cm) wide

£70,000-80,000   **JM**

PAUL McCOBB

A 'Planner' group desk and spindle back chair, by Paul McCobb.

29.5in (75cm) high

£280-320   **SK**

A credenza, by Paul McCobb, with sliding cloth doors and two adjustable shelves.

c1950   *60in (152.5cm) wide*

£800-1,200   **LOS**

A 'Plateau' coffee table, by Paul McCobb, with a single drawer and vitriol top.

32in (81.5cm) wide

£800-1,200   **SK**

A 'Planner' group chest of four drawers, by Paul McCobb, with a walnut finish.

36in (91.5cm) wide

£120-180   **SK**

A contemporary reproduction of a Paul McCobb 'Zither' chair.

34in (86.5cm) high

£180-220   **LOS**

A lounge chair, by Modernage, upholstered in light grey ultra-suede, with loose seat cushion on ebonised block feet, unmarked.

28in (71cm) wide

£180-220   **SDR**

A library table with black lacquered top, by Madame Majeska for Modernage, on a blonde wood base with four quarter-round shelves.

36in (91.5cm) wide

£500-700   **SDR**

A large desk, by Modernage, with open shelves over three drawers with horizontal pulls, the centre one a fall-front with fitted interior, with metal "Modernage" tag.

72in (183cm) wide

£500-800   **SDR**

One of a pair of Art Deco square club chairs, by Madame Majeska for Modernage, upholstered in bias-cut maroon twill, with new cream linen seat covers.

28in (71cm) wide

£280-320 pair   **SDR**

GEORGE NAKASHIMA

A coffee table, by George Nakashima, of English burl oak and walnut, signed "George Nakashima Nov 1969".

58in (145cm) wide

£15,000-20,000   **FRE**

A walnut 'Minguren II' coffee table, by George Nakashima, with one V-shaped end and one expressively figured free-edge end, with a rosewood butterfly key concealed underneath.

55in (137.5cm) wide

£5,000-8,000   **SDR**

An English walnut coffee table, by George Nakashima, marked with client's name.

46.5in (116cm) wide

£4,000-6,000   **FRE**

A 'Minguren II' Persian walnut coffee table, by George Nakashima, the sculptural top with a single rosewood butterfly joint, on a black walnut minguren base.

16.5in (42cm) wide

£5,000-8,000   **FRE**

A black walnut 'Minguren I' coffee table, by George Nakashima, with a free-edge top with natural occlusions and two rosewood butterfly keys, signed "George Nakashima Oct 1979", also marked "Hand & Spirit".

1979   *70.5in (176cm) wide*

£8,000-10,000   **SDR**

An English black walnut dining table, by George Nakashima, of hickory and rosewood, marked with client's name.

81in (202cm) wide

£15,000-20,000 FRE

An English walnut, black walnut and oak dining table, by George Nakashima, marked with client's name.

c1965 68in (173cm) wide

£8,000-12,000 FRE

A 'Minguren I' side table, by George Nakashima, with a freeform Buckeye burl top on a rosewood base, marked with original owner's name.

32.5in (82.5cm) wide

£15,000-20,000 SDR

Two of a set of six 'New' hickory and walnut dining chairs, by George Nakashima, comprising two armchairs and four side chairs, marked with client's name.

Armchair 39in (97.5cm) high

£4,000-6,000 set FRE

A walnut 'Conoid' lounge chair and ottoman, by George Nakashima.

c1975 *Chair 30.5in (77.5cm) high*

£2,500-3,000 SK

A walnut 'Conoid' bench, by George Nakashima, with hickory spindles and free-edge seat with natural occlusion, on tapering dowel legs, unmarked.

1977 *71.5in (179cm) wide*

£10,000-12,000 SDR

An early prototype walnut four-drawer chest, by George Nakashima, with louvered front, of pinned and dovetailed case construction, on a plinth base.

This is a historically important piece that George Nakashima presented to Knoll in the 1940s.

36in (91.5cm) wide

£5,000-6,000 SDR

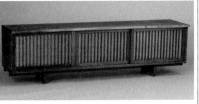

A rare walnut cabinet, by George Nakashima, with dovetailed case, free-edge top, three grilled sliding doors and three interior compartments fitted with dividers and shelves.

84in (210cm) wide

£10,000-12,000 SDR

A walnut wall-hanging shelf, by George Nakashima, with free-edge top, dovetails and two lower drawers, unmarked, some wear.

78in (195cm) wide

£6,000-8,000 SDR

A conference table in rosewood and steel, by George Nelson for Herman Miller, with circular metal tag.

103.5in (236cm) wide

£800-1,200   **FRE**

A home office desk, by George Nelson, with two leather-covered sliding doors over a rectangular top with hinged cabinet revealing a fitted interior, flanked by a leather writing surface with perforated metal basket.

c1950

54in (137cm) wide

£3,000-4,000   **SK**

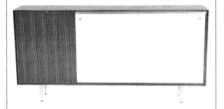

A 'Thin Edge' walnut veneer credenza, by George Nelson for Herman Miller, with a cabinet flanking two cream-coloured sliding doors concealing three shelves, on tapering aluminum legs, unmarked.

67.25in (171cm) wide

£2,000-2,500   **SDR**

A 'Marshmallow' sofa, by George Nelson for Herman Miller, with 18 forest green naugahyde cushions mounted on a tubular steel frame, with circular Herman Miller tag and factory paper label.

Naugahyde is a type of vinyl often used in mid-20thC upholstery.

51in (129.5cm) wide

£8,000-10,000   **SDR**

MIES VAN DER ROHE

A pair of 'Tugendhat' chairs, by Mies van der Rohe, each with two curved arms on a cantilevered flat bar metal frame, S-shaped legs and tufted black leather cushions.

c1930   *34in (86.5cm) high*

£3,000-5,000   **SK**

One of a pair of 20thC 'Barcelona' chairs, by Mies van der Rohe, with black leather cushions on a flat bar base.

29.5in (75cm) high

£3,000-5,000 pair   **SK**

A pair of 20thC 'MR' chairs, by Mies van der Rohe, each with a cantilevered tubular steel frame and green leather padded and upholstered seat.

33.5in (85cm) high

£3,500-4,500   **SK**

A set of four 'BRNO MR50' chairs, by Mies van der Rohe, with green leather upholstery on a steel base.

31.25in (79cm) high

£700-1,000   **SK**

A pair of 'Barcelona' chairs, by Mies van der Rohe, with red leather upholstery on chromed flat metal bar frames.

29.5in (75cm) high

£3,000-4,000   **SK**

A 20thC Tugendhat-style day bed, after a design by Mies van der Rohe, with rectangular black leather cushion and head rest on a webbed wooden frame, raised on four cylindrical legs.

38in (96.5cm) wide

£1,200-1,800   **SK**

A valet chair, by Hans Wegner for Johannes Hansen, made from teak, oak, brass and leather, with branded "JH" logo, marked "Johannes Hansen Copenhagen Denmark".

37in (92.5cm) high

£3,500-4,500   FRE

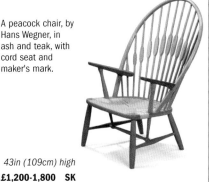

A peacock chair, by Hans Wegner, in ash and teak, with cord seat and maker's mark.

43in (109cm) high

£1,200-1,800   SK

A teak day bed, by Hans Wegner, with natural woven backrest, converts to create an upholstered day bed, with retail label to base.

c1960   *78in (198cm) wide*

£1,500-2,000   SK

A teak lounge chair and ottoman, by Hans Wegner, with a reclining upholstered cushion seat.

c1960   34.5in (87.5cm) high

£2,500-3,000   SK

A teak dining table, by Hans Wegner, with a circular top on a cross-stretcher frame, with metal mounts set into four tapered circular legs.

c1960   61in (155cm) diam

£1,000-1,500   SK

EDWARD WORMLEY

A coffee table, by Edward Wormley for Dunbar.

c1955   60in (152.5cm) wide

£1,000-1,500   LOS

A mahogany coffee table, by Edward Wormley for Dunbar, with partial plank top and brass rods to one end over a low shelf, with yellow "Dunbar" tag.

66in (168cm) wide

£600-900   SDR

A pair of side tables, by Edward Wormley for Dunbar, with round stone tops on mahogany tripod pedestal bases, with metal maker's tag.

c1950   21.5in (54.5cm) high

£1,800-2,200   SK

An easy armchair and ottoman, by Edward Wormley for Dunbar, upholstered in brown ultra-suede, raised on teak supports.

31in (79cm) wide

£800-1,200   ISA

A floating back sofa, by Edward Wormley for Dunbar, fully upholstered in woven black and grey fabric, on an ebonised wooden base with cross stretcher, with yellow "Dunbar" tag.

90.5in (230cm) wide

£2,000-2,500   SDR

FRANK LLOYD WRIGHT

FRANK LLOYD WRIGHT

- American architect Frank Lloyd Wright (1867-1959) studied engineering at the University of Wisconsin before joining an architecture firm in Chicago.
- Wright mainly worked in the Prairie style of architecture, a mid-western interpretation of the Arts and Crafts movement, infused with his own reaction against the historical revivalism that was popular in America at the time.
- Wright designed the interiors to most of his architectural projects, believing in a thematically consistent relationship between interior design and the architectural exterior.
- Rectilinear lines, intersecting planes and simple structures show a strong architectural influence on Wright's furniture. His high-back spindle chair is typical of his take on the Prairie style.
- Wright developed a more Modernist style in the later part of his career, using novel and innovative materials. His work reflected his interest in Japanese art and culture, combined with shapes and motifs that were often Cubist in origin.

A long mahogany bench, by Frank Lloyd Wright for Heritage Henredon, of rectangular form, raised on a pair of board supports with Taliesin motif edges, signed with red monogram.

60in (152.5cm) wide

£1,200-1,800 ISA

A hexagonal mahogany coffee table, by Frank Lloyd Wright for Heritage Henredon, raised on triangular board supports with Taliesin motif edges, signed with red monogram and impressed marks.

42in (107cm) wide

£2,000-2,500 ISA

An eight-drawer dresser, by Frank Lloyd Wright, with overhanging brass pulls, on a plinth base, unmarked.

c1955   *48in (122cm) wide*

£1,500-2,000 SDR

A mahogany buffet, by Frank Lloyd Wright for Heritage Henredon, complete with removable open shelf unit, with Taliesin motif edges, raised on rail legs.

86.5in (220cm) wide

£1,200-1,800 ISA

OTHER DESIGNERS

A highback 'Model 31' armchair, by Alvar Aalto for Artek, with padded seat on laminated beech cantilever supports.

c1935

£280-320 L&T

A pair of birch and plywood tables, by Alvar Aalto for Finmar Ltd., with celluloid "Finmar" tag.

Largest 39in (97.5cm) wide

£300-400 FRE

A 'Pony' chair, by Eero Aarnio for Asko, fully upholstered in black jersey, marked with "Eero Aarnio Adelta Made in Finland" tag.

35in (89cm) high

£1,500-2,000 SDR

A rosewood wardrobe, by Jacques Adnet, with single drawer and three cabinet doors, glass and brass pulls, four original shelves and original keys, marked "J. Adnet".

49in (124.5cm) wide

£1,500-2,000 SDR

A 'Rover' chair, by Rod Arad for One Off Ltd, comprising a salvaged Rover car seat with headrest, covered in black leather, mounted on a tubular steel scaffolding frame, unmarked.

26.5in (67.5cm) wide

£1,800-2,200 SDR

A pair of foam lounge chairs, by Ron Arad for Moroso, fully upholstered in green wool, one with "Moroso" metal tag.

32in (81.5cm) wide

£2,500-3,000 SDR

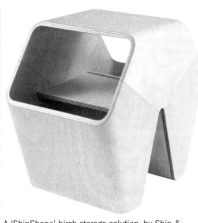

A 'ShipShape' birch storage solution, by Shin & Tomoko Azumi, inspired by the Isokon archives.

2003   *17.75in (45cm) wide*

£300-350   **ISO**

Two armchairs, 'Deko' and 'Müll-Direkt', by Bär & Knell for AEG Berlin, made from black recycled plastic with collage-like applications of plastic household waste, stamped marks "BK 95".

1995   *21.5in (54.5cm) wide*

£700-1,000   **QU**

A bench, by Milo Baughman for Thayer Coggin, with buttoned upholstery and four tapering legs.

c1960   *60in (152.5cm) wide*

£600-900   **LOS**

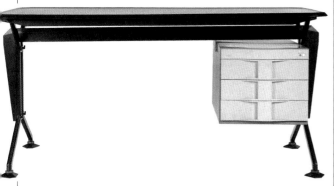

A single-pedestal desk, by Studio BBPR for Olivetti, with clip-corner top and three drawers, on an enamelled metal trestle base, unmarked.

62.5in (159cm) wide

£1,500-2,000   **SDR**

A 'Landscape Chaise', by Jeffrey Bernett for B&B Italia, upholstered in orange felt sewn into segments, with magnetically attached leather pillow.

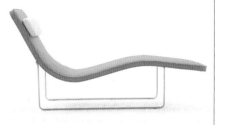

24in (61cm) wide

£1,800-2,200   **BBI**

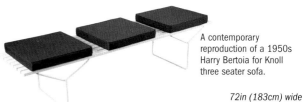

A contemporary reproduction of a 1950s Harry Bertoia for Knoll three seater sofa.

72in (183cm) wide

£800-1,200   **LOS**

A 'Dinette' table, by Osvaldo Borsani for Tecno, with bevelled circular top covered in mottled taupe leather, with embossed design, on four polished curved steel legs, unmarked.

25in (63.5cm) high

£500-700   **SDR**

A lounge chair, by Osvaldo Borsani for Tecno, upholstered in peach, umber, purple, and blue striped fabric, on a steel base with low-slung hard rubber side grips, with "Tecno" metal tag.

26.5in (67.5cm) wide

£700-1,000   **SDR**

An inflatable armchair, by Mario Botta.

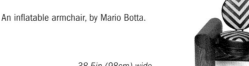

38.5in (98cm) wide

£600-900   **SDR**

A 'Strap Chair', by Boym Partners, with a polypropylene strapping tape seating surface.

'Strap Chair' was featured at the National Design Triennial in 2000.

£2,000-3,000   **BOY**

MODERN FURNITURE

A 'Strap Chair', by Boym Partners, with a polypropylene strapping tape seating surface.

£2,000-3,000   **BOY**

A rolling cart, by Calvin, with a drop-leaf top and casters.

c1965   *34in (86.5cm) wide*

£500-700   **LOS**

A bentwood chair, by Norman Cherner for Plycraft, with orange upholstered seat and partial paper label.

c1955   *31in (79cm) high*

£350-400   **SK**

A 'Torso' armchair, by Paola Daganello for Cassina, with asymmetric fabric upholstered back and leather upholstered seat frame in dark teal, on enamelled steel legs, unmarked.

43in (17cm) wide

£500-700   **SDR**

A satinwood buffet, by Desny, with bevelled black glass insert to top and illuminated interior, flanked by cabinets with chrome hardware, marked "Desny France".

83in (211cm) wide

£4,000-6,000   **SDR**

A wicker chair, by Nana Ditzel and Ludwig Pontoppidan, with a woven barrel seat, mahogany frame and paper label.

c1950   *23in (58.5cm) wide*

£600-900   **SDR**

A Danish coat rack, attributed to Nana Ditzel.

c1960   *65in (165cm) high*

£500-700   **LOS**

A music stand, by Wharton Esherick, with organic bentwood frame, trapezoidal rack and lower shelf.

1962   *46in (117cm) high*

£50,000-70,000   **SDR**

A mid-20thC teak credenza, by Dryland, with rectangular top over four blind drawers and two sliding doors, fitted with sliding shelves and compartments, raised on tapering legs.

82.5in (209.5cm) wide

£500-800   **SK**

A walnut console table, by Wharton Esherick, with freeform bevelled top over a sculptural tripod base, with carved cipher.

c1950   *35in (89cm) wide*

£12,000-18,000   **SDR**

A unique dining table, by Paul Evans, executed in the Queen Anne style, with a rectangular rosewood top on a sculpted bronze base with cabriole legs, unmarked.

This table was from the personal collection of Paul Evans and was used in the artist's home.

103in (262cm) wide

£3,500-4,500   **SDR**

A card table, by Paul Frankl, with undulating laminated cork top, on four tapering legs with ebonised finish, stencilled mark "5002-180".

35.75in (91cm) wide

£400-600   SDR

A CLOSER LOOK AT A LITTLE BEAVER ARMCHAIR

The 'Little Beaver' armchair and ottoman were conceived as part of a project called 'Experimental Edges', in which Gehry used corrugated cardboard to challenge common perceptions of suitable furnishing materials.

This laminated, corrugated cardboard was originally designed for use in the packing industry.

Designs for Gehry's 'Experimental Edges' series were intended for gallery exhibition, and have never been developed commercially. This exclusivity adds to the value of this set.

A 'Little Beaver' armchair and ottoman by Frank Gehry for Vitra, of laminated cardboard construction, marked with brass tag and numbered "54/100".

33.5in (85cm) wide

1987

£2,200-2,800   SDR   SDR

One of a set of four dining chairs, by Paul Frankl, with windowpane backs and black vinyl covered seat pads on ebonised frames, the bases numbered in crayon.

19in (48.5cm) wide

£220-280 set   SDR

A rare 'Skyscraper' chest, by Paul Frankl, asymmetrically configured with drawers, cabinets and shelves, with pyramidal and horizontal brass pulls and metal "Skyscraper Furniture" tag.

36in (91.5cm) wide

£5,000-7,000   SDR

A zaisu chair, produced to an original Kenji Fujimori design by Tendo Mokko, made from a single piece of moulded beech with a zelkova veneer.

The zaisu chair is a legless Japanese interpretation of the Western chair. The hole prevents warping and slipping.

2004   *13in (33cm) wide*

£50-80   TDO

A rare dining table, by Frank Gehry, with a circular plate glass top on a six-cylinder corrugated cardboard base, unmarked.

48in (122cm) diam

£2,200-2,800   SDR

An 'Easy Edges' stool, by Frank Gehry, of masonite and corrugated cardboard, overpainted, unmarked.

12in (30.5cm) wide

£400-600   SDR

A 1950s birch sideboard, by T.H. Robsjohn Gibbings for Widdicomb, with rectangular top, fitted with three cabinet doors, the interior fitted with four drawers and shelves.

72in (183cm) wide

£1,000-1,500   FRE

A mirrored glass, brass and wood step table, by Billy Haines, the upper glass shelf raised on waisted supports rising from a shaped mirrored shelf, all raised on tapering ebonised legs.

1958   *18in (46cm) wide*

£120-180   ISA

An early 'Butterfly' chair, by Bonet, Kurchan and Hardoy, with a leather sling seat on a rod iron frame.

c1950   *34.25in (87cm) high*

£500-700   LOS

MODERN FURNITURE

A unique handcrafted solid black walnut writing table, by Laurence Hendricks.

1972   *30in (76cm) wide*

£1,200-1,800   **LOS**

A wall unit, by Heywood-Wakefield, comprising a top case fitted with shelving over drawers and tambour door compartments, with a walnut colour finish and branded mark.

c1960   *65in (165cm) wide*

£700-1,000   **SK**

A side table, by Wolfgang Hoffmann for Howell, with a rectangular laminate top and chrome trim, on a polished chrome base, unmarked.

27in (68.5cm) wide

£500-700   **SDR**

A harp chair, by Jorgen Hovelskov, made from wood and strung rope.

c1970   *52in (132cm) high*

£1,200-1,800   **SK**

A mid-20thC birch veneer composition desk, retailed by the Interform Collection, with a rectangular top and sides enclosing a suspended bank of three drawers.

64.5in (164cm) wide

£120-180   **SK**

A bent plywood chair, produced to an original Saburoh Inuiby design by Tendo Mokko, in beech with a maple veneer.

2004   *28.25in (72cm) wide*

£320-380   **TDO**

A low table, produced to an original Saburoh Inuiby design by Tendo Mokko, in beech with a zelkova veneer.

48in (122cm) wide

£280-320   **TDO**

A birch 'Monroe' chair, produced to an original Arata Isozaki design by Tendo Mokko.

2004   *21.25in (54cm) wide*

£1,800-2,200   **TDO**

A rosewood coffee table, by Georg Jensen, with a rectangular top inset on one side with abstract patterned studio tiles in olive green and teal blue, unmarked.

23.25in (59cm) wide

£220-280   **SDR**

A 'Swan' chair, by Arne Jacobsen, designed in 1957.

30in (76cm) high

£800-1,200   **LOS**

An 'Egg' chair, by Arne Jacobsen, with blue upholstery, on a metal swivel base.

c1960   *42in (106.5cm) high*

£800-1,200   **SK**

One of a pair of 'No.53' easy Chairs, by Finn Juhl for Niels Vodder, in teak with green fabric upholstery, horn-shaped arms, brass hardware and branded mark.

28in (71cm) wide

£1,000-1,500 pair   **SDR**

A teak 'No. 45' settee, by Finn Juhl for Niels Vodder, with brown vinyl upholstery, sculpted frame and branded mark.

46in (117cm) wide

£4,000-6,000   **SDR**

An early teak 'Chieftain' chair, by Finn Juhl for Niels Vodder, re-upholstered in black leather, with branded mark.

40.5in (103cm) wide

£7,000-10,000   **SDR**

A chair, produced to an original Isamu Kenmochi design by Tendo Mokko, in beech with a maple veneer.

2004   *20.25in (51.5cm) wide*

£220-280   **TDO**

A 'Kashiwado' chair, produced to an original Isamu Kenmochi design by Tendo Mokko, formed from blocks of cedar trunk sanded to reveal the grain.

This wide chair is named after a famous Japanese Sumo wrestler.

2004   *33.5in (85cm) wide*

£2,200-2,800   **TDO**

A low table, produced to an original Isamu Kenmochi design by Tendo Mokko, in beech with a rosewood veneer.

The indentation around the edge of the table top is called a 'mizukaeshi', which means 'water embankment'.

2004   *55in (140cm) wide*

£1,500-2,000   **TDO**

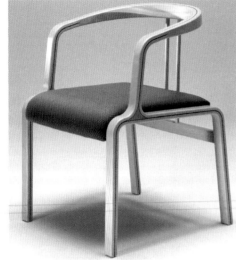

A beech armchair, produced to an original Toshiyuki Kitaby design by Tendo Mokko.

2004

21.25in (54cm) wide

£200-250 TDO

A steel, oak and marble dining table, by Poul Kjaerholm, with a green marble on top of the original oak surface.

80in (200cm) wide

£1,200-1,800　　　　　**FRE**

A conference table, by Florence Knoll, with an oval rosewood top, on a polished chrome pedestal base, with "Knoll International" label.

78in (198cm) wide

£1,200-1,800　SDR

A 'Terrazza' modular lounge sofa, by Ubald Klug for De Sede, consisting of two corner seats, upholstered in chocolate brown leather, with "Stendig" paper label.

27.5in (70cm) high

£2,000-3,000　　　　　**SDR**

A marble coffee table, by Florence Knoll, with a variegated rust-coloured rectilinear marble top on a stainless steel base.

c1975 45in (114.5cm) wide

£300-400　　　　　**SK**

A beech and teak easy chair, by Ib Kofod-Larsen for Christensen & Larsen, with a fabric seat in red and cream on a tapering dowel leg frame, with "Selig Mfg. Co." paper labels.

21.5in (54.5cm) wide

£150-200　　　　　**SDR**

A wood and leather chair, by Kold of Denmark.

c1960 29in (73.5cm) high

£1,200-1,800　　　　　**LOS**

A high-back lounge chair, by Axel Larsson, with sculpted wood frame and reddish-brown leather webbing, missing pillow headrest, branded "SMF" monogram and 1939 World's Fair customs tag.

1937　　　*40in (101.5cm) high*

£3,500-4,500　　　　　**SDR**

A pair of chairs, by Kofod Larsen, with black metal frames, geometric patterned green imitation leather seats and shaped laminated beech backrests.

c1950　　　*29in (73.5cm) high*

£300-500　　　　　**SK**

A 'Fibreglass Group' armchair, by Erwine & Estelle Laverne, with a freeform cutout seat on a steel pedestal base, unmarked.

24in (61cm) wide

£500-800   SDR

A rosewood and amboyna sideboard, attributed to Jules Leleu, with three cabinet doors enclosing interior shelves, with horizontal brass scroll pulls, unmarked.

78.5in (199.5cm) wide

£1,200-1,800   SDR

A pair of box chairs, by Enzo Mari, with tubular frames and perforated plastic yellow and white seats.

c1975   *32.5in (82.5cm) high*

£220-280   SK

An 'Old Point Comfort' club chair, by Warren McArthur, on a tubular aluminium frame with taupe fabric upholstery, remnant of decal.

23.5in (59.5cm) wide

£3,000-4,000   SDR

An 'S534' chromium-plated tubular metal armchair, by Eric Mendelsohn, upholstered with red vinyl cloth, with "Desta" label.

c1930   *78in (198cm) high*

£1,000-1,500   SK

A rare 'Rudder' stool, by Isamu Noguchi for Herman Miller, model number IN-22, in birch with two tubular steel legs, unmarked.

17in (43cm) high

£12,000-18,000   SDR

A pair of high-back armchairs, by Herman Miller, with curvilinear seats in tangerine upholstery, on chrome frames with black armrests and chair supports, with paper labels.

41in (104cm) high

£280-320   SK

A Danish settee, by Borg Mogenson.

64in (162.5cm) wide

£1,200-1,800   LOS

Two of a set of six teak chairs, similar to a design by Neils O. Moller, comprising two armchairs and four side chairs, newly upholstered.

c1960   *31in (79cm) high*

£800-1,200 set   SK

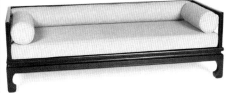

A day bed, by James Mont, with a slatted frame and cushions upholstered in finely woven brushed tan fabric, on bracket feet, unmarked.

76in (193cm) wide

£1,000-1,500   SDR

691

MODERN FURNITURE

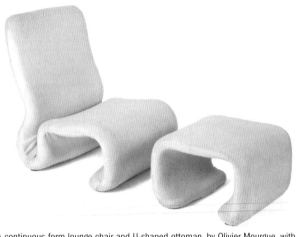

A continuous-form lounge chair and U-shaped ottoman, by Olivier Mourgue, with light grey fabric covering, unmarked.

25in (65.5cm) wide

£700-1,000   **SDR**

A three panel screen, by Peter Niczewski, with trompe l'oeil marquetry, depicting newspaper, photographic images and geometric designs.

48in (122cm) wide

£1,000-1,500   **FRE**

A 'Laminex' beech chair, by Jens Nielsen for Westnofa of Norway, in two parts.

1966   *30in (75cm) wide*

£400-600   **FRE**

OLIVIER MOURGUE

- Born in 1939, Brittany-based Olivier Mourgue produces work firmly rooted in the Pop Art tradition. He owes a debt to the playful Modernism of designers such as Pierre Paulin, whose furniture designs combined comfort with an artistic statement.
- Mourgue's iconic 'Djinn' series, including a two-seat stool, a chaise and a chair and ottoman set, has become a classic. The name is taken from a malevolent spirit in Islamic mythology.
- A magenta Djinn suite was used on the Space Station V set in Stanley Kubrick's film "2001: A Space Odyssey". Its continued cult status has led to its electronic replication for use in the popular computer game "The Sims".
- Another design classic of Mourgue's is the Bouloum Chaise, made in the form of a reclining human figure, complete with head and legs. It is supposedly named after one of Mourgue's childhood friends.
- Ever the eccentric, Mourgue always travelled with a Bouloum Chaise, taking photographs of it in places he visited.

A 'Cone' chair, by Verner Panton for Fritz Hansen.

c1960   *33.5in (85cm) high*

£1,000-1,500   **LOS**

A 'Bachelor' chair, by Verner Panton, with teal blue canvas on a tubular polished chrome frame, unmarked.

29in (73.5cm) high

£150-200   **SDR**

A 'Relaxer 2' crescent-shaped rocking chair, by Verner Panton for Rosenthal, with a blonde wood frame and slatted supports, the cushion covered in channeled rust-coloured fabric, unmarked.

25in (63.5cm) wide

£1,200-1,800   **SDR**

A pair of high-back lounge chairs, by Ico Parisi, with burgundy damask upholstery and brocade trim, on flaring wooden legs, unmarked.

28in (71cm) wide

£1,200-1,800   **SDR**

A brass and enamelled metal coffee table, attributed to Ico Parisi, with a rectangular plate glass top, chipped, unmarked.

36.5in (92.5cm) wide

£600-900   **SDR**

A rare day bed, by Tommi Parzinger, with eight loose cushions upholstered in butter yellow embossed silk fabric, on a dark stained wooden frame, with etched brass details, unmarked.

65in (165cm) wide

£2,200-2,800   **SDR**

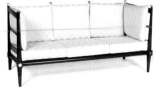

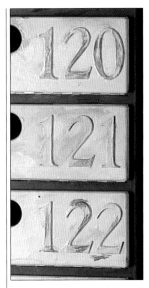

A post-modern storage unit, by Gaetano Pesce, comprising two racks of 13 numbered compartments with hinged fronts, in polychrome wood, on an ebonised frame with open back, unmarked.

1991   24.25in (61.5cm) wide

£1,200-1,800   **SDR**

A green marble and metal dining table, designed by Pasanella & Klein, the rectangular green marble top with white veining, on four tubular steel legs, with flat bar cross and side stretchers.

104in (264cm) wide

£1,200-1,800   **SK**

A single-pedestal desk, by Pierre Paulin for Mobilor, with raised freeform top over two drawers with black laminate surface, on a tubular black metal frame, with "Mobilor" paper label.

47in (119.5cm) wide

£700-1,000   **SDR**

A pair of folding chairs, by Giancarlo Piretti, each with a smoky quartz moulded plastic tub seat, on an aluminum frame, unmarked.

30in (76cm) high

£220-280   **SDR**

A lounge suite, by Warren Platner, comprising three chairs and a table formed of electronically welded steel rods, the chairs upholstered in oatmeal fabric, the table with a circular bevelled glass top, chipped.

1966   Table 54in (137cm) diam

£1,000-1,500   **SK**

A dining table, by Gio Ponti for Singer & Sons, in walnut and brass.

1954   64in (162.5cm) wide

£3,000-4,000   **LOS**

One of a set of four 'Superleggera' dining chairs, by Gio Ponti, each with two horizontal backslats and woven seat, unmarked.

17in (43cm) wide

£1,000-1,500 set   **SDR**

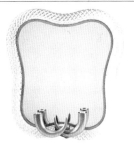

A large and rare illuminated wall mirror, by Gio Ponti for Venini, of scalloped form with braided glass border and two brass crossed horn fixtures, unmarked.

c1940   19.5in (49.5cm) wide

£3,500-4,500   **SDR**

A custom designed walnut dining table, by Phillip Lloyd Powell, unmarked.

c1960   47.25in (120cm) wide

£1,000-1,500   **SDR**

A wood and brass coffee table, by Harvey Probber.

c1960   70.5in (179cm) wide

£1,200-1,800   **LOS**

MODERN FURNITURE

One of a set of four side chairs, by Ernest Race, covered in black vinyl, on black metal legs with chrome capped feet.

19in (48.5cm) wide

£350-400 set   **SDR**

A 'Polar Bear' chair, by Jean Royere, fully re-upholstered in hand-stitched alpaca fabric, on low wooden legs, unmarked.

31.5in (78.5cm) wide

£10,000-15,000   **SDR**

A fine Brazilian rosewood pedestal dining table, in the style of Emile-Jacques Ruhlmann, with a radiating grain pattern to the ivory inlaid top, on four curved supports and a stepped base, unmarked.

72in (183cm) diam

£3,500-4,500   **SDR**

A walnut free-edge dining table, by Gino Russo, with four butterfly joints and terminal supports conjoined by a stretcher, signed "Gino 87".

Gino Russo worked for George Nakashima from the mid-1950s until 1968.

36in (91.5cm) wide

£800-1,200   **FRE**

A post-modern single-pedestal desk, by Peter Shire, with a trapezoidal black lacquered top on an enamelled steel base in yellow, pink and blue, unmarked.

1979   *81.5in (207cm) wide*

£800-1,200   **SDR**

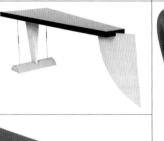

A 'Crazy Horse' table, by Ettore Sottsass for Memphis, with a square laminated top in red and black trim, on a white enamelled steel base, unmarked.

40in (101.5cm) wide

£600-900   **SDR**

One of a set of five chairs, by Philippe Starck for Aleph, comprising one armchair and four side chairs, with bentwood backs and cast aluminium rear legs, stamped "Starck Aleph".

18in (45.5cm) wide

£1,000-1,500 set   **SDR**

An 'M Serie Lang' dining table, by Philippe Starck for Aleph Driade, the circular dyed mahogany veneer top with chrome inlay, on three sharply tapered cast aluminium legs, unmarked.

51in (129.5cm) wide

£700-1,000   **SDR**

Two of a set of four high-back chairs, by Philippe Starck, three in light green and one in dark green vinyl upholstery, all with laced trim on tapering white enamelled wooden legs, unmarked.

15in (38cm) wide

£1,200-1,800 set   **SDR**

A 'Murai' stool, produced to an original Reiko Tanabe design by Tendo Mokko, in beech with a teak veneer.

2004   *17.75in (45cm) wide*

£220-280   **TDO**

A 'Spoke' oak chair, produced to an original Katsuhei Toyoguchi design by Tendo Mokko.

This is an interesting example of a Western form adapted to the Japanese environment, where furniture is traditionally very low.

2004   *32in (81cm) wide*

£400-600   **TDO**

A rare and early asymmetric server, by Russel Wright for Heywood-Wakefield, in a burled wood veneer and black lacquer finish, comprising a single drawer and two-door cabinet with horizontal pulls, unmarked.

45in (114.5cm) wide

£1,800-2,200   **SDR**

Two of a set of four rare and early 'Nikke 9019' side chairs, by Tapio Wrikkala for Stendig, each with vinyl upholstery on a tubular metal base, with "Stendig" labels.

17.5in (44.5cm) wide

£700-1,000 set   **SDR**

A butterfly stool, produced to an original Soir Yanagi design by Tendo Mokko, in beech with a rosewood veneer.

2004   *16.5in (42cm) wide*

£150-200   **TDO**

A drop-leaf dining table, by Stanley Young for Glenn of California.

c1955   *60in (152.5cm) wide*

£2,000-3,000   **LOS**

UNNAMED FURNITURE

Two of a set of five Danish rosewood and leather club chairs, with cotton webbing.

26in (65cm) wide

£800-1,200 set   **FRE**

An Italian cabinet, with an inlaid sliding door over a mirrored interior, on tapering columns, with a glass shelf and marble base, unmarked.

37in (94cm) wide

£700-1,000   **SDR**

An American polished chrome and brass coffee table, with a raised square plate glass top on a base with bracket supports, unmarked.

36in (91.5cm) wide

£120-180   **SDR**

A solid glass cow, designed by Alfredo Barbini for Vetreria Alfredo Barbini, with protruding horns and ears and grey powder inclusions, signed "A. Barbini".

c1955	13.2in (33 cm) long
£3,000-4,000	**VZ**

An amorphous clear glass vase, designed by Alfredo Barbini for Vetreria Alfredo Barbini, of strawberry red cased in clear glass.

c1960	4in (10cm) high
£500-700	**VZ**

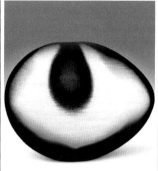

A flat oval 'Vetro Pesante' vase, designed by Alfredo Barbini, of thick transparent smoked and cased cherry red glass, signed on the base "A. Barbini".

c1960	8.75in (22cm) wide
£1,500-2,000	**QU**

A cylindrical black glass vase, designed by Alfredo Barbini for Vetreria Alfredo Barbini, with matt oil spot decoration, etched "Barbini Murano".

c1965	14.25in (36.5cm) high
£320-380	**VZ**

A glass vase, designed by Alfredo Barbini for Vetreria Alfredo Barbini, with a narrow inverted rim and double horizontal band inclusions in ochre, etched "A. Barbini".

1968	12in (30.5cm) high
£2,200-2,800	**VZ**

A turquoise cased glass vase, by Vetreria Alfredo Barbini, with a narrow inverted rim and ochre inclusions in the centre, etched "A. Barbini".

c1970	14in (35.5cm) high
£2,000-2,500	**VZ**

ERCOLE BAROVIER & ERMANNO TOSO

ERCOLE BAROVIER

- Born into a family of glassmakers, Ercole Barovier (1889-1974) abandoned a career in medicine to join his father's firm in 1919.
- In 1929 Barovier created his 'Primavera' series. The distinctive crackled white surface of these vessels was the result of an accidental chemical combination, and could not be reproduced.
- Barovier's experiments with new ways of introducing colour and texture to glass resulted in a technique called 'colorazione a caldo senza fusione'. This literally means 'colouring glass while hot without fusing', and it was widely imitated by other glassworkers on the island of Murano.
- During the 1960s, Barovier produced the 'Intarsio' series, one of his most inventive. The design consisted of a mosaic effect composed of colourful diamond or triangular tesserae and was produced in several different colour combinations from 1963.

A flat ovoid black glass vase, designed by Ercole Barovier for Vetreria Artistica Barovier & Co., with a thick rim and bands of amber aventurine.

c1925	7in (18cm) high
£600-900	**VZ**

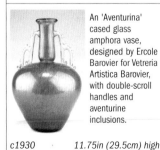

An 'Aventurina' cased glass amphora vase, designed by Ercole Barovier for Vetreria Artistica Barovier, with double-scroll handles and aventurine inclusions.

c1930	11.75in (29.5cm) high
£1,000-1,500	**QU**

A 'Primavera' vase, designed by Ercole Barovier for Vetreria Artistica Barovier, of teardrop form with opaque white craquelure effect and decorative branches in dark green.

c1930	12.5in (32cm) high
£3,000-4,000	**VZ**

A 'Vetro Mosaico' bell-shaped vase, designed by Ercole Barovier for Ferro Toso Barovier, with squared opaque yellow and brown murrines.

c1930	8.5in (21.5cm) high
£4,000-6,000	**VZ**

A 'Lenti' colourless iridescent glass vase, designed by Ercole Barovier for Barovier & Toso, with horizontal semi-spherical bosses.

c1940	8.5in (21.5cm) high
£2,000-2,500	**QU**

A 'Lenti' cylindrical amber glass vase, designed by Ercole Barovier for Barovier & Toso, with hobnail relief, unmarked.

c1940   8.25in (21cm) high
£700-1,000   VZ

An 'A Spirale' clear glass vase, designed by Ercole Barovier for Barovier & Toso, with thick ribbing, purple powder inclusions and a black diagonal spiral band.

c1940   10.25in (26cm) high
£8,000-10,000   VZ

A pale green glass bowl, designed by Ercole Barovier for Barovier & Toso, with applied emerald green flower decorations, painted iridescent gold and petrol blue.

c1940   5in (12.5cm) high
£500-700   VZ

A 'Cordonato Oro' clear glass oval bowl, designed by Ercole Barovier, ribbed throughout with scroll handles and spiral gold foil inclusions.

c1950   3.75in (9.5cm) high
£180-220   VZ

An oval glass bowl, designed by Ercole Barovier for Barovier & Toso, with ochre and opaque orange powder inclusions and irregular bubbles.

c1955   10.25in (26cm) wide
£150-200   VZ

A 'Moreschi' cylindrical glass vase, designed by Ercole Barovier for Barovier & Toso, with alternating rectangular aventurine and amber glass plate inclusions in the 'Pezzato' pattern.

c1955   7.5in (19cm) high
£3,000-5,000   QU

An 'A Canne Multiple' clear glass vase, designed by Ercole Barovier for Barovier & Toso, with spiralling bands in gold, copper, green and black, marked to the base, with remains of paper label.

c1960   17.5in (44cm) high
£1,000-1,500   QU

A 'Efeso' bulbous glass vase, designed by Ercole Barovier for Barovier & Toso, with light blue and dark grey oxide and bubble inclusions.

c1965   16.25in (40.5cm) high
£1,200-1,800   QU

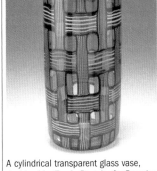

A cylindrical transparent glass vase, designed by Ercole Barovier for Barovier & Toso, with a pattern of woven horizontal and vertical violet, green and white stripes.

c1980   13.5in (33.5cm) high
£1,200-1,800   QU

A 'Morbido' black glass vase, designed by Toni Zuccheri for Barovier & Toso, the applied light grey opaque glass neck with a broad waved rim outlined in black, turquoise interior, marked.

1984   11.75in (30cm) high
£2,000-3,000   VZ

A 'Tessere' cylindrical glass vase, designed by Ercole Barovier, with a pattern of woven-effect stripes and rings, etched "Barovier & Toso Murano" to the base.

c1985   13in (33cm) high
£2,000-3,000   VZ

MODERN GLASS

A 'Tiffany' murrine and amethyst-threaded pietini vase, by Vittorio Ferro for Fratelli Toso.

The wavy rim of this vase is created by the murrines themselves which contract as they cool, pulling the rim downwards.

c1960   11.75in (30cm) high

£1,000-1,500   **VET**

A nerox glass bowl, by Vittorio Ferro, with blue and clear glass rectangular murrines.

This very rare bowl was made for the 'Santi d'Oro' exhibition. By arranging the lined murrines alternately vertically and horizontally, Ferro has created an interesting optical effect.

c1970   9.75in (25cm) diam

£2,200-2,800   **FER**

A 'Pezzato' vase, by Vittorio Ferro for De Majo, with a matte finish.

c1990   9.5in (24cm) high

£800-1,200   **PC**

A rare murrine vase, by Vittorio Ferro.

This vase was made with murrines from another factory on Murano.

1999   7.5in (19cm) high

£700-1,000   **VET**

A red and yellow murrine vase, by Vittorio Ferro for Fratelli Pagnin, with iridescent areas between the murrines.

1998   11in (28cm) high

£1,200-1,800   **PC**

A complex red murrine vase, by Vittorio Ferro for Fratelli Pagnin, signed "2000 Vittorio Ferro".

2000   7.25in (18.5cm) high

£1,200-1,800   **VET**

A gold aventurine and pietina vase, by Vittorio Ferro for Fratelli Pagnin, with blue and gold aventurine murrines, signed to the base "F'lli Pagnin Vittorio Ferro".

This shape is sometimes called 'Dead Man's Bone'.

13in (33cm) high

£3,000-4,000   **VET**

FRATELLI TOSO

A 'Stellato' oval clear glass vase, designed by Pollio Perelda for Fratelli Toso, with encased star-shaped polychrome murrines.

1953   10.5in (26.5cm) high

£3,000-4,000   **VZ**

A 'Farfalle' ovoid transparent glass vase, designed by Pollio Perelda for Fratelli Toso, with dense multi-coloured melted rectangular 'Pezzato'-style pattern.

c1960   14.5in (36.5cm) high

£6,000-8,000   **QU**

A 'Murrine' ovoid clear glass vase, designed by Ermanno Toso for Fratelli Toso, decorated with polychrome murrines, with maker's paper label.

c1960   8.5in (21.5cm) high

£2,000-2,500   **QU**

A 'Kiku' ovoid clear glass vase, designed by Ermanno Toso for Fratelli Toso, with dense polychrome murrine inclusions in flower shapes.

c1960   8.75in (22cm) high

£3,000-5,000   **VZ**

A 'Murrine' glass vase, designed by Ermanno Toso for Fratelli Toso, with a dense pattern of aubergine and opaque white murrines.

c1960   7.25in (18.5cm) high

£3,000-4,000   **VZ**

A baluster-shaped glass vase, designed by Ermanno Toso for Fratelli Toso, with narrow cylindrical neck and a dense pattern of complex coloured flower murrines.

c1960   *9.25in (23.5cm) high*

£2,200-2,800   VZ

A 'Nerox a Petoni' irregular purple glass vase, designed by Ermanno Toso for Fratelli Toso, with star-shaped murrines of various colours and copper aventurine.

c1960   *15.5in (39.5cm) high*

£8,000-10,000   VZ

A 'Nerox a Petoni' slender bottle vase, designed by Ermanno Toso for Fratelli Toso, the cylindrical neck with a slight bulge, with random coloured spot decoration.

The term 'Nerox' is used to describe the opaque black glass used to make this vase.

c1960   *16in (40.5cm) high*

£4,000-6,000   VZ

A 'Nerox a Petoni' slender clear glass bottle vase, designed by Ermanno Toso for Fratelli Toso, with long slender neck and random coloured spot decoration.

c1960   *15.75in (40cm) high*

£2,500-3,000   VZ

SEGUSO VETRI D'ARTE

A 'Vetro Pulegoso' light green cased glass vase, designed by Archimede Seguso, with an internal red spiral pattern.

c1950   *12.75in (32cm) high*

£10,000-15,000   QU

A wide oval clear glass vase, designed by Seguso Vetri d'Arte, with a wavy rim, treated to give a frosted appearance.

c1950   *4.25in (10.5cm) high*

£280-320   VZ

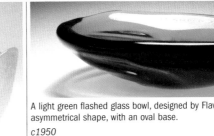

A light green flashed glass bowl, designed by Flavio Poli for Seguso Vetri d'Arte, of asymmetrical shape, with an oval base.

c1950   *12.75in (32.5cm) long*

£180-220   VZ

SEGUSO VETRI D'ARTE

- Seguso Vetri d'Arte began in the early 1930s as a small workshop operated by brothers Archimede and Ernesto Seguso and their father, Antonio.
- After working for various glass manufacturers, Flavio Poli (1900-1984) began a collaboration with Archimede Seguso in 1934. This relationship proved successful for both Poli and Seguso's Vetri d'Arte factory.
- Poli served as artistic director to the Seguso factory for almost 30 years between 1934 and 1963.
- Poli launched the 'Bullicante' range in 1936, which combined clear coloured glass with coloured underlays infused with air bubbles.
- 'Sommerso' glass, designed by Poli in the 1940s and made from the 1950s, brought Seguso Vetri d'Arte international recognition.
- Poli's shell-shaped 'Conchiglie' vases and the 'Siderale' and 'Astrale' ranges, with their concentric rings, won him many accolades and secured his reputation as a glass master.

A 'Valva' sommerso glass vase, designed by Flavio Poli for Seguso Vetri d'Arte, of multi-layered ruby and purple cased glass.

c1950   *9.5in (24cm) high*

£3,000-5,000   VZ

A 'Valva a Forato' sommerso glass vessel, designed by Flavio Poli for Seguso Vetri d'Arte, of cherry red and honey coloured cased glass.

c1950   *8.5in (21.5cm) high*

£1,500-2,000   VZ

A 'Siderale' glass bowl, designed by Flavio Poli, for Seguso Vetri d'Arte, of emerald-green and ochre cased glass arranged in concentric circles, with original factory label.

c1950   7.25in (18.5cm) diam

£3,000-5,000   VZ

A 'Siderale' flat oval glass bowl, designed by Flavio Poli for Seguso Vetri d'Arte, of beige and olive green cased glass arranged in concentric circles.

c1950   6.5in (16.5cm) diam

£1,000-1,500   VZ

A 'Siderale' flat round glass bowl, designed by Flavio Poli for Seguso Vetri d'Arte, of clear and emerald green cased glass arranged in concentric circles.

c1950   5.25in (13.5cm) diam

£1,000-1,500   VZ

A 'Siderale' round glass bowl, designed by Flavio Poli for Seguso Vetri d'Arte, of clear and emerald green cased glass arranged in concentric circles.

c1950   5.25in (13.5cm) diam

£1,800-2,200   VZ

A bulbous glass vase, designed by Archimede Seguso, with a long cylindrical neck, opaque white internal threading and pink and dark purple inclusions.

c1955   7.5in (19cm) high

£5,000-8,000   VZ

A thick oval clear glass vase, designed by Archimede Seguso, with two elongated loop handles and dark purple and amber inclusions.

c1950   12.5in (31.5cm) high

£600-900   VZ

A 'Murrine' ovoid clear glass vase, designed by Archimede Seguso, with short neck and green and white murrine decoration.

c1950   8.25in (21cm) high

£2,500-3,000   VZ

A opalescent sommerso glass vase, designed by Archimede Seguso, with spiralling ribbing and gold aventurine inclusions.

Aventurine has a glimmering finish thanks to the introduction of copper or gold particles to the glass batch. It takes its name from the Italian 'avventura', meaning 'chance'.

c1955   10.75in (27cm) high

£1,800-2,200   QU

A sommerso glass vase, designed by Flavio Poli for Seguso Vetri d'Arte, of beige and smoky brown cased glass.

c1955   8.75in (22cm) high

£1,000-1,500   VZ

A honey yellow sommerso glass vase, by Seguso Vetri d'Arte, underlaid in red and blue, with an arched rim.

c1955   13.5in (33.5cm) high

£1,000-1,500   VZ

A bottle green and orange sommerso glass vase, designed by Flavio Poli for Seguso Vetri d'Arte, of elongated teardrop shape.

c1955   17.5in (44.5cm) high
£500-800   VZ

A fan-shaped sommerso glass vase, designed by Flavio Poli for Seguso Vetri d'Arte, of cased yellow and cherry red glass, with an arched rim.

c1955   10.25in (26cm) high
£1,500-2,000   VZ

A sommerso glass bowl, designed by Flavio Poli for Seguso Vetri d'Arte, of peach and sky blue glass.

c1955   10in (25.5cm) high
£2,000-2,500   VZ

A sommerso glass bowl, designed by Flavio Poli for Seguso Vetri d'Arte, triple cased in purple, red and clear glass.

c1955   21.5in (54.5cm)
£5,000-8,000   VZ

A deep oval glass bowl, designed by Flavio Poli for Seguso Vetri d'Arte, of cased pale turquoise and green coloured glass.

c1955   12.5in (31.5cm) wide
£700-1,000   VZ

An ovoid emerald green glass vase, designed by Archimede Seguso, with fine gold foil inclusions in a spiral pattern.

c1955   3.5in (9cm) high
£1,000-1,500   VZ

A sommerso glass vase, designed by Flavio Poli for Seguso Vetri d'Arte, of cased green glass, with deep amber glass at the base.

c1955   14.25in (36cm) high
£400-600   VZ

A sommerso glass vase, designed by Flavio Poli for Seguso Vetri d'Arte, of teardrop form, in blue and green cased glass.

c1960   2.25in (30.5cm) high
£1,200-1,800   QU

A sommerso funnel-shaped clear glass vase, designed by Flavio Poli for Seguso Vetri d'Arte, with blue and green inclusions.

c1960   9.5in (24cm) high
£300-400   QU

A tall clear glass vase, designed by Flavio Poli for Seguso Vetri d'Arte, with a concave hollow body, in layered cherry red and orange cased glass.

c1960   10in (25.5cm) high
£1,200-1,800   VZ

A flat glass vase, by Seguso Vetri d'Arte, of amethyst glass cased with turquoise.

c1960   7.75in (20cm) wide
£300-500   VZ

A sommerso glass vase, designed by Flavio Poli for Seguso Vetri d'Arte, of cased yellow and turquoise glass, with a squared opening.

c1960   10in (25.5cm) high
£1,500-2,000   VZ

A sommerso glass vase, designed by Flavio Poli for Seguso Vetri d'Arte, of deep yellow glass encased with cherry red.

c1960   6in (15cm) high
£200-300   VZ

A sommerso glass vase, designed by Flavio Poli for Seguso Vetri d'Arte, with funnel neck, of encased honey and chestnut glass.

c1960   7.5in (19cm) high
£200-300   VZ

A sommerso glass vase, designed by Flavio Poli for Seguso Vetri d'Arte, of pale yellow glass cased with light red and orange.

c1960   13in (33cm) high
£1,800-2,200   VZ

A sommerso vessel, designed by Flavio Poli for Seguso Vetri d'Arte, with an asymmetrical opening, of brown and honey cased glass.

c1960   7in (17.5cm) high
£800-1,200   VZ

A sommerso vase, designed by Flavio Poli for Seguso Vetri d'Arte, with flared rim, of cased violet and olive green glass.

c1960   7.5in (19cm) high
£100-150   VZ

A sommerso glass bowl, by Seguso Vetri d'Arte, with diamond-shaped rim, of turquoise glass, encased with amethyst.

c1960   7.75in (19.5cm) wide
£300-500   VZ

A sommerso ashtray, by Seguso Vetri d'Arte, of amber and turquoise glass.

c1960   4.75in (12cm) diam
£80-120   VZ

A sommerso glass bowl, designed by Flavio Poli for Seguso Vetri d'Arte, with convex walls, of turquoise glass double-cased in amber and green.

c1960   3in (7.5cm) high
£400-600   VZ

A sommerso glass bowl, designed by Flavio Poli for Seguso Vetri d'Arte, of ruby cased glass with pale green exterior, with original label.

c1960   12.25in (31cm) wide
£1,200-1,800   VZ

A spiral ribbed glass vase, designed by Archimede Seguso, of cased clear and black glass with shimmering gold inclusions, and original factory label.

c1960   6in (15cm) high
£180-220   VZ

A glass vase, designed by Archimede Seguso, with diagonal lattice decoration of opaque pink squares with opaque white and grey stripes, with label bearing inscription in gold.

c1960   8.5in (21.5cm) high
£7,000-10,000   VZ

A sommerso glass vase, designed by Flavio Poli for Seguso Vetri d'Arte, with flat rim, of green and purple encased glass.

c1960   21in (53.5cm) high
£3,500-4,500   VZ

A turquoise cased glass fish, designed by Archimede Seguso, with dense gold foil inclusions, air bubbles, applied fins and clear glass eyes.

c1960   8in (24cm) long
£1,200-1,800   VZ

A glass vase, designed by Archimede Seguso, of petrol blue and flashed clear glass, with gold and air bubble inclusions.

c1960   6.25in (16cm) high

£800-1,200   VZ

A tapering oval glass vase, designed by Mario Pinzoni for Seguso Vetri d'Arte, with cylindrical neck, of orange glass encased with amber, with factory label.

c1965   13in (33cm) high

£800-1,200   VZ

A long oval rose glass vase, by Seguso Vetri d'Arte, with diagonal ribbing.

c1970   7in (17.5cm) high

£180-220   VZ

A glass horse's head, designed by Archimede Seguso, with wavy mane and applied black glass base.

c1970   6in (15.5cm) high

£500-700   VZ

VENINI & CO.

A moulded red glass bowl, designed by Napoleone Martinuzzi for Venini & Co., with a central rosette, wide flaring rim, the stand marked "Venini Murano".

c1925   14in (35cm) diam

£120-180   VZ

A round oval glass vase, designed by Napoleone Martinuzzi for Venini & Co., with five ribbed scroll handles on each side, of emerald green pulegoso glass.

The pulegoso technique uses a chemical process to place large numbers of tiny air bubbles in the body of the glass.

c1930   14.25in (36cm) high

£8,000-12,000   VZ

A cylindrical glass bowl, by Venini & Co., the wide rim with a trumpet-shaped stand, with spiral ribbing and applied bands.

17.5in (44.5cm) diam

£300-500   VZ

A glass apple, designed by Napoleone Martinuzzi for Venini & Co., of opaque green and clear cased craquelure glass, with burst gold foil inclusions and applied stalk and leaf with relief decoration.

c1930   4in (10cm) high

£800-1,200   VZ

A cylindrical glass bowl, designed by Carlo Scarpa for Venini & Co., with a protruding glass handle on either side and encased air bubbles.

c1935   9.5in (24cm) wide

£800-1,200   VZ

A 'Foglia' leaf-shaped clear glass bowl, designed by Tyra Lundgren for Venini & Co., with iridescent blue band inclusions, signed to the base.

Tyra Lundgren, a Scandinavian designer, was the first freelance artist to work at Venini.

c1940   8.75in (22cm) long

£1,000-1,500   VZ

A tumbler-shaped glass vase, designed by Carlo Scarpa for Venini & Co., of ruby red and honey cased glass.

c1940   4.75in (12cm) high

£1,000-1,500   VZ

A 'Clessidra' hour glass, by Venini & Co., of petrol blue and grey flashed glass, marked to the stand "Venini Murano Italia".

c1950   6in (15cm) high

£500-700   VZ

VENINI & CO.

FULVIO BIANCONI

- After graduating from the art academy in Venice, Fulvio Bianconi (1915-1996) began a career in graphic design, working for large publishing companies.

- His greatest passion was glass, and he designed for great Murano factories such as Seguso Verti d'Arte and Vistosi.

- Bianconi's designs were often witty and playful. He exhibited a flair for caricature from an early age, and this talent found an outlet in his chosen profession within the glass industry.

- Bianconi's meeting with Paolo Venini lead to a magnificent partnership. From 1946, Bianconi produced numerous designs for Venini, including a series of small figures in regional costumes, the multicoloured 'Pezzato' patterned vases and his 'Fasce Orrizontale' and 'Fasce Verticali' series.

- Bianconi's whimsical designs attracted international acclaim at the Venice Biennale Design fair in 1948 and, along with the numerous pieces that he designed for Venini, helped cement his reputation as one of the most inventive designers of Italian glass.

A tall clear glass vase, designed by Flavio Bianconi for Venini & Co., with cylindrical neck, decorated with six opaque red band inclusions, with original label to base.

c1950

£1,000-1,500   VZ

A 'Fazzoletto' clear glass handkerchief vase, designed by Fulvio Bianconi for Venini & Co., with encased bands of opaque pink and turquoise glass, marked to the base.

c1950   5.75in (14.5cm) high

£1,200-1,800   VZ

A tumbler-shaped glass vase, designed by Fulvio Bianconi for Venini & Co., of encased grey, honey yellow and opaque green glass arranged in horizontal layers, marked to the base.

c1950   5in (13cm) high

£5,000-6,000   VZ

A 'Pezzato' flared glass vase, designed by Fulvio Bianconi for Venini & Co., decorated with multicoloured rectangular plates, marked "Venini Murano Italia" to the base.

c1950   9in (23cm) high

£7,000-10,000   VZ

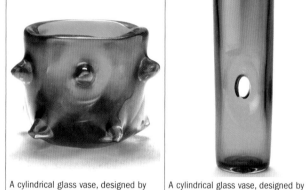

A cylindrical glass vase, designed by Fulvio Bianconi for Venini & Co., of cased emerald and clear glass with matt gold iridescence and prunts.

c1950   3.75in (9.5cm) high

£500-800   VZ

A cylindrical glass vase, designed by Fulvio Bianconi for Venini & Co., of cased turquoise and clear glass with an oval opening in the centre, marked "Venini Murano Italia" to the base.

c1950   10.75in (27cm) high

£1,200-1,800   VZ

A tumbler-shaped emerald green flashed glass vase, by Venini & Co., with regular air bubble inclusions, marked "Venini Murano Italia" to the base.

c1955   14in (35.5cm) high

£800-1,200   VZ

A tapering club-shaped clear glass 'Obelisco', designed by Paolo Venini for Venini & Co., with internal multicoloured spiral band, marked to the base "Venini Italia".

c1955   12in (30.5cm) high

£1,800-2,200   VZ

An 'A Murrina Romana' elongated flat glass dish, designed by Fulvio Bianconi for Venini & Co., with crimped rim and a dense mosaic pattern of fused murrines in various colours.

c1955   11.5in (29cm) long

£3,500-4,500   VZ

An 'Al fasce ritorte e orizzontale' clear glass lantern, designed by Flavio Bianconi for Venini & Co., with three cased glass bands in red, blue and green, signed to the base "Venini Murano Italia".

c1955   12.5in (32cm) high

£1,800-2,200   VZ

A 'Battuto' round glass bowl, designed by Tobia Scarpa for Venini & Co., of cased honey and clear glass, with wavy rim and mark to base.

c1955   3in (7.5cm) wide

£1,000-1,500   **VZ**

An 'Occhi' squared glass vase, designed by Tobia Scarpa for Venini & Co., with dense decoration of blue and green murrines outlined in red and remnants of etched stamp to the base.

'Occhi' is Italian for 'eyes'.

c1960   8.25in (21cm) high

£3,000-4,000   **VZ**

An 'Occhi' conical glass vase, designed by Tobia Scarpa for Venini & Co., with a dense pattern of yellow and grey murrines, marked "Venini 89" to the base.

c1960   13in (33cm) high

£1,500-2,000   **VZ**

A small amber flashed glass vase, by Venini & Co., with regular air bubble inclusions, marked to the base "Venini Murano Italia".

c1960   2.5in (6.5cm) high

£100-150   **VZ**

A conical tapering petrol green flashed glass vase, by Venini & Co., with horizontal veined band inclusions in various colours and remnants of original label to base.

c1960   12.25in (31cm) high

£600-900   **VZ**

An 'Occhi' club-shaped glass vase, designed by Tobia Scarpa for Venini & Co., shaped and pressed on four sides, with a grid pattern of lobster red murrines.

Designed in 1960, this pattern is still made by Venini & Co. today.

c1960   12.5in (32cm) high

£4,000-6,000   **VZ**

A battuto elongated oval grey flashed glass bowl, designed by Ludovico Diaz de Santillana for Venini & Co., with wavy rim and mark to the base.

c1960   8.25in (21cm) wide

£400-600   **VZ**

An 'Ad Incalmo' cylindrical opaque green glass vase, designed by Thomas Stearns for Venini & Co., with applied upper section of clear glass with band inclusions in reddish-black and blue, marked to the base.

c1960   10.75in (27.5cm) high

£800-1,200   **VZ**

A decorative solid glass egg, designed by Ludovico Diaz de Santillana for Venini & Co., with square opaque red murrines speckled in black and dark red, on a bobbin shaft, with engraved mark "Venini Italia".

c1965   11.25in (28.5cm) high

£3,000-5,000   **VZ**

A 'Chiacchera' oval glass vase, designed by Toots Zynsky for Venini & Co., signed and dated.

Toots Zynsky is a renowned American studio glass artist who studied with Dale Chihuly.

1984   10.25in (26cm) high

£800-1,200   **VZ**

OTHER MODERN & CONTEMPORARY GLASS

A fused glass panel, by Dorothy Hafner, entitled "On Call", on a metal stand.

25in (63.5cm) high

£3,000-4,000   **HOL**

A laminated glass sculpture, by Sidney Hutter, entitled "Twisted Solid Vase Form", joined with dyed glue.

2003   16in (40.5cm) high

£7,000-10,000   **HOL**

A glass sculpture, by Kreg Kallenberger, entitled "View at Kelly's Peak".

2003   23in (58.5cm) wide

£6,000-8,000   **HOL**

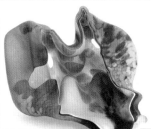

A cut and sandblasted mould-blown glass sculpture, by Marvin Lipofsky, entitled "IGS VII 2000-03 #9".

2003   16in (40.5cm) wide

£8,000-12,000   **HOL**

DALE CHIHULY

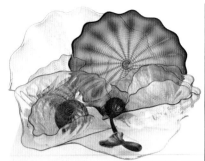

A glass sculpture series, by Dale Chihuly, entitled "Carnival Persian Set", comprising 12 pieces.

2000   *22in (56cm) wide*

£15,000-20,000   **HOL**

A glass sculpture series, by Dale Chihuly, entitled "Carnival Pheasant Macchia", comprising four pieces.

2002   *21in (53.5cm) wide*

£12,000-18,000   **HOL**

A glass sculpture series, by Dale Chihuly, entitled "Harrison Red Basket Set", comprising five pieces.

11in (28cm) high

£12,000-14,000   **HOL**

A glass "Azure and Jade Chandelier", by Dale Chihuly, comprising 130 free-blown elements supported on a steel armature.

This piece is composed of elements similar to those created for the chandelier currently exhibited in the reception area of the Victoria & Albert Museum in Kensington, London.

2002   *48in (122cm) high*

£60,000-90,000   **HOL**

A cut and sandblasted mould-blown glass sculpture, by Marvin Lipofsky, entitled "IGS VI #3", made in three parts, signed.

This piece was made at the International Glass Symposium at Novy Bor in the Czech Republic.

1997   24in (61cm) wide

£15,000-20,000   HOL

A cast glass pâte-de-verre vase, by Charles Miner, entitled "Cleo".

2003   17in (43cm) high

£2,200-2,800   HOL

An 'Ariel' glass bowl, designed by Edvin Ohrstrom for Orrefors, with engraved marks.

7.5in (19cm) diam

£180-220   ROS

A 'Pulcino' orange art glass chick, designed by Alessandro Pianon for Vistosi, with red encrustation accented by eye disks, unsigned.

c1960   9.5in (24cm) high

£1,000-1,500   SK

A glass vessel, by Stephen Powell, entitled "Ignited Lunar Lunacy", made using coloured murrines.

2003   40in (101.5cm) high

£10,000-15,000   HOL

An optical crystal glass form, by Christopher Ries, entitled "Wild Orchid", with cut, ground, polished and engraved decoration.

2001   20.5in (52cm) high

£15,000-20,000   HOL

A cut and laminated glass sculpture, by Martin Rosol, entitled "Radius VI".

2003   11in (28cm) high

£4,000-5,000   HOL

A sommerso grey flashed glass vase, by Dr. A. Salviati & Co, with opalescent finish.

c1950   14in (35.5cm) high

£800-1,200   VZ

A cut and sandblasted blown glass sphere by David Schwarz, entitled "ZAOF 12-19-00", on a metal stand.

2000   13in (33cm) high

£3,500-4,500   HOL

A cut and polished cast glass sculpture, by Steven Weinberg, entitled "Blue Cube", signed.

1996   8.25in (20cm) wide

£22,000-28,000   HOL

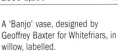

A cut and polished cast glass sculpture, by Steven Weinberg, entitled "Cutty Wow Rock Boat", signed.

2003   14in (35.5cm) wide

£5,000-8,000   HOL

A 'Banjo' kingfisher blue glass vase, designed by Geoffrey Baxter for Whitefriars, moulded with concentric abstract shapes.

12.5in (32cm) high

£1,000-1,500   HAMG

A 'Banjo' vase, designed by Geoffrey Baxter for Whitefriars, in willow, labelled.

The rarest colour for a 'Banjo' vase is ruby red – only one is currently known to exist.

12.5in (32cm) high

£1,000-1,500   TCM

A Dutch wall decoration, comprised of multiple layers of coloured glass forming a landscape scene.

19.75in (50cm) wide

£70-100   FD

707

A blue and brown vase, by Arroyave-Portella.

2003   15.75in (40cm) high
£1,200-1,800   **MOD**

A pair of unicorn bookends, by Waylande Gregory for Cowan, covered in a mottled ochre and mahogany glaze, with stamped flower mark.

7.25in (18.5cm) high
£300-400   **SDR**

A set of four 'Russian Peasant' figurines, by Alexander Blazys for Cowan, with a beige crackled glaze, comprising a Balalaika player, accordion player, tambourine player and female dancer, stamped "Cowan" with numbers.

Largest 11.5in (29cm) high
£2,500-3,000   **SDR**

An Italian majolica jug, by Giovanni DeSimone, decorated with a sun face.

DeSimone is an artist and ceramicist from Palermo who studied under Pablo Picasso.

10in (25.5cm) high
£80-120   **FD**

Five of a set of 12 porcelain plates, by Fornasetti, decorated in gilt with Roman scenes on a white ground, signed in gilt "Fornasetti-Milano".

10in (25.5cm) diam
£350-400 set   **SK**

A rare 'L'Architetto' flared urn, by Gio Ponti and Richard Ginori, printed and filled with a Classical rendering of an architect and a draped urn, marked.

13.5in (34.5cm) high
£6,000-9,000   **SDR**

A white porcelain couple, by Schwarzburger Werkstatten Für Porzellankunst Ebarch, depicted resting while he plays the mandolin, marked.

14in (35.5cm) wide
£700-1,000   **SDR**

An early architectural tile frieze, by Henry Varnum Poor, painted with fig branches flanking a bas-relief panel of pears and a fruit bowl in yellow, green and mauve glazes, mounted in an ebonised wood frame, signed "HVP".

This is one of Poor's most influential commissions, from the Helen Haas house in Nyack, NY.

c1925   34.5in (87.5cm) wide
£3,000-4,000   **SDR**

A hand-made Japanese teapot, by Luo Xiaoping, of Yixing purple clay.

1999   22in (56cm) wide
£1,000-1,500   **MOD**

A hand-made Japanese teapot, by Luo Xiaoping, of Yixing purple clay.

1999   22in (56cm) wide
£1,000-1,500   **MOD**

A hand-made Japanese teapot, by Luo Xiaoping, of Yixing purple clay.

1999   22in (56cm) wide
£1,000-1,500   **MOD**

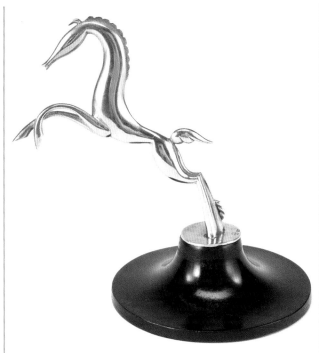

A chrome-plated figurine of a leaping horse, by Hagenauer, mounted on an ebonised circular base, stamped "Made in Vienna Austria WHW".

8.75in (22cm) high

£1,500-2,000   **SDR**

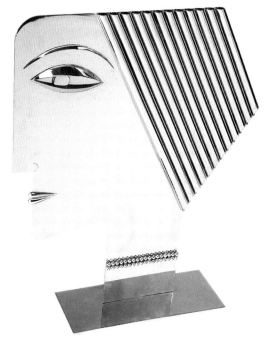

A large polished chrome sculpture of a woman's head, by Hagenauer, in profile with stylized features and locks of hair, wearing a beaded choker and mounted on a flat rectangular base, stamped "WHW Hagenauer Wien Made in Austria".

21in (53.5cm) high

£5,000-8,000   **SDR**

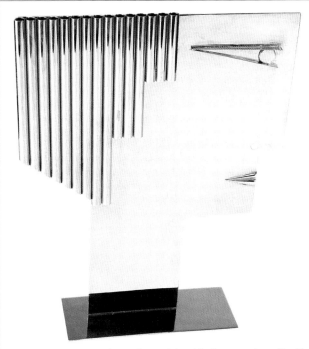

A large polished chrome sculpture of a man's head, by Hagenauer, in profile with stylized features and locks of hair, mounted on a flat rectangular base, with stamped marks.

21in (53.5cm) high

£2,200-2,800   **SDR**

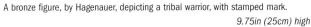

A bronze figure, by Hagenauer, depicting a tribal warrior, with stamped mark.

9.75in (25cm) high

£400-600   **WW**

CLIVE BARKER

An aluminium sculpture, by Clive Barker, entitled "Head of Darth Vader", from an edition of six.

1998   *10.75in (27.5cm) high*

£3,000-4,000   **TCM**

An aluminium sculpture, by Clive Barker, entitled "Superman", from an edition of ten.

1999   *17.5in (44.5cm) high*

£2,500-3,000   **TCM**

A aluminium sculpture, by Clive Barker, entitled "Spiderman".

1999   *19.5in (49.5cm) high*

£2,200-2,800   **TCM**

A bronze sculpture, by Clive Barker, entitled "The Emperor", depicting a Dalek, from an edition of nine.

1999   *6.5in (16.5cm) high*

£1,500-2,200   **TCM**

OTHER SCULPTURE

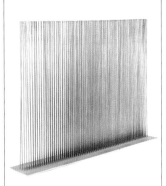

A large sonambient sculpture, by Harry Bertoia, with five rows of alternating beryllium and copper rods, mounted on a long rectangular brass base, unmarked.

36in (91.5cm) wide

£20,000-30,000   **SDR**

A monumental turned burr walnut vase, by David Ellsworth.

1981   *29in (73.5cm) high*

£6,000-9,000   **MOD**

An art glass sculpture, by Jon Juhn, entitled "Rainbow's End", mounted on a base, signed and dated.

c1990   *8.75in (22cm) high*

£2,200-2,800   **SK**

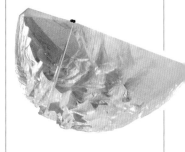

An optical glass sculpture, by Kreg Kallenberger, cast over ceramic fibre.

1986

£6,000-9,000   **JH**

Three pieces of foam sculpture, by Verner Panton, from an exhibition commissioned by Littmann Kulturprojekte of Basel, shown at Gallery Softart in Zurich.

39in (99cm) wide

£1,000-1,500   **TCM**

A rare and early 'Hokus' elephant doorstop, by Russel Wright, from a limited edition of home accessories fashioned after circus animals, unmarked.

c1935   *12in (30.5cm) high*

£8,000-10,000   **SDR**

A bronze sculpture of a camera, by Arman.

This is a limited edition artist's proof.

c1980   *23in (58.5cm) long*

£2,000-2,500   **TCM**

An amethyst, malachite and gold sculpture of an owl, by Andrew Grima.

Grima is primarily known as a jeweller.

c1975   *4.5in (11.5cm) wide*

£1,000-1,500   **TCM**

A Finnish silver pendant, in the form of a woman's profile, possibly by Majja Haavland.

c1965   *1.75in (4.5cm) long*

£150-200   **TDG**

A Canadian silver and enamel pendant.

c1970   *2in (5cm) long*

£60-90   **TCF**

A Scandinavian silver pendant, set with an agate stone.

c1965   *2in (5cm) long*

£30-50   **TDG**

A Scandinavian white metal pendant, set with rock crystal.

c1965   *2in (5cm) long*

£50-80   **TDG**

A Scandinavian silver ring, set with a semi-precious stone.

c1965   *1in (2.5cm) wide*

£70-100   **TDG**

A pair of Scandinavian silver earrings, set with agate stones.

c1965   *0.75in (2cm) long*

£40-60   **TDG**

MODERN METALWARE

A wrought-iron and brass set of andirons, by Donald Deskey for Bennett, with matching fireplace tool set on a stand with a black enamelled metal finish, marked "Bennett" with flame motif.

Tool set 33.5in (85cm) high

£400-600   **SDR**

A silver plated coffee set, by Lurelle Guild for International Silver, with die-stamped marks.

Coffee pot 6.75in (17cm) high

£280-320   **SDR**

A silver water jug, by Stuart Devlin, of flared form with hammered effect and abstract gilt handle, with impressed "SD" seal and hallmarks for London.

1973   *11.25in (28.5cm) high*

£1,500-2,000   **ROS**

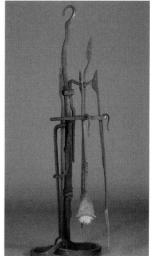

A five-piece fireplace tool set, by Albert Paley, comprising a stand with brush, shovel, poker and log tongs, unmarked.

67in (167.5cm) high

£4,000-6,000   **SDR**

- ▪ Born on the island of Funen in Denmark, Verner Panton (1926-1998) studied architecture at the Academy of Art in Copenhagen before embarking on a remarkable career in design.
- ▪ Panton was interested in holistic design, and would create pieces that complemented each other in an interior setting.
- ▪ Despite being trained in the classic Scandinavian tradition, Panton consistently strove to create innovative and amusing products.
- ▪ The Pantonaef range of modular toys was a collaboration with Kurt Naef. Kits were sold with instructions for making a variety of animals, but the pieces could be assembled into any shape. They have acquired cult status among aficionados of Panton's work.

A Pantonaef modular toy owl, designed by Verner Panton and manufactured by Kurt Naef.

c1975   21.5in (54.5cm) high

£700-1,000   **TCM**

A mounted Mira-Spectrum 'Squares' velvet fabric, designed by Verner Panton.

c1975   47.25in (120cm) wide

£600-900   **TCM**

Pantonaef
Design: Verner Panton
Kurt Naef, CH-4314 Zeiningen
Made in Switzerland

A Pantonaef modular toy fish, designed by Verner Panton and manufactured by Kurt Naef.

c1975   30in (76cm) wide

£700-1,000   **TCM**

OTHER MODERN DESIGN

A length of synthetic fabric, possibly by Pierre Cardin for Dekoplus, printed in shades of blue.

c1970   285in (724cm) long

£120-180   **FD**

A length of printed 'Larch' fabric, by Lucien Day for Heal & Son.

1961   144in (366cm) long

£200-250   **FD**

A boxed 'Shocking' perfume bottle, by Allen Jones for Les Beaux Arts, the stopper in the form of a boot, in shades of red, numbered and signed.

1993   Box 8in (20.5cm) high

£100-150   **TCM**

A boxed 'Shining' perfume bottle, by Allen Jones for Les Beaux Arts, the stopper in the form of a boot, in green and orange, numbered and signed.

1993   Box 8in (20.5cm) high

£100-150   **TCM**

An inflatable plastic cushion, by Peter Max, depicting a running man with butterfly wings, surrounded by flowers and stars.

c1975   12in (30.5cm) wide

£100-150   **TCM**

An inflatable plastic cushion, by Peter Max, depicting a smiling mouth with tulip borders and the motto "Hello".

c1975   12in (30.5cm) wide

£100-150   **TCM**

An inflatable 'Nana' plastic doll, by Nikki Saint-Phalle.

    17in (43cm) high

£70-100   **TCM**

A transparent plastic television set, by Zarach UK.

1978   15in (38cm) diam

£1,000-1,500   **TCM**

'La Comedie', by Jules Cheret, with a dancing girl.

Cheret only designed two decorative series, comprising six images in total.

33in (84cm) wide

£3,000-4,000　　**SWA**

'L'Eldorado', by Jules Cheret, advertising the important Parisian music hall, restored losses in top margin, folds, creases, matted and framed.

c1895　　*32in (81.5cm) wide*

£4,000-6,000　　**SWA**

'Bal Tabarin' in Montmartre, by Jules Alexandre Grun, restored, framed.

This is the original version of the poster.

34in (86.5cm) wide

£3,000-4,000　　**SWA**

'A La Scala', by the caricaturist and painter Albert Guillaume, advertising the opera house, rare.

c1910　　*35in (94cm) wide*

£4,000-5,000　　**SWA**

'Reforme/Le Masque Anarchiste', by Privat Livemont, advertising a novel, restoration along folds and to image, two sheets.

Unlike most Art Nouveau work, this image uses the decorative style to depict a gory scene from the story. Even the floral decorative border contains images of death.

c1895　　*63.75in (162cm) wide*

£2,000-3,000　　**SWA**

'Eugenie Buffet/Ambassadeurs', by Lucien Metivet, with an actress in a snowy scene, rare, trimmed left margin.

c1885　　*31in (79cm) wide*

£4,000-5,000　　**SWA**

'Zodiac', by Alphonse Mucha, restoration and overpainting to top of the image, corners rounded, mounted on paper.

This design for the Zodiac was one of Mucha's most popular, with nine variants. It exists as a calendar, a decorative panel and as advertising for various companies.

c1895　　*19in (48.5cm) wide*

£4,000-5,000　　**SWA**

'Job', by Alphonse Mucha, advertising Job Rolling paper, with a girl in a circle, faded, matted and framed.

c1900　　*38in (96.5cm) wide*

£6,000-7,000　　**SWA**

'Les Etoiles/Claire de Lune', by Alphonse Mucha, with pale moonlight and clouds in a night sky.

c1900　　*30in (75cm) high*

£10,000-15,000　　**SWA**

The Times of the Day, by Alphonse Mucha, the four panels representing 'Nightly Rest', 'Morning Awakening', 'Evening Reverie' and 'Daytime Dash', matted and framed.

c1900   14in (36cm) wide

£25,000-30,000   **SWA**

'Exposition Decennale De L'Automobile', by Georges Rochegrosse, restoration and losses.

This was Rochegrosse's third poster for the organisation, for 10th anniversary exposition.

c1905   45.5in (115.5cm) wide

£3,000-4,000   **SWA**

'La Ligue Vinicole' (the French Wine Guild), by Manuel Orazi, representing the positive attributes of wine drinking, restoration, damage.

c1900   55in (140cm) wide

£6,000-8,000   **SWA**

'Cie Francaise', by Theophile-Alexandre Steinlen, rare, folds, restoration and damage.

c1895   23in (58.5cm) wide

£3,000-4,000   **SWA**

'Chat Noir', by Theophile-Alexandre Steinlen, for the cabaret club, minor tears, paper discolouration.

c1895   16in (40.5cm) wide

£8,000-12,000   **SWA**

'La Revue Blanche', by Henri de Toulouse-Lautrec, advertising the avant-garde magazine, restored losses, tears, framed.

Lautrec's image is uncharacteristically soft and endearing, representing 'Misia', the living incarnation of the magazine.

c1895   36in (91.5cm) wide

£15,000-20,000   **SWA**

'La Chanson du Matelot', by Henri de Toulouse-Lautrec, rare lithograph poster of a British singer performing in Paris, paper skinning, minor creases, slight darkening.

Only five copies of this poster are known to exist. They were possibly intended for insertion into a magazine. The presence of the registration marks implies that the prints were never trimmed for use.

c1900   11.5in (29cm) wide

£30,000-40,000   **SWA**

'Transatlantique', by Jan Auvigne, with the 'Normandie' at sea, early version without text, probably designed for the 1937 Universal Exposition in Paris, rare.

c1935   40in (102cm) wide
£3,000-4,000   SWA

'TWA/Trans World Airlines', by Paul Colin, with a plane circling the globe.

Travel is a rare subject for the artist. He typically depicted Paris's cultural scene.

39in (99cm) wide
£5,000-7,000   SWA

'Cruises Italian Line', by Marcello Dudovich, with a stylish passenger.

Dudovich was awarded the gold medal at the 1900 Universal Exhibition in Paris.

25in (63.5cm) wide
£2,500-3,000   SWA

'Holland America Line', by Willem Frederik Ten Broek, with a view of a ship with an Art Deco curve to its profile, English version.

c1935   25in (63.5cm) wide
£4,000-5,000   SWA

'To New York/Hamburg America Line', by Albert Fuss, with ships sailing side-by-side.

c1930   25.5in (65cm) wide
£800-1,200   SWA

'Forth Bridge/L.N.E.R. to Scotland', by H. G. Gawthorn.

25.5in (65cm) wide
£1,500-2,000   SWA

'Normandie/The world's most perfect ship', attributed to the British painter Herkomer, with the ship at night.

Launched in 1935, the Normandie captured the Blue Ribband on her maiden voyage, making the fastest Atlantic crossing to date. Her interiors exemplified the finest French craftsmanship of the era, reflecting the prevailing Art Deco style.

c1940   24.75in (63cm) wide
£8,000-12,000   SWA

'Westminster from the Thames', by E. McKnight Kauffer, one in a series of three posters for London Transport.

c1935   25in (63.5cm) wide
£2,000-2,500   SWA

'Calcutta', by Philip Kumar Das Gupta, with a fashionable street scene and the Art Deco Metro Cinema.

25in (63.5cm) wide
£1,500-2,000   SWA

'Travel by Imperial Airways', by Tom Purvis, with a plane and elegant disembarking passengers.

c1935   20in (51cm) wide
£1,500-2,000   SWA

'Travel at reduced rates to your favorite winter resorts/Pullman', by Welsh.

This is one in a rare series of Art Deco posters for the Pullman railway company.

c1935   21in (53.5cm) wide
£2,500-3,000   SWA

MODERNIST POSTERS

'Europe/United States Lines', by Lester Beall, with an arrow and a boat.

30in (75cm) high
£1,800-2,200   SWA

'The Chap Book', by Claude Fayette Bragdon, with a stylised allegory of a Juggler and the sun.

c1895   21in (52.5cm) high
£2,500-3,000   SWA

'Now and until next May/Winter Shell', by Maurice Beck and Peter Morgan, with hot water bottles and bed warmers.

c1935   44.5in (111cm) wide
£600-800   SWA

'Persil', designed by Donald Brun, with a little girl against an orange background.

c1950   50in (125cm) high
£200-400   SWA

'A Trip To Chinatown', by The Beggarstaff Brothers, James Pryde and William Nicholson, the orange balanced by a green square, in the Ukiyo-e tradition.

The original design was sold to advertise a musical comedy, "A Trip to Chinatown" by Charles Hoyt, which opened at Toole's Theatre on September 29, 1894. However, the design was altered by the printer, Dangerfield.

c1895   117in (292.5cm) high
£25,000-30,000   SWA

'Cinzano', by Jean Carlu, lithography.

This poster re-works the unofficial emblem created by Leonetto Cappiello in 1910.

c1950   63in (157.5cm) high
£4,000-6,000   SWA

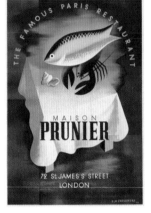

'Maison Prunier', by Adolphe Mouron Cassandre, announcing the opening of Prunier's London branch restaurant.

c1935   117in (292.5cm) high
£20,000-25,000   SWA

'Josephine Baker', by Paul Colin, with Josephine's bust in a slanted frame and free-hand drawings of the dancer in the background.

c1935   30.25in (75.5cm) high
£5,000-7,000   SWA

'British European Airways', by Lee Elliot, with a key made out of the logo and a beam of light.

c1945   39.5in (99cm) high
£300-400   SWA

'Das letzte Stück Brot', by John Heartfield, with anti-fascist propaganda imagery, in an unusual size.

c1930   55in (137.5cm) high
£7,000-10,000   SWA

'Kaffee Hag', by Ludwig Hohlwein, with a character drinking coffee.

c1915   34in (85cm) high
£8,000-12,000   SWA

'Sirenella', by Max Huber, advertising a ballroom in Zürich, depicting a drummer surrounded by colourful circles representing the emanating tempo of Swing.

c1945   53in (132.5cm) high
£1,500-2,000   SWA

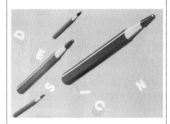

'Design', by Takenobu Igarashi, with flat tones and bold geometric letters.

c1975   40.5in (101cm) high
£600-900   SWA

'Elements of Modern Architecture', by Edward McKnight Kauffer, with asymmetrical typography and post-cubist shapes.

c1940   30in (75cm) high
£1,000-1,500   SWA

'Lubrication by Shell', by Edward McKnight Kauffer, with a Miles M-11 Whitney Straight airplane in photomontage.

c1935   44.75in (112cm) wide
£3,000-5,000   SWA

'Stop', by Pat Cokayne Keely, with a modernist design.

c1940   30in (75cm) high
£150-200   SWA

'Wireless War', by Patrick Cokayne Keely, with airplanes, battleships and an engineer connected by concentric radio waves.

This poster acknowledges the role of Post Office engineers in the field of radio technology. The visual effect has been achieved with an airbrush.

c1945   36in (90cm) wide
£1,800-2,200   SWA

'Museum Rietberg', by Ernst Keller, for the Rietberg Museum, with a stylised eagle and snake engaged in combat.

c1955   50.5in (126cm) high
£1,500-2,000   SWA

'The Truth That Makes Men Free/American Bible Society' designed by Rockwell Kent.

c1940   32in (80cm) high
£600-900   SWA

'Zoologischer Garten', depicting a flamingo, with precise architectural rendering of the zoo buildings.

c1910   26.5in (66cm) high
£800-1,200   SWA

'Lincoln Center', by Roy Lichtenstein, advertising a film festival.

1966   45in (112.5cm) high
£1,200-1,800   SWA

Russische Ausstellung', by El Lissitsky, the two youths sharing a common eye, created with photomontage.

1929   48in (120cm) high
£30,000-35,000   SWA

One of two posters designed by Charles Loupot, this one, 'Mondriaan', paying tribute to the artist.

c1970

£400-600 pair SWA

'Quinquina', designed by Charles Loupot, printed by Gaillard, Paris, for St. Raphael.

c1955   *42.5in (106cm) high*

£2,000-3,000 SWA

'Engelberg', designed by Herbert Matter, printed by C.J. Bucher, Luzern, depicting the immensity of the Alps.

c1935   *39.75in (99cm) high*

£700-1,000 SWA

'Jaarbeurs Utrecht', by Henri C. Pieck, advertising a fair.

Pieck plays with industrial architecture, turning the typography into a building.

c1935   *39.25in (98cm) high*

£1,200-1,800 SWA

'Addo-X', by Ladislav Sutnar, advertising an adding machine.

c1955   *21in (52.5cm) high*

£800-1,200 SWA

'Ladislav Sutnar: Visual Design in Action', by Ladislav Sutnar, to promote Sutnar's book and exhibition of the same name, with the poster mirroring the design on the cover of the book.

1961   *24in (60cm) high*

£600-900 SWA

'Sleeping Murderer', by Tadanori Yokoo.

This poster was made for a poetry volume by Matsuro Takahashi, the character on the poster appears facing forward on the cover.

c1965   *41.75in (104cm) high*

£1,500-2,000 SWA

'A La Maison De M. Civecawa', by Tadanori Yokoo, for the 'Aukoku Buto Ha' dance company, bearing traditional Japanese imagery, including the rising sun, the great wave and a Japanese Bullet Train.

c1965   *40.5in (101cm) high*

£3,000-4,000 SWA

'Hunchback in Aomori Prefecture', by Tadanori Yokoo, for the Tenjo Sajiki theatre company, representing the front page of a newspaper crossed out and 'edited'.

c1965   *40.5in (101cm) high*

£1,000-1,500 SWA

'Kanox', by Tadanori Yokoo, advertising a film and television production company, with images of an Italian Renaissance villa and a bolt of lighting.

c1980   *40.25in (100.5cm) high*

£600-900 SWA

'Janie Marèse', by Jean Chassaing, the face with a dark shadow.

This was the only poster portrait made of this actress who died in a car accident at the age of 23 shortly after filming 'La Chienne'.

c1928   63in (160cm) high

£4,000-5,000   **SWA**

'La Regia', Jean Chassaing, in a caricature style with bold colours.

c1930   62in (157.5cm) high

£600-800   **SWA**

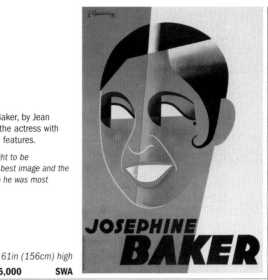

Josephine Baker, by Jean Chassaing, the actress with well stylized features.

This is thought to be Chassaing's best image and the one of which he was most proud.

c1930   61in (156cm) high

£10,000-15,000   **SWA**

A portfolio album by Paul Colin, entitled 'Le Tumulte Noir', with 42 hand-coloured lithographs, one of an edition of 500, complete with double cover and insert, the first half dedicated to the black musicians of 1920s Paris, the second half a satire of Paris under the spell of the Charleston.

1927

£15,000-20,000   **SWA**

'Lisa Duncan', by Paul Colin, depicting the interpretive dancer, the figure intwined with and framed by a grand piano.

The influence of African art can be seen in the neo-cubist, sculptural style of the dancer's limbs.

c1925   47in (119.5cm) high

£15,000-20,000   **SWA**

'Benglia', by Paul Colin, the profile of his head represented in a graphic, realistic way.

This poster depicts the successful Algerian-born screen and stage actor.

c1930   63in (160cm) high

£2,000-3,000   **SWA**

'Sylvie' (Louise Sylvain), by Paul Colin, depicting the actress, with a flat plane and a shadowy, geometric partition.

c1930   63in (160cm) high

£600-800   **SWA**

'Josephine Baker', by Georges de Pogedaieff, depicting the actress, the portrait of her face enclosing the text.

c1930   63.25in (160.5cm) high

£5,000-7,000   **SWA**

'Etoile du Nord/Pullman', by Adolphe Cassandre, with a train on a horizon.

This image was a revolution as it depicted no landscape, no destination and no train. The low angle view of the rails is a signature technique of Cassandre's.

c1925   41in (104cm) high

£8,000-12,000   **SWA**

'SS Côte d'Azur', by Adolphe Cassandre, depicting the boat from the side.

This is the last of Cassandre's 'chimney series'. After this poster, his ship designs began to depict the entire ship rather than just individual design components.

c1930   39in (99cm) high

£8,000-12,000   **SWA**

'La Route Bleue/Autocars Deluxe', by Adolphe Cassandre, the image converging to a point in the horizon where the sun is setting.

c1930   39in (99cm) high

£20,000-25,000   **SWA**

'Brillant bicycles', by Adolphe Cassandre, the composition built around the inline of the bicycle.

This is one of Cassandre's earlier posters and represents one of his more daring attempts to stylise the human body.

c1925   46.25in (117.5cm) high

£20,000-25,000   **SWA**

'Aubucheron', by Adolphe Cassandre, advertising a Parisian furniture store, in an unusual elongated format, with a lumberjack swinging his axe, rare.

c1925   161in (409cm) wide

£30,000-35,000   **SWA**

'Tabarin club' by Paul Colin, depicting three woman united by their dress.

The Tabarin club opened in 1904 and made its name with the cancan.

c1930   63in (160cm) high

£10,000-15,000   **SWA**

'Black Birds', by Paul Colin, advertising a musical revue at the Moulin Rouge by Lew Leslie, depicting three of the show's performers including Adelaide Hall in the centre, unique.

c1930   62in (157.5cm) high

£100,000-150,000   **SWA**

'Bal Nègre', by Paul Colin, advertising an event at the Theatre des Champs-Elysees, depicting Josephine Baker.

Paul Colin produced his album 'Le Tumulte Noir', celebrating the 'black craze' in Paris, to be sold at this event.

c1930   63.25in (160.5cm) high

£60,000-80,000   **SWA**

'St Jean de Luz', by Louis Floutier, with a beach in the Basque country and the Art Deco architecture of Robert Mallet-Stevens' Casino de la Pergola.

Louis Floutier (1882-1936) was one of the major initiators of the Basque Art Deco style.

c1930   41in (104cm) high

£3,000-4,000   **SWA**

'Sables d'Or Les Pins', by Charles Loupot, with a graceful elongated image of a couple, the sand picked out in gold ink.

c1925   41.5in (105.5cm) high

£5,000-7,000   **SWA**

'The Night Scotsman Leaves Kings Cross Nightly at 10.25', by Alexander Alexeieff, published by the LNER.

Alexander Alexeieff (1901-1982) was a well-known ballet set designer and book illustrator. This poster was published in two versions: this one for the London start of the journey and another "To London by Sleeper" used for the Scottish terminal.

c1930   50in (127cm) wide

£12,000-18,000   **ON**

'Olympic/Titanic', by Montague B. Black, with the Titanic in the background.

The poster originally had a green border bearing a caption. After the catastrophic maiden voyage of the Titanic, the White Star Line company over-painted her name, only a few copies have survived.

c1910   39in (99cm) wide

£4,000-5,000   **SWA**

'Atlantic City/Pennsylvania Railroad', by Edward M. Eggleston, with a bustling boardwalk and bathing female.

c1935   25in (63.5cm) wide

£15,000-20,000   **SWA**

'Atlantic City/Pennsylvania Railroad', by Edward M. Eggleston, with a couple and the Atlantic City Boardwalk, the ocean and the Steel Pier in the distance.

c1935   25in (63.5cm) wide

£7,000-10,000   **SWA**

'Yellowstone-Park', by Ludwig Hohlwein, with a Company Coach.

Signed into existence in 1872 by President Ulysses S. Grant, Yellowstone was the world's first national park.

£10,000-15,000   **SWA**

'Rockefeller Centre', By Leslie Ragan, with Long Island City, St. Patrick's Cathedral and the Hudson River, New Jersey in the distance.

c1935   26.5in (67.5cm) wide

£8,000-12,000   **SWA**

'The New York Empire State Express', by Leslie Ragan, the train in an autumn landscape, making the run between New York and Buffalo.

c1940   27in (68.5cm) wide

£10,000-15,000   **SWA**

'Chicago World's Fair', by Weimar Pursell, depicting the Hall of Science.

1933   27in (68.5cm) wide

£3,000-4,000   **SWA**

'Two Days to Europe', by Jupp Wiertz, the Hindenburg Zeppelin LZ-129 pictured soaring over the skyscrapers of Manhattan.

This is the extremely rare English language variation, the poster is also known to exist in German and Italian.

1936   22in (56cm) wide

£8,000-12,000   **SWA**

'Brighton & Hove', by Kenneth Shoesmith, with figures strolling along the boardwalks and the West Pier stretching out over the water.

49.5in (126cm) wide

£1,500-2,000   **SWA**

'The Pool of London', by Fred Taylor, with a bird's-eye view of the river Thames and the surrounding city.

49.5in (126cm) wide

£3,000-4,000   **SWA**

EVERY ANTIQUE ILLUSTRATED in *DK Antiques Price Guide 2006* by Judith Miller has a letter code which identifies the dealer or auction house that sold it. The list below is a key to these codes. In the list, auction houses are shown by the letter Ⓐ and dealers by the letter Ⓓ. Some items may have come from a private collection, in which case the code in the list is accompanied by the letter Ⓟ. Inclusion in this book in no way constitutes or implies a contract or a binding offer on the part of any of our contributors to supply or sell the goods illustrated, or similar items, at the prices stated.

AA Ⓓ
Albert Amor 37 Bury Street, St James's, London SW1Y 6AU
Tel: 020 7930 2444
www.albertamor.co.uk

AAC Ⓐ
Sanford Alderfer Auction Company 501 Fairgrounds Road, Hatfield, PA 19440, USA
Tel: 001 215 393 3000
www.alderferauction.com

ABAA Ⓓ
Abacus Antiques No longer trading

ABIJ Ⓓ
Aurora Bijoux
Tel: 001 215 872 7808
www.aurorabijoux.com

AD Ⓓ
Andrew Dando 34 Market Street, Bradford on Avon, Wiltshire BA15 1LL
Tel: 01225 865 444
www.andrewdando.co.uk

AG Ⓓ
Antique Glass at Frank Dux Antiques 33 Belvedere, Lansdown Road, Bath, Avon BA1 5HR
Tel/Fax: 01225 312 367
www.antique-glass.co.uk

AGO Ⓓ
Anona Gabriel Otford Antiques Centre, 26-28 High Street, Otford, Sevenoaks, Kent TN14 5PQ
Tel: 01959 522 025
info@otfordantiques.co.uk

AHL Ⓓ
Andrea Hall Levy PO Box 1243, Riverdale, NY 10471, USA
Tel: 001 646 441 1726
barangrill@aol.com

AL Ⓓ
Andrew Lineham Fine Glass PO Box 465, Chichester, West Sussex PO18 8WZ.
Tel: 01243 576 241
Mob: 07767 702 722
www.antiquecolouredglass.info

ALL Ⓐ
Allard Auctions P.O. Box 1030, 419 Flathead St. 4, St. Ignatius, MT 59865, USA
Tel: 001 460 745 0500
www.allardauctions.com

ANA Ⓓ
Ancient Art 85 The Vale, Southgate, London N14 6AT
Tel: 020 8882 1509
Fax: 020 8886 5235
www.ancientart.co.uk

ANF Ⓓ
Anfora Glass Factory Contact through Vetro & Arte Gallery, Calle del Cappeller 3212, Dorsoduro, Venice 30123, Italy
Tel: 0039 041 522 8525
www.venicewebgallery.com

AS Ⓓ
Alistair Sampson Antiques 120 Mount Street, London W1K 3NN
Tel: 020 7409 1799

ATL Ⓓ
Antique Textiles and Lighting 34 Belvedere, Lansdowne Road, Bath, Somerset BA1 5HR
Tel: 01225 310 795
www.antiquetextilesandlighting.co.uk

AVW Ⓓ
Circa 1900 Shop 17, Georgian Village, Camden Passage, London N1 8DU
Tel: 0771 370 9211
www.circa1900.org

B Ⓐ
Dreweatt Neate (Formerly Bracketts) Tunbridge Wells Saleroom, The Auction Hall, The Pantiles, Tunbridge Wells, Kent TN2 5QL
Tel: 01892 544500
www.dnfa.com/tunbridgewells

B&H Ⓐ
Burstow & Hewett Lower Lake, Battle, East Sussex TN33 0AT
Tel: 01424 772374
www.burstowandhewett.co.uk

BAM Ⓐ
Bamfords Ltd The Old Picture Palace, 133 Dale Road, Matlock, Derbyshire DE4 3LU
Tel: 01629 574460

BBI Ⓓ
B&B Italia - Maxalto Strada Provinciale 32, n° 15, 22060 Novedrate (CO), Italy
Tel: 0039 031 795 111
www.bebitalia.it

BCAC Ⓓ
Bucks County Antique Center Route 202, PA 18914, USA
Tel: 001 215 794 9180

BEA Ⓐ
Beaussant Lefèvre 32 rue Drouot, 75009 Paris, France
Tel: 00 33 (0)1 47 70 40 00
www.beaussant-lefevre.auction.fr

BEJ Ⓓ
Bébés et Jouets c/o Lochend Post Office, 165 Restalrig Road, Edinburgh, Midlothian EH7 6HW
Tel: 0131 332 5650
bebesetjouets@tiscali.co.uk

BEV Ⓓ
Beverley 30 Church Street, Marylebone, London NW8 8EP
Tel: 020 7262 1576

BIB Ⓓ
Biblion 1/7 Davies Mews, London W1K 5AB
Tel: 020 7629 1374
www.biblion.com

BL Ⓓ
Blanchard Ltd. 86/88 Pimlico Road, London SW1W 8PL
Tel: 020 7823 6310
piers@jwblanchard.com

BLA Ⓓ
Blanchet et Associés 3 rue Geoffroy Marie, 75009 Paris, France
Tel: 00 33 (0)1 53 34 14 44
blanchet.auction@wanadoo.fr

BLO Ⓐ
Bloomsbury Auctions Bloomsbury House, 24 Maddox Street, London W1 S1PP
Tel: 020 7495 9494
www.bloomsburyauctions.com

BMN Ⓐ
Auktionshaus Bergmann Möhrendorfer Str. 4, 91056, Erlangen, Germany
Tel: 00 49 (0)9131 45 06 66
www.auction-bergmann.de

BO Ⓓ
Le Blason d'Or 117 boulevard Stalingrad, 69100 Villeurbanne, France
Tel: 00 33 (0) 4 78 28 01 08

BONM Ⓐ
Bonhams Knowle The Old House, Station Road, Knowle, Solihull, West Midlands B93 0HT
Tel: 01564 776 151
www.bonhams.com

BOY Ⓓ
Boym Partners Inc 131 Varick Street, No. 915, New York, NY 10013, USA
Tel/Fax: 001 212 807 8210
www.boym.com

BRB Ⓓ
Bauman Rare Books 535 Madison Avenue, New York, NY 10022, USA
Tel: 001 212 751 0011
www.baumanrarebooks.com

BRU Ⓐ
Brunk Auctions Post Office Box 2135, Asheville, NC 28802, USA
Tel: 001 828 254 6846
www.brunkauctions.com

BP Ⓓ
The Blue Pump 178 Davenport Road,
Toronto M5R 1J2, Canada
Tel: 001 416 944 1673
www.thebluepump.com

BY Ⓓ
Bonny Yankauer
bonnyy@aol.com

C Ⓐ
Cottees The Market, East Street, Wareham,
Dorset BH20 4NR
Tel: 01929 552826
www.auctionsatcottees.co.uk

CA Ⓐ
Chiswick Auctions 1-5 Colville Road,
London W3 8BL
Tel: 020 8992 4442
www.chiswickauctions.co.uk

CATO Ⓓ
Lennox Cato Antiques 1 The Square,
Church Street, Edenbridge, Kent TN8 5BD
Tel: 01732 865 988
www.lennoxcato.com

CGC/CGPC Ⓟ
Cheryl Grandfield Private Collection

CHA Ⓓ
Charlotte Marler Booth 14,
1528 West 25th Street,
New York, NY 10010, USA
Tel: 001 212 367 8808
char_marler@hotmail.com

CHEF Ⓐ
Cheffins Clifton House, 1&2 Clifton Road,
Cambridge, Cambridgeshire CB1 7EA
Tel: 01223 213 343
www.cheffins.co.uk

CO Ⓐ
Cooper Owen 74 High Street, Egham,
Surrey TW20 9LF
Tel: 01784 434900
www.cooperowen.com

CRIS Ⓓ
Cristobal 26 Church Street, London NW8 8EP
Tel/Fax: 020 7724 7230
www.cristobal.co.uk

CSA Ⓓ
Christopher Sykes Antiques
The Old Parsonage, Woburn, Milton Keynes,
Buckinghamshire MK17 9QJ
Tel: 01525 290 259/290 467
www.sykes-corkscrews.co.uk

CSAY Ⓓ
Charlotte Sayers Stand 313-315, Grays
Antique Markets, 58 Davies Street,
London W1K 5LP
Tel: 020 7499 5478

CSB Ⓐ
Chenu Scrive Berard Hôtel des Ventes Lyon
Presqu'île, 6 rue Marcel Rivière,
69002 Lyon, France
Tel: 00 33 (0)4 72 77 78 01
www.chenu-scrive.com

DA Ⓓ
Davies Antiques c/o Cadogan Tate, Unit 6,
6-12 Ponton Road, London SW8 5BA
Tel/Fax: 020 8947 1902
www.antique-meissen.com

DB Ⓓ
David Bowden Stand 107, Grays Antique
Markets, 58 Davies Street, London W1K 5LP
Tel/Fax: 020 7495 1773

DD Ⓓ
Decodame.com 853 Vanderbilt Beach Road,
PMB 8, Naples, FL 34108, USA
Tel: 001 239 514 6797
www.decodame.com

DJI Ⓓ
Deco Jewels Inc 131 Thompson Street, NY, USA
Tel: 001 212 253 1222
decojewels@earthlink.net

DL Ⓓ
David Love 10 Royal Parade,
Harrogate, North Yorkshire HG1 2SZ
Tel: 01423 565 797

DN Ⓐ
Dreweatt Neate Donnington Priory Salerooms,
Donnington, Newbury, Berkshire RG14 2JE
Tel: 01635 553553
www.dnfa.com/donnington

DOR Ⓐ
Dorotheum Palais Dorotheum,
A-1010 Vienna, Dorotheergasse 17, Austria
Tel: 0043 1 515 600
www.dorotheum.com

DR Ⓓ
**Derek Roberts Fine Antique Clocks &
Barometers** 25 Shipbourne Road, Tonbridge,
Kent TN10 3DN
Tel: 01732 358 986
www.qualityantiqueclocks.com

DRA Ⓐ
David Rago Auctions 333 North Main Street,
Lambertville, NJ 08530, USA
Tel: 001 609 397 9374
www.ragoarts.com

EG Ⓐ
Edison Gallery Susanin's 900, S. Clinton St.,
Chicago, Il 60607, USA
Tel: 001 617 359 4678
www.edisongallery.com

EPO Ⓓ
Elaine Perkins Otford Antiques Centre,
26-28 High Street, Otford, Kent TN15 9DF
Tel: 01959 522 025
www.otfordantiques.co.uk

EVE Ⓓ
Evergreen Antiques 1249 Third Avenue,
New York, NY 10021, USA
Tel: 001 212 744 5664
www.evergreenantiques.com

FAN Ⓓ
Fantiques
Tel: 020 8840 4761
paula.raven@ntlworld.com

FD Ⓓ
Fragile Design 8 Lakeside, The Custard Factory,
Digbeth, Birmingham, West Midlands B9 4AA
Tel: 0121 693 1001
www.fragiledesign.com

FER Ⓓ
Vittorio Ferro at Fratelli Pagnin
See VET

FIS Ⓐ
Auktionshaus Dr Fischer
Trappensee-Schlößchen,
74074 Heilbronn, Germany
Tel: 00 49 7131 15 55 7 0
www.auctions-fischer.de

FM Ⓓ
Francesca Martire F131-137, Alfies Antique
Market, 13 Church Street, Marylebone,
London NW8 8DT
Tel: 020 7724 4802

FRE Ⓐ
Freeman's 1808 Chestnut Street,
Philadelphia, PA 19103, USA
Tel: 001 215 563 9275
www.freemansauction.com

GAL Ⓓ
Gallery 532 142 Duane Street, New York,
NY 10013, USA
Tel: 001 212 964 1282
www.gallery532.com

GCC Ⓓ
Cook's Cottage Antiques at The Ginnel
The Ginnel Antiques Centre, off Parliament
Street, Harrogate, North Yorkshire HG1 2RB
Tel: 01423 508 857
www.redhouseyork.co.uk

GCL Ⓓ
Claude Lee at The Ginnel The Ginnel Antiques
Centre, off Parliament Street, Harrogate,
North Yorkshire HG1 2RB
Tel: 01423 508 857
www.redhouseyork.co.uk

GIL Ⓐ
Gilding's Auctioneers 64 Roman Way, Market
Harborough, Leicestershire LE16 7PQ
Tel: 01858 410414
www.gildings.co.uk

GK Ⓐ
Gallerie Koller Hardturmstrasse 102, Postfach,
8031 Zürich, Switzerland
Tel: 00 41 1445 6363
www.galeriekoller.ch

GKA Ⓓ
Kismet Antiques at The Ginnel The Ginnel
Antiques Centre, off Parliament Street,
Harrogate, North Yorkshire HG1 2RB
Tel: 01423 508 857
www.redhouseyork.co.uk

GMC Ⓓ
Mary Cooper at The Ginnel The Ginnel
Antiques Centre, off Parliament Street,
Harrogate, North Yorkshire HG1 2RB
Tel: 01423 508 857
www.redhouseyork.co.uk

GOL (D)
Nancy Goldsmith New York
Tel: 001 212 696 0831

GORL (A)
Gorringes 15 North Street, Lewes,
East Sussex BN7 2PD
Tel: 01273 472 503
www.gorringes.co.uk

GS (D)
Goodwins Antiques 15 & 16 Queensferry
Street, Edinburgh, Midlothian EH2 4QW
Tel: 0131 225 4717

GV (D)
Galerie Vandermeersch Voltaire Antiquités-
Vandermeersch SA, 21, quai Voltaire,
75007 Paris, France
Tel: 00 33 1 42 61 23 10

H&L (A)
Hampton and Littlewood The Auction Rooms,
Alphin Brook Road, Alphington,
Exeter, Devon EX2 8TH
Tel: 01392 413100
www.hamptonandlittlewood.co.uk

HAMG (A)
**Dreweatt Neate Godalming (Formerly
Hamptons)** Baverstock House, 93 High Street,
Godalming, Surrey GU7 1AL
Tel: 01483 423567
www.dnfa.com/godalming

HBK (D)
Hall-Bakker at Heritage Heritage, 6 Market
Place, Woodstock, Oxfordshire, OX20 1TA
Tel: 01993 811 332

HFG (D)
Galerie Hélène Fournier Guérin 18 rue des
Saints-Pères, 75007 Paris, France
Tel: 00 33 1 42 60 21 81

HMN (A)
Hermann Historica OHG Linprunstrasse 16,
80335 Munich, Germany
Tel: 0049 895 237 296
www.hermann-historica.com

HOL (D)
Holsten Galleries Elm Street, Stockbridge,
MA 01262, USA
Tel: 001 413 298 3044
www.holstengalleries.com

IF (D)
Madame Isabelle Franc Cité des Antiquaires,
117, Boulevard Stalingrad,
69100 Lyon-Villeurbane, France
Tel: 00 33 4 72 44 98 91
Mob: 00 33 6 07 68 17 75

ISA (A)
Ivey Selkirk Auctioneers 7447 Forsyth
Boulevard, Saint Louis, MI 63105, USA
Tel: 001 314 726 5515
www.iveyselkirk.com

ISO (D)
ISOKON Plus Turnham Green Terrace Mews,
London W4 1QU
Tel: 020 8994 0636
www.isokonplus.com

JBB (D)
Jean-Baptiste Bacquart
www.africanandoceanicart.com

JBS (D)
John Bull (Antiques) Ltd. JB Silverware,
139A New Bond Street, London W1S 2TN
Tel: 020 7629 1251
www.antique-silver.co.uk
www.jbsilverware.co.uk

JDJ (A)
James D Julia Inc PO Box 830, Fairfield,
ME 04937, USA
Tel: 001 207 453 7125
www.juliaauctions.com

JES (D)
John Jesse 160 Kensington Church Street,
London W8 4BN
Tel: 020 7229 0312
jj@johnjesse.com

JF (D)
Jill Fenichell, Inc. Suite 333, 55 Washington
Street, Brooklyn, NY 11238, USA
Tel: 001 718 237 2490
By appointment only

JH (D)
Jeanette Hayhurst Fine Glass 32A Kensington
Church St., London W8 4HA
Tel: 020 7938 1539

JHD (D)
John Howard at Heritage Heritage, 6 Market
Place, Woodstock, Ofordshire OX20 1TA
Tel: 0870 444 0678
www.antiquepottery.co.uk

JHOR (D)
Jonathan Horne 66c Kensington Church Street,
London W8 4BY
Tel: 020 7221 5658
www.jonathanhorne.co.uk

JJ (D)
Junkyard Jeweler
www.tias.com/stores/thejunkyardjeweler

JK (D)
John King 74 Pimlico Road, London SW1W 8LS
Tel: 020 7730 0427
kingj896@aol.com

JM (D)
John Makepeace Farrs, Beaminster,
Dorset DT8 3NB
Tel: 01308 862 204
www.johnmakepeace.com

JN (A)
John Nicholsons The Auction Rooms,
'Longfield', Midhurst Road, Fernhurst,
Haslemere, Surrey GU27 3HA
Tel: 01428 653727
www.johnnicholsons.com

KAU
Auktionshaus Kaup Schloss Sulzburg,
Hauptstrasse 62, 79295 Sulzburg, Germany
Tel: 0049 7634 5038 0
www.kaupp.de

KGO (D)
Pauline Guy Otford Antiques Centre,
26-28 High Street, Otford, Kent TN15 9DF
Tel: 01959 522 025
www.otfordantiques.co.uk

L&T (A)
Lyon and Turnbull Ltd. 33 Broughton Place,
Edinburgh, Midlothian EH1 3RR
Tel: 0131 557 8844
www.lyonandturnbull.com

LAN (A)
Lankes Triftfeldstrasse 1, 95182 Döhlau,
Germany
Tel: 0049 92 869 5050
www.lankes-auktionen.de

LANE (D)
Eileen Lane Antiques 150 Thompson Street,
New York, NY 10012, USA
Tel: 001 212 475 2988
www.eileenlaneantiques.com

LB (D)
Linda Bee Grays Antique Market Mews,
1-7 Davies Street, London, W1Y 2LP
Tel: 020 7629 5921
www.graysantiques.com

LC (A)
Lawrence's Fine Art Auctioneers
The Linen Yard, South Street, Crewkerne,
Somerset TA18 8AB
Tel: 01460 73041
www.lawrences.co.uk

LFA (A)
Law Fine Art Ltd. Ash Cottage, Ashmore Green,
Newbury, Berkshire, RG18 9ER
Tel: 01635 860033
www.lawfineart.co.uk

LM (D)
Lili Marleen
www.lilimarleen.net

LN (D)
Lillian Nassau Ltd Lillian Nassau Ltd,
220 East 57th Street, New York NY 10022, USA
Tel: 001 212 759 6062
www.lilliannassau.com

LOS (D)
Lost City Arts 18 Cooper Square, New York,
NY 10003, USA
Tel: 001 212 375 0500
www.lostcityarts.com

LPZ (A)
Lempertz Neumarkt 3, 50667
Cologne, Germany
Tel 00 49 (0)221 925 72 90
www.lempertz.com

LYNH (D)
Lynn & Brian Holmes By appointment
Tel: 020 7368 6412

MACK (D)
Macklowe Gallery 667 Madison Av., New York,
NY 10021, USA
Tel: 001 212 644 6400
www.macklowegallery.com

MB Ⓓ
Mostly Boxes 93 High St., Eton, Windsor, Berkshire SL4 6AF
Tel: 01753 858 470

MGL Ⓓ
Mix Gallery 17 South Main Street, Lambertville, NJ 08530, USA
Tel: 001 609 773 0777
www.mix-gallery.com

MILLB Ⓓ
Million Dollar Babies
Tel: 001 518 885 7397

MJM Ⓓ
Marc Matz Antiques By appointment, 368 Broadway, Cambridge, MA 02139, USA
Tel: 001 617 460 6200 www.marcmatz.com

MOD Ⓓ
Moderne Gallery 111 North 3rd Street, Philadelphia, PA 19106, USA
Tel: 001 215 923 8536
www.modernegallery.com

MTZ Ⓐ
Auktionshaus Metz Friedrich-Eber-Anlage 5, 69117 Heidelberg, Germany
Tel: 0049 6221 23571
www.Metz-Auktion.de

MW Ⓓ
Mike Weedon 7 Camden Passage, Islington, London N1 8EA
Tel: 020 7226 5319/020 7609 6826
www.mikeweedonantiques.com

NA Ⓐ
Northeast Auctions 93 Pleasant Street, Portsmouth, NH 03801, USA
Tel: 001 603 433 8400
www.northeastauctions.com

NAG Ⓐ
Nagel Neckarstrasse 189-191, 70190 Stuttgart, Germany
Tel: 0049 711 649 690
www.auction.de

NBLM Ⓓ
N. Bloom & Son (1912) Ltd.
Tel: 020 7629 5060
www.nbloom.com

NEA Ⓐ
Dreweatt Neate (Formerly Neales)
The Nottingham Salerooms, 192 Mansfield Road, Nottingham, Nottinghamshire NG1 3HU
Tel: 0115 962 4141
www.dnfa.com/neales

ON Ⓐ
Onslows
The Coach House, Manor Road, Stourpaine, Dorset DT11 8TQ
Tel: 01258 488 838
www.onslows.co.uk

PBA Ⓐ
Pierre Bergé & Associés 12 rue Drouot, 75009 Paris, France
Tel: 00 33 1 49 49 90 00
www.pba-auctions.com

PC Ⓟ
Private Collection

PH Ⓓ
Pantry and Hearth 994 Main Street South, Woodbury, CT 06798, USA
Tel: 001 203 263 8555
www.nhada.org/pantryhearth.htm

PIA Ⓐ
Piasa 5 rue Drouot, 75009 Paris, France
Tel: 00 33 1 53 34 10 10

PIL Ⓐ
Salle des Ventes Pillet 1 rue de la Libération, 27480 Lyons la Forèt, France
Tel: 0033 2 32 49 60 64
www.pillet.auction.fr

POOK Ⓐ
Pook and Pook 463 East Lancaster Avenue, Downington, PA 19335, USA
Tel: 001 610 269 4040/0695
www.pookandpook.com

PRA Ⓓ
Pier Rabe Antiques 141 Dorp St., Stellenbosch 7600, South Africa
Tel: 0027 21 883 9730

PSA Ⓐ
Potteries Specialist Auctions 271 Waterloo Road, Cobridge, Stoke-on-Trent, Staffordshire ST6 3HR
Tel: 01782 286 622
www.potteriesauctions.com

PST Ⓓ
Patricia Stauble Antiques 180 Main Street, PO Box 265, Wiscasset, ME 04578, USA
Tel: 001 207 882 6341
pstauble@midcoast.com

PUR Ⓓ
Puritan Values The Dome, St Edmund's Road, Southwold, Suffolk IP18 6BZ
Tel: 01502 722211
Mob: 07966 371676
www.puritanvalues.co.uk

QU Ⓐ
Quittenbaum Kunstauktionen München
Hohenstaufenstraße 1, D-80801, Munich, Germany
Tel: 00 49 89 33 00 75 6
www.quittenbaum.de

R&GM Ⓓ
R & G McPherson Antiques 40 Kensington Church Street, London W8 4BX
Tel: 020 7937 0812
www.orientalceramics.com

RBRG Ⓓ
RBR Group at Grays 158/168, Grays Antique Markets, 58 Davies Street, London W1Y 5LP
Tel: 020 7629 4769
www.graysantiques.com

RDER Ⓓ
Rogers de Rin 76 Royal Hospital Road, Paradise Walk, Chelsea, London SW3 4HN
Tel: 020 7352 9007
www.rogersderin.co.uk

RDL Ⓐ
David Rago/Nicholas Dawes Lalique Auctions
333 North Main Street, Lambertville, NJ 08530, USA
Tel: 001 609 397 9374
www.ragoarts.com

REL Ⓓ
Rellick 8 Golborne Road, London W10 5NW
Tel: 020 8962 0089

RG Ⓓ
Richard Gibbon 34/34a Islington Green, London N1 8DU
Tel: 020 7354 2852
neljeweluk@aol.com

RGA Ⓓ
Richard Gardner Antiques Swan House, Market Square, Petworth, West Sussex GU28 0AN
Tel: 01798 343 411
www.richardgardnerantiques.co.uk

RITZ Ⓓ
Ritzy 7 The Mall Antiques Arcade, 359 Upper Street, London N1 0PD
Tel: 020 7704 0127

ROS Ⓐ
Rosebery's 74-76 Knight's Hill, West Norwood, London SE27 0JD
Tel: 020 8761 2522
www.roseberys.co.uk

ROW Ⓐ
Rowley Fine Arts 8 Downham Road, Ely, Cambridge, Cambridgeshire CB6 1AH
Tel: 01353 653020
www.rowleyfineart.com

ROX Ⓓ
Roxanne Stuart PA, USA
Tel: 001 215 750 8868
gemfairy@aol.com

RSS Ⓐ
Rossini SA 7 rue Drouot, 75009 Paris, France
Tel: 00 33 1 53 34 55 00
www.rossini.fr

RTC Ⓐ
Ritchies Auctioneers & Appraisers 288 King Street East, Toronto, Ontario M5A 1KA, Canada
Tel: 001 416 364 1864
www.ritchies.com

RUM Ⓓ
Rumours 4 The Mall Antiques Arcade, 359 Upper Street, London, N1 0PD
Tel: 020 7704 6549

RY Ⓓ
Robert Young Antiques 68 Battersea Bridge Road, London SW11 3AG
Tel: 020 7228 7847
www.robertyoungantiques.com

S&K/SL Ⓐ
Sloans & Kenyon 7034 Wisconsin Avenue Chevy Chase, MD 20815, USA
Tel: 001 301 634 2330
www.sloansandkenyon.com

SDR Ⓐ
Sollo:Rago Modern Auctions 333 North Main Street, Lambertville, NJ 08530 USA
Tel: 001 609 397 9374
www.ragoarts.com

SF Ⓓ
The Silver Fund 1 Duke of York Street, London SW1Y 6JP
Tel: 0207 839 7664
www.thesilverfund.com

SHF Ⓓ
Steppes Hill Farm Antiques Steppes Hill Farm, Stockbury, Sittingbourne, Kent ME9 7RB
Tel: 01795 842 205

SK Ⓐ
Skinner Inc. The Heritage on the Garden, 63 Park Plaza Boston MA 02116, USA & 357 Main Street, Bolton, MA 01740, USA
Tel: 001 617 350 5400
www.skinnerinc.com

SSP Ⓓ
Sylvie Spectrum Stand 372, Grays Antique Markets, 58 Davies Street, London W1K 5LP
Tel: 020 7629 3501
spectrum@grays.clara.net

STY Ⓓ
Style Gallery 10 Camden Passage, London N1 8ED
Tel: 020 7359 7867
www.styleantiques.co.uk

SWA Ⓐ
Swann Galleries Image Library 104 East 25th Street, New York, NY 10010, USA
Tel: 001 212 254 4710
www.swanngalleries.com

SWO Ⓐ
Sworders 14 Cambridge Road, Stansted Mountfitchet, Essex CM24 8BZ
Tel: 01279 817 778
www.sworder.co.uk

SUM Ⓓ
No longer trading

TA Ⓐ
333 Auctions LLC 333 North Main Street, Lambertville, NJ 08530 USA
Tel: 001 609 397 9374
www.ragoarts.com

TCF Ⓓ
Cynthia Findlay Toronto Antiques Centre, 276 King Street West, Toronto, Ontario M5V 1J2, Canada
Tel: 001 416 260 9057
www.cynthiafindlay.com

TCM Ⓓ
Twentieth Century Marks Whitegates, Rectory Rd, Little Burstead, Nr Billericay, Essex CM12 9TR
Tel: 01268 411 000
www.20thcenturymarks.co.uk

TCS Ⓓ
The Country Seat Huntercombe Manor Barn, nr. Henley on Thames, Oxfordshire RG9 5RY
Tel: 01491 641349
www.thecountryseat.com
www.whitefriarsglass.com

TDG Ⓓ
The Design Gallery 5 The Green, Westerham, Kent TN16 1AS
Tel: 01959 561 234
www.designgallery.co.uk

TDO Ⓓ
Tendo Mokko 1-3-10 Midaregawa, Tendo, Yamagata, Japan Tel: 023 653 3121

TO Ⓓ
Titus Omega
Tel: 020 7688 1295
www.titusomega.com

TR Ⓓ
Terry Rodgers & Melody (Antique and Vintage Jewellery) 1050 2nd Avenue, New York, NY 10022, USA
Tel: 001 212 758 3164
melodyjewelnyc@aol.com

TRIO Ⓓ
Trio L24, Grays Antique Markets, 58 Davies Street, London, W1K 5LP
Tel: 020 7493 2736
www.trio-london.fsnet.co.uk

VDB Ⓓ
Van Den Bosch Shop 1, Georgian Village, Camden Passage, Islington N1 8DU
Tel: 020 7226 4550
www.vandenbosch.co.uk

VEC Ⓐ
Vectis Auctions Fleck Way, Thornaby, Stockton on Tees, County Durham TS17 9JZ
Tel: 01642 750 616
www.vectis.co.uk

VET Ⓓ
Vetro & Arte Gallery (V&A Gallery) Calle del Cappeller 3212, Dorsoduro, Venice 30123, Italy
Tel: 0039 041 522 8525
www.venicewebgallery.com

VS Ⓓ
Von Spaeth Willhelm-Diess-Weg 13, 81927 Munich, Germany
Tel/Fax: 0049 89 2809132
www.glasvonspaeth.com

VZ Ⓐ
Von Zezschwitz Friedrichstrasse 1a, 80801 Munich, Germany
Tel: 0049 89 38 98 930
www.von-zezschwitz.de

W&W Ⓐ
Wallis and Wallis West Street Auction Galleries, Lewes, East Sussex BN7 2NJ
Tel: 01273 480 208
www.wallisandwallis.co.uk

WAD Ⓐ
Waddington's Auctioneers & Appraisers 111 Bathurst St., Toronto, Ontario M5V 2R1, Canada
Tel: 001 416 504 9100
www.waddingtons.ca

WAIN Ⓓ
William Wain at Antiquarius Stand J6, Antiquarius, 135 King's Road, London SW3 4PW
Tel: 020 7351 4905
w.wain@btopenworld.com

WDL Ⓐ
Kunst-Auktionshaus Martin Wendl August-Bebel-Straße 4, 07407 Rudolstadt, Germany
Tel: 00 49 3672 4243 50
www.auktionshaus-wendl.de

WKA Ⓐ
Wiener Kunst Auktionen - Palais Kinsky Freyung 4, 1010 Vienna, Austria
Tel: 00 43 15 32 42 00
www.palais-kinsky.com

WW Ⓐ
Woolley and Wallis 51-61 Castle Street, Salisbury, Wiltshire SP13SU
Tel: 01722 424 500
www.woolleyandwallis.co.uk

NOTE

FOR VALUATIONS, IT IS ADVISABLE TO contact the dealer or auction house in advance to confirm that they will perform this service and whether any charge is involved. Telephone valuations are not possible, so it will be necessary to send details, including a photograph, of the object to the dealer or auction house, along with a stamped addressed envelope for response. While most dealers will be happy to help you, do remember that they are busy people. Please mention *DK Antiques Price Guide 2006* by Judith Miller when making an enquiry.

DIRECTORY OF AUCTIONEERS

This is a list of auctioneers that conduct regular sales. Auction houses that would like to be included in the next edition should contact us by 1 February 2006.

London

Bloomsbury
Bloomsbury House, 24 Maddox Street, London W1 S1PP
Tel: 020 7495 9494
Fax: 020 7495 9499
www.bloomsbury-book-auct.com

Bonhams
101 New Bond Street,
London W1S 1SR
Tel: 020 7629 6602
Fax: 020 7629 8876
info@bonhams.com
www.bonhams.com

Bonhams Knightsbridge
Montpelier Street, Knightsbridge,
London SW7 1HH
Tel: 020 7393 3900
Fax: 020 7393 3905
info@bonhams.com
www.bonhams.com

Chiswick Auctions
1 Colville Road, Acton,
London W3 8BL
Tel: 020 8992 4442
Fax: 020 8896 0541
www.chiswickauctions.co.uk

Christie's
8 King Street, St. James's
London SW1Y 6QT
Tel: 020 7839 9060
Fax: 020 7839 1611
info@christies.com
www.christies.com

Christie's South Kensington
85 Old Brompton Road, SW7 3LD
Tel: 020 7581 7611
Fax: 020 7321 3311
info@christies.com
www.christies.com

Cooper Owen
74 High Street, Egham,
Surrey TW20 9LF
Tel: 01784 434900
auctions@cooperowen.com
www.cooperowen.com

Lots Road Galleries
71-73 Lots Road,
Chelsea, London SW10 0RN
Tel: 020 7376 6800
Fax: 020 7376 6899
www.lotsroad.com

Rosebery's
74-76 Knights Hill, West Norwood,
London SE27 0JD
Tel: 020 8761 2522
Fax: 020 8761 2524
www.roseberys.co.uk

Sotheby's
34-35 New Bond Street,
London W1A 2AA
Tel: 020 7293 5000
Fax: 020 7293 5989
www.sothebys.com

Sotheby's Olympia
Hammersmith Road,
London W14 8UX
Tel: 020 7293 5555
Fax: 020 7293 6939
www.sothebys.com

Avon

Aldridges of Bath
Newark House, 26-45 Cheltenham Street, Bath, BA2 3EX
Tel: 01225 462830
Fax: 01225 311319

Gardiner Houlgate
9 Leafield Way, Corsham,
Bath SN13 9SW
Tel: 01225 812912
Fax: 01225 811777
auctions@gardiner-houlgate.co.uk
www.gardiner-houlgate.co.uk

Bedfordshire

W. & H. Peacock
The Auction Centre, 26 Newnham St,
Bedford MK40 3JR
Tel: 01234 266366
www.peacockauction.co.uk
info@peacockauction.co.uk

Berkshire

Dreweatt Neate
Donnington Priory, Donnington,
Nr Newbury RG14 2JE
Tel: 01635 553553
Fax: 01635 553599
fineart@dreweatt-neate.co.uk
www.auctions.dreweatt-neate.co.uk

Law Fine Art Ltd.
Ash Cottage, Ashmore Green,
Newbury RG18 9ER
Tel: 01635 860033
Fax: 01635 860036
info@lawfineart.co.uk
www.lawfineart.co.uk

Special Auction Services
Kennetholme, Midgham, Nr.
Reading RG7 5UX
Tel: 0118 971 2949
Fax: 0118 971 2420
commemorative@aol.com
www.invaluable.com/sas

Buckinghamshire

Dickins Auctioneers
Claydon House Park, Calvert Rd,
Middle Claydon MK18 2EZ
Tel: 01296 714 434
Fax: 01296 714492
info@dickins-auctioneers.com
www.dickins-auctioneers.com

Cambridgeshire

Cheffins
Clifton House, 1&2 Clifton Road,
Cambridge CB1 7EA
Tel: 01223 213 343
Fax: 01223 271 949
fine.art@cheffins.co.uk
www.cheffins.co.uk

Hyperion Auctions Ltd
Station Road, St. Ives PE27 5BH
Tel: 01480 464140
Fax: 01480 497552
enquiries@hyperionauctions.co.uk
www.hyperionauctions.co.uk

Maxey & Son
Auction Hall, Cattle Market Chase,
Wisbech PE13 1RD
Tel: 01945 584609
www.maxeyandson.co.uk

Rowley Fine Art Auctioneers & Valuers
8 Downham Road, Ely CB6 1AH
Tel: 01353 653 020
Fax: 01353 653 022
mail@rowleyfineart.com
www.rowleyfineart.com

Cheshire

Frank R. Marshall and Co.
Marshall House, Church Hill,
Knutsford WA16 6DH
Tel: 01565 653284
Fax: 01565 652341
antiques@frankmarshall.co.uk
www.frankmarshall.co.uk

Maxwells of Wilmslow
133A Woodford Road, Woodford,
Cheshire, SK7 1QD
Tel: 01614395182
www.maxwell-auctioneers.co.uk

Peter Wilson Fine Art Auctioneers
Victoria Gallery, Market Street,
Nantwich CW5 5DG
Tel: 01270 623878
Fax: 01270 610508
auctions@peterwilson.co.uk
www.peterwilson.co.uk

Cornwall

W. H. Lane & Son
Jubilee House, Queen Street,
Penzance TR18 4DF
Tel: 01736 361447
Fax: 01736 350097
info@whlane.co.uk

David Lay FRICS
The Penzance Auction House
Alverton, Penzance TR18 4RE
Tel: 01736 361414
Fax: 01736 360035
david.lays@btopenworld.com

Cumbria

James Thompson
64 Main Street,
Kirkby Lonsdale LA6 2AJ
Tel: 01524 271555
Fax: 01524 272939
sales@jthompson-auctioneers.co.uk
www.jthompson-auctioneers.co.uk

DIRECTORY OF AUCTIONEERS

Derbyshire

Bamfords Ltd
The Old Picture Palace,
133 Dale Road, Matlock,
Derbyshire DE4 3LU
Tel: 01629 574460

Noel Wheatcroft & Son
Matlock Auction Gallery,
The Old Picture Palace, Dale Road,
Matlock DE4 3LU
Tel: 01629 57460
Fax: 01629 57956
www.wheatcroft-noel.co.uk

Devon

Hampton & Littlewood
The Auction Rooms, Alphin Brook
Road, Alphington, Exeter EX2 8TH
Tel: 01392 413100
Fax: 01392 413110
www.hamptonandlittlewood.co.uk

Dreweatt Neate (Formerly Taylor's)
Honiton Saleroom, 205 High Street,
Honiton EX14 1LQ
Tel: 01404 42404
Fax: 01404 46510
honiton@dnfa.com
www.dnfa.com/honiton

S. J. Hales Auctioneers
Tracey House, Newton Road, Bovey
Tracey, Newton Abbot TQ13 9AZ
Tel: 01626 836 684
Fax: 01626 836 318
info@sjhales.com
www.sjhales.com

Dorset

Cottees Auctions Ltd.
The Market, East Street,
Wareham BH20 4NR
Tel: 01929 552826
Fax: 01929 554916
auctions@cottees.fsnet.co.uk
www.auctionsatcottees.co.uk

Dalkeith Auctions Bournemouth
Dalkeith Hall, Dalkeith Steps, Rear
of 81 Old Christchurch Road,
Bournemouth BH1 1YL
Tel: 01202 292905
Fax: 01202 292931
how@dalkeith-auctions.co.uk.
www.dalkeith-auctions.co.uk

Hy. Duke and Son
Fine Art Salerooms, Weymouth
Avenue, Dorchester DT1 1QS
Tel: 01305 265080
Fax: 01305 260101
enquiries@dukes-auctions.com

Wm. Morey and Sons
Unit 3, Pymore Mills Estate,
Pymore, Bridport, Dorset, DT6 5PJ
Tel/Fax: 01308 422078
www.wmoreyandsons.co.uk

Onslows
The Coach House, Manor Road,
Stourpaine DT11 8TQ
Tel: 01258 488 838
www.onslows.co.uk

Riddetts of Bournemouth
177 Holdenhurst Road,
Bournemouth BH8 8DG
Tel: 01202 555686
Fax: 01202 311004
www.riddetts.co.uk

Durham
Vectis Auctions Limited
Fleck Way, Thornaby,
Stockton on Tees TS17 9JZ
Tel: 01642 750 616
Fax: 01642 769 478
admin@vectis.co.uk
www.vectis.co.uk

Essex

Chalkwell Auctions Ltd.
The Arlington Rooms, 905 London
Road, Leigh-on-Sea SS0 89U
Tel: 01702 710383
www.ridgeweb.co.uk

Cooper Hirst Auctions
The Granary Salerooms, Victoria
Road, Chelmsford CM2 6LH
Tel: 01245 260535

G.E. Sworder and Sons
14 Cambridge Road, Stansted
Mountfitchet CM24 8BZ
Tel: 01279 817778
Fax: 01279 817779
www.sworder.co.uk

Gloucestershire

**Dreweatt Neate (Formerly Bristol
Auction Rooms)** Bristol Salerooms,
St. John's Place, Apsley Road,
Clifton, Bristol BS8 2ST
Tel: 0117 973 7201
Fax: 0117 973 5671
bristol@dnfa.com
www.dnfa.com/bristol

**Mallams Fine Art Auctioneers
and Valuers**
26 Grosvenor Street,
Cheltenham GL52 2SG
Tel: 01242 235712
Fax: 01242 241943
cheltenham@mallams.co.uk
www.mallams.co.uk/fineart

Moore, Allen & Innocent
The Salerooms, Norcote,
Cirencester GL7 5RH
Tel: 01285 646050
Fax: 01285 652862
fineart@mooreallen.co.uk
www.mooreallen.com/cat

Specialised Postcard Auctions
Corinium Gallery, 25 Gloucester
Street, Cirencester GL7 2DJ
Tel: 01285 659 057
Fax: 01285 652047

Stroud Auctions Ltd
The Old Barn, Bear of Rodborough,
Stroud GL5 5EA
Tel: 01453 873800
info@stroudauctions.com
www.stroudauctions.com

Wotton Auction Rooms Ltd
Tabernacle Road,
Wotton-under-Edge GL12 7EB
Tel: 01453 844733
Fax: 01453 845448
www.wottonauctionrooms.co.uk

Hampshire

Andrew Smith & Son
The Auction Rooms,
Manor Farm, Itchen Stoke,
nr. Winchester SO24 0QT
Tel: 01962 735988
Fax: 01962 738879
auctions@andrewsmithandson.com

**Jacobs and Hunt Fine Art
Auctioneers**
Lavant Street, Petersfield GU32 3EF
Tel: 01730 233 933
Fax: 01730 262 323
auctions@jacobsandhunt.com
www.jacobsandhunt.com

May and Son
Delta Works, Salisbury Road
Shipton Bellinger, Hampshire
SP9 7UN
Tel: 01980 846000
Fax: 01980 846600
mayandson@enterprise.net

Herefordshire

Brightwells
The Fine Art Saleroom, Easters
Court, Leominster HR6 ODE
Tel: 01568 611122
Fax: 01568 610519
fineart@brightwells.com
classiccars@brightwells.com
www.brightwells.com

Hertfordshire

Tring Market Auctions
Brook Street, Tring HP23 5EF
Tel: 01442 826 446
Fax: 01442 890 927
sales@tringmarketauctions.co.uk
www.tringmarketauctions.co.uk

Isle of Wight

Shanklin Auction Rooms
79 Regent Street,
Shanklin PO37 7AP
Tel: 01983 863 441
Fax: 01983 863 890
shanklin.auction@tesco.net
www.shanklinauctionrooms.co.uk

Ways
The Auction House, Garfield Road,
Ryde PO33 2PT
Tel: 01983 562 255
Fax: 01983 565 108
ways@waysauctionrooms.
fsbusiness.co.uk
www.waysauctionrooms.
fsbusiness.co.uk

Kent

**Dreweatt Neate (Formerly
Bracketts)** Tunbridge Wells
Saleroom, The Auction Hall,
The Pantiles, Tunbridge Wells,
Kent TN2 5QL
Tel: 01892 544500
Fax: 01892 515191
tunbridgewells@dnfa.co.uk
www.dnfa.com/tunbridgewells

Gorringes
15 The Pantiles,
Tunbridge Wells TN2 5TD
Tel: 01892 619 670
Fax: 01892 619 671
auctions@gorringes.co.uk
www.gorringes.co.uk

**Lambert and Foster Auction
Sale Rooms** 102 High Street,
Tenterden TN30 6HT
Tel: 01580 762083
Fax: 01580 764317
saleroom@lambertandfoster.co.uk
www.lambertandfoster.co.uk

Mervyn Carey
Twysden Cottage, Benenden,
Cranbrook TN17 4LD
Auctions held at The Church Hall,
Church Road, Tenterden
Tel: 01580 240283

Parkinson Auctioneers
46 Beaver Road, Ashford TN23 7RP
Tel: 01233 624426
Fax: 01233 665000
www.parkinson-uk.com

Lancashire

Capes Dunn & Co Fine Art
Auctioneers & Valuers, The Auction
Galleries, 38 Charles Street,
Manchester M1 7DB
Tel: 0161 273 1911
Fax: 0161 273 3474

Leicestershire

Gilding's Auctioneers and Valuers
Roman Way, Market Harborough
LE16 7PQ
Tel: 01858 410414
Fax: 01858 432956
www.gildings.co.uk

**Tennants Co. (Formerly Heathcote
Ball & Co)** Millhouse, South Street,
Oakham, Rutland LE15 6BG
Tel: 01572 724 66
Fax: 01572 72 4422
oakham@tennants-ltd.co.uk
www.tennants.co.uk

Lincolnshire

Eleys Auctioneers
26 Wide Bargate, Boston PE21 6RX
Tel: 01205 361687
Fax: 01205 351091
boston@jameseley.co.uk
www.jameseley.co.uk

Ian H. S. Naylor Auctions
20 St Johns Street,
Wainfleet PE24 4DJ
Tel/Fax: 01754 881 210

Marilyn Swain
The Old Barracks, Sandon Road,
Grantham NG31 9AS
Tel: 01476 568861
Fax: 01476 576100

John Taylors
The Wool Mart, Kidgate,
Louth LN11 9EZ
Tel: 01507 611107
Fax: 01507 601280
enquiries@johntaylors.com
www.invaluable.com/johntaylors

Merseyside

Cato & Crane & Co
6 Stanhope Street,
Liverpool L8 5RF
Tel: 0151 709 5559
Fax: 0151 707 2454
www.cato-crane.co.uk

Outhwaite and Litherland
Kingsway Galleries, Fontenoy Street,
Liverpool L3 2BE
Tel: 0151 236 6561
Fax: 0151 236 1070
auction@lots.uk.com
www.lots.uk.com

Norfolk

Gaze and Son
Diss Auction Rooms, Roydon Road,
Diss IP22 4LN
Tel: 01379 650306
Fax: 01379 644313
sales@dissauctionrooms.co.uk
www.twgaze.com

Horners Auctions
North Walsham Sale Rooms,
Midland Road,
North Walsham NR28 9JR
Tel: 01692 500603
Fax: 01692 500975
auction@horners.co.uk
www.horners.co.uk

Keys Auctioneers & Valuers
Aylsham Salerooms, Palmers Lane,
Aylsham, Norfolk NR11 6JA
Tel: 01263 733195
www.keysauctions.co.uk

Knights Sporting Auctions
The Thatched Gallery, The Green,
Aldborough, Norwich NR11 7AA
Tel: 01263 768 488
Fax: 01263 768 788
www.knights.co.uk

Nottinghamshire

**Arthur Johnson and Sons
(Auctioneers)** The Nottingham
Auction Centre, Meadow Lane,
Nottingham NG2 3GY
Tel: 0115 986 9128
Fax: 0115 986 2139
antiques@arthurjohnson.co.uk

**Mellors & Kirk Fine Art
Auctioneers**
Gregory Street, Nottingham,
Nottinghamshire NG7 2NL
Tel: 0115 9790000
Fax: 0115 9781111
enquiries@mellors-kirk.com
www.mellors-kirk.co.uk

Dreweatt Neate (Formerly Neales)
Nottingham Salerooms, 192
Mansfield Road,
Nottingham NG1 3HU
Tel: 0115 962 4141
Fax: 0115 969 3450
fineart@neales-auctions.com
www.dnfa.com/neales

**John Pye & Sons Auctioneers
& Valuers** James Shipstone House,
Radford Road,
Nottingham NG7 7EA
Tel: 0115 970 6060
Fax: 0115 942 0100
ap@johnpye.co.uk
www.johnpye.co.uk

Northgate Auction Rooms Ltd.
17 Northgate, Newark NG24 1EX
Tel: 01636 605 905
Fax: 01636 612 607
auctions@northgateauction-
snewark.co.uk

Peter Young Auctioneers
The Lord Barnby Memorial Hall
Blyth, North Nottinghamshire
S81 8HD
Tel: 01777 816 609
Mob: 07801 079818
beaconhillside@btopenworld.com
www.peteryoungauctioneers.co.uk

**T Vennett-Smith Auctioneers and
Valuers (FSB)**
11 Nottingham Road, Gotham,
Nottingham NG11 0HE
Tel: 0115 9830541
Fax: 0115 9830114
info@vennett-smith.com
www.vennett-smith.com

Oxfordshire

Holloway's
49 Parsons Street,
Banbury OX16 5NB
Tel: 01295 817777
Fax: 01295 817701
enquiries@hollowaysauctioneers.co.uk
www.hollowaysauctioneers.co.uk

Jones & Jacob Ltd
Watcombe Manor Saleroom
Ingham Lane, Watlington OX49 5EJ
Tel 01491 612810
Fax 01491 614564
saleroom@jonesandjacob.com
www.jonesandjacob.com

Mallams Fine Art Auctioneers
Bocard House, 24a St. Michael's
Street, Oxford OX1 2EB
Tel: 01865 241358
Fax: 01865 725 483
oxford@mallams.co.uk
www.mallams.co.uk/fineart

Mallams Fine Art Auctioneers
Pevensey House, 27 Sheep Street,
Bicester OX26 7JF
Tel: 01869 252 901
Fax: 01869 320 283
bicester@mallams.co.uk
www.mallams.co.uk/fineart

Soames Country Auctions
Pinnocks Farm Estate, Northmoor,
Witney OX8 1AY
Tel: 01865 300626
soame@email.msn.com
www.soamesauctions.co.uk

Shropshire

Halls Fine Art
Welsh Bridge, Shrewsbury SY3 8LA
Tel: 01743 231 212
Fax: 01743 271 014
FineArt@halls.to
www.hallsgb.com

Mullock & Madeley
The Old Shippon, Wall under
Heywood, Church Stretton SY6 7DS
Tel: 01694 771771
Fax: 01694 771772
info@mullockmadeley.co.uk
www.mullockmadeley.co.uk

Walker Barnett and Hill
Cosford Auction Rooms, Long Lane,
Cosford TF11 8PJ
Tel: 01902 375555
Fax: 01902 375566
wbhauctions@lineone.net
www.walker-barnett-hill.co.uk

Somerset

Clevedon Salerooms
The Auction Centre, Kenn Road,
Kenn, Clevedon,
North Somerset BS21 6TT
Tel: 01934 830 111
Fax: 01934 832 538
info@clevedon-salerooms.com
www.clevedon-salerooms.com

Greenslade Taylor Hunt Fine Art
Magdelene House, Church Square,
Taunton TA1 1SB
Tel: 01823 332525
Fax: 01823 353120
fine.art@gth.net
www.gth.net

**Lawrence's Fine Art
Auctioneers Ltd.**
South Street, Crewkerne TA18 8AB
Tel: 01460 73041
Fax: 01460 74627
enquiries.@lawrences.co.uk
www.lawrences.co.uk

The London Cigarette Card Co. Ltd
Sutton Road, Somerton TA11 6QP
Tel: 01458 273452
Fax: 01458 273515
cards@londoncigcard.co.uk
www.londoncigcard.co.uk

Dreweatt Neate (Formerly Wells)
Wells Auction Rooms
66-68 Southover, Wells BA5 1UH
Tel: 01749 678094
bristol@dnfa.com
www.dnfa.com/bristol

Staffordshire

Hall and Lloyd Auctioneers
South Street, Stafford ST16 2DZ
Tel: 01785 258176

Louis Taylor Fine Art Auctioneers
Britannia House, 10 Town Road,
Hanley, Stoke-on-Trent ST1 2QG
Tel: 01782 214111
Fax: 01782 215 283

Potteries Specialist Auctions
271 Waterloo Road, Cobridge,
Stoke-on-Trent ST6 3HR
Tel: 01782 286622
Fax: 01782 213777
enquires@potteriesauctions.com
www.potteriesauctions.com

**Richard Winterton Auctioneers
and Valuers**
School House Auction Rooms,
Hawkins Lane, Burton-on-Trent
DE14 1PT
Tel: 01283 511224

Wintertons
Lichfield Auction Centre, Fradley
Park, Lichfield,
Staffordshire WS13 8NF
Tel: 01543 263 256
Fax: 01543 415 348
enquiries@wintertons.co.uk
www.wintertons.co.uk

Suffolk

Abbotts Auction Rooms
Campsea Ashe, Nr. Woodbridge
IP13 0PS
Tel: 01728 746323
Fax: 01728 748173
auction.rooms@abbottscountry-
wide.co.uk
www.abbottsauctionrooms.co.uk

Durrant's
The Old School House, Peddars
Lane, Beccles Suffolk, NR 34 9UE
Tel: 01502 713490
Fax: 01502 711939
info@durrantsauctionrooms.com
www.durrantsauctionrooms.com

Dyson & Son
The Auction Room, Church Street,
Clare CO10 8PD
Tel: 01787 277 993
Fax: 01787 277 996
info@dyson-auctioneers.co.uk
www.dyson-auctioneers.co.uk

Lacy Scott and Knight Fine Art & Furniture
10 Risbygate Street,
Bury St. Edmunds IP33 3AA
Tel: 01284 748600
Fax: 01284 748620
www.lsk.co.uk
fineart@lsk.co.uk

Neal Sons and Fletcher
26 Church Street, Woodbridge
IP12 1DP
Tel: 01394 382263
Fax: 01394 383030
auctions@nsf.co.uk.
www.nsf.co.uk

Surrey

Clarke Gammon Wellers Fine Art Auctioneers
Tel: 01483 880915
Fax: 01483 880918
fine.art@clarkegammon.co.uk
www.clarkegammon.co.uk
www.invaluable.com/clarkegam-monwellers/

Crows Auction Gallery
Rear of Dorking Halls, Reigate
Road, Dorking RH4 1SG
Tel: 01306 740382
enquiries@crowsauctions.co.uk

Ewbank Auctioneers
Burnt Common Auction Rooms,
London Road, Send,
Woking GU23 7LN
Tel: 01483 223101
Fax: 01483 222171
www.ewbankauctions.co.uk

Dreweatt Neate (Formerly Hamptons) Baverstock House, 93
High Street, Godalming GU7 1AL
Tel: 01483 423 567
Fax: 01483 426 392
godalming@dnfa.com
www.dnfa.com/godalming

John Nicholsons
The Auction Rooms, Longfield,
Midhurst Road,
Haslemere GU27 3HA
Tel: 01428 653727
auctions@johnnicholsons.com
www.johnnicholsons.com

Lawrences' Auctioneers Limited
Norfolk House, 80 High Street,
Bletchingley RH1 4PA
Tel: 01883 743323
Fax: 01883 744578
www.lawrencesbletchingley.co.uk

Kew Auctions and Antiques Ltd
Richmond Station, Kew Road,
Richmond TW9 2NA
Tel: 020 8948 6677
Fax: 020 8948 2021
kewauctions@hotmail.com

P.F. Windibank Fine Art Auctioneers & Valuers
Dorking Halls, Reigate Road,
Dorking RH4 1SG
Tel: 01306 884556/876280
Fax: 01306 884669
sjw@windibank.co.uk
www.windibank.co.uk

East Sussex

Burstow & Hewett
Lower Lake, Battle,
East Sussex TN33 0AT
Tel: 01424 772374
www.burstowandhewett.co.uk

Gorringes Auction Galleries
Terminus Road,
Bexhill-on-Sea TN39 3LR
Tel: 01424 212994
Fax: 01424 224035
bexhill@gorringes.co.uk
www.gorringes.co.uk

Gorringes Auction Galleries
15 North Street, Lewes BN7 2PD
Tel: 01273 472503
Fax: 01273 479559
clientservices@gorringes.co.uk
www.gorringes.co.uk

Raymond P. Inman
The Auction Galleries, 98A
Coleridge Street, Hove BN3 5 AA
Tel: 01273 774777
Fax: 01273 735660
r.p.inman@talk21.com
www.invaluable.com/raymondinman

Rye Auction Galleries
Rock Channel, Rye TN31 7HL
Tel: 01797 222124

Scarborough Perry Fine Arts
Hove Street, Hove BN3 2GL
Tel: 01273 735266
Fax: 01273 723813
info@gsp.uk.com
www.scarboroughperry.com

Wallis and Wallis
West Street Auction Galleries,
Lewes BN7 2NJ
Tel: 01273 480 208
Fax: 01273 476 562
auctions@wallisandwallis.co.uk
www.wallisandwallis.co.uk

West Sussex

John Bellman Ltd
New Pound, Wisborough Green,
Billingshurst RH14 0AZ
Tel: 01403 700858
Fax: 01403 700059
enquiries@bellmans.co.uk
www.bellmans.co.uk

Denham's
The Auction Galleries, Warnham,
Nr. Horsham RH12 3RZ
Tel: 01403 255699
Fax: 01403 253837
denhams@lineone.net
www.catalogs.icollector.com/denhams

Rupert Toovey & Co.
Spring Gardens, Washington
RH20 3BS
Tel : 01903 891955
Fax : 01903 891966
auctions@rupert-toovey.com
www.rupert-toovey.com

Worthing Auction Galleries
Fleet House, Teville Gate,
Worthing BN11 1UA
Tel: 01903 205565
Fax: 01903 214365
info@worthing-auctions.co.uk
www.worthing-auctions.co.uk

Tyne and Wear

Anderson and Garland
Anderson House, Crispin Court,
Newbiggin Lane, Westerhope,
Newcastle upon Tyne NE5 1BF
Tel: 0191 430 3000
andersongarland@aol.com
www.andersonandgarland.com

Boldon Auction Galleries
24a Front Street,
East Boldon NE36 0SJ
Tel: 0191 537 2630
Fax: 0191 536 3875
enquiries@boldonauctions.co.uk
www.boldonauctions.co.uk

Corbitts
5 Mosley Street, Newcastle-
upon-Tyne NE1 1YE
Tel: 0191 232 7268
Fax: 0191 261 4130
collectors@corbitts.com
www.corbitts.com

Warwickshire

Bigwood Auctioneers Ltd
The Old School, Tiddington,
Stratford-upon-Avon CV37 7AW
Tel: 01789 269415
Fax: 01789 292686
auctions@bigwoodauctioneers.co.uk
www.bigwoodauctioneers.co.uk

Locke and England
18 Guy Street, Leamington Spa
CV32 4RT
Tel: 01926 889100
Fax: 01926 470608
valuers@leauction.co.uk
www.leauction.co.uk

Warwick and Warwick Ltd
Chalon House, Scar Bank,
Millers Road, Warwick CV34 5DB
Tel: 01926 499031
Fax: 01926 491906
info@warwickandwarwick.com
www.warwickandwarwick.com

West Midlands

Biddle & Webb
Ladywood, Middleway,
Birmingham B16 0PP
Tel: 0121 455 8042
Fax: 0121 454 9615
info@biddleandwebb.com
www.biddleandwebb.co.uk

Bonhams
The Old House, Station Road,
Knowle, Solihull B93 0HT
Tel: 01564 776151
Fax: 01564 778069
knowle@bonhams.com
www.bonhams.com

Fellows and Sons
Augusta House, 19 Augusta Street,
Hockley, Birmingham B18 6JA
Tel: 0121 212 2131
Fax: 0121 212 1249
info@fellows.co.uk
www.fellows.co.uk

Wiltshire

Atwell Martin
2 New Road,
Chippenham SN15 1EJ
Tel: 01249 449800
Fax: 01249 447780

The Hilditch Auction Rooms
Gloucester Road Trading Estate,
Malmesbury SN16 9JT
Tel: 01666 822577
Fax: 01666 825597
sales@hilditchauctions.co.uk
www.hilditchauctions.co.uk

Woolley and Wallis
Salisbury Salerooms Ltd,
51-61 Castle Street,
Salisbury SP1 3SU
Tel: 01722 424500
Fax: 01722 424508
enquiries@woolleyandwallis.co.uk
www.woolleyandwallis.co.uk

Worcestershire

Andrew Grant Fine Art Auctioneers
St. Marks House, St. Marks Close,
Worcester WR5 3DL
Tel: 01905 357547
Fax: 01905 763942
fine.art@andrew-grant.co.uk
www.andrew-grant.co.uk

Griffiths and Charles
57 Foregate Street,
Worcester WR1 1DZ
Tel: 01906 720160
Fax 01905 745222
rupert@griffiths-charles.co.uk
www.griffiths-charles.co.uk

Philip Laney Fine Art
Malvern Auction Centre,
Portland Road, off Victoria Road,
Malvern WR14 2TA
Tel: 01684 893933
Fax: 01684 577948
philiplaney@aol.com
www.invaluable.com/philiplaney

Philip Serrell Auctioneers & Valuers
The Malvern Sale Room,
Barnards Green Road,
Malvern WR14 3LW
Tel: 01684 892314
Fax: 01684 569832
serrell.auctions@virgin.net
www.serrell.com

East Yorkshire

Gilbert Baitson
The Edwardian Auction Galleries,
Wiltshire Road, Hull HU4 6PG
Tel: 01482 500500
Fax: 01482 500501
auction@gilbert-baitson.co.uk
www.gilbert-baitson.co.uk

Clegg & Son
68 Aire Street, Goole DN14 5QE
Tel: 01405 763140
gooleoffice@cleggandson.co.uk
www.cleggandson.co.uk

Dee Atkinson & Harrison
Agricultural and Fine Arts,
The Exchange Saleroom,
Driffield YO25 7LJ
Tel: 01377 253151
Fax: 01377 241041
exchange@dee-atkinson-harrison.co.uk
www.dee-atkinson-harrison.co.uk

North Yorkshire

David Duggleby Fine Art
The Vine Street Salerooms,
Scarborough YO11 1XN
Tel: 01723 507111
Fax: 01723 507 222
auctions@davidduggleby.com
www.davidduggleby.com

David Duggleby Fine Art
The Paddock Salerooms
Whitby YO21 3DB
Tel: 01947 820 033
Fax: 01947 825 680
auctions@davidduggleby.com
www.davidduggleby.com

Malcolm's No. 1 Auctioneers and Valuers
The Chestnuts, 16 Park Avenue,
Sherburn in Elmet,
Nr. Leeds LS25 6EF
Tel: 01977 684 971
Fax: 01977 681 046
info@malcolmsno1auctions.co.uk
www.malcolmsno1auctions.co.uk

Morphets of Harrogate
6 Albert Street, Harrogate HG1 1JL
Tel: 01423 530030
Fax: 01423 500717
enquiries@morphets.co.uk
www.morphets.co.uk

Tennants The Auction Centre,
Leyburn DL8 5SG
Tel: 01969 623780
Fax: 01969 624281
www.tennants.co.uk
enquiry@tennants-ltd.co.uk

South Yorkshire

BBR Auctions
Elsecar Heritage Centre,
Nr. Barnsley S74 8AA
Tel: 01226 745156
Fax: 01226 361561
www.bbrauctions.co.uk

A.E. Dowse and Son
Cornwall Galleries, Scotland Street,
Sheffield S3 7DE
Tel: 0114 2725858
Fax: 0114 2490550
aedowes@aol.com
www.aedowseandson.com

ELR Auctions Ltd
The Sheffield Saleroom, The Nichols
Bldg., Shalesmoor, Sheffield S3 8UJ
Tel: 0114 2816161
Fax: 0114 2816162
elrauctions@btconnect.com
www.elrauctions.com

West Yorkshire

De Romes
12 New John Street, Westgate,
Bradford BD1 2QY
Tel: 01274 734116

Andrew Hartley Fine Arts
Victoria Hall Salerooms,
Little Lane, Ilkley LS29 8EA
Tel: 01943 816363
Fax: 01943 816363
info@andrewhartleyfinearts.co.uk
www.invaluable.com/andrew-hartley

John Walsh & Co. Auctioneers & Valuers
Ashfield House Auction Rooms,
Illingworth Street, Ossett, WF5 8AL.
Tel: 01924 264030
Fax: 01924 267758
valuations@john-walsh.co.uk
www.john-walsh.co.uk

Scotland

Auction Rooms Ltd.
Castle Laurie, Bankside,
Falkirk, Sterlingshire FK2 7XF
Tel: 01324 623000
Fax: 01324 630343
contact@auctionroomsfalkirk.co.uk
www.auctionroomsfalkirk.co.uk

Bonhams
65 George St., Edinburgh,
Midlothian EH2 2JL
Tel: 0131 225 2266
Fax: 0131 220 2547
edinburgh@bonhams.com
www.bonhams.com

Loves Auction Rooms
52-54 Canal Street, Perth,
Perthshire PH2 8LF
Tel: 01738 633337
Fax: 01738 629830

Lyon and Turnbull Ltd.
33 Broughton Place, Edinburgh,
Midlothian EH1 3RR
Tel: 0131 557 8844
Fax: 0131 557 8668
info@lyonandturnbull.com
www.lyonandturnbull.com

Lyon and Turnbull Ltd. Glasgow
4 Woodside Place, Glasgow,
Lanarkshire G3 7QF
Tel: 0141 353 5070
Fax: 0141 332 2928
info@lyonandturnbull.com
www.lyonandturnbull.com

MDS Auction Co.
15-17 Smeaton Industrial Estate,
Kirkcaldy, Fife KY1 2HE
Tel: 01592 640969
Fax: 01592 640969
sales@scotlandauction.co.uk
www.scotlandauction.co.uk

D.J. Manning Auctioneers
Carriden, Bo'ness,
West Lothian EH51 9SF
Tel: 01506 827693
Fax: 01506 826495
info@djmanning.co.uk
www.djmanning.co.uk

McTear's
Clydeway Business Centre,
8 Elliot Place, Glasgow,
Lanarkshire G3 8EP
Tel: 0141 221 4456
Fax: 0141 204 5035
enquiries@mctears.co.uk
www.mctears.co.uk

Taylor's Auction Rooms
11 Panmure Row, Montrose,
Angus DD10 8HH
Tel: 01674 672775
Fax: 01674 672479
enquiries@scotlandstreasures.co.uk
www.scotlandstreasures.co.uk

Thomson, Roddick & Medcalf Ltd.
44/3 Hardengreen Business Park,
Eskbank, Edinburgh,
Midlothian EH22 3NX
Tel: 0131 454 9090
Fax: 0131 454 9191
www.thomsonroddick.com

Thomson, Roddick & Medcalf Ltd.
Dumfries 60 Whitesands, Dumfries,
Dumfriesshire DG1 2RS
Tel: 01387 279879
www.thomsonroddick.com

Wales

Bonhams
7-8 Park Place, Cardiff,
Glamorgan CF10 3DP
Tel: 02920 727980
Fax: 02920 727989
cardiff@bonhams.com
www.bonhams.com

Bonhams Carmarthen
Napier House,
Spilman Street, Carmarthen,
Carmarthenshire SA31 1JY
Tel: 01267 238231
Fax: 02920 727989
carmarthen@bonhams.com
www.bonhams.com

Evans Bros.
Mart Office, Llanybydder,
Dyfed SA40 9UE
Tel: 01570 480 444
Fax: 01570 480 988
www.evansbros.com

Peter Francis
Curiosity Salerooms,
19 King St., Carmarthen,
Carmarthenshire SA31 1BH
Tel: 01267 233456
Fax: 01267 233458
www.peterfrancis.co.uk

Jones & Llewelyn
Llandeilo Auction Rooms, 21 New
Road, Llandeilo, Dyfed SA19 6DE
Tel: 01558 823430
Fax: 01558 822004
www.jonesllewelyn.freeserve.co.uk

Rogers-Jones & Co.
33 Abergele Road, Colwyn Bay,
Conway LL29 7RU
Tel: 01492 532176
Fax: 01492 533308
www.rogersjones.ukauctioneers.com

Welsh Country Auctions
2 Carmarthen Road, Cross Hands,
Llanelli, Carmarthenshire SA14 6SP
Tel: 01269 844428
Fax: 01269 844428
enquiries@welshcountryauctions.com
www.welshcountryauctions.com

DIRECTORY OF SPECIALISTS

SPECIALISTS WHO WOULD LIKE TO BE INCLUDED in the next edition, or have a change of address or telephone number, should contact us by 1 February 2006.

Readers should contact dealers by telephone before visiting them to avoid a wasted journey.

Antiquities

Ancient Art
85 The Vale, Southgate,
London N14 6AT
Tel: 020 8882 1509
Fax: 020 8886 5235
ancient.art@btinternet.com
www.ancientart.co.uk

David Aaron Ancient Arts & Rare Carpets
22 Berkeley Sq, Mayfair,
London W1J 6EH
Tel: 020 7491 9588

Finch & Co
Suite No 744, 2 Old Brompton
Road, London SW7 3DQ
Tel: 020 7413 9937
Fax: 020 7581 4445
www.finch-and-co.co.uk

Helios Gallery
292 Westbourne Grove,
London W11 2PS
Tel/Fax: 07711 955 997
mail@heliosgallery.com
www.heliosgallery.com

John A Pearson
Horton Lodge, Horton Road, Horton,
Near Slough, Berkshire SL3 9NU
Tel: 01753 682136

Rupert Wace Ancient Art Limited
14 Old Bond Street,
London W1X 3DB
Tel: 020 7495 1623
rupert.wace@btinternet.com
www.rupertwace.co.uk

Architectural

Pattisons Architectural Antiques
108 London Road, Aston Clinton,
Buckinghamshire HP22 5HS
Tel: 0208 5607978
Fax: 01296 631 329
info@ddd-uk.com
www.ddd-uk.com

D & R Blissett
c/o Coutts & Co, 440 Strand
London WC2R 0QS

Joanna Booth
247 King's Road, London SW3 5EL
Tel: 020 7352 8998
Fax: 020 7376 7350
joanna@joannabooth.co.uk
www.joannabooth.co.uk

Drummonds Architectural Antiques
The Kirkpatrick Buildings, 25
London Road, Hindhead,
Surrey GU26 6AB
Tel: 01428 609444
Fax: 01428 609445
info@drummonds-arch.co.uk
drummonds-arch.co.uk

LASSCO
St. Michael's, Mark St (off Paul St),
London EC2A 4ER
Tel: 020 7749 9944
Fax: 020 7749 9941
st.michaels@lassco.co.uk
www.lassco.co.uk

Sweerts de Landas
Dunsborough Park, Ripley,
Surrey GU23 6AL
Tel: 01483 225366
garden.ornament@lineone.net
www.sweerts.com

Carpets & Rugs

Atlantic Bay Gallery
5 Sedley Place, London W1R 1HH
Tel: 020 7355 3301
atlanticbaygallery@btinternet.com

C John (Rare Rugs) Ltd.
70 South Audley Street,
London W1K 2RA
Tel: 020 7493 5288
Fax: 020 7409 7030
cjohn@dircon.co.uk
www.cjohn.com

Gallery Yacou
127 Fulham Road, London
SW3 6RT
Tel: 020 7584 2929
galleryyacou@aol.com

Gideon Hatch
1 Port House, Plantation Wharf,
Battersea, London SW11 3TY
Tel: 020 7223 3996
info@gideonhatch.co.uk
www.gideonhatch.co.uk

John Eskenazi Ltd.
15 Old Bond Street,
London W1S 4AX
Tel: 020 7409 3001
john.eskenazi@john-eskenazi.com
www.john-eskenazi.com

Karel Weijand
Lion & Lamb Courtyard, Farnham,
Surrey GU9 7LL
Tel: 01252 726215
carpets@karlweijand.com
www.karkweijand.com

Lindfield Galleries
62 High Street, Lindfield,
West Sussex RH16 2HL
Tel: 01444 483817
david@orientalandantiquerugs.com

Richard Purdon Antique Carpets
158 The Hill, Burford,
Oxfordshire OX18 4QY
Tel: 01993 823777
antiquerugs@richardpurdon.demon.co.uk
www.purdon.com

Wadsworth's
Marehill, Pulborough,
West Sussex RH20 2DY
Tel: 01798 873 555
Fax: 01798 872 333
info@wadsworthsrugs.com
www.wadsworthsrugs.com

Books

Biblion
1/7 Davies Mews,
London W1K 5AB
Tel: 020 7629 1374
www.biblion.com

Boxes

Alan & Kathy Stacey
PO Box 2771 Chapel Lane,
Yeovil, Somerset BA22 7DZ
Tel: 02076 444 049
www.antiqueboxes.uk.com

Mostly Boxes
93 High Street, Eton,
Windsor, Berkshire SL4 6AF
Tel: 01753 858 470
Fax: 01753 857 212

Ceramics

Albert Amor Ltd.
37 Bury Street, St James's,
London SW1Y 6AU
Tel: 020 7930 2444
Fax: 020 7930 9067
info@albertamor.co.uk
www.albertamor.co.uk

Andrew Dando
34 Market Street, Bradford-on-
Avon, Wiltshire BA15 1LL
Tel: 01225 422 702
andrew@andrewdando.co.uk
www.andrewdando.co.uk

Brian & Angela Downes
PO Box 431, Chippenham,
Wiltshire SN14 6SZ
Tel/Fax: 01454 238134

Clive & Lynne Jackson
Cheltenham, Gloucestershire
Open by appointment only
Tel: 01242 254 3751
Mob: 07710 239351

Davies Antiques
c/o Cadogan Tate, Unit 6, 6-12
Ponton Road, London SW8 5BA
Tel/Fax: 020 8947 1902
www.antique-meissen.com

E & H Manners
66A Kensington Church Street,
London W8 4BY
Tel: 020 7229 5516
manners@europeanporcelain.com
www.europeanporcelain.com

Garry Atkins
Tel: 020 7727 8737
Fax: 020 7792 9010
garry.atkins@englishpottery.com
www.englishpottery.com

Gillian Neale Antiques
PO Box 247, Aylesbury,
Buckinghamshire HP20 1JZ
Tel: 01296 423754
Fax: 01296 334601
gillianneale@aol.com
www.gillannealeantiques.co.uk

Hope and Glory Commemorative Ceramics
131A Kensington Church Street,
London W8 7LP
Tel: 020 7727 8424

John Howard at Heritage
Heritage, 6 Market Place,
Woodstock, Oxfordshire OX20 1TA
Tel: 0870 444 0678
Fax: 0870 444 0678
Howards@antiquepottery.co.uk
www.antiquepottery.co.uk

Jonathan Horne Antiques Ltd.
66c Kensington Church Street,
London W8 4BY
Tel: 020 7221 5658
Fax: 020 7792 3090
JH@jonathanhorne.co.uk
www.jonathanhorne.co.uk

Klaber & Klaber
PO Box 9445, London NW3 1WD
Tel: 020 7435 6537
Fax: 020 7435 9459
info@klaber.com
www.klaber.com

Mary Wise and Grosvenor Antiques
Grosvenor Antiques, 27 Holland
Street, London W8 4NA
Tel: 020 7937 8649
Fax: 020 7937 7179
www.wiseantiques.com

Rennies Seaside Modern
47 The Old High St
Folkestone, Kent CT20 2RN
Tel: 01303 242427
info@rennart.co.uk
www.rennart.co.uk

Robyn Robb
43 Napier Avenue,
London SW6 3PS
Tel: 020 7731 2878

Roderick Jellicoe
PO. Box No. 50732
London NW6 6XW
Tel: 020 7727 1571
Fax: 020 7624 6471
jellicoe@englishporcelain.com
www.englishporcelain.com

Rogers de Rin
76 Royal Hospital Road, Paradise
Walk, Chelsea, London SW3 4HN
Tel: 020 7352 9007
Tel: 020 7351 9407
rogersderin@rogersderin.co.uk
www.rogersderin.co.uk

Roy W. Bunn Antiques
Tel: 01282 813703
info@roywbunnantiques.co.uk
www.roywbunnantiques.co.uk

Steppes Hill Farm Antiques
Steppes Hill Farm, Stockbury,
Sittingbourne, Kent ME9 7RB
Tel: 01795 842205
Fax: 01795 842493
dwabuck@btinternet.com

Stockspring Antiques
114 Kensington Church Street,
London W8 4BH
Tel: 020 7727 7995
stockspring@antique-porcelain.
co.uk
www.antique-porcelain.co.uk

T C S Brooke
The Grange, 57 Norwich Road,
Wroxham, Norfolk NR12 8RX
Tel: 01603 782644

Thrift Cottage Antiques
PO Box 113, Bury St Edmunds,
Suffolk IP33 2RQ
Tel: 01284 702470
www.britishporcelain.com

Valerie Main
PO Box 92, Carlisle,
Cumbria CA5 7GD
Tel: 01228 711342
valerie.main@btinternet.com
W W Warner Antiques
The Green, High Street, Brasted,
Kent TN16 1JL
Tel: 01959 563698

Yvonne Adams Antiques
The Coffee House, 3 & 4 Church
street, Stow on the Wold,
Gloucestershire GL54 1BB
Tel: 01451 832 015
antiques@adames.demon.co.uk
www.antiquemeissen.com

Clocks and Watches

Alan Walker
Halfway Manor, Halfway, Nr
Newbury, Berkshire RG20 8NR
Tel: 01488 657670
www.alanwalker-barometers.com

Baskerville Antiques
Saddlers House, Saddlers Row,
Petworth, West Sussex GU28 0AN
Tel: 01798 342067
Fax: 01798 343956
brianbaskerville@aol.com

Bobinet Ltd.
PO Box 2730, London NW8 9PL
Tel: 020 7266 0783
Fax: 020 7289 5119

David Gibson
PO Box 301, Axminster,
Devon EX13 7YJ
Tel: 01297 631179
www.davidgibson.co.uk

Derek and Tina Rayment Antiques
Orchard House, Barton Road,
Barton, Nr. Farndon,
Cheshire SY14 7HT
Tel: 01829 270429
Fax: 01829 270893
www.antique-barometers.com

**Derek Roberts Fine Antique
Clocks & Barometers**
25 Shipbourne Road, Tonbridge,
Kent TN10 3DN
Tel: 01732 358986
Fax: 01732 771842
drclocks@clara.net
www.quallityantiqueclocks.com

G E Marsh (Antique Clocks) Ltd.
32a The Square, Winchester,
Hampshire SO23 9EX
Tel: 01962 844443
gem@marshclocks.co.uk
www.marshclocks.co.uk

Jeffrey Formby Antiques
Orchard Cottage, East Street,
Moreton-in-Marsh,
Gloucestershire GL56 0LQ
Tel: 01608 650558
jeff@formby-clocks.co.uk
www.formby-clocks.co.uk

Jillings Antiques
Croft House, 17 Church Street,
Newent, Gloucestershire GL18 1PU
Tel: 01531 822100
Fax: 01531 822666
clocks@jillings.com
www.jillings.com

John Carlton-Smith
17 Ryder Street, London SW1Y 6PY
Tel: 020 7930 6622
Fax: 020 7930 1370
www.fineantiqueclocks.com

Montpellier Clocks
13 Rotunda Terrace, Montpellier
Street, Cheltenham,
Gloucestershire GL50 1SW
Tel: 01242 242178
info@montpellierclocks.com
www.montpellierclocks.com

Patric Capon
PO Box 581, Bromley,
Kent BR1 2WX
Tel: 020-8467 5722
Fax: 020-8295 1475
patric.capon@saqnet.co.uk

Pendulum of Mayfair
51 Maddox Sreet,
London W1S 2PJ
Tel: 020 7629 6606
Fax: 020 7629 6616
pendulumclocks@aol.com
www.pendulumofmayfair.co.uk

Raffety & Walwyn Ltd
79 Kensington Church Street,
London W8 4BG
Tel: 020 7938 1100
Fax: 020 7938 2519
raffety@globalnet.co.uk
www.raffetyantiqueclocks.com

Somlo Antiques
7 Piccadilly Arcade,
London SW1Y 6NH
Tel: 020 7499 6526
Tel: 020 7499 0603
www.somlo.com

Strike One
48A Highbury Hill, London N5 1AP
Tel: 020 7354 2790
www.strikeone.co.uk

The Watch Gallery
129 Fulham Road, London SW3 6RT
Tel: 020 7581 3239
Fax: 020 7584 6497

Weather House Antiques
Foster Clough, Hebden Bridge,
West Yorkshire HX7 5QZ
Tel: 01422 882808/886961
kymwalker@btinternet.com

Anthony Woodburn Ltd.
PO Box 2669, Lewes,
East Sussex BN7 3JE
Tel: 01273 486666
Fax: 01273 486644
anthonywoodburn@btconnect.com
www.anthonywoodburn.com

Horological Workshops
204 Worplesdon Road, Guildford,
Surrey GU2 6UY
Tel: 01483 576496
Fax: 01483 452212
mdtooke@aol.com
www.horologicalworkshops.com

Costume Jewellery

Cristobal
26 Church Street, London NW8 8EP
Tel/Fax: 020 7724 7230
steven@cristobal.co.uk
www.cristobal.co.uk

Eclectica
2 Charlton Place, Islington,
London N1 8AJ
Tel: 020 7226 5625
www.eclectica.biz

Linda Bee
Grays Antique Market Mews,
1-7 Davies Street,
London, W1Y 1LP
Tel: 020 7629 5921
www.graysantiques.com

Lynn & Brian Holmes
By appointment
Tel: 020 7368 6412

Richard Gibbon
34/34a Islington Green,
London N1 8DU
Tel: 020 7354 2852
neljeweluk@aol.com

Ritzy
7 The Mall Antiques Arcade, 359
Upper Street, London N1 0PD
Tel: 020 7704 0127

Sylvie Spectrum
Stand 372, Grays Antique Markets,
58 Davies Street, London W1K 5LP
Tel: 020 7629 3501
spectrum@grays.clara.net

William Wain at Antiquarius
Stand J6, Antiquarius, 135 King's
Road, Chelsea, London SW3 4PW
Tel: 020 7351 4905
w.wain@btopenworld.com

Decorative Arts

Adrian Sassoon
Rutland Gate, London SW7 1BB
Tel: 020 7581 9888
ads@asassoon.demon.co.uk
www.adriansassoon.com

Aesthetics
Stand V2, Antiquarius, 131-141
Kings Road, London SW3 4PW
Tel: 020 7352 0395

Arenski Fine Arts Ltd.
The Coach House, Ledbury Mews
North, Notting Hill, London W11 2AF
Tel: 020 7727 8599
arenski@netcomuk.co.uk
www.arenski.com

Art Deco Etc
73 Upper Gloucester Road,
Brighton, Sussex BN1 3LQ
Tel: 01273 202 937
Mob: 07971 268 302
johnclark@artdecoetc.co.uk

Art Nouveau Originals c.1900
5 Pierrepont Row Arcade, Camden
Passage, Islington, London N1 8EF
Tel: 020 7359 4127

Beth
Stand G043/46
Alfies Antiques Market
13-25 Church Street, Marylebone,
London NW8 8DT
Tel: 020 7723 5613
Mob: 07776 136 003

DIRECTORY OF SPECIALISTS

DIRECTORY OF SPECIALISTS

Beverley
30 Church Street, Marylebone,
London NW8 8EP
Tel: 020 7262 1576

Circa 1900
Shop 17, Georgian Village,
Camden Passage, London N1 8DU
Tel: 0771 370 9211
www.circa1900.org

Charles Edwards
19a Rumbold Road (off King's
Road), London SW6 2DY
Tel: 020 7736 7172
Fax: 020 7731 7388
charles@charles edwards.com

Fay Lucas Art Metal
Christie's Fine Art Security,
42 Ponton Road,
London, SW8 5BA
Tel: 020 7371 4404
Fax: 020 7371 4404
info@faylucas.com

**Gallery 1930 - Susie
Cooper Ceramics**
18 Church Street, London NW8 8EP
Tel: 020 7723 1555
Fax: 020 7735 8309
gallery1930@aol.com
www.susiecooperceramics.com

H Blairman & Sons Ltd.
119 Mount Street,
London W1K 3NL
Tel: 020 7493 0444
Fax: 020 7495 0766
blairman@atlas.com
www.blairman.co.uk

Halcyon Days Ltd.
14 Brook Street, London W1Y 1AA
Tel: 020 7629 8811
Fax: 020 7406 7901
info@halcyondays.co.uk
www.halcyondays.co.uk

Hall-Bakker at Heritage
6 Market Place, Woodstock,
Oxfordshire, OX20 1TA
Tel: 01993 811 332

Harris Lindsay
67 Jermyn Street,
London SW1Y 6NY
Tel: 020 7839 5767
Fax: 020 7839 5968
www.harrislindsay.com

John Jesse
160 Kensington Church Street,
London W8 4BN
Tel: 020 7229 0312
jj@johnjesse.com

Keshishian
73 Pimlico Road,
London SW1 W8NE
Tel: 020 7730 8810
Fax: 020 7730 8803

Mike Weedon
7 Camden Passage, Islington,
London N1 8EA
Tel: 020 7226 5319/020 7609 6826
Fax: 020 7700 6387
info@mikeweedonantiques.com
www.mikeweedonantiques.com

Rainer Zietz Ltd.
1a Prairie Street, London SW8 3PX
Tel: 020 7498 2355
Fax: 020 7720 7745

Richard Gardner Antiques
Swan House, Market Square,
Petworth, West Sussex GU28 0AN
Tel: 01798 343 411
rg@richardgardenerantiques.co.uk
www.richardgardenerantiques.co.uk

Robert Bowman Ltd.
8 Duke Street, St James's,
London SW1Y 6BN
Tel: 020 7839 3100
Fax: 020 7839 3223
info@robertbowman.com
www.robertbowman.com

Rumours
4 The Mall Antiques Arcade, 359
Upper Street, London N1 0PD
Tel: 020 7704 6549

Sladmore Sculpture Gallery Ltd.
32 Bruton Place, Berkeley Square,
London W1X 7AA
Tel: 020 7499 0365
www.sladmore.com

Spencer Swaffer Antiques
30 High Street, Arundel, West
Sussex BN18 9AB
Tel: 01903 882132
Fax: 01903 884564
spencerswaffer@btconnect.com
www.spencerswaffer.com

Style Gallery
10 Camden Passage,
London N1 8ED
Tel: 020 7359 7867
Fax: 020 8361 2357
info@styleantiques.co.uk
www.styleantiques.co.uk

Tadema Gallery
10 Charlton Place, Camden
Passage, London N1 8AJ
Tel: 020 7359 1055
www.tademagallery.com

The Coach House London, Ltd.
185 Westbourne Grove,
London W11 2SB
Tel: 020 7229 8311
arenski@netcomuk.co.uk

The Country Seat
Huntercombe Manor Barn,
nr. Henley on Thames,
Oxfordshire RG9 5RY
Tel: 01491 641349
Fax: 01491 641533
www.thecountryseat.com
www.whitefriarsglass.com

The Design Gallery
5 The Green, Westerham,
Kent TN16 1AS
Tel: 01959 561 234
sales@designgallery.co.uk
www.designgallery.co.uk

The Red House Antiques Centre
Duncombe Place, York, North
Yorkshire YO1 7ED
Tel: 01904 637 000
www.redhouseyork.co.uk

Titus Omega
Tel: 020 7688 1295
info@titusomega.com
www.titusomega.com

Trio L24
Grays Antique Markets, 58 Davies
Street, London, W1K 5LP
Tel: 020 7493 2736
www.trio-london.fsnet.co.uk

Van Den Bosch
Shop 1, Georgian Village,
Camden Passage,
Islington N1 8DU
Tel: 020 7226 4550
info@vandenbosch.co.uk
www.vandenbosch.co.uk

Dolls and Toys
Bébés et Jouets
c/o Lochend Post Office,
165 Restalrig Road, Edinburgh,
Midlothian EH7 6HW
Tel: 0131 332 5650
bebesetjouets@tiscali.co.uk

**Collectors Old Toy Shop
and Antiques**
89 Northgate, Halifax,
West Yorkshire HX1 1XF
Tel: 01422 360434/822148
toysandbanks@aol.com
collectorsoledtoy@aol.com

Sue Pearson Dolls & Teddy Bears
18 Brighton Square, 'The Lanes'
Brighton, East Sussex BN1 1HD
Tel/Fax: 01273 774851
sales@suepearson.co.uk
www.suepearson.co.uk

Victoriana Dolls
101 Portobello Rd,
London W11 2BQ
Tel: 01737 249 525
heather.bond@totalserve.co.uk

Furniture
Adrian Alan
66/67 South Audley Street,
London W1Y 5FE
Tel: 020 7495 2324
Fax: 020 7495 0204
enquries@adrianalan.com
www.adrianalan.com

Alistair Sampson Antiques Ltd.
120 Mount Street,
London W1K 3NN
Tel: 020 7409 1799
info@alistairsampson.com
www.alistairsampson.com

Anthemion
Cartmel, Grange-over-Sands,
Cumbria LA11 6QD
Tel: 015395 36295

Anthony Outred (Antiques) Ltd.
Blanchard, Froxfield,
Nr. Marlborough,
Wiltshire SN8 3LD.
Tel: 020 7730 7948
Fax: 020 7730 9509
antiques@outred.co.uk
www.outred.co.uk

The Antiques Warehouse
25 Lightwood Road, Buxton,
Derbyshire SK17 7BJ
Tel: 01298 72967
Mob: 07947 050 552

Antoine Cheneviere Fine Arts Ltd.
27 Bruton Street, London W1J 6QN
Tel: 020 7491 1007

Antony Preston Antiques Ltd.
The Square, Stow-on-the-Wold,
Cheltenam, Gloucestershire
GL54 1AB
Tel: 01451 831586
Fax: 01451 831596
www.antonypreston.com

Apter Fredericks Ltd.
265-267 Fulham Road,
London SW3 6HY
Tel: 020 7352 2188
Fax: 020 7376 5619
antiques@apter-fredericks.com
www.apter-fredericks.com

Avon Antiques
25, 26, 27 Market Street, Bradford-
on-Avon, Wiltshire BA15 1LL
Tel: 01225 862052
www.avon-antiques.co.uk

Baggott Church Street Ltd
Church Street, Stow-on-the-Wold,
Gloucestershire GL54 1BB
Tel: 01451 830 370

Blanchard Ltd
86/88 Pimlico Road,
London SW1W 8PL
Tel: 020 7823 6310
Fax: 020 7823 6303
piers@jwblanchard.com

Brian Rolleston (Antiques) Ltd.
104a Kensington Church Street,
London W8 4BU
Tel: 020 7229 5892

Charles Lumb & Sons Ltd.
2 Montpellier Gardens, Harrogate,
North Yorkshire HG1 2TF
Tel: 01423 503770
Fax: 01423 530074

736

Chevertons Of Edenbridge Ltd.
71-73 High Street, Edenbridge,
Kent TN8 5AL
Tel: 01732 863196
Fax: 01732 864298
chevertons@msn.com
www.chevertons.com

Christopher Buck Antiques
56-60 Sandgate High Street,
Sandgate, Folkestone,
Kent CT20 3AP
Tel: 01303 221 229
chrisbuck@throwley.freeserve.co.uk

Christopher Hodsoll Ltd.
89-91 Pimlico Road, London
SW1W 8PH
Tel: 020 7730 3370
Fax: 020 7730 1516
info@hodsoll.com
www.hodsoll.com

Country Antiques (Wales) Ltd.
Castle Mill, Kidwelly
Carmarthenshire, SA17 4UU
Tel: 01554 890534
info@welshantiques.com
www.welshantiques.com

David J Hansord (Antiques)
6/7 Castle Hill, Lincoln,
Lincolnshire LN1 3AA
Tel: 01522 530044

David Love
10 Royal Parade, Harrogate,
North Yorkshire HG1 2SZ
Tel: 01423 565797
david.love@btconnect.com

Denzil Grant
Drinkstone House, Drinkstone, Bury
St Edmunds, Suffolk IP30 9TG
Tel: 01449 736576
Fax: 01449 737679
nickygrant@excite.co.uk
www.denzilgrant.com

Didier Aaron (London) Ltd.
21 Ryder Street, London SW1Y 6PX
Tel: 020 7839 4716
Fax: 020 7737 3513
didaaronuk@aol.com
www.didieraaron.com

Douglas Bryan
By appointment only.
Tel: 01580 713103

Elaine Phillips Antiques Ltd.
1 & 2 Royal Parade, Harrogate,
North Yorkshire HG1 2SZ
Tel: 01423 569 745
louise@elainephillipsantiques.wana
doo.co.uk

Freeman & Lloyd
44 Sandgate High Street,
Sandgate, Folkestone,
Kent CT20 3AP
Tel: 01303 248986
Fax: 01303 241353
enquiries@freemanandlloyd.com
www.freemanandlloyd.com

Georgian Antiques
10 Pattison St., Leith Links,
Edinburgh, Midlothian EH6 7HF,
Scotland
Tel: 0131 553 7286
Fax: 0131 553 6299
info@georgianantiques.net
www.georgianantiques.net

Godson & Coles
92 Fulham Road, London SW3 6HR
Tel: 020 7584 2200
Tel: 020 7584 2223
www.godsonandcoles.co.uk

H C Baxter & Sons
40 Drewstead Road,
London SW16 1AB
Tel: 020 8769 5869/5969

H W Keil Ltd.
Tudor House, Broadway,
Worcestershire WR12 7DP
Tel: 01386 852408

Heath Bullocks
8 Meadrow, Godalming,
Surrey GU7 3HN
Tel: 01483 422 562
Fax: 01483 426 077

Hotspur Ltd.
14 Lowndes Street,
London SW1X 9EX
Tel: 020 7235 1918
Fax: 020 7235 4371
enquiries@hotspurantiques.com

Huntington Antiques Ltd
Church Street, Stow-on-the-Wold,
Gloucestershire GL54 1BE
Tel: 01451 830 842
Fax: 01451 832 211
info@huntington-antiques.com
www.huntington-antiques.com

Jacob Stodel
Flat 53, Macready House, 75
Crawford Street, London W1H 1HS
Tel: 020 7723 3732
jacobstodel@aol.com

James Brett Ltd.
42 St Giles Street, Norwich,
Norfolk NR2 1LW
Tel: 01603 628171

Jeremy Ltd.
29 Lowndes Street,
London SW1X 9HX
Tel: 020 7823 2923
Fax: 020 7245 6197
jeremy@jeremique.co.uk
www.jeremy.ltd.uk

John Bly
By appointment
27 Bury Street, St James's,
London SW1Y 6AL
Tel: 01442 823030
Fax: 01442 890237
Showroom - The Courtyard
Church Square
Tring, Hertfordshire
HP23 5AE
Tel: 07831 888825/6
Fax: 07092 39194
info@johnbly.com
www.johnbly.com

John Hobbs Ltd.
107A Pimlico Road, London
SW1W 8PH
Tel: 020 7730 8369
Fax: 020 7730 8369
www.johnhobbs.co.uk

John King
74 Pimlico Road,
London SW1W 8LS
Tel: 020 7730 0427
Fax: 020 7730 2515
kingj896@aol.com

Lennox Cato Antiques
1 The Square, Church Street,
Edenbridge,
Kent TN8 5BD
Tel: 01732 865 988
cato@lennoxcato.com
www.lennoxcato.com

Lucy Johnson
PO Box 84, Carterton DO, Burford,
Oxfordshire OX18 4AT
Tel: 07071 881232
Fax: 07071 881233
lucy-johnson@lucy-johnson.com

Mac Humble Antiques
7-9 Woolley Street, Bradford-on-
Avon, Wiltshire BA15 1AD
Tel/Fax: 01225 866329
mac.humble@virgin.net
www.machumbleantiques.co.uk

Michael Foster
118 Fulham Road, London SW3 6HU
Tel: 020 7373 3636
Fax: 020 7373 4042

Michael Norman Antiques Ltd.
61 Holland Road, Hove,
East Sussex BN3 1JN
Tel: 01273 329 253
Fax: 01273 206 556

Norman Adams
8-10 Hans Road, London SW3 1RX
Tel: 020 7589 5266
Fax: .020 7589 1968
www.normanadams.com

Oswald Simpson
The Chapel Maltings, Long Malford,
Suffolk CO10 9HX
Tel: 01787 379287

Owen Humble Antiques
Open by appointment only
Tel: 0191 267 7220

Patrick Sandberg Antiques
150-152 Kensington Church Street,
London W8 4BN
Tel: 020 7229 0373
Fax: 020 7792 3467
psand@antique.net
www.antique.net

Paul Hopwell Antiques
30 High Street, West Haddon,
Northamptonshire NN6 7AP
Tel: 01788 510636
Fax: 01788 510044
PaulHopwell@antiqueoak.co.uk
www.antiqueoak.co.uk

Peter Bunting
Harthill Hall, Alport, Bakewell,
Derbyshire DE45 1LH
Tel: 01629 636203
www.countryoak.co.uk

Peter Foyle Hunwick
The Old Malthouse,
15 Bridge Street, Hungerford,
Berkshire RG17 0EG
Tel/Fax: 01488 682209

Peter Lipitch Ltd.
120 & 124 Fulham Road,
London SW3 6HU
Tel: 020 7373 3328
Fax: 020 7373 8888
lipitcha1@aol.com
www.peterlipitch.com

**Phillips of Hitchin
(Antiques) Ltd.**
The Manor House, Hitchin,
Hertfordshire SG5 1JW
Tel: 01462 432067
Fax: 01462 441368

R G Cave & Sons Ltd.
Walcote House, 17 Broad Street,
Ludlow, Shropshire SY8 1NG
Tel: 01584 873568
Fax: 01584 875050

R N Myers & Son Ltd.
Endsleigh House, High Street,
Gargrave, Skipton,
North Yorkshire BD23 3LX
Tel: 01756 749587
Fax: 01756 749 322
rnmyersson@aol.com

Reindeer Antiques Ltd.
81 Kensington Church Street,
London W8 4BG
Tel: 020 7937 3754
Fax: 020 7937 7199
www.reindeerantiques.co.uk

Reindeer Antiques Ltd.
43 Watling Street, Pottersbury,
Northamptonshire NN12 7QD
Tel: 01908 542407
Fax: 01908 542121
www.reindeerantiques.co.uk

Richard Courtney Ltd.
112-114 Fulham Road, South
Kensington, London SW3 6HU
Tel: 020 7370 4020
Fax: 020 7370 4020

Richard J Kingston
Tel: 01491 574535
Fax: 01491 574535

Robert E Hirschhorn
By appointment
London
Tel: 020 7703 7443
hirschhornantiques@macunlimited.net
www.hirschhornantiques.com

Robert Young Antiques
68 Battersea Bridge Road,
London SW11 3AG
Tel: 020 7228 7847
Fax: 020 7585 0489
office@robertyoungantiques.com
www.robertyoungantiques.com

Roderick Butler
Marwood House, Honiton,
Devon EX14 1PY
Tel: 01404 42169

Ronald Phillips Ltd.
26 Bruton Street, London W1J 6LQ
Tel: 020 7493 2341
Fax: 020 7495 0843
advice@ronaldphillips.co.uk

S J Webster-Speakman
By appointment
Tel: 01502 722252

Stair & Company Ltd.
14 Mount Street, London W1Y 5RA
Tel: 020 7499 1784
Fax: 020 7629 1050
stairandcompany@talk21.com

Suffolk House Antiques
High Street, Yoxford, Saxmundham,
Suffolk IP17 3EP
Tel: 01728 668122
Fax: 01728 668122

Oliver Charles Antiques Ltd.
Lombard Street, Petworth,
West Sussex GU28 0AG
Tel: 01798 344443

Thomas Coulborn & Sons
Vesey Manor, 64 Birmingham Road,
Sutton Coldfield,
West Midlands B72 1QP
Tel: 0121 354 3974
Fax: 0121 354 4614
jc@coulborn.com

Tobias Jellinek Antiques
20 Park Road, East Twickenham,
Middlesex TW1 2PX
Tel: 020 8892 6892
Fax: 020 8744 9298
toby@jellinek.com

Turpin's Antiques
17 Bridge Street, Hungerford,
Berkshire RG17 0EG
Tel: 01488 681886
Tel: 01672 870727

W A Pinn & Sons
124 Swan Street, Sible Hedingham,
Essex CO9 3HP
Tel: 01787 461127

**W R Harvey & Co
(Antiques) Ltd.**
86 Corn Street, Witney,
Oxfordshire OX8 7BU
Tel: 01993 706501
Fax: 01993 706601
antiques@wrharvey.co.uk
www.wrharvey.co.uk

Wakelin & Linfield
PO Box 48, Billingshurst,
West Sussex RH14 0YZ
Tel: 01403 700004
Fax: 01403 701173
wakelin_linfield@btinternet.com
www.wakelin-linfield.com

William H Stokes
The Cloisters, 6/8 Dollar Street,
Cirencester, Gloucestershire
GL7 2AJ
Tel: 01285 653907
Fax: 01285 640533

Witney Antiques
96-100 Corn Street, Witney,
Oxfordshire OX28 6BU
Tel: 01993 703902
Fax: 01993 779852
witneyantiques@community.co.uk
www.witneyantiques.com

General

Alfies Antique Market
13-25 Church Street, Marylebone,
London NW8 8DT
Tel: 020 7723 6066
Fax: 020 7724 0999
www.alfiesantiques.com

Christopher Sykes
The Old Parsonage
Woburn, Milton Keynes,
Buckinghamshire MK17 9QL
Tel: 01525 290259
Fax: 01525 290061

Early Technology
Monkton House, Old
Craighall,Musselburgh,
Midlothian EH21 8SF
Tel: 0131 665 5753
michael.bennett-levy@virgin.net
www.earlytech.com

Grays Antiques Markets
58 Davies St,
London W1K 5LP
Tel: 020 7629 7034
Fax: 020 7499 7034
Email: info@graysantiques.com

Heritage
6 Market Place, Woodstock,
Oxfordshire OX20 1TA
Tel: 01993 811332

Manfred Schotten Antiques
109 High Street, Burford,
Oxfordshire OX18 4RU
Tel: 01993 822302
Fax: 01993 822055
www.schotten.com

**Otford Antiques and Collectors
Centre**
26-28 High Street, Otford,
Sevenoaks, Kent TN14 5PQ
Tel: 01959 522025
Fax: 01959 525858
www.otfordantiques.co.uk

Pantiles Spa Antiques
4-6 Union House,
The Pantiles, Tunbridge Wells,
Kent TN4 8HE
Tel: 01892 541377
Fax: 01435 865660
psa.wells@btinternet.com
www.pantiles-spa-antiques.co.uk

The Ginnel Antiques Centre
Off Parliament Street,
Harrogate, North Yorkshire HG1 2RB
Tel: 01423 508 857

Rellick
8 Golborne Road,
London W10 5NW
Tel: 020 8962 0089

Glass

Andrew Lineham Fine Glass
PO Box 465, Chichester, West
Sussex PO18 8WZ.
Tel: 01243 576 241
Fax: 01243 576 241
Mob: 07767 702 722
andrew@antiquecolouredglass.com
www.antiquecolouredglass.info

**Antique Glass at Frank Dux
Antiques**
33 Belvedere, Lansdown Road
Bath BA1 5HR
Tel: 01225 312367
Fax: 01225 312367
m.hopkins@antique-glass.co.uk
www.antique-glass.co.uk

Christine Bridge Antiques
By appointment only
Tel: 0208 741 5501
Fax: 0208 255 0172
christine@bridge-antiques.com
www.bridge-antiques.com
www.antiqueglass.co.uk

Delomosne & Son Ltd.
Court Close, North Wraxall,
Chippenham, Wiltshire SN14 7AD
Tel: 01225 891505
Fax: 01225 891907
www.delomosne.co.uk

Jeanette Hayhurst Fine Glass
32A Kensington Church St,
London W8 4HA
Tel: 020 7938 1539
www.antiqueglasslondon.com

Mum Had That
info@mumhadthat.com
www.mumhadthat.com

Jewellery

N. Bloom & Son (1912) Ltd.
Tel: 020 7629 5060
www.nbloom.com

J H Bonnar
72 Thistle Street, Edinburgh,
Midlothian EH2 1EN
Tel: 0131 226 2811

Modern

Fragile Design
8 Lakeside, The Custard Factory,
Digbeth, Birmingham, West
Midlands B9 4AA
Tel: 0121 693 1001
www.fragiledesign.com

Francesca Martire
F131-137, Alfies Antique Market,
13 Church Street, Marylebone,
London NW8 8DT
Tel: 020 7724 4802

ISOKON Plus
Turnham Green Terrace Mews,
London W4 1QU
Tel: 020 8994 0636
www.isokonplus.com

John Makepeace
Farrs, Beaminster,
Dorset DT8 3NB
Tel: 01308 862 204
www.johnmakepeace.com

Twentieth Century Marks
Whitegates, Rectory Rd, Little
Burstead, Nr Billericay,
Essex CM12 9TR
Tel: 01268 411 000
www.20thcenturymarks.co.uk

Oriental and Asian

Millner Manolatos
2 Campden Street, Off Kensington
Church Street, London W8 7EP
Tel: 020 7229 3268
Mob: 07900 248 390
info@millnermanolatos.com
www.millnermanolatos.com

Guest & Gray
1-7 Davies Mews,
London W1K 5AB
Tel: 020 7408 1252
Fax: 020 7499 1445
info@chinese-porcelain-art.com
www.chinese-porcelain-art.com

Ormonde Gallery
156 Portobello Road,
London W11 2EB
Tel: 020 7229 9800

Roger Bradbury
Church Street,
Coltishall, Norwich,
Norfolk NR12 7DJ
Tel: 01603 737 444

R & G McPherson Antiques
40 Kensington Church Street,
London W8 4BX
Tel: 020 7937 0812
Fax: 020 7938 2032
Mob: 07768 432 630
rmcpherson@orientalceramics.com
www.orientalceramics.com

Silver

B. Silverman
4 Campden Street,
Off Kensington Church Street,
London W8 7EP
Tel: 020 7985 0555
Fax: 020 7985 0556
silver@silverman-london.com
www.silverman-london.com

C. & L. Burman
5 Vigo Street, London W1S 3HF
Tel: 020 7439 6604
Fax: 020 7439 6605

Didier Antiques
58-60 Kensington Church Street,
London W8 4DB
Tel: 020 7938 2537
didier.antiques@virgin.net
www.didierantiques.com

Fay Lucas Artmetal
Christies Fine Art Securities
42 Ponton Road,
London SW8 5BA
Tel: 020 7371 4404
Fax: 020 7371 4404
info@faylucas.com
www.faylucas.com

Gerald Sattin
PO Box 20627,
London NW6 7GA
Tel: 020 8451 3295
Fax: 020 8451 3295
gsattin@compuserve.com

Goodwins Antiques Ltd
15 & 16 Queensferry Street,
Edinburgh EH2 4QW
Tel: 0131 225 4717
Fax: 0131 220 1412

Hannah Antiques
Tel: 01844 351 935
Fax: 07831 800 774

John Bull (Antiques) Ltd.
JB Silverware, 139A New Bond
Street, London W1S 2TN
Tel: 020 7629 1251
Fax: 020 7495 3001
elliot@jbsilverware.co.uk
www.antique-silver.co.uk
www.jbsilverware.co.uk

J. H. Bourdon Smith Ltd
24 Mason's Yard, Duke Street,
St James's, London SW1Y 6BU
Tel: 020 7839 4714
Fax: 020 7839 3951

Marks
49 Curzon Street,
London W1J 7UN
Tel: 020 7499 1788
Fax: 020 7409 3183
marks@marksantiques.com
www.marksantiques.com

Mary Cooke Antiques
12 The Old Power Station,
121 Mortlake High Street,
London SW14 8SN
Tel: 020 8876 5777
Fax: 020 8876 1652
silver@marycooke.co.uk
www.marycooke.co.uk

Nicholas Shaw Antiques
Virginia Cottage, Lombard Street,
Petworth, West Sussex GU28 0AG
Tel: 01798 345 146
Fax: 01798 345 157
silver@nicholas-shaw.com
www.nicholas-shaw.com

Paul Bennett
48a George Street,
London W1U 7DY
Tel: 020 7935 1555
Fax: 020 7224 4858
paulbennett@ukgateway.net
www.paulbennett.ukgateway.net

Payne & Son (Goldsmiths) Ltd
131 High Street
Oxford, Oxfordshire OX1 4DH
Tel: 01865 243 787
Fax: 01865 793 241
silver@payneandson.co.uk
www.payneandson.co.uk

Peter Cameron Antique Silver
PO Box LB739
London W1A 9LB
petercameron@idnet.co.uk

Peter Szuhay
325 Grays Antiques Markets,
58 Davies Street, London W1Y 2LB
Tel: 020 7408 0154
Fax: 020 8993 8864
pgszuhay@aol.com

Sanda Lipton
28a Devonshire Street,
London W1G 6PS
Tel: 020 7431 2688
Fax: 020 7431 3224
sanda@antique-silver.com
www.antique-silver.com

S & J Stodel
Vault 24, London Silver Vaults,
Chancery Lane, London WC2A 1QS
Tel: 020 7405 7009
Fax: 020 7242 6366
stodel@msn.com
www.chinesesilver.com

Shapiro & Company
380 Grays Antiques Markets,
58 Davies Street, London W1K 5LP
Tel: 020 7491 2710

Smith & Robinson
Tel: 020 8994 3783
cwsmith@ukonline.co.uk

Steppes Hill Farm Antiques
Steppes Hill Farm, Stockbury,
Sittingbourne, Kent ME9 7RB
Tel: 01795 842205
Fax: 01795 842493
dwabuck@btinternet.com

The Silver Fund
1 Duke of York Street,
London SW1Y 6JP
Tel: 020 7839 8935
www.thesilverfund.com

Van Den Bosch
1 Georgian Village,
Camden Passage,
Islington, London N1 8DU
Tel: 020 7226 4550
Fax: 020 8348 5410
info@vandenbosch.co.uk
www.vandenbosch.co.uk

Textiles

Antique Textiles and Lighting
34 Belvedere, Lansdowne Road,
Bath, Avon BA1 5HR
Tel: 01225 310 795
Tel: 01225 443884
www.antiquetextilesandlighting.co.uk

Fantiques
Tel: 020 8840 4761
paulajraven@aol.com

Junnaa & Thomi Wroblewski
78 Marylebone High Street, Box 39,
London W1U 5AP
Tel: 020 7499 7793
Fax: 020 7499 7793
junnaa@wroblewski.eu.com
thomi@wroblewski.eu.com

Vintage to Vogue
28 Milsom Street, Bath,
Avon BA1 1DG
Tel: 01225 337 323
www.vintagetovogue.com

Tribal Art

Elms Lesters
Painting Rooms, Flitcroft Street,
London WC2H 8DH
Tel: 020 7836 6747
Fax: 020 7379 0789
gallery@elms-lesters.demon.co.uk
www.elms-lesters.demon.co.uk

Jean-Baptiste Bacquart
www.AfricanAndOceanicArt.com

Michael Graham Stewart
173 New Bond Street
London W1S 4RF
Tel: 020 7495 4001
Fax: 020 7629 4602
www.graham-stewart.com

Owen Hargreaves & Jasmine Dahl
9 Corsham Street
London N1 6DP
Tel: 020 7253 2669
www.owenhargreaves.com

GLOSSARY

A

albarello jar An Italian tin-glazed earthenware pharmacy jar.

albumen print Photographic paper that is treated with egg white (albumen) to enable it to hold light sensitive chemicals.

ashet A large plate or dish.

astragal Architectural moulding with a semi-circular section.

aventurine A translucent glass given a sparkling appearance by the incorporation of flecks of oxidised metal. Can also be used as a glaze on ceramics.

B

Bakelite An early synthetic plastic which was patented in 1907.

balance An escape mechanism that is used in clocks without pendulums.

baluster A curved form with a bulbous base and slender neck.

Baroque An ornate and extravagant decorative style which was popular in the 17th and 18thC.

bergère The French term for an upholstered armchair.

bezel The groove or rim on the inside of the cover or lid on vessels such as teapots.

bianco-sopra-bianco A technique involving painting opaque white glaze on to a greyish ground.

boulle A type of marquetry that includes tortoiseshell and metal.

brassing Wear to plating that reveals the underlying base metal.

break-front A term for furniture with a projecting centre section.

broderie anglaise White thread embroidered onto white cloth, used after the 1820s.

C

cabochon A protruding, polished, but not faceted, stone.

cabriole leg A leg with two gentle curves that create an S-shape.

cameo Hardstone, coral or shell that has been carved to show a design in a contrasting colour.

cameo glass Decorative glass made from two or more layers of differently coloured glass, which are then carved or etched to reveal the colour beneath.

caryatid An architectural column in the form of a woman.

cased glass Glass encased with a further layer of glass.

celadon A distinctive grey/green or blue/green glaze.

centre seconds hand A seconds hand that is pivoted at the centre of the dial.

chamfered A surface that has been cut with a slanted edge.

champlevé A type of decoration where enamel is applied to stamped hollows in metal.

chapter ring The ring of hour and minute numbers on a clock dial.

character doll A doll with a face that resembles a real child.

charger A large plate or platter, used for display or serving.

chasing The technique of decorating the surface of silver by punching it with small tools.

chinoiserie Oriental-style lacquered or painted decoration featuring figures and landscapes.

chronometer A timekeeper used for calculating longitude at sea.

clock garniture A matching clock and candelabra set.

cloisonné A decorative technique whereby metal cells are filled with coloured enamels.

commode A decorated low chest of drawers with a curved form.

composition A mixture including wood pulp, plaster and glue and used as a cheap alternative to bisque in the production of dolls.

core forming An early form of glass-making where molten glass is wound around a mud core.

D

crackle A deliberate crazed glaze effect used on porcelain.

credenza The Italian term for a side cabinet with display shelves at both ends.

crewelwork A wool embroidery technique used on linen.

cricket cage A small box designed to amplify the chirping of a cricket contained therein.

Daguerrotype An early type of photograph, from c1839 until the 1850s.

Davenport A small writing desk. In America, a large parlour sofa.

dentils Small teeth-like blocks that form a border under a cornice.

Deutsche Blumen Floral decoration found on 18thC faience and porcelain.

diecast Objects made by pouring molten metal into a closed metal die or mould.

Ding A very small dent in metal.

dovetailing A method of joining two pieces of wood together by interlocking mortises and tenons.

dump A doorstop made from left-over glass, often with decoration.

E

earthenware A type of porous pottery that requires a glaze to make it waterproof.

ebonised Wood that has been dyed black to resemble ebony.

egg and dart A classical moulding that incorporates egg and 'v' shapes used to enrich Neo-classical wares.

enamel Coloured glass paste that is applied to surfaces to create a decorative effect.

escapement The mechanical part of the clock or watch that regulates the transfer of energy from the weights or spring to the movement of the clock or watch.

escutcheon A protective plate, as for a keyhole

F

faïence Earthenware treated with an impervious tin glaze.

fairing A small porcelain figure made in Eastern Germany and given away as prizes or sold inexpensively at fairs.

Fazackerly A style of floral painting found on English delft.

Fazackerley colours The bright enamel colours used to decorate pieces of English delft. The name probably derives from a pair of Liverpool delft mugs, dedicated to Thomas and Catherine Fazackerley, which were destroyed in WWII.

festoon A decorative motif in the form of a garland or chain of fruit, flowers and ribbons suspended on a loop.

figuring A natural pattern created by the grain in the wood.

finial A decorative knob on a terminal or cover of a vessel.

flatware Any type of cutlery.

free blown Glass blown and manipulated into shape without the use of a mould.

fretwork Geometric pierced decoration.

frieze A piece of wood supporting a table top or cornice.

frit Powdered glass added to white clay to produce a soft-paste porcelain. Also describes impurities found in old glass.

fusee A grooved device found in clocks that offsets the force of the spring as it runs down.

G

gadroon A decorative border of flutes or reeds.

gesso A paste mixture applied to timber then carved and gilded.

gnomon The part of a sundial which casts the shadow.

Greek key A Classical motif of interlocking lines.

grosse point A stitch that crosses two warp and two weft threads.

guilloché An engraved pattern of interlaced motifs, sometimes with translucent enamels.

H

hard-paste porcelain Porcelain made from kaolin, petuntse and quartz.

harlequin set A set of ceramics or furniture, in which the pieces are similar rather than identical.

hiramakie A Japanese decorative technique whereby a powdered charcoal design is coated with a layer of transparent lacquer.

honey gilding A decorative technique using gold leaf mixed with honey for a reddish tinge.

hotei The Japanese god of contentment and happiness.

I J K

intaglio Cut or engraved decoration on glass.

japanning The process of coating objects with layers of coloured varnish in imitation of lacquer.

knop The knob on lids and covers and also the bulge on the stem of a candlestick or glass.

kovsh A Russian shallow drinking vessel with a handle.

kraak ware Late Ming Chinese blue and white porcelain exported by Dutch traders in ships known as 'carracks.'

L

lacquer An oriental varnish made from tree gum with a gloss finish.

lead glass or crystal A particularly clear type of glass with a high lead oxide content.

lead glaze A clear glaze with a lead based component.

longcase clock A weight-driven, free-standing clock.

lustre An iridescent finish found on pottery and produced using metallic oxides.

M

manganese A mineral used to produce a purple glaze.

maiolica Italian tin-glazed earthenware produced from the 14thC.

marqueterie sur verre A method of decorating glass in which a hot glass shape is pressed onto the surface of a shape.

marquetry A decorative veneer made up from coloured woods.

married A term uses to describe a piece that is composed of parts that were not originally together.

Meiji A period in Japanese history dating from c1868-1912.

Mon A Japanese family crest. A common example is the 16 petal chrysanthemum flower.

movement The entire time-keeping mechanism of a clock or watch.

N O

netsuke A small toggle used to secure pouches and boxes hung on cords through the belt of a kimono.

ogee An S-shaped shallow curve.

okimono A Japanese ornamental carving.

opalescent An opal-like, milky glass with subtle gradations of colour.

opaline glass A translucent white glass made with the addition of oxides and bone ash.

ormolu Bronze gilding used in 18thC and early 19thC France as decorative mounts.

overglaze Enamel or transfer-printed decoration on porcelain that is applied after firing.

ovolo A quarter-circle shaped moulding.

P

parian A semi-matt type of porcelain, made with feldspar, that does not require a glaze.

parquetry A variant of marquetry where veneers are applied in symmetrical designs.

parure A jewellery set usually comprising a matching necklace, pair of earrings, bracelet and a brooch.

paste The mixture of ingredients that make up porcelain. Also a compound of glass used to make imitation gemstones.

patina A surface sheen on objects that is produced over time through polishing and handling.

pavé setting A method of mounting jewels so that each stone is set close to the next.

pearlware English earthenware with a blue tinted glaze, developed by Wedgwood.

penwork Indian ink decoration applied with a pen.

petit point Finely worked embroidery with stitches that cross one warp or weft thread.

pinion A small toothed gear within a clock movement.

piqué A decorative technique where small strips or studs of gold are inlaid onto ivory or tortoiseshell on a pattern and secured in place by heating.

plique-à-jour Technique where enamel is set into an openwork metal frame to create an effect similar to stained glass.

porcelain A mixture of china clay and china stone that becomes hard, translucent and white when fired. Hard-paste porcelain is fired at a higher temperature than soft paste.

pounce pot A small pot for gum dust used to prevent ink from spreading.

press-moulded Ceramics formed by pressing clay into a mould. Pressed glass is made by pouring molten glass into a mould and pressing it with a plunger.

Q R S

repoussé A French term for the raised, 'embossed', decoration on metals such as silver.

sabot The metal 'shoe' on the end of cabriole legs.

sabre leg A leg shaped like the curved blade of a sabre.

scagliola Imitation marble made with plaster.

sgraffito A pattern of scratched decoration that reveals a contrasting colour beneath.

slip A mixture of clay and water used to decorate pottery and to produce slip-cast wares.

soft-paste porcelain Porcelain made from kaolin, powdered glass, soapstone and clay.

splat The central upright in a chair back.

squab A stuffed cushion.

sterling silver A standard of silver where the silver content is 92.5 per cent pure silver.

stretchers The bar between two legs on tables and chairs used to stabilise the structure.

stuff-over seat A chair with an upholstered seat rail.

T

tin-glaze An opaque tin oxide glaze used on earthenware.

transfer printing A method of printing ceramics that involves transferring a design from an inked engraving to a vessel.

transitional The Chinese period around the transition from the Ming to the Qing dynasty.

U V W Y

underglaze Decoration painted on to a biscuit body before glazing.

veneering A technique used in furniture making which involves using fine woods to cover or decorate the surface of less expensive woods.

vermeil Gold-plated silver.

wheel engraving A method of engraving into the surface of glass by holding a rotating wheel of stone or metal against it.

white metal Precious metal that is possibly silver, but not officially marked as such.

yellow metal Precious metal that is possibly gold, but not officially marked as such.

INDEX

INDEX